To my friend
in England
I hope you enjoy it

Naomi Lee
Oct/09

Politics, Religion and Love

Politics, Religion and Love

The Story of H. H. Asquith, Venetia Stanley
and Edwin Montagu, Based on
the Life and Letters of
Edwin Samuel Montagu

Naomi B. Levine

NEW YORK UNIVERSITY PRESS
NEW YORK AND LONDON

Library of Congress Cataloging-in-Publication Data
Levine, Naomi B., 1923–
Politics, religion, and love : the story of H. H. Asquith, Venetia
Stanley, and Edwin Montagu, based on the life and letters of Edwin
Samuel Montagu / Naomi B. Levine.
p. cm.
Includes bibliographical references (p.   ) and index
ISBN 0-8147-5057-5 (cloth)
1. Montagu, Edwin Samuel, 1879–1924. 2. Politicians—Great
Britain—Biography. 3. Montagu, Venetia Stanley, 1887–   —
Marriage. 4. Politicians' wives—Great Britain—Biography.
5. Asquith, H. H. (Herbert Henry), 1852–1928. 6. Prime ministers—
Great Britain—Biography. 7. Great Britain—Politics and
government—1901–1936. I. Title.
DA566.9.M56L48   1991
941.082′092—dc20
[B]   90–26382
CIP

New York University Press books are printed on acid-free paper,
and their binding materials are chosen for strength and durability.

c 10 9 8 7 6 5 4 3 2

Dedicated to my daughter Joan and my granddaughters, Chloé and Olivia, to remind them that a woman can do anything she wants to do—at any age and any time.

And to my husband, Leonard, for understanding this. His contribution in the preparation of this book was invaluable.

Contents

Preface   xi

Introduction: Who Was Edwin S. Montagu?   1

1 The Beginning   7

2 Childhood and Early Education, 1879–1898   27

3 Cambridge and the Beginning of a Political Career   42

4 The Liberal Party and the Landslide of 1906   67

5 Asquith before 1906   74

6 Parliamentary Private Secretary to the Chancellor of the Exchequer, 1906–1908   82

7 Venetia and the Beginning of a Romance, 1908–1910   102

8 The Political Scene, 1909–1911   115

9 Under Secretary of State for India: First Two Years, 1910–1912   128

10 A Love Triangle Begins, 1911–1912   165

11 The Trip to India, October 1912–March 1913   180

12 The Triangle Is Now in Place, March 1913–January 1914   198

13 As the War Clouds Gather: Financial Secretary to the Treasury, 1914   210

14 Five Months of Military and Naval Disasters, August 4–December 31, 1914   238

15 Prelude to Political Disaster, January–May 1915   254

16 Venetia Announces Engagement to Montagu; Asquith Forms Coalition Government, May 1915   278

17 Venetia's Escape to France—the Conversion and Marriage, May, June, July 1915   301

18 The Coalition, May 1915–December 1916   327

19 Montagu at Munitions, July–December 1916   350

20 The Fall of Asquith, December 1916   361

21 Marriage: The Beginning, 1915–1916   386

22 Montagu and Reconstruction, January–June 1917   394

23 Zionism: The Balfour Declaration   422

24 Secretary of State for India, July 1917–December 1918   450

25 The Marriage, 1917–1918   484

26 The Best and Worst of Times, 1919   492

27 The Marriage Continues to Deteriorate, 1919   527

28 Censure and Shame, 1920   538

29 Reading and Montagu, 1921   573

30 The Resignation, January, February, March 1922   609

31 Some Private Notes: Pearl and the Birth of a Daughter, 1921–1922   652

32 Alone at Eventide, March–December 1922   656

33 Personal and Political Darkness, 1923   670

34 Despair and Death, 1924   682

35 Venetia without Edwin, 1924–1948   703

Epilogue: The Cycle Is Complete: The End   730

Appendix: The Genealogy of Edwin S. Montagu   731

Manuscript Sources and Abbreviations   735

Notes   737

Bibliography   807

Index   811

Illustrations appear as a group following p. 370

Preface

In April 1984, I met Michael Brock and Eleanor Brock, shortly after the publication of their compilation of the love letters of Prime Minister Herbert Henry Asquith to Venetia Stanley, a young woman more than thirty-five years his junior. The book was widely acclaimed as an extraordinarily moving account of the last days of Liberal England.

Edwin Samuel Montagu, a member of Asquith's Cabinet, one of the Prime Minister's closest friends and confidants, and a rising political star, had also been in love with Venetia Stanley at the time the Prime Minister, who was already married, was pouring out his passion to her in his love letters. Montagu, a son of Lord Swaythling, the founder of Samuel Montagu and Company, one of England's largest and most respected financial institutions, had been educated at Cambridge, where he was elected President of the Cambridge Union, the undergraduate debating society whose presidents often went on to distinguished political careers. With the finest education possible, an enormous family fortune, and a seat in Parliament at the age of twenty-five, Edwin Montagu should have had a glittering future. Two factors worked against him: his personality and the fact that he was a Jew. Anti-Semitism was a powerful force in Great Britain. It affected Montagu's life from his earliest days in public school to his final hours as a Member of Parliament.

The juxtaposition of H. H. Asquith, the paragon of the British establishment, and Edwin Samuel Montagu, the son of an Orthodox Jew, men of different backgrounds yet bound together by a strong obsession with the same young woman, intrigued me. I asked Dr. Brock if any biography of Edwin Montagu existed. He told me that one brief biography did exist, written by a member of the family, Sir David Waley, but he encouraged me to do a more extensive study, because he thought Montagu's contributions to British history might warrant such an effort. Thus, at the age of sixty, having never written anything more complex than a legal brief, I began this book. The five years I spent working on it—encouraged and assisted by my husband, Leonard Levine, who is an accountant—turned out to be one of the most exciting intellectual adventures of my life.

Beginning as a biography with heavy emphasis on the triangle of Asquith, Venetia Stanley and Montagu, the book quickly became a historical biography, for as my research progressed it became clear that Edwin Montagu had little meaningful life outside of his political career. Even his love for Venetia was secondary. He lived and breathed politics and was passionately involved in nearly every political issue of his day. The history of the period in which he lived became an absolutely essential component in recounting the story of his life.

In writing this book I drew primarily upon Edwin's correspondence with Asquith, Lloyd George, Beaverbrook, Balfour, Curzon, Reading and Diana and Duff Cooper; upon Edwin's letters to Venetia; and on their extensive private memoranda and diaries. I also drew heavily upon the secondary literature listed in the Bibliography at the end of this book. The most important sources, in addition to the Brock compilation of the Asquith letters, are the biographies of Asquith written by Roy Jenkins and Stephen Koss and *Edwin Montagu* by Sir David Waley.

I acknowledge with gratitude the assistance I received from the India Office, Library and Records, the Bodleian Library at Oxford; from the University Library at Cambridge, where the majority of Montagu's correspondence and other written materials are stored; and from the Bobst Library of New York University, whose section on English history is superb. Additional material about the Montagus has been kept by Milton Gendel, husband of the late Judith Montagu Gendel (daughter of Venetia Stanley Montagu), and by their daughter Anna (Venetia's grandchild).

Wherever possible, I have deliberately quoted directly from the letters of the people involved on the assumption that letters reveal personality, attitudes and feelings better than do other sources. As the biographer James Atlas has pointed out: "There is something incredibly moving about reading a collection of letters from beginning to end. Nowhere else does the passage of time, the sense of life bracketed by birth and death, so palpably convey itself."[1] Fortunately, Edwin Montagu, Venetia Stanley, Asquith and their contemporaries were prodigious letter writers. This, along with their penchant for gossip and their reporter's eye and skill, have left us a treasure house of information.

Milton Gendel and his daughter, Anna Gendel, have permitted me to examine and quote from these letters even though some present a less than flattering picture of the players. They have recognized that such revelations do not detract from the substantive contributions that Edwin Montagu made to the history of Great Britain. Nor do they detract from the fact that Venetia Stanley was an exciting, brilliant, liberated woman—years ahead of her time.

I owe an enormous debt of gratitude to Milton Gendel and Anna Gendel for recognizing this and permitting Venetia and Edwin, through their letters and diaries, to speak for themselves. I am grateful, too, to Dr. John Brademas, President of New York University, who introduced me not only to Dr. Michael Brock and Eleanor Brock, but to his many friends at Oxford University who were extraordinarily generous with their ideas and assistance; to Dr. L. Jay Oliva, the Chancellor of New York University, who shared his historical expertise with me and guided me in understanding the role of history in biographical writing; to Dr. Mary Moore, principal of St. Hilda's College at Oxford, from which I received a Senior Research Fellowship, permitting me to finish my research in England; to Carlton Rochell, Dean of Libraries at New York University; to my daughter, Joan S. Kiddon, who patiently edited the first draft; to my secretaries, Eva Burch, Bonnie Burns, Muriel Castro and Ray Weiss; to the Reprographics Department of New York University and its Client Services Supervisor Jim Gibby; to Andrew Adonis of Oxford University and Rengui Yu of New York University, who helped me immeasurably with my research; and to my editors Ann Mandelbaum, Pat Woodruff, Despina Gimbel, and Colin H. Jones, Director of the New York University Press, without whose help this book could not have been published.

I want to thank, too, the following for permission to use copyrighted books and documents: The Rt. Hon. the Lord Bonham Carter (the letters of H. H. Asquith in the Bodleian Library, including his letters to Sylvia Henley, and excerpts from the Diaries of

Margot Asquith); Mr. Milton Gendel and Anna Gendel (the letters of Edwin Montagu and the letters of other members of the Montagu family); Dr. Stephen Waley (the biography *Edwin Montagu,* by Sir David Waley); the Rt. Hon. the Lord Jenkins of Hillhead (the biography *Asquith*); the University of Chicago Press and Paul Barton Johnson (*Land Fit for Heroes,* by Paul Barton Johnson); the *Jewish Chronicle Publications* (*The Balfour Declaration,* by Leonard Stein); Weidenfeld and Nicolson and David Higham Associates Ltd. (*Lord Reading,* by Dennis Judd); Harper and Row (*The Unquiet Souls,* by Angela Lambert); Hamish Hamilton Ltd. and Columbia University Press (*Asquith,* by Stephen Koss); D. M. Cregier *(Bounder from Wales);* Lady Cynthia Asquith (for permission to reprint excerpts from *Diaries,* by Lady Cynthia Asquith, copyright © 1968); Franklin Watts Inc. (*A Durable Fire,* by Artemis Cooper); Macmillan, London, and Sir Lawrence Jones (*An Edwardian Youth,* by Sir Lawrence Jones); Alfred A. Knopf Inc. (excerpts from *Diana Cooper,* by Philip Ziegler, copyright © 1981 by Philip Ziegler); Patrick Leigh Fermor for his essay on Judith Montagu Gendel; Odhams Distribution Ltd. (*War Memoirs,* by David Lloyd George); Curtis Brown Ltd. (*The Rainbow Comes and Goes,* by Diana Cooper); Penguin USA (*John Maynard Keynes,* by Robert Skidelsky); and Little, Brown & Co. (*The Last Lion,* by William Manchester).

Acknowledgment is also given for permission to use extracts taken from *War and the State,* by Kathleen Burk, reproduced by kind permission of Unwin Hyman Ltd.; for permission to use excerpts from *Lord Reading,* by H. Montgomery Hyde (copyright © 1967 by Harford Productions Ltd.), reprinted by permission of Farrar, Straus and Giroux, Inc.; and excerpts from *The Cousinhood,* by Chaim Bermant (copyright © 1972 by Chaim Bermant), reprinted with permission of Macmillan Publishing Company.

I wish to thank, too, the Rt. Hon. the Earl of Oxford and Asquith, the Hon. John Jolliffe, and Messrs. Collins for permission to reproduce part of a letter from Raymond Asquith to Conrad Russell that appears on p. 202 of *Raymond Asquith: Life and Letters* (1980); and Dr. Michael and Mrs. Eleanor Brock and the Delegates of the Oxford University Press for permission to use a number of quotations from *H. H. Asquith Letters to Venetia Stanley* (1982), and from the paperback edition of the same (1985).

Introduction: Who Was Edwin S. Montagu?

On May 17, 1915, in the midst of the most devastating war his country had yet known, the Prime Minister of Great Britain, Herbert Henry Asquith (known as H. H. Asquith), sat in his paneled study at 10 Downing Street and wrote to King George V, "After much reflection, & consultation today, with Lloyd George and Bonar Law, I have come decidedly to the conclusion that, for the successful prosecution of the war, the govt. must be reconstructed on a broad and non-party basis."[1] With this one line Asquith informed the King and the country that he was replacing the Liberal Party's control of the war with a coalition government—an act that for all practical purposes eliminated the Liberal Party from British politics. His colleagues were utterly amazed.

What made Asquith agree hastily, and with little or no Cabinet consultation, to form a coalition government with members of the Tory Party, for whom he had nothing but distaste? What made him agree to share with his adversaries the power that the Liberal Party had fought so fiercely to achieve? What made him willing to sacrifice in this reorganization his dear friends Richard Haldane and Winston Churchill?

Asquith had always been a man who acted slowly and with care. He was a man for whom consultation was an imperative in the political process. As a brilliant lawyer and parliamentarian, he took particular pride in his ability to settle difficult problems through reasonable discourse—not precipitous action. "Wait and see" was his response to a crisis. Yet, with hardly any warning, with behavior that startled and angered most of his colleagues, he acquiesced quickly and unexpectedly to a request for a coalition government. Why did he behave so uncharacteristically?

I

While there were many reasons for Asquith's decision to form a coalition government, the announcement of the engagement of Venetia Stanley, the woman he deeply loved, to Edwin Samuel Montagu was the factor that tipped the scale. That announcement so shocked him that he had no heart for the parliamentary struggle that he undoubtedly would have faced if he had resisted the pressure for a coalition.

Who was Venetia Stanley, over whom a strong and powerful Prime Minister was so distraught at the announcement of her marriage?

Who was Edwin Montagu? Why did Venetia Stanley, one of the most intelligent and attractive women in Great Britain, decide to marry him, even at the cost of ending her love affair with the Prime Minister of England? Why is so little known about Edwin Montagu when his voluminous correspondence, diaries and personal memoranda, and the letters and records of Asquith, Lloyd George, Lord Curzon, Lord Beaverbrook and other political leaders of the day show that he was deeply involved in nearly every major issue of his time?

Montagu was a Member of Parliament for the West Division of Cambridgeshire from 1906 to 1918, and for the consolidated area of Cambridgeshire from 1918 to 1922; Parliamentary Private Secretary to Asquith, when he was Chancellor of the Exchequer (1906–08), and later when he was Prime Minister (1908–10); Financial Secretary to the Treasury (February 1914–July 1916); a Privy Councillor from January 1, 1915; Chancellor of the Duchy of Lancaster and a member of the Asquith Cabinet (February–May 1915); Minister of Munitions (July–December 1916); Chairman of the Reconstruction Committee (January–July 1917); Under Secretary of State for India (1910–14); Secretary of State for India and a member of Lloyd George's Cabinet (1917–22).

As Financial Secretary to the Treasury, during the first two and a half years of World War I, Montagu helped prepare the nation financially to shoulder the economic burdens produced by the war. He was called the "Father of the War Savings Certificate,"[2] a financial innovation that proved invaluable to Britain. He also suggested and helped draft the arrangement Britain made with J. P. Morgan & Company, which not only increased the Allies' supply of munitions and war materials from the United States but saved them millions of dollars on their American purchases. In its obituary of Montagu, *The Sunday Times* wrote that this had been a "genuine act of commercial statesmanship and it was one for which Mr. Montagu neither claimed nor received the credit that was due to him."[3]

Montagu's contributions to the war effort were not limited to financial matters. As Secretary of the Shell Committee created by Asquith in 1915 and as Minister of Munitions in the second half of 1916, Montagu helped cope with the difficult problem of providing weapons to the British Army at a time when inadequate supplies were threatening the survival of the British Expeditionary Force. Commenting on Montagu's role, Lord Beaverbrook said that Montagu "supplied much of the hard executive work which this Committee contributed to the problem set before it and Montagu's abilities were extraordinary."[4] Beaverbrook added that in Montagu's early days he "was capable of becoming the successor to Lord Rosebery as the head of the Liberal Party," but unfortunately "Montagu achieved his success at almost too early an age for the hope of morning to last the afternoon."[5]

After the war, Montagu was a member of the British Empire delegation in Paris and participated in the peace negotiations, especially as they related to Turkey. His objections to the Treaty of Sèvres, signed with Turkey in 1919, and his fear that it would aggravate Muslim unrest in India proved prescient. The Treaty of Lausanne, finally signed by Britain on July 24, 1923, repudiated the Treaty of Sèvres and incorporated nearly all the suggestions Montagu had made five years earlier. It came too late, however, to heal the bitterness in India engendered by the Sèvres treaty and the anti-Turkish policy it represented—a policy against which Montagu had long fought and for which he sacrificed his political life.

As Under Secretary of State for India, and later as Secretary of State for India, Montagu made invaluable contributions to the concept of self-government for that country. If the Montagu-Chelmsford Reforms of 1919 had been carried out in the spirit in which Montagu had conceived them, the tragedy that developed between Britain and India might not have taken place, or at least might have occurred with less bloodshed. Many Indians viewed Montagu as their country's finest Secretary of State. On November 15, 1924, the day of his death, all of India went into mourning in a moving demonstration of their admiration and affection for him. The native

Princes, the Legislative Councils, the Indian universities, the Indian press and Indian political leaders, radical and moderate alike, were lavish in their praise. In language rarely used by Indians to describe their British rulers, they saluted Montagu as one who would "go down in posterity, linked with the affectionate gratitude of the Princes and people of India for all times," who "gave India her promised and honored place within the Empire," a man who was a true Liberal, who "abhorred racism and prejudice," who was "an ardent champion of India's rights, prerogatives and dignities" and, above all, was India's "faithful friend."[6]

As part of India's tribute to Montagu, statues of him were erected in the center square of Jamnagar and in Calcutta.[7] These statues of Montagu are among the few of Englishmen that stand in India today. In unveiling the statue in Jamnagar, the Maharajah Jam Sahib proclaimed Montagu "intellectually, the most brilliant statesman and best friend India ever had since, perhaps, Edmund Burke. England and the Empire are poorer today for his loss."[8]

As sensitive as Montagu was toward Muslim religious feelings and Indian nationalism and self-government, he opposed the concept of a Jewish homeland in Palestine. As the only Jewish member of Lloyd George's Cabinet, he almost single-handedly defeated the Balfour Declaration. Some of his fears about a Jewish home in Palestine were misplaced, but his argument against the Zionist concept of Jews as a "people" and a "nation," and not merely a religion, raises issues that thoughtful Jews are still debating.

In spite of his contributions, Edwin Montagu is almost totally forgotten—bypassed by historians, he earns only a brief line or footnote in most biographies or histories of the period. The story of his life, his love affair with and marriage to Venetia Stanley, and the role he played in the history of India, Zionism and English politics, before, during and after World War I, deserve more than such perfunctory recognition.

There is still another reason the story of Edwin Montagu is of continuing interest. England's image is that of a great and civilized nation, without a history of pogroms and genocide. But England is also a country with a deep vein of prejudice and bigotry; some of its most cherished leaders were themselves bigots with strong anti-Jewish feelings. British anti-Semitism was not, in most cases, virulent. It has been described as "civil and good-mannered,"[9] but it existed everywhere, "at school, at Oxford and Cambridge, in clubs and pubs and in the government, especially in the Foreign Office."[10] Yet, while condoning such prejudice and anti-Semitic attitudes, England is also a country that has permitted Jews to climb to the pinnacle of economic and political success and has rewarded those who reached the top with some of its highest honors.[11]

Edwin Montagu's life is a vivid and sad commentary on this paradox in English society. His life also exemplifies an important fact of Jewish history: that even so assimilated a Jew as Edwin Montagu, with learning, power and inherited wealth, to whom Judaism was at best an irritant and at worst a burden, was not safe —even in so enlightened a nation as Great Britain—from the humiliation and evils of anti-Semitism.

1

The Beginning

They must at my death be professing the Jewish religion and not be married to a person not professing the Jewish religion.

The last will and testament of Samuel Montagu

Twelve Kensington Palace Gardens, in the heart of London, is a beautiful, splendid, mid-Victorian mansion, solid and elegant, in Kensington Gardens, with a large, manicured garden, protected from public view by high hedges, stone pillars and an imposing iron gate. One hundred years ago, it was the home of Samuel Montagu (Lord Swaythling), one of the pillars of the Jewish community and one of England's great bankers and financiers. On February 6, 1879, it became the birthplace of his second son, Edwin Samuel Montagu.

Today Kensington Palace Gardens houses foreign consulates. Number 12 is owned by a Saudi Prince. When Edwin was born there, however, Kensington Palace Gardens was known as "Millionaires' Row," a street lined with the opulent homes of the very rich, including some of the "Cousinhood," that small group of successful Jewish financiers and bankers, related by marriage and money, that dominated Jewish life in England for more than a century and a half. These included the Montefiores, Rothschilds, Solomons, Cohens, Goldsmids, Waleys, Samuels and the families related to them.[1]

Edwin's father, Samuel Montagu, and his mother, born Ellen Cohen, were both part of the Cousinhood. By the time Edwin was born, Samuel Montagu was a millionaire several times over. Ellen Cohen, the granddaughter of Levi Barent Cohen, known as the "Father of the Cousinhood," and grandniece of Sir Moses Montefiore, who, for sixty-five years, from 1820 to 1885, was the most powerful and respected Jew in England, had brought to the marriage an impeccable pedigree.[2]

The interior of 12 Kensington Palace Gardens was as solid as its occupants. The furniture was huge and heavy, "so solid," Edwin's nephew, Ivor Montagu, recalled in his autobiography, "that it was impossible for my puny strength to budge it."[3] The rooms were large and softly carpeted, the mahogany side tables were covered with family photographs and bibelots, while the fireplaces burned brightly day and night in season, casting a warmth and amber glow that added to the sense of comfort and luxury permeating the house.

Like other mansions of the day it had its nursery, special children's rooms and servants' quarters, a master bedroom and at least five or six other bedrooms on the second floor. On the main floor were an elegant entrance foyer with cut glass chandeliers, a drawing room, a dining room large enough to seat sixty, a formal living room, a sewing room, and a study and library with shelves from floor to ceiling filled with not only books but also old magazines. "She [Edwin's mother]," Ivor recalled, "gave me chocolate-meringue finger-biscuits . . . and let me read the old *Punches.*"[4]

The house was filled with an eclectic collection of paintings, tapestries, mazer bowls, crystal, old china and old English silver, all reflecting Samuel Montagu's broad interest in art and his love of collecting. He was fond of saying, "Collecting must continue in heaven even if the object of the collection might be a rare cherub."[5] As an Orthodox Jew, Samuel Montagu had little interest in Italian madonnas, but he owned several oil paintings of the Dutch masters and a number of paintings by Constable, Gainsborough, Turner and Van Dyck, which hung prominently in his home. He was an authority on old silver, owned an immense collection of antique silver artifacts and was a member of the Burlington Fine Arts Club and the Society of Antiquarians.[6]

Landed Gentry: South Stoneham

The Montagus also had a country home, a splendid Queen Anne mansion built in the midst of a parklike setting of twelve hundred acres at Swaythling in South Stoneham, with vast, rolling gardens designed originally by Lancelot (Capability) Brown, one of the leading landscape artists of the eighteenth century. By the standards

of the Cousinhood, however, this was not a large estate. The Rothschilds, for example, held thirty thousand acres in Buckinghamshire,
while other members of the Cousinhood owned country seats surrounded by fifty thousand acres. Land occupied a special place in the
hierarchy of English values. Money was, of course, important, but
ownership of land conferred respectability. Beginning in the nineteenth century, as soon as the law permitted, Jews bought country
estates as symbols of their economic ascendancy.

The Montagus were no exception. As soon as they could afford it
they bought a country home, elegant and distinctive enough to be
described in the November 1889 issue of *Gardener's Magazine:*

It is a substantial red brick building in the Elizabethan style, walls partly
clothed with creepers. A raised terrace surrounds the house on the south-
east sides forming a broad walk with a good green turf on which are flower
beds. On the north-east side of the mansion is a spacious lawn tennis court
surrounded by grass banks on top of which is a flower border planted in
ribbon form backed up with ornamental trees and shrubs.[7]

The estate had a well-stocked salmon pond, rose and fruit gardens,
magnificent old trees and "tidal waters which formed a reservoir."[8]

Ivor Montagu provided a more intimate description, one that
demonstrates how desperately the wealthy Jews of the period sought
to emulate their Gentile neighbors:

The house was long, and colored dark rose red. At the entrance side,
beyond the shrubbery, was the village, where you could get brandy-balls.
Inside were stone passages and the same heavy comforts as at his [Samuel
Montagu's] house in London. To one side was croquet, and the rear
windows gave on to a vast lawn with mighty cedars on it, stretching . . .
down to . . . the salmon pool. This pool was tidal. The bottom end of the
gounds was bordered by that famous trout stream, the Itchen . . . At high
water, first my grandfather [Edwin's father], then my father, with fa-
voured guests, would fish for salmon. The proper costume was tweedy.
With knee breeches and stockings turned down at the knee, a tweed cap
and a carefully selected batch of multi-coloured flies or silver minnows, my
father and later my brother too would cast . . . a keeper beside them to net
and gaff. . . .

Once a year there was a big fete, when tents covered the lawns and you
could drink lemonade and get your fortune told.[9]

On Saturday mornings Samuel Montagu would take his children
for long walks through the country surrounding the South Stone-

ham house. They examined the garden, noting new topographical details, studying whatever wildlife appeared—butterflies, birds and small animals—with excitement. This love of nature, of country living and the delight in its flora and fauna was one of the few interests which Edwin shared with his father. He never lost it. It would become his principal form of relaxation.

Dress Balls, Elegant Weddings and a Coat of Arms

Samuel Montagu not only liked the peace and quiet of the country, but also enjoyed entertaining there. He was a gracious and generous host. Like the English landed gentry, the Montagus used their homes in South Stoneham and Kensington Palace Gardens for elaborate parties and dress balls, as well as special family occasions. One of these was the wedding of their daughter Henrietta. "It was a brilliant spectacle," according to the *Bayswater Chronicle*. "Seldom is seen such an imposing gathering of our Jewish neighbors."[10] The *Ladies' Pictorial,* the leading fashion magazine of the day, reported:

The bride wore a dress of rich white terry velvet, handsomely trimmed with old Spanish pointlace, her jewels being diamond pearls. She carried a lovely bouquet composed of orange blossoms, orchids and gardenias, and her train was borne by her two little brothers dressed as pages in rugby velvet. About one hundred guests were present. The presents, over one hundred and twenty in number, were varied and costly; including many articles in modern and ancient silver, objects of art and needlework from sisters and personal friends.[11]

By the last decade in the nineteenth century, the Montagus had been granted their own coat of arms, with a crest of a stag and the motto "Swift yet sure," and two spear bearers, one on either side of "a tent of Judah."[12] Now the Montagus had it all: money, a London townhouse, a country estate, their own coat of arms, a distinguished collection of art and artifacts, and a large family to bring them increased fame and fortune in the years to come. It was into this world that Edwin Montagu was born and where he spent his childhood and youth.

For Edwin's father, life had not always been a series of beautiful homes, or a round of costume balls and salmon fishing in tweed knee britches. His eighteenth-century forebears had not lived in the luxury of Kensington Gardens but rather in the ghettos of Poland and later in the crowded port city of Liverpool.

The Beginnings

Expelled from England by Edward I in 1290, the Jews did not begin to trickle back into the country until some four hundred or so years later, initially under Oliver Cromwell (1653–58). Cromwell, a pragmatist, was interested in encouraging English commerce. Jewish merchants had been responsible for the prosperity of Livorno, Hamburg and Amsterdam. While an insignificant infiltration of Maranos from Spain into England had been going on for some time, with Cromwell's approval Jews now started returning to England in larger numbers, this time from Amsterdam and Hamburg. They tended to settle in London and were mainly wholesale merchants trading with the cities of the Mediterranean and the new colonies in the Caribbean. Their immigration was accepted de facto but never incorporated into law.[13] Fearing the uncertainty of such status, the Jews petitioned the Crown in 1664 for a more definitive ruling and were assured that they could both live in England and maintain their own places of worship.[14] No special legislation was passed, however, thus giving them no further privileges but also imposing no penalties. Their position would continue to be defined case by case.

During the reign of Charles II (1660–85), persecution of the Jews increased in Europe, resulting in a slight rise in immigration into England. By 1663, census records show that fifty-seven families were added to the Jewish community in London and a rabbi was summoned from Amsterdam. A new chapter in the history of the community began with the coming of William of Orange in 1688. As one historian has noted, his expedition "which led to the Glorious Revolution, inspired as it was by Englishmen and executed by Dutchmen, was to a large extent financed by Jews."[15]

The cost of the expedition was largely underwritten through an interest-free loan of two million crowns to William from a Dutch Jewish merchant, Antonio (Isaac) Lopez Suasso. William's horses and troops were fed with bread and forage provided by another Jewish financier, Isaac Pereira.[16] It is not surprising, therefore, that William favored Jewish immigration. For the next fourteen years (1688–1702) when he headed the governments of both England and

Holland, Jewish immigration from Amsterdam to London increased.

In the course of the seventeenth century, the Jews of England progressed from traders and sellers of clothing and other merchandise, to bullion dealers, brokers on the exchanges, and bankers skilled in international finance. With England's trade expanding and her need for capital on the rise, the Jews saw greater opportunities in money and credit than in merchandising. As word of such opportunities spread, even more Jewish immigrants arrived in Britain to partake of this promise of prosperity and freedom.[17]

In 1669, the Jewish community in London was large and secure enough to buy land for a new synagogue—and first built in England since the thirteenth century, still standing in Plough Yard, Bevis Marks, in 1991. By the close of the seventeenth century, Jewish businessmen, many of whom were to play a leading role in Anglo-Jewish history, had established themselves in England's commercial life—thus achieving one of the objectives of William of Orange in encouraging their migration to England.

In the beginning of the eighteenth century, persecution of Jews in Germany and Poland led to increased Jewish migration, and, by the early 1800s, there were some twenty to thirty thousand Jews in England—two-thirds in London and the remainder in the port cities, such as Bristol, Plymouth and Liverpool.[18] The Jews who settled the port cities were generally more adventurous, peddlers who dared to leave the relative security of London to sell their wares in the provinces. They became silversmiths, pawnbrokers, glass manufacturers, shoemakers, watchmakers and suppliers to the Royal Navy. Vessels from the Orient, Africa, North and South America, unloading the riches of the world, made these ports turbulent and exciting places, attractive to those with an instinct for trade. Jews, in particular, thrived in these port cities where breeding and formal education were less valued than initiative, daring and hard work.

Thus, by the end of the eighteenth century there were enough Jews in Liverpool to require rooms for a synagogue and enough bourgeois Jews to require synagogue members to maintain "certain minimal standards of deportment."[19] The head of the synagogue was listed in the Liverpool Directory as the "Jewish High Priest." In 1790, he was Rabbi Benjamin ben Elijakim Getz, who took the name Benjamin Yates. He had come to England from the German town of Strelitz. The lay head of the Liverpool community at this time, a clothier named Ralph Samuel, had also come from Strelitz. The two families intermarried and eventually included another family named Samuel who arrived in Liverpool from London. In time they were joined by the Franklin family which had settled in London in the eighteenth century and then moved to Liverpool. The Yates-Samuel and Samuel-Franklin unions, from which so many distinguished English Jews descended, were thus created.[20]

Louis Samuel: Edwin's Grandfather

The Samuel family that had made its way from London to Liverpool was descended from Menachem Samuel, Edwin Montagu's great grandfather, who had been born in Breslau in the Austro-Hungarian Empire and who later settled in Kempen en Posen, a small village in the pale of settlement, the Jewish ghetto of Poland. He came to London in 1775 following the persecution of the Jews under Empress Maria Theresa who ruled the Austro-Hungarian Empire from 1740 to 1780. His son, Louis Samuel (1794–1859), Edwin's paternal grandfather, left London as a young man and moved to Liverpool. He was a watchmaker, as well as a sometime pawnbroker and silversmith. He married Henrietta, daughter of Israel Israel of Bury Street in the town of St. Mary Axe, outside of London. Israel Israel was a London bullion dealer of considerable means.

By 1819, when Louis Samuel was twenty-five, he was described as having achieved "moderate prosperity."[21] Whether he arrived at this prosperity through his work as a watchmaker and silversmith or through his wife's inheritance is unclear. The Samuels were Orthodox Jews, as were most of the Jews of Liverpool, regularly attending the services conducted by Rabbi Yates. They kept kosher homes, strictly observed the Sabbath and the Jewish holidays, and rigidly obeyed as many of the mandates of Jewish law as they could in the primitive, rough-and-tumble world of Liverpool. Louis Samuel and his wife Henrietta, as was the practice of Orthodox families, took seriously the biblical mandate to "multiply and be fruitful." They had seven children. The youngest (their second son) was born in 1832 and was named Montagu Samuel.[22]

Samuel Montagu: Edwin's Father

At school Montagu Samuel's family name was incorrectly recorded as Montagu instead of Samuel, and this was said to have suggested to his parents that since the Samuel family was so large, it was to their son's advantage to change his name to Samuel Montagu. This change was made in 1842, when their son was ten years old. He obtained a royal license for the change in 1894 when he became a baronet. In 1907 he was made a baron. He was only the second Jewish peer in English history; the first had been Rothschild.

Samuel's change of name inspired Hilaire Belloc, the British novelist, poet and virulent anti-Semite, to compose one of his well-known limericks when Samuel Montagu was elevated to the peerage. Like much of Belloc's work, it quickly made its way around London and was quoted to chuckles of delight in many an elegant drawing room:

> Lord Swaythling, whom the people knew,
> And loved, as Samuel Montagu,
> Is known unto the fiends of hell
> As Mr. Moses Samuel.[23]

As an intelligent, sensitive child, Samuel Montagu was no stranger to anti-Semitism. In those days, although Jews were making significant strides toward integration into British economic and political life, there continued pronounced anti-Jewish feelings throughout English society, especially in the Tory Party. Jews were not as yet fully emancipated in the political life of the country. They were still not permitted by law to sit in Parliament. Jewish children in the public schools were often taunted and abused, and the writings of social commentators such as William Cobbett and Charles Lamb, distinguished academicians like Thomas Arnold, head of Rugby College, and politicians like Sir Robert Ingles, Member of Parliament for Oxford University, were filled with anti-Semitic barbs and strong statements on the need to merge church and state and keep England "Christian." These were widely circulated and contributed significantly to keeping political emancipation for the Jews from becoming a reality until the middle of the nineteenth century, when Jews finally were permitted into the House of Commons (1854) and the House of Lords (1866). Their political acceptance, however, did little to reduce the social stigma that still attached to being Jewish.

Overseas, these were the days of the Damascus Blood Libel and renewed persecution of Jews in Eastern Europe. These were topics that were reported in the *Jewish Press* and read by the young Samuel Montagu who as a boy was passionately fond of reading and study. It was said of him that "he could vanish from view for hours on end in one of the city's libraries, and could, on occasion, smuggle a novel into a synagogue to read between the sober covers of a prayer book."[24]

While life for the child of a watchmaker in Liverpool in the 1830s and 1840s was far from the luxury that Edwin enjoyed at Kensington Palace Gardens, the Samuel children had a relatively comfortable life. Their parents worked hard and lived frugally, but the children had a good home and a supportive family, and were encouraged to read and study and to take their places in the life of the nation. England was viewed as a wonderful land of opportunity where Jews could practice their religion, earn a good living, rely on the courts for justice, and send their children to the secular schools in London and some of the provinces.

As a child, Samuel Montagu attended one such school, the Mechanics Institute, now the Liverpool Institute. The Mechanics Institute of Liverpool was an outgrowth of the London Mechanics Institute, founded as a private college by a Dr. Birbeck in 1832. It provided technical education and courses in science and mathematics, as well as a smattering of languages and history. Lily Montagu, describing her father's experience in school, wrote that he was forced to "fight many battles in order to extort respect for his community." This did not lessen his respect for learning or his lifelong support for education.

In addition to a modest secular education, Samuel Montagu was also given a Jewish education both at home by his father and in a Hebrew school. Jewish communal day schools, as well as after-school Hebrew and Talmud classes run by the synagogues, were well established by the middle of the 1800s, not only in London but also in the provinces. Liverpool had a Jewish communal day school by 1840, the largest of the day schools outside of London, with eighty pupils. It also had two synagogues, a Jewish choral society and various Jewish welfare institutions.

At fourteen, Samuel Montagu left school to start his business career. While this was the end of his formal education, it was far from the end of his self-education. In the years ahead, while he was beginning his business career in London, he would study the classics each evening after work and, through translations, became conversant with the great writers in Latin and Greek, as well as nearly all the English classics.

As for his Jewish education, he never stopped studying. As an observant Orthodox Jew, it was a religious commandment that he read the Torah and Talmud at every opportunity. And he did so with a fervor and religiosity that permeated every aspect of his long life.

Samuel Montagu: The Banker

Samuel Montagu's first job, at the age of thirteen, was with a firm of foreign merchants on Lombard Street in Liverpool. Adam Spielmann, a foreign banker who was married to Montagu's sister, Marion, brought him into the firm. When Montagu realized that his prospects for advancement were slight, he moved to London at the age of seventeen, where his parents had been living since his father retired. Although Samuel had originally wanted to go to Australia, his family persuaded him against it.

Samuel was soon manager of the London branch of the French bank Monteaux. Here, too, advancement seemed slow for him. He was a young man of great energy and ambition, with an extraordinary gift for numbers, and at an early age he had acquired an understanding of foreign exchange that was rare among London bankers of any age.

In February 1853, still underage, he persuaded his father to advance five thousand pounds on his behalf to his brother Edwin (Edwin had kept the name Samuel) to begin a new foreign exchange and banking house. Edwin became a partner but not an active one. Samuel was the driving force, pulling Edwin with him to greater and greater success. The firm became known as Samuel & Montagu, and later as Samuel Montagu & Co., with offices first on Leadenhall Street in the heart of London's growing financial district and later at 60 Old Broad Street, also in the center of the financial district. (The present Samuel Montagu & Co. Limited still has premises at this address.)

Montagu began his banking business at a time when the British economy was booming. With a taste for foreign exchange dealings born in his adolescence among the sailors on the Liverpool docks, he was drawn to this field and even at a young age could foresee its potential. He brought to it a brilliance, creativity and drive that soon made him the country's leading expert in bullion and foreign exchange and contributed significantly to making London the chief clearinghouse for the international money market. By the time Samuel Montagu was in his late twenties he had amassed a considerable fortune, and when Edwin was born in 1879 he was a millionaire many times over. He was then forty-seven.

As an employer, Montagu was demanding but paternalistic. No detail of his business was too small for his interest.[25] While the partners were all members of his family and the rest of the staff could not aspire to enter this circle, "they were in some respect part of the family too, sharing the bank's disappointments and rejoicing in its successes."[26] When in 1903 Samuel Montagu & Co. reached its fiftieth anniversary, it seemed only fitting "that the celebrations take place not in some anonymous West End banqueting hall . . . but at the banker's own home, 12 Kensington Palace Gardens. And the staff, some sixty all told, who gathered round the U-shaped table, showed their appreciation by composing a poem of twenty stanzas long, in praise of the founder,"[27] as a token of their genuine pride in being part of the company and their affection for Montagu. The September 1885 *Bankers' Magazine*'s description of Montagu illustrates the esteem in which he was held:

His quick perception of profit extricable from the most round-about exchange operation involving the conversion and reconversion of foreign currencies, is a marvel and nothing less. Unlike many men who have made a great deal of money, Mr. Montagu has not been a speculator in the ordinary sense of the word; that is to say, he has never borrowed the money of others with which to play a game of pitch and toss. Persons who follow his method of "business" pocket the profit in case of a lucky result and leave their creditors to bear the loss in the other event. Money— probably more than half a million—has been acquired by hard work, ability and perseverance beyond all praise. His commercial character is one of the best, and if he only bore the name of a great old house, instead of being the founder of a new one, there would be none whose position was higher in the city.[28]

The article concluded that "the nobility and uprightness of Mr. Montagu's character are reflected in his face. He is a credit to the Jews, generally, and we are glad to claim him as an English man of business acting up to and fully sustaining the traditions of energy, caution and extreme shrewdness, on which the wealth of the city and of the city men has been built."[29]

Samuel and Ellen

When he was thirty, Samuel Montagu was not only a successful businessman with enormous self-confidence but also tall, handsome and strong-willed, with a powerful personality. He married Ellen Cohen, a member of one of the most prominent Jewish families in Liverpool, the daughter of Louis Cohen, a respected investment banker; sister of Benjamin Louis Cohen, first baronet; a great grand-niece of Sir Moses Montefiore; and granddaughter of Levi Barent Cohen, one of the leading figures of Anglo-Jewry. Ellen's father was, like other members of the Cohen family, deeply religious, a man of great wealth and a highly respected member in the Anglo-Jewish community of England.

Samuel Montagu and Ellen had ten children, four sons and six daughters. Edwin was the second son and seventh child. The children older than Edwin were Henrietta, Florence, Marion, Louis, Ethel and Lillian. The younger children were Gerald, Elsie and Lionel.

Ellen was overshadowed by the strength of personality of her husband: The chapter on Samuel Montagu in *The Cousinhood,* the story of the great Jewish families of Britain, devoted nine pages to Samuel, seven and a half to his daughter Lillian, more than twenty-five to Edwin, and but a single paragraph to Ellen.[30]

The clearest portrait of Ellen comes to us from the letters of her son, Edwin, who wrote to her daily, as long as she lived. The letters portray a warm and concerned mother trying to provide some perspective and support to offset the rigid standards of a demanding father. While her husband ostensibly left to her the details of running the house, including the health and education of their children, he was too strong a man to make this a complete delegation. She consulted him on all matters affecting the children and his wishes invariably prevailed. She attempted to act as a mediator when conflicts arose. This was especially true with Edwin, who never seemed able to do anything that pleased his father and, from an early age, refused to follow his father's strict Orthodox practice of Judaism.

In later life Ellen was described as a "kind, placid soul, squat and heavy like all the family women, black-clad with a white cap over her white hair, a full face with velvety lined cheeks and a twinkle behind her pince-nez."[31] She lived until 1919, eight years after Samuel's death. Edwin was forty years old.

Samuel Montagu: Politics and Religion

While Montagu was rigidly conservative in matters of religion and was clearly an authoritarian father and husband, he was a radical-liberal in politics. In 1885, when he was fifty-three and Edwin was seven, Samuel Montagu entered politics as a Liberal and was elected a Member of Parliament for Whitechapel. He associated himself throughout his parliamentary career as part of the radical wing of the Liberal Party.

On entering Parliament, he was described as "tall, robust, with broad shoulders, a magnificent head, long, flowing beard and piercing eyes."[32] The fact that he was an Orthodox Jew, whose attire and manner underscored his religious affiliation, was not lost upon the anti-Semitic press, which frequently called him the "Hebrew Candidate" and attacked him in clearly anti-Semitic references.[33]

An editorial in the *Topical Times,* for example, during his first election campaign, wrote of him:

When a small boy [Samuel Montagu] used to polish up the handle of Spielman's front door, changed his quarters from Liverpool to London and his name from Montagu to Samuel to Samuel Montagu, considers himself the best of his kind since Moses the prophet, for he has a good conceit of himself. He has plunged wildly into politics as an out-and-out Radical and spouts like a sperm whale. An upright, downright clever man of business and of no account in politics. A rich banker and a poor orator; a pillar of the city and a pebble—uncut—in society. Unpolished. Very small beer; but thinks himself important.[34]

The anti-Semitism of the *East London Observer* was more subtle: It attacked Montagu not for his religion or lack of Christian manners but for his lack of experience. The fact that scores of non-Jewish candidates also ran for Parliament without experience was not mentioned:

Because he has carried on business in Old Broad Street in the City of London for thirty-seven years is sufficient reason, Mr. Montagu thinks, for urging his suit to sit in Parliament for Whitechapel. But if such a plea could be accepted what an ugly rush might we not expect in the East-End Boroughs of successful men of business. That he is active in community is certainly news to the East-End public. Mr. Montagu's light has evidently been under a bushel, but where? Mr. Montagu has tried to please everybody, but like the old man and the ass, pleases nobody.[35]

The *London Figaro* was one of the few non-Jewish newspapers that both praised and supported Montagu, calling him:

a popular candidate because he professes the ancient faith. He esteems it an honor to be described as a self-made man who by means of hard work has made his way from small beginnings to success far exceeding his anticipations. He has spent much of his wealth for the benefit of his race. He is an advanced Liberal . . . a trifle ambiguous on Ireland . . . a determined Free Trader.[36]

The *London Figaro,* however, was the exception. The anti-Semitic barbs against Montagu and the practice of calling him the Hebrew Candidate were so prevalent that it prompted the *Eastern Post,* a newspaper published for the Jewish community, to protest: "It seems to be exquisite humor in certain Tory quarters to refer to Mr. Montagu as the Hebrew Candidate for the new borough of the Towe-Hamlets. We protest against the injustice of attempting to affix religious labels to political candidates."[37] After Montagu's victory, the *Jewish World* and the *Jewish Chronicle* reported that his opponent, a Colonel Le Poer Trench, blamed his defeat on "the ignorance and partisanship of the Jewish electors."[38]

Fortunately for Samuel Montagu, the anti-Semites did not influence the election. He maintained strong support in his district, which had a significant Jewish constituency, and held his seat in Parliament for fifteen years. His political ideas were an outgrowth of his religious convictions. He took literally Judaism's deep concerns with social justice, with the care of the poor, the ill, the homeless, the widows and orphans, and with the belief that we are indeed "our brother's keeper" and must contribute time and energy and part of our financial wealth to help the less fortunate.

According to his daughter Lily, "he found in the Old Testament the expression of his faith in the separation of the Church and State, in the liability of employment, in the State responsibility for human life and health, in the limitation of the hours of labour, . . . primogeniture, and the accumulation of lands."[39]

In Parliament and out he advocated the provision of evening classes and state guardianship for neglected children. He wanted legal aid for the poor . . . and municipalization of public utilities, like water. He was a keen supporter of death duties, and preferred a higher direct tax to purchase tax, which, he felt, weighed most heavily on the poor. He believed that the hereditary peerage was a serious obstacle to social reform and was treasurer of the League for the Abolition of the House of Lords.[40]

He was also a strong advocate of free trade, reform of the tax systems to help the poor, aid to the small farmer, and even compulsory acquisition of land by local councils, on fair terms, to be sold cheaply to farm workers to stem the tide of migration to the cities. He supported the decimalization of the currency and the adoption of the metric system. In 1894 he persuaded the government to exempt from death taxes works of art and gifts to museums, universities and art galleries.[41]

He was a loyal supporter of Prime Minister Gladstone. When the Liberal Party split over Gladstone's Home Rule for Ireland, Montagu remained faithful to Gladstone, although he disagreed with the Prime Minister over Turkey in its conflict with Russia. Gladstone was anti-Turk and pro-Russia. Montagu was pro-Turk and anti-Russia because of the Russian persecution of the Jews.

Although Edwin disagreed with his father on most issues, they agreed on political ideology. Like his father, he was a radical-liberal and favored free trade, tax and land reform and a pro-Turkish foreign policy. Unlike his father, however, his pro-Turkish policy was based on his concern for Muslim sentiments in India, not on Russia's anti-Jewish pogroms.

Samuel Montagu retired from Parliament in 1900 in favor of his nephew Sir Stuart Samuel at a time when it was thought that a younger man was needed to keep his seat for the Liberals. Later the same year, Samuel Montagu ran for Parliament, at the request of his party in the Leeds Central District against Gerald Balfour, and lost. It was reported that he was not particularly pained by the defeat, which was predictable. After Gladstone's death in 1898, he lost much of his interest in the politics of the House of Commons.[42]

In 1894, on the recommendation of Lord Rosebery, Samuel Montagu was made a baronet and was raised to the peerage in 1907. He enjoyed his seat in the House of Lords and was proud that he was one of the few Lords in the country who came from and belonged to the people. "He took a real pleasure in publicly taking the oath with his head covered," his daughter Lily wrote, and "[h]is first speech in the House of Lords was to champion the small Jewish shopkeeper."[43]

Samuel Montagu and Philanthropy

At the same time that Samuel Montagu fought in Parliament for social and economic reform, he generously used his own financial resources, without publicity, to help those in need, both Christian and Jew. C. B. Fry, the English cricketer, after receiving a substantial gift from Montagu for establishing a training ship for poor boys, said: "He was the kindest of men, and with his splendid white beard accorded with one's idea of Moses. All the kinder of him in that we were nominally a Church of England training ship and he was a strict Jew."[44]

In addition to giving financial support, Samuel Montagu found time to sit on numerous boards of Jewish and non-Jewish philanthropic institutions, including, among his scores of affiliations, the Council of the United Synagogue, the Jewish Board of Deputies and the Russo-Jewish Committee. He helped build a magnificent temple in St. Petersburg Place in the West End of London, described as "a cathedral . . . lofty, pinnacled, and splendid."[45] He traveled to Russia and Poland to examine the situation of the Jews and helped facilitate throughout Europe the movement of Jewish refugees from areas where they were persecuted. At times his trips placed him in danger, but this never stopped him. The *Jewish Chronicle* reported that Montagu and Dr. Asher Asher, the Director of the United Synagogue, went to Russia together to investigate Jewish problems.[46] During the journey, when their passports were checked, they were told to leave Russia within twenty-four hours. He also went to America in 1882 to soothe the Hebrew Immigration Aid Society of New York that sought to stop the immigration of the Jews from England to the United States.

In 1887 he brought all the small synagogues in the East End that had been founded by Russian and Jewish immigrants when they arrived in England into a single Federation, the Federation of Synagogues, and acted as its first President—although most members of the Anglo-Jewish leadership opposed the Federation and were embarrassed by the customs, dress and rituals of the newer immigrants and their dilapidated, tiny synagogues. The story of this monumental effort underscores Montagu's sensitivity to the poor immigrant from Pinsk or Plotsk and his sympathy for the Orthodox religion they were determined to preserve in spite of the opposition of the richer and more established Jews.

He supported Jewish colonization in Palestine and visited there in 1875, but had no sympathy with "political Zionism" and the idea of a Jewish people or a Jewish home. As an Orthodox Jew, he also believed that without the Messiah there could be no Palestine and he did not view any of the Zionist leaders as the Messiah.

Samuel Montagu's belief in a personal Messiah would surprise no one who knew him. He obeyed and believed in the sanctity of every word and every mandate in the Old Testament, the Talmud and the *Shulchan Aruch*, the codification of Jewish law. His Judaism was not confined to merely attending synagogue, fasting on Yom Kippur or inviting his family to dinner on Passover. He believed in obeying all the rules of the *Shulchan Aruch* "in all its aspects and all its minutiae, from the intricacies of the dietary laws to separation from his wife during her unclean period."[47] From these rules, there could be no deviation, no change, no modification. The Bible and Jewish law were sacred; they were given by God and subject to change only by God.

In the face of this rigid position, it took great courage for Edwin to reject his father's orthodoxy and his sister Lily to become one of the founders of Liberal Judaism in England and one of its most important leaders.[48]

Samuel Montagu died of a heart attack on January 12, 1911, at the age of seventy-eight. Thousands of Jewish mourners followed his coffin to its burial place in the cemetery of the Jewish Federation of

Synagogues at Edmonton. He chose not to be buried among his fellow pillars of the Anglo-Jewish community, who were usually buried in the Willesden Jewish Cemetery. Of his grandfather's death, Ivor Montagu wrote: "There can be little doubt of the 'people's love' for my grandfather, whose funeral cortège was followed—so I understand, I was not present—by thousands in Whitechapel, where for many years he had sat as a Liberal member of Parliament."[49]

In spite of the love, warmth and generosity that Samuel Montagu extended to the poor, to the immigrants and to those in need, he was, according to his daughter Lily, "remote . . . and had an almost morbid abhorrence of failure." In spite of himself, she wrote, *"he despised the individual to whom he gave money . . . As he himself had carved his way through very hard circumstances, he had little sympathy with the man who failed to get on"*[50] (emphasis added). How difficult it must have been to be a child of such a man, to grow up in the shadow of someone of remarkable achievement, who abhorred failure, who was rigid in his religious views, who expected his children to be as motivated as he was and at the same time to be docile enough to accept his religious creed exactly as he saw it.

Montagu was not only disappointed in his children's attitude toward religion, but he was also dismayed that only one of his sons, his eldest, Louis Samuel (the second Lord Swaythling), showed any talent for banking. He joined his father's firm immediately after school. Gerald also joined the firm at an early age but was more interested in playwriting than in banking. Lionel, the youngest son, was a playboy for much of his early manhood. He married late and was a man who enjoyed a rich social life and the company of women. He was a great horseman, a member of the Jockey Club, and he kept a stable. When his father asked him to join the family firm, he asked, "On what terms?" "Precisely the same as the rest of the family," his father replied, "five percent of the profits." "In that case," replied Lionel, "might I have two and a half percent and leave at lunchtime?"[51] Lionel chose not to join the Montagu firm until 1927, sixteen years after his father's death.

Edwin, however, may well have been his father's greatest disappointment. He showed no predilection toward banking but wanted to become first a doctor and then a politician. To make matters worse, at an early age he showed open hostility to religion. Unlike his sisters, Marion and Lily, he did not want to reform or change Judaism. He wanted to escape it. Religious dogma and organizations were anathema to him. He never belonged to any Jewish organization and had no sense of responsibility to the Jewish community. He spent his life trying to flee what he called the "ghetto mentality" and pleaded with his father for the right to choose his own religious expression. "Religion," the nineteen-year-old Edwin wrote to his father, "concerns only the individual and can be no man else's concern."[52] Samuel Montagu never agreed with his son. The more they argued over this issue (and over Edwin's choice of a career and money), the more hostile father and son became.

Samuel Montagu was not content to try to influence his children's attitudes toward religion during his lifetime: Even after death he sought to control their religious practices. In his will, he provided that if any of his children married outside the Jewish faith or ceased "professing the Jewish religion," they would lose their inheritance. Of his daughters, Marion and Lily, his will said, "They have, contrary to my wishes, promoted and assisted a movement known as Liberal Judaism, the object of which I strongly disapprove." He directed his executors to withhold three-quarters of their share of the estate, "if they should persist in their efforts."

These provisions in the will, while legally valid, were sharply criticized in England at the time as an example of "one generation [trying] to limit the spiritual freedom of another."[53] Commenting on the public's fascination with Montagu's will, G. K. Chesterton, an outspoken anti-Semite, thought it strange that Englishmen were concerned with Montagu's will, rather than with Jewish power, which he viewed as far more dangerous.

Many Englishmen, and I am one of them, do seriously think that the international and largely secret powers of the great Jewish houses is a problem and a peril. To this, however, you are indifferent. You allow Jews to be monopolists and wire pullers, war makers and strikebreakers, buyers of national honours and sellers of national honour. The one thing you won't allow Jews to be is Jews.[54]

Samuel Montagu's effort to control his children from the grave was not successful. It did not stop his daughters from continuing their support of Liberal Judaism. Indeed, Lily increased her activities for the Liberal movement, traveling throughout England and the

United States on its behalf and earning the title of Judaism's first "Lady Rabbi."

Edwin, in a supreme act of rebellion against his father's orthodoxy, married—soon after his father's death—Venetia Stanley, a Gentile, intellectually an agnostic, outspoken against orthodoxy of any kind and openly critical of the rituals of Judaism. Her conversion to Judaism for no apparent reason except to save Edwin's inheritance was the scandal of her day.

2

Childhood and Early Education, 1879–1898

Of course you take no notice.

Edwin's comment about the teasing
Jewish boys received at Clifton

Edwin Montagu's childhood was spent in the twilight years of the Victorian era, the so-called Indian summer of British aristocracy, the final two decades of a century of British political and economic preeminence. The spectacle of the Queen's Jubilee in 1887, when Edwin was eight years old, with its dazzling procession of royalty from every state in Europe paying tribute to the venerable ruler of the Empire, reinforced the image of a nation at the zenith of its power. The glitter was, however, only skin-deep. Beyond the call of the trumpets was a nation precariously divided between rich and poor, a society that afforded very substantial luxury and comfort for a privileged few but deep and pervasive poverty for the vast majority. The gap between capital and labor was growing, making more apparent the glaring disparities between the extravagances of the rich and the hardships of the poor. Sobriety, family and religion, the trinity of values championed by Queen Victoria, were observed more in the breach than in practice. Religious ties were loosening, and drunkenness and sexual promiscuity were widespread, especially at the extremes of the economic spectrum.

Adulterous house parties, where hostesses arranged sleeping partners as well as dinner partners, and bedrooms were assigned accordingly, had become a de facto part of upper-class English life.[1] It was frequently expected that hunting, shooting and parlor games made up one part of the weekend, and recreational and clandestine sex at night the other, the latter carried out with appropriate and stylish concealment. Thus, marriage was for family, convenience and public occasions; love and passion were often reserved for mistresses, lovers and country weekends. As long as discretion was observed and the rules followed, the charade was enjoyed more or less enthusiastically by all.

As Jews became increasingly assimilated into English society, the Jewish community did not remain immune to these influences. While drinking among Jews seemed less pervasive than among non-Jews, and while marriage and the family seemed still viewed as sacred covenants, the younger, wealthier Jews were prone to engage in the same social and sexual experimentation as their Gentile friends and were increasingly skeptical about the importance of religion and Jewish law in their lives.

As with English society generally, Jewish society was sharply divided between the rich and the poor, with a small number enjoying lavish luxury while the majority was fighting for its survival in the slums of London's East End and in other urban centers.[2] For all classes, it was a world of rapid change. Industrialization, new towns, advances in medicine, public health and education, railway and steamship expansion and voting reform were affecting every aspect of people's lives, irrespective of class. It was a world in which the working-class poor were beginning to express their discontent more stridently and even violently, in which the Toryism of Disraeli, as paternalistic as it tried to be, was giving way to the more liberal philosophy of Gladstone and the Liberal Party.

While thoughtful people could see the signs of danger on the horizon, for those like Edwin Montagu who were lucky enough to be born into families that were rich and powerful, it was still a time of relative peace and prosperity and of great pride in the indisputable supremacy of the British Empire. For Edwin, as for most children of the Cousinhood, it was also a world of the extended family—grandparents, aunts and uncles, nephews and nieces, all ready to help one another by opening doors—a world in which nepotism was the first principle of business, often stifling in its parochialism and sharply regulated by custom and tradition. It was also a world of untold opportunities and horizons.

Money, powerful connections, a devoted family, a natural intelligence and opportunities for the best education combined to give Edwin Montagu a head start that only a privileged few enjoyed. Yet from his earliest days he was an insecure, overly sensitive child, shy, frail, morbid, fearful of the dark, endlessly worrying about his health and desiring constant affection and attention. One of his earliest letters, written to his mother when he was six years old, makes special mention of the fact that his sisters had decorated the nursery, "when we came upstairs we kissed each other."[3] Even at so young an age, affection was something he noticed and thought important enough to be included in a letter to his mother. His early letters frequently mention his German governess, Rosie, with whom he spent a great deal of time and whom he loved dearly. He never failed, in any of his letters home, which he wrote regularly throughout his life, to mention her, thank her for a gift or letter and express his love for her. It was reported that her name was the last word he spoke before he died.[4]

Doreck College: 1887–1891

In 1887, when he was eight, his parents enrolled Edwin in a preparatory school, Doreck College, not far from his home, at 63–64 Kensington Gardens Square. He remained there until he was twelve. Edwin's conduct was excellent and in most subjects he was in the top half of his class, doing especially well in science and languages. His penmanship was atrocious—almost illegible—and continued to be so his entire life. While he was shy and timid, his report cards indicated that in his early years he was working "well and happily," and he was described as "a gentleman in behavior." His homework, however, was not always good, his fingernails were often unclean, and he took no care with his appearance. But overall, he was a "pleasant pupil."[5]

By the time he was ten, his report cards said that he was "disposed to be dictatorial" and that he was "not always kind to his younger brother."[6] He was timid, shy and a gentleman but at the same time could be imperious, callous and unkind.[7] The conflicts in his character were already present.

There were contradictions, too, in his schoolwork. By and large he did well in Latin, algebra and science, but was only average in other subjects. And as the years passed, his report cards would indicate that "he did not always do on exams what he was capable of doing."[8]

During these early years, other lifelong traits began to surface: He was a complainer and very concerned about his health and the health of those around him. In his letters home during these years, he would write, for example, that he went on a trip but did not join the group on their walk because it was "very long." Elsie had "tight boots and could not walk" and "Mina had a cold" and the Empress of Austria was supposed to come to the city he was visiting "but most likely she will not come as she had a cold."[9] On a more positive side, this period of his life also saw the development of his lifelong interests in nature and shooting. He wrote home asking for a bow and arrow and he wanted to be certain his sister Marion was watering his ferns.[10]

By the time Edwin was almost twelve his parents decided that he should go to a boarding school. The opportunity to live with other boys might be a healthy experience for this frail and fearful child. His father chose Clifton College, a preparatory school which since 1878 had had a special Jewish House run, since 1890, by the Reverend and Mrs. J. Polack. Edwin needed special tutoring before he could take the admissions test, since he feared examinations and became anxious and ill when faced with them. As a result his testing did not reflect his intelligence. The tutoring helped. He passed the examinations and his parents enrolled him in Clifton in the spring of 1891.

By the time Edwin entered the Jewish House, it had an excellent reputation and had prepared many of the children of the Cousinhood whose parents wanted them to have a secular education within a Jewish environment. At first Edwin was happy, writing to his mother that he was enjoying himself and that "Mr. and Mrs. Polack are very kind and all, rather nearly all, the boys are nice."[11] In the middle of May he was still happy, bragging that he was good at cricket and while he entered the grade "as 20th in the class; Bob entered 13th. Today Bob is 16th and . . . [I am] 9th."[12] He was clearly proud of this achievement and as a reward "*wants* a full-size bat" and "*wants* a ball" (emphasis added).[13] In the imperious manner observed in his Doreck College report cards, he demanded what he believed was his due.

But by the end of May he was homesick and pleaded with his mother to visit. He chastised her for refusing to tell him exactly when she was coming and copied the train schedule in full in his letter to her as an extra enticement.[14] By June, his loneliness and homesickness had become acute enough for Edwin to end one of his letters with the poignant sentence "So with best love I remain your very lonely son dying to see you."[15]

As the spring wore on, his unhappiness and loneliness increased and he developed headaches that at times became so acute that it was impossible for him to attend class. "Mr. Glazebrook," he wrote, "is commonly known as the Bogey-man. He is not very charming." And to make certain his parents understood he added "in fact he is very horrid."[16] In the same letter, he described the evening activities at the Polacks: each night, two boys would have a bath; at 7:50 P.M. all the boys were given their prayer shawls and prayer books; by 7:55 P.M. they had to stop talking; and at 8 P.M. Mr. Polack would lead them in prayer.[17]

For the first time, Edwin told his parents that the Jews were teased by the other boys. "Of course, you take no notice" was his response,[18] one that would become characteristic of his dealings with anti-Semitism. Throughout his life Edwin would try to "take no notice" of the subtle and often not so subtle anti-Semitism that surrounded him. He would seek to ignore it, turn the other cheek, pretend it did not exist, and hope that by taking no notice it would go away. But Edwin was far too sensitive a child to believe this or truly to take no notice. It is more likely that he did notice, that he internalized his discomfit with it, and that his lifelong concern with the discrimination suffered by Indian students at English universities was a reflection of his own experiences.

Whatever their cause, Edwin's headaches throughout the summer of 1891 became "too awful to bear." "Sometimes," he wrote, "I think I have done something wrong and these headaches (come from overworking and . . . they are the retribution.) Please try and console me in the reply."[19] And again: "I am sorry my happy term should end this way. I can do nothing but cry and console myself by sleep when I feel very bad about crying which however does no good and by the doctor saying that he is sending fifty boys home early this term which is no better."[20]

Edwin's worry about being sent home was an important factor in exacerbating his headaches, as was his fear of ending the term with poor grades.

Here is a pretty state of things. I am utterly miserable. I don't know what to do. I have tried all sorts of remedies but in vain. My headache is unbearable but I must correct your error in thinking I eat too much sweets. I am utterly dejected and half mad with pain and can scarcely bear the sorrow of ending the term in such a poor way.[21]

It was a vicious cycle. Fear of failure increased Edwin's headaches, which prevented him from doing well in school, which in turn caused the headaches to become even more acute. By August 11, 1891, he confessed to "a horrible case of loneliness which makes me feel miserable . . . could not Gerald, Lee or Rich stay with me here."[22]

Even during these dark days Edwin got some pleasure, albeit not enough to overcome his general unhappiness, from trips to study butterflies and jellyfish, and from making bird cages for his friends. During the fall his grades improved. On October 28, 1891, he made "first" and seemed, for the moment, to feel better. But his headaches continued. He wrote to his mother:

I begin to despair of getting rid of them. Please don't worry or be miserable about me, *but try and come down to see me very soon.* I do so want to be comforted. I must work. I shall never be able to get on and I shall never be able to get any scholarships. . . . Please don't show this to anyone. . . . I must get over being so miserable.[23] (emphasis added)

It is not possible to tell from the surviving letters how frequently, if at all, his parents visited him. One thing is certain: His mother did not visit him enough to satisfy him. Nearly all his letters were written to his mother and reveal an overwhelming need for her attention. He had no relationship with his father, of whom he lived in fear. His only letters to his father during this period were those asking for something, accounting for money or reporting his grades.

The decision to send him to Clifton may have been made primarily to end his dependence on his mother, and her decision not to visit him as frequently as he wished may also have been part of a purposeful effort to sever his reliance upon her. She faced heavy burdens at home, with all of Edwin's nine brothers and sisters, ranging in age from eight to twenty-six, still living at Kensington Palace Gardens. All required her attention and care. Lily, who was eighteen, had recently recovered from what we would now call a nervous breakdown and was in constant disagreement with her father about her role in Liberal Judaism.[24] Edwin's father had, only four years earlier, entered politics and this, too, added to the pressures on Edwin's mother. She could not give any single child her sole attention but had to divide her time among ten children, a demanding husband with communal and political responsibilities and the management of two homes and her own activities in the Jewish community.

Edwin's brothers and sisters seemed able to cope with their mother's divided attention more successfully than did Edwin. Louis was eleven before his father went into politics and, as the oldest son, had had his father's attention for five years before Edwin's birth. In temperament he was like his father and they always got along well. The girls had one another and this seemed to substitute for their parents when they were occupied with other responsibilities. Lionel and Gerald, as the babies, had the attention of all the sisters and seemed to develop other interests early on, Gerald in playacting and Lionel in sports. Edwin was caught in the middle: He was too old to be treated as a baby with Lionel and Gerald, and too young to compete with Louis.

Edwin's brothers, moreover, were all robust and generally healthy; Edwin was thin and sickly from birth. By the time he was twelve, his illnesses, whether physical or psychological in origin, became more acute. He suffered not only from headaches and colds but also from anxiety, depression and hypochondria. He had also perfected the ability to use his "headaches" and "illnesses" to attract the attention, if not the time, of his parents.

As his first year at Clifton drew to a close, Edwin's headaches had become so serious that his parents decided to take him out of school for four months, from December 1891 to April 1892, in the hope that a sea voyage around the world would help. He was accompanied by a Hebrew teacher, J. D. Israel, who had the task of not only supervising the details of the trip, as well as Edwin's education, but also making certain that Edwin rested on the Sabbath and the Holy Days and ate only kosher food the entire trip. Assuring that Edwin observed the laws of kashruth was extraordinarily difficult, but Samuel Montagu would have it no other way.

Although the physicians were worried about Edwin's health, the family did not accompany him on the trip, but instead seemed comfortable in trusting Edwin to the care of a young tutor. No one seemed to think that a little more maternal and paternal attention might be as important as sea air. To compensate for his separation from home, Edwin continued his habit of writing to his mother at every opportunity, sometimes twice a day. He explained that he preferred to write to her because in that way "everybody in the family" will see his letters "including Rosie."[25]

His letters were perfunctory, revealing no signs of the talent for writing he would later show in some of his letters to Venetia and in his Indian diary. They report rather cryptically his impressions on seeing New Zealand, Queenstown, Honolulu, Malta, Port Said, Israel, San Francisco, Salt Lake City, Denver, Chicago, Niagara Falls and New York City—only a few of the places he and his tutor visited. Sites of natural grandeur, such as the volcanoes in New Zealand, the rainbows in the water at Niagara Falls and the hot lakes in Israel, were more exciting to him than the cities. "If you have seen one city you have seen them all"[26] was his reaction to Chicago.

His health improved, with Mr. Israel writing at various points along the way that "Edwin's color has returned," the headaches were "much less," and even after a rough passage across the Bay of Biscay, during which Edwin was "very brave," he seemed "happy and well," "hasn't complained of headaches" and now seemed "thoroughly recovered."[27] Mr. Israel did report that earlier in December Edwin had had a cold and fever.[28] He had also had a headache on entering the Red Sea;[29] he occasionally developed "slight headaches but nothing serious."[30]

Throughout the trip Mr. Israel, as instructed, made certain that only kosher food was eaten, even if he and Edwin "had to do without meat for a couple of days." Edwin, he reported, is "none the worse for it . . . he had a mild headache, nothing more."[31] He also made certain that for Passover they stayed at a "Jewish House" in New York City, at 167 East 82nd Street, so that Edwin could participate in the Seder.[32]

On February 6, 1892, while touring Australia, Edwin celebrated his Bar Mitzvah, his thirteenth birthday, one of the most solemn occasions in the life of Jewish boy. It is a time when a young man assumes his responsibilities in the Jewish world. It is the first time he may wear phylacteries (tefillin)—two little black boxes containing special prayers (Exod. 13:1–10, 13:11–16; Deut. 6:4–9, 11:13–21) attached to leather bands. During prayer, the boxes are strapped to the forehead and the arm, as a covenant between God and the Jewish people. The strap and the box on the arm symbolize the commitment of one's body; the box and the strap on the head, the commitment of the mind.[33]

In England, and in most Jewish communities in Europe at the turn of the century, the Bar Mitzvah was not celebrated with the elaborate observance that is prevalent in the United States today. On his thirteenth birthday, a Jewish boy merely put on his tefillin and joined his father in the Synagogue service on the day of his birthday. This was usually followed by a small lunch or dinner for family and friends.

It is curious that the Montagus did not plan a shorter trip for Edwin, one that would have brought him home in time for his thirteenth birthday. Instead, he spent it alone with Mr. Israel, in Australia thousands of miles from home. Mr. Israel, in his regular report to Edwin's father, wrote: "He [Edwin] had his phylacteries on for the first time this week. We intended to celebrate his birthday today with a picnic but bad weather compelled us to lunch at home."[34] As for Edwin, there is no evidence that reaching thirteen made any impression upon him. He made no mention of it in any of his letters, which by and large support Mr. Israel's reports that he was feeling much better and was happy.

He found Mr. Israel "very, very nice," and liked him and the trip very much. This did not keep him from complaining that in Malta he developed a fever and cold and "had to stay in bed,"[35] that Americans think a lot about themselves,[36] and that he was sorry that he would not be home for Passover.[37] He wrote his mother that while traveling was "very nice and it is good to see everything . . . I will be glad to be with you again."[38] He then added, in anticipation of returning to Clifton, "the only pity is I shall have to leave you so soon."[39]

Edwin's parents reenrolled him in Clifton during the summer of 1892. To their dismay, he continued to be miserable. If anything, his letters reflected even greater unhappiness than before his trip. He informed his mother that he was very nervous in class: He feared he would catch the measles, since everyone had it.[40] He regretted she could not visit but added, "However what can't be cured must be endured and I am perfectly content and reconciled."[41] In truth, he was far from reconciled. His letters continued to express unhappiness, loneliness and depression.

Sometime in June or July 1892, his mother reprimanded him on the quality of his work, which brought a rather acerbic response from Edwin: "I do not think your letter was calculated to cheer me up. . . . It is unkind of you to say I don't try. . . . Do I not work as hard as possible. . . . Please don't scold me because it makes me so much more miserable."[42] That July, when his father was reelected to Parliament, Edwin expressed his pleasure at this in a letter—to his mother, not his father. He also asked for some fresh and preserved fruit, ginger, honey and blackberry jam, to be sent "as soon as possible."[43] By the fall, his headaches returned with such virulence that his teachers did not see much of him and reported that "he seems so exceedingly delicate."[44]

His father was very unhappy about his work at school, and this prompted Edwin to write to his mother: "I am very unhappy about Pappa's letter as he seems to think that I lack courage and perseverance and do not do credit to your name? I try very hard to do everything to please you . . . but it is very difficult not to be despondent."[45]

By the winter of 1892 he had clearly made up his mind that Clifton was not for him. He urged his family to visit and relieve his loneliness. On February 6, 1893, he wrote home, "it's not been a very happy birthday." No one in the family visited. The next month, Edwin, whose homesickness and headaches were becoming increasingly serious, had decided that he wanted to transfer to the City of London, a day school on the Victoria Embankment not far from his parents' home. When in April 1893 his report card from Clifton concluded "it's a demoralizing waste of time to keep him at Clifton; in his present condition nothing can be done; his poor health has increasingly made him irregular [in attendance]" and suggested a new school "at which he might make more headway," his parents finally agreed to take him out of Clifton. On April 7, 1893, he was removed from Clifton and admitted to the City of London School, which he officially began in the summer of that year.

The City of London School was founded in 1837 and was one of the few middle-class preparatory schools that admitted Jews. In 1851, out of a total of six hundred boys, seventeen were Jews. By 1893, when Edwin entered, it had a slightly larger Jewish enrollment, but Jews were still a small minority.

This did not bother Edwin. He was now living at home with his parents, sisters and brothers. His headaches vanished and his health and grades improved. After six months, the headmaster gave him permission to take extra science courses as well as to continue his classical studies, so that he would be in a position to take the exams to enter Cambridge when he was ready. Thus, five years before he entered Cambridge, it had already been decided that he would not go into his father's business; he would continue his education at Cambridge in the sciences.

During his adolescence, Edwin's sharp likes and dislikes and his tendency to be hypercritical of others—traits he had exhibited since childhood—became even more pronounced. "Tell Gerald," he wrote in September 1893, that "I don't like Abraham at all and he made a great fool of himself and was idiotic the whole time." [46]

Even his family was not spared his sharp reactions and his sharp pen. Thus, writing about his aunts and cousins to his mother on July 17, 1893, "Ida and Stella arrived last night. I do not like her at all and I do not think she's at all pretty. She, May and Aunt Clara have talked dresses all night and I can't read so it was awful. How can three people talk about dresses for two hours?" In one of his letters in 1895, he expressed anger at his younger sister, Elsie, for doubting that he had written home. "Elsie might have known it was not my fault and her letter was most unkind and unnecessary." And in his imperious tone, he added, "I do not want letters of that kind!"

As a student, Edwin made no particular mark at the City of London School. His report cards there, as at Clifton, frequently noted that he was not fulfilling his potential. His headmaster, interviewed at Edwin's death, only remembered him as a lad "devoted to beetles." A classmate later recalled that he caused an inordinate excitement in class by bringing a snake to school.[47]

Here at the City of London School, Edwin first experienced the pleasure of seeing his writing published. His trip around the world had inspired him to write some articles, "Impressions of a Circumnavigator," which were accepted by the school magazine.[48] The most important contribution the City of London School made to Edwin's development, however, was not increasing his interest in writing or zoology but encouraging his interest in politics. At the age of fifteen he began to take an active part in the School Parliament, holding the office of "Chancellor of the Exchequer."

In this Parliament, which was really a debating society, Edwin began to develop his ability to speak before an audience. In this endeavor, "young Montagu was following in the footsteps of another statesman, to whose influence and help he afterwards owed so much. At exactly the same age, nearly thirty years before, this man was also practicing the gift of oratory."[49] His name was Herbert Henry Asquith.

Edwin left the City of London School in December 1895, at sixteen, to enroll in University College, London, to specialize in biology. This college had a good science curriculum, and if he was going to pursue a career in the natural sciences it was not too early to accelerate his studies in these disciplines.

The curriculum at University College was far more demanding than that at the City of London School, and once again Edwin was unable to withstand pressure without developing physical illnesses. Although he continued to live at home, he often wrote to his mother whenever his parents went to South Stoneham or when they or he went on holidays outside of London. During the first year and a half at the University, his letters were, by and large, cheerful, but by 1897 they were again filled with complaints: He "felt very frightened before exams"; he was "very nervous although I know all the things"; on the morning papers he "did magnificently . . . on the afternoon papers . . . I did very badly. I lost my head."[50] He reported, "I am not feeling very cheerful . . . my stomach is upset."[51] He was again "miserable" and feeling "terribly ill."[52] "Another catastrophe. I went into zoology this morning with a most violent headache which rapidly became worse"; he was "sure" that he failed.[53] Despite his worst fears, in June 1896, Edwin had placed in the First Division of his class (top group), obtained an Exhibition in Biology (an award that qualified him for entering a university) and won the gold medal of the year, given to the candidate who was first in Biology in the Bachelor of Science Examination.

The only relief from tension Edwin found was in the occasional trips he took to study birds. In July 1896 he went on a particularly memorable expedition, a month's walking tour through Scotland and the Orkney Islands, during which he studied hundreds of birds as well as other wildlife, fished, hunted, skinned and mounted several birds of rare species and took extensive photographs of all that he saw. His letters during this trip, unlike the ones written during the school term, were filled with enthusiasm, his joy at spending "another happy day on the moors and among the hills"; and his appreciation of the natural beauty around him. Nothing ever relaxed Edwin as much as exploring wild areas, shooting and studying birds. He could watch a bird in flight for hours, enthralled by the sight of it and its sounds, watching it soar upward with both awe and envy.

None of the other trips Edwin took during these years—to Nice, Monte Carlo, Sweden and Rome with his father or one or another of his brothers or sisters—ever thrilled him as much as his tramps through the wilderness and his ornithological expeditions. On his trips to the great cities he was likely to write: "Louis has a temperature of 97 and a half. His feet are all right but his knees are worse"; "I had a considerable headache this morning"[54]; or "I do not feel any more fit for work than before I went away."[55] But when he was fishing in Ireland in August 1898, his letters were again ecstatic and enthusiastic; he wrote he had a "pleasant journey," with neither headache nor fever.[56]

Although Edwin's father spent a little more time with him during these years, their relationship was not warm. In July 1896, for example, when Edwin took his walking tour through Scotland, he was accompanied by a young man named Jenkinson, who had the responsibility of organizing the trip and making certain the dietary laws were observed. Apparently Edwin's father wrote to Jenkinson, concerned that his son was not having enough meat. Edwin replied angrily to his father that arranging for the kosher meat was entrusted to him, not to Jenkinson, and his father should have written directly to him.[57] He went on to explain that they had brought meat from home and that, as soon as they arrived at a place to which meat could be sent, they placed their order for more meat with Furst's, a kosher butcher in London; as a result, they had meat nearly every day. He added, "In the first place regarding to the utmost possibilities, my *mother's* wishes, we have obtained meat on every occasion on which it was possible."[58] No mention is made of his father's wishes, although it was his father, not his mother, who had insisted on the kosher meat.

Edwin's feelings that his father did not respect him or have confidence in him were expressed often and openly to his mother. On August 4, 1897, he was indignant that his father had asked him to write home at least once a week and complained to his mother: "This is a bad reward for my regularity hitherto. His advice all through makes me regret the bad opinion my father has of my intelligence."[59] In that same letter he told his mother that he might have made "an admirable businessman." But apparently his father did not agree. "He never offered me a place in his business."[60]

In one respect, Edwin was correct. His father did in fact offer to take his other sons into his business as partners or secure for them partnerships in other banking houses. He did not do this for Edwin. But he thought enough of Edwin to send him to college and entertained the hope that he would become a scientist or a doctor. He may not have believed Edwin would make a good financier, but he did not, despite Edwin's belief to the contrary, have a bad opinion of Edwin's intelligence. He was critical, however, of the fact that Edwin was still uncertain about his career.

At seventeen, Samuel Montagu had known exactly what he wanted. He was already working in a bank, living on his own and supporting himself. Edwin, on the other hand, was still supported by his family and utterly uncertain about his future. When he arrived at University College, he was almost sure that zoology would be his chosen career, but two years later he changed his mind. He had not done well on the zoology exam. He tried to pass the Inter-Science Degree exam in July 1897 but failed. "However," he wrote to his mother, "I am not a bit disappointed. I am now getting to see that Zoo is not everything and begin to see that after all I should like to become a doctor."[61]

This, too, did not last long. Briefly, while at University College, he attended University College Hospital as a medical student but, as with zoology, was not ready to make the necessary commitment. He needed more time and more exposure to other disciplines. Finally, he had the credentials to apply to Trinity College, Cambridge, to which he was admitted in October 1898 at the age of nineteen. It was the turning point of his life.

3

Cambridge and the Beginning
of a Political Career

The bar offers the shortest road to Parliament. I must try and go there.

Edwin to his mother, Aug. 10, 1900

Like many of his classmates then and since, Edwin was instantly caught up in the mystery and romance of Cambridge. It was a love that lasted twenty-six years and ended only with his death.[1]

When Edwin entered Cambridge, the University had already undergone major changes because of the educational reforms of 1870 and 1880: Its doors were open to a larger number of Britons; religious tests had been removed in 1871; and teaching had, to some degree, been modernized, with the introduction of more courses in the sciences. Despite the changes in curriculum and admission policies, Cambridge and Oxford were of course still predominately schools for the aristocracy, and their primary goal was the transmission of tradition and to some extent the preparation of men for a life of public service. Trinity College could be especially proud that by 1898 it had produced more leading statesmen than all the other colleges of Cambridge together: two Prime Ministers, Lords Melbourne and Balfour (a third in 1906, Sir Henry Campbell-Bannerman) and nine of the twelve Chancellors of the Exchequer. It was also the college of Bentley, Dryden, Byron, Thackeray, Newton and Tennyson.

While the removal of religious tests had meant the loss of their exclusive Anglican character, Cambridge and Oxford did not lose their Anglican atmosphere. Chapel was still compulsory; life was cloistered; meals, preceded by a Latin grace, were served at long medieval tables; and a midnight curfew was rigidly imposed. This traditional Anglican environment, along with the fact that only a handful of Jews were enrolled at Cambridge, made Edwin's father fear that Edwin would move away from or, worse, reject his Judaism. Samuel insisted, therefore, at the time Edwin entered Cambridge, that he join a synagogue, keep the dietary laws and observe the Sabbath and the other High Holy Days. After a few weeks at Cambridge, Edwin told his father that he strongly objected to these demands and that he did not believe in ritual, which he believed was not a necessary part of being a Jew.

His father was furious, and on October 23, 1898, an exchange of letters began between father and son that expressed more dramatically than any of their other correspondence the chasm that existed between them over Judaism. Samuel wrote:

Dear Edwin:

Your letter has grieved me very much. I have not discussed it with your mother since she is concerned at present with Lily. . . . Nothing can reconcile me to the casting off of religious observance by any of my children. . . . If you are in such a haste to kick over what it has taken thousands of years of sacrifice and self-restraint to maintain, it would be hopeless to think of your returning. . . . It is so easy . . . to get rid of restraints, however beneficial. . . . I only remember one or two cases of return to orthodoxy. *Now I want no other reply to this than one of acquiescence.* [emphasis added]

I should not feel justified in visiting any child of mine whose household was not conducted on Jewish lines (illness of course excepted). Now what I propose is this: That while you remain at Cambridge you keep the Sabbath festivals and dietary laws and when you leave we will discuss your future. . . . It would be a great grief to me to be obliged to keep your younger brothers away from your influence. . . .

I would like you for my sake to enroll in the Cambridge Synagogue on Friday.

This is indeed a serious crisis in your life. You may think it heroic to sever yourself from the observants of your family. I would rather see my children in the humblest walks of life keeping the Jewish observances than reaching the highest positions without religious faith. I attribute my health and success to my observance and feel convinced that you would suffer in many ways by discarding them. I have however a gleam of hope. Your letter is frank and plain spoken and I feel sure you will [feel] honor bound not to sever from our great observance. I have made great sacrifices in my young days and older to keep my religion. I have always looked upon Judaism as a sacred trust . . . handed to me from my late father and which I hoped would be safeguarded by my children. If they reject those principles which I hold as of vital import they will bring down upon my grey hairs much sorrow.

What will your so-called friends think? That Jews . . . have not a Jewish name or Jewish appearance and are now endeavoring to conceal their race by abandoning Jewish observance?

I have written to you at great length and as frankly as possible because I am convinced that a Jew who does not take up his ancestral responsibilities and rejects the ten commandments on which alone society exists commits an unworthy act.

Your loving father,
Samuel Montagu
October 23, 1898 [2]

Edwin was not ready to surrender without arguing his case further. Edwin was a young man who, in the face of a father who implied the threat of dire punishment and who desperately needed his father's financial support, was willing to face his personal Goliath with nothing more than a slingshot. On November 11, 1898, he replied, confirming his allegiance to his Jewishness but rejecting its ceremonies and traditions. He recognized that this would anger his father and threaten his "monetary advantage," but he would "not be false" to the principles in which he believed. He would not reject his Judaism, but he would practice it as he saw fit.

My Dearest Father,

The righteous of every creed have a share in the Kingdom to come.

This is one of the most beautiful truths in the Jewish religion and I would urge you not to forget it or limit its application. Religion concerns only the individual and can be no man else's concern. By race I am an Englishman and my interests are mainly in England but I will never forget that I am a "Jew" and the son of a Jew and I will always be a good Jew according to my sights, my description of a good Jew differing from yours.

I cannot have much opinion of a religion which places as I think, ceremonial in a position it should not occupy and will not stand the test of any [objections] and with regard to your creed you have confirmed this in your letter.

I chose to write when . . . I ought to have spoken but I cannot keep my temper when arguing with you. We have tried it so often. You, just as you did in your letter, leave many questions unanswered and go on to side issues. You will not see it my way. I cannot see yours and further reflection is not useful.

I see my duty clearly and must act by it. You do not see that what I consider is my duty is so, but there is nothing to do about it. No one is to blame for doing what he conceives to be his duty and indeed he is bound to do so.

I fully realize how much I am forfeiting by acting as I contemplate. First of all it is an awful thing to lose a father's love as I fear I am doing now and how I shall live without it I cannot think. But I must not and will not consider the benefits or the monetary advantages. I should by doing so despise and demean myself. I am old enough to think for myself and will not be false to my honour or to myself. However much it grieves me or my relations I must try and be true and honest . . . let us drop the subject for my mind is quite made up.

When you have resisted all temptation to swerve from your duty you have acted rightly and so shall I act rightly, now and always acting up to my convictions. You worry my motives will be misunderstood. I must learn to care nothing for what others say and let them think what they like, strong in my own convictions.

I will never disguise my Jewishness or be ashamed of it (for why should I), but I must leave its ceremonial ritual and law excellent in their way but not parts of a religion.

If I think differently in the future I will change.

As for my brothers, until they come to a reasonable age I will never while with them or you in your houses act in religious matters in any way contrary to the faith in which they were brought up . . . this much I promise.

This then closes the discussion. It grieves me terribly to write like this to a father who does so much for me. I can't help it. Try to forgive me. I must do my duty.

Your very affectionate son,
E.S.M.[3]

Edwin may well have wanted to "close the discussion," but his father was not ready to concede. The subject was too important to him. His response, written immediately on receiving Edwin's letter, revealed the depth of his feelings. It was not, however, the reply of a tyrannical parent. It was softer in tone than his previous letter and sought to convince Edwin that his judgments were "immature." It neither threatened nor bullied him.

The first sentence revealed Samuel Montagu's simple but absolute faith. "Fear God," he wrote to his son. "Keep his commandments, for this is the whole duty of man."[4] To Samuel Montagu God was real. He existed. He had spoken to the Jews at Mount Sinai. He had given them the Law, and they in turn had been chosen to implement and safeguard those sacred words. Such a view of Judaism permits no doubts, no modifications and no picking and choosing among the commandments one wishes to follow. Samuel Montagu continued:

Your letter of the tenth contains such evidence of immature judgement that I feel bound to point them out. You start with a quote from the Talmud. It is an admirable tenet of our faith adopted by the whole Jewish nation in accordance with its broad-minded and general view and also from the fact that the man who wishes it was an Orthodox observant Jew. But what does it mean that a man following the creed in which he was born . . . is not personally responsible if he erroneously [rejects] that creed. [Only] if he acts righteously he will have a share in the kingdom to come. Surely this is quite opposed to what you advance, as it condemns a man who renounces his religion.

No religion can stand the strain of materialism presumably based on science attacking everything that cannot be mathematically proved. . . . That is the peril to which all young people of every sect are exposed. Believe me I do not give too prominent a place to observances. They are necessary for the well being and preservation of the nation. *I cannot however understand how anyone can pick and choose in the Commandments. How can he accept that which prohibits murder and theft and yet reject those which enjoin keeping the seventh day holy and honouring parents?*[5] (emphasis added)

Samuel Montagu closed by expressing more of a hope than a fact: "It appears to me that very little separates us. I ask you to observe the Sabbath Festivals and Dietary Laws while you are at Cambridge."[6]

Samuel Montagu was mistaken. A great deal did separate Edwin and him and an attempt to reconcile their differences by argument or persuasion was fruitless. They each started from totally different premises. Samuel Montagu had made a leap of faith: All the rest followed logically and with ease. Edwin had not. Whatever "God" meant to his father, He did not exist for Edwin. The Ten Commandments and Jewish law, in Edwin's mind, were man-made; what man could make, man could change. To his father they were immutable mandates given to the Jewish people by God. The differences could not be bridged. Lily Montagu understood this and her involvement in the development of Liberal Judaism as a separate branch of Judaism was her response to the problem.

The argument between father and son subsided after this exchange of letters, with each man compromising and neither happy with the result. Edwin agreed to observe the Sabbath whenever he was home for the weekends, to spend Passover and the High Holy Days with his family whenever possible and to attend synagogue on these occasions, in spite of his distaste for what he called "public worship." On March 18, 1900, he wrote that going home for Passover "is a great nuisance," but he did plan to go home for the holidays "and as a result will have to come to Cambridge a few days before Passover."[7] On March 19, 1900, he explained that he didn't know exactly when he would come home. "Sabbath was out much earlier." He then explains that the time of the Sabbath does not concern him "except when I have to come home."[8]

As for the High Holy Days, the Jewish New Year and Day of Atonement, Edwin wrote to his father on October 14, 1902, that if he knew his father wanted him home for the holidays, he would come. "I will never spend a Festival or Holiday away from home without your consent and will go the Synagogue the first and last days of every festival and whenever you ask me." He hoped his father would forgive him for failing to come home for this holiday.[9]

This was a far cry from the rebellious and hostile tone of his exchange of letters with his father three years earlier. He had acceded to his father's wishes to attend synagogue on the Jewish holidays and had agreed to observe the Sabbath, at least when he was home. There is no evidence, however, that he joined a synagogue in Cambridge or observed the dietary laws except when he was in his parents' home. One of his bills from Cambridge for tuition and other items, dated March 25, 1901, reveals that he paid not only tuition but also £4 13s. 9d. for "Dinners."[10] This suggests that he was eating in the Trinity Dining Hall which was, of course, non-kosher. When he became active in various clubs and in the Union, he often ate his dinners with the club members, which was another impediment to Edwin's observing the Jewish dietary laws.

All in all, he seems to have resolved his conflict over religion with his father by compromise: He obeyed some of his father's wishes and ignored others. This continued to grieve Samuel, who came to recognize what Edwin's political adversaries would learn in years to come: Edwin was a very stubborn man whenever he felt deeply.

Illness

Religion was not the only area about which Edwin continued to worry his parents. His letters, as in the past, were filled with reports of accidents and ill health, including coughs,[11] headaches,[12] despondency,[13] a swollen ankle,[14] lack of energy,[15] colds and fever,[16] fainting from fatigue,[17] falling down the stairs and fracturing his toe,[18] and suffering from influenza, which caused him to be "seized with a fit in the night." "I can't get warm at night," he wrote to his mother, "and hardly sleep at all."[19] He even suffered carbon monoxide poisoning from a stove that was poorly installed and as a result, required oxygen "every four minutes" to regain consciousness.[20]

If he was not suffering from an illness himself, he was writing home about measles epidemics, scarlet fever and other calamities which, according to Edwin, were threatening the very life of the student body at Cambridge. His symptoms always became more acute before an exam or a speech. As in the past, he was invariably certain that he would do poorly, that he would fail and that life would hold nothing for him save disaster and misery.

Sense of Paternal Rejection Grows

Throughout his years at Cambridge, Edwin felt that even when he did well on exams no one in the family seemed to care. He was especially hurt that his father "for some unknown reason" took no interest in his school work.[21] He believed he had "forfeited" his father's love, and "a father's love is higher than a mother's because he can withhold it. . . . In spite of his great kindness I can't help feeling that it [his father's love] is being withheld from me," he wrote to his mother on December 12, 1898.[22] By the time Edwin was nineteen, his sense of paternal rejection was nothing new; he had expressed this in his earliest letters. Nor was it imagined. A healthy, robust man like Samuel had little patience with this frail and sickly son, filled as he was with fears and phobias. Samuel was a reserved and unemotional man, who admired strength and success and abhorred failure. He did not understand a child like Edwin, who craved affection, was constantly fearful and showed no evidence that he could successfully navigate the challenges of life. To Samuel, Edwin was a great disappointment. Edwin felt this keenly.

Politics As a Career

By December 1899, Edwin had decided against becoming a doctor, since he was not clever enough in the sciences. A public career in Parliament, he wrote to his mother, "was the highest career a man can seek" and the "law was the best route to reach Parliament."[23] Having chosen the law and politics, Edwin continued to have doubts and fears about his future. On January 7, 1900, at the age of twenty-one, he wrote to his mother that he was "miserable to think of the failure my life has been hitherto." He reported further that he had "failed to get a first in my Tripos. . . . I am not good at science. I shall fail to keep myself alive I suppose. If only I had the means, I believe I might do something by travelling and collecting, but it would be a very mean fate for all my ambitions." He then wrote: "Could I farm I wonder: I feel it must be the Bar but how shall I succeed there after all my failures. . . . I have just been refused a part in the Greek play next term, a thing I desired above all things." But he ended the letter: "It must not be thought that I am unhappy at being a miserable failure. I try to be, but this place and the people are so delightful it is impossible."[24]

By summer 1900 his doubts seemed to have vanished. He had made up his mind to make politics his career, with membership in Parliament his goal. "The Bar," he wrote his mother on August 10, 1900,

offers me the shortest (and it is long enough) road to Parliament. I must try and go there, not because the work is likely to be congenial but because I believe it to be possible and I hope to persuade my father to let me begin eating dinners next October. Had I been born to possess riches I think my ideal would have been to possess land, to work and farm it myself and to represent the neighborhood in Parliament. That dearest mother is the dream of one who loves the country and the country pursuits but is tinged with some not inconsiderable ambition and self-conceit—a dream none-theless beautiful and comforting because it is impossible because of the

dismal horizon of failure which stares me in the face. . . . Please show this
to my dear father and try to help him to understand me for I think he
fails.[25]

Samuel Montagu was strongly opposed to politics as a career for
Edwin. His opposition appears to have been based on the fact that
Edwin did not demonstrate to his family that he had the personality
to win the support of electors and never showed any interest in
cultivating people and attracting friends, both important traits for a
successful politician. Father and son were again at loggerheads, with
Edwin convinced that his father totally failed to understand him.
"What you say about my father," he wrote to his mother on August
13, 1900,

confirms me in saying that he does not understand me. To all who know
me and who are capable of judging it is obvious that I can't be a surgeon or
a doctor. Not only am I not fitted for it but I hate the idea of disease too
much. . . . Further, father can't understand that one may be devoted to
zoology as I am without wishing to make it a profession.

He explained again that he liked natural history more than zoology
in a laboratory.

The country is what I want but I must satisfy my ambition as well and
have the conviction, which as you know I have had for a long time, of
going to the Bar where I might succeed in earning money to go to Parliament. One must begin young in politics, my father knows that—why then
does he prevent me? How Louis dares to counsel opportunities when he
laments that he himself did not become a barrister, I cannot conceive, but I
am too tired and awakened now. . . . So we must postpone discussions till
I return home.[26]

A week later, he wrote again: "No use talking about my future. It is
so useless to try and make you and father understand what you can't
and won't understand and so I give it up."[27]

In fact Edwin did not "give it up." He continued to try to make
his case repeatedly. After two months of persistent pressure, his
parents capitulated. In October his father finally agreed to permit
Edwin to study law. He assured his father that he would "never
regret this," that he would "work very hard" and become "a Bencher
of the Inner Temple."

Even as Edwin argued with his family about his career in politics and law, he had already entered into the political life of Cambridge. In 1899, a few months after entering Trinity, he was invited to join the Liberal Club, one of the most important clubs at Cambridge, where budding politicians had the opportunity to debate the great issues of the day at dinners sponsored by the Club and meet some of the prominent figures in Liberal politics. At one of the dinners held by the University Liberal Club in 1901, the chairman was Mr. Asquith who was at the time a Member of Parliament, a former Home Secretary in the Gladstone government, and a rising star in the Liberal firmament. Edwin delivered his first speech in the presence of the future Prime Minister, and he made enough of an impression for Asquith to congratulate him afterwards and for a writer for the *Manchester Guardian* ten years later, when Edwin became Asquith's Parliamentary Private Secretary, to recall a particular line that Edwin used in that speech. "I am not an ordinary undergraduate," Edwin had declared. Mr. Asquith's eyebrows had risen slightly. "No undergraduate is," continued Edwin, to the amusement of the group.[28]

Edwin rose to become Secretary of the Club in May 1902, when Sir Edward Grey was the principal speaker, and was the President of the Club in 1903, when Lloyd George visited Cambridge. At that dinner, Edwin was the chairman and described the University Liberal Club as:

A body mainly composed of youthful students who have no dire concern with practical politics, who are voteless for the most part, are unrepresented and who feel the burden of the rule of government of the University and its impositions far more than the government of this country and its impositions. From this sheltered outlook we have considered the questions of recent times and we have laid by a store of political maxims which we hope to submit to the test of time and the test of maturer criticism.[29]

Lloyd George not only congratulated Edwin on "managing so successfully to keep order" but, in what was meant to be a humorous aside, suggested that he was qualified for the speakership of the House of Commons. It may have been a humorous aside for Lloyd George, but one can be certain that Edwin took it very seriously. Even at the age of twenty-four he was driven by ambition.

Edwin also became a member of the prestigious Union Society, at the cost of £4 a year. For this fee, he received daily newspapers, had access to a good library and had the chance to participate in a debate a week. He spoke in more than thirty debates in the Union, was responsible for at least six motions before the House of the Union, led the opposition two or three times and was the second supporter or opponent on several other occasions. The *Cambridge Independent Press,* in its obituary of Edwin, commented:

This is a striking record when one considers the comparatively short period that an undergraduate is associated with the Union and the large membership it possesses. I imagine that few statesmen who have been at Cambridge or Oxford for that matter, can show a similar record of activity. Mr. McKenna, one of the Cambridge men who have risen to the Chancellor of the Exchequer, has confessed that he only took part in one debate.[30]

It was at the Union Club that Edwin developed his speaking abilities, which even then were impressive. He was soon recognized as one of the best speakers in the Union. There was scarcely any subject on which he did not have something to say, and he seemed equally successful whatever the topic of debate. The *Cambridge Independent Press* reported too that Edwin's maiden speech, delivered with wit and humor, was hailed by one scribe whose duty it was to record the debates for an undergraduate journal as "the best maiden speech heard for a long time."[31]

While he appeared poised and self-confident in delivering his speeches, Edwin was in fact very nervous and suffered from his characteristic illnesses and headaches before each delivery. Immediately after his maiden speech, he wrote to his mother:

I was suffering from an awful headache and felt very ill. I had nothing to eat all day. I began quietly amid absolute silence. The House was asleep, but I soon roused them. More by my voice which was truly pathetic than anything, I succeeded actually in awakening and moving a Union audience. I saw that they had all come down to vote against me and I resigned myself to tub-thumping. The Union rose as one man and hissed Smuts and Schreiner, who I held up to them as examples of Cambridge men. I could hardly help laughing at them.[32]

Two weeks later, Edwin delivered his second speech and the comments were even more glowing. "'His delivery," according to the *Cambridge Independent Press,* "is easy and confident and his voice clear and pleasant." He treated his subjects "in a light and original manner" and showed himself capable "of dealing seriously with serious questions."[33]

One of the first debates in which he took a leading part was on the eve of Queen Victoria's eighty-second birthday, when Edwin supported a motion "that the abolition of Monarchy will soon be a necessity."[34] The motion was an unpopular one, but Edwin motivated a vigorous defense on its behalf. In those years, he was a harsh critic of the monarchy—a position which he shared with his father who had strongly opposed hereditary privilege. Edwin argued that the monarchy had no purpose other than to "furnish a convenient anthem with which to close popular entertainments." The monarchy, he argued further, "hindered progress, it was expensive and it was merely ornamental. . . . Surely the time is coming when everyone will realize that charity on the large scale cannot be undertaken by the British Government and that the charity as at present exercised is an ignorant piece of childishness."[35] Defending a resolution to abolish the monarchy was just the sort of topic Edwin loved to debate. It gave him a chance to shock, to be disrespectful of authority and to bring to bear the full range of his cynicism, wit and humor, which could often be both sharp and trenchant. At Cambridge, such style enlivened what generally were boring and dull student presentations. In the real world of Parliament that Edwin would soon enter such a style did not win friends and attract supporters to his side. It antagonized and infuriated the opposition. But at Cambridge it brought him wide attention and a reputation as one of the Union's most articulate, effective and amusing speakers.

In 1902 Edwin debated a motion in which he urged that "a very hearty welcome [must] be given to Indians wishing to take part in the government of India."[36] This expressed a deeply felt hostility against discrimination of any kind, especially against Indians studying at the universities in England, who, he believed, would always carry back to India the sense of hurt and humiliation they received at the hands of bigoted English students. Even after he left Cambridge this was a point Edwin made repeatedly in later years as Under Secretary of State and later as Secretary of State for India, as he pleaded for the integration of Indian students into English university life.

During 1902 the Cambridge Union, on Edwin's recommendation, invited John Maynard Keynes to speak. Keynes at this time had just entered Cambridge and had brought with him from Eton the reputation of being a brilliant scholar. Keynes later said that accepting the Cambridge Union invitation was "the bravest thing I ever did." One of Keynes's biographers adds: "*Granta,* the undergraduate newspaper, thought it [Keynes's speech] excellent. So did the President of the Union, Edwin Montagu. . . . Montagu, a rising Liberal politician, was Keynes' first and most important political patron. . . . Maynard [Keynes] had much reason to be grateful to him in the early part of his career. At the Union, Montagu was more taken by Keynes' logic than by his delivery."[37] This visit would mark the beginning of a long and important friendship for both men.

Despite his success at the Union, Edwin continued to feel rejected by his father, envious of his brothers' success, anxious about his future, and convinced he was doomed to failure. When his brother Lionel did well in school, Edwin wrote his mother: "It is gratifying to me to think that my father will find in Lionel someone who will be successful in school and position and also in life. I work hard but the prizes go to real ability . . . I get nothing."[38] When Lionel was told by his father that he was not going on to the University but directly into the banking business, Edwin found cause to feel depressed, blaming himself for Lionel's plight. "Can't you help him?" he pleaded with his mother: "He ought to go to the University. . . . I feel as though I were to blame and though he never reproaches me, I think he thinks so too . . . Poor Lionel. It is a pity."[39]

Edwin need not have worried. Lionel, after working in banking for three years, eventually persuaded his father to permit him to go to Oxford, promising that upon graduation he would return to the banking business. He received his B.A. from New College in 1905 and an M.A. in 1911. He kept his word and after graduation became a partner in A. Keyser & Co., founded by Ellis Franklin, Lionel's uncle, with money supplied by Samuel Montagu. He joined Samuel Montagu & Co. in 1928, long after his father died. Edwin's third brother, Gerald, also went into banking, joining his father's firm as a partner in December 1900 at the age of twenty.

While he was happy for his brother Gerald's partnership, it triggered again Edwin's great fear that everyone but he was moving forward with their lives and only he, almost twenty-one years old, was still a student, uncertain of his future and dependent on his father. "Now," he wrote to his mother on December 26, 1900,

two of my brothers are prospering and there is an offering for a third while I—oh mother my situation, coupled with my ambition, I have perhaps more ingrained than any member of my family, love of what money can procure such as comfortable surroundings, travel and especially sport. And neither my ambition nor my financial hopes are any nearer to realization and I am getting very old. What is to become of me?

Edwin asked his mother to help him: "to find out what my financial prospects are, how long my present allocation is likely to continue and whether there is a prospect of an increase, and more important still, a decrease at any distant date, how far my father will help my parliamentary ambition and so on. Help me get this information."[40]

His mother was unable to help. She had little or no influence on her husband's attitudes toward money. Although by now Samuel Montagu was extraordinarily rich, he was not generous to his children, particularly his sons. He expected them to work and earn their own way as soon as they were old enough to do so. Of his four sons, Edwin at twenty-one was still requiring the support that his father gave only grudgingly and with many strings attached. Edwin's hostility by this time knew no bounds. On October 2, 1900, while still at Cambridge, he lashed out in a letter to his mother about his "father's constraints." "He demands of me," Edwin complained, "that I obey the letter of *his* law. He never shows parental pleasure or affection and I won't do it anymore. I'm sick of it."[41]

Such outbursts were of little avail. Samuel Montagu was as rigid about money as he was about religion. As long as he lived, he doled out money to Edwin sparingly, demanding detailed monthly accounts of every penny Edwin received. Samuel Montagu's grandson Ivor described his grandfather's attitude toward giving Edwin money as cruel and humiliating, a noose around Edwin's neck almost until he became a Cabinet member.[42]

By 1901, Edwin had found time to become firmly entrenched not only in the Union, but in many of the other extracurricular activities offered at Cambridge. He found great pleasure in amateur theatricals. He became a member of the Actors Dramatic Club and took a strong interest in its activities. For a time he filled the office of librarian and was later Acting President.

Each undergraduate at Cambridge was required to perform at least once in a Greek play. In November 1900 Edwin appeared in the student production of Aeschylus's *Agamemnon*. During one of the performances Edwin was also scheduled to speak on behalf of a motion at the Union. He left the performance hurriedly but arrived at the Union late. He apologized by explaining that he had come a long way—"from Argos"—and that his lateness was due to the fact that "Troy had been taken." He received "a loud round of applause for converting a possible disaster into a resounding success."[43] It was this occasion to which a local supporter referred several years later when alluding to Montagu's abilities as a candidate for Parliament: "A man who can reel off the opening oration in a Greek play before an audience which includes the Regius Professor of Greek, and twenty minutes later be seen in modern evening dress speaking to a pleased and applauding audience must be blessed with a resourcefulness which is urgently needed in Parliament."[44]

Edwin was also a member of the most celebrated of all the college debating societies, the Magpie and Stump. This society, founded in 1866, counted among its members some of Trinity's most distinguished alumni. It was founded to offset the seriousness of the Union and to provide a platform for debating light topics. For Edwin, it was another outlet for his wonderful sense of humor, which by this time was recognized throughout Cambridge. In addition, Edwin was elected for four terms co-editor of *Granta,* the University's humor magazine, a great and unusual honor.

Unlike most Cambridge men, who viewed group athletics, especially rowing, cricket and soccer, as being almost as important as their academic studies, Edwin cared little for sport. The great event of the year was the Inter-University Regatta and the boat crews were the heroes of the University. While Edwin occasionally participated in the boat races and mildly enjoyed them, he was totally disinterested in this aspect of University life.

While at Cambridge Edwin does not appear to have had any serious love interests. If he did, his letters gave no hint of it. In the hundreds of letters that have survived from his Cambridge days, only one mentions a young woman. In a letter to his mother, sent at the end of 1901, he wrote: "Hannah is staying at Somerville and we got on surprisingly well. I liked her enormously, so that I was not surprised to receive an invitation, although it is rather soon. I'd like to go but if they truly wanted me they shouldn't have given me such a ridiculously short notice."[45]

Here again Edwin evinced the familiar conflict within his personality: On the one hand, there is arrogance in his comment that he was not surprised to receive an invitation from Hannah and her family. On the other, there is insecurity in his uncertainty that they really wanted him, since they gave him such short notice. A less insecure man might have believed that the shortness of notice showed Hannah's genuine impatience to see him as soon as possible. But Edwin could only draw the most negative conclusions from any set of facts that involved a judgment about himself.

Being a Jew at Cambridge

Edwin paid little or no attention to his Jewishness at Cambridge and was successfully assimilated into the University culture. The fact that he became President of the Union Society and the equally prestigious Magpie and Stump and co-editor of *Granta* is evidence of his success. It is evidence, too, of the spirit of religious tolerance that seems to have prevailed within these University clubs.

But attitudes within these student organizations did not represent the views of all clubs at Cambridge or of the Cambridge administration. There the intrinsic snobbery and old boy network that was part of Cambridge and Oxford still prevailed. Jewish students would be tolerated but never given genuine acceptance.

In later years, in his speeches on India, he strongly condemned the prejudice and discrimination Indian students experienced while attending English universities. His plea that the universities "extend a hand of friendship not patronizing tolerance" and his poignant descriptions of the "loneliness and unhappiness" of the "friendless, sensitive young Indian boys" exposed to the "insular reticence and prejudice" of Oxford and Cambridge strongly suggest that while speaking on behalf of the Indians, he was referring as well to his own experiences.

Sir Lawrence Jones, in his autobiography *An Edwardian Youth*, recalls his first meeting with Edwin and the reaction of one of the deans of Trinity when Edwin's parents invited Lawrence to spend a vacation bird watching at Stoneham. Sir Lawrence recalls that the dean referred to Montagu's parents as "very rich Jews" but refused to take the responsibility for encouraging such a weekend: "So, I missed the chance of making friends with an older man whose subtle and sensitive mind would, I cannot but think, have brought me nothing but good. I was indignant, but can hardly, in retrospect, blame my parents."[46]

Appearance: His Eyes Dominate

Edwin was not a physically attractive young man. According to Sir Lawrence, he had a "long, ugly, bony face marked like a photograph of the moon." He appeared "unbelievably mature, almost world weary . . . his eyes held me, sombre, patient, unhappy eyes, of extraordinary intelligence. He held the talk: he was sophisticated and mocking, more amusing I thought than anyone I had met."[47]

Montagu's physical characteristics did not change over time. He continued to be described as ugly, ungainly, with piercing eyes, tall and somber, with a pockmarked face. Later in life, at about the age of thirty, he began to go bald and also to wear a monocle over his right eye, which made him look both fearsome and scholarly.

His eyes were the central feature of his face: remarkable, expressing both intelligence and compassion, and sparkling with humor and kindness. When he wanted to be, he was "the warmest and most amusing of companions, a man whose ugliness was obliterated by his charm."[48] At other times, he was moody and solemn, and his eyes looked dark and foreboding.

Completing His B.A.

In April 1902, Edwin finally received his B.A. degree. He proudly wrote to his father, "My scientific education has now been completed and on Tuesday next I shall have my Bachelor of Arts from the University of Cambridge."[49] With his typical sense of humor, he added; "Instead of them paying me for getting through the examination I have to pay them for my degree twelve pounds." He asked his father to pay this sum "before midday on Sunday."[50]

Although Edwin's grades were only average, he did achieve both recognition and respect among students and faculty. As he wrote to his father in 1903:

My achievements will then [at age twenty-two] be

—1 honours degree, two parts Science
—1 Presidency of the Union
—1 Acting Presidency A.D.C.
—1 Secretary Cambridge University Liberal Club
—1 Presidency Magpie and Stump
—a certain amount of fame
—a certain amount of notoriety
—a certain number of friends
—a few enemies
—and a glorious time of four years and a term.[51]

Having convinced his father that he had a future in politics, Edwin remained at Cambridge and began the study of law. His mother suggested that he might prefer to live at home and take his advanced degree at a university in London to save the cost of living at Cambridge. This he could not do. His conflicts with his father were too disturbing for him to consider living at home, although he was still dependent on his father for support. He wrote to his mother:

Much as I love all at home, yet I realize that it will be difficult for me to fit in as a resident there. We must, I suppose, try, but the strain, the terrible friction, the different interests and the difference of religions will be terrible. Here [at Cambridge] God knows there is worry enough to drive me mad, but it is with things and not with people—all is peace. At home I think it is primarily a difference of education and a difference of religion that will make things difficult. . . .

. . . You say things worked smoother last vac—only because most of the friction landed against Nettie. Under the circumstances, I think I must be allowed now and always my solitary breakfast that I love as opposed to the letter-reading food scramble of K.P.G.[52]

And so he remained at Cambridge, preparing for the political goal he had now set for himself.

As early as 1902 he had begun to accept engagements at meetings when the Liberal Party needed a speaker. On June 30, 1902, for example, he wrote to his mother that he had on his schedule three speeches in Cambridge, one in Oxford, one in Edinburgh and six others in the provinces. He was rated as "the most brilliant speaker on the Liberal side among the students of his day at the Union and his services were eagerly sought and readily given. In this way he was brought closely in touch with village life and acquired valuable experience in rural problems which was afterwards to stand him in good stead."[53]

By 1903, it was generally acknowledged that he probably would be the next candidate for the West Division of Cambridgeshire. An official designation would not take place until 1905, which gave him two years to assure his adoption.

The Law and Edwin's Entrance into Politics

While working to assure his political nomination, Edwin began in April 1902 to prepare for the Bar and to clerk in a solicitor's office —Messrs. Coward, Hawksley & Chance at 30 Mincing Lane. Working in a solicitor's office was common practice for young men studying for the Bar. It also gave Edwin some additional insights into the problems of the residents of the area, while earning some extra money for his political activities.

His father had been instrumental in getting him this employment. While Edwin was grateful for the job and the money, he despised practicing law. "No work has ever bored me more," he wrote at the time. Several years later he said scornfully of the law:

It is a profession which I would never recommend to, or willingly see adopted by, anybody I was fond of. It is a bloodsucking, all-domineering profession, which takes a man who practices it, twists him and distorts him, and demands from his youth, energy, vigour, long years of disappointment and despondency, waiting for practice and bitter regret when the practice arrives; work from morning to night, without excitement, without reward, not allowed to choose the subjects which engross you, with a hidebound etiquette and a cynicism which is not even surpassed by the medical profession itself.[54]

In the autumn of 1903, Edwin convinced his father that he and a friend, another active young politician, Auberon (Bron) Herbert should to to Canada to see for themselves how the Canadians felt toward free trade and whether the Tory Party and Joseph Chamberlain's proposed "Imperial Preference" had the support of Canada, an important dominion within the British Empire. Free trade was a major tenet of the Liberal Party philosophy and was at this time under serious political attack.

Edwin and Bron Herbert left for their fact-finding mission in December 1903. They worked hard, paid all their own expenses, interviewed hundreds of Canadians and published their findings in a book, *Canada and the Empire,* in which they concluded that Canada did not want Imperial Preference but supported free trade.[55] Popular interest in the book was heightened since Lord Rosebery, intellectual leader of the Liberal Imperialists at the time, wrote the introduction, in which he said:

The authors are two young men, sincere and convinced Imperialists, who went to Canada last autumn with the earnest desire to ascertain the truth for themselves and on the spot. They have here laid bare before the public the results of their inquiries, which will tend to strengthen the position of those who see in the new fiscal policy not a probable bond, but a possible dissolvent of the Empire.[56]

With the publication of this book, Edwin gained considerable stature within the Liberal Party. He learned at a young age that being a well-received author was an excellent way to gain public attention.

It was now only a question of time until he was officially chosen as the representative of the Liberal Party in West Cambridgeshire to run for Parliament. His father had in the meantime gotten him another job, again as a lawyer, to begin in 1904. Edwin disliked this as much as his first job and struggled for a year to convince his father to release him from this arrangement and give him sufficient support so that he could concentrate on running for office. "I am struggling. You have allowed me to embark on a political career and I think I have shown you that I have great enthusiasm and ambition in the field. But I need funds. . . . I won't give up politics."[57]

By December 1904 Edwin was not only devoting every spare moment to politics but also working and continuing his studies for the Bar, which required that applicants first pass a difficult Constitutional Law Examination. He found this exhausting and was often sick and lonely. In a letter in 1904, he wrote:

Oh mother darling, you have no notion of the unhappiness in my life. You and all my brothers and sisters have always been able to live at home in plenty. I am so terribly lonely seeing no friend or relation from week to week and talking nothing but politics. The work I like immensely, the life I like, but it is so terribly, so maddeningly lonely, and I am driven mad

with money troubles. . . . It was assumed that I was not to be a businessman when I was twelve and since then I have had to find my own way
more and more each step onward.[58]

Finally, after months of continued arguments and pleading, Edwin's father agreed to release him from work as a lawyer and to pay
his political expenses (but only his political expenses) if Edwin agreed
to submit detailed accounts to his father each month, justifying each
expense as a political necessity. Edwin reluctantly accepted this humiliating arrangement. He was now free to move into an even more
active political life, free from the burdens of legal work. Every
penny he received from his father was given by a man who despised
failure and had respect only for those men who could make it on
their own. His father's attitude only served to aggravate Edwin's
anxieties and sense of failure. On June 14, 1905, he wrote to his
father:

I fully realize that I am, and must be for the rest of my life, in an uncomfortable position with regard to my two younger brothers. You placed
them in positions which assured them, eventually luxurious incomes and
great material prosperity. You placed me in a position to spend such
income, if I had it, with the possibility of making a few odd shillings with
a profession which is over-crowded and which completely saps a man's
energy and prevents his doing other work. . . .

I fully realize that the gift you gave me was the more valuable, for it
must have cost you more pain to give it to me in that I fear I have not in
any way and in nothing that I undertake [gained] much of your approval.
. . . the chances of partnership in two flourishing financial concerns . . .
although financially more valuable, cost you both financially and morally
less than the possibility of notoriety which you gave me. . . . I leave no
stone unturned to get called to the Bar, although if in moments of impatience you wish that I should practice, that in my opinion somewhat a
degrading profession, I remind you that . . . my sole reason for desiring to
be called was to know something of the Law. . . .

There is of course assistance . . . from political organizations, but this
means you lose political independence.[59]

Edwin wrote that he was trying to earn some money "by taking
writing assignments" but this was both difficult and time-consuming. As an aside, he asked his father if he might be permitted to
"send in his accounting quarterly, not monthly." He considered the
cost for renting his rooms in Cambridge a "political expense" and

as such should be paid out of his father's allocation. He also defended the fifteen pounds he had given a friend in financial trouble:

With regard to the 15 pounds you, I believe, have never been in financial difficulties—I have. And when a man comes to me and tells me of the ruin and disgrace which are staring him in the face, of the widowed mother, and a ne'er-do-well brother depending on him, when I know that his story is true, when I know him to be respectable, and when I know that perhaps by privation I can one day make up the possible loss—I am sorry if you consider it extravagant but I cannot resist the appeal.[60]

It was particularly difficult for Edwin to plead for money every month, knowing his father's attitude toward men in need. Only the strongest motivation could have kept him on this track in the face of such an impediment. What joy he must have felt when, in 1905, he not only received his M.S. but in November passed the Constitutional Law section of the Bar Examination. He wrote to his father:

If you have read your *Times* this morning, as I suppose you did, you will have noticed that, as I had hoped, despite my protestations I have succeeded in passing the Constitutional Law Exam. This was the chief obstacle to my being called to the Bar and I hope now to get through without further failure.

I am glad, I know it will please you. I did more than I had to as I was among the top ten or twelve.[61]

Edwin's Nomination

A month later, in December 1905, Edwin's efforts came to fruition: The Liberal Party in West Cambridgeshire adopted him as its candidate for the upcoming election in 1906. His selection was uncontested.[62] By 1905, Edwin had lived in Cambridge for seven years. He was a much sought after speaker throughout the district, and he had won a reputation for being knowledgeable and concerned about the local problems, particularly concerning the small farmer.

Liberal candidates were chosen from a wider range of classes, religions and occupations than their Conservative counterparts. They included more nonconformists (Christians who were not members of the Anglican Church), Jews, professionals and businessmen. Liberal candidates in the 1906 election were also, on the whole, younger than their Conservative counterparts. The electoral defeats of the

Liberals in the 1890s and the withdrawal of some wealthy patrons left a vacuum for these younger, more radical members of the Liberal Party to move into electoral spots and party leadership. Of the 401 Liberals elected in 1906, 205 were new to the House of Commons. Sixty-two percent of the Liberal candidates were between thirty and fifty years of age. Fifty-six percent of the Conservatives were over sixty. Since the Liberals started with so few M.P.'s before the election, this too is not surprising. Running younger candidates has tended to be a feature of landslide victories after years in the wilderness. This was exactly what happened to the Labour Party in its landslide victory in 1945.

Edwin was typical of the new breed of Liberal. He was radical, articulate, young, reformist, energetic and intelligent. To the world outside his family, it appeared that he had a private source of income sufficient to support his candidacy. The speeches at the meeting at which Edwin was chosen were most flattering. It was said that "he had many excellent qualities for membership in Parliament. He had ability, he had ambition, he had energy, he was devoted to the cause of Liberalism,"[63] and according to one story in the *Cambridge Independent Press,* "he had sufficient money to provide for his political career and not enough to demoralize his constituency."[64] They knew nothing, of course, of the restraints imposed upon him by his father. The speeches also noted that Edwin "was not trammelled with business or a profession; he was prepared to dedicate his life to political work and to the Liberal cause."[65] Edwin told his supporters that he had no intention of being a "sleeping candidate." He intended to meet nearly every elector in his district. It was not an idle promise made in the heat of the moment. It represented a plan of campaign he methodically carried out and that was largely the secret of his success in the campaign.

West Cambridgeshire then had the reputation of being a constituency in which Conservatives and Liberals took turns representing. (In 1900, for example, the Conservatives won with 4,190 votes out of a total population of 10,352; the Liberals had 3,691 votes.) Edwin could thus not take victory for granted, although by 1905 the tide seemed to be turning toward Liberalism.

Determined to win and leave no stone unturned, from 1903 on, Edwin traveled up and down his district, speaking at every available meeting, luncheon or dinner, getting to know the area, answering questions, shaking hands and meeting with the voters. He devoted so much time to the problems of rural Cambridgeshire that he was soon able to talk with the authority of a native on the subject of fruit growing and the manufacture of fruit jam.

Off and Running

Finally, on December 9, he wrote to his mother that although he didn't know the exact date of the election, "Unless anything occurs to the contrary I intend to accept adoption on the 23rd to begin work immediately after Christmas." Like any other politician running for office, Edwin had to concern himself with such matters as addressing envelopes and writing cards. His mother volunteered her services for both tasks, which he gladly accepted:

There is therefore plenty of work for you to do, and in addition being a bachelor it seems to me that it would be a great advantage if I had some lady relative to go about with me.

Buckmaster, a grass widower, is to be accompanied by his sister . . . it would be most useful if one of my sisters or preferably, my Mother could be with me for the whole time.

I know this is a great deal to ask but I don't want the people here to get hold of the idea that I have quarreled with my family. You, mother, have been kind enough to come to one of my meetings, — *My Father has been to none, and I do earnestly trust he will succeed in getting down once at least, if it's impossible to hope for more.*[66] (emphasis added)

During December, Edwin's mother came to Cambridge frequently. She accompanied him on his round of speeches, wrote letters, folded envelopes, licked stamps—with such zeal that Edwin's political aid "couldn't believe it." His father was "happy" with the reports he received of the campaign, eventually visited and spoke in the area a few times and even made the family's horses and carriages available to help Edwin canvass his entire district.[67]

Edwin at twenty-six was now off and running for his first elected political office, just six years to the day after first writing to his mother that a career in Parliament "was the highest career a man can seek," and that law "was the best route to reach Parliament."[68] His opponent in the election was Major W. Raymond Green, a diehard Conservative, a gentleman farmer and longtime resident of Cambridgeshire.

Edwin devoted most of his speeches to economic issues—free trade, unemployment, land and tax reform and the condition of the poor. He invited his friend John Maynard Keynes to join him on the campaign trail and to speak on these issues. Keynes spent several days with Edwin and, according to Keynes's biographer, "the fiscal question was the only one capable of bringing Maynard to political life." [69] With Keynes's expertise, Edwin was able to develop sophisticated answers to some of the controversial economic issues of the day. Their friendship and Keynes's influence on Edwin's ideas would continue throughout Edwin's life.

4

The Liberal Party and
the Landslide of 1906

It is the the duty of the State to secure for all its members, and all others whom it can influence, the fullest possible opportunity to lead the best life.

Herbert Samuel, Liberalism

It was no accident that Montagu chose the Liberal Party as his political home. Not only his father but the overwhelming majority of the Jewish community at the time were firmly committed to the Liberal Party, the party of emancipation, nonconformists, dissenters, religious liberty and the rights of the individual. It was the party of the middle class, of private enterprise and of the bourgeoisie, of which Jews had now become an important part. The Tories, on the other hand, were seen as the party of the time-honored interests of England, of land, aristocracy and the Anglican Church.[1]

As Jews became increasingly assimilated into English life, the Jewish attitude toward the Liberal Party became less absolute. Wealthy Jews now found they shared social and economic interests with their Christian neighbors and this commonality of concerns became a factor in their political choices. Of the five Jewish members elected to Parliament in 1880, four were Liberals, one was Conservative. Thirteen Jews had run for Parliament; of these eight were Liberals. However, by 1900, "11 of the 23 Jewish candidates were Unionists, of whom 7 were elected as against 3 Liberals."[2] Gladstone's support of Russia against Turkey in 1877 and his advocacy of Irish Home Rule in 1886 were the principal causes of this defection. The Home Rule issue split the Liberal Party, and a new group of "Liberal Unionists" that identified with the Conservatives was formed. Lord

Rothschild, who before his elevation to the peerage had been a staunch Liberal, joined the group. It thus became respectable for Jews to join the Conservative ranks, although their number remained small. When Montagu entered politics, Jews were still overwhelmingly members of the Liberal Party.

The Liberal Party: A Loose, Diverse Alliance

The Liberal Party was not a monolithic organization with a prescribed party platform. Rather, it was a loose alliance, an umbrella for so many different ideologies as to make a clear definition of its goals almost impossible. Born of the seventeenth-century struggle for freedom of conscience and the resistance of Parliament to the arbitrary authority of the King, it soon came to include other traditions and ideas in its developing philosophy: individualism, the importance of morality in politics, self-government, civil and religious liberty, dislike of authoritarian government and free trade.

By the time Montagu joined the Liberal Club at Cambridge in 1899, a new belief was gaining currency among a growing number of Liberals: that liberty notwithstanding, the government had an obligation to help the underprivileged—"the poor, the ill and the less fortunate."[3] To the radicals within the Party this became the central doctrine of Liberalism or, as some called it, "The New Liberalism."[4]

These Liberals believed that freedom must not permit individualism to limit the opportunities of all people to enjoy a better life. Nor should it limit the responsibilities of government to provide those services and opportunities that some were unable to achieve by themselves. How to reconcile the two basic tenets of Liberalism, "individual liberty" and "state action," became the principal philosophic debate among Liberals in the last years of the nineteenth century and the first of the twentieth.

This was only one of a score of issues that divided the Party, which in reality was a conglomerate of three distinct groups, with three distinct agendas. The Whigs represented the right wing of the Party, including the aristocratic core of the Party. They were committed to Liberalism more out of tradition and history than support of a specific philosophy. The Radicals on the left consisted of intellectuals, journalists and some wealthy businessmen. These were the ideologues of the Party and provided whatever advanced political ideas the Party developed. Montagu was firmly in this camp. The third sector was the Moderates, consisting of landlords, middle-class businessmen, lawyers and army and navy officers. They were at the center of the Party and could be influenced by either the right or left, depending on the issue.

It was these three divergent elements that William Gladstone's political skill united into a Party strong enough to achieve the Liberal victory of 1869, a precursor of the 1906 landslide. It was that victory, built not only on Gladstone's skills but on discontent with Tory rule and the growing desires of the working class for social and economic change, that turned an amorphous coalition into a single victorious political Party. In addition, it was Gladstone's first premiership, which lasted till 1874, and to a lesser extent his second administration, from 1880 to 1885, that added cohesion and strength to the Party and produced what has come to be called "the heyday of political liberalism."[5]

But even under the astute political leadership of a master politician like Gladstone, the Liberal Party often lacked a consistent program, was internally at odds and was unprepared as a Party to support programs that would directly affect the working class: pensions, wage and hour legislation, unemployment insurance and tax reform. While these measures were often supported by individual members of the Party, they were not endorsed by the Party as a whole.

Despite the Party's reluctance to adopt a program of expanded state responsibilities, Gladstone's twenty-year administration was able to adopt some legislation, albeit on a modest scale, that sought to remedy some of the social ills of the time. It did try to lighten tax burdens, improve education, extend the franchise and expand the powers of local government. This was not enough, however, either to satisfy the electorate or consolidate the Party. Divisiveness continued. Conflict over foreign policy, Home Rule and the defeat of the government in 1885 over the budget all helped to return the Tories to power in 1886 and elect Lord Salisbury Prime Minister.

The defeat of the Liberal Party in 1886 is often called the point which "marked a divide in the evolution of the party."[6] The Whigs, for all practical purposes, left the Party, and many of the remaining

Liberals believed that only by developing a more radical program and winning the support of the workingman could their party return to power.

This was a time when the workingman, strengthened by the extended franchise, began to develop as a political force. Impatient with Parliament's seeming indifference to their plight, workers began to develop their own organizations, leaders and tactics. Most members of the Liberal Party did not foresee the long-range effects of these developments, but a vocal and significant segment of the Party was wise enough to recognize that the Liberal Party's strength was bound to be affected if it lost the support of labor. The demand for what was called the radicalization of the Liberal Party was their response.

Unfortunately, most Party members in Parliament seemed oblivious to these threats and continued to ignore social issues. The Party seemed doomed by its own internecine political power struggles and by the composition of the Party itself, which prohibited it from moving either to the left or to the right. Outside of Parliament, however, the rank and file of the Liberal Party were restive. Joseph Chamberlain, seizing upon this unrest, organized the National Liberal Federation (N.L.F.), a coalition of Liberal Party clubs and associations demanding a comprehensive program to alleviate the hardships of the poor, assure greater democracy in government and less church influence.

The Newcastle Programmé was the result. Adopted in October 1891, fifteen years before Montagu ran for office, it advocated church disestablishment in Wales and Scotland, one man–one vote, land and tax reform, employer's liability and a formula for limiting working hours. This did not quiet the growing discontent of the workers who, in January 1913, formed the Independent Labour Party, a momentous event in British history.

While Gladstone never fully endorsed the Newcastle Programmé and was not comfortable with this new radical "socialist" approach, the new, younger leadership of the party—Asquith, Campbell-Bannerman, Richard Haldane, Lord Rosebery, Edward Grey, Arthur Acland and John Morley—did support it. The defeat of the Liberals in 1885–86 and the shake-up it caused in the party leadership provided these younger men with the opportunity to rise to new positions of power within the party. As a consequence, new "radicalization," with its concern for social ills, became a larger part of the Liberal Party agenda.

These were the men with whom Montagu would spend the majority of his political life, although by the time he entered Liberal politics, they were the old men of the Party and had lost a good part of their reformist zeal. He would often find himself to their left, urging new and innovative government action, to alleviate the problems of the poor and the poverty that many workers and farmers endured.

Poverty

During the sixty years from 1841 until 1901, four million people left the English countryside and moved into the cities, where conditions for the workers "were utterly miserable."[7] The 1891 census showed that the towns were chronically overcrowded, sanitation almost nonexistent and crime and disease rampant. About one-third of the population was living below the poverty line. Unemployment, famine and ill health were widespread. In 1892 in Manchester, during the Boer War, eight thousand men out of the pool of twelve thousand were rejected by the army: Only twelve hundred were accepted "as fit in all respects, though the army measurements had been reduced to the lowest standard since Waterloo."[8]

Robert Blatchford, editor of the *Clarion*, a socialist newspaper, described the condition of the poor in a pamphlet called "Merrie England," first published as a series of open letters in 1893:

Go out into the streets of any big English town, and use your eyes, John. What do you find? You find some rich and idle, wasting unearned wealth to their shame and injury and the shame and injury of others. You find hard-working people packed away in vile, unhealthy streets. You find little children famished, dirty, and half naked outside the luxurious clubs, shops, hotels and theaters. . . .

You find men and women overworked and underpaid. You find want and disease cheek by jowl with religion and culture and wealth. You find the usurer, the gambler, the fop, the finnikin fine lady, and you find the starveling, the slave, the drunkard, and the harlot.[9]

As the British workers became more knowledgeable about the nature and extent of their poverty, and more demanding that the government assume some collective responsibility to help alleviate it, their support for imperialism and the Empire grew less enthusiastic. They believed that money spent on arms, the Navy and the administrative costs of the Empire could better be spent on social improvements. Joseph Chamberlain's 1903 program to strengthen the Empire through protective tariffs was not, therefore, received well by the average worker. It not only split the Conservative Party and drove Winston Churchill into the Liberal Party, but it also gave the Liberal Party its rallying cry for the 1906 election. "Free trade" became its principal election slogan. Concerned by the rise in the cost of living that would be caused by the imposition of duties on foreign imports, the working class voted overwhelmingly to reject Chamberlain's program. This was the central issue in the 1906 campaign, which ended in the largest landslide in British history, giving the Liberal Party an astounding victory and electing Edwin Montagu to Parliament.

The Liberal Landslide

The Liberals returned 377 Members to Parliament, the Irish Nationalists 83, Labour 53, and the Conservatives 157. Since the Liberals could often count on the support of the Irish Nationalists and of Labour, they now effectively controlled 513 seats, with the Opposition reduced to 157.

The 1906 Parliament was the first truly middle-class Parliament, the first in which a majority of members worked for a living. Lawyers, journalists, teachers and self-made businessmen appeared in force. Only one Liberal member in three had attended public school.

It set a new record for the election of members of churches other than the Church of England. It elected 56 Methodists, 65 Congregationalists, 18 Baptists, 10 Unitarians, 6 Quakers, 3 Presbyterians, 16 Jews, 80 Irish Catholics and a handful of English Catholics.

This extraordinary Liberal victory, the last the Party would ever receive, also thrust the Labour Party onto the political scene with 29 of the 53 Labour representatives sitting as an independent party. Of the remaining 24, 13 were miners, 4 represented other trade union members, and seven were classified as "Lib-Labs" (supported by both the Liberal and Labour Parties).

To Balfour the Liberal victory was the forerunner of socialism in Britain—"a faint echo of the same movement which had produced massacres in St. Petersburg, riots in Vienna and socialist processions in Berlin"—the beginning of a new era, one in which English politics "would never be the same."[10] In truth, the election was neither a forerunner of upheaval, nor a "St. Petersburg style massacre" nor a revolution. It was, rather, a victory for the center. But it did lay the groundwork for the welfare state, which had within it the seeds of socialism. More than that, it ushered in a new era in British politics. In that new era Herbert Henry Asquith would now become a key player.

5

Asquith before 1906

The greatest pleasure and the greatest honour I have ever known have been to serve you.

Montagu to Herbert Asquith, Apr. 7, 1908

Edwin Montagu's life was inextricably tied personally and politically to that of Henry Herbert Asquith from the time of the election of 1906 until Montagu was driven from Cabinet office in 1922 and from the House of Commons the following year.

Asquith was Prime Minister for eight years and two hundred and forty-one days, one of the longest tenures held by an English Prime Minister. The nearly nine years of Asquith's stewardship were among the most challenging in English history. He was the key player in the constitutional crisis that resulted in limiting the role of the House of Lords through the Parliament Bill of 1911; he played a critical role in the struggle from 1909 to 1914 over Home Rule for Ireland; he was largely responsible for mustering support for Britain's entry into World War I; and his administration is credited with laying the groundwork for the modern British welfare state. On the negative side, he was accused of poor leadership during the first year of World War I, resulting in the death of thousands of young Englishmen; of causing irreparable damage to British-Irish relations because of his procrastination; and of contributing significantly to the decline and ultimate demise of the Liberal Party in Great Britain.

When Montagu and Asquith met in 1901 it was inconceivable that such disasters, or indeed any disasters, would one day be laid at Asquith's door. At forty-nine, Asquith was a rising star in Liberal politics, a recognized leader, a Member of Parliament for East Fife, a former Cabinet member in Gladstone's government, and a respected barrister, with an enviable record of academic achievement at Oxford. Montagu, twenty-one and a struggling student, was immediately impressed by the older man. Asquith was a brilliant self-made man, versed in the classics, seemingly effortless in his intellectual achievements, with an extraordinary memory and an organized and methodical mind. He exuded an air of superiority, natural leadership and assurance.

It is not difficult to understand how Montagu, filled as he was with self-doubt and insecurity, would be attracted to such a man. Asquith was everything Montagu wished he could be. Asquith, moreover, had achieved this with neither family connections nor support. His father had died when he was twelve and his mother was chronically ill. He had been raised by a grandfather and an uncle, and at an early age was boarded out with other families. For all practical purposes he had been treated as an orphan.

In spite of his bleak childhood, he had a generally optimistic and cheerful attitude, the very antithesis of Montagu's. He had been a very bright young boy and his intellectual gifts were recognized even in elementary school. He and his brother attended, as Montagu later did, the City of London School. Headmaster Edwin Abbott would later comment that he did little to help Asquith but "to place before him the opportunities of self-education and self-improvement . . . simply to put the ladder before him, and up he went."[1] Abbott added that Asquith developed the ability to write and speak early on, in "beautifully balanced and lucid English diction."[2] His speeches for the school debating society "exhibited all the *gravitas* and massive precision which were later to become recognized as the most notable Asquithian oratorical characteristics."[3]

In 1869 at the age of seventeen, Asquith won a Classical Scholarship to Balliol College, Oxford. Only two were awarded each year. To receive one of these awards was itself a great honor. To receive it when you came from a relatively unknown school, which had never before gained a Balliol scholarship, made the achievement particularly noteworthy.

Even at an early age Asquith was intellectually intolerant and had contempt for what he regarded as inferior disciplines outside the mainstream of traditional classical learning. At school he had little interest in subjects other than the Classics, English and anything involving public affairs.[4] He often visited the House of Commons and wrote long accounts to his mother of some of the great Parliamentary debates to which he listened intently.[5]

At Oxford his academic achievements were dazzling. "He worked with a steady and proficient ease which brought results of almost unbroken excellence."[6] Outside of his class work, his main interest at Oxford, like Montagu later, was the Oxford Union, where he took part in nearly every debate. Immediately after completing his undergraduate work he tutored the son of the Earl of Portsmouth and saw, at first hand, how the very rich and powerful lived. He would later write, "I thus obtained a glimpse of a kind of life which was new to me."[7] It was a life he learned to like very much. Perhaps because of his stark beginnings, Asquith was always attracted to the comforts and accoutrements that money can buy. He was personally extravagant, always enjoying the good life—good food, good companions, good conversation and attractive women.

While Asquith's beginnings were far different from Montagu's, their attitude toward money and extravagant living were very similar. Montagu, while having a rich father, was in some ways as economically deprived as Asquith and spent his early life always needing money and pleading for more. Perhaps as a reaction, both men were not only attracted to the grand and luxurious life but determined to enjoy it, even if at times neither could afford it.

Early on at Oxford Asquith, like Montagu, chose the law as his route to politics. Here the similarity ended. Asquith enjoyed the law; Montagu despised it. Asquith was called to the Bar; Montagu was not. Asquith opened an office with two other young lawyers, practiced law before and after entering politics and handled several important legal matters that gave him both a reputation and a source of income. Montagu, except for his brief sojourn in the solicitor's office and with Mr. Pollack, went into politics almost immediately after graduating from Cambridge. He had, as a result, no source of income except politics and his father.

In 1883 a friend of Asquith's, Sir Robert Samuel Wright, another Balliol man, became Junior Consul to the Treasury and asked Asquith to handle some of his practice while he was involved with the Treasury. He also introduced Asquith to Sir Henry James, the Attorney General, for whom Asquith prepared various memoranda, all of which were well received. Asquith also drafted for Sir Henry the Corrupt Practices Act of 1883 and a guide to its implementation.

This brought him to the attention of many Members of Parliament and was the start of his reputation for intellectual prowess.

At the same time, his dear colleague and friend Richard Haldane, also a fellow Balliol man, who had recently been elected to Parliament,[8] persuaded him to run for Parliament from the neighboring district of East Fife, where the incumbent, a Liberal, had been rejected by the local association for refusing to follow Gladstone on Home Rule. Asquith agreed and with little effort won his first seat in Parliament, by the modest majority of 2,862 to 2,487—a slight margin of 375 votes out of 5,349 votes cast.[9]

During these early years in Parliament, Asquith spoke only two or three times a year, but when he did, his speeches were applauded and even his opponents conceded that they were eloquent and powerful.[10] He worked closely with others who entered Parliament with him. Asquith was not the oldest of this group but seems from the start to have taken charge as their official leader. He often spoke at Liberal Party meetings throughout the country and gained the reputation as a dependable and persuasive speaker.

When Montagu met Asquith, he was already married to his second wife, Margot Tennant. His first marriage, to Helen Milland, when he was nearly twenty-five, had lasted fourteen years. She had died of typhoid fever, leaving Asquith with five children, the eldest twelve years old, the youngest eighteen months. Asquith had first met Margot in 1891, while Helen was still alive. From the first, an attraction developed between them, resulting in a long and intimate correspondence that began immediately after they met. Several of Asquith's letters expressed deep love for Margot, even during Helen's lifetime, which raised the question of his devotion to Helen and his ability to sustain a monogamous relationship.

After Helen's death, Asquith and Margot saw each other frequently, but they did not marry until 1894. The wedding was a splendid affair held at St. George's Church in Hanover Square. Hundreds of dignitaries from the political world and social register attended, including former Prime Minister William Gladstone, the current Prime Minister Lord Rosebery, and a future Prime Minister, Arthur Balfour. The Cabinet postponed its meeting that day and crowds of excited people waited outside the church to "see Margot Tennant married."[11]

Margot Tennant, who was thirty years old at the time of her

marriage (Asquith was forty-two), was one of the five Tennant sisters: Charlotte (Charty), who married Thomas Lister, the fourth Baron Ribblesdale; Pauline, who married Thomas Gordon Duff; Lucy, who married the dashing Thomas Graham Smith; and Laura, who married one of the most handsome men in the society in which they moved, Alfred Lyttelton. The sisters and their father, Sir Charles Tennant, were known as "highly gifted, of totally unconventional manners, with no code of behavior, except their own good hearts." [12] Sir Charles Tennant was a successful businessman, bold and energetic, who had amassed a great fortune, enormous estates and a massive library of rare books and works of art. "By 1881 his money, and the way he spent it . . . had made him one of the new, socially acceptable entrepreneurs who were invading the world of the landed aristocracy." [13]

Margot Tennant was a vital, driving and exciting woman. She was, in her youth, the center of a glittering social world called "The Souls" that had included politicians, artists, writers, intellectuals and other young men and women characterized by their wealth, social status, intelligence and wit. She was a brilliant conversationalist who loved entertaining extensively and extravagantly, a prominent member of London society and a woman of great ambition for her husband. As time progressed, she became an unpleasant and domineering woman, snobbish and intolerant, acerbic, difficult, subject to long bouts of illness, candid to the point of rudeness—one who lost as many friends as she made. Pamela McKenna told a friend in September 1912: "She criticizes everything incessantly . . . and always in the unkindest way; . . . but I know she never means to be wounding and I do feel sorry for her, as she makes herself so terribly unhappy." [14]

Gladstone's Cabinet

In 1892, two years before he married Margot, at the age of forty, Asquith had been reelected to Parliament and had entered Gladstone's Cabinet as Home Secretary. He remained in that position when Lord Rosebery became Liberal Prime Minister in 1894. As Home Secretary, Asquith has been described as "cool and decisive," [15] self-confident, a man who inspired confidence among his colleagues and "among uncommitted opinion throughout the country." [16] His record in that office was superb. While he may not have been the most innovative minister, he ran a sound and well-functioning department and was singled out by Sir Robert Ensor in his analysis of the Liberal government of 1892–95 as "the most brilliant Home Secretary within living memory." [17] He had the ability to do well in any role or assignment given to him. Years later Campbell-Bannerman would dub him "the Sledgehammer" because of his power in debate. "He would pile argument upon argument in flowing, lucid sentences crushing his opponents by weight of logic." [18]

He was also, however, accused of lacking "a sense of vision, of creative imagination . . . and his skill was the lawyer's skill in handling and presenting the ideas of others." [19] But from his earliest days in Parliament he had the uncanny ability of "making the maximum of impact . . . with the expenditure of the minimum of effort." [20]

Liberals Turned Out of Office

Whatever skills Asquith had were not enough to help the Liberal Party remain in power. The Rosebery government was turned out of office in a crushing defeat in 1895. Asquith, however, was returned with an increase in his majority from 294 to 716. With little effort he was soon recognized as the leader of the Liberal Party. He himself believed that it was only a matter of time until he would be Prime Minister.

In the meantime, with the Tories in power and Lord Salisbury Prime Minister, Asquith was without Cabinet position. He gave more time to the practice of law and participated in the rich social life that Margot provided. He appeared to spend less time on parliamentary duties than in drawing rooms and at dinner parties, enjoying feminine company, light conversation, parlor games with his daughter's young friends and too much wine and liquor. The serious stern young politician became a man less given to thoughtful conversation than to the enjoyment of London society. Some of Asquith's friends, like Haldane, blamed Margot for this transformation, but it is more likely that Asquith himself "yearned to be corrupted," [21] if such a life can properly be called "corrupt."

Although Asquith may have given the impression of frivolity and lack of concern for his work, in fact he was never ill-prepared and always had the capacity to do his work quickly and efficiently. What may have appeared as a lack of discipline was in reality the effortless manner in which he could solve complex problems and do his work well in less time than most of his colleagues. If he enjoyed escape from work, it may well have been that his style of work—brief but intense—required an escape valve.

By 1899 Campbell-Bannerman had assumed titular leadership of the Liberal Party, with Asquith second in command. In spite of Campbell-Bannerman's conciliatory personality and his attempt to lead from the center, disunity within the Liberal Party increased. The election of 1899 showed that the public took seriously the slogan that "a vote for a Liberal is a vote for the Boers." [22] As a result, most Liberals lost. Asquith, however, was reelected, even increasing his margin of victory from 716 to 1,431.

From 1899 to 1902, the Conservatives remained in power, but by the summer of 1905, under the leadership of Balfour, they began losing ground. The economy began to falter, labor discontent was rising and the Education Act of 1902 (which used government taxes to help religious schools including Anglican and Roman Catholic schools) aroused the ire of the nonconformists. It was only a matter of time before Balfour was forced to resign. He did so, however, anticipating that the Liberals would be unable to form a government because of the conflict within the Party. He was wrong. Campbell-Bannerman was confident that the Liberals had the majority of the country behind them. On December 5, 1905, he accepted the King's invitation to form a government and immediately dissolved Parliament, which had been sitting for five years. A special general election was scheduled for January 1906.

The result was the 1906 landslide victory for the Liberals. The Conservative Party, which had ruled the nation for eleven years, was shattered. Balfour, Lyttelton, Walter Long and Bonar Law all lost their seats. Britain would not see a genuine Tory government again until 1922.

Montagu's Victory

Through extraordinarily hard work and a backbreaking speaking schedule that took him all over his district, Montagu rode the wave of the Liberal victory, winning in his district by 513 votes. Montagu received 4,829 votes, his opponent, Major W. R. Green, 4,316 votes. [23] The press had little to say about Montagu's victory except to comment that he was "the son of Sir Samuel Montagu, the London banker who sat in the House of Commons for fifteen years as a member for the Whitechapel Division of the Tower Hamlets." [24] Even in victory, Montagu walked in his father's shadow.

Three days later, on February 22, *The Times* ran an election story about a meeting of the new Cabinet at 10 Downing Street. Buried in that story, almost as an afterthought, was the report that "the Chancellor of the Exchequer, Herbert Asquith, has appointed Edwin Samuel Montagu MP to be his [unpaid] Parliamentary Private Secretary." [25] This may have been an insignificant announcement for *The Times,* but for Montagu it was a watershed. By this one act, Asquith brought Edwin into the inner circle of power. He was now not merely an obscure M.P., but the Parliamentary Private Secretary to a man presumed by most of the leadership of the Liberal Party to be the next Prime Minister.

Edwin had achieved this entirely through his own merit—not through the help of his father or any of his family and friends. He had achieved it because of his reputation in Liberal circles as a thoughtful and impressive speaker, a serious young man who did his homework and who had made a lasting impression on Asquith by a speech he delivered at a dinner of the Cambridge Union five years earlier. The appointment as Asquith's Parliamentary Private Secretary was not just a political plum for Montagu. It also was the beginning of a relationship with Asquith that would bring happiness and sadness to both their lives. But that was in the future. For now, the Liberal Party was back in power. And Montagu had achieved his deepest desire—he was in Parliament and at the center of Liberal Party politics.

6

Parliamentary Private Secretary to the Chancellor of the Exchequer, 1906–1908

Just as you are bound by no pledge of secrecy on Government Affairs to your private secretaries so it seems to me I have the right to disregard the confidential nature of the information concerning the welfare of the Government when reporting confidences to you.

Montagu to Herbert Asquith, Feb. 4, 1908.

Promises to Keep

In 1906, Henry Campbell-Bannerman, a sturdy, conciliatory, shrewd and experienced politician, loyal to his party and to its commitments to social justice, assembled one of the strongest Cabinets in English history. In addition to Asquith at the Exchequer, it included Lloyd George at the Board of Trade, Haldane at the War Office, and Edward Grey at the Foreign Office; John Burns, a Labour Member and hero of the London dock strike became President of the Local Government Board. Herbert Gladstone was at the Home Office, John Morley returned as Secretary of State for India and Augustine Birrell became the Minister for Education. At the junior level, Winston Churchill became Under Secretary of the Colonies and Herbert Samuel, Edwin's cousin, Under Secretary for Home Affairs.

Apart from such notable exceptions as Churchill, this was a middle-class Cabinet, both in character and in values. They sought to respond to the discontent of the electorate by using the existing structure of government to correct the ills of society through innovative legislation. Two-thirds of the Liberal candidates, including Edwin Montagu, had pledged support for such measures during the campaign. While their support was often expressed in general terms, their intent was clear: Social and economic reform must be the first order of the new government.

Such reforms almost always involved changes in fiscal and budgetary policies. They were, therefore, of direct concern to Asquith as Chancellor of the Exchequer and to his secretaries, particularly Montagu, who as a member of the Radical wing of the Liberal Party was strongly committed to such ideas. While Montagu was not a socialist or a collectivist, nor even as extreme in his radicalism as Lloyd George, he did believe that even within a system of free enterprise and with the restraints of a balanced budget more could and must be done to redistribute income and to improve social and economic conditions.

As such he saw taxation not as an evil, but as an instrument of social policy, and like his friend John Maynard Keynes, he believed that poverty and unemployment deprived the masses of the capacity to purchase goods, which in turn reduced production causing unemployment and a general decline in economic activity. Put differently, Montagu and the so-called Radical wing of the Party believed that the real enemy of economic health was underconsumption by the masses. This, they believed, could be remedied by the reallocation of purchasing power—pumping more money into the system. In that process the government must play an active role. Reform of the tax system was essential and a balanced budget, while desirable, was not sacred.

Such policies broke sharply with the traditional Gladstonian-Whig belief in government retrenchment, modest budget expenditures and the notion that taxes were an evil that should not be used as a means of reallocating income. In subsequent years this "New Liberalism" came to be accepted, moderately and slowly, as the mainstream of Liberal economic policies. In 1906 it was viewed with suspicion and fear not only by the Conservatives, but by large segments of the Liberal Party.

Montagu's Role as Parliamentary Private Secretary

As Parliamentary Private Secretary to the Chancellor of the Exchequer, Montagu was in a unique position to influence the development of economic policy during the formative years of the new Liberal government. He could not have asked for a more exciting role. In his desire to see the government adopt new economic policies, he was far more radical than Asquith and the government in power. Underlying his approach was his belief that unless the Liberal Party made good on its economic promises, the workingman would turn to the Labour Party, and the ability of the Liberals to retain power would thus be threatened.

As Parliamentary Private Secretary to the Chancellor, Montagu had the responsibility of briefing him on all issues involving finance and budget, and, with the Chancellor and the Treasury officials, of devising the strategy for presenting these matters in Parliament. Montagu, however, viewed his role in broader terms: as an advisor to help Asquith develop long-term fiscal and budgetary policies. Always brimming with new ideas, Montagu transmitted these on a regular basis in long, weekly memoranda to Asquith, urging him at every opportunity to take more vigorous positions on "the glorious principle of taxing the rich for the benefit of the poor," on "Land Values, Local Taxation readjustment etc."[1] and Old Age Pensions. He also took it upon himself to alert the Chancellor to any criticism leveled against him and to act as Asquith's eyes and ears in and out of Parliament. His memoranda were, like Montagu himself, wise but often impolitic: witty and sarcastic, occasionally expressing pleasure at the response in Parliament to Asquith's leadership, but more often showing worry and pessimism.

The *Daily Mail* described Montagu as "a tall reflective young man, practically a silent member who could come unobtrusively from behind the Speaker's chair, seat himself on one of the back benches and get through hours of debate with a faraway expression on his face. Politics always seem distant from his thoughts. As a matter of fact he was taking in all that was said and was losing no opportunity of adding to his equipment, being probably quite determined that his opportunity was coming."[2] He was, according to the *Daily Mail,* shy and diligent:

Unlike many unambitious young members he did not make frequent attempts to catch the Speaker's eye. He seemed rather to be a young member who would be embarrassed to be called upon to speak. Diffidence and diligence appeared to be his predominant characteristics. Those who knew him privately said he was possessed of high capacity. His silence in debate gave no evidence of it.

Of striking personal appearance, he was always a notable figure on the back benches, but it would have been difficult for the most acute parliamentary observer to have discerned outstanding qualities in this studious, silent man.[3]

The *Daily Mail* congratulated Asquith for having seen Montagu's great capabilities behind his quiet and reserved exterior:

Mr. Asquith was aware of his ability, for he quickly picked him out as Parliamentary Secretary to himself, a post which calls not only for wide knowledge but also for tact and quick decision. The P.M. is, by virtue of his experience, a pretty good judge of men. In his silent and unobtrusive way Mr. Montagu soon demonstrated his power. He did so in the Prime Minister's private room, in the informal conferences behind the Speaker's chair, in the House itself when during debate he was seated just behind Mr. Asquith ready to support a line of argument with references or quotations from books or documents. Somehow the House grew to have a higher estimate of Mr. Montagu though he hardly ever said a word in debate.[4]

Montagu may have been silent in the House, but he was hardly that with Asquith and other key officials, at committee meetings and in his memoranda and letters to Asquith. In writing he had the courage to say what he could not say in person. He was aware of this and commented to Asquith in one of his long letters, written in January 1907, that "a wise man once told me never to write what I had not the courage to say."[5] Montagu never followed this sage advice. Behind the illusory protection afforded by pen and paper, Montagu became strong, combative and outspoken.

This January letter was a typical Montagu letter: a combination of gossip, political wisdom and parliamentary reporting. Montagu not only conveyed to Asquith his opinions of the major personalities of Parliament but, as in most of his letters, he pleaded with the Chancellor to deal more vigorously with the economic issues, to change the tax structure "to help meet social needs," provide old age pensions and begin an examination of local taxes and land values. He urged Asquith not to be satisfied with "piddly changes and compromises but to think big and with courage."

There is nothing so important to the Liberal Party as this next Budget. Every Member of Parliament relies on this Budget to substantiate the popularity of a Party whose claim to the affections of the Electorate is at present based upon anticipation . . .
    . . . [F]or eleven years Liberals and Radicals have preached the good things to come from a Liberal Budget—"the free breakfast table" is becoming rickety with old age; the re-adjustment of taxation; the strict application of the glorious principle of taxing the rich for the benefit of the poor; and the materialization of such projects as Land Values, Local Taxation re-adjustment, etc., etc., are dear to them. What are they to get? . . . It may well be that nothing big in the way of finance remains to be done; and those that have promised and whetted appetites will have to pay the penalty of irresponsible promises. But the scape-goats of the Party will not be those that are to blame—the men who failed to satisfy the demands will be the scape-goats of other people's faults.[6]

Montagu's letters were brutally frank. In the same letter, he warned Asquith that "the people will not wait another year," that they viewed Haldane and Asquith as Whigs, and that the "majority of the Party hardly trust you and only tolerate you because of the enormous capacity, ability and power of the leaders in the wing."[7]

Anyone less secure than Asquith would not have encouraged such comments. But Asquith, whatever his faults, was a man utterly secure in himself, blessed with that self-assurance that stopped just short of arrogance. Montagu's own brutal frankness did not ruffle him. He not only accepted the sharpness of Montagu's comments, even when directed at himself, but actually encouraged them and found Montagu's political astuteness, his candor and his tidbits of gossip useful political tools.

Montagu, for his part, was smart enough to dilute his criticism with praise, and nearly all his letters contained compliments to balance the harshness of his condemnations. In the January 1907 letter, for example, after telling Asquith that the "party hardly trusts you," he added the explanation that "the new Parliament hardly knows you. They were impressed, however, with your powerful speeches on the Trade Bill and on Education. They were brilliant speeches."[8] He also praised Asquith for seeing a deputation on old age pensions, for this too was "very popular. Once the Parliament gets to know you," Montagu assured Asquith, they will understand "what a remarkable leader you are."[9]

Asquith's long-range financial policies were not yet developed. Montagu warned him that this was "dangerous." With a rare gift for political prophecy he wrote:

If you cannot provide . . . material for their Social reforms by Free Trade methods, you will rivet together the quakes and the dupes into a concerted effort to raise money by other means: you will drive the Labour Party into the arms of Chamberlain's successors; and those who have the intelligence to see that the people themselves will pay the taxes, will say that they are willing to pay them because they will see that they are spent for the benefit of the people.[10]

He also pressed again for the imposition of death duties—an idea he had suggested "sometime ago"—and for a "popular" Budget. "Threats against the House of Lords are not enough." He ended by enunciating that he viewed his function as "to try and inform you of the opinions of your Party . . . and I want so much that it shall not be said that Harcourt was the last great Liberal Chancellor of the Exchequer."[11]

Montagu: A Part of the Asquith Family

Private Secretaries often play far more important roles in government than their titles suggest. They spend an inordinate amount of time with their superiors, who come to depend upon them for the detailed analyses of problems that the pressures of their high political office often preclude them from undertaking themselves. This was certainly the case in Asquith's relationship with Montagu, which in a short time became not only professional but personal as well.

By 1907 Montagu had virtually become a member of the Asquith family, spending more time with them than with most of his other friends and certainly more time than he spent with his own family —a fact that chagrined his parents, particularly his father. "To a remarkable extent his [Asquith's] social life was organized around a few of the younger members of his government. . . . Montagu [although] treated in correspondence [by Asquith] as a figure of fun, but one to whom an almost obsessive attention was paid, was the most central. He was constantly staying at the Wharf [Asquith's country home on the Thames at Sutton Courtney, Oxfordshire] and in and out of Downing Street."[12]

Montagu not only saw the Asquiths in London and at the Wharf but spent time with them at Archerfield, a splendid house on the Firth of Forth in Scotland that the Asquiths often borrowed from Frank Tennant, Margot's uncle, and at The Glen in Peebleshire, in Scotland, a baronial mansion belonging to Margot's father. Montagu was delighted to accept their invitations. He was in turn a superb house guest, a much sought-after bridge partner, a poker player of considerable skill and a scintillating conversationalist. He had a great capacity for friendship, especially with women. Until his relationship with Venetia Stanley, he received scores of long letters from several women friends, including Margot Asquith, in which they revealed their most intimate of thoughts.

In the spring of 1907, after one of Margot's frequent illnesses during which Montagu was most attentive to her, sending flowers and letters that contained, in Margot's words, "constant kind thoughts," she wrote to him: "Write to me a nice long letter very distinctly as I read your writing badly and oblige your very grateful and affectionate Margot."[13] They became dear friends.

Most of the women with whom Montagu corresponded were, like Margot, married, and since they considered Montagu a most interesting although a physically unappealing man, it is unlikely that their relationships were anything other than platonic. This was certainly so for Margot, who adored her husband but was often ill and alone and craved company and attention. Montagu, with no family responsibilities, was always available with the kind of political gossip, bright conversation and humor that Margot loved. He was also kind, generous and loving to friends, traits Margot found endearing. Early in their friendship she felt comfortable enough to tell him:

I had no idea you ever either disliked me or thought that all my beloved friendships with interesting people would be bad for me—make me spiky and over critical or unhumble. . . . I am horribly impatient and restless and irritable, but I am very near the earth and not really tamed or harnessed, but sensible enough to conform. My life has not been at all easy, I can assure you. Henry has pulled me through and all you say of him touches me very much—more than you will ever know. The kind of things you minded at Rothes I have always minded. I get so tired of brains! I value

heart a hundred times more. All my clever friends had profoundly sympathetic natures. I soon dropped those that hadn't.[14]

By this time Asquith, like Margot, looked upon Montagu as a
dear friend as well as a political confidant. He had not only affection
for him but also the deepest respect for his judgment and advice.
Montagu was not being immodest when in May 1908, he wrote to
Asquith, who had just become Prime Minister, how pleased he was
that so many of the ideas he had proposed to Asquith had been
enacted into law.

I have turned up the first letter I wrote to you on political matters after
leaving Rothes [where he had stayed with the Asquiths] in October 1906
and find that I urged as our goal a scheme of Old Age Pensions, the
remission of the Sugar Tax and the reduction of the debt contracted by our
predecessors. I am grateful to you that I have been allowed to share in your
triumphant achievement of this programme and, though I shall long lament the fascination of the Treasury and the seething schemes it begets,
and although I find much difficulty in getting interested in the vortex of
patronage and the claims of the "on-the-makers" at No. 10, yet the past
three years and your achievement is something to be proud of.[15]

When Asquith was named Chancellor of the Exchequer, he was
viewed with suspicion by many in his own Party. His principal
goals were to reduce expenditures and reform the income tax—
hardly radical objectives. "His cleverness was admitted," wrote Lord
Snowden, "but it was the tendency and character of the cleverness
which were not approved. He was regarded as cold and unsympathetic, as autocratic and reactionary."[16] It was during his term as
Chancellor of the Exchequer, one historian has noted, that "the
Radical majority had come to form a different opinion of him. He
had largely defined himself with their views on social and economic
questions, and as a result greatly advanced his Parliamentary position."[17]

There is strong evidence that Montagu's advice and his persistent
pleading both in letters and in conversation for a more vigorous
economic policy to help the poor played a role in convincing Asquith to identify himself with these views. But neither Asquith nor
other leaders of his government accepted these ideas with Montagu's
zeal and commitment or that of other leaders of the Radical wing of

the Liberal Party. As a result they permitted the Labour Party, as Edwin Montagu had warned, to co-opt ideas and programs that could have legitimately stayed within the Liberal Party.

The Budgets of 1906, 1907 and 1908

As Chancellor of the Exchequer, Asquith was the principal architect of the budgets submitted from 1906 to 1908. Montagu made extensive recommendations and pushed hard for his pet proposals: the "super tax" (a surtax), full gradation in the tax structure, a differential in taxing earned and unearned income, and the imposition of death taxes. In 1906 Asquith was not yet ready to accept these ideas. His first budget of 1906 was not an innovative one. The only social welfare provision it contained was a state grant of £200,000 toward the 1905 Unemployed Workmen's Act.

His budgets of 1907 and 1908 were different. They reflected, to a modest degree, some of the suggestions in Montagu's weekly letters as well as the pressure from other Radicals, including Lloyd George. The second budget "made an important break of new fiscal ground" and the third "laid the first brick of the welfare state."[18] While they did not satisfy all the demands of either Montagu or the Radicals, they achieved, in characteristic Asquith fashion, "a maximum radical result . . . while arousing the minimum of conservative opposition."[19]

The most innovative section of the second budget was the differentiation in the size of the tax on earned and unearned income, which Montagu strongly supported. The Treasury bitterly opposed this. In an effort to win support, Asquith created a select Committee on which Montagu served to study the problem. After a long and heated debate, often provoked by Montagu, the majority of the Committee supported differentiation over the objections of the Chairman, Sir Charles Dilke, a leading Radical. The House of Commons also voted its support and differentiation was incorporated into the 1907 Budget. Montagu paid a heavy price for this victory: He aroused Dilke's animosity and that of his supporters, who thereafter always viewed him with suspicion and dislike. They would become powerful adversaries in the debates over India.

This budget marked a change from the old Gladstonian view that a reduction in expenditures was itself a laudable goal. Haldane's savings at the War Office had contributed to a surplus of more than £5 million. Ordinarily, this would have been partly returned to the taxpayers by lowering taxes and applying the balance to the Sinking Fund (a special fund set aside from budget surplus) to pay off past debts. Asquith did not do this. Instead, he decided to set aside a portion of the surplus (i.e., £4 million) for noncontributory old age pensions—paving the way for a pension program in 1908. By this act, he was making a dramatic statement: It was perfectly acceptable to cut back on expenditures for the military and to spend the savings on social programs. As commonplace as such a policy is today, it was revolutionary in 1907.

As early as 1906, Montagu had been pressing Asquith to use some part of the budget surplus in this way. Like Asquith he was especially interested in old age pensions. Asquith did not need much persuasion. In fact he felt so strongly about the Pension Bill that he insisted on introducing the budget of 1908 (in which funds for a modest pension program were allocated) even though Lloyd George was Chancellor of the Exchequer. Old age pensions "occupied his [Asquith's] mind throughout the period of his Chancellorship . . . it was the single most important piece of social legislation for several decades past and it brought England more or less in line with Germany, Denmark and New Zealand, countries which had hitherto led the way in this field."[20]

Land Reform

While Montagu's chief concern during these years was the budget, he also considered himself a champion of land reform. His constituency was largely composed of small farmers, and he firmly believed, as had his father before him, that if farming could be made more profitable farmers would be deterred from deserting the country for the cities. He never liked the big cities, as his earliest letters show, and he had an almost romantic attachment to the land and country. He never doubted that by strengthening the farmers the economic health of England would improve.

The agricultural system in England at the time was divided into three classes: landlords, tenant farmers and hired laborers. Most of the land was owned by landlords, who farmed very little themselves and divided their estates into holdings occupied by tenant farmers, who held their land by leases of varying terms. Most tenant farmers in England, unlike those in Scotland, were tenants at will whose leases could be terminated at six months' notice. The tenant farmers, in turn, hired laborers to help them. Laborers owned no land and were dependent on wages.[21]

Montagu believed that the landlords often lacked the money, ability or desire to ensure the proper upkeep of their estates, a state of affairs that harmed not only the individual farmer but the agricultural production as well. At every opportunity, he joined with other Radicals in Parliament to make changes in the system and give the farmers greater protection. This was reflected in a series of small but significant changes made initially in 1906 and expanded in each successive Parliament. In 1906, for example, landlords were made liable for compensating tenants for damage brought about by game, for ending a tenancy for any reason other than for bad farming, and for repairs made by the tenant because the landlord had failed to make them.[22]

During the 1906 debate on the Agricultural Holdings Act, Lord Londonderry had published a letter in *The Times* that attacked those supporting this Act as persons "who wished to create ill feeling between landlord and tenant." Montagu, a strong supporter of the Act, took it upon himself to respond. His exchange of letters with Lord Londonderry revealed not only his strong pro-tenant feelings, but the style he was developing to deal with his adversaries: a style at once sharp and devoid of political civility. He characterized the Lord's comments as "a disgusting allegation" and added, "I should be glad if you would furnish me with the motive for and the evidence" for this statement. When his Lordship responded that he could not imagine any reason for advocating such legislation except to exacerbate landlord-tenant relations, Montagu suggested that his "imagination would not be strained by indulging in the correct supposition." He ended by asserting, "I can assure you that your statement is doubtless unintentional, but nevertheless, offensive; and, on behalf of my colleagues, who are endeavoring to promote the welfare of those engaged in Agriculture and on my own behalf, I cannot but emphatically state the strong resentment which your statement has caused."[23] Such letters may have merely startled their recipients in the early years of Montagu's career, when he might have been excused as a rash young man who had not yet learned the rules of the game. Later, they were received with anger and irritation and helped to create the army of critics that stood ready to cry for his head and do him in when the right moment arrived.

Montagu dispatched a similarly acid letter to Lord Rosebery on March 27, 1907, six days later. Rosebery had delivered an anti–land reform speech before the Liberal League that infuriated Montagu: "I am a Radical and I believe that the policy of Land Reform upon which the Liberal Party is now only just embarking, is vital to the prosperity of our country, and, therefore vital to the best interests of our party."[24] He was indignant, he wrote, at Rosebery's suggestion that the Liberal League should reject such reform.[25] He called Rosebery and others who dared attack Campbell-Bannerman "libellers and detractors" and suggested that the purpose of the Liberal League should be to strengthen Liberalism, not to attack policies of the Liberal Party such as land reform.[26] On land reform, he wrote: "I attach more importance to the land policy of the Government than to anything else and there is no more loyal supporter within and without this House, of the Prime Minister, than myself. I desire also to remain a member of the League."[27]

In substance, Montagu was correct: The Liberal League *was* causing mischief for the Liberal government and becoming increasingly antagonistic to the New Radicalism. But Montagu could have conveyed that same message in less hostile language to Lord Rosebery, a former Prime Minister, who had been kind enough to write the introduction to Montagu's book, *Canada and the Empire,* years earlier when Montagu was a young and unknown political aspirant. It was language that Rosebery and the other "libellers and detractors" would never forget. It demonstrated Montagu's inability to bridge the gap of political differences with conciliatory language. He learned much from his long political apprenticeship with Asquith but could never emulate Asquith's ability to gloss over conflict with the hope that time and the "unexpected in politics" would reconcile opposing views. If anything, Montagu seemed to relish his ability to sharpen the differences and to exacerbate conflict.

Montagu had now begun to work more closely with Winston Churchill, who, like Montagu, had become a champion of the poor and the small farmer. These were Churchill's radical days. And although he, like Montagu, was controversial and outspoken and frequently made enemies, unlike Montagu he had a great capacity to win political friends who often protected him from himself. Unlike Montagu, moreover, Churchill did not use his pen to fight his battles. He was a marvelous speaker, unafraid of the mob, fearless on the platform and able to capture an audience with a remarkable phrase or facial expression. Montagu, who was a solid and persuasive speaker when he was prepared, was not comfortable as an extemporaneous speaker. Nor did he have an exciting personality. He envied those who did and had nothing but admiration for Churchill's skills as an orator. This skill was particularly striking in a land policy speech Churchill made at a rally on April 25, 1907, before four thousand people representing three hundred organizations at the Drury Lane Theatre. Montagu was among the members of Parliament on the platform who joined the cheers that greeted Churchill's accusations that agriculture was "blighted and restricted," that the rural population was "melting fast into the great cities," where their health was "deteriorating fast."[28]

Following Churchill's presentation, a motion was passed urging the government to introduce drastic land reform. It urged revision of rating and land values, compulsory purchase of land by public authorities for public purposes at a fair price, regulation and planning of urban areas and more power to a central authority to promote housing and small holdings. Churchill concluded by telling the cheering crowd that the movement of land reform "had no intention of plundering the landlord and they had no intention of allowing him to plunder them."[29]

From the son of Randolph Churchill and a descendant of the great Duke of Marlborough, this argument was acceptable. When voiced by Montagu, it was attacked as the worst form of radicalism, and later in Montagu's career it would give the Tories the additional ammunition to call him a "Bolshevik."[30] But Montagu continued to speak out on land reform with the same passion as Churchill, both in and out of Parliament.

Montagu Betrays Confidences

Beginning in February 1908, Montagu's letters to Asquith take on a new tone. On the night of February 12, Campbell-Bannerman suffered his second heart attack; he was never able to leave his home again. In just a little more than a month Asquith became Prime

Minister. Montagu felt that it was now important not merely to write to Asquith about financial matters, but "that it would be of advantage to you to hear, through me, weekly, some report of the opinions expressed by private members on Parliamentary events."[31] He told Asquith that since this information would be confidential, he would ask Asquith's confidential secretary to type it. He would divulge the names of those "from whom I derive the information. Just as you are bound by no pledge of secrecy on Government affairs to your Private Secretaries, so, it seems to me I have the right to disregard the confidential nature of information concerning the welfare of the Government when reporting confidentially to you."[32]

Montagu thus placed himself in a position in which he spied on his colleagues and transmitted their confidential comments to Asquith. Montagu said that his primary purpose was the welfare of the government. While the desire to serve the government may have played some role in his motivation, it is more likely that he was impelled by a far more personal reason: his fear that Asquith would not reappoint him as his Parliamentary Private Secretary when he became Prime Minister, and his belief that by offering information Asquith could not get elsewhere, he would improve his chances.

Montagu did not have to do this. Vaughan Nash, one of Asquith's four Private Secretaries, wrote to him on April 12, 1908: "Asquith told me this morning that your name was to be included with the rest of the Private Secretaries in the announcement this morning. My impression is that he never regarded it as an open question at all."[33]

Montagu's anxiety that he would not be reappointed was entirely characteristic. His terror of failure and fear of his father's criticism, as well as the fact that by then he had no means of supporting himself except through politics, only exacerbated his anxiety. Montagu ought to have known that there are no secrets in politics. Sooner or later it was bound to become known that he was spying for Asquith, and his own trustworthiness would suffer. But in the agitated state in which he saw his choice as being rejected by Asquith (and facing an irate father who would doubtless view this as yet another of his failures) or earning the scorn of his colleagues for acting as an informer, Montagu chose the latter. In time, even his friends became critical of his "foolish gossip." On November 13, 1911, Margot Asquith, who was still a dear friend of Montagu, recorded in her diary that "Montagu who might have been Lloyd George's Under Secretary by his foolish unmanly gossip about McKenna and others has made himself suspected so L[loyd] G[eorge] said he 'wd. not have a sly man' in his office . . ."

—Apparently Montagu had 1st told H[enry] that Mc.Kenna wd. be pleased [Margot writes] to go back to this post where he had done so well under Henry in consequence of this Mc.K. was sounded as to this to his amazement—Montagu also told H that Mc.K. [with whom he had been staying as guest at the Admiralty] had said he cd. not stay the course & added "Poor fellow he is quite off his head do you know what he said one night alone with me à propos of yr. letting Winston wind up the vote of Censure Debate—'I can only imagine Asquith is jealous of Grey not to have asked him to do it.' When H. told me this vile gossip of Montagu's he added 'can you imagine anything so grossly disloyal as Montagu telling me this!' "[34]

Seemingly unaware of the consequences that would follow from the reputation he would gain as a gossipmonger, Montagu sent his weekly reports to Asquith for two years, beginning in February 1908.

On April 7, 1908, Edwin wrote his last letter to Asquith as Chancellor of the Exchequer. Campbell-Bannerman had already announced his retirement and the King had asked Asquith to form a new government.

Your four Private Secretaries dined together to mark the end last night, and although many, besides those who worked for you, desired nothing more than to see the country under your Premiership, the breaking up of the old order to make room for something more glorious is an uncomfortable period. May I add a personal word of my own. The greatest pleasure and the greatest honour I have ever known have been to serve you. It is perhaps not unnatural that I should not desire so much to congratulate you on becoming Prime Minister of England as to want to congratulate you on achieving success which you are certain to obtain in the time that is to come. You will be able to count on the devoted loyalty of your Party, and, as I hope you know and believe, on me, wherever and whenever you want my services.[35]

Despite Montagu's penchant for the dramatic, it was not an exaggeration when he said that the three years he had spent as Secretary to the Chancellor of the Exchequer had been formative and exciting years for him. He had become a part of Asquith's inner circle. He had seen many of the ideas to which he was committed become law and budgetary policy, and he had gained the respect, admiration and friendship of the most powerful leader in England.

Most young politicians would have been pleased by such developments. Not Montagu. His letters home continued to say that he was "awfully depressed," that his health was poor, that he was overworked and lonely, short of money, and misunderstood by his father. He had never been physically strong and the grueling work schedule was taking its toll. "I was saying this morning," he wrote to his mother in January 1907:

I have rarely seen anybody as ill as I look, but I think it is just nerves. Fits of awful depression are merely produced in me by the inevitable solitude in which I live, either living quite in silence or with acquaintances and strangers. I do not suppose I shall have a long life because I look sixty today, but I intend to do all I can to keep a life which, unhappy as it is, is on the whole very precious to me. I know, dearest mother, you want to help, but believe me there is nothing you can do.[36]

Montagu was twenty-eight when he wrote this letter, expressing his premonition that he would die young, a fear that would haunt him all his life. The following year, he wrote to his mother that "Dr. Rose Bradford says I am still suffering from much the same functional disturbance of the heart action, but that is much better. . . . I don't get as many headaches as I used to, but they last much longer."[37] Illness and fear of death were his constant companions.

To add to his anxieties, his father continued to exercise control over Edwin's ability to remain in politics by stopping the salary of his son's political aide in Cambridge. As usual, Edwin protested vehemently but did not move his father. Edwin then tried a new tactic, apologizing profusely, and pleading for a yearly allowance "of a suitable size" that would "permit me to go on with my work, which I truly enjoyed. . . . We have been living recently," he wrote his father, on so "much better terms than in the old days, that I am sorry this has risen. If only I could induce you to make me an inclusive allowance of a suitable size these things could never arise. . . . Whatever may be said against me and however I may enjoy my work, I never spend your money or my time on pleasure. I never go to the theatre, hardly ever to a dinner. It is all work, direct or indirect, and from morning to late night I lead an absolutely lonely life, cut off from all but casual acquaintances."[38] Edwin's pleas were of no avail. As long as his father lived, he was never given "an inclusive allowance of suitable size" for his wants and needs. He had to beg for every penny.

His refusal to be called to the Bar continued to anger his father, who believed that Edwin had broken his promise by turning his back on the practice of law. In July 1907, Edwin received an especially harsh letter from his father, which he described as "abounding in affectionate terms" but filled with "accusations of dishonesty and broken vows, of selfishness and the gorging of food, of avoiding his family, and running through a catalogue of misdeeds" since he had left school. This provoked another angry quarrel and Edwin was again "plunged into further depths of misery."

He continued to find some escape from daily pressures in visiting wild and remote areas, either abroad, as when, in May 1907, he went to Hungary to study birds, or in Scotland and Ireland, where fishing, bird watching and shooting ducks and snipe gave him some relief from the tensions of work and from his ever present feelings of exhaustion. Montagu's family never understood his need to escape and viewed these trips and his collecting rare birds as but other examples of his extravagance and his unwillingness to spend his leisure time with his family.

Edwin was especially unhappy when he had to spend the Jewish holidays in London attending synagogue with his parents. But his father remained adamant. The religious debate with his father was no different now that he was an important national figure than it had been when he was a small schoolboy. To Samuel Montagu, his sacred trust to the Jewish community required that his son accompany him to the High Holy Day services as a matter of honor. To Edwin, this was an invasion of his privacy and of his conscience. There never could be and never was a resolution.

In October 1907, Edwin was enjoying a much needed rest and holiday in Ireland when his father commanded him to return for the Yom Kippur and Rosh Hashanah services. Edwin obeyed but found his father angry and filled with complaints. "Why do I put up with it?" Edwin asked in a letter to his mother.

Because I am at present too great a coward to throw up everything and leave "home" to make my own life . . . let me urge you to remember that the biggest coward can be goaded to acts requiring courage. I am sorry to write like this. A blank despair is coming over me. You love me and I love you deeply, devotedly, passionately. But you can't constitutionally write without digging at me. It does hurt me. I love and admire my father and am grateful for his moneys, but can't he grease the wheels by a little more kindness?[39]

Edwin's mother felt that if he were called to the Bar, his father's criticism might be stemmed. Edwin was adamant in rejecting this course of action. He hated the practice of law and wanted no part of the profession. He was annoyed that his mother was again raising a subject that he had spoken to so many times before. He sent her a typewritten response in place of his usual handwritten one so that he could keep a copy "in order that I may not again have to write to you on the subject." He explained that he had become a student of law solely to help him achieve his political goal. He could not carry on his political responsibilities and practice law at the same time. He believed, moreover, that ultimately he could earn more in politics than in law. "Besides that," he wrote, "may I say that I can see no connection between my passing the Bar exams and the finances of this constituency: as to gratifying my father, that would seem to be impossible."[40]

During these years Montagu frequently expressed his desire for a country home of his own "with a garden and small farm." He was tired of renting rooms, or staying at Kensington Gardens or at a club or depending on invitations to spend weekends at other people's country estates. "I have no interests in a town and love the country . . . oh, to have a home, and not live in lodgings, permanently camping out,"[41] he wrote home in January 1908.

While, from Edwin's perspective, it seemcd that by withholding the money Edwin could use to buy a small country home and refusing to give him a regular allowance, his father was being cruel and manipulative, Samuel Montagu's view of the situation was quite different. To Samuel Montagu his son was a twenty-nine-year-old man who refused to take the necessary steps to support himself. Other young politicians, like Asquith when he first entered Parliament, managed to practice law and engage in politics at the same time. Asquith did not depend on a rich father for support. To add to Samuel's chagrin, his son not only could not support himself but indulged himself in expensive habits that included extensive travel, hunting, collecting rare birds, and elegant and excessive dining. He refused, moreover, to live at home, although he could not afford separate living quarters. He was totally divorced from the Jewish religion, played no role in the Jewish community and rarely attended synagogue, except under the sternest orders from his father.

Samuel Montagu also believed that Edwin had broken his promise to him to become a practicing lawyer. He had also promised to spend the Sabbath and the Jewish holidays with this family, but now did so only under coercion. From time to time he had promised to supplement his income, but he had never followed through. Yet in spite of these broken vows, Edwin continued to expect his father to support him with an income that would allow him to live well. Viewed in this way, one can understand (and even have sympathy for) Samuel Montagu, who took pride in his family, his religion and the fact that he was a self-made man, and who was being asked to support a son who rejected all of these values.

Women

Edwin's parents were also chagrined that he rarely spent time with his relatives or friends within the Cousinhood. He preferred the company of non-Jews like the Asquiths, Churchill, Walter Runciman, Edward Grey, Asquith's daughter, Violet, and Lady Dorothy Howard, daughter of the Duke of Norfolk. In fact, Edwin had no qualms about telling his parents that he disliked most of his relatives. He rarely courted the Jewish women to whom his mother often introduced him. She was concerned that at twenty-nine, Montagu was not only unmarried but without any discernible love interest. Montagu was concerned about this too, agreeing with his mother that he was lonely.[42] But, he wrote to her, it was no use pressuring him about this, "as it is no good wishing for what cannot be. I have just got to put up with it and live alone."[43]

The fact that he was a Member of Parliament, Private Secretary to the Prime Minister, and son of one of the wealthiest and most respected Jewish leaders of his day should have made him a most eligible prospect within the Cousinhood, even if he lacked physical attractiveness. But he went out infrequently, explaining that his schedule at work gave him little or no time to pursue women seriously. And when he did, they were usually not from among the

Cousinhood. His desire to escape from what he often called the "Jewish ghetto" and his hostility toward his father and all he represented contributed to his preference for non-Jewish women.

One of his favorites was Lady Dorothy Howard, with whom he corresponded and went out for a time during 1908. She shared his love of both nature and politics and wrote to him regularly. Walter Runciman, who had become a friend of Montagu, told him that Lady Howard liked him and that her mother seemed to approve. Runciman urged Montagu to move quickly to solidify the relationship: "She [Lady Howard] told Hilda [Runciman's wife] that you are the only young politician who has interested her mother for two or three years. So that impression is all right. Then she at another time said some excellent things of you, but with all proper restraint. From what I know I am certain that so far you have done well there. Her heart is not at present captured by *anyone*. I am inclined to think that you cannot be too direct. The sooner you see her the better."[44]

There is no evidence that Montagu acted on Runciman's advice. But even if he had wanted to court Lady Dorothy and marry her, and even if she had reciprocated, the fact that she was not Jewish would have been an obstacle. Montagu's father made clear not only in his will, but during his lifetime as well, that if Edwin or any of his other children married out of their faith, they would forfeit whatever financial support they were receiving. Edwin could not afford to be disinherited and did not love Lady Dorothy enough to take the risk.

The engagement of Montagu's younger brother, Gerald, in 1908 provided yet another occasion for Edwin to reflect on his unhappy state and engage in the kind of self-castigation and self-pity that were now characteristic. "Here is Gerald," he wrote to his mother, "my father's partner and trusted son, wealthy, healthy, and happily settled. Here I am, untrusted and often tolerantly condemned, poor, unhealthy, unsettled. No one would care to look out for a wife" for someone who is "bad-tempered, cynical, uncouth, *poor,* with nothing to offer."[45] Any man who viewed himself in this manner, with such a mixture of disdain and self-contempt, was the ideal target for the arrows of unrequited love that would soon be directed at him by a young and exciting woman—Beatrice Venetia Stanley.

7

Venetia and the Beginning of a Romance, 1908–1910

Venetia permitted herself, in the morning of her youth, no recourse to her femininity. She carried the anthologies in her head, walked the high garden walls of Alderley with the . . . stride of a boy . . . a splendid virginal creature reserving herself for we knew not what.

Sir Lawrence Jones, An Edwardian Youth

Many years in a life blur together and leave no special mark. There are other years, because of an event or a person or an emotional upheaval, that stand out clearly and dramatically and forever hold a special place in our memory. For Edwin Montagu, 1909 was such a year. This was when he met Venetia Stanley.

Venetia was a most unusual woman. No ordinary twenty-year-old could handle an intense love relationship with the Prime Minister of England, almost three times her age, while at the same time encouraging the amorous attentions of his private secretary, dear friend and political confidant. No ordinary woman would have converted to Judaism, although she had nothing but scorn for all religion, or married Montagu on terms that permitted each to have extramarital affairs. And no ordinary woman, while married to Montagu, would have lived openly as the mistress of the powerful newspaper magnate, Lord Beaverbrook, who played a major role in the overthrow of her former lover, the Prime Minister.

Venetia's lovers were brilliant and powerful men whose lives were enmeshed in politics. Venetia held them not by her beauty—

she was an attractive woman, but far from a stunning one—but by her intelligence, excitement, force of personality and political sophistication. Without any formal education she was able to discuss politics with any Cabinet member of her day as well as discuss the classics and modern literature with equal depth and insight. Indeed, men not only enjoyed talking to Venetia but listened respectfully to her advice and opinions. And at least two, Prime Minister Asquith and Montagu, sought this advice and came to rely heavily upon it. Sir Harold Acton, art connoisseur and writer, himself skilled in the art of repartee, considered Venetia one of the wittiest and best conversationalists of her day.[1] When a friend of Lord Beaverbrook's was challenged to demonstrate that Venetia was a brilliant talker, he replied, "The other day someone said to her—'Where is Max?' and she answered 'Oh, he's with Maurice Woods trying to re-assemble his split infinitives.' "[2]

Venetia was a fascinating woman not only because she was a witty conversationalist with unorthodox views on religion, marriage and sex, but also because there was at least as much ambiguity and conflict in her personality as in Montagu's. On the one hand, she was a rebel and a radical urging change and nonconformity; yet, in her own life, she exploited the status quo and came to epitomize the worst values of the British aristocracy. She believed women should be sexually liberated, yet she showed no interest in their efforts to achieve political or economic equality. In fact, she was always content to have men speak for her politically and take care of her financially. She was not interested in a career of her own or in supporting herself. She had great warmth and the capacity for friendship but was cold and indifferent as a wife and mother. And while she was often described as an attractive woman with many male friends she was also described as "rather masculine," lacking "in seductive charms," with a reputation for making virile men "impotent."[3] Raymond Asquith went so far as to suggest that she had a lesbian affair with Diana Cooper.[4] Venetia's one quality about which everyone agreed was her indifference to convention and to the opinion of those around her. She was always her own person.

Venetia's Family: Early Records

Venetia came to her unconventional ideas, intelligence and independence naturally. Her family was filled with independent, strong-willed men and women and sprinkled generously with eccentrics and political radicals. She was the daughter of Lord and Lady Stanley of Alderley and of Sheffield, one of the oldest families in the English aristocracy. Born on August 22, 1887, she was named Beatrice Venetia (Montagu at this time was eight years old, already an unhappy boy; Asquith was thirty-five).

The earliest records of Venetia's family tell of a William de Audithley from Audithley in Normandy, who with his two sons, Lyulph and Adam, came to England with William the Conqueror. "From the elder son Lyulph, came the famous Lord Audley who," it was recorded, "performed . . . feats of valour at the battle of Poitiers."[5] Adam, the younger son, settled in Staffordshire on lands granted to him by the King. His grandson, a second Adam, married Mabella, the daughter of Henry Stanley, Lord of Stoneley, from a small hamlet near Leek in Staffordshire. Adam, being a younger son, made Stoneley his seat and adopted the name of his father-in-law, Stanley, as was the custom at the time.[6] His son, Sir William de Stanley, was the father of Sir John Stanley, who in 1385 was created Lord Deputy of Ireland. In 1406 he was given a grant to the Isle of Man from Henry IV, and in 1413 he was made a Knight of the Garter. He married Isabell, daughter of Sir Thomas Lathom of Lathom and Knowsley in Lancashire. It was their son, Thomas Stanley of Knowsley, who, after fighting bravely for the Tudors, was given the honor of crowning Henry VII on Bosworth Field. Two months after the battle, he was created the first Earl of Derby. Sir Thomas's second brother, John, married Elizabeth, daughter and heiress of Thomas Weever of Weever and Alderley. It was through this alliance that the Stanleys came to Alderley. Sir Thomas's great grandson, another Thomas, served as High Sheriff of Cheshire in 1572 and made Alderley his principal seat.[7]

In the late seventeenth century the Stanleys built Alderley Hall, which was the family seat for almost a hundred years. When the house burned down in 1779, nearly all of its contents were destroyed, including the entire library, containing irreplaceable family records and priceless paintings, including one of Sir John by Gainsborough. Another house, also called Alderley Hall but larger and grander, was built on the same site in 1818 and remained the home of the Stanleys until 1936. With forty bedrooms, six large halls, a brewery, a laundry, a mill house, and a farm, it was practically self-supporting. It was filled with portraits of members of the family and furniture "that would make a collector's eyes glitter," such as a pre-Reformation oak refectory table, a Sheraton table "with a patina of glass-like brilliance and beautiful Hepplewhite chairs."[8] It was in Alderley Hall that Venetia was born, a place she loved dearly all her life.

The garden and park at Alderley were its most charming features. It had magnificent trees, some seldom seen in England, such as tulip trees, mulberries and beech. Some of the mulberry trees were given to the Stanleys by King James I when he was trying to encourage the silk industry in England. Alderley's gardens were copied from the great gardens of Italy, with ponds and covered bridges, fountains, a tea house covered with wisteria, rare plants and an "air of remoteness . . . and quiet peacefulness" that made it an especially beautiful retreat.[9] It was there that Venetia spent much of her youth reading, daydreaming, and enjoying its quiet. She never lost this love of the country, one of the few qualities she shared with Edwin.

In the early years most of the Stanleys married wealthy women from the same background as they and from the same areas. The fifth baronet, however, departed from this custom and married the heiress of a London banker, a Miss Ward. His son, who succeeded him in 1775, did the same, marrying another heiress, Margaret Owen of Scotland, who brought the Welsh estate, Penrhos (which Venetia adored even more than Alderley Hall), into the family. Both Miss Ward and Margaret Owen were not only wealthy women but also highly intelligent. The tradition of accepting and respecting bright women in the family had begun.

The son of Margaret Owen, the first Lord Stanley of Alderley, married still another intelligent and wealthy woman, Maria Josepha Holroyd (from whom the Sheffield title came). Their son, Edward (Venetia's grandfather), married the Hon. Henrietta Maria Dillon (Venetia's grandmother), also bright, wealthy and exciting.[10] Edward and Henrietta Maria had nine children, among whom was Venetia's father, Lyulph.

Venetia's Father, Mother, Aunts and Uncles

Lyulph was the third son and his mother's favorite. He had a brilliant career at Oxford, but his radical ideas were too far ahead of his contemporaries to be accepted by the politicians of his time. He was unconventional in his ideology, a nonbeliever and prepared to take unpopular positions if he believed in them. At one time in his life he was a Liberal Member of Parliament, primarily interested in higher adult education.

One of his older brothers, Henry, was the most difficult and eccentric of the brood. Henry developed a passion for the Middle East, traveled extensively there dressed as an Arab, became a Muslim, and married a Spanish woman who was still married to her first husband at the time of her bigamous marriage to Henry. Henry and his brothers and sisters quarreled incessantly. At his funeral, which was conducted according to the Muslim faith, his younger brother, Algernon, commented of Henry that he "lived like a dog, [and would be] buried like a dog."[11]

The other two sons of Henrietta and Edward were equally offbeat. Algernon became a Roman Catholic priest but always retained a certain skepticism toward religion in particular and life in general. He accumulated a fortune despite his vows of poverty. John, the second son, was a delicate boy and man. He fought in the Crimean War and in India and was a gifted writer.

The girls—Alice, Blanche, Maude, Kate, and Rosalind—rounded out the family, each as different from the others as were the sons. Maude was described as:

goodness itself; she and Kate Amberly were the two most human members of the family. . . . She did her best to keep on good terms with her brothers and sisters and whenever possible, to reconcile them with each other. . . . Apart from her missionary work in the family, she did a great deal for the poor, invented and founded a girl's club and helped her mother to forward the cause of women's education and rights. She seems to have been in love with Sir Henry Rawlinson, later Lord Rawlinson, and when he married another she evidently gave up the idea of marriage.[12]

Blanche married Lord Airlie and was the grandmother of Clementine Hozier, who married Winston Churchill. Venetia and Clementine were cousins once removed.

Kate was the mother of Earl Russell, better known as Bertrand Russell. The youngest daughter, Rosalind, married George Howard, later the Earl of Carlisle, an artist of considerable distinction, and founded a large family which she ruled with an iron hand. From this brief description of Venetia's ancestors, especially her father and her aunts and uncles, one can easily see how Venetia acquired some of her more distinctive characteristics. As one reads the vignettes of their lives, one finds over and over again, words like nonconventional, irreligious, liberal, radical, strong-willed, intelligent, well read and well versed in politics. One can also understand more readily Venetia's later conversion to Judaism and her total lack of concern in rejecting Christianity when one recalls that her father was a nonbeliever, one uncle a Muslim and another a Roman Catholic bishop, who remained a skeptic all his life and was able to accumulate a fortune while ostensibly performing his bishop's duties. Neither should one be surprised at Venetia's skill in conversation which was encouraged at her father's dining table. Not only was the conversation of the highest level, but all the children, girls and boys alike, were expected to read the hundreds of books and periodicals that Lyulph collected and share their thoughts with one another. Venetia was a voracious reader, enjoying books on every subject, but especially literature, history and politics.

The best picture of Venetia's family and the luncheons at Alderley are captured in Bertrand Russell's autobiography:

Lyulph [Venetia's father] was a free thinker, and spent his time fighting the church on the London School Board. . . . Algernon was a Roman Catholic priest, a Papal Chamberlain and Bishop of Emmaus. Lyulph was witty, encyclopedic and caustic. Algernon was witty, fat and greedy. . . . At the Sunday luncheons there would be vehement arguments, for among the daughters and sons-in-law there were representatives of the Church of England, Unitarianism and Positivism. . . . I used to go to these luncheons in fear and trembling, since I never knew when the whole pack would turn upon me.[13]

Venetia's mother, Margaret, was the antithesis of her outspoken, opinionated and radical husband. She was a gentle, soft-spoken, beautiful woman, described by Bertrand Russell as "the only friend [Bertrand Russell] could count on"[14] when he visited Alderley, and by Sir Lawrence Jones, a family friend, as "speaking low among the

clear, challenging voices of her children and children-in-law . . .
looking like an eighteenth-century marquise . . . with dark eyes and
brows beneath silvery hair. She could hint; she could confide; she
could glance obliquely; she was wholly different from her downright brood in manner, though sharing their unwinking vision. She
gave me her friendship and won my heart."[15] She and Lyulph had
eight children—five girls and three boys.

Of the Stanley family and Alderley itself, Sir Lawrence recalls
Alderley "as not just another hospitable country house offering all
the pleasures of riding, swimming, and lawn tennis. It had its own
peculiar atmosphere since all the Stanleys were 'characters,' diverse,
outspoken, independent."[16]

Lord Sheffield [Venetia's father], a bearded sage, only emerged from his
library at meal-times, to take the head of the enormous table and to tease
his family and guests with a severe *viva voce* examination. Denying the
existence of an omniscient Deity, he was himself omniscient. A younger
brother of this skeptic was a Monsignor, the Bishop of Emmaus *in partibus
infidelium*. This plump, rosy, rather greedy worldling, who knew his elder
brother to be damned but approved of the table he kept, was excellent
company. He liked young people and demanded no respect for his sacred
office.[17]

Alderley was ahead of the times "in the candour, the open-eyed
down-to-earthiness of its inmates. The table talk among the brothers
and sisters was robust and disputatious."[18]

Venetia

It was to Venetia, Sir Lawrence wrote, that he owed "the fun and
friendships of Alderley, that spacious home that reflected in its large
simplicity and strength the generous, no-nonsense character of its
inhabitants."[19] The family not only enjoyed political arguments at
dinner but also practical jokes and pranks. In this, Venetia and "her
gang of smart young friends," as her cousin Adelaide Stanley Lubbock described them, were the family leaders.[20] Venetia also kept a
menagerie of animals: a monkey, several dogs, a fox, a penguin and,
for a short time, a bear—all helpful props for pranks and mischief.

No occasion was spared from Venetia's irreverence. Even the
christening of the daughter of Venetia's sister, Sylvia Henley, at the

church at Alderley became the occasion for raucous behavior that characterized the Stanley family get-togethers—with Venetia and her animals turning a solemn religious ceremony into another opportunity for irreverence. All the dogs got loose:

after having been carefully shut up, and had to be hurrooshed back from the church with the usual yells and stone-throwing. Two strangers—tourists—were looking at the church when we arrived and were evidently petrified with astonishment at the levity of the christening party—especially when Venetia made a remark in a stentorian voice about "drowning the young gorilla." They also seemed to think it much out of order that Bibs (myself) should be installed in the middle of the aisle in her perambulator. She was asleep for most of the service but woke towards the end and started a long and loud conversation with Ellen (my nurse) whose attempts to try and quiet her "silently" were most humorous.[21]

Not only was Venetia a prankster but there was a tomboyishness about her that prompted Sir Lawrence to describe her as having not only "dark-eyed aquiline good looks," but a "masculine intellect." And while she and he were good friends, Venetia "permitted herself," he wrote, "in the morning of her youth, no recourse to her femininity. She carried the Anthologies in her head, but rode like an Amazon, and walked the high garden walls of Alderley with the casual strides of a boy. She was a splendid, virginal, comradely creature, reserving herself for we knew not what use of her fine brain and hidden heart."[22]

Sir Lawrence was not alone in noting Venetia's lack of femininity. While men often relied on Venetia as a confidante, there is no evidence that she was romantically involved with any young man of her age or circle. She was, according to Dr. Brock, "in the simple, psychological categories used in her circle . . . classed as rather 'masculine' in outlook. When she helped at a summer camp for a Hoxton boys' club in 1913, she 'played football for the first time' and wrote to Edwin, 'It's I think far the most thrilling game I've ever played: it intoxicated me!' "[23]

Venetia has also been described as "tall, strongly built, formidably intelligent," but "lacking in seductive charm. She had the reputation of rendering even the most virile man impotent. She was handsome in her way."[24] While "her upbringing had given her enough independence to defy stuffier conventions," she lacked a sense of independence "to strike out decisively on her own. Unlike another of her cousins, Gertrude Bell, she had not the self-confidence of a 'college girl.' She would never have emulated the actress Lillah McCarthy in scribbling 'Votes for Women' across the PM's blotter. With all her strong intelligence, she had a curious lack of determination and initiative; she would drift pleasantly with the stream until action was imperative."[25]

Put differently, she was not prepared to discipline herself or devote her time and effort to convert her ideas to action. With all her interest in politics, for example, she preferred to remain on the sidelines of the political scene. She did not become active in Liberal politics, but was content to express her opinions privately to the Prime Minister, to Montagu and to other political leaders over lunch or dinner, or in more intimate surroundings. She never campaigned for candidates of her choice. In several of Asquith's letters, he chided her on the wasteful days she spent at luncheons, gossiping with her friends, at the theater, nightclubs, parties, riding, golf, tennis and the like.

In London, in the years before the war, Venetia became a member, indeed, one of the dominant members, of a clique that called itself the "Coterie" and that was dubbed by others "The Corrupt Coterie." They "met constantly, at balls and dinners in town and leisurely country house parties, and they cultivated all the pleasures of civilization. They indulged their high spirits in treasure-hunts, fancy dress balls, and deliciously illicit evenings playing poker. They held riotous parties that went on till dawn and their doings were written up by a shocked and delighted press. . . . Their company was always in demand by the great hostesses and the eminent politicians."[26]

Venetia was hedonistic and while she may have been a committed Liberal, she had no qualms about enjoying the life of privilege. Although she did enlist for service as a Red Cross nurse during World War I, her own letters from the front make clear that her motivation to serve was at least in part her boredom in London, when all of the eligible young men in her circle were on the fighting front. She craved excitement, writing while at a hospital in France that she wanted to get even closer to the front, not to be of greater service to the wounded, but "because it would be a 'new sensation.' "[27] In another letter, she wrote that "two of the orderlies were nearly drowned while bathing today and another came near to dying of heart failure running for help so we've had a little excitement but not much to live on for a whole week."[28]

It may have been this quest for excitement that made her especially attractive to men, not necessarily in romantic terms but as someone with whom one could enjoy a good adventure, a hearty laugh and witty conversation. She showed interest in the problems of her friends. She listened and sympathized and was able to provide comfort and solace to a degree quite remarkable in so young a woman.

It was her remarkable ability to give comfort that first brought Venetia to the attention of both Prime Minister Asquith and Edwin Montagu. The year was 1909 and Violet Asquith, the Prime Minister's daughter, had just lost her dearest beau, "Archie" (Archibald) Gordon, who had died after a car accident. Venetia was Violet's closest friend. In fact, the two were almost inseparable.

"This pair of rarities," observed Sir Lawrence, "the dark (Venetia) and the fair (Violet) were as interlocked as night with day."[29] Violet was slender, had a warm and gentle voice, and like Venetia, was extraordinarily intelligent, with a wide circle of friends and an overriding passion for politics and political discourse. She adored her father but was indifferent and at times even hurtful to her stepmother, Margot.

Sir Lawrence described his first impression of Violet as "Waves of shadow across a wheatfield"; her voice had "clear tones" and a "cooing note," holding the attention of those about her. "Even then," he reminisced, "Violet, the compeer of trained minds, veiled in her femininity the bright blade of her intellect." She was never girlish, "but she was very much a woman, and unconsciously exacted, as Venetia did not, a touch of diffidence, a shade of deference, in our masculine approaches."[30]

Violet took the tragedy of her beau's accident very hard and spent the week before he died at his hospital bedside. Venetia, as Violet's closest friend, was never far from her side. The Prime Minister, who loved his daughter as much as she adored him, also spent as much time as he could with Violet during this crisis and was thus in Venetia's company frequently. It was during this week that Asquith began to feel a particular admiration for Venetia as he watched her comfort and console his grief-stricken daughter.

Venetia and Asquith

Actually, Venetia was no stranger to the Prime Minister. Even before 1909, as Violet's friend, she spent enough time with the Asquiths for Margot to view her, as early as 1907, as part of what she called, the Prime Minister's "little harem."[31] Asquith enjoyed the company of clever, attractive young women and during these early years Margot accepted this with grace, or at least she pretended to. Asquith had a need for the company of young women, enjoying their beauty as well as their conversation. Winston Churchill's daughter, Mary, later wrote that her mother, Clementine, disliked "Mr. Asquith's predilection for peering down 'Pennsylvania Avenue' (the contemporary expression for a lady's cleavage) whenever he was seated next to a pretty woman."[32] It was well known in the circles in which they moved that Asquith had a roving eye, with, as he himself had written, "a slight weakness for the companionship of clever and attractive women."[33]

In January 1908, for example, Pamela Jekyll, one of the members of Asquith's "little harem," noted in a diagram she sent to Asquith that his heart was divided among five young women: "Viola [Tree], Dorothy [Beresford], Lillian [Tennant], Venetia and me."[34] While most of his time with such young girls was spent in conversation and harmless flirting, a kiss, an intimate touch, and a hug were not unheard of. During November and December of 1910 Venetia accompanied the Prime Minister and Violet in his election travels through "Bluey's" (Harold Trevor Baker's) constituency—Accrington and Burnley—prior to the second election held that year. The trip made a lasting impression on Asquith, who, four years later, reminisced longingly to Venetia:

Do you remember the night, years afterwards when Bluey led us astray thro' the wilds of Lancashire & we arrived near midnight at Gawthorpe, and were entertained by the same great man & his 2 daughters? What fun we had! I think, if I remember right, that we started the evening in the company of Ottoline at Burnley. How little we any of us foresaw of the future—least of all I, my darling.[35]

By 1910, the other women in his life were being displaced by Venetia.

Venetia and Montagu: A Relationship Begins

Venetia's relationship with Edwin Montagu began at the same time that Asquith began to focus his attentions on her as well. For Montagu as for Asquith, Archie Gordon's death was the catalyst. Montagu had known Venetia before 1909, since both were often guests of the Asquiths at Archerfield. Venetia was exactly the kind of woman that Montagu found most attractive. She was vivacious, witty, articulate, politically knowledgeable—and not Jewish. He, however, was not the kind of man to interest Venetia. He was serious and solemn, neither handsome nor exciting, and was only a lowly Member of Parliament.

Sometime in the spring of 1909, Edwin had in fact invited Venetia to dinner on the pretense of having her meet Runciman, an invitation Venetia politely declined, ostensibly because she had a prior engagement. It was not until the day after Archie Gordon's funeral, almost seven months later, that Montagu had the courage to write again:

December 21, 1909

Dear Miss Stanley,

Your kindness to me in the past makes me bold to break in on the grief which you, like the rest of us who are Violet's and Archie's friends, must feel.

I have never seen anything like the collected helpless sorrow of yesterday's service and it has but served to emphasize the sense of reality of our loss and the sad plight of those who survive.

I have just written the letter I shrank from the impossible stereotyped banalities of sympathy.

While you may be a friend to one [Violet] who feels thus helpless and anxious please tell me at some time how she is and whether the courage which she has shown is helping her to bear the intolerable.

Yours ever,

EM[36]

Venetia answered immediately, thanking Edwin for his note and telling him of Violet's condition. The letter was a formal one, dealing almost exclusively with Violet's condition, but it had a friendly tone and an invitation to continue corresponding, "My dear

Mr. Montagu," Venetia wrote, "I'm glad you thought of writing to me." She told him how courageous Violet was on the last day of her beau's life, making it "the most gloriously happy last day." But Venetia worried how Violet would react when she returned to Archerfield and "her usual life begins and she feels that everything is indeed over."[37] Near the end of December Venetia wrote again, asking if she and Montagu might meet for lunch so that she could get his opinion about Violet's condition. Unlike Edwin, Venetia was never shy about asking for a date, even in the opening stages of a relationship.

In the early months of 1910 the letters between Venetia and Montagu showed their growing affection, with Montagu openly expressing his pleasure at receiving Venetia's notes and sharing with her some political comments. On January 25, 1910, a month after their last exchange of letters, Montagu wrote again: "Dear Miss Stanley, I wonder whether you will acquit me—as I deserve—of any exaggeration when I say that of all the telegrams I received on Saturday [on the occasion of his re-election to Parliament] none pleased me so much as yours. Thank you so much for sending it."[38] This letter was sent from the Hotel Sea View, a favorite resort of Montagu in Mayo County, Ireland, where he had gone for a rest after a most strenuous election campaign. He addressed ninety-seven meetings in three weeks. This resulted in his feeling "rather knocked to pieces," but he "still kept a seat for the Prime Minister." He ended his letter admitting that he had been reluctant to write to her until she had written to him. "I have often thought of writing to you again but always hoped to hear from you."[39]

Venetia answered promptly, explaining that she too had wanted to write before but that there was "so little to say." Violet had been ill, a result of "stress." Violet, Venetia, and Venetia's mother planned to go to the south of France and that "should do her [Violet] good." The letter ended again with the formal "Yours, Venetia Stanley."[40]

Either because of Montagu's shyness or Venetia's indifference, very little progress had been made in the year since their correspondence had first begun. But Venetia's letters, by implication at least, seemed to invite a more serious relationship and Montagu, shy or not, was eager to pursue.

8

The Political Scene, 1909–1911

This year has been occupied with the Budget. This has been hotly fought in the House where the members have been teaching an imaginative and an almost illiterate Chancellor [Lloyd George] the elements of practical finance.

Montagu in a letter to a friend, Nov. 1, 1909

While 1909 would be remembered by Edwin as the year in which he began his relationship with Venetia, for Britain it was the year of the "People's Budget" and the constitutional crisis it triggered, resulting in the enactment of the Parliament Act of 1911, which would change forever the political system of England.

As the year began, Montagu continued as Private Secretary to the Prime Minister. His main political concern was the mood of the country and the need for Asquith to do something dramatic to spark enthusiasm among the constituents—to light some "fireworks" and bring excitement to the political scene.[1] Edwin's nerves were again causing him some form of cardiac irregularity, but his doctor had assured him "that there is as yet (I hate these words, I am such a coward), nothing wrong organically but the nerves are again all wrong though nothing as bad as two years ago."[2] His cardiac and nervous condition did not stop him in January 1909 from undertaking a speaking tour for the Central Liberal Association, which covered thirty-two "dreary little village meetings absolutely essential to the County member, but at the same time boring and irksome in the extreme. At each place I have to address men who will not read, and therefore must be told the whole political story, so that I repeat the same speech every night, twice, without any opportunity of saying something original and inspiring."[3]

Montagu worried about the prospect of the House of Lords veto-
ing the budget when it was presented in April, and he urged Asquith
to appeal to the country against the recent use of the veto by the
House of Lords and not to permit the Conservatives to maneuver
him into two General Elections—"the first on the Budget (which
the Tories will be glad to lose) and a second on the House of Lords,
(which the Tories would hope to win)."[4] Montagu wrote to Asquith:

Your opponents are concentrating their efforts and even determining the
action of the House of Lords on a conviction that they can force you to
two General Elections in this issue, and it is their victory in the second
upon which they are calculating. They will say . . . that your victory, if
you achieve one, in your first election, means that your Budget is wanted,
and that the abolition of the veto of the House of Lords received no
mandate and must be referred once again back to the electors. This is what
is buoying up Arthur Balfour who hopes that the eventual passage of the
Budget will rescue him from his tariff Reform friends. This is the line of
action: [two elections: one on the budget and a second on the Lords] which
will commend itself most to H. M. [King Edward VII] who will see in this
an easy way out of all the constitutional changes which he dreads.[5]

Montagu pleaded with Asquith to "employ every weapon that pres-
cience offers to defeat this maneuver by a clear presentation of your
action to the country *before* the election[6] . . . you should focus public
opinion, supply the necessary drama for the campaign of your creation under your leadership by a series of resolutions moved immediately after the rejection of the Bill."[7]

Earlier in the year, Montagu had urged Asquith to set forth "a
program for tomorrow."

We are wandering like sheep without a leader . . . you have only addressed
your followers in the House and are still silent to the country. Winston is
not yet P.M. . . . [he, Winston] delights and he tickles, he even enthuses
the audiences he addresses—but when he has gone, so also has the memory
of what he has said. . . . We want to know the plan of action.[8]

Montagu's propensity for brilliant analysis of the political condition
is nowhere more sharply revealed than in these letters. He read the
political tea leaves perfectly.

Hoping that Violet might be able to influence her father to take
this course of action, Montagu wrote to her as well:

Things are not well in London. . . . The Constituencies are in excellent heart, ready and eager to be led. The fireworks of last Session are to be succeeded by soaked squibs this Session. People are complaining of your father's silence, and it almost looks as if your father did not know what to do. Politicians are getting weak-kneed, constituents are getting more and more enthusiastic. As my confidence in your father grows, my lack of confidence in his colleagues grows too. I hope to goodness history won't say they proved too strong for him.[9]

Violet was no more successful with her father than was Montagu.

The People's Budget

The "fireworks" that Montagu believed were necessary to stimulate excitement and sustain support for the Liberal government did take place. They were provided, however, not by an immediate fight on the House of Lords veto, but by the presentation of the People's Budget by Lloyd George in April 1909. On this budget, which contained many provisions attacked as radical and as the forerunners of socialism, the Prime Minister did not remain silent, as Edwin had feared. The budget had Asquith's complete support. During the forty-two Parliamentary days necessary to get it through the Finance Committee and the seventy days of floor debate in the House of Commons, Asquith stood firmly behind the budget. "He several times came across from Downing Street at the end of an all-night sitting and took over for the last hour or so before breakfast; and he moved the minor but permanent procedural changes which, at the end of July the Government decided were essential if the bill were ever to get through. . . . The Prime Minister," Lloyd George re-called, "was as firm as a rock."[10] All through these days and long nights Montagu, as Asquith's Parliamentary Private Secretary, was right beside him. He almost lost his voice, while his headaches, nervous tension and cardiac problems grew worse.

The principal goal of the budget was to raise £16 million to meet a prospective deficit that included, among other things, funds for the old age pensions that had begun modestly in 1908 and the dreadnoughts sought by the Navy. Lloyd George and his supporters believed that the burden of this increased taxation should fall on the rich. This had been a principle championed by Montagu for years in his memos to Asquith beginning in 1906. In this he was as radical as

Lloyd George, and he never swerved from this belief. Lloyd George also needed new sources of income for state insurance against sickness and unemployment and to implement his land reform program.

Under the proposed budget, the new revenue would be raised by increasing death duties on estates over five thousand pounds, raising the income tax slightly on both earned and unearned income, and increasing duties on tobacco, whiskey and stamps. New taxes were introduced on motor cars and gasoline, the proceeds of which would be devoted to road building, and a tax was levied on mineral royalties to be applied to miners' welfare benefits. The budget also created, for the first time, the "super tax," fixed at a low rate, on incomes over three thousand pounds. The last of these, it was estimated, would bring in no more than a half million pounds. It was a modest beginning but established a principle for which Montagu had fought long and hard from the moment he became Secretary for the Chancellor of the Exchequer.[11]

Although each of these increases was small and, individually, probably would have been adopted without controversy, the land value duties (a form of capital gains on the transfer of land), that were also part of the budget, caused an uproar because in order to impose these taxes, the government had to value, or appraise, all the land in the entire country. This, the Conservatives feared, was likely to lay the groundwork for larger property taxes in the future. Moreover, the program raised the philosophic question of why land should be selected for a capital gains tax while other forms of property remained exempt.

The response of the Liberals was one that had large-scale appeal: Land was a divine or natural gift, while all other property was created by man. Thus, land should be treated differently. As Churchill put it, land was a "perpetual monopoly . . . the mother of all other forms of monopoly. . . . Land, which is a necessity of human existence, which is the original source of all wealth, which is strictly limited in extent, which is fixed in geographical position—land, I say, differs from all other forms of property."[12]

Lloyd George was less diplomatic. His speeches, delivered throughout the country in defense of the budget, often included vitriolic attacks against the aristocracy and the large land barons, "the Dukes," as he called them. In his attacks he often used the specific names and examples of landlords who exploited huge sums from the common people.

Such tactics were bound to inflame the Conservatives and strike fear among the landowners, who could see in the campaign the shape of a radical society and the beginning of a movement that would ultimately deny them the free use and control of their land. There was another reason for the strong Conservative opposition to the budget: They saw it as a reinforcement of the principle of free trade. If extra money could be raised from increased taxes, there would be no need for protective tariffs as a source of extra revenue.

Debate on the budget was intense not only within Parliament but throughout the country. Even Lord Rothschild, who was a Liberal, sent the Prime Minister a protest signed by the heads of the leading financial houses of England. A month later, he chaired a crowded meeting of agitated financiers, mostly Liberals, opposed to the Financial Bill. Lord Rosebery also entered the fray denouncing the budget as "inquisitorial, tyrannical and socialistic."[13]

Lord Swaythling, Montagu's father, always true to his radical politics, supported the budget. Although he was seventy-eight years old, he attended a Liberal city meeting addressed by Asquith and supported a pro-budget demonstration attended by two hundred fifty thousand Britishers who marched on Hyde Park. For once father and son were on the same side of an argument.

Montagu wrote on November 1, 1909, that the budget "has been hotly fought in the House where the members have been teaching an imaginative and almost illiterate chancellor the elements of practical finance." Montagu concluded that Lloyd George was a "marvelously clever pupil," that "a good and nearly watertight bill" had been hammered out by Commons and that "the party is solid and in high fittle." He foresaw, however:

the House of Lords will throw the budget out without any conviction as to results but from a high sense of duty to their class . . . I think we should then ask the country to assert that the House of Lords

(1) has no rights at all in financial matters
(2) should not be permitted to reject bills
(3) should be reconstituted to form a revising committee of Parliament reporting to the Commons.

Tacticians among the Tories will try and force two elections in rapid succession on these issues. They will be helped by the King. We shall be fools if we don't see this and prevent it. [14]

Constitutional Crisis

Montagu's warning that early on the government should have endorsed a definite plan to limit the powers of the House of Lords and should have sought a mandate for such a plan as soon as possible was prescient. This was not, however, the course followed by Asquith. Throughout the fall he held to the position that it was unthinkable that the House of Lords could violate a 250-year-old rule and reject a budget adopted by the House of Commons. By publicly emphasizing the impossibility of rejections, Asquith hoped he could bring the Lords to their senses. He preferred, as was his style, "to wait on events which he did not wish to accelerate by any bold pronouncement or even by an acknowledgement of the gravity of the situation." To his critics, this was an example of Asquith's penchant for inexcusable delay and of his lack of leadership. To his advocates, it illustrated his "refusal to be stampeded into the excitement of the moment." [15]

There were several reasons for his reluctance to attack the issue. The Liberals were geared for a general election in the fall of 1910 and he was uncertain an early election would serve the Liberal cause. More importantly, the Cabinet could not itself agree on how it wanted to "smash the veto." Montagu's suggestion that the House of Lords be reconstituted "to form a revising committee of Parliament reporting to Commons" [16] would never have been accepted by the Cabinet, many of whom would have resigned if such a drastic step were taken.

With the Liberals so divided Asquith saw no point in forcing an election. But by the end of November he had no choice: On November 30, 1909, the House of Lords, exactly as Montagu had predicted, rejected the budget, 350 to 75, after the House of Commons had passed it by 379 to 149. Within twenty-four hours the House of Commons adopted a resolution submitted by the government that framed the issue in the sharpest possible constitutional terms: "That the action of the House of Lords in refusing to pass into law the financial provision made by the House for the service of the year is a breach of the Constitution and an usurpation of the rights of the Commons."[17] The issue was now joined. Three days later Parliament was dissolved and the people would be asked to express their opinion.

First Election of 1910

This was just the kind of issue the lawyer in Asquith liked best. He held British law and its institutions in great reverence and never wavered in his position that the House of Lords could not extend its power and thus change the nature of the British parliamentary system. Asquith may not have been a crusading reformer, but he was a staunch traditionalist and, on this point, inflexible.

A week after Parliament was dissolved, Asquith gave a rousing speech at Albert Hall that set the tone of the Liberal Party's campaign. "The will of the people as deliberately expressed by their elected representatives must within the lifetime of a single Parliament be made to prevail,"[18] he declared. The Conservatives ran an equally energetic campaign arguing that the Liberals were trying to introduce a single chamber and destroy the structure of British government. It was a hard fought campaign.

Montagu Wins Again

Even before Parliament was dissolved, Montagu anticipated the January election and began "perfecting" his organization.[19] He had hoped that his mother would campaign for him, but since his father wanted her to join him on a trip abroad, he wrote to her, "I shall have to do without you, but this will be very difficult."[20] He added, "I am torn in my desires between the want of you and a strong belief that my father ought to be allowed at this time of his life to do exactly what he likes." He told her too that the weather was "horribly cold" and driving around in a motor "would not be very good for you."[21]

Earlier Montagu had suggested that his father take his Aunt Clara on the trip and leave Montagu's mother free to help him. Montagu's father had objected, wanting the company of his wife on what turned out to be his last trip abroad. Even at thirty, Montagu was still arguing with his father over the attention and time of his mother.

In addition, Montagu found himself in disagreement with the family over the use of its automobiles in his campaign. By now motor cars had become of considerable importance in rural campaigns, especially in a district as geographically diffuse as Montagu's. On December 17, he complained to his mother that Lionel had told him the cars were not available, since they were being used to help his cousin Herbert Samuel who was up for reelection as well. "I am most anxious," he wrote:

to help preserve Stuart's seat; but really that the claims of an enormous Constituency 30 miles long by 20 miles wide with 11,000 electors should be weighed against a tiny place with about 3,000 electors concentrated in a very small area is difficult to understand. Just in the same way that Herbert with his 1,500 majority obtained this year should put the desirability of getting ten or twelve extra votes one way or another against the chance of keeping a seat with only a majority of 500 four years ago, is past my comprehension.[22]

From such letters as this, it is apparent why Montagu was not a favorite in the family.

He alerted the family to the fact that he would be "adopted" by the party "next Thursday" and needed his bank account opened as soon as possible to pay campaign expenses. As for his opponent, he described him as:

very ignorant, not very clever but quite honest and nice. I do not think he enthuses his supporters much and he certainly cannot make a speech. Their organization is in a terrible muddle and all this counts in my favor. On the other hand, there are more Tariff Reformers than there used to be and it is difficult to interest them in constitutional issues and we are very short of motor cars![23]

As usual, Montagu worked around the clock, attending two or three meetings a day, never relaxing, pushing himself to the limit and ending each day in a state of nervous exhaustion plagued by tension, back pains, diarrhea, headaches and feelings of loneliness. Even months after the election, in explaining his general fatigue to his mother, he blamed it on this election, complaining that he could not be out all day (hiking, shooting, etc.) "as I used to without begetting a splitting headache and lower back stabs—as an old man and this at 31. . . . I regard this . . . as the result of the last election which cost me too much in health. . . . I won't go through it again for anything at that price."[24] His doctors, he told his mother, used to say that his "vital organs were less worn than most men of twenty but now doctors say everything is weak and terrible and I fear so."[25] In the same letter, he added that his "eyesight is also failing" and his hair and portions of his beard were turning grey.[26]

Montagu won his difficult constituency by a majority of 505, which was slightly less than his majority of 513 in 1906. In a sense, this was a far greater personal victory for him than his win in 1906. In that year he was carried by the Liberal landslide; this time he had no such help. This victory was truly his own. In the election, the Liberals lost 104 seats and their margin over the Conservatives dropped to 2. Asquith was now totally dependent on the Irish Nationalists and on Labour for his majority. It was a disappointing election for both the Liberals and the Conservatives.

Under Secretary of State for India

Montagu had now been serving Asquith as Parliamentary Private Secretary for almost four years and was becoming increasingly eager for a change and a promotion. He expressed this to his colleague, Vaughan Nash, who replied: "It grieves me to know that you are feeling overlooked and slighted by the P.M. Please try to be patient and next time you see the old man, you will be sunny and serene— or as near it as your gloomy, but lovable nature will allow you."[27]

As Nash had predicted, Asquith, grateful for Montagu's loyalty and hard work and pleased that he had kept his seat for the Liberal Party, appointed Montagu Under Secretary of State for India, in February 1910. This would mark a great turning point: With this appointment Edwin's involvement and fascination with India began. It was a bond and affection that lasted the remaining fourteen years of his life, and it was the only love in his life that rivaled his obsession with Venetia.

It was with pride that he was able to write to both his parents on February 17, 1910: "I have ceased to be Asquith's Secretary and have accepted the distinguished and responsible office of Under-Secretary of State for India."[28] Yet even while he was pleased with the importance of his new appointment, he expressed regret that he was leaving Asquith and going into a "branch of politics divorced from the ordinary turn of political life."[29] He was fearful that he would fail, since he knew nothing of India and would have to represent the India Office in the House of Commons and introduce the India budget, "a responsibility of the office of which I doubt my courage." "Had I no ambition," he wrote, "I should never have moved."[30]

But as always his ambition was stronger than his fear, and he gladly accepted his new promotion, "pleased to have achieved recognition" and the congratulations of his parents. At thirty-one, the approval of his parents still mattered intensely, as did the congratulations of Venetia. During the first months of his new appointment he was so absorbed in his work that he had little or no time for correspondence. But Venetia had not forgotten him. With his new appointment he became a slightly more important member of the government and thus of greater interest to her.

Montagu's responsibilities at the India Office were both more demanding and exciting. The political scene around him, moreover, had become fraught with danger for the Liberal Party and he was deeply concerned that it would not be able to retain its majority. The margin on which Asquith could rely was small and the possibility of yet a second election in 1910 was imminent. As the new Parliament convened, its immediate agenda was still the budget and the curbing of the House of Lords. The composition of the new Parliament gave the Lords more confidence than before. They viewed the election as having seriously weakened the Liberals and their intransigence became even more pronounced.

To add to Asquith's woes, there was still no unanimity in the Cabinet over how the veto problem should be handled and what, if any, reorganization of Parliament should be proposed. His Irish support was shaky and their dislike of the budget well known. The morale in the Cabinet was so low and the conflict so severe that during the early weeks of 1910 there was every reason to believe that the government would fall at any moment.

The Parliament Act

Asquith had no intention of seeing his government resign. "To him surrender was never a viable policy. His primary need was to secure the regular backing of the Irish vote and, with great tactical skill, this was what he set out to achieve."[31] As a first step in salvaging his agitated and disputatious Cabinet, he appointed a Cabinet Committee to draft a proposal on the House of Lords. Within a few weeks it issued a report favoring a series of resolutions under which any bill would become law if passed by three successive sessions of the House of Commons. The Lords could neither reject nor amend a money bill, and the Speaker of the House could determine, subject to established rules, what was or was not a money bill. On behalf of the Cabinet, Asquith informed the King that if the House of Lords rejected this proposal, the Government "would either resign or advise a dissolution of Parliament." In somewhat veiled language, Asquith told the King that the advice to dissolve Parliament would not be given unless the King guaranteed that he would create enough peers "to swamp the House of Lords."

Asquith went public and spoke to the House of Commons "in that wonderful language of his," the Chief Whip wrote, "and with a dignity that abashed some of the ruder spirits. . . . It was a stirring scene."[32] Finally, he "bit the bullet"—almost a year after Montagu had pleaded with him to develop a program that would tell the country what plan he proposed to curb the House of Lords. Now he did so. The resolutions of the Cabinet Committee were the core of the plan. If Lords rejected them, Asquith would dissolve Parliament, and after an election that he was certain of winning, he would push to implement the resolutions, knowing he had the King's assurance in his pocket. He still hoped that the hotheads among the Lords would act reasonably and not push him to take this course.

After Asquith's speech, the government felt strong enough to reintroduce the budget, and it was passed in Commons on the third reading. On the following day the Lords passed it without amendment, thus acknowledging that the January election had settled the budget issues. However, the Lords were not prepared to concede that this settled the constitutional issues. Montagu's early letters to Asquith had warned that the Lords would determine the strategy unless Asquith preempted the issue. Asquith had failed to do so. The Liberals would now have to face another election before the constitutional issue would be solved.

A New King

To further complicate the matter, on May 6, 1910, while Asquith was vacationing aboard the naval vessel *The Enchantress,* King Edward VII died suddenly; some believed that the anxiety caused by the struggle over the House of Lords contributed to his death. Because of his inexperience, the new King, George V, was a far more difficult man to deal with on this issue. He was also less worldly, less informed and less willing to "pack the Lords." He insisted on further negotiations and was deeply troubled when these failed. On November 10, in the face of this failure, the Cabinet called for dissolution. Before Asquith implemented this, he was determined to obtain his needed guarantees from the new King, which he did, with extraordinary cleverness.[33] Dissolution took place on November 28, 1910, and the campaign was over before Christmas.

The Second Election of 1910

Montagu won his seat again and wrote to Asquith on December 12, 1910, that he was pleased to be able to keep his seat "for the Party which you lead." In spite of the lackluster campaign, the Liberals performed "the feat unprecedented since 1832, of winning three successive general elections."[34] But the House of Lords was not easily impressed. The die-hards, known as "the Ditchers," were determined to fight on to the "last ditch." The more reasonable and moderate among them, "the Hedges," knew the battle was lost, although for weeks controversy ensued. But the Hedges won. The final vote was taken in August 1911, and the Parliament Bill became law. The long constitutional crisis was over, with no bloodshed, a revolutionary change wrought by peaceful means: words and legal maneuvers. If Asquith achieved nothing else as Prime Minister, history should rank him among England's great political leaders for this achievement alone. Its enactment was the crowning glory of his career.

The remaining months of 1911 continued to be filled with unrest and crises. The year was marked by a series of industrial strikes unparalleled in the nation's history and an international controversy involving Germany and France, the Agadir incident, that was a minor precursor of the war that lay only two years ahead. Montagu's involvement in the Agadir crisis and the efforts to solve the menace of the strikes was only peripheral. While he continued to warn the Liberal Party that it could not ignore the plight of the workingman and the small farmer, his major concern had now shifted from the struggle for social justice at home to the struggle for democracy in India.

9

Under Secretary of State for India: First Two Years, 1910–1912

A new force in English politics.

Daily Mail, *July 27, 1910*

Montagu assumed his new responsibilities as Under Secretary of State for India at a propitious time. This was a period in English history when a new interest in Indian affairs had developed. On the platform, in the press and in general literature, increasing attention was being focused on India, sufficient for one newspaper to devote a full page to a speech by Montagu in which he proclaimed that, "everywhere we find a dawning realization that what has been called the 'brightest Jewel in the British Crown' is no mere ornament but an Imperial charge involving great and growing responsibilities."[1]

There were many reasons for this. Europe had become increasingly interested in what was poetically called "the spirit of the East." At the same time the growing movement of nationalism in India, accompanied by sporadic outbursts of violence and police brutality, was beginning to filter through the equanimity of British rule. The fact that the Secretary of State for India was Lord Morley, a distinguished leader of the Liberal Party, also added to the new political prominence given to India. His appointment put an end to the habit of regarding India as "a dumping ground for mediocrities"[2] and announced that India was important enough to have as its Secretary at Whitehall one of the leaders of Liberal England.

Morley, for his part, increasingly involved himself in the administration of India, especially in trying to assuage Indian grievances, thus making Indian problems of more immediate concern to the Home government. This was applauded in some circles within the Liberal Party on the grounds that only the parliamentary spirit, as expressed by the Secretary of State, could nourish democracy in India. Left to itself, the Indian government, it was believed, would only become more authoritarian. There were some who disagreed, believing that Indian affairs should be left to the Indian government with the Secretary of State involving himself only in overriding questions of constitutionality, national policy and budget.

This was only one of the conflicts facing Montagu as he entered the India Office. Other questions were even more difficult: how political unrest should be handled in India; how to distinguish between "legitimate" political aspirations and "illegitimate" unrest aimed at overthrowing British rule; and to what extent Indians should be represented in the Councils of government without impairing British control. These were questions that had been posed from the beginning of the strange relationship between India and Britain, although at different times the questions took different forms and were advocated with varying degrees of intensity and even violence.

India and Britain: The Beginning

By 1910, England had maintained a presence in India for more than three hundred years. It began not from an imperial wish to conquer and colonize but rather from a desire to trade for spices. It began when Queen Elizabeth granted a royal charter in 1600 to a group of London merchants to form the East India Trading Company. The charter provided that the Trading Company was not to annex territory; its purpose was to buy, sell and make a profit. To carry out this commercial purpose, it was given certain quasi-sovereign rights: to enter treaties and agreements with native princes; to raise troops to protect its workers; to build forts from which to conduct its trade; to adopt rules and regulations to govern its employees; to wage war, but only for the purpose of eliminating the competition of the French and the Dutch; and to protect employees of the company from hostile local rulers following the disintegration of the

Mogul empire. In theory, such warfare was permitted only to secure the peaceful environment needed for the free flow of trade.

Greed and power came to interfere with theory. Wars were often fought and territory acquired ostensibly to achieve "a peaceful environment," but in fact to satisfy dreams of power and to line pockets with gold. In the early years, even as its servants were becoming rich, the profits of the East India Trading Company were slight. In fact, it almost went bankrupt. It only became profitable when it expanded its trade to include silk and tea from China, paid for with opium grown in India. The history of the trading company as ruler of British India from the 1600s until 1858, when Britain took direct responsibility for governing India, is a story that in many ways is a rare adventure story of remarkable men—some motivated by concepts of British trusteeship and the white man's burden, others by money and power. But all were swept up in an exotic world that both mystified and intrigued them.

When the British government took over the administration of India in 1858, it replaced the Board of Directors of the East India Company with an India Office in London under a Secretary of State responsible to Parliament. His responsibilities were to be executed in India by a Governor General, known as the Viceroy, who was to be advised by an Executive Council and a Legal Council in India. Financial control remained with the Secretary of State in London. Few, if any, Indians sat on the Executive or Legal Councils. Thus, as with the East India Company, policy and financial control were held by those in Britain, with the British in India responsible for administration and implementation. Whatever powers the Indians had were given to them by the British.

During the eighteenth century this had not been a major problem, since there was little interest in India at home. As a result, British control was implemented loosely. In the latter part of the nineteenth century British political and military interests as well as economic interests became more pronounced, sufficient for Lord Curzon to announce on the eve of becoming Viceroy in 1898 that "India is the pivot of Empire, by which I mean that outside the British Isles we could . . . lose any portion of the Dominions . . . and yet survive as an Empire; while if we lost India, I maintain that our sun would sink to its setting."[3]

Curzon's view of the importance of India was an accepted part of

British economic and geopolitical policy, which demanded greater consolidation of British interests and control. As these controls had increased, Indian dissatisfaction and resentment had increased as well, especially among the educated. Englishmen who were knowledgable and concerned with India were aware of this. In an effort to meet this political awakening while, at the same time, maintain control over the country, Parliament had adopted the Indian Councils Act in 1861, providing for local legislatures in Madras and Bombay, and empowering the Governor General and his Council to establish similar local legislative bodies in Bengal and other small provinces. At the same time, the power of the Governor General and the Executive Council was strengthened; the number of Indians actually involved was still minimal. The Act was more symbol than reality and was intended to demonstrate that Britain was responding, albeit in a limited manner, to the aspirations of the Indian people.

The new structure failed to satisfy the Indian leaders. Many regional political organizations were formed to express Indian discontent, such as the Indian National Congress, formed in 1885. Several British leaders in India encouraged these organizations as a "safety valve" for British rule. No one anticipated the role that they would ultimately play in ending British rule in India.

As the unrest continued, the British government took two simultaneous approaches: It enacted strict measures to suppress disorders, and it tried to quell the forces of nationalism by expanding Indian involvement in the Indian government by the passage, first, of the Indian Councils Act of 1892 and later by the Morley-Minto Act of 1909. The first act merely increased Indian representation in the work of the government; the second was far more substantive. It has been described as the "first great step in the constitutional development of India,"[4] introducing representative government with greater Indian involvement, and recognizing the principle of election, although the vote was restricted to men of property. The number of nonofficial Indian members of the central government and the local councils was thus increased, as was the opportunity for debate.

Indian leaders found the legislation both too little and too late. They believed it did not give them representative government but rather benevolent despotism. It showed that Britain was willing to consult with Indians but not to transfer any real political power to them.

The notion of granting India real political power, much less independence, could not have been further from British thinking in 1909. Britain's overriding concern was to develop a policy that would diminish Indian political agitation while retaining British control. The result was a policy that has been described as no policy at all, unclear, perplexed, uncertain, ranging from sternness to compassion and from totalitarianism to democracy.[5]

Lord Morley

This was the state of Anglo-Indian affairs when Montagu became Under Secretary of State in 1910. Lord Morley[6] was still the Secretary of State for India, but he remained in that post for only ten months of Montagu's four-year tenure at the India Office. They were a critical ten months for Montagu.

The Viceroy at this time was Lord Minto,[7] who had been Governor General of Canada before assuming the Indian post in 1905. He, Morley and Montagu worked well together. Morley was a first-rate administrator with imagination and intelligence as well as a concern for the implementation of policy. He was a Liberal who took seriously the aspirations of the Indians for greater involvement in their own government. He was committed to the rule of law, and at the same time he was determined to preserve British rule in India. His was the task of walking the fine line between giving more political representation to India and maintaining British power. In this, he had the wholehearted support of Lord Minto.

Lord Morley and Montagu developed an almost father-son relationship, the older man helping his protégé to understand the staggering numbers of facts and figures as well as the issues and personalities he would face in his new office. Much of the information as well as many of the ideas and attitudes about India that Montagu expressed with such brilliance and erudition in his early days at the India Office came from Morley. At the end of 1909 Morley had left the House of Commons to take his place in the House of Lords. Thus, when Montagu became Under Secretary in 1910, he found himself the spokesman for the India Office in the House of Commons. He was thirty-one years old.

In his first six months at the India Office, in addition to his two-hour presentation of the Indian budget, Montagu answered orally almost two hundred questions on the floor of Commons and scores of written questions[8] covering almost every conceivable issue involving India. This barrage of questions came from both the left and the right: those who felt the government was being too repressive, led by Keir Hardie of the Labour Party, and those who believed the government was not repressive enough. The latter group's spokesman was Sir John D. Rees, a Liberal by party affiliation but a Tory on imperialism and India. At nearly every session of Parliament from February through July these members, among others, badgered Montagu, repeating their questions, challenging his responses and criticizing the India Office.

Montagu's handling of these questions earned him the praise of not only his colleagues but also the press. He consistently supported the government of India and refused to condemn the police accused of specific brutality until the courts of India found them guilty. At times he was tough and curt and used language not likely to endear him to his adversaries. But he always did his homework and was thoroughly prepared. Even the press noticed this, and it was not uncommon to read in the newspapers during 1910, even in newspapers hostile to his positions, that "Mr. Montagu . . . takes his duties at the India Office very seriously. Few of his predecessors have applied themselves so assiduously to the work of mastering the problems of India as he has done."[9] His performance on the floor of the House of Commons reflected this. There is no question but that India, its people and problems fascinated Montagu from the moment he entered the India Office. As a result he brought to his new responsibility even more than his usual intensity and study.

It was often said at the time that Montagu's fascination with India was the result of his "Jewish descent . . . which made him an Oriental."[10] Waley properly dismisses this. There was nothing "Oriental" about Edwin Montagu or his interest in India. Jews like Edwin Montagu, whose ancestors had been in England for more than three generations, and whose lineage went back several hundred years in Central Europe, were no more Oriental than Lord Curzon or Lord Morley, whose fascination and absorption in India were no less intense than Montagu's.

But it is true that being a Jew probably did make Montagu

especially sensitive to prejudice, racism and snobbery. It also may
have accounted for his hostility toward persecution, authoritarian
government and police brutality, about which he worried more and
more, the longer he remained in office. In 1910 his sympathies by
and large were still with the efforts of the Indian government and
the police to maintain order and prevent incitement to riot. But the
problem was not simple. His first experience with its complexities
surfaced in June of 1910 during the controversy surrounding the
banning in India of a pamphlet entitled *The Methods of the Indian
Police in the 20th Century,* written by Frederick Mackarness, a former
Liberal M.P. for Newbury.[11]

The Mackarness Pamphlet

The Indian government and Lord Morley deemed the Mackarness
pamphlet so dangerous that it was banned in India under the Press
Act of 1910.[12] It professed to be based on the Blue Book issued at
the end of 1902 by Lord Curzon's Commission of Inquiry and other
official documents. It contained lurid descriptions of several cases of
alleged police brutality and torture committed by the Indian police.

The banning of this pamphlet was brought to the attention of the
House of Commons by Keir Hardie, who "in a rather blustering
mood" according to the *Yorkshire Daily Post,*[13] asked Montagu if he
were aware of the fact that the pamphlet had been banned in India.
Montagu told Hardie in language that left no room for doubt concerning his position that the pamphlet was intended to bring the
Indian government into "hatred and contempt," that Lord Morley
himself supported the action of prohibition, seeing no reason why
"obnoxious matter" sent from England to India should be treated
differently from similar material produced in India.[14] Montagu said
that the Indian government believed the pamphlet to be "a dangerous document" and the government's opinion must be respected.
He invited Hardie to meet with him after the question period so that
Montagu could personally show him the "enormous number of
inaccuracies contained in every page."[15] Mr. Hardie declined the
offer and appeared embarrassed.

Montagu's response was greeted with a "general cheer at this
frank declaration but Mr. K. Hardie and his friends were anything
but pleased."[16] Mr. Montagu handled the incident in a manner

which showed that his lethargic style had under it spirit."[17] The Liberal press was less enthusiastic and more cautious than the Conservative. It expressed concern at detention without trial, the curtailment of free speech and the reports of police brutality, which Montagu did not deny, although he did assure Parliament that they were being corrected. It was not pleased with Montagu's sharp rebuke of Mackarness, a devoted and long-time member of the Liberal Party. The seeds of Montagu's isolation within his Party were already being sown.

The Budget of 1910: A Masterful Presentation

In July 1910, barely a month after the Mackarness Report was raised in the House of Commons, and while the press was still debating both the issue itself and Montagu's response to it, Montagu delivered his first Indian budget speech.[18] It was the single most impressive speech of his career, a tour de force. Normally, speeches involving India were delivered to an empty House. This time, the galleries were filled with family and friends of Montagu and curiosity seekers eager to see the performance of a new minister, especially the son of Lord Swaythling. The speech, which lasted more than two hours, covered a wide range of topics and was not limited to financial matters.

On the whole, Montagu's economic overview of India was an encouraging one; most of the speech was devoted to political unrest. Here Montagu's eloquence soared. He told his listeners of India's diversity and that "in India . . . under a single rule [are] varieties of races far wider than can be found in the whole of Europe, as many different religions as Europe contains sects of Christianity. Stages of civilization range from the Hindu or Mahomedan gentleman on the Bench of the High Court to the naked savage in the forest." The Indian population then numbered nearly three hundred million, with Europeans fewer than two hundred thousand, "numerically insignificant" but with power that is "wholly disproportional to its numbers."

The demands for self-government, he believed, "are confined to a very small portion of the Indian population. One must never lose sight of the remarkable fact," he warned, "that nine-tenths [or over 200 million], of the vast population of India are still uneducated and illiterate. All talk of unrest . . . is the talk of the small fraction of a vast number of the people which has been educated, and within this small fraction are to be found all those divergent forces which are classed together as political unrest. We must remember, however, that the amount of yeast necessary to leaven a loaf is very small; when the majority have no ideas or views, the opinion of the educated minority is the most prominent fact in the situation."

"May I say," he continued, "how strange it seems to me that a progressive people like the English should be surprised at unrest. We welcome it in Persia, commend it enthusiastically in Turkey, patronize it in China and Japan, and are impatient of it in Egypt and in India!" One cannot touch an ancient civilization with Western ideas "without disturbing its serenity, without bringing new ideas into play, without infusing new ingredients, without, in a word, causing unrest . . ."

When you came into India you found that the characteristic of Indian thought was an excessive reverence for authority. The scholar was taught to accept the assurance of his spiritual teacher with unquestioning reverence; the duty of the subject was passive obedience to ruler; the usages of society were invested with a divine sanction which it was blasphemy to question. To a people so blindly obedient to authority the teaching of European and particularly of English thought, was a revelation. English literature is saturated with the praise of liberty, and it inculcates the duty of private and independent judgement on every man. . . . The Indian mind was at first revolted at this doctrine, then one or two here and there were converted to it. They became eager missionaries of the new breed of private judgement and independence, and the consequence is that a new spirit is abroad wherever English education has spread, which questions all established beliefs and calls for orthodoxy, either political, social, economic or religious, to produce its credentials.

"The condition of India at the moment is one which, handled well, contains the promise of a completer justification of British rule; handled ill [it] is bound to lead to chaos." The principal task of the government thus must be to distinguish between unrest which is legitimate and that which is illegitimate. It must be sympathetic to differences of opinion but must never excuse illegal agitation or anarchy.

Montagu's speech also contained a moving plea to the British universities to help Indian students overcome their loneliness in

England, a condition often exacerbated by prejudice. He urged the English to extend the hand of friendship, "not patronizing tolerance." If the Indians were treated decently, he argued, they would return to India with warm feelings about England; if treated badly, they would take such attitudes home with them. Recalling the snobbery he had encountered and the discrimination he had felt as a young boy, he added: "Many a friendless, sensitive lad looks back, I fear, on the period that he spent in England as one long spell of loneliness and unhappiness. Nothing that the India Office can do will remedy that. The remedy lies in the endeavor of those among whom their lives are spent to overcome insular reticence and prejudices." This was a recurring theme in Montagu's speeches.

The budget was adopted overwhelmingly.

Montagu: A New Force in English Politics

With this single budget speech, Montagu became a figure of national importance. The press was overwhelmingly positive, responding not only to the substance of the speech but to Montagu himself as a new political force in the Liberal Party. On July 27, 1910, for example, the *Daily Mail* described him as "one of the ablest young men of the House of Commons," who had his first opportunity "and employed it to such advantage that he is sure of promotion if the Liberal Ministry should continue in office. . . . Whether in office or not, he is certain to leave his mark on parliamentary life."[19] The article described Montagu as a "tall, reflective young man . . . of striking personal appearance, always a notable figure, a studious, silent young man." When he was appointed Under Secretary of State, "many questioned his experience for such an important post. Would he be able to resist the extremists on his side? These questions and others received a complete and indeed a dramatic answer this week. Mr. Montagu is fully capable."

The article observed that as Under Secretary he did not take a position (in the House of Commons) as near to the Prime Minister as possible, as some Under Secretaries do. He sat at the end of the Treasury bench, "in the obscurity of the Speaker's chair where he could be seen by few." But "if those who stimulate Indian unrest imagined from this that they had an Under Secretary who could be bullied or hustled, they soon found out their mistake." He answered questions "with deliberate force and faced his critics with firmness and control. On the whole the House was pleased." "Delivering his budget speech," the article noted, was his "great occasion. The Prime Minister was on the Treasury bench; in the gallery was Lord Morley and Montagu's father, Lord Swaythling, an old man with a long white beard eagerly watching his son seated among the Cabinet Ministers."

There are no records or letters to indicate Lord Swaythling's response to his son's resounding speech. In the face of the almost universal acclaim Montagu received for his budget speech, however, his father may finally have been proud of Edwin and pleased at his choice of politics as a career. So well was Montagu able to hide the nervousness and inner tension he had all his life when called upon to speak that the *Daily Mail* described him as exuding "quiet confidence" with "not a trace of agitation." It also described him as "tall rather ungainly with long black hair surmounting" a white overhanging forehead with a "single eyeglass" that gave him an "intense student-like face." But "when he speaks," the *Daily Mail* article continued, his whole personality changed:

He becomes at once a person to whom it is necessary you should pay attention. His speech, long, comprehensive, forcible, was marked by modesty. He was brimming with incontrovertible facts. . . . He "wiped the floor" with certain mischievous busybodies. And the House of Commons, the most critical Assembly in the world, was deeply interested in his speech. At the end of it, Mr. Montagu took his seat, *having established himself in the course of an afternoon as a new force in English politics.*[20] (emphasis added)

Other press reports were equally glowing. The *Glasgow Evening News*,[21] the *News of the World*,[22] the *Observer*,[23] the *Englishman*,[24] *Punch*,[25] and *London Opinion*[26] hailed the speech as "brilliant," "remarkably clever," "trenchant," "vigorous." Montagu had delivered his speech "with a powerful voice"; "he gripped his subject," and was "vivid," "bold" and "dramatic." The *Observer* reported that Montagu's speech "justified promotion over the heads of so many seniors." It was "a remarkably clever and trenchant speech. It is altogether too soon to call Mr. Montagu a possible Liberal Disraeli but the impression he made was that he may go very far."[27] The *Englishman* characterized the speech as "remarkably eloquent" and found Montagu himself a "picturesque personality" with a "face pale and long, the eyes dark and luminous, the jet black hair smooth and prematurely thin," with a "brow high domed and thoughtful, the voice deep and musical. Like his relative, Herbert Samuel, he is immaculately groomed and garbed."

Everybody was struck with the bold and dramatic way in which the young minister, flinging out his eyeglass, fell upon the sedition-mongers and the somewhat notorious author of the Mackarness pamphlet. Yet there was dignity behind it. . . . While Montagu was making his two-hours' review, a bearded, massive figure gazed down from the Peers' Gallery. It was Lord Swaythling, the Minister's father. He must have been deeply gratified by the Under-Secretary's achievement.[28]

The *News of the World* reported not only on the speech, but on the two other Jewish members of the Ministry who were in the audience:

The House witnessed a brilliant performance when Mr. Edwin Montagu, the Under Secretary for India, took in hand the task of unfolding the Indian Budget. Mr. Montagu is only 31, and has not hitherto played a very important part in debate. His handling, therefore, of a difficult and delicate task took the House by surprise. Listening to the young Minister in the Peers' gallery were two men who are intimately interested in his career— Lord Morley, his chief, and Lord Swaythling, his father. Two Jewish members of the Ministry were on the Treasury bench observing the first ambitious effort of their young Jewish colleague—his cousin, Mr. Herbert Samuel, and Sir Rufus Isaacs.[29]

The *London Opinion* also commented on Lord Swaythling and the large number of Jews in the Asquith government:

Mr. E. S. Montagu, the Under Secretary for India, who made a remarkably noteworthy speech in the House of Commons last week, is one of the youngest members of the present Ministry. He is only 31, and is a first cousin of Mr. Herbert Samuel, Postmaster General. Mr. Montagu acted for some time as private secretary to the Prime Minister, and he is the son of Lord Swaythling, who before his elevation to the peerage, sat for many years as Sir Samuel Montagu. The Montagus are great bankers, and Lord Swaythling has always been regarded as the leader of the Jewish Liberals, as Lord Rothschild is the leader of the more conservative element.

Lord Swaythling is a grey-bearded, venerable looking man and perhaps his two most dominant characteristics are good nature and an appealing courtesy which is shown equally to the distinguished and to the obscure.

It is rather remarkable that the present Government should contain no fewer than three Jews among its members, Sir Rufus Isaacs, the Solicitor General, being the third. [Montagu and Herbert Samuel being the first two.]

Of course, Lord Beaconsfield will always remain the most famous Jew numbered among the governors of Great Britain; but Lord Beaconsfield did not retain the Jewish faith, and since his death there has been no conspicuous Jewish minister until the present time.

It is interesting that the Permanent Secretary of the Post Office, now presided over by Mr. Herbert Samuel, is a fellow Jew—Sir Matthew Nathan. Lord Swaythling is one of the four Jewish members of the House of Lords, the others being Lords Michelham, Rothschild and Wandsworth [plus Swaythling].

There are also four Jewish Privy Councillors—Lord Rothschild, Mr. Samuel, Sir Edgar Speyer, and Mr. Arthur Cohen, K.C.[30]

Making Enemies

Montagu's speeches and responses to questions during these early years of his political life not only reveal the sources of his brilliance and meteoric political rise, they also presage the causes of his ultimate political failure. While the press lauded his directness, force and candor, these were precisely the traits destined to make enemies. He was often unnecessarily sharp in rebuttal, sufficiently acerbic and curt for the *Wednesday Review* to refer to "the almost vindictive manner in which Mr. Montagu allowed himself to refer to the writings of a veteran Liberal worker [Mr. Mackarness]" and his excessive zeal in condemning "an old political friend"; the *Review* concluded that this manner was "keenly resented by those who know how sincere and whole hearted Mr. Mackarness' services have been to the cause of freedom at home and abroad."[31]

The *Manchester Guardian* similarly noted that in attacking Mackarness, Montagu did not merely disagree with his conclusions, but was unduly harsh and brought "a number of charges of grave personal misconduct against Mr. Mackarness, accusing him of false statements, of garbling documents and otherwise of falsifying evidence . . . accusations which anyone familiar with Mackarness would find hard to believe."[32]

Discretion should have impelled Montagu to let the Mackarness issue cool down. He did not. After his attack against Mackarness in

Parliament, he repeated his charges in even stronger language in a major address delivered before the League of Young Liberals at Cambridge in August. It was a "matter of personal honor," he told the audience, for his constituents to understand the facts.

In addition to his style of debate, the substance of Montagu's position was bound to place him in an untenable position. To many Liberals, Radicals and Labourites he had turned his back on two of the most sacred tenets of the Liberal Party: free speech and self-government. As the debate continued, important organs of Liberalism such as the *Nation,* the *Daily News,* and the *Morning Leader* all came to the defense of Mackarness. The Tories, on the other hand, while supporting Montagu's position on the Mackarness Report, were never supporters of Montagu himself, convinced as they were that he and Morley were destroying British control of India and were too sympathetic to the traitors and agitators. Their hostility increased after Montagu's speech at Bishop Auckland on November 3, in which he attacked extreme opinions, "on both sides" which he classified as "irresponsible."[33]

During his early days in office Montagu had the unswerving support of Lord Morley, who became not only a close working colleague but also an admiring friend. Unfortunately for Montagu, Morley was on his way out. On November 7, 1910, Morley held his last Council meeting. With his departure Montagu lost an important ally and champion.

Venetia and Montagu: The Friendship Continues

During the spring and fall of 1910, Montagu wrote to Venetia Stanley more often and in more personal terms and took her to lunch and dinner whenever their calendars permitted. In Montagu's letters to her, he had begun to express his feelings about himself and about Venetia. In one note, he even confessed: "1. That I'm still a little frightened of you. 2. That I talk a great deal. 3. Often very nakedly. 4. That an attractive sentiment sometimes really just made out to fill a gap in conversation becomes developed irresistibly to astounding proportions."[34] The praise Montagu received on his Indian budget address was not lost on Venetia. She was among the many friends who filled the galleries of Parliament to hear his maiden address. They dined together after the end of the session.

Pressure to Marry Jewish Cousin

While Montagu was beginning to deepen his relationship with Venetia, his parents were increasing their pressure upon him to marry a young cousin, one of the few relatives he liked. In none of Montagu's letters at this time, or in the letters of his mother, is the name of this cousin mentioned. She is only referred to as "my young cousin."

In the autumn of 1910 Montagu seriously considered marrying this "young cousin" but was not certain he wanted to:

I am very much inclined [he wrote his mother] towards my young cousin and find it difficult to forget her even here. But, my dear, be patient with me. I must be sure of myself and her before I do anything. After all, she ought to look round before joining herself to morose old me even *if* I want her and of that I am not quite sure.[35]

Montagu's father was seventy-eight at this time and in failing health. The family hoped that Montagu would marry before his father died. But he would not be rushed. He was thirty-one and his cousin only nineteen. "I cannot," Edwin confided to his mother:

discover whether I am thinking about the matter because of my own feelings or because the idea is being so constantly presented to me by some of my people and hers. . . . The trouble is that I can never be sure one way or another. I do not see how one is to, particularly with so young a character.[36]

When, two years later, he fell seriously in love with Venetia, he had no doubts. He was a man who quickly formed strong likes and dislikes. The fact that he was unsure of how he felt about his young cousin could only have meant he was not in love. But his family and hers maintained their pressure and the courtship, such as it was, continued.

During these months Venetia continued to write to Montagu, unaware of the situation with his cousin, although surprised that he could find so little time for her. Montagu merely acknowledged her letters, thanking her for her invitations and, in a noncommittal tone, conceded in a letter of December 1910 that "it makes me believe it's my fault and not yours that I haven't seen you for 654 years."[37] He did not mention his cousin, to whom a few months later he did, in fact, propose marriage.

Suddenly, on January 12, 1911, Montagu's entire life changed when his father died. He was now a rich man, with an annual income of ten thousand pounds, a sum equal to at least a quarter of a million American dollars in the last decade of the twentieth century. He no longer had to plead and account for every penny. He now had a regular source of financial support and was rich enough to take a wife.

In March 1911, a little less than three months after his father's death, and six months after he had told his mother that he was not certain that he loved his cousin, Montagu proposed to her. Family pressure and his own loneliness had won out. She rejected him "definitely and finally."[38] In the letter to his mother in which he conveyed this news, he casually mentioned that he had accepted an invitation from Venetia's mother, Lady Sheffield, to visit Alderley. "Alderley was quite good fun," he later wrote, "altho' the presence of three Hungarian musicians did not help to amuse me very much. But the Sheffields are pleasant people."[39] In truth, Montagu found the Sheffields far more than pleasant: They were the kind of politically sophisticated people he enjoyed. And they were part and parcel of the old English aristocracy that the assimilationist in him always found attractive.

There is no evidence that at this time Montagu was thinking seriously of seeking Venetia's hand in marriage. All through his adult life he had longed for financial independence and had chafed at living on the five hundred pounds a year his father had doled out to him for his political career. It would take nothing short of an emotional earthquake to make him risk the substantial sum of ten thousand pounds a year for the love of a non-Jewish woman. For the present his relationship with Venetia would continue as a mild flirtation and a most enjoyable friendship.

Lord Crewe: Cold, Courteous, and Conservative

At the India Office, Montagu faced new problems. Morley's successor was Lord Crewe.[40] He was very different from Morley, who described him as "assiduous, accurate-minded and careful."[41] Montagu described him in the very early days of their relationship as "kind," "patient, courteous, essentially conservative."[42] Margot Asquith wrote in her diary that five years later, reflecting on his relationship with Crewe, Montagu described him as the ablest man in the Cabinet. This surprised her because earlier he had described Crewe "as a bloodless man merely registering Hardinge's will & a chief impossible to get into close touch with or to impress or influence in any way—pigeon-holing his (Montagu's) schemes for India —In fact he [Montagu] told me once he felt suffocated & inclined to commit suicide as a result of this."[43]

Crewe was patient and courteous and, at the same time, cold and aloof and not easy to get close to. He was also efficient and hard-working, and if he pigeon-holed Montagu's ideas, it was not because he was a poor administrator but rather because he actively disapproved of them. He was, as Montagu aptly described him, far more conservative than Morley.

Unlike Morley, Crewe was unwilling to disturb the status quo. His goal was not to restructure or change constitutional relations, but to provide efficient, peaceful government in India under "fair and firm British rule." The recent rise in Indian unrest, as well as the loss of Lords Morley and Minto (who left at the same time as Morley and was replaced by Sir Charles Hardinge), made Montagu's task a more difficult one. The Montagu-Morley-Minto team would have faced the challenging conditions in India quite differently from the Montagu-Crewe-Hardinge team. Before, Montagu had had ideological allies; now he was often a third man out.

Police Brutality

During 1911, Montagu was increasingly uncomfortable with the charges of police brutality in India, which were becoming almost daily occurrences in the House of Commons. Montagu found it more difficult to defend the police and to excuse the government of India for its failure to act promptly to punish the perpetrators of torture. "Criticism of the police in the House of Commons," he wrote to Hardinge on April 5, 1911, "is running very strong and it is more difficult to meet than it was last year, because it is now in good faith and honest."[44] In fact, he had come to agree with the critics that torture and other abuses could and must be eliminated by a vigorous campaign that would include the death penalty for police officers whose victims died because of torture.

By October 1911 Montagu was able to thank Hardinge for his

help in minimizing police brutality through a variety of new rules and regulations. He believed the matter was "on a satisfactory basis."[45] In spite of the progress made and of Montagu's strong positions on police brutality, he could not satisfy his "radical" critics, who continued to view him as an apologist for police brutality and as a Radical who had abandoned his political roots.

The 1911 Budget

Montagu's second budget presentation in July 1911[46] was generally well received. It was acclaimed as "very sensible," "more cautious than his first one," "a repetition of those wise, firm, and thoughtful statements previously made by Lord Morley," a "decidedly superior performance," with "utterances of far reaching importance which we do not generally hear from official lips," "a most compendious essay upon the condition of India," which should "enhance the reputation he [Montagu] made in a single afternoon by his India budget statement a year ago."[47] Despite the overwhelmingly positive press response, several newspapers attacked the speech as "too optimistic," "too long," and filled with "lies about prosperity . . . and the contentment of the populace and beneficence of British rule."[48] The anti-Semitic *Justice* used the occasion to call Montagu "an impertinent, ignorant Jew, who owes his position wholly and solely to the weight of the money bags behind him [and whose] ill bred impudence to Mr. Mackarness is still remembered . . . with the puffed up superiority of his race."[49]

The 1911 budget was different from the one Montagu presented the year before, concentrating far more on the economic and social problems of India than on the political scene. He reaffirmed the policy of Lord Crewe and Lord Hardinge, which continued the policy of Lords Morley and Minto: "immovable determination to punish . . . anarchy and crime with strict sympathy for orderly progressive demand for the peoples that they govern." Then the visionary in Montagu took over:

India is changing as fast as, if not faster than, the West and our views must keep pace with the change. India has been given peace, unity and an Occidental education, and they have combined to produce a new spirit. It is our duty to watch that movement and to lead it, so far as it may be led from without, into right channels. When a change is produced in the political organization of a great Empire, it must not be regarded as the result of an inspiration of a philosophic Secretary of State . . . It must originate from within not from without. Social conditions, slowly developing, stir public opinion and public demand which move unformed and uncertain at first, gathering strength and shape later, and it is the duty of those in charge of the machine of Government to lead them into the channels of altered policy by means of Statutes, Orders in Council, etc. . . . And here lies true statesmanship—to watch the manifold and complex currents, to diagnose aright the signs of the times, to await the moment, and, when the moment comes, to step in and mould into proper shape aspirations and demands which are feeling and groping for expression.[50]

Montagu again paid tribute to Lord Morley and to the Morley-Minto Reforms, which he said were "a complete success."[51] Montagu advocated industrial development in India. "Indians must turn their attention to organizing an industrial population which can reap the agricultural and industrial wealth of the country, and attain a higher level of education and a higher standard of living."[52] India needed more men trained in finance, business and management. Her agriculture and industry required modernization and diversity, which in turn depended on broadening the opportunities for education and expanding science, hygiene and technical instruction as well as education in business and finance. More education would not only help in strengthening the economy but would bring with it a higher standard of living and help ameliorate social ills and poverty. Montagu argued that India wanted mass education and must be prepared to pay for it. Sanitation must be improved and housing expanded. And while India was developing industrially, he said, she must protect her workers from capitalist exploitation and tariff protectionism and make certain that they receive decent wages and enjoy decent working conditions.

Montagu also discussed the Hindu caste system, a subject most politicians of his day assiduously avoided. It was, the *Indian Daily Telegraph* noted, "unusual for a Secretary or Under Secretary to bring religious and social questions within the purview of a Budget speech," but, the *Telegraph* continued, Montagu's "appeal to Hindus to consider whether their caste system is compatible with modern social progress, will be received in a good spirit, especially as the speaker admitted that he had been emboldened to make the suggestion by . . . the leaders of Hinduism, to bridge the gulf between the depressed classes and the twice born."[53]

Montagu recognized in his speech that Hindu-Muslim relations was a "subject of great delicacy," but he believed it was important enough to be raised. He underscored that he hoped that nothing he said would be construed as offensive to the beliefs of any religion. "Every religion has forms and ceremonies which it is difficult for those outside its pale to appreciate and to understand." Montagu then referred to his special sensitivity to this, as a Jew. "If the House will forgive a personal allusion," he said, "I was brought up in a denomination which attaches great importance to quasi-religious ceremonial institutions . . . and I should be the last to question the religious usages and semi-religious usages which are dear to our Indian fellow subjects. But I wish to suggest to the leaders of Hindu thought that they might, if they thought fit, look carefully into certain of their institutions and consider whether they are compatible with modern social conditions and modern industrial progress. Of the 220,000,000 of the Hindu population 53,000,000 form what are known as the . . . untouchables."[54]

The industrial history in England demonstrated, Montagu asserted, how important it was for the "captains of industry to have fresh blood infused into their ranks." Fluidity is essential for progress. To keep fifty-three million people frozen in a caste and prohibited from marrying between castes is a condition that could only hamper India's industrial growth.

Montagu appealed to both Muslims and Hindus to unite for the good of India. "The Government would be the first to welcome and help the cooperation we all desire." Antagonism within Hinduism and between Hindus and Muslims was bound to hamper the growth of national feeling in India. "Now of course it would be criminal to foster this difficult antagonism, but not to recognize its existence is to be blind to facts in a way which must enhance the evil."[55] Montagu did not foresee that one result of such Hindu and Muslim cooperation would be to create a unified force against British rule in India. Indeed, the first task that faced Lord Reading when he became Viceroy in 1921 was to destroy this cooperation as a step in restoring law and order in a country that was plagued by that time by violence and noncooperation.

Montagu called on Parliament to become better informed about India and to accept well-ordered progress. "There are the pessimists," he declared, "who spend a useless life, mourning a past which can never return, and dreading a future which is bound to come. Then there are those who, filled with antediluvian Imperialism, cannot see beyond domination and subjection, beyond governor and governed, who hate the word 'progress,' and will accuse me of encouraging unrest. I bow submissively in anticipation."[56]

Montagu believed there was nothing dangerous in what he said. "I have pointed a long path, a path perhaps of centuries, for Englishmen and Indians to travel together" he concluded. "I ask the minority in India to bring along with it—for there is room for all—by education in the widest sense, by organization and by precept, all those who would be good citizens of their country. And, when at intervals this well-ordered throng show to us that they have made social and political advance at another stage, and demand from us in the name of the responsibility we have accepted, that they should be allowed still further to share that responsibility with us, I hope we shall be ready to answer with knowledge and with prudence."[57]

One does not have to be a prophet to know that such an approach, a plea for shared responsibility between India and Britain, expressed with all the passion Montagu was capable of bringing to issues about which he felt deeply, was bound to bring him into conflict with Crewe, Tory opinion, the Tory press and Lord Curzon. It was only a matter of time.

Durbar of 1911

The Budget of 1911 also allocated approximately £71 million from Indian revenues for the Coronation Durbar of the British King and Queen to be held in Delhi in December 1911. (The term *Durbar* was used in India to describe an audience or reception held by a native prince or by the British ruler. Technically the Coronation Durbar was a gigantic reception given by the King for his Indian subjects to celebrate his Coronation.) The event was spectacular, intended to demonstrate to India and the world the importance Britain placed on "the jewel in her crown." Parades, visits with ruling Princes, receptions for three to four thousand representatives of British India, Durbar ceremonies before an assembly of eighty thousand people, a review of ninety thousand troops with maneuvers "on a scale never before found possible,"[58] and all the pomp and ceremony the British Crown was capable of devising were part of a week-long visit of their royal majesties. It was a spectacular demonstration intended to display British power and glory and dazzle and overwhelm its spectators. The India Office at home, the Viceroy and his staff, as well as Crewe and Montagu—all played roles in designing the event. It received universal acclaim and went off flawlessly.

No one expected, however, that the King would use the Durbar for an announcement that the capital of India would be transferred from Calcutta to Delhi, that a new Lieutenant Governorship would be created for Behar, Oressa and Chota Nagput, that a Governor in Council would be created for Bengal (a change that in effect would reunify Eastern Bengal with the old province) and that Assam would once more be reduced to a Chief Commissionership. (Bengal had undergone partition in 1905 by Lord Curzon, which had resulted in fierce popular agitation that took several years to subside.) These changes announced by the King were not insignificant tokens to mark the occasion. They were important changes in borders and governance and produced widespread astonishment. The British defended moving the capital to Delhi on the grounds that the consolidation of British rule in India and the development of the railway system made it no longer necessary for the seat of government to be a seaport. They explained the creation of new Lieutenant Governorships as an effort to give the subordinate provincial governorships autonomy and the reunion of Bengal was said to be "not a reversal of the partition but a rearrangement after experience."[59]

In spite of these explanations, these changes were criticized not only on substantive grounds but for the way in which they were presented. Since they were announced by the King-Emperor speaking ex cathedra from his Indian throne, it was impossible for Parliament to refuse to adopt them without damaging the prestige of the Crown. Critics noted that the trouble caused by the Curzon partition had subsided and that it was a grave error to reopen the question. Further, it appeared as if the government had made these changes as concessions to agitators who had long urged reunification for Bengal.[60]

The announcement by the King of these changes came, moreover, as a complete surprise. Planning and formulation had been carried out in total secrecy and had leaked neither to the press nor to Members of Parliament. That this was achieved within the gossipy atmosphere of London politics was extraordinary. Montagu, who played an important role in developing the changes, and who was addicted to gossip, also managed to keep this information secret. He did not mention it in any of his letters to Venetia, which indicates the importance he placed on the element of surprise in the plan.

Press and Curzon's Reaction

Since Crewe was in India at the time of the King's announcement, the task of dealing with the press fell to Montagu. His strategy was to convince the press that, taken as a whole, the changes were merely adjustments and not intended to undo Curzon's work. In a telegram to Lord Crewe on December 12, 1911, Montagu reported that by and large press reaction was "very friendly."[61]

"*The Times,*" he wrote the next day, "was almost enthusiastic; most Conservative papers welcome the transfer to Delhi, and several of them the Assam arrangements, but some regard the rest as a reversal of the Partition, which they decry as a yield to clamor and sedition." Montagu believed that this reaction was "merely in tribute to Curzon," and when the time came, he and Crewe "can prove it was not a reversal but a reorganization."[62] Montague underestimated the opposition. "The only disquieting features," he wrote, "in a chorus of approval . . . are the telegrams sent from India . . . which tell us that, although Military India and the Chiefs are pleased, the Mohammedans . . . consider they have been left, and the Bengalis [believe] that the reversal of the Partition will not make up for the degradation of Calcutta."[63] Again, on December 14, Montagu wrote that "the Policy goes swimmingly here. . . . Liberal members of Parliament are very ignorant about India and simply say 'Is this a slap in the eye of Curzon and a reversal of Partition?' When they satisfy themselves that it is so, they approve. This was also the view of most of the Liberal Press."[64] As for the Conservative press, Montagu continued to believe that their criticism arose "only out of loyalty to Curzon."[65]

Montagu conceded that Curzon was very angry,[66] and although "by energetic handling I think we may flatter ourselves that we are getting the Press here to commit itself to the Policy and more or less to isolate Curzon . . . I detect symptoms of a growing criticism of the method described in some quarters as 'Anti-parliamentarian' by which we have chosen to accomplish it. People are beginning to say, if it was good we need not have used the King, and if it was bad we ought not to have used the King. In argument, I have taken the line that we have not used the King to help us to carry the plan, but we have used the plan to make a success of the King's Durbar announcement. I think Curzon is being very active behind the scenes, but I am glad to be able to say that your colleagues in the Government . . . and our friends in both Houses, are on the whole delighted with everything."[67]

Montagu's assessment that Curzon was "very angry" was no exaggeration: Curzon was livid. He took the changes announced at the Durbar as a personal affront and a deliberate attempt to destroy the Partition he had worked so long to achieve. He saw Montagu's fine hand in devising this scheme and never forgave him. Montagu, for his part, seemed relatively unperturbed by Curzon's reaction. He was singularly unimpressed with him. In a letter to Crewe on December 26, 1911, in which he assured Crewe that there would probably not be any great debate in Commons on "the Policy," Montagu wrote:

In your House [of Lords] you will probably enjoy a contest with Curzon. I cannot yet, I fear, and I know I am wrong, count myself as one of Curzon's admirers. He has oratorical methods which irritate me and would always make me inclined to vote against him. . . . He has indomitable pluck, and energy, but where are his breadth of view, his intelligence, which is not commonplace, or his farsightedness? Was it the act of a statesman to rush impetuously into opposition to the changes without looking round?[68]

This letter illustrates one of the propensities that kept Montagu from the great political career he so desperately wanted. He was open and candid to the point of foolishness. He was tactless and prepared to say things in writing that were bound to come back to haunt him. In the case of Lord Curzon, Montagu had chosen a formidable foe. In the duel that would ensue between them, Curzon would never forget and would be merciless in the punishment he would inflict upon Montagu.

Montagu and Crewe: Discord Develops

In his letter of December 26, discussing the press reactions to the Durbar, Montagu also wrote to Crewe that it was Crewe's duty to turn down financial requests from the Viceroy who usually asked "far too much," and that Crewe had failed in this responsibility because his "Finance Department is useless . . . Schuster is no good, Newmark is not a great man and Abrahams does not understand this part of his duty."[69] Montagu was not only critical of Crewe's lack of firmness in rejecting some of the Viceroy's requests, but he also accused Crewe of falling down on his duty to obtain sufficient funding for the legitimate needs of India. This was unusually harsh criticism of Crewe by his subordinate.

Montagu, as busy as he was, also found time to develop recommendations on court reform for India, proposals to change the Secretary's Indian Council to bring to it more expertise and a proposal for the creation of a Royal Commission to examine the Indian Civil Service. He also worked on plans for a graduated income tax for India, developed a program to improve the integration of Indian students into English universities and continued to struggle with the problems of police brutality in India. Earlier in the year he had supported capital punishment for a policeman who had killed a prisoner by torture, even though the death was accidental. By April 1911, after reflection, he had spoken against this in the House of Commons, saying that "such a departure from accepted principles of British and Indian justice seems neither necessary nor practicable."[70]

The Hardinge Dispatch: Conflict with Crewe

On August 25, 1911, Lord Hardinge issued what appeared to be an innocuous dispatch about the transfer of the capital from Calcutta to Delhi. It was published in December 1911 and contained a paragraph on constitutional reform supporting gradual self-government of India. It read:

The only possible solution would appear to be gradually to give the Provinces a larger measure of self-government until at last India would consist of a number of administrations, autonomous in all provincial affairs, with the Government of India above them all and possessing power to interfere in cases of misgovernment but ordinarily restricting its functions to matters of Imperial concern.[71]

The dispatch at first went unnoticed. It contained nothing that Morley, Minto, Montagu and Hardinge had not said in one form or another over the preceding years. Two months later, in early February 1912, the matter came to the attention of Curzon, who had not yet recovered from the Durbar incident and was looking for some way to strike back at Montagu and the India Office. Supported by Lord Lansdowne, the fifth Marquess of Lansdowne, who had been Viceroy of India from 1888 to 1893, he accused Hardinge and the government of India of planning Home Rule for India.

Crewe assured the House that nothing of the kind was contemplated. The issue would probably have died except that Montagu chose to raise it again in a speech he delivered at Cambridge. "That statement," he said of the Hardinge dispatch, "shows the goal, the aim toward which we propose to work—not immediately, not in a hurry, but gradually. We cannot drift on forever without stating a policy." Montagu pointed to a new generation of young Indians who were asking, " 'What are you going to do with us?' The extremists had published their Swaraj; the 'moderates,' . . . look to us to say what lines our future policy is to take. We have never answered that and," Montagu warned, "we have put off answering them far too long. At last and not too soon, a Viceroy has had the courage to state the trend of British policy in India and the lines on which we propose to advance."[72]

Curzon and his supporters in the House of Lords found this in total contradiction to Lord Crewe's interpretation of the Hardinge dispatch. They attacked Montagu on the substance of the Delhi changes, on the hurtful effect these changes would have on the Muslims and on Montagu's interpretation of the Hardinge dispatch.[73] Montagu stood his ground firmly. The day before the Curzon attack in the House of Lords, Montagu told the House of Commons that "if a microscopic examination can detect any difference of meaning in the words that I used at Cambridge and the words which my chief used in the House of Lords, I will ask the House to attribute the difference to the obvious difference of atmosphere between the other place and the platform in my own constituency."[74]

Curzon, responding in the House of Lords in June, attacked Montagu's interpretation as "nationalistic." Crewe denied this, stating emphatically in the House of Lords "that he saw no future for India on the lines of colonial self-government."[75] *The Times* reported this with approval the following day.[76]

Thus Montagu found himself rebuffed not merely by Curzon but by his own Chief. As was his style, he refused to remain silent and let time heal the breach. Immediately upon reading Crewe's comments on June 26, he wrote him a long letter expressing his dismay at *The Times*'s report. "I am more than unhappy because I have always hoped that even if I did let you down you would be certain in public to come to my assistance. That is an incentive to do his best which any member of the Government however subordinate may feel. I am not concerned now to argue that my interpretation of the passage in dispute is accurate. History will judge the importance to Indian policy of the words as printed and published. I am rather inclined to believe that we are in agreement as to the matter."[77]

He expressed his regret that Crewe's speech seemed to disagree with him and that it looked as if his statement had been rejected by his superior. "I have never said one word as to federalism and indeed I contrasted at Cambridge our ideals with B. Pal's [Bepin Chandra Pal, an extremist follower of Tilak] ideal of colonial self-government. I do not think therefore it would have been difficult to say what you did say with some protecting words for me. As made, however, I submit respectfully that your speech will be construed to mean that I have been thrown over and that hurts."[78]

Montagu wrote to Crewe again on June 28, that "time does not diminish the dismay. I hate to be acclaimed as the friend of the extremist or to be told that I have been over-ruled."[79] Montagu was not alone in his dismay. The Indian press, led by the *Times of India*,[80] was harshly critical of Crewe's position and the Honorable Sachedaranda Sinha, a barrister, a friend of Britain and a member of the Imperial Legislative Council, regarded Crewe's repudiation of Montagu as "disastrous. It will probably deepen discontent."[81]

Faced with such a reaction, Crewe continued to search for words to satisfy both Montagu and Curzon. On July 29, he told the House of Lords that there was no difference among the government of India, Montagu and himself.[82] The policy of all three was the same, namely: "the supremacy of British rule in India, because the maintenance of British rule was the best method of securing the happiness of the people of India." Crewe then asked: "Was it conceivable at any time [that] the Indian Empire could succeed on the lines of Australia or New Zealand?"[83] Crewe responded to his own rhetorical question with a resounding "No." Montagu would have answered emphatically "Yes." The differences in policy between the two men could not have been clearer, in spite of Crewe's efforts to gloss over the conflict. Lord Courtney concluded the debate by diplomatically saying, "no one could pretend to pronounce a final judgement in regard to the future of India and of the Asiatic races."[84] And with that, the matter was closed, for the time being at least.

This conflict was a precursor of what lay ahead, for, in fact, Montagu was developing a vision for the future of India that was not that of Crewe and was certainly a far cry from Curzon's. He foresaw more self-government for India. He envisioned a development in the future, in line with Hardinge's dispatch, under which India would consist of "a number of administrations, autonomous in all provincial affairs, with the government of India above them, able to interfere in cases of mismanagement and on foreign policy." Montagu could even see a relationship with Britain similar to that of Australia and New Zealand. The fact that these countries were white and India nonwhite did not matter to him. On this and other issues he was color-blind.

In defending the changes announced at Delhi or discussing his interpretation of the Hardinge dispatch, Montagu, unlike Crewe, made no effort to find language to appease Curzon. Indeed, it often appeared that he went out of his way to take on Curzon. In his speech at Cambridge he praised Curzon's work in India, but then attacked him mercilessly:

Admiring what he has done, not looking and saying, "We have done this," but saying, "This is my work." It is not "Hands off India" which he preaches: it is "leave Curzonian India as Lord Curzon left it. . . ." These are not the grave and weighty criticisms of a statesman; they are the impetuous, angry fault-findings of a man thinking primarily of himself.[85]

In that same speech he also characterized Curzon as "a chauffeur who spent his time polishing up the machinery, screwing every nut and bolt of his car, ready to make it go, but never driving it or knowing where to drive."

Later, in the House of Commons, when Montagu was explaining how the new borders would help India, he added gratuitously that although Curzon was one of Britain's "greatest Viceroys" he had "no policy of any sort" on the future of India.

I do not mean it disrespectfully of one of the greatest Viceroys we have ever had when I say that Lord Curzon in this matter had no policy of any sort or kind. He was a great administrator. He was the administrator who produced an efficiency which is one of the most cherished possessions of the Indian Government at the present moment. But his concern was with an unwieldy province. He found it too big and determined to divide it. He moved nationalities about and he moved individuals about as though they were automatons: that was the root of the evil.[86]

Muhammadans and Their Religion

Montagu's proclivity for bluntness was evident again in his comments on the second reading of the Government of India Act, on April 22, 1912, when he discussed the Muhammadan reaction to the new borders, and said: "It would be a mistake . . . to talk of the Mahomedan people of India as though they were a homogenous people of one nationality. The Mahomedans of Eastern Bengal are the descendants of Hindu converts, or are Hindu converts themselves and have little or no relation except that of their religion."[87] While such a statement may have been historically and geopolitically accurate, it brought a barrage of criticism from Muslim leaders who questioned Montagu's right to conclude that Muslims were not a homogenous people. It gave Curzon and the Tory press yet another weapon with which to discredit government policy in India, in general, and Montagu, in particular.

The *Observer* called Montagu's remarks on the Muslims "disparaging," but the *Times of India,* while charging that Montagu spoke "as usual with a light hearted indifference to fact," concluded he "was correct when he pointed out the various conflicts among the Moslems." In spite of this, *The Times* expressed the hope that "the incident will teach him [Montagu] to be less careless in the future in his handling of the truth."[88] Only two years after the acclaim he received following his first budget speech, Montagu now was being described as "tactless," "overconfident," and "indiscreet," having made a powerful enemy of Curzon and the Tory press. Even his superior, Lord Crewe, had put some distance between them. To make matters worse, Montagu seemed disinclined to learn the rules and oblivious to the studied politeness of the British politicians. As a result, the bright future Montagu had enjoyed in 1910 now seemed to be losing its glow; his enemies were increasing and his political friends were few.

The Marconi Scandal

During 1911 and 1912, "the Marconi affair," as it became known, added to Montagu's political unhappiness. The Marconi incident grew out of a resolution of an Imperial Conference of Prime Ministers in May 1911 calling for the establishment of a network of government-owned wireless stations to improve communications between London and the Empire. With Cabinet approval, Herbert Samuel, the Postmaster General, opened negotiations with Marconi's Wireless Telegraph Co., Ltd. (a British firm) to construct the necessary stations. He later accepted, subject to parliamentary approval, the contract tendered by Godfrey Isaacs, managing director of the Marconi Company, a brother of Sir Rufus Isaacs, the Attorney General, and a friend of David Lloyd George. Rumors immediately began to circulate that the contract under discussion was especially favorable to the Marconi Co. and that this was due to Rufus Isaacs's pressure on his coreligionist Herbert Samuel.

In April 1912, it was revealed that Rufus Isaacs, David Lloyd George and Alec Murray, Secretary to the Liberal Party, had purchased shares in the American Marconi Company, later claiming to have thought that there was no connection between the American and British companies. (In truth, the British company owned half of the shares of the American company.) During negotiations between British Marconi Ltd. and the British government, the value of the stock in both the American and British companies rose dramatically, and three days after Isaacs, Lloyd George and Murray purchased stock in the American company it increased 100 percent.

When Lloyd George and Murray sold their stock, with Rufus

Isaacs acting as their agent, each made a profit of £743. A few days later, on May 3, Rufus Isaacs sold all of his shares. On May 22, Lloyd George bought three thousand additional shares of American Marconi. Alec Murray was even more excited at the possibility of a quick profit. He began investing (secretly) some £9,000 of Liberal Party funds as well as considerable sums of his own money.

On July 19, Parliament tabled the agreement between the Postmaster and Marconi Ltd. as the controversy over the propriety of the conduct of Samuel, Isaacs and Lloyd George heated up considerably, becoming bitter, acrimonious and anti-Semitic. In fact, when the debate on the contract resumed on August 7, the Speaker had to adjourn early when Parliament became too boisterous to conduct business. The anti-Semites had a field day. The anti-Semitic weekly *Eye Witness,* edited by Cecil Chesterton, printed the most spurious anti-Semitic slander against Samuel and Isaacs, accusing Jews in government of conniving with their coreligionists outside to make a quick profit from inside information.[89] So outrageous were their attacks that Samuel considered a lawsuit; Asquith persuaded him against it.[90]

The Tory press, for its own political reasons, jumped on the bandwagon, charging corrupt relations between the British Marconi Company and the government, with Samuel as head of the Post Office improperly giving Marconi a favorable contract. There was never a real case against Samuel. He had dealt in no shares and made no profit, and no proof was ever offered that the contract was in fact "an improperly favorable one." The pretense of a case against Samuel was sustained "in order that the anti-Semitic overtones . . . might be exploited to the full. . . . To bring together one Samuel and a couple of Isaacs in a skein of transactions bordering on the world of high finance was an irresistible attraction for Belloc and Cecil Chesterton."[91]

How experienced politicians such as Samuel, Isaacs, Murray and Lloyd George could have acted so foolishly with so little concern for propriety and public opinion is difficult to understand. They may have honestly believed that purchasing stock in the American Marconi Company, after a fair contract had already been concluded with the British company, did not harm the British government or the British public. And they may have believed that the attacks upon them were motivated only by politics and anti-Semitism. But the conflict over their behavior became so bitter that the Cabinet was forced to appoint a Select Committee to investigate the case against the two ministers, Lloyd George and Isaacs.

After nine months, in June 1913, the Committee divided along political lines, the majority finding Isaacs and Lloyd George not guilty and finding no grounds for censure. The Conservatives issued a minority report that, while exonerating Lloyd George and Isaacs from wrongdoing, condemned the ministers' "grave impropriety."[92] After the Committee Report was given to the House of Commons, a vote of censure was taken on June 18 and 19, and lost, 346 votes to 268. Asquith, while privately disapproving of the behavior of the ministers, stood by them publicly, believing that they had violated the "rule of Prudence" but had acted "with complete innocence of intention."[93] In private, however, Asquith was critical of their lack of judgment but, as always, was tolerant of human foibles.

He refused to accept the resignations offered by Lloyd George and Rufus Isaacs and, in fact, later in 1913, appointed Rufus Isaacs Lord Chief Justice of England. Alverstone, the incumbent Chief Justice, had resigned. The Attorney General traditionally was next in line for this position. If Asquith had denied Isaacs this promotion, it would have appeared to be an acknowledgment of his belief in Isaacs's guilt. He refused to do this and Isaacs became the first Jewish Lord Chief Justice of England. This caused another outcry in the Tory and anti-Semitic press and provoked Kipling's anti-Semitic poem "Gehazi."[94]

The anti-Semitism unleashed by the Marconi Affair was especially troubling to Montagu because it involved his cousin, Herbert Samuel, and his good friend Rufus Isaacs. This episode undoubtedly added to his distress and anxiety when he found himself, barely a year later, enmeshed in another crisis, the Silver Scandal, which also involved Jews. In this, the anti-Semitic attack would strike much closer to home, implicating Montagu himself, his cousin Sir Stuart Samuel, and his father's firm, Samuel Montagu & Company.

Women's Suffrage

In 1911 and 1912 there was another issue adding to the domestic unrest that characterized the decade before World War I: the struggle

of women for the right to vote. This was an issue over which
Montagu broke with Asquith, something he rarely did. Montagu
supported the vote for women, while Asquith did not.

While the Marconi incident demonstrated Asquith's acceptance of
human foibles and his generally tolerant attitude toward life and
people, he was rigidly intolerant and hostile to the demands of the
suffragettes. On the surface, it would appear contradictory for a
man like Asquith to have taken this position. He always admired
and loved intelligent women and was married to a woman of keen
political interests and involvement. He encouraged his daughter in
her political pursuits and repeatedly asked Venetia for her political
advice and guidance.

In Asquith's official biography his son, Cyril Asquith, and J. A.
Spender explain that Asquith:

had a profound respect for the mind and intelligence of women. . . . But
he considered politics to be peculiarly the male sphere, and it offended his
sense of decorum and chivalry to think of them as engaged in the rough
and tumble of this masculine business and exposed to its publicity. He
always vehemently denied that the question had any relation to democratic
theory or that the exclusion of women from the franchises was any reflection on their sex.[95]

In some ways Asquith's attitude toward women paralleled his attitude toward Jews. Jews, like Montagu, were fun to be with, smart,
helpful in government, especially in financial matters, but not to be
considered as truly equal to their Christian colleagues. While Asquith's attitude toward Jews could be kept private and revealed only
in personal correspondence, his attitude toward women could not.
Women's rights were now an important item on the political agenda
of England. Attitudes toward Jews were not.

The majority of the British public and their leaders were as hostile
to women's rights as was Asquith. The only way women knew of
keeping their agenda before the public was by violence. Asquith's
cherished values of "old fashioned chivalry and courtesy" were of
no help in motivating the politicians to support their cause. The
increasing use of violence by the women, beginning in 1905 and
growing in intensity in the years that followed, proved in the early
years, however, to be counterproductive. While keeping the issue
alive, it also alienated a large segment of the public, including other

women. It infuriated Asquith and made him an increasingly vocal antagonist. "The idea of converting a human being's reason by parades, marches and fighting the police was incomprehensible to him [Asquith]. The more the women marched, the less his reason marched with them." [96]

He was strongly supported in his attitudes by his wife and daughter. They opposed the women's movement and frequently had to be restrained physically in their desire to respond to Asquith's hecklers. But, in spite of Asquith's hostility, the women had enough support in Parliament for a number of women's suffrage bills to be introduced throughout 1910–11. They never mustered a majority since most of the bills included restrictions on age and property that some Liberals, such as Lloyd George and Winston Churchill, believed would help the Tories.

In 1912 the Cabinet proposed, over Asquith's objections, that the women's vote be included in a major voting reform bill that would abolish plural voting (the right of an elector, with property in several constituencies, to vote in more than one) and extend the male franchise from 7½ to 10 million. Asquith had no alternative but to announce in July that the Cabinet would accept any amendment adopted by the House that would add the vote for women to the Reform Bill. While women's leaders had mixed feelings about the bill and some wanted a separate bill for symbolic reasons, most Liberals, including Montagu, supported it.

The amendment came up for discussion in late January 1913 while Montagu was in India, and on January 22, the Cabinet was prepared for debate. Two days later, the Speaker (James W. Lowther) took everyone by surprise by deciding that if the women's amendment was adopted it would so change the bill as to necessitate its withdrawal. A new bill would have to be introduced, and it could not be carried in that season. "This is a totally new view of the matter," Asquith wrote to the King, "which appears to have occurred for the first time to the Speaker himself only two or three days ago, and is in flat contradiction of the assumptions upon which all parties in the House hitherto treated the bill." [97]

While Asquith would have voted against the amendment (as his subsequent vote in May 1913 confirmed), he disagreed with the Speaker on procedure. But he was also relieved. In a letter to Venetia on January 27, 1913, he revealed his true feelings: "The Speaker's *coup d'etat* has bowled over the Women for this session: a great relief."[98]

Venetia wrote to Montagu in January that if the amendment had been passed by the House of Commons, Asquith would certainly have abided by it, although she was certain he had "some plan."[99] Whether or not this "plan" was, in fact, the Speaker's ruling is not known. In all public utterances, however, Asquith appeared as surprised as anyone by the ruling.

Montagu, too, disapproved of the Speaker's tactic. "Poor Old Prime" he wrote to Venetia from India. "The speaker seems to me to have behaved very ill to the Government about the Franchise Bill and I can't believe he announced his decision at the right moment. If he had kept quiet and the amendment had been defeated, the bill could have gone forward. But, it was obviously right to withdraw the bill at all costs as soon as he had spoken for the decision would not have been a real one."[100]

For the moment, the only thing the Cabinet could do without infuriating the suffragettes was to drop the Voting Bill. To proceed without the Women's Amendment would have violated the assurances they had given to the women's movement. A new bill would be introduced in the next session which would incorporate the vote for women.

This bill came up for a second reading on May 6, 1913. Grey spoke for it, Asquith against, making clear that he would vote for such legislation only if he believed a majority of women favored it or if he believed the rights and needs of women were being neglected because they could not vote. He saw no such evidence. Neither did 268 members of the House of Commons, who defeated the bill, with 221 members, including Edwin, voting for it.

1912 Budget: Focus on Education

In July 1912, Montagu made his third India budget presentation.[101] It was shorter than his other two speeches and, in Asquith's words, was "very good, tho from the nature of the principal topics— Education, etc.—rather more juiceless than last year . . . I think." "His delivery," Asquith wrote to Venetia, "improves and gets easier, but it is a pity to say 'reel' and 'ideel' when you mean real and ideal. But, it is a depressing ordeal to have to talk at such length on a hot afternoon to a tiny audience of somnolent men."[102]

In discussing education Montagu concluded that the time was not ripe for free, compulsory primary education in India. He believed instead that the "greatest expansion of education can be secured not by making it free or compulsory at the present moment, but by the improvement and multiplication of the schools . . . It has been demonstrated that the surest way of increasing the school attendance is to increase the number of schools. . . . Compulsion really can only be worked where education is popular."[103] In India this was not the case. While free primary education was increasing, it was only the beginning. Britain must continue to encourage its development and must also help in strengthening secondary education, residential colleges, independent universities and technical education.

In this speech Montagu also announced the King's appointment of a Royal Commission to study reform in the Indian Civil Service. The last such Commission had been created in 1891. Montagu had been urging a new one since shortly after coming to the India Office. As for the Indian Civil Service itself, Montagu conceded that it was the most efficient in the world, but that more "is wanted—humanity, capacity to deal with men, statesmanship, and above all the quality which is increasingly wanted as the keynote of British rule in India—sympathy."[104]

Returning to a cause which he had advocated repeatedly, Montagu once again summoned the British to recognize their special responsibility to Indian undergraduates in England. They would be the administrators of India in the future, "and if we allow our Indian visitors to be segregated, isolated, or rudely treated, we are sowing seed which will sprout and fruit long after we have repented of the carelessness which allowed it to germinate."[105] He warned the House of Commons that it would be a "calamity producing blunder" to adopt a policy of reaction and repression for India.

England must not accept advice on India from men who are "out of date with what is happening":

. . . If we are to do our duty . . . we must move forward cautiously; nobody can possibly foretell what will be the eventual characterization of the population we shall form in India; the India which must be a heritage not of its Asiatic population alone but of the small handful of Europeans who have unified it, giving it its trend, brought to it its traditions and its ideals which must be reckoned with in its destiny.[106]

Montagu called for "East and West to meet 'at the altar of humanity' . . . not with clash or discord but in harmony and amity. There need be no enmity or competition; the forces are not mutually destructive, they are mutually complementary. Each has learnt much and has much to learn from the religion, the art, and the philosophy of the other. The quietism of the East qualifies and is in its turn qualified by the restless spirit of the West." He concluded:

The asceticism of the Oriental, the simplicity of his code of life, and the modesty of his bodily needs, are meeting the restless spirit of progress in material things, the love of realism, the craving for the concrete, and the striving towards advancement which come from the West. The golden thread of Oriental idealism is being woven into and embellishing the drab web of our scheme of life, and our science of government, which we have so laboriously inherited and are handing down, is being offered to the oriental to help him in material progress, and the East and the West together, united and assisting one another, are constructing in India, let us hope successfully, the lasting temple of their joined ideals.[107]

The newspaper *India* reported that the speech may have been long and "read in slow and laboured fashion, from closely written manu-script. . . . But if the manner left something to be desired, . . . the matter was magnificent."[108] It revealed the idealist in Montagu that his often blunt and tactless manner often hid. His were the ideals of a genuine Liberal, a man who truly believed in human rights, self-government and freedom, and who, unlike so many in the Liberal Party, also abhorred snobbery, prejudice, discrimination and racism and believed that people, regardless of their origins—be they Christian, Jewish or Muslim—must meet "on the altar of humanity." The words were Edwin Montagu's; the spirit came directly from his father.

10

A Love Triangle Begins, 1911–1912

I want you, more and more.

Edwin to Venetia, Sept. 8, 1911

Suddenly, in a single instant . . . the scales dropped from my eyes . . . and I dimly felt . . . not at all understanding it, that I had come to a turning point in my life.

Asquith's recollection of the day he fell in love with Venetia, 1912

By the middle of 1911, Montagu's feelings for Venetia Stanley had begun to change. She shared his interest in politics; she loved the outdoors and bird watching; she was the kind of woman with whom he could relax comfortably and recharge his vitality.[1] She was also a good listener, sensitive to his moods, and capable of providing comfort and care. To Montagu, always in need of a shoulder to cry on, such qualities were especially attractive.

For different reasons, these qualities were attractive as well to Asquith, whose relationship with Venetia also had become more serious by early 1912. Thus, Montagu and Asquith both became active suitors of Venetia at approximately the same time.

In 1911, Venetia was twenty-four years old, still not married and a little more receptive than at first to Montagu's overtures. At this time in his life, Montagu was described as "an imposing, almost fearsome figure, with an overlarge head, a dark, saturnine, pock-marked complexion, black moustache. His mouth was large, sensual and slightly twisted. A gleaming monocle in his eye gave an impression of fierceness which bore no relation to his character."[2] At other times, his eyes "sparkled with humour and kindliness."[3]

In relation to Venetia, Montagu was never either "fearsome" or "imposing." He was kind and gentle, witty, sophisticated, highly intelligent, eager to please, generous, a rising star in politics and wealthy enough to entertain her lavishly. Such redeeming features compensated, in some measure, for his physical unattractiveness. He was also a fount of political gossip and a splendid addition to any party.

As a result, by the spring of 1911, Montagu found himself the recipient of scores of invitations from Venetia, for luncheons, dinners and weekends at Alderley and Penrhos. Often her invitations lured him with the extra inducement that no one else will be present,[4] except, of course, Venetia's family, and on other occasions, the promise that Venetia alone would be there.[5] Montagu accepted eagerly.

Between visits, Venetia and Montagu began an extensive correspondence. Nearly all of her letters followed the same pattern: They extended invitations and recited a daily routine that invariably included shopping, bridge, visiting friends, reading, fencing, playing pranks, traveling, and practicing chess so that she could beat Montagu and Asquith.[6] She may have been a brilliant conversationalist, but her letters were dull and repetitive.

Rarely did any personal revelations intrude. Once she chastised Montagu for telling Violet that she had thought him priggish, and added, "probably it is another of your tortuous deductions taken from two stray words and as usual wrong."[7] Montagu apologized profusely. He would never, he wrote, "say anything to reflect negatively" upon her character. He added that she had been "wonderfully good" to him and that he would become a bore if he "repeated his real conversation [about her] to Violet."[8] In another letter, she remarked that she had seen a picture of him with another woman in the *Daily Mail* and she asked him who his friend was,[9] suggesting that she was jealous. Aside from such minor breaches in her wall of privacy, her letters were devoid of any suggestion of how she felt about Montagu or about anything.

Montagu's letters, by contrast, were replete with personal revelations. He was not ashamed to share with Venetia descriptions of his various illnesses, depressions and anxieties. Nor was he ashamed to admit that he left for Spain to avoid the coronation of George V, because he "feared the bodily fatigue, strain, panic or what you will of five hours in the Abbey," that he had "eccentric impulses," lacked "moral courage," and was "usually imbued with coming disaster." "Oh," he wrote, "I wish I could get out of that habit."[10]

Venetia had little patience with illness, including her own. When a few months later she was plagued with jaundice, she viewed it merely as a boring nuisance. To her, Montagu's illness and fears were part of his peculiar personality. She listened to him politely and solicitously; she alternately teased and comforted him; but she never took him seriously. She was more interested in his social calendar than in his health. Nor did she take seriously his protestations of growing affection, which began to appear in his letters in the spring of 1911. By then he felt comfortable enough to express openly his desire and need for her: "I want you more,"[11] he wrote after a June weekend with her. And again in September, after another weekend, he confessed that he could not get her out of his mind. Writing from Archerfield, where he was vacationing with the Asquiths, he told her how much he enjoyed the long talks with her and that it made him "want more and more as soon as possible."[12]

It was during September that Venetia had her bout with jaundice, an illness Montagu described as "beastly"[13] but which Venetia found "pleasurable,"[14] since it forced her to rest at both Alderley and Penrhos, where Montagu, always at her beck and call, joined her frequently. After each weekend, Montagu's letters waxed more and more ecstatic. Venetia was described at this time as "a post Victorian young woman who displayed alarming symptoms of modernism . . . a pagan . . . with no sense of sin . . . a beguiling mixture of beauty, candor and seductiveness."[15] Yet, it is not likely that Edwin and Venetia were lovers since, in 1912, when Venetia first rejected Montagu's proposal for marriage, she made it clear that she did not want to sleep with him because she found him sexually unattractive. She was prepared to play with him, but no more. And Montagu, eager for her acceptance on any terms, was prepared to abide by her rules. Later, he would come to regret such a torturous bargain, but for the present he acceded to her every wish.

He told Venetia that her last letter was on his mantelpiece and that it compensated for the frequent tedium of political life. "I see a corner of your handwriting," he wrote, "it induces a wish you could materialize. I am looking forward to Penhros with no Pauls, or Jonahs—or even Bakers or Craigs—just you in a setting."[16] Montagu was in love.

Although his feelings had become intense, he was uncertain of Venetia's. When in November he addressed her in a love letter as "My dear Venetia," he immediately pulled back and added parenthetically, "I have somehow slipped into addressing you by the most beautiful name in the world (which happens to be yours)—if you dislike it you will of course some time or other say so (please don't) —it is I suppose because I think of you thusly." He then berated himself, not only because of his familiar salutations but because in carrying out his duties on behalf of the India Office he thought himself "a coward through and through—physical and I fear moral. I venture little and I win about as much. . . . Nevertheless I am having fun and am rather myself with fight and energy and it's always fun writing to you."[17] It was characteristic that Montagu would call himself a coward. This time he was referring to his not speaking out more vigorously against the accusations of police brutality in India, which were making headlines almost daily.

One could argue that Montagu could not, as an Under Secretary of State, take a different position from the government and the Secretary of State, even if he was becoming uncomfortable with the behavior of the police in India. His responsibility was to represent the government's policy in the House of Commons—not to attack it. There was nothing cowardly about such behavior. But, as was Montagu's style, he seemed happiest when he was berating himself.

As Christmas drew near, not even the pressures of his political responsibilities interfered with the time he spent trying to find for Venetia a gift that would express his feelings. He spent two hours in search of such a present and finally gave up. "I wanted to express," he told Venetia, "our relationship as I understand it at the moment by finding something personal, different to anything else you would receive, different to anything I was giving to anybody else. . . . Well it was hopeless. . . . [T]he fact of the matter is that giving a present is too sacred when they mean much to be trammelled by seasons. And so I abandon my right to give you a X'mas present and claim a right in substitution to give you one whenever I can find one which I think will be a real message of what I want. . . . Meanwhile will you take this letter in all its crude floundering," he continued, "to mean that at this, the end of one year and the beginning of the next, I am thinking much of you and hoping for you every sort of happiness and fun."[18]

Venetia replied from Archerfield, where she was visiting the Prime Minister, that "it was very nice" that Montagu wanted to buy her a present but she regretted that it caused him "such an unpleasant and unprofitable morning. You must have," she added, "a very high standard." She found that her greatest difficulty was to "stop buying."[19]

Such a cold response to his effort to find her a special present should have been a signal to Montagu that his feelings were not reciprocated. But he was too much in love to notice. His next letter, on December 27, told her again that he wanted her "now . . . very much indeed. That is literally true." To mask his feelings, he then hid behind some mild humor:

But there is a more negative quality which you possess that makes my longing for you more strident than all your positive ones. It is that you do not play golf. I am rather lonely. Not that I'm not enjoying myself hugely but I want company for my now solitary walks to the sea, while everyone chases golf balls and talks about them.[20]

Montagu switched from the personal to the political, confessing that he was "rather unhappy about women's suffrage *despite* my belief in it—because I care for the P.M. more than all and I think he must beware." Two days later, in a letter to Lord Crewe he reaffirmed his support of women's right to vote, telling Crewe that he opposed "any amendment of franchise laws . . . which do not give women votes on the same terms as men." He dreaded, however, any referendums which he viewed as "the end of Parliamentary government."[21] He worried about the attacks against Asquith by the suffragettes and their supporters and found himself "profoundly depressed over the whole matter."[22]

The Trip to Sicily

Montagu would have been even more depressed if he had known that while Venetia was accepting and encouraging his attentions, she was also spending more time with Asquith, both at Archerfield and at Downing Street, and frequently taking drives with him to the country on Friday afternoons. Recalling this time with Venetia, Asquith wrote in 1915 that "long intervals of absence and separation" characterized their friendship, but always, when they came together, they "resumed, without effort, as though it had never been broken off, the old delightful attitude of true companionship. . . . The only new things I noticed in particular were her interest in and knowledge of poetry, and her really remarkable memory, not only for words but for things and places."[23]

The so-called companionship Asquith felt for Venetia was strong enough for him to ask her to leave a skiing trip she was enjoying in Switzerland and to come with Violet to join Montagu and him in Sicily. The two men were on vacation enjoying the ruins of the Greek temples, but decided that they would enjoy the temples more in the company of the two women. After Violet and Venetia joined them, the trip became a truly memorable one for all, although, according to Asquith, love and romance had not as yet entered the picture. "The first stage of our intimacy (in which there was not a touch of romance and hardly of sentiment) came to its climax when I went to Sicily with Montagu . . . at the . . . beginning of 1912. Violet and Venetia joined us there and we had together one of most interesting and delightful fortnights in all our lives."[24]

By early January 1912, before the vacation in Sicily, Margot Asquith knew that the Prime Minister's wide-ranging eye had focused on Venetia. When she saw him off to Sicily, "she wept" and "confided in her diary that she was jealous of those who had gone with him."[25] This would imply that she surmised that Asquith intended to invite Venetia and Violet before leaving for Sicily or had already done so. Margot not only loved Asquith deeply, she also strongly disliked Venetia and Violet. She was critical of the amount of time the girls spent together, and called Venetia "Violet's squaw." She always believed that the girls were "conspiring" against her in their pranks and jokes and was suspicious early on of Venetia's relationship with her husband.[26]

Asquith in Love

The vacation in Sicily was the turning point in Asquith's feelings for Venetia. A few weeks after they returned, Venetia was Asquith's weekend guest at Hurstly, a house borrowed by the Prime Minister from a cousin who described it as "a nice little villa" on the edge of New Forest, near Lymington. It was here that Asquith realized that his feelings for Venetia had turned to love. He wrote:

It was when we got back to England [after Sicily] and I was spending most of my Sundays in the late winter and early spring at a house lent to me on the outskirts of the New Forest (I remember it was on the eve of the Coal Strike which gave me one of the most trying experiences—up to then—of my public life) that she came down with us for the usual "week-end."[27]

He was sitting with Venetia "in the dining room on Sunday morning—the others being out in the garden or walking—and they were talking and laughing just as on our old accustomed terms," he wrote. Then suddenly, "in a single instant, without premonition on my part or any challenge on hers, the scales dropped from my eyes; the familiar features and smile and gestures and words assumed an absolutely new perspective; what had been completely hidden from me was in a flash half-revealed, and I dimly felt, hardly knowing, not at all understanding it, that I had come to a turning point in my life."[28]

Asquith had no idea that Montagu shared his love for Venetia. The idea that this moody, gloomy, unattractive Jew could share the same love never entered his mind. He was aware that Montagu visited and entertained Venetia, but he probably paid no serious attention to this, either because he believed that Venetia could never fall in love with so unattractive a man as Montagu, or because he felt so superior to Montagu that it was inconceivable to him that the two could be in the same ring, competing for the same prize.

Edwin Begins a Courtship

Inconceivable or not, Montagu had become a serious contender. In 1912, he wrote more than thirty letters to Venetia, each expressing repeatedly his desire for her. Venetia wrote forty letters to Edwin, including, for her, a revealing note in which she told Edwin that she too had "delicious thoughts" about Sicily.[29]

On February 6, Venetia's letter to Edwin, inviting him to lunch and telling him of the "extract" she sent him for his birthday, addressed him as "My dear Tante." *Tante* was a popular novel written by Anne Douglas Sedgwick, published in 1911, about "the most famous of living pianists who sees life as a dark riddle and counts herself as of the entombed."[30] Montagu had frequently announced that "he had all sorts of hidden affinities and resemblances to the moody and tempestuous genius."[31] Montagu seemed not to be offended by being called "Tante" by both Venetia and Asquith, both of whom used the term affectionately.

In February, Montagu did something that was the antithesis of cowardly behavior: He spoke on behalf of Home Rule in Belfast. It was a village meeting of about a hundred people with more than two-thirds booing when he entered. But after the initial heckling, he told Venetia, "the audience settled down and listened courteously." He found the people of Belfast provincial, petty and badly educated. After the speech, his car was mobbed by twenty people, but he escaped unhurt.[32]

It took courage to make such a speech in Northern Ireland but Montagu never viewed anything he did as worthy of praise. If anything, his self-deprecation increased as he became older. Nor did he believe that he could make a good speech; he always envied the abilities of others, especially Asquith, Grey and Churchill. The last of these, he wrote to Venetia, was "a great asset to the Liberal Party . . . fearless, not afraid to express unpopular ideas."[33] In this letter, Montagu thanked Venetia for lunch and assured her that he would "come back to dinner Sunday. . . . Sicily has spoilt me. I miss you tremendously the days I can't see you. I wonder how much you realize this. If you do you'll make your summons as frequent as you can tolerate."[34]

If Venetia did realize this, she gave no hint of it in her response, which was a brief note bearing no salutation and asking whether her father could borrow Montagu's "Sicilian Baedeker", since Lord Sheffield was of an "economical turn of mind, and doesn't like the idea of getting a new one," an attitude Venetia described as "strange." She also expressed regret that Montagu was unhappy with his speech (the budget presentation of 1912). Everyone had thought it good, she wrote, including the Prime Minister and Margot. She closed with another invitation.[35]

Montagu was delighted with her comments about his speech, but disagreed with her. "I am not shamming in what I say about the speech," he wrote to her. "I don't pretend it was bad and I make all allowances for the horrible condition of the House and the fact that no preceding speech had fired me," but the speech "lacked courage, resource, crispness, alertness, and it didn't help much. But it did reveal the kindness of my friends and when I remember the large gathering of people who came on to the Treasury Bench and into the Ladies gallery away from dinner—I am rather happier than usual."[36] In spite of Montagu's complaints about being lonely and friendless he did have a large enough circle of friends, including women, who felt close enough to him to crowd the galleries to hear his budget presentations.

Montagu: I Don't Like Jewesses

During February 1912, Edwin's mother again urged him to marry, pleading with him to marry a Jew. She probably had heard of his attentions to Venetia; their world was too small for such gossip to have escaped her. He responded, "I fear it can't be done. It is not only that I don't as a rule like Jewesses. It is also that I firmly believe to look for a wife in one set of people is as wrong as it would be to say you must look for a wife among blue eyed women."[37]

A year after his father's death, Montagu felt free enough to confess that he did not like Jewish women and would not marry one. How Montagu intended to reconcile his interest in non-Jewish women with his father's will was not clear, unless at this early stage in his relationship with Venetia he thought that her disinterest in all religions would make it easy for her to convert to Judaism, if she ever wanted to marry him. By the end of February 1912, this thought was very much on his mind. In spite of his love for his mother, he ignored her pleas and continued his pursuit of Venetia, awaiting each "summons," as he accurately described her invitations, and counting the days until he could be with her. By springtime his pursuit was intense. By this time Venetia must have been aware of his feelings and desires. His letters left no room for doubt.

A Memorable Night with Asquith

Venetia's knowledge that Montagu was very much in love with her did not stop her from spending the night with Asquith in April, at Ewelme Down in Oxfordshire, the home of a friend, Frank Lawson, an occasion Asquith later described in a letter to Venetia as a night which "perhaps you have forgotten but I never forget it."[38] It was this night that confirmed the love he had felt at Hurstly when the "scales dropped from his eyes," and his love for Venetia had been revealed "in a flash."[39]

There are few other letters that have survived from Asquith to Venetia from 1912. In the spring he had asked her whether she could guess "with what pleasure and hope he looks back upon last Sunday."[40] He acknowledged that "it is no good snipping the bud if its place is to be taken by a mere excrescence on the stem." He asked her to "try and be suggestive about tomorrow. I am quite free."[41] In another letter he told her he wanted to see her and "must" see her before she left London, that he hoped she could stay to hear the budget presentation and afterwards come for tea in his room. He wrote that Montagu, who in this letter he calls "Cassandra-Tante," is having "his (or her) annual Budget dinner."[42] Late in April Asquith also wrote about the "horror and heroism" of the *Titanic*, quizzed Venetia about two literary riddles and ended, "I only wish you were here, dear love."[43] He was again at Ewelme Down, the scene of their "unforgettable night."

Edwin's Courtship Continues

March and April were busy for Venetia. She not only gave the Prime Minister "unforgettable memories," but she also found time to see Montagu with increasing frequency and exchanged more than a dozen letters with him. Hers were short, giving no hint of any change in her affection for him, and devoid of substance. But she encouraged Montagu to write to her "about . . . more important and vital issues" in his life "rather than permanently to stick to such questions as whether Cynthia is nicer than Katharine and Cys cleverer than Raymond." And she added "if as you say, it made a difference to you to talk about it to anyone, I am glad that it should have been . . . to me."[44]

In April 1912, Venetia spent ten days in London taking writing lessons. Her letters showed no improvement and continued to be boring. This may have been deliberate. Short, noncommittal letters were enough to keep Montagu interested and dangling; they were not intended to heat the flame.

If Montagu was troubled by Venetia's letters or by her lack of response to his expressions of affection, none of his letters reflected this. They were generally more critical of his own behavior than of anything she said or did. On March 11, for example, he confided to Venetia that he was "miserable" because he thought he "lied in spirit, if not in words (and I think the latter) in the House of Commons and that I am going to be, as I have indeed been all along, the tool of a bureaucracy which despises politicians and which has put words into my mouth which I would have never used if I knew the objects for which they had been carefully chosen."[45] Venetia, never one to shrink from a white lie, was sympathetic. Although she acknowledged that Montagu may have "intentionally misled the House," she consoled him by concluding that "only the force of circumstances," caused him "to go back on given pledges and assurances." In such circumstances, "an intentional lie," by Venetia's standards, was not a sin.[46]

Aside from this questionable advice, Venetia's letters continued to avoid anything that might give Montagu a glimpse into her feelings or thoughts. Finally, after three years, Montagu commented upon this. Gently and cautiously he asked:

Dearest Venetia, if you will do me the great favor of answering this, I should like you to tell me what you think about these things . . . you are most frighteningly reserved about yourself. All self centered people are and the greater they are the more frightening it is. And asking isn't much good but I sometimes feel rather mournful when I reflect that the inner you is as hidden from me (except at moments oh so rare) as it was a year ago.[47]

And then, fearing that even this mild inquiry might be taken as a rebuke, he added: "P.S. Please forgive this letter being hypercritical, boring and I fear a little too impertinent."

Venetia responded with a five-line note, even shorter than her norm, thanking him for a present that he had sent, promising to wear it, and agreeing to answer his questions when they next met.[48] Such meetings became much more frequent during the summer of 1912, with Venetia expressing genuine disappointment when Montagu was unable to see her. "I'm miserable," she wrote on July 15, "when you can't come."[49] She seemed finally to be taking a greater interest in him.

Two days before writing this note to Montagu, Venetia had received a long letter from Asquith in which he expressed deep

disappointment that she did not have the time to take their customary ride through the countryside on Friday afternoon. He discussed
the marriages of her sister Blanche and of Viola Tree. Viola married
Asquith's secretary, Alan Parsons. He referred to some lines from
Medea that Venetia sent to him and that he wrote are "not intended
for Tante," who "made quite a good speech on Thursday."[50]

At the end of July, Montagu, encouraged by some of Venetia's
comments about "missing him," and her barrage of invitations,
began to think seriously of marriage. On July 22, he asked for the
opportunity to visit her for about an hour. "If you will let me talk
to you once more I'll try not to be a nuisance and I'll try and make
it final. I—well I think I'd rather say it."[51] From this letter, it
appears that Montagu had begun to discuss the possibility of marriage with Venetia even before July.

Eight days later Asquith wrote to Venetia that "Tante's" budget
presentation "was good, that his delivery improves but that his
Jewish intonation is distracting." He also hopes he may "somehow
see her."[52] Pressure on Venetia from both sides was now increasing.

Edwin's Marriage Proposal

Sometime before August 4, Edwin mustered enough courage to
propose marriage. Venetia rejected him, for on August 4, 1912, he
wrote that when she turned him down he thought of severing all
ties with her. But he changed his mind. Why should he lose her
friendship, which meant so much to him? Also, he clung, uncharacteristically, to optimism. As long as she was unmarried there was
hope. He added, "so in one month I lose you and all hope of politics." (He thought his budget speech poor.) He was leaving for India
but would go to Penrhos first to say goodbye. Although he had
been rejected, he could not break off the relationship.[53]

Montagu did not keep his proposal a secret from the Prime Minister. It did not dawn on him that Asquith was in love with Venetia.
To Montagu, Asquith was only a friend of Venetia's—someone
who, like himself, enjoyed her company and brilliance, nothing
more.

Asquith, on the other hand, was now beginning to pay more
attention to Montagu as a competitor, but still could not conceive
that Venetia would take him seriously. But he was beginning to

worry. "It is an age since I heard from you or of you," he wrote to her on August 14, 1912,"—or even about you. It is time you made some sign. Have you been cultivating new acquaintances, or (what would be much worse) playing fast & loose with old ones. Step into the confessional & let me know the worst. I know (for he spent Monday night here) that the Assyrian has been coming down among you like a wolf on the fold. Did the 'sheen of his spear' dazzle your vision? and what happened? Tell me all about it."[54] This was the first time in his letters to Venetia that Asquith referred to Montagu as "the Assyrian." This and the name "Mr. Wu" were used frequently by Asquith and his family as well as Venetia as nicknames for Montagu, suggesting that Jews were not real Englishmen but were foreigners, aliens, mysterious Orientals.

Asquith's reference to Montagu as "the Assyrian" came from Byron's poem "The Destruction of Sennacherib."[55] Stephen Koss, in his biography of Haldane, suggests that such nicknames were a form of anti-Semitism. Such attitudes were "closer to the surface in some cases than in others. This sentiment was always particularly prevalent among those who aspired to social station; it was usually purposeless and sometimes sportive, as when his colleagues referred to Edwin Montagu as 'The Assyrian.' "[56] Ted Morgan, in his biography of Churchill, added: "Behind his back, Asquith and Venetia cruelly mocked Montagu, laughing at his attentions, and writing anti-Semitic doggerel about him."[57]

If such nicknames bothered Montagu, he "took no notice," the attitude he developed when teased by the non-Jewish boys at Clifton. But Montagu was too sensitive not to understand the underlying significance of them. One of the tragedies of Montagu's life was that he accepted such teasing, internalized his reactions and never fought back. This is understandable in a young boy of twelve. It is much harder to accept in a grown man, a political leader, of thirty-three.

A Compromise Affair

On August 18, 1912, Montagu wrote to Venetia that he hoped she would reconsider his proposal. He pleaded with her not to close the door. He would take her on any terms. Later that month he wrote again, to wish her happy birthday. She was twenty-five.[58]

By August 26, Montagu had not yet left for India. He was vacationing in Scotland and still pleading with Venetia to "think about
his proposal again." He was especially disturbed by her vacillations.
First, she refused even to consider his offer. Then she said she
"might." Now she had decided to reject it outright. He tried to
understand what caused these changes of heart and sadly concluded
in a letter to Venetia, that maybe "this was due either to the fact that
me in the flesh was less possible than me when you thought of me
in my absence, or to the fact that I was too much really in love and
should demand too much for what may be called a 'compromise
affair'. This latter is what you state it to be."[59]

Venetia had first suggested that she might accept him, but only if
their relationship would be what they had called a "compromise
affair"—no sexual relationship, only friendship. When it became
clear that Montagu loved her too much and could not be satisfied
with a sexless relationship, she rejected his proposal. He was in a
quandary. She wanted an affair without passion, but his love made
it difficult for him to control his physical desires. "Now it seems a
rum way to win a lady's affection," he wrote to Venetia, "to try
and convince her that you do *not* really love her but that seems my
only chance." But in spite of her rejections he still wanted to make
her his "wife and not lose [her] thereby as the best friend man ever
had." He urged her to write again and ended "Till then, my Venetia."[60] Thus we see Montagu, a man rich, intelligent, sophisticated,
worldly, and politically successful, prepared to accept a woman on
any terms that she dictated, knowing full well that she did not love
him and found him physically unattractive.

In 1913, when Lady Dorothy Howard finally married another,
Montagu told his mother, who was still urging that he marry, that
"if it had not been for my father's wishes, I should have married
long ago and now, God bless her [Lady Dorothy Howard], and may
she [be] very, very happy. . . . I feel it would be wicked to choose a
wife because of my father's will," he continued, "or any Jewish
woman whom I did not love as I have loved. I have not yet, though
I have tried desperately, found one such."[61] In truth, Montagu did
not "try desperately" to find a Jewish woman. His self-hatred and
his concomitant dislike of Jewish women made it easier for him to
accept Venetia's insults and rejections rather than look for a Jewish
woman.[62] And no matter how coldly Venetia treated him, he re-

turned for more. He pleaded to see her before he went to India because, he wrote, "I've got a craving irresistible."[63] He went to Scotland to rest but could not get her out of his mind and begged her to join him.[64] She turned him down but that did not stop him from going to Penrhos to say goodbye in person. He even considered canceling his trip, fearing that putting distance between them would eliminate any chance he might have of making her change her mind again.[65] Whatever he did, wherever he turned, he thought longingly of her and the life they could have together. Her rejection of his marriage proposal did not cool his ardor.

In the midst of such heavy correspondence with Montagu, Venetia sent "two delightful letters" and a lovely box to Asquith, who answered her letters promptly on September 14, on his way to Edinburgh. He regretted that she could not join him. Montagu had also not joined him, or, as Asquith put it, "The Assyrian after many vacillations, also played us false."[66]

Sometime in mid-September, Venetia wrote to Montagu and once more gave him hope that she might reconsider his offer of marriage. This letter is not available. He was in ecstasy: "Oh my dear Venetia what made you change again? It can hardly be any new revelations about my character or defects. . . . Will you let me at least believe that you would like to hope that you could find it possible."[67]

His joy was short-lived. Venetia either did not mean what she wrote or Montagu misread her letter, for on September 29, he wrote again, acknowledging that Venetia had now made it clear that she would not marry him. He ended on a note of finality. "Goodbye," he wrote, signing this farewell letter with nothing more than "ESM."[68]

Venetia's vacillations would have been hard on any man, even one with a strong self-image. For Montagu, they were devastating. But he could not make a clear break. Even on the eve of his departure he wrote to her so she would know "where his thoughts still lie."[69] Finally, on October 4, 1912, after receiving no further encouragement, he left for India. A new chapter in his life now opened and a new love began, one which almost rivaled Venetia.

11

The Trip to India,
October 1912–March 1913

The infection of this country has become so acute I doubt I shall ever get over it.

Montagu, Diary, Nov. 12, 1912

Montagu's trip to India was not a spur-of-the-moment decision. From his earliest days in the India Office, he had expressed the desire to visit the country and see Anglo-Indian relations for himself. Such a trip would make him the first Under Secretary of State to visit India during his term of office. In July 1912, after some persuasion, he received the approval of the Prime Minister and Lord Crewe and spent three months organizing the itinerary, which he wanted to be as extensive as possible.

He planned to leave London October 3 for Dover, to go on to Marseilles, where he would board the P&O *Simla* for India with his brother Lionel and his secretary, Mr. H. Peel. He would spend six months in India, sightseeing, gathering facts and meeting as many Indians in and out of government as possible, and he would attend the first meeting of the Legislative Council in Delhi. The press reactions to the announcement of his plans reflected their mixed attitudes toward Montagu. The Indian press was pleased. The Anglo-Indian press was hostile and skeptical and used the occasion, according to the Indian newspaper *India,* to "have some ill-mannered flings at the Under Secretary of State for India. . . . The Anglo-Indian papers have affected a supercilious dislike for Montagu, because Mr. Montagu has dared to be sympathetic and show courage in dealing with affairs of India."

. . . the Anglo-Indian Press would have preferred Mr. Montagu to be a dummy Under Secretary crossing the "t's" and dotting the "i's" of Sir John David Rees. . . . As he has, however, elected to be a statesman with individuality of his own and with broad progressive sympathies he must be made light of and ridiculed.[1]

Montagu was described by the *Englishman,* another Indian newspaper, as someone with "brilliant intellectual gifts. His wide sympathies and his personal charm will ensure him a hearty welcome from the public men with whom he will be brought into contact with a great many of whom he is already acquainted."[2]

India, in an open letter from its Madras correspondent to the Under Secretary on September 20, 1912, asserted that Montagu's unwarranted and impetuous condemnation of Mr. Mackarness and his pamphlet on police brutality "embittered our feelings against you, but your Cambridge speech censuring Lord Curzon's Indian policy palliated your initial . . . ignorant error and blunder. You earned a lasting remembrance in India's grateful heart for the interpretation you gave to the now famous paragraph 3 of the Government of India's dispatch of August last, though unhappily Lord Crewe gave you the audacious go-by." The newspaper letter continued:

As a great and rich financier's son and ex-private secretary to Mr. Asquith we have great hopes of your preferment and advancement in the Liberal ministry. I beg of you most earnestly to see all India with an open eye. Lord Crewe, when he came here last year, maintained a dignified but regrettable aloofness which modern India resented as a slight to her. I don't mean to say we want from you mob pleasing speeches. No doubt you will give one ear to Anglo-India, but I pray you to give the other ear willingly to Indian-India. I beg you to attend the Congress and the Social and Industrial Conference sessions. Pray, see for yourself what India is, what India wants, and what India observes.[3]

On the other hand, the *Times of India,* epitomizing the Anglo-Indian attitude toward Montagu and his trip, expressed concern that the trip represented encroachments by Whitehall on the government of India and called Montagu "an ambitious Parliamentarian who has made himself conspicuous by the comprehensiveness of the claims to direct and carry out policy and administration in India which he has set up on behalf of the India Office. Mr. Montagu's claim to

departmental omnipotence so often seems to carry with it an assertion of personal omniscience that there is some danger lest people
should do less than justice to him."[4] The *Pall Mall Gazette* called
Montagu patronizing "even in the days when all he knew about
India was derived from books."[5]

Even Montagu had mixed feelings about going to India, afraid
that his absence would remove him from the center of political
action and from Venetia's thoughts. He was in one of his bleak
moods, when he wrote to Venetia on August 4, 1912:

I have to confess things look very black. I was a fool to say I'd go to India.
I think the P.M. thinks so too. It means I shall never get what my ambition
yearns for—more important work to do and I'm very very miserable to
think no one wants my services. But I'm still going because I think it
would be still worse to change my mind and because if they don't want me
—and they don't—it's no use thrusting myself on them. This is based on
fact!

So in one month, I've lost you and all hopes of politics. It's pretty black
isn't it.[6]

Montagu was correct in feeling that no one else wanted him. His
tactlessness and sharp tongue were frequently reported in the press
and his criticism of Crewe and their disagreements were no secret.
Few political leaders would voluntarily add such a personality to
their staffs. Going to India, moreover, would remove him from the
important debates in London that year on women's rights, industrial
strife, Home Rule for Ireland, and clashes over the Plural Voting
Bill.

Whatever ambivalence Edwin felt about the trip dissolved almost
instantly when he landed in Bombay. It was, he exclaimed in his
first letter home, "the single most thrilling experience" of his life.
His fascination with India from behind a desk in Whitehall was one
thing; but to see the country, to be caught up in its mystery, its
opulence and splendor, its physical beauty and its people made India
not merely the subject of academic and political concern, but a part
and parcel of his whole being. As Montagu wrote on November 12,
"the infection of this country has become so acute I doubt I shall
ever get over it. . . . I cannot think of anything but this country, its
people just awakening, its possibilities so marvelous that America
with its capital development seems small, its difficulties and mistakes so vivid that even I can pronounce them."[7]

Montagu was determined to see everything. His tour included visits not only to thirty cities and provinces, but also to tiny villages, jungle outposts and military installations. He was interested in everybody and everything, the rich and the poor, the powerful and the powerless, the rulers and the ruled, judges, soldiers and civil servants. He wanted to meet the educated, the illiterate, the rickshaw carrier and the Maharajahs, the extremists and the moderates, the government officials and the members of the press. He wanted to understand India's industry, agriculture, irrigation, hospitals and medical services, visit her museums and forests and observe her animals and, of course, her birds of every variety.

He had enormous energy and a habit of asking innumerable questions. He wanted to understand Indian customs, the ways of worship and the attitudes of Muslims and Hindus toward each other. He wanted to meet the men who ran the government, especially those in the Indian Civil Service, and to form his own judgment of them. He was open and relaxed in his relationship to people and most of them responded honestly to him. To each encounter he brought a sense of wonder and adventure. As he did on his first trip around the world with Mr. Israel, he sent a letter home each week to his mother, an excerpt from the diary in which he recorded his impressions and ideas. As in the past, his mother read these letters aloud when the family gathered for the Friday evening Sabbath. He also wrote, although not as frequently, to Venetia, sending her only six letters during the first three months of the trip. She sent seven. For the first time in their correspondence, most of his letters were short and impersonal and hers long and chatty. Near the end of October, for example, she wrote an eight-page letter about her life at Alderley. She was busy and involved in local service groups like the Girls' Club and sewing classes. She was directing a children's play and making costumes for it. She had become more concerned with contributing her time to useful projects and reported that her character "has completely changed."[8] This was quite different in tone than Edwin's one-line letter of October 17: "Nothing to tell you but we reach Bombay tomorrow. Good luck."[9]

Venetia herself recognized the difference in Montagu's letters and complained that "while your letters get shorter and shorter mine seem to lengthen every time I write."[10] It was as if Venetia were trying to compensate for the hurt she had inflicted upon him and

Montagu, in turn, wanted to demonstrate by his short, curt notes that he had accepted the inevitable. He would now view Venetia as a friend to whom one drops a line and not as a lover to whom one bares one's soul.

Diary Notes

Montagu's diary was filled with his awe of the physical beauty of India. The naturalist often overshadowed the politician. He wrote with ardor about "the flowers with a misty smell of which the whole of India seems to smell, people, scenery and places," of "cool moon-lit nights," and the "sounds of crickets," the "yellow grass dotted with trees," "the motionless pheasant, bronze and white, elegant and so peaceful to the reverent man who comes to salaam," "the jewelled elephants and wild stallions," "the snow hills rising 23,000 feet" and the sunsets, "the most gorgeous I have ever seen in my life."[11]

His tour included Bombay, Alwar, Simla, Peshawar, Charsadda, Kashmir, Canal Colonies, Lahore, Amritsar, Meerut, Algarh, Agra, Cawnpore, Lucknow, Benares, Calcutta, Udaipur, Bikaner, Delhi, Gwalior, Jodpur, Jabalpur, Madras and Mysore and ended with a return to Delhi and Bombay. Edwin and his party had a special train with a sitting room, three bedrooms, a kitchen, and a bathroom, as well as servants and a cook. But he also traveled by ordinary train, by automobile, and six hundred miles by elephant, and he went down the Ganges by boat.

Most of his travel was in the more populous cities, but he drove over the Khyber Pass, visited tribal villages on the border of Afghanistan and did big game hunting in various jungles throughout India, spending ten days in the Kheri forest shooting from an elephant. He was particularly taken by the jungles in Mysore, which he described as:

far more beautiful than anything I have ever seen. Nestling at the foot of the Nilgiri hills, the little marshy rivers, glorious clumps of giant bamboos, scarlet-flowered trees called, I believe, "the flame trees of the forest," and others covered with bright salmon-colored flowers, teak trees with withered brown leaves falling now and then with a tremendous clatter, and bright-colored butterflies made up a splendid scene.[12]

Montagu shot bison, panthers, crocodiles and tigers, as well as demoiselle crane, black buck, sand grouse and chinkara. He could not shoot elephants; having ridden six hundred miles on one, he had developed such a genuine affection for it that he could not kill any of its family.

While he was in fact a superb sightseer, missing nothing, he viewed himself as only an amateur in his interest in, and understanding of, architecture and art. As a naturalist, however, he considered himself an expert. "Would a genuine student of Indian architecture or history," he wrote in his diary, "have found the time at the Taj to be really thrilled by the sight—the first I have ever had—of a hoopoe sitting on a marble balustrade and emitting its well-known cry? I notice that the Indian hoopoe has a four-syllabled cry and puts its beak straight down and its crest straight up to emit it."[13]

In January 1913, he shot a panther measuring 6 feet 3½ inches. "The method of shooting was to watch, absolutely motionless, in a shelter," a method unique to India. Montagu was intrigued with this as it "gives one an opportunity of seeing the panther and watching it; and so makes it especially interesting in the not very attractive performance of the actual shooting of big game."[14] It would appear from such comments that while big game hunting was exciting to Montagu, studying and observing animals and birds was often more pleasurable.

Throughout his recollection his profound appreciation of India's beauty is evident:

I cannot go on raving about Indian sunsets and sunrises, but I do not feel at the moment I shall ever get tired of them; the play of colour is so wonderful. . . . There is a beautiful sunset every night . . . the dark comes suddenly and there is no twilight; but the purpling hills and fading lights an hour before the sun goes down are indescribable.

Of the Taj Mahal he wrote:

when one stands near it, when one sees the light on it, when one sees the beauty of its carving and its inlaid design, there is no reason for criticism. And I know of nothing more wonderful that I have seen in my life than the dawn on the Taj on that misty day, or the effect of the interior, with its rolling echoes, lighted by a single lamp, and the pierced screens of unequalled beauty with which the tombs were surrounded.[15]

But Montagu's diary was more than a travelogue and a description of sunsets, flame trees, panther shoots and wild birds. Its chief importance lies in its political observations and warnings. The language of the diary was often sharp and brutally frank and included Montagu's evaluation of the Indian Civil Service, the military, the police, the Viceroy and the Council, Muslims and Hindus, the abject poverty that existed side by side with the extraordinary luxury of the British raj and the Indian ruling classes and the attitude of the Muslims to Turkey. Most importantly, the diary was a condemnation of British snobbery and racism and the hostility it was creating among educated Indians, which Montagu correctly foresaw as encouraging extremism and ultimately destroying British rule.

Of the men in the Indian Civil Service, Montagu found that the opinions he had formed at home were confirmed: They were efficient, hardworking and able, but interested in statistics and "progress of the material kind. . . . They were not interested in men as individuals; they want progress reducible to statistics; the men [Indians] are pawns."[16] He bemoaned their inability to relate to the Indians as individuals to bring Indians and Englishmen closer together, and he feared that this would lead to disaster.

The well-meaning of it is so pathetic. . . . An Indian official never explains; there are no rules to show him how. He does his duty and at that he is better than any man of any age—but to explain things and thereby to bring us and the people together in the light of humanity is to them impossible. . . . One sees in Lahore the type of what I fear exists in India, which, if it goes on, will lead us to disaster—the resentment of the educated Indian and his claims.[17]

Perhaps, Montagu mused, the inability of members of the Indian Civil Service to treat the Indians as human beings was due to the fact that they were conservative and racist. This lack of innovation was particularly evident in the lackluster policy of the Finance Department in India which was not developing the vast resources of India. "A paternal government with its land, its salt, its railways and its canals cannot be financed on Treasury lines, but as a business. . . . We limit progress because we worship Treasury traditions."[18]

Many of the Englishmen in positions of importance, Montagu found, were old, snobbish, and racially intolerant. Some, such as Lord Nicholson, Montagu described as "very senile. . . . He urged me never to talk to my servants, as this was very harmful to prestige."[19] The men of the Indian Civil Service were, of course, no different in their attitudes from most of the Englishmen in government positions in India at the time, including most of the Governors of the Provinces, members of the Councils and the Viceroy himself. As a group, Montagu found them unhappy with the thought of change, determined to preserve the status quo.[20]

As for the Viceroy, Montagu found Lord Hardinge unenthusiastic about his visit, cold and aloof to him, proper but not eager to share ideas and confidences. Montagu confessed in his diary, "I cannot of course feel any resentment at his lack of any sort of personal enthusiasm or desire to assist me. I do not suppose he has ever found occasion to realize or appreciate me; but I certainly regret it, and it will make it all the more difficult to focus what seems in India a very intangible personality."[21]

The Silver Scandal

In November 1912, while Montagu was in India, a crisis occurred in England that caused him much grief. It also afforded the anti-Semites another opportunity to attack the Jews, especially those in government. This time their attack was directly on Montagu himself and his family's firm, Samuel Montagu & Company. The firm had been appointed by the India Office to get a cheaper price for the silver to be used in Indian coinage and to break the monopoly of the "Indian Silver Ring," which, it was alleged, was taking advantage of the government.

Montagu was accused of using his influence to obtain this contract for the Montagu firm, although, in fact, he had never been involved in this negotiation or in any questions involving currency and exchange in the India Office. Montagu was deeply disturbed by these attacks but grateful for the loyalty of his friends. Asquith staunchly defended him, as did his friend, John Maynard Keynes. Keynes wrote a forceful letter to *The Times*[22] refuting the allegations contained in a series of articles published in *The Times* on what was now being called "The Silver Scandal." Keynes was already recognized as an expert on India's monetary policy and was at this time employed by the India Office. His knowledge of the facts was indisputable.

Montagu, as well as Samuel Montagu & Co., were completely exonerated by a parliamentary committee, but this did little to stop the anti-Semitic attacks. Men like Major Glyn, a Conservative Member of Parliament who strongly disliked Jews, used the incident to attack the Liberal Party for permitting Jews to become an influence in the government and in the Party. "What a party," Glyn said in a speech in North Bedfordshire, "which has two members of the family in the Government, another brother who is a Member of Parliament and another who is a member of the House of Peers and all of them making money out of Indian finance. The Under-Secretary of State is a Mr. Samuel; the Postmaster General is a Mr. Samuel and there is Lord Swaythling, a pretty name for one who was a Samuel—the Infant Samuel—and also a Sir Something Samuel, all of whom were created by the Radical Party. All the silver for India is financed by the House of Samuel." [23]

At one point Montagu was so outraged that he urged his family to bring a libel suit against the *New Witness,* a particularly vitriolic anti-Semitic publication that accused Edwin of "duplicity . . . characteristic of Jews." His family did not take this course, correctly believing that legal action would keep the issue alive long after it was of interest to the public. The anti-Semites, while not successful in driving Montagu from office, did succeed in forcing the resignation of his cousin, Sir Stuart Samuel, as Member of Parliament for Whitechapel, because of his membership in the Montagu firm. Stuart later ran for Parliament again and regained his seat.

Although Montagu was cleared and vigorously defended by the Prime Minister and others, he believed that the episode would be fatal to his career. If he were promoted out of the India Office it would appear that his superiors thought him guilty; if he remained, there was no hope of political advancement. In India, moreover, he felt isolated and unable to answer the charges against him directly. He expressed his unhappiness and fear that his career was doomed in his diary:

each English mail at present makes me shudder with only too well-justified apprehensions about the "Silver Scandal." I am driven to regret my visit of India altogether, and feel very isolated. It is not only what people write, but the fact that they do not write at all (not a single member of the House of Commons—not a single Downing Street man or woman) makes me feel as though even those in England who do not believe in the corruption charges, think it ought not to have happened, and that any defense that I knew nothing of it shows, as I suppose it does, a culpably limited interest in India Office work. The only alternative would seem that, because I am the brother of my brother and the son of my father, there is no room for me in politics. A desperate desire to rush home aimlessly and to curse desperately has been conquered; but I am lastingly depressed by the silence of my friends and the perverseness of Liberal newspapers. The bright and grateful feature is the splendid sympathy of the Secretary of State and the whole Office. It will, I fear, colour the future and limit any possibilities for good work I may possess.[24]

There is an irony in the anti-Semitic attacks against Montagu. He was a Jew who did not care about Judaism, who disliked Jewish women, who spent most of his time in the company of non-Jews, and yet he was subject to the same anti-Semitic tirades as his Orthodox brethren in the East End. As with the Marconi Scandal, there clearly was no escape.

The Trip Continues

Montagu was troubled, as well, by the opulence he found among the British officials in India. He thought their homes were too elegant, the offices palatial and the entertainment on too grand a scale, especially when the "poor masses are beginning to think." Only a Viceroy who dared to be unconventional could make changes in this matter and he would be very unpopular. "I think I could do it," Montagu concluded, "and I would give the money I saved to charity."[25] Montagu was critical too of the snobbery of the English women. He placed substantial blame upon them for many of the attitudes he found.

Our women will not like the Indians and will not try to. They deteriorate very quickly here in everything, except courage and their wonderfully good quality of loyalty to their men does not make up for their selfish smartness and short sightedness which makes them the most wearisome company. They infuse the air of *de haut en bas* and cynical resentment, which is so common among the men and which the sensitive educated Indians hate so much.

Such attitudes he believed infused hatred into Indian women, who in turn imparted it to their children. The British "know . . . that the

Indian does not respect them, or approve the way they dress and live; and they [the British] take no pains to explain things. And the Indian does not really like them and his women hate us and do not really like to talk to us, even when they are not Purdah. I believe it is true that the mothers of India are the future heads of real sedition; that the women are almost completely alienated; and that they are powers in their own homes and in affairs generally, and work through the men."[26]

The Muslim Issue

Montagu's trip and the opinions expressed to him by several officials whom he respected also influenced his belief that what happened in Turkey with its large Muslim population would have repercussions in the Muslim community of India. "Ross-Keppel [Chief Commissioner, North West Frontier] says it will be very serious if the Turks are turned out of Constantinople . . . that it would be followed by a series of crusades and an outbreak of Ghaziism, or private assassinations by fanatics."[27] The Aga Khan reinforced the belief that trouble in Turkey would trigger trouble in India. Montagu wrote that the Aga Khan had told him "if anything happened to Turkey in Asia, there would be serious trouble . . . and some declaration ought to be made of our determination to maintain Turkey's independence and integrity."[28]

His trip also revealed to Edwin the complexities of the problems the government of India faced. He understood more than ever before that quick solutions did not exist. "We have in India," he concluded, "every century from the twentieth to the fifth, and the same machinery for all. It is too rigid and unimaginative for the twentieth, too conventional and elaborate for the fifth; and we train our officials to go into partnership with the twentieth by making them administer the maze of rules applied to the fifth."[29]

He left India not only overwhelmed by these complexities but also saddened that no one listened to his warnings of the failure of the British to understand the inadequacies of their rule. "India is absorbingly interesting and difficult," he wrote on March 8, 1913, as he prepared to leave Bombay. "Would that I had more opportunity to help! One feels so much that one is shrieking like Cassandra . . . no one seems to disagree with or to take my advice."

. . . what with no Parliamentary opportunity, the censure-like action of Asquith and Crewe in regard to the Commission . . . I go home without zest and rather depressed. India ought to have a great official purifying and it does so want energy. Almost a revolution of ideal and method is needed to avert a revolution of its people. One cannot feel optimistic after being there and discussing almost every problem with nearly everybody of importance.[30]

Venetia and Edwin: The Relationship Resumes

By the end of November, Montagu's determination to forget Venetia began to ebb and his letters expressed anew his desire for her. "You would love the jungle," he wrote, "if I could induce you to come and see it."[31] Venetia did not respond.

The letters to her became longer and a little more personal. In early December he complained that no one had written to him, including the Prime Minister and "not a single member of the Government."[32] He continued to believe that this was because of people's suspicions about his role in the Silver Scandal.

Venetia, while not responding to Montagu's invitation to visit India, continued her long and newsy letters. She commented on his remark that something she said was obscure or cryptic. "It probably was nothing. Get it into your head that my simple and foolish comments are just that." She said she was glad he was enjoying India. England was very dull. She saw a lot of Violet and a little of the Prime Minister, who was:

in grand spirits whenever I see him; one night dining with Bluey he was at his very best—most lovable and foolish. His Muse has come into song which means "he has superabundant spirits." Violet is planning to go to America for three weeks; Margot is not well—seems crusty and edgy. The family is planning a vast Christmas party. . . . This letter will reach you between Christmas and New Years. I hope 1913 will bring you masses of good luck.[33]

Montagu's last letter in 1912 was dated December 18, probably written before he received Venetia's New Year's greetings. The letter ended with another expression of his new love:

If you want a living sight of entrancing interest come to India and drift slowly down the Ganges, in front of Benares and look at the people bathing in hundreds. To see an old man standing knee deep or waist deep in the water saying his prayers with his hands lifted to heaven, to see a man standing on one leg while he shouts his . . . hymns—to see them men and women and children, dipping, praying, washing their clothes and themselves in the sacred stream. . . .

It wants more than a few months to understand the mixture of idolatry, superstition, philosophy and God worship.[34]

India may have become Montagu's new love but it did not replace Venetia, for he ended his letter confessing that he still wanted "so badly to talk to" her.

Venetia's Christmas day letter tried to dissuade him of the notion that any of his friends might have believed him guilty of the Silver Scandal.

I can't bear the idea that you should think for an instant that anyone who knows you at all has *ever* imagined that you were remotely responsible for anything that has occurred lately. Everyone knows that you have nothing and would have nothing to say or do in the matter. It's horrible not having any letters (though by the time you get this you will probably have had two from Violet, I know and several from Margot).[35]

Venetia was absolutely correct. None of Montagu's friends suspected him of wrongdoing in the Silver Scandal. During this time Lady Dorothy Howard also wrote:

Are you an old donkey or has the sun hurt you, or have you not taken enough exercise, that you write me so gloomy a screed? I don't believe you think so horribly badly of your friends and colleagues as to think that they have been callous—let alone credulous—whilst guttersnipes have chirped out their nasty cries! Outsiders have shrugged shoulders and disbelieved and said, "Just like politicians to throw mud at each other." Insiders have been furious and stamped on the faces of the guttersnipes.[36]

But Montagu, sensitive and gloomy as usual, was difficult to convince.

In her Christmas letter, Venetia also urged Montagu to "hurry" home because she believed he should be involved in the Indian Finance debate and not let "Bluey" do it for him. She was genuinely solicitous about this. "I hear you are thinking of staying to April," she wrote:

Is that a good idea? Why don't you hurry up and come home by March 10. If they knew you were going to be back by then perhaps they would postpone the Indian Finance debate (it will be a great crush won't it to get it in before the February adjournment and your return would be an excellent reason for delaying it a little). Wouldn't it be much more satisfying for you to be there for Bluey, good as he is he can't know much about it. . . .

We've just come to the end of a most strenuous Christmas Day. . . . I've done very well in the way of loot.[37]

Montagu took her advice and returned in March, a month earlier than he had planned.

Asquith and Venetia: While Montagu Was Away

During the early months of 1913, Venetia and the Prime Minister spent a great deal of time together. The Prime Minister's feelings were becoming more serious and his letters, which he wrote with increasing frequency, clearly reflected this. During January and February of 1913, Asquith wrote seven long letters to Venetia, as well as seeing her nearly every Friday afternoon and many weekends. His letters were filled with political gossip as well as love. They discussed "the intrigue and counter-intrigue" of the suffragettes and his abhorrence of the movement, his pleasure at Alderley, his desire to spend more time with Venetia, his remembrance always of the "mist—& rain—blurred survey of the three counties thro' wh. we drove on Saturday" and the depression he felt "at the thought of absence & separation" from her. He wrote also of the fact that he "purposely" held himself in check when they were together "so much: more, I dare say, than you suspect."[38] And he wrote during the debate on the Silver Scandal, "Bluetooth" and he "championed the far-away Assyrian, who was left without a stain on his character."[39]

As Asquith began to think of Montagu as a potential rival, his letters began increasingly to refer to the negative qualities in Montagu's personality and to his religion. His comments about Judaism are particularly revealing. In a letter to Venetia, he told her of a dinner party at which the guests discussed H. G. S. de Blowitz, "the great *Times* correspondent in Paris from 1875 to 1900," who, according to Brock, was a "Roman Catholic of Jewish extraction, born in Bohemia. He became a French citizen during the Franco-Prussian War and was decorated for helping the French Government deal with the Commune in Marseilles in April 1871."[40] Discussing

Blowitz, Asquith wrote, "We had some quite good talk; amongst other things & people, of Blowitz. . . . I quoted Gambetta's remark about him—that he was the *four* worst things: 'Juif, Polonais, Catholique, décoré' [Jew, Pole, Catholic, decorated]. Which do you think the most objectionable of the four? I am afraid, the first?"

Only one of Venetia's letters to Asquith survives, and it does not show whether, and if so, how, she responded to his question of which she thought the most objectionable. The only letter that remains from Venetia to Asquith was written on January 20, two weeks after Asquith's remarks. The only comment about Montagu in Venetia's letter is her reference to a story in the *Times,* which prompted her to write: "Do you see that the Assyrian has 'acquired' [in the words of *The Times*] a house in Queen Anne's Gate? Do you think," she asks Asquith, "he will entertain us there lavishly? I fear not."[41]

It is difficult to tell what Venetia meant by this comment. Montagu was known to be a lavish host and there is no reason to assume he would be less expansive in entertaining now that he had finally bought his own home. He loved expensive food (a source of great dismay to his late father) and enjoyed good company and conversation. Was Venetia trying, in her desire to preserve the triangle, to downplay any relationship she had with Montagu by suggesting to Asquith that *she* did not anticipate being entertained by Montagu in his new home? She knew better.

Venetia also wrote regularly to Montagu of the increasing amounts of time she was spending with the Prime Minister. Asquith had now become, she told Montagu, one of "her favorite people,"[42] and she wrote, in a matter-of-fact tone, of her pleasure in being in his company, her first visit to the Wharf, and the conversations in which they engaged. "I motored down with the Prime Minister," she wrote on November 12, "to the Wharf."

It was delicious seeing him again. I hadn't any kind of talk with him since the end of the summer. He was in very good spirits I thought in spite of the crisis. He didn't as you can imagine talk much about it and our conversation ran in very well worn lines, the sort that he enjoys on these occasions and which irritate Margot so much by their great dreariness. I love every well known word of them—with and for me the familiarity is a large part of the charm.

Venetia commented on the Wharf, which she had never seen before, and which she believed was not very suitable for a large gregarious family and "is full of drawbacks." They talked about the trip to Sicily and "it left the most delicious after impression."[43] She protected the triangle, however, by telling Montagu that she some-times doubted the Prime Minister even enjoyed her company. "I spent most of last week . . . at Downing Street," she wrote in November 1912, and "saw not very much of the Prime Minister. Do you remember me saying how much he varied in his liking for me and that sometimes he quite liked me and at others not at all? Well, this was one of the not at all times. He was horribly bored by my constant presence at breakfast, lunch and dinner."[44]

Venetia by this time knew how the Prime Minister felt about her. The excursions on Friday afternoons, the trip to Sicily, the time spent at Hurstly, the "memorable" night at Ewelme, and his letters, clearly conveyed his feelings. It is more likely that, while she openly told Montagu of the enjoyable times she spent with Asquith, she thought it best to minimize the romantic nature of their relationship, in much the same way that she made light of her relationship with Montagu when writing to Asquith. It is on such deceptions that triangles are built.

Margot

By this time, the health of the Prime Minister's wife, Margot, had seriously deteriorated; she often suffered from nervous disorders, many brought about by illnesses resulting from pregnancies and miscarriages. "She criticizes everything incessantly," Pamela Mc-Kenna, wife of Reginald McKenna, a leading Liberal politician and close personal friend of the Asquiths, wrote, "and always in the unkindest way . . . but I know she never means to be wounding and I do feel so sorry for her, as she makes herself terribly un-happy."[45] Her strained relationship with her step-children, espe-cially Violet, who made no effort to hide her dislike, did not help. "I always tell everyone of temperament," Margot wrote in August 1912, *never* to be a step-mother."

The fault was not all Margot's. Asquith's children were difficult and intellectually snobbish, and they made Margot feel inferior and unwanted. Violet became increasingly hard to please. The more time she and Venetia spent with Asquith, the more they made Margot feel like an intruder, an outsider to their fun and games. As Asquith's feelings for Venetia increased and Margot found herself excluded from their trysts, her dislike of Venetia increased as well.

The fact that she tolerated Venetia's company as much as she did is a tribute either to her open-mindedness or to the fact that Asquith would have it no other way. In later years she wrote: "Some of my friends . . . wondered why I was not jealous of the women he was fond of. On the contrary, I welcomed them, as they fitted the theory I have always held about wives. . . . No woman should expect to be the only woman in her husband's life. The idea of such a thing appears to me ridiculous. . . . I not only encouraged his female friends, but posted letters to them if I found them in our front hall." [46]

This was only partially true. Margot accepted Asquith's young women friends when his relationship with them was confined to conversation and tea; she was justifiably jealous when his relationship with Venetia became serious. Margot's subsequent letters to Montagu and to Venetia's mother clearly show this. But her feelings did not deter her husband. As 1912 drew to a close, Venetia was rarely far from his thoughts. Even as the New Year approached, his plans were not to be with Margot and their family but to join Venetia "almost as soon as the New Year has struck." [47]

Edwin Winds up His Trip

At the beginning of 1913, while Asquith's pursuit of Venetia was intensifying, Edwin wrote to her, "Calcutta at Christmas was one of the liveliest places." [48] He then described his rising at six A.M. to go to the races or watch polo and the busy schedule he kept. He was totally absorbed in seeing, learning and reading about India.

He expressed unhappiness about Margot, in response to a comment in one of Venetia's letters about Margot's deteriorating relationship with her husband and stepchildren. "I have noticed the state of things being very bad before I left London and I fear it will get worse." What Montagu did not know was that the more troubled the relationship between Margot and Asquith became, the more the Prime Minister would seek escape and solace with Venetia. Ignorant of this, Montagu began to think of renewing his relationship with Venetia, although he assured her that he would not pursue marriage. He wrote that he had thought about it and in retrospect recognized how foolish he had been. He promised not to behave in such a manner again. "One does occasionally get opportunities for thought in India," he wrote, "and one of my pious resolves has been that I will no longer be a d——d nuisance to those to whom I have been so in the past." He assured her that he would not make "immoderate demands" upon her "patience and sympathy" and ended "with renewed thanks and every sort of affectionate remembrance expressible and in-expressible."[49]

12

The Triangle Is Now in Place, March 1913–January 1914

Oh, how I pant for you.

Edwin to Venetia, Nov. 11, 1913

Montagu returned from India on March 23, 1913. He had been away almost seven months and returned "tanned and fit"[1] with considerably more knowledge and understanding of that country, its people and its problems. He went to India with a growing sympathy for the pleas of Indian leadership for more education and self-government. He returned with this sympathy intensified and confirmed. He went to India with a growing discomfort at the bigotry of the British ruling classes, the Indian Civil Service and the police. He returned with his opinions confirmed. And he went to India with a fledgling understanding of Muslim religious and political fears, their identification with the independence of Muslim Turkey and the importance of Muslim loyalty to the British. And again, he returned with a deeper understanding.

With a Liberal government in power, he continued to believe that he could persuade his colleagues of his ideas about more education for the Indians, more sensitivity to them as a people, and more self-government. As for the Muslim issue, this was a subject not really understood in England and viewed as too esoteric and on the fringes of political interest. Only the debate between Curzon and Montagu the year before, inspired more by Curzon's political aims than by his ideology, made the Muslim problem of sufficient interest even to be raised in Parliament. But to Montagu, it became a major item on his Indian agenda.

He came home "bursting" with new ideas and impressions and with a deep foreboding about future problems in India. Venetia, knowing him well, urged him during his visit to the Wharf the day he returned not to "pour out all the juice and vitriol which you must have collected during the last six months."[2]

She would be back in London the day after his return and urged him to visit her before dinner, since she was "dining at Downing Street." She added that it would be "fun" to see him again. Venetia had no qualms about seeing one suitor for cocktails and another for dinner. It was "fun" to be with Montagu and "fun" to be with the Prime Minister. Love was not part of her script.

Asquith, now fully aware of Venetia's involvement with Montagu, not only continued to comment about Montagu's Jewishness at every opportunity but began to express his jealousy more openly. For example, on March 22 he wrote, "I go back Monday and hope to see you unless you are monopolized by Assyrian redux."[3] In April, in a poem he composed for her, Asquith reminded Venetia that she was a Christian and that Montagu was not.

> Venetia, though a Christian child,
>   Sprung from an Aryan stem—
> Frequents—too easily beguiled!—
>   The silken tents of Shem[4]

Both Venetia and Asquith referred to Montagu's home at 24 Queen Anne's Gate as "The Silken Tent," in part because of its silk curtains.[5] Asquith added the descriptive name of Shem to underscore again Montagu's Jewishness. Jews were supposed to have descended from Shem, the eldest of Noah's three sons; hence the word "Semitic."[6]

Again, on April 7, Asquith wrote to Venetia that Montagu was visiting the Wharf and was "in an introspective and sombre mood," that "he had never known what it was to be free from physical and mental pain: and complained that he amused nobody and nobody amused him. Apart from this," Asquith continued, "[Edwin] seemed to be in quite good spirits, and played Bridge with zest & determination. . . . We drove back . . . in Tante's Rolls Royce which devours the ground. . . . Come soon. Dear love."[7] Between the lines was Asquith's message: Why should you, dearest Venetia,

become involved with a somber, moody Jew, never free from physical and mental pain.

During May, June and July 1913, Montagu became more depressed than usual. He was disappointed that the Prime Minister
vetoed the idea of visiting India "next winter." India was still very
much on his mind. He reported that he made a great speech, "a real
triumph for Liberalism," but one that received "the usual boycott
by the Liberal papers."[8] By this time, the Liberal press was not
friendly toward Montagu. They were disappointed in his policy
toward police brutality in India, believing that he had failed to take
a firm enough position. Nor had they forgotten the Mackarness
affair. The Tory press was even more hostile and rarely mentioned
Montagu, except in criticism.

Although he was trying to put some distance between himself
and Venetia, he was not succeeding. Even when he was on the road
making speeches, he thought of her and wished he were "sitting in
the garden with her."[9] He found too that the Prime Minister was
not confiding in him as he had in the past, his present job did not
give him any scope and yet he was not wanted "elsewhere." Politically and personally, he saw himself "gloomy" and without much
hope.[10] The Prime Minister confirmed this by reporting to Venetia
on June 11: "The Assyrian was with us at the Wharf on Sunday—
full of gloomy retrospection and fitful gleams of suggestions and
even hope. But all the books of Moses are nothing but supposes."[11]

During July Montagu's depression continued and his inability to
develop a deeper relationship with Venetia added to his gloom. He
wrote to Venetia that she was "very and pathetically difficult to get
hold of," and that "that's the worst of liking people other people
like." He had not seen her for a long time; nor had he seen the
Prime Minister. It seemed his friends were "slipping away."[12]

Venetia's only letter to Montagu in August, while not responding
to his plea for a closer relationship, was one of the few in which she
revealed some part of herself.[13] She wrote that she had just turned
twenty-six the day before, which she found depressing, and so
wanted to assure that her future life would be "permanent fun." To
Venetia, the word "fun" was more than a casual term to describe
the things, occasions and people she enjoyed. It was the actual
principle that guided her life. A friend wrote:

If asked whether she had any guiding principles, she would in some moods declare that it was to get the "maximum of fun" out of life. In other moods, perhaps more often, she was inclined to doubt whether (in the words of a friend) "the query was worth the quest." She was preserved from cynicism, and from living at haphazard by the native energy of a healthy temperament, and by a capacity for real devotion where she really cared.[14]

Neither Asquith nor Montagu was critical of Venetia's desire for fun. On the contrary, they applauded it and each in his own way encouraged it. Early in July of 1913, Asquith composed a poem describing a day in Venetia's life, filled with fencing, eurythmics, luncheons, "tête a tête—where the Assyrian's groaning board is spread at Queen Anne's Gate," gallery hopping, going to the hairdresser, listening to gossip and scandal, dinner, bridge, "a rout, a dance—a supper, still remain; . . . to bed at half past three. To do it all again."[15]

Budget Presentation: 1913

Montagu presented his fourth and final Indian budget in August.[16] Much of the speech showed what Montagu had learned in India about the conflict between Muslims and Hindus and the marked differences between these two peoples, with Hindus interested largely in India and Muslims interested in Islam, wherever it was practiced. British foreign policy, Montagu warned, must consider the international character of the Islamic religion. To ignore it would doom their relationship with the Muslims of India and jeopardize British rule there.

The Muslims, he reminded his audience, were a proud people, keenly aware that they had once been a great world power. They remembered the history of Spain under the Moors and looked sadly upon their present condition:

I think the Indian Mussulmans realize that they have, as a whole, too long neglected the educational opportunities that the British Government wishes to offer as freely to them as to the Hindus, with the result that in those spheres of public employment, the doors of which are opened by Western education, they have not attained a position proportional, either to their achievements in the past or to the numbers at present.

Montagu expressed the hope that the Muslims would take advantage of the educational opportunities the British now offered, and in this way become a more powerful force in the politics of India. Montagu's interest in and understanding of the Muslims in India and their concern with Islam in North Africa and the Ottoman Empire was now beginning to take hold.

Montagu discussed the Royal Commission to investigate personnel in India, regretting that its purpose had been misunderstood. He believed that it was increasingly important to get the best possible men to India. To do so, pay must be increased, pensions improved in order to attract "young, intelligent and sensitive men," rather than those who "regret the old days" and who lamented "that we must cooperate with the Indians." They must be ready to help the Indian "in the development of his capacity for local government." This statement is a clear precursor of the principle of dyarchy, the basis of the Montagu-Chelmsford Reforms of 1919.

"The old era of a hard and fast division between government and governed in racial lines has long ago disappeared," he said. "The watchword of the future is cooperation. We are pledged to advance, and we mean to advance, but it must be steadily and prudently. . . . The Commission will advise us as to what changes, what reforms are necessary to take us far forward on this new road as we are now justified in going."[17] Both sides must act "in the spirit of the underlying principle," with "a gentleness of application and an endeavor to interpret,"[18] not a rigid adherence to the letter of the law. Rigidity, he believed, would doom future relations.

Speaking of the police, Montagu's tone was very different than it had been before his trip. He now recognized that while there were exceptions, there were many good police about whom "we don't generally hear." We "should relax no effort to improve the condition of the police"; we should not abolish records "of confessions prior to trial. We have two duties; one is to avoid and prevent torture, . . . but we are not justified in hampering ourselves against the other side of our duty—the punishment of crime and the protection of law abiding citizens."[19]

His last words were "a plea for devolution, not necessarily by a redistribution of duties and powers, but by the liberty to exercise a wise discretion in the use of duties and powers as they now are. If we make cooperation and devolution our guiding principle, I am convinced that we shall be on the right lines."[20]

This was Montagu's final budget speech and his last major address on India to the House as Under Secretary. He wrote to Venetia that it went well. "Winston and Birrell were very appreciative. The PM rather sleepily but he listened to most of it. Bonar Law very flattering, as also Morrell."[21] Edwin Montagu had come a long way. In the four years he had held this post he had educated the House on the problems of India, he had become the most knowledgeable man in the House on India, and he had established his reputation as a political leader of brilliance and insight. But he had also made enemies, angering powerful forces in British politics, both to his left and to his right, antagonizing Tories, Liberals and Radicals alike.

Conflict with Crewe and Asquith

Montagu now found himself disagreeing more frequently with Lord Crewe and even with the Prime Minister. Asquith had agreed to the creation of a Royal Commission to look into the financial problems facing the India Office, including its overall financial organization. Montagu's letters to Crewe and Asquith express his "dismay" and "disappointment" at this decision. While he appreciated Asquith's loyalty in defending him personally in the Silver debate, he felt strongly that a Royal Commission would put an end to the ideas of reform of the financial organization of the India Office, for which he had been working for almost two years and which he had hoped could be adopted quickly on his return as a simple parliamentary bill. A Royal Commission would cause unnecessary delay and be "an obstacle to reform."[22] Not only did Crewe disagree[23] but so did the Prime Minister, who saw Montagu's telegrams and wrote to Crewe: "I return these [Montagu's telegrams]. Montagu's final attitude is quite unreasonable; he ought to realize that for the time being we are in closer touch with public opinion and parliamentary condition here."[24] This was very strong language for Asquith, who rarely criticized colleagues. In writing to Venetia, Asquith, using Montagu's sensitivity on the issue against him, displayed his irritation. "By the way," he wrote, "Crewe tells me today that Tante is already firing off neurotic telegrams on the subject of the proposed inquiry. He sent me a series of silhouettes—etched in vitriol—of the members of the Viceroy's Council, a few days ago."[25]

Montagu was also at odds with Crewe and Asquith, as well as with his old mentor, Lord Morley, and with Lord George Hamilton —both former Secretaries of State for India—over Montagu's proposals for reform of the India Council and the reorganization of the India Office.[26] As in so many other instances, he was incapable of leaving things alone, preserving the status quo. He believed strongly that the structure of the India Office was cumbersome, antiquated and unbusinesslike. It was slow to function, delaying important decision making, and was the subject of much criticism in India.

Montagu did not suggest that the India Council be abolished, a recommendation he was later accused of making. Instead he had suggested that the Council be made smaller, that its members have more independent power and that it consist of people recently returned from India or those still in India who were knowledgeable about India. Montagu believed that neither Lord Morley nor Lord Hamilton, both experts on India, understood his recommendation. With no support from his superiors, his suggestions were not adopted, which caused Montagu great frustration. This is probably one of the reasons why, by the summer of 1913, he had become increasingly restless and unhappy with his position, convinced that no one cared for him or for his ideas, and certain that his career was over and that he would never find another position in government.

The Triangle Is in Place

During the summer of 1913, Montagu had little opportunity to visit Penrhos; the responsibilities of the India Office were overwhelming. He complained that he was "awful rushed," but added in a letter to Venetia that "perhaps it's as well for I find I want to see you dangerously much."[27] The Prime Minister was also very busy, giving Venetia reason to complain to Montagu that one of the sad aspects of the summer was not seeing either him or the Prime Minister, "the two people I have most fun with and enjoy talking to most, you and the Prime, until you all come back from Scotland."[28] She also told Montagu that she had heard from the Prime Minister that Montagu's budget speech was "of remarkable excellence."[29]

Montagu was delighted and for once agreed with the evaluation of his speech. He also discussed his restlessness and his desire to move on but realized that if someone is doing poorly in a job no one wants him, "and if you are a success . . . nobody wants to move you. . . . One must be wanted elsewhere, and that is not [the] case with me." Part of him did not really want to move on, since he was "most interested in India," but preferred to do something for India, "doing not speaking, and also have my fingers in other pies, e.g. land reform." He was also playing tennis and enjoying it but wished he was younger.[30]

His love for Venetia, in spite of the promise he made in India, began to show again. He told her, "you are not I think aware how many times in the day I want to talk to you and if only you'll write to me you will be sending your delicious letters to one who appreciates them enormously."[31] Asquith now was aware that Montagu was seriously pursuing Venetia again, and his letters mentioned this frequently. On August 19, he wrote to Venetia that while Ireland may have been a new milieu, it was "peopled, I fear, by the same familiar figures. . . . One, perhaps the most interesting to you of these is expected here on Friday. I can already here the distant rumble . . . of his 'thundering' Rolls Royce." He told her that he had listened to Montagu's speech on the budget and felt it was good with "some notable patches tho at times too light, ragged and uneven."[32]

A few days later he wrote again to Venetia, informing her that "The Assyrian writes (with characteristic cold-bloodedness) that the sudden death of his host 'rather complicates' his plans: he still hopes to be with us to-morrow."[33] Montagu's letter to Venetia about the death of this friend was far from cold-blooded, telling her that he had had "an awful time: my poor friend . . . died literally in my arms. . . . This is a wonderful family believing . . . that death is but an incident. I like death less and less the more I come to it and my friends' faith does not inspire me: it frightens me."[34] Montagu had many unpleasant characteristics but "cold-bloodedness" was not among them. His friends found him warm and tenderhearted. Asquith's characterization of him to Venetia as cold-blooded was yet another indication of the Prime Minister's own growing jealousy.

In his letter about the death of his friend, Montagu referred to Venetia's letter telling him about her twenty-sixth birthday and her desire for permanent fun. If what she desired was fun, he wrote to

her, she must learn to concentrate her affections on one person. "As
of me," Montagu complained, "the years as they go on make matters and things grow worse and more dismal. Hopes and aspirations
become failures, doors close with a bang and I remain, and I fear,
forever a celibate, boycotted unused U[nder-Secretary] of S[tate] for
India. When you are inclined to curse streaks of your luck—please
remember mine."[35] He also wrote that he had received a highly
agitated communication from Margot and he feared things must be
bad. "Goodbye dearest Venetia. If you knew how satisfying writing
to you was, you'd wonder I did not do it oftener. If you knew how
yearning producing it was, you'd wonder I ever did it at all."[36]

Asquith celebrated Venetia's birthday with another poem, this
time writing about "the secret of Venetia's spinsterhood." In it, he
condemned all the men who dared not rise "to risk the gain or loss
of such a prize" and wrote of his envy of those younger than he.[37]

On September 3, Asquith wrote about Lady Dorothy Howard's
engagement to the Honorable Francis Henley, a brewer who was
Venetia's brother-in-law. Lady Dorothy Howard was Venetia's first
cousin. Asquith, with his usual elitist attitude, repeated Violet's
description of Henley as "Sylvia's discard . . . a brewer" and wondered if he was going to "confine his energies in the future to the
production of ginger pop."[38] Venetia also commented on Lady
Dorothy Howard's fiancé in a letter to Montagu. "I think it's larks
[very amusing] his being a brewer and a Conservative and an anti-
suffragist."[39] Montagu replied, but in a tone far different from
Asquith's and Venetia's. He had once loved Lady Dorothy and was
not prepared to laugh at her choice of a husband. While he wrote
that he was surprised, he said he believed her choice was "partly
revolt and partly a physical attraction. I agree with your description
of him. You never liked her as I did but I think you can understand
what it means to me the engagement and marriage of my friends—
the sense of loss not unlike death, the shrinkage of my world, the
enhanced value of those that remain."[40]

Montagu's gloom and depression over his failure to be married
was not restricted to his own letters. On September 16 the Prime
Minister wrote to Venetia from Hopman Lodge in Morayshire that
"the Assyrian" was visiting, and although the Prime Minister found
him in good form, he was "full of sighs and grousings when he

found himself alone with any of our Does. He hates this place like poison and says frankly that a fine day was wasted on it."[41]

Marriage may have been foremost on Montagu's mind; but it was not on Venetia's. She was still pursuing fun on the Admiralty yacht, the *Enchantress,* and wrote to Montagu that she loved life at sea, "long intervals of drifting about and then one goes to divine inaccessible places."[42] This was the opposite of Montagu's reaction to the sea. He hated it and found it monotonous and dull. "Praise of the sea," he once wrote, "maddens me. It isn't the sea people like, it's the coast lines."[43]

By the end of September, Montagu again proposed, causing a crisis for Venetia. Word of this was relayed to Asquith who lost no time in writing to Venetia to discover what the real facts were and to tell her that Montagu looked "slightly shattered."

The offhand reference in your letter seems inadequate, according to all my accounts . . . there was at one moment something very nearly approaching to a *crise du coeur.* Why didn't you give me a full and veracious narrative of this interesting incident? Was your conscience perchance still suffering from the after-swell which is apt to follow an emotional storm? The other personage in the drama [Montagu]—tho looking slightly shattered—is as well as could be expected.[44]

Venetia may have "shattered" Montagu, according to Asquith's description, but this did not stop her from continuing her letters and invitations to him. On November 1, she asked him to come to Alderley with the Prime Minister and asked: "Are you still cuckooed out of your mind."[45] If he was, she obviously was not taking it seriously. She wrote that she hoped she could see him in London and expected that their relationship would continue as in the past. Her expectations were fulfilled: Even her most recent rejection had failed to cool Montagu's ardor. When he could not see her in London or at Penrhos because of a speech, he ended his letter, "Oh how I pant for you."[46]

He later elaborated on his feelings for her, telling her that seeing her was difficult. He felt jealousy and despair. "There comes a time when my lack of success becomes very hard to bear. And the yearning for what I cannot have becomes so poignant that I dare not trust myself to behave naturally. . . . The years are slipping" and he

had yet "to accomplish anything or win power." But he assured
Venetia that he would not give up the struggle to win her. If he
failed, together with his other failures, it would kill him. "I shall
make a fight and if I go on failing it will not be either because I have
given in or that I was aware that the fight was going against me. So
my friend accept the grousing as the bleating of a bruised but
undaunted soul."[47]

As 1913 drew to a close, the die was cast. As long as Venetia
remained unmarried, Montagu would keep trying to win her hand.
Her repeated rejections would not deter him. As for Asquith, he too
would continue his pursuit of Venetia and, whenever the opportunity arose, he would make Venetia aware of any flaw in Montagu in
the hope that this would preclude Venetia from becoming too serious about his rival.

On December 15, Asquith wrote to Venetia that Montagu had
spent the weekend with the Asquiths at the Wharf, during which
time Montagu had confided to Margot that Viola Tree was "the sort
of woman whom he ought to have married & . . . compared her
favorably with the unsatisfying and elusive young females who have
so far played . . . the part of pole-star to his rather vagrant heart. I
hope," Asquith coyly added, "this won't rankle too sorely your
susceptible bosom. . . . You know how I long to be with you—
don't you? *Dearest Love*."[48]

Two days later Asquith wrote to Venetia that Margo had talked
with Montagu in her bedroom, "informing our Oriental friend
(among other things) that he had the qualities of his race, which do
not include courage. He seems to have taken this quite meekly."[49]
It was one thing for Montagu to believe that he personally lacked
courage. It was quite another for him to permit such a description
to be imposed on all Jews. If the slur had been directed against
Hindus or Muslims, he would not have remained silent or meek.
Whether Montagu accepted these insults against Jews because he had
come to believe them, or whether he accepted them in silence because he dared not disturb his standing with the Asquiths and the
world they represented, is less important than the mystery of how a
man so outspoken in his condemnation of discrimination and prejudice against Indians and other nonwhites in Kenya, South Africa and
India could be so indifferent to the same prejudice against his own
people and himself.

As 1913 ended, Montagu was more determined than ever to win Venetia, although the odds seemed great and the chances slight. He was determined, too, to make a change in his political career, although here, too, he could see no clear way to achieve this. But as Asquith often said, "the unexpected often happens in politics." On February 13, 1914, six months before the outbreak of World War I, the unexpected did happen. To his surprise and delight, Montagu was made Financial Secretary to the Treasury.

13

As the War Clouds Gather: Financial Secretary to the Treasury, 1914

Oh! If only Venetia would marry—how I loath girls who can't love but claim and collect like a cuckoo for their own vanity—Venetia's head is completely turned.

Margot Asquith to Montagu, Mar. 21, 1914

Montagu's appointment as Financial Secretary to the Treasury may have come as a surprise to him, but Asquith had been considering it for some time. He had become increasingly concerned with the hostility Montagu was engendering on Indian policy, not only among the Tories, but also within the Liberal Party and in the Liberal press. The vacancy in the post of Financial Secretary gave Asquith an ideal chance to accomplish several goals with a single stroke: to reward Montagu for his loyal service with a promotion; to use the experience Montagu had acquired as Parliamentary Private Secretary to the Chancellor of the Exchequer and in preparing the Indian budget; and to remove Montagu's abrasive manner from the debate over Indian policy.

The first hint of Asquith's plan to promote Montagu came in a letter to Venetia in early February when he told her that he had informed Lord Crewe that "he [Crewe] might have to part with the services of his Assyrian Curate—called by Providence to a higher sphere—*strictly entre nous*. I am not sure that after all it may not be the Treasury."[1] Even at this stage in Asquith's relationship with Venetia he revealed information to her that was not yet public, a practice that would extend even to wartime military information, when the stakes were much higher.

On February 12, Asquith again wrote to Venetia that "the fate (immediate not ultimate) of Shem will be decided this afternoon."[2] To Asquith's credit he did not allow his growing jealousy of Montagu over Venetia to interfere with a promotion that he believed Montagu deserved. And so, on February 14, 1914, just eight days after Montagu's thirty-fifth birthday, he was officially appointed Financial Secretary to the Treasury. This came only eight years after he was first elected to Parliament.

Montagu was delighted and welcomed the promotion. As usual, he was worried that the did not have the financial expertise to do justice to his new responsibility. He never understood how or why he had developed a reputation for being knowledgeable about finance and money. "There never was anything more fraudulent in all public reputations," he wrote to Lord Chelmsford several years later, "than the reputation, which is the only one ever given to me, for financial ability. I was designated for the Treasury . . . because there is a public opinion which I cannot correct and which haunts me still, that I was once in the City." With characteristic self-deprecation, Montagu wrote: "On that pretence I obtained as it were a forged passport into the conclave of City men, and when in the Treasury I behaved as all Financial Secretaries do, clutching at the economic advice given me by Civil servants and spending my time in saying 'You must not' to angry Government Departments who wanted six-pence to spend."[3]

Montagu always believed that being the son of Lord Swaythling and being a Jew contributed to this "fraudulent image." All Jews were supposed to have some uncanny instinct for finance, and a financial genius like Lord Swaythling surely must have a son especially gifted—or so people thought. But despite Montagu's protestations, he did have skills in this area—perhaps not as great as his father's, but enough to establish a reputation in financial circles. His record as a first-rate Parliamentary Private Secretary to the Chancellor of the Exchequer, his speeches on taxes and the grasp of broad monetary policies that he brought to budget problems in India, all earned him respect among financiers, even when many did not agree with his Radical views.

John Maynard Keynes confirmed Montagu's lack of knowledge

about the intricacies of finance as well as his disinterest in money, but praised his sound financial judgment:

Others [memoir writers], judging from his [Montagu's] parentage and from his entering the City in the last two years of his life, make out that he was, naturally, a financier. This also is far from the truth. I saw him in the Treasury and in the financial negotiations of the Peace Conference, and, while his general judgment was good, I do not think he cared, or had great aptitude, for the problems of pure finance. Nor—though he loved money for what it could buy—was he interested in the details of money-making.[4]

While Montagu, by Keynes's standards, may have lacked an aptitude for figures and the technical questions of exchange and the working of the monetary system, he did have strong opinions on national and local taxes, grants in aid and land valuation, and he was deeply concerned with long-range government financial policies and how these affected social programs. He gave considerable thought to these subjects and his memoranda to Asquith and the contributions he made to the innovative provisions of the budgets of 1907, 1908 and 1909 bear witness to this. More importantly, he was prepared to study hard, do his homework and devote to his new assignment his characteristic zeal. A willingness to work long and hard was an absolute prerequisite for this new appointment.

The Treasury

The Treasury is one of the most respected departments of the British government. Although financial policy is set by the Chancellor of the Exchequer, the day-to-day operations of the Treasury were, in Montagu's time, conducted by three Secretaries: the Financial Secretary, who was the Deputy of the Chancellor in the House of Commons and responsible for a large part of ordinary Treasury business, being the workaday political chief of the Department; the Parliamentary Secretary, who took no part in Treasury business but was the Chief Government Whip and distributed the patronage of the Treasury; and the Permanent Secretary, who was the permanent operating officer of the Department. The first two changed with the Government, the third did not.[5]

The Financial Secretaryship was one of the most important and challenging of all non-Cabinet offices. In the days when Ministers went through a training period, "the Financial Secretaryship was regarded as the office *par excellence* qualifying the holder for promotion for Cabinet rank; and it has probably trained more Cabinet Ministers than any other. . . . The opportunities which the Financial Secretary has of influencing Treasury policy and administration throughout are unlimited."[6]

An Exciting Challenge

In preparation for this new responsibility, Montagu took a brief trip to Seville and Guadalquivir in Spain to relax in the only way he knew how: by studying birds. He had a glorious time, he wrote to Venetia, enjoying "bright sun and great fun" but he was "longing to see her" before "his vigor and buoyance" is displaced "by the horrors of London."[7] He told her too that her letter to him in Spain was "the best he had received. . . . [Y]ou have that divine gift of knowing the kind of letter one is longing for." He returned to London in excellent spirits, buoyed by the trip and the excitement of a new political challenge. He immersed himself in his new work. Even weekends and social occasions were used for Treasury business, which he found all consuming.

On February 26, shortly after Montagu assumed office, Asquith wrote to Venetia that when he returned to the House of Commons (after spending time with her) he "found the Assyrian lying in wait, with a number of dullish business problems. Not that he [Montagu] finds them dull: for the present at any rate every sum in Treasury arithmetic is irradiated in his eyes with a special glamour—'the light that never was on sea or shore.' "[8] And later he wrote: "The Assyrian came down [to the Wharf] in the afternoon and spent the night here. . . . Amidst the open derision of the family (i.e., Violet and Cys) he & I solemnly retired after breakfast to the Barn and there discussed for the best part of an hour Budget figures and fantasies (for Ll.G., who has forgotten all about land and housing, is in one of his most imaginative and audacious fiscal moods: going to 'sweep the country' etc.)."[9]

The Financial Secretary, like the Under Secretary of State for India, was faced in the House of Commons with a daily barrage of written and oral questions. The interest among the Members in Treasury matters was always high; the quality of Montagu's answers, even during the first months after he assumed his new role was equally high—reflecting the intensity of his preparation.[10]

Montagu had less than one month in which to prepare for his first appearance in Parliament as Financial Secretary and become knowledgeable about thousands of facts involving Treasury activities and only two months to be ready to respond to questions on the complicated 1914 budget. His unusual intelligence, retentive mind and enormous ability to study and comprehend quickly issues of extraordinary complexity helped him become highly informed on budget and finance.

Lloyd George's Ignorance

Montagu's task was made more difficult because the Chancellor of the Exchequer, David Lloyd George, was woefully ignorant of financial matters. This had become clear during the Marconi affair to the embarrassment of the Liberal leadership when Lloyd George had to be given a cram course on the operations of the stock market before he could testify before the Committee created by Parliament to investigate the matter.[11] Keynes wrote during the war that "Lloyd George never had the faintest idea of the meaning of money," and during a trip to Paris with Lloyd George for the first Inter-Allied Conference during the opening days of the war, Keynes "did not hesitate to tell Lloyd George to his face that his views on French finance were 'rubbish.' "[12] Basil Blackett, who had been Secretary to the Indian Currency Commission and who served at the Treasury during 1914, was equally critical. He had very serious misgivings about Lloyd George's capacity during the early days of the war and wrote: "If Sir Edward Grey is indispensable, at the Foreign Office the first few days suggest Lloyd George could be dispensed with at the Treasury." As a token of disdain for Lloyd George, Blackett reports that among Treasury officials Lloyd George was known as "The Goat,"[13] because he was always jumping from one point to another. "Less kind souls," writes Bruce K. Murray in his analysis of the People's Budget of 1909, "have suggested that it was his agility in leaping from bed to bed that earned him the epithet."[14]

Keynes and Montagu

Keynes's attitude toward Montagu was quite different. He liked him, respected his judgment and always appreciated the fact that Montagu had not only brought him into government service but was responsible for all his promotions or, as he put it, for all his "steps up in life." In 1924 Keynes wrote:

In 1913 when he [Montagu] was at the India Office, it was he who got me put on the Royal Commission on Indian Currency, which was my first step into publicity. . . . It was he who got me called to the Treasury in 1915 during the War. It was he who got me taken to Paris in February of that year for the first Inter-Ally Conference and so established me in my war work. It was he who introduced me to the great ones. (I first met with Lloyd George in a famous dinner party of four at his house; I first met McKenna through him; I first met Margot [Asquith] sitting next to her at dinner in his house.) It was he who got me invited to the dinner of inner-secretaries during the early part of the war (private gatherings of the secretaries of the Cabinet and of the chief ministers who exchanged the secret news and discussed after dinner the big problems of the War).[15]

Montagu and Lloyd George

Montagu's feelings toward Lloyd George were more ambivalent than Keynes's. He agreed that Lloyd George had little or no financial acumen, but at the same time he had the highest regard for the Chancellor's drive and determination and his ability to excite and move an audience. He was drawn to Lloyd George's charismatic style but was never sure of his trustworthiness and instinctively knew, as Keynes had observed, that "Lloyd George was, of course, the undoing of his political career." Yet Montagu "could not keep away from that bright candle. But he knew, poor moth, that he would burn his wings."[16]

For his part, Lloyd George never liked Montagu. According to Frances Stevenson, Lloyd George's mistress and later wife, he mistrusted Montagu and thought him "insincere," a "hanger on" and "a spy" for Asquith.[17] "Of all the Cabinet worms," she wrote, "I think Montagu the wormiest. He writes the soapiest and most groveling letters to D[avid Lloyd George] but all the time is doing his best to secure D's downfall."[18] At another time, Miss Stevenson wrote: "Montagu has been making an analysis of the Cabinet. I loathe Montagu, but he is rather amusing at times. I don't know what class Montagu puts himself in, but I should call him one of the most insignificant but most ambitious Cabinet Ministers, differing from the majority of the others in that he has an enormous degree of the 'push' which is characteristic of the Jew."[19]

Lloyd George never forgot that during the debate on the National Insurance Bill in 1911, when intense opposition to this Bill was developing, Montagu came to him to urge him to drop it. "Drop it!? Never! Fight for it: Yes!" the Welshman had roared at Montagu who was then Under Secretary of State for India. "Dirty coward. *Men of that race always are,*" muttered Lloyd George as "Montagu fled, literally fled, from the room" (emphasis added).[20] Three years had passed since that exchange and Lloyd George, always the pragmatist, was not one to hold a grudge against anyone who could help him. And so, when Margot Asquith asked him in March 1914 after Montagu had been at Treasury for a month, "How do you like my friend [Edwin]?" he responded, "Oh very much, he has got excellent brains and he should get on well."[21]

The early months of 1914 thus began on a bright note for Montagu. His relationship with Lloyd George was harmonious. His quest for Venetia seemed to be gaining strength. And while he still missed India, the challenges of his new appointment were exciting and gave him little time for regret. For once the sun seemed to be shining on Edwin Montagu.

War

Although signs of war were appearing on the Continent, they were the farthest thing from Montagu's thoughts. He was not alone. Europe seemed more quiet and less dangerous than at other times in the decade. Relations between Britain and Germany appeared more relaxed; the naval question seemed dormant; the Balkan question seemed to have been settled by the Ambassadors' Conference in 1913; the Moroccan question had ceased to be of concern; and compromise settlements between Britain and Germany over colonial and Asian issues had been finalized and only awaited Germany's signature. The German Ambassador to England, Count Lichnowsky, was a friendly, moderate man, eager to cooperate with the

British government. The Liberal Party, by and large, and especially its Radical wing was, by philosophy and tradition, opposed to war and still committed to Campbell-Bannerman's 1906 pledge "to put Liberal England at the head of a league for peace." It was suspicious of any entanglements with France; indeed, many of its members were in far greater sympathy with Germany than with the government in Paris. For Montagu, as for most Englishmen, it was the domestic scene that was more threatening than the potential squabbles overseas. It was the budget of 1914, the increases in naval expenditures, the urgent need for more social services as well as the perennial problem of Home Rule in Ireland—not the age-old rivalries of dying empires—that seemed to threaten peace and tranquillity.

The Budget of 1914

The most immediate of these issues, the budget of 1914, was of direct and immediate concern to Montagu and the Treasury. Each department of the government was required to submit an estimate of anticipated income and expenditures for the coming year to the Treasury, which in turn had the responsibility of preparing a cohesive document. Montagu, as Financial Secretary, was not only involved in implementing this process but also had the principal responsibility for shepherding the budget through Parliament.

While the budget was to be presented in May, Montagu began working on it as soon as he assumed office. This budget was of particular importance to the Liberals because it would be introduced when a General Election was in the offing. It had to be framed so as to correct a deficit of at least £5 million resulting from the large increase in Navy expenditures agreed upon in January by Churchill and Lloyd George less than a month before Montagu went to the Treasury. Such a projected deficit would require heavy tax increases, especially if the Liberals wanted to make good on some of their promises for improved social services. The challenge thus facing the Liberals, especially Lloyd George, Montagu and the Treasury, was to devise a formula that would raise this additional revenue from the rich and not the poor.

The centerpiece of the budget, the section that achieved the most praise from the Radicals, was a plan to provide £11 million in grants to local authorities for education, health services, expanded aid to children, road and sanitation improvements and other social needs. To raise the funds for these grants and to offset the deficit caused by the increase in naval allocations, the proposed budget increased the income tax by 11 percent, added a graduated surtax beginning with incomes of three thousand pounds instead of five thousand, raised death duties by 1 percent on all estates worth over £60,000, while for estates over £250,000 the scale went as high as 20 percent. Previously it was 15 percent. It also raised inheritance taxes by 3 percent. The Finance Bill in which the budget was presented also included a provision for "site value" ratings to lay the groundwork for a national system of local property tax rates intended to make local taxation less onerous for the less affluent.

These provisions reflected Montagu's love of innovative tax schemes and his belief that the rich should be taxed to carry the costs of expanded programs for the poor. These ideas were totally compatible with those of Lloyd George who believed that soaking the rich and helping the poor was not only sound government policy, but would show to the electorate that Radical reform, as he espoused it, was still alive in the Liberal Party. This was one occasion when the Chancellor of the Exchequer and the Financial Secretary to the Treasury were in complete accord.

The Tories and many middle-of-the-road Liberals were not pleased with what they viewed as a radical anti-Gladstonian approach to government spending and taxes. Reluctant, however, to attack Lloyd George, they made the main culprits the Treasury and Montagu, who had to defend the budget for the Chancellor in the House of Commons. The "extravagant approach to spending" that they charged characterized the budget was scornfully called the "Treasury's view." It was attacked as an example of fiscal irresponsibility with the cost of social reform too expensive and the increase in taxes too high.[22]

Radicals in and out of Parliament, on the other hand, enthusiastically welcomed the budget. They rejected the notion that heavy direct taxation injured trade and asserted the state's responsibility for basing the tax system on principles of social justice. Haldane believed the adoption of this principle in the 1914 budget, more than in preceding budgets, marked a fundamental change in English party politics. "You could not have had this budget ten years ago," he told the National Liberal Club.[23] Such sharp differences on tax policy were expressed in the bitter debate and the hundreds of questions that barraged Montagu in Parliament. Answering these questions occupied a great deal of Montagu's time from the moment the budget was introduced in May through June when it suffered an ignominious defeat.

Montagu argued eloquently for the budget, concluding that:

Our Budget . . . is a way of relieving unjust taxation and improving local services. Local services are at the root of national health and prosperity. The figures of our revenue, the figures of our national wealth, are ample and abundant evidence that we can afford to devote the money necessary to alleviate and prevent the remediable distress which is a blot upon our national reputation, and I am perfectly certain that the people of this country are willing to join *in the war against ill-health and avoidable poverty as a valuable investment for the taxpayers of this country, provided that this House assists them in placing the burdens, local and national and Imperial alike, upon the broadest and most vigorous shoulders.*[24] (emphasis added)

Montagu also defended the difference between taxing earned and unearned income arguing that "earned income, which has not been saved and invested is a precarious income, dependent upon the earning capacity and the health of the man who earned it, whereas the savings not dependent upon the man's health or upon whether he is capable of earning them or not is different and less precarious." It should be taxed, therefore, "at a higher rate than the earned income of the worker."

On July 23, 1914—the last day of budget debate—Montagu closed the discussion with another appeal on behalf of the poor, the ill and the aged, and a sharp attack on his Conservative adversaries. He observed that:

The Conservative of today is the Liberal of two generations ago. He remains petrified. Liberalism being, in my opinion, a live creed, goes on! I think this extolling by Conservatives of Liberals of past generations is the extolling of bygone ideals. The old policy used to be to arm against the foreign foes, to maintain a Navy and an Army, and to leave the great social evils which exist in this country without any attempt to meet, to deal with them, or to make any progress in dealing with them.[25]

Once again Montagu called for a war against poverty and illness "as real a war as was ever carried on against a foreign foe."[26]

Commenting on Montagu's role during these early years at the

Treasury, Lord Beaverbrook observed that Montagu never received the recognition he deserved for so many of the innovative ideas in the budget and in other projects because "unrivaled in his mental equipment, he seemed to lack the courage to take the responsibility for his own projects, sound as they invariably were, and as a consequence tougher but less able men reaped where he had sown."[27]

Keynes attributed this to Montagu's "violent fluctuations of mood" which made him act with "reckless courage" at times and "in panic and dejection" at others, adding that because Montagu viewed himself as a coward "it was easy for the spiteful to convict him out of his own mouth."[28] Montagu's own self-hate, his own sense that he had been rejected by a powerful and omnipotent father, his fear of sickness, death and failure—all supported his image of himself as weak and cowardly. This self-image was reinforced by the society in which he moved, which also believed Jews were cowardly. Since Montagu had come to believe this and expressed it openly, it was easy for friend and foe alike "to convict him out of his own mouth."

Montagu Fears Budget Defeat

Neither Montagu's "excellent brains," nor his defense of the budget in Parliament, nor Lloyd George's extensive tour to advocate the budget to the people seemed able to gather enough support to save the budget from its opponents. Many of its provisions were too complicated to win public support, and as the session wore on, even Lloyd George seemed to lose interest. Montagu was becoming increasingly concerned, complaining to Venetia on April 12 that Lloyd George was finding it impossible to focus his attention for more than half an hour; his attention wandered; he rejoiced at interruptions and avoided making decisions. In spite of this Montagu said he liked Lloyd George "tremendously."[29]

Asquith also recognized Lloyd George's inability to concentrate on one issue for any length of time. He referred to his meetings with him as "a baffling kind of amusement"[30] and on April 18 he wrote to Venetia:

I had a whole hour (!) with Ll. G. attended by the faithful Assyrian, and we played about with millions and tens of millions with good humour & even gaiety. No one can hop with greater agility from one twig (or even one tree or forest) to another. Meanwhile the land campaign, housing, repeopling the deserted glens, getting fair play from the ground landlord for the Gorringes etc.—all these have receded into a dim background & are for the moment as though they had never been.[31]

While Lloyd George had lost interest in the budget, Montagu could think of little else. On May 3 Asquith wrote: "We found the Assyrian and Mikky [R.S. Meiklejohn, a Principal clerk in the Treasury, who worked for the Prime Minister] here: the former left early this morning to spend a happy day budgeting with the Chancellor of the Exchequer at Walton Heath."[32]

During this time, Montagu continued to write regularly to the Prime Minister and to Lloyd George sharing his thoughts and observations. He wrote to Asquith that he was especially concerned with reports that Lloyd George did not want to proceed with a Housing Bill at a time when housing was seriously needed. Such a decision, Montagu believed, would "be disastrous politically."[33] And to Lloyd George, he expressed his concern that prospects looked dim not only for the budget but also for the vast array of new Liberal legislation. He warned the Prime Minister and Lloyd George that with the excitement of Home Rule on the horizon it would be very difficult to get the House to focus on "dull technical Rating Reforms." He asked Lloyd George to consider what would happen. "You will have raised enormous sums of money which you will not be able to spend and if you are succeeded . . . by . . . the Conservative Party you would see the funds . . . devoted . . . to finance and popularize the Edinburgh brand of Tariff Reform."[34] (He had warned Asquith of the same prospect in March 1908, when he told him that it is a "mistake of Liberalism to leave too much for dissipation by Conservatives at a future time.") Montagu also suggested that they proceed only with a basic Finance Bill and leave local tax reform rates and grants to localities for a future time. This was almost exactly what eventually was done—but not until almost two months were spent in bitter argumentation on the floor of Commons.

By May 5, 1914, Asquith confirmed Montagu's distress, writing to Venetia that the budget debate was collapsing "in a well (or luckily) contrived morass of obscurity in which for the moment every one was bogged."[35] And, on June 22, in spite of the efforts to the contrary of Montagu, Asquith and Lloyd George, the Speaker of the Commons ruled that the part of the Finance Bill relating to grant proposals was out of order and the Finance Bill must be confined to taxation, forcing the Chancellor to drop his site value rating clauses and several other sections—a suggestion Montagu had made two months before. On June 23, the Cabinet had no choice but to accept this decision. The Cabinet decided, too, to drastically cut the Finance Bill, not only abandoning the grant provision (except for insurance and education) but also reducing the income tax increase by one penny on the pound.

This was a far cry from the "Radical Budget" proposed on May 12. Asquith was reported as "writhing" under the indignity of the Government having to "take back one half of the Budget." "The whole thing has been a shocking muddle," McKenna complained to Riddle, who noted in his diary on July 12, "L.G. has had a bad week. His stock stands low with the party. The Budget has been a fiasco."[36]

The 1914 budget was Lloyd George's worst parliamentary defeat. He totally misread the will of the House. He misread the will of the public. He ignored the warnings of men like Montagu and he did not concentrate on the specifics of the budget, which only he could sell. As hard as Montagu worked, he was no substitute for Lloyd George. The Chancellor's lack of leadership and interest contributed greatly to the loss. Lloyd George did not see it that way. He was quick to blame "the parliamentary draftsmen" who, he complained, "let me down badly. They should have found out beforehand what the Speaker's decision would be."[37]

Typically, Montagu blamed himself. "I am so miserable," he wrote to Venetia after the budget defeat. "I was sent to the Treasury to prevent this sort of thing and I have failed."[38] The budget presented in May was now dead. Only a shadow of its radical self survived. The Cabinet was tired and drained and its attention was now turning to Home Rule for Ireland, which was reaching crisis proportions.

The Irish Question

As frustrating as the budget debate had been, it paled compared with the problems Asquith faced with the Irish question. Since 1886 the Liberals had been committed to Home Rule for Ireland—giving the Irish their own Parliament. They had no chance of achieving this since a majority of the House of Lords was strongly opposed to it. With the passage of the Parliamentary Act of 1911, the situation changed. The Liberals now had the power to enact a Home Rule Bill but continued to face Unionist opposition which became ever more strident in 1912 and 1913.

In spite of such opposition, Asquith had no alternative but to introduce the third Home Rule Bill in April 1912. He had promised this to John Redmond, the leader of the Irish Nationalists, and his followers for their support of the Parliament Act of 1911 and he had no intention of reneging on his promise. It would become law in 1914 under the provisions of the Parliament Act.

The Cabinet was severely split on this issue with at least three strong Ministers—Churchill, Lloyd George and Grey—disagreeing with Asquith. They believed that it would be impossible to coerce Ulster even if the Bill were almost on the statute books and that some provision for individual (Protestant) counties to opt out must be part of the Home Rule Bill.

Montagu's views on Home Rule had evolved over the years. On March 31, 1908, he had written to Asquith: "As regards Home Rule . . . I do not know what to say. . . . I joined the Liberal League and 'swore off' Home Rule, at a time when, theoretically, I was a Home Ruler. If I am no longer a Home Ruler, it is because I have looked at the Nationalist Party in the House of Commons, spent two winters in Nationalist Ireland, and grudge the enormous time and electoral energy dissipated on Irish matters. So far as I know English constituencies, although interest in Home Rule is practically negligible, so also is opposition to Home Rule." By September 1913 he had become convinced that some form of Home Rule was necessary, but he wrote to Asquith that he found the problem "insoluble." By 1914 he had come to believe that a compromise must be found that would exclude Ulster for some prescribed period of time but would guarantee to Southern Ireland that Ulster's exclusion would not be permanent.

Although Montagu was not part of the Cabinet, the Prime Minister invited him to participate in many of the meetings (which were often held at his home in Queen Anne's Gate) to search for some acceptable compromise. Asquith continued to hope that one could be found, never truly believing his adversaries would take up arms against the government. The sanctity with which he viewed the law

and constitutional government made it impossible for him to contemplate a situation in which violence could be substituted for rational discourse among reasonable men.

In 1912 Asquith preferred to delay the concessions for two years
until 1914, in the belief that once Home Rule was imminent the
Protestants of the north would become more reasonable. Here his
"wait and see" policy proved wrong. The Ulstermen, with the
support of the Conservatives, became only more intransigent with
the passage of time and only more determined to establish their own
government with the use of armed force if necessary.

All through 1913 and into the spring of 1914, efforts to find a
solution to the crisis continued with one meeting following another.
As a participant in these negotiations, Montagu offered several ideas
for consideration, including an Irish Federation in which Catholic
Ireland and Ulster would be autonomous within a federation.[39] For
a time, Lloyd George supported this "federal solution"; he also
thought there was merit in another of Montagu's ideas, that Pres-
byterian Ulster, settled largely by Scotsmen, should be united with
Scotland.[40] Ultimately, none of these plans was adopted. Each side
held rigidly to its own plans, with passions so aroused that concessions on either side became impossible to make.[41]

In the meantime, the threat of civil war increased daily. New
secret negotiations were undertaken in late June by Montagu, Lord
Rothermere and Lord Murray of Elibank, with Asquith's blessing,
in one final attempt to bring the sides together: They failed mainly
because there was no agreement on the question of excluding the
northern counties. The first meeting of Montagu, Rothermere and
Murray took place at Claridge's Hotel on June 24. Montagu wrote:
"Rothermere has seen Bonar Law (Colonial Secretary and Tory
leader) recently and learned of him that it was only in the last three
weeks that he had persuaded Lansdowne (Conservative leader in the
Lords) that Home Rule was inevitable."[42] Montagu was convinced
that in spite of the difficulties they faced, Rothermere must continue
to talk to Bonar Law and Sir Edward Carson (the leader of the
Ulster Unionists), who Montagu believed were anxious to settle,
although Carson was unsure of his power to control the Ulster
volunteers.

On June 25, Montagu conveyed these thoughts to the Prime

Minister, who agreed with him and urged that the secret negotiations continue and that Rothermere meet with Carson and Bonar Law, as Montagu had suggested.[43] Rothermere met with Carson and Bonar Law and, on June 27, lunched with Montagu, who later wrote: "Bonar Law will support any reasonable settlement with Carson, even to the smashing of the Tory Party—and his own political life,—hinted that he would see the Government through, if the Irish kicked, even to taking office under Asquith."[44]

But there was such a strong Tory opposition to a settlement, not only on ideological grounds but because a settlement would be a triumph for the Liberal government, that these efforts, which in retrospect seem so reasonable, also failed. The Unionist leaders believed that faced with strong opposition, Asquith would back down. Perhaps, if they had not viewed Asquith as an old-fashioned gentleman who abhorred confrontation and would "never pull his stroke through"—the Irish question might have taken a different tack at a time when the options were still open. But it did not. Carson continued to hang tough. He and his followers were adamant that the six Protestant counties be permanently excluded from any Home Rule settlement.

Montagu believed that the real problem was the disposition of the two counties of Tyrone and Fermanagh, where the presence of Catholics made a solution even more difficult than in the four other northern counties.[45] Asquith agreed but had nothing new to suggest to break the deadlock.[46] On June 28, 1914, in the middle of these discussions, the Archduke Francis Ferdinand, heir to the Austro-Hungarian throne, and his wife were murdered by Serbian terrorists in Sarajevo in Bosnia. This event caused indignation and sympathy, but few in England thought it likely that Britain would be drawn into the great struggle that the assassination might provoke. The concern of the English at this time was civil war in Ireland, not regicide in Bosnia.

By July, the Irish situation had become critical. The time had run out in Parliament for the 1912 Home Rule Bill, which did not exclude the Protestant counties of Ulster. The Bill awaited only the royal assent to become law. How could the government permit the enactment of a bill that was certain to provoke a civil war? Negotiations were now imperative. In desperation Asquith agreed to the

King's suggestion that a conference be held at Buckingham Palace with the Speaker (James Lowther) as chairman and both sides represented.

The conference met from July 21 to July 24; it broke down on July 24, again over the boundaries of two of the counties that were to be excluded, Fermanagh and Tyrone. Asquith's sense of utter frustration is revealed in his letters to Venetia. On July 22, after the second meeting, he wrote:

We sat again this morning for an hour & a half, discussion maps & figures and always getting back to that most damnable creation of the perverted ingenuity of man—the County of Tyrone. The extraordinary feature of the discussion was the complete agreement (in principle) of Redmond and Carson. Each said, "I must have the whole of Tyrone or die; but I quite understand why you say the same." The Speaker who incarnates bluff unimaginative English sense, of course cut in: "When each of two people say they must have the whole, why not cut it in half? They wd. neither of them look at such a suggestion. . . . I have rarely felt more hopeless. . . . Isn't it a real tragedy?[47]

The day of the final meeting (July 24) he wrote: "The last meeting this morning was in some ways dramatic, though the actual business consisted merely in settling the words to be publicly used. At the end the King came in, rather *emotionné* and said in two sentences . . . farewell, I am sorry and I thank you. . . . I must go on with an Amending Bill *without* the time limit." Commenting on the mysteries of the Irish people, he concluded: "Aren't they a remarkable people? And the folly of thinking we can ever understand, let alone govern them!"[48]

War on the Continent

On the day the Conference broke up, the government was informed of the terms of the Austrian ultimatum to Serbia. As July ended, Serbia seemed ready to accept these terms, but it was becoming increasingly clear each day that nothing would satisfy Austria-Hungary. The British people and the Cabinet were still hopeful, however, that they would not be drawn into the conflict.[49] As Asquith wrote to Venetia on July 24:

Austria has sent a bullying and humiliating ultimatum to Serbia, who cannot comply with it, and demanded an answer within 48 hours—failing which she will march. This means, almost inevitably, that Russia will come on the scene in defence of Serbia and in defiance of Austria; and if so, it is difficult both for Germany and France to refrain from lending a hand to one side or another. . . . Happily there seems to be no reason why we should be anything more than spectators. But it is a bloodcurdling prospect —is it not?[50]

This was twelve days before Britain entered the war.

The Business Community Panics

On July 28, Austria-Hungary declared war on Serbia. The bankers and financiers were thrown into a panic, fearing financial chaos at home and the collapse of international trade if the war spread:

London was not only the world's principal foreign exchange market; it was also paramount in the spheres of deposit banking, acceptance and discount. At the mere prospect of war, the system had more or less broken down. By 1 August, "the foreign exchange market had practically ceased to operate, the Stock Exchange was closed, it was impossible to get bills accepted or discounted, the accepting houses and bill-brokers were both in grave danger of having to stop payment, and the Bank of England itself found the demands upon it increasing alarmingly, and its reserves very near exhaustion."[51]

That day, Montagu summoned a group of financial and business leaders to meet with Lloyd George, and Treasury staff to discuss what could be done to calm the City and bolster confidence in financial circles. Without immediate action, the whole economy could be thrown into bankruptcy. While the War Office and Admiralty had some plans and a subcommittee of the Committee of Imperial Defence had considered the economic problems of war in 1911 and 1912, the "Treasury was unprepared to administer a great war"[52] and was not equipped with an emergency plan. Contingency plans had to be developed at once.

When Britain's entry into the war seemed imminent, a more structured committee of advisors was created, which included McKenna; Runciman; Austen Chamberlain; Sir John Simon; Sir Walter Cunliffe, Governor of the Bank of England; Lord Chief Justice Reading (upon whom Lloyd George relied heavily); Sir George Parish (a leading economist and the joint editor of the *Statist*); and

Montagu. Their quick and decisive actions stemmed the panic and stabilized the market.

The Pursuit of Peace: Home Rule Shelved

While the Treasury and other departments of government worked on contingency plans, every effort was still being made to pursue peace. Even at this late date, the Asquith government and most of Britain did not want war. Britain was, however, prepared for war. Churchill had the Navy in a "precautionary stage," and the Cabinet began to review Britain's obligations under the Treaty of 1839 to maintain Belgian neutrality. Asquith made clear to France that England would give no declaration of support if France attacked. England preferred to wait and see what developed concerning Belgian neutrality before making a commitment.

It was during these strained days that Bonar Law suggested that the second reading of the amended Irish Home Rule Bill be postponed indefinitely. Asquith and his Cabinet agreed. Their intention was that the Home Rule Bill be permitted to become law, "but that its operation should be suspended until a new amending bill could be passed,"[53] when the international crisis had been resolved. Thus, for the moment at least, the Irish question was solved. As Asquith liked to say, "the unexpected" in politics had happened again.

Steps Leading to the War

To Asquith the issues concerning the war were clear-cut. As he wrote to Venetia:

Happily I am quite clear in my own mind as to what is right and wrong. I put it down for you in a few sentences.

1. We have no obligation of any kind either to France or Russia to give them military or naval help.
2. The despatch of the expeditionary force to help France at this moment is out of the question and would serve no object.
3. We mustn't forget the ties created by our long-standing and intimate friendship with France.
4. It is against British interests that France should be wiped out as a great power.

5. We cannot allow Germany to use the channel as a hostile base.
6. We have obligations to Belgium to prevent her being utilized and absorbed by Germany.[54]

Although Belgium's neutrality was important to Asquith and the government, it was not the only issue that propelled Britain into war. It was, however, the major rallying point around which Asquith and his supporters built the propaganda that moved Britain in a single month from disinterest in war to eager participation. Equally important was Britain's determination to keep Germany from replacing France as the principal European power. Nor would Britain permit Germany, with a dramatically enlarged Navy, to use the English Channel as its own lake. The Channel had always been England's security. She would not easily concede control.

While the Cabinet was discussing the implications of these principles, Austria declared war on Serbia on July 28. A day later, Sir Edward Grey tried without success to convene a four-power conference to mediate between Austria and Serbia. Britain still hoped that she would not be drawn into war, although on July 29 Lloyd George —an opponent of entering the war—joined his Cabinet colleagues in approving the opening of the "War Book," a detailed series of precautionary plans drafted by the Committee of Imperial Defence. The drift toward war accelerated when, at the end of July, Russia began to mobilize against Austria. France began to pressure Britain to make clear that it would not stand by in the face of a German attack on any of the Entente powers; at the same time Germany demanded a statement of British neutrality.

The Cabinet would not give either; it would not give France the guarantee it wanted and it instructed Grey to advise the German ambassador that Germany should not count on British neutrality. Grey had already done this informally, but his warning now represented a mandate from the British Cabinet. This was all the Cabinet could agree upon. It was divided with many gradations of sentiment, from Churchill's desire to enter the war at once to John Morley's isolationism.

On July 31, Germany issued a call for mobilization, on the same day Grey urged France and Germany to respect the neutrality of Belgium, although the Cabinet was still divided on whether Britain's obligation toward Belgium, arising out of past treaties, was one of policy or one of law. Indeed, when Asquith wrote to the King about this he made certain to state that "if this matter arose it would be handled as a matter of policy rather than a legal obligation." At this point, Lloyd George was still against intervention and was supported by Lewis Harcourt and John Morley. Montagu strongly believed in Britain's entering the war at once.

On Sunday, August 2, Asquith spent the day with his family and Montagu. Margot Asquith wrote in her diary:

Mr. Montagu dined with us that night. Though gloomy and depressed he was less excited than he had been on the previous Friday. "Till last night," Montagu said, "I had hoped against hope that we might have been able to keep out of this war, but my hopes have vanished. All the men I've seen feel like me except X [Lloyd George], who is intriguing with that scoundrel Z [Simon]. I asked the Attorney General yesterday what was going to be said . . . in the House tomorrow and he answered: 'Don't worry! None of us can say at this moment what resignations the Prime Minister may or may not have in his hands at tomorrow's Cabinet.' "[55]

By this time, despite Lloyd George's attitude, Asquith's mind was made up: An invasion of Belgium would trigger England's entry into the war. For this position he had complete Tory support but his own Cabinet was still divided. On Monday, August 3, Belgium rejected Germany's ultimatum and England received a letter from the King of Belgium saying that the German invasion of his country was imminent and that he was determined to fight. It was a letter that deeply moved the Cabinet.

Lloyd George began to shift toward intervention and urged those members of the Cabinet who had announced that they would resign if England entered the war to remain. All but Morley and Burns agreed. Britain sent an ultimatum on Belgian neutrality to Germany, announcing that if it received no assurance from Germany on Belgian neutrality by 11:00 P.M. (12 midnight, German time) on August 4, Britain would enter the war.

By 11:00 P.M. there was no response from Germany. Earlier in the day the Cabinet had received word that Germany had in fact invaded Belgium. The ultimatum expired. By midnight Britain was at war in western Europe for the first time since the Napoleonic Wars one hundred years before. The lamps of Europe were about to go out. When they were lit again, Britain and the countries of

Europe would be far different. The worlds of Asquith and Montagu would never be the same again.

Through the Looking Glass

Throughout the eight months leading up to Britain's entry into the war, months of crisis upon crisis, Asquith became increasingly dependent on Venetia, showering her with love letters and demanding more of her time. As his political troubles became more complex, his need to escape into the fantasy world that a love affair affords became essential to his ability to function. Or, as Brock put it, "When a man falls in love and moves through the looking-glass, where 'the familiar features assume an absolutely new perspective' that need of escape is met."[56]

Love and passion, like any narcotic, have the capacity to induce a sense of escape that appears to make the pain of reality more bearable. Asquith had a history of seeking solace from the pressures of his work in outside stimuli, not only in the conversations he enjoyed with young women, but in alcohol, as well. As early as 1904, he was reprimanded by Haldane for his heavy consumption of champagne, and over the years his colleagues would remark on his "free use of wine which he cannot carry."[57] Even friends like Churchill noticed. And there were incidents in Parliament during which Asquith appeared to be under the influence of liquor, to the embarrassment of his colleagues.

After 1912, Venetia seemed to take the place of the wine and champagne. By 1914, Asquith's need for her was intense. His letters show that his feelings had become almost obsessional, and he made no effort to hide them. He "longs" to see her (February 4); he consoles himself "with the thoughts of Friday" (February 11); he pleads with her to be "dear and kind" (March 10); he is distressed if she does not write (April 11); he describes the time he spends with her as "delicious" (May 11) and "divine" (June 17); and he worries that he is boring her (June 18), but continues to write daily, sometimes even twice a day. He longs for her, misses "the touch" of her hand (April 17) and by July confesses, "My darling—you are dearer to me than I can tell you" (July 8); talking to her makes him "happier & more hopeful. . . . Blessed are the life-givers, of whom there is none to equal you" (July 18).[58]

Venetia's feelings in this make-believe world were almost irrele-vant to Asquith. His feelings, his needs, his desires were primary. It was his need for someone to play with, to listen to him without argument or discord—and to provide comfort and adoration—that became the fulcrum of the relationship and the escape it provided. Margot could no longer provide these things. She had grown acer-bic, cranky, argumentative, unpleasant and no longer interested in sex. This was as much a contributing factor to Asquith's need for an extramarital relationship as was the pressure of the premiership.

Many historians believe that while Asquith was deeply in love with Venetia and their relationship may have included sexual fore-play, the relationship did not reach physical consummation. "Not being a love affair in the physical sense," Brock states, "it did not follow any sequence of passion and satiety."[59] And a biographer of Churchill states from a confidential source: "His [Asquith's] love was never consummated, for Venetia was repelled by his drooling, high stroking advances, but for the sixty-three-year-old Asquith, physical fulfillment was less important than the emotional comfort Venetia provided in her letters."[60]

Contemporaneous writers and some of the intimate friends of Asquith and Venetia had a different impression. Angela Lambert, author of *Unquiet Souls,* wrote, based on her own private sources: "Asquith had not the temperament for unconsummated love—cer-tainly not platonic love. He was too full-blooded to have been a Balfour, palely loitering; especially as Margot became disinclined for sex after twenty years of marriage. As women soon found out, to be left alone with him was to invite immediate and bold approaches, admittedly playful to begin with, for hand-holding, touching, fon-dling and kissing. He was simply, an importunate lecher. . . . If he found no resistance to his advances—or even active encouragement—he would take the relationship to its fullest conclusion."[61]

Lady Diana Cooper, Venetia's closest friend for many years and a member of Asquith's "harem" before Venetia, seemed, according to a remark her husband Duff Cooper made in 1915 in his *Diary,* "quite certain that Venetia was his [Asquith's] mistress."[62] In the same *Diary* account, Duff wrote that Diana told him Asquith had made overtures to her (in a letter) to take Venetia's place. Duff was furious and wrote:

This letter, which was rather obscurely expressed, seemed practically an offer to Diana to fill the vacant situation. She [Diana] was in great difficulty as to how she was to answer, partly from being uncertain as to its meaning and partly from the nature of the proposal it seemed to contain. She was anxious not to lose him but did not aspire to the position of Egeria, which she felt sure would entail physical duties that she couldn't answer or wouldn't fulfill. I advised her to concoct an answer which would be as obscure as his proposal and leave him puzzled.[63]

Angela Lambert spoke with Lady Diana Cooper in February 1984 and confirmed categorically that Diana believed the Asquith–Venetia relationship "must have included some sexual contact."[64]

The publication of the Asquith letters in the Brock compilation unleashed a rash of speculation on what A. J. P. Taylor called, in his own review of the book, "the burning question: did they or didn't they?" The answers were split, with half certain that they "did," and the other half equally certain "they did not."[65] "The editors of his letters [the Brocks]," Taylor wrote, "are almost certain that Asquith never became Venetia's lover in the physical sense. I agreed with the editor's judgment until I came across a letter ending 'You know how I long to. . . .' Now what are we to make of that— merely that Asquith wanted to hold Venetia's hand under the carriage rug? I doubt it."[66]

Godfrey Hodgson, an English literary critic who reviewed the Brock book for the *New York Times,* took a different view, concluding that "there was no physical intimacy between Asquith and Venetia Stanley," although there is no evidence presented in Hodgson's review to support this conclusion.[67] Peter Clarke, an historian and fellow of St. John's College, Cambridge, who reviewed the Brock book for *The* London *Times*'s Education section, was uncertain. While classifying the letters as clearly "love letters not merely sentimental" with a strong "erotic charge," he was not prepared to conclude Venetia was Asquith's mistress. "It may have been so, who can tell—but the tenor of the letters suggests otherwise."[68]

Clarke believed that the relationship was "an implicit tradeoff between sex and power, mutually titillating in the way that each fed off the other. Thus, the phases of the affair had a private and public synchronization." Developing this interpretation further, Clarke concluded that it was no accident that the affair began at a "time of political tension in March, 1912 (i.e., the Coal Strike). What Asquith seems to have done was to sublimate political tension into sexual fantasy, finding the release which was impossible with Margot in his ejaculations for Venetia."[69]

Alastair Forbes, a long-time friend of both Venetia and Diana, has disagreed with Angela Lambert's certainty that Diana Cooper believed Venetia was Asquith's mistress. In a letter to the editor of *The Times* he wrote:

As one having enjoyed for a decade the friendship of Mrs. Edwin Montagu and for nearly half a century that of Lady Diana Cooper, I was surprised to see in Stephen Koss' incisive review of *H. H. Asquith's Letters to Venetia Stanley* . . . the claim repeated that Diana Cooper naturally assumed that Venetia had been Asquith's mistress. [I note in passing that A. J. P. Taylor had now begun to assume this too.] The Brocks refer in a footnote to a passage in Philip Ziegler's *Diana Cooper* where Lady Diana has clearly been misunderstood and misreported. She certainly never suspected such a thing of Asquith and Venetia at the time and the subsequent highly circumstantial account the latter gave her of the disagreeable brutal defloration to which she was subjected by her husband on her wedding night could scarcely have caused her to revise her opinion.[70]

The Brocks agreed with Forbes, having written that when their book appeared, Diana Cooper said that Venetia had told her, as she had told Forbes, that she was a virgin on her wedding night. "Thus," Brock continued, "Lady Diana revised the view she had held in May 1915 when, sometime after July 1915 she had an account from Venetia of that wedding night."[71] This would confirm the conclusion that while there may have been a sexual component in the Asquith–Venetia Stanley relationship, it was never consummated.

Forbes and Brock were challenged by another letter to the editor of *The Times,* from the son of a man who had had a love affair with Venetia, who wrote:

I hesitate to trespass on Alastair Forbes' own territory of personal gossip reported several removes after several decades, but I must question his confident denial that the relationship between H. H. Asquith and Venetia Stanley seventy years ago was physically consummated. . . .

My father, W. Grey Walter, who was one of Venetia Montagu's young lovers fifty years ago (he makes a brief appearance as such in Virginia Woolf's Diary for July 21, 1934, and I inherited the Cartier cigarette case he was given for services rendered), told me in the 1970's that she told him in the 1930's that Asquith had indeed been her lover in the full sense in the 1910's. He was interested because during the First World War his father Karl Walter had been a minor supporter of Lloyd George . . . whereas his father-in-law, S. K. Ratcliffe had been a minor supporter of Asquith. . . .

It seems that she may have told different people different stories at different times for different reasons, about a relationship whose true nature, as Stephen Koss says in his review of Asquith's letters to her (November 26), seems to be impossible to ascertain, though tempting to speculate about as long as the only available evidence is second-hand gossip.[72]

Thus, there is no clear-cut evidence to support a firm conclusion that Venetia was Asquith's mistress. Probably Nicholas Walter, the young man whose father had had an affair with Venetia, came closest to the truth when he wrote that Venetia may have told different stories at different times for different reasons to different people, and it is impossible to come to any certain conclusion since all the evidence is "second-hand gossip." But the nature of the Prime Minister, his reputation as an importunate lecher, his need to touch, to talk with and to be with women, Margot's illness and subsequent disinterest in sex, Venetia's totally unconventional and liberated views of life, sex and sexual experimentation, her lack of any sense of sin or morality, and some of the language used in the letters themselves strongly suggest that the affair had a strong sexual component, even if actual consummation may not have taken place.

To raise the question of whether Venetia and Asquith were physical lovers is not merely "prurient curiosity." Enoch Powell points out in another review of the Brock book that this question goes to a verdict on the very nature of the relationship and the way in which its ending affected Asquith personally and politically.[73] For that reason it is relevant to this story and is not merely a titillating excursion into an area that deserves privacy.

Margot and Venetia

By the beginning of 1914, Margot was well aware of the seriousness of Asquith's relationship with Venetia and as a result had come to detest Venetia, pouring out her heart to Montagu, whom she viewed as a dear friend and member of the family:

If Venetia ever does talk to you about me [Margot wrote to Montagu], the thing I wd. really love best wd. be if you said to her "I wd. much rather you never spoke of Margot to me for hers is a character you don't and never wd. understand." Candour and truth simplicity and courage of the kind I want to have she doesn't try to have—she despises and mocks at. Her head is slightly turned—poor Venetia I ought not to be unkind about her . . . but I'm so disappointed in the young ones that I've watched now for so many years! they are so incurably flimsy & idle & quite without any power to love or to stay the course. I hate to be misjudged and deceived, I wd. rather be hit across the face. Do ask me to go for a motor drive with you next Friday I wd. lunch with you and we'd only be driving 1½ back for tea and your work.[74]

On March 21 she wrote again to Montagu:

I suppose you won't come tomorrow now Venetia and Violet and Henry are in London.

I told you that every Friday I suffered *tortures*. I had a vile night and while I was struggling to eat dinner in bed I knew in my bones Henry was with Venetia. Violet just telephoned what fun they had dining with the Sheffields. I rang off as I feel suffocated with tears. Deceitful little brute! Why should she [Venetia] have said to me that they wanted H. to dine last night if his cold kept him in London—wh. they knew it most probably would.

As I've said before to you—if Venetia had an ounce of truth and candor like Violet Mouche Dorothy (a girl you never heard of) (and two other women whose names I shan't tell you) have got and have always shown me I shd. smile but she is even teaching Henry to avoid telling me things. My step-family think all this *very* good fun and that I wd. be a fool to mind. I'm far too fond of H. to show him how ill and miserable it makes me it wd. only worry him at a time he sd. be free. Good God! to think you proposed to her! a woman without refinement or any imagination what-ever. . . .

—Oh! If only Venetia would marry—how I loathe girls who can't love but claim and collect alike a cuckoo for their own vanity—Venetia's head is completely turned.[75]

Margot did not know at this time that Montagu was still pursuing Venetia and that he was still hoping she might change her mind and accept his offer of marriage. Six days before Margot sent the March 21 letter, Montagu had written to Venetia expressing his strong regret that Treasury business had kept him from being with her because his "desire" of her company "increases,"[76] and on March 22, Asquith wrote to Venetia: "Thank you darling for your sweet little pencil letter. . . . I have never wanted you more."[77] The triangle was now firmly in place.

14

Five Months of Military
and Naval Disasters,
August 4–December 31, 1914

I object strongly to spending a single penny that can be avoided . . . the country will win in this war whose purse is the longest.

Montagu to Herbert Samuel, Oct. 1, 1914

The thought of a love triangle was far from Asquith's mind as he awakened on the morning of August 5 and found himself, at the age of sixty-one, the leader of a nation at war. It was not a happy thought. He was aware from the start that he and his colleagues faced the prospect of "days—more trying, perhaps, than any body of statesmen for a hundred years had to pass through."[1]

He did not exaggerate. World War I was a far different war from any the world had ever faced and brought devastation that none of its participants could imagine. They were prepared for a different kind of war, one that would be over in a year. The strategy and initial planning of the British and their allies reflected this miscalculation. Montagu was no exception in believing this. On October 28, 1914, two months after the war began, he bet Margot Asquith that the war would be over by June 8, 1915.[2]

Asquith's first act after war was declared was to resign as Secretary of State for War (a post he had held since the Curragh Mutiny) and to offer this post to Lord Kitchener of Khartoum, the hero of Omdurman, who accepted only reluctantly. Kitchener was adored by the public, was a national hero and, during the early months of the war, had the total confidence of the Cabinet. Unlike most of the other military leaders in Britain and France, Kitchener did not believe the war would end quickly. In his view it would last at least three years, and he could see no chance of its being won by the allies unless Britain was prepared to raise a mass army.[3] He based his conclusions on three observations: The French were outnumbered, the Germans well-trained and the Russians ill-equipped and badly led.

While his colleagues were skeptical of his pessimistic outlook, they accepted his conclusion and authorized him to direct a massive effort to recruit a volunteer army of five hundred thousand men. This would be only the beginning, Kitchener warned. "We must be prepared to put armies of millions into the field," he told the Cabinet, "and to maintain them for several years."[4] He did not yet urge conscription: The opposition among the Liberals would have been too vehement.

With the declaration of war, the Cabinet met daily and politics in and out of Parliament were minimized. To supplement the Cabinet, the Committee of Imperial Defence was summoned whenever deemed necessary by the Prime Minister. The structure was cumbersome, the lines of authority too confused and the Cabinet too involved in the details of the war. Even Asquith's official biographers concede that the Cabinet did not delegate enough, and as a result "too many subjects were discussed by too many people"[5] causing the decision-making process to be too slow to meet the exigencies of total war.

Three months later, in November 1914, a War Council was formed, responsible for overall military strategy. It was a Cabinet committee, with Asquith as Chairman, and included Kitchener, Lloyd George, Churchill, Grey, Crewe and the chiefs of staff. Balfour was also a member, the only permanent one outside the Cabinet. The lines of responsibility between the War Council, the Cabinet, and the Secretary of State for War were never clearly defined. This undoubtedly added to the confusion in strategy that marked the first year of war. As the year ended, the news from the battlefields and the battleships was grim: defeats, retreats, sunken ships and unexpectedly heavy casualties. It became clear that this war would be a long and bitter struggle.

Financial Problems

While the War Council tried desperately to cope with the military crisis, Montagu and the Treasury were facing a crisis of their own. They had the responsibility for developing plans to stabilize the financial markets and also to raise sufficient funds to wage the most expensive war in history. Nor did the exigencies of the war permit them the luxury of time. Speed was of the essence, with programs and projects that would ordinarily take months to prepare condensed into days. Montagu and the Treasury staff worked tirelessly with Montagu reporting that he was "utterly worn out," working "practically all night," and "ready to drop."[6]

From the start Montagu recognized the importance of the financial side of waging a war and its relationship to Britain's postwar survival, but as usual he downplayed his role. "My position," he wrote to his mother on August 2, "is only that of scullery maid to the Government and the City. Panic follows panic, foreign office telegrams come hourly, hopes vanish and revive . . . nothing but blackness ahead." He conceded that while he was involved in what appeared to be the "unromantic side of war," it was "by no means the least important and on it really depends the continued existence of our country after the war."[7]

As busy as Montagu was, he found time to continue writing regularly to his mother and to express his concern and condemnation of the anti-German hysteria that was sweeping the country and affecting the security of those who, like his own childhood nanny, Rose Reidel, had been born in Germany but had lived in Britain nearly all their lives. Rosie was touched by his concern and wrote to Montagu in August 1914: "I was very touched by your more than kind letter to me and thank you with all my heart for your sympathy. It is indeed a great comfort to me in this time of trouble and anxiety to know I have so many kind friends to feel for me."[8]

The Keynes Memorandum

On August 3, at the height of the financial crisis, with the support of Montagu and the Treasury, John Maynard Keynes submitted a crucial memorandum in which he argued against "suspending specie payment before it was absolutely necessary."[9] He took the position that gold reserves were to be used, not "hoarded," and that "the City would be jeopardised if it suspended specie payments [coin, as opposed to paper money] at the first sign of emergency. . . . Keynes suggested that gold payments be restricted internally, but retained for international transactions. This was the opinion which, more or less, carried the day."[10] Gold reserves held by the banks were centralized in the Bank of England, and the Treasury was empowered to issue emergency currency of one and ten pound notes. The Bank of England supported Keynes's position. Other banks and bankers, however, were not happy at the prospect of paying their debts with gold. They preferred the creation of new assets and the suspension of liabilities.

On August 6, 1914, the Currency and Bank Notes Act was passed, incorporating the Keynes recommendations. The Bank of England was authorized to issue the notes not backed by gold. In effect, Britain was now off the Gold Standard. Gold payments for external debts were kept, the Bank rate was returned to 5 percent on August 8, and the immediate banking crisis was over.[11]

Keynes's role and his brilliant memorandum did not change Lloyd George's attitude toward him. He viewed Keynes as part of Montagu's intellectual crowd at the Treasury, a group with which he was never comfortable. He preferred his own advisors and in the early days of the war did not give Keynes an official Treasury appointment, although Montagu pleaded for it and Keynes wanted it badly.

It was to Montagu that Keynes wrote frequently during these days about his distrust of Lloyd George, his terrible fear of inflation and his anger at being kept out of the Treasury. "As one of the few people who combine special knowledge of these things, with not having their personal future at stake, I chafe at being a purely passive observer."[12] He sent Montagu several memoranda outlining his recommendations for the war and his opposition to hoarding gold.[13] From the start Montagu recognized Keynes's genius and was never too proud to listen and learn from him. Keynes's ideas strongly influenced Montagu and helped considerably in defining Montagu's own approach to financing the war.

Emergency Financial Matters

By August 7, as a result of the government's quick action, matters were sufficiently under control for the banks to open again. The financial condition of the country, however, was uncertain. The Stock Market was still closed and the moratorium had only just been lifted. Credit had been restored by emergency measures but it was still shaky and the outlook for trade and industry was unclear.

By the end of August the Treasury recommended and the House adopted a War Loan Act permitting the government to borrow "as it saw fit for war purposes on the security of the Consolidated Funds." Commons voted a line of credit of £100 million. On November 16 a further vote of credit for £225 million was obtained, since the first £100 million had been exhausted in less than three months. On November 17 Lloyd George introduced the first war Budget, the second budget for 1914.[14]

In his address, Lloyd George noted that two million men were already in uniform, a figure that was likely to rise to three million within the next months. To feed, clothe and equip such a force, provide £65 million a year for separation allowances and to pay for other costs of war, the government needed £328 million over and above the usual government expenses, bringing the total request for estimated expenditures to about £535 million. Subtracting the revenue expected, the amount to be raised before March 31, 1915, was nearly £340 million. To meet this, the budget proposed to double the income tax, double the supertax, and increase the duties on tea and beer. Because this new taxation could only apply for one-third of the year, its impact on revenue in 1914 was estimated to produce no more than £15.5 million. The balance had to be raised by borrowing, which became a major source of war finance, even though taxes continued to increase substantially.

The budget met with little opposition. Montagu answered more than 125 questions on the third reading of the bill; by and large they were friendly. The bill quickly became law. In retrospect, it has been suggested that the budget should have contained larger increases in taxation to avoid extensive borrowing for the war. The experience with the earlier budget of 1914 may have made Montagu, Lloyd George and the Treasury too cautious. They could not afford another defeat on a budget when so much was at stake.

To make up the difference between the income to be raised by the new taxes and the war needs of the country, a £350 million war loan was floated, enough to carry the country through July 1915. The loan was a spectacular success. When Lloyd George announced it in Parliament, £100 million had already been pledged by the banks and the rest of the loan was soon oversubscribed. Lloyd George and the Treasury were now heroes, receiving universal plaudits for their "sound financial planning."[15] The measures adopted during the first weeks of the war have been described as "the most novel and far reaching which had ever been taken in the field of public finance."[16] When the crisis had subsided, by the middle of November 1914, Lloyd George told Reading that "he thought the Government's financial arrangements the most remarkable of all its operations."

Lloyd George's lack of any technical knowledge of finance and banking made him of little value during the early days of the war, when these measures were being designed and implemented. His friend Tom Jones acknowledged that "with the advent of war the Treasury immediately became the centre for the determination of urgent questions of monetary policy, of which neither the Chancellor nor his able staff, with Sir John Bradbury at its head, had any previous experience."[17]

"The Chancellor had to learn in the midst of a raging financial crisis. . . . [T]he Chancellor had never seen a bill of exchange and knew little or nothing of the delicate and complicated mechanism by which international trade is regulated."[18] He, was, however, a quick study and in a short time mastered the broad outlines of the problem. But details continued to bore him and he had no hesitation in delegating them to others. In such circumstances, the role of the Treasury, of Montagu and of special advisors like Lord Reading was critical. It was their financial acumen and innovation that devised the measures that stemmed the panic.

In the books written about the Treasury during this period, Montagu's name is rarely mentioned. Henry Roseveare, for example, author of *The Treasury*, wrote that the financial innovations taken during the early days of the war were the result of Lloyd George's efforts, aided by "The Governor of the Bank of England . . . other city leaders . . . also by two former chancellors of England, Austen Chamberlain and Lord St. Aldwyn," and "above all . . . the Treasury under Sir John Bradbury, Permanent Secretary at the age of forty-one." [19] Roseveare omitted Montagu and ignored the fact that Lloyd George had a very poor opinion of Bradbury, who was regarded as having as little experience as George himself. [20]

Roseveare, as did Harrod in his biography of Keynes, also gave Basil Blackett the credit for bringing Keynes into the Treasury, and he concludes that with Blackett's help "he [Keynes] helped draft papers which began Lloyd George's education in high finance." [21] Roseveare did not mention Keynes's letter that credits Montagu for bringing him into the Treasury nor the close working relationship Montagu had with Keynes. In Katherine Burk's essay "The Treasury—From Impotence to Power," on the effects of World War I upon the Treasury, there is also no mention of Montagu, although he was Financial Secretary to the Treasury for almost two out of the four years about which Burk wrote. [22]

One of Lloyd George's biographers did concede that the programs to calm the panic in financial circles during these early days of the war "were suggested to Lloyd George by his Treasury advisors and by Reading," and it was "their success in averting disaster [that] suddenly changed the chancellor's status in the City from pariah to hero. It was a strange turnabout for the 'Marconi Ministers.' " [23] In this account too, while "Treasury advisors" are mentioned, the Financial Secretary of the Treasury, who was more than a "Treasury advisor," is not.

Lloyd George himself gave neither recognition nor thanks to Montagu in his *War Memoirs,* upon which so many other books of the period have depended, although he went out of his way to thank many others profusely, including Reading, Sir George Parish, Chamberlain, and Lord Cunliffe, Governor of the Bank of London. [24] It was as if the Financial Secretary of the Treasury did not exist, although Montagu's letters to Venetia made clear he was working "practically all night" on Treasury plans to meet this emergency. [25]

Nor did Lloyd George in his *War Memoirs* give any recognition to Keynes. In fact, not a word is mentioned about the August 3 memo and Keynes's vigorous support of retaining specie payment, which was a pivotal part of the emergency measures adopted at the outset of the war. One must keep in mind that Lloyd George's *War Memoirs* were written after Keynes had left the Government in 1919 and had blasted Lloyd George's role in the struggle over reparations, and after Lloyd George had forced Montagu's resignation as Secretary of State for India and Edwin, like Keynes, had publicly attacked him. Lloyd George was not the kind of man to give recognition, deserved as it might be, to those who had become his bitter political enemies. In fairness to Lloyd George, it is not likely that any other politician would have been magnanimous in the same circumstances.

A few writers, though not many, such as Reading's biographers, Dennis Judd and H. Montgomery Hyde, recognized both Montagu's role during this period, acknowledging him as "the brilliant young Financial Secretary," and his capabilities.[26] In his own writings, Keynes not only acknowledges that Montagu brought him into the Treasury, but often mentioned Montagu's tireless work with the Treasury staff in formulating the wartime financial policies that were eventually adopted. Whether history would remember him was never a principal motivation for Montagu's indefatigable work. Applause from his colleagues, advancement, power, pride in achievement, and the approval of friends and family motivated him far more than the thought of historical recognition. It may have crossed his mind as it does the minds of all those who work for a cause, but it was not his guiding light. By nature he was far more concerned with the present than the future. For the present his only concern as Financial Secretary was to help give England the financial wherewithal to win the war. Toward that end nothing was too much for him and virtually no part of the war effort escaped his scrutiny.

Treasury Control

One area that troubled Montagu from the outset of the war was the absence of financial controls over the departments directly involved in the war, especially the War Office and Admiralty, which were growing quickly. He viewed with alarm the helplessness of the Treasury in trying to limit their hiring and expenditures and offered suggestions to bring accountability and economy into their administration. He feared that unless this was done the nation would face an inflation that would destroy its capacity to finance the war. He suggested that each department involved in the war have a board of inquiry, consisting of three businessmen, to check on the department's expenditures. He believed a panel of inspectors should be created in the Treasury to prevent departmental extravagances.[27] Both ideas were rejected.

The attempt of the Treasury to exert control over spending, regardless of which department was involved, had in fact predated the war. It was an accepted practice that departments were expected to submit projected expenses to the Treasury, which had ultimate responsibility. The Treasury investigated the pay and the number of staff employed by any governmental department.

It was almost impossible to exert such controls during war when each department became a fiefdom of its own. *A Report of the Royal Commission on Civil Service,* published at the end of 1914, revealed what Montagu had recognized as soon as the war had begun: that "the influence exercised by the Treasury fell short of real control."[28] This was the case not only in the War Office and Admiralty, but in the new "mushroom ministries"[29] that had developed during the war, such as the Ministries of Labour, Food, Shipping and the Air Board. They were not subject to Treasury control at all, and their staff multiplied according to the whim of their ministries.

Montagu struggled with this problem throughout his tenure at the Treasury. The departments in question vigorously opposed any of the controls he tried to impose, claiming that during war they were unable to "find time to explain our expenses to outside persons."[30] Responses such as these further convinced Montagu that there existed no satisfactory controls. His view was that one "can't expect economy inside a department." It must come from the Treasury or from special boards of outsiders created in each department.[31] His pleas went unheeded. Commission after commission was created to study the problem as the war progressed, and scores of recommendations were offered. It was not until after the war that the Treasury was reorganized and given again its power to control the Civil Service and departmental spending. During the war such controls were not imposed, despite Montagu's continued efforts.

The War Will Be Won by the Nation
with the Longest Purse

Montagu's fear of inflation made him not only one of the chief advocates for economy in the government's operation but also an opponent of any expansion of social services during the war. This often brought him into opposition with other Radical Liberals, including his cousin Herbert Samuel, who saw the war as an opportunity to increase not only state control and centralization but also state spending for social needs.

In October 1914, Montagu chastised Samuel in a sharp letter responding to a column in the *Daily Chronicle* in which Samuel had written: "The State has sanctioned the expenditure of several million £ sterling to provide employment wherever industry has been relocated by reason of the war."[32] "You will perhaps forgive me," Montagu wrote Samuel, "for saying that I do not think that this is carrying out the spirit of the arrangement which you made with the Chancellor. It is of the utmost that we limit expenditures. We do not want to encourage anybody to spend anything unless it is absolutely inevitable to provide employment for people who are out of work."[33] Montagu added:

Why encourage people to think that the more they spend, the more praiseworthy they are? You would have had a right to boast if you could have circulated in the newspaper the statement that, having regard to the war, local authorities had been so public spirited as to postpone things they stood much in need of . . . *I object most strongly to spending a single penny that can be avoided . . . the country will win in this war whose purse is the longest.*[34] (emphasis added)

The last sentence expresses better than any other Montagu's attitude toward finance and the war. He always believed that Britain's ability to keep her financial and economic position strong was as important as anything she did on the battlefield. This would require a combination of higher taxes, government loans, economy in administration and a tightening of civilian belts. The slogan "Business as Usual," which was coined by the big shopkeepers during the first months of the war, was anathema to him.

Even on the emotionally charged issue of separation allowances for the wives of servicemen and pensions for the wives of those killed in action, Montagu held firm to his belief in strict government economy. Early in the war he had served on the Committee of Pensions that had explored this issue. He sent a long memorandum to Asquith explaining the options available to him and presenting the arguments for the various scales of payments to women whose husbands were on the front or had been killed. Montagu suggested to Asquith and Lloyd George a conservative formula, which Lloyd George supported. He and Montagu took what appeared to be a hard line, not because they were heartless but because they had the responsibility both for financing the war and fighting inflation. They felt strongly, too, that women who were able should work, and that government pensions should not encourage such women to be subsidized by the government. They were overruled by a majority of the Cabinet, with Asquith writing to Venetia that the Cabinet had had a long meeting and finally decided "the much vexed question of 'separation allowances' wh. we have settled I think on a very generous scale—a minimum of 12/6 [12s.6d.] a week for a childless wife & a maximum of 22/ [22s] for a wife with 4 or more children with an intermediate sliding scale."[35] This was more generous than Montagu had urged.

As for the rate of pensions for childless war widows who could work, the Cabinet also voted a larger payment than Montagu had supported. Although he lost on the separation and pension issues and many others involving the economy in government spending, Montagu continued to press the point whenever he could. The specter of inflation was a fear he carried with him throughout the war. He had learned well from his friend Keynes. The penuriousness of his father may have also been a subliminal influence.

Edwin, Venetia and Asquith—Love in Wartime, 1914

The difficulties and frustrations of these early months of the war were assuaged for Montagu by the increasing attention Venetia gave him. In turn, he was becoming a more aggressive suitor and pressing again his proposal of marriage. On September 2, 1914, he wrote to her that merely seeing her was "heavenly," to hear from her "a pleasure," and to be able to do anything for her "is just a taste of all the joy I have had if . . . Oh . . . Why not. I wish you were here and I most sincerely wish I were not."[36]

But even with the emotional support (slight as it was) that he received from Venetia, he continued to be racked by insecurity and feelings of inadequacy: "I work harder and get more discouraged every day,"[37] and again, "I'm in the depths of despair. . . . Everything seems to be going wrong in my office and I am suffering from a reputation of incompetence, untrustworthiness, and unconstructiveness. I wish I could disappear."[38] Venetia's letters continued to give him "great joy" but not enough to stop him from "mourning" his own incompetence. "How I wish I knew how to be more useful."[39]

No letters or memoranda from Asquith, Lloyd George, Keynes or any of the key players at the Treasury confirm Montagu's negative evaluation of his own performance at the Treasury. The comments that have survived, especially from Keynes and Asquith, express just the opposite view. When Asquith appointed Montagu a Privy Councillor in January 1915, he told both Venetia and Montagu what a superb job Montagu had done.[40]

That the Prime Minister and Montagu's colleagues approved of his performance did not relieve his anxieties. By the middle of October he was falling into a state of deepening depression, writing that "the war news is not good, if not bad," and he continued to complain that he was becoming "no more competent—hence happiness is rather impossible. But just at present I am getting on very well with [Lloyd] George—I nearly went to Paris with him tomorrow but did not do so because I did not think I could stand Sir C. Henry and Simon. I made a speech last night to about 4,000 people at Cheltenham—got several recruits and made Belgian refugees present weep salt tears. But I hate having Tories on the platform."[41]

While Montagu's letters to Venetia were filled with self-depreciation and complaints, and with an occasional expression of love and need, Asquith's letters exuded confidence and sureness. They also contained secret details of the war, descriptions of the people, pressures and problems involved in his day-to-day leadership responsibilities, as well as personal trivia, poetry and passionate expressions of his love and devotion. His letter to Venetia on the eve of her birthday, August 21, 1914, is a characteristic example of the Asquith style—poetic and filled with open expressions of his love and need:

It will be 27 years to-morrow since you opened your eyes on this sinful world, and it is not yet quite 3 since I made my great discovery of the *real* you. I sometimes wonder, looking back, whether you would rather that I had *not* made it, and that things had continued between us as they were in the early days of Venetiad. I believe—indeed I know what you have told me, and you never lie—that it has made a difference to the interests & pleasures (perhaps also at times to the anxieties) of your life. I cannot tell you, for you might think I was exaggerating—the length & breadth &

depth of the difference it has made to mine. It has been given I suppose to few men to go through such a succession of 'crises' in the same space of time; you have been a stay and refreshment to me in them all; and during this last 12 months with its almost miraculous series of emergencies I have come more & more to rely and rest upon you and you have never failed me either in counsel or in love. So I bless you darling with all my heart, and pray for you every boon that the years can bring.[42]

Mixed with these expressions of love was information found in no other source: Lloyd George was concerned that the Russians were not taking the Allies into their confidence; the British captured thirty-five ships on the high seas by the second week in August; by October 1914, Churchill wanted to be relieved of his present office and "put in some kind of military command," but he was told he couldn't be spared from the Admiralty; the British recognized the French strategy had failed them; and the Belgian field army was "quite untrustworthy." He further revealed that there was "nothing to be done but to order their naval men to evacuate their trenches . . . Rawlinson will meet them . . . at Ghent, after which point they are safe"; that Churchill's decision to send green naval brigades to save Antwerp was a "wicked folly"; that German mines were responsible for the sinking of the *Audacious,* one of the best and newest of Britain's dreadnoughts with a crew of about a thousand; that "the losses in the 7th Division which . . . was the last to go out have been terrific—at least 4,000 out of about 12,000 men and 200 officers"; that the Indian troops were having a bad time with the Germans in East Africa; that at one point Hankey had suggested the immediate arrest of the twenty-five thousand or so German and Austrian subjects at large in London—but that Asquith firmly rejected this suggestion; that by the end of December, Britain was planning to have nine hundred thousand soldiers on the front; that Kitchener was gloomy about the Russian position; and that the ambassador in Washington "is convinced that both the German and Austrian ambassadors there are working for peace."[43] In several of the letters, Asquith warned Venetia that the information was "secret," "very secret," and for her eyes only.[44]

Thus we see a Prime Minister of England at a time when the nation was involved in a life-and-death struggle, sharing the most intimate details of military strategy, Cabinet meetings, political intrigue and personal gossip with a young woman whose guiding principle in life was having "fun." In 1913 Asquith wrote Venetia fifty letters, and beginning in July 1914, in spite of the burdens of war, he wrote every day, often during Cabinet meetings. Asquith himself calculated one night in bed in July 1914 that "roughly speaking since the first week in December I have written you not less than 170 letters."[45] An examination of the Asquith letters shows that he wrote 133 letters in that eight-month period, with 151 additional letters before the end of that year, an average of more than one a day. In January 1915, he wrote 45; in February, 48; and in March, 58. Ted Morgan, one of Churchill's biographers, believed that this behavior was Asquith's way of keeping "his hold on Venetia by bringing her into the decision making process."

"What do you think, my darling" was a frequent refrain. What did she think of sending troops to the Dardanelles, or of Kitchener's New Armies, or of Winston's conduct at the Admiralty? She was treated in government matters like a consultant. If he could not have her as a mistress he would make her an accomplice, for she gave him the lifeblood of all that he did.[46]

Asquith often wrote these letters, which were longer and livelier than his daily account of Cabinet business to the King, in the middle of Cabinet meetings. "A messenger would come into the Cabinet room with a letter from Venetia and he would read it in great concentration and then settle down to reply at length, ringing for the messenger, who would then take the reply for dispatch. Other members of the Cabinet, particularly Lloyd George, were dismayed at the time he spent on his personal correspondence during meetings over which he should have been presiding, lost in his private thoughts while grave wartime manners were being discussed."[47]

The sharing of sensitive military secrets with Venetia in letters that went by ordinary post and could have easily fallen into the hands of the enemy has been severely criticized as endangering the lives of British soldiers,[48] "incredibly indiscreet,"[49] a "terrifying indifference to the rules of discretion on national security,"[50] verging on "a national scandal,"[51] hair-raising, a risk "to national security,"[52] an act of "recklessness,"[53] the behavior of a "deranged" mind.[54] While the last characterization may be extreme, Asquith's disregard of the possibility that the letters might fall into enemy hands or that Venetia might show them to other people (in fact, she did show them to Edwin, who was not known for his discretion) deserves the opprobrium it received.

The letters reveal that during these difficult days the Prime Minister continued to spend a good deal of time with Montagu—not only discussing business but at luncheons, dinners, golf, bridge and other social and family affairs. Yet in spite of Asquith's own closeness to Montagu, he continued to point out Montagu's less appealing traits to Venetia. On September 4, 1914, he wrote Venetia: "I am sorry the Assyrian has been 'grousing' to you. I am always saying 'something nice' to him & he has really no reason to complain of want of appreciation. He is *very* efficient, but I wish of him (as of others) that he was rather more self-dependent. The young men . . . of the present day seem to need such a lot of cosseting."[55]

By October Asquith's jealousy of Montagu had become more explicit. "I hate you lunching to-morrow with the Assyrian—not that I should have had any real talk with you here; but to *see* you is so much. Damn!" he wrote to Venetia in October,[56] and on November 21 he wrote, "I feel very jealous of the Assyrian."[57]

It was during this time that Asquith mentioned to Venetia that he planned to make Montagu a Privy Councillor on New Year's Day 1915. In his letter to Montagu bestowing this honor, the Prime Minister praised Montagu's work at the India Office and the Treasury, especially his "strenuous and inestimable service since the outbreak of the war." The letter ended: "It is . . . the greatest of pleasures to me to be able to offer a public mark of distinction to a friend whose loyalty and affection have never failed me."[58] Montagu was elated, writing to Venetia that the letter was "the best thing I have ever had. This is far more than even an 'honour' . . . it is a glorious possession."[59]

Montagu continued throughout the closing months of 1914 to have the closest relationships with the Asquiths—not only with the Prime Minister, but with Margot and Violet. He continued to be virtually a part of the Asquith family, although by now he was courting Venetia with persistence, knowing full well of the Prime Minister's love. The Prime Minister, for his part, continued to include Montagu in his family's social and familial life with no hint that he thought his "friend" would win the hand of the woman he loved.

As the year drew to an end, not only was Asquith's personal life becoming more demanding but the war was becoming a military nightmare. Asquith's letter of December 30 spoke of the "existing deadlock" that had developed in the "West and East," which was "likely to continue," and that the losses involved "in the trench-jumping operations now going on both sides are enormous and out of all proportion to the ground gained."[60] On midnight December 30, Asquith wrote a second letter to Venetia, calling 1914, in spite of the tragedies of the war, what the "ancients used to call 'annus mirabilis,' " a wonderful year, and concluding:

I thank you, my darling, from the bottom of my heart, from the very source of my being, for what you have been to me. Without you I must often have failed & more than once gone down. You have sustained & enriched every day of my life.

That is my New Year's greeting. . . . Perhaps you don't always realize that I am as fully conscious as you can be of the great apparent difference and disproportion: you in the full tide of your glorious youth: I—according to the Calendar—on the threshold at any rate of the later stages of life. Whatever comes or goes, I am & must be the debtor: hugely overdrawn, often ashamed of what I owe; but—I can't say more tonight.[61]

On December 31, Asquith pleaded with Venetia to "send me a *nice* New Year's message, which I can remember and treasure." And then he asked: "Where and what shall we be this time next year? My last word to you *this* year, my own darling, is one of untellable gratitude and unalterable love. Bless you."[62] On New Year's Day, he wrote again, quoting Shakespeare's ninety-first sonnet: "Thy love is better than high birth to me, Richer than wealth, prouder than garments' cost. . . . Wretched in this alone, that thou mayst take, All this away, and me most wretched make."[63]

Asquith and Montagu were now both hopelessly in love with Venetia, who was still enjoying this outpouring of affection from both suitors while returning just enough to keep them both happy. But the situation could not hold. Edwin, Venetia and Asquith, like the soldiers on the battlefields of Europe, knew that in love, as in war, the status quo cannot endure.

15

Prelude to Political Disaster,
January–May 1915

The War which had begun so dramatically had missed its climax. It had ceased to be either a tragedy or a triumph. It had become a wearisome thrusting against . . . evils.

H. G. *Wells,* Mr. Britling Sees It Through

New Year's Day 1915 was a day of neither sunshine nor joy for the British people. It was a day of pouring rain, freezing temperatures and blistering wind. It was a day that matched the disheartened mood of the public: dark, cold, depressed and dreary.

The course of the war during the last five months had gone from bad to worse, and during 1915 it would become even more desperate. As if to presage the tragedies that lay ahead, five hundred men and officers were lost on the British warship *Formidable,* which was torpedoed in the Channel by a German submarine when the New Year was barely twelve hours old.

For Prime Minister Asquith, 1915 would be the worst year of his life, both politically and personally. For the Liberal Party, 1915 signaled the beginning of its end. For Venetia Stanley, this would be a year of deep and troubling soul-searching and painful decisions.

Only for Edwin Montagu was 1915 to be a year that brought some personal happiness. It was marred however by the pain the announcement of his marriage to Venetia inflicted on Asquith and by the disastrous course of the war, as well as by the political conspiracies that began to destroy the Prime Minister he truly loved.

The prospect of a long war was now apparent to any thoughtful observer. "The war which had begun so dramatically," H. G. Wells wrote, "missed its climax . . . it had ceased to be either a tragedy or a triumph. It had become a wearisome thrusting against a pressure of evils. . . . Under that strain the dignity of England broke . . . the British spirit . . . wasted its energies in a deepening and spreading net of internal squabbles and accusations."[1]

At the center of these squabbles and accusations stood Asquith, now sixty-two, in office seven years, still physically strong, a war leader who remained as committed to constitutional government as he was to winning the war. As such, he was not and could not be a demagogue, in speech or in action. He could not readily restrict personal liberties even when the exigencies of war seemed to call for greater governmental control and less individual freedom. He was a lawyer trying to win a war with the skill and style of a man of reason. He was a gentleman of the old school, prepared to listen to opposing points of view and to search for compromises when necessary. He was first and foremost a lawyer: slow, deliberate and logical as he tried to cajole and convince.

In the early months of the war, no one demanded that this trusted leader, this scholar from Oxford, this respected lawyer, this brilliant Parliamentarian, change his style. But the frustrations that accompany defeat and mounting casualties on the battlefield demand a scapegoat, and Asquith suddenly found himself not the trusted and indisputable leader but the target and repository of a nation's bitterness and rage. Criticism poured forth from both the Left and the Right. The Left was uncomfortable with the war and not ready to sacrifice its liberal principles even to assure victory, and the Right was dissatisfied with what it perceived as a lack of vigor in the prosecution of the war. Added to Asquith's woes were the constant and vitriolic attacks by a small clique within the Tory Party who saw the problems of the war as providing an ideal chance to advance its own political objectives.

The Tories had never liked Asquith: They had not accepted with equanimity the Liberal landslide of 1906 and they did not believe a Liberal could execute a war with sufficient vigor and toughness to assure victory. They despised some of the key players in Asquith's government: Haldane, whom they attacked as the "German-lover"; Churchill, whom they viewed as a deserter of party and class, and who became for them the arch-villain of the Dardanelles fiasco; and Montagu, the Jew now at the Treasury, whose religion and policies on India and tax reform were anathema to the Right. Now was the time to even the score.

As 1915 began, the Tory attacks against Asquith had not yet reached down to Montagu. For Montagu, now thirty-five, the year began on an especially happy note. His relationship with Venetia was more serious than ever and his inclusion as a Privy Councillor in the New Year's Honours filled him with enormous satisfaction. While the Privy Council, made up of leaders from all fields, was primarily ceremonial, it was the "badge of importance in the nation."[2] To complete his honors on February 4, 1915, Montagu was appointed Chancellor of the Duchy of Lancaster, which automatically elevated him to the rank of a Cabinet Minister.

Traditionally, the Duchy was a way of bringing someone into the Cabinet without giving him departmental authority. It was a ministry without portfolio. "His actual duties were to manage the property held by the King in his Duchy of Lancaster, which had never been surrendered to the Treasury. This took about two hours of office work a week."[3] The rest of the time could be spent on special assignments from the Prime Minister or service on Cabinet committees. The Duchy was often given to a loyal party member as a reward for service. When Churchill was given this post in May 1915, it was said that it "was humiliating [for him] to take such a lowly post, which had been given to party hacks like Charles Hobhouse and protégés like Edwin Montagu."[4]

For his part, Montagu did not view this post as a humiliation. It brought him into the Cabinet and thus involved him more broadly in decisions involving the war. He was physically exhausted from his work at the Treasury and an easier position was most attractive. He felt frustrated at what he viewed as his failure in achieving the passage of the 1914 budget. Yet he recognized the importance of his work at the Treasury and had misgivings about leaving it at a time when devising wise fiscal policies was as important as developing effective military strategy. With his usual anxiety and suspicion, he put the worst face on the appointment, seeing it as part of a plot by Lloyd George: "So I go to the Cabinet," he wrote to Venetia, "with conviction that I am deserting my post, pushed therefrom by the man I have served for a year, who I thought trusted and liked me, and encircled by those who will see in me the greedy supplanter of Masterman."[5] Masterman had been his predecessor at the Duchy.

In fact, Lloyd George had nothing to do with the appointment, nor was Montagu responsible for Masterman's displacement. Masterman had been the Chancellor of the Duchy of Lancaster and the Minister of Insurance. As a Minister he had to be a member of Parliament. He was scheduled to run in Norwich but, as Asquith told Venetia on January 24, "the local people won't hear of Masterman and have already got . . . a candidate. . . . Shipley—Illingsworth's old seat—also refuses to look at Masterman. He has now been nearly a year out of the House and there is no prospect of his getting back again. This is intolerable in the case of a Cabinet Minister who is responsible for important administration like the Insurance Act. So I have come to the conclusion that he must go."[6]

Asquith also confided to Venetia that if he was successful in maneuvering Masterman out of his position he would "promote the Assyrian to the Cabinet, giving him the Duchy and charge of Insurance, wh. I think he would do quite well, tho Lloyd George (who likes him) seems to think he might fail in quickness of decision."[7] In telling this to Venetia, Asquith told her to keep this "*strictly* between you & me."[8]

Venetia believed this was an important promotion for Montagu and assured him it was not a "plot," since Asquith was "very fond" of him and wanted him in the Cabinet.[9] "I am certain too," she told him, "you won't stick in the Duchy for long and I am very ambitious for you (!) I welcome this step very greatly."[10]

Asquith also believed Montagu should take the Duchy post but acknowledged to Venetia that Montagu "is *really* sorry to leave the Treasury, especially at this time when it is full of interesting war problems, for wh. the little ripples of the Insurance backwater are a poor substitute."[11] Asquith reminded Montagu too, of "Mr. Gladstone's sound dictum: 'no man shd ever refuse Cabinet office for the first time; it is the great chance of his life; and it matters nothing what particular place for the moment he holds.' "[12] Asquith continued, "He [Edwin] is of course fully alive to this, & didn't hesitate. He was very emotionné & began to say all sorts of nice things about my friendship for him etc., etc.—wh. I cut short. . . . I am sure he has gone back to his tent—for once in his life—a genuinely happy man."[13]

In spite of his initial suspicions, Montagu was pleased with the prospect of a Cabinet post. He viewed the post of Chancellor of the

Duchy as Venetia did: an interim appointment, another step to a higher position. He was never offered the task of heading an Insurance Ministry as Asquith's letter to Venetia had suggested. If he had been, he probably would have turned it down since he was primarily interested in becoming Viceroy of India, succeeding Lord Hardinge, whose term was almost over.

The idea of becoming Viceroy was an idea with which Montagu had toyed as early as 1912, during his first trip to India. He thought of himself as eminently qualified for this position and even went so far as to mention it early in 1915 to Lloyd George, who immediately passed it on to Asquith. Hearing this, Asquith wrote to Venetia, "Our friend [Montagu] had confided to [Lloyd George] his Indian ambitions. Ll. G. says he was never so staggered in his life. I am sure he would be wise not to nurse that dream, and I shall take some opportunity of telling him so."[14]

Ten days earlier, Asquith had discussed Hardinge's successor with Lord Crewe and told Venetia that he "then threw a fly about the Assyrian, but it did not lure Crewe at all; he thought it quite an impossible idea, wh. wd. arouse the resentment of the whole Indian Civil Service, be badly received by the leading Native Princes, and be regarded here at home as in the nature of a party job. At the same time he was full of appreciation of our friend's qualifications & merits—in the abstract."[15] While Crewe was correct in his assessment of the reaction of the Indian Civil Service, he was wrong about the Indian Princes. They were the staunchest supporters of Montagu; many had become his dear friends and admirers.

Montagu himself raised the idea of his appointment as Viceroy directly with Asquith in March. The Prime Minister did not discourage him but instead sent him an "affectionate but non-committal reply," indicating that the choice of Hardinge's successor was the thorniest of problems and ending with the question, "And who is to do Education, I suppose there is nothing you would loathe more?"[16]

Montagu still believed, therefore, that he had a chance of realizing this goal and saw his new Cabinet position as yet another step toward achieving it. In December, Montagu wrote again to Asquith that he would not be doing his duty "if I did not again put forward my own claims. . . . I have no other ambitions save to go to India and I have had no other since I entered public life." He believed that a conventional appointment "will lose the moment." The Viceroy should be someone who can invigorate the administration rather than surround himself with "out of date and rather tawdry pomp."

Montagu raised the question of his "race"—which he believed was a "serious obstacle" and one the Prime Minister must "balance against other considerations." He pointed out that he had dear friends among the Indian Princes who all supported him, including the Aga Khan and their Highnesses the Princes of Bikaner, Alwar and Gupta. He hoped the Prime Minister would not just choose someone whom he might want to get rid of, like "Kitchener or McKenna," or "reward like Beauchamp." That would not be worthy, he argued, "of a great Liberal Prime Minister."[17]

Keynes Joins the Treasury

Before Montagu left the Treasury, he succeeded in having Keynes made assistant to Sir George Parish, who was serving in the Treasury as Special Advisor to Lloyd George. Keynes stayed at the Treasury for the duration of the war and became one of its brightest lights. Over the next few months, as secretary of a Cabinet committee, Keynes worked with Montagu in organizing government purchases of Indian wheat at below market prices—a policy made possible by the embargo on private Indian wheat exports. Montagu's knowledge of the politics and economy of India made him of special value in developing this policy.

In early February, Keynes and Montagu accompanied Lloyd George to Paris for the first Inter-Allied Conference to discuss the international aspects of financing the war. Keynes was given the opportunity to go as a representative of the Treasury—again on Montagu's recommendation, because Lloyd George had little regard for his two permanent secretaries, Bradbury and Ramsey. "I have no use," Lloyd George wrote to Montagu, "for such men in a conference."[18]

It was at this conference that the complex system of inter-Allied credits was designed. It was largely the works of Keynes and led by stages to a centralized buying system, with Allied orders abroad placed by Britain, and paid for by British credits earmarked for Allied accounts at the Bank of England. In return, Allied nations deposited gold in London as partial collateral.[19]

Montagu worked closely with Keynes in devising this system. Each man continued to enjoy the other professionally and person-

ally. Keynes's relationship with Lloyd George never improved. Keynes
viewed him as totally ignorant on financial matters and believed that
it was against "the spendthrifts like Lloyd George that the system of
Treasury controls had to be invented."[20]

Venetia Becomes a Nurse

During January 1915 Venetia began training as a nurse. Most of her
friends and women of her class were now involved in some way in
helping the war effort, many volunteering for hospital duty at home
and overseas. Venetia was candid in admitting that she was not
motivated by any sense of duty or morality. Rather, working as a
nurse seemed exciting, life at home was a bore, most of her male
friends were at the front and she needed some new dimension to add
to her pursuit of "fun."[21] Her relationships with the Prime Minister
and Montagu were no longer enough.

Her training was in London, and Montagu lost no opportunity in
intensifying his pursuit. He opened his home at 24 Queen Anne's
Gate to Venetia and her friends and entertained them lavishly. His
home became a haven from the horrors of the war, a place in which
to escape and relax.

While no letters survive from December 1914 between Venetia
and Montagu it is clear from later letters that during that month
Montagu had decided to press again his proposal of marriage. His
letters beginning in 1915 are far more personal, both in salutation
and content, shifting from "My dear Miss Stanley" in 1914 to "My
Dearest Venetia" in January 1915.

For Christmas 1914 Montagu gave Venetia a dress especially
designed for her and sent it with glowing words of love. He gave a
similar dress to Katharine Asquith, Asquith's daughter-in-law; Asquith made a snide comment about it to Venetia: "As a matter of
fact, I could have spotted in one guess his present to you: for last
night Kath. came down to dinner in a wonderful *confection*—designed I imagine by the same hand—at any rate proceeding from
the same source. Do wear yours on Monday evening: & we can
compare notes & criticism."[22]

By February, Montagu, encouraged by Venetia's attention, visits
and letters, finally had the courage to suggest marriage once more,
although in a jocular vein: "God bless you Venetia. You have been

an angel friend to me, why not a wife? I can't guess. Have you ever thought again of that?"[23] Venetia may have thought about the proposal but she was still not ready to say "yes." She did not, however, reject it outright as she had in 1912. Instead, she equivocated in her response and permitted the relationship not only to continue but to deepen considerably.

Her attitude toward Montagu was changing. She was in her late twenties; most of her friends were married; few eligible men remained at home; many had been killed. Suddenly, Montagu did not look as unattractive as before. His poor health made it certain that he would not be called to the front. He was advancing politically and was now a Cabinet member—no small achievement for a man of thirty-five. He might even become Viceroy of India. And he adored her, had lots of money and was willing and eager to lavish it upon her. While she still had many doubts, she was not ready to close the door upon him as she had done three years before.

Montagu for his part had no serious romantic attachments at this time and was free to concentrate all his emotions and time upon her. With good humor, Asquith wrote to Venetia: "The Assyrian got a lot of telegrams of congratulations today on his P.C. [Privy Council]. We have been chaffing him at dinner (after drinking his health) on the sources from wh. they came. So far as we cd. extract disclosures from him the only feminine senders were Fr. (Frances) Horner & the ever-faithful Pamela McKenna."[24] Both Frances Horner and Pamela McKenna were married. There is no suggestion that they were anything but platonic friends.

By the middle of March 1915, Montagu felt comfortable enough with Venetia to complain that she had time to see Violet and Bongie but could not find time to see him. "Yet do I give in. *Never*. I love you more than love. Come to lunch tomorrow! Yrs. tremendously and however foolishly devoted, E.S.M."[25] Venetia was not pleased with this expression of mild jealousy and must have replied with a rebuke, for Montagu's next letter on the following day apologized profusely for his "quasi reproach," explaining that he was "desperate" concerning her, must hear her voice and see her for his "love grows and can't be killed by cold letters."[26]

Although Montagu had thought that when he left the Treasury his work schedule would become lighter, it did not. He was still working long hours. In a letter to his mother on March 20, he said that he had "never worked so hard" in his life, "not even in the first weeks of the war. I have the Cabinet," he wrote, "three Cabinet committees, my own two offices, the labour and contracts things with George Runciman. I have been there [Treasury Chambers] all day for four days on that, doing other work all night and Acland is so ill so I am also at my old job. I am however, fairly well." [27] One of the most time-consuming committees on which Montagu served was the Committee on Food Prices, an extremely important committee chaired by the Prime Minister. This letter is one of the rare ones Montagu ever wrote to his mother in which he said that he was feeling "fairly well." Perhaps the excitement of his romance with Venetia helped him not only psychologically but also physically.

Another committee on which Montagu served was one concerning requests for "war bonuses" for railway men and extra overtime pay for postal servants and other workers. While Montagu accepted the war bonus for railway men, he opposed extending this to other workers. If the government had to grant such increases, he warned, "the process will go on indefinitely, with the result that money will be depreciated to such an extent as to seriously disorganize our overseas trade and dislocate the foreign exchanges." [28] On matters of this kind, as in the case of pensions and allowances for wives and widows of soldiers, Montagu continued to fear inflation and oppose expanding the base of government expenditures.

Pressure upon Venetia

Overwork, new government responsibilities and the disastrous course of the war did not stop either Montagu or Asquith from courting Venetia with persistence and ardor throughout the first months of 1915. While Montagu's letters expressed his growing adoration and passion, so did those of the Prime Minister. During these months, Asquith continued to write daily, sometimes as often as two or three times a day. His letters became increasingly filled with expressions of dependency and an all-consuming need to be with Venetia, to hear from her, to spend time with her. "I long more than words to see you again: *twice* a week is a meagre & *irreducible* minimum." [29] He fussed when she couldn't see him, dreamed of her, longed for her, begged her to write even if it is only a "scrap of paper," [30] read and reread her letters, began to worry when she missed writing even for a day,[31] confessed that he had written to her more freely than to anyone he had ever known,[32] and called her the "pole-star of his life."[33] He longed to hear every detail of her life (as trainee at the London Hospital) and thought of her "every hour." Her love was "the *best* thing" in his life.[34] The intensity of Asquith's feelings was evident:

My darling—it is just after mid-night & the bells have only just ceased ringing. Your dear Xmas present is on my knees & I am writing with it as a support.

I don't the least know, nor can I guess, what this year is going to bring. But my first thoughts & my first words are for you.

I wrote to you last night & this morning about 1914—a year of many agitations & anxieties—which through you has been transformed for me.

Will you be the same in 1915?

My loyalty & love will never grow paler or fainter.[35]

That evening, Asquith sent another letter that ended, "I must go to bed—with your dear letter under my pillow. Good night—most dear—never more dear, or so dear, as on this first night of a New Year."[36]

Of particular interest is Asquith's analysis of Venetia's character in a letter of January 9 in which he confessed that she had far more influence on him than he had on her.

I have been thinking . . . of what Sylvia said to me . . . of my being both a good & a bad influence upon you. I can see now that I ought to have replied: "You make a great mistake about the whole situation. The truth is that I have *less* influence upon Venetia than she has upon me. She is one of the least influenceable people in the world. I can say so, because no one knows her better, or has tried harder to understand her mind & character & temperament."[37]

Asquith then went on to compare Venetia to a mountain. After describing different classes of mountains, he wrote:

But there is a third class—the rarest, most difficult, most stimulating—wh. cannot be ascended except by *rock-climbing*. Now & again there is a narrow cranny . . . often, what seems a practicable face is found to be covered with a surface of ice; and . . . you are lucky if you can secure sufficient hold for hand or foot, while a false step means not only failure but destruction. Of the last class there is no more conspicuous example than Mount Venetia!

There my own sweet darling, you see what I *sometimes* feel. But I mean
to persevere and wd. far rather fall into the abyss than cease to climb. I
won't ask you what you think of my chances.[38]

Even to Asquith, Venetia is "a narrow cranny . . . covered with a
surface of ice."

This did not stop him from loving her, pouring out his most
intimate thoughts to her and continuing to share with her the most
sensitive military information. On January 11, 1915, he wrote to
Venetia that General Murray did "not believe in the possibility of a
successful German offensive in Flanders or France, even if we send
no more troops. He hinted (this is *most secret*) that the points at wh.
the French hope sooner or later to break through are at Arras and
East of Rheims."[39] And on January 25 he wrote: "While we were at
dinner last night a messenger arrived from the Admiralty with a
letter to me from Winston, giving a narrative of the naval battle in
the North Sea. The *Lion*—Beatty's flagship—was a good deal damaged. . . . None of this appears in the official account published
today—from which one wd. gather that none of our ships had been
touched. Don't you think this kind of secrecy quite puerile?" In the
same letter Asquith wrote:

You know how I value your judgment: I put it *quite first* among women,
and there are only 2 or 3 men to my mind in the same class. And you have
now shared my inmost confidence so long & with such unsurpassable
loyalty that I can speak to you really *more freely* about the most important
things than I can to any other human being. . . . For 13 months now you
have never failed me & I know you never will.[40]

But by February, Asquith was beginning to fear that perhaps
Venetia would "fail him," that perhaps she would find someone
else. He wrote:

Sometimes a horrible imagination seizes me that you may be taken from
me—in one way or another; with you would vanish all the colour and
"point" of my life; and tho I might struggle on for a time from habit, or a
vague sense of duty, or the instinct to finish off a half-done job—that
would be all.[41]

This was a critical letter. Asquith's comment that if Venetia left him
he "would struggle . . . from habit . . . and duty" but his heart
would no longer be in his work would come into play in under-

standing Asquith's reaction to Venetia's announcement of marriage three months later. On February 9, Venetia quieted Asquith's fears by sending what he described as "the most delicious letter" she had ever sent, assuring him that she did not ever want him to stop loving her and wanting her.[42] This was written eight days after Montagu's proposal of February 1.

Margot was distraught. She knew by now that her husband was deeply in love with Venetia; this was no passing flirtation. Oddly, she seemed not to blame Asquith but vented all her spleen on Venetia. "[She] is even teaching Henry to avoid telling me things," Margot wrote to her confidante, Ettie Desborough. "I am far too fond of H. to show him how ill and miserable it makes me." She attacked Venetia as "a woman without refinement or any imagination."[43]

Still unaware of how serious Montagu's relationship with Venetia had become, Margot wrote to him:

I am *fundamentally* humble & without any form of vanity (I know as well as Blanche that tho' I'm well made & have an alert expression I'm plain, severe, crisp and candid). I have as you know often wondered if Venetia hadn't ousted me faintly—not very much—but enough to wound bewilder and humiliate me—(I have been chaffed about her more than once). Venetia as I said to Henry has many fine points: she is unselfish & kind but she leads (not in Hospital) the kind of life I hate (after being out 10 years) and she is not *candid* with me—She has not much atmosphere of moral or intellectual sensibility & in old days she always made mischief between Violet & me just when Violet was *most* devoted to me but in spite of all this I really have no sort of personal dislike and *always* suggest Venetia for everything . . . Meetings (Newcastle), Walmer, W[h]arf, Debates, dinners, etc. etc. My jealousy is *not* small as from *wounded vanity,* it is *Love* for Henry.[44]

Margot continued with candor and poignancy, explaining that she not only felt hurt because of her love for Asquith but from "the *knowledge* alas! that I am no longer young and I daresay—in fact I always observe—as men get older they like different kinds of women."[45]

She told Montagu, in a manner suggesting that she was protesting too much, that she and Asquith continued to have a unique relationship, that he told her everything, that he was moved by her letter to him (in which she obviously complained about Venetia), that he told her he had lunch with Venetia and "spoke of her with great sweetness."[46] She ended with a plea to Montagu. "*Your* part to play is to persuade both Violet and Venetia that if they don't marry they will be miserable formidable egoists and amateurs."[47]

The letter from Asquith that Margot referred to in her note to Montagu was clearly intended to calm her suspicions. In it Asquith had assured her that she had *"no* cause for . . . doubts and fears," that it was untrue that he was transferring his confidence from her to anyone else and that his "fondness for Venetia has never interfered and never could" with his relationship with Margot. Venetia, he wrote to Margot:

> . . . has *au fond* a fine character as well as great intelligence, and often does less than justice to herself (as over the Hospital business) by her minimising way of talking. She is even now trying to arrange for a fresh spell of what is to her not at all congenial work.
>
> I wish, with you, that Violet had rather more of the same sense of the futility of much of the life they have been leading.
>
> But to come back to the main point, *I never consciously* keep things from you & tell them to others.[48]

Honorable as he may have been, Asquith was not telling Margot the truth. He was indeed keeping things from her. He was not sharing with her the information and intimacy he was sharing with Venetia. Nor did he hint to her in any way the intensity of his love of and dependence on Venetia. He blamed his irritations and curtness to Margot on the terrible and "perpetual strain" under which he had been living for the past three years and reassured her that "it has not been due to want of confidence and love."[49] It is at least as likely that the strain he was under and his curtness and irritability to Margot were caused by his guilt over Venetia as by the problems of the war. Such a relationship could not but affect the quality of his marriage. In her letter to Montagu, Margot communicated that she clearly sensed this but did not know how to handle it.

In fairness to Asquith, it may have been that in spite of his passion for Venetia he did continue to love Margot. Men in positions of power, faced with extraordinary pressures, seem especially prone to such relationships. Gladstone once said that he had known eleven Prime Ministers and seven of them had been adulterers.[50] Whatever may have been the case of the Prime Ministers cited by Gladstone,

Asquith's conduct caused Margot the most intense pain and embarrassment, especially when his relationship with Venetia had become by March 1915 an open secret in London society. "Everyone was gossiping about it," according to Adelaide Stanley Lubbock, Venetia's niece. Venetia's mother was deeply distressed too, but "had no influence over Venetia—indeed, she was rather afraid of her daughter. She was subjected to scenes from Margot who railed at her for not putting a stop to Venetia's affair with her husband.[51]

Lady Sheffield never could control Venetia. As early as November 15, 1914, in desperation, she wrote to her sister, Blanche, for advice but received no help. Her sister believed there was no way she could stop Venetia's relationship with Asquith which she believed was probably only "a delightful friendship."

I feel distressed that you should have had such an upsetting episode with Margot and it is difficult to know how to take such violent outbursts which I fear *are* caused by jealousy of the P.M. and also largely by wounded vanity and humiliation at not being able to retain the position and influence she once had. She will *never* know any peace of mind, I am sure, until . . . perhaps, our V. is married.

I don't think it is possible for you to do anything as regards V.'s friendship for the P.M., even if it causes you anxiety. The only thing which could do any good would be that V. should realize that her friendship for the P.M. was the source of annoyance and unhappiness to Margot —when I believe her generosity and large nature would induce her to avoid giving Margot pain and distress by being less intimate and seeing less of the P.M.—though it would no doubt be very difficult now to break off what is, after all, a very delightful friendship. . . . As for the dear old P.M. you will never get him to see things from your point of view, I am certain. And there is always rather a fear of putting oneself in the wrong by any suggestions (however delicately thrown out) that you don't quite approve of his friendship for her. . . . I always feel that V. is very safe, which is the main thing, as it is her cleverness and intellectual side that is involved much more than her affections, though no doubt she is very fond of P.M.—But you don't think there are any signs of her being too fond of him, do you?[52]

Lady Sheffield's sister's analysis that Venetia enjoyed and was flattered by Asquith's attentions but that she was not in love with him seemed to be accurate. This did not make Margot feel any less threatened nor did it make the gossip more palatable to her. Asquith's feelings had by now become obsessive. He fretted when

Venetia's letters came late;[53] he continued to write letters to her during Cabinet meetings, so she could receive them "before the last post"[54]; he kept her letters under his pillow, reading them over and over again;[55] he worried constantly about the unpleasantness she faced in the Hospital, more concerned about her "hands and health" than the condition of the soldiers to whom she ministered;[56] he envied Montagu the "innumerable little opportunities he seems to find or make for seeing you"[57] and bemoaned the fact that Montagu was spending weekends at Alderley.[58] Asquith's vision of Venetia had become increasingly idealized. "My darling," he wrote, "you have just left me and I feel very desolate. You were (as you always are) your real self to-day: sweet, resolute, undeceiving. I know no woman . . . who could be in any comparable degree all three things at once."[59]

Such an inaccurate picture of Venetia prompted one writer to suggest that Asquith was not in love "with a woman but with an idealized *feeling* of love."[60] Asquith even excused and minimized Venetia's indifference to morality as a touchstone of behavior, something he would never excuse in others. He wrote as part of a portrait of Venetia:

It was characteristic of her [Venetia's] tendency to minimise moral dimensions, where she herself was concerned, that even when she took up unpalatable tasks (like hospital nursing), she quite sincerely disclaimed the imputation of "high-mindedness." She attributed her action not to unselfishness, or a sense of duty, or a desire to relieve suffering, but to the joint operation of two purely self-regarding motives: the one positive and the other negative. The positive motive . . . was her calculation that she would emerge, after three months of drudgery, with a whetted appetite and zest for the pleasures of the world. The negative motion was that, during the three months, she would at any rate escape the more tiresome routine of daily life under war conditions in a country house. . . . There is a want of proportion, and therefore of accuracy, in minimising, just as there is in exaggerating: . . . Self-deception takes a thousand different forms: with most people it tends to make them idealize their own motives and conduct; with her it moved in the exactly opposite direction.

Nor was this attitude of hers towards herself due in any way to a cynical temper. She had a rich capacity for admiration, was intensely ambitious for her friends, and was beyond measure rejoiced at any recognition by the world of the qualities and faculties in them.[61]

In this letter he confessed to Venetia that for the preceding two years he "lived *literally* every day" in her company, "sharing with you things great & small, big political issues, little social gossip, stories & jokes & odd bits of poetry or biography. . . . The most ideal comradeship that a man 'immersed,' as they say in affairs, ever had with a woman since the foundation of things. And from being first a luxury, then a recurring pleasure, it has become to me . . . a necessity. I cannot imagine a day passing in wh. I would not tell you my doings & my thoughts & my hopes and fears; with the certainty of sympathy & understanding & response, the wisest counsel, the most tender & unselfish help." An *"unspeakable blankness—"* he wrote, *"the tragic pall of black unrelieved midnight darkness,"*[62] would come over him if she left (emphasis added).

By March 1915, Margot was not the only one becoming uncomfortable with Asquith's behavior. Montagu, too, was finding the triangle untenable. Venetia had shown him some of Asquith's letters and he realized that the situation had gotten out of hand. He felt that Venetia could not let the situation continue and must tell Asquith that she was now seriously considering marrying Montagu. Although he did not know precisely how she could end it without hurting Asquith, he was not prepared to be part of a relationship in which Venetia's attentions were so divided. He wanted Asquith to have "fun" and enjoy himself with Venetia but, as he asked Venetia, "can a lover who means business put up with it?"[63] He urged Venetia to break off with Asquith for he saw the relationship as "unsatisfactory for Venetia" and for Asquith, for whom such a relationship could only "cause an absorption and possible loss of grip eventually. . . . I love him"; he added, "I have every reason to; but I believe I write in his interests."[64]

Early in April, Asquith seemed again in need of special reassurances from Venetia of her love and asked unabashedly for it. She apparently said or did whatever was needed to give it to him, for on April 4 he wrote that she never was "more sweet" or "sincere!"[65] She may have been sweet, but "sincere" does not describe her dealings with Asquith. On April 13, nine days after she had assured Asquith of her love, she wrote to Montagu: "Don't fail me on Friday. I want you very much . . . write to me one line to say you still love me. Can you? Love, Venetia."[66]

She confessed to Montagu that she was distraught about Asquith. "I . . . know that this Sunday has made it very difficult for me to go on writing to the P.M. as tho nothing had happened. Darling, what am I to do."[67] She was prepared, she explained, "to carry on as I've been doing," not believing there were any hard and fast rules "of right and wrong." And since she did not feel "what people call duty towards themselves," "the simplest plan" would be to carry on as before.[68] She was clearly upset, confiding to her sister, Sylvia Henley, that the relationship with Asquith had become too difficult for her to control. At first it had been fun, but now it was a burden. Montagu's pressing for marriage did not help. Not even Venetia could continue to juggle two relationships of such intensity.

One way to escape was to put some distance between herself and her pursuers and she decided, therefore, to accept an assignment in a hospital in France. This did not stop the pressure. Not knowing what to do, she asked Montagu, "why can't I marry you and yet go on making him happy?" But she concluded, "neither of you think that fun and I suppose my suggesting it shows how peculiar I am emotionally. I am so perplexed and wretched. . . . Go on loving me and above all make me love you."[69]

Her desire to maintain her relationship with Asquith and "make him happy" after her contemplated marriage to Montagu was, to use Venetia's own description, "peculiar" (or, as Katharine Asquith described Venetia, "queer").[70] It was one thing for Venetia to enjoy the triangle when she was single, but quite another to suggest a threesome after marriage. Venetia herself tried to explain it by acknowledging that she was a cold and detached person with a "thin and meager" supply of emotion, "completely cold-blooded," making it possible for her to accept love without emotionally reciprocating. "Please darling," she wrote to Montagu on April 30:

. . . don't be too ready at once to think that because I don't see you every day and can contemplate going to Boulogne that I don't any longer like you. I told you over and over again that I'm no fun to be in love with, that my supply of emotion is a thin and meager one. . . . And you mustn't always be examining it under a microscope . . . because it won't last.

We can have fun together and I'm sure could be so really happy and if that can't be made a good basis for marriage I don't know that I shall ever find a better. . . . I'm completely cold-blooded—detached from all interest in my own life. . . .

Katharine was quite right in telling you I was "queer." [71]

In this explanation of her inability to respond with the same passion and intensity Montagu felt for her, Venetia was as straightforward as she could be. Her love, she confessed, would be "thin and meager," but she believed that that need not preclude a life of fun and happiness.

It may be, as Raymond Asquith wrote, that Venetia had within her latent lesbian tendencies. Raymond expressed this in a letter to Diana Cooper on December 18, 1915, four months after Venetia and Montagu married. Raymond, although married to Katharine Horner, was in love with Diana and she with him. He wrote to her regularly from the trenches in France. "I had an obscure and scandalous letter . . . from Venetia," he wrote:

. . . from which I gather that you have been enjoying a nice glass of wine yourself lately; were you riotous at Ardley Square? I hope so. . . . Then Vinney [his nickname for Venetia] tells me also of what she calls *"a little Sapphic dinner"* where you and she alone made merry over an egg and a bottle of the Boy. There is something rather loathsome and lovely in the wedding of your whiteness and Vinney's blackness! Your pink and gold under the beetling menace of those raven locks, that insight and inexorable nose and Edwin across the road in Parliament complacently droning away about the Budget, the unconscious cuckold of a Virgin Goddess! Was it Alcephron once or Arisbe? Male ringlets or feminine gold? [72] (emphasis added)

If Raymond was correct, it would provide one explanation of Venetia's ability to remain so aloof and detached in her relationship with both Montagu and Asquith. She could flirt, pet, engage in foreplay and even consummate the sexual act and still feel no gratification, remaining emotionally uninvolved, "a surface of ice," as Asquith had described her. For that reason, she chose two men who agreed to be satisfied with a minimum of sexual activity. Asquith may well have been sexually satisfied by kissing, touching and the various levels of intimacy—short of actual consummation—which Venetia could provide. As for Montagu, although he desired Venetia sexually, there is no evidence in the written records of his life to show that sex was important to him. A man filled with such self-denigration and hatred was gratified with whatever crumbs Venetia cared to toss his way.

By the second week in April, Venetia was almost certain she would marry Montagu, although she had not yet told Asquith. With the tragedies of the war battering him daily, no time seemed appropriate. Montagu had suggested at first that Venetia gradually detach and free herself,[73] which he thought might make it easier for the Prime Minister. Venetia did not feel she could carry out such a plan; Asquith's feelings were so strong that this would not work.

Venetia then decided that she would tell him during the weekend that Montagu, Asquith and she were planning to spend together at Walmer Castle, April ninth to the eleventh, 1915. As the weekend unfolded, she could not bring herself to do it and developed, instead, a crushing headache and took to bed. Both men were upset and annoyed. A few days later, Asquith asked: "So you think that I was 'unsympathetic' with your afflictions last Sunday? Do you? And that all I cared about was being deprived of the selfish pleasure of companionship? I know you don't mean it. I was really *very* anxious about you; it seemed such an unnatural kind of temporary paralysis."[74] Montagu's reaction, which he wrote the night Venetia became ill, was one of utter frustration. "Glowing with happiness at staying with you it has resulted in my being like a caged beast raging up and down at a delectable being separated by the bars of a cage. . . . Yrs. separated, yearning, anxious E. S. Montagu."[75]

He and Venetia quarreled after the weekend. Venetia wrote, "[W]e mustn't quarrel, but you were bloody to me."[76] Montagu asked forgiveness, not quite sure what he had said to upset her. "All I know," he wrote, "is that you hardly spoke" and "carefully arranged [the evening so that] I could not possibly drive you home (as I had hoped to do) . . . and went off with hardly a goodnight."[77] The following day, after a wakeful night, he concluded that while he never loved her more, the proposed marriage "is bound to fail: we had better agree to abandon it." By the end of the letter he thinks the better of this, suggesting they should still try it. And yet, "he confessed, I fear."[78]

As for Asquith, the weekend at Walmer Castle may have been a fiasco but it did not cool his ardor. He continued his barrage of letters, mixing expressions of the deepest love and need with gossip and war secrets. On April 14, regretting his inability to spend the weekend with her at Alderley, he sent her—*"to keep secret or destroy"*—a letter he received from Kitchener after Kitchener had interviewed General French. Kitchener had written that *The Times* had lied, that the lack of ammunition was not holding back our army. "Of course," Asquith warned Venetia, "you won't breathe a word of it."[79]

Asquith also wrote that he and Crewe had met to discuss the next Viceroy and "had again, with many sighs of sympathy & regret, to pass over Mr. Wu."[80] By any objective standard, Asquith should not have dismissed Montagu as a potential candidate for Viceroy. While the Tories and the Indian Civil Service would have objected to his appointment, Montagu's attitudes on most Indian issues were no different from Asquith's. His competence, moreover, was never in question and his relationship with many of the Indian Princes was excellent.

Montagu was doubtless correct in believing that his religion was a key factor. It certainly was a subject of discussion in the meetings Asquith held to consider his appointment. Margot Asquith recorded in her diary a conversation she had had with her husband about this.

H. Montagu thinks it is entirely because he is a Jew that he is not going (I told H. how Montagu had in confiding his ambition to be Vice Roy of India to me more or less asked me what I thought—I had never talked to Henry on the matter tho I knew from the gossips Violet & Venetia that he wanted it. I told him I didn't think it wd. be possible as he was a Jew—he took it very well as he always does anything I say to him—I love Mr. Montagu—he has never given me away & he is the only person in the whole world that I have ever mentioned certain aspects of my life to!). . . . We've decided nothing about India.[81]

Montagu's religion came up again in a letter from Asquith to Venetia in December 1914: "Why should Beauchamp's High Churchism unfit him for Viceroy in India? Ripon was a full-blown Papist who took with him a father Confessor, and the whole bag of tricks. Do you think an 'Ebrew Jew' better qualified religiously than an Anglo-Catholic?"[82] Venetia's response has not survived, but one can be certain that her answer would be a resounding "yes," if she were seriously considering Montagu as her husband. The idea that she might be the Vicereine of India surely occurred to her.

Whether Montagu would make a good Viceroy concerned Venetia far less at this time than how she should tell the Prime Minister that she might marry Montagu. This she could delay no longer. She had tried several approaches but he had become so upset at the mere suggestion, always begging her not to leave him, that she retreated time and time again. Rather than breaking off the relationship she would instead reassure him of her love and all would be well, at least for the moment.

On the sixteenth day of April, Asquith reiterated his desire to be near her: "If only you were always near me," he wrote, "how much stronger & wiser I should be."[83] On the morning of the nineteenth, he wrote that he would rather have her in the audience to hear his speech at Newcastle than "any one of the 3 or 4 or 5000 who may be there."[84] On the evening of the nineteenth, he confessed that she had "(as no one else ever had or could have) 'the potentiality of making me wretched.' . . . But . . . you have given me . . . ," he wrote, "the supreme happiness of my life."[85] And on April 20, he wrote, "I will try and make my love for you more *unselfish,* and more worthy of you, my darling."[86]

Montagu's position by this time had become unbearable. He "simply can't face . . . hurting the P.M.," he wrote to Venetia. He also blamed himself "night and day for landing him [Asquith] in this munitions evil. In a way," Montagu continued, "that's his fault for ever trusting my judgement or giving me any position of responsibility. . . . I owe all to the P.M. I love him. I can't be guilty for my own happiness of hurting him."[87]

Montagu was referring to the inability of the Cabinet to formulate a plan to increase and control the manufacture of munitions. Montagu was Secretary of the Shell Committee that Asquith had created to solve the problem. The shell shortage had become not only a disaster for the army, but a daily weapon for the Tory press to use against Asquith. Montagu knew from the start that the use of a Committee to solve the problem was the wrong approach. From the outset of the war, he had offered alternative suggestions. He was not able to convince Asquith. Blaming himself for the failure of the Shell Committee was yet another example of his misplaced guilt and self-flagellation.

Unlike Montagu, Venetia was devoid of any sense of personal guilt. By the end of April 1915 she had made up her mind to marry

Montagu, although there were moments during which she was still plagued with doubt. She had convinced herself that breaking off with Asquith would not cause him too much grief since, as she saw it, "if it hadn't been me it would have been someone else or a series of others."[88] It was comments such as this that caused one writer to describe Venetia as superficial and a "heartless political adventuress who settled down comfortably with a Montagu fortune."[89] She candidly told Montagu that all of her family and friends would be "annoyed" at the marriage, but that their reactions would not deter her.[90]

And while her letters became increasingly loving to Montagu she continued to turn away from his kisses and advances. He in turn yearned for a lover "who surrenders herself to him body, mind and being." "Is it," he asked, "because you feel so little trusting that you turn your head in alarm each time I might take advantage of you?" "Don't you trust me?" "The only explanation you give me is personal distaste. Or is it that you are not giving me your all?"[91] He urged her to explain and be as honest with him as he had been with her.

While one may admire Venetia's honesty one is still taken aback by her openness in telling Montagu that she turned from his embrace from "personal distaste." Raymond Asquith's comments about Venetia's potential lesbianism raise the question of whether it was personal distaste for Montagu or for sex with any man. Venetia's later sexual liaisons with Eric Dudley and with Lord Beaverbrook make it more likely that while she may have been a cold woman with some latent lesbian tendencies, when the "right" man came along, she was prepared for and enjoyed sexual relationships. Montagu was not such a man and her letters confirm that she did not desire sex with him.

Later, she and Montagu discussed the question in detail and she agreed to have some relationship with him whenever she chose, while retaining her right to have sex outside the marriage. This was satisfactory to Montagu, and finally, on April 28, 1915, they made a firm commitment to marry. The following day, Montagu wrote ecstatically to the "most desperately beloved of all women. . . . Yesterday was the greatest day of my life. Its net result was that the most wonderful woman in the world delivered herself into my safekeeping, into my hands for better or worse, in the hope that with me she could lead a happier life than was possible without me, or with any other man."[92]

The letter was filled with Montagu's love. "I am in earnest more than I can say in promising that despite all my gloomy warnings and safeguardings I will do my best—I will try to alter lifelong and crusted habits and adopt all your suggestions to fashion myself into the husband of your desire. . . . Such a love my darling you have. I never thought I had in me to give so much. I have. Every moment that goes by convinces me more of that. Sometimes in the past I have had doubts, based on desire for other women's company, on vacillation, or fears for the future generally. One by one they go and I want no higher task, no more satisfactory mission than to give you the fun you sometimes pursue."

Montagu told Venetia that he wanted her to become a Jew and that the process was a simple, meaningless one:

Just as a woman who marries a Frenchman becomes a Frenchwoman, but in this case you become naturalized before. As to the religion, it seems always to me the easiest of religions and makes no demands of me save a very rare visit to synagogues and Passover at my mother's (do you remember how amused you would be at that!!) You have no use for formulated religion, nor have I, still less for ceremonial masquerading as religion.

Montagu continued:

As regards our children, I have always believed that no religious teaching was the right thing and I mean to stick to that. If they want to know they shall be told that their father was born a Jew and remained throughout life a Jew—that their mother was a Jew by adoption and they are therefore born Jews. If you want a religion to practice, although you and I practice none, they can choose their own.

You are right in saying that they are likely to have more non-Jewish than Jewish friends and therefore they are likely to care nothing about their label. *If they want to marry Xians or Hindus they will have no criticism from me, nor shall I think any the worse of them for wanting to. But if they choose to stick to the flag (which I do not think likely because I would regard [it as] unloving to try and influence them in any way) I shall be pleased. That's all, and it's a feeling that I shall never express again, which I confess to you and which is of no importance because it leads to no positive and indeed no negative action.*

I never think of myself as one. It's a thought which does not intrude. You won't find it will. But all I ask is that when we are attacked or scorned, that you regard yourself as one of us by adoption, that you have thrown in your lot with us, and that honestly is the only time I find one ever thinks about it at all. If people never thought of us as Jews, Jews like myself would forget all about it. You don't think of yourself as black-haired. You would think of yourself as red-haired by adoption if you dyed your hair red.

This is really all. If you can do this I shall be more than satisfied.

Will you take my advice? It is this. Think of the fun we shall have together, think of our lives from happiness to happiness, think of the things we can do together, I think of the possible great happiness of the children we have so often discussed, think of having a wonderful life.

Venetia darling, I want you tonight, always. Come to me soon. I agree about money. Let them say what they like. We won't increase our difficulties by poverty. Just dismiss the matter by saying to me "I will go through with it and do it." I can't part with you for my abstract morality. "Whatever happens" has made me miserable. Don't say this again. (emphasis added)

This is the letter of a man deeply and passionately in love, an unattractive man who after almost five years finally wins his beautiful princess. His joy knew no bounds. All the obstacles that their marriage might face were brushed aside. Even her conversion to Judaism became, in his mind, "painless and meaningless," only a minor hurdle that could easily be crossed. On the other side awaited only happiness and fun.

And so in April 1915, Venetia finally said yes to Montagu. She had not yet told Asquith, and the stage was now set for the personal and political crisis the Prime Minister would face in May. As his relationship with Venetia began to deteriorate, so too did his political fortunes.

16

Venetia Announces Engagement to Montagu; Asquith Forms Coalition Government, May 1915

The poor Prime Minister is absolutely broken-hearted; that it is stimying all public troubles. Perhaps, if truth were known it is really the cause of the Coalition.

Cynthia Asquith, Diaries, 1915–1918

As the stalemate continued in France, criticism of Asquith as a war leader became more vocal and angry. Now the very traits that had won him accolades and admiration as Prime Minister for seven years were described as a danger to a nation at war. His calm and deliberate style, his willingness to hear both sides and take time to make decisions—these attributes, his critics claimed, did not project an image of a tough, decisive warrior who could mobilize a nation for victory. All the skills that made him a master of parliamentary maneuvers were the traits most derided when disaster followed disaster on land and at sea.

Asquith's need to escape from the pressure of political office in trips to the country in the company of lovely women, in bridge and lighthearted conversation, in social weekends, and dinner parties— all of the diversions that had been tolerated in peacetime added to the image of a man too frivolous to be the leader of a country now caught in a life-and-death struggle. That Asquith could not lead in war was not just the conclusion of the hostile Tory press; by 1915 it had become the opinion of many of his own colleagues and friends as well. The calm and deliberate Asquith style that had been strong enough to strip the House of Lords of its power only two years before was now forgotten. Forgotten, too, was the Asquith style that had been powerful enough to lead a divided nation into war less than a year before, no easy task in the face of powerful opposition to the war, including strong opposition within Asquith's own Party.[1]

During all of the crises he faced in his seven years in office, his method had been no different than it had been at Oxford. He absorbed issues with extraordinary speed; he read and wrote with great skill and dexterity; his scholarship was extraordinary, his concentration intense; and his ability to cut through an issue and get to its heart was always amazing, even to colleagues who had worked with him for decades. But such enormous concentration always required a safety valve to relieve the pressure. The weekends in the country, the flirtations, the parties and alcohol seemed to be an important component in his ability to maintain his style of work. It is not likely that he could have carried the heavy burden of office for as long as he did without them. The added pressure of the war exacerbated his need to escape and thus added to the ammunition his enemies were now accumulating against him.

As 1915 dawned, someone had to be accountable for British losses on the battlefields, the bad intelligence, the incompetent military strategy, the thousands of men sent to France, in Churchill's vivid phrase, to "chew barbed wire in Flanders,"[2] and the casualties that were increasing daily. By February, sixteen thousand British soldiers had been killed, twenty thousand were prisoners, twenty-seven thousand were wounded and incapacitated, and forty-one thousand wounded and returned to action. On one day, February 10, 1915, it was recorded that Sir John French lost a hundred officers and two thousand men. The horror of war now hit the British with a "traumatic force, leaving bitterness and cynicism in its train."[3] Since Kitchener was still above reproach, the blame fell to the Prime Minister.

Yet it is not likely that by January 1915, or even in the six critical months that followed, Lloyd George or any other leader could have changed the military predicament in any significant way, or would have been prepared to solve the munitions problem, had it required dismissing Kitchener. Kitchener still had enough support throughout the country to temper the criticism against him. His dismissal, even after his administrative skills were found lacking, would have caused a nationwide outcry and would have added another divisive blow to the nation's shaky morale.

Nor was it personality that persuaded Asquith not to press for a compulsory draft in the face of the strong opposition of the Liberals, supported by Kitchener. Kitchener always believed that voluntary recruitment would provide all the soldiers he needed. Again, Asquith decided to be guided by Kitchener, although he recognized that a time might come when conscription would be needed. By January 1915, Kitchener had been able to mobilize almost one million soldiers from Britain alone, as well as four hundred fifty thousand from Ulster, Canada and the Naval Division. This seemed more than enough at the time. Here too, it is unlikely that a different personality would have made a different decision.

Although his decision on conscription may have been correct, it added to the image of Asquith as a weak leader, subordinate to Kitchener and reluctant to contradict the service chiefs on controversial military strategy—although the losses on the battlefields continued to mount in staggering numbers. Asquith's slowness in handling conscription, the shell shortage, his failure to solve the increasing tension and incompatibility that had developed between Lord Fisher and Winston Churchill, and his inability to control the generals and their resistance to new ideas and technical innovations were all used as examples of his inability to make hard and unpleasant decisions.

The Shell Shortage

The allegations of a shell shortage—and the image of British soldiers helplessly killed in their trenches for lack of ammunition—was an especially incendiary issue. It was one in which Montagu had a particular interest, from the earliest days of the war.

At the outset of the war, munitions came from two sources: the complex of state-owned munitions factories and a number of private firms sometimes called the War Office List companies. Procedurally, the supply of munitions to the Army involved a labyrinth of bureaucracy.[4] The system was cumbersome and not organized to meet the extraordinary demands of trench warfare. To make matters worse, the ordnance and military specialists never seemed to understand the kind of war in which they were involved or the need to improvise new methods to increase the speed with which the supply of munitions reached the front.

After only a month of war, Lloyd George requested that a Cabinet Committee be appointed to examine the "guns, shells, and rifles question." Kitchener strongly opposed; he resented civilians butting into military matters. Lloyd George was not one to be put off and continued to press for such a committee.

Montagu Urges Two Secretaries of War

At the beginning of October 1914, Montagu began to press Asquith for some action to cope with this problem. He urged that the responsibilities of the Secretary of War be divided into two Cabinet positions: "Call them, if you like," he wrote Asquith, " 'The Military Secretary of State for War' and 'the Civil Secretary of State for War.' "

I think they must both be in the Cabinet or otherwise there will be no way of keeping the watch necessary by the one on what the other does. The suggestion as to the way it would work is, Lord Kitchener would want 30 guns, 500 blankets, 10,000 men—or whatever the military needs of the War require; he would have the whole control of policy, and the disposition of troops, but the recruiting of his men, the clothing of his men, the placing of his contracts should all be in the hands of the Civil Secretary of State; and I believe only by this means will you get somebody who realizes the organization necessary and sets the machinery at work to obtain it.[5]

Montagu warned Asquith that he was "running into a most awful morass with regard to the War Office." Normally, it had to deal with approximately forty thousand soldiers; it now needed to "create, to arm, to maintain an Army of 2 million roughly speaking." It was not qualified to do this task. Part of the fault was Kitchener's, who did not know "how to persuade people to work for him; he and the soldiers whom he preferred to civilians did not know how to cajole recruits or to treat decently offers of help."

Everybody is getting in turn disgusted with the Office [Montagu wrote] and I cannot help think that very large problems are never dealt with at all by the War Office because they never occur to the plain, simple hero who is at the helm. He believes that if he bangs the table and asks for anything from a blanket to a howitzer, it can be materialized out of thin air.[6]

But even if Kitchener had been an "educated politician," Montagu continued, there was just too much work at the War Office for one man to supervise. It had to be divided into two Secretaryships. He suggested that perhaps Runciman, McKenna or Harcourt could become the new Civilian Secretary of State for War. "Everywhere one hears of shortcomings—recruiting, clothing, arming; and not only shortcoming but reversals of accepted decisions either of the Cabinet or of the Office itself. The Treasury has completely lost financial control of the War Office."[7]

Kitchener Shell Committee Created

Asquith rejected Montagu's suggestion of two Secretaries of State, creating instead, as Lloyd George had suggested, a Shell Committee of the Cabinet consisting of Lloyd George, Churchill (Admiralty), Runciman (Trade), McKenna (Home Office), Lord Lucas (Agriculture), and Haldane (Lord Chancellor), with Kitchener as Chairman. It was called the Kitchener Committee. It met only six times before it was disbanded in January 1915, largely because of Kitchener's hostility to civilians interfering in what he viewed as a military matter. The Committee's most important achievement was revealing the inadequacies of the Ordnance Department, which helped convince Asquith and the Cabinet that something drastic had to be done. The industrial capacity of the entire nation had to be harnessed if the Army was to be provided with the munitions and arms it needed.

Even before this Committee was disbanded it was clear that it could not do the job. It was then suggested to Asquith that he put a civilian, perhaps a businessman, in the War Office to supervise procurement and contracts. Montagu disagreed, writing to Asquith early in December 1914 that "nothing is to be gained by putting a civilian in the War Office to look after Kitchener," since he would pay no attention to a civilian. "It is a ministerial responsibility and only a minister can do the job."[8] Enclosed with that letter was a memorandum to Asquith which stated that the organization of the War Office is "wholly insufficient" with Kitchener's popularity shielding "the War Office from criticism." Its staff saw itself as "above reproach." They "do not know or understand politics, recruitment or purchasing at home or abroad." Unless they did, he warned, the supply of munitions would continue to fall short of need. The overlapping of functions in the War Office, Montagu wrote, its ignorance of finance and its distrust of civilians were additional problems. "This is particularly so," because the cast of mind of the staff in the War Office "is of the Civil Service type, which is rather inclined to leave things as they are and to resist the disturbances of existing machinery or of the application of invention, resource and increasing effort in order to find new and more expeditious methods."[9] Montagu was always a critic of the "civil service mentality"—at home and in India. While he respected the diligence and commitment of members of the Civil Service, he decried their lack of imagination and innovation, and their reluctance to ever threaten the status quo.

Three months later Asquith recognized that the armaments problem was still a major concern: "So far as things at home are concerned, the thorniest question" the government faced, he wrote to Venetia, was "to get more labour & plant for making armaments & other things needed for war. I think we shall have to 'take over' the principal firms, leaving the management in its present hands, but keeping the whole business, especially the division of profits during the war, the distribution of work & labour, and the wages paid to the workmen, under Government supervision."[10] Asquith conceded: "We shall want a special Minister to look after it, if this is done, & I incline to the Assyrian." Asquith told Venetia that Montagu had sent him that morning "an excellent mem. on the subject . . . a letter of gigantic proportions wh. dealt with his own personal aspirations, the relative claims of colleagues, & other delicate matters of the same order."[11]

In his letter Montagu had described a scheme for an Army Contracts Directorate with a Minister in Charge to provide administrative machinery for the Shell Committee. By the middle of March Asquith had still taken no action concerning the munitions problem and the idea of a Special Minister, with perhaps Montagu in that role, seemed now to have been rejected. Instead, Asquith was considering relieving Lloyd George of his present duties and creating "a new office for Ll. George (Director of War Contracts' or something of the kind)."[12] But Lloyd George continued to refuse such a posi-

tion unless he were given power over Kitchener on munitions supply. Kitchener remained adamant in his opposition to such supervision.

During these discussions, Montagu sent Asquith what Lloyd
George called in his *Memoirs* "a very trenchant memorandum"[13] on
the subject. In describing Montagu, in relationship to that memorandum, Lloyd George called him "a man of exceptional insight and
grasp of realities"—the only favorable comment about Edwin in the
entire 2,045-page *Memoirs*. "This memorandum [by Montagu] is
worth reading as a contemporaneous statement of the difficulties
experienced in dealing with the War Office."[14]

Montagu's memorandum stated in no uncertain terms that Kitchener and the War Office were incapable of handling the production
and procurement of munitions and that any Committee structure
that left Kitchener responsible for this function was doomed to
failure.

It is not for me to suggest [Montagu wrote] any explanation of the War
Office's . . . continued, bigoted, prejudiced reluctance to buy rifles or to
increase the munitions of war, but that the solution of the suggestion above
is most unsatisfactory can be supported by the evidence that:—

1) Lord Kitchener, as he says, knows nothing about the problem.
2) Lord Kitchener is overworked.
3) Lord Kitchener admits that it would have been better to take the advice
   (and he did not take it) of the Committee in September.
4) Lord Kitchener views with complete complacency figures which *mean
   nothing* unless labour is obtained, looks with complete satisfaction at
   machinery provided at Government expense which is idle because there
   is no labour, and works quite happily at a maximum of 350,000 shells a
   month, a maximum not yet by any means in sight. If you assume that
   an Army Corps wants 100 guns and each gun wants 17 shells per day,
   that shows a requirement of 1,700 shells per day per army corps, or
   51,000 shells per army corps per month, which means that 350,000 will
   supply shells for seven Army Corps and we are talking of an Army of
   one million men.

On the other hand, Montagu continued, Asquith could appoint a
Committee that would not report to Kitchener and would have
complete responsibility for munitions "and take the blame for any
shortage of munitions of war from this time forward." Such a
Committee must have "not only existence but power." Montagu

recognized that Kitchener was adamantly opposed to such a Committee, but he concluded that "the situation is serious," that delay could be disastrous and that Asquith had "no alternative" but to create such a Committee, in spite of Kitchener's objections.[15]

Second Shell Committee: Lloyd George, Chairman; Montagu, Executive Secretary

Later in the month, Asquith, acting on Montagu's suggestion, created a new and more representative Munitions Committee with very broad powers. Lloyd George was made chairman. Writing to Venetia on March 22 following the meeting at which this decision was made, Asquith said: "I think we came to some rational (and unanimous) conclusion. But we may have some difficulties with K, and I am going to suggest to Ll. G. (who is to be Chairman of the new Committee) that he sh. take on the Assyrian as his curate."[16] Writing to Lloyd George, Asquith said, "I am disposed to think that (on the political side) in addition to yourself and A.J.B. [Balfour] you should have a financier."[17] Montagu was to be the "financier."

While Asquith is subject to criticism for his slowness in establishing this Committee, one must remember that he was faced by the constant threat of Kitchener's resignation if such a Committee were ever created. It took all of Asquith's power of persuasion to hold Kitchener in his post when the Committee was finally created on April 8, 1915, eight months after the war had begun. The Committee was given the power to: "take all steps necessary for the purpose of ensuring the promptest and most efficient application of all the available productive resources of the country to the manufacture and supply of munitions of war for the Navy and Army."[18]

There were many besides Kitchener, in and outside of the government, who were suspicious of the Committee's mandate. It was a clear break with the old tenets of laissez-faire to use whatever state power was necessary to get the needed munitions to the soldiers. It reflected the acceptance of the principle that "only the central organization of the nation's power and a commitment to state control of the nation's productive capacity could supply the tools needed for this war."[19] It thus became a principal contributor to the movement toward British collectivism, which has characterized British social and economic policy since 1914, and "thus has a special place in modern British history."[20]

When it was created, no one thought of the Committee's ultimate place in history. It was viewed as serving but one purpose: to increase the production of munitions for a distraught Army facing a growing threat of military defeat. Montagu acted as Executive Secretary of the Committee and, according to Lord Beaverbrook, "supplied much of the hard executive work which this Committee contributed to the problem set [before] it. Montagu's abilities were extraordinary."[21] Beaverbrook also wrote that the increase in the supply of shells, which did in fact appear in France during the late summer and autumn of 1915, was claimed by some to be the result of the work of this Committee.[22]

Beaverbrook, never one to be effusive, wrote after Montagu's death that Montagu "became the rising hope of liberalism, the visible successor of Lord Rosebery at almost too early an age for the hope of the morning to last into the afternoon. At 20 he had almost ceased to be young; at thirty he was middle aged; at 40 he already represented a maturity of judgement which accompanies real age." Beaverbrook characterized Montagu's intelligence as "unrivalled" and bemoaned the fact that "his early death was an irreparable loss to the State in this dreadful age of mediocrities."[23]

In spite of the fact that Lloyd George subsequently minimized Montagu's role on the Shell Committee,[24] he and Montagu worked closely and effectively. As he had demonstrated when he was Chancellor of the Exchequer, Lloyd George was superb at painting with a broad brush. He needed someone with Montagu's administrative skill and concern with detail to carry forward his ideas. Both worked tirelessly on their new responsibilities but both soon came to the conclusion "that no Cabinet Committee, no matter how broad its charge, could ever overcome the munitions shortage."[25] Nothing short of a separate Ministry that would shake up the entire procurement structure as well as the War Office could work. And hard as they tried they could not satisfy the Tory press, which throughout April kept the rumors alive that munitions were dangerously low and were responsible for the staggering losses in France.

On April 14, the same day that the new Shell Committee was announced, Kitchener reported to Asquith that General French had told him the army had sufficient munitions for their next advance.[26]

On the strength of this assessment (which had been based on assurances by General French), Asquith delivered his now infamous Newcastle-upon-Tyne speech on April 20, in which he denied that there was a shell shortage. The Tory press was not convinced. They attacked the speech as yet another effort to lull the nation.

Beginning in May the Tory press increased its agitation still further, and on May 14, *The Times* carried a damaging story by Colonel Charles à Court Repington (a war correspondent for *The Times*) that the shortage of "high explosives was a fatal bar to our military success," concluding that the failure of British troops to pierce the German lines (at Fromelles and Richeberg) was due to these shortages.[27] Repington was given this information by French himself. The effect was disastrous and other newspapers soon joined in sharp criticism of Asquith and the Liberal government. Kitchener himself was now included in these attacks.

Lord Beaverbrook disagreed. In his analysis he puts the blame squarely at the door of General French and his staff, concluding that they not only gave Kitchener and Asquith the wrong information but should not have entered into offensive battle if they did not in fact have enough ammunition. "The commander who miscalculates," Beaverbrook states, "is surely to blame. . . . It is quite true that the Army had not enough ammunition, especially high explosives; it is by no means clear that the military authorities at the front were not as much responsible for this . . . as the War Office."[28]

Lloyd George, on reading Repington's story, which confirmed information French had sent him a few days earlier, wrote to Asquith that he could not continue as Chairman of the Shell Committee if critical information was being withheld by Kitchener. A new approach to the munitions problem had to be found—or the slaughter on the battlefield would continue.[29]

The Dardanelles

The same day, May 14, that the Repington story broke, Admiral Lord Fisher resigned to protest the actions of Churchill. The Fisher resignation was long in coming. While Churchill had been responsible for Fisher's appointment, there was little upon which the two men agreed. The clash of two such strong, almost megalomaniac personalities was virtually inevitable. The issue that precipitated the clash and ultimately led to Fisher's resignation was the Dardanelles expedition.

By the end of 1914, a divided Cabinet had been desperately searching for some alternative to the bloody stalemate in France. The "Easterners" wanted a new front in the Baltic or the Dardanelles, and the "Westerners" wanted more troops on the French front. Asquith was in the middle. He did not resist a new front but was not prepared to force the military leaders to lessen their support of the French front.

At the end of December 1914, Churchill had written to Asquith of Lord Fisher's scheme for forcing open the Baltic with the aid of Russian troops and of landing behind the German lines, ninety miles north of Berlin. Montagu and Lloyd George also sent New Year's Eve letters stressing the need for some victory to overcome the spreading sense of defeat. Lloyd George wanted to open a new offensive, preferably in Salonika. Montagu had no special plan but stressed the need for a victory to give the public a lift. "The future of the Government," Montagu wrote, "is at stake."[30]

Kitchener, depressed at the imminence of another German drive in France, suggested that an alternative theater might be found, such as the Dardanelles, which he thought "to be the most suitable objective, as an attack here could be made in co-operation with the Fleet. If successful, it would re-establish communications with Russia; settle the Near Eastern question; draw in Greece and, perhaps, Bulgaria and Rumania; and release wheat and shipping now locked up in the Black Sea."[31] Hankey agreed. Fisher was as skeptical as Churchill, since Kitchener waffled when questioned about sending troops and seemed to view this as a naval engagement "to force the Narrows and capture the Gallipoli Peninsula and Constantinople by a purely naval force."[32]

In the closing hours of 1914, after conferring with Hankey, Churchill had dropped his and Fisher's Baltic plan and agreed on the Dardanelles strategy, aware that Kitchener was not prepared to divert troops from France. Lloyd George also expressed the hope that the Army would not be required to pull the chestnuts from the fire for the Navy. Churchill himself, at this point, did not press for military support; he would have liked nothing better than a great naval victory. Fisher remained unconvinced. He preferred his Baltic plan. If the Dardanelles plan was to work at all he believed it would

need the support of the Army. As plans for the expedition progressed he became "increasingly apprehensive and sulky."[33] He did
not resign but often threatened to do so.

By this time, Asquith firmly supported the Dardanelles expedition but, as was his style, he did not order Kitchener to send the
needed troops. He tried instead to persuade Kitchener and not over-
rule him. It was not until March 12 that Kitchener finally ordered
the 29th Division under the command of Sir Ian Hamilton to the
Dardanelles.

In spite of this internal bickering the expedition had started out
well. By March 18 the fleet had carried out a major bombardment
and advanced to within a few miles of the Narrows. If troops had
been available for a major assault or if the Navy had renewed its
bombardment, the day might have been won. But the British Admiral de Robeck did not move forward. On March 22 he conferred
with the newly arrived Hamilton, who convinced him to wait until
the expeditionary force was ready to attack. Churchill tried to over-
rule de Robeck but was stopped by Fisher. This delay gave the
Turks the necessary time to fortify their position. As a result, when
they finally took place in April, the Gallipoli landings met the stiffest
opposition. The casualties were heavy.

Meanwhile, the fleet could do little except become a target for
U-boat torpedoes. Finally on May 12, at the price of Kitchener's
bitterness, the Navy decided to withdraw the flagship of the Dardanelles fleet, H.M.S. *Queen Elizabeth,* because of the U-boat threat.
Her withdrawal signaled the failure of the mission. Had there been
troops for a large-scale landing earlier in the expedition, or had the
Navy pushed ahead with its own attack earlier, the outcome might
have been different. As it was, the Dardanelles expedition was a
costly and humiliating failure. For Fisher it was a confirmation of
his hostility toward the Dardanelles strategy. Churchill believed its
failure was caused by Fisher's resistance to his order that de Robeck
move ahead and attack earlier in the campaign. Both men were at
loggerheads.

Finally, on May 14, Fisher resigned, making it clear that he could
not work with Churchill. After sending his resignation letter to
Churchill, Fisher told him he was leaving for Scotland. In fact, he
went into hiding at the Charing Cross Hotel, where Asquith tracked
him down and sent him a letter demanding, in the King's name,

that he come to 10 Downing Street to discuss the issue further. Fisher did return to speak with Asquith, but the Prime Minister failed in his effort to persuade him to remain. Under no conditions would he serve under Churchill or Balfour. Nor would he accept any civilian control for the war's duration. Kitchener's position as a Cabinet member had always rankled him. But the immediate target of his fury was Churchill, whom he and his Tory supporters now blamed for all the war's failures: the torpedoed cruisers, the fiasco at Antwerp, the dispatch of the untrained naval brigade, and now the Dardanelles. Fisher did not blame Kitchener, whose failure to send the troops to the area earlier had played a major role in the disaster. Nor did he blame de Robeck or Hamilton for misjudging the need for continued naval attack—before the Turks had a chance to fortify. To Fisher and the Tories, there was but one villain: Winston Churchill.

Fisher would not stay if Churchill remained. Nothing Asquith could say would change his mind. He would stay only if Churchill and the entire Board of the Admiralty were dismissed and he himself were put in complete control, without civilian oversight. These terms were unacceptable to Asquith.

Asquith Accepts Coalition

On May 17, to the surprise of many of his own colleagues, Asquith wrote to the King: "After much reflection & consultation today with Lloyd George and Bonar Law, I have come decidedly to the conclusion that, for the successful prosecution of the War, the Gov't. must be reconstructed on a broad and non-party basis."[34] A Coalition government was now to replace the Liberal Party's control of the war. The Tories' price for coming into the government was not only more representation in a Coalition Cabinet but Churchill's removal from the Admiralty and Haldane's from the government.

Few people challenged Haldane's competence as Lord Chief Chancellor or his long years of service to England. It is widely accepted that he was the victim of a libelous press campaign because of his enjoyment of German philosophy and culture and his generally pro-German sympathies. There is no evidence that once war was declared he was unpatriotic or did or said anything to indicate lack of support for his country.[35] This did not stop the attacks against him; he had to go.

Churchill was a different matter. His competence, unlike Haldane's, was seriously questioned. He was bitterly disliked by the Tories and also by many Liberals. He was too much of a "hawk" to be loved by the Liberal Party, who still viewed itself as a party of peace that unfortunately had found itself in a war. *The Times* reported on May 22, 1915, that Liberal Members of Parliament, "look[ing] upon Mr. Churchill as the author of all their party ills," were "petitioning their chiefs to exclude [him] from the new Ministry altogether."[36] W. M. R. Pringle, a lifelong friend of Asquith, warned him that:

a number of your supporters have been driven to the conclusion that the present crisis has been brought about by the actions of Mr. Churchill. I do not only refer to his differences with Lord Fisher but we believe he was privy to the intrigue which resulted in the Repington disclosures.

In these circumstances we regard his presence in the Government as a public danger.[37]

The Tories were even more hostile, agreeing with the *Morning Post* that Churchill's characteristics "make him in his present position a danger and an anxiety to the nation."[38]

Even members of the Cabinet began to have second thoughts about Churchill. Frances Stevenson wrote that after Fisher tendered his resignation Lloyd George said:

If Fisher's resignation is accepted, Churchill will have to go. He will be a ruined man. "It is the Nemesis," said C. to me, "of the man who has fought for this War for years. When the War came he saw in it the chance of glory for himself, & has accordingly entered on a risky campaign without caring a straw for the misery and hardship it would bring to thousands, in the hope that he would prove to be the outstanding man in this war."[39]

What Churchill's enemies forgot was that it was Kitchener and Hankey, not Churchill, who had originally suggested the Dardanelles operation; that Lloyd George approved it but saw it completely as a naval operation—a hope shared by Churchill; and that Asquith and the Cabinet had all accepted the plan. The only critic was Fisher. All such reasonable arguments were lost; Churchill had now become the scapegoat, responsible for everything that was going wrong in the war.

When the restructuring of the government took place, Asquith believed he had no choice. In spite of Churchill's pleas (and those of his wife), he was removed from the Admiralty. It had been the Tories' single most important condition for a Coalition.

Why Asquith Agreed to a Coalition

Historians still debate whether Churchill's quarrel with Fisher and the latter's resignation or the shell crisis was the principal cause of the formation of the Coalition government. Lord Beaverbrook argued persuasively that the conflict at the Admiralty and the Tory attack it would stimulate in the House of Commons, and not the shell shortage, caused the crisis. He argued that the Northcliff attacks in *The Times* against the government for failure to supply enough munitions to the soldiers at the front began in earnest only after the Coalition was formed, although the Repington story in *The Times* appeared on the same day as Fisher resigned. The Northcliffe attacks, according to Beaverbrook, did not bring the Government down; rather they made certain that a new Ministry of Munitions would be formed with Lloyd George at its head.[40]

Others disagree, placing greater, or at least equal importance on the shell shortage. Koss maintained that a debate on munitions would have caused a serious crisis for the government, while a debate on the Admiralty "would have been a relatively harmless diversion." The crisis between Fisher and Churchill he believed "became a smokescreen which historians as well as contemporaries have mistaken for the real conflagration."[41]

But storms are seldom the result of a single cause. The formation of the Coalition was no exception. It had several causes: the shell shortage, the Fisher resignation and a nation's frustration and grief at the loss of hundreds of thousands of its young men in a war that seemed to be going from bad to worse.

There was another factor that played an equally important role: Asquith's reaction to the engagement of Venetia to Edwin. While many problems set the stage for the Coalition, it was Asquith's personal problem that tipped the scale. The shell shortage, the resignation of Fisher and even the military losses would have been unlikely individually to have led Asquith to acquiesce so quickly to a Coalition government.

Asquith had handled equally difficult problems before. After almost eight years as Prime Minister, often in turbulent times, he was well equipped to handle a Conservative attack in the House of Commons against the retention of Churchill and the resignation of Fisher. He was accustomed to criticism, and continued to take pride in his position as an arbiter between ideological camps and a skilled and proficient mediator. In the past, he had mended rifts between Lloyd George and Kitchener, Kitchener and Churchill, Fisher and Churchill, and Lloyd George and McKenna, among many others.

He had good arguments that would justify his letting Fisher go. Fisher had now taken the position that he would not continue as First Sea Lord if any civilians were to be his superiors. This attitude would not have sat well with the House of Commons, which guarded zealously its own prerogatives and the concept of civilian oversight. In fact, Asquith had earlier decided to support Churchill and had agreed to the creation of a new Admiralty Board with Sir Arthur Wilson as its head; he planned to announce this to the House of Commons early in May.

Neither the Conservatives nor the Liberals were eager for a Coalition. Many Conservatives would have preferred to continue to be critical of the government from the backbench rather than join in the administration of a war whose outcome no one could predict. Nor was the prospect of having a few Tories in the Cabinet enough to make them eager to pull Asquith's chestnuts from the fire. From their point of view, it would have been better to have the Liberal government fall and have a Conservative government back in power with full responsibility for the war than to share the responsibility of a Coalition.

The Liberals were equally hostile to the idea of a Coalition. "The party was profoundly shaken in May 1915 by his [Asquith's] decision, at Conservative insistence, to form a coalition ministry; it required a twenty-minute exhortation from him [Asquith] to dissuade a meeting of over a hundred liberal M.P.s from passing a resolution hostile to the change."[42] Liberals were also unhappy to see a change in government that they believed was in part attributable to the yellow journalism and rabble-rousing tactics of the Tory press. Many Liberals, moreover, could see no connection between the Admiralty crisis and the decision to reconstruct the government. "Why the fact that Winston quarrelled with Fisher should mean your giving up the L[ocal] G[overnment] B[oard]," Masterman wrote to Samuel on May 26, "is a *non sequitur* which today and tomorrow will find difficult to understand."[43]

As for the attack against him over the shell crisis and his Newcastle speech, Asquith could have explained that his speech and the munitions information on which it was based came from Kitchener and that he had been "the victim, . . . the unwitting perpetrator of a gross deception."[44] The Tories would not have wanted that kind of attack against Kitchener, or General French, debated publicly. In a letter to Venetia in February, Asquith himself had been strong in his criticism of a Coalition government. As recently as May 12, 1915 (five days before he wrote to the King informing him of the formation of the Coalition), on being asked whether "he will consider the desirability of admitting into the ranks of the Ministers leading members of the various political parties in this House," Asquith had answered unequivocally that such an arrangement "was not in contemplation."[45]

What happened to make Asquith change his mind after expressing such hostility to coalition? What happened to him during this period that made him begin to appear to his colleagues as "a shattered man"? Why did he agree so quickly to a Coalition that would require him to dismiss Haldane and Churchill, two men he genuinely admired, and to admit into his Cabinet representatives of Tories he disliked so intensely? Why did he not follow his usual "wait and see" tactic? What had happened to his slow, deliberate style of decision making?

It is neither "outrageously melodramatic"[46] nor a position insufficiently supported by evidence,[47] as some have claimed, to conclude that the answer to these questions lay in Venetia's announcement of marriage. Nor is it melodramatic to assert that he was "reeling under the impact of 'a stunning personal blow.' "[48] All through April and during the first two weeks of May, he was worried and anxious about Venetia, sufficiently so that some of his colleagues observed that he seemed less efficient than normal.[49] The announcement of Venetia's marriage plans came as the final blow and led him to take the path of least resistance, listlessly agreeing to the formation of a Coalition.

Asquith received word of Venetia's engagement on Wednesday, May 12. On the same day he wrote to her:

Most Loved
> As you know well *this* breaks my heart.
> I couldn't bear to come and see you.
> I can only pray God to bless you—and help me. Yours.[50]

This was only five days after he had written to Venetia on Friday, May 7, after one of their "heavenly drives" that only she or an act of God could get rid of him as Prime Minister, not the Tory press.

I will undertake to say that, in the hundred or more of our drives, there has never been a greater interchange of 'Fun,' in the best & widest sense, than has even happened in our time, or perhaps my time, between any man and any woman. (This will rather amuse you: George Moore, French's friend said to Margot (apropos of *The Times* attacks): "Northcliffe thinks he can get rid of the P.M.: there is only one person who can do that." M: "Who?" Moore: "God.") Very simple isn't it, darling? *Whoever possesses that power, can exercise it effectively & without a moment's delay, when any veil is dropped between me & you—soul of my life.*[51] (emphasis added)

At that time Venetia must have been trying to hint to him of her forthcoming engagement—but to no avail. His letter continues:

Whatever the future has in store for you in the way of companionship and intimacy (with some undisclosed person, whom in advance I loathe more than words can say) I shall be ready at the day of judgment to mention that I had the best of it! "Poor darling" (I almost hear you say) "he has for once, at any rate, rather a swollen head."
Perhaps: but my conviction is unshaken & unshakable. "For the time being"—you said to-day. God knows how long or how short a time that means. Long or short, it measures out the supreme and crowning happiness of my life. The rest will be silence.[52]

Only two days before receiving her May 12 announcement, Asquith had written: "I walked back with the Assyrian from Mansfield St. and we had (as always) good conversation. I don't honestly believe that, at this moment, there are 2 persons in the world (of opposite sexes) from whom I cd. more confidently count, whatever troubles or trials I had to encounter, for whole-hearted love & devotion than you & he: of course, in quite different ways & senses."[53]
One can only imagine the shock to Asquith of learning that these two whom he loved so much had, in a sense, deceived him and that the woman he loved was to marry—not any man, but his dear

friend and confidant whom he believed he could count on for "whole-hearted love and devotion."

Even under normal circumstances, most men would find such a revelation traumatic. For Asquith, to whom Venetia had become not only the object of the deepest and most idealized love but an important escape from excruciating pressures, the news was shattering. He had told her several months earlier that if she ever left him, "the tragic pall of black unrelieved midnight darkness"[54] would descend upon him. Now that the dreaded separation did occur he was thrown into the depths of despair. He was dealt, in his own words, "a death-blow"[55] and felt "as tho' the world stood still; and . . . everything was upside down; and that all values had lost their meaning."[56]

The fact that it was Montagu, whom he never took seriously as a romantic rival, a Jew of ungainly appearance, whom he described to Venetia's sister Sylvia Henley on May 12, the same day he received Venetia's announcement, as "not a *man*—a bundle of moods & nerves & symptoms"[57] made the news especially shattering.

I don't believe there are two living people, who, each in their separate ways, are more devoted to me than she and Montagu [Asquith wrote to Mrs. Henley]: and it is the irony of fortune that they two shd. combine to deal a death-blow to me. . . .

But (I say again) *this!*

It is not merely the prohibitive physical side (bad as that is)—I won't say anything about race & religion, tho' they are not quite negligible factors. But he is not a *man:* a bundle of moods & nerves & symptoms, intensely self-absorbed, and—but I won't go on with the dismal catalogue. . . . She (Venetia) says at the end of a sadly meagre letter today, "I can't help feeling, after all the joy you've given me, that mine is a very *treacherous* return."

Poor darling! I wouldn't have put it like that. But in essence it is true: and it leaves me sore and humiliated.[58]

As he told Venetia on May 14, it was "too terrible. No hell can be so bad."[59]

As stated earlier, even before receiving news of Venetia's engagement, Asquith lived in dread of losing her. Dr. Brock reports that as a result of this there developed, during April and early May "a notion in governmental circles" "that something must have lessened his [Asquith's] capacity to grapple with problems."[60] Brock dismissed the idea that Asquith was physically ill at this time, but conceded that "his personal worries may have given some of those close to the Government an impression of impaired performance for which a bout of ill health seemed the only explanation."[61]

Throughout the period when he [Asquith] was in dread of losing Venetia he was thus faced also with acute governmental difficulties. His friendship with her seems up to this point to have enhanced his efficiency. Now he had to envisage the withdrawal of the prop on which he had come to depend.[62]

"Though the Prime Minister's private anxieties may have produced some such effect," Brock continues, "it would be absurd to regard them as the chief cause of the Government's weakness."[63]

It is not suggested here that Asquith's personal problems were the chief cause of the Government's "weakness" or of his decision to form a coalition. Rather, it is suggested that his personal problems seriously influenced the way he handled these problems. He did not bring to this crisis his usual deliberation and caution. He acted out of character and with haste, sufficient for Churchill to subsequently criticize him "for not allowing a few days' delay."[64] It is not "absurd" to believe that he was vulnerable, apprehensive and distracted.

The Koss biography of Asquith gives even less credence than does Brock to the idea that the crisis with Venetia played a critical role in Asquith's decision to form the Coalition. After calling this conclusion "outrageously melodramatic," he wrote that Asquith could always divide his public and private life sufficiently "into separate compartments, which were never permitted to impinge on each other."[65] While the separation of the public and private man could often take place on the surface, it is rare that such separation can hold in matters of deep emotional impact.

Koss's description of Venetia as just another friend with whom Asquith corresponded ignores the intensity of Asquith's feelings, which were not the same as his feelings for his other female correspondents. The five hundred letters he wrote to Venetia clearly reveal a deep attachment, quite different from any he had with other women. While the three hundred and more letters he wrote to Sylvia Henley after Venetia's marriage also expressed his love for her and his compulsive need to convey his thoughts to an attractive female correspondent, they did not contain the obsessive infatuation and idealized adoration that filled his letters to Venetia.

Jenkins, another of Asquith's biographers, unlike Koss, acknowledged to some degree the impact of Venetia's announcement of marriage on Asquith's behavior during the crisis, writing that Venetia's support of Asquith "collapsed at a time when he was in particular need of it."[66] He suggests that the speed with which Asquith rushed to accept the Coalition was unusual and out of character as was his (Asquith's) dismissal of Churchill and Haldane. If he waited a few days, moreover, there was a good chance that Italy would enter the war. (She did so on May 23.) Brock expressed some doubt about the validity of these conclusions, writing, "the evidence cited by Jenkins is not conclusive."[67]

Perhaps most historians are reluctant to believe that heartache caused by love can be blamed for decisions that change the course of history. "How outrageously melodramatic," Koss has written. William Manchester, on the other hand, in his biography of Winston Churchill accepted this "romantic" and "melodramatic" conclusion, believing that the marriage announcement drained Asquith's strength and destroyed his will to fight back. He wrote:

Asquith's emotional stability, unknown to his colleagues or even his family, had just been dealt a cruel blow. All these months he had been sustained by his love for Venetia Stanley. It was a sign of his dependence upon this sophisticated but shallow young woman that he had disclosed every state secret to her; indeed, it is arguable that she had become England's greatest security risk. And Venetia, unlike Lloyd George's Frances, was not constant. She had finally decided that the disparity between her age and Asquith's—thirty-five years—was too great. That Friday, May 14, she told him their relationship was over. She intended to marry Edwin Montagu, a future Cabinet minister. Only the week before he had written her, "You give me the life blood of all that I do, or can ever hope to do," and that if anyone wanted to destroy him, he could do it "effectively & without a moment's delay, when any veil is dropped between me and you—soul of my life."[68]

When Bonar Law confirmed Fisher's elopement and threatened a major debate in the House, Asquith refused to pick up the gauntlet. He lacked the strength. . . . Bonar Law proposed a Coalition and Asquith listlessly agreed.[69]

On May 17, in response to a second note from Venetia telling him how disturbed she was to hear nothing from him since her announcement on May 12, Asquith broke his silence by telling Venetia how miserable he was and how torn he was between his desire to see her and the heartbreak he knew this would cause him:

Darling your most revealing and heart-rending letter has just come. What am I to say? What can I say? I was able to keep silence for the two most miserable days of my life, and then it became unbearable; and like you I felt that it was cruel and unnatural, and that anything was better. So I scrawled my 2 or 3 agonised sentences, and thank God you once more speak to me and I to you.

When I think that, only a week ago, I should never have thought twice about what I was saying & writing to you, but put down every word & thought that came into my head, while now I dread lest, without knowing it, I may give you acute pain by anything I write—I am able to measure the distance wh. it has taken so short a time to travel.[70]

Should he see her? He was not sure.

How right you are when you say that one of the most hellish bits of these most hellish days was that you *alone* of all the world—to whom I have always gone in every moment of trial & trouble, & from whom I have always come back solaced and healed & inspired—were the one person who could do nothing, & from whom I could ask nothing. To my dying day, that will be the most bitter memory of my life. Don't think, darling, that I am reproaching you (that I *never will,* nor have I any reason): but you well understand.

Do you want to see me before you go on Thursday? Are you sure? I cannot make up my mind whether it would be wise and right for either of us: I tremble to think that in a moment of weakness I might strike a jarring note, or, from selfishness, be disloyal to my ideal of what I have tried to be, and shall always try to be, to you. You will believe (I know) when I say that I would rather pluck out my eyes, and end my career, and lose the whole world (this and the next), than in this searching and scorching trial for both of us add to your perplexities or increase your suffering.

And you may imagine what that means, knowing as you do what the sight of your face and the sound of your voice has always meant to me.

So I won't yet say Yes or no.

I am on the eve of the most astounding and world-shaking decisions— such as I would never have taken without your counsel and consent. It seems so strange and empty and unnatural; yet there is nowhere else that I can go, nor would I, if I could.

Tell me quite frankly, after weighing it all, whether it would make you happier to meet.

But for the past, on which "Heaven itself has not power" I should be the most miserable of men. Darling I am *till Death, Yours.*[71]

This letter was written on May 17, the day that Asquith had informed the King that he had decided to reconstruct the Government. It is another piece of evidence that from May 12, when he had first heard of Venetia's engagement, until May 17, when he announced the Coalition, he was in a state of intense emotional turmoil.

Cynthia Asquith, who was married to the Prime Minister's son, Herbert, had no doubt that it was Asquith's inability to handle Venetia's announcement of marriage that was the cause of the Coalition. She wrote in her diary that "Bluetooth" (Harold Baker, Financial Secretary to the War Office in 1914–15) had told her in utmost confidence " 'that Venetia is really going to marry Montagu and, so that he may not forfeit his fortune, she is formally to become a Jewess.' He said, 'The poor P.M. is absolutely broken-hearted, that it is stymying all public troubles. Perhaps if truth were known, it is really the cause of the Coalition.' " [72]

From this and other descriptions of Asquith emerges a portrait of a Prime Minister who was and looked "bruised," "shattered," "broken hearted," "ill and distracted," "sore and humiliated," "depressed and dejected." In this state he would have been superhuman if he had been able to divorce his personal problems from his public responsibilities. His actions, precipitous and out of character, had been foreshadowed when he wrote to Venetia on February 7, 1915, that if she left him, "I might struggle for a time, from habit or a vague sense of duty, or the instinct to finish off a half-done job . . . that would be all." [73]

17

Venetia's Escape to France— the Conversion and Marriage, May, June, July 1915

I shall never think of myself as a Jew anymore than I think of you as one.

Venetia to Edwin, May 27, 1915

Tout passe, tout casse, tout lasse.

Asquith to Venetia, June 3, 1915

Even after Venetia's announcement of her engagement on May 12, Asquith continued to nurse the hope that perhaps she might change her mind. Venetia wrote to him several times asking that they meet before she left for her hospital duty in France, so that she might explain her decision, but he could not face her. "I feel that we should both suffer. Perhaps you think I am . . . a coward. At any rate don't despise me. Nothing can efface the past."[1]

He pleaded with her "by all the sacred and unforgettable memories that must bind us together," that she "take time: do not allow yourself . . . to be hurried: get things into a true perspective: and then use what . . . I have always thought the best judgment of any woman of our time."[2] Of himself, Asquith wrote: "My heart—as you know—is broken."[3]

After he sent this, Asquith received another letter from Venetia on May 21, criticizing him for judging her by harsh standards. He was hurt that she was angry with him. He was sorry he had upset her. He was still uncertain whether to see her. The problems he was facing politically were the worst of his career.

Venetia was not to be put off. She wanted to see him. She wrote again on that same day, a letter he described as "one of the dearest you ever wrote." It soothed his "sore heart"[4] and made him reconsider his decision not to see her. "I think I *must* see you on Monday before you go," he concluded. In that same letter he wrote that he had received "a most characteristically noble and generous letter from E.S.M. I love him."[5] He wrote a third letter in which he said he was now certain that "after all I have said and thought in a contrary sense I *must see you* before you go. I know it will be painful, but I must tell you why. I think both you & I ought to face it."[6]

The balance of the letter, written during the most critical days immediately following the formation of the Coalition, reveals Asquith's misery at losing Venetia and at the same time his unhappiness in having to bring the Tories into the government and dismiss friends like Haldane and Churchill.

Our relationship has been in every way unique. When your first letter came today, if I had had a pistol at hand, I should without hesitation have blown out my brains. To end such a *glorious* experience in a dim, almost poisonous, cloud of misunderstanding & reproach, would have been worse than anything one cd. conceive of Hell.

But then came the other, and I saw you once again (as I know you so well) in the noon-tide of our sunlit understanding & sympathy, yet shadowed a little for the moment by what you thought I had done or said to dull, or even to smirch it. That I *can't* endure. It is so unlike us.

So, at whatever cost to both of us, I feel that in loyalty to our past, I must come and tell you the real & whole truth. I go to the Wharf for Sunday—late Sat.—but I shall be back fairly early on Monday. Have you then a spare half-hour?

I don't know yet whether we (you & I) have a real future. That will become clearer in time. But I am quite resolved that our *past* shall not be spoiled, but "orb into the perfect star." . . .

. . . I have just got your sweet little letter. Please send a line *tomorrow,* Sat., to the Wharf to tell me what time I can see you Monday—and anything else.

Is there anyone—even yourself—who knows *how much* I love you?
It will *never* be told.[7]

On Saturday, May 22, Asquith wrote again, reaffirming his desire to see Venetia before her departure. He also told her how difficult his interview with Churchill had been and how tragic it was to have

lost her support when he needed it most "in this most tragic fortnight of my life." He knew he must not be selfish and hoped she
would be happy. "For God's sake," he warned again, "take time."[8]

Finally, on May 23, Asquith met Venetia. It was not a happy
meeting. He continued to urge her "to take her time" and reconsider
her decision to marry; she, in turn, resented what she sensed was his
hostility to her choice of Montagu. While Asquith had written of
his "love" of Montagu in his letter of May 22 to Venetia, his
comments in a letter to Venetia's sister, Sylvia Henley, on May 12,
were different. In this letter, he was angry with Montagu for asking
Venetia to convert and found the idea of Montagu marrying Venetia
"utterly distasteful."

On the surface, however, Asquith was the perfect gentleman,
showing no signs of anger or distaste, although Montagu wrote to
Venetia that "unfortunately, he [Asquith] finds it difficult to talk
with me. At dinner last night, he was sweet but quickly left after
bridge."[9] From the moment he received Venetia's engagement announcement, Asquith's letters to Montagu became perfunctory and
formal. On May 18, for example, he wrote:

My Dear Montagu,
    Many thanks for your letter, which contains some very sound truths, I
greatly value what you say as to your own readiness to help, though I
know I can always count on that in any emergency, or (which is perhaps
better) when there is no emergency to make any special call.
    I have been engaged all morning in the most dismal of all occupations—
whetting the pole-axe, and marking down the victims. I am glad to hope
and think that you are not one of them, though you may have to shift your
quarters.
    I will have a talk with you on these matters sometime tomorrow: today
I am very full.

Yrs. affly.
H.H.A.[10]

For his part, Montagu was more worried about Venetia than he
was about Asquith. He recalled all too vividly his experience with
her three years earlier when she had agreed to marry him and then
changed her mind. He lived in terror that she would behave the
same way now.

Her desire to continue her relationship with Asquith also troubled
him. He must have told her so, for on May 24 she felt it necessary

to reassure him that regardless of what she may have said about "the P.M. . . . I want you to remember that nothing really matters to me but you." On the other hand, she wrote: "It would be absurd to pretend that his [Asquith's] unhappiness doesn't affect me very deeply, how could it not? For three years he has been to me the most wonderful friend and companion and to see him just now made wretched by me is, and should be, if I pretend to any heart at all, a real sorrow."[11] She urged Montagu to protect Asquith "not only for his sake but for mine."

Montagu assured her he needed no "special stimuli" to do all he could for Asquith. "Margot," he told her, "thought I loved him as much as I do you. . . . Of course that is not true." But he continued, "I love him more than any other man."[12]

On May 24, Venetia left for France. The trip was uneventful, she wrote to Montagu, "not a vestige of a submarine" disturbing the crossing. She found the hospital at Wimereux "a rather squalid hotel —in a stretch facing onto a small river." The sea was about three hundred yards away. The railroad was only twenty yards away which made "the place very noisy." She began her work feeling neither excitement nor fear, but instead "resigned and detached."[13]

Five days later, on May 30, Asquith also went to France to confer with Generals Joffre and Foch and to see firsthand the British Army in the field. Colleagues abroad commented that he looked tired and weary. Montagu became immediately concerned again, asking Venetia if she planned to see Asquith, and telling her that he too planned to arrive in France. He plaintively asked, "Tell me how to see you Thursday or Sunday."[14] Venetia managed to see them both, despite her nursing schedule.

Asquith wrote to her from the General Headquarters of the British Army near Boulogne on June 3 before he saw her. It was merely a short note, reaffirming his "one prayer" that she be happy and commenting on her wish that he be successful. *"Success!"* he asked, "I wonder in what. I have made up my mind to try (with whatever I have left) to push this war through. Apart from that, *'tout passe, tout casse, tout lasse* [everything passes, everything breaks, everything wears out].' "[15]

Things Can Never Be the Same

Since Asquith was near Boulogne, not far from her hospital, Venetia persuaded him to see her, on that day, June 3. At their meeting, she made clear her determination that her marriage not change their relationship. He was not persuaded and wrote on June 11:

Most loved—Your letter written on the night of the Thursday [June 3], when I last saw you wandered about & did not reach me till Tuesday in this week. My impulse . . . was to reply at once; but I thought it better for both of us that I should think about it and the whole agonizing problems [*sic*] wh. it raises before writing an answer. . . . You talk of your "gross selfishness." My darling I am . . . more selfish for you than I could ever be for myself. You were the centre and mainspring of my life: everything in it hung upon you: there was not an act or a thought (as you know well) wh. I did not share with you.

No one—not even you, who know me so well—can ever imagine what your letter on the 12th May (exactly a month ago!) meant to me. Believe me, I have never in word or even in thought reproached you. I know why you were silent; you were undecided, you were considerate. . . . I think it might have been easier if you had taken your courage in both hands and— But I love and honour you so much that even now I don't dare say that you were not right. You have given me so much more than I can give or could give to you . . . that in all the terrible & heart-rending hours that made my life a veritable hell, I have never . . . felt that I had any title to complain.

Say *beloved* that you believe me.

But your letter . . . is addressed not to the unforgettable past, but to the undisclosed & impenetrable future. . . .

You say that your old love for me is not impaired or altered by what has now come to you, and that in spite of what you contemplate, with all that it involves, that love will persist, constant and unchanged. You don't need to be told that mine will never cease or wane, until I die.

. . . But how can you think it possible—you don't, I know—that things can ever again be as they were? I had the *best* that a man had or could have . . . I told Montagu the other day in the only talk I have ever had or wish to have with him on the subject that I don't care what happens to me or to him—that I wouldn't lift a finger to save either him or myself from instant death if I could be sure . . . you would be happy.

. . . You say, & I devoutly pray that you are right, that you believe you love him enough to make sure of your happiness with him. . . .

Don't force me to sadder and adamantine resolutions. Don't think me hard if I seem for the time to stand aloof. Don't press me now to say anything—except that I love you, always, everywhere.

Your broken-hearted and *ever-devoted*.[16]

Venetia told Montagu of the visit and her exchange of letters with Asquith. She seemed to believe that her request that their friendship continue after her marriage "must have shown him [Asquith] more clearly than anything else I've written how little I really cared for him. Bongie was right, I suppose I oughtn't to have gone to see him. I shall urge my daughters to marry young, if they can . . . before they've had time to make friends who they'll regret. They can do that afterwards."[17] It is difficult to believe that Venetia cared for Asquith as little as this letter implies. If she was telling the truth, then the descriptions of her as cold, unfeeling and calculating are true. If she wrote this merely to assure her future husband, it is less reprehensible, but not much.

The Jewish Factor

There is no doubt that Asquith's shock at Venetia's marriage plans was exacerbated by her decision to convert to Judaism. While in his own conversation with Montagu on May 29, Asquith assured him that the religious issue was subsidiary and his real concern was his fear that they did not love each other and would not be happy,[18] many of Asquith's later letters and comments, especially to Sylvia Henley, reveal the opposite. He was appalled at the thought of Venetia becoming a Jewess, and found it "repugnant and even repulsive."[19] In this he was expressing an opinion that most Englishmen would probably have shared.

Calling Montagu "the Assyrian" and "Mr. Wu," referring to his home as the "Silken Tent of Shem," making frequent snide comments and jokes about his Rolls Royce and his extravagant feasts, all combine to confirm Asquith's image of Montagu, the Jew, as a rich Oriental potentate, not a true-blue Englishman. Asquith rarely commented, if ever, on the extravagant lifestyles and elegant homes of his Gentile friends, although many were far more elegant than Queen Anne's Gate. While the nicknames and jokes might be viewed as reflecting a subliminal anti-Semitism, there is nothing subtle or subliminal in Asquith's feelings as expressed in his letter to Venetia of January 3, 1913, in which he asked Venetia which she thought "worst," being Jewish, Polish, Catholic or decorated. He had come down squarely in finding that "being a Jew is the worst!"

Nor was there anything subliminal in a short note Asquith had written, marked "Private" and addressed to Lord Crewe on October 4, 1913. It listed the names of Jews who then held high office in the government:

India Office	*P.O.*	*Island Roads*
Montagu	Samuel	Abraham & Nathan

On the bottom of the note Asquith wrote: "I don't think this will do. Ever yours, H.H.A."[20] When Asquith expressed concern that as a nurse Venetia might be sweeping rooms and doing what he called "slut's work," he added that this was a thought he could not endure and compared it to his being employed "to run errands, & call taxis, and calculate percentages for Lord Swaythling. It would be about the same disproportion."[21]

During January, Asquith received a memorandum from Herbert Samuel on the future of Palestine, arguing with much vehemence in favor of British annexation of Palestine and suggesting that "we might plant in this not very promising territory 3 or 4 million European Jews." Asquith commented to Venetia, "I confess I am not attracted by this proposed addition to our responsibilities. But it is a curious illustration of Dizzy's [Disraeli's] favorite maxim that *'race is everything'* to find this almost lyrical outburst from the well-ordered and methodical brain of H[erbert] S[amuel]" (emphasis added).[22]

A year before, on November 3, 1914, Asquith described a dream he had "in which (with the concurrence of my colleagues), I was supplanted," he wrote, "by Herbert Samuel, as Prince Hal says, 'A Jew, an 'Ebrew Jew.' Do you think," he asked Venetia, "that is going to be my fate? I wonder. I take refuge in the Beatitude: 'The meek shall inherit the earth'—and *no Jew was ever meek!''* (emphasis added).[23] Aside from the clearly anti-Semitic slur this letter contained, it is also interesting to see that in the dream Asquith was supplanted by the Jew Herbert Samuel, as Prime Minister, at a time when one of his greatest fears was that the Jew Edwin Montagu would replace him not as Prime Minister but in Venetia's affections.

When Asquith learned that Venetia planned to convert to Judaism, he spewed forth his disdain for Judaism with a passion he rarely expressed about political or ideological issues. In a letter to Venetia's sister, Sylvia Henley, he wrote how "repugnant and even repulsive" he found the thought that Venetia planned to substitute Judaism for Christianity. He was bewildered that anyone could so blithely turn upon Christianity, "the main force wh. has created the West, . . . has remoulded & transformed the world & made us what we are." To reject Christianity for Judaism, which he called a "narrow, sterile, tribal creed wh. has . . . kept alive and separate the Israelite sept" was even more bewildering. "And that *this* should be the fate of our darling noble Venetia!" he wrote, made him sick.[24] In another letter to Mrs. Henley on May 18, 1915, he asked her whether she had ever heard the following saying about Jews: "Sometimes they are at one's feet; sometimes at one's neck; but never at one's side."

After Venetia's conversion, Cynthia Asquith wrote in her diary on July 2, that "Bluetooth says, in a letter I got this morning, Bongie is avoiding Montagu; and Mr. Asquith has told Venetia that, if she persists [in her conversion], he will never speak to her again."[25] If his letters expressed his real feelings, and there is every reason to believe that they did, Asquith viewed Jews as foreigners, Orientals, given to conspicuous consumption in the Silken Tents in which they lived in Oriental splendor; they were aggressive, disloyal, "at one's feet and neck," the antithesis of "the meek," a race apart, committed to a religion that is "sterile and narrow," and a "tribal creed," which has "kept Jews separate" from the rest of Western civilization, a civilization made great through "the remarkable contributions of Christianity."

Other political leaders of both the Tory and Liberal Parties, including two of Edwin's major adversaries, Lloyd George and Curzon, shared similar feelings toward Jews. They were more outspoken about their anti-Jewish feelings than even Asquith. Lloyd George believed that "men of Edwin's race" were always "dirty cowards," and Frances Stevenson said she and Lloyd George distrusted and disliked Montagu, found him loathsome and groveling and the "most ambitious of Cabinet Ministers" with "an enormous degree of 'push' which is characteristic of the Jew."[26] One of Lloyd George's biographers, John Grigg, added: "While he [Lloyd George] respected the Boers, he had nothing but contempt for the Uitlanders, and this was due, unfortunately, in large part to anti-Semitism. One of the more striking ironies of his life is that he, who made possible the Jewish nation's return to Palestine, and some of whose best friends were, later, Jews, should have had a distinct, even a venomous prejudice against Jewry":[27]

"The people we are fighting for, [Lloyd George said] those Uitlanders, are German Jews—15,000 to 20,000 of them. . . . Pah!—fighting for men of that type!" Most of them, he [Lloyd George] said, ran away when the trouble started. He shared the popular Gentile belief that the Jews were natural cowards. In 1916 he said of Edwin Montagu, who succeeded him as Minister of Munitions, that he "sought cover as was the manner of his race, grew hollow-cheeked under the strain." As well as being prejudiced against them on ethnic grounds, Lloyd George may have had another, but subconscious, ground for resentment against the Uitlanders. They were, after all, men who had struck [it] lucky with gold, and to one of the promoters of the Welsh Patagonian Gold Mining Syndicate (that failed) their prosperity must have been galling.[28]

The fact that Lord Curzon's first wife had been the daughter of an American whose family was Jewish and converted to Christianity did not stop him from harboring anti-Jewish prejudices, which can be seen most dramatically in Curzon's battle with Montagu over India and Turkey. While it is true that Asquith, Lloyd George and even Curzon were more polite and discreet in their prejudices than the Whites and Bellocs, in the long run their attitudes were equally damaging to Jewish security. They gave the vicious and open anti-Semitism of the Whites and Bellocs the respectability it needed to gain wider acceptance. For this reason, it has been said by students of anti-Semitism that the respectable classes of English society, of which Asquith was a prototype, were as much to blame as the more venal anti-Semites in laying the groundwork in England for the anti-Semitic fascism that erupted in the 1930s.

The Scandal of the Day

Asquith was not the only person disturbed by Venetia's impending conversion and marriage. Many members of Venetia's family and many of her friends were equally shocked and troubled. To add to their discomfort, the English gossip magazines were filled with stories about the engagement and the conversion, treating the event as the "scandal" of the day.

According to Adelaide Lubbock, Venetia's niece: "When the next batch of English periodicals arrived I, as usual, read them through surreptitiously. They were full of Venetia's engagement and photographs. The story was so obviously scandalous, even to my eyes, that I had to confess to reading the paper in order to find out more about it." [29] Mrs. Lubbock quoted a letter from her mother, Margaret Stanley, Venetia's aunt, to a friend, Mrs. Evans Gordon, on September 28, 1915:

Adelaide has gotten hold of the *Tatler,* unknown to me . . . and reading the heading "Bride changes her Faith as well as her Name." She immediately wanted to know whether she (Venetia) had given up being a Christian. I found it a little difficult to explain, as the thought evidently shocked her very much, but I sheltered myself by saying that sometimes people adopted their husband's or wife's religion when they married. She said, "Well I think it is *horrible* and very hard on poor Christ." Edwin [Edwin Stanley, her brother] said "I don't suppose He will mind much!" with comfortable philosophy, but Adelaide cannot get over it. [30]

Of all Venetia's friends it was Violet Asquith, her dearest friend, who reacted with the most intense hostility. Not expecting this, Venetia had written to Violet as soon as she had decided on the marriage and conversion. "I think," she explained:

I have quite made up my mind to be married to E. in such a way as not to separate him for ever from his family. . . . It won't change me, I shan't live religiously or spiritually a different life than if I'd married any complete free thinker, the only thing is that by this very formal compliance I make two people (of whom-[Edwin]-is very fond, his mother and his brother) reconciled & happy and myself live in greater comfort. Of course there would be absolutely no difficulty about doing it if this bloody money weren't involved, but I do admit I mind the fact that nearly everyone will think it has been done for that alone. It doesn't sound convincing when one says the other thing. They won't quite believe it & you who love me must (if you believe it too) try & reconcile yourselves to the idea. [31]

By May 28, Venetia thought Violet had become reconciled and told her that she was able to leave London "with real joy and relief." She confided to Violet that she was becoming increasingly nervous and "miserable . . . every day things seem more difficult and I feel less and less energy to face them." [32]

It was fortunate that Montagu did not see this letter; it would have added to his anxieties over Venetia's attitude toward their marriage. He knew that she still harbored serious doubts and uncertainties. Although she recognized how understanding Montagu was and how deeply he loved her, her own ambivalence and confusion were undiminished.

If Venetia left for France believing that Violet had accepted her conversion, she was wrong. Violet still vehemently opposed it. Like her father, she was far more hostile to Montagu than to Venetia, putting the blame squarely on him. In a long angry letter, she told him that she viewed his asking Venetia to convert as "contemptible," and quoted her father as speaking of the conversion "with horror." "What matters," she wrote in a letter to Montagu on May 24, 1915, "is not the criticism to which she [Venetia] will be exposed but the fact that those who love her most will feel it to be deserved." Violet concluded, "It is too high a price to pay even if the price includes not only your yearly income but also the peace of mind of your relations."[33] She refused to accept Edwin's excuse that Venetia offered to convert. Violet wrote:

You have said to me in the past that it would be impossible to ask anyone you loved and respected to do what she is willing to do & you base your change of attitude to the whole matter entirely on the ground that you haven't *asked* but that she had *offered*. This seems to me the pettiest of distinctions—almost a matter of social etiquette. Why haven't you asked? Why *couldn't* you ask her to do it? Because you regard it as a demeaning act —something untrue and a little ugly—an antic—the cynical purchase for all at the expense of her falsehood—(Qualify if you like.)

Yet you are ready to *accept* all this from her—so long as she will go through the form of offering it herself.

To take it from her—to bear it for her—for *Her* for whom you want only the greatest, finest, loveliest things that Life can yield—for whom your standards must be so inaccessibly high, your demands so insatiably ambitious—your fastidiousness so exacting—so delicate, so intense. This is to be your first touch on her life—which she is giving you. You speak of going through it like an operation—it is a bad simile. An operation may hurt but it does not discredit.

The merely *painful* consequences, the (very hypothetical) "obloquy, segregation, etc." are trivial to the point of non-existence as compared with the intrinsic quality of the action itself.

What matters is—not the criticism to which she will be exposed—but the fact that those who love her most deeply and seriously will feel it to be deserved. You will feel it yourself.[34]

Violet then concluded:

If you knew that it [Montagu's family's peace of mind] would be sacrificed, & if you knew that you cared about it too much to be prepared to sacrifice it—you had surely no right to ask her or any woman you loved with any chivalry to marry you? To put as selfless a woman as Venetia in such a position almost amounts to blackmail—especially if she cares for you. Your first duty is not to sacrifice *her*—and it is a duty which becomes even more imperious if she doesn't mind being sacrificed.[35]

You speak of "being loyal to your agony." It is a phrase which conveys nothing to me. Be loyal to it by all means—but not to the extent of making it someone else's agony too, & that Venetia's.

If you mean that by refraining from forcing a Xian [Christian] into your church you are somehow dodging the stigma which you think attaches to your race—I assure you that that stigma will continue to exist for those for whom it does exist (Belloc!) whether you practice yr. religion in this detail or not. . . .

Goodbye—God bless you. Forgive me if I have hurt you by anything I have said. It would have been treachery for me to keep silence—for I feel the truth of my conviction in this matter as deeply & as passionately as the biggest things of my life. I think of Archie—& Rupert—& Father and Cys—& it stands the stronger—oh, ever so much stronger for the thought of them. And I do love you both—bless you, Your V. Write to me please.[36]

Montagu was upset by the letter and sent a copy to Venetia. He urged her not to be angry with Violet, because "I think she is a little mad. Remember," he added by way of reassurance, "the multitude of our friends are on our side."[37] Venetia was not angry. She took a rather philosophical attitude toward Violet's diatribe, writing:

I am going to write to Violet. I shan't tell her you've shown me her letter, the difference in our outlook on her actions and words is that I think she is really fond of us both; and wants us to be happy, but she is and always has been ridiculously influenced by abstract moral principles which she has laid down and which make her judge everyone by a narrow standard, though at the same time, owing to her marvelous power of dialectics [approve] everything she wants to do.

If she were in my place she would be able to prove quite incontrovertibly that what she was doing was for the most splendid thing that had ever been done. . . . All I mean to say is that she is not, as you think, resentful because we have settled our lives while hers is still in the melting pot. Don't let us have "pride," I mean don't let us resent anything she may say, I wish I minded things more, but darling I do love you very much and that's the chief thing.[38]

Other members of Asquith's family were less harsh in their judgments than Violet. Arthur Asquith, one of the Prime Minister's sons (nicknamed "O.C."), who was fighting in Gallipoli, wrote to Violet: "I hate the whole business; but my social self-indulgence is such that the crimes of my friends rarely make me wish to forgo their society."[39]

Raymond Asquith, another of the Prime Minister's sons, and his wife Katharine strongly supported the marriage. Katharine was, in fact, the only member of the Asquith family who attended the wedding. Raymond's letter to his friend Conrad Russell about the marriage, written from the battlefields of France, supported the "Stanley-Montagu match," as he called it, for several reasons. First, he believed "for a woman any marriage is better than perpetual virginity which after a certain age (not very far distant in Venetia's case) becomes insufficiently absurd." Second, Venetia "had a fair chance of conceiving a romantic passion . . . for the last twelve years and has not done so and is probably incapable of doing so." For that reason she was "well advised to make a marriage of convenience." Her marriage to Montagu, Raymond concluded, is clearly a marriage of convenience for "if a man has private means and private parts (especially if both are large) he is a convenience to a woman." Third, "because it annoys Lord and Lady Sheffield," and fourth because "it profoundly shocks the entire Christian community."

Raymond goes on to discuss Edwin's ugliness and Venetia's (and other women's) lack of squeamishness when faced with the prospect of sleeping with an unattractive man. He wrote:

Of course I see your point when you say you wouldn't like to go to bed with Edwin. I don't mind admitting that I shouldn't myself. But you must remember that women are not refined, sensitive, delicate-minded creatures like you and me. None of them have much physical squeamishness and Venetia far less than most. You say she must have weighed the consequences and so she did, quite carefully: but what frightened her most was not the prospect of the bed being too full but of the board being too empty.

She was afraid that her friends might give her up in disgust; but after sounding a few of them—Katharine e.g., and Diana—she concluded that it would be all right and decided to flout the interested disapproval of Mr. H.H. and the idiotic indignation of Miss V. Asquith.

Raymond described Edwin's personality and also the extramarital relations upon which he and Venetia had agreed, and which their friends discussed quite openly. He tells Russell:

Your character sketch of Edwin is done in much too dark colours. You are obviously prejudiced against him by the fact (if fact it be) that he steals birds' eggs, a vice utterly immaterial in a bride-groom. I agree that he has not a drop of European blood, but then neither has he a drop of American. I don't agree that he is a wet-blanket in Society. He is moody certainly, but is capable of being extremely amusing and (especially during the last year) has succeeded in attracting some very critical and some very beautiful women. He is broad-minded, free from cant, open to new impressions, tolerant of new people. I do not think he will be either a dull or a tyrannical husband, *and I understand that the terms of alliance permit a wide licence to both parties to indulge such extraconjugal caprices as either may be lucky enough to conceive.*[40] (emphasis added)

Margot Asquith was also supportive of the marriage and conversion, not because she was more tolerant of Judaism than her husband, but because she was relieved that Venetia was finally going to be married and might leave her husband alone. She wrote to Violet on June 7: "They [Edwin and Venetia] are both old enough to know their minds and no one must tease them now. There's a good deal of bosh in the religious campaign *au fond* tho' superficially it takes one in."[41] Her real feelings about Judaism were expressed more candidly to her diary after Montagu joined Lloyd George's Cabinet. "I felt ill," she wrote, "with indignation & said 'one xpects a Jew to have no faith but this does not necessarily imply he has no judgment!' "[42]

In Venetia's family, as among her friends, there were differing attitudes toward the marriage. Lord Sheffield, then seventy-seven, was furious at his daughter's conversion and in the days following the announcement refused to talk to either Venetia or Montagu. He "boycotted" them, to use Venetia's term for her father's reaction. His daughter-in-law, Margaret, recalls that he once mentioned the possibility of such a marriage and conversion and was "very vehement in his denunciation of it."[43]

Venetia's brother, Oliver, by contrast, was supportive. With his help, Lord Sheffield finally agreed to talk to Venetia and Montagu and to recognize their marriage. He did so, however, with "deep distaste." By July, he seemed to have become a little more accepting of it, according to Montagu.

Lady Sheffield's reaction was mixed. On the one hand, she was not overjoyed at Venetia's converting to Judaism; on the other, as her sister wrote, she was relieved that Venetia "is settled at least and that she will not be harassed by her vagaries anymore."[44] That Montagu had money and could care for Venetia in style and comfort was probably important enough to overcome, to some degree, Lady Sheffield's distaste for the conversion. That Venetia was twenty-eight and had no other suitors at the time except a married Prime Minister forty years her senior also helped to reduce whatever doubts and discomfort she may have felt.

Lady Sheffield's main concern was her fear that Venetia did not love Montagu and was marrying him only to escape Asquith's mounting demands. In a letter to Venetia, Montagu told her that he had assured her mother that he:

often thought as she did and had put it to you that if you were marrying me to end difficulties and an unsatisfactory life as a good way out and pretending to yourself that you were in love, deluding yourself, it would be disastrous because in a partnership that lasts for years the delusions will not be kept up. I said you agreed and satisfied me that you were being honest with yourself and that you were marrying for love. I pray most earnestly that you are not deceiving yourself, that you are right, for otherwise! . . . But I am radiantly confident that it's all right. Bless you. And your mother was quite comforted, I think by my confidence. She said your Aunt Blanche had told her you ought to get married and that although she had never met me, she thought I was the right person and that Jews were very respectable people. I feel as though the Pope had approved.[45]

Lady Sheffield and her sister, Blanche, may have approved but the rest of Venetia's family, according to her niece, Adelaide Lubbock, were far less forgiving. "The whole family," she wrote, "censured Venetia for her ruthlessness, and for 'turning Jewish for the sake of £8,000 a year!' Her cold-blooded acceptance of 'the Assyrian' . . . for his money, shocked them all, including my mother [Margaret Stanley], who shuddered at the alliance."[46] In a letter Margaret Stanley sent to her own mother, Mrs. Henry Evans Gordon, on July 28, 1915, she had written: "He is such a repugging creature, and how she brought herself to accept him I cannot think. I had a very unhappy letter from the P.M."[47] Mrs. Stanley continued: "I cannot help feeling very sorry and regretting that she had acted unworthily—as according to my ideas she has. I don't mind her having rejected Christianity as she never professed to be a Christian, but I do regret her having assumed the profession of a faith that she equally doesn't believe in, and this for the sake of money. *That* is the ugly thing."[48] Venetia's brother, Arthur, Mrs. Stanley wrote:

is also very sorry over it, but has not taken the line of that ferocious old P.-in-law [Venetia's father], has, who will neither see her at present (tho' he says he will, by-and-by), nor give her a present or any money for a trousseau. Venetia's future has always been rather a problem, and if she is going to be really happy and settled, one must shut one's eyes and swallow the ugliness of her marriage—(and the bridegroom!)[49]

Since Venetia was going to convert, Montagu's family, unlike the Sheffields, was less critical. Lionel, Edwin's older brother (Lord Swaythling), and his sister, Lily Montagu, were especially helpful in arranging the conversion and the marriage ceremony, which was to be performed by the Rev. Morris Joseph, a member of the Liberal branch of Judaism, of which Lily was a leader. Because of the lack of study and ritual involved in Venetia's conversion, no Orthodox rabbi would perform it.

Montagu's mother, an Orthodox Jew, would have preferred her son to marry within the "Cousinhood," something she had urged for many years. But he was getting on in years—he was thirty-seven at the time of his engagement to Venetia—he was not well and he surely needed a wife to care for him. The fact that Venetia was prepared to convert helped, of course, to offset any objections she felt.

The Dowager Lady Swaythling was not well. Just a month before the engagement she had suffered an acute case of bronchitis. Montagu was deeply concerned about his mother, and, as always, was most solicitous of her health and well-being. His statement to Venetia that he wanted her to convert not merely to insure his inheritance but to spare his mother pain and anguish was true. If Montagu loved anyone in his family, it was his mother. Even at this stage in his life, he continued to write to her regularly and she responded with the same kind of letter every Friday. "I love them," he said of his mother's letters, "They are so very early Victorian in tone." [50]

Venetia Avoids Coming Home

Montagu's real problem during the weeks following the marriage announcement was not the approval or disapproval of friends or family but Venetia's ambivalence, the tenuous quality of her commitment, his fear that she did not love him, and her refusal to set a date for the marriage or for her return to England. She was also flippant about her responsibility to read some of the books assigned to her in preparation for her conversion. Montagu feared she would never get through the process, as simple and undemanding as it was.

His letters while she was at Wimereux were filled with worry, but also with love and passion, and a great desire to grant her every wish and need. He pleaded with her to come home; he promised her he would try to change his personality, to give her a life of "fun, and fun and fun." He sent her lavish gifts and hampers of food enough to feed sixteen nurses with truffles, chocolates, champagne and pineapples. He was distraught when she suggested she might stay till the middle of August or maybe until the end of the war. His life, he wrote, was "intolerable" without her. He was "counting the hours." He loved her "physically, animally as well as mentally and morally." He loathed the people who saw her, "even the soldiers who talk to you." He prayed that she really loved him too, but said that he understood the limitations in her emotional makeup. He confessed that she was "the only thing in the world that matters" to him; and he counted the days until she returned. [51]

Venetia's letters contained genuine appreciation for Edwin's generosity and his patience with her moodiness. Unlike her earlier letters, they were warm and often loving, although devoid of any desire or passion for him, and lacking any awareness for the horrors of the war that surrounded her. Although she was now at a hospital through which hundreds of wounded and dying soldiers passed, she rarely even mentioned them. She appeared to be more concerned by the "dreadful" condition of her hands, caused by the "acids and disinfectants," and by the freckles or pimples that developed on her face. The hospital, she complained, "was hot, crowded and dirty." And then she added, "There is one real tragedy about the place," that it wasn't possible to have a hot bath. "Isn't that dreadfully squalid?"[52]

Every so often, in spite of herself, the horror of the war caught up with her and she wrote "it's very hard not to be depressed about the war out here." She added quickly, as if to keep her reputation for fun, "one hasn't other fun to think of."[53] Some days she worked long and grueling hours; others she was bored and listless. But in spite of her complaints, she found the experience sufficiently exhilarating for her to write to Edwin on June 9, "I just can't come home, my desire for a new sensation is too strong." She then added, "Why is it that no one thinks it unreasonable for Anthony to desert his wife and children and go first to France and then the Dardanelles and yet he is doing it for his own fun only."[54] The next day she wrote that "there might be an element of shrinking" in her desire to remain, since she found the hospital, even when dull, "very peaceful and impersonal."[55] It provided her with an atmosphere she found soothing. It was the sense of imminent excitement that held her there, almost against her will. "I'd come home if I could," she wrote on June 12, "but then I should *never* forgive myself if I were to leave France & then something very exciting came to happen & I'd missed it all! Just imagine my horror?"[56]

To Montagu, and to most people, Venetia's desire to remain in France could mean only one thing. She did not

really feel that getting married is important and cannot be compared to the thrill of a hospital crowded with [wounded patients]. By that I don't mean that I am humble enough to feel that I don't play much part in your life. But really London means to you the old life and no very great difference. It's true that I shall be there, but I have been there for you and I am there now, so really from your remarkable but intelligible point of view there is not much to come home for. . . . I should expect you, to postpone a disagreeable return than rush over it. That's really an incentive to keep you away. The act of getting married is going to be disagreeable. Some people might say 'I mean to do it, so let's get it over with.' You say 'I mean to do it some day, but let's put it off as long as possible.'[57]

Montagu was correct in believing that Venetia did want to postpone the return and the marriage as long as possible. Her doubts continued to plague him. At one point she wrote that perhaps she was "too dreary a woman to marry, that I probably wasn't in the least in love, that I didn't care what happened to anyone including myself and that generally it wasn't worthwhile bothering about me."[58]

In response, Montagu crossed the Channel again to plead with her to set a date for her return. She could not, he told her, postpone this indefinitely. She also had to submit her application for conversion by July 12, since two of the rabbis involved in her conversion were themselves leaving for the front.[59]

The Decision Is Made

Finally, after much letter writing and off-again-on-again arrangements, Venetia made up her mind to return to London on July 10. Montagu's joy knew no bounds.

When word reached Asquith, he wrote to Venetia:

I hear that matters with you are rapidly approaching a climax. It seems so strange that I can't and don't wish to, realize it all and what it means, more closely or directly. . . . You know me too well to think that I can ever be forgetful or callous or disloyal. I pray with my whole soul that you may be truly and lastingly happy. Don't answer, or wish me now to say more. Your ever loving.

The letter was dated "14 July 1915, Midnight."[60]

The Conversion

Now the only obstacle standing in the way of the marriage, which was officially set for July 26, was Venetia's conversion. She made no bones about the fact that she cared not at all for religion, including Judaism. Her primary motive in converting was to save Edwin's fortune and, secondarily, to help him avoid estrangement from his mother and those members of his family whom he loved, such as Lionel and Lily. From a religious point of view, it was a travesty. Yet, in spite of Montagu's willingness to accept what was clearly a meaningless conversion and his own indifference to religion, he had written to Venetia in April that if their children "want to marry Christians or Hindus, they will have no criticism from me . . . But if they choose to stick to the flag . . . I shall be pleased." And he had added that all he asks of Venetia is that "if we [Jews] are attacked or scorned you regard yourself as one of us by adoption."[61]

Edwin's last two sentences may reveal one of the mysteries of Jewish survival. Here was a man with no interest in Judaism, for whom Judaism represented, at best, Passover at his mother's and a rare visit to a synagogue, a man prepared to participate in a conversion that was a total deceit, who had no identity with the Jewish community. Yet he could say, "I will be pleased if my children marry Jews," and he hoped that if Jews were attacked, his nonbelieving, falsely converted wife would stand with the Jews attacked and not with their persecutors. Why? Why should he care and be pleased if his children married Jews? Why should he care if his wife cast her lot with the Jews in a time of Jewish persecution? Why would it not be equally satisfying to him if she sought refuge and safety with the Christian community rather than suffer the indignities and dangers of Jewish persecution? There was nothing in Montagu's life to indicate that he cared to find the answers to these questions.

In this failure, he was not and is not alone. In every age and country there have been and are Jews who, like Montagu, practice no religion, who do not believe in God or prayer or ritual, who attend synagogue only on the High Holy Days, who may even call themselves "secular humanists," who cannot explain their Jewishness, who are illiterate in the Jewish tradition, law and literature, and yet they still cling to some thread of Jewish identity, even if they can neither explain nor define it. It is this almost mystical sense of identification with their Jewish heritage that has contributed to the preservation of the Jewish people in the face of thousands of years of persecution and dispersion. And in Montagu's own way, in letters that seem so callous and indifferent to his religion, he, too, reaffirmed this mysterious bond to his Jewish past that he could not explain but that slipped seemingly from nowhere into his letters.

Venetia was baffled by his attitude. "You . . . say that if your sons were to marry Christians you would feel that they had deserted. Is it race or religion you care about or merely label? If it is race," she continued, "you are declassing it by marrying me, whatever I do. Religion you know I care nothing about and shan't attempt to bring up my children in any."[62] Venetia continued:

There only remains the label. And will it stick do you think? If we have children how do you think they will be brought up? Amongst Jews or amongst Christians? Won't their natural friends be Arthur's children, Anthony's Geoffrey's and not your relatives? And this is not because I shall be separating you from your family because you have never really belonged to them by ties or friendship except with your mother and one brother. The whole of what it amounts to is this—I shall nominally call myself one of you; but that is the limit of what will happen. I am sure that your children will not in any way regard themselves as any different from their friends.

And, in response to Montagu's hope that after her conversion, she would "stand by" the Jews, if they were persecuted, Venetia responded:

Perhaps you don't care a damn but after what you said I felt I had to make it clear to you that I shouldn't lift a finger to keep all the inhabitants of Przemyal (I don't even know how to spell it) from going over to the enemy. But I want to ask you honestly if this most superficial acquiescence is enough. Darlingest don't think I am being influenced by what anyone has said. This is only a question between you and me. I don't want to deceive you about my intentions. It is not whether I am right or wrong to change my label, but whether I am changing it enough, I can't do it more. I shall *never* think of myself as a Jew any more than I think of you as one.[63]

Venetia was absolutely honest with Montagu about her attitudes and feelings about Judaism. "Were I to be washed one hundred times in the waters of the Jordan and go through every rite and ceremony the strictest Jewish creed involved, I should not feel I had changed my race or nationality," she told him. "I go through the formula required," she continued, "because you want it for your mother's sake and because I think one is happier rich than poor."[64]

Montagu could not have been surprised at these attitudes. Venetia had always been open in her rejection of traditional religious observance. Early in 1915, when Asquith was trying to write parts of his autobiography, which included a portrait of Venetia, he wrote,

From the point of view of technical "religion" she offered little encouragement to preachers and evangelists. She had no "sense of sin"; no penitential moods; no waves of remorse, no mystic reveries; no excursions (after the fashion of St. Paul) into the Third Heaven, and hearing of "unspeakable words that it is not lawful for a man (or a woman) to utter." She was no subject for William James. The wings of her imagination—and it had wings as well as feet—when it left the ground took quite a different light. Poetry and music fed & sustained it.[65]

In many ways Venetia's attitudes were no different from Montagu's save for the fact that he had some inexplicable feeling about defending Judaism, when it was attacked, and a desire he could not explain, even to himself, of having his children remain Jewish and marry Jews.

Nor was Montagu troubled by the fact that if any rabbi, even from the Liberal wing of Judaism, had read Venetia's letters, they never would have performed the conversion. His only concern at this time was Venetia's reluctance to do her homework and study the material she needed for the conversion. As minimal as these were, they required reading and preparation. Venetia's responses to his inquiries as to her progress were not encouraging.

On May 28, she complained that she couldn't study the book that "Old Joseph" (the Rev. Morris Joseph, who was to conduct the conversion ceremony) had sent her, because it was "too boring." "I am afraid it would be useless as I should have forgotten it all by the time I got home. I shall mug up all about the Paschal Lamb when I get home."[66] On June 14 she wrote: "As for old Joseph and all his tribe we'll settle with him in half note time. . . . I wish I could be spared by writing, it would save time, but I suppose he can't."[67]

Montagu became increasingly anxious and warned her in a letter that "a breaking point might come—when they may say . . . you are not in earnest." With this letter he sent some additional books.[68] Venetia replied: "I'm not sure a little judicious cramming of old Joseph's at the last moment won't be more efficacious . . . and I'm then very likely to remember it. Also as I have a fairly good verbal memory I might *hope* to flatter the old boy by some verbatim quotations."[69]

On June 9, Montagu wrote that his sister Lily "urges speed as the best way to cut the cable." He agreed and added: "I asked her again what is demanded of you afterwards. She agreed wholeheartedly nothing but the avowal if *challenged* that you have adopted citizenship of our citadel and a steadfast refusal to propose yourself a Christian."[70] Given this assurance, Venetia buckled down and did her homework; on her return home she was tested by Rabbi Joseph and his assistants on July 12 and was received into the Jewish faith.

Prewedding Days

In the days before their wedding, Venetia and Montagu made plans for their honeymoon, began remodeling 24 Queen Anne's Gate, shopped for clothing, and met with friends and family. As late as June 15, Venetia had written that she had never met Montagu's mother or sisters. "I might be humpbacked for all they know to the contrary."[71]

As for other plans, Venetia suggested that Montagu meet her in Folkestone when she returned from France on Sunday, July 10, that they drive to London, have dinner and stay at 24 Queen Anne's Gate. They would then spend Monday shopping for clothes for a honeymoon in Russia (the disastrous course of the war in Russia prevented this), spend Tuesday meeting with Rabbi Joseph for her conversion and then visit a few days with her mother at Alderley. After the wedding she wanted to spend a long weekend at Penrhos. "Penrhos will be peaceful and not full of people."[72]

Montagu's joy was clouded by his constant worry about Venetia's true feelings. Her ambivalence seemed to show itself even during the excitement of the prewedding days. Cynthia Asquith wrote that two weeks before the wedding she dined "with Montagu and his bride and her family—Sylvia, Blanche, and Oliver Stanley. Dinner was leavened by Nellie and Bongie. I enjoyed it very much, but it was a trifle strained and Venetia certainly doesn't look completely happy. . . . The house was delicious and comfortable. I found Montagu delightful to talk to and I think he will give Venetia exactly the life she wants when once she has taken the plunge."[73]

Venetia's moods may have troubled Montagu, but they did not diminish his adoration. Diana Cooper wrote that a week before the wedding Raymond and Katherine, Montagu and Venetia and she and Duff spent a Sunday at Brighton. "Edwin was at his most cheerful and appreciative, his noble eyes softer than usual with love for Venetia."[74]

Three days before their wedding, with his sense of his own early death always on his mind, Montagu wrote a touching letter to Venetia:

My darling Venetia,
    This letter is written to you on the eve of our marriage, and will not be

read by you till I am dead. You will not be surprised that it does not contain much that isn't business, but I look forward with such joy and certainty of success of our married life that I also shrink more than ever from the inevitable ending thereof. It is a wonderful thing that you have consented to marry me and I can only hope most devoutly that this letter will not reach you till you have enjoyed many years of happiness with me. To that end I shall devote what remains of my life.

I want you to give some presents to my friends. I have left you all I possess. I have left you as much of what my father gave me as I legally could, and all else I have left you absolutely.

My father's wishes have been a sacred trust. He was a splendid father and a great man. But with his example before me I take no steps to enforce my wishes. I only ask you to do what I pray you to do, and I know you will.

Please give some keepsake to whoever of the following are still alive, and if you can find nothing, buy something for them. But I had rather you found for them something I had in my possession.

Katharine, (let her choose), Asquith	Bongie
Diana Manners	Raymond
Nan Herbert	Alan
Viola Parsons	Duff
Ruby Peto	P.M.
Hazel Lavery	E. Grey
Violet Asquith	Eric Drummond
Margot Asquith	Bron
Lady Gwendoline Churchill	Conrad
Lady Horner	Winston
Lady Wimborne	Masterton
Sylvia Henley	E. A. Sommers
Pamela McKenna	H. W. Malkin
	Gen. Mathews
	Buckmaster

All my brothers sisters and nieces, (these can be bought). Anybody else you think of.

You know my friends, just let them have something to think of me with.

I don't want to be buried in a graveyard. Please see to that. I hate it.

I would prefer, of all places, P   Hill, Crayborough + + + + + + + I'll show you where or Will Malkin will know.

If this is impossible bury me on Mill Island, Penrhos, you know where.

If this is impossible bury me at Whiteslea, Hickling? anywhere.

PLEASE see to this. I am very keen about it. Let there be no funeral service. Let anybody come who likes, and say any prayers they like *silently* with no word, and let no parson say anything.

Bless you my darling Venetia. I hope I shall have so conducted myself that you will think well of me.

Yours most gratefully,
Edwin S. Montagu[75]

On July 24, Venetia visited with Asquith the last time before her marriage. On returning he wrote:

I thought it was better for both of us not to say goodbye to-day. It was not (as you know well) want of feeling, or of a sense of the full meaning of your new departure, now approaching within a measurable number of hours.

"Not heaven itself upon the Past has power."

But when (as is inevitable now) I have to survey the past, in the light (if it is light)—perhaps I ought rather to call it twilight—of the impending and unescapable future, I should wish you always to remember that I am conscious of many things, on my part, which fell short of what I should have wished them to be: that I treasure, as among the best things that any companionship could give, unforgettable and undying memories: and that I pray without ceasing to "whatever gods there be" that you may have a complete, and (so far as may be) an unclouded life.

Will you always also remember an old & favorite text of mine (on which I never found it necessary to preach to you): "It is the Spirit that prevaileth."

Always & everywhere
Your loving[76]

The Wedding

Finally, the wedding day, July 26, 1915, arrived. The ceremony took place at the estate of Edwin's brother, Lionel, the second Lord Swaythling. It was an elegant occasion. The bride was dressed in a specially designed Parisian wedding gown of extraordinary beauty; and the groom looked uncomfortably fashionable in the formal attire of the day. The vows were exchanged under a "Chupah," a traditional Jewish wedding canopy.

The bridegroom made the following declaration:

Be thou my wife according to the law of Moses and of Israel. I faithfully promise that I will be a true husband unto thee. I will honour and cherish thee; I will work for thee; I will protect and support thee, and will provide all that is necessary for thy due sustenance, even as it beseemeth a Jewish husband to do. I also take upon myself all such further obligations for thy maintenance, during thy life-time, as are prescribed by our religious statute.

And the bride, according to Jewish law, "plighted her troth unto him, in affection and in sincerity and has thus taken upon herself the fulfillment of all the duties incumbent upon a Jewish wife." The Covenant of Marriage was duly executed and witnessed on the second day of the week, the fifteenth day of the month of Ab in the year 5675, A.M., "according to the usage of Israel." At the end of the ceremony, also in accordance with Jewish tradition, Montagu stepped on a drinking glass, shattering it—a symbol to remind Jews throughout the ages of the destruction of the Temple in Jerusalem and to renew the dream of regaining a Jewish home in Palestine.

No one at the wedding, least of all Montagu, could have imagined that the opportunity to restore Palestine to the Jews would be offered in their lifetimes, with the help of British leadership and the Balfour Declaration. Ironically, it was Edwin Montagu who would almost defeat that effort. Had he succeeded, the shattered glass would have remained not only the symbol of yesterday but the reality of today. But he did not succeed and the history of the Jewish people changed dramatically.

Prime Minister Asquith did not attend the wedding. He sent Venetia two silver boxes (chosen by her sister, Sylvia) with a brief note: "with all my love and more wishes than words can frame for your complete and unbroken happiness."[77] A chapter in his life and in hers had closed. For Venetia and Edwin a new chapter began.

18

The Coalition,
May 1915–December 1916

It is essential that you should strike before you are struck—that you should strike dramatically.

Montagu to H. H. Asquith, Oct. 22, 1915

In the months following the announcement of Venetia and Edwin's engagement, Montagu's happiness was marred by the fact that he was omitted from the Coalition Cabinet. His position as Chancellor for the Duchy of Lancaster, which had given him his place in the Cabinet since February 1915, was given in May to Winston Churchill to compensate him for his loss of the Admiralty. Montagu had hoped he might be considered for the Chancellor of the Exchequer, since he felt especially qualified for this post. Instead, he was asked to return to the Treasury as Finance Secretary under Reginald McKenna, the new Chancellor of the Exchequer, whom he considered "as undistinguished as any man I have ever served and I have not much respect for him as a politician."[1]

Even McKenna's wife was surprised at the appointment and sent Asquith "a letter of almost amazed gratitude."[2] Montagu's disappointment was made all the more acute because in the weeks preceding the announcement of the Cabinet, Prime Minister Asquith had talked with him about various other appointments which, as Montagu wrote to Venetia, included: "1) Ireland, 2) Education, 3) Munitions, 4) Board of Trade, 5) ultimately (?) Exchequer and has offered me definitely P.M.G. or Board of Agriculture. Net result Under Secretary to McKenna!!"[3]

The Tory dislike of Montagu, which had been growing, was one major reason he did not get a more senior appointment. Asquith, faced with so many problems, was unwilling to add another to his list of controversies with his new Tory partners. It was easier to bypass Montagu, although he was better qualified than McKenna, than to face yet another conflict.

Montagu had also asked Lloyd George to permit him serve in the new Ministry of Munitions whose creation he had urged as early as October 1914, but, here too, he was rejected. "He pretends to want me," Montagu told Venetia, "but really wants McKenna. Latter pretends he doesn't want it but does really. Between the two I have not much chance."[4] And so, given no choice, Montagu returned to the Treasury.

At first, he found McKenna easy to work with, plodding conscientious and honest, someone who compensated for his modest intelligence with hard work and trustworthiness. "I have gotten on very well with McKenna, so far." Montagu wrote to Venetia on May 28, "He shares things with me more than [Lloyd] George even though I feel how small he is compared with George. I think we shall be happy and it is so glorious to see how happy the civil servants are. They at last believe they can trust this Chancellor not to give them away and to do business instead of avoiding it."

Montagu was especially pleased that his friends in the world of finance and his old colleagues at Treasury welcomed him back enthusiastically. "I have several good experiences," he continued in his letter to Venetia. "One is their joy at my coming back, another is a warm letter of gratitude from one of the Governors of the Bank of England, Cole, who once refused to eat with a Liberal!" Montagu was also pleased that Grey, without Montagu suggesting it, offered to continue to send him Foreign Office telegrams "just as if I was still in the Cabinet."[5]

Montagu believed that Asquith did "magnificently" in forming the new Government. "In all things that matter," he wrote to Asquith, "in all the crises that frighten, in all the apprehensions that disturb, you show yourself clear-sighted and self possessed, ready to help, elucidate, respond, to formulate, to lead, to inspire. That's why serving you and following you is so easy and profitable, it's worthwhile all the time."[6] And to Venetia he wrote that Asquith "fought for his friends, unasked (George didn't) and none served the Liberal party as he has done the last week. The Tories have been properly dished. They occupy only one war post . . . A.J.B.'s and he by no means reckoned as a proper official Tory."[7]

In this evaluation, as was Montagu's wont in evaluating his friends, he went overboard and exaggerated. While Asquith may have been unhappy about removing Churchill and Haldane, there is no evidence that he fought hard for them (or for Montagu). His treatment of Haldane was unpardonable and has been called "the most uncharacteristic fault of Asquith's whole career."[8]

As for the composition of the cabinet, Montagu's assessment was correct: the major positions were still held by the Liberals. Grey remained at the Foreign Office; Lloyd George became Minister of the Ministry of Munitions; and McKenna went to the Exchequer. Kitchener remained at the War Office. The only Conservative who received a key appointment was Balfour, who replaced Churchill at the Admiralty.

The other Tory appointments were of lesser importance: Curzon was appointed to the Privy Seal, and Carson became Attorney General, a strange post for a man who had been ready to lead an Irish rebellion against England. All told, when the Coalition Cabinet was announced, it had twelve Liberals, eight Unionists, one representative of Labour and Kitchener. Bonar Law became Colonial Secretary, a relatively insignificant post for the leader of the Conservative Party.

Asquith, according to Montagu, "hated"[9] the Coalition and was genuinely distressed at having men like Carson and Walter Long (who became President of the Local Government Board) part of the Cabinet. Asquith viewed the Coalition as a "temporary abandonment" of the two-party system "that ruled England from 1832 and was under normal circumstances" the best adapted "to the needs of the country." He accepted the Coalition, he explained to his Chief Whip John Guilland, only because he believed that "a non party Government" was the "most efficient instrument for the successful prosecution of the War," even though it caused him "infinite personal pain." He hoped that when the war was won, the country would return to its usual party system and that the Liberal Party would be able to finish the course it had set for itself.[10]

Montagu and McKenna

Montagu became increasingly disenchanted with McKenna and found him difficult to work with. Under Lloyd George, Montagu had been left relatively free to manage the Treasury as he saw fit. Mc-Kenna, however, wanted to be involved in everything, while bringing little or no experience or creativity to the job.

By June, Montagu was complaining to Venetia: "My work is very heavy, heavier than ever. Reggie is getting a little rattled and overwhelmed by the magnitude of the task. I hope he will keep his head. You see L.G. had completely lost interest and has let things slide shockingly since I left. I had no idea the [Department] was in as bad a condition as it is, and I really think financial matters are worse than in August [1914]. George has relied largely on greatly organized newspaper enthusiasm. He's doing it again now. He is talking at large about labour just as he did on drink and he is being idolized by the whole press, but he will be found out. . . . We had a War committee this morning, P.M. in chair. . . . McKenna stated the facts well but in his economies he was confused through sheer nervousness and rattledness."[11]

The Second War Budget

During June and July, Montagu was deeply involved in helping McKenna shepherd the Second War Budget, which Lloyd George had brought to the floor in May, through Commons. While Lloyd George, in introducing this budget, had painted a gloomy picture of the nation's economy, the budget provided no way to meet the problem. It did not add new taxes, it did not increase old ones, it did not tax excessive war profits, and it made no effort to examine increasing expenditures in the multitude of new offices that proliferated because of the war. Worst of all, it projected a deficit of almost £800 million.[12] It was totally inadequate. And since Lloyd George's proposals to raise taxes on alcohol and beer had been defeated, these sources of new income were now foreclosed.

McKenna made no effort to change or amend the budget. Instead, he and Montagu weakly defended it, although Montagu, in response to criticism from the floor of Commons, did say he would soon give Parliament "a watertight proposal for getting at the extra income made during the War and for taxing it substantially."[13]

Second War Loan and War Savings Certificate

In June, McKenna proposed a Second War Loan (of £250 million) to help meet the deficit. By this time, the war was costing £3 million a day. Montagu helped in the drafting of this loan, writing to Venetia on June 15: "Beloved, I've had an awful time preparing the new loan which will be issued next week. We've found a good plan and rather original." [14] He told Venetia that he was also "busy hammering out a scheme against time by which the working man may invest in [the] War loan. I sit presiding over a committee on which Arthur Henderson and G. [Lloyd George] are remnants. I think I have a scheme." [15] He also told her that he had been "very busy with a part of a scheme to which I attach much importance and have devised what I think is a workable scheme to enable working men to subscribe." [16] This was the War Savings Certificate that played so important a role in World War I and World War II and that Montagu's fertile mind devised and developed.

Montagu not only helped to create these certificates but spent an inordinate amount of time popularizing them and establishing Voluntary War Savings Associations. These and the War Savings Certificates permitted the average Britisher to invest in this loan and, at the same time, encouraged him to save—a help in limiting inflation. The *Dictionary of National Biography (1922–30)* credited Montagu with both ideas, the War Savings Associations and the War Savings Certificates, and concluded that they were indispensable in raising enough cash to close the gap between tax revenue and the rising deficit.

Although Asquith did not appoint Montagu to the Cabinet, he continued to seek his advice and appreciated Montagu's loyalty and hard work. When Montagu praised Asquith for a particularly successful speech, Asquith replied, "You know well how high I rate your appreciation of anything I say or do. . . . I am very fortunate to have such a friend." [17]

Shadow Cabinet

Asquith's Private Secretaries, Maurice Bonham Carter, Eric Drummond, Masterton Smith, and Montagu were all friends and they saw one another frequently. These four men, along with Lt. Col.

Fitzgerald and Colonel Hankey, formed a "Brain Trust" that Asquith called "The Shadow Cabinet." They usually met at Montagu's home on Friday evenings. Their conversations covered every topic of interest to the group, but generally concentrated on the war and the problems it raised. Usually Montagu reported back to the Prime Minister if any ideas of special interest resulted from the discussions. His letter of July 3, 1915, following one such evening of conversation, was typical: It was sixteen pages long, brimming with ideas and suggestions.

Montagu addressed the military situation, concluding that not only had the 1915 Anglo-French offensive failed but the plan to drive the Germans from France through existing strategy was also doomed to failure. A frontal attack, he noted, usually required a ratio of three attackers for every one defender, and the French and English together did not have the requisite numbers. Those who based their hopes on substantially increasing the use of high explosives by the British Army "have not profited by the lesson to be learnt from the fact that the French have such equipment, have expended it lavishly, and found it useless." He was critical of French optimism, which he believed ignored the real factors against them and "is bound to produce disappointment, deterioration of morale and distrust of judgement." He was supportive of "mechanical inventions" (especially tanks) but warned that "whatever scientific surprises we have for the German must not be used until available in large numbers."

By now Montagu was certain that the war would be a long one and would become a "war of endurance." In such a situation, he concluded, finance would play a very important role. This was the theme he had been repeating since the war began. He was critical that one year into the war, the British people had not yet felt the pain of a war economy; the war had been waged "on the principle that no one ought to feel it if we can avoid it." He admonished the Prime Minister, writing, "that will not do." A war economy must include efforts to limit consumption and the importation of nonessential goods. It must limit supplies for civilians and must include the rationing of "bread, meat and other things." Government departments must also cut back, practice "rigid economy" and "increase taxes." It was not until after the fall of the Asquith government that some of these principles were put into effect and accepted by the politicians and the people. In World War II, they were immediately adopted, with hardly a whisper of objection.

Montagu saved most of his wrath for the Joint Stock Banks, which he accused of being selfish by trying to make a profit from the war and not helping in the War Loan. "Their selfishness is beyond belief and even now while they are asking concessions from the Chancellor of the Exchequer as a price of cooperation in the Loan, I hear that it is their intention—one bank has already carried it out—to keep their dividends as usual, notwithstanding the serious depreciation in capital values." [18] The letter ended with sharp criticism of the way manpower was being recruited and used. While Montagu did not express an opinion on whether enlistment should be voluntary or compulsory, he did state his concern that the allocation of men had ignored the nation's production needs. Not enough men were being assigned to produce the equipment, munitions and other supplies for the Army and to increase Britain's export trade, which he viewed as essential for Britain to sustain herself financially. France was heavily in debt with no financial plan to solve her predicament. He suggested a novel idea: Perhaps France should "hold the German" this winter (not attack) and let England not increase her armies but use her men to produce materials from the sale of which Britain could make money. "We can only finance them, we can only make munitions, we can only find the money if we can make more money; and we can only make money by selling abroad, as we alone of the Allies are able to do, because we have command of the seas." [19]

He said he had no objections to recruiting young men who reach eighteen for the Army, but he would not recruit men who were essential to other work. He suggested that recruitment should be under the direction of Lloyd George since recruitment was connected with munitions. He repeated again the need to manufacture only articles for profitable export. The government must either take over these firms or tax them heavily. No one, he wrote emphatically, should be allowed to make a profit in the war. He believed that England was capable of equipping an army of no more than 1,250,000 men. The number of men in training should thus not be more than two million. The rest should be sent back to work in essential industries.

Montagu was wrong about the number of men needed in the

Army. But he was correct in his criticism of how manpower was recruited and allocated. In this criticism he was not alone. By the autumn of 1915, many people already believed that voluntary recruitment could not meet the needs of the Army. Nor could it provide enough manpower for various segments of the economy, especially the industries producing munitions and other war materials and equipment. The cost of the war was now rising to almost £5 million a day, and the tax system and the industrial infrastructure were not adequate to meet expenditures of this magnitude.

The Third War Budget

From the moment he returned to the Treasury in May 1915, Montagu, the Treasury staff and McKenna began grappling with the problem of designing a budget that, unlike Lloyd George's last one, would provide enough revenue through taxation to meet the needs of the war. They were firm believers that only increased taxation, not continued and expanded borrowing, could save England from the threat of bankruptcy that faced the European nations. Borrowing must supplement the tax system, not replace it.

The budget introduced by McKenna and vigorously supported by Montagu in September 1915 was a reflection of that philosophy. It increased the income tax by 40 percent; it reduced exemptions and raised land assessments; it increased the super tax; and it placed a 50 percent tax on profits. This was the famous Excess Profits Tax that Montagu had promised Parliament during the debate on the Second War Budget in July 1915. Duties as high as 33½ percent were placed on luxury goods to discourage spending on extravagances and to help maintain a balance in foreign exchange. A new tax was placed on gasoline and postal rates were also increased.

The debate on the budget was intense, with Montagu and McKenna sharing the responsibility of convincing the House of Commons of the merits of its various proposals. The criticism of the protective duties was especially severe and Montagu spent a great deal of time trying to convince his adversaries that such duties were only "temporary measures" and that they were in no way intended to conflict with the doctrine of free trade.[20] This was not entirely true. The imposition of such tariffs was the first breach in the free trade doctrine, and it was an example of how the war was whittling away

"sacred articles of mid-Victorian faith and nineteenth century abso-
lutes."[21]

This budget laid the foundation of British war finance as it related
to taxation. "If England escaped financial ruin," the *Report on British
War Budgets,* prepared by the Carnegie Endowment for International
Peace, stated, it was because "a shuffling of offices gave us a Chancellor of the Exchequer who clapped on the taxes and set an example
which was followed to the end, making the revenue keep pace with
the debt charges."[22] The *Report* should also have said that the re-
shuffling of offices also gave Montagu back to the Treasury. His
strong feeling about the importance of increased taxation to carry
the burden of war, his belief in strict government economy, and his
adamant belief in the Excess Profits Tax and the taxes on luxury
goods, all helped McKenna not only to conceptualize these ideas,
but also to translate them into legislation and to help push them
through Parliament.

Conscription and Government Control

The Coalition found itself embroiled in a bitter controversy between
those who believed in voluntary enlistment with a minimum of
government intrusion and those who supported conscription and
more government control over the allocation of citizens in the war
effort. This controversy was causing a major rift within the Cabinet,
one over which Cabinet members often threatened to resign.

Englishmen were not accustomed to the idea of universal and
compulsory national service for war; they had a strong traditional
objection to the creation of large armed forces as potential instruments of tyranny and as infringements of personal liberty. The wars
they had waged in the past required only small professional armies
filled with volunteers attracted by the glamour of a uniform and the
King's shilling. They found it difficult to believe that the five million
men who had volunteered for the Army and the crucial industries
from Britain, the Dominions and India, between 1914 and 1915, or
were on waiting lists ready to be called, would not suffice.

Yet this new war of attrition, and the economic and production
needs it created, made an all-volunteer army obsolete. The inability
of the Asquith government and the Liberal Party to understand this
reality was a major factor in its ultimate fall. By October 1915, even

Kitchener acknowledged in a memorandum to the Cabinet that the volunteer system had failed to produce the manpower the country needed. He was not yet ready to endorse conscription but suggested instead a cumbersome system that mixed volunteer recruitment and compulsion. Conscription had become not only a serious military issue but also a political hot potato that threatened to topple the Coalition.

As early as August 16, 1915, Montagu concluded that it would be better if Asquith yielded to the demand for compulsory military service than risk the fall of the government. In a letter to Asquith, he acknowledged the importance of the issue and how it was being used as an opportunity "for putting an end to the present government and trying to get another." In his usual pragmatic manner, he expressed his view that the issue was philosophically not important. The volunteer system had failed, not because it was inherently wrong but because it had not been presented effectively or intelligently: "The volunteer system brought in enough men but brought in the 'wrong men.' " He advanced an opinion he had expressed earlier, that an effective compulsory system should not necessarily increase the army beyond a size that the country could properly arm and equip, but it should harness the total manpower of the nation and allocate men where they were needed most. The current system was leading to deplorable waste and mismanagement of available manpower. He did not consider the matter of compulsory recruitment serious enough to endanger the government. Conscription "may be unnecessary, it may be foolish, it may produce little result, but I doubt very much that it is sufficiently serious to plunge us into the fatal delays and friction caused by another change in government."

He pleaded with Asquith to understand the dimensions of the problem: "Please forgive me for troubling you," he wrote, "I want it to be said that you not only led the Liberal Party triumphantly for nearly ten years, but that you carried the War to a successful end." Always the "eyes and ears" of Asquith, he continued: "and it has come to my knowledge that this [compulsory recruitment] is to be made a test question." In ordinary times, he observed, Asquith's wait and see policy, to delay the decision until the storm blows over, might work. But these were not ordinary times. The opposition "is determined to prevent this and the material is so explosive that *one man* may precipitate the situation."[23]

Asquith did not act decisively. Instead he sought ways of reconciling the divergent opinions through compromise. He appointed Lord Derby the Director of Recruitment; his "Derby Scheme" sought to deal with the problem through an elaborate system of national registration requiring that every man of military age (eighteen to forty-one) register and "attest" to his willingness to serve. The men were divided into two groups, single and married, and then subdivided into categories by age and skill. The scheme failed. Only two million men out of a possible five million registered. About half of the two million single men took the trouble to attest, and many who did so were either rejected for medical reasons or were in jobs from which they could not be spared. Lord Derby estimated that the final number of men he would actually get for the Army from the entire effort would be 343,386 new recruits. This would not be enough to meet the needs of the Army and the home front.

The failure of the Derby Scheme merely intensified the conflict within and without the Cabinet, not only over recruitment but over the general failure of the war effort. It became another symbol, as Montagu had warned, of Asquith's inability to provide the Army with the fighting power it needed to break the stalemate and achieve victory. Montagu became increasingly worried and on October 22, 1915, in a most unusual letter that foresaw, with uncanny accuracy, what lay ahead, he urged Asquith to take the offensive to "strike before you are struck."[24] He warned Asquith that the Coalition would fail without a united policy and confidence among its members and that a general election in wartime was unthinkable. Therefore Asquith should not come near the House of Commons until he was prepared to state his policy; he should introduce a bill to prolong the life of Parliament and "use that occasion to make a statement and get a vote of confidence."[25] Montagu felt that Asquith should ask his critics and those of the war—for example, Churchill and Curzon—to resign "not from hostility but with regret on the ground that their action shows they are not in accord with you and your colleagues on war policy."[26] He warned Asquith that he should not let them resign first because then their colleagues, like Long and Law, "must, out of loyalty to the belief they share, go too. . . . The loss of a colleague by resignation," he wrote, "leaves you weaker (e.g. Curzon). The loss of a colleague by dismissal must leave you stronger."[27] Montagu believed too that Churchill and Curzon should be dismissed from the Cabinet "for the Cabinet which will be left to deal with departmental matters can't have loquacious people who have no departments left in it."[28]

He urged that Asquith take action against the press: announce

that what is impossible in the Cabinet is impossible in the Press. Discussion there is all right when it can be answered, but not now. You have taken administrative action by which *The Times,* the *Daily Mail,* and the *Evening News* would not appear again except under guarantee of good behavior. You were going to ask for an Act of Indemnity and powers to treat any other newspaper similarly. But act before you get the power—drama and suddenness is absolutely essential.

Montagu suggested that "the War be conducted by a committee of three—Asquith, Balfour and Lord Kitchener," with Asquith having the right to call in others as necessary. This recommendation by Montagu was made at least a year before such a small War Cabinet was suggested by Lloyd George and Hankey. It was, in fact, the argument over the establishment of this committee that eventually ended the Asquith regime.

Lloyd George was not included in Montagu's suggested "Committee of Three" because: "If you have a larger Committee you get involved in questions of balance of parties in coalition and who to leave out. Put in any one person and you can't stop him. . . . George is not a war minister but a supply minister."[29] Montagu also urged Asquith to "tell Bonar Law you will not appoint his nominees when vacancies occur. Parties are now fused and you want the best man of which you must be the judge."[30]

Montagu would have liked to see Lloyd George entirely dismissed from the Cabinet because of his criticism of Asquith, but he concluded that this was "impossible," because Lloyd George was still too strong in the country and the army.

So for sheer expediency I suggest you keep him, shorn of his press and after a very straight talk about his conduct. His appointment of Lee and Money just now are most impudent. But I still do not think him treacherous at all. He is panic-stricken. He must be told to pull himself together, to work loyally with his colleagues, etc., and he must be appealed to on his sentimental side, reminded of all he owes to you, etc., etc., He is an asset and would be formidable still outside.[31]

The letter concluded with a plea that Asquith "strike before you are struck—that you should strike dramatically."[32] This letter was probably the most important Montagu ever sent to Asquith, whose failure to follow its advice helped to doom his government.

With the failure of the Derby Scheme, the Cabinet began to inch toward conscription and on December 28, 1915, introduced a bill to draft all single men. McKenna, Runciman and Grey resigned despite Margot Asquith's plea: "Do you love your opinions more than you love him?"[33] On hearing of the resignations, Montagu implored McKenna to stay.

The P.M. has told me of your interview with him to-day and its purport.

I am more miserable than I can say. We have worked six months in perfect happiness so far as I am concerned . . . think what you will of me, . . . I feel that I must above all else stick to the P.M. to the end.

I would implore you to take the same view whatever sacrifice it may involve. I believe that by so doing you would earn his support in resisting the demands of the War Office and obtain it.[34]

In spite of Montagu's unhappiness with McKenna's decision to resign, he believed that McKenna was correct in concluding that the General Staff's demand for fifty-four divisions, plus thirteen divisions for home service (which necessitated compulsion), was excessive. To the Prime Minister, Montagu wrote: "McKenna ought to win. The General Staff only needs according to my calculations 4–5 divisions for home defense [in addition to the 54 divisions for overseas]. If they could agree on this, there would be no need for a compulsory draft." Concerning the number of men needed to fight the Germans, he wrote, "there is no difference between McKenna and the General Staff."[35] On the basis of such calculations, a compromise for limited compulsion for single men was worked out, and the ministers who resigned, including McKenna, came back into the Cabinet. Asquith told his wife that no praise was too much for Lord Reading, Montagu and Hankey, whose skill and patient persuasion had helped to produce the compromise.[36]

Raymond Asquith on Trench Warfare

In February 1916, the Germans launched their offensive at Verdun. For five months, they battled Allied forces day and night but made few, if any, real advances. While the gains were slight, the slaughter was immense, with almost as many deaths from the diseases and

filth of the trenches as from shells and bullets. Few descriptions of
trench warfare were as graphic and heartbreaking as those contained
in Raymond Asquith's letters home, in spite of the cynical detachment he tried to affect. "Mud and water are well above the knee and
the cold intense. . . . An unpleasant feature is the vast number of
rats which gnaw the dead bodies and then run about on one's face,
making obscene noises and gestures. Lately a certain number of cats
have taken to nesting in the corpses but I think the rats will get them
under in the end; though like all wars it will undoubtedly be a war
of attrition."[37] Raymond continued:

The trenches are so filthy that there is a temptation, hard to resist, even by
the most lily-livered, to walk about on top of them instead of the bottom.
One has to remind oneself that Mr. Don't Care was eaten by the lions.
Rifle bullets, as long as they don't come in great numbers are rather more
exciting than alarming; Shells I believe can be terrifying. . . . [T]he noise is
rather irritating. . . . [T]here is hardly a minute of the day and night when
one or another . . . is not banging away.[38]

At other times, Raymond wrote about the long walks in rain and
mud which the soldiers had to make "most of the time," and, if one
was lucky, "one can lie down for a couple of hours in the mud or
better still on a plank the width of a knife board."[39]

Occasionally, he confessed, there were moments of excitement,
even of happiness, "when one marches in late at night after a week
of dirt and bullets and finds a feather bed and a bottle of Boy
waiting." But most of the time the soldier's life is boredom, nausea,
discomfort, danger, terror and death—"one's mind collapses . . .
with no visible horizon . . . looking no farther ahead than the next
meal."[40]

Raymond mourned for his friends who had been killed, "moving
from the Lido to the Styx," and quoted Omar Khayyám:

> And some there be, the loveliest and best
> That rolling Time has from his Vintage pressed
> Have drunk their cup a round or two before
> And one by one crept silently to rest.[41]

Most of the soldiers did not die silently. They died crying in
agony from injuries caused by shells and mortars powerful enough
to rip a body to shreds. The worst part of the tragedy was the

enormous supply of men needed to keep the war machine alive. Anything short of conscription could no longer suffice.

Compulsory Draft Becomes Law

On March 28, 1916, Montagu telegraphed to Asquith at a conference in Paris that the conscriptionists were again demanding immediate legislation to provide compulsory military service for all able-bodied men, married and unmarried alike. He urged that Hankey return to Britain at once and not go with Asquith to Rome, where the Prime Minister was to try to convince the Italians to join the Allies.

A Cabinet Committee on Military Manpower and Finance was appointed. Its report was a victory for Asquith and for those who opposed conscription. It concluded that there was no case to be made for extending compulsion to all men of military age. The present system with some modifications was adequate. Montagu believed it was a first-rate report and that the Prime Minister was now "clear of that ditch" and should be congratulated on his chairmanship of the Committee.[42]

Montagu misjudged the intensity of feeling that conscription generated. The manpower crisis was far from over. The Cabinet was still sharply divided and was not satisfied with the compromise suggested by the House Committee. A majority of the House of Commons and the public, inflamed by the press, were pushing hard for total conscription. Asquith was furious both at the press and those Cabinet members who took this position. He believed they were reacting with hysteria and that if they waited until June (the date of the scheduled Somme attack), as he wrote on April 18, they would discover that their arguments had been "purely academic." He was especially angry with Lloyd George, whom he viewed as the "villain of the piece"[43] and the one responsible for agitating the press.

Asquith's anger became irrelevant. Pressure for conscription became too strong for him to withstand, and on May 2, he succumbed by asking the House to support a measure for general and immediate military service for all men between the ages of eighteen and forty-one, except those needed for economic reasons. Asquith's request received a cold reception but met with little opposition. It went through all stages of the parliamentary process by May 25; on the third reading, only twenty-seven Liberals and ten Labour representatives voted against it. Immediately after its adoption, the War Committee of the Cabinet appointed a Committee on Manpower to implement the act and direct the assignment of the men who would now be drafted. It was a monumental administrative job. The Prime Minister asked Montagu to become the Chairman. He declined on the grounds that he could not do this without neglecting his work as Financial Secretary to the Treasury. That Asquith was prepared to give this responsibility to Montagu was a significant tribute to him and to the role he had played in trying to solve the conscription problem, a role Asquith called "indefatigable." [44]

Montagu's Criticism of Diplomatic Service and the Contract with J. P. Morgan

One of the Montagu's pet peeves throughout his political career had been the inadequacies of the civil service mentality, whether at the Treasury, in India, or, as on February 26, 1916, in the British Diplomatic Service. He wrote to Eric Drummond, then Grey's Private Secretary, that the Diplomatic Service was "at the root of all our ailments, past and present."

Look at Persia, Turkey, Bulgaria, France, Italy. Give yourself the pleasure of an interview with any of our moth-eaten Ambassadors who have returned from belligerent countries: and I do not even yet despair of getting you to agree with me that the diplomatic service, with its predilection for promotion by seniority, its method of recruitment, its concomitant of divorcing the ambassadors from everything the Home Government is thinking, its practice of refusing to speak English but of communicating among themselves or at home in the language of diplomatic telegrams— all these have robbed our diplomacy of life. In the early part of the War I tried, having enlisted the sympathies of Lloyd George, to get Edward Grey to take Balkan Diplomacy into his own hands on the spot. I wonder what the result would have been had we done that. [45]

Montagu also expressed his concern with the contract Britain had signed with J. P. Morgan & Company in the United States. Under this contract, negotiated in 1915, Morgan would coordinate all arms purchases in America. According to the *Dictionary of National Biog-*

raphy (1922–1930), Montagu had initiated this agreement, which saved the Allies many hundreds of millions of pounds on their American purchases of munitions and arms.[46] When the agreement was completed, Montagu had been assured that "Spring Rice, however amiable and delightful he undoubtedly may be," would not be given the responsibility to oversee the implementation of the agreement in the United States because, according to Montagu, he had "no influence in America." Montagu had suggested "that Lord Rosebery should be asked to take his place or Bryce sent back on special mission. I never heard it argued that Spring Rice was satisfactory, but of course nothing has been done." Montagu suggested that "Crewe or Hardinge on his return from India" be sent "at once to America," adding, "I know things are pretty bad at Paris, but you can trust Bertie to gossip amiably and it is possible to ascertain exactly what is going on in Paris by sending someone under 150 and not so fond of dinner-table gossip from time to time to see what is actually going on. Yours in great anger E. S. M."[47]

Such sweeping attacks against the Diplomatic Corps and against men such as Spring Rice and others did not endear Montagu to the vast number of men involved in the British Foreign Service. Word quickly spread that Montagu was a critic and an enemy. It would come to haunt him when he became Secretary of State for India.

The Fourth War Budget

On April 4, 1916, the fourth War Budget was introduced. Like its predecessor, it included large increases in income tax, a new entertainment duty and more increases in taxes on sugar, cocoa, coffee, and motor cars, as well as some new duties on matches, mineral waters and other nonessentials. In addition, it raised the Excess Profits Tax from 50 percent to 60 percent. This time there were few complaints.

In fact, the budget received widespread praise: "Practically every speaker during the discussion congratulated McKenna on its clearness . . . and nearly all approved of the Budget in general."[48] Raising a large part of the costs of war by taxation was viewed as a courageous and sensible policy, unlike Lloyd George's previous budget. Montagu was pleased, finding the "reception of the Budget very gratifying."[49] Montagu was never troubled by what some people viewed as an intrusion of government into the lives of its citizens through increased taxes and compulsory conscription.

In a speech in Cambridge on February 21, 1916, he pleaded for an open mind on state control of fiscal policy in light of the experiences derived from the war. "Look back," he said, "and see the use which Germany has made of her trade, and ask yourselves whether we can afford or dare to let that happen again."[50]

Montagu's attitude was closer to that of Lloyd George and the Labour Party than to Asquith's, whose traditional Liberalism made it difficult for him to accept extensive government control. But traditional Liberal methods could no longer win this nontraditional war. Montagu was supported by others in the Liberal Party and by many Tories who had become outspoken "proponents of greater State control over the nation's material and human resources in the interest of victory."[51]

Little did they know that such controls would not end with the war: They would remain a fundamental part of British governance and transform the economic and social structure of Great Britain in a manner utterly antithetical to Tory and Liberal philosophy.

The Easter Rebellion (April 1916); Montagu Asked to Serve As Irish Secretary

On July 10, 1916, the country was faced with another major crisis, one as bitter as any that the Cabinet had ever faced: rebellion in Ireland.

"In the early summer of 1914," Lloyd George wrote in his *Memoirs:*

. . . the Protestant North had reached a state of incipient rebellion, and was arming and drilling for resistance to the decision of the imperial Parliament. The Catholic South had begun to copy these tactics, and raise National Volunteers to match the Ulster Volunteers of the North. There was gun running at Larne to supply Ulster with guns from Germany; and then one at Howth to supply South Ireland. The paradox of the situation was that Ulster's rebellion was acclaimed by a powerful section of British opinion as loyalty, while Southern Ireland's preparations to defend the decision of the Imperial Parliament were denounced as sedition.

At the outbreak of the Great War, the Home Rule Act was suspended . . . to procure a measure of unity, in face of the common danger. For the moment this action achieved its purpose, but it may be doubted whether in the long run it proved profitable. For Southern Ireland, seeing its hopes dashed at the moment when they were about to be realized, at first sulked in resentment and soon became a mass of seething disaffection.[52]

On February 7, 1916, two months before the Easter Rebellion, Montagu had written to Sir Thomas Heath, Permanent Secretary to the Treasury, of Montagu's recent trip to Ireland. What he saw there convinced him that the Government's policy was not only wrong "but on dangerous lines," that anti-English feeling was growing, and "that every opportunity was being taken to gain recruits to foster the separatist movement."[53]

He left Ireland "frightened" by the situation. While the war lasted, he believed the best way to keep Ireland from rebelling or joining the Germans was to "keep them sweet on money matters and £10,000 spent to avert a row is far better than £10,000 saved at the cost of a row."[54] He believed that the Government must pay careful attention to the administration of Ireland, not to create difficulties for the Irish Government or for the Nationalist Party, "for they are our weakening bulwark."[55] By April 1916, encouraged by Germany and by Irish Americans, the Sinn Fein leaders in Dublin decided on open rebellion, to occur on Easter Day, April 23, two days after the arrival of the Irish revolutionary leader Roger Casement by boat from Germany.

Although the British captured the boat, on Easter Sunday small disturbances took place in Dublin and in some other parts of the country. In Dublin, it took several days to quell them; in other places they were easily suppressed. Several of the rebel leaders were tried by court martial and shot.

Shortly after the Easter Rebellion, and on the same day on which the Prime Minister accepted Birrell's resignation as Chief Secretary of Ireland, Asquith held a dinner party attended by Montagu and Venetia, Maurice and Violet Bonham Carter, Eric Drummond and Maurice Hankey, at which the Prime Minister raised the question of who should succeed Birrell. By then, his anger and shock at Venetia's marriage to Montagu had softened to the point where they were again part of his inner circle.

After the dinner discussion on May 1, Asquith offered the post of Chief Secretary of Ireland to Montagu, who was both "surprised and disconcerted." Montagu refused, saying that being a Jew would be a deterrent, since the Secretary of Ireland "had to deal with religious questions in a creed," he explained, "in which I do not believe."[56] He felt that he was too much of a coward to assume responsibility for a situation fraught with the seeds of violence and revolution. In addition, he told Asquith, he knew very little about Ireland.

When he heard Montagu talk about his cowardice, Hankey commented, "I never saw any sign."[57] As for Montagu's knowledge of Ireland, he had in fact a lifelong interest in the country and its people and, as an intimate friend of Birrell, was very well informed on the Irish problem. During the Irish crisis of 1913, he had played an active role in trying to bring both sides together. Nor had he ever believed that being a Jew was a deterrent to his becoming Viceroy of India, where he would have had to make major decisions affecting Muslims and Hindus. Why was this any different from making decisions involving Catholics?

The real reasons for his refusal are contained in a letter he wrote to the Prime Minister the following day, May 2, in which he explained that the Irish post would take him away from the conduct of the war with which he was profoundly concerned. It was, moreover, a no-win situation and a political dead end. He wrote:

1) I put first the fact that my personal relations with Birrell are so intimate and affectionate that the idea of stepping into his shoes when he retired in something like disgrace is repugnant to me in the extreme. I think this personal consideration applies to Birrell more than to any other member of the Cabinet after—and a long way after—yourself.

2) I am, as you know, profoundly interested in the conduct of the War and what is to come out of the War; . . . I cannot contemplate, without abandoning most of my political interests, being taken away from any connection with any of these topics to undertake work in no way connected with the War. . . .

3) There is no possibility of doing Ireland well. It must mean, it seems to me, for me an approximation to political death. . . . It is hard to contemplate this before one has ever enjoyed the task of attempting to do any of the things one has wanted to do.[58]

In this letter, Montagu analyzed his qualifications and concluded he could not administer any situation that would involve repression and coercion. He shrinks "with horror from being responsible for punishment," he wrote. Nor could he bear the criticism of the press, although he had done his best to fight against this. He had not succeeded in overcoming it. He knew that these qualities "set a fearful limit" on his political aspirations, but "to nervous and sensitive persons these limits must exist."[59]

Montagu suggested that one day he might make a "Chancellor of the Exchequer," or an "imaginative administrator of the Board of Trade" or a "good Minister of Munitions"; he might be able to handle "the problems of the local Government Board," or the "civilian side of the War Office or Admiralty." But, he concluded, the offices he could never hold were the Home Secretary of Ireland, the Colonial Secretary, or Secretary of State for India. As for the last, he modified his statement by adding that "I frankly admit that my enthusiasm for Indian affairs might have led to an obscuring of the disadvantage by the absorbing interest which I should find in the functions of the office."[60]

Montagu's analysis of himself was on the mark. When his "absorbing interest" in India led him in 1917 to accept the post of Secretary of State for India, his sensitivity and abhorrence of punishment made it impossible for him to administer a policy of repression and persecution. Instead, in the face of widespread opposition he steadfastly sought to solve the problems in a noncoercive fashion. This brought him only condemnation and ultimately failure.

Asquith did not press Montagu. He understood his reluctance to go to Ireland and this in no way lessened his appreciation of Montagu's loyalty and service. "For ten years," he wrote to him at Easter, 1916, "your friendship and devotion have never failed me; and each successive trouble in these harassing times brings me fresh proof of the value of your affection and counsel."[61]

Lloyd George Attempts to Find a Solution

Until a new Secretary could be appointed, Asquith sent the Permanent Secretary of the Treasury, Sir Robert Chalmers, to Ireland to hold the fort. In the meantime, he did what he had done in the past: He temporarily added the Secretaryship of Ireland to his own burdens and, on the night of May 11, went to Dublin himself to examine the situation.

He met some of the most "hard bitten Carsonite leaders," toured the country, examined the administration of justice, and visited the men in jail, releasing those against whom the evidence was slight. On his return to London, he wrote that he "was inclined to put much of the rebellion down to economic conditions. Some 12,000 families in Dublin lived in single rooms."[62] Keeping Home Rule in limbo was no longer a workable arrangement. A new solution had to be found. He asked Lloyd George, whose sympathy with the Irish was well known, to try to negotiate a settlement. He would have preferred that Lloyd George become Chief Secretary, but Lloyd George, like Montagu, did not want a permanent position in Ireland. The most he would do was to agree to find some solution.

Asquith's request that Lloyd George try to negotiate an Irish settlement and the latter's acceptance may have saved his life. Lloyd George had planned to accompany Lord Kitchener to Russia to develop closer military cooperation with the Russians. After his decision to accept Asquith's offer to try his hand at an Irish settlement, Kitchener left without him on the H.M.S. *Hampshire,* which sank after hitting a German mine in the North Sea. Kitchener and the staff with him were all killed.

Lloyd George assumed his new responsibilities to seek an Irish settlement with his usual vigor, creativity and determination. He met with all the key players in the Irish drama and, after much discussion, he and they accepted by mid-June a settlement that would provide immediate Home Rule for all of the six disputed counties until the end of the war. The ultimate solution for the area and the future of the Irish government would be determined by an Imperial Conference. In the meantime, all eighty Irish Members of Parliament would continue to sit at Westminster.

Both sides in the North and South had accepted these terms. But when they were published, the Unionists (not the Ulstermen, but the bulk of the English Conservatives) revolted. Asquith was able to work out a modified version of Lloyd George's proposals that satisfied the Cabinet. When the House of Lords met on July 11, however, the Marquess of Lansdowne, who had seemed reluctant to accept the terms in the Cabinet, now spoke strongly against them. He emphasized that Ulster must be permanently excluded and that Southern Ireland must be governed by a strengthened Defense of the Realm Act, with which the Dublin Parliament would have no right to interfere. The whole agreement fell apart and, by August 24, Asquith wrote that he thought the proposal was dead.

With the leading players at one another's throats, Asquith stopped the process of negotiations, appointed a new Chief Secretary for Ireland and reverted to the old system of governance and control. This decision has been strongly criticized. If Asquith had stood firmly behind Lloyd George's proposal, he might have marshaled enough support in Parliament to get the agreement passed. Instead, he gave in without a fight. As a result, the rebellion and Lloyd George's efforts achieved nothing. Ireland was again left to fester and become further dissatisfied and rebellious. The old-line Tories had destroyed a good opportunity to find a settlement—"They had the bulk of Conservative opinion with them."[63] With their eradication of Lloyd George's proposal, they not only destroyed the chance of finding a solution for Ireland but the conflict they generated within the Cabinet and Parliament added to the criticism of the Coalition. Its days were now numbered.

19

Montagu at Munitions, July–December 1916

We are out; it can only be a question of time when we shall have to leave Downing Street.

Margot Asquith, Diary, *July 1916*

On Kitchener's death Lloyd George became Secretary of War, and on July 1, 1916, Asquith appointed Edwin Montagu the Minister of Munitions. Lloyd George had suggested that Winston Churchill be given the Ministry.[1] The good feelings that Lloyd George may have had about Montagu in their early collaboration at the Treasury were not sufficient in 1916 to warrant his recommending Montagu as his successor at Munitions.

For his part, Montagu continued to admire Lloyd George's creative mind and drive, and even as his distrust of him increased, Montagu recognized his extraordinary value to the war effort. Asquith had similar feelings. Lloyd George had not been his first choice for the War Office. For three weeks he had searched for another appointee, but for one reason or another, none of his choices were available. He even considered holding the post himself. Indeed Lord French "on behalf of the whole Army,"[2] fearing the appointment of Lloyd George, pleaded with Asquith to consider doing this. For political reasons Asquith concluded that this would not be a wise decision. Moreover, like Montagu, Asquith had great respect for Lloyd George's talents, in spite of his distrust. In the past, he had given Lloyd George many difficult tasks to perform and was generally pleased with the results. He also thought that the Allies would welcome such an appointment.

Margot Asquith, unlike her husband, saw the appointment as the beginning of the end of Asquith's Premiership. She recorded in her diary: "We are out: it can only be a question of time now when we shall have to leave Downing Street."[3] Montagu did not share her fears. He thought it was a good appointment, not only because of Lloyd George's popularity, but because Lloyd George expected the appointment and would probably make political mischief if it were denied him. Also, he believed it would be useful to have Lloyd George at the War Office "during the announcement of heavy casualties and a possibly unfruitful offensive."[4] The letter in which Montagu made this remark was found, according to Frank Owen, by Lloyd George's secretary, J. T. Davies, in a drawer at 10 Downing Street long after Asquith had gone and Lloyd George had become Prime Minister. "Some people wonder if it had been left deliberately."[5]

Montagu was delighted with his appointment as Minister of Munitions. The appointment gave him a Cabinet post again, something which he had sorely missed. The problem of providing the necessary amounts of ammunition and equipment to wage the war successfully had intrigued Montagu from the start. He always believed that this responsibility should be taken away from the War Department and handled separately. He had written to Asquith as early as May 1915 describing a scheme for an Army Contracts Directorate with a Minister in Charge. At other times, he had suggested two Secretaries of War, one a Civil Secretary to handle recruitment and munitions purchases. His services as Executive Secretary of the Shell Committee also brought him into close contact with this problem. He thus came to his new position with considerable interest and background.

The enormous scope of this Ministry was captured in Montagu's address to Parliament on August 16, 1916, in which he said that in one day he had had to deal with a "friendly controversy with a government office about the transport from the . . . Arctic Circle to a neutral country of a mineral which name is unknown to me but which . . . was needed in the output of certain . . . munitions"; the need for pressing India for the construction of a railway "in the interest of Munitions supply"; the question of gold in South Africa; the allocation of certain chemicals "to meet the competing needs of the Army, the Navy and the Air Service"; discussion of contracts in America "valued at over £10 million sterling"; consideration of

"ingenious artificial legs"; and the "quickest means of manufacturing gun carriages" plus "a hundred and one topics which must
confront any body of men who spend their whole days watching
curves which ought always to go up and figures which ought always
to swell; reading reports from all parts of the world, and confronted
always with the cry, 'more, more, more,' and 'better, better, better!' "[6]

Montagu went on to say that there were five hundred different
munitions manufacturing processes in which women were now engaged, two-thirds of which had never before been performed by
women. Women were now indispensable to the war effort, working
not only in munitions, "but in hospitals, agriculture, in transport
trades and in every type of clerical operation. When the time and
occasion offer," he suggested to the House, "it will be opportune to
ask 'Where is the man now who would deny to women the civil
rights which she has earned by hard work?' "

The Radical Liberal in Montagu came to the fore now as he ended
his speech praising "the new spirit in every department of industry"
which he believed "is not destined to disappear" when the war
ended. Rather, he hoped the system of controls now in place and the
"General Staff of British Industry" which had been organized would
be used after the war and "all this moral and material energy can be
turned to peaceful account instead of being dispersed in peacetime."
State control of economic planning, Montagu believed, was a healthy
and progressive development that should not be dismantled at war's
end. On this, he went much further than Asquith and his traditional
Liberal colleagues. They viewed such control as a necessary wartime
expedient—an evil that interfered with economic freedom. The
sooner it could be removed, the better.

A Brief but Productive Tenure

Montagu was fortunate that much of the preliminary work of creating the Munitions department had been performed by Lloyd George
in the year in which he held that position. Lloyd George had started
with no organization and a tiny staff. Within a year, his drive and
genius not only built a huge and complex organization but brought
into Munitions an unusual cadre of men of action and experience
from the business community. His "men of push and go" seemed

to perform miracles. He was also able to persuade workers to join this crusade to become "soldiers in England's defense," a feat he accomplished through extraordinary effort. Without the participation of Labour, there could be no victory.

When Montagu arrived at the Ministry, it had nineteen departments and a staff of five thousand. During Montagu's tenure, the staff increased to eight thousand, with new responsibilities added and new departments created. When the Department was handed over by Montagu's successor, Addison, to Winston Churchill only a year later, it had fifty departments and fifteen thousand employees.

While Lloyd George was enormously successful in increasing the production and distribution of munitions, he had little patience with accepted principles of organization and had given little thought to creating even a semipermanent departmental structure. Under his direction the various sections of the Ministry "constituted a confederation of separate units, tied together through the person of the Minister and his staff."[7] It had many administrative weaknesses; it suffered from poor coordination and depended heavily on Lloyd George's personal style of operation. "When the house is on fire," Lloyd George quipped, "questions of procedure and precedence, of etiquette and time and division of Labour must disappear."[8]

Montagu's first task, therefore, in assuming his new post was to bring order to the Ministry. In August, six weeks after becoming Minister, Montagu summoned the heads of each Ministry department to discuss the best means of "securing relief for the Minister in his arduous duties and ensuring smooth working and cooperation throughout the department."[9] He recognized that the Ministry of Munitions must be organized differently from the old-line departments in the government. Red tape must be kept to a minimum and department heads must be given freedom to do their jobs, unfettered by restrictions and controls. A contemporary source wrote: "Speaking as an 'unprejudiced observer' and after testifying to his growing appreciation of the work of the Ministry," Montagu explained that he recognized that the organization of "an old established government department manned by civil servants with a well-established organization hierarchy" could afford to be bureaucratic and slow. Munitions, by the nature of its responsibility, had to be organized differently. "The keynote of the Ministry is putting responsible people at the head of responsible departments and leaving them to conduct their businesses just as the head of a business in the commercial world would conduct it."[10]

But Montagu told his department heads, "this makes the position of the political head of the Ministry extraordinarily difficult."

He cannot regard himself, as he does in an old-established office, as a transitory fount, a telephone for communicating the activities of the department to the House of Commons. He has got to regard himself as a sort of epitome in himself of the permanent head of the department and the political head of the department, the sole focus for the coordination that exists. Well—I do not say that is fair to him, and I do not think, it is the best way of securing coordination between the departments and the Ministry.[11]

Montagu outlined to his staff two alternative methods of operation, either a Board of Directors, or, borrowing from the organization of the French Ministry of Munitions, an office of *Chef de Cabinet*. "*The Chef de Cabinet* is a personal assistant to the Minister who has his own department, in a way a kind of Board of Directors, but much more analogous to a Staff in an army."[12]

Montagu explained in great detail how both systems would work, concluding that:

Both of these schemes have this in common, that there is no suggestion of putting anybody with executive responsibility over departments. Both of these schemes have the one feature in common that they should form the machinery for bringing departments together, and for making sure that inter-departmental questions which ought to be considered are not forgotten.[13]

The *History of the Ministry of Munitions* concludes that the "whole of the subsequent history of the centralization of the Ministry may be regarded as commentary of the above speech."[14]

A year was to pass before an organization satisfying Mr. Montagu's requirements was set up, though the Munitions Council organization as framed by Mr. Churchill, followed on the experiments inaugurated by Mr. Montagu and continued by Dr. Addison, in the development of which, as will later be seen, the idea of a *Cabinet du Ministre*, though not formally adopted, had important influence.[15]

The department heads met unofficially with Montagu on August 22. While not accepting the idea of a *Cabinet du Ministre*, all agreed that the existing organization was defective and that Montagu should reinstate the meetings of the department heads, which Lloyd George had abandoned. They agreed that a small advisory committee be appointed, with a secretary to advise and consult with the Minister.

The first newly inaugurated regular meeting of the department heads was held on October 22, 1916. Montagu made it clear that the group would meet regularly every two weeks; he would prepare an agenda for each meeting; and only those departments involved in the agenda items would be invited. At the first meeting, Montagu set the tone for his administration.

The first consideration is now no longer the desire to harness energy and speech in developing the sources of production; what we have now to do is to consider the best use to make of our mobilized resources. The disadvantage of mobilization is that, when you have mobilized what you have got, there is less to be mobilized in the future and, although I have not the slightest doubt that we are in a better position than any other country in the world, enemy or ally, yet the fact remains that, both in materials and manpower, the more we do, the shorter we become, and our chief aim, if we are going to husband these resources, ought to be to act collectively, so that there shall be no overlapping, as little competition as possible in our desire to supply all we can for the Allies and our own cause.[16]

On October 3, 1916, even before the department heads met, Montagu set up a small Advisory Committee. The Chairman, Sir Arthur M. Duckham, K.C.B., and Vice Chairman, Sir James S. Barth, had no department duties. The other five members were heads of departments chosen for their personal qualifications. Duckham, thirty-eight, was an engineer by profession and had been in charge of the department responsible for the production of rifles and machine guns and the ammunition for both. The following month, when Asquith wanted to appoint Duckham as Food Controller, Montagu objected, writing on November 27, 1916:

When I reorganized the Ministry, I started an Advisory Committee of my six best men to view the Ministry as a whole and investigate each problem as it came up. I refer them to the Committee and the Committee suggest references of its own. They have already produced invaluable reports on many subjects and have helped to construct an ordered Ministry in which departments are kept related to one another. The Committee is already much overworked. It really constitutes a "General Staff." Duckham is Chairman. This work and his work on inventions keep him more than fully occupied, and he is the principal man here to whom I am looking for advice on our own very important reconstruction problems.[17]

The Advisory Committee was at first viewed with skepticism and concern, since department heads feared it would become yet another department and usurp their power. Montagu spent considerable time allaying these fears. The Committee was given no executive powers; it would not relieve the Minister of his responsibilities or stand between him and the department heads. The responsibility of all officers would remain the same. The Committee would be restricted to specific assignments, given to it by the Minister after conferring with department heads. Montagu was so successful in designing the Committee so it would not infringe on departmental duties that Sir Alexander Roger, a Committee member, later wrote that he had been amazed to see "the camaraderie and esprit de corps" that permeated its meetings.[18]

As he had expected, Montagu found that one of the most difficult questions he and his Ministry faced was the problem of manpower and industrial unrest.

The Army was desperately short of recruits, munitions factories were desperately short of workers, and there was profound and widespread unrest among industrial workers, led by the shop stewards, due to the belief that the pledged word of the Government was being violated; that dilution was being used to force skilled men into the army, and to exempt those who had taken up munitions work to evade military service.[19]

To meet the complaints of Labour and the ends of the War Office, Montagu devised scores of formulas that he believed could provide the Army with the number of men it needed, consistent with the demand for the manufacture of munitions. He saw no room for differences between the War Office and the Ministry of Munitions; both were working on the same problem. He believed, however, that the manpower needs of the Ministry of Munitions should not be under the control of the Manpower Board of the War Office.[20] Eventually he won his argument, but not before some hostile words were exchanged between him and the War Office. He made no friends in this conflict. The results gave him the flexibility to work successfully with both Labour and Business. Montagu's six months at Munitions were always viewed by him as "the most satisfying and enjoyable of his career."[21] The Ministry grew; new responsibilities were undertaken; the output of all kinds of munitions multiplied and, most important, coordination became "the watchword of administrative policy."[22] When Montagu's tenure was over a colleague at the War Office wrote:

I cannot tell you how sorry I am that you are leaving your present post. If at times during our official acquaintance I may have seemed obstructive, it was only in my desire to get the War Office on its proper footing in regard to Munitions, which it had certainly lost in days gone by. *But I can honestly say that since you have been at the head of the Munitions Department, I always felt that I was dealing with one who had the interest of the Nation at heart.* [emphasis added]

Yours ever sincerely
General Sir C. F. N. Macready[23]

Montagu, Churchill and the Tank

While at Munitions, Montagu and Churchill became increasingly friendly. Both men had imaginative minds that were never happier than when contemplating a new strategy, idea or invention. Early in the war, both had become intrigued with the idea of the tank. On January 5, 1915, Churchill had sent Asquith a memorandum suggesting that it would be simple "to fit up a number of steam tractors with small armored shelters, in which men and machine guns could be placed, that would be bullet proof."[24] Asquith allocated £70,000 to develop a design for a prototype for such a machine. When the first one was completed, the War Office, calling it "Winston's Folly," said that "tanks were not wanted; they would be unable to cope with mud."[25]

From the start of the war, Montagu had also pressed Asquith to encourage new methods of conducting the war, including the tank: Guns and men would never be enough. "The future of the War," he had warned Asquith in July, "depends largely on mechanical inventions."[26] Montagu was especially pleased, therefore, when in November 1916 Churchill wrote to him about a "new conception of the method of attack by mechanical agency which I should be glad to unfold to a select and secret audience."[27] Churchill and Montagu became colleagues in lobbying for reconsideration of a new tank design that might break the deadlock and the slaughter of the young men at the front.

When Montagu became Minister of Munitions, he continued to press for the tank and the airplane, as well as other new inventions. Money was allocated for these innovations, and when Churchill took over Munitions on July 20, 1917, the design for the tank was well on its way. Under Churchill's direction, 456 tanks were ready for a major "tank offensive" east of Amiens on August 8, 1918. In retrospect, "this was the turning point in the War's last convulsion. . . . 'the black day of the German army.' "[28] While the offensive gained little and the position of both sides remained the same, the Germans had been stopped and their faith in their own invincibility was shattered. From then on, they knew they could not win. The significance of the tank was profound.[29]

Montagu's and Churchill's instincts had been correct, and their persistence paid off. To Churchill belongs the honor of being "the father of the tank." But when the tanks rolled into battle at Amiens, Montagu had the satisfaction of knowing that he, as well as Churchill, had had the vision to see the importance of this weapon and to encourage its creation.

Conflict with McKenna

While Montagu's relationship with Churchill and with most of the men in his own Ministry were good, he continued to make enemies in the broader political world. For example, he told Arthur Henderson, one of Labour's most respected leaders, that Henderson's suggestion that he be named an Under Secretary in Munitions was "impertinent,"[30] although he would like him to be "Labour Advisor to the Ministry of Munitions."[31] He complained to Asquith that McKenna had deliberately not taken him to the Allied Conference in London, at which the Russian and French Ministers of Munitions were present, and that McKenna was not telling the truth when he said that Montagu would have nothing to say about his scheme for purchasing in common by a Central Bureau. In fact, Montagu had never seen "the scheme in writing."[32] He had seen the plan and he had many objections to it. McKenna, moreover, gave the War Committee a distorted picture of the plan. "Therefore," Montagu concluded, "I think the Chancellor of the Exchequer is misinformed."[33]

His relationship with McKenna went from bad to worse. Apparently, McKenna had told the War Committee that if contracts were made abroad without Treasury sanction, "he could not discuss the matter" or be responsible for their payment. "I submit with great emphasis," Montagu wrote to Asquith, "that it is the Chancellor of the Exchequer's business to find the means of paying what the Government needs, that for thirteen months he has done so, that it is his duty to do so, that there has been no change in the procedure of the Ministry since I have been there . . . I will give him all the information he requests when I can—my business is to buy goods —his to pay for them and I have enough to do without doing his work."[34]

Montagu believed that McKenna had lost the confidence of the Treasury staff as well as of Lords Reading and Cunliffe and even if his current problems were resolved, the difficulties would only arise again. "It is tragic," he wrote to Margot Asquith:

to think it is not really a question of ability; it is a question of method and manner. If this were all it would be bad enough, but we are face to face with inter-Ally difficulties of McKenna's making. They concern Russia, the most popular of our Allies. They are holding up departments like the War Office and the Ministry of Munitions. They would not be tolerated apart from the merits of McKenna's position, which are very real, by public opinion at the present stage of the War, and yet the difficulties have been created, the impasse has resulted without McKenna's consulting any of his colleagues—indeed I fear from my own experience that there is great reason to believe that he has misrepresented the case to his colleagues. . . .

The fact emerges that despite efficiency and ability of great value to the Government, McKenna is a bad colleague.

It has always seemed to be my duty despite my personal likings and disliking to work with any colleague whom it pleased the Prime Minister to ask me to work with, but I cannot regard as loyal to the Prime Minister the difficulties which McKenna makes with Lloyd George.

It is well known that they dislike one another personally; it is well known that they make the fatal error of doing their work surrounded by their own particular choice of press-men: but McKenna shows himself small in his everlasting objections, often petty and always badly stage-managed, to anything that Lloyd George proposes.[35]

Montagu concluded that the only solution was McKenna's resignation:

Things cannot go on as they are at the Treasury. I cannot see how to retrieve them with McKenna as Chancellor of the Exchequer. I cannot bear to see Lloyd George's complaints of bad colleagueship absolutely substantiated, despite the enormous errors of Lloyd George's conduct and policy, but this is going on from day to day, and I cannot see any sort of light on the situation except McKenna's resignation, which for reasons of friendship I am more than loathe to contemplate, or the following:

1) That the Prime Minister should come to an understanding with McKenna that he will not tolerate his policy of enmity with Lloyd George.
2) That the Prime Minister should see Lloyd George and McKenna together, tell Lloyd George that he has stated this to McKenna ask them there and then to shake hands in the determination of maintaining unity.

That it should be a condition of peace that McKenna should be reinforced by a representative committee of his colleagues which he should be instructed to keep informed of matters of importance.

I know that the Prime Minister will hate these steps. They cannot be done on his behalf by anyone else. It is the only alternative I can see to McKenna's resignation.[36]

Montagu never sent this letter. The draft has survived among his private papers. If Asquith had read it, and if Edwin could have convinced him that McKenna's hostility was causing irreparable dissension in the Cabinet, the events of the next few months might have taken a different course.

20

The Fall of Asquith, December 1916

I desire to place on record that I have not received any offer to join the Lloyd George Government.

Montagu, private memo, Dec. 9, 1916

Montagu was never able to persuade Asquith that McKenna's bitterness to Lloyd George and the bad blood it created would, in the long run, bring irreparable damage to the government. By 1916, Montagu's own relationship with McKenna had degenerated so thoroughly that Asquith may well have viewed Montagu's evaluation as too subjective to be of value. By the summer and fall of 1916, moreover, Asquith's major problems were far more serious than the squabbling between McKenna and Lloyd George. The war was continuing to go badly and although the supply of munitions and men had increased, this did little to improve the military situation. While the Russians had been successful against the Austrians, and the Italians won a modest victory in August at Gorizia, all the other news from the battlefields was disastrous. Romania, an ally of three months, was defeated; the Germans were outside Bucharest; the French continued to "bleed themselves white"[1] at Verdun and the British casualties on the Somme were astronomical. In the first twenty-four hours, twenty thousand British soldiers died and ten thousand were wounded. Within three weeks, the casualties had reached one hundred twenty thousand.

This added considerably to the tension in the Cabinet. Lloyd George was becoming increasingly obstreperous, not only arguing with his Cabinet colleagues, but also second-guessing the generals, criticizing the overall military strategy and demanding ever more men for the front. This brought him into open conflict with Montagu, who needed manpower for the production of munitions. On several occasions, the conflict became so intense that Montagu had to threaten to resign to assure the supplies he needed.

Without the other pressures, such interdepartmental conflict would not in and of itself have been disastrous. But the arguments between the War Office and Munitions were only one of a series of quarrels between Cabinet members—all acted out against the hostile backdrop of criticism of the government's conduct of the war, orchestrated by the Northcliffe press, *The Times,* and the *Daily Mail.* Their attacks were vicious and unrelenting and increased in proportion to the military disasters. In September the Somme attack became new grist for their mill. Four hundred thousand casualties were reported —with little or no ground gained. The need for more men and new strategy became critical.

The failure of Somme was the final straw. The nation was frustrated and war weary. With or without the fury unleashed by the press, the British public could no longer endure the status quo. Acrimony, recrimination, and mistrust were the weapons of attack. In this war, Montagu assumed one of the most important roles of his political career: mediator in the effort to prevent the fall of Asquith.

Raymond Asquith Killed

Early in the fall of 1916, Asquith was still unaware of the political machinations that were beginning to take shape against him. For the moment, at least, political problems were secondary to the personal tragedy he endured in September, when his eldest son, Raymond, "the symbol of the talent of a generation,"[2] was killed in the first wave of the Somme attack. The blow to Asquith was a heavy one. "Whatever pride I had in the past, and whatever hope I had for the far future—by much the largest part of both was invested in him. Now all that is gone. It will take me a few days more to get back to my bearings," Asquith wrote in his *Memories and Reflections* on September 20.[3] It took him longer than a few days. He mourned deeply throughout the autumn, missing several Cabinet meetings and withdrawing into himself at one of the most crucial times in his political life.

Montagu, Venetia and other members of the Coterie grieved almost as deeply as Asquith. Raymond was everyone's favorite, the star of the group, the best and the brightest. He was a scholar of Winchester and Balliol and a winner of the Ireland, Craven and Derby scholarships. He had also won a First in Greats and a Fellowship at All Souls:

With these towering academic achievements went indifference to worldly success . . . preferring to cultivate friendships and his intellectual pleasures. John Buchan described him as a demi-god: "a scholar of the reputed Elizabethan type, a brilliant wit, an accomplished poet, a sound lawyer— these things were borne lightly, for his greatness was not in his attainments but in himself. . . . Most noble in presence and with every grace of voice and manner, he moved among men like a being from another world, detached from the common struggle." Demi-gods are by definition inhuman; Raymond Asquith could appear so to his acquaintances but to his friends he was warm, sympathetic, and an exhilaratingly good companion. Posterity may fairly doubt the qualities of many members of the lost generation but about him there can be little dispute.[4]

All of the Coterie empathized with Diana Cooper's reaction to Raymond's death when she wrote that the pain was physical: "A sensation never before felt. . . . [M]y brain is revolving so fast screaming 'Raymond killed, my divine Raymond killed' over and over again. . . . I have lost with him my energy and hope and all that blinds one to life's horror."[5]

By October 22, Asquith was able to attend a Cabinet meeting and wrote: "This has been a great blow to me and I am much shaken by it. . . . Today I braced myself up to propose a vote of credit in the House of Commons; a trying and difficult speech, especially that latter part of it. I got on better than I expected as everyone was very kind and sympathetic."[6] Not everyone was kind and sympathetic. *The Times* and the *Daily Mail* continued their merciless attacks with no respite. Quarrels in the Cabinet continued, going from bad to worse. Nothing seemed to be going right, either at home or abroad.

The War Cabinet, seeking new strategies, now met more frequently. It included nine members and Montagu who was often invited. The meetings, according to Hankey, were "dreadful." Montagu agreed, writing that "there was conviction among all the Prime Minister's colleagues that he was a bad Chairman of the Committee. I cannot," Montagu continued:

charge myself with disloyalty to him, and yet I agree that among disputants he is too patient. Long Cabinet training and experience made him treat the War Committee as a Cabinet, giving all persons the right to express their opinion as lengthily as they liked, and not paying sufficient attention to the paramount necessity of getting decisions as quickly as possible and getting through the agenda.[7]

Roy Jenkins was probably closer to the mark when he concluded that it was not the Chairman alone who was at fault. "It was rather that the lack of trust between members was so great, and the external pressures so demoralizing, that agreement had become impossible."[8] In this situation, factors that in normal times would have been viewed as mere irritants assumed mammoth proportions, each putting another nail into the coffin of the Asquith government.

Dardanelles Commission

The establishment of the Dardanelles Commission was one such factor. Pressure by Churchill and others to have an investigation of the Dardanelles expedition and the Mesopotamian failure had been festering in the House for several months, after Bonar Law, on June 14, had agreed—without consulting Asquith—to put before the House all the available documentation about the Gallipoli fiasco. Churchill was especially eager that this take place, since he believed it would exonerate him and place the blame instead on Asquith, Kitchener and other generals, as well as on other members of the Cabinet. Asquith had been reluctant to agree to an investigation because it would open a can of worms at a time when criticism of the Army and Navy could only hurt the war effort. The pressure was so intense, however, that he and the Cabinet felt obliged to agree. Hankey believed that the Coalition "never recovered from (this) decision." From then on, the Supreme Command functioned under a shadow of "mutual suspicion. . . . Such homogeneity as the Government had . . . weakened. . . . Before long . . . the power of decision in difficult questions was affected."[9]

Nigerian Land Debate

Montagu did not put as much blame on the Dardanelles Commission for the government's troubles as did Hankey. His choice for the linchpin in the fall of Asquith was a comparatively unimportant debate on Nigerian Land Sales. This issue was of import to Bonar Law, who was Secretary of the Colonial Office. To Law's dismay, the position he took on this subject was rejected, and during the debate he was bitterly attacked by Carson, threatening his role as Conservative Leader in the Coalition. In Montagu's view:

> Bonar Law's position in the Ministry was always, to my mind, beneath contempt. He was there as a delegate of his Party. He alone of all my colleagues based all his arguments in Council on the effect on his Party in the House of Commons. Having formed this estimate of his own position, he lived in daily fear of Carson whom he regarded as a man destined to lead from its allegiance to him the Conservative Party . . . and he never felt secure in his chair or worthy of occupying his position if he did not reflect in every opinion the Conservatism as organized in the House of Commons. When therefore, an acrimonious debate—in which he and Carson were opposed—took place in the House of Commons, followed by a remarkable division in which a substantial proportion of the Conservative Party voted against the Government, he began to think that it was all up with the Coalition.[10]

Bonar Law's concern that he was losing control of his Party made him especially susceptible to Lloyd George's suggestions for change. In Montagu's view, this was "the origin of the trouble."

The Lansdowne Memorandum

As part of a general examination of the war, Asquith asked each member of the Cabinet to express his views about the war and the conditions under which the nation should consider peace. In response, on November 13 Lord Lansdowne distributed a devastating memorandum. It said the war was "killing the best of the male population," that it was producing financial burdens "almost incalculable," and that England should not discourage "any movement, no matter where originating, in favor of an interchange of views as to the possibility of a settlement."[11]

These were not Asquith's views. Only four days earlier, he had made it clear that the war must go on, even if it were a long war. In a speech at the Guildhall,[12] Asquith had said that the time was not ripe for peace. The Northcliffe press insisted, however, that the Lansdowne memorandum had been distributed as a "feeler" for

Asquith and that it was yet another example of Asquith's ambivalence in the war. Nothing Asquith said could convince the press otherwise. Their goal was to see him and the Coalition replaced; accuracy in reporting was not important.

Asquith never understood the power of the press. It was a relatively new force in politics—not part of the world he knew or respected. He gave few, if any, interviews and never bothered, as did Lloyd George and Churchill, to cultivate friends in the fourth estate. Rarely did he invite editors or publishers to dinner, although social dinners were an integral part of his life. In Asquith's worldview, politics included Parliament, the King, the Army, the electorate, business, the Church and the Party. Newspapers were not included in his circle of power. He paid a terrible price for this lapse.

A New War Committee

While the Lansdowne memorandum was fueling the fires of the press, Asquith left London to attend a war strategy conference in Paris. On the last evening of the Conference, Lloyd George and Hankey, who had accompanied the Prime Minister abroad, took a walk together. Hankey suggested that a new and smaller War Committee be created independent of the Cabinet. He urged too that the Prime Minister not chair the Committee.

Lloyd George had thought of this himself before he had left for Paris and had asked Max Aitken, who had become his friend and political advisor, to try it out on Bonar Law. Aitken, who later became Lord Beaverbrook, like Lord Northcliffe, believed his position as a newspaper czar gave him special insight into political issues. At first Bonar Law was lukewarm to the idea, always certain that Lloyd George was only interested in his own advancement. But he slowly began to accept the proposal. Still haunted by the embarrassment of the Nigerian Land Sales debate, he became fearful that if he did not, Lloyd George would turn to Carson. When he heard the idea from Bonar Law, Asquith rejected it as yet another example of Lloyd George's desire for the Premiership.

But Lloyd George and Max Aitken were not so easily discouraged. They drafted a proposed reorganization of the War Committee in a memorandum for Asquith's signature. The reorganization would provide for a new civilian General Staff with Lloyd George as Chairman, the Prime Minister as President, and two other members of the Cabinet, without portfolio. There was a blank space for the other two names but it was understood they were to be Carson and Bonar Law. This new body would have executive authority over the conduct of the war, with Asquith retaining the right to bring disputed issues to the full Cabinet.

Bonar Law brought the document to Asquith on Saturday, November 25. Asquith, as was his style, did not immediately react, saying instead that he would study the document over the weekend. As promised, he provided a written reply on Monday, November 27, in which he rejected this proposal. He believed it a mistake to have a War Committee without the Ministers of War and of the Admiralty; he could not promote Carson over Balfour, Curzon or McKenna; and finally—perhaps most importantly—he opposed Lloyd George as Chairman. "He has many qualities that would fit him for the first place," he wrote, "but he . . . does not inspire trust. . . ."[13]

Even then, Asquith failed to recognize the gravity of the crisis. Only when the *Morning Post,* on November 30, carried a banner headline urging that Lloyd George become Prime Minister, did Asquith finally see that he faced a major threat. To his dismay, the same suggestion was echoed by the *Daily Express,* the *Daily Mail,* and *The Times.*[14] This reinforced Asquith's determination not to give Lloyd George the Chairmanship of a War Committee, since it could not, in his judgment, be "carried out without fatally impairing the confidence of loyal and valued colleagues and undermining my authority." He was prepared, however, to establish a small War Committee with himself as chairman.[15] "Everybody had begun to agree," Montagu later wrote:

that a new War Cabinet was necessary. The Prime Minister would have proposed one on Friday, December 1st. The Cabinet had adopted [on November 29th], a proposal of Robert Cecil's [Parliamentary Secretary for Foreign Affairs, 1915–1916] which I thought was a bad one, for a Civil Committee, and the Prime Minister had determined to have a new War Committee on which McKenna would not have had a place, even at the risk of McKenna's resignation. He had also agreed that the Cabinet should not meet again during the War and that the Heads of Departments should not regard themselves as responsible for policy.[16]

But Lloyd George jumped the gun. On Friday, December 1, he met directly with Asquith and proposed orally and in writing that there be a three-man Cabinet consisting of the War Secretary, The First Lord of the Admiralty (who should be Carson, not Balfour) and a Minister without portfolio. One of the three members would act as chairman. Montagu wrote in his December 9 record of these events that he and Bonar Law, as well as Carson and Lloyd George, were to be members of the committee. Montagu also recorded that he had told Asquith that he had had no part in drafting this proposal and would not serve on such a Committee. Lloyd George was thus proposing a War Cabinet that Asquith was not to chair and on which the Prime Minister was not even to serve.[17]

Asquith replied in writing that same afternoon that a small War Cabinet should be established, but that the Prime Minister must be its Chairman. The Prime Minister cannot be relegated to the position of "an arbiter in the background or a referee to the Cabinet."[18] He agreed that the War Secretary and the First Lord of the Admiralty were necessary members. He was "inclined to add the Minister of Munitions (Montagu) and one other member with or without portfolio." He suggested a Vice Chairman perhaps as a way of bridging the differences, for the position would probably be filled by Lloyd George. And since the War Cabinet would meet every day, Lloyd George would thus play an increasingly important role. Asquith continued to disagree with Lloyd George over Carson replacing Balfour.[19] Lloyd George found the reply "entirely unsatisfactory" and vowed to fight.[20] The issue was now drawn. Either a compromise could be devised to satisfy both parties, or the government would fall.

Montagu and Reading: Mediators in Search of a Compromise

Montagu and Lord Reading were the only Liberals who kept their lines of communication open with both sides and they thus assumed the role of mediators. Montagu felt strongly that a government without either Asquith or Lloyd George was unacceptable. He believed that each had special qualities that complemented the other and that both were needed to successfully prosecute the war. He never believed that urging Lloyd George to remain in the Coalition, or urging Asquith to compromise with Lloyd George was disloyal to Asquith. In his mind, this would serve both Asquith and the war effort.

During the last days of November, Montagu was in daily contact with Asquith, hoping to persuade him to work out some arrangement with Lloyd George. On December 1, after Lloyd George had told Asquith he wanted to be Chairman of the proposed three-man War Cabinet, Montagu and Venetia, Lord Reading and Cunliffe met with Lloyd George for dinner as his guests. Their goal was to convince him to compromise. They failed. Montagu later wrote that he had found Lloyd George "very disturbed and distrait . . . very little conversation occurred between us and he was called away."[21] It was Lord Beaverbrook who beckoned to him from across the room. The two left shortly in a taxi in which Bonar Law was waiting. The following day Montagu had breakfast with Lord Reading and in the afternoon Reading and Montagu went to see Lloyd George but "could not shake him from the determination to insist upon the Chairmanship of the War Cabinet and the removal of Balfour from the Admiralty."[22] He would not budge in his determination to fight.

In the meantime, Asquith kept to his routine, going to Walmer Castle for the weekend, prompting Hankey to remark: "It was very typical of him that in the middle of this tremendous crisis he should go away for the weekend!" This was typical "both of his qualities and of his defects. . . . and of his easy-going habits."[23] Before going to Walmer, Asquith had lunch with Hankey, who suggested a solution, "but it was not well received." After lunch, at Mrs. Asquith's request Hankey had met with Bonar Law and had learned that he had called a meeting of Unionist Cabinet members for Sunday and would probably resign so that it would not appear that he was being "dragged at the heels of Lloyd George."[24] Neither Hankey nor Reading, whose help Hankey had requested, was able to persuade Bonar Law to postpone the meeting until Monday. So Hankey arranged for Bonham Carter to go to Walmer Castle and escort Asquith back. At this point, Bonham Carter himself believed Asquith should accept Lloyd George's proposal.

Hankey walked home with Lord Reading, and they agreed that "the whole crisis is intolerable. There is really very little between them." They also agreed "that the methods of the War Cabinet call for reforms . . . that the Prime possesses the best judgement." The

obvious compromise, Hankey and Reading thought, was "for the
Prime Minister to retain the Presidency of the War Cabinet with
Lloyd George as chairman, and to give Lloyd George a fairly free
run for his money."[25] This was Montagu's solution too but he
believed that if such a compromise could not be agreed upon it
would be better for Asquith to accept Lloyd George's proposal than
to wreck the government. His letter to Asquith of December 2,
while not saying this explicitly, certainly implied it. He argued that
the situation had become "irretrievably serious," and that he had
just come from an hour of hard fighting with Lloyd George, who
he feared "has committed himself" and will not budge.

He [Lloyd George] says that you as Prime Minister, with the House of
Commons on your shoulders, with appointments to attend to and with the
thousand and one duties of the Prime Minister, should be relieved of the
day to day work of the War Committee but should maintain supreme
control of the War, seeing the chairman of the War Committee every
morning before it met, receiving their reports and conferring with them
when you thought fit. He says that your duties prevent sufficiently frequent sittings and that by this means quicker decisions would be arrived at.
He does not for one moment regard it as possible for the War committee
without the Prime Minister to challenge the Prime Minister's supreme
control of the War, but he regards it as essential that the small War
Committee should sit so frequently and act with such rapidity that the
Prime Minister, whoever he were, ought not to have a place upon it, but
he is loud in his assertions that you are the right Prime Minister in the right
place. He will not budge from this position and I cannot do anything
more.[26]

Montagu told Asquith about "the very bitter letters" he had
received from Margot. "She, like McKenna, attributes everything
that has appeared in the press to L. G. notwithstanding the fact that
the views in the press are nearly all inconsistent with L. G.'s
scheme."[27] He warned Asquith that if Lloyd George left the Government "it will be impossible for the government to carry on, but
will plunge this country into recrimination and public debate in the
face of the enemy which will hearten them up and shake to its
foundations the Alliance."[28]

He believed that if Lloyd George resigned, Lord Derby and Bonar
Law would also be forced to go and this would bring about the
downfall of the Asquith government. "It is a nightmare to me,"

12 KENSINGTON PALACE GARDENS   *The home of the first Lord and Lady Swaythling and Edwin's birthplace. (Picture taken by the author, 1988).*

SIR SAMUEL MON-
TAGU, THE FIRST
LORD SWAYTH-
LING *The father of
Edwin Montagu. (Bett-
mann-Hulton).*

LILY MONTAGU *Ed-
win's sister, one of the founders
of Liberal Judaism, and a dedicated social worker and humani-
tarian, earning the title of Judaism's first "Lady Rabbi."
(Jewish Chronicle Publications,
London).*

EDWIN MONTAGU
*Taken in 1919. (Bett-
mann-Hulton).*

EDWIN AND VE-
NETIA *Canvassing
in the 1915 election.
(Milton Gendel).*

INDIA OFFICE, MARCH 1921   *The Marquis of Crewe, Edwin Montagu, Lord Islington and Sir William Duke (left to right), at the unveiling of a War Memorial at the India Office in March 1921. (Bettmann-Hulton).*

RALLY AND MARCH IN 1919 TO PROTEST POGROMS IN PO-
LAND   *The persecution of the Jews in Russia and Eastern Europe added to the clamor
for a homeland for the Jews in Palestine, which Edwin vigorously opposed. (Bettmann-
Hulton).*

VENETIA STANLEY   *Venetia Stanley with Anthony Morton Henley (future brother-in-law), on a picnic in 1902. (Anthony Pitt-Rivers).*

VENETIA STANLEY
In 1908. (Anthony Pitt-Rivers).

PENRHOS   *Penrhos, one of Lord Sheffield's country homes on the Anglesey coast near Holyhead. Venetia adored Penrhos, spending many happy moments of escape in this isolated coastal country. Montagu and Asquith were frequent visitors here during their pursuit of Venetia. (Anthony Pitt-Rivers).*

ALDERLEY HALL   *In Alderley, Cheshire, the family seat of the Stanleys built in 1818, after the first Alderley Hall built in the fifteenth century burned in 1779. It remained their home until 1936. It was in Alderley Hall that Venetia was born; it remained throughout her life a place that, like Penrhos, she loved dearly. (Anthony Pitt-Rivers).*

VENETIA STANLEY   *In 1907, with her pet monkey, Pluto, and some friends including Cynthia Charteris, later the wife of Herbert Asquith (Bob), second son of Prime Minister Asquith, standing at her right. On the far left is Harold T. Baker ("Bluey" or "Bluetooth"), a young member of the Asquith Government. (Anthony Pitt-Rivers).*

CYNTHIA AND VENETIA   *Close-up of Cynthia (left) and Venetia in 1907.*
(Anthony Pitt-Rivers).

VENETIA WITH FRIENDS   *Venetia (second from left), Violet, Asquith, and Edwin Montagu to his left, 1909. Venetia's sister Sylvia is on the far left. (Anthony Pitt-Rivers).*

VENETIA STANLEY   *With H. H. Asquith, February 1910. By this time Venetia and Asquith's relationship had become a more serious affair. (Anthony Pitt-Rivers).*

VENETIA STANLEY   *With Winston Churchill at Penrhos, 1910. (Anthony Pitt-Rivers).*

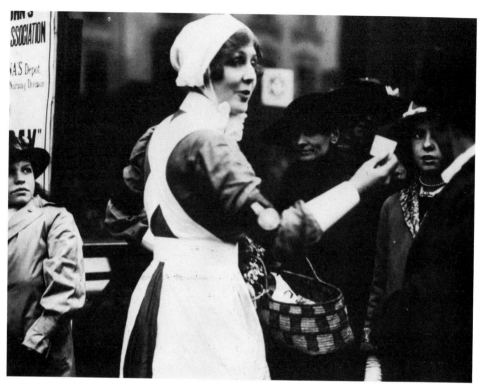

LADY DIANA MANNERS   *In 1916, as a nurse before she married Duff Cooper; unconventional, a fine actress and a reigning London beauty for almost a quarter of a century. During World War I, she and Venetia became very close friends. (Bettmann-Hulton).*

LADY DIANA COOPER AND HER HUSBAND, ALFRED DUFF COOPER
In 1923, on the Riviera. (Bettmann-Hulton).

THE ASQUITH FAMILY   *With friends, Easter, 1904. (Anthony Pitt-Rivers).*

H. H. ASQUITH
*In 1908, when on
Campbell-Bannerman's
death, he became Prime
Minister. (New York
Public Library).*

H. H. ASQUITH AND MARGOT ASQUITH   *At Penrhos, Venetia's family estate, in July 1912. (Maurice Bonham Carter in the rear) (Anthony Pitt-Rivers).*

H. H. ASQUITH *Asquith leaving the War Office in October 1915, after he had conceded to the formation of a Coalition Government in May 1915, and after Venetia had announced her engagement to Montagu. The strain of almost two years of military and naval disasters were beginning to show. (Bettman-Hulton).*

H. H. ASQUITH   *In 1907 with Venetia's sister, Sylvia, (who married Anthony Henley). Sylvia became his confidant to whom he wrote almost 300 letters after Venetia's marriage. They were not love letters in the sense that his earlier letters to Venetia were. She was the friend of his twilight years. (Anthony Pitt-Rivers).*

EDWIN MONTAGU MONUMENT   *Statue of Montagu in Jamnagar, India, unveiled two weeks after his death, on December 1, 1924. The statue was planned before his death, as a tribute to him for his role in advancing political freedom in India. In unveiling the statue, the Maharaja Jam Sahib called Montagu "the greatest friend India has ever had, since perhaps Edmund Burke. England and the Empire—are the poorer today for this loss . . ."*

DAVID LLOYD GEORGE   *In 1922, the year in which he asked for Montagu's resignation as Secretary of State for India. (New York Public Library).*

MONTAGU WITH LLOYD GEORGE AND M. ALBERT THOMAS

Montagu as Minister of Munitions in 1916 with Lloyd George and M. Albert Thomas. Montagu succeeded Lloyd George to this position (during the Coalition Government), and always claimed that his six months of service in this capacity (July to December, 1916), were among the happiest and most productive of his life. (Milton Gendel).

WINSTON CHURCHILL AND CLEMENTINE CHURCHILL   *In 1916, inspecting airplanes while he was First Lord of the Admiralty. As Minister of Munitions in 1916, Montagu was a strong supporter of Churchill's desire for the development of the "tank," and increased airplane production. Clementine was Venetia's cousin. (Bettmann-Hulton).*

WINSTON CHURCHILL   *In 1916, with French army officers in France. (Bett-mann-Hulton).*

GEORGE NATHANIEL   *First and last Marquess Curzon of Kedleston, in his robes as Viceroy of India. (Bettmann-Hulton).*

LORD READING *Rufus Isaacs, First
Marquis of Reading, at the time of his elevation
to the peerage, when he was appointed Lord Chief
Justice. He was Viceroy of India from 1921 to
1926. He and Montagu worked closely and har-
moniously from 1921 to 1922. Reading's desire
for permission to publish the Government of India's criticism of British policy toward Turkey
precipitated Montagu's removal from office. (New
York Public Library).*

LORD BEAVERBROOK *On the French
Riviera in 1920. (Bettmann-Hulton).*

MOHANDAS GANDHI AND MRS. GANDHI   *In 1921, a year during which Gandhi's influence, his non-cooperative movement, and his call for "Swaraj" (self-government), became a critical factor in Anglo-Indian politics. (Bettmann-Hulton).*

Montagu concluded, because the issues were not policy but procedure. "I am willing to do anything you suggest, but I can do
nothing more without your orders."[29]

The following day another compromise was formulated by Eric
Drummond and Lord Reading with slight changes added by Montagu. It was based on the earlier suggestion made by Reading and
Hankey under which the Prime Minister would act as President of
the War Committee and Lloyd George as Chairman. When Asquith
lunched with Montagu that day he said he would accept the compromise. He thought that it might break down over personnel, since
he would not remove Balfour, but in principle the suggested formula was acceptable to him.

Asquith was unaware that earlier that day Bonar Law had met
with the Unionist Ministers and that they had adopted a resolution
calling for a change in government, concluding that the publicity
given to "the intention of Lloyd George" (which they found offensive) made "reconstruction from within no longer possible." They
urged that "the Prime Minister should resign."[30] If he felt unable to
do so, they authorized Bonar Law to tender their resignations.

There are sharp differences of opinion among contemporary ob-
servers and among historians over the intention of the Unionist
Ministers. Beaverbrook held that the Unionists, thoroughly annoyed with Lloyd George, believed that when Asquith resigned,
Lloyd George and his friends could not form a new government and
would be thrown out of the new one that Asquith would subsequently form. If that was their intent, Jenkins has concluded, they
acted with "unbelievable ineptitude" and were "extraordinarily
foolish."[31] In light of later events, he believed that it would have
made greater sense to agree with Curzon and Chamberlain that the
Unionist leaders assumed that Asquith could not form another government and that Lloyd George could do so only with Unionist
help, giving them an opportunity to shape and influence that government in a way they could not with Asquith.[32]

Later that day, Bonar Law met with Asquith. He did not show
him the resolution, which was also critical of Lloyd George's publicity. He summarized it. From this conversation, Asquith inferred
that all the Unionist Cabinet Ministers were now opposed to him
and were asking him to resign. (If he had been shown the resolution,
he might have come to a different conclusion.) Then he asked to see

Lloyd George. According to Montagu, this was a friendly meeting at which Asquith agreed to a substantial number of Lloyd George's demands, even agreeing that Lloyd George should be chairman of the War Committee with "the Prime Minister to have supreme and effective control of War Policy."[33] The agenda of the War Committee would be submitted to the Prime Minister and the Chairman would report to him. The Prime Minister would also have veto power over decisions of the War Committee and at his own discretion attend meetings of the War Committee.

Lloyd George accepted this and he and Asquith discussed the other members of the proposed new War Committee, without reaching any conclusions. Lloyd George seemed prepared to keep Balfour at the Admiralty and to allow Winston Churchill to be a fourth member of the Committee, thus not restricting it to three. After that meeting, Bonar Law joined them and informed Asquith that the Unionists had agreed that all the ministers should tender their resignations except the Prime Minister, and that Asquith should reconstitute the government on the basis of the proposed new War Committee. Lloyd George later wrote that at the meeting with the Unionist leaders they insisted that he become the Prime Minister but he refused and insisted he would serve only under Asquith. As Jenkins commented: "Thus is history quickly confused by even the most intimate participants—or misreported by even the most reliable witnesses."[34]

After this meeting with Lloyd George, Asquith dined with Montagu at Queen Anne's Gate. Venetia was in the country. Crewe and Reading joined them after dinner. Montagu urged Asquith, as did Bonar Law, to commit his agreement with Lloyd George to writing. This was not done, but Asquith did issue a brief statement to the press at 11:45 that night that "the Prime Minister, with a view to the most active prosecution of the war, has decided to advise his Majesty the King to consent to a reconstruction of the Government."[35] Asquith thought that this "disagreeable crisis" was over, and he wrote,

I drove down to Walmer yesterday afternoon hoping to find sunshine and peace. It was utterly drab and cold, and for my sins (and other persons) I had to drive back soon after 11:00 this morning. I was forced back by Bongie & Montagu and Rufus to grapple with a "Crisis,"—this time with a very big "C." The result is I have spent much of the afternoon in colloquing with Messrs. Ll. George & Bonar Law, & one or two minor worthies. The "Crisis" shows every sign of following its predecessors to an early and unhonored grave. But there were many wigs very nearly on the green.[36]

Asquith's political judgment was wrong. The crisis was far from settled.

Montagu also thought that a compromise had been reached, but he continued to be worried. He saw Lloyd George after the latter had worked out the agreement with the Prime Minister and recorded his impressions of that meeting.

I joined George at the War Office, where he expressed his great gratification at the fact that he was going to work with Asquith . . . and see [him] every day. He recognized my share in this happy issue and urged me to persuade Asquith to put the agreement in writing that night, in order that there might be no watering down or alterations, and in order that it might not be misconstrued. I told him I would do my best.

As I came away I saw, with fear and foreboding in my heart, Northcliffe waiting in his [Lloyd George's] Private Secretary's room. This secret has been locked in my knowledge ever since; I have told nobody but Primrose that I knew George did see Northcliffe that night.[37]

The next morning, December 4, Montagu saw Lloyd George and said that he had "breakfasted with Derby and Carson and that they agreed that I ought to be Chancellor of the Exchequer. I told him that I did not think I could do this job, and that I did not wish to leave the Ministry of Munitions."[38]

Montagu then visited Asquith and found him very disturbed. He had now completely changed his mind. Asquith had read the story in *The Times* that morning, which bitterly attacked him and in which it appeared that he had completely surrendered to Lloyd George. The article could only have been written by someone with facts that had been provided by a person privy to the discussion of the Sunday afternoon meetings. The Prime Minister was certain that the story had been leaked by Lloyd George himself. Asquith was furious and wrote at once to Lloyd George:

December 4

My dear Lloyd George,

Such productions as the first leading article in today's *Times,* showing the infinite possibilities of misunderstanding and misrepresentation of such

an arrangement as we considered yesterday, make me at least doubtful as
to its feasibility. Unless the impression is at once corrected that I am being
relegated to the position of an irresponsible spectator of the War, I cannot
go on.

The suggested arrangement was to the following effect:

The Prime Minister to have supreme and effective control of War
policy.

The agenda of the War Committee will be submitted to him; its Chairman will report to him daily; he can direct it to consider particular topics
or proposals; and all its conclusions will be subject to his approval or veto.
He can, of course, at his own discretion, attend meetings of the Com-
ittee.

Yours sincerely

H. H. Asquith[39]

The letter did not repudiate the agreement reached on Sunday. It
hinted and warned of repudiation. Within an hour, Lloyd George
replied that he had not been responsible for the story and that
Northcliffe wanted a "smash" but that he did not. (The fact that
Montagu had seen Northcliffe with Lloyd George the night before
the story was published makes Lloyd George's denial less credible.)
He, Lloyd George wrote, fully accepted "in spirit" the summary of
their arrangement as set forth by Asquith, subject to future discussions on personnel. It was a conciliatory note.

This was Montagu's view as well, and he continued to try to
bring the parties together.

I left George [December 4] and went to Downing Street where I found
Asquith very angry about the Northcliffe article. He said that Henderson's
name was known only to George and himself. I reminded him that Bonar
Law also knew it and had communicated it to his friends. He said he was
just about to see the King. I urged him not to be put off by the Northcliffe
article; he had never paid any attention to newspapers, why should he give
up now because of Northcliffe? He said it was because the Northcliffe
article showed quite clearly the spirit in which the arrangement was going
to be worked out by its authors. I told him I felt certain he was wrong, and
that Lloyd George meant to work it honestly and in the spirit as well as the
letter. He promised to write to Lloyd George before he went to see the
King, as in fact he did.

I do not understand why he should have gone to see the King if he had not at the moment, about mid-day Monday, still [been] determined to carry the matter through.[40]

Since Montagu had his own suspicions about Lloyd George and the Northcliffe story, it is difficult to understand how he could have believed that Lloyd George was eager to have the new agreement work smoothly. He was either deceiving himself in his eagerness to bring the parties together or was misrepresenting the facts.

Asquith's audience with the King took place at 12:30 P.M. on December 4. He submitted the resignations of all his colleagues but not his own, a normal procedure when a general reconstruction is planned, and he received authority to form a new government. He then returned to Downing Street for lunch and went to the House of Commons to ask for a three-day adjournment.

In his recollection of these events, Beaverbrook wrote that while at the House of Commons, Bonar Law asked Asquith if he still favored the agreement reached on Sunday. Asquith replied that he was not as keen as on Sunday because Lloyd George was leaking stories to the press. Many of Asquith's Liberal colleagues had begun to express their unhappiness with the agreement. Asquith did not continue his conversation with Bonar Law, since he was called to the floor to answer questions and soon afterward he left and went to Downing Street. Bonar Law followed. When he arrived, Grey, Harcourt and Runciman were outside the Cabinet Room. McKenna was closeted with the Prime Minister. When Bonar Law finally saw Asquith, he urged that he stick by the agreement and made it clear that if he did not, he would resign. Asquith remained silent.

After these meetings with his Liberal colleagues, Asquith declined Lloyd George's request for a meeting and sent his letter of December 4, telling Lloyd George that he had met with the King and received authority to form a new government, and that he had been thinking about the Sunday agreement and had come to the conclusion that it was not possible for a small War Committee to be effective without the Prime Minister as Chairman. At times when the Prime Minister had "other calls upon his time and energy," he might "delegate from time to time the chairmanship to another Minister," but the Prime Minister, if he was to retain his authority, must be its "permanent head."[41] In this letter, Asquith reaffirmed his opposition to Balfour's replacement at the Admiralty and his opposition to Carson's appointment to a War Committee. He agreed, however, to appoint a small War Committee, as had been suggested earlier. Asquith thus made it clear that if he was to remain as Prime Minister, he would reconstitute the government as he saw fit. After dispatching the letter, Asquith dined, as he had the evening before, with Montagu at Queen Anne's Gate, but "refused to discuss the situation."[42] Montagu feared the worst.

Lloyd George received the letter on Tuesday, December 5, and replied at once that Asquith's proposal was not acceptable and that he would resign.[43] At the same time, Balfour wrote to Asquith from his sick bed that he did not want Asquith's support for his post at the Admiralty. "The mere fact the new Chairman of the War Council *did* prefer, and as far as I know, *still* prefers, a different arrangement is, to my mind, quite conclusive, and leaves me in no doubt as to the manner in which I can best assist the Government which I desire to support."[44] Asquith, if he comprehended the meaning of this letter, must have been stunned. For weeks he had been vigorously defending Balfour and insisting that he not be replaced, and now Balfour was saying that the did not want such support and was assuming that Lloyd George would be the new chairman of the War Council. Jenkins commented: "It is doubtful whether Asquith fully assimilated the shift of allegiance which this letter quietly announced. He saw Balfour and Lloyd George in such different lights . . . the idea of an alliance between them hardly entered his head."[45]

On December 5, the Liberal Ministers met with Asquith to consider what steps he should take in the face of Lloyd George's resignation. With the exception of Montagu, they urged that Asquith resign too. They said that would meet "head on" Lloyd George's resignation and the outcome would then turn on the attitude of the Unionists. Even at this stage they could not believe that the Tories and Unionists would support Lloyd George.

Montagu vehemently disagreed. He suggested that the King be asked to call a conference among Asquith, Lloyd George, Bonar Law and Henderson to try to settle the crisis by continued negotiations. Montagu later wrote that his idea was "derided and McKenna most helpfully asked me if I wanted four Prime Ministers, or, if not, which one I wanted."[46]

Asquith asked the Unionist Ministers, who had resigned when Lloyd George resigned, whether they would work with a new government from which Lloyd George and Bonar Law were absent. They said they would not. Would they serve in a Lloyd George administration? They said they would.[47] To add to Asquith's consternation, Balfour wrote again, indicating that he too would offer no opposition to Lloyd George. When word of these developments reached Montagu, he wrote in great distress to Asquith: "I am shortly going to see you, but I imagine in the company of my colleagues, and in case I do not have an opportunity of talking with you, I must trouble you to read the following."[48] Montagu underscored his belief and hope that Asquith should and must remain Prime Minister, "because I am certain that any other Prime Minister cannot succeed."[49]

Montagu, unlike most of the other Liberal Ministers, expressed the opinion that he "could not think of a Government conducting the War without Lloyd George. Whatever office he had held, and despite his defects, during the war he has rendered services to the country which cannot be minimised . . . he has achieved at least one thing in the War Office which, if the war goes on next year will save our armies from destruction; . . . his belated success in getting the army to attend to their railway communications."[50] Montagu also pointed out that Lloyd George was invaluable on the War Council: "His ever active brain had suggested . . . policies . . . in which you [Asquith] have been in agreement with him." His "uncontrolled conduct of the War," without Asquith, Montagu wrote, "is unthinkable," but a combination of the two, Montagu repeated, is "what every thinking man in the country requires."[51]

The letter argued repeatedly against the Prime Minister's resignation. "A government which you do not lead means disaster. A split country means victory for the enemy." Montagu told Asquith what he had done to avoid this, because "I want to do nothing behind your back." He had spent time on December 4 with Lloyd George, whom he found was also "very unhappy. . . . He does not want to be Prime Minister and does not want a victory for Northcliffe and wants to work with Asquith."[52] As this letter and others show, Montagu strongly believed throughout this controversy that both Lloyd George and Asquith must both be kept in the Government and that Lloyd George was prepared to do this—if he were made Chairman of the War Council.

Montagu ended by explaining that he had seen Lord Derby after

Lloyd George and had urged that the King bring Lloyd George and Asquith together.

That is all I can do. I ask your forgiveness for my part in all this. I may have given advice which you think to have been wrong now or in the past. I am sorry that I have failed, but looking back through the whole history of your government, I can charge myself with never having taken any action which I did not, from the bottom of my heart, think was in your interest.[53]

Asquith did not take Montagu's advice. The strong feelings of his key Ministers, the attitude of Balfour and the knowledge that the Unionist Ministers would not serve under him without Lloyd George and Bonar Law, added to the Northcliffe attacks and other critical articles in the press, proved too much for him to ignore. In the face of these circumstances, Asquith decided to resign "not as a tactical manoeuvre, but because he did not have sufficient support to carry on."[54] He had been Prime Minister for eight years and two hundred and forty-one days.

The King wrote later in his diary that Asquith had told him he had truly tried to work out the differences with Lloyd George over the War Committee but was unable to do so. All his colleagues, moreover, had urged him to resign. The King expressed concern that there would be panic in the financial community in America, and harm done to the Allies. "It is a great blow to me & will I fear buck up the Germans."[55]

After Asquith resigned, the King summoned Bonar Law and asked him to form a government. Bonar Law went to see Lloyd George and conferred with him. He asked Asquith also if he would serve under him or Balfour. Asquith demurred, saying he did not think it would work, but "did not close his mind on continuing consultation."[56] A Buckingham Palace conference took place that afternoon with Asquith, Lloyd George, Bonar Law, Henderson and Balfour.

Balfour took the position that no one could be the Prime Minister, the leader of the House of Commons and the Chairman of the War Committee at the same time. Asquith disagreed. He reaffirmed his position that only the Prime Minister could preside over the War Committee. He also denounced the press. The result of the meeting was that Asquith agreed to think about the proposals put to him and to let Bonar Law know if he would serve in a government under him. If his answer was no, Lloyd George would be asked to form a government.

Asquith met again with his Liberal colleagues. Crewe, Grey, McKenna, Runciman, Buckmaster and Wood all urged him not to serve in a subsidiary role. Harcourt, Samuel and Tennant silently agreed with their view. Montagu and Henderson dissented. Again, Asquith did not follow Montagu's advice and agreed with those who urged him not to serve. At 7:30 P.M. the commission to form a new government was given to Lloyd George. Within twenty-four hours he had discharged it.

Lloyd George's Government

The new government was primarily a Unionist one, with Curzon, Milner, Bonar Law and Henderson holding the same Ministries as they had under Asquith. In addition, Carson went to the Admiralty and Balfour to the Foreign Office. No Liberal members of the Asquith Cabinet were asked to join the new Cabinet. Two other lesser-known Liberals were brought in, as well as two Labour leaders and Henderson.

Thus Lloyd George, the radical "outsider from Wales," achieved the pinnacle of power through the help of the Tories, who had often been his most outspoken critics. They had not only been critical of his policies and ideology, but they also looked down upon his background and education. Haldane reflected this when he said of the new Lloyd George government: "[T]o tell the truth . . . [he did] not think the new govt. will make as much difference, one way or the other as, people think. *Only it is very low class*" (emphasis added).[57] Harold Macmillan put it in a broader perspective: "For me—much as I admired Asquith's intellectual sincerity and moral nobility—Lloyd George was the rebel, the revolutionary; and above all the man who would get things done. Asquith represented, as it seemed to me, the qualities, but also the faults of the old world. Above all, he had tolerated too long the mistakes of the High Command."[58]

Lloyd George was not only the rebel revolutionary who could get things done, but he was also "a man with no feelings or respect for the past, void of historical association, hardly with memories—living altogether for the future, which he is anxious to fashion anew out of the vigour of his own brain."[59] It was these qualities in Lloyd George that were attractive to Montagu, in spite of his love and admiration for Asquith. For Montagu, too, had little respect for tradition or for England's inherent conservatism and bigotry against those who did not come from the privileged classes. Montagu, the Jew, with all his money and influence, was as much on the periphery of English society as was Lloyd George, the workingman's hero from Wales. A. J. P. Taylor, in his introduction to Frances Stevenson's *Diary*, called Lloyd George "the man from the outside."[60] This is perhaps the key to Lloyd George's appeal to Montagu. Montagu, even while entertaining and being entertained by the powerful of England, always knew that behind his back they were making snide comments about his Jewishness and looking upon him as they did upon Lloyd George, as a "man from the outside."

Montagu: Honest Broker or Disloyal Jackal

Throughout the long days and nights of negotiations, Montagu always believed that Asquith and Lloyd George—different as they were—could be kept together and their differences reconciled. He was not "openly equivocal," as some have held. Nor was he "keeping a foot in both camps" to assure his position regardless of which side won, as others have accused him of doing.

His letters show clearly that in spite of his deep attachment to Asquith, he did not believe that the Prime Minister would have made a good chairman of the War Committee; he often said that the Prime Minister was "too patient" with Cabinet members and permitted them to argue incessantly, thus preventing the Cabinet from reaching the critical questions of war strategy. As early as March 1915 he had written to Hankey, raising this issue:

You do not get discussions in the War Council differing materially from those of the Cabinet; you have the same protagonists in both and all you do is to substitute a different set of spectators.

The War Council should be used by its political members to get a frank opinion of the military experts, but . . . this is not done and will not be done unless the Council is reconstituted, or unless the president lays down this as its specific duty.[61]

Montagu never went public with his criticisms, but he did believe that a change was necessary, as his letter of December 2 to Asquith made clear. Until the last moment, he hoped that a reorganization could be devised that did not appear to threaten the Prime Minister's overall responsibility for directing the war. But he also believed the status quo could not continue and that Lloyd George's style was indispensable to the functioning of a government involved in a life-and-death struggle. He was never either ambivalent or equivocal about this. It was to this end that he worked indefatigably.[62]

Montagu knew that because he did not join McKenna and the other Liberal Cabinet members in urging Asquith to reject any compromise, he would become a pariah, derided by them and accused of disloyalty. The fact that he believed "the best form of Government was Asquith and Lloyd George; failing that the best form of Government is George" added to their accusations of infamy. "A jackal . . . who howls in sympathy with any camp," he was called.[63] On December 9, two days after Lloyd George became Prime Minister, Montagu decided "to put down as clearly" as he could "the . . . events which have ended so disastrously for the Nation and have resulted in the fall of the Asquith Government."[64] Aware of the accusations of disloyalty that were being made against him, he wanted his role in this story, as he saw it, stated for posterity.

When the crisis began in November 1916, Montagu wrote, many Liberals and Unionists were not eager to see Lloyd George become Prime Minister. They disliked him and were suspicious of him; and there were no plans to make him Prime Minister. Yet within a few weeks he was Prime Minister and Asquith was out. How did this come about?

In addition to the immediate causes that had precipitated the crisis, such as the Nigerian Land Sales debate and the attacks by the Northcliffe press, Montagu blamed Asquith's fall on three fundamental factors: the deep depression in England caused by discontent with the war, Asquith's failure as chairman of the War Council, and the folly of friends of both men who exacerbated the situation and drove Asquith and Lloyd George apart. Montagu placed particular blame on Carson and Northcliffe for encouraging Lloyd George to refuse to compromise, and on the Liberal Ministers, led by Mc-

Kenna, who was very vocal in his hatred of Lloyd George. Margot
Asquith was also to blame. She despised Lloyd George and was
equally vocal in her condemnation of any form of compromise.
Duff Cooper wrote in his diary on December 8:

Dined with Diana, Edwin and Venetia at Queen Anne's Gate. Edwin was
in the depths of depression and could talk of nothing but the political
situation. He is miserable that he had to resign and thinks he might have
avoided it. I don't think he could have. He is very fond of Lloyd George
and hates all the other Liberals. He was especially bitter about McKenna.
He says that all might have been well if it hadn't been for McKenna and
Margot on the one side dragging Asquith away from Lloyd George and
Harmsworth and Hedley Le Bas dragging Lloyd George away from Asquith.[65]

Left to themselves, Montagu wrote, Lloyd George and Asquith
could have worked out their differences. They complemented each
other, "Asquith with his incomparable capacity for mastering a
particular case, detecting the vital considerations, discarding the bad
arguments and giving a clear and right decision," and Lloyd George,
who brought his "fertile and ever working imagination and con-
structive power"[66] to a problem. Montagu saw Asquith and Lloyd
George working together "in complete harmony. Lloyd George's
ideas were nearly always acceptable to Asquith. George yearned for
Asquith's confidence and was never happier than when working
with him or when alone with him." This was an exaggeration.
Neither man liked or trusted the other. The most that can be said is
that both Asquith and Lloyd George were thorough professionals
who knew how to put aside their personal feelings in order to get a
job done. They did complement each other and worked well together. But "harmony" is too strong a word to describe their relationship.

According to Montagu, McKenna was a man of "no vision, no
clarity of judgment, great ambition; great jealousy and a very petty,
mean mind." Montagu recognized however, that he was "unswerv-
ingly loyal to Asquith but his loyalty took the form of endeavoring
to create a quarrel between Asquith and George . . . and of pursuing
from fear of George, the very policy which Asquith had deliberately
discarded, that of separating the two men."[67]

Montagu ended his narrative with a plea that history understand his role. He tried to keep Asquith and Lloyd George together not because he would benefit, but because he felt that it would be good for the country. He opposed the policies of his colleagues in refusing to join the Lloyd George government for the same reason. He was never promised a role in the new government. If offered, he would have declined. Whatever he did, he did out of conviction, not desire for political advantage.

I desire to place it on record that I have not received any offer to join George's Government, but I know that this is because George did not want a refusal, and if at any time I had sent him a message to say that I would come in, I should have been invited to join. I fear that I would not have been offered to remain where I am [Munitions], but I gather that as Bonar Law insisted on the Exchequer, I was to go to the India Office. I should not have cared to do this, because it has no connection with the War. Meanwhile, I find no common cause with my colleagues for refusing to join George's government. They do not believe in George. I do. They felt that their resentment at the methods by which the Government had been formed ought to make them keep out of it. I felt the resentment too but did not feel it ought to weigh with me in refusing. The one reason that I can put forward as a justification for keeping out is that my relations with Asquith and my affection of him would prevent me from doing my work in the new Government if I were haunted by the fear that I had deserted him in his needs.[68]

Montagu criticized his colleagues in the Liberal Party, who not only jeopardized the Party's future but destroyed it. By their behavior, the "center" of British politics was destroyed; only the poles of Conservatism and Labour remained. A compromise might have prevented this, as Montagu was aware. His Liberal colleagues did not see this, and England paid the price.

In closing, Montagu wrote that he regretted leaving Munitions, which was moving ahead very well, and was now better organized. "We have had plenty of disputes with other departments. We have always won. . . . We are on the way to solving a considerable problem. I wish I had been there to finish."[69] In her diary, Cynthia Asquith wrote about Montagu's sorrow at not being in the government:

The P. M. is wonderfully unbroken by the storms of state. I have got quite a lump in my throat about him.

Went to see Venetia about 4:30. She said Montagu had had dozens of frenzied letters from Margot full of insults, "I hear you are going with them—where is friendship? Where is loyalty?" However, poor dear, he is not going in with them, though I believe suffering tortures in refusing. Apparently he is *sous le charme* of Lloyd George and could quite well go in with him as regards his own intellectual conscience, so it is a real sacrifice to personal loyalty.[70]

On December 13, 1916, on behalf of Lloyd George, Bonar Law offered Montagu the position of financial Secretary to the Treasury. He refused.

It is with great regret that events of the last fortnight have placed me in such a position that I do not think I would be of much use if I accepted. For this reason I must decline, but I need, I hope, not assure you that I wish you and the Government the greatest possible good fortune and that I hope to find means of proving my support and desire to assist.[71]

Whether Montagu would have said "no" to a more prestigious position is difficult to discern. Lord Beaverbrook noted that this post was offered Montagu after all the principal positions had been filled.[72] At the time that Montagu turned down this position, he had begun to undertake special assignments for Lloyd George, writing to him on December 18 that he had just come home from delivering "a day's talk on national service. I hope by Wednesday or Thursday to be ready with the detail."[73] He apparently was working on a scheme to implement the new National Service Act.

Lloyd George subsequently offered him the Directorship of National Service. Again, he rejected the offer, but this time not because he was uncomfortable with joining the new government but because he felt that he was not the man for the job. He was "too green and plastery," he wrote, and not strong enough for such a difficult assignment. "It is not true patriotism," Montagu wrote:

. . . to attempt tasks for which you are not fitted. I do not lack conceit or self-confidence, I do think I am of service in council or as an administrator, but to create a new office or to dragoon a nation you want sterner stuff. I would much prefer at present to help in Hankey's office with a view to assisting in administration, suggesting action, attending to reconstruction, pending a job more likely to be successful.

I think you agree with me. . . . I am too green and plastery to be a rod of iron, too soft to breed a brood of dragons. It isn't that I don't want to, it is that I know I can't.[74]

Even turning down the positions offered to him by the Lloyd George government did not change the opinion of Margot and the other Asquithians who continued to believe that Montagu was a turncoat more interested in protecting his own political flank than in remaining loyal to friends and party. The fact that Montagu was so close to Asquith, so dependent on him for his political advancements and so much a part of the Asquith family made him more suspect. Margot also believed that by urging a compromise with Lloyd George "he [Montagu] and Bongie [Bonham Carter] and Eric [Drummond] had given H. [Asquith] the most rotten advice."[75] She and Violet Asquith, relentless in their accusations and anger, were totally unforgiving.[76]

21

Marriage: The Beginning,
1915–1916

Montagu is called "Shylock, the Merchant of Venetia."

Cynthia Asquith, Diaries, 1915–1918

During this most turbulent period in Montagu's political life, he was also adjusting to a very difficult marriage. While he knew from the start that Venetia did not love him or find him sexually attractive, Montagu hoped that in time this might change. He hoped that the strength and passion of his own love might infect Venetia. It did not. In spite of this, their marriage in the early years did seem to give both of them some happiness. Venetia now had the money to have "fun" and marriage provided her with a cloak of respectability to mask her unconventional behavior. And Montagu, for his part, had the pleasure of her company, which, even with minimal sexual fulfillment, seemed in the beginning at least to satisfy him. In time, he discovered that unrequited love was not a happy situation. He became increasingly morose and irritable. While he had always displayed such traits, a good marriage might have diminished them; a bad marriage only made them worse. The fact that his pre-nuptial agreement with Venetia permitted them both extra-marital relationships was no consolation. He loved Venetia too much to be happy with another woman.

Venetia was quite open about the intimate details of her marriage and made no effort to conceal her feelings toward Montagu. On November 12, 1915, only four months after the wedding, Cynthia Asquith wrote that "Bluetooth" (Harold Baker) told her a "funny story of Venetia sitting in front of a fire and soliloquising in a

386

dreamy voice 'I wonder if that old swine is still in bed' (Montagu has a habit of going to bed after lunch)."[1]

In October 1915, Raymond wrote of the rumor that the marriage had not been consummated.[2] A story Venetia had told a friend, Alastair Forbes, years later, about the "brutal defloration to which she was subjected by her husband on her wedding night"[3] presents a different picture. It seems, however, to be so much at odds with the picture of Montagu's subservience toward Venetia and his constant fear of upsetting or losing her, that it appears more likely that Venetia was either exaggerating or completely fabricating a story for her own purposes. In any case, whether the consummation took place early or late in the marriage, there is strong evidence that Venetia did not enjoy Montagu in bed. She did enjoy, however, the money he provided for her to travel, gamble, entertain, attend the theater, the ballet, the opera, weekend parties—to live the kind of happy-go-lucky, hedonistic life that had always appealed to her. Montagu's money and indulgence also gave Venetia the opportunity to shop at the most expensive stores in London and Paris and to change her style of dress dramatically, going from a rather simple, indifferent appearance to one of high fashion. Cynthia Asquith reported that on meeting Venetia one afternoon shortly after her marriage, she found her "looking [like] a magnificent Jewess in her fabulous bird of paradise hat . . . I felt [like] a country bumpkin. . . . How she has changed since her old days when she used to be so brutally careless of her person!"[4]

Five months later, Cynthia wrote: "I dined with the Montagus. Venetia resplendent in a home-made tea gown self-embroidered with beads, really extraordinarily pretty. The Parsons, Diana, a temporary soldier called Cripps, Duff and a nice fat brother of Montagu's were the party."[5] And again the same month, Cynthia observed as she watched Venetia dress: "She has become the most dainty and *recherché* of women about underclothes, and has the most lovely things. It seems so anomalous and foreign to one's conception of her."[6] Marriage and the adoration of two men, Asquith and Montagu, as well as the most luxurious clothing money can buy, had converted the careless tomboy into a sophisticated woman, aware of her attractiveness and enjoying the opportunity of showing it off.

Montagu also gave Venetia carte blanche to redecorate Queen

Anne's Gate, and she converted it into a luxurious and ostentatious home. Cynthia Asquith's description of her bedroom gives a sense of the opulence that Venetia liked. "Her abode is almost Elinor Glynish—magnificent, impersonal, green lacquer room. . . . Her bedroom is that of a courtesan."[7]

With Queen Anne's Gate redecorated, Venetia used it to entertain lavishly, taking great pains not only to have the house look beautiful, but to provide sumptuous food, scintillating conversation, the finest wines, bridge, poker, and other forms of relaxation. It was not unusual for the parties and the poker and bridge to continue until early dawn. Her dinners were attended by some of the most important men in the government, who were carrying the heaviest responsibilities of the war. Venetia's parties catered to the needs of such men and their wives, to allow them to escape from the almost unbearable burdens they shouldered. That she succeeded is evident in the reputation her home earned as a "haven" from the terrors of war.

Asquith apparently forgave Venetia and Montagu sufficiently by the end of 1915 to become a frequent guest in their home until the fall of the Asquith government. Until then, he and his family, Margot, Raymond and Katharine, Cynthia and Violet, and their spouses and friends regularly enjoyed the Montagus' hospitality and found their company both entertaining and relaxing. Diana Cooper described a typical evening: "Venetia had brought two of the old flower-sellers' baskets from Piccadilly Circus, packed high with spring flowers for the drawing room. Mr. Asquith at his happiest, asked a riddle: 'What is it God never sees, kings rarely see and we always see?' Raymond improved on the real answer 'An equal' by guessing 'A joke.' "[8]

Queen Anne's Gate quickly became not only a haven for the war-weary politicians but also the headquarters of the Coterie. Venetia and Edwin, Duff and Diana Cooper, Alan and Viola Parson, Iris Tree, Nancy Cunard, Claude Russell and Katharine and Raymond Asquith were the core of this unconventional, faintly wicked and daring crowd, whose sole purpose in life was to amuse themselves in a fashion described as "daring to the point of outrage, exotic, almost corrupt."[9] Drugs, alcohol and sex were all part of the scene. Morphia and chloroform were especially easy to obtain and most frequently used. Diana Cooper confessed that the Coterie's "pride was to be unafraid of words, unshocked by drink, and unashamed of 'decadence' and gambling—Unlike-Other-People, I'm afraid."[10]

In the early years, Raymond Asquith was the leader, and although the group enjoyed wild and riotous parties and pranks, dress balls and poker, they also "took pride in their learning and erudition. Politics and ideas were discussed with serious concentration, and plays, prose and poetry were often read aloud."[11] As many of the Coterie's members left for the front, and as the war began to take its toll, a different spirit overtook its remaining members. In an effort to escape the tragedies that surrounded them, the Coterie parties became wilder, the drink flowed more copiously and sex was freer and more promiscuous.

Raymond had been the symbol of the prewar Coterie, but now Diana Cooper became the symbol of the new Coterie. Raymond had been an intellectual; Diana was not. She had no formal education but was well read and immensely curious; she wrote well and knew a great deal about literature, art and music. Her fame, however, did not come from these accomplishments. She was one of the most beautiful and unconventional women of her day, wild, tempestuous, with a fierce love of life, and acknowledged as a fine actress as well as a reigning London beauty.

Diana married Duff Cooper who was equally unconventional, handsome and daring. Cooper had a war record of courage and leadership and was a career diplomat. He adored Diana and was as wild, unpredictable and promiscuous as she. Diana and Duff had been lovers during the war (they did not marry until 1919). Since Duff did not go overseas until 1918, he and Diana were partners in the Coterie during most of the war years. Their love letters from 1915 to 1919 give a rare and intimate glimpse of the life of the Coterie and include some of the most insightful comments about Venetia and Montagu that have survived.

Since they had no home of their own and Duff was not welcome at Diana's home—her mother, the Duchess of Rutland, did not think a penniless member of the Foreign Office staff good enough for her daughter—the Montagu homes, both Queen Anne's Gate and their country home, Breccles (bought in 1916 in Norfolk), became, in Duff's words, "ever-open havens of hospitality" for them. Diana and Duff spent as many as three to four nights a week with the Montagus and many weekends. Montagu was welcomed by the Coterie in spite of his age and more solemn demeanor, not merely because of his hospitality, his house and his wife, but because he was genuinely appreciated for his wit, intelligence and his kindness to friends. "Edwin," wrote Diana, "was a new Coterie member who, being 'very old' (not forty) and very eminent, we called 'Mr. Montagu.' We had to struggle to change to Edwin . . . but he felt that the 'Mr.' put him out of our category." [12]

Duff wrote: "He was a man whose ugliness was obliterated by his charm. He had a huge, ungainly body, a deep soft voice and dark eyes that sparkled with humour and kindliness . . . He was very nervous and absurdly pessimistic. Whenever he talked about the future he would interject: 'But, I, of course shall be dead by then.' " [13] Diana added: "In his face shone a benevolence that made me think he must be under some spell and that a magic word, the fall of a sparrow, would allow him to cast his cruel disguise and turn into a shining paragon." [14]

"In this summer of 1915," Diana continued, "he would say 'My fires give no heat.' That was his attitude to all things, but they blazed brightly enough for us. At his house we saw not only unadulterated Coterie but the Prime Minister and Margot, Winston and Clemmie, Augustine Birrell and most of the Government, politicians, new bloods of the town, and Edwin's brother in the Naval Brigade 'Cardie' Montagu. But of all these Edwin liked us best." [15] And in return, "we had given Edwin all our affection," wrote Diana:

ragging him for his gloom and forcing him sometimes to be carefree. We seem by letters to be there (at his house) several times a week. Hospital goodnights said (Diana worked at a hospital during the war) I would tear out of the house . . . and run down St. James Street to Duff. There we would split a half-bottle of champagne and then stroll past the birds and the swans of St. James Park to 24 Queen Anne's Gate (the "Green Griffon" Mr. Birrell called it), to the stimulating company and all that was left of the loveliest and the best. [16]

Cynthia Asquith also wrote of the affection felt for Montagu and the charm that his friends were permitted to see and which was so absent in his political life. "Mr. Wu [Montagu] is a great success here. Papa and Angela both think him 'charming.' Venetia is in good form and seems very happy now." [17]

The affection his friends had for him, however, did not deter them from describing him, physically, in most unflattering terms. "His long, bony features were so pock-marked," Diana Cooper wrote, "that Katharine Asquith, playing tennis on a particularly dilapidated asphalt court, remarked that it reminded her of Edwin's face";[18] she also wrote that he, Edwin, had "no thread to his personality."[19] Still other friends remarked that he "yawned like a hyena,"[20] took a long joyride from London to Oxford in a motor car despite the poster campaign of his own Treasury Department that urged Britons "Don't motor for pleasure!"[21] and that while he was a generous host, he was not generous in sharing his wealth. Duff wrote to Diana on November 16, 1916:

Edwin said the other day he wondered why "rich" people didn't give themselves the pleasure of suddenly giving a poor friend £10,000. That is the kind of pleasure you could give tomorrow by suddenly forgiving me and letting me lunch with you. You probably won't, just as the rich never give people £10,000 and just as Edwin never gives one £10.[22]

Cynthia Asquith thought it was a joke when someone called Montagu "Shylock, the merchant of Venetia."[23] The Coterie affection for Edwin may have been strong, but the undercurrent of anti-Semitic prejudice that permeated their class was even stronger. They saw nothing strange in loving Montagu and at the same time calling him "Shylock, the merchant of Venetia."

Even Duff and Diana Cooper, some of whose dearest friends were Jewish, were not immune from this bigotry. Before the war, Diana had traveled extensively, spending time in Paris. Commenting on that visit, she wrote, "A thought from an Englishman is worth ten years' devotion from these squalid, misshapen, Jewish, vulgar, loud-tongued, insult-asking Frenchmen."[24] Ziegler, a biographer of Diana Cooper, has written that epithets against Jews were part of the common slang used by young boys and girls in England and Diana probably gave no more thought to them than she gave to other slang expressions. She "grew up with the instinctive anti-semitism of her class and race. When George V acceded she wrote to Patrick Shaw-Stewart that 'he represents to me all that I most heartily dislike . . . except that I thank God that he hates the Jews.' "[25] Ziegler continued: "Such jibes never meant much to her. . . . In youth . . . she grew up as intolerant as the majority of her friends.

Acquaintances were condemned for their accents, their clothes, their stupidity, their hair style. Jewishness was just another to be added to the category of vices; venial certainly, but a blemish all the same."[26]

Diana and Duff had among their closest friends Hilaire Belloc who, in spite of the nastiness with which he expressed his anti-Semitism, was admired by the Coopers. In this they were not alone. He was viewed by most of the Coterie as a "true poet" of distinction.[27] Under the influence of alcohol, Diana once wrecked a weekend party by reciting for her dinner partner, Cardie Montagu, Edwin's brother, Belloc's malicious verses.[28] Duff was not much different from Diana. While enjoying the home and hospitality of the Montagus, he was heard to snarl, "these bloody Jews are all the same," when not allowed to borrow Philip Sassoon's Rolls Royce one rainy night.[29] When Duff thought of becoming a "rich" lawyer, the only one that came to his mind was Rufus Isaacs (Lord Reading), although there were scores of lawyers as rich or richer than Isaacs. Duff wrote to Diana on July 11, 1918, "So after the war, darling, I go straight to the Bar and shall soon become as rich as Isaacs."[30] That same month, he wrote Diana:

My dear, have you read the *Morning Post* these days about Edwin's [Montagu-Chelmsford] report? It is really too insulting but rather funny. On Monday it says that when the Indians see Mr. Montagu coming to India they argue with themselves. "Why does the British Raj advance this person of ignoble birth"—for there is unhappily a prejudice against the Montagu type in India. . . . "Mr. Montagu . . . is to them merely a symbol of the decadence of the British Empire." Does Edwin read it and wince, read it and laugh, or not read it? Good bye, baby. Are you going to marry me? Duff.[31]

There was no indignation in Duff's reaction to the insulting comments about Jews and Montagu in the article. He merely found it "rather funny."

To his credit, in his later years, Duff became "an ardent champion of Zionism," a hater of Hitler and "an enemy of every kind of persecution, a man who was to dedicate his book *David* to the Jewish people."[32]

Diana, too, changed dramatically as she grew older. "Many years later, when her son was describing the virtues of his latest friend, he was rash enough to qualify the catalogue with '. . . though he's a Jew.' He can still remember the stinging box on the ears which his mother administered while asking: 'And what, pray, is there wrong with that?' "[33] Not only did her attitude change but "many of the greatest pleasures in Diana's life came to her through Jews whose affection she cherished and to whom she was utterly loyal."[34] Venetia and Montagu were two such people. She became Venetia's closest and dearest friend. They shopped, dined, played and traveled abroad together and for many years were inseparable. She replaced Violet Asquith as Venetia's best friend since Violet's friendship for Venetia cooled considerably after Montagu joined the Lloyd George government.

This change signaled a change in Venetia's lifestyle. While she loved fun and pranks, friends such as Violet and Raymond added a quality of seriousness to her life. They were unconventional but they were also proper and restrained and had some social conscience. With their leveling influence gone and Duff and Diana's carefree, devil-may-care attitude casting its spell, Venetia's life became almost totally devoid of any purpose except fun and pleasure, with drugs, sexual promiscuity and experimentation high on the list of her preferred activities. It is no wonder that friends began to talk about the marriage as "doomed." It is no wonder that Montagu spent more and more time at work and became more irritable with each passing day.

22

Montagu and Reconstruction, January–June 1917

To design a country fit for heroes.

Lloyd George to the Second
Reconstruction Committee, Jan. 1917

Immediately upon taking office, Lloyd George drastically over-hauled the whole machinery of the government. As had been expected, Grey was replaced by Balfour at the Foreign Office, Derby took over the War Office and Bonar Law became Chancellor of the Exchequer, an office Lloyd George had dangled before Montagu during the discussions before the fall of Asquith. A new War Cabinet was created, consisting of Bonar Law, Milner, Curzon, Henderson and Lloyd George. Maurice Hankey continued as Secretary. The Cabinet was small enough to act quickly and decisively. During its first year, it met more than three hundred times.

The Conservatives were now firmly entrenched in the key positions of the government, thus producing the strange spectacle of a so-called Liberal Prime Minister, whose government was composed mainly of Conservatives, while the leaders of the Liberal Party, supported by the majority of the Liberals, sat on the opposition bench. In spite of the bitterness between the two groups, an uneasy truce did exist until the end of the war. Liberal hostility toward Lloyd George was strong, and although Asquith took the high road and promised not to imperil national unity and the Lloyd George government, his heart was never in it.

By taking this position, Asquith put his followers in a most difficult position. Were they really in opposition? How intense should their attacks be against specific measures? Should they feel free to attack Lloyd George? Would this imperil national unity? How could they lead an opposition when their leader, Asquith, assumed the role of the responsible statesman and remained aloof and silent? They could not. Asquith, by occupying a political no-man's-land—not really supporting Lloyd George and not truly opposing him—may have avoided an out-and-out break within the Liberal Party and may have helped foster the appearance of national unity, but his position doomed the Liberal Party to impotence.

Montagu had feared this from the beginning. As he had written to Asquith on January 25, 1917:

Nobody can predict if the split occurs, in what direction it will occur. It may be that the Lloyd George part of it will be very small. It may be that it will be very big. Nobody, I think, thinks, that it will be a majority. But whatever its size, it will be a pity of the first magnitude if and when parties resume the normal peace avocations. At any rate it ought to be a split upon policy, for I am confident that whatever the Liberal Party in the country thinks of the way in which the Government was formed, nobody now is interested in what to us is a personal question. It would be terrible to have party strife based on persons, however great our respect or affection may be for those who have been wronged.

If I am right in all this, we ought, in my opinion, to avoid accepting a challenge or forcing a split. I hear that the Liberal Whip's Office is forcing upon Associations and upon candidates the question "Are you an Asquith-ite or a Lloyd Georgeite?" Now as I understand the Reform Club policy, there is no room for this antithesis. It is not a question that anybody ought to be asked to answer. Asquith is leader of the Liberal Party and the Liberal Party is supporting Lloyd George's Government.[1]

Montagu's pleas fell on deaf ears. Asquith was too bitter to listen, and Lloyd George was too involved with his own personal ambitions and the war to care about the long-range health of the Liberal Party. His immediate concern was harnessing the resources of the Empire to turn stalemate and defeat to victory. Toward that end, he applied all his enormous energy and imagination. In addition to the new War Cabinet, he created new departments almost overnight: shipping, labor, food, and national service. The first three became Ministries at once; national service became one in March 1917.[2]

The public responded with confidence to Lloyd George's almost dictatorial style. Their concern, like his, was to win the war. If in the course of this effort old rules and ideas about parliamentary government and freedom from state control were distorted and destroyed, it mattered not. Niceties of style were not to interfere with the end result; victory on the battlefields would justify almost any means.

The War Grinds On

But victory was as elusive for Lloyd George in 1917 as it had been for Asquith. At the beginning of 1917, the Germans had retreated along a wide sector of the British front from Arras to Soissons, but the British did not take advantage of this. The retreat had given the Germans the opportunity to regroup along the Hindenburg line—a better fortified line of defense. But the Germans retreated toward Germany and this gave the British some comfort.

The Canadian capture of Vimy Ridge, taking twenty thousand prisoners and two hundred and fifty guns, also convinced some that the Germans were tired and were showing signs of strain. This was not so. The Germans may have been tired, but their fighting spirit persisted. They announced unrestricted submarine war against neutrals in barred zones, giving no advance warning to passengers, and inflicted a major defeat on Italy at Caporetto, where two hundred and fifty thousand Italians were captured and three thousand guns lost.

To add to the woes of the Allies, the Russian Revolution was nearing a climax. The Czar and his government were collapsing, and by August 1917 the Russians were out of the war, having signed a separate peace treaty with Germany. This freed the German troops at the eastern front, who were then sent to increase the pressure on the British-French lines.

Lloyd George continued to have the same difficulties with Haig, Robertson and the other generals as had Asquith, and he was not able to move them away from their all-out commitment to the Western front. On July 31, Haig launched the third battle of Ypres (also called Passchendaele), which Lloyd George accurately called "the battle of the mud."[3] It was here that the final episode of the battle was waged. It was a disaster: Everything went wrong. This was the rainiest August in many years; men, guns and tanks sank knee-deep and sometimes neck-deep in the mud, which quickly became a graveyard for hundreds of thousands of British and German soldiers. The slaughter was horrendous. The British advanced only four miles, an area from which they retreated in the face of the German offensive of March 1918. The campaign had cost Britain another four hundred thousand casualties.

The Homefront

Nineteen-seventeen was also a bitter year for civilians. Rationing of bread, wheat and sugar was put into effect; food and fuel were running short; railway fares rose by 50 percent; the queue became a new British institution; industrial conscription was not popular; and Henderson was dismissed from the War Cabinet for supporting the Labour Party's desire to attend a Socialist Popular Front Peace Conference in Stockholm. Economic discontent was festering and critics of the war became more overt.[4]

This was the year too of the Corn Production Act, which fixed prices for wheat, oats, and potatoes, provided necessary subsidies to encourage production, fixed wages for agriculture and limited landlords' right to raise rents. It was the year of the Irish Conscription Bill and the Representation of the People Act, a voting bill that simplified the franchise, requiring only a six-month residency, and gave women the vote, although on a more restrictive basis than men. It also disenfranchised conscientious objectors for five years after the war. One hundred and six Liberals, led by Herbert Samuel, voted against the last two provisions, while Asquith and Montagu voted with the government, causing great irritation within the Party.

The divisions within the Liberal Party that Montagu had predicted were now growing. The general mood in the country and among its fighting men had turned from the naive romance of the first years of the war to a quiet sense of endurance, a numbness and a resolve to get on with this unpleasant matter. The soldiers were no longer dewy-eyed poets and white knights. They were now more professional; they had seen the real horrors of war and were not ashamed to sing:

> Oh my
> I do not want to die
> I want to go home. . . .

The only bright spots in 1917 were Allenby's victory over the Turks, his capture of Jerusalem and, most importantly, the American entry into the war on April 2, 1917.

Montagu Becomes Vice-Chairman of the Reconstruction Committee

In January 1917, after Montagu had rejected the posts of Financial Secretary and Director of National Service, Lloyd George asked him to act as Vice-Chairman and Acting Chief of a second Reconstruction Committee. Lloyd George himself would be titular Chairman.

Hankey had originally suggested to Lloyd George that he appoint Montagu "joint secretary of the War Cabinet." Lloyd George, according to a letter Hankey wrote to Montagu on January 21, 1917, had said, "No, it's too dangerous." Hankey commented: "I am afraid he must think you are too much in with McKenna and Co. The Reconstruction Committee has not yet been touched by the War Cabinet and there would soon to be an opportunity there."[5]

Such a letter must have pained Montagu. It revealed how little Lloyd George knew of Montagu's feelings toward McKenna. Montagu was as hostile to McKenna as Lloyd George was and, indeed, blamed him for destroying any hope of compromise. The letter showed that Lloyd George never understood Montagu's role during the last days of the Asquith government in trying to reconcile the differences between Asquith and himself. In Lloyd George's mind, Montagu was too identified with the Asquith forces, including McKenna, to be trusted with a sensitive position, such as Junior Secretary of the War Cabinet.

Montagu, out of political action for a month and a half and miserable at his exclusion from the government, eagerly accepted the offer of Vice-Chairman of Reconstruction. He had always been interested in Reconstruction and had served on the first Reconstruction Committee created by Asquith in March 1916. And since the Reconstruction Committee to be created by Lloyd George was advisory and not executive, serving on the Committee would not make Montagu an official part of the Lloyd George government. This seemed to Montagu to be less threatening to Asquith than if he had accepted a role more directly involved in the administration of the new government. Indeed, he felt sufficiently comfortable with the position to write to Asquith a few days after Lloyd George's offer that he could not visit him at Freshwater since he was busy trying to get the Reconstruction work started. "Lloyd George says that, subject to the consent of the Cabinet, he will hand it over to me." Lloyd George "is delighted at the prospect of having 'Bongy' work there." Montagu added, "Nash assures me that the idea of my doing it meets with your approval and I think we shall be a very happy party and do useful work."[6] There is no indication of Asquith's reaction.

The First Reconstruction Committee

A Reconstruction Committee had first been created by Asquith in 1916 as a committee of cabinet ministers, chaired by the Prime Minister. Montagu had served on it as Chancellor of the Duchy of Lancaster. When he established the Committee, Asquith wrote, "I propose to set up, on the analogy of the Committee of Imperial Defense, a Committee over which I shall preside, to consider and advise with the aid of sub-committees upon the problems that will arise on the conclusion of Peace, and to co-ordinate work which has already been done by the Departments in this direction."[7]

The Committee worked through scores of subcommittees, some already in existence in the established Departments, some newly created. While investigating problems of postwar employment, demobilization, housing, the special problems of women and other issues the nation would face after the War, the Committee mainly concentrated on devising plans to prevent Germany from regaining economic power after the war. Germany was to be viewed as the enemy even after peace and would be denied access to foreign supplies and raw materials. This might entail a new kind of economic protectionism alien to the free trade philosophy of the Liberal Party, but it did not deter the Committee from exploring these methods of punishing Germany.

Although the Asquith Reconstruction Committee lasted only ten months, it made important contributions. "In some ways it outranked and outperformed both of its successors."

It launched reconstruction [Johnson, a major historian of Reconstruction, states]; it gave the task a breadth of conception which it never lost. . . . the only reforms achieved in wartime were due to it. No measures that were

recommended by the later committee or the ministry became law until
1919. By contrast, the Corn Production Act, the forestry program, and the
Whitley Council program were adopted or passed in 1917. . . .[8]

The Reconstruction Committee of 1916 made important contributions
to its successors. The training of its staff was directly carried over. Eight
active sub-committees worked on into 1917, helping preserve continuity;
and sub-committee reports left their mark on the final results.[9]

Montagu, who became Vice-Chairman of the Second Reconstruction Committee, and Hammond, who was Assistant Secretary
of both Committees, received their training and experience on Asquith's first Reconstruction Committee: This helped in getting the
Second Reconstruction Committee off to a speedy start.

The Second Reconstruction Committee

In creating his Reconstruction Committee, it was Lloyd George's
aim to create a Committee representing "more advanced thinking,"[10] including that of Socialists, Fabians, Liberals, Liberal Conservatives—all "persons of ideas,"[11] who were prepared to examine
the breadth of British society and not be afraid to recommend
fundamental changes when necessary. Lloyd George made this clear
at the first meeting of this Committee. He said that while under
Asquith the Reconstruction Committee had been a Committee of
ministers too busy to give it their full attention, his Committee
would not be made up of ministers; it would be composed of
experienced men and women with ideas and imagination who he
expected to devote their full energies to surveying the whole field of
power, to assist in painting "a new picture which would arise immediately after the war with fewer grey colours in it."[12]

The Committee would continue to study areas explored by the
first Reconstruction Committee as well as begin exploration of new
areas: demobilization, questions of labor, land, wages, employment,
housing, the machinery of local and central government, education,
the relationship of the state to industry, agriculture, industrial production and all the other problems involved in the transition from a
war to a peacetime economy. "Conditions before the War were
often impossible and stupid," Lloyd George told the Committee at
its first meeting. "The Committee must advise the Government
what steps could be taken to make a repetition impossible."[13] "No

such opportunity has ever been given to any nation before—not even by the French revolution":

The nation now was in a molten condition: it was malleable now and would continue to be so for a short time after the War, but not for long. It was for the Committee to advise the Government on the way to give to the nation a shape which would endure to the advantage both of the nation itself and of the whole Empire. [14]

Lloyd George gave the Committee a mandate to develop new social and economic policies that would create a stronger economy for Britain and a better life for all the people and would design "a country fit for heroes to live in." [15] It was a radical's dream, and an ideal vehicle for Montagu.

Lloyd George was Chairman of the Committee and Edwin Montagu, Vice-Chairman. [16] Since Lloyd George did not attend any meeting after the first, Montagu was, for all practical purposes, the Chairman, and Chief Executive Officer. [17] He prepared memoranda on the agenda, assigned papers to be researched, brought in new staff and Committee members, recommended panels and took upon himself the responsibility to act as a liaison with departments involved in the problems analyzed by the Committee.

After assuming the responsibility for Reconstruction, Montagu tried throughout January and February to see Lloyd George. [18] He was unsuccessful and finally resorted to a seventeen-page letter in which he said that in addition to reporting on Reconstruction, he would now send Lloyd George weekly letters commenting on current political problems, as he had done with Asquith from 1906 to 1910. He sent the letters until July 1917 when he became Secretary of State for India.

In the first of these letters, Montagu gave his views on Carson's appointment to the Admiralty, commenting that Carson's speech in the House was good and that, in spite of his face, Montagu found him kindly and sympathetic. He suggested that a system of convoys and a Ministry of Supply be considered and that subsidized industries should be liable to heavy excess profits taxes. He reported that he was disappointed with the government's slowness in implementing compulsory National Service and suggested that Lloyd George form his own National Labour Party and not be co-opted by Conservatism. The younger Liberals and young Conservatives, Mon-

tagu believed, "coupled with the best elements of Labour, which
has so long sought intelligent leadership and policy, ought to make
a fine National Party under your leadership. Such a Party would not
contain Massingham and McKenna; such a Party would not, I think,
contain Curzon, Chamberlain and Salisbury. But such a Party would
contain all the people who want to get a move on." Montagu also
pleaded for a new attempt to settle the Irish problem along the lines
that Lloyd George had suggested but that Parliament had rejected in
1916.[19]

There is no evidence that Lloyd George ever read this or any of
the other long letters Montagu sent to him. Unlike Asquith, he did
not have the patience to conduct government through memoranda.
He preferred face-to-face exchanges, where instantaneous decisions
could be made and his persuasive personality could invariably cajole
the responses he wanted.

Montagu was aware of this and knew that the memoranda he was
sending were only a last resort and not likely to be read. He therefore continued to plead for meetings, even resorting to writing
fawning and obsequious poetry:

> Dear Prime Minister
> As the desert sand for rain,
> As the Londoner for sun,
> As the poor for potatoes,
> As the landlord for rent,
> As Drosera rotunderfolio for a fly,
> As Herbert Samuel for Palestine,
> As a woman in Waterloo Road for a soldier,
> I long for a talk with you.
> *Will you breakfast or dine tomorrow?*[20]

Neither his poetry nor his prose helped. After acting as Vice-
Chairman for more than five months, he was still writing notes to
Lloyd George, begging "for a conversation . . . of learning your
views[,] on how things are going, that breakfast, dinner, visit to
you in the country have all seemed equally unattractive to you. . . .
What am I to do?" He wrote: "You will not permit me to act on my
own responsibility, and we are awaiting decisions of a series of what
seem to me to be small points. The appointment of Committees is
hung up, and actions on Reports are delayed because of the impossibility of getting to you or to the Cabinet."[21] He soon learned that

he would have to act on his own, with or without Lloyd George's specific acquiescence.

He was determined to be more than a pro forma chairman and sought "to give a strong lead; he went beyond the routine function of summarizing the past situation and supplied the second meeting of the Committee with a major policy paper on future work." This document, Paul Barton Johnson states, *"was one of the most coherent and broadly conceived statements that wartime was to produce"* (emphasis added).[22]

In spite of the testiness of his colleagues and the difficulties in managing such an independent and often unruly group, Montagu persevered. He continued to have little or no support from Lloyd George, rarely seeing the Prime Minister and complaining: "Every day that goes by makes me more and more anxious to have a talk with you. . . . I want to prepare and propound big schemes and I employ too experienced and conservative a staff for investigative machinery."[23] Montagu's radicalism came to the fore when he wrote, "I want nationalization of many things, mines, railways, and land, reorganization of government, and Parliament, etc. But I must have more access to you. You ought to know, half an hour's talk would set you at rest, and I hope stimulate you. But it must be soon for difficulties loom ahead."[24]

Although Lloyd George could find no time to discuss policy with Montagu, he objected when Montagu gave an interview to the press expressing his own ideas about Reconstruction. Montagu had to reassure him at once that this had not been a deliberate slight:

Since writing to you this morning I heard it rumored that you think I have "rigged" the press on the subject of reconstruction. This would be a serious matter if it were true, and I will give you the facts. I know no journalist and the reference to the matter in the press can only refer to the *Observer* and the *Daily Chronicle*. As regards the former I *did* meet Garvin before the article on the subject appeared. But it was at the invitation of your secretary Waldorf Astor at his house at lunch. It was to discuss reconstruction but I did not give the impression of advocating any policy. . . . If only we met these misunderstandings would not arise.[25]

During July 1917, Montagu prepared "a major policy statement on industrial controls," which has been described as "new and remarkable."[26] Its basic premise was that "the state must control food and shipping and imports and exports after the war; the needs of home industries must come first."[27] Montagu's rationale was simple: "The case for control is that the transition period is bound to present conditions which it would be impossible for private trade to contend with without grave danger to the interests of the community."

If the various systems of control . . . were suddenly abolished, merchants, manufacturers and financiers might indeed rejoice, but we should have . . . intolerable confusion, with freights and prices soaring up. . . . The only safe forecast is . . . of insufficient food, materials, and above all of shipping, and this means that the stampede would, if it were unregulated, be tremendous; that articles of necessity would be elbowed out by luxuries; . . . bricks and timber and girders needed for building workmen's houses might be used up in building great houses or theatres. . . . Control is not advocated because a crippled community will require crutches, but because with the depletion of necessary stocks and the deterioration of works and services of all kinds . . . and the limited supply . . . some temporary system of State guidance, information and direction is indispensable before free methods of trade can be relied upon again.[28]

Johnson continues: "Many times warnings against swift decontrol were to be voiced. This exposition by Montagu was second to none."[29]

Montagu's New Approach to Postwar Commercial Policy

During July 1917 Montagu prepared a paper, originally for Albert Stanley, who was then President of the Board of Trade and later Lord Ashfield, which provided a new outlook on Britain's postwar commercial policy. Until then, the British attitude toward postwar economic policy had been focused on Germany, based on the notion that "the undefeated enemy remained, in British eyes, a potent threat to economic recovery"[30] and plans for postwar British economic policy were geared to protecting Britain and the Empire from Germany which was viewed as the "chief danger to British recovery."[31] Montagu disagreed. His paper examined British postwar commercial policy and concluded that the likelihood of world scarcities, *"not* Germany *per se,* . . . made joint Allied control over supply and distribution essential. Germany would not be in a position to disrupt the economic transition: 'To put it at its lowest, many months must elapse before German manufacturers will be able to produce on a large scale for export or to compete as previously with their rivals in the markets of the world.' "[32]

Thus, the prospect of Germany's dumping goods, which had been "held to be a danger" at the time of the Paris Economic Conference in 1914, Montagu no longer considered a likelihood in the summer of 1917. Indeed, according to Montagu, the overriding factor in economic plans in 1917 "is a probable world-shortage for some time to come in important raw materials and food-stuffs, accentuated by the recent bad harvests of last year and by the increasing shortage of shipping."[33] He concluded that the circumstances called for "concerted action" among the Allies for the short-term purpose of making "skillful use" of their economic powers, and so to have the leverage to influence "the enemy both during the War and in any peace negotiation."[34] Beyond that, the interest of Britain and her Allies was "not so much to defend themselves against German aggression as to provide cooperatively rather than competitively for their own postwar needs."[35]

Peter Cline, an economist and historian has written: "In the succeeding twelve months, this understanding of the postwar recovery problem [developed and pushed by Montagu] came only gradually to prevail in government."

Early among those moving to Montagu's view was Christopher Addison, newly appointed Minister of Reconstruction, who was then, together with Montagu and Albert Stanley, appointed to the Economic Offensive Committee. And it appears that they influenced Carson's thinking, as they made of the Committee a "sounding board" for their viewpoints and reconstruction proposals. They seemed to have cooled Carson's ardor for a "trade war" and diverted him from the issue of protectionism. *They encouraged Carson instead to pursue their common interests in post war materials control. Thus it seems, it was under their influence that the focus of the economic offensive shifted from Germany as the chief danger to British recovery, towards the more diffused menace of world shortages and dislocations.*[36] (emphasis added)

The Reconstruction Committee, as well as the Economic Offensive Committee created by Lloyd George to develop postwar trade and economic policies, accepted Montagu's thesis. Their "strong recommendation that the government renounce most favored nation treaties reflected their evolving strategy. Britain and her Allies had to free their hands before they could ration materials. In addition, their report on postwar prospects for raw materials, which the government took with it into its consultations with the Allies made a strong case for controls."[37] Montagu also called for an American-Allied Conference on economic policy, "adding the disconcerting thought that the dawning prospect of total Allied triumph rendered obsolete the assumptions that underlay all extant studies of trade."[38]

Although Montagu was Vice-Chairman of the Reconstruction Committee for only six months, he not only was its chief executive officer, directing and supervising the staff, acting as the driving force behind the preparation of many of its reports, especially those on housing and the Poor Law, but he also prepared policy papers on the major goals of Reconstruction. His paper on state control of industrial policy after the war profoundly influenced British attitudes toward postwar commercial policy, moving Britain away from viewing Germany as its major problem and toward an understanding that the likelihood of world scarcities was the real problem.

Johnson, in placing the Reconstruction Committee in historic perspective, calls it a "unique chapter in British history. . . . The Reconstruction Committee, for all its conflicts and diversities, . . . had nevertheless set to work with a will. No other papers and memorandum pulse with such dogmatic conviction." Johnson queries whether it was Lloyd George or the spirit of 1917 that "called forth this spirit."[39] Since Lloyd George only came to the first meeting, and since Montagu organized, administered and directed the Committee, it is reasonable to conclude that it was Montagu and the members of this Committee, rather than Lloyd George or the spirit of 1917, that made the work of the Committee so unique.

Montagu Longs to Enter the Lloyd George Government

In April 1917, Lloyd George suggested that Montagu accept a Cabinet post. Concerned as he was with the reaction of the Asquiths, Montagu was seriously interested. He longed to get back into government more directly than his work in Reconstruction permitted. And although he had never lost his interest in India, he preferred a position more clearly connected with the war—something like Chancellor of the Exchequer. "I am intimately acquainted with the Exchequer, now for ten years," he wrote to Lloyd George, "indeed I think this Budget [1917] which is to be introduced tomorrow is the first Budget since 1906 which imposes taxation with the preparation of which I have had no concern whatever. I have been at the Treasury, too, during the war . . . and one of my pleasantest recollections is the degree of confidence which I seem to have established among the people in the City with whom the Treasury had to deal."[40]

Montagu explained why Chamberlain should not go to the Treasury. When the war ended, he told Lloyd George, finance must be tackled in an "unorthodox way." "A generous Treasury may be our only method of avoiding a revolution," he wrote. "You must not have so Conservative a Conservative in charge of the Nation's purse,—a man with so few ideas as Chamberlain possesses. His efficient, humdrum mind will, I think, tend to make him a public danger at the Treasury."[41]

Montagu believed that a Liberal, a radical Liberal, should be Chancellor of the Exchequer. He also explained why he thought he should not be Secretary of State for India. This position, he wrote, is "tied, swaddled, swathed, manacled by legislation, and by the existence of the Council of India."[42] There would be little more he could do as Secretary of State than he was already doing from the outside. Any legislation he might suggest, moreover, he was sure would be rejected by Curzon. He believed Chamberlain would be better suited to be Secretary of State for India than Chancellor of the Exchequer.

He recommended creating a Ministry of Reconstruction, similar to the one the Germans had developed. He suggested that he could be involved in this as a Minister without Portfolio with the opportunity to attend War Cabinet meetings when matters concerning reconstruction were on the agenda. He repeated his belief that Lloyd George needed new Liberal blood in his government and offered his services, friendship and loyalty.

I am anxious to be the fore-runner of young Liberals who will flock to your standard. After all, my friendship with Asquith is well known. I am prepared to leave him because I find that I am in agreement with you in your aims and objects and in disagreement with those whom I now find to be my colleagues in the House of Commons. When I come to you, you will be my only political friend in the Coalition Government. Let us have an opportunity of working and sticking together.[43]

If Margot Asquith had seen this letter, she would have had every reason to be even more incensed than she already was. It portrays

Montagu at his worst, ready to swallow his past distrust of Lloyd George, forego his friendship with Asquith and make Lloyd George not merely a working colleague but his "only political friend" in the Coalition government. By early May, Montagu had definitely decided to accept a place in the Lloyd George government if the opportunity presented itself. He dictated a memorandum on May 10, 1917: "Since last week I definitely made up my mind to take office in the Government. I have had no conversations whatever with anyone in the last Government and I have not seen the Prime Minister."[44]

He wrote that he tried to see Lloyd George but had been unable to do so. He believed Lloyd George did not want to see him. He also recorded that Freddy Guest, new Chief Whip, had asked to see him. He did not think much of Guest, who seemed to him to be "a stupid man." Guest had spoken with him of the need to bring Asquith back into the Cabinet and thought Winston Churchill could do this. Guest had also told him that "Neil Primrose, who asked Freddy to be Whip, said that I [Montagu] would be joining the Government."[45]

Montagu added that he had spent the weekend at the Wharf with Asquith and Margot, who continued to be annoyed at his role during the last days of the Asquith government. Lloyd George would not take his calls; Winston Churchill urged him not to join the government and Rufus (Lord Reading) told him that Lloyd George was annoyed at Guest's suggestion that Asquith should join the government, as it would appear that his "Government has failed."[46]

Montagu Suggests a Ministry for Reconstruction

By the middle of May, Montagu was convinced that the Reconstruction Committee should be a Ministry. He wrote to Lloyd George that the organization of the Reconstruction Committee:

is not adequate for the vital purposes it has to achieve. I say nothing against my colleagues. The harmony in which they work and the eagerness with which they are throwing themselves into the struggle, are far better than I ever dreamt could have been possible. But I believe that if you were to ask them (or the majority of them) privately their own opinion, they would agree with me that they are conscious of their own shortcomings for the purpose for which they were appointed. A committee is really and truly not the proper organization through which to tackle reconstruction problems.[47]

He recommended that the Minister of Reconstruction be a member of the Cabinet, "with the understanding that he not take part in military or naval questions."[48] He would have public status, access to the Cabinet, "for Reconstruction will loom larger as peace comes nearer."

During May and June of 1917, Montagu continued to have conversations with various members of Lloyd George's "inner circle" and finally with Lloyd George himself over his possible roles in the government. Negotiations had advanced to the point that Montagu felt comfortable in writing to the Prime Minister on June 11, 1917, that he would gladly be either the head of the Ministry of Munitions or a Minister without Portfolio in charge of Reconstruction. He preferred Reconstruction.

I have naturally to thank you [he wrote to Lloyd George] for a very enjoyable afternoon yesterday, for the business you found rare leisure to transact, and for the gratifying suggestions which were the outcome of our conversation and about which I promised to write to you today.

It was suggested by you either I might return to the Ministry of Munitions on the promotion of Addison—Labour being handed over to the Ministry of Labour so far at any rate as disputes were concerned—(an excellent reform, if I may say so).

As an alternative it was suggested that you would agree to make me a member of your Cabinet as a Minister without Portfolio ["or salary"—deleted] to take charge on behalf of the Government reconstruction matters in particular and to assist in domestic policy generally. It is not an easy choice to make, but notwithstanding my affection for the Minister of Munitions and the joy with which I would welcome being associated with those there again and notwithstanding the difficulty of seeing a suitable appointment to the Ministry (I think W.E. [Worthington Evans] is not a good idea) the second alternative seems to me to be the one which I would prefer. . . .

I have become so absorbed in reconstruction matters that I should welcome the opportunity of continuing the work under even more favorable conditions, while the chance of rendering service in the Cabinet is sufficiently attractive to outweigh the attractions of the Ministry of Munitions.

You told me yesterday that you proposed to add Smuts to your Cabinet especially for war purposes. I would suggest with great respect that it would be very preferable if the two additions to the Cabinet could be announced together!

With my real thanks for the new expression of confidence,

I am, Yours sincerely,
Edwin S. Montagu[49]

By June 18 he was so confident that the job at Reconstruction was his that he wrote to Lloyd George requesting "substantially increased staff . . . particularly financial and commercial experts."[50] He also wrote to Asquith of his plans, with the hope that Asquith would understand his great desire to return to an active role in the government. He was not happy, he told Asquith, about the new government and its strained relationship with Asquith. He felt, however, that Reconstruction was so important that it justified his joining Lloyd George:

Believe me I am under no misapprehension as to the position and I am very unhappy. I hope you know the anguish which separation from you causes me. . . . I have been so closely connected with you, and have so much, indeed everything, to thank you for, that if I felt I was free to choose I would do now what I did in December rather than separate myself from you.

I am also under no illusion as to the position of the government which I propose to join. Its very weakness however seems to me to throw a grave responsibility on any Liberal who at the present time refuses an opportunity of helping it. That responsibility I was not prepared to take when it was a mere question of helping to administer an office like the Treasury or going back to the Ministry of Munitions.

But reconstruction is another matter. I am just beginning to get a sort of an idea of the scope of the policy which must be ready for any government faced with the problems of peace. There is nobody else that I know of who can be brought in safely at the moment to begin all over again and after consultation with those who knew I came to the conclusion that it was my duty from the point of view of reconstruction alone to accept the offer.

The reconstruction work must be done and the Government are right in my opinion and in the opinion of those here in coming to the conclusion that Cabinet decisions can only be obtained and Government departments helped by a member of the Cabinet.

The organization which the Prime Minister set up three months ago has proved . . . itself inadequate. . . .

That is the whole story. When the matter was first being discussed my

first inclination was to ask you to advise me and to consult you before I
made a decision of which I was afraid. But I felt that I ought to think for
myself in this matter, that it would not be fair to you to consult you, to
throw upon you any responsibility in the matter. I accordingly, again to
my great sorrow, was forced to fight the temptation to talk it over with
you.

Although the matter has now reached a stage where I can tell you of it,
it is not I am told to be regarded as settled. . . .

It has been very difficult to write this letter and I send it to you with
assurances that my anger at the events of December, my appreciation of
your leadership, and my hopes for your return remain undiminished. The
only new position is that I do not feel I can refuse at this moment to assist
in this way the Government now in office. I am glad to think that there is
no difference in principle in their policy and yours.[51]

Asquith responded curtly and made no effort to mask his discomfort:

Thank you for your letter of yesterday. In view of our past relations, it is
not unnatural that I should find it difficult to understand, and still more
difficult to appreciate, your reasons for the course which you tell me you
propose to take.

But in these matters every man must be guided by his own judgement
and conscience.

I need not assure you of my real gratitude for what you have done for
me in the past or my sincere good wishes for you in your new future.[52]

As Montagu later wrote, he "had definitely accepted the Office of
Minister without Portfolio in charge of Reconstruction, and that
this appointment was to be announced together with the appointment of Hayes Fisher at the Local Government Board during Mr.
Lloyd George's visit to Glasgow."[53] "In my letter of acceptance,
however," he wrote, "I asked leave for its postponement until after
the Mesopotamian Debate because of my interest in India. The
Prime Minister assented to this."[54]

Montagu outlined the advice he gave Lloyd George on India. He
had "begged him" not to send Austen Chamberlain as Viceroy to
India and asked him to consider Lord Grey instead, an idea that
appealed to Lloyd George. "I told him that I proposed to give
Chamberlain orders as to the way I thought Indian Government
ought to be reformed in the Mesopotamian Debate. He told me he
thought Hardinge would resign, that Chamberlain, he was glad to

say, was full of reforms and had no idea of resigning [as Secretary of State for India]."[55]

This was not the first time that Montagu had expressed his opinion about India, although he had had no official connection with it for three years. On April 21, 1917, in the midst of preparing for the first meeting of the Reconstruction Committee, he submitted a memorandum to Sir Maurice Hankey in his role as Secretary to the War Cabinet, in which he urged that India be given some recognition after the war in appreciation for her loyalty. He argued that economic concessions would not be enough, and that some announcement of a future policy goal for India must be made once peace was won. "Surely the right aim and object is a federated series of states and provinces, possibly with completely different constitutions and varying degrees of liberty and self control at varying times, suited to the conditions of each state and province."[56] Montagu urged that the Cabinet establish a Committee to examine Anglo-Indian policy. The Committee members should be "chosen from a wide field of men accustomed to problems of Government, and not solely from among those who are or have been directly connected with the administration of India."[57] Montagu always was critical of those involved in the administration of India, viewing them as too conservative and committed to preserving the status quo.

The Mesopotamian Report

While Montagu and Lloyd George were discussing the announcement of his appointment as Minister without Portfolio in charge of Reconstruction, the Commission established to study the military disaster at Mesopotamia released its report. It was a devastating condemnation of military ineptitude in India, blaming many in India, including the Viceroy and the Commander in Chief in India for the terrible disaster.

What had begun as a series of victories by the Indian divisions against the Turks at Kurna and Kut in battles waged in Mesopotamia, from November 14, 1914, through September 1915, had ended in the surrender of six thousand Indian soldiers as well as two thousand other British soldiers, in a humiliating defeat by the Turks, whose mistreatment of the surrendered soldiers was one of the war's most terrible chapters. Lloyd George called this disaster an example of "stupidity, criminal neglect and amazing incompetence of the military authorities who were responsible for the organization of the expedition" and who "caused the horrible and unnecessary suffering of the gallant men who were sent to failure and defeat through the blunders of those in charge."[58]

The Report of the Commission appointed by Lloyd George to investigate this tragedy shared his view that the Indian military were guilty of criminal neglect. It found inadequate planning, the wrong transport boats, incorrect clothing, inadequate fighting equipment, lack of airplanes, no wheeled ambulances and a total breakdown of medical care on the battlefield, leaving thousands to die on the field in excruciating pain. The Commission concluded that all the authorities involved in the expedition performed not only badly—but negligently, "to the point of incredibility."[59] Not until London took over from India were measures taken to remedy the disaster. A new fighting force was organized under Sir Stanley Maude, proper equipment and supplies were provided and, ultimately, the British recaptured Kut and captured Baghdad on March 18, 1918. By November 3, 1918, Turkey had been utterly defeated and was suing for peace.

The publication of the Mesopotamia report was a critical factor in Montagu's career. His response to it and his participation in the debate it engendered in Parliament changed forever the direction of his professional life. The publication of the report caused Montagu to write to the Prime Minister in July that not only did he hold very strong views about India, but he was more interested in this question "than any other question I have ever known."[60] He blamed the disaster in Mesopotamia on the failure of British policy in governing India. He used the occasion to project his own vision of British-Indian relations, criticizing Chamberlain for having made "inadequate" suggestions before the Mesopotamia report had been issued. He argued that it was not enough to say that the British goal is self-government for India. "The goal must be clearly stated to be a federation or collection of self-governing provinces, in order that all those who administer India may know that the strengthening of the provincial Governments is in harmony with the carrying out of this policy. . . . Mr. Chamberlain is right in this but he does not go far enough."[61] As a result of the publication of the Mesopotamia report, there now existed an opportunity to convince Great Britain that the machinery by which the Viceroy governed was inconsistent with efficient government; that the organization of the India Office was "indefensible and ludicrous"; and that the position of the Secretary of State for India vis-à-vis the House of Commons was "impossible in a democratic country."[62]

Montagu also criticized Chamberlain and the Anglo-Indian conduct of the war, because "they never set themselves at the outset to do more than to obtain for India itself a position of benevolent neutrality. They never attempted to fit Indian organization to [be] a part in the world war. . . . They showed—and India knows that they showed—fear of Indian loyalty. But it was unpardonable, I think, having pursued this policy then to embark on the wholly inconsistent policy of a Mesopotamian campaign."[63]

The criticism contained in Montagu's letter of July 5 was included in a speech he made the following week on the floor of Parliament on the Mesopotamia report, in which he placed the blame for the Mesopotamian tragedy squarely on the British government of India: "The Government of India is too wooden, too iron, too inelastic, too ante-diluvian to be of any use for the modern purposes we have in view. . . . The whole system of the Indian Office is designed to prevent control by the House of Commons for fear there might be too advanced a Secretary of State."[64] He chastised the House of Commons for its lack of interest in Indian affairs. He pointed out, as he had repeatedly before, that the Secretary of State did not really control his department since he could be overruled by a majority of the Indian Council and that the Executive system of India must be overhauled with less control by Westminster and Whitehall and more responsibility given to the people of India. He did not believe there was any demand for complete Home Rule in India—a point of view to which he adhered in spite of increasing evidence to the contrary:

As a goal, I see a different picture: I see the great self-governing Dominions and Provinces of India organized and coordinated with the great Principalities—not one great Home Rule country, but a series of self-governing Provinces and Principalities, federated by one Central Government. But whatever the object of your rule in India, the universal demand of those Indians whom I have met and corresponded with is that you should state it. Having stated it, you should give some installment to show that you are in real earnest; some beginning of the new plan which you intend to pursue that gives you the opportunity of giving greater representative institutions in some form or other to the people of India, of giving them greater control of their Executive—that affords you the opportunity of giving the Executive more liberty from home because you cannot leave your harassed officials responsible to two sets of people.

Responsibility here at home was intended to replace or to be a substitute for the responsibility in India. As you increase responsibility in India, you can lessen that responsibility at home.[65]

Immediately after the debate, Chamberlain resigned. Montagu claimed that he had never intended to drive Chamberlain from office. None of his friends had given him a hint that this might occur and it never entered his head that if it did, he could be offered Chamberlain's position.

Even as late as July 14, two days after his speech and Chamberlain's resignation, Montagu still believed he would be appointed to head Reconstruction. Writing to the Prime Minister that day, he acknowledged the great hostility among certain leaders in the House of Commons to his becoming a Minister and expressed his willingness to accept Reconstruction without a Ministry. It was a sad letter. It shows that Montagu recognized the "strong personal condemnation" and "rancorous animosity" that existed against him, but he did not understand why his colleagues and the press reacted as they did. "All your other colleagues are respected by the House of Commons. However much the House may differ from their policy, no personal animosity embitters their relationship."

"Some people object to me," he wrote to Lloyd George, because "I am an Asquithian." Others object "because I have no commercial or industrial experience." Still others claim "I am a Capitalist," and still others "because I am a Socialist." And, *"Nearly all of them object to me because I am a Jew.* This is a view which finds particular favour in the organs of freedom of religious opinion! (The *Morning Post* is not, I think, worthy of notice)" (emphasis added).[66]

If Montagu knew his Jewish history, he would have known that the contradictions in the attacks against him were similar to the irrational responses Jews have experienced throughout their history. They have been cursed as capitalists and at the same time as socialists and communists; as radicals stimulating labor unrest and as businessmen supporting the exploitation of the worker; as too aggressive and as too meek; as separatists wishing to preserve their separate "tribal rites" and as pushy assimilationists trying to infiltrate Gentile society. In Montagu's case, however, there was more than anti-Semitism, although that was clearly a factor. He was unkind in his criticism of his colleagues; he could be sharp and arrogant; and his gloomy, forbidding appearance did not help. The anti-Semitism was, however, pivotal.

But politics was Montagu's life: He had no alternative but to dismiss the anti-Semitism as an evil aberration and to keep pleading with Lloyd George to keep the Reconstruction Committee and appoint him as Chairman, even without creating a Ministry.[67] Montagu never sent this letter. Hankey advised him to withhold it for two days.

Secretary of State for India

On Monday, July 16, Montagu wrote a memorandum for his files saying that Hankey had sent for him from the House of Commons and informed him that Lloyd George had told Hankey the day before that he was planning to offer Montagu the post of Secretary of State for India. *"I told him that I could not believe it"* (emphasis added).[68] On the same day Guest, the Chief Whip, told Montagu that Lloyd George would give Montagu the choice of India or Reconstruction with Addison going to the one Montagu refused. "I told Guest that I should ask the Prime Minister not to offer me India because I should prefer Reconstruction even as it was (i.e., without creating a Ministry) but I could not refuse India if it was offered to me."[69] The next day, Tuesday, July 17, the Prime Minister asked Montagu to come to Downing Street before 10 A.M.

Montagu went to Downing Street "where the Prime Minister was just going to see the King," Montagu wrote.[70] The Prime Minister told Montagu that he had made up his mind that he wanted Montagu at the India Office. Montagu asked about Reconstruction and the Prime Minister told him it was going to Addison, that Lloyd George had no choice since it was the only position Addison would take. Addison wrote in his memoirs that his appointment to Reconstruction, which would now become a Ministry, was made before Montagu made his speech during the Mesopotamian debate.[71]

The Prime Minister also told Montagu that Curzon and Balfour were protesting Montagu's speech on the Mesopotamia report; he felt it would make Montagu's position at the India Office "difficult" and that if "I [Montagu] was appointed after that speech, that speech would be taken to be the policy of the Government. I said of course it would, it could mean nothing else."[72] Lloyd George agreed; he had read the speech carefully and was surprised that it contained many "cautious phrases."[73] He wrote to Balfour on July 16, 1917:

I carefully read through Montagu's speech. It is much more cautiously worded than I feared. He did not commit himself to "self-governing institutions" and even in the matter of reform he indicated a gradual improvement of the present system.

I found the King this morning strongly for his appointment. What do you think after further reflection.[74]

Balfour was not prepared to object. He found Montagu clever, knowledgeable about India and popular with the Indians. According to Balfour, he would be disliked by the Anglo-Indians, "partly because he is too much (in their opinion) of a 'reformer'; partly because he is a Jew."[75] With Balfour's less than enthusiastic approval, Lloyd George was prepared to move forward. He asked Montagu to write him a letter about his ideas on India which he could read to the Cabinet, largely to soothe Curzon's fears.

Montagu, although he agreed to write such a letter to restate what he had said during the Mesopotamian debate, made it clear that "it was quite impossible" for him "to make any alterations" in what he had said publicly.[76] Lloyd George gave Montagu an hour in which to write the letter. Montagu began writing at 10:45 A.M.; the letter reached Downing Street at 12:30, "a quick time to formulate an Indian policy!" Montagu wrote.[77] He had time to consult only with Henderson and Nash. With their help he was able to formulate and send the letter in time for Lloyd George to receive it the day he appointed Montagu as Secretary of State. It was a clear, straightforward, unambiguous statement leaving nothing to doubt or speculation. It restated much of what Montagu had previously said on the subject:

My dear Prime Minister,
    The speech which I made in the House of Commons on the 12th of July was delivered, as you know, without the faintest suspicion that there would be in a few minutes a vacancy in the India Office.

You have now offered me the Secretaryship of State, and as I told you this morning, I am proud to accept that offer.

Of course it will be taken as a general acceptance by the Government of the policy outlined in my speech. Anyone who reads the speech will see to what extent the Government is committed if I become a member of it.

The main principles are:

1. An immediate *exploration* of the system of governing India at home and in India with a view to devising greater elasticity and greater efficiency, and

2. A statement that the *ultimate* end we have in view for the Indian Empire is a series of self-governing Provinces united to one another and to the principalities by one Central Government, together with some install-ment of the policy as a start. . . .

I definitely expressed my belief that Home rule for India is not possible. I asked that the goal for which we were aiming should be stated to be a federation of great self-governing provinces and principalities, in order that both the people of India and those who control its destinies might have the trend of policy explained to them. The policy should be safe-guarded as to time. Before that goal is achieved many years and indeed many genera-tions, will have been spent, and different parts of India can be treated at a different speed. I asked for a statement of goal and some installment as an earnest. I have not the slightest intention of urging my colleagues, if I become a member of your Government, to embark upon precipitate ac-tion. I should not dream of suggesting touching the great fabric of the Government of India without careful investigation.

Yours sincerely,
Edwin Montagu[78]

Montagu later heard that Lloyd George had not been pleased with the letter and *"after I was appointed on Wednesday I heard rumors that led me to think that he* [Lloyd George] *never showed the letter to Curzon or Balfour"* (emphasis added).[79] But Montagu's conscience was clear. "The history that I have chronicled accurately above shows that I am on firm ground in stating that that speech or the letter a copy of which I attach is my charter, and that no one will have any reason to complain if at a subsequent date my resignation is caused by a refusal to adopt any part of that letter as the policy by the govern-ment."[80]

Lloyd George knew that he was asking Montagu to step into an arena in which he would meet strong and determined opposition from powerful adversaries. Not only would Montagu face the ideological opposition of Curzon and Balfour, but he would also face the enmity of those who believed that a Jew should not be given the responsibility to rule over India. Lloyd George, fearing such opposition, appointed Montagu to the India Office on the same day that he appointed Winston Churchill to the Ministry of Munitions, consulting neither the War Cabinet nor his colleagues.

Lord Derby was "furious at being kept in ignorance," and commented, "The appointment of Montagu, a Jew, to the India Office has made, as far as I can judge, an uneasy feeling both in India and here, but I personally have a very high opinion of his capability and I expect he will do well."[81] Derby regarded the appointments of both Montagu and Churchill as clever political moves that brought into Lloyd George's government two men who had been most important in the Asquith government and who were both powerful platform speakers. Weakening Asquith's political circle could well have been a principal reason for Lloyd George's move.

Not only were Curzon, Balfour and their Tory colleagues, as well as the anti-Semites, unhappy with Montagu's appointment, but Margot Asquith was furious. How could Montagu do this to her husband? How could he lend his name to a man whose treachery had destroyed her husband's premiership? How could someone who was more than a friend to her husband and herself—who was a member of their "family"—desert his dearest friend and join the enemy?

She reported in her diary that when she saw Montagu in the House of Commons during the Mesopotamian debate, he told her that he had not joined the Government and "may not do so after all —After this he seems to have tagged on all the nonsense of if he did join it it wd. be *pure* unselfishness! etc. Patriotism!! that glorious word for covering all self-seeking. To do him justice he never once hinted at this tosh to me when he was so hysterically melancholy at being out of munitions! *Poor devil! How sad to be born a Jew—*" (emphasis added).[82]

After Montagu was appointed Secretary of State for India, Margot wrote: "Mr. Montagu accepted & wrote a sort of farewell letter to Henry wh. I have not seen but wh. I shall see. He told me it had hurt him very much—I felt ill with indignation & said *'one expects a Jew to have no faith but this does not necessarily imply he has no judgement!'* [emphasis added] To think of any man preferring his private & public ambition to serving his fallen chief & greatest private & political friend is to me an act of political suicide. *For days I cd. think of nothing else.* I only wrote to Peggy Crewe & Beatrice Granard but au fond I felt it and still *feel it deeply."* [83]

And on July 21, 1917, Margot wrote that she had "not seen either of the Montagus or been in the same room with them. Venetia came up to me in the Bath Club looking very uncomfortable," and "beyond a greeting we said nothing to each other. I do not want to see them. I hear from McK. [also through a friend from Montagu] that McK. had talked to Montagu earnestly and kindly begging him to think well what it meant deserting his Chief and going to fight in the opposite ranks—McK. (to me last night 20th July 1917) I assure you if he [Montagu] had been my son I cd. not have been more open, more wise and more patient—You do not see what I've *always* seen—The love and glamour he felt for Asquith disappeared when he [Asquith] fell; *no Jew cd. behave differently.* [emphasis added] *M.* I see it perfectly now but it has been a *great* shock—if he were to crawl back to us I sd. *never* feel the same about him again! As far as I am concerned I have washed him out." [84]

Thus, at thirty-eight, as Montagu became Secretary of State for India, he entered the final chapter of his political career not to cheers, but to a chorus of anti-Semitic criticism. In accepting this position, his break with Asquith and the Asquith wing of the Liberal Party became official. To the Asquithians, and not only to Margot, he became persona non grata. At the same time, his new political allies viewed him with apprehension and suspicion. He never found in their ranks the friendship and support he enjoyed with his old comrades. He would never find a political mentor like Asquith. Hard as he tried to reach out to Lloyd George, he could never convince him of his loyalty. Lloyd George may have respected his ability but he never grew to like him or make him a confidant, a role Montagu sought with unabashed eagerness. He would always be a distrusted stranger in the strange coalition Lloyd George held together with his special kind of political magic and mirrors.

Frances Stevenson recorded Lloyd George's distrust of Montagu and her own intense dislike of him. On February 1, 1917, she wrote:

Personally I hate the idea of Montagu hanging around. He is not to be trusted & I feel sure he is a spy. I spoke to D. [David Lloyd George] about it and he said 'Don't you worry; I know my Montagu; I only tell him things that I want Asquith to know!' I think D. knows what he is about too, but you cannot be too careful of these people.[85]

On May 20, 1917, just two months before Lloyd George appointed Montagu Secretary of State for India, Stevenson criticized Montagu for deserting Asquith and emphatically declared that Lloyd George would never have him in his government:

Montagu is doing his level best to get into the Government by hook or by crook, but D. says he will not have him. D. says he does not like his readiness to turn his back on Asquith. He says that if it had not been for Asquith, Montagu would never have been heard of—that he is purely a man who was made by Asquith. But Montagu has no scruples in deserting his benefactor and going over to the other side as soon as it suits his interests to do so. He is as treacherous as a man could be.[86]

Nowhere in Frances Stevenson's *Lloyd George,* or in Margot Asquith's diaries, is there a similar attack on Winston Churchill who also joined Lloyd George's government, nor is there the slightest note that there might have been anything reprehensible about Lloyd George's seizing power from Asquith, after Asquith had given him the appointments he needed to become a national figure. Churchill's and Lloyd George's behavior is accepted by both women as political necessity; Montagu's was seen as the treachery of a Jew.

Neither Frances Stevenson nor Lloyd George ever changed their minds about Montagu. Montagu was not aware of the intensity of Lloyd George's hostility to him until the final months of his career. He may have been wise to the political machinations that permeated the Lloyd George government, but he was utterly ignorant of how Lloyd George really felt about him. In 1917, he still believed that he and Lloyd George could become friends and political confidants. He put aside his disappointment at not becoming Minister of Reconstruction and eagerly accepted his new responsibilities for his great love, India.

23

Zionism: The Balfour Declaration

No form of words should be used by . . . the British Government which implies there is a Jewish people . . . and that any Jew who happens to live in England, France, Italy or America is in exile.

Montagu to Lord Cecil, Sept. 14, 1917

In the months before Montagu assumed his new role as Secretary of State for India, he found himself embroiled in one of the most bitter conflicts of his career. It was a struggle in which he became known as the renegade Jew who almost single-handedly defeated the Balfour Declaration.

In his hostility to the Balfour Declaration and the concept of Jewish nationalism upon which the Declaration is based, Montagu was not alone. He was in fact, supported by the majority of the leadership of the Jewish community of England, who were outspoken critics of the idea of a "Jewish people" with a "homeland" in Palestine. This was probably the one issue upon which Montagu and the Jewish leadership of his day ever agreed.

As early as 1879, the chief Rabbi of England and one of its most distinguished scholars, Dr. Herman Adler, had expressed what came to be viewed as the classic Anglo-Jewish doctrine opposing Zionism and Jewish nationalism:

Ever since the conquest of Palestine by the Romans we (Jews) have ceased to be a body politic. We are citizens of the country in which we dwell. We are simply Englishmen, Frenchmen or Germans, as the case may be, certainly holding particular theological tenets and practicing special religious ordinances; but we stand in the same relation to our country-men as any other religious sect, having the same stake in the national welfare and the same claim on the privileges and duties of citizens.[1]

The majority of British Jewry endorsed this position.

In the face of the overwhelming opposition to the concept of the Jews as a separate people, it remains an anomaly that a relatively insignificant number of British Zionists were able to persuade the British government to support the establishment of a Jewish homeland in Palestine.

England's Early Interest in Palestine and the Jews

As early as 1832, Lord Palmerston, the great Foreign Secretary and later Prime Minister, had instructed the British representative in Turkey to encourage the Jews to look to Great Britain for protection in Palestine and even tried to persuade the Turks to permit Jews to settle in Palestine.

In his interest in the Jewish resettlement of Palestine, Palmerston had the support of many of the English intelligentsia of the time: writers, publishers, travelers, archaeologists, religious leaders and political theorists. Their interest had several bases: their knowledge and respect for the Old Testament, admiration for the achievements of the Jews, sympathy for the Jews in face of their long history of persecution, a belief that Britain had a historic mission to lead the suffering Jews back to Palestine, and British political and military interest in keeping the lands of the Ottoman Empire (which was on the verge of collapse) from falling into the hands of Germany and France. The Russians posed no immediate threat to British interests at the time.

Thus from the start, British self-interest, while a major factor, was not the sole reason for British involvement. The genuine solicitude of this small segment of English leadership for the welfare of the Jews also played a role. Lord Palmerston failed in his efforts to persuade the Sultan to permit a Jewish settlement in Palestine or to permit Great Britain to have a special relationship to the Jews in that land. But the weakness of the Ottoman Empire kept the discussion of Jewish settlement in Palestine alive throughout the nineteenth century. When in the 1880s, Jewish immigration began to trickle into Palestine from Eastern Europe, their struggle again attracted sympathetic attention in England, but even their supporters did not believe it was realistic to expect Great Britain to take steps to help in the restoration of the Jews to Palestine.

During this period, Zionism continued to develop and gain adherents, slowly but steadily in the ghettos of Eastern Europe, among Jews caught in the intellectual ferment of the times, and in the associations for the promotion of Jewish emigration to Palestine that sprang up in Eastern Europe. But it failed to develop as a major movement or as a political force. Particularly in England, Zionism not only had little support but was looked upon as "a travesty of Judaism," "a mistake," a "peril," "a blow and an injury to the development of Judaism as a religion"; "in the long run [it] will be prejudicial and deleterious to the best interests and truest welfare of the Jews themselves."[2] it was also viewed as a program designed by foreign Jews with no understanding of the freedom and equality the English Jew enjoyed.

Herzl

It was not until a Jewish journalist from Vienna, Theodore Herzl, published his pamphlet *Der Judenstaat (The Jewish State)* in 1895 that the Zionist movement began to gain some recognition and momentum. His efforts, like those of his predecessors in England, were aimed at persuading the Sultan of Turkey that a Jewish homeland in Palestine would be economically and politically useful to the Ottoman Empire. When he failed, he shifted his activities to London in the hope of persuading British Jewry and British political leaders that such a state would not only help Jews but be an instrument that would weaken Turkey and enlarge British influence in the Middle East. Here too he failed; he had no more luck with British Jewry and British political leaders than he had had with the Sultan. A few affluent Jews like Walter and Charles Rothschild and Mrs. James Rothschild supported his cause, but they were in a small minority. Neither assimilated Jews like Lionel and Leopold Rothschild, Claude Montefiore, Sir Philip Magnus, Robert (later Sir Robert) Waley Cohen, nor Orthodox Jews like Samuel Montagu, were receptive to Zionism. To the majority of the British Jewish leadership, Jews were not a race or a people. England was their only home. They were first and foremost Englishmen whose religion happened to be

Jewish. They believed in universal liberalism and emancipation, not a return to an ancient homeland.

While vehemently disagreeing with political Zionism, Samuel Montagu had long been interested in Palestine. As early as 1875, he and Lord Rothschild had founded a school in Jerusalem and had supported various efforts at colonization in Palestine for Jews forced to flee persecution in Europe. As an Orthodox Jew, he believed that the reestablishment of a Jewish state in Palestine must await the coming of the Messiah and no Zionist leader qualified for that position. He believed that the notion of establishing a homeland for Jews in Palestine would raise questions of dual allegiance and only serve to increase anti-Semitism.

Herzl became so angry with Samuel Montagu that in 1900 he tried to persuade Sir Francis Montefiore, a Zionist, to run against Montagu for Parliament. Sir Francis decided that this would be a losing battle and refused to run. Samuel Montagu retained his seat but his feelings toward Herzl and Zionism did not improve.

Herzl was undeterred. While Montagu and the other leaders of Anglo-Jewish society continued their opposition, the Zionists continued their efforts at organization, especially among immigrant groups from Eastern Europe. By 1902, a fledgling Zionist organization began to function in London and the debate on Herzl and Zionism had grown important enough to become a major item of bitter discussion on the agenda of the organized Jewish community.

Edwin Montagu had not yet joined the debate. He was finishing his undergraduate education at Cambridge, still arguing with his father about religion, still determined to keep his religion a private matter. He was divorced from any concern with Jewish problems or Jewish issues, totally committed to escaping from his father's "orthodox ghetto," and hostile to anything that could be classified as sectarian or viewed as strengthening the barriers between Jews and Christians.

When in 1902 his mother asked him to speak to his sister Lily about her interest in Liberal Judaism and the club for Jewish women she was forming, he refused, making clear that her interests in Judaism were abhorrent to him. While he loved and respected her and knew she, of all his family, saw his possibilities, "her life and my life," he wrote to his mother in April 1902, "are destined always to be apart, for she works for sectarian purposes—I abominate them. She strengthens the barriers, I want to abolish them. So I cannot take an interest in her club."[3]

These were the years of British hostility to the increased Jewish immigration and of the anti-Semitism that accompanied the debate on the Aliens Act of 1902. Herzl was beginning to gain some modest support and had sought and obtained the right to testify before a Royal Commission appointed to investigate the problem of increased immigration.[4] Lord Rothschild (Nathan), a member of the Commission, was distressed. He believed that "Herzl's appearance before the commission, . . . could only have two effects: the anti-semites would be able to say that Dr. Herzl . . . maintained that a Jew could never become an Englishman; and if Herzl harped on the bad situation of the Jews in eastern Europe and their need to emigrate this would lead to restrictive legislation."[5] Herzl was keenly aware that his testimony could be used in this fashion. In his testimony, therefore, he walked a fine line, opposing any limit on immigration but at the same time urging a Jewish home in Palestine, on the assumption that even the most liberal immigration policy could not answer the needs of Europe's persecuted Jews.

Exactly as Rothschild had predicted neither Herzl's testimony nor that of other Jewish leaders changed the opinion of the royal Commission of Parliament. Restrictive legislation was adopted in the summer of 1905, a year after Herzl's death. It was adopted with the support of Balfour over the opposition of Churchill. The debate from 1902 through 1904 did, however, give Herzl increased public visibility although it was not yet enough to gain any significant support for Zionism.

In the meantime, the plight of Jews in Eastern Europe worsened and some Zionist leaders, including Herzl, began to wonder if it was wise to wait for Palestine. Perhaps, in the face of pogroms and persecution, some other place might temporarily be a safe harbor. In this frame of mind Herzl discussed the possibility of a Jewish home on Cyprus with Lord Rothschild; a Jewish colony in the southeastern corner of the Mediterranean, with Joseph Chamberlain (who then was Colonial Secretary); and a possible settlement in the El Arish of Egypt, with Lord Lansdowne, Foreign Secretary, and Lord Cromer, Viceroy of Egypt. He finally spoke with Joseph Chamberlain again, who suggested Uganda as a potential colony for the Jews.

During these discussions the urgency of the need to provide some haven for the Jews was dramatized still further by the Kishnev pogroms. Herzl later met with the Russian leadership, who would, he thought, support him, if only to get rid of its Jews. This, too, came to naught and resulted only in the condemnation of Herzl by many Jewish leaders, including Chaim Weizmann, who by this time was already a leading younger Zionist.

A week after his Russian trip, in August 1903, Herzl left for Basel to attend the sixth Zionist conference. It was there that Herzl received a message from Sir Clement Hill, chief of the Protectorate Department in the Colonial Office, informing the Zionist movement that the British government was "interested in any well considered scheme aimed at the amelioration of the position of the Jewish race."[6] The British government was willing to look into the establishment of a Jewish settlement in Africa if the Zionists would establish a commission to recommend suitable land. "If the result were positive, and the scheme commended itself to the government, there would be a good chance of a Jewish colony or settlement being established under a Jewish official as chief of the local administration in which the members would be able to observe their national customs."[7] This was the first time a major power had recognized the Jewish people and offered its help in achieving a colony or settlement for them.

Herzl was prepared to accept Uganda only as a "temporary shelter" to help Jews forced to migrate immediately.[8] Most delegates at the Basel Conference opposed this suggestion. Palestine was their original home: It had a mystical and religious meaning. By a biblical mandate they were obliged to return only to Palestine. No other land would do. The Zionist movement now faced the most important decision of its history. While the resolution establishing the Commission to look into Uganda was passed 295 to 178 (largely out of respect for Herzl), the East European Jews made it clear they would never go there. Herzl was called a traitor, and Max Nordau, one of his principal supporters, was shot and almost killed by a Zionist student. With great effort, a semblance of harmony was achieved. But Herzl was deeply disturbed and depressed. His health began to deteriorate and on July 3, 1904, he died at the age of forty-five.

Post-Herzl

While the Zionist movement did not die with Herzl, it became
noticeably weaker in the years immediately following his death.
Interest in Zionism had dwindled in Britain to the point that in
1909–10 no one could be found to act as Chairman of the English
Zionist Federation. It was not until 1912, with the appearance of a
new generation of young Zionists, that Zionism seemed to recover
its momentum. By 1914 the Zionist Federation of Great Britain had
some fifty branches and during the war, as nationalism gained as an
acceptable creed and Jewish migration from Russia increased, "it
gained many new adherents."[9] But as the Zionist movement grew,
so too did the conflict between it and the majority of Anglo-Jewish
leaders. While the actual arguments against Zionism were relatively
unchanged from those made in the middle of the last century, the
intensity and hostility of the debate had escalated. The Zionist concept that the Jews were a dispersed nation awaiting a home in
Palestine, and not merely a religious sect, was repeatedly attacked
from pulpits, at meetings, in resolutions, and eventually in the War
Cabinet and before the full Cabinet. The major questions included
whether the Zionist approach to Judaism would adversely affect the
status of British (or American, or French) Jews. The majority of the
Anglo-Jewish leadership answered with a resounding "yes." Should
the Jews be viewed as part of a scattered Jewish nation, discharging
their civic obligations in the country in which they lived but never
identifying themselves with its national life? The answer was a clear
"no." Perhaps the idea of a Diaspora Nationalism, the concept of a
Jewish nationality sharing a common citizenship with other nationalities but living a separate national life, could work in multinational
empires like Russia and Austria, but it had no place, the Anglo-
Jewish leadership declared, in a heterogeneous country such as England.

By the early 1900s, the debate had spread beyond the Jewish
community, with twenty-five "graduates and members of Oxford,
Cambridge, and London Universities"[10] on April 9, 1909, sharply
attacking Jewish nationalism in a resolution widely circulated in
political circles and in the press. By this time Montagu, as Parliamentary Private Secretary to Prime Minister Asquith, was very
much at the center of British politics but not as yet involved in the

Zionist debate. He was more concerned with budgets, tax reform, agriculture, Ireland, and Venetia Stanley than with the notion of Jewish nationalism.

Herbert Samuel

Coincidently, another member of the Samuel family, Montagu's cousin Herbert Samuel, played a key role in persuading the British to accept the Balfour Declaration, while his cousin Edwin Montagu by 1916 became his principal antagonist. Herbert Samuel's father had died when he was very young and Montagu's father, Lord Swaythling, became his guardian and mentor. While Samuel Montagu had a strong influence upon Herbert Samuel's commitment to Radical Liberalism, it would appear that he had no influence on his relationship to Judaism or the Jewish community in which, as a young man, he (Herbert) showed no interest. Nor was the young Herbert Samuel interested in Palestine or Zionism.[11]

In November 1914, when Great Britain declared war against Turkey, Herbert Samuel, at the age of forty-four, held a seat in the Cabinet as President of the Local Governing Board. The declaration of war was the turning point in his life and in the history of Zionism. In a speech at the Lord Mayor's Banquet on November 9, 1914, Prime Minister Asquith made it clear that in light of its declaration of war, Great Britain had abandoned her traditional Eastern policy and now included among her war aims the dismemberment of the Turkish Empire. Discussing the Turkish question at the meeting, Lloyd George referred to "the ultimate destiny of Palestine." After the meeting, Herbert Samuel raised the subject of a Jewish state with Lloyd George, who assured him that "he was very keen to see a Jewish state established in Palestine."[12]

Later that day Samuel discussed this further in a conversation with the Foreign Secretary, Sir Edward Grey. He suggested that "British influence ought to play a considerable part in the formation of such a State" since "the geographical situation of Palestine, and especially its proximity to Egypt, would render its goodwill a matter of importance to the British Empire."[13] Noting that the "jealousies of the great European powers would make it difficult to allot Palestine to any one of them," he suggested that "perhaps the opportunity might arise for the fulfillment of the ancient aspiration of the Jewish people and the restoration there of a Jewish state."[14] "If a Jewish state were established in Palestine," Samuel told Grey, "it might become the centre of a new culture. The Jewish brain is rather a remarkable thing, and under national auspices the State might become a fountain of enlightenment and a source of great literature and art and development of science."[15]

While Grey was sympathetic, Prime Minister Asquith was not. It seemed incredible to him that Zionist "fantasies" should have found their way into Samuel's "well-ordered and methodical mind."[16] Lloyd George, while not prepared to accept Samuel's ideas, was not as unreceptive as Asquith. During 1915, Samuel further developed his arguments, emphasizing the strategic importance of a British annexation of Palestine. Annexation by France or another European power would be a menace to the Suez Canal and to Britain's influence in Egypt and the Middle East.

During this time, Chaim Weizmann, a brilliant young scientist who was an instructor in chemistry at Victory University in Manchester, was emerging as the new Zionist leader in England, having come to London in 1904 from Poland. He, too, believed that Zionist aspirations must be shown to be in accord with Britain's strategic and political interests. His friendship with C. P. Scott, editor of the *Manchester Guardian,* influenced Scott to become a strong Zionist supporter and gave Weizmann access to political figures such as Samuel and Lloyd George. Weizmann's success in developing an economical method of producing acetone, needed in the manufacture of munitions, also brought him into close association with Lloyd George and provided an additional reason for the personal relationship that developed between them.[17]

Montagu Enters Debate

Debate in the Jewish community continued to rage, and by 1916 Montagu had entered the controversy. He adamantly opposed the idea of Jewish nationalism, writing to a friend:

It seems to me that Jews have got to consider whether they regard themselves as members of a religion or of a race, world-wide in its habitat and striving to maintain in spite of geographical distribution an entity for political as well as religious consideration.

For myself I have long since made the choice. I view with horror the aspiration of national unity. Did I accept it, as a patriotic Englishman, I should resign my position on the Cabinet and declare myself neutral, or at any rate not primarily concerned in the present war. Nobody is entitled to occupy the position that I do unless he is determined to consider, and consider only, the interest of the British Empire.[18]

Four months later, in December 1916, the Asquith government fell and Lloyd George became Prime Minister. The Zionists were elated. Asquith was gone and they had gained four sympathizers in the Cabinet: Lloyd George; Balfour as Foreign Secretary; Lord Alfred Milner, a member of the War Cabinet; as well as Lord Robert Cecil, Assistant Foreign Secretary and a strong Zionist. On the negative side, they had lost Herbert Samuel, their strongest ally. Asquith never believed that Lloyd George was truly a supporter of Zionism, writing in his diary on March 13, 1915, that George "does not care a damn for the Jews or their past or their future, but thinks it will be an outrage to let the Holy Places pass into the possession or under the protectorate of 'agnostic, atheistic France.' "[19]

Invasion of Palestine: Zionism Gains in Strength

The change in government coincided with a military offensive in the Near East. The British Expeditionary Corps from Egypt had occupied the Sinai Peninsula since late 1916, and the War Cabinet decided on April 2, 1917, to invade Palestine. In the meantime the Zionists were consolidating their strength and defining their strategy. The result was an aggressive campaign to infiltrate Jewish organizations in England and to wrest control from the leaders of these organizations with the help of the poorer immigrant Jews. By the fall of 1917, relations between Zionists and non-Zionists had reached a peak of animosity and distrust.

Conjoint Committee Statement

In the summer of 1916, Lucien Wolfe, a journalist and historian, Secretary for the Conjoint Foreign Committee of Foreign Affairs of the Jewish Board of Deputies and the Anglo Jewish Association, and generally regarded as the community's oracle on diplomatic affairs, was chosen to represent the group in talks with the Zionists to explore whether an accommodation could be reached. A correspondence began in October 1916 and ended in April of the following year with Wolfe's announcement that no agreement was possible and that his Conjoint Committee must be free to take whatever action it deemed necessary.

Wolfe then began discussion with Balfour, the new Foreign Secretary, repeating his Committee's insistence that a Jewish state in Palestine not claim the allegiance of the Jews of Western Europe. His committee believed that the status of the Jews and their integration into the national life of England was at stake. To the Conjoint Committee, Zionism would cause a kind of rejection and disinheritance—"perpetual alienage"[20] in the country in which they felt at home and at peace.

These sentiments moved the Conjoint Committee to issue a statement in the spring of 1917, expressing these principles. It was signed by the President of the Board of Deputies, David L. Alexander, K.C., and Claude Montefiore, President of the Anglo Jewish Association—the two most powerful Jewish coordinating committees in Great Britain. It was published in *The Times* on May 24, 1917.

Their statement was carefully drafted to rebut Rabbi Moses Gaster, principal Minister of the Sephardic Congregation in London and a devout Zionist, that "the claim to be an Englishman of the Jewish persuasion—that is, English by nationality and Jewish by faith, is an absolute self-delusion" and to rebut Weizmann's comment that "the efforts of the emancipated Jew to assimilate himself to his surroundings . . . deceive nobody but himself."[21] The statement of the Conjoint Committee was vehemently attacked in the Jewish press, and a major battle took place in the Council of the Anglo-Jewish Association and the Jewish Board of Deputies.

By a vote of fifty-six to fifty-one, the Board of Deputies adopted a resolution expressing "profound disapproval" of the statement, influenced as much or more by the lack of process involved in issuing the statement as by its substance. Shortly thereafter, the Conjoint Committee was dissolved. The rank and file were now voicing their discontent with the autocratic style of governance with which a number of old Jewish families ran the Jewish community— a style in which, they believed, democracy played no part. With this change in attitude and leadership within the Jewish organizations, came increased support for Zionism.

Zionist Statement on Palestine: Montagu Enters the Fray

In June and July of 1917, the Zionist leaders began to draft a statement supporting "the reconstitution" of Palestine as a Jewish state as one of the key aims of the war. They hoped that the British government would issue it, even though Nathan Sokolow, a Russian-Polish member of the Zionist Executive Board, sent to London to help, thought it too ambitious. "If we ask for too much we shall get nothing."[22] The Foreign Office under Balfour was sympathetic and began drafting its own declaration. It used such terms as "asylum," "refuge," and "sanctuary," for "Jewish victims of persecution." This was rejected by the Zionists, who insisted that the declaration would have no value unless it supported a Jewish state.

On July 18, 1917, the second Lord Rothschild (Walter), who had always been sympathetic to Zionism, submitted a compromise to Balfour. It referred not to a Jewish state but to Palestine as "the National Home of the Jewish people." Two days before Rothschild sent this letter Edwin Montagu had rejoined the Cabinet. Panic gripped the Zionist ranks and several leaders, including Rothschild, believed the Zionist cause had suffered a setback that might be fatal.[23] "Do you remember," Rothschild wrote to Weizmann some months later, that "I said to you in London, as soon as I saw the announcement in the paper of Montagu's appointment, that I was afraid we were done?"[24]

Immediately after the announcement, Sokolow in a letter to Rothschild told him that he had spoken about it to Mark Sykes, another Zionist leader in London. "I asked [Sykes] if he thought that the appointment of Mr. Montagu might affect our cause adversely . . . to which question he answered in the negative. Let us hope, therefore, that there will be no difficulty in the way of getting the proposed Declaration."[25]

In July the War Office announced its plan to establish a Jewish Legion to fight in Palestine.[26] This was as inflammatory as the Zionist idea and sharply divided not only the Jewish community but also the Zionist movement. It almost caused the resignation of Chaim Weizmann, and it enraged Montagu.

By 1916, approximately twenty thousand Russian Jews were living in the East End of London. Many had not been naturalized and thus could not serve in the British Army. Nor could they serve in the Russian Army without being deported. The fact that this large body of men who had sought refuge in Britain was not fighting on her behalf was bitterly resented by both the Jewish and non-Jewish British public.

Even Herbert Samuel was outraged, writing to Lucien Wolfe on August 30, 1916: "If the mass of the Russian Jews in this country refuse to lift a finger to help, when the country is making immeasurable sacrifices in a war with which the cause of liberty all over the world is bound up, the effect on the reputation of the Jewish name everywhere will be disastrous."[27] Samuel felt so strongly that he enthusiastically supported the Military Service Act adopted in July 1917 requiring that immigrants enlist or face deportation. While discussions were taking place concerning the implementation of this Act, some Zionists convinced the War Office of the value of a separate Jewish Legion to help in the liberation of Palestine. Samuel as well as many other Zionists vehemently objected.

In the non-Zionist community the opposition was even more intense. Why should there be a Jewish regiment anymore than a Roman Catholic or a Methodist regiment? Thousands of British Jews were already in the British Army. Should they be pulled out of their regiments and reassigned in the new Jewish regiment? The anti-Zionists saw this as a victory for the Zionists, whose cause they viewed as gaining momentum.

Writing to Weizmann, who supported a Jewish Legion, Lord Rothschild said that the "origin of the whole misfortune arose from the fact that the Jewish regiment and all its consequences were too hastily entered upon by the Government, and I fear Mr. Jabotinsky was the wrong man to advise on the subject owing to his fanatic enthusiasm."[28] Jabotinsky had long harbored the dream of a Jewish legion in the belief that Jews must fight for Palestine. Ultimately the idea of a Jewish regiment was dropped, but a de facto Jewish battalion, as part of the Royal Fusiliers, was formed—with no special Jewish emblem (the 38th Royal Fusiliers). Weizmann did not resign. The Zionist leaders closed ranks and turned their attention once more to the declaration concerning Palestine which they were negotiating with Balfour.

Early in August, the Rothschild draft was submitted to the War Cabinet, but discussion was postponed. It reappeared on the agenda on September 3. Montagu, now a Cabinet member although not a member of the War Cabinet, was invited to express his views. He had already made his opinions known in a memorandum he had circulated on August 23, with the provocative title "The Anti-Semitism of the Present Government."[29] It was a powerful polemic against the philosophy of Zionism.

Montagu explained that he had deliberately chosen the title not to suggest that the British Government was anti-Semitic but rather because he believed that the declaration to establish a homeland for Jews in Palestine would result in anti-Semitism "and prove a rallying ground for anti-Semites in every country in the world." "This nation [Palestine]," he wrote:

will presumably be formed of Jewish Russians, Jewish Englishmen, Jewish Roumanians, Jewish Bulgarians, and Jewish citizens of all nations—survivors or relations of those who have fought or laid down their lives for the different countries which I have mentioned, at a time when the three years that they have lived through have united their outlook and thought more closely than ever with the countries of which they are citizens.

Zionism, Montagu continued, is a "mischievous political creed, untenable by any patriotic citizen of the United Kingdom. If a Jewish Englishman," he wrote:

longs for the day when he will shake British soil from his shoes and go back . . . to Palestine, he has . . . aims inconsistent with British citizenship . . . and [is] unfit for a share in public life in Great Britain or to be treated as an Englishman. I have always understood that those who indulged in this creed were largely animated by the restrictions upon and refusal of liberty to Jews in Russia. But at the very time when these Jews have been acknowledged as Jewish Russians and given all liberties, it seems to be inconceivable that Zionism should be officially recognized by the British Government, and that Mr. Balfour should be authorized to say that Palestine was to be reconstituted as the "national home of the Jewish people." I do not know what this involves, but I assume it means that Mohammedans and Christians are to make way for the Jews, and that the Jews should be put in all positions of preference and should be peculiarly associated with Palestine in the same way that England is with the English or France with the French, that Turks and other Mohammedans in Palestine will hereafter be treated as foreigners in every country but Palestine. Perhaps also citizenship must be granted only as a result of a religious test.[30]

Montagu laid down three basic principles:

1. *I assert that there is not a Jewish nation.* The members of my family, for instance, who have been in this country for generations, have no sort or kind of community of view or desire, with any Jewish family in any other country beyond the fact that they profess to a greater or less degree the same religion. It is no more true to say that a Jewish Englishman and a Jewish Moor are of the same nation than it is to say that a Christian Englishman and a Christian Frenchman are of the same nation: of the same race, perhaps, traced back through the centuries—through centuries of the history of a peculiarly adaptable race. The Prime Minister and M. Briand are, I suppose, related through the ages, one as a Welshman and the other as a Breton, but they certainly do not belong to the same nation.

2. *When the Jews are told that Palestine is their national home, every country will immediately desire to get rid of its Jewish citizens,* and you will find a population in Palestine driving out its present inhabitants, taking all the best in the country, drawn from all quarters of the globe, speaking every language on the face of the earth, and incapable of communicating with one another except by means of an interpreter. I have always understood that this was the consequence of the building of the Tower of Babel, if ever it was built, and I certainly do not dissent from the view, commonly held, as I have always understood, by the Jews before Zionism was invented, that to bring the Jews back to form a nation in the country from which they were dispersed would require Divine leadership. I have never heard it suggested, even by their most fervent admirers, that either Mr. Balfour or Lord Rothschild would prove to be the Messiah.

I claim that the lives that British Jews have led, that the aims that they have had before them, that the part that they have played in our public life and our public institutions, have entitled them to be regarded not as British Jews, but as Jewish Britons. I would willingly disenfranchise every Zionist. I would be almost tempted to proscribe the Zionist organisation as illegal and against the national interest. But I would ask of a British government sufficient tolerance to refuse to endorse a conclusion which makes aliens and foreigners by implication, if not by law, of all their Jewish fellow-citizens.

3. *I deny that Palestine is today associated with the Jews or properly to be regarded as a fit place for them to live in.* The Ten Commandments were delivered to the Jews on Sinai. It is quite true that Palestine plays a large part in Jewish history, but so it does in modern Mohammedan history, and, after the time of the Jews, surely it plays a larger part than any other country in Christian history. The Temple may have been in Palestine, but so was the Sermon on the Mount and the Crucifixion. I would not deny to Jews in Palestine equal rights to colonisation with those who profess other religions, but a religious test of citizenship seems to me to be only admitted

by those who take a bigoted and narrow view of one particular epoch of the history of Palestine, and claim for the Jews a position to which they are not entitled.

If my memory serves me right, there are three times as many Jews in the world as could possibly get in to Palestine if you drove out all the population that remains there now. So that only one-third get back at the most, and what will happen to the remainder?

Montagu lashed out at the government and the Jewish community, not only for the Balfour Declaration but for contemplating a Jewish regiment, and sarcastically added:

I can easily understand the editors of the Morning Post and of the New Witness being Zionists, and I am not in the least surprised that the non-Jews of England may welcome this policy. I have always recognised the unpopularity, much greater than some people think, of my community. We have obtained a far greater share of this country's goods and opportunities than we are numerically entitled to. We reach on the whole maturity earlier, and therefore with people of our own age we compete unfairly. Many of us have been exclusive in our friendships and intolerant in our attitude, and I can easily understand that many a non-Jew in England wants to get rid of us. But just as there is no community of thought and mode of life among Christian Englishmen, so there is not among Jewish Englishmen. More and more we are educated in public schools and at the Universities, and take our part in the politics, in the Army, in the Civil Service, of our country. And I am glad to think that the prejudices against inter-marriage are breaking down. But when the Jew has a national home, surely it follows that the impetus to deprive us of the rights of British citizenship must be enormously increased. Palestine will become the world's Ghetto. Why should the Russian give the Jew equal rights? His national home is Palestine. Why does Lord Rothschild attach so much importance to the difference between British and foreign Jews? All Jews will be foreign Jews, inhabitants of the great country of Palestine.

. . . I am waiting to learn that my brother, who has been wounded in the Naval Division, or my nephew, who is in the Grenadier Guards, will be forced by public opinion or by Army regulations to become an officer in a regiment which will mainly be composed of people who will not understand the only language which he speaks—English. I can well understand that when it was decided, and quite rightly, to force foreign Jews in this country to serve in the Army, it was difficult to put them in British regiments because of the language difficulty, but that was because they were foreigners, and not because they were Jews, and a Foreign Legion would seem to me to have been the right thing to establish. A Jewish

Legion makes the position of Jews in other regiments more difficult and forces a nationality upon people who have nothing in common.[31]

He concluded by chastising the British government for allowing itself to be:

. . . the instrument for carrying out the wishes of a Zionist organisation largely run, as my information goes, at any rate in the past, by men of enemy descent and birth, and by this means have dealt a severe blow to the liberties, position and opportunities of service of their Jewish fellow-countrymen.[32]

At the War Cabinet meeting on September 3, Montagu expanded on this, passionately insisting that the phrase "home of the Jewish people" would "prejudice the position of every Jew elsewhere." The vehemence of his protest made an impression. While the pro-Zionist Declaration was not rejected by the Cabinet, Montagu was successful in getting the issue postponed pending comments on it by President Wilson. Wilson's first reply, in September 1917, was non-committal. This encouraged the non-Zionists and Montagu, who was now their principal spokesman in the Cabinet, to believe they still had a chance to defeat the Declaration. Montagu began at once to accelerate his campaign. On September 14, he wrote to Lord Robert Cecil, a strong Zionist sympathizer, pointing out that Zionists were not in a majority and non-Zionists had the support of at least half the Jews of England. Zionism had a foreign origin, and he, Montagu, was "impelled to urge once more that no form of words should be used by any spokesman of the British Government which implies that there is a Jewish people in the political sense and that any Jew who happens now to live in England, France, Italy or America is an exile in belonging to the English, French, Italian or American people among whom he dwells at present." Montagu continued: "Such a declaration would be felt as a cruel blow by the many English Jews who love England, the birthplace of themselves and their ancestors for many generations, who wish to spend their lives working for her, and whose highest aspiration is to continue to serve her."

Montagu offered an alternative to the Balfour Declaration:

But I am particularly anxious to avoid a refusal to respond to Lord Milner's generous intention. There has been brought to my notice a body formed some years ago called "The Jewish Territorial Organisation," which adopted the following words to explain its object: "To obtain a territory" for those Jews who cannot or will not remain in the land in "which they live at present." If it is desired to say anything, would this be any use?:

> His Majesty's Government accepts the principle that every opportunity should be afforded for the establishment [of a land] in Palestine for those Jews who cannot or will not remain in the lands in which they live at present, will use its best endeavors to facilitate the achievement of this object, and will be ready to consider any suggestions on the subject which any Jewish or Zionist organisations may desire to lay before it.

N.B. I do not wish to limit the suggestions which are invited to the Zionist organisations.

I should of course prefer that the Government as a Government should say nothing, but I do hope they will not go further than this.

Yours sincerely,
Edwin S. Montagu[33]

Weizmann and his colleagues responded with their own memorandum, which was distributed to the War Cabinet on October 3. They were determined that Montagu not succeed in again postponing a vote of the Declaration. In fact, Weizmann believed that another postponement might be fatal.[34] He and Lord Rothschild now pressed for prompt action and indicated their concern that "rumours . . . seem to foreshadow that the anti-Zionist view will be urged at the meeting of the War Cabinet by a prominent Englishman of the Jewish faith [i.e., Edwin Montagu] who does not belong to the War Cabinet."[35] They concluded by characterizing Montagu's presentation as "strikingly one-sided."[36] Their presentation tied Zionist interest not to the "Jewish people" argument but rather to the needs of British foreign policy. They asserted that the Zionists "have entrusted national and Zionist destiny to the Foreign Office and the Imperial War Cabinet in the hope that the problem would be considered in the light of Imperial interests."[37]

Over the Zionists' objections, Montagu was invited to the October 4 War Cabinet meeting, before which he had circulated a second memorandum, entitled "Zionism." It reminded the Cabinet that the India Office received "a series of valuable papers on Turkey in Asia from the pen of Miss Gertrude Lowthian Bell, the remarkable woman who, after years of knowledge gained by unique travel in these regions, is acting as Assistant Political Officer in Baghdad."[38] Bell had written that the Jews of Palestine made up, at most, one-quarter of the population and the Christians one-fifth, while the remainder were Muhammadan Arabs. "Jewish immigration," she wrote:

has been artificially fostered by doles and subventions from millionaire co-religionists in Europe: the new colonies have now taken root and are more or less self-supporting. The pious hope that an independent Jewish state may some day be established in Palestine no doubt exists, though it may be questioned whether among local Jews there is any acute desire to see it realized, except as a means of escape from Turkish oppression: it is perhaps more lively in the breasts of those who live far from the rocky Palestinian hills and have no intention of changing their domicile. Lord Cromer took pleasure in relating a conversation which he had held on the subject with one of the best known English Jews, who observed: "If a Jewish Kingdom were to be established at Jerusalem I should lose no time in applying for the post of Ambassador in London." Apart from the prevalence of such sentiments two considerations rule out the conception of an independent Jewish Palestine from practical politics. The first is that the province as we know it is not Jewish, and that neither Mohammedan nor Arab would accept Jewish authority; the second that the capital, Jerusalem, is equally sacred to three faiths. Jewish, Christian, and Moslem, and should never, if it can be avoided, be put under the exclusive control of any one local faction, no matter how carefully the rights of the other two may be safeguarded.

Montagu continued:

This extract shows fully the extent today of the Jewish population of Palestine. Again I ask, is it conceivable by anyone who knows the country that there is room in Palestine for a large extension of the population? If this does not occur, what part of the existing population is it proposed to dispossess? Having regard to the geographical, geological and climatic conditions of Palestine, is it worth while jeopardising the position of all Jews who remain in other countries for the insignificant fraction of the Jewish population that can conceivably find a home in Palestine? I yield to no one in my admiration of the distinguished Russian, Professor Weizmann, who looms so large in our discussions. His services to the Allied cause have been great. He is a scientist of repute, but on this matter he is near to being a religious fanatic. His enthusiasm for this cause has been the guiding principle of at any rate a large part of his life. It is his overwhelming enthusiasm. How often do such enthusiasms lead to complete disregard of practical potentialities! How little likely is such an enthusiasm to take into account the susceptibilities of those who differ from him among those of his own religion, or of those of other religions whom his activities, if successful, would dispossess.

. . . The Cabinet has been informed that the French Government are in sympathy with Zionist aspirations. It has recently come to my knowledge officially that the French ambassador has approached our Foreign Office with a proposal to establish a Jewish nation in El Hasa in Arabia, oblivious of the fact that although this is technically Turkish territory, we have concluded so recently as 1915 a treaty which roughly promises to support Ibn Saud and his followers in the occupation of the country. I quote this to prove that the French are anxious to establish Jews anywhere if only to have an excuse for getting rid of them, or large numbers of them.[39]

Montagu listed the names of forty-seven prominent anti-Zionists, who he asserted "include every Jew who is prominent in public life in England, with the exception of the present Lord Rothschild, Mr. Herbert Samuel, and a few others."[40] "These are all men," Montagu wrote, "who lead an English life as well as acknowledging and rendering their services to their fellow-religionists in this country and abroad. They contain among them ultra-orthodox as well as certain heterodox Jews."[41] Montagu added:

I submit again that the Cabinet's first duty is to Englishmen, to citizens of the British Empire of British traditions. I would submit with them great respect that it is not their business to espouse the cause of Americans, Russians, Austrians, and Germans, naturalised though they may be, in the teeth of the ardent wishes of those who have lived for generations in this country, and who feel themselves to be Englishmen. At this moment Jews are constantly being attacked for being outside the great national feelings which the war has engendered, and of being cosmopolitan in their sympathy and international in their aspirations. This is a gross libel on the Jewish Briton. It is true of the Zionist. I hope that the British Government of which I am a member, will pause before ignoring the British feeling which I represent in this matter in favour of that section of the community which is international in its views.

. . . the opinion of the present Chief Rabbi is quoted. I would quote the opinion of the late Chief Rabbi who held that office amid great respect for many years, and only died a few years ago.

"When we dwelt in the Holy Land we had a political organisation of our own; we had judges and kings to rule over us. But ever since the conquest of Palestine by the Romans, we have ceased to be a body politic; we are citizens of the country in which we dwell. We are simply Englishmen, or Frenchmen, or Germans, as the case may be, certainly holding particular theological tenets and practising special religious ordinances; but we stand in the same relation to our country men as any other religious sect, having the same privileges and duties of citizens. To Mr. Goldwin Smith's question 'What is the political bearing of Judaism?' I would reply that Judaism has no political bearing whatever."[42]

Montagu took issue with the claim that the Jews of America were Zionists. He wrote:

It is asserted that the American Jews are in favour of Zionism. The President of the Twenty-Eighth Annual Convention of the Central Conference of American Rabbis, held in Buffalo, New York, on 28th June of this year, said:

"I am not here to quarrel with Zionists. Mine is only the intention to declare that we as rabbis, who are consecrated to the service of the Lord, whose lips are to guard knowledge, and from whose mouth the people are to seek the Law, because we are messengers of the Lord of Hosts, have no place in a movement in which Jews band together on racial or national grounds, and for a political state, or even a legally assured home. . . . The religious Israel, having the sanctions of history, must not be sacrificed to the purely racial Israel of modern planning. . . . The time has come for this Conference to publish the statement that it stands for an Israel whose mission is religious, and that, in the light of this mission, it looks with disfavour upon any movement the purpose of which is other than religious."[43]

Montagu quoted the position of Jacob Schiff, who was considered one of the most eminent Jews in America:

The breaking down of the Ghetto walls [Schiff wrote] in Russia and the dispersing of, and the radical change in, the social status of one-half of our entire race, cannot but have a far reaching effect upon the Jewish problem everywhere. One thing appears certain, that the feeding, from the late Russian Pale, of Jewry outside of Russia, and especially of Jewry in our own country, both in numbers and in the product of the great Jewish mind, is sure to become greatly reduced if it is not going to cease entirely.

The danger is great that this may, in coming generations, lead to disintegration, and I have asked myself what can be done to counteract this. Now, we cannot, and must not, close our eyes to the fact that Palestine has a peculiar attraction for the Jews; more so now even than in bygone ages. This, I feel, in the face of what has taken place in Russia, should be taken advantage of to establish in Palestine, not a Jewish nation, but the seed for a large, if not almost exclusive Jewish population, among which Jewish religious life, Jewish thought and Jewish learning would develop in all its primitive purity and become a reservoir, out of which would flow the stream to stimulate Jewry wherever it may exist among the nations of the world. The Mississippi and other great rivers would run dry, and the countries dependent on these rivers would go to waste, if the fountainheads of these streams became closed up and so, notwithstanding what may be said to the contrary, Jewry will disappear and its mission will cease, if somewhere there is not a centre or central reservoir from which it can be ever and ever fed anew.

Schiff opposed a Jewish nation and asserted:

From 50 per cent to 75 per cent, of the so-called Jewish Nationalists are either atheists or agnostics, and . . . the great majority of the Jewish Nationalist Leaders have absolutely no respect for the Jewish religion. Conditions in this respect are already now—before a Jewish nation has actually been established, as is the desire of these Jewish nationalists—the same as those which existed when the Jewish state was an actuality and when priest and prophet were ever in disagreement and feud with kingdom and state, and which led in the end to the state's destruction. This would surely happen again were a Jewish state again established.[44]

Finally, Montagu alluded to Jewish opinion in Italy and France:

(1) Italy
Signor Luigi Luzzati, the eminent Italian Statesman who was Prime Minister in 1910, writes "Jewish Exponent." 18th May 1917:—

"Jews must acquire everywhere full religious liberty as existing in the United States and in Italy. In Palestine, delivered from Turks, Jews will live, not as sovereigns but as free citizens, to fertilise their fathers' land. Judaism is not a Nationality but a Religion."

(2) France
M. Joseph Reinach, the well-known French Deputy and Polybe of the Figaro, writes under date of 12th April 1917:—

"Patriotism is the first of our duties. It is the duty of every country to accord the same rights to all citizens without regard to their beliefs. In this respect Rumania will certainly follow the example of Russia.

"I am a resolute adversary of Zionism. Jerusalem belongs to all the religions. We know its history for 3,000 years. The Jewish Kingdom endured scarcely five centuries.

"Judaism is a religion.

"The absolute duty of the Jews, as of the Catholics, Protestants, and

Orthodox, is to serve their country as good citizens and loyal soldiers. Zionism has been a dream. Tomorrow it will be nothing more than an archaeological snare."[45]

Not only did Montagu bombard members of the War Cabinet with memoranda and letters, but he also argued with the deepest conviction and passion at Cabinet meetings. So heated were his attacks against the Balfour Declaration that he felt obliged to send a letter of apology to Lloyd George: "Please," he wrote, "do not resent my expression with all the vigour of which I was capable of views which I cannot but hold."[46]

In his struggle against Zionism, Montagu had the support of Curzon, who raised a number of questions including the problem of the Arabs in Palestine and their relationship to large-scale Jewish immigration. This was one of the few times Curzon and Montagu were on the same side of an argument. Curzon's support did not help. Nor was Balfour moved by either one. In his support for Palestine, Balfour was probably influenced at least as much by religious conviction as by Imperial considerations. While he was generally described as cyncial and detached, he had a profound curiosity about philosophy and religion and a special interest in the Old Testament and in the Jews.

By the middle of October, when President Wilson sent a note giving "unequivocal support" to the establishment of a Jewish homeland in Palestine, Balfour's resolve that the Zionist Declaration be adopted became stronger than ever. In dismissing the arguments made by the anti-Zionists and Montagu, Balfour insisted that only a handful of wealthy English Jews opposed the Declaration, while the majority of Jews in America and Russia "and probably in other countries," supported it, and he saw nothing inconsistent between the establishment of "a Jewish national focus in Palestine and the complete assimilation and absorption of Jews into the nationality of other countries."[47] Balfour is quoted as informing the War Cabinet "that the German Government were making great efforts to capture the sympathy of the Zionist Movement."[48] This argument was taken seriously by the Foreign Office and undoubtedly influenced it in the pro-Zionist position it espoused.

While Montagu recognized the role of the Foreign Office and its influence on Lloyd George, Balfour and Milner and knew they were immovable in their support of the Zionist Declaration, he doggedly held his ground and secured enough support at the October 4 meeting to postpone the decision once more. As a result of his stubborn resistance, the Cabinet decided to give both sides a final hearing by inviting selected leaders from each side to present their views in writing. Letters requesting these position papers were sent on October 6 to the Chief Rabbi Joseph Herman Hertz, Lord Rothschild, Nathan Sokolow, Chaim Weizmann, Louis Cohen (President of the Jewish Board of Deputies), Sir R. Magnus, M.P., Claude Montefiore (President of the Anglo Jewish Association) and Sir Stuart Samuel, M.P. (newly elected president of the Board of Deputies of British Jews).

When Weizmann heard this, he interpreted it as yet another concession to Montagu and angrily wrote to Philip Kerr, Lloyd George's secretary, denouncing the importance the Cabinet placed on the opinions of "so-called British Jewry." In his opinion, those British Jews who opposed Zionism were a small minority "of wealthy half assimilated Jews who have been in this country for the last three or four generations . . . and have cut themselves adrift from Jewry." The majority of British Jews, on the other hand, he wrote, "are in favour of Zionism." Zionism was intended for "these masses." Once the Declaration was adopted, the others "will fall in line quickly. . . . No amount of talk by Mr. Montagu or people like him will stem the tide."

Concluding his letter to Philip Kerr, Weizmann again stressed "Imperial interests" as a reason for the Balfour Declaration. "It is true that British help, if it comes now, will be invaluable to us, but it is equally true that a reconstructed Palestine will become a very great asset to the British Empire."[49] Concerned that Montagu's arguments might sway the War Cabinet, Weizmann also urged the local Zionist chapters to adopt resolutions supporting Zionism. As a result, three hundred Zionist and other Jewish organizations throughout the country adopted such resolutions and sent them to the Foreign Office.

On October 9, the text of the proposed Declaration was sent to Herbert Samuel with the names of those already consulted and an explanation that it was felt "your opinion should also be ascertained, the more so as the War Cabinet has already received two memoranda on the subject from Mr. Montagu."[50] As expected, Herbert

Samuel again expressed his support of the draft Declaration, emphasizing his concern that "If the Turks are left ostensibly in control of Palestine, the country is likely to fall in course of time under German influence."[51]

By the middle of October, Montagu realized he was fighting a losing battle. Scott wrote to Weizmann on October 14: "I think the thing will go through all right. Montagu, when I saw him last Sunday at Alderley, seemed to have come to that conclusion. He said Lloyd George and Balfour were immovably favorable and, if I remember rightly, Milner is favorable too. . . . Bye-the-bye, Montagu sails next Saturday, so he won't be in at the finish!"[52]

At the War Cabinet meeting on October 31, the fateful decision was finally made. Balfour was authorized to write Lord Rothschild the following letter with the request that he bring it to the attention of the Zionist Federation.

Dear Lord Rothschild:

I have much pleasure in conveying to you, on behalf of His Majesty's government, the following declaration of sympathy with Jewish Zionist aspirations, which has been submitted to, and approved by, the cabinet.

"His Majesty's government views with favour the establishment in Palestine of a national home for the Jewish people, and will use their best endeavours to facilitate the achievement of this object, it being clearly understood that nothing shall be done which may prejudice the civil and religious rights of existing non-Jewish communities in Palestine, or the rights and political status enjoyed by Jews in any other country."[53]

This version was not the same as the original Rothschild draft that had contained the sentence: "Palestine shall be *reconstituted* as *the* national home of the Jewish people." The version finally submitted used the phrase *"a* national home" instead of *"the* national home" and substituted the word "constituted" for "reconstituted." Chaim Weizmann always believed that Montagu's strong opposition played an important role in effecting these changes.[54] There were other changes made in the Declaration. During the drafting of the final document, Balfour and some members of the Cabinet used the phrase "Jewish race." The Zionists succeeded in changing this to "Jewish people."[55] The final Declaration also includes some reassurances for the non-Jewish population of Palestine, which had not been present in the original Rothschild document, and reference to the protection of the rights of Jews living outside of Palestine. It has been asserted that the first was included at the insistence of Curzon[56] and the latter to satisfy Montagu.[57]

In spite of the bitter debate that had divided the Jewish community on the Declaration, on November 2, 1917, its adoption was greeted with jubilation throughout the Jewish world. Even its opponents recognized that a new chapter in Jewish history had now begun. Lloyd George wrote in his *Memoirs of the Peace Conference:* "Urgent diplomatic and military reasons at last ensured complete unanimity on the subject. Even Mr. Montagu surrendered his opposition and accepted the declaration as a military expedient."[58]

This did not accurately reflect Montagu's feelings. He was defeated but he was not reconciled. He was angry and confused, and he took the Declaration as a personal rebuke. "I see from Reuters telegram," he wrote from India on November 11, 1917, "that Balfour has made the Zionist declaration against which I fought so hard. It seems strange to be a member of a Government which goes out of its way . . . to deal this blow at a colleague that is doing his best to be loyal to them, despite the opposition. The Government has dealt an irreparable blow at Jewish Britons, and they have set up a people which does not exist; they have alarmed unnecessarily the Mohammedan world. . . . Why we should intern Mahomed Ali in India for Pan-Mohammedanism when we encourage Pan-Judaism, I cannot for the life of me understand."[59]

Montagu's feelings on the subject never changed. He never recognized the concept of Jewish nationalism; he never believed it was in Jewish interests or in British interests to establish a Jewish state or homeland in Palestine. More importantly, he always believed that such a state would unnecessarily alarm the Muslim Arab world. This view of British geopolitical interests, contrary to that of Lloyd George and Balfour, was fundamental to his position on British postwar policy in the Middle East, Turkey and India.

These views were espoused before Hitler. Today, whether one agrees or disagrees with the concept of a Jewish people, one cannot disregard the central historic fact of contemporary Jewish history: that six million Jews were destroyed in Europe and that the existence of Israel made the rescue of those who remained possible.

To Jews who understand the horror of the genocide and the miracle of the rebirth of Israel, Montagu's arguments, as cogent as they are, seem like an exercise in semantics—with no relationship to the real world. For, in the post-Holocaust period of Jewish history, the question of whether Jews are a people or a religious group pales in the face of the belief among Jews that the existence of Israel stands as an assurance that the mass murder of Jews will not happen again. The Israeli army, navy and air force, not the sticks and stones of the Warsaw Ghetto fighters, will defend Jewish lives. In 1917, no one in his wildest imagination could have conceived of Hitler's determination to destroy the Jews. Without such knowledge and on the basis of the facts before them, Montagu and the other anti-Zionists were arguing entirely within Anglo-Jewish religious tradition.

In spite of his feelings Montagu came to believe that Britain had an obligation to keep its promises to the Jews. During the summer of 1922, when Britain began to waver in her commitment, he wrote to Herbert Samuel:

As you know, I regarded the Balfour Declaration with strong opposition and disapproval, and even to-day would give anything that it should not have been made. . . . But it seems to me that conflict of opinion on the basis of the policy must have ended when the Declaration was announced and endorsed, . . . It is almost a platitude to say that Great Britain's promises . . . ought to be kept and honoured without hesitation and made as successful as human effort can make them.[60]

The promises Britain had made to the Jews were only part of the commitments she had simultaneously made to the Arabs and the French after the Turkish surrender on October 30, 1918. The nest of conspiracies, distrust and conflicting interests that surrounded these promises, as well as the increasing opposition of the Conservative press to the Balfour Declaration, doomed from the start the British mandate for Palestine that Britain received at the San Remo Peace Conference on April 25, 1920. By that time the seeds of tragic conflict between the Arabs and the Jews had already been sown. Britain was powerless in the face of forces she had unleashed but could not control. She finally accepted the harsh reality that what began as a golden moment in British and Jewish history had become unworkable. All that remained was the official acknowledgment of this failure. This the British did when they issued their *White Paper on Palestine* in 1939 which canceled all further Jewish immigration into Palestine. At a time when immigration was a matter of life or death to the Jews fleeing Hitler's Europe, the gates of Palestine, which Britain had opened, were now tragically closed. This could not have come at a more perilous time. "Now, there," Winston Churchill said, "is the breach; there is the violation of the pledge; there is the abandonment of the Balfour Decision; there is the end of the vision, of the hope, of the dream."[61]

Montagu regretted that he had to leave for India before the debate on Palestine was over. But from the moment he was appointed Secretary of State for India in July 1917, that country and its problems became his primary concern. The man who had fought so hard against the concept of nationalism for the Jewish people was now to begin his struggle for the national rights of a people three thousand miles away from the shores of England.[62]

24

Secretary of State for India, July 1917–December 1918

We cannot devote more than a century to the tilling of the soil and then refuse to plant the seed.

Montagu's budget speech, 1918

One can only imagine the thoughts that ran through Montagu's mind as he walked into his office as the new Secretary of State for India on his first morning there, July 18, 1917. It was a regal office, furnished magnificently with thick Oriental rugs, an elegant hand-carved desk and chair, and oak-paneled walls decorated with Indian miniatures and with the oil portraits of former Secretaries of State. These looked down upon him, stern and stately, staring, perhaps incredulously, upon this rather unattractive Jew, the first of his religion to hold this office. Here was Edwin Montagu, the great-grandson of a man born in a small village in the Jewish ghetto of Poland, grandson of a watchmaker from Liverpool, son of an Orthodox Jewish banker to whom the Jewish Sabbath was more sacred than the Magna Carta, following in the footsteps of the Earl of Derby, Lord Salisbury, Lord Randolph Churchill and the Duke of Argyll, to mention only four of the great British aristocrats who had held this post.

It was only seven years since he had been appointed Under Secretary of State for India in February 1910 by Prime Minister Asquith, but politically it had been an eternity. During those seven years, the foundations of British political life had fundamentally changed. Asquith had been driven from power; the Liberal Party divided; Lloyd George was now Prime Minister, with strong Tory support; and Great Britain and her entire empire were engaged in a bitter war of worldwide dimensions that had become a life-and-death struggle.

The declaration of war against Germany and the King's call for the support of the empire had temporarily quieted the cries of discontent in India. The Indian Imperial Legislative Council had not only unanimously passed a resolution affirming its "unswerving loyalty and enthusiastic devotion to their King Emperor,"[1] but had sent troops and pledged financial support. The presence of these troops on the Western front during the early days of 1914–15 had been critical in restraining the German advances as Kitchener tried desperately to recruit and train enough manpower to hold back the German onslaught.

In the long course of the war, India sent forth more than six hundred thousand combatants and four hundred thousand noncombatants in nearly all the theaters of war; fifty-three-thousand Indians were killed or died of wounds. By July 31, 1918, India had lent £100,000,000 to the war and was in the process of raising another £20,000,000 through a new war loan. Nearly all the tanned hides used in Army boots were made in India, as were the much-needed Army blankets.[2]

The Native Princes were equally loyal, many leading their own troops into battle. Indian leadership seemed, in fact, during these early months, "to take Lord Hardinge's word for anything that he declared to be necessary for the winning of the war."[3] But this lull was temporary and delusive. The war lasted too long; victory seemed ever more distant; the empire, which had seemed eternal and impregnable, now appeared weak and floundering; and the list of Indian sons dying on the battlefield was growing. People were now beginning to question not only the war but India's role in it.

By the beginning of 1916, the call for Indian Home Rule was again gaining respectability. It was no longer the cry of extremists, but had sufficient moderate support to be incorporated in a resolution adopted by the Indian Council in 1916. And in 1917, the Indian Council elected Mrs. Annie Besant, a national leader in the fight for Home Rule, as its president.

The Mesopotamian disaster added to Indian disillusionment. The surrender of Kut on April 29, 1916, and the terrible tales of mismanagement and unnecessary suffering of the predominantly Indian troops added to the growing unhappiness. As discontent with the war grew, so grew the clamor for self-government. Among the advocates of more self-government were not only the Indians themselves but now also the Viceroy himself. Lord Hardinge, resigning as a result of the Mesopotamian disaster, had no hesitation in affirming in his farewell address to the 1915–16 session of the Legislative Council in Delhi: "I do not for a moment wish to discountenance self-government for India as a national ideal."[4]

This occasion was marked by another significant event: a joint Hindu-Muslim dinner. From now on, the demand for Home Rule and self-government would be a joint effort of Hindu and Muslim, moderate and extremist, a far more formidable and united front than in the past.

Bal Gangadhar Tilak, a Brahman and the acknowledged leader of the Hindu extremists, whose motto "Home Rule is my birth-right, and I will have it" had become the rallying cry of the educated and more articulate Indians, now joined Mrs. Besant, adding his inflammatory rhetoric to an already incendiary situation.

Lord Chelmsford: New Viceroy

Against this background Lord Chelmsford arrived in April 1916 as the new Viceroy and Montagu assumed his duties as Secretary of State, one year later. Chelmsford was a tall, cold, reserved and handsome man, who looked more like a schoolmaster than a politician or Viceroy. After spending two days in Delhi with Chelmsford in 1917, Montagu described him as not having "the dignity of Hardinge or the pomposity of Curzon, but he is quite good to look at, with a fine, athletic figure, square shoulders, small hips . . . thoroughly nice, but unfortunately cold, aloof—reserved. He seems to me strongly prejudiced." Montagu continued:

Oh, the fact of the matter is—and it is borne in on me every moment of the day, every hour, but it is of no use because nobody will believe me— the sort of man we seek to make a Viceroy is wholly wrong. . . . They approach their problem from the wrong side; they do the work they are called upon to do; they wade through files; they think of their regulations; and then as to the social side—precedence, precedence, precedence. . . . Informal discussion, informal conversation, they do not know. Political instinct they have none.[5]

Chelmsford confirmed the accuracy of Montagu's judgment when his first dispatch to Whitehall whittled down Hardinge's proposal for self-government by urging that "the rate of progress towards the goal [of self-government] must depend upon the improvement and wide diffusion of education, the softening of racial and religious difference and the acquisition of political experience."[6] To achieve this goal, Chelmsford and his Council advocated that local government bodies be more democratic and that more Indians be brought into the higher branches of the public services. A storm broke out in the Imperial Legislative Council in India. On one side, Sir Reginald Craddock, a member of the Imperial Legislative Council, thought Chelmsford's proposals went too far, and on the other, Sir Sankaran Nair, the Council's only Indian member, thought they did not go far enough.[7]

Thus from the outset, Chelmsford was caught up in the conflicts inherent in Anglo-Indian relations. He learned quickly that trying to hold the center was not easy. It was a lesson that Montagu was still learning. In spite of his rocky start, Chelmsford persisted in believing that some statement about Britain's goal for India was absolutely necessary. While he continued to believe that the demands of the Home Rulers were out of the question, he did believe that it was necessary to give India "the largest measure of self-government compatible with the maintenance of the supreme authority of British rule."[8] In the autumn of 1916 he wrote to Chamberlain, who was Secretary of State, urging some promise of constitutional reform.

Chamberlain was sympathetic and brought Chelmsford's proposals to his India Council, which debated the issue from December 1916 to March 1917. There was no agreement in the Council and the fear of making a wrong move resulted in no move. Rather, the Council suggested that a Royal Committee be established to examine the matter and make recommendations. The War Cabinet could find no time to deal with India, despite Chelmsford's pleas that the situation was deteriorating.

Finally, on May 22, Chamberlain, after continued pressure and pleas from Chelmsford, recommended to the War Cabinet that some statement on Britain's goal for India must be made. The first step, he said, should be to implement the India Council's suggestion that a Royal Committee be created to investigate the situation. Lord Curzon favored this but recommended that Chamberlain alone go to India, rather than an entire committee. Balfour agreed that something should be done but thought it a mistake to believe that India could be self-governing like Australia or South Africa. Because the Prime Minister was absent and the War Cabinet thought it important that he participate in the debate, the discussion was adjourned until July 5 and then again until July 12. A week later Chamberlain resigned and Montagu became Secretary of State.

Proclamation on Goal for India: August 20, 1917

One month after Montagu's appointment, on August 29, 1917, a proclamation of British goals for India was issued. The fact that this was achieved at all and was done in thirty-four days is a singular tribute to Montagu's obsessive determination. In a steady flow of memoranda and letters that Montagu wrote to key Cabinet Ministers, including Lloyd George, he lobbied, begged, persuaded, and would not take no for an answer. He made Chamberlain his ally and advisor and, in spite of his personal dislike for Curzon, did all he could to win him over.

On August 7, three weeks after taking office, he wrote to Lloyd George: "I have got to beg and entreat you to turn your attention to India." Chelmsford and Chamberlain agreed "that action is necessary at once . . . if you do not act soon, you will be led irresistibly along the lines of repression, coercion, imprisonment—compared with which I am certain that the recent history of Ireland will be placid and peaceful."[9] "The old antagonisms between Hindu and Mahommedan, upon which certain short-sighted statesmen relied to keep order in India," he continued, "is gone, and they are uniting in their demands. Extremists are receiving recruits from day to day from the ranks of the Moderates. The Princes like Bikaner and Aga Khan, the educated Indians like Sinha, are all on the same tack."[10]

Montagu warned that Britain must tell India that she hoped for self-government one day. "This is what Chamberlain reluctantly felt was necessary. This is what Chelmsford advocates in every telegram he sends me. This is what all those connected with the Government of India want, even my Council here."[11] He urged again that the word "self-government" be used. "Unless you use the word 'Self-government,' " he warned, "you had better not make a pronouncement at all."[12]

Montagu also told Lloyd George that he planned to go to India in October. He assumed he had the Minister's approval. But a pronouncement must be issued first. Montagu wrote to Chamberlain, again on August 7, telling him that time was passing and that he could not get the Cabinet to consider the problem. If the government did not make a statement, it would see "grim repression on a growing scale and the alienation of many, if not all, the Moderates."[13]

On August 9 he wrote to Curzon expressing his distress that the issue was not before the Cabinet and had been postponed yet again. He needed a decision. The Prime Minister agreed to put it on the agenda and Montagu hoped that Curzon would consent in principle to a statement.[14]

Two days later, he told Lloyd George why he, rather than Chamberlain, should go to India. Although Chamberlain had been kind and helpful, "I do not think that I should like to entrust the formulation of your policy to Chamberlain. He is much too likely to let it be the policy of the Indian machine rather than . . . the spirit which animates you . . ."[15] While Montagu may have been correct in his judgment of Chamberlain, it was with his characteristic bluntness that he characterized Chamberlain as one he would not trust. Surely Montagu could have found other arguments with which to convince Lloyd George that he should go to India. It was this tendency, which seems so at odds with Montagu's otherwise sensitive nature, that contributed to his having, with the passage of time, fewer and fewer political allies.

Finally, on August 14, the Cabinet considered the Indian proclamation. Montagu had lobbied "every member of the Cabinet first."[16] It was adopted and announced by the Cabinet on August 20, 1917, and was a simple sentence proclaiming: "The policy of H.[is] M.[ajesty's] Government, with which the Government of India are in complete accord, is that of increasing association of Indians in every branch of the administration and the gradual development of self-governing institutions with a view to the progressive realization of responsible government in India as an integral part of the British Empire."[17]

Originally Montagu had written, "His Majesty's Government and the Government of India have in view the gradual development of free institutions in India with a view to the ultimate self-govern-

ment within the Empire."[18] Curzon preferred, however, the words
"responsible government" to "self-government," and the final pronouncement expresses Curzon's preference. Montagu never understood Curzon's reasons. In a letter to Chamberlain the day after the
Cabinet adopted the proclamation, Montagu noted that he had explained the importance of "self-government" to Lloyd George, who
promised to "back him up." But three minutes into the debate,
Lloyd George "chipped in with an objection to quarrelling about
words and a statement that 'Self-government' was really what Lord
Curzon . . . described it as being. Fortunately Lord Curzon was
more helpful than the Prime Minister and did not take this view."[19]

In discussing why Curzon insisted on "responsible government"
over "self-government," one of his biographers shared Montagu's
confusion: "If this substitution, with its emphasis on the eventual
emergence of *responsible government* did not mean the eventual emergence of *parliamentary* Government there, what did it mean? Surely
Curzon could not be woolly-minded over, of all things, India?
Surely he realized what he was saying."[20]

Before the drafting of this paragraph, Curzon caused Montagu
more grief. Although he had originally agreed to consider the words
"self-government" or "responsible government," when the completed draft was sent to him, Curzon reversed his previous stand.
"He had decided, for reasons of his own, to change his mind and
now insisted that he did not want 'self-governing institutions' or its
corollary 'responsible government' at all, and that the reforms envis-
aged would take India along the path to democracy far too fast."[21]

Montagu was in a panic and felt that if he could not settle this
clash with Curzon, he would have to resign. In a fight with Curzon,
the "great Indian panjandrum,"[22] what chance did he have? But as it
happened, while Curzon continued to voice concern over the proclamation, he was prepared to accept it in the modified form in which
he had redrafted it.

Curzon may have drafted the paragraph as finally adopted, but
without Montagu it would not have been adopted. No one but
Montagu thought it important. It was his persistence and determination that finally made the Cabinet, by and large disinterested in
India, understand the significance of their issuing a proclamation,
something that Chelmsford and Chamberlain were not able to do,
and something that Curzon and Balfour, left on their own, would

not have done. Montagu was able not only to get the matter before the Cabinet, but to get a Conservative Tory Government to adopt it.

It is, therefore, disheartening to read a historian-journalist such as Durga Das say that "Montagu's own inspiration in this pronouncement was transparent; but in Simla and Delhi the knowledgeable were aware that Curzon had played a crucial role in winning the Conservatives over to making this gesture in response to the political aspirations of the Indian people at a time when the fortunes of war were in a state of stalemate."[23] Curzon is also given credit for the proclamation by Sir Valentine Chirol, another distinguished Indian historian, who writes that Montagu was only the "mouthpiece"[24] of the Cabinet on the proclamation. The truth is that Curzon did not play a significant role in winning over the Conservatives in the Cabinet. He was ambiguous, changing his mind repeatedly, and only at the end, after he had redrafted the proclamation to suit his own style, was he prepared to vote for it. While this may have influenced his fellow Conservatives, there is no evidence that he went out of his way to gain their support for the pronouncement. That this proclamation was issued at all was due to the constant pressure and repeated telegrams and warnings from Chelmsford, and, most of all, to Edwin Montagu's doggedness and his eloquent presentation of the rationale for its adoption. Montagu was anything but "the mouthpiece" for the Cabinet. He believed in the Proclamation; he insisted it be brought to the Cabinet; he lobbied endlessly on its behalf; he pressed Curzon for support and he wrote the first draft.

Preparation for the Trip to India

Montagu recognized from the start the enormous difficulties he would face in attempting to implement the August 20 proclamation and in developing self-governing institutions in India. "How far can we go in this direction safely?" he asked Chelmsford in a letter of September 21, after the proclamation had been issued. Schemes on paper, he conceded, were easy to formulate; the real test is in translating them into workable administrative machinery. "We are discussing":

. . . a problem of the administration of an important part of the world and are not considering an abstract matter for debate. . . . Is there any country in the world that has attempted a half-way house in this, or a quarter-way house? An autocratic and independent executive is common. Self governing institutions are now . . . accepted as the only proper form of government. How can you unite the two? Can you have a form of government administered by an alien agency partly responsible to the people of the country itself?

You have got a democracy at home, ignorant of Indian conditions, a Central government in India naturally jealous of the efficiency of the Government of which it is the custodian, local governments growing in importance with the civilization of the countries over which they preside, and an Indian opinion . . . which is now absolutely impossible to ignore. *How can we reconcile all these things at a time when no complete solution is possible and everything must be another step upon the slope which we started on a hundred years ago?*[25] (emphasis added)

Montagu Returns to India

Whatever answers England tried to propose were generally viewed by Indians as both too little and too late. The difficulty of the problem served only to spur Montagu to a greater determination to devise a solution. He resolved to go to India himself to develop a scheme that would implement the proclamation and please both the Indians and the British. With this as his goal, Montagu left London on October 20, 1917, for what would be a historic trip to India.

Montagu had spent a good deal of time during September and October selecting a delegation to accompany him. His group included Lord Donaughoure, Under Secretary of War, a Conservative and a friend of Curzon, and several members of the Round Table, a group of intellectuals interested in imperial problems, especially in India, such as Sir William Duke, Sir Malcolm Seton and Charles Roberts, a Member of Parliament, as well as Sir Cecil H. Kisch and Alan Parsons, Montagu's Private Secretaries. It included Mr. Bhupendranath Basu, a former president of the Indian Congress, Sir William Vincent (a member of the India Council), Mr. F. C. T. Halliday, a member of the Indian police, and George Franey, a stenographer.

Montagu had invited Chamberlain to join the mission to provide continuity in Indian policy, but Chamberlain had declined. Montagu made certain to tell Chelmsford that Chamberlain had been most useful to him in getting the proclamation adopted and that even Curzon was "sympathetic about the difficulties of my position." He assured Chelmsford he would not embarrass him during his trip to India. He would "be governed by the support that I can give to the Viceroy."[26]

Before sailing, Montagu had lunch with King George and Queen Mary and reported to Chelmsford that the King was "anxious to be associated by name with any great pronouncement about Indian Reforms, but he knows that Curzon is opposed." They discussed Mrs. Besant, and Montagu assured their majesties that she had been released from jail only on assurances that "she meant to behave herself." The King expressed concern that the Yacht Club in Bombay refused to admit natives.[27]

Montagu departed with the good wishes of the King and Queen, and he was also feted at a farewell dinner given by his friends. According to Diana Cooper, Montagu spoke glowingly of his two years of marriage to Venetia and his hope that Diana would look after her if anything happened to him on the trip. He also wrote a letter to Venetia, to be opened only after his death, in which he told her she had made him happy "beyond belief . . . almost too good to last," that she had been "wonderful" to him, that they had "enjoyed" one another and that if anything happened, she should do whatever she wanted to do that would bring her fun and happiness. "[T]hink of me sometimes," he concluded, "but all I ask of you is to enjoy your life for my sake."[28] On this note, his party left for Folkestone, from whence they were then escorted by two destroyers to France.

Montagu and his party arrived in France, went on to Paris and then Rome, and then boarded a light cruiser that took them to Port Said. They spent some time in Egypt as the guest of Sir Reginald Wingate and then sailed on another P & O boat, arriving in India in November 1917. The journey was not a safe or easy one. They were traveling in wartime; they sighted submarines; they required two Japanese escorts as they moved into the Indian Ocean aware of the large number of Allied vessels already sunk by the enemy. But Montagu's determination to tackle this problem by himself was so strong that even the thought of traveling in mine-infested waters did not deter him. The adjective "cowardly," that he so often used to describe himself, was certainly not applicable to his making this voyage. His diary included no word of fear or trepidation but instead was filled only with anticipation of the adventure ahead.

While Montagu was probably sincere in assuring Chelmsford that he was going to India to support the Viceroy and would do nothing to embarrass him, he also viewed his mission in the broadest geopolitical terms, recognizing the heavy responsibilities he bore in finding the ways to make major changes in the administration of India without appearing to force his schemes upon the government of India, the Viceroy or the Indian leadership.[29] Montagu and his party arrived in Bombay on November 10, 1917. He would remain in India six months. He wrote regularly to Venetia, sending his diary notes with each letter, just as he had written to his mother during his India trip in 1912. Montagu's diary was not only filled with the business of each day and his comments on the men with whom he worked but also expressed the awe and excitement he continued to feel at the physical beauty of India and its people. There was something about "one's first introduction to India," he wrote as he sailed into Bombay, that was "one of the wonders of the world, and just produce exuberance, enthusiasm, even to the most prosaic nature."[30] His love of India had not diminished: In fact, it seemed to have increased.

A Formidable Task

This time Montagu was in India not as a quasi-tourist but rather in an official capacity to develop a form of governmental structure that would implement a proclamation of the Parliament of His Majesty's government—to increase the role of India in "every branch of the administration," to give India the opportunity to gain the experience needed for "self" or "responsible" government and at the same time to preserve the rights and interests of Great Britain. He would be required to listen to and to reconcile hundreds of different opinions and ideas, to study in minute detail how the government of India actually functioned on the local as well as national level, to meet and work with the Viceroy and scores of governmental funtionaries, along with the Princes of the Native States. He was constantly aware that forcing his own opinions on the government of India would doom the process. Most difficult of all, he had to continue to walk the fine line between expressing sympathy for the Indians' desire for more self-rule and the reluctance of Great Britain and the government of India to transfer important powers to a people they believed ill-equipped for democratic government.

It was an enormous task, not one that it is likely any statesman could have completely achieved at that time. Ten years earlier such a goal might have been reached. But at this point in India's history, the Home Rulers had become too strong and vocal and the Conservatives in control of the government in Parliament were decreasingly inclined to part with any real measure of British control.

Montagu was aware of the magnitude of the task he had undertaken and the difficulties he faced. Characteristically, he feared that he was inadequate: The task before him required "the tact, the courage of the greatest of English statesmen."[31] If only he were Asquith or Lloyd George. He trembled with the fear of failure because "if the Indians believe we are fiddling with the existing order of things," they "will never believe us again—a vast Continent, whose history is our glory, and whose hopes and aspirations, fears and tribulations it is pathetic to see."[32]

Montagu had an informal, open, relaxed manner in dealing with the Indian leadership. There was nothing cold or reserved or elitist about him. His hatred of snobs and prejudice was evident, and as a result, Indian leaders talked to him "as they never dare talk to anybody else." "Perhaps there is some truth," he wrote, "in the allegation that I am an Oriental. Certainly that social relationship which the English people seem to find so difficult comes quite easy to me."[33]

Montagu's attitude had nothing to do with his being an "Oriental." It had everything to do with his disdain for elitism and racism and his own unhappy experiences with the prejudices of the English. Montagu has been described in this mission as "the antithesis of Chelmsford, a politician to his fingertips, quick, mercurial, imaginative, charming but also erratic and arrogant."[34]

All of these observations were probably just. On his good days Montagu was charming, optimistic and imaginative; on his bad days, arrogant, impatient and pessimistic. But regardless of mood, he pressed on. He found Chelmsford courteous and honest but without "any vigour or personality." Chelmsford rarely showed "spirit" or "came up with ideas or criticism." He found the original proposals of the government of India "dreadful," and were such that they would be shouted down "in derision" by the Indian leadership.[35]

Montagu met with Jinnah, Gandhi, and Mrs. Besant, "the real giants" of the Indian political world, and worried about the kind of government they would create if they succeeded in achieving Home Rule. "Owing to the thinness with which we have spread education," he wrote, "they have run generations away from the rest of India." If they were in control, they would create "another and indigenous autocracy."[36]

Whatever his private thoughts, his relations with the Indian leadership were excellent. Mrs. Besant, in fact, pleaded with him to address the Indian Congress that was to meet in Calcutta during his visit. He declined the invitation bemoaning the fact that were he Lloyd George, he could dash off to the Congress and make an extemporaneous speech with the demagogic flourishes Lloyd George used to such splendid effect to bring a crowd to its feet. Montagu knew he was not Lloyd George: It took him days, even weeks, to prepare a speech, and while his were often stunning in scope and substance, he did not have the kind of delivery that brought an audience spontaneously to its feet. Montagu was, moreover, spending "weary hours" listening to the views of "people and parties of secondary importance."[37] But every base had to be touched and every opinion considered.

Between Montagu's exhausting meetings, he attended round upon round of "appalling dinner parties,"[38] where he found himself making meaningless conversation and shaking hundreds of hands. Of all his tasks, he disliked this the most. During the course of his visit, his relationship with Chelmsford improved, although it too varied day-by-day—even hour-by-hour. On December 12, 1917, he wrote: "I like Chelmsford more than ever. Fatigue cannot stale the courtesy of his manner or the inherent honesty of his character."[39] On other days, he was irked by Chelmsford's inability to generate enthusiasm or ideas or be a critical partner in the search of the elusive compromise.[40]

He also found to his chagrin that in certain parts of India, certainly in Madras, Anglo-Indian relations had deteriorated badly during the previous seven years. The change "was simply appalling." Before, "it was a peaceful country, inhabited by men and women on amiable terms with one another, differing from the whole of the rest of India in being happy. Now the English hate the Indians; the Indians hate the English, and this new violent opposition of the Brahmins to the non-Brahmins has become the guiding principle of the place."[41]

Montagu became increasingly worried about India's ability to work with representative institutions and was fearful that full transfer of powers of law and order would lead to "anarchy, revolution, bloodshed and starvation [like that] which has resulted in Russia. It is this use of power which they must be taught and which they must learn by experience and which we cannot risk. I cannot see there is anything offensive in telling them this."[42]

No people enjoys hearing that it must learn how to govern before it assumes power. This was especially offensive to the educated Indians, who believed that such ideas were an expression of white supremacy and racism. Surely their culture and tradition, they believed, made them as capable as the English of governing themselves.

Montagu's moods ranged from elation on some days to gloom on others: joy when Chelmsford praised him in a letter to Islington, depression after meeting with the Conference of Governors. He spoke eloquently to the Conference of the need to make India a political country with parliamentary government. But the Indians' desire for greater control of their government continued to preclude any harmony or accord. At the end of the Conference, the participants signed their names to Montagu's proposals but did so with skepticism and heavy hearts. Montagu knew this and continued to worry that Indian opinion would not be satisfied with halfway measures. Shrinivasa Shastri, a moderate Indian leader with whom Montagu consulted, wrote that the "Moderates were all profoundly impressed with Montagu's personality, his honesty, earnestness and sincerity of purpose. . . . If they were only half-converts to his scheme, they had become full converts to Montagu himself."[43]

Dyarchy

Montagu's notes show that he was now moving closer to accepting the idea of "dyarchy," originally conceived by Sir William Duke, a member of Montagu's delegation, who was a member of the Secretary of State's India Council in 1915. Duke had conceived of this idea in a memorandum for the Round Table issued under the title "Suggestions for Constitutional Progress in Indian Policy" and later called the Duke Memorandum. Duke and the members of the Round Table believed that the solution to the Indian problem was to find a method of "introducing true responsible government in a limited and manageable field of administration, which could be contracted or extended in accordance with the practical results attained, without imperiling the structure of the government itself. The method by which this gradual and safe advance to responsible government could be made in India . . . was nicknamed 'dyarchy,' "[44] a name that it retained.

Montagu found time, too, for a few short holidays. Hunting panthers, wild pigs and tigers; shooting ducks; bird watching; enjoying the wildlife and jungle scenic wonders of India continued to enthrall him. By January 24, 1918, Montagu wrote to Venetia that he believed that they were all getting along "famously," and that the government of India seemed to "have agreed to my approach."[45] By February 28, 1918, he wrote in his diary that he had grown weary with fatigue. "I cannot describe," he wrote, "the weariness of my flesh. I am tired of conciliating, cajoling, persuading, lobbying, interviewing, accommodating, often spoiling my own plans to quell opposition."[46]

He was disturbed that he was away from the war in a place "where people do not feel it." He was also angry that while he had been working day and night, the Government "has never sent me, in answer to my telegrams, one little line of encouragement. If I have failed, what have I done? I have kept India quiet for six months at a critical period of the War."[47]

By March 19, the pressure of his work schedule had caught up with him. He developed a fever. He continued to work while in bed and by March 26 was well enough to move to the Viceroy's summer quarters at Dehra Dunn, which Montagu found "one of the prettiest spots" he had ever seen.

From the last week in March until mid-April, everyone in the delegation worked on the report from ten in the morning until eight at night, with no exercise: editing and revising draft after draft, with Chelmsford, according to Montagu, confining himself to such inconsequential nonsense as "whether the Government of India is a plural or singular noun."[48]

The Montagu-Chelmsford Report

Finally, on April 21, 1918, the report, which came to be known as "The Montagu-Chelmsford Report," was completed. The report was based on the principle of dyarchy, under which the functions of government in the nine Governor's provinces would be divided into two sections. Functions such as the police, the administration of justice, irrigation and land revenue were reserved exclusively for the jurisdiction of the Governor and his Executive Councillors (some Indian and some British). Other responsibilities, such as those for education, public health, agriculture, local government and public works were transferred to the control of ministers chosen from and responsible to the local legislature or Legislative Council. At least 70 percent of the Legislative Council members were to be elected. The Governor could, as a last resort, make financial and legislative decisions in the category of reserved subjects against the will of the Legislature. "It was, however, contemplated that if the new system worked satisfactorily the range of transferred subjects would be extended until ultimately the whole [local] administration should be handed over to responsible ministers."[49]

The principle of dyarchy was not extended to the Central or Supreme Government, to which 47 "central" government functions, for example, defense, foreign affairs, customs, coinage of currency, police and civil and criminal law, would continue to be reserved. Executive authority would still be vested in an Executive Council consisting of seven heads of departments approved by and responsible to the Crown. The Central Administration would also have a Central Legislature consisting of two Houses—the Council of State and the Legislative Assembly or Lower House. The Council of State would consist of 60 members, 34 elected on a restricted franchise and the rest nominated. The Assembly was to consist of 144 members, of whom 104 would be elected. In this way the Central Legislature became larger and more democratic. The scheme also provided for a Chamber of Princes to form a link between the British government and the Indian States.

The Montagu-Chelmsford report recognized that the arrangements were transitional—"temporary expedients for training purposes," that would provide "progressive realization of responsible government." After the first ten years, and thereafter at intervals of twelve years, a royal commission was to consider the possibility of further progress on the road to complete self-government. The report concluded with a call for support:

We believe that the announcement of August 20th was right and wise; and the policy which it embodies is the only possible policy for India. . . . We are not setting about to stir 95% of the people out of their peaceful conservatism and setting their feet on a new and difficult path merely at the bidding of the other 5% . . . Our reason is the faith that is in us. We have shown how step by step British policy in India has been steadily directed to a point at which the question of self-governing India was bound to arise; how impulses, at first faint, have been encouraged by education and opportunity; how the growth quickened nine years ago and was immeasurably accelerated by the war. We measure it not by the crowds at political meetings or the multiplication of newspapers; but by the infallible signs that indicate growth of character. We believe profoundly that the time has now come when the sheltered existence we have given India cannot be prolonged without damage to her national life; that we have a richer gift for her people than any we have yet bestowed on them; that nationhood within the Empire represents something better than India has yet attained; that the placid contentment of the masses is not the soil on which such Indian nationhood will grow, and that in deliberately disturbing it, we are working for her highest good.[50]

For Montagu, this was not mere rhetoric: He may have been a practical politician on scores of issues, but on India he was an idealist and dreamer. He also loved the country and wanted her to enjoy those fruits of freedom and democracy to which he was so strongly committed.

During the final days of his visit in April 1918, he wrote in his diary of his fear that the report would be meaningless unless its principles came to inform the Government's actions:

The main principle [of the report] is that instead of founding the Indian Government on the confidence of the people of England, we are gradually to found it on the confidence of the people of India. We are, beginning in the Provinces, maintaining the Government of India as now, but subjected, I am glad to think, to more criticism, and future progress will depend on the creation of an electorate.[51]

Montagu confessed that while it "is good to be going home," after six months of India he regretted "their coming to an end. *I love this country, it is where I am happiest.* The circumstances are cheerful, we have got an agreed report. We have kept India quiet for six critical months" (emphasis added):

> When I came out, Moderates were rushing to join the Home Rule League: on leaving, the secession of Moderates from the Home Rule League is making marked headway.
>
> *In the future . . . the principles of the report, are dead unless they are acted upon, unless they animate the governments.* Will they do anything when I have gone? Do they want someone to drive them before they will move? These are the anxieties. Shall I be allowed to carry out the proposals? That is another anxiety. On the other hand, I have gone through the winter feeling that I exercised a very great influence with educated Indian opinion. Certainly, I got out of them what nobody now in India could have got out of them, but the question I go away with is, have I done anything to establish the confidence of the officials or led them to agree that I have influence with the Indians? The events of the past week [when the Government officials would not invite Montagu to the Durbar] lead me very much to doubt it.[52] (emphasis added)

Unfortunately, this report and the Government of India Act of 1919 that incorporated its salient points did not prevent future conflict and bloodshed, nor did they lessen the unrest and violence that convulsed India in the decades ahead.

From a personal perspective, however, these were Montagu's most important contributions. They showed how one man's determination could, against enormous odds, develop a plan acceptable both to Indian leaders and the British government of India—an achievement no one thought possible. It was a brilliant piece of constitutional reform: unprecedented, creative and innovative.

When adopted, the Montagu-Chelmsford report was described as "historic," of "revolutionary spirit," "a watershed in British-Indian relations," and a "development of great moment."[53] One historian went so far as to view it as the beginning of the end of "the Second British Empire and the beginning of the Third British Empire, the transformation of the Empire into a Commonwealth of Nations . . . a landmark in British Imperial history. . . . it marks the definite repudiation of the idea that there can, under the British flag, be one form of constitutional evolution for the West and another for the East, or one for the White race and another for the non-white."[54]

While this was Montagu's dream, it never was the intention of the Tory government that adopted the report or the view of the British public. They never viewed their nonwhite possessions in the same way they did their white colonies. They were racist to the core. Had they viewed the report as Montagu did, as a step toward bringing genuine constitutional government to India (in the way in which they were prepared to permit such developments in Canada, Australia and New Zealand), the course of Indian history might well have been different.

There were other reasons why the report never had a chance. It came too late. The extremists in both England and India had grown too strong, Curzon and Balfour were too powerful, and the Prime Minister, despite his protestations to the contrary, was not prepared to oppose his political supporters for the sake of India. The Tories' dislike of Montagu was another factor. But for Montagu, as he returned home in April 1918, these problems were veiled by his optimism and hope. In his eyes, the report was a heroic victory, achieved through his perseverance and skill. He was determined to see it become law.

Curzon: Stumbling Block Again

His principal adversary in this effort continued to be Curzon who, on matters relating to India, was still viewed as the resident authority and spokesman in the Cabinet. He was a difficult man to reach. He was variously described as aloof, arrogant, ill-tempered and pompous; he had a grand manner, "lacked vision and was incapable of understanding other people's psychology . . . an eighteenth-century aristocrat born out of his time."[55] Curzon also had an almost compulsive concern with detail which to him was "all-important."[56]

On May 31, Montagu wrote to Chelmsford: "Curzon has very little complimentary to say about the Report and has not committed himself to any criticism of its proposals. He thinks it is a confused document, difficult to follow. . . . But that is only the manner of the Grand Mogul, and at any rate he is in favor of its immediate release." Montagu added that H. A. L. Fisher, "who is at least [as] good a judge of style as Curzon," thought the report was "admirably written."[57]

Unlike Curzon, Chamberlain was of invaluable assistance to Montagu, not only in advising him on substance and strategy but in calming him in the face of Curzon's difficult behavior. Since it had been Montagu's speech on Mesopotamia that had precipitated Chamberlain's resignation, his willingness to help Montagu was a tribute to his decency. On June 15, Montagu wrote to Chelmsford that "Chamberlain is a tower of strength" and that he could not "have done without him . . . he is always ready to advise and suggest and to do it in so nice a way that I have got into the habit of seeking his advice whenever I can."[58]

He found that Curzon continued to be amusing, interesting and irritating.[59] The truth is that Curzon was more than irritating; he was a genuine threat. In a clash of opinions between Montagu and Curzon, either one or the other would have felt compelled to resign. With the Conservatives holding the key to Lloyd George's government, Montagu realized it would have to be he.

As it turned out, while Curzon continued to object to various parts of the report, he did not vote against it. As one of his biographers noted: "All that the clash served to demonstrate . . . was that, even on the subject of India, Curzon did not always know his own mind."[60] And so on July 1, 1918, in spite of Curzon's hesitations, the Cabinet agreed to the publication of the report, but without any specific endorsement of its proposals, and left it to Curzon, Chamberlain and Montagu to settle the question of appointing two committees, one to look into the question of the franchise in India as it related to the report's proposals, and the other to further investigate the division of functions between the government of India and the local governments.

Report Published

Later in the month, Curzon took it upon himself to write to Montagu to remind him that the Cabinet had merely agreed to publish the report and nothing more, and that hardly anyone actually understood it. He told Montagu he was particularly annoyed at the pressure Montagu was exerting upon him. "In many respects," he wrote, "I have gone very far, but the sense of being perpetually pushed does not heighten one's zest in going further." Moreover, Curzon warned Montagu, "haste and confidence are liable in Indian undertakings to rude disappointment."[61]

Montagu's immediate reaction was to respond with another long and angry diatribe. Chamberlain calmed him and advised him not to press further, to let the matter rest for a while, to send a shorter letter and be less disputatious in his correspondence with Curzon. Montagu had still not learned to mask his emotions or to let time take its course. He was unable to control himself from pressing others on any issue of concern to him. And so, despite Chamberlain's prudent admonitions, he wrote a nine-page letter in response to Curzon, going over the same ground again and again, repeating all the arguments for the proposals in the report and continuing to press Curzon in precisely the way that Chamberlain had urged him to avoid. And yet, without Montagu's pressure, it is unlikely that the Montagu-Chelmsford report would have been published. With the Cabinet engrossed in the war and Curzon ambivalent and, at times, hostile, it could easily have been pigeonholed in committee.

In preparation for the publication of the report, Montagu had organized a propaganda committee within the Indian Office to begin to meet with the press to explain the report, answer questions and persuade the press of its value. On July 8, after the report was published, he analyzed for Chelmsford the press reaction, which, as was expected, broke along party lines. The Liberal press praised it, the Conservative press was hostile, and the anti-Semitic newspapers were particularly virulent.

Montagu was especially disturbed at the *Morning Post,* one of the most anti-Semitic of the newspapers, which attacked not only the report, but him personally. "I hate that sort of thing [Montagu wrote] and it wounds me more than I can say. It would appear that our proposals are going to suffer by my connection with them— encouraging, isn't it? [T]o one who has only one purpose in the world, to get something like them through."[62]

Montagu never overcame his shock and dismay at how anti-Semites always looked for ways to denigrate the efforts of Jews. But while he may have expected the Conservative and anti-Semitic press to object to the report, it is unlikely that he expected the criticism the report received in the Indian press. The response of the *Bombay Chronicle* was typical.[63] It directed its criticism against the concept underlying dyarchy, which the newspaper asserted was based on the notion that Indians were as yet unfit for self-government and thus must be accorded it only gradually.

Similarly, the leaders of the Indian Congress, which met in special session to discuss the report, found it "disappointing and unsatisfactory"[64] in that it gave them less than they expected and showed that Britain did not have enough faith in them to transfer more power to them. In spite of its criticism, the Indian Congress recognized that the report was "more in consonance with the announcement of August 20th" and decided to accept it in its broad outline and "to urge modifications and improvements" that were necessary "to make it a substantial first step towards responsible government in India, that is, both in the Central and Provincial Governments."[65] The All-India-Muslim League also adopted this view. Its response was a tribute to Montagu and his efforts to woo the Indian leadership. It was a testament, as well, to their faith and trust in him.

Indian Budget of 1918: Reforms Not Finance

On August 6, 1918, Montagu delivered the annual budget message to the House of Commons[66] for the first time since 1914. As in his last presentation, he used the occasion to deliver a speech on the problems of India, concentrating on the constitutional reforms contained in the Montagu-Chelmsford report. Montagu reviewed his arguments in support of the need for change in the government of India, urging the members of the House of Commons to read the report and to come forward with their ideas and criticism. He warned that, since the British have "steadily inculcated into some, at least, of the Indian people, love of liberty and self-government," they should not be surprised if the Indians now say: "You have taught us the value of self-government; set us on the road to obtain it."[67]

If you criticize this scheme because you are not willing to give responsible Government to India, then you are denying the principle embodied in the announcement of August last.

If you criticize it because you want to do it at once . . . then again you are denying the principle of this announcement.[68]

Montagu put the report in its historic perspective—it was not "a conspiracy" which he had "hatched," but a natural development from the days of Lords Morley and Minto, "quickened by the War" and by "the statements of our own ideals," pursued by Lord Hardinge, "taken up immediately by Lord Chelmsford" when he took

office and supported by his (Montagu's) predecessor Chamberlain.[69]
To accuse him (Montagu) of instigating this report and dragging an
"unwilling and unfortunate Viceroy" along is "a travesty of the
facts."[70] "For six months Lord Chelmsford and I worked together
. . . as colleagues. . . . We are together responsible for our proposal.
I could not drag him along if I tried; we both walked together side
by side."[71] Montagu ended with a plea for constitutional change—
not revolution or anarchy: "We cannot devote more than a century
to the tilling of the soil and then to refuse to plant the seed. . . . You
cannot . . . leave things as they are in the Government of India."[72]

Montagu also attacked the racial considerations that in the past
had prevented Indian soldiers from acquiring commissions in the
British Army, applauding the new policy that overturned the effects
of that discrimination:

It is said sometimes that it is an intolerable thing to risk British soldiers
being commanded by Indian officers. Those racial considerations are, I
hope, wholly out of date. When different principles have long since been
established for the civilian population, when Indians are eligible for the
highest positions in their own country in civilian life, when Indian officers
command large hospitals in Mesopotamia at this moment, it is idle to say
that racial considerations should continue to debar Indians from obtaining
his Majesty's commission and becoming officers in His Majesty's Army.
That controversy . . . extending through many years—is now, I hope, at
last settled with the approval of the overwhelming majority of people of
this country.[73]

Racial prejudice and discrimination were never far from Montagu's
thoughts.

Implementation of the Report

For Montagu, the remainder of 1918 was a time for consolidating all
the support he could for the report and for its implementation in
Parliament, in India and in the press of both countries. His major
antagonist in Parliament continued to be Curzon. Their first meeting to discuss Committees to implement the report, on July 11,
1918, at which Chamberlain was also present, began so badly that
Montagu had to leave the meeting in the middle.[74] He wrote to
Chamberlain the next day complaining of Curzon's ambivalence and

seeming unwillingness to confront him on the issues: "It seems to me to be a non-courageous attitude, the attitude of a man who intensely dislikes my proposals, daren't say so, and clings desperately to the noncommittal attitude of the Government as a means of avoiding indicating even to me what his real view on any proposal is."[75]

Montagu never sent the letter, since he received one first from Chamberlain in which he wrote that after Montagu left the meeting, Curzon had agreed to the appointment of two Indian Committees "on the understanding that in respect to the Committee on devolved and transferred subjects we are not committed to more than the principle, and in respect to that on franchises that we were not committed to the particular framework and constituency of the Councils in the Provinces and Government of India."[76] Chamberlain urged Montagu to accept the two Committees even with their narrow scope, not to press for "your India Office Committee or for the immediate Indianization of the services." He asked that Montagu try to be patient and conciliatory.[77]

Montagu replied immediately, thanking Chamberlain profusely. But, as was his wont, he could not leave well enough alone. He explained how much compromising he had already done to please Curzon, that he had tried to be loyal to Curzon, but that nothing he had done satisfied him.[78]

And so it went. The balance of the letters between Montagu, Curzon and Chamberlain during September, October and November of 1918 repeat this theme: Montagu pressed, Curzon objected, and Chamberlain stepped in and tried to keep peace. Montagu kept stating that he wanted to cooperate and compromise, but at the same time his letters continued to be argumentative and written in such a tone as to produce hostile replies. He was unable to leave a single point raised in a Curzon letter unanswered, and each reply turned into a major rebuttal. At the same time he constantly assured Curzon that he was most anxious to avoid controversy.[79]

Montagu also wrote regularly to Chelmsford, some days optimistically, to the effect that reforms were moving ahead, on other days dismayed at the snail's pace. During October, he reported to Chelmsford that the House of Lords debated the reforms for two days. "The Lords were very hostile."[80]

Before the meeting of the House of Lords, Montagu tried again to persuade Curzon to support the reforms. The farthest Curzon would go was to conceal his doubts, but he told Montagu not to expect him to express enthusiastic support. But, as was so often the case with Curzon, in the end he changed his opinion to the point of withdrawing his opposition to the appointment of a Joint Cabinet Committee to consider translating the report into law. Montagu was right in thinking this a tactical victory—and necessary to prevent the report from being debated and amended to death in both Houses of Parliament.

Even the preliminary debate on the report in the House of Lords had already, Montagu reported to the Prime Minister, depressed the opinion of the moderates in India who now "think their chances of getting anything through are small."[81] Montagu had every reason to be concerned about opinion in India: The mood among politically oriented Indians was turning increasingly sour; rioting and violence were on the rise. The more the Indians studied the reforms, the less they liked them.

Despite Indian discontent with the Montagu-Chelmsford report and the increase in unrest in India, Montagu forged ahead, determined to see the reforms become law. He continued to believe that if the reforms were adopted and implemented, there existed a chance for peace. Two committees under the Chairmanship of Lord Southborough were finally sent to India to define the electorate in areas where voting was involved and to settle the lines of division between the "reserved" and "transferred" subjects. Montagu's schedule for converting the reforms to legislation was proceeding on time.

As 1918 drew to a close, Montagu had much to be grateful for. His trip to India had been a success; he and Chelmsford, despite many difficulties, had agreed on a report, as had many segments of the Anglo-India government and the Indian leaders, albeit with varying degrees of skepticism. The report had been published by the Cabinet, Curzon's criticism had been restrained, and the two Committees necessary to elicit more information to introduce legislation were en route to India. Their recommendations, along with the report itself, would become the basis of an Indian reform bill that would be presented to a Joint Committee of Lords and Commons, chaired by Lord Selbourne. It would eventually be enacted into law at the end of 1919.

The War Ends

Nineteen eighteen also saw the end of World War I. The year had not started well for the Allies. The Germans had decided to make one final major effort on the Western front before the Americans arrived in large numbers. General Erich Von Ludendorff, in charge of German strategy, determined to break through Flanders and swing around behind the fortified trenches. He began his offensive on the Somme to strike at a point where British forces had been drawn away. His plan was to attack weak spots in the line by surprise.

Accordingly, on March 21, 1918, the Germans did exactly that. They attacked on the Somme at the weak spot where British and French forces were joined. It was a complete surprise, aided by an unusually heavy fog. Commander in Chief Sir Douglas Haig faced defeat on the field, as German troops and artillery moved ahead in large and threatening numbers. As an emergency measure, Lloyd George took over the War Office from Lord Derby. He found that eighty-eight thousand men were home on leave and another eighty thousand were stationed, for one reason or another, in Britain. Transports were rounded up and the number of men rushed to Haig increased from eight thousand to thirty thousand a day. It was the kind of crisis that Lloyd George handled best. He short-circuited the Foreign Office and appealed directly to President Wilson for immediate use of American troops on the battlefields. Wilson agreed, overruling General John Pershing.

The Allies were still retreating and falling apart. No combined strategy among the British, French and American commanders existed. An emergency conference was held, with Sir Alfred Milner representing Lloyd George. It was agreed on April 18, 1918, that General Ferdinand Foch should become Commander in Chief of the Allied Armies.

The Germans were within forty miles of Paris. The decisive thrust into Flanders, however, was still delayed. In the meantime, the Allied Armies grew stronger. A half million men were added to the British Army and, by the end of July, the Americans had sent more than a million men overseas. This did not stem the despair sweeping across Britain: The war still seemed endless. British military leadership, in fact, believed the war would not be won in 1918. Jan Smuts and Milner were pressing for a compromise; labor strikes, the problems in Ireland and the Maurice Affair (in which Lloyd George was accused of being responsible for the shortage of troops needed at the front)[82] were taking more and more of Lloyd George's time.

To compound the misery, on July 15 the Germans began another offensive against the French, one that would be their last. Ludendorff was already in Flanders, poised for the final blow, when the news arrived that the Germans had suffered a defeat in the south. Suddenly the initiative seemed to pass to the Allies and Foch issued his battle cry: "Attack—Attack—Attack."

Victory

On August 8, the British attacked in front of Amiens. Haig's strategy was to attack with a sharp jab, prevent an unwieldy salient from forming and then attack again at another point in the line. The Germans began falling back. Foch used the same technique repeatedly. The Germans continued to fall back, in one place after another. Meanwhile, at Foch's insistence, the Americans had been split up and were being used piecemeal to help stem the German attack wherever they were needed. As a result, Americans saw action at Aisne, Nayon-Montdidier and Champagne-Marne. In these engagements "American troops made a notable contribution to the ultimate defeat of Germany by checking their advance at the Marne and preventing the enemy from taking Paris. At Chateau-Thierry, they resisted one of the heaviest German assaults of the entire war."[83]

As a result of the "fighting qualities that the American soldiers showed, Foch agreed to Pershing's demand to have an independent American command created, and finally, in August, 1918, the First American Army was formed and given responsibility for holding part of the Allied line; by the end of the war the Americans were holding one quarter of the front, or more than the British."[84] The tide was now turning. After the German defeat at Champagne-Marne, the Allies intensified their counterattack. On September 28, the British and the Belgians attacked in the extreme north, and within the first day, Messines Ridge, which had been fought over in a week-long battle earlier that year, was recaptured. The German strength had now been broken. The entire Allied line was moving forward. German prisoners were being taken by the tens of thousands and their guns at the rate of a thousand a day. October was a month of advance and capture for the Allies.

Signs of Allied victory had in fact appeared earlier, when Commander in Chief Edmund Allenby had destroyed the Turkish Army at Megiddo, entering Damascus a week later. On October 3 the Ottoman Empire signed an armistice. Bulgaria surrendered too, and another door opened for the Allies to break into Central Europe. Ludendorff did not have enough men to stop them. On September 29, he asked the German government to seek an armistice; it refused. On October 4, German fortunes on the battlefields began to worsen and the German government approached President Wilson to begin to discuss peace. They thought they could receive a better deal from the Americans and thus could drive a wedge among the Allies. For three weeks, Wilson negotiated with the Germans alone. He was successful in persuading them to accept his Fourteen Points. He then intended to convince Britain, France and Italy. While these countries were indignant at Wilson for moving alone, Lloyd George "damped down the discontent."[85] He did not want to risk a breach with the United States and thought the Fourteen Points, including the idea of a League of Nations, should be accepted. Wilson's proposal was not significantly different from the ideas put forth by the Prime Ministers of Britain, France and Italy at a meeting held in London on Christmas Day 1916, and "as a magician with words himself," Lloyd George "was confident that the Fourteen Points could be made to mean everything or nothing according to the ingenuity of their interpreter."[86]

The Germans accepted the Fourteen Points on October 23. The Supreme War Council considered them on November 4. They were finally agreed upon, with certain reservations by the British and the French, reservations they resolved to raise at the Peace Conference. "In this roundabout way," A. J. P. Taylor has written, "the British and the Allies generally, having failed to lay down precisely their war aims against Germany, had their terms defined for them by the American President, a commitment which some of them later regretted."[87]

The terms of the armistice were also arrived at in a haphazard manner, when Wilson referred the Germans to the commanders in the field, as soon as they had accepted the Fourteen Points. Not all the Allied generals had the same idea of what the terms should be, and weeks passed in argument while soldiers continued to be killed. On November 3, the Austro-Hungarian high command finally signed an armistice with the Italians, and on November 7, a German armistice team passed through the Allied lines and was received by Foch and Admiral Rosslyn Erskine Wemyss, Supreme Naval Commander, in a railroad train in Rethondes, France. The terms of the armistice were handed to them. They returned to their lines to consider the terms, although they had no alternative. The Hohenzollern Reich was collapsing, William II had abdicated and fled to Holland and a new German Republic was proclaimed on November 9. At 5 A.M. on November 11, the German delegation signed the armistice, which went into effect at 11 A.M.

Peace

Sirens screamed in London and guns roared in tribute. People poured into the streets, singing and dancing with joy. Bewildered soldiers on the blood-soaked battlefronts sat silently or wandered about, dazed with relief. When he entered the House of Commons, Lloyd George received a standing ovation. It was his finest hour. His voice was close to breaking as he read the terms of the armistice. "This is no time for words. Our hearts are too full of gratitude, to which no tongue can give adequate expression."[88] The Speaker led the members of the House of Commons across the street to Westminster Abbey and on to St. Margaret's for a service of thanksgiving. Lloyd George walked with Bonar Law on one side and Asquith on the other. It was reported that at this moment, a watershed in world history, Asquith and Lloyd George talked quietly about their daughters.[89]

The Montagus were among the dignitaries at St. Margaret's, giving thanks with the Prime Minister at the announcement of peace. But, as for many of their friends, the day was as much a day of grief as of rejoicing; so many of their friends had died—Raymond Asquith, Billy Greenfell, George Vernon, Patrick Shaw, Edward Horner, Rupert Brooke—to mention only a few. More than half of the Coterie's thirty or forty members had been killed in the war. Many of the officers lost were close friends or relatives. They were among the 37,452 British officers killed in battle, a very large percentage of the young men of the upper class. And since this was a relatively small class to begin with, everyone had experienced either a death in the immediate family or in that of a friend or relative.

Duff Cooper's reaction to the armistice could have been written by Venetia or Montagu:

It was past eleven o'clock when we reached Liverpool Street, the armistice had been signed and the town was in an uproar. As we drove from the station I felt unable to take part in their enthusiasm. This was the moment to which I had looked forward for four years, and now that it had arrived I was overcome by melancholy. Amid the dancing, the cheering, the waving of flags, I could think only of my friends who were dead.[90]

"One will have to look at long vistas again . . . and one will at last recognize," Lady Cynthia Asquith reflected, "that the dead are not only dead for the duration."[91]

Montagu was so busy with his political responsibilities and with the prospect of starting a new election campaign that his usual melancholy and preoccupation with death, which the end of the war invoked, did not last long. Two weeks after the armistice was signed, he wrote to Ronaldshay in India:

The end of the war has come quicker than any of us dared to expect, and the acceptance of the Armistice terms—onerous as they are—is a measure of the enemies' collapse. The Germans managed to keep their shop windows well dressed till the last moment, and their troops fought . . . with an obstinacy which hardly justified one anticipating such an immediate breakdown. But there was nothing behind, and we are assured that had the war continued a few days more there would have been a German disaster on a scale for which history affords no parallel.

The new German government will have immense difficulty in holding the country together, but they seem to be setting about their work with characteristic Teuton thoroughness, and with the spectre of Bolshevism and all its horrors on their borders, the German people may be able to withstand that menace to society.[92]

To Montagu, the problem was now "the spectre of Bolshevism." There was no way he could know that the Germans would fight Bolshevism with Nazism and the "Teuton thoroughness" he admired would be responsible for the death of six million Jews. His letter continued:

You can imagine the feeling of relief that spread over London as soon as news of the Armistice was known. The offices were closed and crowds paraded the streets clambering on the buses, cabs, and any kind of vehicle that was handy. Speaking generally, people behaved themselves well, but there were some unfortunate incidents leading to damage, mainly, I understand, due to the exuberance of Australian troops. As I write spirits have somewhat abated, and we are now engaged on the formidable task of restoring normal conditions of life. In some ways this is even harder than waging war.

I am off to Cambridge to start my Election Campaign. I dislike it intensely, and it will be a great relief to me when it is over.[93]

The Coupon Election

The 1918 election would be very different for Montagu. During November, Lloyd George and Bonar Law had decided to maintain the Coalition and hold a General Election as soon as the war ended. On November 5, George V agreed that Parliament should be dissolved. It had exceeded its statutory term by three years. The electorate had more than doubled; nearly all men and a majority of women now had the vote and the "government needed popular endorsement before they negotiated the peace settlement."[94]

Lloyd George was eager to keep the Coalition. He urged Labour to remain; he offered to make Asquith Lord Chancellor and to include at least two Liberal ministers. Both refused. Labour was determined to become a second party with socialism as the core of its program.[95] The Liberal Party was in an even more difficult position. Throughout the war, Liberal Party members believed that the truce would be continued and that in the Coalition government with the Labour Party they would play an important part in the postwar Parliament. They had urged Lloyd George early in November to run in alliance with Asquith and the Liberals, not with Bonar Law. Lloyd George had been noncommittal. All evidence seemed to point to the conclusion that he had already made a deal with Bonar Law and the Conservatives, probably in the belief that the mood of the country augured well for a Conservative victory. Those "favored" Liberals—the 150 who pledged to support the Coalition government—were spared the risk of defeat by Conservatives: No Conservatives ran against them. Asquith claimed that "the coupon," as he called it, was "a device for slaughtering the Independent Liberal Party"[96] and punishing those who voted against Lloyd George in the Maurice debate.

It was a bitter campaign. Montagu had to decide whether he would remain in the Coalition with Lloyd George. If he took this course, the breach with Asquith and the Liberal Party would be complete. He believed the old Liberal Party and Asquith were politically dead. If the principles in which he believed were going to be carried forward by Lloyd George, he could join his ranks comfortably.

At a meeting with Lloyd George on November 6,[97] to which Lloyd George invited not only Montagu but also Winston Churchill, Montagu raised the matter of "principles and program" directly. He discussed Home Rule, free trade, finance and taxation. Lloyd George's responses on all these issues satisfied Montagu, who was nonetheless still concerned with how Lloyd George could carry out a Liberal program without the Liberals or Asquith. In a note for his files, on November 6, 1918, he wrote:

My own perplexities are increased. There is no doubt whatever in my mind that a change of Prime Minister at this moment would be fatal. . . . He [Lloyd George] appears before us as responsible for all the great achievements of the war. . . . He has dominated the Versailles Council . . . we must have the same man there. On the other hand, I do not see now, after Asquith's unfortunate declaration of war [against the Lloyd George government], how he (Lloyd George) is likely to maintain a Liberal policy. . . . On the other hand, if he can stick to his policy as he announced it at lunch yesterday, I have no quarrel with him at all.[98]

In another note, Montagu recorded that he had had dinner with Lloyd George, Winston Churchill, and others and that Lloyd George took the position that "there would be no difficulty at all with the Conservatives about a very advanced programme, Housing, Land, something far better than had ever been done before in this country, transportation and so forth."[99] They also talked about India, and Lloyd George said he would help Montagu in advancing his reforms. This prompted Montagu to write to Chelmsford:

The Prime Minister [Lloyd George] yesterday and the day before gave before witnesses explicit assurances that, whatever happened, he was going on with the intention of carrying out our Reform policy. This is important because it will qualify and effect decisions which I have got to take during the next few hours. You may be sure that I will not lightly abandon this prospect of bringing our ship to harbour. On the other hand, for it I may be called upon to make sacrifices greater than I can make. Asquith has hoisted a party flag and the old Liberal Party in which I was brought up, in which I thoroughly believed, appears to me to be dead. It looks as if I shall become a member of a so-called Coalition which consists of the whole Conservative Party, a few Liberal members disowned by their organization, and a few Labour members repudiated by the Labour that they represent. This doesn't matter, but Liberal principles will, thank goodness, survive. If the differences remain, as they seem to me to be now, those of persons, my course is clear. If they become differences of principle, it remains for me to decide how many I can temporarily abandon or still in order to support a Government, which I think ought to remain in charge of our destinies and in order to get an Indian bill through. The perplexities will have been solved before this letter reaches you.[100]

There is no doubt that Montagu's desire to get his India Reform Act passed was a major motivation for staying with the Lloyd George Coalition. But there were other reasons: He believed that Lloyd George was very important to the coming peace negotiations and that he was in the best position to carry forward Liberal policies on social and economic issues. He believed, too, that Lloyd George and his new Coalition would win.

Montagu worked hard on this election campaign. A brief note in his files, dated December 16, 1918, written after the election, recorded that his election district (now consolidated into Cambridgeshire) consisted of 130 parishes, an area of 800 square miles, mostly rural and agricultural, without a single town. The farmers in the area continued to be small; there were no large landholders. His adversary was an ex-farmer, a member of the Labour Party; no Conservatives ran. As he had in the past, he visited and spoke in nearly every parish. His diligence paid off once more. He won by a plurality of nine thousand votes, which greatly pleased him.

Lloyd George won a stunning victory. Asquithian Liberals won only 26 seats; Labour won 5 and the Coalition 474 (338 Conservatives and 136 Liberals).

Asquith Defeated

Asquith lost by some two thousand votes, a crippling blow. Even without a "coupon" against him, his constituency of thirty-two years refused him their support. He was left with a crumbling party and no power. He had hoped to play a part at the Peace Conference, but Lloyd George had made it clear that if he wanted to go to Paris, he had to join the Coalition government. If he refused, he would have no part in the peace talks. Asquith refused. He thus lost not only his seat in Parliament but also any opportunity to contribute to the peace process.

Many Englishmen felt a sense of shock and shame at Asquith's defeat, and many wrote to him expressing their profound sadness. Some people believed that women, whose suffrage he had opposed for many years, had made the difference. But it is more likely that after thirty-two years his constituents wanted a change, someone younger and more dynamic. Posters saying "Asquith nearly lost you the War. Are you going to let him spoil the peace?" also expressed a general dissatisfaction with the fallen hero. His friends felt differently. Hankey wrote to Asquith, "When times are less breathless and the public perspective is restored, the people will learn . . . the tremendous burden you carried through the first half of the War, and that it was you who saved the Empire from absolute disaster."[101] And Montagu wrote:

I mourn greatly the disappearance of old political friends from the House of Commons. They had much ability, which can ill be spared, and a modus vivendi with them would have immeasurably strengthened the Government. Charles Robert's disappearance is deplorable from the Indian point of view, while, from an Imperial and International point of view, the imposing figure, the sterling reputation, the dispassionate judgement, the concise speech of Mr. Asquith is something that we can ill do without.[102]

This would be the first term in his political career that Montagu would serve in Parliament without Asquith.

25

The Marriage, 1917–1918

Venetia, having essentially married him [Edwin] "for her days not her nights" was now . . . tortured by real repugnance and . . . Edwin appeared plunged in doom.

Diana Cooper in conversation with Cynthia Asquith, June 1918

The novelty and excitement of redecorating her London home and buying and renovating their Norfolk country home, Breccles, kept Venetia relatively content during their first two years of marriage, but by 1917 she had become restless and bored with Montagu. Increasingly, her weekends and attendance at dinner parties were without him (even before his trip to India), and her letters to him while he was in India often recounted her emotional involvements with other men.

Alan Parsons, who accompanied Montagu on his trip, told to Diana Cooper on his return:

Venetia's letters were so unbelievably dreadful that no one an inch less besotted with love than Edwin could have tolerated them. Beginning always with the warm gambit of "darling I wrote you a frightfully good letter, but have already lost it, so must write another one, a bad one. Last night I dined with . . ." then follows a long, long succession of dinners and their guests, without even a peroration of love; nothing in fact that Edwin could not give Alan to read.[1]

In the seven of Venetia's letters to Montagu that survive (from January through March 1918), Venetia, as she had in the past, merely recited her daily schedule. Occasionally, she reported on the prog-

484

ress Lutyens, the great architect who helped to design New Delhi, was making on the renovations and restoration of Breccles, on the death of dear friends, on items she had bought for the house, gifts Montagu had sent her, or her winnings at cards. Like most of her earlier letters, they contained nothing intimate, no expressions of love or concern for him, none of the jottings of a caring or loving wife. The only sign of some affection was in a salutation she occasionally used, "My darling Ted," a nickname which she and some of her friends had given him.[2]

She had no hesitation in telling Montagu that she might "go to the Wharf (Asquith's home) for Easter"[3] and had "a latest passion, Sidney Herbert . . . tho this is rather on the wane as I have not seen him from Monday and his leave is up on Saturday. I have to tell you all about my vagaries in the emotional realm, as if I didn't I'm sure some one else would and I'd rather disarm suspicion by being open about it."[4] She reported of the "gay life" she had been leading:

. . . owing to Sidney Herbert's leave . . . balls, 2 parties . . . I'm sure you would like him, he has such marvelously high spirits, enjoys himself much . . . has natural fundamental sweetness which makes him very kind. I like him very much, more than any of the other young men, tho I'm bound to confess that during these months I've come around to Michael (Sidney's brother) very much. But I think Sidney has really far more independence of character than he has, the way he has stuck to poor old Sybil is a very fair indication.[5]

In a letter of March 7, 1918, she wrote of a lunch with Eric—Eric Ednam, later the third Earl of Dudley, a dear friend of Venetia, Diana and Duff. Eric, according to the Duchess of Marlborough in her autobiography *Laughter on a Cloud,* would later have a serious affair with Venetia.[6]

Montagu's letters to Venetia from India were quite different: They continued to reflect the intensity of his feelings. They were filled with longing and love. The salutations range from "my own perfect darling"[7] to "my own beloved and most perfect."[8] He would count the days until he would be home. "Darling mine," he wrote:

do take care of yourself. I long every moment for you and all you mean to me but if you could come to me here, I should never I think want to leave

India. So take care of yourself who are all the world to me and I know that I am counting the days, the minutes till I can get back to you.[9]

And again:

Many many kisses. I wonder if there has ever been so marvelous a marriage as ours is *to me*—It is *[sic]* brought into my life something I could never have imagined in my wildest dreams—something which is everything— which unites passion, comradeship, friendship, understanding gratitude love—all of which grow—it produces ecstasy to think of—oh I wish you were here and your picture was not so sad.

Near the end of the trip he wrote, "I kiss you across the bloody seas —but so passionately and lovingly that you must feel it."[10] And on April 1, 1918: "I'm not going to write any more—if things go well we shall be together when you read this—if we're not, well I've never been without a presentiment and you will know that my last thoughts were of Venetia—my own, my love who has been and is *all* the world to me."[11]

When Montagu returned, he found that absence had not made Venetia's heart grow fonder. On the contrary, he found her cold and unresponsive. By June 1918, just two months after Montagu's return, Cynthia Asquith wrote of a conversation she had had with Diana Cooper, who now took a gloomy view of the Montagu marriage, "opining that Venetia—having essentially 'married him [Edwin] for her days not her nights'—was now (after her interval of grass widowhood) tortured by real repugnance and that Edwin appeared plunged in gloom."[12] (A grass widow is one whose husband is alive but has been absent from his wife.) Other friends also thought that the marriage was nearing its end and that there was little they could do. Katharine Asquith, for example, wrote: "It is no use our trying to put the Montagus right, as they don't exist at all."[13]

According to gossip, moreover, Venetia was having an affair with Sir Matthew ("Scatters") Wilson,[14] whom she had known for several years. As early as 1914, Diana Cooper's letters noted that the Montagus, Duff and Diana and Scatters were spending considerable time together. In 1917, especially when Montagu was in India, Scatters was often seen in Venetia's company and at dinners at her home.

Wilson had a reputation as a flirt. For three years, from 1916 until

1919, he carried on a love affair with Curzon's second wife, Gracie, while both were married—a situation which, it was reported, "must have wounded Curzon's pride intolerably."[15] Cynthia Asquith described him as a "funny ebullient bounder, with his blue eyes and hoarse whisper,"[16] and wrote that he:

Played bridge—assisted by Venetia, mercifully I liked Scatters: he and Barbara drove me home. Either the scandal as to him and Venetia is—as I believe—purely legendary, or he is the most consummate misleader, because we discussed Venetia in the taxi and he diagnosed her as a jolly "Long-haired chum" not "out for a fling"—and quite out of the siren class and argued the point with Barbara who disagreed. But I can't understand Venetia's strange burst of beauty.[17]

Diana Cooper found Scatters: "a dashing soldier." He was a "baronet from Yorkshire via India . . . [who] had married an elder sister of the beautiful Laura Lister, by now Lady Lovat. I had thought as a child he was funnier than any of the clowns and he could still keep the table of all ages in a roar."[18]

While it is an unanswered question whether Venetia and Scatters were lovers, there seems no doubt that by July 1918, three months after Montagu's return from India, she was not sleeping with her husband. Duff, in a commonsensical and explicit letter to Diana, suggested that even if Venetia had no interest in Montagu, she should "not be an ass," let him have sex with her and "simulate excitement if necessary." Duff wrote:

Your interview with Edwin is sad. I think their troubles are unworthy of them both. If Edwin's only trouble is Venetia's lack of interest in politics tell him not to be an ass—if it is rather her lack of interest in him tell her not to be an ass but if necessary to simulate.[19]

Duff also wrote of Montagu's concern with the debts he and Venetia were accumulating. "If it is debt tell them both not to be bloody fools but to sell Breccles which they need never have bought."[20] Duff could not understand how "a pair so worldly wise and so money wise starting married life two years ago in affluence can *really* now be in financial difficulties. We must remember how Edwin invariably magnifies misfortune and foresees disaster."[21] But Montagu was not exaggerating. Venetia was spending money on a scale that surpassed even his inheritance.

The renovations and redecoration of 24 Queen Anne's Gate and Breccles, the beautiful clothes Venetia was buying, the ornate furniture and art work, the travel and the elaborate dinners kept Montagu in constant debt. Venetia was especially attracted to Oriental furniture and clothing. Diana Cooper wrote that at one party, "V. was dressed like an elephant in 'howdahs' and sham Eastern spoils."[22]

It was not only Venetia who was extravagant. Montagu, too, loved food, entertaining, good wines and gambling. Margot Asquith was not far from the mark when she wrote in one of her more acerbic letters, "If Mr. Montagu would eat less, lower his gambling stakes, and drink paraffin, he would be a much richer man."[23] And it was Montagu, as much or more so than Venetia, who was responsible for the purchase of Breccles Hall, an estate in Attleborough, Norfolk, about a hundred miles from London.

Breccles Hall had been built in the tenth century. During Queen Elizabeth's reign it became a refuge for Jesuits. After passing through many hands, it had fallen into total decay by the late nineteenth century. It became a working farm, but the buildings continued to be neglected. At the end of the nineteenth century, Charles Bateman Hanbury bought Breccles and with the architect Detmar Blow began reconstruction, using antique pink brick for the exterior to match the original color and design and making no changes that were not historically authentic. At the front of the house, partitions that had not been part of the original were removed to permit the reconstruction of a great hall eighty-seven feet long. The only change Hanbury and Blow made was to remove old pictures of former owners from the great hall and replace them with a large mural of Bacchus astride a beer barrel, painted by Rex Whistler shortly before he was killed in World War I. When the Montagus bought Breccles in 1916 the renovations Hanbury had begun were only partially completed and most of the house was still in bad shape.

Montagu adored Breccles. He had always dreamed of having a country home and now at least this one dream had come true. It was he who had hired Edwin Lutyens to supervise the Breccles restoration and renovation, although Lutyens was one of the most expensive architects in England. It was a monumental and costly job supervised by Venetia, entailing new bathrooms, a new kitchen, structural changes, painting, new rugs, draperies, furniture and scores of decorative additions inside and out.

When Montagu and Venetia first bought Breccles, they fell in love not only with the house but also with the natural beauty surrounding it: trees and ponds, a moat, lush bushes and wild flowers that had the feel of wilderness and seclusion, a sense of "a distant fen or mere." Diana Cooper wrote:

So beautiful and so hot . . . I see at last the charm of Norfolk. It's so demoralized. The fields are half tilled only, so that poppies and wild blue torches fight with the corn and some acres are given up to them. It is thinly populated because Norfolkians can't or won't propagate, so that the birds have it their own way and reign unmolested, except by love and in gratitude even the high building species in this country nest on the ground, presumably out of consideration for the inhabitants.[24]

There were many species of birds in the area, which made it especially exciting for Montagu: lapwings, plovers, snipe, redshank and duck. There also were forty different kinds of butterflies. Montagu also leased a piece of wild land a few miles from Breccles called Hickling Broad, which he converted into a bird sanctuary, bringing in vast numbers of foreign species of ducks and other birds, which he never tired of watching. Montagu was also an enthusiastic gardener, adding to the shrubbery, planting new trees and flowers and building small bridges over the streams and the moat.

Cost did not deter him. He never regretted a penny he invested in Breccles. Unfortunately, whatever problems he and Venetia had were not to be solved by the peace and beauty of Breccles. Unable to face time alone with Montagu, Venetia used every available weekend at Breccles for a house party—some wilder than others, but all geared to fun and frolic. Neither war nor a distasteful marriage had changed the one goal in her life.

The house at Breccles was rough and rustic, described by Diana Cooper as "impossible" with moths, few lamps, "creakings and belfry smells." She quoted Birrell as saying: " 'This is a house for the young' as his head cracked on a beam, showering him with wormwood dust." But, Diana continued, "with all its inconveniences, it had the advantage of transfiguring Edwin"[25] who was never so happy as when he was relaxing and entertaining there.

Generally, weekends consisted of hiking, good talk, pranks, bridge and chess, at which Venetia was a master. Sometimes Montagu or his guests would discuss books or read poems or stories aloud.

Extramarital sex was always one of the major pastimes at these parties. Mrs. Patrick Campbell, one of the "most outspoken women in polite society," succinctly expressed the group's attitude: "It doesn't matter what you do in the bedroom as long as you don't do it in the street and frighten the horses."[26] Breccles was a fine place "to do it"; its isolation and the free and easy spirit that Venetia projected gave it a special feeling of escape, not only from convention but from the horrors of the war. It was, as Diana and Duff Cooper often called it, "the ultimate escape."

Diana spent nearly the entire month of August 1918 at Breccles between her rounds of service at Rutland Hospital. This gave her every opportunity to see Montagu and Venetia intimately, and her portrait of them is a sad one. While both tried to lose their unhappiness in the groups of friends with which they surrounded themselves, Diana could still see it. As she wrote to Duff on August 9, 1918, Montagu was becoming increasingly moody and in despair had made advances to her. She rejected him gently and suggested to Viola Tree that she sleep with him, since Montagu seemed so desperate:

Edwin insists on staying out till 10:30 p.m. which makes the servants bad-tempered and really now it's a mute point which is the most moodily unreliable, he or his wife. Tonight I played chess with Edwin and got left behind with him, he drew me on the sofa and said, "Must you go to bed? or will you stay and love me a little—" "I must go to bed, but I always love you." "Not in the way I want though." Silence and an almost imperceptible drag away on my part. "Go to bed then"—and he sprang up, walked sharply to his room and banged the door. *I think Venetia refuses him and he is half mad with desires. Poor baboon. I've told Viola she must sacrifice herself.*[27] (emphasis added)

Duff was furious, answering Diana at once:

A very slow letter came from you today. . . . It told me of Edwin's overtures which made me shudder a little. And it shocked me that you should tell Viola to sacrifice herself. Damn the man—he's got a wife and if he can't tame her let him pay a mistress. Don't let's be too tolerant of silly weakness in our friends.[28]

But Diana continued to be forgiving, increasingly worried, and, ultimately, "terrified" at what was happening to the Montagu marriage. She wrote on August 16, 1918:

The train [to Breccles] took two hours longer than scheduled on account of most of the U.S. Army, and ill mannered curs they are, jeering and booing and even insulting us as we passed their windows. The hundred German prisoners drawn up further on I found far decenter. The relationship of the Monts [Montagus] is worse daily—he had preceded us and was out shooting when we arrived, and returning in the middle of dinner beaming and keen with an evening walk and many kills, he kissed my hands first then Viola's fervently and in fond anticipation of Venetia's at last, but smilelessly she did not let it meet his lips and with an irritated gesture asked a gruff question about a bailiff. *I am not magnifying, and I am terrified.*[29] (emphasis added)

The fall of 1918 saw no change in the situation and Diana had every reason to be upset. But the prospect of peace and Montagu's success with the India Reform Act made life look more cheerful for the Montagus, despite their personal problems. They opened Breccles for Duff's leave in October and it was there that they, with Diana and Duff, heard of the Kaiser's abdication. On November 11 all domestic discord was put aside as they joined the members of Parliament at St. Margaret's with the Prime Minister, grateful for peace, but keenly aware that such peace was sorely lacking in their lives.

26

The Best and Worst of Times, 1919

The treaty will be a disaster. I do not see how as Secretary of State for India, I can sign it.

Montagu to Lloyd George on the Turkish Treaty, Nov. 1919

The year 1919 was both the best and the worst of times for Edwin Montagu. The year began in a glow of expectation and exhilaration; it ended in darkness and despair. In between, Montagu managed to have one of the most productive years of his life.

Montagu had been reappointed Secretary of State for India, as Lloyd George had promised, immediately after the December election. On January 9, 1919, he wrote an effusive letter to the Prime Minister, expressing appreciation not only for his reappointment but for Lloyd George's having agreed that the King would mention the proposed India reforms in his speech opening the new Parliament.[1] In a letter to Chelmsford on January 10, Montagu exclaimed with obvious delight that "the Prime Minister in offering me the post of Secretary of State for India . . . agreed to include a promise of legislation in the King's speech contingently upon the Reforms Committees having finished their work. . . . So I think we can say from the point of view of the Government that our chances are rosy, but one has yet to see what our chances are from the point of view of the Houses of Parliament."[2] While India was the consuming passion of Montagu's life, it was not, however, a major agenda item for Lloyd George, whose immediate concern was negotiating a peace settlement and whose attention was taken up by putting together the delegation to represent the British Empire at the Peace Conference, scheduled to open in Paris on January 18.

India at the Peace Conference

The British Empire delegation consisted of fourteen representatives: Lloyd George and Bonar Law, as leaders of the Coalition, Barnes (representing Labour), Balfour as Foreign Secretary, one Dominion Prime Minister (not always the same), as well as independent representation for Australia, Canada, South Africa, India and New Zealand. India was to be represented by Montagu, who would be accompanied by two additional representatives chosen by the Viceroy, the Maharajah of Bikaner, from one of the largest of the Rajput States, and Satiandra P. Sinha, a moderate in the Indian government. Both were dear friends of Montagu. Montagu was viewed as the senior spokesman, with the power to sign any treaty or document affecting India.[3]

The fact that India was not a Dominion led some members of the Cabinet to object to India's having the same representation as the Dominions. But Montagu persisted. The generous and important role that India played during the war, he reminded his colleagues, entitled her to the same status at the Peace Conference as the Dominions. After much bickering, he won.

Early in January 1919, Montagu achieved another first: He was successful in having Sinha appointed as Under Secretary of State for India. No Indian had ever held as high a position in the British government. He also received a promise from the King and from Lloyd George that Sinha would be presented for the peerage. This was done in 1919, at which time Lord Sinha became the first Indian peer. "It will be a fine thing for India and for our position vis-a-vis India in such countries as America to have the Indian Government defended in Parliament by an Indian," Montagu happily wrote Chelmsford on January 10. "It will be a fine thing for Lord Sydenham and all those who wish to indulge in racial obloquy to have to do it in the presence of an Indian, and it will give the best earnest it is possible to give of the reality of our intentions with regard to the future status of India."[4]

In his next letter to Chelmsford, he wrote that he wondered "whether you ever have the time to reflect upon the profound, irretraceable changes that have been made in the Constitution of the British Empire during the last few months?" He was elated that the Prime Minister invited the Dominions to become members of the

Imperial War Cabinet, that the Secretary of State for India had been appointed a member of the Imperial War Cabinet, and that the Dominions and the Indian representatives were invited to accompany the Prime Minister to Paris. "An attempt is made to invite only our nominees, but I claim they cannot represent you without me and this claim is granted."[5]

He believed that all of these changes would in time lead to India's acceptance as a self-governing Dominion, despite the fears expressed by many political leaders and ex-proconsuls, who were:

holding up their hands with horror at any substantial efforts toward self-government, and at the same time we have gone . . . into a series of decisions which put India so far as International affairs are concerned on a basis wholly inconsistent with the position of a subordinate country. Her status has soared far more rapidly than could have been accomplished by any of our reforms, and this trend is strengthened by the Prime Minister's appointment to a parliamentary position of Lord Sinha.[6]

The British Delegation Arrives in Paris

The British delegation at the Peace Conference was supported by a staff estimated between three hundred and six hundred, a phalanx of experts, advisors and secretaries who descended upon Paris. The principals were housed at the Majestic Hotel, using the Hotel Astoria as office space. While the panoply that accompanied the British delegation was impressive, its role was, in fact, ambiguous and often irrelevant. Lloyd George, with his usual dictatorial style, represented Great Britain at the meetings of the so-called Big Four— Lloyd George, Georges Clemenceau of France, Woodrow Wilson of the United States and Vittorio Orlando of Italy. All the major decisions were made by this group, with the really difficult questions decided upon by Lloyd George and Clemenceau, although Wilson's Fourteen Points were often used as a framework to guide the discussions.

Clemenceau's goal was to cripple Germany territorially, militarily and financially; Orlando's interests were to get as much as he could for Italy. Wilson was viewed as an enigma—a scholar who was impressed with the formulas he framed alone in his study but which often turned out to be inapplicable to the real world. However, he was also seen as a man genuinely interested in world peace, and he represented a country that was not interested in territorial gains.

Lloyd George was difficult to read. No one trusted him and no one was sure of the positions he would take. The French thought he was pro-German; the Italians thought he was pro-Serbian; the Serbians, pro-Italian. They may all have been correct. His positions changed daily, depending on political pressures.

Montagu arrived in Paris with the British delegation on January 11 and stayed at the Majestic Hotel. He remained until the middle of February when he had to return home to begin to shepherd the India Reform Act through Parliament. For the rest of the year he shuttled back and forth between London and Paris to represent Indian opinion on issues involving the Peace Treaty, especially those concerned with Turkey and the Sultan, and to chair the British Finance Committee and represent that Committee on the Inter-Allied Finance Committee.

On January 20, 1919, the British delegation came to an agreement on a major procedural point on which Montagu would rely in his arguments with the Prime Minister, Balfour and Curzon. The delegation agreed that the Dominions and India could submit memoranda to the Inter-Allied Conference, expressing their opinions separately from positions taken by the British delegation, even though the Dominions and India took part in the deliberations which led to the decisions adopted by the delegation.[7] Montagu always read this to mean that if he and the Indian delegation took a position on the Turkish peace terms, they could submit it to the Inter-Allied Conference, after it was discussed by the British delegation, even if it differed from the position of the British delegation. He would soon learn that this interpretation was not acceptable to the Prime Minister, who read the document differently. He believed that only the position of the British delegation should be presented to the Inter-Allied Conference.

The first two months of the Conference were spent preparing preliminary papers, outlining recommendations and trying to develop machinery to move the Conference forward. In spite of the brainpower assembled and the inordinate manpower used to develop guidelines and procedures, the Conference was slow and disorderly, sometimes verging on chaos and often appearing as though it might break down completely. But Great Britain and France pushed assiduously ahead and, with Wilson's help, kept the Conference on a respectable timetable.

Documents Drafted for the Peace Conference

One of the first documents that Montagu helped prepare was distributed in early January 1919 to the British peace delegation and was entitled "The Ottoman Empire and Financial Conditions of Peace."[8] The recommendations in this memorandum reflect Montagu's general attitude to questions relating to the Peace Treaty. He believed in moderation, a tough but just and reasonable peace. Anything that would produce economic or social upheaval would in the long run push the enemy into the hands of the Bolsheviks and would not be in the long-term interests of the Allied cause. In this memorandum on Turkey, Montagu's approach, which he took in all the ensuing debates, reflected this. His approach was simple: With Turkey close to bankruptcy, the Allies must prevent her becoming economically destitute. They must alleviate her stress and reestablish her credit; tight control of her finances by the Allies was essential. A Council of Debt and a Currency Board should be created by the Allies, and European financial advisors brought in. Such provisions, Montagu urged, should be incorporated into the Peace Treaty. A treaty based on revenge, he believed, could not last; while it would satisfy the passions of some countries at the peace table in 1919, it would not provide for long-range security for Britain or for the rest of Europe.

For the same reasons, Montagu was also opposed to military action against the Bolshevists, believing that an economically strong Europe, not military action, was the best way to defeat Communism. "It seems to me there are two kinds of Bolshevism," he wrote to Lloyd George on February 14, 1919:

There is first and foremost the Russian Bolshevist Government, supported by a military organization, . . . formidable in strength . . . if you want to deal with it, there is only one way . . . namely to declare war on it and beat it. This is a formidable undertaking, costing men, which no country has to spare, and money, at a time when we want every penny. If you declare war . . . you must be prepared . . . to put all your strength into the war.

Montagu disparaged the idea that war and money and matériel could defeat the Bolshevists. "I maintain," he said, "that there are not in sight forces in Russia . . . able to profit by the munitions and money we send them." The second kind of Bolshevism, Montagu wrote, "is not the Bolshevism of the Russian Government, but the Bolshevism, the 'smash everythingism' to hell with the existing order of things . . . which arises out of overstrain and economic conditions." He believed that the best way to fight Bolshevism was, therefore, not by military means, "which enforces the circumstances which promote international or spontaneous Bolshevism," but by "spending our money on ourselves" and strengthening Britain's economy.[9]

In this position he was adamantly opposed by Winston Churchill who was the Secretary of War in the new government, and supported war against the Bolshevists and was now the Bolshevists' "most vehement British foe."[10] Lloyd George was somewhere in the middle, neither happy with Churchill's pro-war stance, nor ready to stop all aid to the anti-Red forces. For the present, Lloyd George was content to put Russia on the back burner and concentrate on the negotiations at Versailles.

The Peace Treaty with Turkey

While Montagu was interested in every aspect of the Peace Conference, he believed that his main responsibility was to make certain that the treaty Great Britain ultimately signed with Turkey did not upset the Muslims in India and thus exacerbate Anglo-Indian tensions. He stated his views early in the peace process, beginning in January 1919, and repeated them in hundreds of letters and memoranda written between 1919 and his forced resignation in 1922. Several of his early memoranda set the tone of the struggle that later ensued between Montagu and his opponents.

"We should observe that from the Indian point of view," Montagu wrote in January 1919, a treaty with Turkey, "should not be a peace of destruction and that there should be nothing in the peace terms demanded of an enemy who was only a victim of German machinations and designs, which would prevent the restoration of friendly relations after retribution has been exacted."[11] Turkey was important to India because Turkey was Muslim. The Sultan was not only the secular leader but also the Khalif, the religious leader. Hedjaz was a holy place and should not be removed from the custody of the Khalif. Countries that were Muslim before the war should remain so afterward, "in the interests of nationality and in accordance with the principle of self-determination." Areas that were Turkish should remain Turkish. This should not apply to Armenia where the Armenian population had been reduced by Turkish massacres. Montagu warned that one should not interfere with sovereignty.

Montagu reminded those preparing the peace treaty that the Muhammadans in India were loyal to Great Britain and the Allies during the war and were largely responsible for the military victory over Turkey:

We would remind the Prime Minister that throughout the war, despite every temptation the Mohammedans remained steadfastly loyal and Mohammedan troops fought for us. Over a million Indian troops were raised. The defeat of Turkey was mainly brought about by Indian troops and Indian resources. We therefore claim the voice which you have been good enough to give us in the settlement of this question.[12]

"The non-Moslem Indians," Montagu pointed out, were in sympathy with "their Mussluman fellow subjects." This was "evidenced by the fact that in the recent riots in India, very largely caused by Moslem unrest, for the first time in the history of India, the Mosques were thrown open to Hindus and Hindu orators were asked to speak to the people from the pulpits never before occupied by non-Moslems. . . . This is a serious matter." Montagu urged that Syria, Arabia and Mesopotamia should remain Muslim; that Palestine, which "for over one thousand four hundred years has been Mohammedan should not be given over to a non-Mohammedan government; and the Allies should declare that they have no desire to interfere with the Khalifite who is the spiritual leader."

Supplementing this memorandum, Montagu wrote another arguing that Turkey should "remain in possession of all those territories in Asia Minor and in Thrace which are predominantly Turk in race, with its capital at Constantinople. *This was the Prime Minister's statement in January 1919.*"[13] Montagu suggested that an International Commission be established to administer Constantinople and the Straits "under the nominal sovereignty of the Sultan." This would not preclude the mandate that "the Turkish government . . . accept European advisors in all departments of its government." Mesopotamia, Arabia, Syria, Palestine and Armenia should be separated from the Turkish Empire. Arabia should become independent; Palestine and Mesopotamia should be put under British mandate; France should have a mandate over Syria and the United States should have a mandate over Armenia.

If these recommendations were acceptable, plebiscites should be held. If Adrianople were removed from Turkish sovereignty, a promise should be given that all the Holy Places must be under Muhammadan guardianship. The memorandum had a note to remind Lloyd George: "This was agreed by you at a Breakfast some weeks ago and recorded by Sir Maurice Hankey."[14]

Montagu also wrote a testy letter to Curzon taking issue with his position on Turkey and clearly indicating that he was prepared to go to the mat on this subject:

I would remind you that the majority of the Eastern Committee, the War Office and the Admiralty representatives and Lord Robert Cecil definitely agreed it was better to leave the Turk in Constantinople than to accept any other solution except so far as Lord Cecil was concerned . . . that he would prefer the American to the Turk. I do not see this stated in your Paper and although I don't want to say anything controversial I am afraid I must address the Cabinet on the subject if you see no objection.[15]

Montagu also circulated a memorandum to the Cabinet on the future of Constantinople. He disagreed with a Curzon memorandum and wanted "to offer a few observations."

1. I think Indian Mohammedan opinion is entitled to greater consideration. The very fact that the misfortunes of Turkey during the war have been borne by them without excitement is only testimony to their loyalty to the British Throne and does not mean in the least that there has not been a conflict between their temporal and spiritual allegiance which has placed upon them a severe strain. . . .
2. . . . in making peace with Turkey we have got to teach the Turk that he is beaten. We have got to deal with him firmly. . . . But we are not turning the Austrians or the Germans out of their capital. . . . It is not that the Indian Mohammedan has sanctity or reverence for Constantinople; it is that we ought not to deal this blow to a Muslim Power when we have achieved victory over it with the assistance of Muslim arms and I would remind the Cabinet that the Prime Minister has stated, "We

are not fighting to deprive Turkey of its capital" and again "Great Britain did not challenge the maintenance of Turkey or of the Turks in the homeland of the Turkish race with its capital of Constantinople."

3. I agree with Lord Curzon that if the remedy which he suggests were adopted, it would probably entail the return of San Sophia to Christianity . . . that to interfere with the Mosque of San Sophia or any other mosque must be regarded as a deliberate anti-Muslim Act.

4. [Is it worth while] to remove the Turk from Constantinople, to embark upon new anti-Muslim action which will be resented by those who have stood by us loyally in India . . . in order to adopt any of the solutions which have been suggested by Lord Curzon and others who have written on this subject?[16]

This memorandum was Montagu's definitive statement on the Turkish problem. Although Montagu was willing to agree to the substitution of an international authority for the Sultan in the actual administration of Turkey, he consistently held to his original position—that to move the Sultan out of Constantinople would increase unrest in India and was thus a foolish and unnecessarily cruel approach to the Turkish problem, with no benefit for Great Britain.

San Sophia Mosque

Something happened early in February that should have alerted Montagu that the support on Turkey he thought he had from Lloyd George was not there. A group called the San Sophia Redemption Committee wrote to Montagu to ask his help in their efforts to rededicate this Constantinople mosque as a Christian church.[17] Montagu responded: "As Secretary of State for India and representative of 80 million of our Mohammedan fellow subjects, I can only assure you that the movement you are promoting will cause the greatest dismay among those I represent."[18] To his great surprise and consternation Lloyd George and the entire Cabinet refused to approve this letter. On February 24, Montagu wrote to Lloyd George:

Davies tells me you cannot approve of my reply with regard to San Sophia. I do not want you to approve the letter, but only to allow me to send it. India has been given separate representation at the Peace Conference and this as I understand your ruling gives us the right to express our views, not, of course, as the views of the Allies nor even of his Majesty's Government nor the British Delegation, but as the views of the Indian Delegation.[19]

Montagu was not prepared to go further and ended his letter by adding meekly, "If you want, I will keep the matter over until the fate of Turkey comes to be decided."

On February 28, now more aggressive, he wrote to the Prime Minister that he had heard the Cabinet was unanimous in opposing his letter since they believed that any views he expressed would be deemed the views of the Cabinet. He did not understand that conclusion. He reminded the Prime Minister that India had expressly been given its own representation precisely to assure that such separate views would be heard. But he conceded, as he had in his earlier letter, that it would probably be better to argue the issue at the Peace Conference than to convey Indian opinions in a letter, although he felt an obligation to present them.[20]

Montagu was unaware that whatever Lloyd George had said in the past about Turkey or India's right to express its own views, he was no longer prepared to support Montagu's views or his right to press them if they did not reflect Cabinet consensus or his own views. Yet the pressure upon Montagu from India, from the Viceroy and other government officials, as well as from the Indians themselves, was so intense that even if he had realized the futility of the struggle, he could not, as their representative, fail to fight on their behalf. Aubrey Herbert, a member of the Indian Civil Service, sent Montagu a letter he had received from an Indian friend saying, "The Moslems of India are getting into a state of frenzy. No amount of political reform will conciliate the Moslems if Turkey is broken up."[21]

On February 5, 1919, the entire Indian component of the British delegation prepared another memorandum on the future of Constantinople, reaffirming Montagu's views and asserting that these views represented the unanimous opinions of the Viceroy and his colleagues in the government of India. As Montagu had already done many times before, they pointed out that the Muslims had been unstintingly loyal in the war. They had given men and money and, at the same time, "prayed for their Kaleph who is the Sultan of Turkey,"[22] which caused a terrible strain. The Prime Minister, moreover, had assured them that Britain was not fighting to deprive

Turkey of its capital city, Constantinople, which for four centuries had been Muslim. Surely the same principles of national unity and freedom should be maintained for Turkey as for the European countries. "Do not interfere with the Caliphate; do not touch the mosques." In his Fourteen Points, President Wilson had stated that the Turkish portions of the Ottoman Empire should be assured sovereignty, conditioned on a guarantee of the interests of the subject nationalities and of the freedom of the Bosporus Strait. "We urge that the Turks be left in Constantinople with such provisions against misgovernment as the mandatory principle can afford."[23] Unfortunately, British policy was moving in a different direction; neither the unanimity of Indian opposition nor the passion with which it was presented could redirect it.

Reparations

In addition to representing India at the Peace Conference, Montagu was also on the Financial Drafting Committee with the responsibility for drafting those sections of the peace treaty involving financial matters. For a time, he was chairman of the British group that worked on these problems. Montagu, with his lifelong belief that he had no financial acumen, found serving on the Financial Drafting Committee of the Peace Conference irritating and detestable. "I know nothing of political economy," he wrote to Chelmsford,[24] "not even so much as I know of music. International Finance bores me as much as it frightens me. I spend my time in Paris committing myself to nothing until a Treasury official tells me what I am to say and trying hard to invent excuses for getting somebody to take my work."[25] This was likely an exaggeration. While international finance may have bored him at times, the memoranda on the international aspects of the postwar economy that he prepared as chairman of the Reconstruction Committee were widely acclaimed.

In financial matters, especially reparations, Montagu took the same moderate position that he took on other aspects of the peace treaty. He believed the Allies should take steps to help Germany recover economically and that reparations should not be excessive and should be based on what Germany could realistically pay. The payment should be apportioned among France, Great Britain and the other Allies and should be paid over a period of as long as thirty years. This approach accorded with the position that John Maynard Keynes had taken at the Treasury as early as December 1916. A paper written by him and the historian W. J. Asley on the collection of indemnities had taken the stand that payments from "losers to victors would be favorable to the victors provided they took place over a period of years rather than all at once."[26]

Again, on October 31, 1918, less than two weeks before the armistice, Keynes had asserted that reparations against Germany must take into account what Germany could pay. "It must not be so severe as to crush Germany's productive power; for, in the end, moveable property, gold and foreign securities apart, Germany could pay only by exporting goods to earn foreign currency."[27] The capacity of Germany to pay, Keynes argued, was as important in calculating reparations as the amount of damage Germany had perpetrated.[28] President Wilson had suggested that the measure of reparations be limited to material war damage (i.e., 'restoring' the invaded territories) and not include indemnities. But the armistice agreement the Germans had signed included an addendum inserted by France and Great Britain to the effect that by "restoration" the Allies understood that "compensation will be made by Germany for all damage done to the civilian population of the Allies and to their property by the aggression of Germany, by land, sea and from the air."[29]

In a Treasury memorandum in November 1918, based largely on Keynes's October recommendations, it was estimated that "a round figure of £4,000m might be taken as representing the preliminary claim of the Allies under the head of 'reparations.' The Treasury document emphasized that this represented damage 'done *directly*' to the civilian population . . . However, the maximum Germany could pay was estimated at £3,000m; and an actual payment of £2,000m would be 'a very satisfactory achievement.' . . . The assumption was that Germany would pay this over a number of years in the form of an annual tribute. 'If Germany is to be "milked" she must not first of all be ruined,' the memorandum concluded."[30] Montagu completely agreed with Keynes and the Treasury's conclusion.

While Montagu and Keynes took this moderate approach, much of the British public, including many British businessmen, Conservatives and Protectionists, as well as the French leadership at the Peace Conference, took a much harder line. Germany must be "bled white." One of the loudest voices in support of this position was the Prime Minister of Australia, William Morris Hughes.

Lloyd George was of two minds on this issue, sometimes breathing fire against Germany to accommodate the public's cry for revenge, and at other times responding to the call for moderation. To help him resolve this issue, which had become a political hot potato, he took the politician's classic escape: He appointed a Commission. He assured, however, that its recommendations would be anti-German by asking Hughes to serve as chairman and by stacking the Commission with Conservatives. Keynes and Montagu were invited to only certain of the Commission's meetings.

The Commission's report, issued on December 10, 1918, had concluded that Germany was liable to pay £24,000 million as the cost of the war; Germany would be asked to pay this in annual installments of £1200 million. Even the War Cabinet rejected this as "a wild and fantastic chimera,"[31] but at the same time it appointed Hughes and Lord Cunliffe (Governor of the Bank of England), the authors of this report, to represent England on the Reparations Committee at the Peace Conference. As was to be expected, this Committee could not reconcile the differences between the moderates and the hardliners, with Lord Cunliffe, at one point suggesting that "Germany could pay £25b, but finally agreeing to recommend £8b, if the Americans would agree."[32]

The French Minister of Reconstruction, Louis Loucheur, told Norman Davies, the American Assistant Secretary of the Treasury, that Germany could never pay that amount. But he, like most French and British politicians, could not make this assertion publicly. To add fuel to the fire, everyone knew that Wilson undoubtedly would veto such a sum.

Lloyd George was now claiming, however, that Wilson's comments notwithstanding, "he did not think it could be argued that President Wilson had ruled out indemnities." Montagu was shocked at this distortion of the facts and Wilson's clearly stated position:

I do not think at any period of my incumbency of any office I have been so much depressed. There we were, the trusted of the Empire, the custodians of the future, the translators of victory, the instruments of lasting peace. And what was our attitude? It seemed to me that we were apprehensive of the arrival in our midst of a really disinterested man who might, although we all hoped that he would not, want to apply the principles for which he had fought, actually might (O heaven forbid) really have meant what he said on more than a hundred occasions! What was to be the effect of his coming upon us, who did not dare confess this morning that flushed with victory we meant to insist upon terms of peace which had no justification in our war aims and which were based, not on brotherly love, on the healing of wounds, or international peace, but on revenge on our enemies, distrust of our Allies, a determination for swag.[33]

On February 24, Montagu wrote to Lloyd George:

It does not look to me as if there is any way of bridging over the divergences of view between the Americans and the rest of the Allies as to whether the cost of the War is or is not to be an item in the bill of costs presented for payment to Germany . . . Theoretically it is a matter of the supremest importance; but unless people contemplate obtaining annual payments from Germany for let us say 50 years, it does not seem to be . . . a matter of practical importance, for the reparations which Germany can pay and the cost of reparations is likely to be so large as to absorb all her resources. . . .

It would seem therefore as if the prolonged scientific investigation into bills of costs and actual claims which the Reparations Committee is considering . . . are likely to lead to no practical results, are likely to take much too long and are likely to lead to unnecessary international disputes.

It is therefore suggested that the first decision to take is how much Germany can pay. As soon as that is decided the five great Powers should allot on some principle . . . the available booty. . . . It would seem that this is the quickest way to obtain a quick decision. . . . [T]he fundamental [question] is how much she can pay.[34]

Montagu also addressed the anomaly of the role he was playing. "May I add as I told Chamberlain last week, reparations is part of finance . . . all our Allies have seen this. France, Italy, Belgium, Japan and America have put their Financial Representative on the Reparations Commission. England alone is represented by a man who is not concerned with the most important financial question— reparations. It is from no reluctance to be of service to you that I would earnestly suggest that when the Finance Drafting Committee has done its work and if the method suggested above of solving reparations questions were adopted, the terms of reference to the Reparations Commission should be enlarged to deal with other financial questions and I should cease to concern myself with them."[35]

Three days later, on February 27, Montagu again wrote to Chamberlain complaining of the sloppy structure the British had created to handle the financial problems of the peace treaty and to urge that he be relieved of his responsibilities, now that Keynes had been appointed to the Economic Committee, representing Chamberlain:

I was nominated by the Prime Minister to represent the British Government on a Financial Commission. This was eventually proceeded by a Financial Drafting Committee for which the Prime Minister nominated Mr. Hurst of the Foreign Office, but when it transpired that the representatives of all the other nations would be Ministers, he asked me to do the preliminary work. I have done it.

. . . I told you . . . I was more than ever convinced that all our Allies were correct in having . . . one head of the financial section of their work . . . I suggested your finding someone who would discharge this function . . . You told me to return to Paris and go on with the work and I agreed. . . .

Today I am informed Keynes was appointed . . . to represent you on the Economic Council . . . it does not seem to me that I can act for Keynes or in subordination to his decisions.[36]

Chamberlain apologized for not telling Montagu about Keynes, explaining that the Prime Minister had suggested that he, Chamberlain, be the British Delegate on the Economic Council, with Keynes as his alter ego, "since it was impossible for me to spend any length of time in Paris. I am afraid that I did not properly appreciate how this affected your position." Chamberlain assured Montagu that he was certain they could work this out and that he and the Prime Minister would soon be in Paris to discuss it further.[37]

Chamberlain and Lloyd George persuaded Montagu to continue his help on financial matters, and on March 10, Lloyd George, Clemenceau and Col. House, representing Wilson, appointed a secret committee consisting of Montagu, Davies, and Loucheur to try and break the deadlock that had developed over reparations, and to determine what amount could realistically be collected from Germany and how it should be divided among the Allies.[38] The committee agreed that the most Germany could pay over thirty years was £3 billion, a sum close to the figure Keynes had suggested in October 1918. This was a far cry from the Hughes Committee's recommendation of £24 billion and the recommendation of the Reparations Committee of £6 billion to £9 billion. They also suggested that this should be paid over thirty years, with 55 percent going to France, 25 percent to Great Britain, and 20 percent to the other Allies. Loucheur told Montagu that even £3 billion was high, that "Germany could not . . . pay more than £2 b. which would have to be supplemented by . . . 'monkey's money'."[39]

Lloyd George seemed to accept this, telling Davies on March 15 that he would "have to tell our people the facts."[40] But by March 18, after having been assured by Lord Sumner that Germany could be pressed for at least £11 billion, Lloyd George postponed going to the public. On March 26, Lloyd George again decided that the time had come to tell the people the truth but he could not bring himself to face the public response. As in so many critical moments in his life, he was saved by a fortuitous suggestion, this time by Louis-Lucien Klotz, the French Secretary of the Treasury, that an Allied Reparation Committee be created and that it report by 1921 on what Germany owed, "subject only to the proviso that it [Germany] pay £1 billion on account."[41] To the chagrin of Keynes and Montagu, Lloyd George had found a way out of his conflict without having to make an ideological commitment.[42]

On April 1, Lloyd George, Smuts, and John Foster Dulles met to discuss another aspect of reparations—whether pension and separation allowances should be part of reparation damages. They had before them a recommendation by Keynes and Montagu advocating a Commission to arbitrate such questions "provided that the capacity of the enemy was not exhausted without the inclusion of such item." Lloyd George disagreed and insisted that pensions and separation allowances be included in reparations and he was able to convince Wilson of this position.[43]

The final defeat for Montagu and Keynes came on April 5, when, in spite of their efforts to limit Germany's reparations bill to thirty years, the Big Four agreed to extend the time limit "if it turns out that all [of the reparations] cannot be paid in this period."[44] Keynes and Montagu had lost on every point. Although Lloyd George had consulted them and had placed them in key positions, they were not part of the Prime Minister's inner circle. He never thought of taking their advice.[45] Keynes later told Margot Asquith that the British had the best equipped delegation in Paris, but that for all the use the Prime Minister made of them "we might have been idiots."[46] For while Keynes and Montagu were searching for solutions, Lloyd George was looking for devices. They were moved by economic and ideological concerns, Lloyd George by political needs.

Keynes became as depressed and exhausted as Montagu and, like him, could not wait to leave Paris and "the nightmare" it represented.[47] He felt the peace was "outrageous and impossible and can bring nothing but misfortune,"[48] and he felt no compunction about blaming Lloyd George for "leading us into a morass of destruction."[49] While in later years Keynes modified his attitudes and conceded that some of his judgments might have been wrong, he never forgave Lloyd George for the treatment he received during these months.

More Frustration about Turkey

In March, Montagu discovered that not only could he not persuade his colleagues to his position on reparations, but he also had to fight for permission merely to express his opinion on the Turkish problem to the British delegation and the Peace Conference. He pleaded in a letter to Hankey on March 3 for the right "to lay before the Peace Conference" the views of the Indian delegation on the future of Turkey.[50] Hankey replied that he would have this opportunity, but as late as March 14 the issue was still not on the agenda. Montagu pointed out that it was "all the more urgent because of the report of the Commission on Greece which deals with Smyrna, a subject which cannot be treated separately from the future of Constantinople."[51]

He also told Hankey that "the Minutes of The British Delegation" agreed that "the opinion of the Dominions and Indian Delegations might be communicated to the Peace Conference,"[52] but that they should first be brought before the British delegation for discussion. On March 28, he reminded Hankey that the Prime Minister had promised at the last meeting of the British delegation that the views of the Indian delegation, on the future of Constantinople, would be communicated to President Wilson.[53] Even at this stage, Montagu still believed that Lloyd George would honor his commitment. For an experienced politician, Montagu demonstrated a surprising naïveté; he had totally misread Lloyd George's character and method of operation.

On March 15, 1919, Montagu's mother died. Although Lady Swaythling was in her late seventies and her health had been failing, her death was doubtless a heavy blow to Montagu: She had been his one protector, patient with his endless complaints and illnesses, supportive of his ambitions and tolerant of his peculiarities; most importantly, she had been the intermediary between him and his father. He loved her deeply. The absence of any comment about her death in the many letters that Montagu wrote during this period suggests that he found her death too painful to discuss, even in writing. As usual, he found solace in his work, and after the Jewish "schiva" of ten days of mourning, he returned to Paris on March 25.

The situation had changed. By the end of March, it had become clear to Montagu that because his opinions on Turkey were not shared by Curzon and Balfour, and because Lloyd George seemed unwilling to oppose them, Montagu was being deliberately excluded from meetings in Paris in which he had a legitimate interest. On March 25, he wrote to Balfour that he had heard "by accident" that a committee would be appointed to go to Palestine, Armenia, Mesopotamia and Syria and that its journey would postpone a treaty with Turkey for six months. Milner, he wrote, "a newcomer in Eastern affairs has been conducting some negotiations with somebody, I cannot find out what they were. . . . At some stage or another . . . I have to communicate to the Government of India the decisions arrived at without consultation with them on matters in which they are vitally interested."[54] He urged that a meeting be called of those "who have been entrusted with . . . these affairs" as soon as possible.[55]

He wrote to Hankey that while the Prime Minister "is aware of views as to Turkey," it was not the same as giving the Indian delegation a chance to discuss these views. The Prime Minister was moreover pledged to make the Indian delegation's position known to Wilson. "How can I best see that this pledge is carried out?"[56]

Hankey told him that if India were consulted, every small power like Greece or Belgium would want to be consulted. Lloyd George was well aware of the Indian position, Hankey wrote. He urged Montagu not to send Lloyd George the long letter he had prepared on the subject and had shown to Hankey. "Lloyd George has immense problems," Hankey told Montagu diplomatically; the "letter will rather annoy him at a time when he really ought to be left alone."[57]

By the first week in April, Montagu was utterly demoralized. Although he had worked tirelessly for three months on every assignment given him, he now found that Lloyd George did not want to see him or even to receive any other memoranda from him. He was denied any part in the drafting of the peace treaty. Lloyd George felt no responsibility to fulfill his pledges on Turkey, and no progress was being made on a treaty with that country.

Montagu expressed his sorrow in a private memorandum on April 4.[58] It is a sad indictment of Lloyd George's attitude toward his own ministers and of the dictatorial manner with which he conducted the negotiations for peace. Lloyd George, on his part, may have come to dislike Montagu, his positions and his persistent pressure and may have felt that conversations with him would be of little or no value. "I have not at any stage or any time been allowed to express an opinion, been informed officially, been consulted upon affairs in Mesopotamia, Syria, Arabia or Palestine," wrote Montagu. "I do not know what is occurring. I cannot accept responsibility." He continued:

I undertook for a time to represent the Financial interests of the British Empire here. The work of the Financial Committee was limited by the Committee of Ten to the answers to a series of questions. . . .

We have reported on. . . . the financial clauses which are *not economic* or *reparations,* of the treaty of Peace with Germany.

As regards the Peace . . . I had no share in, nor was not consulted on policy.

As regards indemnities, I made it clear that my financial responsibilities did not cover the question of indemnities. I was asked by the Prime Minister to discuss this with the French (Loucheur) and the American, Norman Davies. . . . Everyone agreed privately that the Germans could not pay more than £200,000,000 which would have to be supplemented for public consumption, by what he elegantly called "monkey's money."[59]

And yet, Montagu wrote, Lloyd George would not allow the report of this small committee to be made public. He concluded: "I then had to go to London for the funeral of my mother"; conversations continued on reparations but "led to nothing." During these talks, he said, "we negotiated on instructions" but "had no responsibility."[60] This was precisely the complaint that Keynes had made.

On April 4 Montagu left for London, informing the Prime Minister that the reports of the Indian Committee had arrived and he "must proceed to complete the Bill for introduction into Parliament." He would leave the question of Turkey to his Indian colleagues. "As for Mesopotamia and other affairs of the Middle East, I have not been consulted, so I do not think you will require my assistance."[61]

By April 15, Montagu acknowledged in a letter to the Prime Minister that the kind of peace treaty Lloyd George proposed for Turkey "will be hateful to the Indian Mohammedans." "What ought I to do?" he asked. He could not sign it. Yet he did not want to resign. An Indian Reform Bill was necessary. "All the ambition I possess," he wrote, "is centered on achieving the passage of such a Bill; every moment is important . . . I would not contemplate resignation lightly. . . . But if I cannot accept the peace with Turkey, the Mohammedan population of India. . . . will become more difficult to deal with."[62] This was a dilemma genuine enough to make Montagu sick, physically and psychologically.

What added to his grief was that nearly all of the Eastern experts agreed with him, as did the military. Yet, Curzon, Balfour and Lloyd George disagreed. "But if you turn the Turk out of Constantinople," he pleaded again, "and also cut him off from the Sea of Marmara, and deprive him of Smyrna," no one in India would support the Treaty. There would be terrible disorders in Asia; "Mohammedan unrest is at the root of the troubles in India."[63] Nothing that Montagu could say seemed to influence Lloyd George. Nor was Montagu even able to get the issue before the British delegation, although on April 27 Kerr told him that Lloyd George did hope that the British delegation would get to the issue "shortly." This was almost four months after the peace conference had begun.

Amritsar

During April, Montagu was affected by yet another crisis, although it is doubtful that at the time he realized the profound effect it would have upon his future. The problem centered neither in Paris nor London, but thousands of miles away in the Jallian Wallah Bagh, a small yard in the town of Amritsar in the Indian province of the Punjab. It came at a time when, as Montagu had written to Chelmsford as early as January, India was being recognized increasingly on the international scene not as a subordinate country but as a Dominion, an equal partner in the British Empire.

As a protest against the Rowlatt Act,[64] in February 1919 Gandhi had launched his campaign of "Satyagraha," or noncooperation. Chelmsford had written to Montagu on April 19, with typical British blindness to colonial matters: "Dear me, what a d——m nuisance these saintly fanatics are. Gandhi is incapable of hurting a fly and is as honest as the day, but he enters quite lightheartedly on a course of action which is the negation of all government and may lead to much hardship to people who are ignorant and easily led astray."[65]

The result of Gandhi's campaign was far from a mere "nuisance." By April, it had caused riots in Bombay, the Punjab and Delhi. In Delhi the riots lasted three weeks "in defiance of the Chief Commissioner and indeed of the Viceroy himself."[66] Writing of Satyagraha, Sir Valentine Chirol said:

When Gandhi travelled all over India preaching *Satyagraha* and administering the vow, Mohammedans and Hindus flocked in their thousands to hear him, and though they knew little or nothing of the Rowlatt Acts, they readily succumbed to the magnetism of the frail and emaciated figure which . . . seemed to tell the cruel story of his long suffering for those of their own race. . . . The *Satyagraha* movement spread like a prairie fire, and even Indian legislators who had helped to pass the Acts took fright and joined the popular outcry against them. . . . Government, however, showed no signs of yielding and Gandhi proceeded to proclaim the 6th April 1919 as *Satyagraha Day,* on which a complete *hartal,* or abstention from ordinary business and the demonstrative closing of all bazaars, was to be observed throughout India and mass meetings held for the taking of the vow. . . . Of the sincerity of Gandhi's injunction to refrain from violence, there is no reason to doubt, but no one can work up ignorant and emotional masses to a high pitch of religious frenzy without creating a temper which the slightest incident will provoke to violence and behind Gandhi there were many who did not share Gandhi's aversion from violence.[67]

In spite of Gandhi's promises to the contrary, violence did follow. In some cases, mild disturbances took place, in others, rioting, pillage, arson and murder. Soon the Punjab was in flames. Sir Michael O'Dwyer, a tough, hardheaded, old-fashioned administrator of the kind Montagu had often criticized, was in charge. For his part, O'Dwyer had been highly critical of the Chelmsford-Montagu reforms. On January 2, 1919, Montagu had noted in his diary that he had received "a violent note from O'Dwyer [Lt. Gov. of the Punjab] damning our scheme all the way up hill and down dale."[68]

Later, a month before Amritsar, on March 8, 1919, in a long letter to Chelmsford, Montagu urged reforms of the Indian legal systems and a policy that would distinguish legitimate "social reformers" from the extremists "with no particular political wisdom . . . disguising under a pretended desire for progress . . . real conservatism battening on race hatred and prejudice," and raised serious questions about O'Dwyer's tough approach and his alleged success in the Punjab:

There is nothing so easy at any particular moment as to govern through the police. It is far simpler than any other method. It requires less thought, less circumlocution. Take every man on his police record, use intercepted correspondence and exceptional powers and you have an easy time. But you sow the whirlwind for your successor to reap and you bring down the Government in God's own time as certainly as it was brought down in Russia. *That is why I have always thought O'Dwyer's success in the Punjab so cheap a success.*[69] (emphasis added)

O'Dwyer's rule, as Montagu always feared, was a failure. While he was able to keep order through tough regulations and police enforcement, discontent was brewing and ready to explode at the first opportunity.

On April 13, 1919, in an incident that has come to be known as the Amritsar Massacre, violence erupted. For Montagu, it would be the beginning of the end. It has been described as an event that in "a few minutes" irrevocably "changed the future of India and the future of the United Kingdom."[70] It had begun with some local agitation that the government officials viewed as just another disturbance. On the morning of April 10, as was their custom, they deported two of the chief agitators, in the belief that this would curtail further agitation. The effect was exactly the opposite. Later in the day, an angry crowd tried to force its way across a bridge and threaten the Deputy Commissioner. The two British soldiers and two Indian policemen who tried to stop them were stoned. One of the soldiers fired, three or four people were killed or wounded, and the crowd stopped and dispersed. A larger crowd soon assembled and tried to rush the bridge, stoning the defenders. This time twenty to thirty people were hurt as the soldiers tried to hold the line. The crowd surged forward, wrecking the Telephone Exchange and the Telegraph Office, seizing the Telegraph Master and brutally beating a guard to death.

Meantime in the City a Sergeant was murdered and Miss Sherwood, a lady missionary, was knocked down by blows on the head and beaten while on the ground: when she got up to run, she was knocked down again more than once; in the end she was left on the street because she was thought to be dead. She was afterwards picked up by some Hindus and her life was saved. Many buildings were burned down and looted and telephone wires were cut.[71]

On April 11, 1919, General Reginald Dyer, arrived on the scene to take charge of the military, although by now the ten who had been killed were buried and the rioting had stopped. On the twelfth, Dyer's troops made some arrests, read a proclamation that imposed an 8 P.M. curfew and forbade any further processions or gatherings. But the demonstrators had issued their own proclamation, calling for a meeting in a yard called the Jallian Wallah Bagh on April 13.

At 5:00 P.M. on April 13, General Dyer marched 50 troops to the yard, in which upwards of 20,000 Indians had gathered. They were listening to speeches and were unarmed. Dyer ordered his troops to open fire at the people—without warning of any kind. The Indians tried to escape in panic through the yard's few exits. Dyer continued firing till his troops ran out of ammunition. At least 379 Indians had been killed and 1200 wounded.[72]

Amritsar has been called "the decisive moment" when "Indians were alienated from British rule."[73] From this moment, Gandhi's noncooperation movement grew larger and larger. Although the disturbances ultimately died down and the government of India continued as though nothing had happened, the British government suffered a psychological, moral and political defeat at Amritsar from which it never recovered.

At the hearings later held on the massacre, General Dyer would not repent. He reaffirmed that he did what he thought he had to do and if lives were lost, it was the result of Indian disobedience not of his indiscriminate firing upon an unarmed mass. He explained that he had a responsibility not merely to disperse the crowd but "to produce a sufficient moral effect, from a military point of view, not only on those who were present but more especially through the Punjab."[74]

After the shooting, martial law was declared in Amritsar under General Dyer, who added his own harsh and humiliating orders to existing police regulations. These included his infamous "crawling order," which prohibited Indians from 6:00 A.M. to 8:00 P.M. from walking through the street on which Miss Sherwood had been attacked. If they wanted to move through that street between 6:00 and 8:00, they had to crawl.[75]

To many members of the Indian government and the military, to the Indian Civil Service and to the Tories in and out of Parliament, General Dyer was "only doing his duty." His conduct (except for the crawling order) was supported by his immediate military superiors, including Lieutenant Governor Michael O'Dwyer, who promoted him and who felt that while his behavior may have cost hundreds of lives, it saved thousands of others from more rioting and pillaging. Dyer's conduct only reinforced Montagu's determination to press ahead for the adoption of his Reform Act; it also increased his anxiety that these "distressing occurrences" might cause a "retreat from the . . . proposals we have made." He wrote to Sir George Lloyd, Governor of Bombay:

I cannot help thinking that what the asses call strong government is very largely responsible for what has occurred. Sitting on the barometer, stifling discussion, interfering with the free movement of people, eases the situation at the moment, but brings its reward.[76]

Montagu restated his objection to "strong government" in a letter to Chelmsford in May, suggesting that it would "be necessary to have an enquiry into the causes of and the treatment of the riots that have occurred in India. . . . The more I read of these occurrences the more I am struck by the fact that there is every reason to believe that they are the inevitable consequences of that easiest of all forms of government, firm strong government."[77]

The Committee under Lord Hunter that had been created six months after Amritsar, in November 1919, to investigate the incident, held extensive hearings and concluded that General Dyer's action was wrong, that he should have taken only the steps necessary to prevent further rioting and that he should not have fired indiscriminately on the crowd, which at the time was not riotous. The Committee held that he used excessive force "beyond what a reasonable man could have thought necessary." Montagu censured General Dyer, and the Commander-in-Chief required him to resign. This decision was upheld by the Army Commissioner.[78]

The parliamentary debate the following year on Amritsar and the Hunter Commission report was one of the most bitter on record. Montagu's enemies used the occasion to whip him publicly. Although Montagu's defense of the Hunter report eventually won in Parliament, the long-term effect of the attack upon him was devastating. It confirmed his sense of his lack of public support and the role that prejudice played in judgments of individuals and nations. He confessed in a letter to Chelmsford that he felt unhappy that he had not achieved the confidence of the public, especially that of the British in India. Somehow he had developed a reputation for "double dealing, falsification of records and untrustworthiness."[79] He did not understand this. "I am confident of its baselessness." He added:

Public men get a reputation well-founded, more often than not, which no act of theirs can remedy. That sly, sloppy sentimentalist, Mr. Asquith, as full of affectionate impulse as a potato is full of starch, had a public reputation for cold austere aloofness. For many years there was in England a belief that Edward Grey could do no wrong and it was almost indecent to criticise him.[80]

As for himself, he concluded:

Perhaps people judge nations as they judge individuals, on prejudice. And perhaps after all they are better judges of individuals than the individuals concerned [are] of themselves. And that is enough to make me melancholy, for as I see myself portrayed in public discussion at home and in India, I find myself not only unamiable but disreputable. Never mind, I still hope that by the end of this year our Bill will be through and that by next spring I shall be watching the birds nesting and the spring flowers budding with all the mixed feelings of a man who has done his work, ill or well or both.[81]

The Reform Bill

The enactment of the Reform Bill was one wish Montagu lived to see fulfilled. He wrote to Chelmsford on May 14 that the Cabinet "had agreed that I be allowed to introduce the Bill with general Government second reading support, have it read a second time and sent to Joint Committee. This leaps another fence. I hope to introduce it in the beginning of June and get a second reading before Whitsuntide."[82]

While Montagu was optimistic about his Reform Bill, he continued to suffer intense anxiety over Turkey, writing to Chelmsford that Greek troops had been sent to Smyrna. "If this is to be permanent, it is in opposition to the policy which I have been advocating, but would seem to me to make the retention of Constantinople by the Turks stronger."[83] A week later his hopes rose again; he was going to Paris where "the Council of Four is to hear the Indian delegation on Moslem Affairs. Aga Khan and another Moslem have been invited by the Prime Minister to Paris. Please keep secret for the present in case it does not come off."[84]

While Montagu was absorbed with Turkey and the Reform Bill, he wrote to Chelmsford that he would have had a more difficult time in the budget debate on May 22, because of the riots in India and especially Amritsar, but for the fact that he had made "very vague promises of enquiry."[85] He urged Chelmsford to submit his proposal for this inquiry. He congratulated Chelmsford on his condemnation of public flogging. On the Reform Bill he noted that "events are . . . moving with lightning speed with regard to Reforms."[86]

This was a far cry from his memoranda and letters of February and March, filled as they were with his fears that Curzon would reject a Reform Bill,[87] that he would not help draft such a bill and would not even meet with Montagu to discuss his criticism of the Report.[88] Curzon ultimately changed his mind, without further explanation. In the debate on the India Reform Act, Montagu wrote, neither Curzon nor his supporters "showed their heads."

I am a little puzzled by their silence. Dear old Colonel Yate, woollied a bit, rather incoherently, but whether the opposition is suddenly going to appear in all its force when the Bill is introduced, whether they hope to kill it in Joint Committee, throw it out in the Lords, or accept it, I don't know. As at present intended, the Bill will be published tomorrow and read a second time next week.[89]

Two days after his return from Paris, on June 5, Montagu spoke in the House of Commons on the second reading on the India Bill:

"I implore this House to show to India to-day that Parliament is receptive of the case for self-government and only seeks an opportunity for completing it by the demonstrable realisation of the success of its stages."[90] He said that he recognized that in the Cabinet and the House there was controversy over dyarchy, and he acknowledged that he himself saw its flaws but knew of no alternative.

He wrote to Chelmsford a week later that there was nothing further to report on the Bill. Curzon seemed prepared to help, or at least be neutral.[91] Montagu anticipated a difficult time for the Bill in committee. "I am not going to have an easy time," he wrote to George Lloyd, the Governor of Bombay.

My Committee [on the Reform Bill] is going to contain Selborne, Middleton and Harris. Selborne, of course, is an honest fellow, as honest as daylight, but very stupid; and dear old Sir John is more steeped in prejudice than a sardine in oil, whilst the idea of leaving modern Indian problems to be solved by a Lord Harris is really too ludicrous. The Committee may be fatal to me. But of one thing I am certain, that is, that my Bill would have been thrown out by the House of Lords without a moment's hesitation if the Committee device had not been adopted.[92]

If only "I could get our bill through quickly," he wrote to Ronaldshay, "we might devote our attention to the things more directly affecting the everyday life of the people than constitutional reform," and that, he said, would make him a "happier man."[93]

Montagu could not speed the process. All through July and August the Joint Committee on the India Bill met, argued, heard testimony and gathered evidence. On August 15, Montagu wrote that the Joint Committee was interviewing Mrs. Besant and scores of other witnesses from the Indian deputation, trying to gather as much evidence as possible before adjourning for a brief holiday. Montagu continued to push but admitted "there are really not enough hours in the day to get through it all."[94] His letters during September and October show the strain under which he was working as well as the fatigue, depression, exhaustion and crankiness that resulted. He seemed to be fighting the battle alone, with few allies and intense opposition.

On September 8, he wrote to George Lloyd that the Indian Civil Service "are wholly against us in trying to transform India from an estate which they manage to a living entity." They failed to recognize that while they would lose some of their powers of local government, they still have "the Seditious Meetings Act, the Press Act, and the Right to Search." He worried that the more they believe their powers to be weakened, the more they would use these other laws.[95]

During this period, Montagu's relationship with Chelmsford had deteriorated sufficiently for Montagu to write to him on September 11 of his wish that "they could get back into smoother waters."[96] Montagu may have "wished" that their relationship would improve but he did little to achieve this goal. His long, critical letters to Chelmsford contained innumerable suggestions that Chelmsford invariably rejected. The letters were also filled with doom, anticipating the worst. On October 2, he told Chelmsford that he felt depressed, that everyone seemed to turn down his suggestions, and that even when they accepted them, they seemed to be "dissatisfied with them." He had tried, wherever possible, to defer to Chelmsford's views, to minimize their differences rather than increasing "any tendency to any unbridgeable gaps," yet on "some subjects and some times, I feel grave apprehension."[97] Even his dear friend Willingdon seemed annoyed with him. Montagu wrote to him in October: "I now notice in your letters that I am becoming as unsatisfactory to you as he [Chelmsford] is. Well, I must grin and bear the loss of your confidence and can only hope and pray that the time will come when you will reconsider your judgment in light of fuller knowledge."[98]

Finally, the Joint Committee on the Reform Act finished gathering evidence in mid-October and began drafting its report. Montagu wrote, "I am anticipating one of the most unrestful times even of my experience at the India Office."[99] A month later, he wrote: "We are getting near the final stages on the Joint Committee of our work. It has been for me, as you will understand, in some respects an exhilarating, and in all respects an exacting time. I must own to a fair amount of satisfaction at what has already been decided."[100]

On November 20, the Bill with the Joint Committee's Report was finally signed. Montagu expected a bitter fight over it in Parliament, but in a sense he was looking forward to it "if only for the sake of a change from having to debate the whole thing point by point for hours at a stretch in the Joint Committee where the atmosphere was not congenial to scrapping of the give and take in which one can indulge in the House."[101]

Reform Bill Passes: A Victory for Montagu

To Montagu's surprise, the Bill had a much smoother passage than he anticipated. On November 20, the day it was signed by the Joint Committee, it was delivered to the House of Commons and within two weeks it passed on its third reading. Montagu was ecstatic, although totally exhausted, and did not exaggerate when he wrote to Chelmsford:

I am so tired and pleased and irritated and altogether exhausted. . . .

This afternoon it passed the Third Reading without any dissentients after a couple of hours. . . . The real hero of the occasion was Whitley in the Chair, who made quite audacious but very comforting use of his power of selecting amendments. If it had not been for him, I should still be in the House getting on my feet every five minutes to go through the usual torture of arguing down amendments, for hours in succession, and sinking deeper and deeper into the nightmare sensation of being condemned to watch an unending and execrably bad cinematograph film in which in some mysterious way I also had to play a number of parts. That is an ungrateful thing to say when it really and honestly was one of the most thankful moments of my life to see the response of the House when it put its final endorsement on the Bill. But I am writing for the mail and do not pretend that I have altogether shaken off the nightmare sensation as I write.[102]

Montagu had every reason to feel proud and exhilarated. To get such a liberal and controversial measure through the House of Commons in normal times would have been remarkable; to get it through a Conservative government was even more so, especially when the interests of the Prime Minister and the Cabinet were in concluding the peace treaty in Paris, and when India seemed to many to have become more of a liability than a precious jewel.

Montagu was utterly without allies in this struggle. By this time his obsession with this issue, the irritating manner in which he often dealt with his colleagues and his alienation from most of the Tories within the Lloyd George government had lost him many of the allies and friends he had made earlier in his career. The passage of this Act, like the Proclamation of 1917, was achieved almost single-handedly by Montagu, in spite of the government, rather than with its help. It was Montagu's persistence, single-mindedness, irritating doggedness, and the inexhaustible energy he brought to bear on this subject that achieved what at the time was perceived as a great victory.

Neither Montagu nor those who contributed to the passage of the Act could foresee how long a shadow would be cast on Indian affairs by Amritsar—one so strong as to negate all the good they envisioned would flow from the passage of the Reform Act. But in 1919, the implications of Dyer's actions in the Punjab and of Gandhi's growing strength were not yet fully understood. Without knowing the ultimate influence of Amritsar, Montagu was justified in viewing "his Bill" as a "major step forward in India's march to self-government."

Turkey and Greece

Even as Montagu worked tirelessly on the Reform Act, he continued to make trips to Paris to plead for a compassionate peace for Turkey. But no one listened. On May 8 he wrote to Chelmsford that it seemed that he could not do anything about British policy toward Turkey. "Greek troops have been sent to Smyrna . . . it is in opposition to the policy I have been advocating."[103] On May 20 he wrote to Ronaldshay that the entire Muslim delegation had the opportunity to explain their position to the Big Four directly, something Montagu had long been pleading for. To his dismay their presentation failed to change the opinion of a single person in the room, certainly not Lloyd George, who remained strongly anti-Turkey and pro-Greece.

British policy toward the Ottoman Empire had not always been hostile. During the Crimean War and the Eastern Crisis of 1877–78, when Russia was perceived as a menace to European stability, English policy and English statesmen like Palmerston and Disraeli supported Turkey. This began to change in the late nineteenth century. The Turks had a series of incompetent, weak and corrupt Sultans who reduced the Ottoman Empire to a state of decline. The growing strength of nationalism in Greece and the Balkans gave England, France and Russia—now allies—an excuse to support these countries in their aggression against Turkey, and, at the same time, to gain a new source of commerce and new Mediterranean sailing and commercial rights.

The Turks did not help matters. The terrible massacres they perpetrated upon the Armenian Christians, who were butchered by the thousands in 1896–97, gave the Europeans yet another reason for despising the "savage" Muslim heretics. In a single day in 1896, six thousand Gregorian Armenians were slaughtered in Constantinople. Gladstone's vehemently anti-Turkish sentiments were shared not only by the British public but by all of Europe.

Germany, on the other hand, while it may have shared these views, did not let them stand in the way of its courtship of Turkey. It financed a railroad across Anatolia, sent German officials to train Turkish soldiers and provided loans and advice. Turkey fought fearlessly and fiercely on the German side in the war.

Turkey: After the War

In July 1918, three months before Turkey signed the armistice, a new Sultan succeeded to the throne. On December 8, an Allied military administration was established in Constantinople; Allied troops occupied most of the city; and on February 8, 1919, "the French General Franchet d'Espérey, like Mehmed the Conqueror centuries before, rode into the city on a white horse, a gift of the local Greeks."[104]

Arab provinces that had been part of the Ottoman Empire were already in Allied hands. French troops had advanced from Syria into Silesia and the Adona district. British forces occupied the Dardanelles, Samsun, Ayntab (Mesopotamia) and the entire length of the Anatolia Railroad. Even Italy had managed to take possession of areas of the Turkish Empire that had been assigned to her by secret wartime agreements.

While Montagu pleaded for a compassionate peace and urged that a treaty be signed expeditiously, the Allies delayed and wavered in their approach. They were prepared to make concessions to the Germans but refused any suggestion of leniency to Turkey. They never considered that German leaders be driven out of Berlin or that other lands belonging to Germany be allocated to other powers.

Yet, they had no qualms about considering such a position in regard to Turkey, in spite of the pleas of the Muslims in India.

Lloyd George and His Ministers

In May, Montagu and some of the other Ministers had been summoned to Paris by Lloyd George to discuss not only Turkey but also the proposed peace terms for Germany, which were now in the final drafting stages. On Monday, June 9, as part of these meetings the Prime Minister invited Montagu to breakfast with Bernard Baruch to discuss reparations and to ask Montagu to become involved again. Montagu, who would reject the offer, described the breakfast:

The Prime Minister put to Baruch his alternative proposal for indemnity. Baruch plainly told him it was no damn good. Then the Prime Minister turned to me and said that he thought that Loucheur, Baruch and I should have a conversation about the indemnity. I said that I had tried before and counter-proposed that Baruch and Loucheur should talk. When Baruch had gone the Prime Minister asked me what on earth I meant by leaving it to an American and Frenchman, that he must bring me there to protect British interests. I looked him very straightly between the eyes and said: "Prime Minister, I am sure you don't want me to explain to you again why nothing will induce me to renew the service which I had once tried to render you in this direction." He said no more, but expressed a hope that I would come to the [meeting on the] Austrian Peace Terms and that then we would fix up a lunch elsewhere.[105]

Montagu had the courage of his convictions. He wanted no part of the discussions on reparations. His views were well known. The Prime Minister had rejected them for political more than economic reasons. It would be futile for Montagu to try again. In a memorandum for his files on these meetings, Montagu wrote:

I went to the Austrian Peace Terms, a show that was interesting but not important and seemed to me to be treated by the Austrians as a joke, that is to say as though they were thinking, we have been a joke, it is very amusing to see what you are going to do with us now,—and after all there is nothing had in breaking up an Empire of that kind. I was not surprised to receive no renewed invitation to lunch and I spent the afternoon in considering the India Bill.

To my surprise I was bidden to breakfast on Tuesday morning. The Prime Minister was alone and seemed to have forgotten the dramatic little incident of yesterday morning. I told him again that the only possible way of solving the indemnity question was to fix a sum to be paid by Germany by handing over bonds to that value to the Allies, and that we should have an agreement with the Allies as to the division of that sum. My own view was five thousand millions from Germany, of which two thousand five hundred should go to France, one thousand five hundred to us and a thousand to the others. I then urged that if these things were accomplished our experts should discuss with the German experts the methods and details. I don't think I had the slightest effect and he has asked me to go back on Friday.[106]

Having rejected Lloyd George's offer to help again on reparations, Montagu found he had little to do in Paris. His opinions on Turkey continued to be ignored. He was appalled that Lloyd George was breaking his word on this issue, which Montagu believed was inexcusable for a British Prime Minister; Montagu was kept out of meetings where Turkey was discussed. "I arrived in Paris," he wrote to Balfour:

but find nothing to do. . . . [Al]though . . . the fate of Turkey is under active discussion I can find no opportunity of participating. . . . in Turkey. To us [the Indian delegation] everything we hope for hinges on the Peace with Turkey. . . . More than that even is involved—the reliability and the importance to be attached to the word of the Prime Minister of Britain.[107]

It was not difficult for Lloyd George to say one thing at one time and conveniently ignore or forget his commitment at another. For Montagu, however, the fact that Lloyd George had made a pledge to the Muslims to retain the Sultan and Turkish rule in Constantinople was something that could not be ignored. He felt so strongly that in August of 1919 he distributed a memorandum to the Cabinet called "Lest We Forget," in which he quoted Lloyd George's promise of 1918.[108] This did not endear him to Lloyd George.

Peace Treaty Signed at Versailles

While peace negotiations with Turkey were floundering in indecision, the peace treaty with Germany was finally signed in the Hall of Mirrors at the Palace of Versailles on June 28, 1919. After Versailles, other treaties were signed: with Austria on September 19, 1919; with Bulgaria, November 27, 1919; and with Hungary, June

4, 1920. During this time the controversy continued over the terms
of the peace treaty with Turkey, and Greece continued her march
eastward into Turkey.

The fact that Lloyd George was reneging on his pledge to the
Muslims in India continued to upset Montagu. He faced a quandary
and needed guidance. Lloyd George had made a pledge. Everyone
in the Cabinet, except Curzon and Balfour, agreed to leave the
Turks sovereign in Constantinople and parts of Thrace, yet the draft
of the treaty would take Constantinople from Turkey. Of course
this would please the French; they had always been jealous of Britain's relationship with the Muslims. The treaty, Montagu felt, would
be a disaster. He did not see how as Secretary of State for India he
could sign it.[109]

While Montagu was increasingly becoming a pariah with Lloyd
George and his Tory coterie, his reputation among the Indian leadership was rising—to the point that on November 15, 1919, Annie
Besant wrote to Montagu urging him to become the Viceroy, a
suggestion that had already been made by the Maharajah of Bikaner
and the Aga Khan. He was, as one might expect, pleased with this,
but at the time he said nothing to Lloyd George. He had yet to get
his Reform Bill enacted and to convince Lloyd George to reconsider
his position on Turkey. The military men in the War Office were
reporting that the rebel forces in Turkey were growing and the
national movement of Kemal Pasha, later known as Kemal Ataturk,
Father of Turkey, was keeping the peace—not the Sultan or the
British government.[110] Surely, Montagu thought, this would persuade Lloyd George to reconsider his Turkish policy. It did not.

It is difficult to understand how the British government could
have ignored these warnings and continued to negotiate with the
Sultan, while permitting itself to be lobbied so masterfully by the
Greek Eleuthérios Venizélos. Yet this is precisely what Lloyd George,
Balfour and Curzon did. They either underestimated the growing
strength of Kemal or were so sure of ultimate victory by the Greeks
—or so ignorant of what was happening in Turkey—that they
blithely continued their negotiations with the Sultan. They failed
completely to recognize that his power was slowly slipping away
and any treaty signed by him would be worthless. They were prepared to take the opinion of Venizélos over the judgment of the
military who were on the scene or that of the Muslim leaders, or

that of Montagu and Chelmsford, who presumably knew more about Muslim reactions than did the self-interested Venizélos.

On December 11, Montagu wrote to the Prime Minister that he could not accept the proposed treaty. On December 18, he circulated a long memorandum to the Cabinet pointing out that his opinion on the Peace Treaty had the unanimous support of Indian opinion—Hindus, Muslims, the government of India, the Viceroy, and the Native Princes.[111] Lloyd George, Balfour and Curzon were not moved by his arguments. They continued to support the Greek advance into Turkey. This was now official British policy and there was nothing Montagu could do. Thus, the year 1919, which had begun with such hope and exhilaration for Montagu, was ending in despair. He was tired and physically exhausted, his nerves were shattered and his spirit depressed. On December 29, as the year ended, he wrote to Chelmsford informing him that, on his doctor's orders, he would soon be entering a nursing home.

27

The Marriage Continues
to Deteriorate, 1919

If you aren't happy with me, tell me so.

Edwin to Venetia, Apr.15, 1919

The year 1919 was not just a difficult one politically for Edwin: For his personal life, it was a disaster. This was the year during which Venetia openly became Lord Beaverbrook's mistress. She also became a prominent member of a decadent crowd described by Asquith as "a rotten social gang . . . who lead a futile and devastating life."[1] While Venetia had led such a life for several years, this new "gang" was more promiscuous, more open in flaunting their privilege and more obscene in their extravagance than even the "Corrupt Coterie." Although Diana Cooper continued to be the star of the group, it was Lord Beaverbrook's power and money, as well as his penchant for publicity, that added notoriety to the group. Money, power and political influence were always attractive to Venetia. Beaverbrook had them all and he became increasingly appealing to her.

The Montagus had become friendly with Beaverbrook as early as 1915. At that time he was still Max Aitken. He was not elevated to the Peerage until the following year. By 1918, they were seeing him so frequently that in May 1918 Diana Cooper wrote:

I do not remember how Max Beaverbrook became so woven into this period. It was during Duff's time in France that the Montagus and I saw him almost daily, this strange attractive gnome with an odour of genius about him. He was an impact and a great excitement to me, with his humour, his accent, his James the First language, his fantastic stories of his

Canadian past, his poetry and his power to excoriate or heal. We went a lot to his house at Leatherhead, to his rooms and offices in London and my letters to Duff are full of admiring references.[2]

Later that spring, Diana wrote: "Great success and fun at Max Beaverbrook's last night. He lives at the Hyde Park and we had an amazing meal in a sitting room—Edward, Nellie, Mr. Means, the Canadian representative at the Conference, host and self. Edwin really stimulated with argument and Beaverbrook terribly attractive."[3]

Beaverbrook was an exciting and attractive man, not only to Diana and Venetia but to many other women. Yet he was not physically imposing. He was slight, with a head too big for his body, piercing eyes, short legs, a slight paunch and a sardonic grin. He was a self-made man, a financial wizard who was a millionaire by the age of thirty. A Canadian by birth, he came to England in 1910 at the age of thirty-one and spent the rest of his life contributing his money and energy to British journalism and politics. He called himself a journalist on his passport, and he seemed proudest of that designation. He bought the defunct *Daily Express* and turned it into one of the most powerful newspapers in England. This newspaper, as well as the *Sunday Express* and the *Evening Standard*, gave him enormous opportunity to influence public opinion. Next to Northcliffe, he was the most powerful journalist and publisher in England and a much feared political adversary.

Beaverbrook was elected to Parliament in 1910 and was a force in unseating Asquith in 1916. He helped to elevate Lloyd George to power in that same year; he also helped to unseat him in 1922, thus paving the way for his dear friend Bonar Law to become Prime Minister. He was a member of Lloyd George's government during World War I as Minister of Information and Chancellor of the Duchy of Lancaster, and of Churchill's government during World War II.

Like Montagu, he was always ahead of his time with new ideas and programs, bringing to politics the same creativity and eccentricity he had brought to business. In business these traits helped catapult him to success and power; in politics they were often a hindrance. His image as an unconventional mischief-making power broker was no deterrent in business; in politics, it was. It has been said that he did not go as far as his talents could have taken him in politics because "people regarded him as indescribably wicked, an evil man."[4] Beaverbrook was michievous, quick, temperamental and tyrannical with his staff, but he was also inordinately generous and kind to his friends. For example, in his old age, Asquith needed financial help and Lord Reading undertook to raise an annual endowment of £3500 for him in 1927. Beaverbrook immediately contributed £1000. Margot Asquith thanked him profusely for his "acts of generosity." "When I think of the behaviour of our Liberal friends," she wrote, "men who ʹowe us not only their political reputation but their political salvation and contrast it with what you have done, I can only say I am stunned. Bonar Law always said you were the best friend in the world and he was right." Asquith was equally moved, writing on August 3, 1927: "I have been much touched by, and more than grateful for, your kindness to me during the last fortnight. I shall always remember your generosity and your delicate consideration."[5]   The public rarely saw the "generous" Beaverbrook. They saw instead the rash, tyrannical business tycoon, too clever to be trustworthy, with his roving eye and his penchant for mischief and ostentatious living. "If Max gets to Heaven," said H. G. Wells, "he won't last long. He will be chucked out for trying to pull off a merger between Heaven and Hell . . . after having secured a controlling interest in key subsidiary companies in both places, of course."[6]

This was as true of Beaverbrook's behavior in politics as it was of his financial dealings. He admired both Lloyd George and Bonar Law, both Churchill and Birkenhead, as later he admired Aneurin Bevan and Brendan Bracken. Of course he expected them to contend in public, but underneath, he supposed, they all wanted much the same as he did—dynamic, creative policies. The politicians he disliked were the staid and cautious, above all the complacent planners.[7]

His taste in women reflected this same inclination. He was attracted to brilliant, creative and dynamic women who enjoyed excitement and fun and liked to flirt with danger. Although married from 1906 to 1927, he had mistress after mistress and was as restless with his women as he was with politics.

David Farrer's description of Beaverbrook's relationship to women after his wife's death in 1927 could as well have been written before her death since her existence in no way deterred him from his sexual liaisons. Farrer, who worked closely with Beaverbrook, wrote:

Often two or three women were present at his dinner table. Since the death of his wife fifteen years earlier there had been many women in Beaverbrook's life. They satisfied him in the need not just for sex but for uncritical admiration. Most of them gave it in full measure. They found this, by normal standards, ugly man almost irresistible. Where women were concerned he was a whole magnetic field to himself.[8]

He was exactly the kind of man that Venetia found exciting. By 1919, she was not only dining with him, accepting gifts and financial advice, but also sleeping with him.

During the Peace Conference in Paris in 1919, while Montagu was working around the clock on reparations, international economic policy and India, and sleeping alone at the Majestic Hotel, Venetia was living at the Paris Ritz with Beaverbrook. Diana Cooper wrote that Venetia was living with Beaverbrook "in open sin" at the Ritz in "a tall silk suite with a common bath, and unlocked doors between while poor Ted [Edwin Montagu] is sardined into the Majestic, unknown and uncared for."[9] Diana reported also that when she visited Venetia at the Ritz, she could hear "Crooks' [a nickname for Beaverbrook] ablutions next door."[10] "Crooks and Venetia turned up just as we [Diana and her mother] were turning out. It's a disgusting case—her face lights up when that animated little deformity so much as turns to her." Later in the day, Diana "dined with Crooks and the Montagus at the Ritz Grill. The shocking, shocking Crooks said to me 'Don't you think she's very attentive to Edwin nowadays?'—a bad, bad sign. . . . I've just left Crooks and V. in their luxurious nest and expedited Ted to his Etoille."[11]

Even Diana was shocked, and there was a note of disapproval in her letters about Venetia's behavior. She was clearly in sympathy with Montagu's plight and found Venetia's behavior to be in bad form. Coming from Diana, who was no prude, this was quite a condemnation.

Montagu seems to have accepted the situation. He could not have been ignorant of the facts. He knew Venetia was staying at the Ritz, and he knew her room was next to Beaverbrook's. He must have heard the gossip about their relationship and yet he seemed to have acquiesced, and, in fact, he dined with Beaverbrook and Venetia at the Ritz Grill and let Diana, not Venetia, take him home to the Majestic.

Duff Cooper believed that by this time Montagu had lost his love for Venetia:

I spoke to Edwin seriously about the desirability [of Venetia joining Diana on a trip to the south of France]—and he against all expectation encourages it. I think he is mad keen to get rid of Venetia—who he undoubtedly loves less daily. He said she had not been happy for three years and that she might be so there—he became petitionary. Looks bad baby.[12]

Montagu's letters, however, do not bear this out. They continued to be filled with love and yearning for Venetia and obsessive fear that she was bored with him. He was prepared to do anything to make her happy and to keep her his wife.

On February 5, he pleaded with her to be honest with him. If she were bored, he asked her to tell him. If she wanted him near, he would be near; if she wanted him away, he would oblige. He told her he would try to be as interested in her as he was in India and other political issues. He wrote:

It goes to my heart when you tell me the review of your life. Sweetheart don't I know how difficult it seems to you to review when you are down. You see I think it really is that you are wanting change and that without it you are restless and above all I am desperately afraid that often you cannot get as much fun as I want you to have out of me, alone—it's boring for you and you give way to gloom. I'm either not available when you want me or too much so. What I think we want is my new strict frankness. I'm conceited enough to think, God I shall be miserable if it were not so, that sometimes I can give you what you want. What's wanted is that you should learn to tell me when domesticity is going to bore you when you want somebody else, when you want change, when if it isn't me you want me to go away. And I must learn not to mind but to show if I do so that we thoroughly understand. You must learn not to say "I don't mind" for fear you may propose something which I don't like. I must learn not to howl if I don't like it. For the rest I must learn to be . . . more considerate, to be more thoughtful, to be more amusing and stimulating and less absorbed in my stunts and not to subordinate everything to Indian reforms and shooting and fishing. We must do more things we like more things together and then by *frankness* I shall cope with your moods . . . and you will cope with mine.[13]

He knew she would never be satisfied with the activities that fill the lives of most women. And he knew, too, that for her, he was not the most exciting of men. He told her he loved her more each day and repeated his pledge that he would do anything to make her happy:

But darling mine, you are not the stuff ever to occupy yourself with your embroidery, your herb garden, your store cupboard, your hospital, your creche or even your children, or any other one thing and you'll never find happiness by trying to—you're too sparkling, too electric, too alive. As for me I'll never have the unfailing vitality of Diana, or Scatters, or the even placidity of Sidney, or [   ] but I have this to fortify these wonderful resolutions on the eve of my fortieth birthday (God what an age, how short a time I've got—how gloomy it feels) that my love for you is immeasurable and growing. I never thought that how ever divine one's wife that as one went on being married as one knew more of her as one had less to discover love would grow—mine does every day and with it an everlasting prayer that yours may too, a desire to continue courtship, to disclose and cultivate new charms. Angel mine if this makes me too explorative, too desirous of looking at the roots, too morbid, forgive me bear with me—realise the cause and let's be *frank*.

I wonder whether instead of Venice in the autumn you would like to be feted in America? Let's travel and change environment—coming to rest in Breccles from time to time.

On don't let's waste time apart. Let's be together that's all I want. That's frank enough. I won't be without you for it's hell.

I must see you at once tonight and never leave you again. That's how I feel.

Klotz sends his love to Madame!

Goodnight my darling. If this reaches you I hope it will find you happier. [14]

This letter was written only a few weeks after he had seen her living in a suite adjacent with Beaverbrook's in Paris.

On February 24 he wrote to her as, "My own most perfect," telling her that he was bored with his work on the Finance Committee. He hated "the finance," believing himself to be "an incompetent." He hated Paris, but it was "better than it used to be because I can get access to Balfour and Milner," although not the Prime Minister. But most of all he was "miserable" to think that she was "bored in bed" and that he could not be with her. [15]

And on May 15, in a letter opening "Oh my beloved," he continued to express his deep concern about her:

My darling I am still worried about *you* and that's far worse than anything else in the world. I am haunted by a fear that when we are alone you find me difficult to talk to—you *make* conversation and that you only *bubble* as you can with wit and spriteliness to your friends Diana, The Unspeakable, and the others. Why darling I love being alone with you so much—I long to see you happy so awfully that I can think of nothing else. If you aren't happy with me tell me so and I'll discuss it with you and after having causes out, decide on a remedy whatever it costs me. But I feel now that I in response to your questions tell you at infinite length what I am doing—never hear your delicious accounts of your own doings.[16]

He was even prepared to sell his beloved Breccles for her sake:

Now I want to ask you a tremendous question. Do you want to sell Breccles? Tell me darling. Of course I love it but if it's a bore to you I'd far rather chuck it without minding without feeling it a bit. It's so funny to me. I like old things, things I have done all my life, plans I know well, you don't—you seem to get sick of them; I like new people you like the old ones! But my angel I realise to the full that all the fag, furnishings, blinds, housekeeping, servants, electric light, gardens fall on *you* and if they are a nuisance to you, we'll chuck it. I don't want you to think I don't mind. I would but I've never done anything for you yet and if I was convinced you would be a happier woman, I would do it with a glad heart.

Am I a nuisance to write like this. Well my angel, I love you so that I worry about you, when I am away particularly and this letter as so often is the appeal for your help in making you happy from your impotent, helpless, feeble but passionately devoted husband who hates the "small unhappy voice" and loves your glorious smile.[17]

By fall, matters had become worse with Venetia rarely writing to him. "Darling, Darling," he asked, "Why oh why don't you write to me?"[18]

These are not the letters of a man who has come to dislike his wife, as Duff had suggested. They are rather the letters of a heartsick man, still in love with a woman who was bored with him, the letters of a man desperately trying to understand what he could do to keep his wife. If ignoring the fact that she was sleeping with Beaverbrook and others was one way to keep her, he was prepared to do this.

While he was baring his soul to Venetia and pleading for her attention and her letters, she was busy writing twenty-eight letters from March through December 1919 to Beaverbrook. She did write to Montagu occasionally, once in January 1919, telling him she is going to have an Aarons operation to take care of a "little thing wrong with me."[19] An Aarons operation was not an operation; it was a treatment developed by one of London's leading gynecologists to treat conditions which would interfere with compatible coital activity. She had had such treatment in 1916 as well. While Cynthia Asquith wrote that Venetia had an Aarons operation to permit her to carry out "her marital obligations," it is more likely that she had it to assure her ability to carry out her extramarital liaisons.

Most of her letters in 1919 were to Beaverbrook, and unlike her short notes to Montagu, in which she continued merely to report on her social engagements, her letters to Beaverbrook were far more interesting. The letter she wrote to Beaverbrook from Paris on April 2, 1919, in which she discussed Lloyd George's relationships with members of the peace delegation, is especially perceptive:

I arrived to find that Edwin was no longer the Pearl of the Hareem, tho' the first night I was here we had L.G. to dine, Wilson (not President but C.I.G.S.) and Balfour being the others. Conversation at dinner when not directed against Wilson (President) and what they chose to call his Sermon on the Mount manner (which is intensely irritating not only to all the English but also to Clemenceau) was chiefly occupied by recollections of Gladstone & Dizzy. I know this line so well it's one into which weary statesmen fall with alarming facility. The Majestic presented a scene of real gaiety as it was Saturday night, on which evening the typists have their weekly ball. We went and looked on after. The P.M. is obviously the idol of all of them as they keep on coming up to him and saying "I think I got a smile all to myself just now, was it really all for me? Am I being good tonight" in high voices of most loving awe. I think he adores the role. That horrible old "Procureur" Riddle was oiling around the whole time. I saw your charming friend Orpen who is lunching with us Thursday, he asked most tenderly after you.[20]

She discussed how hard Montagu and Keynes worked and how frequently their work was ignored by Lloyd George, after he had ostensibly approved it.

Edwin had had some characteristic dealing with LLG. About 10 days ago he was suddenly told he must see to indemnities (the job having been given officially to Hughes, Sumner, and Cunliffe) so he and Keynes work away like blacks, see LLG. daily (the others don't know they are on the job or aren't supposed to) draw up a memorandum which on Sat. they give to LLG who says he approves it; on Saturday afternoon Smuts arrives and he is at once put on the same job without Edwin & Keynes being told a word and they are dropped & told nothing. They do no more work on the matter till Monday morning they are sent for to go to President Wilson's house, they arrive, are told they aren't wanted, are just leaving when LLG comes out and says "We want you to go up and arrive at an agreement with the finance delegates upstairs": "On what lines, what about" they ask, "Oh they'll tell you, you must arrive at an agreement." Up they go, find Baruch & 3 other Americans, 2 French & 2 Italians (who have all been in close touch with their Govts) sit down and try and disentangle indemnities. To make matters worse Edwin can understand what (Loucheur) says, but not what Klotz does, he can understand one Italian & the Americans can understand no one, the French spend half the time having violent quarrels together which no one can follow, but it's a jolly life.

This has gone on for 3 days. From time to time Edwin & Keynes fight a point, which they think particularly damnable, very bitterly and then are told, perhaps by the Americans, that LLG. has come to an agreement on this point already and never told them. This actually happened and they were so astonished that Edwin sent Keynes to ring him up to find out: the answer came back "the P.M. believed there had been some talk about this but he couldn't remember what he had said."[21]

Venetia complained that she never saw Montagu who was spending all of his days with the financiers, so she was coming home on Wednesday. She invited Beaverbrook to the Coq d'Or on Friday, "Will you come to it with me, we'll either dine first or after, we can arrange that later"; she cautioned him not to exhaust himself in "riotous living" before Friday.[22]

The letters to Beaverbrook continued in this warm and chummy tone throughout the spring and fall. Venetia even asked Beaverbrook to "get rid of yr. [your] hang up" and visit Breccles for a weekend even though Montagu might be at home.[23] Beaverbrook may have had some sensitivity and scruples about coming to Breccles—the home of the husband of the woman with whom he was sleeping. To Venetia, who had none, these sensitivities were merely "hang ups." She not only continued to invite Beaverbrook to Breccles while Montagu was there, but discussed Beaverbrook openly with Montagu, with neither qualms nor embarrassment.[24]

During the rest of 1919, Venetia continued a steady flow of letters to Beaverbrook, in which she discussed the proofs of articles and books that Beaverbrook was writing, including his account of the fall of Asquith, Gallipoli, and other events before and during the war. Her comments were usually positive. These letters also revealed that Beaverbrook finally overcame his scruples and visited Venetia at Breccles. During this time, she provided Beaverbrook with some of the letters Asquith had written to her between 1913 and 1915. Beaverbrook used the information in these letters in the books he was writing, not indicating the source.[25]

By June 1919, Venetia was beginning to hint to Beaverbrook that he make certain gifts to her by subtly telling him that she was "looking for a small 2 seater American car which the Cadillac people are selling for £370."[26] In another letter, she asked whether she should pay a certain bill to the Rover people and recover it from him.[27] By June, too, she felt comfortable enough with Beaverbrook to tell him that she had an estrangement from "the black man" (a name they used for Scatters), but that it was "nothing definite merely the action of time on his inconsistent character so I am thrown rather onto my own resources which are few but increasing. Lady Wilson [Scatters's wife] . . . is blindly in love with the old boy. . . . Don't spend too much time in Canada, come back quickly. We miss you very, very much."[28]

Time would show that Beaverbrook's sexual interest in Venetia, like Scatters's, also would diminish: He was as inconsistent as Scatters and changed women regularly. His friendship and generosity to Venetia, however, would not change. He was always solicitous, generous, and caring. His financial advice, loans, stock investments and bank guarantees to both Montagu and Venetia were constant.

By the summer of 1919, he had not yet grown bored with Venetia, although her letter to him of August 21, 1919, revealed that he had become a little careless in his obligations to her. She wrote: "I think you might have taken just a small amount of trouble necessary to send me a telegram saying you weren't coming. As it was I stayed at home alone as you had repeatedly assured me you would turn up before the end of the week." She retreated a little from her irritated tone, continuing: "However I daresay it's not done me any harm I was really looking forward so much to your visit and I am disappointed about it."[29] In spite of his seeming neglect, her ardor for him had not cooled. She wrote on September 26:

Our lunch together remains with me as one of the most delightful I can remember. Out of my friendship for you there are 3 or 4 outstanding talks which remain, one or two at Cherkley during a walk after tea, one in Paris in a cold wet rain, one afternoon when we walked to Notre Dame, one lunch at the Hyde Park H. another walk up the Champs Elysées, but this last one ranks high with the best. So looking forward to Wed. Love V.[30]

Most of her earlier letters bore no salutations. By October 1919, she was addressing him as "My dearest Max." She sent him a present that "carries with it much love and gratitude" and told him that she could not have gotten through "this last fortnight without you and this fortnight is only a further proof that you are the most wonderful friend that was ever known."[31]

These were difficult days for Venetia, Montagu and the marriage. During the summer and fall of 1919, Montagu had become increasingly depressed, as well as angry and frustrated over his failures at the Peace Conference. Venetia was now spending more time away from him and "has too much time to think of one's [her own] real shortcomings."[32] She became more discontented with her life and less interested in Montagu's political and personal problems, even though Montagu's health was deteriorating rapidly.

On December 23, she wrote to Beaverbrook that she was preparing for a large Christmas party; she sent him a gift and a poem and commented that the author "has an even lower opinion of women than you have." She wished him "fun and success" in 1920 and urged that he not "let Scatters lead you astray in Monte Carlo."[33] Venetia did not mention a word about Montagu's health or political frustrations, although by now she must have known that he would soon be entering a nursing home. Nothing in her behavior or her letter indicated that she had done or was planning to do anything to help him through a most trying time in his life. On the contrary, her letter revealed that a few weeks before he entered the nursing home, she was planning a large Christmas party, sending Christmas gifts and warning Beaverbrook about his behavior at Monte Carlo. Perhaps Montagu's obsessive concern for his health had made Venetia callous to his dire messages of ill health. Or, perhaps, by the end of 1919 she really did not care.

28

Censure and Shame, 1920

If he is Mr. Gandhi's friend he has not the right to be Secretary of State for India.

Rupert Gwynne speaking of Montagu, July 8, 1920

For Edwin Montagu, the twelve months from January 1919 to January 1920 felt more like a millennium than a year. By 1920, Lloyd George's Coalition was coming apart. The Conservatives were growing tired of their Liberal allies and began openly to attack those Liberal Ministers associated with reforming policies: Christopher Addison (Reconstruction), Edward Shortt (Ireland) and Montagu (India).[1] Of all of these, they disliked Montagu the most. To them, he was the Jew who had dared to condemn the gallant British soldier, General Dyer, their hero at Amritsar. Montagu-baiting soon became an accepted practice of the ultra-Conservatives in the House of Commons. The tone of the attacks upon him began to increase in anger, hostility and personal vindictiveness. "Thick-skinned as a hippopotamus," "a grave peril to the country," "he would do anything to save his own skin"; "there he sits unmoved and it is impossible to drive home to him that it was time he went"—such were the barbs directed against him throughout 1920 and in 1921.[2] At the same time, unrest and rebellion were increasing in India and Montagu was being accused of inciting such unrest by his Liberal policies and his alleged friendship with Gandhi. To add to Montagu's sense of failure, Lloyd George, always sensitive to the political barometer, now saw Montagu as a political liability, a minister who had become an irritant whom the Conservatives were determined to drive from office. He had also lost confidence in Montagu's judgment on Turkey, calling him "too pro-Turk." The state of Montagu's political health now matched that of his physical and emotional condition.

His health was so bad that on his return from two weeks in Paris on January 21, his doctor ordered him to enter a nursing home at once. He had been warned earlier in December. But now he could no longer ignore the doctor's verdict. He was a very sick man in the throes of a nervous breakdown. "I hate it," Montagu wrote, "but I find myself so hopelessly tired that there is positively nothing for me to do but acquiesce."[3]

Montagu remained in a nursing home for two months, February and March 1920. The only personal comment that survives among his letters concerning this stay is a line in a letter to his friend Lord Willingdon, Governor of Madras, whom he had known since Cambridge, in which he wrote that he had shaved off his mustache "when I was in bed to find something to do with my time and my wife would never let me grow it again."[4]

On the first of January 1920, before entering the nursing home and before leaving for Paris, he circulated a confidential memo to the Cabinet on the proposed peace treaty that had been prepared by the Anglo-French Conference on the Turkish settlement (to which he had not been invited) and which Montagu described as "disastrous and incredible," and a "complete surprise" to him. He understood that the majority of the Cabinet, in spite of the objections of Curzon and Balfour, had agreed to keep Constantinople under Turkish rule, and that the Prime Minister, Curzon and Balfour had agreed to present new proposals to reflect that decision; they did not do so. He expressed his shock at their disregard of the Cabinet's directions.[5]

He hoped, too, that the War Office would be consulted. It would, in his opinion, be disastrous for Great Britain to dictate a peace which the Allies had not the military strength to enforce. Nor did he believe that Great Britain "will be found willing to indulge in a prolonged War in semi-tropical climates in order to enforce a peace, which, reading it from end to end, I cannot see of any advantage to us."[6]

The same day, Montagu wrote to Chelmsford to tell him that he would resign if Curzon's tough anti-Turkish plan were adopted. This anti-Turkish attitude, as Montagu knew only too well, was not only Curzon's: It was shared wholeheartedly by Balfour and Lloyd

George, who took every opportunity to attack the Turks as cruel and barbaric with absolutely no "capacity to rule over alien races"[7] who had the misfortune to find themselves under Turkish sovereignty. "The Turk in Constantinople," Curzon argued, "has been an ulcer in the side of Europe."[8]

Those who supported the proposed Turkish treaty also argued that the Peace Conference had an obligation to liberate non-Turkish nationalities from Turkish rule and return them to their own national states. This was the principle being used in Europe and should be applied to Turkey too, especially in those provinces with a Greek majority. Britain was not anti-Islamic; if Turkey were now made to suffer for her misdeeds, it was because her rulers had proved themselves corrupt and ruthless, not because they were Muhammadan.

These were all arguments that, under most circumstances, Montagu might have supported. He had always opposed brutality, murder and religious and political persecution, and he could not have been blind to the corruption and misrule that had characterized Turkish rule for generations. Yet Montagu opposed this position. One Indian historian, Sir Valentine Chirol, has suggested that Montagu's pro-Turkish position was the result of the tolerance that Turkey extended to Jews when Judaism "was proscribed by Christendom."[9] In view of Montagu's disinterest in Judaism, it is not likely that this affected his views. It is more likely that the real reason was his concern for India. He was absolutely certain that the proposed treaty would aggravate conditions in India. Nothing could persuade him otherwise.

Curzon's plan to force the Turks from Constantinople was finally rejected by the Cabinet, although the Prime Minister and Balfour supported it. Montagu should have been pleased, but he was not. He continued to be concerned with Curzon's attitude and his implementation of the treaty, writing to Bonar Law that if the Treaty was carried out in a way that would upset the Muhammadans in Egypt and India, even if Constantinople remained under Turkish rule, the "Cabinet will lay much blame on me."[10] Montagu himself was beginning to sense that he was annoying people with his persistent hammering away on this point. "I hate to be a nuisance," he wrote, "I loathe to cause people trouble and worry and I am very nearly as anxious to spare the feelings of All Highest as I am to spare my own."[11]

He may have wanted to spare the feelings of Curzon, Balfour and the Prime Minister but nothing in his behavior suggests that he made any effort to put this wish into practice or that he restrained himself from writing long letters arguing his case. His letter of January 20 directed to the Prime Minister was yet another long harangue against the treaty, this time warning that if the Allies treated Turkey too harshly it would turn to Bolshevism. He reminded the Prime Minister, not for the first time, that he had been asked to draw up an outline for a proposed peace treaty with Turkey; he had done so but it was never discussed by his colleagues even though "we sat up all Sunday night to have it ready by Monday morning."[12]

Viceroy to India

Just before entering the nursing home, Montagu wrote a final very long letter to the Prime Minister on a subject very close to his heart: his desire to be appointed Viceroy to India. He reminded Lloyd George that when he had been offered the position of Secretary of State for India in 1917, he had hesitated only because he had always been anxious "to serve India in India." Lloyd George had responded by reassuring Montagu that if he were successful as Secretary of State, he would have no hesitation in sending him to India, although there existed no precedent for a Secretary of State later to become the Viceroy. Montagu went on to make a most persuasive case for his appointment.

He had carried out the policy outlined in his Mesopotamian speech, which had prompted Lloyd George to appoint him in the first place. The India Act, which he had shepherded through the Parliament, reflected this, "in the spirit and in the letter." He wanted more than anything to be the one to translate that Act into a new constitutional government for India and believed he was better qualified to do this than anyone else.

The imagery in this part of the letter revealed the intensity of his personal feelings for India and the Reform Act:

I feel very much as I would conceive a mother to feel after she had more or less successfully borne a child. Proud, happy, weak, relieved of a great weight that had been carried about with more or less fortitude for a great length of time, but consumed with anxiety for the future of the offspring. Good fairies of great benevolence but of considerable weakness and some apathy have pronounced many benedictions. Bad fairies have prophesied ill, cursed and indulged in gloomy foreboding. The child is not strong, the weather in which it has seen the light has been inclement and the mother feels that everything depends on not being compelled by the doctor to put the child out to some other and less loving hands to nurse and is eagerly anxious to do the nursing herself. You are the doctor—and not only the doctor but indirectly interested in the welfare of the child yourself.[13]

He wrote that much depended on what would be done in the early stages before the Prince of Wales arrived in India (the Prince was due to make a state visit in 1921). He feared that the government of India would give what they had to "grudgingly." This would be "fatal," as "everything depends upon persuading, enlisting upon your side all sorts of forces, governing politically as well as administering efficiently. I cannot," he wrote, "trust it to those in India."[14]

The new constitution would give India more responsibility for its own taxation. This would require careful handling. Montagu believed that he had the financial experience to do this. His administrative skills and knowledge of the new constitution would also be useful, he wrote, in handling problems of the Army in India, in involving local governments in the new structure, in providing a better news service and in reexamining the Law Courts which needed improvement.

Montagu's letter ended on a poignant note, acknowledging that the Prime Minister "may have misgivings" about his relationship with the civil and military services and with the Europeans in India. He believed he could get along with the Europeans, having found them "easy to handle" on his last trip. He believed the younger men in the Civil Service "are on my side."[15]

This desire to become Viceroy of India was not new for Montagu. He had hinted at it to Lloyd George earlier. Sir Henry McMahon (Lord Kitchener's replacement in India in 1910) had told Violet Asquith that he had met Montagu in India in 1912 and "had diagnosed his ambition, i.e. to become the future Viceroy." In response to Violet's question on how he knew this, McMahon replied, "I noticed a glint in his eye which I have learnt to recognize."[16]

The "glint in his eye" in 1912 had, by 1920, became a burning desire in his heart. He was not yet aware of the depth of hostility that had developed toward him in the Indian Civil Service and among the Tories at home and he still believed he had a chance for the appointment. He entered the nursing home hopeful that Lloyd George would give serious consideration to his request. To go back to India, a land he truly loved, as its Viceroy, and to have the chance to implement the Reform Act and help India move toward self-government—what a wonderful way to cap his career. What a wonderful dream.

His Stay in the Nursing Home

In the nursing home, Montagu was under strict orders to relax, rest, read and free his mind from his political responsibilities. But he was, of course, emotionally incapable of following such orders. He was incapable of closing his mind to the political problems in which he was involved. He was incapable of forgetting about Turkey or India simply because a doctor prescribed it.

Instead, he spent two months in the nursing home running the India Office from his bed and writing to anyone he thought might listen or help, "with the tears of the sick . . . to fight the battle of the Turks. . . . I am very suspicious," he wrote to his friend H. A. L. Fisher, the Vice-Chancellor of Sheffield University and a member of the Royal Commission on Indian Public Service:

We came to a decision of the Cabinet. Curzon says he will try and get it reversed. Lloyd George, at any rate, ostensibly is loyally sticking to it, and the new French Government is of our view. But if you will look at the telegram from the War Office of the 29th of January C.P. 538, you will see why I am anxious.[17]

Fisher responded beginning with the admonition: "It is very wrong of you, is it not, to be governing India from your sick bed?" He chastised Montagu for believing that Curzon and the Foreign Office would not carry out the mandate of the Cabinet to keep Constantinople under Turkish rule. "I have received no indication that the Foreign Office intends to reverse the decision which the Cabinet has reached with respect to Constantinople." He confessed, however, that Curzon had "only recently returned and he may open the question." But, he assured Montagu, "you may rely on me to fight as well as I can the battle for Moslem Peace."[18]

Montagu's instincts were better than Fisher's, for even as Fisher was writing to Montagu, Lloyd George was doing everything he could to reverse the Cabinet's position on Constantinople. He eventually changed his vote on this question only because, he wrote in his *Memoirs,* "of the invincible opposition of our Allies,"[19] not because he agreed with their position or with Montagu's.

On February 14, continuing to ignore the doctor's orders, Montagu again raised the question of his appointment as Viceroy with the Prime Minister.[20] In this letter, unlike the January one, Montagu asked only to be named temporary Viceroy for three years, so he could be present when the Prince of Wales inaugurated the new Constitution and "to begin the organization" of the "new order of things" in India. He would come home when a new Viceroy was chosen.

"I have done a good job," Montagu wrote, openly pleading for the appointment. While India was not peaceful, he argued that its situation was better than that of either Ireland or Egypt. A tolerable peace with Turkey would help. "Sinha says the reforms have been received well and only a noisy minority profess to be disappointed with the measure."

Montagu examined other potential candidates, noting that Willingdon had the requisite temperament and political instincts but lacked the necessary administrative skills to deal with the minute details that the reorganization of the government would entail. It would take a new person two or three years to get to know the Constitution, the country and the people, and that length of time would be fatal. He wrote:

I have been associated with the India Office now for 6 years. . . . That whole atmosphere of India at the present moment is, I fear, inclined to give to the Indians as much as they must under the law, but to give it grudgingly, fighting over every detail, and then gloating over the increase in the size of the extremist party. . . . No act of Parliament is any use unless it is worked in the spirit as well as in the letter. And it is because I do not want the policy to fail because of the way it is worked that I want to go to India for which I care more than anything else in the world.[21]

Montagu acknowledged two objections to his appointment: that of the English community in India and that of Lord Curzon. Concerning the first, Montagu argued that the English community was not as hostile as the press made it appear. To balance that, he pointed out that the Indians respected him and wanted him. As for Curzon, "he has of course no interest in the fierce nationalism and proved patriotism of the educated Indian. He has no sympathy in what other people think."

Montagu truly believed he could do the job better than anyone else. While he was usually his own worst critic and was generally unsure of himself and insecure, on this issue—his ability to be an effective Viceroy at this time in English history—he had no doubt. "Most men . . . can make a success of something that they love so much as I love the cause of self-government in India and its continued loyalty to the British Empire. I have never felt certain of my success in any other office that has been suggested to me."[22] He told the Prime Minister that he planned to give up his seat in Parliament in the next election, believing that he could no longer perform useful work as a Member of Parliament. He ended by arguing that the policy he had set forth in his speech on the Mesopotamia Report was now the policy of the government. It was "now your policy." He asked for the opportunity to move that policy forward. The Prime Minister did not reply to this impassioned plea. Instead he asked Kerr to respond for him, in a noncommittal note on February 27, stating merely that the Prime Minister had not yet come to a decision.[23] Given Lloyd George's method of operation, it is more likely that he had already come to the conclusion that Montagu was too much of a political liability to retain him in any position involving India or even to keep him in the Cabinet.

Venetia and Beaverbrook

While Montagu was in the nursing home, Venetia's relationship with Beaverbrook intensified. In addition to the time she spent with him and the emotional support he provided her, she also became more dependent upon him for financial advice and support. Several of her letters to Beaverbrook during this period raise questions about investments he had made on her behalf with her money and sometimes with his own. She did not hesitate to ask for his help. He had once indicated that he would be pleased to do this. She took him up on it immediately and in her usual coy way asked:

A little while ago you told me that it was unwise of me to speculate in my own name and at the same time you said that if I have some money I was speculating with you would do it for me. Was this a joke or would you be bothered with it? I can't think you really would and I'm ashamed to bother you and if you say "No I'm afraid I can't" and if you never meant to be taken seriously . . . don't think ill of me for asking you.[24]

Nor was Venetia shy in making clear to Beaverbrook how much she enjoyed his company, and, as with Asquith and Montagu, she did not hesitate to suggest dates and weekends for them to spend together. In March, while Montagu was still in the nursing home, she told Beaverbrook that she would soon be in London, and asked "Do we meet at all? I long to see you. . . . I will ring you up at 4:30 and find out your plans."[25] And on March 22, 1920, writing from the nursing home at which Montagu was staying, she told Beaverbrook she would be back in London in a few days. "Will you dine, Mon., Tues., & Wed.?" She was planning a party for some of the people he "loves much."[26] This letter reveals that Venetia did visit Montagu at least once while he was recuperating in the nursing home but that even while there, she continued to think about Beaverbrook and felt the need to write to him.

Montagu also sought Beaverbrook's advice, not only on financial matters but on his political problems. These were some of the bleakest days of his career and he was desperately in need of guidance and direction. Should he disobey his doctors and leave the nursing home to answer the attacks against him in Parliament? "For God's sake tell me," he wrote in a letter to Beaverbrook on March 15, 1920.[27] "I can see no one and get any advice. Give me yours by wire." Beaverbrook and the doctors advised that he remain at least through March, and Montagu, as unhappy as he was, acquiesced.

Turkey: Still in Flux

While Montagu was in the nursing home, the problem of the Turkish treaty continued to grow. By this time France and Italy had begun to express objections similar to Montagu's, causing Lloyd George to be "a minority of one"[28] in support of a tough Turkish policy. This came to a head at the Allied Conference on the Turkish Peace Treaty held on February 12 at 10 Downing Street. The cast of characters had changed dramatically. Clemenceau had retired and

France was now represented by Alexandre Mitterand and the French Foreign Secretary, Philippe Berthelat, both far more conservative and right wing than Clemenceau. Italy was represented by Francesco Nitti and Tittoni, in place of Orlando and Sonnino. This meant a fundamental transformation in Italian and French foreign policy. France had greater financial interests in Turkey now than did any other country. At the same time, Wilson's policies and America's involvement had been rejected by the Senate; America was now represented by an observer who took no part in the proceedings.

The change in representation from those countries produced an unmistakable change in attitude toward Turkey. Wilson, Clemenceau and Orlando had been determined to confine Turkey to Asia. The new leadership did not share this desire. They believed, as had Montagu, that Constantinople should remain the Turkish capital and that the Sultan should remain in that city.

While the proposed Turkish treaty was being debated at the conference in London, the Turks, led by Kemal, were growing stronger, successfully attacking the Greeks and compelling them to flee. By now, the Foreign Office, the War Office and the Tory Members of Parliament were increasingly sympathetic to the Turks and were urging that the Greek Army be withdrawn. Even in the face of this, Lloyd George remained the champion of Venizélos and refused to consider such a move.

By the middle of February, the terms of the proposed peace treaty had been leaked to the press and Curzon, writing to Montagu on February 18, told him it would now be permissible for him "to tell it to India." Curzon was clearly unhappy with the part of the treaty that would keep Constantinople in Turkish control. "I deplore the decision. . . . you will live to see," he wrote Montagu, "that you have won a Pyrrhic victory."[29]

In fact, Montagu had not won this victory. His opinion on this subject had been of no importance to Lloyd George. It had been France and Italy that had forced the Prime Minister's hand and won the battle. The proposed treaty contained other provisions that Montagu still opposed, such as giving Smyrna, Thrace and the remaining Turkish islands in the Aegean Sea to the Greeks and continuing British aid to the Greek army in its march eastward into Turkey. Montagu did not view the treaty as a personal victory.

He left the nursing home in April. His first letter on April 1, to

Chelmsford, showed the extent to which their relationship had deteriorated. Neither man was now concealing his feelings toward the other. Chelmsford had written letters while Montagu was in the nursing home indicating his irritation with Montagu, who now made no apology for his "methods of work" or his "mentality." He was certain that the culprit in their problems was the English press in India and some of Chelmsford's associates, "who try to make mischief between us." [30]

Montagu was still unaware of the intensity of the feeling that had grown against him among the Tory ranks at home and in the Indian Civil Service, as well as in some sections of the Anglo-English community in India. To these adversaries he had come to symbolize "reform and democracy" in India, which they took to be the cause of Indian unrest. Nor was Montagu sufficiently aware of the political problems now facing Lloyd George and how irritated he had become with Montagu's Turkish policies, which he thought had exacerbated his own problems with his Tory supporters. Ignorant of these developments, Montagu wrote to Hankey on April 8, asking whether Lloyd George would like him to go to the San Remo Conference on the Turkish peace treaty. He had been invited to the Paris Conference in January 1920, where the issues had not been addressed. He also requested that his suggestions for the treaty be distributed to the Cabinet and, alluding to his rights under the resolution of the British delegation, he asked that it also be distributed to the Peace Conference.

Hankey acknowledged this letter, on instruction from the Prime Minister, noting that the British Empire delegation no longer existed, that the representatives of the Dominions had gone home and that any resolution adopted by that group was not binding. "You will remember on a previous occasion," he reminded Montagu, "on which you proposed to circulate a memorandum to the Peace Conference, the Prime Minister's view was that it was for him, as senior British representative, to represent the British case as a whole and that it would not be in order for the Indian delegation to address the Peace Conference direct. In these circumstances I hardly see how I can take any action in regard to the second communication [i.e., the distribution of the memorandum to the Peace Conference]." [31]

The letter also informed Montagu that "the Prime Minister proposes that Lord Curzon should be the only British minister to accompany him to San Remo." The issue was now firmly stated: Only Lloyd George's policy on Turkey was to be presented to the Peace Conference and only Curzon, who shared his views, would accompany him. The message could not have been clearer.

On April 15, 1920, Montagu wrote again, this time to the Prime Minister, in a manner that would have infuriated any Prime Minister, but particularly Lloyd George. It was the letter that sealed Montagu's fate. In it he enclosed his exchange of correspondence with Hankey and, despite the firmness of Hankey's reply, told the Prime Minister: "I must with great respect insist that my Memorandum be forwarded to the Supreme Council. I claim this as a right."[32]

He offered as evidence to support this conclusion the fact that he held his appointment as "Plenipotentiary in respect of our Empire of India" from the King, and this gave him "all manner of Power and Authority to treat, adjust and conclude with such Ministers, Commissioners or Plenipotentiaries as may be vested with similar Power and Authority. . . . I cannot doubt that this includes the right to address a Memorandum to the representatives of the four Great Powers which are considering the Treaty with Turkey."[33] At Paris, on January 20, 1919, "the British Empire Delegation agreed that the Dominions and India were. . . . entitled to put forward memoranda for the Peace Conference." While Hankey on the Prime Minister's instruction, had taken the position that the British Empire delegation had ceased to exist because the principal representatives had gone home, Montagu did "not see how this affects the situation and I always understood that when the Dominion Ministers went away, they appointed representatives to act on their behalf."[34]

Montagu questioned the conclusion that only Lloyd George was empowered to represent "the British case as a whole." Montagu's recollection of the resolution was quite different. He recalled that when the discussion of Adrianople was taking place, he withdrew his memorandum on this subject only because the Prime Minister had agreed that he would present the arguments of the Indian delegation. "It is inconceivable," he concluded, "that you could have reversed the decision of the British Empire Delegation, thus depriving the Dominions and India of the position given them in respect of the Germany Treaty as States with particular interests."[35]

Montagu's letter infuriated Lloyd George, whose response, written on April 25,[36] not only rejected the substance of Montagu's argument but also included a personal rebuke. The Prime Minister's letter signaled the beginning of the end of Montagu's career.

The Prime Minister told Montagu that not only had he read the Montagu-Hankey exchange but he had also discussed the issue further with Balfour and Curzon and "regrets" that he "cannot comply." Most importantly, he refused to believe that Montagu's position was supported by the documents he quoted. If Montagu were correct, every one of the five Plenipotentiaries of Great Britain would have had the right to submit conflicting memoranda.

Lloyd George chastised Montagu for being deceitful in not quoting the full resolution adopted by the British delegation on January 20. "I think it is a pity," he wrote, "that you did not quote the whole of the resolution which entirely changes its significance, for misquoting is a fruitful cause of misunderstanding." The paragraph to which Lloyd George referred was: "It was further agreed, however, that the Plenipotentiaries of the United Kingdom, the Dominions and India should send their memoranda in the first instance to the Secretary of the British Empire Delegation with a view to joint discussion and agreement before being sent to the Peace Conference."

Lloyd George disagreed with Montagu's conclusion that unless he had the right to forward his memorandum, "India will not have had its views properly presented and considered. . . . I do not understand," Lloyd George wrote, "how it is possible for you to make such a statement." He reviewed all the meetings at which India had had its view presented, both in London and in Paris:

Both Balfour when he was Foreign Secretary, and I had repeated interviews not only with the two Indian representatives . . . of Mohammedan opinion in India, in order that we might be satisfied that we really understood the Indian Mohammedan view about the Turkish settlement. At my request, President Wilson, M. Clemenceau and Signor Orlando, held a special sitting of the Supreme Council in order that the Indian Delegates . . . should present the case of India with regard to the Turkish Treaty to the Peace Conference. Throughout the January sitting of the Peace Conference, you were present in Paris and attended every meeting of the British Delegation which discussed the Turkish Treaty. Not only at the Conference, but in the intervals, I have received from you a constant stream of letters and arguments urging me to make concessions in favor of the Turks. Unfortunately during the recent meetings of the Conference you were away ill, but even so you received copies of the whole process verbal (a privilege not granted even to the heads of independent states with particular interests) and that you were able to concern yourself with the affairs of India is shown by the fact that you wrote letters about many aspects of the negotiations, and were able to send me a long and closely reasoned letter asking that you should be appointed immediately as the next Viceroy. Finally at your urgent request within the last few weeks, I had a long interview with the Caliphate Deputation which had come straight from India purporting to represent the latest phases of Indian Moslem opinion. . . . And so, India far from not being heard, its representatives have occupied a position more privileged than that of any other powers.

In light of this background, Lloyd George questioned whether Montagu should have the right to continue to press his view upon the Peace Conference, "a view that differs profoundly from that of the British Government and Delegations." He wondered whether Montagu's "strongly pro-Turk views" were his own or "represent the views of the Government and people of India." He was certain that as long as Britain was responsible for India, the decision on Turkey to be pressed upon the Peace Conference "must be that arrived at by the British Cabinet."

To make certain that Montagu understood how strongly he felt, Lloyd George wrote: "A situation in which a member of the British Cabinet appears before the Peace Conference in its final stages either in person or writing, to oppose the policy of the rest of his Government is clearly impossible and absurd." Underscoring his anger and disapproval, he characterized Montagu's attitude "as being not so much that of a member of the British Cabinet but of a successor on the throne of Auranazeb." As to the policy that Montagu advocated, Lloyd George believed it was not representative of India as a whole but rather of the Muhammadan "minority." He accused Montagu of being too pro-Turk and not paying "sufficient regard to the rights of the nationalities oppressed and massacred by the Turk in the past."

The Prime Minister warned Montagu not to encourage agitation in India by supporting those Indian Muslims who were "subverting Indian interests to Turkish politics."

I have felt for some time grave doubts as to whether steps ought not to have been taken long ago to make clear to Indian Mohammedans that the British Government, while anxious to give the utmost weight to the representation of reasonable men, was not to be deflected from its considered policy by agitation. I believe that the reform proposals associated with your name constitute the greatest hope for both peace and progress in India. Nothing . . . is more calculated to imperil these reforms . . . and India's unity and future than that Indian Moslems should be encouraged to subvert Indian interests to Turkish politics.

The next lines must have been even more devastating to Montagu: Lloyd George implicitly blamed him for the unrest in India:

I am not sure that in your advocacy of the case as viewed by yourself, you have not given encouragement to an agitation in India which, if it were to continue, might not undermine the edifice of Indian Constitutional Government which you have so carefully reared. I therefore, trust that you will now take immediate steps to make clear to Indian opinion that the decision of the British Government and its Allies. . . . is final and must be accepted as such. I believe that the decisions . . . are wise and just and that scrupulous regard has been paid to the religious feelings of Indian Mohammedans, and that as such the peace would commend itself to the judgment of the overwhelming mass of the Indian people if they could be sufficiently informed.

A subdued Montagu responded on April 29.[37] As a disciplined Cabinet Minister, he "accepts the decision" that Lloyd George expressed. But there were certain points in the letter he could not let pass without comment. He noted that he had been appointed Plenipotentiary not on behalf of Great Britain but on behalf of India, "an appointment similar and analogous to that, let us say, of Mr. Hughes of Australia." He had joined the delegation not as a member of the British Cabinet but as a representative of India. He recognized the difficulties of his dual responsibility and did not wish to argue further. He was disturbed that the Prime Minister had "some harsh things" to say about him. While he did not want to encourage discord, he felt he must respond.

He had not intended to misquote the resolution. In his original letter to Hankey, he had, in fact, cited the entire resolution:

I thought it unnecessary to quote the second resolution in my letter to you, because I do not read it to mean that a Memorandum so sent, but not discussed and not agreed upon by the Imperial Empire Delegation was to be withheld altogether from the Peace Conference without further reference to its author. For the latter purposes I was ready, as I informed Sir Maurice Hankey, to hold myself at your disposal at San Remo, as at your invitation I had placed myself at your disposal in Paris earlier in the year.

In short, he did not believe that the section quoted by the Prime Minister in the resolution precluded his forwarding a memorandum to the Peace Conference, if the memorandum was not discussed or agreed upon by the imperial delegation. While he appreciated the fact that the Indian delegation had the opportunity in the past to express its views, he believed it was important to present them anew because Wilson, Clemenceau and Orlando had gone home and new principles were entitled to a fresh hearing.

He insisted he was not pro-Turkish. "I have no interest in a country who at the invitation of Germany fought against us and prolonged the war. But I had the deepest interest and deepest concern to present a case on behalf of a part of the British Empire for which I am responsible and whose peace and well being may be so profoundly affected by the Turkish Treaty." He was distressed that Lloyd George thought this was his personal view: He had evidence that it was the opinion of the government in India, that of Indian local government and the consensus of opinion of all India, Hindus and Muslims alike.

He ended on a conciliatory note. He hoped that before the treaty was announced, "we could let India know" that "the terms . . . are in harmony with their religious beliefs. . . . We should invite the French, Greeks, British and Italians to agree that a deputation of loyal Indian Mohammedans should visit these Holy Places and satisfy themselves that the custody and rule of the Holy Places will remain in Mohammedan hands." This would be "of great assistance in keeping order in India. Is it a possible suggestion?"

At the time, it would not have been unreasonable to conclude that Lloyd George was correct, that Montagu's pro-Turkish stance had exacerbated the tensions in India and that his interpretation of the January 20 resolution of the British delegation was ludicrous. It would also have been reasonable to hold that Montagu was correct —that Lloyd George's anti-Turkish policy was the major cause of Indian unrest. With hindsight, it is now evident that both men were wrong. Unrest in India was as much or more the result of the racial attitudes of the British, postwar economic problems and the worldwide forces of nationalism that developed after World War I, than of Britain's policy toward Turkey.

At most, Turkey was only an excuse for the growth of Gandhi's noncooperation movement. Hostility to British rule went much deeper. Had Turkey not existed, there would have been another catalyst. Montagu himself only provided an excuse for the Conservatives to give vent to their anti-Liberal anti-Semitic sentiments. If they had not found India, they would have found another issue; if Montagu had not provided them with a scapegoat, they would have found another.

Recognizing at last that he had no chance of becoming Viceroy (even his friend Beaverbrook told him he had but one chance in a thousand), Montagu wrote to the Prime Minister on April 30, 1920, that there was no urgency in choosing a Viceroy; the choice could wait until October and by then he promised to suggest some other names. "Will you please therefore consider . . . the matter postponed until the autumn."[38] And during June 1920, Montagu suggested that the Office of Viceroy be divided between two people: someone like the Prince of Wales to handle the ceremonial aspects of the job, and someone like Harcourt Butler, Governor of the United Provinces, to handle the political problems.[39]

Lloyd George rejected both the idea of the Royal Prince and the name of Harcourt Butler. Montagu then suggested other names for the Viceroyalty, among them those of Winston Churchill and H. A. L. Fisher. Churchill, Montagu wrote, "might result in a great failure. It might be a great success. Whichever it was, it would be great."[40] He had finally recognized how controversial he had become. To withdraw his name from consideration for a post he wanted so much and to be forced to submit the names of men he believed inferior to himself in their knowledge of and feeling for India must have broken his heart.

Report on Amritsar

The report of the Hunter Commission on Amritsar, released to the Cabinet on April 7, 1920, dealt Montagu's already failing spirit a near fatal blow. The intensity of the feelings generated by Amritsar was so great, and opinions on it so divided, that the Commission of Inquiry had to issue both majority and minority reports.[41] The majority report characterized Dyer's conduct as "an error in judgment." It rejected Dyer's excuse that he acted out of fear that another insurrection might occur and because he wished to set an example that would deter such an eventuality. It was critical of the fact that he had fired without warning into the crowd and continued to fire although it was unarmed. The duty of an officer in such circumstances, the report concluded, was only to take such measures as were necessary to save lives and to prevent the destruction of property, and not to "strike terror" into the populace. The minority report signed by the three Indian members of the Commission did not dispute the facts, but it placed greater emphasis on its belief that Amritsar was not a rebellion but only a disorder, that the harshness of the Rowlatt Act had triggered it, and that the blame for the incident lay not merely with Dyer but with the behavior of the Indian government, which had engendered the mood that had set off the riots. The minority report also concluded that Dyer's order prohibiting public meetings had not been adequately published.

While Montagu publicly supported the majority report, his sympathy lay with the minority. He had always predicted that government repression would provoke rebellion. The government was thus more to blame than the people were. He expressed this opinion in a letter to Chelmsford on April 8:

I do not regard the Report of the Hunter Committee, on first reading as having exonerated Sir Michael O'Dwyer. On the contrary they are inclined to say in guarded language what I would say about the sort of rule for which he was responsible. . . . I was not at the India office during most of O'Dwyer's regime. Whether the ring-fence policy, which he to some extent advocated, was necessary or not, I do not choose to say. I have not the material. But let all people beware that when they contemplate executive action, deportation, suppression of Press, prohibition of public meetings, prohibition of free movement, they are bound, sooner or later, to reap the reward. It is an expedient which perhaps tides them over for the moment. I am convinced that it does not tide them over in the long run. . . . Do not let us shut our eyes to the fact that there must be a harvest. The greatest administrator and the greatest Governor is the man who keeps his Province quiet and orderly without recourse, or with the minimum of recourse to those powers with which he has been entrusted.[42]

When the report was first circulated within the Cabinet, Lloyd George appointed a Committee to examine it, to suggest how and when it should be published and how its differences with the government of India could be reconciled to give the appearance of unanimity on this very sensitive issue. Montagu was named Chairman. It was a thankless and arduous responsibility. Weeks were spent ironing out differences among the positions held by the Indian government, Montagu and this Committee. Language and tone were often debated more than substance; reconciling these was not easy.

The report was finally published on May 26, 1920, with a resolution by the government of India and a dispatch by the Secretary of State for India. Most differences had been worked out, and the resolution by the government of India gave that body the opportunity to express comments that were not part of the report or of Montagu's dispatch. The resolution warned men like Gandhi that they could not urge that laws be broken and then deny responsibility for the total breakdown of law and order. "These warnings," the resolution stated, "have gone unheeded. The question has now been put to the test and the answer written in . . . flame and blood."[43]

This was a direct rebuke to Gandhi and the image of peace and nonviolence he espoused. But by now Gandhi was beyond reproach. His influence was enormous; he was now revered not only as a leader but as a saint. And if the result of his message of nonviolence and peace was "flame and blood," his followers either did not see the connection or did not care.

Montagu was apprehensive about publishing the report, fearing that it would please "no one because as usual we have had to hold the balance between the conflicting schools of thought."[44] His fears were justified. Within two weeks of its publication, the report was attacked by the Indians for not going far enough and by the Conservatives for going too far in condemning "a gallant soldier just trying to do his duty."

The *Morning Post* took up the cudgel for O'Dwyer and Dyer by publishing a letter by O'Dwyer in which he claimed that he had been denied a hearing before the Cabinet, that the five "European" members of the Hunter Commission had never served in India and that the three Indians on the Committee belonged to that class of people who were now making the trouble. He suggested that the delay of six months between the disorder and the inquiry had prejudiced the hearing, that agitators had taken advantage of the delay to intimidate witnesses and that the riots in Amritsar were part of an organized conspiracy. General Dyer, he wrote, had smashed the rebellion at its source and thus prevented widespread bloodshed and the murder of Europeans in the Punjab and probably elsewhere. The Hunter Commission report contained no condemnation of those who had fomented the disorders and were the ones really responsible for the bloodshed.[45]

O'Dwyer also took on Montagu and the India Office. He was in London in June 1919, he stated, two months after the riots, and claimed to have given Montagu all the facts. He was also in London in November and could have answered questions. Therefore, he was shocked when he returned to India in December and saw the December 16 cable from Montagu saying he had not known the details of Amritsar until he had read them in the newspapers.

The O'Dwyer letter inflamed the Conservative community. Montagu was now vilified as the man who had kept the Amritsar story from the House of Commons, as the one whose bad management and failure to support the brave soldiers who were trying to keep order was placing in jeopardy British rule in India. Although Montagu tried to give his side of the story in a letter to the *Morning Post* on June 14, 1920,[46] the damage had already been done.

In his letter, Montagu rejected O'Dwyer's claim that he had given Montagu all the details of the Amritsar massacre. When Montagu talked to O'Dwyer in June 1919, he had not been told that the firing had been without warning nor that it had been done not to disperse the crowd but, as Dyer had said later, to set an example—"to strike terror" in the hearts of the people. O'Dwyer himself probably did not know this and it was not until Dyer attempted to justify his actions that this information became known. No one had this information until August when Dyer reported to his military superiors. It was to gather all the information that Montagu had established the Commission on Inquiry. When he talked to O'Dwyer, he repeated, he did not have all the facts.[47] The Tories did not believe Montagu on this point and would make it the subject of heated debate in the House of Commons in the months ahead.

Kemal Marches Forward

By May 1920, in the middle of the outcry over Amritsar, it was clear that Montagu had lost not only his parliamentary leadership on India but also the struggle to achieve a moderate Turkish treaty. The terms of the proposed treaty were given to the Turks on May 20, and they were told they had no choice but to accept. No further negotiations were to be held. In their rush to conclude the treaty, the Allies underestimated the strength of Kemal who was gaining support daily. He now threatened to march on Constantinople and had announced that he and his supporters would repudiate any treaty signed by the Sultan.

The Allies hastily reconvened, this time at Lympne on June 20, 1920, to devise a strategy to stop Kemal. Venizélos offered to put the entire Greek Army at the disposal of the Allies. While France and Italy were reluctant to continue the war in Turkey, Lloyd George persuaded them that the Allies had no alternative. The proposal of Venizélos was accepted, and additional Greek soldiers were dispatched to Turkey. They marched into East Thrace and occupied Adrianople, meeting no opposition. Kemal had withdrawn to regroup his forces and redesign his strategy. Montagu continued to object to Britain's role in this war, but Lloyd George was not to be moved in his determination to assist the Greeks and, once and for all, to destroy Turkish opposition to the proposed Allied peace treaty. He had given in on Constantinople, but that was all.

Debate on Hunter Committee Report

If Lloyd George had given Montagu half the support he gave Venizélos, the disgraceful debate on the Hunter Committee report, the personal attacks it engendered against Montagu, as well as the deterioration in Anglo-Indian relations that ensued, might not have occurred. But he did not. In his political judgment, it was better to throw Montagu to the Tory wolves than to jeopardize his pro-Greek policy. From the moment the report was leaked to the press in April (it was not officially presented in the House of Commons until July 8, 1920), not only did Montagu become the target of the Conservative press, but he also found himself the brunt of intense harassment in the House of Commons.

The parliamentary debates, beginning in mid-April and continuing through July 8, demonstrate a vindictiveness that had rarely been seen in Parliament. Throughout, Montagu had no support from Lloyd George and very little from his Liberal colleagues or from the Cabinet. The more personal the attacks, the more isolated he became.

Churchill made the strongest statement in support of the Hunter Committee report in a brilliant and eloquent speech that called Dyer's action "monstrous" and "tragic." It played a decisive part in determining the outcome of the vote:

However we may dwell upon all this, one tremendous fact stands out—I mean the slaughter of nearly 400 persons and the wounding of probably three or four times as many at the Jallian Wallah Bagh on 13th April. That is an episode which appears to me to be without precedent or parallel in the modern history of the British Empire. It is an event of an entirely different order from any of those tragical occurrences which take place when troops are brought into collision with the civil population. It is an extraordinary event, a monstrous event, an event which stands in singular and sinister isolation.[48]

By his indiscriminate shooting of innocent people, Churchill asserted, Dyer had failed to demonstrate the compassion and concern for human beings that distinguishes Englishmen from Bolsheviks who practice "bloody . . . terrorism . . . this is not the British way of doing business." Churchill made a point of complimenting Montagu: He was the only colleague to do so. He reminded the House that if Indian relations with Britain had ruptured as relations had in Egypt, it would have been "one of the most melancholy events in the history of the world." That they did not rupture was attributable to Montagu, who risked the hazards of a voyage to India during the height of the war to spend six months there trying to reconcile differences:

I was astonished by my right hon. Friend's sense of detachment when, in the supreme crisis of the War, he calmly journeyed to India, and remained for many months absorbed and buried in Indian affairs. It was not until I saw what happened in Egypt, and, if you like, what is going on in Ireland to-day, that I appreciated the enormous utility of such service, from the point of view of the national interests of the British Empire, in helping to keep alive that spirit of comradeship, that sense of unity and of progress in co-operation, which must ever ally and bind together the British and Indian peoples.[49]

On July 8, Asquith too condemned General Dyer's actions as "one of the greatest outrages in our annals," and Bonar Law spoke halfheartedly in defense of the Hunter Commission report. But aside from Churchill, no one said a single kind word on behalf of Montagu or uttered a word of recognition for what he had accomplished for India. On the contrary, Sir Edward Carson, Sir William Joynson-Hicks (later Lord Brentford), Rupert Gwynne and Col. Charles Edward Yate, among others, were determined not only to harass and embarrass Montagu but to drive him from office.

No matter what Montagu responded, nothing satisfied his adversaries. They were not interested in the answers. They not only objected to Montagu's substantive position on Amritsar but spent an inordinate amount of time trying to show that Montagu had lied when, in December 1919, six months after Amritsar, he had told the House that he did not have all the facts.[50] Montagu attempted repeatedly to explain that while he had some information from the reports he received from India, he was awaiting the full report of the Commission of Inquiry before judging or commenting on the case.[51]

This did not satisfy his Tory opponents. Lt. Col. F. Hall asked whether Montagu believed that "the manner [in which] the gallant soldier [Dyer] had been treated will assist in dealing with other outbreaks."[52] The meeting became so unruly at this point that the Speaker called the last question out of order. But the Tories sensed that they had Montagu on the run and pursued him ruthlessly, hurling the same questions at him repeatedly.

Montagu's position was supported by a letter dated June 30, 1920, and put into the record of the parliamentary debates by T. W. Holderness, a member of the India Office. He rejected O'Dwyer's recollection of how much information he had given Montagu. He pointed out that O'Dwyer's interview with Dyer on April 16 was limited to "a quarter of an hour and that when Sir M. O'Dwyer left India (for London) in May the Punjab Government was still awaiting Gen. Dyer's Report," which "was not made until August 1919. It was this report, that contained the passage which gave the key to Gen. Dyer's action and which is the centre of the controversy to which his action has given rise. It was no longer a question of merely dispersing the crowd but one of producing a sufficient moral effect . . . not merely on those who were present, but more especially throughout the Punjab. There could be no question of undue severity."[53]

It was Holderness's conclusion that if he had been called upon during the summer or autumn of 1919 to prepare a statement on the Jallian Wallah Bagh incident and had framed it on the information received from O'Dwyer, it would have "been of a different complexion from the account of the facts given by Gen. Dyer. It would not and could not have included the critical features on which discussion has since centered."[54] Holderness also said that the India Office would have been criticized if it had issued incomplete information while a Committee was making an investigation. Holderness's letter was given little or no attention and the attacks continued unabated.

Stronger men than Montagu would have cracked under this barrage of criticism. He had just been released from the nursing home when the attacks began and was still not entirely recovered from his illness. It is not surprising that by the end of April he was again deeply depressed. He wrote to Chelmsford: "I have failed to produce a decent Turkish Peace. . . . I have isolated myself from my colleagues and such is the racial bitterness in India that nobody who tries can satisfy either Indian or European. The whole thing looks gloomy. . . . I wonder when the sun will ever shine again?"[55] In his political life, the sun would never shine again for Montagu.

During a series of questions on July 7, Montagu was asked whether Dyer had accepted the accuracy of the evidence against him. Montagu said he did not know. Dyer's statement to the Army Council was to be published shortly, he said, and would be presented to the House of Commons during the July 8 debate. Churchill was then asked if the Army Council was prepared to publish Gen. Dyer's statement. He responded in the affirmative and then told the House that in spite of the great difficulties in which Dyer found himself, Dyer "cannot be acquitted of an error of judgement." He added gratuitously that the Commander in Chief in India had removed Dyer from employment in India, that he had been informed that he would not be employed further and, as a result, was reduced to half pay.[56]

The reaction of the House to this statement was a prologue to the rowdy and hostile debate that would begin the next day. Members began shouting "Why—Why," then "Shame—Shame."[57] The Speaker had difficulty achieving order. This provoked Churchill to rise and announce, "this is very improper and disorderly." Cries of "Why—Why" continued to echo through the House. Churchill responded that the Army Council considered all the facts and "does not feel called upon . . . to take any further action."[58] Joynson-Hicks queried whether Churchill was prepared to defend that position. Churchill replied loudly and clearly, "Certainly." And with that, some order was restored in the House.

With this background, it is no wonder that Montagu dreaded the official debate, which was to begin July 8. The formal debate began on a motion inquiring whether Parliament should contribute to the salary of the Secretary of State for India. This was a historic motion, the first time that Parliament had considered such a contribution. An amendment was introduced to reduce the salary of the Secretary of State by £100 as a gesture of dissatisfaction with Montagu.

The debate could not have been more unpleasant. It provided a unique opportunity to attack not only an outspoken Liberal but a Liberal Jew. Here was a chance at a double-barreled victory, to attack and reject the Hunter Committee report and to force Montagu to resign for incompetence.

Although Montagu's speech on behalf of the report has been characterized as a "Parliamentary failure"[59] and was disparaged by Montagu himself, the speech was a sound, factual presentation. Under the pressure of interruptions and rude catcalls, Montagu did at times respond emotionally and with a raised and impassioned voice, which was characterized by one Member of Parliament in a letter to Lloyd George as "more racial and Yiddish in screaming tone and gesture," which resulted in a "strong anti-Jewish feeling."[60] In his biography of Churchill, William Manchester called Montagu's response, "a calamity." Manchester continued: "He was a Jew and there were anti-Semites in the House. He had been warned to be quiet and judicial. Instead, he was sarcastic; he called Dyer a terrorist; he worried about foreign opinion"; and he thoroughly roused most of the latent passions of the stodgy Tories.[61] In Manchester's view, because he was a Jew, Montagu should not have called Dyer a terrorist or spoken with such passion, although he felt strongly about the issue and had been criticized mercilessly.

While Montagu frequently turned the other cheek to anti-Semitic insults, this time he could not do so. The issues meant too much to him not to strike back with all his emotion. Montagu began his response by explaining that the dispatch based on the Hunter Commission report, which was now the object of censure, "was drawn up by a Cabinet Committee and approved by the whole Cabinet. Every single body, civil and military which has been charged with the discussion of this lamentable affair has come to the same conclusion. The question before the Committee this afternoon is whether they will endorse the position of his Majesty's government, of the Hunter Committee, of the Commander in Chief of India, of the Government of India and of the Army, or whether they will desire to censure them." And then, hoping to avert personal attacks that he knew would follow, he added: "I hope the Debate will not take the shape of a criticism of the personnel of any of them. It is so easy to quarrel with the judge when you do not agree with his judgment."[62]

Montagu framed the issue as a condemnation of terrorism:

The real issue can be stated in one sentence, and I will content myself by asking the House one question. If an officer justifies his conduct, no matter how gallant his record is—and everybody knows how gallant General Dyer's record is—by saying that there was no question of undue severity, that if his means had been greater the casualties would have been greater, and that the motive was to teach a moral lesson to the whole of the Punjab, I say without hesitation, and I would ask the Committee to contradict me if I am wrong, because the whole matter turns upon this, that it is the doctrine of terrorism.

If you agree to that, you justify everything that General Dyer did. . . .

I say, further, that when you pass an order that all Indians, whoever they may be, must crawl past a particular place, when you pass an order to say that all Indians, whoever they may be, must forcibly or voluntarily salaam any officer of His Majesty the King, you are enforcing racial humiliation.

I say, thirdly, that when you take selected schoolboys from a school, guilty or innocent, and whip them publicly, when you put up a triangle, where an outrage which we all deplore and which all India deplores has taken place, and whip people who have not been convicted, when you flog a wedding party, you are indulging in frightfulness, and there is no other adequate word which could describe it.

If the Committee follows me on these assertions, this is the choice and this is the question which the Committee has put to it today before coming to an answer.[63]

Montagu acknowledged publicly the harassment and indecent personal attacks that he had endured with relative calm in the House of Commons during the two preceding months:

Dismiss from your mind, I beg of you, all personal questions. I have been pursued for the last three months. I have been pursued throughout my association by some people and by some journals with personal attacks. I do not propose to answer them to-day. Are you going to keep your hold upon India by terrorism, racial humiliation and subordination and frightfulness or are you going to rest it upon the . . . growing good will of the people of your Indian Empire?[64]

In defense of Dyer, Palmer shouted, "It saved a mutiny." Captain W. Benn put in, "Do not answer him." Montagu continued:

The great objection to terrorism, the great objection to the rule of force, is that you pursue it without regard to the people who suffer from it, and that having once tried it you must go on. Every time an incident happens you are confronted with the increasing animosity of the people who suffer, and there is no end to it until the people in whose name we are governing India, the people of this country, and the national pride and sentiment of the Indian people rise together in protest and terminate your rule in India as being impossible on modern ideas of what an Empire means. There is an alternative policy which I assumed office to commend to this House and which this House has supported until to-day. It is to put the capping stone on the glorious work which England has accomplished in India by leading India to a complete free partnership in the British Commonwealth, to say to India: "We hold British lives sacred, but we hold Indian lives sacred too."[65]

Rupert Gwynne attacked Montagu for having misled the House and for having no pity on Dyer, condemning him for taking two hundred or three hundred lives when he thought this would save thousands of others, and concluded that Montagu was "not fit to be Secretary of State." He accused Montagu of keeping information about the Amritsar outbreak from the House on December 16, 1919, in order to get the Reform Act passed. On May 22, 1919, he asserted, Montagu made some reference to Amritsar and then dropped the issue. On May 20, the First Reading of the Bill took place, and on June 5 the Second Reading. In August, General Dyer was requested to send his report to the government of India. Why did Montagu not read the report at that time? Gwynne also accused Montagu of pressuring the Indian government into accepting the Hunter Committee report. Montagu tried to respond, repeating again that in May "we decided to appoint a Committee and I thought that it would be best to wait for its Report." Gwynne was not finished. He quoted a statement made by Montagu in 1919 in which he described Gandhi as a "very great and distinguished Indian . . . a man of the highest motives and one of the finest character."[66] This was the man, Gwynne continued, who:

is at large, spreading pernicious doctrines. If he [Montagu] is Mr. Gandhi's friend he has no right to be Secretary of State for India. . . . If the right hon. Gentleman continues we are going on the right road to lose India. The most graceful thing he could do now would be to resign. I would even prefer that the usual method of the Government should be proceeded with and that he be given, if necessary, a more important appointment rather than be allowed to ruin India.[67]

Gwynne did not mention the fact that the Hunter Committee report had been approved by Lloyd George, the Cabinet, the Army, the Secretary of War and the Viceroy, in Council. The matter was now a personal vendetta against Montagu.

Finally, after standing by in silence while Montagu was attacked, abused and insulted for almost four months, and for seven consecutive hours on July 8, for a policy and report approved by the Cabinet, Bonar Law came to the rescue. Always the gentleman, he objected to the unfair treatment accorded Montagu by Members of the House. The policy of Great Britain toward India had been taken before Montagu had become Secretary of State. As for Dyer, the dispatch criticizing him was not Montagu's opinion alone. It was "the work of a Committee of the Cabinet, which drafted and advised it and *we are all responsible for it*" (emphasis added).[68]

Law's speech painted a very sympathetic picture of Dyer's action but concluded that in spite of his sympathy for this brave soldier, Dyer was "entirely wrong."[69] He should have given notice before he opened fire. Here, there was laughter from the House, as if to suggest that giving notice to thousands of Indians was a ludicrous and laughable suggestion.

Bonar Law ignored the laughter and continued to point out, as

Montagu had done, that Dyer was not in danger of being attacked, that he continued to fire long after he ought to have stopped; and that he used more force than necessary. It was difficult, Law admitted, to draw the line in such cases, but the evidence was clear that he fired not to disperse the crowd but to produce "a sufficient moral effect." That, Bonar Law concluded, "is a principle which ought to be repudiated."[70] Again he reminded the House that the Cabinet took this position, as did the government of India, the Army Council and the Commander in Chief of India. All the Army people "to whom I have spoken . . . have taken the view that General Dyer was wrong."[71]

Bonar Law said nothing that Montagu had not said. However, he spoke in a voice of quiet confidence, and, most importantly, he was a man the Conservatives liked and respected. He was "one of them." He could be trusted, unlike Montagu, the Liberal Jew. While he may not have changed any of the votes of the diehards, at least he brought order to the House. He was not, however, a friend of Montagu. He disliked him and the Liberalism he represented. Whatever he said in Commons that day he said to save the face of Lloyd George's Cabinet, not to help Montagu. As one historian has noted: "Although Bonar Law had thus as in duty bound rallied to the defense of Edwin Montagu, his private opinion of the Secretary for India was not high. Three months earlier, he had written to Lloyd George a letter whose precise context is not clear but which evidently refers to the Dyer case. It said: I saw Max yesterday. Edwin Montagu is going to do nothing. With all his cleverness he has evidently some of the poorest qualities of his race."[72]

After Bonar Law's presentation, at 10:49 P.M., the vote was taken on the motion to reduce Montagu's salary by £100: 137 voted for and 247 against. The next day, July 9, 1920, Freddy Guest reported to Lloyd George:

The unpopularity of Montagu amongst Unionists is undoubtedly responsible for at least half of the voting.

The debate could not have had a worse start . . . and this is entirely due to Montagu's speech. He had evidently been greatly overwrought for the last three weeks on this subject and made exactly the wrong kind of speech . . . the Whips had the greatest difficulty on account of this, many members insisting that they were voting more against Montagu than in favor of

Dyer. . . . Winston made an amazingly able speech, but Bonar is reported not to have been so effective as usual.[73]

While Montagu's enemies may have lost this vote, ultimately they won the battle. In the House of Lords, Dyer's actions were condoned by a vote of 121 to 86. But more importantly, Montagu's opponents had now brought into the open their intense dislike of him and had made clear to Lloyd George that they wanted his resignation. The fact that he was Jewish was now openly acknowledged as an important factor in their dislike.

To Lloyd George, already losing his control of the Conservatives and his grip on the Coalition, Montagu had become yet another source of political trouble that he could ill afford. The fact that Montagu was defending a report of a commission that Lloyd George himself had appointed became irrelevant; the fact that Montagu's attackers were influenced as much or more by their anti-Semitism and anti-Liberalism as they were by the substance of the report was equally irrelevant. To Lloyd George the issue had become his own political survival. If Montagu's head had to fall to achieve that end, then it would fall.

Montagu was devastated by the attacks upon him and what he perceived as his own failure to frame the issue properly. In a letter to Chelmsford on July 15, 1920, he wrote:

You will see that up to the end of my letter I have been shirking any mention of that dreadful debate. I find myself in a frame of mind in which I either write nothing at all or inflict on you in full the speech which I now think I ought to have made. I am not going to do the last and I must not do the first. But what I do say is this. Many allegations have been and are being made against me personally, and many attacks have been and are being made on me. There is only one sort of allegation or attack which gives me real and deep concern at the moment, and that is the sort of attack which is directed, intentionally or not, against you and your Government. I ought to have said a great deal more to make your position quite clear. I failed to say it; and if the result is that I have left unanswered any charge which reflects on you, my first obligation is to set it right. My dear Chelmsford, if you think I have done anything of the kind, don't be afraid, don't conceal it, don't add it to your score against me—though I have no right to talk like that—but remember that you are dealing with a man who feels it to be his debt of honour to help you.[74]

Montagu was seriously concerned about Gandhi and in the same
letter wrote to Chelmsford:

Now they are getting very pertinacious about Gandhi. They want to know
why you don't lock him up at once because they disapprove of him. This
may be more serious for us than the other charges. At present it is all my
fault because I once said that Gandhi was my friend. At question time
yesterday I repeatedly explained that I was going to leave the methods of
maintaining order to your discretion. I am most certainly going to adhere
to that; but I have got to confess that one of the results of the dead set
which is being made against me is likely to be a running cross-examination
of what steps you are taking to handle the Khaliphat and the non-cooperation movements.

To make matters worse, Chelmsford agreed with some of the
criticism directed against Montagu's presentation before the Commons. He objected to some of Montagu's language that he found
too inflammatory, especially Montagu's use of the words "frightfulness and terrorism" to describe Dyer's action. He told this to Montagu in a letter July 14. Montagu had felt badly enough already, now
to have the Viceroy join in the criticism was a blow he could barely
endure. To his credit, he did not back down. Instead he reaffirmed
the positions he had taken in his presentation, including the word
"frightfulness," which he believed was absolutely necessary to show
that it was the principle on which Dyer acted and that it deserved
condemnation. The crawling order was "frightfulness," and shooting to produce a moral effect was "terrorism." He stood firmly
behind his position. "I have had," he concluded, "a hard and bitter
time, harder and more bitter than can be imagined. I do not ask for
sympathy. . . . Looking back now the thing I regret more than
anything else, now that I know the sort of man he is, is that we did
not deal more severely with O'Dwyer."[75] As for India, he told
Chelmsford, he was "infinitely depressed," and "nothing but a
determination to appear to desert the policy for which you and I
stand gives me the heart to go on." He believed Amritsar did terrible
damage and "we are in for a bad time in India."[76]

As Montagu had predicted, the repercussions in India of the
debate were very serious. Educated Indians were humiliated by the
slurs and insults directed against them in the course of that debate.
It reinforced the Indian belief that Britain had no real desire to treat
them as equal partners in the British Empire, that the lives of Indians

meant nothing to the British, who were racially prejudiced and indifferent to the problems of nonwhites. The launching of a pro-Dyer fund by the *Morning Post,* inspired by Sir Edward Carson, for the "Man Who Saved India," to which ten pounds was donated by Rudyard Kipling, only added to Indian outrage. Rabindranath Tagore, the Indian poet who had recently been knighted for his contributions to literature, returned the honor, informing the Viceroy that "I wish to stand shorn of all special distinctions by the side of those of my countrymen who, for their so-called insignificance, are liable to suffer a degradation not fit for human beings."[77]

Throughout the rest of 1920, the Tories continued their attacks on Montagu, giving him no respite during the almost six months that remained after the official Amritsar debate concluded on July 8. The attacks on Montagu were particularly difficult on July 23, when he moved for the adoption of draft rules relating to the election of provincial legislative councils and to the Indian Legislature under the Reform Act. Only after several hours of argument and the offering of scores of nit-picking amendments involving a word or phrase were the rules finally adopted.

Questions were again raised about Amritsar, the Khalifat movement and Gandhi. A shouting match broke out on why Gandhi had not been imprisoned and why so many prisoners were being pardoned. Montagu held his ground with astonishing calm. On these last two questions, he continued to take the position that responsibility for law and order rested with the government of India and that he would not interfere.

Later in the year, Gandhi was the subject of yet another heated debate. Montagu placed in the record an official report of a resolution by the government of India addressing the need to beware of taking action that would make Gandhi a martyr, of impairing freedom of the press and of speech at a time when India was on the threshold of instituting its new reforms.[78] The best minds in India condemned noncooperation, the resolution stated. The government of India preferred to refrain from repressive action and to depend on the good sense of most Indians.[79]

The resolution gave rise to another nasty debate between Gwynne and Yate and Montagu, with Gwynne demanding that Montagu answer the question "What steps are being taken to restrain Gandhi?" Montagu gave his stock reply, that it must be left to the

Government of India.[80] Only once did Montagu display his personal feelings. Following a question by Yate on the Indian Civil Service, Montagu responded: "All that that means is that my hon. and gallant Friend is not satisfied. I am afraid that to satisfy him is a task to which I do not aspire."[81]

Amritsar, as Montagu had rightly feared, had doomed any efforts to implement effectively the Reform Act of 1919, and it gave Gandhi new ammunition for his campaign of noncooperation. The British government was now denounced by Gandhi as "unscrupulous, immoral and unjust."[82] He called for a general boycott of all institutions, urging the Muslim League to join him. He now was clearly recognized as the leader in India, rising to full power in the aftermath of Amritsar.

The real tragedy was that before Amritsar, the chances of India becoming an equal, self-governing partner in the Empire were real. It was Amritsar and the attacks it prompted among the Tories that doomed such a goal. They, not Montagu nor the Reform Act, had made Gandhi a hero and had encouraged the movements for noncooperation and Home Rule. They, not Montagu, had precluded the possibility of evolution toward self-government in India.

This was the legacy of Curzon, Yate, Carson, Joynson-Hicks and their colleagues. This was the legacy of Lloyd George's silence during the attacks upon Montagu and upon the policies that Montagu had come to symbolize. Montagu may have been the immediate victim, but British rule in India was the ultimate loser.

The Treaty of Sèvres

The treaty finally signed with Turkey by the Allies (except the United States and Russia) on August 20, 1920, in Sèvres, France, did not improve Montagu's physical health or mental condition. It was based largely on the anti-Turkish recommendations made at the Conference in San Remo in mid-April, to which Lloyd George had refused to take Montagu. It was a harsh treaty, the kind that Montagu had long urged Lloyd George to reject. While Constantinople and the strip of territory along the Chatalja line remained Turkish, as did the rest of Anatolia, the remainder of Turkey was dismembered, and the Turkish government was required to relinquish all claims to non-Turkish territory.

Venizélos was delighted, exclaiming, on the signing of the treaty: "By combining the culture of her old civilization with the vitality and spirit of her younger generations, Greece will become a factor of progress, of peace and order in the Near East, and will thus prove that you have not given her your invaluable support in vain."[83] By this time, Montagu was so beaten by the harassment in the House of Commons that his public criticism of the treaty was muted. He had fought bitterly against it, his position had been rejected, and now he seemed resigned to the worst.

Indians Support Montagu for Viceroy

The one bright spot in Montagu's life was the support he now received from his friends in India for his appointment as Viceroy. Sinha wrote to the Prime Minister not only supporting Montagu for the post, but informing Lloyd George that the Maharajah of Alivar and Jam Sahib of Nawanayar, leaders of India, also strongly supported Montagu.[84]

Even with this support, Montagu could read the handwriting on the wall. He knew he had no chance. In a sad letter to the Prime Minister on August 4, 1920, while acknowledging that the Maharajah of Alivar had suggested that he be considered for Viceroy, Montagu asked that the Prime Minister ignore this suggestion. And then, moving to a subject even more painful and humiliating, the attacks upon him in the House of Commons, Montagu pleaded with the Prime Minister to "please deal vigorously with this small group that is attempting to drive me from office."[85] At this point it is unlikely that the Prime Minister wanted to do anything and, if he did, he probably would not have been able to stop the attacks. This wing of the Conservative Party was not under his control.

While Montagu removed himself from consideration as Viceroy, a replacement for Chelmsford continued to weigh on his mind. During the next two months he submitted other names to Lloyd George, none of which the Prime Minister approved. On December 7, Montagu wrote that Austen Chamberlain would not accept. "Reading is probably the best man, then Winston, then Lytton, then Willingdon."[86]

Apparently Lloyd George had been considering Reading for at least a month. There is a letter dated December 3 in Montagu's files

from Bhupendranath Basu, a former president of the Indian Council, and a member of the delegation that visited India with Montagu
in 1917, to Lloyd George, responding to the Prime Minister's request for his opinion of Lord Reading as Viceroy: "You thought he
would be good as he had nothing to do with Reforms and could
begin with no prejudice from people represented by the *Morning
Post.*" Basu disagreed. The *Morning Post,* he told Lloyd George,
"will have as much objection to Lord Reading as to Montagu."
Basu was referring to the fact that Reading was a Jew and that the
Morning Post would object to him on that ground regardless of
whether he had been involved in the Reform Act. Since this was the
case, Basu suggested that Lloyd George consider Montagu. He was
respected; he had a good reputation and, if he were appointed,
Indians would feel reassured of Britain's goodwill. Basu enclosed a
cable from S. R. Bomanjie, a wealthy merchant in Bombay who
supported Montagu, as did the Native Princes, who "feel the same
way." To disregard this would be "fraught with grave peril."[87]
What Basu did not know was that Lloyd George was prepared to
face an Indian peril far more readily than the specter of a disgruntled
Tory opposition.

On December 7, Montagu again wrote to the Prime Minister
urging the appointment of a Viceroy as quickly as possible, since
Chelmsford's mother was ill. "Austen won't accept," he said, "and
Reading is probably the best."[88] By December 16, Montagu waffled
on Reading and suggested instead Lytton or perhaps bringing Hardinge back, who was "undoubtedly the most popular Viceroy of
modern times."[89] Montagu may have had second thoughts about
Reading, but Lloyd George did not. On January 19, 1921, he appointed Lord Reading the fifteenth Viceroy of India.

29

Reading and Montagu, 1921

I shall want your advice badly to know how to avoid sudden humiliation.

Montagu to Lord Beaverbrook, Dec. 9, 1921

With Reading's appointment as Viceroy, Montagu now had a friend at the head of the government of India, and Britain, for the first and last time in its history, had a Jew as Viceroy. Reactions in English society, in government circles, and in India were mixed. Was England prepared to let two Jews, Reading and Montagu, rule the largest country in her Empire? Was she prepared to let a Jew occupy a post that bestowed upon the incumbent a power second to none in the whole of Asia or throughout the British Empire?[1]

Because of Reading's outstanding reputation, the reaction of the majority seemed to be favorable, albeit with some hesitation. Reading's distinction at the bar, his remarkable success during the war as Ambassador to the United States and as personal advisor to Lloyd George, his reputation for cautious and sound judgment, his personal charm, his mastery of detail, his administrative skills and nonconfrontational politics, all seemed to offset the fact that he was Jewish.

Lord Birkenhead summed up the general reaction when he said, "Everyone feels that he would be better if he was not a Jew, but is willing to give the Jew a trial."[2] The press by and large shared this view, with the exception of the *Morning Post* and other anti-Semitic newspapers and magazines, which unanimously wrote that no Jew should be permitted to rule India, and if Montagu was an example of a Jew with political power over India, the future of India was doomed.

Indian opinion was mixed. Some Indian newspapers and leaders believed that Reading's Jewish background would enable him to better understand the Oriental mind. The shibboleth of the Jew as an Oriental was as widespread in India as in England. Others believed that it was a disadvantage to have a Jew as Viceroy because it would antagonize some of the Muslims and certain of the Native Princes, although they begrudgingly agreed that Montagu's religion had not been a deterrent to his warm relations with both groups. In fact, Montagu's popularity with the Indians, both Hindu and Muslim, and with the Princes probably made Reading's Jewishness appear to be an asset rather than a liability.

Some people still remembered Reading's "indiscretions" in the Marconi scandal, and while the House of Commons had acquitted him, as they had Lloyd George and Herbert Samuel, some segments of the British public, especially the Conservatives, were never satisfied. The Viceroy, they believed, must be above reproach; and the taint of the Marconi scandal made Reading suspect. They remembered too the anti-Semitic poem "Gehazi," that Kipling, whose dislike of Jews was well known, wrote when Reading was appointed Lord Chief Justice in 1913.[3] In spite of slurs and condemnations, the majority viewed Reading as a man of exceptional talent. Even Lord Curzon magnanimously conceded that he was "quite prepared . . . to overlook [Reading's] race, because of the enormous importance of securing a *first rate* man."[4]

Lloyd George had no trouble with Reading's Jewishness. He and Reading were old and dear friends, their friendship going back to 1909 when Lord Reading, then Rufus Isaacs, an up-and-coming solicitor, had represented Lloyd George in a libel suit against the newspaper the *People,* which had accused Lloyd George of committing adultery with a married woman. Reading won the case; the *People* apologized and Lloyd George had received a thousand pounds in damages.

During the days when Lloyd George was Chancellor of the Exchequer and knew little or nothing about finance, Reading had helped and advised him. This close relationship of advisor and friend continued throughout their professional lives. Both men were pragmatists, not passionate ideologues, and both appreciated the ambition, talent and drive of the other.

The anti-Semitic slurs that Lloyd George frequently used in his comments about Montagu were never present in his remarks about Reading. When a man was useful to him, as Reading was, his religion became irrelevant. When he was not, Lloyd George's latent anti-Semitism surfaced. Beyond that, Reading was the personification of the assimilated Jew in his dandified appearance, demeanor and speech. When one was in his company, it was easy to forget that he was Jewish. Montagu's Jewishness remained stamped on his appearance and in his speech, despite his efforts to escape the past.

Montagu and Reading

Montagu was as pleased as Lloyd George with Reading's appointment, for he and Reading had become friends when they worked together during the early war days, when Montagu was Financial Secretary of the Treasury and Reading was financial advisor to Lloyd George. They both played bridge with the Asquiths and moved in the world of Liberal politics and, to some degree, in the smaller world of upper-class English Jewry.

Both had Orthodox Jewish fathers who had fought and pleaded with their errant sons to practice Judaism in the traditional ways. Disinterested in religion, both had rejected it, held no formal religious beliefs and were strongly anti-Zionist. Reading's second wife was not Jewish and he accepted with no conflict—some said he even encouraged—the Anglican baptism of his grandson. Most importantly Reading shared Montagu's desire for self-government in India. He had the legal and administrative skills to begin the implementation of the Reform Act and he supported Montagu's views of the Treaty of Sèvres.

But here the similarities ended. Montagu came from a rich and affluent background. When he was born, his father was already a millionaire, and Samuel Montagu & Co. was a worldwide institution with an impeccable reputation. Reading's father, Joseph Isaacs, was in the wholesale fruit business and, while able to provide his family with middle-class comforts, he could not match the Montagus' wealth or social standing. Reading had no university training; he left school when he was fourteen. Montagu was a product of Cambridge, and his presidency of the Cambridge Union was an honour he took pride in all his life.

Montagu had been interested in politics as a career and became a lawyer only as a method of entering politics. Reading's earliest interest was in making money. His first job was in a stock brokerage house; his first independent business venture was also the selling of bonds and securities. When the stock brokerage house went bank-rupt, Reading then entered upon the study of law, with some hesi-tation, as had Montagu. In Reading's case that hesitancy quickly disappeared. In a short time he became a brilliant lawyer and there-after, in quick succession, a very successful and respected solicitor, a Queens Counsel, a Solicitor General, Attorney General and then Lord Chief Justice.

Reading was by nature a restless and ambitious man who began dabbling in politics on the local level as an avocation. In 1900, he ran for office as a Liberal in North Kensington and lost. He kept in touch with the Liberal Party and ran again in 1904. He was never a radical Liberal like Montagu, who had entered politics with a deep-seated passion to correct the ills of the world. But Reading was known as a decent man with a genuine concern for social problems and a commitment to liberty, tolerance and equality. He supported all the planks of the Liberal program. It was on this platform that he ran successfully for Parliament in 1904 from the town of Reading. In this election, he had the support of Montagu, as well as that of other bright Liberal stars, including Lloyd George and Winston Churchill, both of whom campaigned for him. He probably needed all the help he could get from these fiery young orators, since his own speeches, according to Beaverbrook, were "dignified and dull. He was deliberate, cooperative, and so cautious that he never gave an opinion until he was forced to do so."[5] His whole demeanor was the antithesis of Montagu's. He was described as tall, dignified, splendid-looking and especially attractive to women. Reading was the epitome of tact and charm and had great patience. He was a born diplomat and conciliator. When Reading entered Parliament in 1904, he was forty-three years old. Montagu was twenty-seven when he became a member of Parliament, two years later.

During the 1904 election, when Reading encountered a heckler who had shouted "Down with the Jews," he responded: "When I came to Reading I said and I say now I am a Jew and proud of it." He then spoke of the suffering of the Jews and reminded his audience of Britain's reputation for justice and fair play. The heckler was silenced. Thus, while Reading had no great interest in his Judaism (and never entered a synagogue except for a wedding or memorial service), he, like Montagu, never publicly renounced it.

Montagu and Reading shared one other similarity: The careers of both men were given their initial impetus by Prime Minister Asquith. It was Asquith who had appointed Reading Solicitor General in 1910 and Attorney General seven months later and who brought Reading into the Cabinet as Attorney General in 1912. And it was Asquith who went out of his way to protect Reading (as well as Lloyd George and Herbert Samuel) during the Marconi scandal. Margot Asquith later asserted that Asquith did this only because of his high regard and affection for Reading.[6]

But Montagu's relationship with Asquith was very different from Reading's. In the early years of their association, Montagu adored Asquith and viewed him as his dearest friend. And while their relationship soured after Montagu joined the Lloyd George government, he never ceased to have the deepest feelings for Asquith. When he joined Lloyd George, he did so not out of affection for Lloyd George but because he desperately wanted to get back into politics. He never felt toward Lloyd George as he did toward Asquith, where a father-son relationship existed from the start.

Reading, on the other hand, viewed Lloyd George as his best friend. When he worked for Lloyd George it was not only from the deepest admiration but from genuine affection. During the leadership struggle of 1916, it was Reading who acted as peacemaker on behalf of Lloyd George; Montagu represented Asquith. This relationship between Reading and Lloyd George, Montagu believed, would be of great importance to India. It would mean that not only would Montagu have a friend and ally as Viceroy, but also that the Viceroy would now have the ear of the Prime Minister as well as his respect.

Reading would certainly need all the support and assistance he could muster. He was coming to India at a most difficult time. He had been appointed in January 1921 and spent the two months before leaving for India reading as many books as he could, picking the brains of civil servants in the India Office and of anyone he could find associated with India and spending as much time as possible talking to Montagu. "I am delighted with Rufus," Montagu wrote. "We spend much of the day together. No one can say who is going to make a good Viceroy, but one can confidently predict that Rufus ought to make a good one."[7]

Agitation Increases

Reading arrived in Bombay on April 2, 1921, and was greeted by large, cheering crowds. After two days of ceremonies, speeches, receptions and parades with body guards resplendent in red and blue uniforms, he left for Delhi on the magnificent Viceregal train.[8] The railway line to Delhi, 845 miles away, "was guarded at twenty-yard intervals by soldiers holding flickering torches—a lavish deployment of manpower"[9] and, one might add, an extravagant exhibition of the majestic and regal lifestyle that surround the Viceroy.

But the pomp and glitter masked an ugly mood. Gandhi and his followers were moving toward civil disobedience, which, in turn, was encouraging more riots and more rebellion. The moderates were becoming increasingly hard-line. All through January, February and March of 1921, before Reading's arrival, Chelmsford's telegrams to Montagu were bleak and discouraging. In Bengal the Khalifat movement and the noncooperative movement were growing; boycotts were being organized to embarrass the Duke of Connaught, who was to arrive in February 1921 to open the first Indian Legislative Council elected as part of the Reform Act of 1919. Strikes were spreading in the colleges. Stone throwing and looting occurred daily.

On January 26, Chelmsford sent Montagu a telegram, the uncharacteristically forceful language of which expressed the serious concerns he and his colleagues felt over developments in Turkey. "One of the most dangerous factors in problems which confronts us is however Moslem unrest over the Turkish peace terms. Whatever may have been origin of the Khalifat movement, it is now preeminently a religious one which has secured very general support."[10] Chelmsford urged that the Duke of Connaught make an important statement on his arrival on Moslem concerns about Turkey, "to mitigate the bitter feelings which now prevail."[11]

Montagu agreed, and since an Inter-Allied Conference on Turkey was then meeting in London, the time was propitious. With the Prime Minister's approval, Montagu wrote a moving statement which the Duke read on his arrival in India on February 9 at the opening of the new Indian Legislative Assembly. The statement referred "with the deepest regret" to the "shadow of Amritsar having lengthened over the fair face of India," but the Duke reassured the audience that they now had "the beginning of *swaraj* [the Hindi word for self-government] within my Empire." This was the first time the word *swaraj* had been used in a royal message and, according to one Indian journalist, Durga Das, "an emotional wave" rose from the Indian section of the House.

Montagu outdid himself with the eloquence and "generous spirit" of the statement he had prepared for the Duke. In addition to acknowledging the inevitability of *swaraj,* the statement reaffirmed the British commitment to democratic government step-by-step in India, which in time "will lead to self-government within the Empire." "For years, it may be for generations, patriotic and loyal Indians have dreamed of *swaraj* (Home Rule) for their Motherland. Today you have the beginning of *swaraj* within my Empire and the widest scope and ample opportunity for progress to the liberty which my other Dominions enjoy." [12]

Commenting on the speech, Das acknowledged that Montagu had written it and said that "Montagu used the occasion . . . to. . . . to touch the hearts of the Indian people." Das reported that he "felt a thrill" as the Duke read the speech. Another Indian newspaper reported it as "one of the most impressive public utterances which was ever delivered." [13]

If beautiful words could have soothed troubled waters, Montagu's statement, as read by the Duke, would have surely brought a halt to the agitation in India, for it was a stirring presentation written in the spirit of the new reforms. It was a typical Montagu peroration, a heartfelt expression of hope for India's freedom and self-government. But Gandhi, the Ali brothers and their followers were not to be quieted by the magic of words or promises of freedom. In fact, their agitation increased after the Duke's visit, fueled in part by the continued intransigence of the Lloyd George government over Turkey.

Yet another conference on Turkey was scheduled for February 21 in London, and Chelmsford and Montagu thought it might be useful to invite a delegation of Muslims from India, including the Governor of Bombay, to present their own case to the conference. Chelmsford had also suggested that a member of the Viceroy's Council, Sir William Vincent, accompany the delegation. Montagu rejected the idea in a response that shows how sensitive he had become about his role in this issue. "From the day of the Armistice," he told Chelmsford, "I have left no stone unturned." [14] Chelmsford quickly apologized and abandoned the idea of sending Sir Vincent.

On February 24, [15] Montagu admonished Chelmsford in a cable for not taking the opportunity to tell the press that he, Montagu, had done everything possible on the Turkish issue. "It is not that I care for my personal credit," he wrote, "but it is bad for India to think that a callous Secretary of State has been 'bombarded' with your views. You are fully aware that I have made representation and taken action to the point of resignation." [16] It was clear that by now Montagu was deeply disturbed by the attacks in Parliament and in the Tory press. Montagu never sent his telegram since the Prime Minister agreed that the Indian delegation should appear before the Conference and that no final decision should be taken on Turkey before their arrival. The Conference listened respectfully to the delegation, but neither their presentation nor the barrage of memoranda Montagu and Chelmsford sent during February and March changed Lloyd George's position.

Montagu was still undeterred. If the Prime Minister refused to listen to him, perhaps evoking the name of Reading would help. On March 11, 1921, he wrote to Lloyd George that he had talked to Lord Reading, who "will tell you if I cannot that the reforms are working." If the Turkish treaty could be satisfactorily settled, *"there is every prospect of profound Peace and the cessation of all our troubles."* He corrected the Prime Minister, as he had chastised Curzon in the past, that when referring to the Governor of Smyrna, "instead of describing him as a Christian would you describe him as non-Turkish." [17] The French by now had evacuated Silesia which made the British position even more inexplicable in India. [18] Lloyd George not only continued to reject these arguments, but on March 18 and 19, 1921, he met with a delegation of Greek ministers and, without discussing it with the Cabinet or Curzon, encouraged their plans for a new advance into Asia Minor and supported their request to raise money in England.

The Cabinet was by now in utter disarray over the issue. Curzon had finally decided to part ways with Lloyd George and the conflict between them was in the open. Word of Lloyd George's encouragement of the Greeks spread quickly. The Indian delegation wrote to Montagu, expressing their pain that decisions had been made about Turkey before they had had the opportunity to explain their case.

Italy was trying to stop Greece, and Britain, with a million Muslims, was encouraging it; "the Prime Minister does not seem to fully realize the intensity of the feeling in India over this question and the magnitude of the unrest prevalent here."[19] Montagu, now totally discouraged, could only say, "Believe me, time will bring out and not before long, the rightness of our view and then it must prevail."[20]

Reading's Agenda in India

Although friction had developed between Montagu and Chelmsford during their last month working together, Montagu wrote Chelmsford a warm farewell. "So ends the Chelmsford-Montagu period of India history," he wrote nostalgically:

Not only can it be said that you have done your best, but it can also be said that the best was of great profit to India. I am delighted to think that we shall still be brought into contact through the Joint Committee, and I am still more delighted to think that in a few weeks time now, I shall have the joy of grasping you by the hand.[21]

When he did see Chelmsford in April, it was disappointing. He found Chelmsford as usual "courteous and subdued . . . a curious fellow. He studiously refrained from expressing any personal opinions. There was no trace of cordiality, criticism or antagonism at any moment. It was just rather sloppy ice."[22]

Reading, meanwhile, arrived in India with a carefully thought-out agenda, and three specific goals:

First, he was determined to give dyarchy and the new reforms a fair chance, and, as he later wrote, "to guide the first steps of this vast and heterogeneous population along the path toward ultimate self-government which had been marked out by the Government of India Act of 1919."[23]

Second, he must restore law and order. Here he faced the age-old problem of how much firmness a government can apply before stimulating increased unrest and how much freedom does it tolerate if the freedom is used to undermine the goals of the government? It is the traditional "which comes first, the chicken or the egg" riddle. Does a tough administration of the law produce agitation? Or does agitation result from a lack or failure to firmly administer the law?

Third, Reading was determined to separate the Hindus from the Moslems—to drive a wedge between the Moslem Ali brothers and Gandhi and his Hindu followers. The Ali brothers, Mahommed and Shaukat, were the leaders of the Khalifat movement and were calling for complete independence. They were far more radical than Gandhi.

Reading never wavered from his commitment to the implementation of the Chelmsford-Montagu Reforms, and especially to the principle of dyarchy. In a letter to Chelmsford in May 1924, when Chelmsford was First Lord of the Admiralty in the Labour government, Reading wrote:

We must strive to the utmost of our human capacities to ensure the success of the Reforms, strive genuinely and honestly to prevent a breakdown, and never allow ourselves to fall back upon the difficulties and obstacles India has put in our way until she has succeeded, by her Extremists (Heaven forbid!), in bringing the Dyarchy and the Constitution generally to a complete standstill.[24]

Surprisingly, Montagu had developed serious doubts about dyarchy and about the policy of granting self-government by stages. As early as September 9, 1920, he had written to Lord Willingdon that perhaps it would have been better to have let the Indians run their own government. Nor did he believe that:

The Dyer incident was the cause of the great racial exacerbation which is now in existence and which has got to be levied through and down before we can get a more hopeful atmosphere. . . . This racial consciousness is inevitable. As soon as the Indians were told that we agreed with them and they were to become partners with us, it instilled into their minds an increased feeling of existing subordination and a realisation of everything by which this subordination was expressed. Similarly, when the Europeans were told that, after driving the Indians for so many years, that regime was to be over and they might find themselves forced to cooperate with the Indians, or even forced to allow Indians to rule India, their race consciousness sprang up afresh. I am convinced in my own mind that that has been the fatal mistake of our policy in India. We ought to have let Indians run their own show from the beginning, with all its inefficiency and imperfections. Development would have been much slower, but the inevitable transition would have been less difficult.[25]

He ended on a prophetic note:

I am, however, satisfied that the temper of democratic countries such as ours is increasingly against remaining in a country where we are not wanted, and we have either got to make our peace with the Indians, or, as the educated classes grow, we shall find a strenuous desire in this country to get rid of India and all its bother.[26]

Whatever concerns Montagu had developed about dyarchy he kept to himself or discussed only with his closest friends. Publicly, he continued to press for its implementation and gave Reading his complete support.

When he first became Viceroy, Reading suggested to Montagu the convening of a Round Table to discuss the constitutional issues involved in the reforms and to make concessions to the nationalists if necessary. Instead of the Round Table Conference, bowing to Montagu's suggestion, Reading "agreed to meet Gandhi and other national leaders face to face for discussions."[27] Reading believed he could use these discussions to separate Gandhi from the Ali brothers. He met Gandhi on May 21, 1921. It was the first of six interviews. In a series of lengthy letters to his son, Reading wrote that he was impressed with Gandhi, that he found him knowledgeable and deeply religious, frank, honest, insecure about Hindu-Muslim cooperation[28] and eager to continue to talk in an effort to find solutions.[29]

On Amritsar, Gandhi told Reading he was bitter against all the British officers who were involved in the incident, particularly O'Dwyer and General Dyer. He "demanded the cancellation of their pensions. As for the Treaty of Sèvres, aware that he was not an accredited spokesman for Muslim opinion," he made only perfunctory comments.[30]

Eventually Reading was able to persuade Gandhi to agree to try to convince the Ali brothers to cease inciting violence and to apologize publicly for their provocations. In return, Reading undertook to ensure that the charges of sedition against the brothers would be dropped. "Although Gandhi subsequently tried to insert in his draft letter to the brothers some passage supporting non-cooperation, Reading would have none of it, and finally fixed a time-limit for an accommodation to be worked out. Gandhi deluged the Ali brothers and at last obtained their agreement to Reading's demands."[31] Montagu was ecstatic with Reading's strategy and its results. "We are delighted," he wrote to Reading, "with your skillful treatment of Gandhi. You gained a great victory."[32]

Reading believed he had found a friend in Gandhi and had, at the same time, "undermined the influence of the Ali brothers." In this assessment, Reading was overly optimistic. The Ali brothers were soon explaining away their apology and Gandhi resumed his attacks on the Raj. Beyond that, Reading's public interpretation of their meetings had irritated Gandhi and caused a widening of the breach between him and the British. Speaking at a banquet in Simla on May 30, 1921, Reading dramatized the Ali brothers' apology and made it appear as if it had been the main outcome of his six meetings with Gandhi. Das, the journalist, reported: "Sapru [Sir Tej Bahodur Sapru, member of the Viceroy's Executive Council who had brought Gandhi and Reading together] was unhappy but Sarma [Sir B. Nar-simha, Member of the Viceroy's Executive Council and a lawyer] said: 'What else did you expect. Don't you see he has failed to pull off a deal with Gandhi. *He is a Jew*. He does not want it to be said he parleyed with a rebel and made things difficult for the Prince of Wales' visit. He had to show it was Gandhi who sought an interview and that he had scored over Gandhi by remarking that the interview was not entirely fruitless' " (emphasis added). Das concluded that the interview had embarrassed Gandhi and had given the noncooperation movement "fresh impetus." [33] Gandhi felt that Reading had sought his support only to assure peace during the visit of the Prince of Wales, Das continued, and that he saw "no change of heart" in the British Viceroy; nor could he assure peace during the Prince's visit until there was "a political settlement." [34]

Such criticism did not deter Reading, who persisted in his efforts to isolate the Ali brothers and to woo Gandhi. He stood firm in his refusal to arrest Gandhi, in spite of the growing clamor for the arrest in Parliament. On June 9, 1921, he wrote to Montagu: "So long as Gandhi pursues his policy of less virulence and refrains from preaching active hatred of the Government and all its works, it is plain that no action should be taken by the Government." [35]

This reflected not only Reading's cautious and deliberate style and his belief in rational discourse but also his expectation that Lloyd George would support him. With such confidence he was not likely to be pushed into premature action even in the face of escalating criticism in the Tory ranks. What he did not know was that his intransigence would inflame Parliament, not against him but against Montagu, with Lloyd George not raising a finger to stay the assault.

Africa and the Political Rights of Indians

Reading and Montagu faced another crisis during Reading's first three months in office, one that illustrated more clearly than any other issue the intensity of British prejudice, and especially Tory prejudice, toward nonwhites. The issue arose at the Imperial Conference held in June and July of 1921, which had been called to discuss the refusal of South Africa to extend political rights, including the franchise, to Indians and the refusal of Kenya to permit Indians to own land in the Kenyan uplands.

In both battles Montagu was the principal exponent of equal rights and led the fight almost single-handedly. In both battles his chief opponent was Winston Churchill, who at the time was the Secretary of the Colonial Office, with jurisdiction over South Africa and Kenya. The conflict centered around the interpretation of an agreement between the original white settlers in northern Kenya and the government that prohibited grants of land to non-Europeans. Montagu and many lawyers argued that there was a difference between a grant of land and the right of a seller to sell his own land, and therefore a seller had the right, if he so chose, to sell to an Indian. Montagu believed, moreover, that the principle of equal rights had to be upheld with no compromise and under all circumstances. He argued that the agreement made by the white settlers to deny Indians the right to buy land had been signed before India had been granted Dominion status. Few civil rights advocates have spoken more eloquently than did Montagu in a letter addressed to "My dear Winston," on June 17, 1921:

I exist in politics only for one purpose—the application of the principle of equal status for Indians within the British Empire and the removal from our system of Government of all limitations placed upon Indians because they are Indians, irrespective of whether they are good Indians, bad Indians or indifferent Indians. If I do not compromise this principle, I am absolutely convinced that thru bad weather and good weather, India can be kept within the Empire more and more contentedly. If I compromise this principle I am convinced that the row will begin very soon and rightly.

I cannot defend a position . . . in which the Aga Khan, merely because he is an Indian and not a European has to go to the Governor for permission to buy land in the Uplands from a willing seller whereas Captain

Malone, Perberton Billing and Michael Collins can buy land at any moment merely because they are Europeans. I cannot defend it. You cannot defend it.

. . . I cannot help it . . . if the Europeans . . . swear that they will never sell to an Indian. I cannot help it, if you choose to lay down stringent sanitary regulations, so that no Indian who does not live completely in European fashion can live in the Uplands. And I cannot help . . . it if you legislate against absentee landlords . . . land speculation . . . but I must continue to protest so long as there is upon the statute book a regulation which differentiates between European and Indian subjects of the King.[36]

He reminded Churchill that the British Government had not to promised Dominion or equal rights to the Somalis or Arabs, but that it had done so to the Indians. (Churchill had pointed out that if Britain gave equal rights to Indians, they would have to do so to Arabs and black Somalis.) He urged Churchill to reconsider his position, and on June 21, 1921, asked Churchill not to publish anything on this issue because "it would have a disastrous effect in India."[37]

The issue in South Africa was slightly different. There the problem was the denial of the franchise to the Indians, not based on an agreement but rather on the whites' fear that giving blacks and Indians the vote would end their control of the country. Underlying the problems in both Kenya and South Africa was racism. To most Englishmen, blacks, Indians, or any nonwhites were inferior and not equal to His Majesty's white subjects. This was the central issue. Montagu saw this clearly, and, unfortunately, even decent men like Churchill were too prejudiced to accept so radical a principle as equal rights for nonwhites. As a result, Churchill supported General Smuts, who, while he expressed sympathy for the principle of equal rights for Indians at the Imperial Conference, could not apply it to South Africa. He argued that it would lead to open rebellion.

Montagu recommended a compromise to Churchill: a resolution that would accept the principle of equal rights with an exception that would read: "And while recognizing the adoption of this principle [of equal rights] is for the present impossible in the greater part of the Union of South Africa, owing to exceptional circumstances, they [the Imperial Conferees] recognise its adoption in the other parts of the Empire as a matter of urgent importance."[38] Churchill replied by telling Montagu that Smuts would accept the amendment without the phrase "for the present," since he would not agree to give guarantees of what would be done in the future. "I think you must take it on trust," he added, since Smuts is "more with you than the other S. African statesman."[39] Later, Churchill wrote to Montagu that by insisting on the phrase "for the present" he was "splitting hairs"; Smuts "would resent being pressed further" and he should have accepted Smuts's position.[40] Churchill suggested that Montagu add a paragraph about future negotiations between India and South Africa, but that was as far as he should go.

If Montagu had been less of an ideologue and more of a pragmatist, he would have accepted Churchill's advice. But he could not. As he had said to Churchill in his letter of June 17, he now existed in politics only to fight for India's equal rights. This had become an obsession to which he was totally committed.

He responded to Churchill in the spirit of this commitment. While he wrote that he was grateful for Churchill's advice, he believed that it was Smuts who was unreasonable, not himself. He said he was sorry that Smuts thought he was splitting hairs, but to take the phrase "for the present" out of the resolution removed all hope for the future. "I propose to press them in full Conference, as the only means open to me . . . The repudiation of his [Smuts's] attitude is to my mind infinitely more important to the Empire than any wounding of his susceptibilities or feelings."[41]

Montagu's persistence kept the resolution from dying. But his unwillingness to compromise made it impossible to get the resolution adopted in even a modified form. The Conference was deadlocked. Lloyd George, the eternal pragmatist, entered the fray and took the floor. It was one of his shining moments and demonstrated how the political process, while requiring the conscience of the idealist, cannot function without the pragmatist. "No greater calamity could overtake the world," he told the Imperial Conference on August 2, "than any further accentuation of its divisions on the lines of race. The British Empire has done a signal service to humanity in bridging the divisions in the past; the loyalty of the King Emperor's Asiatic people is the proof. To depart from that policy, to fail on that teaching would not only increase the danger of international war, it would divide the British Empire against itself. Don't let India go home believing that 'the British Empire has failed us. . . .' We must do our best. We want to build an Empire not on force but on mutual trust."[42]

Having thus said the right thing to assuage the Indians and the
Liberals in the audience, Lloyd George pleaded not for Montagu's
position, which in fact would have eliminated the divisions along
the lines of race, but rather for the Churchill and Smuts compromise. "Don't blame Smuts," he urged, who was trying to find a
"middle ground. . . . At least let the Indians know we listened to
them, we heard their message, we cannot give them everything they
want but we must give them something."[43]

The Prime Minister's speech seemed to melt the opposition on
both sides, and on August 9 the Conference agreed upon a compromise similar in substance to the one suggested to Montagu by Churchill on July 22, which supported equal rights but exempted South
Africa from such a statement. It read:

> The Imperial Conference while reaffirming the Resolution of the Confer-
> ence of 1918 that each community of the British Commonwealth should
> enjoy complete control of the composition of its own population by means
> of restriction on immigration from any of the other communities, recog-
> nized that there is an incongruity between the position of India as an equal
> member of the British Empire and the existence of disabilities upon British
> Indians lawfully domiciled in some parts of the Empire. The Imperial
> Conference accordingly is of the opinion that in the interests of the solidar-
> ity of the British Commonwealth it is desirable that the rights of such
> Indians to citizenship should be recognized. The representatives of South
> Africa regret their inability to accept this Resolution in view of the excep-
> tional circumstances of the greater part of the Union.[44]

Montagu's suggestion that the exemption given to South Africa be
limited "to the present" was defeated. Churchill and Smuts had
won.

While the representatives of India appreciated the principle expressed in the resolution, they recorded "their profound concern"
with the position of Indians in South Africa and the hope that the
governments of South Africa and India could, through negotiations,
find a better solution. Grateful for Montagu's efforts, they recognized that without him there would have been no resolution at all.
They were also moved by the Prime Minister's words and especially
pleased by the support they received from New Zealand and Canada.

For their part, the non-Indian representatives were impressed
with the quality of the Indian delegation. The Prime Minister wrote
to each of them, as well as to Montagu, a warm letter of thanks,

telling them how important the Conference had been and with what "satisfaction he heard India's views expressed so clearly. The cogent appeal by Indian delegates was very impressive." He added, "The resolution shows how much we recognize the importance of India." He hoped that someday "India will be represented in the Conference by her own Prime Minister." He wrote exactly the same letter to each Indian delegate and to Montagu, ending each with the sentence: "I greatly enjoyed our association as colleagues in the Conference and shall always remember with pleasure the spirit in which you approached our common tasks."[45] This was eight months before he would ask Montagu for his resignation.

The Indian delegation sent an equally gracious letter on August 3, expressing its appreciation to Lloyd George. "It is profoundly gratifying to us that the whole Empire except South Africa has recognised in unequivocal language the principle of citizenship. The matter is now in principle at any rate . . . a question between the Governments of South Africa and of India."[46]

Churchill's Position and East Africa

Churchill's position on East Africa was equally unworthy of a great statesman. The Kenya issue was removed from the agenda of the Imperial Conference and held for further discussion by a Committee of the Colonial Office at a time when Lord Delamere, representing the Kenya settlers, would be in London. In the interim, Churchill continued to reaffirm the contractual right of the British in Kenya to prohibit the sale of land to non-Europeans, a euphemism for nonwhites. He never budged from this position. In a letter that expressed considerable racial prejudice, Churchill wrote to Montagu: "The Indians in East Africa are mainly a very low class of coolies, and the idea that they should be put on an equality with the Europeans is revolting to every white man throughout British Africa."[47] He went on to suggest that the Cabinet would "have to decide how far this policy is to be pushed." He also recommended that Gandhi be deported and informed Montagu that his idea for Dominion status for India was alarming to the European community because of the absence of firm government in India.

Montagu was appalled by the letter. "I am almost in despair," he wrote to Churchill. "Your attitude changes so fast. The statement you make that 'the Indians in East Africa are mainly of a very low class of coolies and the idea that they should be on an equality with the European is revolting to every white man throughout British East Africa' might have been written by a European settler of a most fanatical type." Montagu also expressed surprise at Churchill's comments about Dominion status for India, as he had always assumed that Churchill accepted this policy. "The imprisonment or nonimprisonment of Gandhi," Montagu added, "has nothing to do with Dominion status."[48]

Nothing that Montagu said could change Churchill's attitude. The pressure on Churchill from the European settlers in Kenya was too strong. A secret society of Europeans had already formed in Kenya to seize the railroads and government buildings if any resolution were passed to require them to sell land to Indians. While precautions had been taken to prevent such civil disobedience, Churchill was not eager to have a rebellion on his hands. The feelings of the Indians were of no importance in the face of such threats. Reading was grateful for Montagu's efforts but was concerned over the reaction of the Indians to Smuts and Churchill. The noncooperation movement now had new ammunition in its war against the British.

Arrest of the Ali Brothers

Beginning in the middle of 1921, Reading thought that the Khalifat movement had lost some steam and that the Ali brothers were having trouble asserting their leadership. Reading also thought that Mahommed Ali had become "very high-handed" and was "upsetting his own followers"; the time was ripe for him to arrest the Ali brothers.[49] Reading's judgment and timing were perfect. In September, the Ali brothers were arrested and hardly any commotion followed. Reading was able to write to Montagu: "I believe generally throughout the community, except of course the extremists, there is a feeling that the Ali brothers have been incarcerated and are to be prosecuted."[50]

Reading's strategy of driving a wedge between the Muslims and the Hindus was succeeding. His other goal of restoring law and order by arresting major troublemakers was also moving forward, albeit very cautiously, in true Reading fashion. His goal of influencing Lloyd George to modify his Turkish policy, however, was futile. In this he was no more successful than Montagu.

Reading and Turkey

The Greeks, who had begun their new offensive with Lloyd George's approval in July, had lost an important battle on August 24 but had won a few skirmishes. Montagu's anger at Lloyd George increased as his frustration mounted. On September 15, he wrote to Reading:

A letter which means peace or war in Ireland is on its way. God knows what is going to happen. Meanwhile the Great Prime Minister becomes greater every day. He is delighted with himself at the defeat of the Turks. What foresight he showed! How great is Venizelos! How contemptible are the Military advisors on the General Staff! What brutes the Turks are! How eminently desirable it is that the Government of India be firm! All the time I feel that it is a thousand pities that the Prime Minister has not a little more confidence in his Secretary of State, and how bad a thing it is for India that the Secretary of State has so little confidence in the Prime Minister, so far as India is concerned.[51]

On the subject of Turkey, Reading felt as strongly as Montagu and was equally critical of the Prime Minister, at least in his letters to Montagu. On October 11, 1921, Reading wrote to Montagu as impassioned a condemnation of Lloyd George's policy as any composed by Montagu:

I wish it were possible to impress on his Majesty's Government how important it is to re-establish the British position in the Moslem world. The longer we avoid doing this moreover the more we disturb the Moderates who are our friends and the Hindus who are in a sense disinterested but who made common cause. Moslem agitation is the dominant factor in Indian politics today, especially since reports are circulating that France and Italy are in favor of restoring Thrace and Smyrna and are generally pro-Turk but that Britain raises the objection for her own purposes, being determined to make Christian influence predominant in these parts and to weaken or destroy Moslem influence.[52]

Reading urged the government to make some statement. "Nothing is so important in India at this moment, nothing would so counteract the machinations of our enemies, nothing would so quickly help in the restoration of the position of the British Government in India."[53]

Montagu immediately sent this to Lloyd George on October 12, 1921, writing:

I beg to enclose for your information the accompanying private telegram from Lord Reading and earnestly commit it to your notice. I have voiced my views so long and so unsuccessfully on this subject that I despair of making any impression upon my colleagues by reiteration of arguments. Lord Reading comes fresh to the situation and does not, I think, exaggerate in any degree the difficulties caused to India by British foreign policy. I content myself with asking you to give the consideration to his views which the difficulties of his task justifies.[54]

Reading's friendship with Lloyd George did not deter him from taking this adversarial position; but neither did it influence or change Lloyd George's anti-Turkish feelings which were even stronger than his admiration and friendship for Reading.

Indian newspapers were also outraged at Britain's role. A column in the *Islamic News,* which was published in London, declared under the headline "Mr. Montagu's Task" that Montagu was the only British leader who had questioned British policy. "He is the most valuable friend the Muslims possess in the British Cabinet."[55]

Reading, too, was generous with his praise of Montagu. On April 26, 1921, he wrote to Montagu telling him that he had informed the press about "all that you have done"; again, on June 11 he made a point of telling Montagu that things were going well and that this was due not only to his own efforts but to all that Montagu and Chelmsford had done.[56] The two months that Reading had spent with Montagu before coming to India had probably alerted him to Montagu's need for this kind of reassurance and recognition. He sincerely appreciated what Montagu was doing and thoroughly enjoyed working with him.

Pressure on Montagu Mounts; Reading Stands Firm

By now Reading was aware that the incessant attacks to which Montagu was subjected in Parliament were being exacerbated by his own refusal to arrest Gandhi. There is no evidence, however, that Reading appealed to the Prime Minister or to any of his friends in Parliament to try to stop the attacks. Nor did he accelerate his strategy to arrest Gandhi.

The attacks against Montagu intensified in October, when Gandhi openly advocated strikes and boycotts during the visit by the Prince of Wales scheduled for November. Beaverbrook's *Sunday Express* was sufficiently concerned to urge that the visit be canceled. On October 9, 1921, Montagu wrote an angry letter to Beaverbrook protesting this, arguing that Reading and his aides had decided to go through with the visit and that the *Sunday Express* article would only make it more difficult for them. Montagu was also distressed that Beaverbrook had not shown him the article before it went to press.[57] Beaverbrook responded with an apology. Neither he nor Blum, the editor, had seen the article. They claimed that they would not have published it if they had seen it.[58]

While the controversy was growing in Parliament, Reading continued to meet with Gandhi and with Muslim leaders, in the hope that he could negotiate some concessions in order to avoid hostile demonstrations against the Prince. In all of these conversations, especially with Muslim leaders, the question of British attitudes toward the Turks was always in the forefront. After a meeting with Mohammed Ali Jinnah in November 1921, Reading wrote to Montagu:

He (Jinnah) left me on the understanding that if better conditions prevail with regard to Greece and Turkey, and I find that I can give greater hope, I should let him know and he would come again at any minute I called him. I am left under the impression that there is a real desire to arrive at a settlement, particularly as he told me he had seen both Gandhi and Malaviya before he left [Bombay] for Delhi. . . . I was not particularly desirous of encouraging him in his role as broker, as he termed it, for I see little if any prospect of agreement between Gandhi and myself.[59]

Although Reading saw little prospect of influencing Gandhi's behavior and was anxious "to banish illegal and substitute constitutional agitation," he was not "prepared to make substantial sacrifices" in the strategy he was following in order "to arrive at it."[60] Reading preferred to continue his efforts to drive a wedge between the Muslims and the Hindus. He wanted no broker to try to heal the rift. He was not prepared to make concessions to Gandhi, but he also was not ready to arrest him.

Pressure in Parliament to arrest Gandhi became so intense that on October 20 the Prime Minister himself wrote to Reading that in view of Cabinet opinion on Gandhi's arrest, he wanted Reading to have his "personal opinion." He believed that

the time has passed for patience and toleration toward direct incentives to assault upon the very foundations of government. We have shown the utmost readiness to meet Indian feeling by. . . . giving Indians power and responsibility never dreamed of even five years ago. The majority of Indians are cooperating loyally. . . . they should not be allowed to doubt which is strongest, Gandhi, or the British Raj. . . . The British Empire is passing through a very critical phase and it will not survive unless it shows now, in the most unmistakable fashion, that it has the will and the power . . . to deal conclusively with any challenge to its authority. . . . I have absolute confidence in your firmness as in your judgment and you may rely upon my whole-hearted sympathy and support.[61]

Even in the face of this plea from the Prime Minister, Reading was not going to be pushed and wrote to Montagu that he hoped he was not being given "an order" or "informal direction." "I am glad to have the support of the Prime Minister, yourself and the Cabinet in the arrest of Gandhi when it takes place," but, he wrote, he hoped that he would be trusted to choose the right time.[62]

Reading also told Montagu that Gandhi's inability to make good on some of his promises had weakened his influence. If Reading had arrested Gandhi a few months before, there would have been violent disturbances. He did not think that would happen now. When the right moment came, he would not hesitate to do so. "Can you not influence pressure at home not to exaggerate the importance of Gandhi's recent pronouncements."[63]

Although defending Reading's position caused Montagu only greater difficulties in Parliament, he stood by Reading, convinced that he must be left to handle the matter as he saw fit. On October 25, Montagu wrote to the Prime Minister, "I do not think we can press Reading any further." He "firmly claims the right to exercise his own judgment."[64]

Montagu Pleads for Help

Montagu implored Lloyd George to use his personal influence "to prevent a debate on India in the House. Information which reaches me shows that the main objective is to pursue still further the vendetta of a small but determined group against myself. But I speak with every sense of responsibility when I say that a debate just now would be really disastrous and would let loose a torrent of comment and cross comment in England and India."[65]

Montagu gave the reasons a debate would be so disastrous: The Viceroy's policies would be attacked, conditions in India were touch and go; negotiations with Gandhi and the Muslims were ongoing; and the success of the Prince of Wales's visit depended on the Viceroy's negotiations, which would be upset by attacks in Parliament. "An appeal from the leader of both Houses to the ultra-conservative forces, with private assurances of our reasons and motives, would . . . avert what I believe would be disastrous."[66]

There is no record of what Lloyd George did when he received Montagu's plea. His relations with the ultra-Conservatives were then so poor that any efforts he might have made to stop a debate were likely to fail. As Montagu expected, on October 25, the day he had written to Lloyd George, the attack against him began with Lord Sydenham requesting a full debate on India in the House of Lords.

Sydenham told the Lords that the situation in India "had grown menacing" and that the causes "were clear." "Since the present Secretary took office," Lord Sydenham said, "we have seen a long series of disastrous mistakes, illusions and concessions and even attempts to create an artificial atmosphere favorable to impossible policies." Not a word was said about Reading. No one was as yet prepared to take on the Prime Minister's dear friend.

Montagu had also alerted Curzon to the potential of such a debate and urged him to try to postpone it. Curzon, probably with the approval of Lloyd George, did ask for a delay of the debate, noting that negotiations with the Viceroy on critical matters were now taking place, plans were being made for the Prince of Wales's trip to India scheduled for late December, and it would be disastrous if anything were said "to mar the harmony of his departure."[67] Curzon refuted Sydenham's assertions, telling the Lords that Sydenham's view "does not altogether tally with the information I have." He emphasized the importance of letting the Viceroy and his Council handle the situation because he "knows far better than we can"[68] what must be done.

Curzon was not able to stop the debate entirely, since several

Tories insisted on being heard, including Lords Salisbury and Ampthill who made long speeches complaining of conditions in India and implying that Montagu was to blame. Again, Reading's name was never mentioned. Ampthill warned that to disturb "the placid contentment of these masses" was bound to lead to trouble. "The Moplahs," he declared, "are great, jolly, cheery sportsmen full of humor . . . at times a wild fanatic. When he becomes fanatic he becomes exactly like a wild dog and the only way to treat him is to treat him in much the same way as you would treat a mad dog. His only object at such time is to die . . . and if he gets killed in fighting against the Infidel he goes straight to Paradise . . . [This] makes him desirous of getting killed."[69] He added that the British must protect the Moplahs against themselves. "Disturbing delicately the placid pathetic contentment of the masses for their own highest good" can only lead to trouble.[70]

One of the few who defended Montagu was Chelmsford, himself now a Lord. Always a gentleman, he would not remain silent in the face of such unfair attacks even though he had had some very difficult times with Montagu. At least as much as Montagu, he had been responsible for the policy in India now under attack, Chelmsford told the House of Lords, and it was unfair to put the blame solely on the Secretary of State. "It has once or twice been mentioned this evening," he told the Lords:

that the Secretary of State for India is a sinister figure in connection with the policy in India. May I say this, and say it most emphatically, that as regards the question of our policy with reference to Non-cooperation, the Secretary of State from beginning to end has had no part or lot in it except to be kept fully informed by myself and my Government of all we were doing and the policy we were pursuing. *I think it is only fair, when a great public servant is being continually attacked for a policy which is not his, though he may have accepted it, but did not initiate [it], that I who am responsible for it should most distinctly say where the responsibility lies. It lies on my shoulders.*[71] (emphasis added)

Lord Lytton, Under Secretary of State for India, also came to Montagu's defense. He told the Lords they were "all wrong" if they thought Montagu had told the Viceroy what policy to follow and that "the Secretary of State at no time sought to interfere with his [the Viceroy's] discretion or to send him instructions as to how he was to behave in purely administrative matters."[72]

This debate and the attacks on Montagu had little influence on Reading, who still refused to be pressured into changing his strategy. He continued his meetings with Muslim and Hindu leaders, becoming convinced that "the Gandhi movement could never have gained its strength but for the Treaty of Sèvres, which made the Mahommedans so frantic that they joined up with the Hindus."[73] Neither Reading nor Montagu could sway Lloyd George as the Greek army continued its march into Asia Minor, claiming victory after victory. The trouble was that the Turks were also claiming victory, prompting Curzon to write: "We are reminded of the battle of Jutland which was simultaneously celebrated as a triumph in London and Berlin."[74] The truth was that both sides, Greece and Turkey, had achieved only a stalemate.

Curzon was desperately trying to achieve some diplomatic settlement. He knew that the more ground the Turks gained, the less likelihood there was of achieving a new treaty that would be acceptable to them. But he had little support from Lloyd George who continued to conduct foreign affairs in his own personal, dictatorial fashion, with no regard for either Curzon or the Foreign Office. By now, he disliked Curzon as much as he did Montagu and made no attempt to conceal it.

By November 3, Montagu and Curzon had a new ally in Churchill who reported that the Greek Prime Minister, Gounaris, was favorably disposed toward peace. Reading, too, was intensifying his pleas, writing to Montagu on November 9, 1921, "There will, sooner or later, be outbreaks of disorder and serious bloodshed."[75] Reading urged settlement of the Thrace and Smyrna issue as "absolutely necessary" to forestall disaster in India. Nothing was of greater importance, he warned, than "the appeasement of the 70,000,000 Mohamedans in India," and this was of "gravest danger to the whole Indian Empire."[76] Montagu circulated this telegram to the Prime Minister and the Cabinet reporting that he was being bombarded by the Viceroy, urging that the British government issue a statement on the Greek-Turkish war. He reported that the Prince of Wales's visit continued to go well and the antics of noncooperation "have created a revulsion in feeling in favour of the Government."[77]

The Prince's Visit

Montagu's comments about the visit of the Prince of Wales did not give an accurate picture of what was happening and were aimed at putting the best face possible on a visit that had many difficulties. In truth, the visit was not a success, if the measure of success was the lessening of agitation and the rejection of Gandhi. The Prince's visit, in fact, increased the agitation.

The Prince arrived in Bombay on November 17, 1921, to learn that only a hundred feet from where he was speaking sixty thousand Indians were gathered to hear Gandhi. When his speech was over, Gandhi set fire to a huge pile of foreign clothing. This, along with Gandhi's speeches encouraging boycotts and strikes, set off a wave of riots and attacks against Europeans that began on the day of the Prince's arrival and lasted two full days. Fifty-three died and four hundred were injured. The first speech the Prince made on Indian soil, "I want you to know me; I want to know you," was lost in the din of the stampede of the rioting crowds.[78] Agitation became so heated that during the first ten days of December the Indian Government was forced to arrest the top leaders of the noncooperation movement. It did not arrest Gandhi.

Reading continued to believe he could find some solution if he could negotiate with Gandhi, and he reported to Montagu that Gandhi was also appalled at the outbreak of violence. "Gandhi has again called forth a spirit which he could not control, as he now admits. I am told that in several quarters in which he appeared to quell the trouble, he was powerless. He admits that his emissaries came back having been badly assaulted, and he is so disappointed that he expresses himself now against civil disobedience for the moment."[79] Gandhi called off *swaraj* and undertook a fast until November 22.

The rest of the Prince's visit was slightly better. The riots were quelled, but the Prince wrote to Reading on December 23: "The non-cooperators have prevented thousands of natives from turning out to see me. You will no doubt have had reports from Bombay, Poona, Ajmer, Lucknow, Allahabad, Benares and Patna. The cases of each have been the same—hartals [boycotts]—and more or less emptied streets."

The Prince also complained of overprotection by the police, who crowded the people together like sheep, with the police facing the crowds, and prohibited him from driving through Indian neighborhoods. "In my opinion, such severe police tactics can scarcely be conducive to encouraging even loyal natives to come and see me."[80] He was especially angry at the universities of Lucknow, Allahabad and Benares, where nearly all the students refused to meet him. In Calcutta his reception seemed a little better.[81]

On January 1, 1922, on his way home, the Prince wrote to Montagu telling him that "the newspaper accounts at home of the various visits, ceremonies and receptions have almost invariably been hopelessly exaggerated, and reading these accounts from this end, I feel that camouflage is almost invariably the dominant feature." He believed that these reports had given the impression that the tour had been a success, when it had not been. He found that the British did not want their sons in the Indian Army or the Indian Civil Service. "The reason for this," he wrote, "is that India is no longer a place for a white man to live in. I am sorry to have to paint you such a gloomy picture, but I cannot refrain from doing so, as I know that, as Secretary of State you want to, and should, know the truth."[82]

In his reply Montagu tried to paint a more positive picture, noting that Indian crowds are "habitually silent" and that the Civil Service always grumbled. He wrote to the Prince:

Please believe me when I say that I do not underestimate their [the Civil Service's] difficulties and troubles. I have never been able to convey to them how much I sympathise with them, and I know that their task is made the more difficult by the campaign of misrepresentation and calumny which would lead them to believe that they cannot be sure of support from the Government of India—at home or in India. Of course it is easy to see their troubles. A population wholly ignorant and uneducated is far easier to deal with than a population which contains elements at any rate with political aspirations, moved and stirred by world conditions. They have to do their daily work in a chorus of calumny, misrepresentation and abuse, and the seriousness of their position is aggravated, apart from the complexity and difficulty of their task, by financial stringency which we would be only too glad to remedy or alleviate if it were not for the grave financial position in which India, not unlike other countries, finds herself involved to-day. Not a day passes but what I spend a part of it in trying to think of some step to take to help them, and I know that Reading is in the same position. . . .

I know it must have crossed your mind from time to time in the inevitable moments of reaction and fatigue, to wonder why we asked you to expose yourself to this. I feel sure, Sir, the argument is familiar to you, but let me repeat it. It was not only an easily intelligible desire that His Majesty's Royal promise should be kept; it was not only because we thought of the effect throughout the world if we let it be believed that the conditions of India were such that the Heir Apparent to the Indian throne could not visit the Indian Empire; it was not only because we conceived that the highest Imperial interests made it essential that we should not countenance the disloyal resolutions and feelings of the extremists; but it was because, and particularly at difficult times it was thought right that those who govern and those who are governed in His Majesty's name, should be inspired by a visit from the most popular Prince in the world. I do not under-estimate the troubles and difficulties in India to-day, but I believe in the country as it has been made and moulded by British effort, and I believe that if we pursue our purpose firmly, keep our promises, support our friends and help them against our enemies, we shall win through to more peaceful times.[83]

In fact, Montagu was deeply troubled by the situation in India. The "unavailing insults" as he called the hostilities shown the Prince were not only embarrassing to His Majesty's Government, but they aggravated the attacks against Montagu in Parliament. Indeed they set the stage for the final act in the tragedy that would end his political career in 1922.

By December, the Cabinet was more divided than ever on Turkey. Curzon, Lloyd George and Balfour were overruled on ejecting the Turks from Constantinople and Curzon was dispatched to attend yet another peace conference, scheduled for January 8. Curzon was to present the following proposals, which Montagu described on December 21, 1921, in a telegram to Reading:

1. Smyrna was to be restored to Turkey
2. Greek Army to be withdrawn from Smyrna and Asia Minor
3. Greeks to leave Eastern Thrace
4. A predominance of Moslems to serve on the Executive Committee for the government of Adrianople
5. Constantinople to be evacuated by the Allied Army and returned to British control
6. Demilitarized zones to be reduced and placed under the League of Nations
7. Abolition of Allied control over Turkey.

Montagu had won: These were the proposals he had advocated for more than three years. Neither Lloyd George nor Curzon was happy with these instructions and Montagu wrote to Reading that they continued "to oppose the new provisions on Constantinople and Thrace." But Montagu had the satisfaction of having the support of the rest of the Cabinet, in spite of the intransigence of Curzon and Lloyd George.

Although the Cabinet was resolving its differences on Turkey, this did not help in the deteriorating relationship between Curzon and Montagu. They hardly ever agreed on anything, procedural or substantive, trivial or important. These disagreements only increased as 1921 progressed.

In April 1921, for example, they argued not only about Turkey but about Afghanistan and Palestine, with Curzon writing to Montagu: "I am afraid you are one of my colleagues to whom I am least successful in giving satisfaction. For whenever I pen a telegram or write a dispatch I have an uneasy fear that . . . you will some-how or other find cause for complaint."[84] Montagu responded, complaining that the letter was filled with "sweeping complaints and generalizations." He characterized other aspects of the letter as "inaccurate" and "unfortunate."[85] In May they argued over Reading's suggestion that the Berar be returned to Nezan. Curzon was "horrified" that the subject was being reopened. He had closed it in 1902 and saw no reason for another Viceroy to raise it now.[86]

In September, Curzon was angry over Montagu's accusation that the Foreign Office was responsible for France's refusal to bestow a French decoration upon the Maharajah of Kapurthala. In November, Montagu was concerned that Curzon was losing confidence in Reading and was unhappy with the handling by the Foreign Office of Egypt. By the end of November, relations between the two men had reached its lowest ebb. During a Cabinet meeting on November 22, Montagu remarked that Curzon was so convinced "that he knew what the Mohammedans of India ought to think that it angered him to learn what they did think."[87]

Curzon was furious. "I do not know," Curzon wrote to Montagu, "what impelled you to make a wholly unprovoked and as the Prime Minister remarked, unfounded attack upon me at Cabinet this afternoon. It was all the more unjustified because during the past three years I have written you scores of letters in reply to appeals from you endeavoring to find formulas or to present facts with which you could assuage the wrath of Indian officials. I have noted on several occasions [that] these appeals for private assistance are [not] compatible with great asperity of tone and pronounced hostility in Cabinet."[88]

Montagu drafted a response at once saying that he was deeply wounded by the Curzon letter.

I am sorry that you should find it necessary to complain of my demeanor at the Cabinet and towards you generally. Had I agreed with the Prime Minister or you that I had made an attack upon you that was unprovoked or unfounded I would have withdrawn it at once. But I had not the slightest intention of making an attack upon you and nobody was more astonished than myself that you responded to it as an attack.[89]

Montagu did not send this letter. Instead, he sent a less inflammatory response explaining that his "remark in the Cabinet was intended as banter," and if it caused offense, he was sorry. He praised their work together on Afghanistan. "Would it not be possible to institute some similar cooperation on other matters in order to avoid differences between us in the Cabinet?"[90]

Curzon sent a conciliatory reply and agreed that cooperation would be helpful. He blamed his inability to find time for such cooperation on "the work of the Foreign Office," calling it "positively crushing."[91] This gracious exchange of letters did not end the hostility between the two men but merely quelled it for the moment.

By December, Montagu may have forgotten his pledge of cooperation with Curzon when he sent a note to a member of the Foreign Office staff, which he had every reason to know would infuriate Curzon:

I learn that you are engaged in drafting a reply to my letter asking the Prime Minister's permission to assure Lord Reading that. . . . the Viceroy should be asked to invite an Indian Mohammedan to attend the Conference. I also learn that the Foreign Office are against this. . . . They know . . . of the difficulty in India, and every suggestion that I make to them . . . to ease the situation is criticized . . . Without the intervention of the Prime Minister. . . . I would have made no progress. The suggestion that it would lead to a request for a Roman Catholic or a Protestant Delegate is too ludicrous. There are plenty of Roman Catholics in the Foreign Office and Lord Curzon has been described as the representative of British middle class non-conformity. . . . Finally, it is no use disguising from ourselves the fact that Lord Curzon of all diplomats is regarded with the greatest suspicion in India.[92]

On December 27, Montagu wrote to Winston Churchill in total frustration to ask him to plead with the Prime Minister to at least permit the Aga Khan, who was in Paris, to remain for the peace conference, since Curzon continued to oppose an Indian delegation at the conference to discuss Greece and Turkey. Montagu told Churchill that on the subject of Turkey neither the Indian Civil Service nor the Indian leaders trusted Curzon.[93]

Montagu never understood how dangerous his feuds with Curzon would be. He regarded Curzon merely as an "obstructive survival from the Salisbury period."[94] No two men could have been more different. Curzon prided himself on being an aristocrat, putting great store in breeding, heritage and the divine right of the chosen few to rule. (He had, however, no compunctions about marrying an American, Mary Victoria Leiter, whose father, Levi Ziegler Leiter, a wealthy Chicago millionaire, made his fortune in dry goods and real estate, and whose family had converted from Judaism to Episcopalianism. It was Levi Leiter's money that made it possible for Curzon to live in the grand style.) Even as he was supported by the money of a real estate entrepreneur, Curzon had contempt for bourgeois and middle-class businessmen and wrote of Joseph Chamberlain that "his lack of the finer finish must be attributable to his origin and education, both narrow, municipal and a little sordid."[95] He was equally contemptuous of Liberals, Jews and the Liberal doctrine; as one of his biographers remarked, "His was not a liberal mind, but a feudal one."[96]

Curzon has also been described as arrogant, intolerant, supercilious, "unstable and unpredictable" and as one who never forgot a slight. He was a proud and confident peacock who viewed himself, and was viewed by others, as a "most superior person."[97] He saw himself as the font of all knowledge about India and could not accept Montagu's increasingly important role in India, the Liberal policies Montagu advocated or the affection with which Montagu was held in India. Although Montagu's policies were no different than Reading's, he rarely attacked the Viceroy. He knew an open attack against Reading might antagonize the Prime Minister, a situation he preferred to avoid. Montagu was the easier and less protected mark.

Economic Issues and Reparations

Although Lloyd George made no effort to stop the attacks against Montagu in Parliament and disagreed vehemently with him on Turkey, he continued to seek his advice on economic and financial matters and had even asked Montagu's help on the reparations crisis that had developed in 1920. During that year, Montagu sent various notes to the Prime Minister in response to his inquiries, and often when no inquiry was made, opposing the lifting of controls after the war, supporting the nationalization of the coal mines and the railroad, opposing the cutting back of social services, supporting Addison's program to build low-cost housing and urging the Prime Minister's support of free trade. And while Montagu voted for the taxation of goods coming into England that would undersell comparable English goods—known as the Anti-Dumping Bill—he did so only with "great disgust" and because Coalition politics demanded it. On May 12, 1921, he wrote to Reading:

To anybody who understands political economy, or pretends to, nothing is so disgusting as the Anti-Dumping Bill now going through the House of Commons. . . . I have got to grin and bear it, but it does disgust one with political life to know that we Liberals in the Government have got to defend this Bill, and that even the Conservative leaders realize that it is ridiculous but have got to play up to their man. Asquith made the best speech yesterday that he has made since his return to House—vigorous, humorous, incisive, splendid. I felt myself in cordial agreement with everything he said, and went dismally into the Division Lobby against him.[98]

On broader economic policy, Montagu prepared a draft memorandum for the Prime Minister on December 9, 1921,[99] which Lloyd George agreed to send for consideration to the Cabinet Committee on Finance. The memorandum addressed the proposed 1922 budget. The Conservatives, led by Chamberlain as Chancellor of the Exchequer, had framed a budget that cut expenses and provided "microscopic" reductions in taxes. Montagu urged a different approach. He noted that retrenchment and government cutbacks are "unwelcome and irritating in that they deprive . . . that section of the community interested in that particular department of amenities and desiderata which they are reluctant to forego. The country is not interested in economies; it is only interested in reduction of taxation."

Nor did he believe that "microscopic reductions" in taxation would provide the psychological relief needed to stimulate the economy. "The only proposals which are really worth while are . . . of such dimensions as to have an immediate effect: 1) in increasing the purchasing power and therefore the capacity for employment of those with money; and 2) of a substantial reduction in the value of money which will enable ultimate funding operations and any necessary borrowing to be accomplished at cheaper rates than obtained today. Imperceptible reductions in taxation gradually achieved will not have this effect."

Montagu acknowledged that his proposals were unprecedented, but argued that the financial position Britain faced was also "novel" and "alarming." He would "take this opportunity of getting rid" of what always seemed to him to be Britain's "indefensible system of double taxation. If we charge supertax on a man's net income after he had paid income tax," Montagu argued, "the supertax would become far less irritating to the taxpayer, would appear to me to be more obviously fair, and in the future the supertax yield to the Exchequer would be increased every time there was a reduction in the income tax."

Then Montagu asked the difficult question: Where will the money be found to support social services and tax reductions? He estimated that with the projected deficit for 1922, including nothing from German reparations or interest from Allied debts, £165 million must be found. £60 million would come from Geddes Committee reductions, and £20 million from the Washington Conference. That left £85 million, which he urged the Government to raise by borrowing, either by increasing the floating debt or by issuing a loan.

Montagu knew that orthodox financial opinion was against borrowing and especially against increasing the size of the floating debt. This did not faze him. "Our debt is so large now," he argued, "that an additional eighty-five million pounds will be negligible, in comparison with the huge benefits to the economy." As to the morality of borrowing, Montagu justified it because "the exceptional gravity

of the financial situation warrants it" and, in a sense, "such borrowing can be justified to *meet war expenditure. It is nonsense to assume that
war expenditure ceases with cessation of hostilities.* . . . I am perfectly
convinced that at least one hundred million of expenditure in our
budget, on analysis and investigation, would be proved to be war
expenditure properly charged in part at any rate to posterity, arising
directly and wholly out of the war."[100]

He urged that the Financial Commission explore these ideas. He
recognized that "all these proposals are undoubtedly connected with
reparations and Inter-Allied indebtedness." If Germany could pay
her reparation debt and inter-Allied debts could be adjusted to British advantage, the situation would change.

Montagu also made a suggestion similar to the one he had made
in a major policy statement in 1917, when he had urged that the
Allies shift the focus of their economic offensive from war against
Germany to "the diffused menace of world shortages."[101] Montagu
included Germany in these international efforts. On this Montagu
remained utterly consistent. In 1921 as in 1917, he believed that
postwar Germany must not be viewed as the eternal enemy: Her
economic recovery was very much related to the prosperity of Europe and Britain.

It was this macroeconomic view that colored Montagu's approach
not only to British postwar economic policies but also to reparations. On both issues he continued to have the complete and passionate support of Keynes, who wrote:

To what a different future Europe might have looked forward if either Mr.
Lloyd George or Mr. Wilson had apprehended that the most serious of the
problems which claimed their attention were not political or territorial but
financial and economic and that the perils of the future lay not in frontiers
or sovereignty but in food, coal and transport.[102]

Keynes, like Montagu, would not only have limited German damages to £2 to £3 billion, but would have canceled inter-Allied debts,
created a European free trade area to offset the economic disorgani-
zation of "innumerable political fronts" and established an international loan to stabilize the exchanges and to encourage Germany's
natural organizing role in Eastern Europe, including Russia.

Like Montagu, Keynes argued that Germany could not "pay
more than it itself accepted as reasonable and just, without a perma-

nent army of occupation. More generally, the attempt to collect debts arising from the war would sour international relations and damage social order."[103] Capitalism in the long run would suffer, the result would be "convulsions of revolution. . . . which will destroy. . . . the civilization and the progress of our generations."[104]

Lloyd George created the Allied Reparations Commission in 1919 with a mandate to find an acceptable figure by 1921. All through the years 1920, 1921 and 1922, conference after conference was devoted to the problems arising from reparations and the security of France, problems intimately linked. The collapse of Wilson's power in the United States, along with mounting unrest and acute inflation in Germany made the prospect of a final agreement less and less likely.

By the late spring of 1921, the situation had become so critical that Lloyd George, on May 5, reported to the House of Commons that Allied troops would move into the Ruhr by May 12 unless Germany met its commitments. Finally, on May 11, the Germans agreed to another arrangement and to make regular payments. For the moment, the reparations crisis was settled.

Montagu played an important role in designing the May 11 agreement with the Germans. On May 12 he wrote to Ronaldshay that he had been working "day and night at arriving at the scheme which has now been accepted by Germany. The whole matter has been a triumph for Great Britain, and mainly for the Prime Minister. We did our best to keep the French out of the Ruhr and we succeeded. I am now up to the eyes in the industrial situation. That is the life we lead."[105]

While Montagu frequently complained of the difficulties and frustrations of politics, in truth he loved the intensity of political life. Juggling ideas about Turkey, India, dyarchy, tax reform, reparations, South Africa, Kenya and Muslim agitation all at once exhilarated him and gave his life a purpose and meaning. But most of all, he enjoyed developing innovative and novel schemes for economic recovery, for achieving peace in Asia Minor, for containing the Bolsheviks and for running his department more efficiently.

These hectic days, which were to be among Montagu's last in politics, were marred by his unhappiness over the vitriol of the attacks upon him in Parliament. At first he thought that he was overreacting and being too sensitive. Perhaps, he thought, his sense that a "small group of ultraconservatives"[106] was trying to push him out of office was only a suspicion and a delusion. He often met with and wrote to Beaverbrook during these months, soliciting his advice. Beaverbrook confirmed that Montagu's suspicions were "genuine and true and not the delusions of a suspicious mind."[107] Montagu was crushed, writing to Beaverbrook: "If one is stigmatised as bad at one's own job and useless outside of it, it proves that one's position is very precarious. I shall want your advice badly to know how to avoid a sudden humiliation and how to end or amend so dangerous a state of affairs. For the moment I see no daylight. If I was regarded as useless outside my subject I would bide my time. Besides, if I am regarded as useless in it too, I am naked."[108] There would be "no daylight." He was "naked." His fears, for once in his life, were real. Beaverbrook had no advice that could save him from the humiliation and heartache that lay ahead.

30

The Resignation,
January, February, March 1922

I am doubtful whether I ought to let Edwin go into the wilderness . . . we are both children of Israel and both anathema to certain people.

Lord Reading to his son, Mar. 1922

January, February and March 1922 were the worst months of Montagu's life. They had many characters and situations reminiscent of Shakespearean tragedy: an evil ruler, Lloyd George, struggling to retain his kingdom; a vindictive, arrogant henchman, Lord Curzon, always eager to attack a vulnerable opponent; a hero, Lord Reading, whose action precipitated the tragedy; a white knight, Montagu, defending his beloved India with courage but not always discretion; and a coven of witches, the Die-hard Tories, determined to destroy the white knight and have his head for their cauldron of political intrigue and prejudice.

As the curtain rose in January 1922, there were few signs of the disaster soon to unfold. While Montagu was continuing his fight with Curzon and Lloyd George over Turkey and Greece, the Cabinet's decision in December 1921 to modify the Sèvres treaty along the lines he had suggested gave Montagu a sense of vindication and renewed hope for a treaty that would mollify Muslim sentiments. He continued to find Reading an able and determined ally, while Churchill became a new partner in the Turkish debate. And he found enormous praise and appreciation in India for the role he was playing in the Turkish and Kenyan debates.

A new conference on Turkey had been scheduled for January 6 in Cannes, for the British, French and Italian ministers to resolve their differences before the Allies met with the Turks in Constantinople. Although Lloyd George and Curzon were not pleased with the Cabinet's instructions on new proposals on the Turkish treaty, they were prepared to carry them out. Lloyd George was especially eager to resolve the "Eastern problem," which had become a thorn in his side. He also hoped to retain French Prime Minister Briand in office, realizing that any successor would be even more pro-Turkish. In this spirit, Lloyd George went so far as to inform the Greek Prime Minister that no settlement of the problem was possible unless Greece withdrew from Smyrna, that British support of Greece had diminished as a result of King Constantine's return to power and, under these circumstances, the Greeks would receive no help from Britain if they renewed their war against Turkey. Lloyd George urged the Greeks to place themselves in Curzon's hands and let him find a diplomatic solution.

At the conference, Lloyd George also convinced Briand to agree to a World Conference at Genoa, to explore the problems of Europe, Turkey, and relations with the Bolshevik government. These were steps of which Montagu strongly approved. But there were straws in the wind to suggest that despite these positive developments, all was not well for Montagu.

Montagu's correspondence with Curzon was becoming increasingly testy, with Curzon freely expressing his irritation. On January 2, for example, Curzon had written, "Your letters always leave on me the impression that everything I do is in your opinion wrong, and I consequently feel considerably disheartened."[1] This was in a letter rejecting Montagu's suggestion that the Aga Khan meet with the three foreign ministers at Cannes, while agreeing with Montagu that the Aga Khan should be invited to the larger meeting of the Allies in Constantinople to represent Muslim opinion. In that letter Montagu had begged Curzon to invite the Aga Khan to both meetings in Paris so that the foreign ministers who were to decide the terms to be suggested to Greece and Turkey, could hear Muslim opinion directly from a Muslim.[2]

Curzon then agreed to have the Aga Khan meet with him informally in Paris and "keep him *au courant* with what passed and profit by his advice."[3] To his dismay, however, he had heard that the Aga Khan had been asked by Montagu and Churchill to "try and settle the Turkish question on his own"; he "semi-officially sent proposals of [the] British Cabinet to the Turks."[4] Curzon was furious. He could not, he told Montagu, now employ the Aga Khan, even informally as a "counsel."[5] Both Montagu and Churchill vehemently denied any culpability,[6] but their responses did not lessen Curzon's anger.

To add fuel to the fire Montagu also circulated a memorandum to the Cabinet from the Governor of Bombay that irritated Lord Curzon.[7] The Governor had written that things were bad in India, that Montagu must hold fast, that the Muslim question must be handled promptly and that the faith of Islam in the British Empire must be restored. "I hope you will not think," the Governor had written:

that I have misread either this situation or the home difficulties but I have spent most of my life in studying Islam in Turkey and elsewhere and I am absolutely confident that a continuation of our present policy toward Islam or what appears to the public to be our policy . . . will lead to results fatal to our rule in the East.[8]

This was directly contrary to Curzon's analysis. While he was never as anti-Turkish as Lloyd George, he did not believe that British policy toward Turkey would affect British rule in India. He believed that the Kalifate movement in India was unconcerned with the Sultan and with Turkey and that it was using the Turkish problem as an excuse to increase anti-British agitation. Curzon was incensed that the Governor of Bombay had the audacity to believe that he was more a student of Islam than Curzon, "the superior person" who viewed himself as England's most distinguished and knowledgeable Viceroy. He was equally irritated that Montagu had had the temerity to distribute the Governor's memorandum to the entire Cabinet.

But Montagu was not one to be intimidated by a man whose ideas he viewed as feudal. The more Curzon objected, the harder Montagu fought back. On January 12, he sent Curzon a copy of correspondence between Stanley Reed, editor of the *Times of India,* and Lord Lytton, the Under Secretary of State for India. Reed had forwarded to Lytton extracts of an article he had written for *The Times* that had been reproduced in many Muslim papers. The article reviewed the reasons Britain's anti-Muslim position was actually helping the noncooperation movement and urged Reading to go public with the position of the Indian government on the Greek-Turkish conflict.[9] When he forwarded the correspondence to Curzon, Montagu could not know that Reed's suggestion that Reading go public would encourage Reading to seek permission to do so in a telegram he sent on February 28, the act that precipitated Montagu's dismissal from the government. All Montagu knew at this time was that Reed's article and its wide acclaim in India supported his views, and he wanted to make certain that Curzon knew of this.

By the middle of January, while his letters to Curzon continued to express a firm and determined policy, Montagu's correspondence with Churchill was beginning to betray a gnawing fear that his policies for India might not be correct. Montagu wrote that maybe Churchill and Curzon were right. Perhaps a tougher and more authoritarian posture would do more to quell the uprisings than a policy that advocated liberties and reforms and attempted to placate Muslim feelings for Turkey.

He confessed to Churchill that every minute of his time was spent worrying about India. He did not think he was to blame, but he was "haunted" by the thought. On balance, however, he still believed he was right and that if Britain could only take "the lead" in winning the goodwill of Turkey "instead of allowing ourselves to be dragged at the heels of France . . . you would be startled at the improvement in the Indian situation." He bemoaned the fact that the French crisis had delayed further action, that the Greek and Turkish treaty and his Indian policy were being influenced by "British policy in the Middle East, which in his mind serves no British end at all."[10]

The British press was of no help. Nothing sold more newspapers than headlines heralding killings, rapes and violence in India. Exaggeration was rampant and the bloodier the report the more space it received on the front pages. The *Daily Express,* for example, on January 16, 1922, reported on the Prince of Wales's trip under the headline "Bayonet Work in Madras," with the subheadline "Grim Scenes Off the Royal Route." It then wrote about Ghandhist organizers who "worked hard . . . to impose a complete hortal [day of mourning]." The story itself reported that there was some rioting off the royal route but "the violence failed to touch the actual reception and welcome of the Prince of Wales."[11] In fact, *The Times* of the same day reported that the Prince had been greeted by "happy crowds" on the same route.[12] This may have been an exaggeration as well, with the truth lying somewhere in between.

Montagu was concerned enough to complain to Beaverbrook about the *Daily Express*.[13] He sent a copy of a letter he had received from Lord Ronaldshay, which described the Prince's visit as:

passing off with a measure of success for which I had not dared to hope. The complete hortal . . . did not come off. Trams and other vehicles piled all day as people again gradually were reassured . . . increasing numbers flocked into the streets. . . . The reception in Bombay went well; without rioting. Since the 24th tremendous crowds of Indians have been out daily to see his Royal Highness and have cheered him lustily.[14]

The *Daily Express* stories, Montagu wrote to Beaverbrook, gave a "wholly wrong impression." While he expected some of the newspapers to do this, as they were out for 'sensational journalism,' " he was surprised "that the *Daily Express* was doing the same."[15]

A few days later, Montagu again called Beaverbrook's attention to the yellow journalism of his newspaper, enclosing clippings of a story in the *Daily Express* under the headline reading "Gandhi Butchers— Strong Hand Necessary at Bangalore." The story in fact pertained to "butchers who supply meat" (not killers, as the headline had implied), who had been warned not to strike. Nothing in the story justified the headline.[16] But Beaverbrook would not apologize. Selling newspapers was more important to him than the journalistic responsibility to tell the truth, or the fact that such misleading headlines were adding to Montagu's grief. The most he would do was suggest that Montagu write directly to the editor: "He will not resent a strong attack from you."[17] In spite of this attitude, Montagu continued to view Beaverbrook as a dear friend, and on January 27, 1922, just four days after Beaverbrook's callous reply, invited him to join him on February 10 to celebrate Montagu's "hundredth" birthday.[18] Montagu may have felt like a hundred, but in 1922 he was only forty-three.

In the meantime, Briand had been replaced as Prime Minister of France by Raymond Poincaré. And although Poincaré was anti-Greek and pro-Turkish, Montagu continued to fear that the unsettled political situation in France would defer any prospects of arriving at any Turkish settlement. "Poincaré is . . . very difficult, . . . more pro-Turk and anti-Greek than Briand." Curzon suspected him of "playing for delay" in hopes of further Turkish overtures.[19] Curzon's suspicions were correct; the more delay in the diplomatic efforts to secure peace, the greater the chance of Turkish victories. And the greater the chance of Turkish victories, the more isolated Lloyd George stood in his pro-Greek sentiments and the more insecure his foreign policy became.

The Die-Hards were only too eager to take advantage of the situation, attacking not only the delay in working out a new Turkish treaty, but the delay in arresting Gandhi. For the failure in the Middle East, they blamed Lloyd George. For the failure to arrest Gandhi, they blamed Montagu. The fact that Montagu agreed with them on the Turkish problem and that it was Reading, not Montagu, who was responsible for Gandhi's freedom did not matter to them.

Montagu, faced by increasing hostility, became nervous enough to press Reading to arrest Gandhi in the hope that this might stem the attack. "You are of course aware," he telegraphed to Reading on January 26, "that public opinion here is becoming even in the circles most favorable to the Government and in Cabinet itself more and more perplexed by the non-arrest of Gandhi."[20] But Reading continued to bide his time. He would arrest Gandhi when he, not the Cabinet or Montagu or even Lloyd George, thought the time was right. The fact that Montagu might pay a heavy price for this neither distressed him nor influenced his strategy.

Churchill Ignores the Cabinet on Kenya

By the end of January the Kenya issue had erupted again, and Montagu found himself in direct conflict with one of his few remaining political friends, Winston Churchill. Churchill, as one of his contemporaries commented, was more Tory on some issues than the Tories themselves. But he was honest, open and courageous and had defended Montagu brilliantly in the debate on Amritsar. Recently, moreover, Churchill had supported Montagu on the Turkish treaty, and the last thing Montagu needed now was to alienate so eloquent an ally. Characteristically, however, this did not stop him from continuing his argument with Churchill over Kenya. For Montagu, it was a matter of principle; he could not remain silent, regardless of the personal cost.

On January 27, 1922, Montagu wrote to Churchill, telling him that he knew Churchill would be addressing a Kenya dinner and he hoped that Churchill would not commit himself on this issue, since it must be decided by the Cabinet. "I have steadily tried . . . to avoid any conflict with you. I hope . . . that . . . we shall avoid it altogether." And then he wrote, showing how sensitive he had become to the attacks of his enemies: "I hope, in any generalization that you make . . . that there is some saving clause which will not let my enemies and the *Morning Post* believe there are dissensions in the Cabinet."[21]

The next day, he wrote to Churchill again,[22] urging him to remember that India would never agree to a restriction on immigration into Kenya based on race. Such a restriction would be insulting and unacceptable. He told Churchill that he would not object if the immigration deposit were raised to five hundred florins for all. His only concern was racial discrimination. He continued to believe that Kenya should accept the resolution of the Imperial Conference adopted in 1921. "We have had two and a half years of correspondence and nine months of conference."[23] The time had come, he concluded, to settle it.

In spite of these pleas, at the dinner Churchill reaffirmed all the positions that Montagu had urged him to avoid. He made it clear that Kenya would remain a white British colony, that contracts against selling land to non-Europeans would be enforced and that immigration on the basis of race would be restricted. Alluding to the resolution adopted by the Imperial Conference, Churchill offered a sop to India by concluding that "wherever practical equal rights will be protected." *The Times* of January 28, 1922, commented: "How he can reconcile this statement with the paragraphs above where he urges that Kenya be kept a white colony, baffles the imagination."[24]

All Montagu's pleading had been for nought. In the midst of Cabinet consultations, Churchill had publicly espoused a position on which the Cabinet had never agreed. Montagu wrote to Churchill accusing him of "a grave breach of the ordinary conventions of political life between colleagues and Ministers of the same Government" and a breach of Britain's promises and policy toward India. He was "amazed" that when Churchill had shown him the speech before he delivered it, he "did not at the same time give me an indication of the other pronouncements of policy that you were about to take." Montagu was referring to the fact that Churchill had repeated the pledge to reserve the Highlands of East Africa exclusively for European settlers, "and we do *not* intend," Churchill had stated, "to depart from that pledge. That must be taken as a matter which has been definitely settled in all future negotiations." "I would ask you, how can you," Montagu asked, "possibly harmonize this announcement with the usual conduct of a Cabinet Minister. I do not know who you mean by 'we' but I assume you mean H.M. Government. But you surely cannot deny that this matter has been specifically reserved by us throughout long months for ultimate decision by the Cabinet in case we could not come to an agreement about it and that *the Cabinet never considered it.* You must know that I do not accept and cannot accept and never have accepted your interpretation of the pledge." [25]

Montagu reminded Churchill that he, his advisors and the government of India all believed that the pledge made by Lord Elgin in 1909 permitted only Europeans to receive grants of land but that it did not prohibit the Europeans from voluntarily transferring their lands to Indians. To prohibit such a voluntary transfer, they argued, would be equivalent to racial discrimination in violation of Lord Elgin's pledge to India. They did not demand that grants of land be made to Indians. "What we did say," Montagu wrote Churchill, "was that so long as a willing owner of land in the Uplands was prohibited from selling his land, if he so chose, to a willing purchaser who happened to be an Indian, the existence of that prohibition was a racial discrimination which was a violation of Lord Elgin's pledge to the Indians. On that you and I have never been able to agree and that was a subject we were going to submit to the Cabinet when in due course we had gone so far as we could agree." [26] Montagu wrote that he and Churchill had agreed that together they would await the arrival of a delegation from Kenya and then "suddenly . . . without consultation . . . without any reference to the Cabinet, you have made a further pledge to the European settlers which brushes aside all the suggestions I have made. In the circumstances this seems to be unjustifiable and indefensible." [27]

On February 1, 1922, Churchill responded to this long, impassioned and well-reasoned document with a five-line note that said, "Sorry to receive such a long scolding letter." Churchill said that he had consulted officials in the Colonial Office and concluded, "I don't think you have any cause to complain."[28] Churchill felt secure in his belief that most of the Cabinet would support his position, racist as they were.

He was correct. No one took him to task but Montagu. No one in the Cabinet but Montagu objected to his taking a position while the Ministers were debating the issue. And no Cabinet minister, including the Prime Minister, raised the specter of a breach of Cabinet collective responsibility, an issue that would be raised to the level of a constitutional crisis in the case of Montagu only a month later.

Montagu was infuriated with Churchill's reply and responded the same day that Churchill had not gotten his point. He pointed out that two Ministers (he and Churchill) had been debating an issue. The first suggested a compromise. One, Churchill, went public. He was astonished. "And how can you say I have no grounds for complaint?"[29]

Churchill not only opposed Montagu on the issue of Kenya, but he also began to take India to task for its rebellious behavior. India could not expect to be accepted as an equal partner in the Commonwealth, he argued, or to be granted equal rights, if it continued to agitate against the British Empire. Riots and rebellion, he warned, would not succeed in getting the British government to acquiesce to its demands.

Montagu was amazed at this change in Churchill's attitude, from supportive to critical of the policies of the Indian government. "I find it difficult to understand what I have done which has made you quite suddenly and without any warning adopt a new method of dealing with this question," he wrote. But then, afraid to have Churchill as an enemy too, he added, in an uncharacteristic tone, "but I do not complain of it."[30]

By now the Die-Hards had so intimidated Montagu that he was running scared. He assured Churchill that he had told the Indians that disorder in India had made it more difficult to deal with the Kenya issue. He also told Churchill that the Indians in Kenya were not disorderly and should not be made to suffer for the behavior of their compatriots on the subcontinent.

Churchill's argument attacking the behavior of the Indians in India was, in fact, a red herring. Even if the Indians in India had been behaving in an exemplary fashion, the Europeans in Kenya would not have conceded equal land-owning rights to Indians in Kenya. The issue was not agitation in India but racism in Kenya. Churchill was too clever not to have realized that.

Writing of Churchill's attitude toward India, William Manchester, one of his biographers, has said that even as a young man in Cuba, fresh out of Sandhurst, "he had distrusted 'the negro element among the insurgents.' He never outgrew this prejudice."[31] Churchill was a racist and this attitude always influenced his position in India. Manchester added that the term "racism" had not yet been coined and was not in the *Oxford English Dictionary* or in *Webster's,* and that prejudice was not only "popular" at the time and "acceptable in polite society," but was "fashionable, even assumed."[32]

It was never either "fashionable" or "acceptable" to Edwin Montagu. It was anathema to him. Regardless of the political consequences, and as terrified as he was of the mounting attacks on him in Parliament and in the Tory press, Montagu would not and could not compromise this principle—even if it meant antagonizing Churchill. The Viceroy, the Indian press, and representatives of the Kenyan Indians were equally angry with Churchill, reminding him that his Majesty's Government had never said that the Europeans came first and claiming that Churchill's speech was open support of "white racial supremacy."[33]

Montagu, concerned that Reading might think he had not done enough to stop Churchill, wrote to him explaining that he had not known that Churchill was planning to make this speech and that he was trying to induce Churchill to qualify his statement.[34] Montagu delivered a rebuttal before the Coalition Liberals at the 1920 Club, making clear that Churchill's opinions were his own and not those of the Lloyd George government. He spoke of the need to enforce law and order (a remark ridiculed as the comments of a Johnny-come-lately by his adversaries in Parliament) but expressed the belief that this condition did not warrant discrimination against Indians in Kenya.

Tensions Mount in India; Reading Moves Cautiously

In the meantime, Churchill became increasingly outspoken in his criticism of conditions in India, complaining that Reading and

Montagu were being too lenient and raising the question of whether "the democratic principles of Europe" were suited to "the development of Asiatic and African people."[35] Reading was moving slowly and evenly, while Montagu was growing increasingly uncomfortable with his pace. Montagu was also annoyed with the Indians, who were, he felt, unjustified in their agitation and anti-British conduct. On February 1, 1922, he wrote to Reading, suggesting that force might have to be used:

I do not know what the future of India will be and how we shall get through our new troubles. I am convinced they would have been much worse if it had not been for reforms and I suppose some way out will be found eventually. In the meantime, it looks to me as if there was nothing for it but a vigorous attempt to smash the organization against us and to deal with sedition wherever it shows itself. That is the opinion here and it looks as if it is the opinion in India. . . . I am rather pessimistic and think that force will have to go on for some time before talk is possible.[36]

He pleaded with Reading not to dismiss his concern with the need to take firmer action to enforce the law and arrest those responsible for the agitation, including Gandhi:

The fact of the matter is, Rufus, that people here are fed up with India, and it is all I can do to keep my colleagues steady on the accepted policy, let alone new installments of it. The Indians are so unreasonable, so slow to compromise, so raw in their resentments, and the insults to the Prince of Wales have made fierce feeling in this country. If the Government were thinking only of their political well-being, they would show much greater impatience than they have done. That is one of my great difficulties with Winston over Kenya; he can snap his fingers at me, and know that the whole of public opinion, Liberal and Conservative, would be on his side of the subject. If only Indians could be got to realize that they could have everything they wanted for loyalty and that there never was a more unjustified unrest than theirs![37]

The Viceroy would not yield. He was waiting for the propitious moment and nothing would take him off his cautious track, not even the attacks against Montagu that his policy caused. With three thousand miles between him and Parliament, and secure in the Prime Minister's backing, Reading could afford to wait it out.

On February 1, Gandhi issued a manifesto threatening further civil disobedience unless certain of his demands were met. The government of India drafted a response and sent it to Montagu who urged the government to take tougher action. He said that civil disobedience, partial or total, must be prohibited and that the leaders of civil disobedience, including Gandhi, must be dealt with promptly, if they had not already been arrested.[38] He told Reading that His Majesty's government was very anxious, that each telegram added to the impression that the situation was very serious and that allowing Gandhi to remain free to organize civil disobedience "must lead to disaster."

In your telegram of the 25th of January you said that the Government of India wished to wait [the] next move of Gandhi which it seems clear must be of a kind involving a more direct challenge to the Government than any hitherto attempted.

In his [Gandhi's] letter to you dated February 1, he has now given you the most direct challenge possible. You owe it to those who would otherwise become his tools or dupes to protect them.[39]

Montagu repeated this theme in another letter sent to Reading on February 7, in which he warned that Reading "can't beat Gandhi by debating, with explanations and refusals. You must with immediacy accompany your communiques, with action against the man who is the head of the organization responsible for all the trouble." On a more positive note, he added that Curzon had sent the new proposals on Turkey to the French, that they were "much along the lines" that he had been suggesting and that he was striving to prevent the British from appearing to lag behind the French.[40] "If the Allies are too tough and Kemal rejects their proposals, a Conference will become necessary." He had "high hopes" that a conference would soon take place. Montagu's main Turkish proposals now seemed destined for acceptance at a conference on the Greek-Turkish war, and Reading seemed ready to arrest Gandhi. The sun, at long last, seemed about to shine on Montagu.

An Appeal to Lloyd George

On February 9, Reading sent what seemed at the time to be an innocuous cable, offering "to formally place on record the view of the Government of India, Local Governors, Ministers, Councils, on the need to alter the Treaty of Sèvres." This would amount, Reading wrote, "to the final act that the Viceroy and governors could take, to enforce his policy, short of actual resignation to enforce a policy they think imperative."[41] Montagu did not know that Reading would subsequently ask that these views be made public and that they be released to the press; Reading's request that the views of the Indian government on Sèvres be made a matter of record seemed innocent enough to Montagu.

Montagu was facing a far more disturbing matter. Churchill had delivered a speech before a Ministerial Conference in which he had again criticized the agitation in India, called for a tougher Indian policy in order to enforce law and order and repeated his belief that the Indians could not expect to get equal treatment in Kenya or anywhere else if they continued to engage in rebellion. Montagu decided that the issue was important enough for him to write directly to the Prime Minister. On February 10, he told Lloyd George that Churchill's speech left him very uneasy and "in consequence I feel it necessary to ask for an assurance that nothing will be said in the approaching debate in the House of Commons that would be inconsistent with the solemn declaration of Parliament we have made gradually to convert India from a dependency to a self-Governing partner in the British Empire. . . . I cordially agree that during this difficult transitional period, which cannot in the nature of things be a short one, order must be maintained."[42]

Montagu assured Lloyd George that he agreed that sedition and violence must be dealt with and that progress toward Indian democracy would be impaired if the disorders continued. He was distressed that Churchill was now challenging this and, at the same time, speciously connecting this issue to that of the rights of Indians in Kenya. Lloyd George did nothing when he received this plea, and no arguments from Montagu, Reading or the Indians in Kenya could change Churchill's mind. No pleading would move Reading to arrest Gandhi either. On February 11, Montagu again wrote to Reading: "We have, I think arrived at a moment when a larger body of Indian opinion will accept Gandhi's arrest than at any time hitherto."[43]

Reading replied three days later, explaining his resistance to arresting Gandhi. "I hope," he wrote to Montagu, that "the Cabinet will understand why I felt bound to postpone arrest." He wrote that there seemed to be a change in the attitude of the noncooperation movement and "difficulties in their carrying out Civil Disobedience" and he did not want to lose the support of the Indians on his Council because this would "sway other Indians." Sapru had already asked for a delay of several days to explore what was happening and "then he would support Gandhi's arrest."[44]

Motion to Censure Montagu

Then the bomb fell. On February 14, the day that Reading told Montagu he would soon arrest Gandhi, Sir W. Joynson-Hicks introduced an amendment on the floor of the House of Commons, which he himself defined as "one that is in effect a vote of censure upon the Secretary of State [for India] for his actions during the last two years."[45]

If Reading had heeded Montagu's pleas and arrested Gandhi would that have made a difference? One cannot be sure. The Die-Hards' dislike of Montagu was so great that they might have found some other reason to censure him. But one cannot minimize the effect that Gandhi's arrest would have produced. It would have eliminated one of the major thrusts of the attack.

With Gandhi in prison the Die-Hards' cry against Montagu for tougher enforcement of the law in India would have lost its effectiveness. This in turn might have quieted their immediate opposition to Indian policy and turned their attention away from Montagu, for the moment at least. But this is surmise. Reading did not arrest Gandhi at this time, in spite of all Montagu's pleas, and the Die-Hards decided that the time had come to attack.

The substance of Joynson-Hicks's charges against Montagu was not unexpected. He accused Montagu of using his position as a Liberal Minister in the Coalition government to govern India "in accordance with liberal and Home Rule ideas" and that he was prepared to give India a "free and democratic government," although such a government could not "keep law and order." He also charged that the situation in India was "menacing" and "besieged by rioting and killing," that Montagu, as a friend of Gandhi, had supported civil disobedience and that the Reform Act of 1919, which was pushed by Montagu, had been a "disaster." From the moment Montagu became Secretary of State, the charges continued, "trouble began to brew in India." He had broken the heart of the Civil

Service and was guilty of the criminal betrayal of every white man and woman in India, all through 1919, 1920 and 1921.[46]

Joynson-Hicks was followed by Rupert Gwynne, who had led the debate in Parliament against the Hunter Commission report and continued to blame Montagu for the report's condemnation of General Dyer. He disliked Montagu with a passion, and his speech was as vitriolic, personally abusive and replete with anti-Semitic innuendos as any ever made in the House of Commons. It was Montagu, he told the House, who bitterly criticized Chamberlain's administration of India and who, within a few weeks of becoming Secretary of State, began to remodel India; the "disastrous bloodshed and disturbances of today is his doing." He accused Montagu of being personally responsible for the turmoil in India. He could not blame the government of India, although it was Montagu's style "to put on other people the blame which he ought to take for himself." "It is not fair. . . . It is not English. If you attempted to do that sort of thing at school you were considered a sneak."[47]

He reminded the House that when Chamberlain felt that he was responsible for the "uncomfortable muddle" in Mesopotamia, although he was not directly responsible, he resigned. Not Montagu. The problems in India would have "caused any ordinary individual to resign 20 or 30 times but he sits there unmoved, putting the blame on anyone he can, breaking a soldier here, sacking a civilian there, doing anything to save his own skin."[48] At all times "the right Honorable Gentleman remains in the background. He is working underground. His methods remind one of a mole. . . . His skin is not too thin. Indeed I doubt if a hippopotamus has a thicker skin."[49]

Ninety-three members of the House had signed a petition, urging that the Prime Minister dismiss Montagu, and yet he remained. He pandered to extremists, brought disgrace upon the government and now, suddenly, at a meeting of the 1920 Club he had become a disciple of law and order. He asked again why Gandhi had not been arrested, implying that Montagu was responsible for Gandhi's continued freedom and agitation.

Montagu's response to these attacks was remarkably calm, given that he had just been described as a sneak, a mole, a thick-skinned hippopotamus and an extremist who had single-handedly brought riot and rebellion to India. He defended his early friendship with Gandhi, who was not then the mischievous agitator he would later become. He said that the decision to arrest Gandhi must rest with the Viceroy and the government of India. This was the policy that had always been followed by the Secretary of State. He reviewed the reasons for unrest in India and the development of race consciousness, but he believed that such racial awareness, "if carefully used add[s] to the strength and vigor of the Indian people." The economic situation of the world, high taxes, high prices, poverty, the propaganda of the Bolsheviks, dissatisfaction with the Turkish peace treaty, the aftermath of Amritsar and the general unrest in the world, all contributed to the situation in India. He emphasized that law and order in India could not be enforced from Great Britain. It must be left to the government of India. They had responsibility for law and order. This had never been in doubt.[50] He also reminded the House that he did not invent the declaration of August 20, 1917. It was drafted by the Cabinet and issued on their authority.[51] But nothing that Montagu said could sway his antagonists.

Only a single member of the House of Commons, the Right Honorable Francis D. Acland, had the courage or the decency to rebut the anti-Semitism in Gwynne's attack. "I believe," Acland said, "that these personal attacks on the Secretary of State are based very largely not on sober and careful consideration of the position in India, but on religious prejudices which ought to be unknown when serious matters of this kind are at issue."[52] No one, including the Speaker, tried to stop the "deep-throated and dramatically sustained outbursts of cheering" from the Conservative benches and the derisive shouts of "Resign," "Move him out" and "Shame to him" that accompanied what one observer called the "bitterest and most crudely personal taunts."[53]

Sir J. D. Rees, while refraining from commenting on the anti-Semitism of Gwynne's attack, did assert that Montagu was not to blame for unrest in India or for the reform movement. He reminded Commons that Lord Chelmsford, Reading and the entire Cabinet supported reform. Persia, Iraq, Palestine and Mesopotamia were all in ferment, and Montagu was not responsible for that.[54] As for Gandhi's arrest, Rees remarked that he was prepared to await Reading's decision, for in Reading, he said, "we have someone who was an extremely capable Attorney General, . . . Ambassador in

Washington and he was Lord Chief Justice of England. If Reading thinks it is wise to wait I for my part am prepared to accept [his] opinion."[55]

Then Lloyd George spoke. He said not a word against the personal attacks against Montagu. But he went out of his way to congratulate and compliment Joynson-Hicks, "a fellow lawyer," who had made a very able speech delivered with "moderation and restraint."[56] Regardless of how Lloyd George felt about Montagu, it was indecent for him to leave unanswered the accusations that Montagu was a "sneak," a "thick-skinned hippopotamus," somehow "un-English," someone who had behaved like a "mole." Even if Montagu had not been a member of the Cabinet, or if he had not labored long and hard on behalf of India for a policy putatively supported by Lloyd George, he deserved to have the Prime Minister step forward and slap down these virulent slurs against him, as a Jew, an Englishman, a Member of Parliament, and as a member of Lloyd George's own Cabinet.

But Lloyd George calculated that he needed the Die-Hards more than Montagu, and if the price of their support was to ignore their gutter insults against Montagu, he was prepared to do so. The most he would do was to say that Montagu was being attacked from both sides, and it was an unpleasant situation for anyone to "try to walk a moderate path between two extremes." He noted that Montagu had not created the troubles in India. They were there when Morley had been Secretary of State. Whenever you try to bring Western ideals to the East it is unsettling: "It was putting the new wine of the West into the older bottles of the East." In such cases one must expect "the bottles to burst, the wine to leak and the intoxication to sweep over the East."

He agreed with Montagu that the causes of unrest were poverty, high taxation, increasing burdens and diminished means. He agreed, too, that it was unfortunate that England had to fight "the greatest Islamic Power in the world." It would be advantageous to have peace with Turkey but it must be "a just peace and balance the rights between various religions." He covered his flank with the Conservatives by declaring that India had never been a democracy. If democracy were to succeed it must be a gradual process, he said, quoting Macaulay that "laws exist in vain for those who do not have the courage and the means to defend them."

Montagu had also quoted Macaulay in his speech, but it had been a far different citation:

By good government we may educate our subjects into a capacity for better government; that having become instructed in European knowledge, they may in some future age, demand European institutions. Whether such a day will ever come, I know not, but never will I attempt to avert or retard it. Whenever it comes it will be the proudest day in English history.[57]

The difference between the quotations chosen by Montagu and Lloyd George illustrates how far the latter had come from the days when he had supported the 1917 Declaration and how far he was now going to placate the Die-Hards. In the same vein, Lloyd George urged that authority be strengthened in India and that civil disobedience be met with sternness and severity, a position advocated, he added, by Lord Reading.[58]

While Lloyd George presented Reading as someone who was aware of the need for law and order, he deliberately ignored the fact that Montagu, not Reading, had been urging Gandhi's arrest, and that Reading, not Montagu, was dragging his feet, reluctant to take such action. Lloyd George did, however, support Montagu in concluding that "you cannot do this [i.e., enforce law and order] at a distance. We must leave this to the government of India." And then, to clearly impress upon the Conservatives his commitment to the Empire, he assured them that Britain had no intention of leaving India: The results would be disastrous. He closed with a quotation from Morley, referring to Morley as a man who believed in reform but "knew the dangers of the course which has been pursued by some of the leaders of India. These are the words which we adopt as a declaration of our task: How should we look in the face of the civilized world if we turned our back on our duty and our task? How should we bear the savage scorn of our conscience when, as assuredly we should, we heard in the dark distance the storm and confusion and carnage in India?"[59]

Lloyd George's remarks were sufficient to defeat the censure amendment by a vote of 248 to 64. Ninety-three members of the House had signed the censure resolution; 29 were thus convinced by his words to change their vote. The vote took place at almost 11 P.M., after a long and grueling debate. In spite of the viciousness of the debate, Montagu was elated with the final vote. He had come through victorious, with the censure motion defeated by a substantial majority. "Of course I hate these attacks as anyone would," he wrote to Reading, "but I don't think they really matter much in the sense of embarrassing you or weakening our position or our policy. . . . At any rate even the die hards admitted that they did not desire a reversal of policy."[60] If Montagu had been more perceptive concerning his own political future, he would have seen that the debate did indeed "matter much." It revealed his vulnerability, the intensity of the Die-Hards' dislike of him, the anti–Semitism that not only existed but was tacitly accepted in Parliament, the absence of any real support in his favor among his Cabinet colleagues and Lloyd George's open courting of Die-Hard support.

While at first he may have failed to see the direct relationship between this debate and his political future, he did see, as he wrote to Reading, on February 23, 1922, that the debate revealed that the Conservative Party was getting "more and more restive at the existence of the Coalition" and that the "trend of events is by no means closer alliance but rather towards separation, and what-ever happens it looks as if Liberalism at the moment is not in a bright position, hopelessly split, more so than ever between the fires of Ultra-Conservatives on the one hand and Labour on the other."[61] Lloyd George might appear imperturbable, "but, if anything is endeavouring to right himself with the Conservatives." As for Winston, "He jumps from the diehard to the Liberal camp as he works from Egypt or India to Ireland."[62]

In the face of Lloyd George's courting of the Conservatives and the anti-Indian mood among the British public, Montagu now told Reading that no new proposals concerning India should be presented in Parliament and that Gandhi must be arrested. "No statement," he concluded "seems to convince the public that your Government and the Local Governments have been dealing vigorously and effectively with disorder."[63] Only Gandhi's arrest would achieve that.

Reforming Liberals Must Go

Trevor Wilson, a British historian of the period, has interpreted the censure vote far more negatively than did Montagu. He viewed the debate on censure not only as evidence of the restiveness of the

Conservative Party but as part of a deliberate effort of the Party to drive the Liberal Ministers from government, especially "those ministers associated with reforming policies: Addison (whom Lloyd George jettisoned at their insistence in June 1921—an ill-reward for loyal service), Fisher, Montagu and Edward Shortt."[64]

Montagu they hated most of all, as a Jew, who in July 1920 had presumed to condemn the British perpetrators of the Amritsar massacre. On his own side of the House, Montagu-baiting became a regular sport of reactionaries like Joynson-Hicks and Rupert Gwynne, who applied to him expressions like: 'Thick-skinned as a hippopotamus', 'A grave peril to the country', 'Anything to save his own skin', 'There he sits unmoved but it is impossible to drive home to him that it was time he went.'[65]

If Montagu had any doubts of his standing with Lloyd George after the censure debate, the Prime Minister's conduct in another episode that month should have put those doubts to rest. When Lord Lytton, the Under Secretary of State for India, announced that he was leaving, Montagu suggested as his replacement Lord Winterton, Ormsby Gore or Samuel Hoare. Chamberlain and Lloyd George liked these suggestions but Curzon and the Lord Chancellor did not. Montagu then suggested "a popular Conservative," Lord Lovat. "To my surprise," Montagu remarked, "I learnt from Chamberlain that you decided to appoint Edward Wood and gave him a peerage in order to meet the objections of Lord Curzon." Curzon believed that the Under Secretary should be in the House of Lords, since the Secretary was in Commons. "I always understood," commented Montagu, "that a Minister at the head of a Department is consulted as to the appointment of an Under-Secretaryship,"[66] a courtesy that was always done in such cases. Instead of making an issue of the discourtesy, Montagu, who by now realized the insecurity of his position, merely added: "I have no doubt that Wood will render greater assistance. I have no doubt also that the fact that I was not consulted was due to your knowledge that this would be my attitude."[67]

This was the first public sign that Montagu had lost his spirit and confidence. Before the censure debate, he would not have accepted such an appointment without a long and bitter harangue. In this case, Montagu would have been perfectly justified. It was a serious breach of ministerial collegiality for Lloyd George to appoint an

Under Secretary of an important Ministry, indeed any Ministry, without consulting the Minister himself. It was an open slap at Montagu.

Not only did Montagu quietly accept this insult, but a few days later his wife invited Lloyd George to a dinner party to be held on February 24 to meet a "beautiful French Princess." Lloyd George had met this woman in Paris, and she was now marrying an Englishman and intended, according to Venetia, "to make him take an active role in English politics, I hope and believe as a supporter of yours, as she has fatal Circe charm. It would be so nice to see you again."[68] It is certain Venetia sent this invitation at the request of her husband in the hope that a warm social gesture might help him reestablish his rapport with the Prime Minister.

Montagu's desire to retain his position in the government was stronger than nearly any other emotion. His enemies called him "thick skinned," "insensitive" and capable of "doing anything to save his own skin." But one could also say that politics and India were so central to his life that he was prepared to accept any indignity to carry on the work he loved most and in which he fervently believed.

An Innocent Telegram from Reading

With the vitriol of the censure debate still ringing in his ears, Montagu faced his final month in office, March 1922. It began no differently than previous months. In some ways, it was even a little better. While Montagu was now fully aware of the intensity of the feelings against him among the Die-Hards and could no longer be blind to Lloyd George's attitude, his victory over the censure amendment still buoyed his spirits. The fact that a settlement of the Turkish problem along the lines he advocated seemed imminent also added to his sense of relief. But suddenly the scene changed with no warning.

It began, innocently enough, with a telegram Reading sent to Montagu, dispatched from Delhi on February 28 urging that the Treaty of Sèvres be revised:

On the eve of the Greco-Turkish Conference we feel it imperative to lay before His Majesty's Government the intensity of the feeling in India regarding the necessity of revising the Treaty of Sèvres.

The Government of India are fully alive to the complexity of the problem, but India's services in the war, in which Indian Moslem troops so largely participated, and the support which the Indian Moslem cause is receiving throughout India, entitle her to claim the extremist fulfillment of her just and equitable aspirations.

We are conscious that it may be impossible to satisfy India's expectations in their entirety. But we urged upon His Majesty's Government three points which, due provisions having been made for safeguarding the neutrality of the Straits and the security of the non-Turkish population, we ourselves regard as essential:

1. The evacuation of Constantinople
2. The Sultan's sovereignty over the Holy Places; and
3. Restoration of Ottoman Thrace including the sacred Moslem city of Adrianople and the unreserved restoration of Smyrna.

The telegram continued: "We earnestly trust this Majesty's Government will give these aspirations all possible weight, for their fulfillment is of the greatest importance to India." But the critical sentence was: "So important is it for the Government of India to range itself openly on the side of Moslem India that we press for permission to publish the forthgoing . . . forwith." [69]

Reading had offered to send this telegram three weeks earlier on February 9, "to finally place on record" the view of the government of India, adding, in his letter to Montagu of that date, that this would amount to "the ultimate statement which the Viceroy could take to enforce his policy, short of resigning." Montagu had encouraged Reading to issue such a statement, believing it might be useful at the conference being planned in Paris, at which the Greek-Turkish war was to be discussed again. Reading completed the document, which he now requested to be published.

As Reading's biographer Hyde has written: "There was nothing new in the contents of the telegram which had not been expressed before by Reading in his replies to various Moslem deputations which he had received from time to time, except perhaps that the telegram was phrased in more formal and succinct terms." [70] "Of course, I know that the Greco-Turkish Treaty [of Sèvres] was one of international complications," Reading explained in a confidential message to the Prime Minister. "I was, however, with my Government definitely of opinion that, having regard to the situation in India, it would be great value if we as a Government, together with the provincial Governments, could impress upon the Mohammedan population by our action and by publication of the telegram of 28th February that we had done all in our power to present their views as forcibly as possible to His Majesty's Government." Reading believed that publishing such views before the arrest of Gandhi "would be of special importance."[71]

Montagu received the telegram on Wednesday, March 1, at 8 A.M. At that time, he knew, as Reading had written, that Reading was planning to arrest Gandhi at any moment. The need to placate Indian leadership by some affirmative gesture, such as a strong pro-Turkish statement, had become in Montagu's mind, as in Reading's, an urgent necessity.

When he received the telegram, Montagu asked his staff to circulate it. There is no evidence that he told them it was "urgent," and it was dispatched for circulation in the ordinary way. As a result, the order for circulation was not officially acted upon until Friday, March 3, with Cabinet members receiving it on Saturday afternoon, March 4.

Many, including Montagu, were in the country for the weekend. On Saturday, Montagu received another telegram from Reading pressing for an immediate answer to the first, since Gandhi's arrest was expected within the next several days. The telegram added that reports from the provinces made clear that violent disturbances which had broken out there "had been largely attributed to the turbulent and fanatical element among all the Mohammedans."[72]

Montagu immediately cabled permission to Reading to publish, without consulting any of his colleagues or the Prime Minister, who was also in the country due to illness. He did this, Montagu later explained, because he believed that the telegram contained nothing new, that everyone knew the position of the Indian government on the Treaty of Sèvres, that Mohammedan delegations had been given this information orally by Reading and that Gandhi's arrest, which would occur at any moment, necessitated such a public statement at once. In addition, since Lloyd George was ill, Montagu did not expect an early Cabinet meeting.

On his return to his office on Monday, March 6, Montagu sent an additional telegram to Reading, amplifying his authority to publish. This telegram is crucial for it affirms that Montagu had no intention of hiding the incident from his colleagues. It began by stating: "I am glad to have your views as to the Turkish Peace, which I shall at once bring to the notice of my colleagues." In truth, he had already circulated Reading's telegram, and by Monday all the Cabinet members had had their copies for at least forty-eight hours. He asserted that while India's views must be heard, "India cannot dictate the terms of peace." He softened a phrase in the first telegram, referring to suggested modifications in the Sèvres treaty, from "we ourselves regard as essential" to "we urge as first importance." In case Reading had to urge India to accept terms different from the ones suggested, the second phrase, he explained, would give him more leeway. And he explained that it was not within the Allies' power to assure the Sultan's suzerainty over the Holy Places. "The Prime Minister," he said, "in his interview with the last Mohammedan Delegation assured them that the Treaty would be amended so as to avoid any obstacle to the religious suzerainty of the Khalifat over the Holy Places but the actual achievement of this religious suzerainty depends upon its acceptance by the King of Hedjaz and the King of Iraq. It is not a matter with which the Allies ought to interfere, and it was not a matter which can now be imposed upon King Hussein or King Feisul."[73]

This telegram was not that of a man who believed he was doing something surreptitiously. It was simply a matter-of-fact recitation of facts. This telegram and the one Montagu sent on Saturday, March 4, were not distributed to the Cabinet, which, in spite of Lloyd George's illness, did meet on Monday, March 6, with Austen Chamberlain in the chair. The telegram from Reading, which the Cabinet members had had since Saturday, was not discussed at the meeting. Instead Curzon spoke privately to Chamberlain, who agreed that it should not be published, and then to Montagu, remarking that he supposed Montagu would not authorize the publication without Cabinet discussion. "I have already done so," replied Montagu, according to Curzon's description of what took place, "on Saturday last."[74]

Curzon later wrote that he was so dumbfounded that he had had to return to his seat. "Had Mr. Montagu given the slightest hint that there was still time to cancel or postpone the order which he had sent to India by telegram two days before, or had I regarded such a suspension as possible, I should at once have brought the matter before the Cabinet, but I presumed that publication had already, under Mr. Montagu's authority, taken place in India."[75]

Montagu told the story differently, asserting that during the Cabinet meeting he took Curzon aside and privately informed him he had authorized the publication of the telegram. "If he [Curzon] had wanted to," Montagu wrote, "he could have resumed his seat in the Cabinet, which was still in session. He could have urged his colleagues to object to publication. I should have had something to say on the other side, and if the decision had gone against me, it is an irony to reflect, that there was ample time to send a telegram reversing my orders and stopping the publication of the telegram."[76]

Curzon did not raise the issue in the Cabinet. In fact, he remained totally silent in the Cabinet. Instead, he wrote a letter to Montagu that evening, which Montagu described as "one of those plaintive, hectoring, bullying, complaining letters, which are so familiar to his friends and colleagues."[77] Nowhere in that letter was there the slightest indication that Curzon would request that Lloyd George ask for Montagu's resignation. Instead, he merely recited his displeasure with Montagu's behavior. He informed Montagu that if he had ever authorized such public statements about British policy in Egypt when he was Viceroy, he would have been recalled. Chamberlain and Lloyd George both agreed that publishing the Reading telegram would make his task at the conference more difficult, and India had no right to "dictate" British foreign policy. He ended by saying he hoped that this would be "the last of these unfortunate pronouncements and if any other is contemplated," he hoped Montagu would give him "the opportunity to discuss it in the Cabinet before sanction is given."[78]

The letter was marked private and Curzon kept no copy. Montagu was correct in reading the last sentence as a reprimand and as a directive not to repeat this breach of Cabinet responsibility in the future. In no way can it be interpreted as suggesting that Montagu resign.

Dennis Judd, one of Reading's biographers, has noted that "Curzon's righteous indignation was particularly ironic in view of his own conflict with the Balfour government over exactly the same issue several years earlier. Balfour had fought a protracted campaign to limit Curzon's high-handed approach to Indian foreign policy," and "had also remarked wryly that Curzon, if unbridled, 'would raise India to the position of an independent and not always friendly power.' "[79] Curzon conveniently forgot these events in his own condemnation of Montagu. His letter to Montagu was incorrect in suggesting that by publishing the telegram the Viceroy was "dictating to the British Government." The Viceroy's telegram was not dictating policy: It was expressing the opinion of the Indian government—an opinion it had expressed since the war to Great Britain, to the Peace Conference in Paris and to the Big Four at their numerous meetings. The Indian press had often carried stories about the Treaty of Sèvres and the efforts of Reading and Montagu to get it modified. The *Islamic News* of June 10, 1921, for example, had carried a story headlined "Mr. Montagu's Task," which concerned Montagu's position on the Turkish treaty and the difficulties he was having persuading the British to change their views. It had criticized the British government "for destroying herself to save Greece" and described Montagu as "the most valuable friend the Moslems possessed in the British Cabinet." Thus, as early as 1921, the Indian press was aware of the Montagu and Reading position. Reading's telegram of March 1, 1922, contained nothing new.

In December 1921, the Cabinet had in fact instructed Curzon to negotiate with the goal of returning Constantinople to the Turks and Eastern Thrace to Turkey. For all of these reasons, Montagu had continued to believe that he did "right in granting the Viceroy permission to publish part of his telegram with certain alterations when he asked me for it." As he wrote to Curzon on March 7, 1922,

I do not . . . accept your description of the Government of India's telegram as being a dictation to His Majesty's Government nor am I influenced by what was or was not permissible when you were Viceroy. India has been given direct representation in the settlement of the questions arising out of the war and the right to express its views . . . comparable to the right expressed by the Dominions. . . . You do not seem to realise in the least either what changes have been made in the constitution of India . . . nor I venture to say, do you realise the enormous difficulties which you have put in the way of the Government of India by your foreign policy. . . . If you have any complaints to make on my conduct I should be glad if you would express them in Cabinet when I shall have an opportunity of answering them. I am getting tired of your everlasting opposition to every proposal that comes either from this Office or from the Government of India.[80]

Montagu did not mail this letter.[81] On March 9 the Prime Minister returned to London, read the story in the press, spoke to Curzon and asked Montagu to see him at once.

Montagu Forced to Resign

While the Prime Minister was critical of Montagu (and, according to Montagu, critical of Reading as well), at their meeting he did not ask for his resignation. Immediately following the meeting, Montagu sent a letter to Lloyd George in which he sought to justify his behavior. He wrote that the Viceroy pressed for a reply, that he believed he was completely justified in the action he took, that India's views had been stated and published repeatedly and that it had every right to express its views. "I understand that an attempt will be made [in the House] to move the adjournment in order to debate it. I propose on the motion for adjournment to justify the proceeding on the lines that I have justified it above."[82]

Montagu concluded that he did not know how to react to Lloyd George's accusations that he and "Reading have muddled India in a way that it was 'almost impossible that it could be muddled' " and that he (Montagu) did not have "the courage to carry through any decision and now by a gross act of treachery on the part of you [Montagu] and Reading, you are trying to throw the 'blame on somebody else.' " Since this statement involved Reading, Montagu wrote that he wanted "to consider it."

As Montagu wrote this reply to Lloyd George, he was unaware that the Prime Minister would request his resignation in a letter sent immediately after their meeting but before he received Montagu's first letter of the day:

My dear Montagu,

I had rather anticipated that before this I should have received a communication from you on the subject of our conversation of this morning. No letter, however, has so far reached me, and as there are questions in the House on the subject of the publication of the Viceroy's telegram, to which an Answer cannot be delayed, I feel bound at once to indicate the view I take of the situation.

That you were actuated in the course you pursued solely by a sense of public duty I do not for a moment doubt. Nevertheless, the fact remains that without being urged by any pressing necessity and without consulting

either the Cabinet or Foreign Secretary or myself or anyone of my colleagues, you caused to be published a telegram from the Viceroy raising
questions whose importance extends far beyond the frontiers of India or
the responsibilities of your Office.

A conference on the Near East is about to take place. The questions that
will be there discussed are of the utmost delicacy; the weight of responsibility which the Foreign Secretary will have to carry must in any case be
most serious; and your action has rendered a task which was already
difficult almost impossible. This was done, so far as I can see, without
reason or excuse. It was on Sunday that, on your sole responsibility, you
authorized the publication of the telegram in India; though there was a
Cabinet fixed for Monday which you could have consulted but which, as a
matter of fact, you did not even inform. The public consequences of this
course of action must inevitably be serious; its effect upon your colleagues
is, I need hardly say, painful in the extreme. *In these circumstances, I cannot
doubt that you will share my view that, after what has occurred, we cannot usefully
co-operate in the same Cabinet.*

I need not tell you that this severance of our official connection is a
source to me of deep regret, but I am confident that everybody, and not
least you yourself, will feel that, however painful, circumstances have
made it inevitable.[83] (emphasis added)

This was the first indication that Montagu had that Lloyd George
wanted him to resign. One can imagine his shock and consternation.
But Lloyd George's letter was clear and straightforward: He and
Montagu could no longer "usefully co-operate in the same Cabinet"
and Montagu's "severance" from the Cabinet was essential, "as
painful" as that might be.[84]

Montagu had no option. On that same day, March 9, 1922, he
wrote to Lloyd George tendering his resignation. His letter repeated
the reasons he had agreed to publish the telegram, repeating all the
language he had used in his earlier letter, only this time more formally: "When I was assured the Government of India regarded the
matter of the deepest urgency, I felt I was justified in the action I
took." He wrote that he believed his policies in India "will win
through to success."[85] He asked that his letter of resignation and his
telegram to Reading on Monday, March 6, be given to the press.

The Prime Minister acknowledged this letter immediately. By
not consulting his colleagues, Lloyd George wrote, Montagu "raised
questions whose importance extends far beyond the frontiers of
India or the responsibilities of your office. . . . Such action is incom-

patible with the collective responsibility of the Cabinet, to the Sovereign and to Parliament and I cannot doubt that on reflection you will share my views that, after what has occurred we cannot successfully cooperate in the same Cabinet." Lloyd George also refused Montagu's request that the telegram he sent to Reading be published, because the publication "would obviously aggravate the bad effects of the manifesto already published, and the Government therefore cannot consent to such a course."[86]

Lloyd George also wrote another short note to Montagu, on that same day, adding that he (Lloyd George) "must however at once say that your account of my references to Lord Reading are gravely inaccurate."[87]

Was Lloyd George trying to protect Reading? Or did Montagu really exaggerate Lloyd George's comments at their morning meeting? The evidence that survives does not provide a definite answer. It is not inconceivable, however, that Lloyd George, in the heat of the argument that morning, did attack both Reading and Montagu for the publication of the telegram but, when he thought about it calmly, decided he did not want to involve Reading. It was wiser politically to put the blame solely on Montagu. To force Reading to resign as well would jeopardize conditions in India, a situation Lloyd George could ill afford. It would also destroy a lifelong friendship with a man who was still politically useful to him. With Montagu, the situation was different: In one move, he could rid himself of a thorn in his side, as well as satisfy his Tory supporters. It was the perfect set-up for a master politician like Lloyd George. He seized the opportunity at once—totally indifferent to the morality of his course of action and to the grief it caused Montagu.

After tendering his resignation to Lloyd George, Montagu wrote to King George:

Mr. Montagu, with his humble duty to Your Majesty, would ask to be permitted to express to you the regret with which he leaves Your Majesty's service. During the eight and a half years it has been his privilege to serve Your Majesty, first as Under Secretary of State and then as Secretary of State for India, he has derived inspiration from Your Majesty's continued and anxious interest in the well-being of Your Indian subjects and the Princes of India. He recognizes fully the difficult position in which India is to-day; but, just as it has been his purpose throughout his term of office to further and secure the ties which bind the peoples of India to Your Majesty's Throne, so he ventures to predict that the storms will pass away, and that India will remain a source of pride to Your Majesty and to the British people.[88]

One can be certain that writing this letter broke his heart.

Montagu Goes on the Offensive

Angry, shattered and despondent, Montagu believed that his being asked to resign had little to do with Cabinet responsibility. Rather, he believed he had been sacrificed by Lloyd George in the Prime Minister's effort to stem some of the criticism mounting against him in the Conservative Party. Lloyd George needed a scapegoat and Montagu was an easy victim. Montagu was furious, too, that Lloyd George had refused to send a copy of his letter of resignation and his telegram to the Viceroy to the press. Montagu decided to go public on his own, to take his case to his constituents on March 11 at Cambridge.[89]

It was a long and impassioned speech that pulled no punches. He had a most receptive audience, including not only his Liberal constituents but also a large number of Indians. To this audience, he laid bare his anger and emotion. No, he told them, he had not been forced to resign because he had published the Viceroy's telegram. That was merely an excuse. "An accusation of the breach of the doctrine of Cabinet responsibility from the Prime Minister . . . is a laughable accusation. It is grotesque," Montagu told his audience. Since Lloyd George had been in control, there had been "the total, complete, absolute disappearance of the doctrine of Cabinet responsibility. . . . the thing is a joke. . . . It is a pretext. . . . We have been governed by a great genius — a dictator who has called together from time to time conferences of Ministers, men who had access to him day and night, leaving out those who, like myself, found it sometimes impossible to get to him for days together. He has come to epoch-making decisions, and over and over again it is notorious that members of the Cabinet had no knowledge of such decisions, and if such knowledge came to them it came at a time when they could make no effective use of their knowledge."[90] Laughter and cheers greeted this comment.

Montagu gave other examples of Cabinet members who had

expressed themselves on issues without Cabinet clearance: Winston Churchill, when he took a stand on Indian rights in Kenya before the Cabinet had discussed the issue; Lord Milner, who issued his report on whether Egypt should remain part of the Empire without the authority of the Cabinet:

Was Lord Milner asked to resign? He remained in the Government for months afterwards and by his remaining there, prejudiced and I think decided the fact that the Cabinet became responsible for the principle at any rate of the report which he had presented. Have you heard of the Army memo of the Geddes Committee Report? Where was the doctrine of Cabinet responsibility then?

No. Cabinet responsibility is not the cause. What then is the cause? The fact that, with or without consulting my colleagues, I consented to the publication of this telegram? Well, I did. Why should it not be published? The Government of India were parties to the Treaty of Sèvres. It was signed on their behalf. Had it produced some peace the Government of India would have loyally accepted it but when it showed—as I knew it always would show—that it could not produce peace, they pleaded for its revision, and as a party to the first Treaty they had every right to express their views—having been given separate representation on the Peace Conference—as to what they thought best in the interests of the country, and, on behalf of those for whom they spoke, ought to be the guiding factors in the new peace.[91]

Montagu argued that the real reason he had been forced to resign was that he had "been pleading, arguing, cajoling, urging against the Prime Minister's policy in the East ever since the Peace Conference. I have never been able to understand from what motive his [Lloyd George's] pro-Greek policy was dictated. . . . I do not know in whose interest it is. I am certain that it is calamitous to the British Empire." Montagu went into great detail about why he gave permission to publish the telegram, reviewing all the facts as he had presented them to the Prime Minister. He repeated his accusations of Curzon and disclosed the private letter Curzon had sent him, which did not ask for his resignation but ended by urging him not to allow such publication in the future without Cabinet clearance.

Curzon was infuriated at Montagu for revealing this letter, not only because it was not customary to reveal the contents of a private letter, but also because it showed that when he had written to Montagu he did not think the sin of permitting publication war-

ranted a forced resignation. Asking Montagu to resign clearly came
as an afterthought, when Lloyd George and Chamberlain realized
what a splendid opportunity the situation offered. It was tailor-made
for a politician like Lloyd George. Montagu was a sufficiently astute
politician to see this, and his Cambridge speech reflected his anger
at being treated by the Prime Minister in this way.

"The Prime Minister gave them [the Die-Hards] an appetizer of
what was coming when on the occasion of the last Indian debate
. . . getting up to defend me, a member of the Government, the
exponent of a policy which, on the doctrine of collective responsibility, he was responsible for, he paid compliments to the men who
attacked me but said not a word in defense of me." And now Lloyd
George was giving them "the scapegoat they sought."

There he stands, the greatest strategist in the world, scenting the air,
waiting for the pursuit, and thrown into the wolves the most convenient
cargo. . . . The Die Hards tried to get rid of me [through the censure
motion] and failed, but the great genius who presides over our destinies
had done for them what they could not do for themselves and presented
them with what they so long desired, my head on a charger.[92]

Montagu continued:

They have made against me wild and baseless charges and accusations.
They have shown, as I think, in Indian affairs . . . a complete lack of
political sagacity and political vision which is characteristic of them. They
represent the desperate demand of foolish but unhonest people to crystallize
against the march of time every anachronism in the world. They have
unwittingly instigated a riot and revolution by their lack of sympathy with
humanity and progress. . . . They have fomented unrest in the Indian
Service by baseless rumours. . . . They have invented speeches by me
belittling the Indian Service . . . distorted their meaning. . . . They have
asserted that the Government of India was prevented from maintaining
order from home. My successor . . . will find ample evidence of the
support given by me and my council. . . . I believe that this Die-Hard
Party, honest and sincere as they are, is the most dangerous element in the
political life of this country.[93]

Montagu turned to Indian policy, expressing his belief that his
resignation would not change British policy toward India, for the
vast majority of the British people were in sympathy with the
people of India. "I beg of the Indians to remember that race hatred

will only delay the day . . . of common action and common coop-eration. . . . I do not believe my disappearance means any alteration in Indian policy."[94] In closing, he commented on the sad state of affairs within the "suffering" Liberal Party, which saw its colleagues disappearing one by one. His forced resignation was part of this plot to eliminate Liberal ministers from the government. Looking to the future, he expressed his hope that cooperation between Liberals and Conservatives could continue:

Whether the government will adjust its own initial difficulties is not for me to say; whether it will be easy to create a national party without leaving out a single Die Hard and with as few Liberal Ministers . . . is not for me to say. But it does not mean that an honest cooperation between Liberals and Conservatives is not one of the things we ought to strive for, in the difficult times in which we live. . . . I propose to take my seat in the House as a Liberal believing in honest cooperation with that part of the Conservative Party which has demonstrated its willingness to cooperate.[95]

As Montagu and Lloyd George were soon to discover, coopera-tion between Liberals and Conservatives was a dream of the past. Few Liberals retained any faith in the Coalition and hardly any Conservatives were willing to continue their cooperation. For all practical purposes, the Coalition was at an end.

Two days after Montagu's speech, on March 13, Austen Cham-berlain, still representing Lloyd George in the House of Commons, was asked to comment on Montagu's resignation and the charges Montagu had made at Cambridge. Montagu's speech had received wide press coverage. Chamberlain refused to comment on the sub-stance of the Reading telegram but focused instead on the procedure of permitting its publication without Cabinet clearance especially since a conference on Turkey was to take place in a few days in Paris.

Chamberlain acknowledged that the government of India was entitled to put its views before His Majesty's government and to ask that they be published. But this request should have been denied by the Secretary of State. It was Montagu who was responsible; and it was he, not Reading or the government of India, who was wrong.

Since the Muslims were very disturbed at Montagu's resignation, Rees asked whether the government should issue a statement reaf-firming its sympathy with Muslim sentiment. Chamberlain responded that the Prime Minister's letter accepting the resignation made clear that it had nothing to do with the merits of the policy advocated by the government of India. Chamberlain reviewed the circumstances surrounding the publication of the telegram:

The late Secretary of State for India gave no hint to my Noble Friend that there was still time to stop publication of the telegram. Had he done so, of course, my Noble Friend would have consulted me and we should, if necessary have consulted the Cabinet, or acted on our own responsibility, and at once sent a telegram stopping publication. I imagine the Secretary of State for India did not suggest that there was still time to stop publication because he himself did not believe it. The Indian Government had asked leave to publish immediately, he had given that authorization on Saturday, and it was only afterwards, for reasons into which I do not go, that the Government of India delayed publication.[96]

Chamberlain criticized Montagu for "the very unusual course of referring to a private letter sent to him by Lord Curzon." Following this, Colonel Wedgwood asked the pivotal question: "Is it not a fact that the Noble Lord, the Foreign Secretary [Curzon] in writing to the ex-Secretary of State for India did not protest against the lack of Cabinet solidarity in publication, but asked that in the future any such despatch should not be published without Cabinet authority and would he [Chamberlain] therefore get permission from the Noble Lord to have that letter published so that we can see exactly what attitude was taken towards this shocking breach of tradition before it was found advisable to get rid of the late Secretary of State."[97]

This was a legitimate question and undeserving of the hostile and unresponsive answer that Chamberlain gave. In an indignant tone, Chamberlain asserted that Colonel Wedgwood was "not entitled to make insinuations of that kind" when he was supposedly seeking information. "What was the insinuation?" asked Wedgwood. Chamberlain, revealing his own discomfort with how the Montagu incident had been handled, responded that Wedgwood was implying that the reasons given for Montagu's resignation "were a mere pretext."[98]

Wedgwood replied that since it had been Chamberlain who suggested that he had made such an insinuation, he would like to pursue it. "May I ask," he continued, "how he [Chamberlain] reconciles the action taken towards the late Secretary of State for India and the action taken in exactly similar circumstances towards the speech the Secretary of State for the Colonies [made] in connection with a similar subject."[99] This too, was a legitimate question.

Chamberlain's response confirms that the reason given for Montagu's dismissal was a pretext and that the government did not want to discuss it. His reply was evasive and irrelevant: "the hon. and gallant Gentleman having made an unfounded allegation, now tries to cover his action by an argument. I state that his allegation is unfounded."[100]

Asquith was present during the debate. He made no effort to defend Montagu. His only contribution was to suggest that the matter be held over for a full discussion when Montagu was present. Chamberlain agreed and also suggested it be postponed until Curzon had spoken in the House of Lords the following day, March 14.

Curzon arose from a sick bed to deliver his peroration against Montagu. He was in intense physical pain but was determined, after Montagu's attack at Cambridge, to respond. "When he received the telegram on Saturday, I knew," Curzon stated:

there would be a Cabinet meeting on Monday. I never believed he would publish it. When, during the Cabinet meeting he told me privately he had published it I was dumbfounded. I thought it was too late to cancel. Nothing would be gained by raising it in the Cabinet. I wrote to him deploring his actions and protesting a repetition. I thought he would answer me in Parliament where we could debate the issue. Instead he went before a political club and vilified me and attempted to shift the blame to me. My letter made clear that in the future he should give me the opportunity to discuss a matter of such importance before he took action, in the Cabinet.[101]

Curzon's response leaves unanswered the key question: If he was so disturbed by Montagu's response, why did he not raise the issue at the Cabinet meeting and make his position clear then and there? Why did he merely write a letter telling Montagu not to do it again? An examination of the letter confirms Montagu's claim that while Curzon was angry at the publication of the telegram, he did not want to make a Cabinet fight over it. He might not have won. Therefore, he did not demand Montagu's dismissal. A reprimand was all he felt necessary. It was Lloyd George who had seized the opportunity to get rid of someone the Die-Hards despised, whose defense of the Hunter Commission report still rankled them and whose attacks on the Prime Minister's Turkish policy had become an irritant. Montagu's belief that the issue was purely political—to placate the Die-Hards—was correct. A dismissal over a technical breach of the kind he made might not have been sustained within the Cabinet.

This was implicit in Lord Crewe's remarks in the House of Lords after Curzon spoke. While conceding that Montagu's conduct was not technically correct, he pointed out "that action of this kind on the part of a Minister, surprising as it may be, is less surprising than it would have been from a member of a Government in which the old tradition of collective responsibility had been more uniformly respected." Crewe agreed that the telegram expressed views that India "was known to hold." He did not excuse Montagu but continued: "We cannot help recalling other cases in which His Majesty's Ministers—I do not name any—seem to have arrogated to themselves the right to make speeches either on the platform or sometimes even in Parliament, conveying views distinct from and opposed to, those which were understood to be entertained by the government as a whole. If this particular Minister has gone too far, as we all think he has, in the assertion of this independence, I am afraid he has been encouraged to do it by the manner in which No. 10 Downing St. had conducted the system of Government." [102]

Removing Montagu from the India Office had been in Chamberlain's mind for some time before the telegram episode. On March 6, for example, Chamberlain had written to Walter Long after the censure debate: "Egypt and India have caused great uneasiness in the Party but the recent announcement about Egypt and the debate on India have done much to restore confidence and to clear the air. Much of the mistrust of Montagu is unfair, but I confess I should be glad if other work could be found for him." [103]

As early as 1921, Chamberlain had been concerned over the opposition that was developing in the Conservative Party and was eager to have Lloyd George placate the Tories who now wanted to bolt the Coalition and go it on their own. It was he who advised Lloyd George in April 1921 not to back Addison, whose housing programs were being bitterly attacked by the Tories, because the Tories were becoming restless and the Coalition was in jeopardy. Lloyd George followed that advice, severely ridiculed Addison in

Commons with "insults and innuendo" and eventually forced Addison, a trusted and respected colleague, to resign.

Both Chamberlain and Lloyd George were increasingly fearful of the Die-Hards, and although Chamberlain did not share their extreme right-wing ideology, by 1921 he was prepared to make serious concessions to them and to support the dismissal of ministers with Liberal reputations. In Montagu's case, Lloyd George had yet another reason to seize the first opportunity to dismiss him: He doubted Montagu's loyalty. As early as 1920, word had reached him in a written report from the Tory Central Office that Montagu and Venetia had voted against the Coalition candidate at a by-election in South Norfolk.[104] Lloyd George had also heard that Montagu had been involved with Birkenhead and Churchill in an alleged plot to overthrow him, although there was and is no evidence to support this.

Neither Addison nor Montagu, moreover, had the kind of personalities that endeared them to their superiors. A list of Addison's characteristics describes Montagu's qualities as well: "stubbornness, quiet but persistent and personalized reproach, a maddening memory for pledges, and an idealist's devotion to causes precisely where subtler courtiers would choose silence or flattery. Only those with unassailable popularity or an inherited position can afford such virtues when policy and place are at stake."[105]

Like Addison, Montagu was not a "subtle courtier" and did not have "unassailable popularity" or "inherited position." He could never use flattery or remain silent in the face of what he perceived to be an injustice. His speech to the House of Commons on March 15, defending his instructions to publish the Reading telegram, is pure Montagu. He pulled no punches; he would not go quietly into the night.

He told the House that the Cabinet had had ample time to raise the problem of the telegram on Monday, Tuesday or Wednesday. No one thought he had committed a "constitutional outrage." The reasons given for his dismissal were a mere pretext. He had every right to use the Curzon letter. He had no other evidence to support his case. He did not misquote the letter. He could gain nothing from a misquotation, since the letter itself was available for public verification. "Lord Curzon," Montagu emphasized to the House, "ended his letter with a request—a request to do what? Not to hand my resignation to the Prime Minister, not to recognize that it was impossible that I should continue in office with him; a request not to come with him to the Prime Minister, and discuss a matter which would render continuation in office impossible, but merely and only a request not to do it again."[106] Montagu ended with words that truly expressed his heartbreak:

I longed for nothing better than to devote myself so long as I could to these all absorbing problems, and not to leave undone or half done at a most critical moment the work in which I glorified. I have parted this week from colleagues in the India Office and in India with whom I have worked for a term of years with uninterrupted accord, and I have laid down the proudest title that in my belief an Englishman can hold, the title of the Secretary of State for India, which means the right in particular to serve the King, this Parliament and India, and this is the unhappiest moment of my life.[107]

Chamberlain was testy and defensive during the debate, demonstrating that old wounds never die. "My right hon. Friend is not the only Minister who has had to resign," he reminded the House. "He is not the only Secretary of State who at a certain moment has found it is not compatible with his duty to remain in office. I sympathize with him."[108] Chamberlain was referring to the debate on Mesopotamia and Montagu's speech of 1917 that had caused his own resignation.

Asquith, whose own scars may have been equally painful, was still gentlemanly enough to remind the House that, while he did not excuse Montagu for breaking the rules (although he had personally excused Lloyd George, Reading and Samuel for breaking far more important rules in the Marconi Case), he regretted that "a career which has been associated with so much good, remarkable and I believe fruitful work in the interests of India and of the Empire should for the moment be checked."[109] Asquith had the gift of magnanimity in both politics and personal relationships. He had a remarkable capacity to see things in their proper perspective, understand foibles and human error and not stand in judgment.

Venetia was in the Speakers Gallery of the House of Commons when Chamberlain announced that Montagu's resignation had been accepted by the King and "had the mortification of hearing the loud cheers which this piece of news evoked among the die-hards on the Tory benches."[110] Lloyd George was not present. He was still recuperating from his illness. His Secretaries kept him informed daily, one of them writing to him on March 15: "I will let you know tomorrow how the Montagu debate goes off tonight. He was here this afternoon, and his eye did not reveal the triumphant gleam of the confident gladiator."[111] The next day Lloyd George was informed "that the Montagu debate was a complete fizzle. Every single speech was poor and did not last long. Asquith looked very tipsy and the Speaker interrupted him (rather unfairly) to tell him to keep nearer the subject which completely knocked him off his perch."[112]

The anti-Semites continued their venomous attacks. Sir Walter Lawrence, for example, wrote to Curzon: "You have been very much in our thoughts lately, as we feel as do all your friends, very bitter against that malicious and dangerous Jew. My inference is that he deliberately created this situation to get out of office before the crisis came to India. He suggests intrigue—he who has intrigued with his agents in India, British and Indian, to be made Viceroy. It ought to be emphasized that the problems that are coming to India are due, not so much to our policy, as to the intrigues and methods of this mischievous Jew."[113] Sir Walter Lawrence, the author of this letter with its insinuation of an international Jewish conspiracy, was a respectable member of British society and a dear friend of Curzon. He had served Curzon with great devotion as Private Secretary while Curzon was Viceroy. It it not likely that he would have written in this fashion unless he believed that his anti-Semitic views would meet with Lord Curzon's approval.

Reading's Reaction

Reading was horrified at the news of Montagu's resignation and wrote to him the next day expressing his distress, especially because the resignation had been "occasioned in connection with the telegram from my Government and the request for sanction to publish. I have always recognized and admired your enthusiastic devotion to India and Indian problems. I feel I am sustaining a grave personal loss of association, which I cannot adequately express. The relationship between us has been so intimate and we have acted so much in accord that I am profoundly moved by your departure."[114]

Nowhere in this letter, however, did Reading offer to resign, although in writing to his son that same week he confided: "I am very doubtful whether I ought to let Edwin go into the wilderness without following him, not merely because we are both children of Israel and both anathema to a certain section of people, but because I find it very difficult to understand why he should have [been] drummed out of the Cabinet, post haste."[115] On March 11, after Chamberlain's report to the House of Commons, Reading sent a more formal telegram to the new Secretary of State for India, Lord Robert Peel, expressing his deep personal loss at Montagu's resignation. In this telegram, he made a point of noting that in the twelve months he had been Viceroy there had been no difference of opinion between them:

Whatever comments and criticism may be passed here or in England upon the discharge of his duties as Secretary of State of India, his devotion to the cause of India, according to his views cannot be doubted. I have been Viceroy nearly twelve months and during that period have been in the most constant and intimate communication with Mr. Montagu. Rumours have been circulated that there were differences of opinion between him, representing His Majesty's Government, and myself and my Government regarding the policy to be pursued toward non-cooperation and its leaders. There never has been the faintest ground for those rumours.[116]

Reading was anxious to avoid the impression that Montagu had been dismissed because the government was opposed to his Indian policies. He telegraphed suggestions for Montagu to use in a message he was then preparing to explain his resignation to the people of India. Reading wanted Montagu's statement to include the following sentence: "Another point I must emphasize is that my resignation involves no change in the policy of His Majesty's Government on the subject of Reforms, as announced in the Declaration of August 1917 and as later embodied in the provisions of the Government of India Act [of 1919]."[117] Montagu refused. It was completely contrary to what he believed. Chamberlain told Reading two days later that he was unable to authorize publication of Montagu's proposed message with or without this addition, but he emphasized that "the resignation of Mr. Montagu had nothing whatsoever to do with the Government of India policy."[118]

The controversy continued for several more days, sufficient for Reading to complain to Lloyd George on March 13 that press reports were suggesting that some "particular cunning" underlay Reading's initial request for a revision of the Treaty of Sèvres and that he "owed it to his self-respect to resign with Montagu. I am very distressed by the resignation," he wrote to Lloyd George:

first because it arose from the reply of Montagu to my application for leave to publish, and secondly because of my close connection with him since I became Viceroy. Ever since I began to understand Indian affairs, I have been convinced that Mohammedan attitude in relation to the Treaty of Sevres was of cardinal importance. Communications were published by me on instructions from Home Government setting out substance of modification of Treaty it was hoped to obtain. Since then I have at various times received deputations from Mohammedans and have made replies that I would support their views to best of my power . . . There is little if anything in the telegram published that is new and has not already received approval.[119]

Reading was adamant that the impression that Montagu had been sacrificed to the hard-liners should be avoided.

Montagu did not agree with Reading. In all his public statements, Montagu took the line he did at Cambridge and in the House of Commons, blaming his dismissal on hard-line opposition to him and to his Liberal Indian policies. On March 13, Reading again wrote to Montagu, explaining that while he had contemplated resigning he had decided to stay on because "my departure from office simultaneously with you would have a remarkably bad effect in India, not because of my own personality but because I had become identified in Indian minds with the Liberal policy you have pursued."[120]

Montagu replied on March 15: "May I say how much I hope you will stick to it and continue your wise rule."[121] Montagu felt so strongly about this that he pleaded with Beaverbrook to have his newspapers leave Reading alone. On March 13, in the midst of his own crisis, he had written to Beaverbrook:

The views which Lord Reading has expressed now have been expressed over and over again, before. This telegram and everything connected with it is a subterfuge of the Prime Minister's. I believe it will be a calamity if Lord Reading were to resign. I have not the slightest doubt that he thinks so too and my prayer to you would be to leave him alone.[122]

Montagu need not have worried; it is not likely that Reading was prepared to give up a position he loved so much to demonstrate solidarity with Montagu. He was encouraged, moreover, to remain by Lloyd George and Chamberlain who went out of their way to explain that he had every right to ask that the telegram be published. He had done nothing wrong. Montagu was the culprit for breaking with the policy of Cabinet collective responsibility. Assuaged by this reasoning and Lloyd George's personal pleas, Reading remained in office. Montagu's attitude toward Reading's resignation was remarkably unselfish and showed him to be far more generous than his opponents made him appear.

The Indian Princes, the Legislative Council of the Provinces and Montagu's many friends in India were utterly dismayed at his resignation and unanimous in their grief. They deplored his being "thrown to the wolves" for fighting on their behalf and heaped upon him warm, almost idolatrous praise as the greatest Secretary of State in India's history. The Aga Khan, the Governor of Madras, Annie Besant, Mukerji, the President of the All India Conference of Indian Christians, Basu, the Maharajah Bikaner, Sir George Lloyd, the Maharajah Alwar, the Bengal Legislative Council, the Muslim Members of the Indian Legislature, the Council of Bombay, the Maharajah Kapurtmala, the Indian Merchants Chamber and Bureau, the Executive Committee of the Legislative Council of Punjab, the Delhi Legislative Council, and scores of other official and unofficial governing bodies and institutions, all wrote the warmest letters of praise coupled with expressions of deep sadness at his leaving.[123] Many of Montagu's friends in India believed that his separation from India would be temporary. It was not. It was permanent.

Gandhi's Arrest: Too Late to Help Montagu

On the day after Montagu's resignation, March 10, 1922, Gandhi was arrested and sent to prison for six years. Even more ironically, Montagu's resignation gave rise to far more vehement outcries and protestations than Gandhi's arrest did. When Gandhi emerged from prison—two years later—the scene in India had changed dramatically. The alliance between Hindus and Muslims had been shattered and killings between the two groups occurred daily. Driving a wedge between Hindus and Muslims had been a goal of Reading's, supported by Montagu. Neither foresaw the bloodshed that would follow.

On the positive side, by 1924, at least three of Montagu's and Reading's other goals were being implemented: Britain had repealed the Rowlatt Acts, the Indianization of the Indian Civil Service was under way, and the British government was urging that India be admitted to the League of Nations. But by then Montagu was mortally ill and could gain no pleasure from these achievements. By 1924, too, the Treaty of Sèvres had been replaced by the Treaty of Lausanne, which incorporated nearly all of Montagu's suggestions. Lloyd George was out of office, and Curzon had been denied the Premiership of Great Britain to his dismay and humiliation. But that was two years hence. In 1922, all Montagu knew was that he had been removed from office without just cause and that all the tears shed for him in India could not erase the pain of his bitter vilification.

31

Some Private Notes: Pearl and the Birth of a Daughter, 1921–1922

Pearl has just given me a little daughter and we are very happy about it.

Montagu to Lord Reading, Oct. 1921

Neither Montagu's nervous breakdown nor the bashing he suffered all through 1921 and 1922 in any way affected Venetia's style of living. She continued in her addictions to travel, lavish entertaining and gambling at the casinos in Nice and Cannes and in her love affair with Lord Beaverbrook and her flirtations with other men.

Montagu accepted, at least to some degree, his wife's vagaries and her need for Beaverbrook and other men to satisfy her sexual desires. This did not dampen his own friendship with Beaverbrook whose company he sought so frequently that he felt obliged to apologize, fearing that "there must be limits to your [Beaverbrook's] patience."[1] He also felt comfortable enough to ask Beaverbrook to guarantee a seven thousand pound bank loan Montagu was forced to take for his campaign in 1921. Beaverbrook's generosity knew no bounds; it extended even to his lover's husband. He guaranteed not only the original note but also its renewal six months later.[2]

While Beaverbrook was clearly a favorite of Venetia, he was not the only man in her life. This was not a secret from Montagu, who wrote to Venetia on January 31, 1922: "Lord Charles is a new star in your constellation. . . . Who is he and what is he like?"[3] And on February 7, he wrote:

By the by I asked Valentine if he knew the Charles Hope who looms so largely in your correspondence. His reply was, "Oh yes, very well; I like him very much but he is a typical old woman's darling." I told him that I should at once repeat this description of you, and him and I have faithfully done so.[4]

Did Montagu have a mistress or some other woman to answer his needs? His letters are silent, except for one written to Lord Reading on October 11, 1921, in which it appeared that not only did he have a mistress but that he even had a child by her. This was not substantiated in any other letters that Montagu wrote before or since. Nor do Venetia's or Montagu's friends ever mention this woman or child in any of their letters, autobiographies or biographies of the period.

In this astonishing letter, Montagu first congratulated Reading for the "successful commencement of a most arduous office in a most difficult period." He assured Reading that "everyone here is confident that you will pilot your ship well and bring it into safe port." He then added, in a matter-of-fact tone: *"Pearl and I are thinking of coming out to India arriving at Bombay about January 6–8. . . . Pearl has just given me a little daughter and we are very happy about it"* (emphasis added).[5] In no letter had Montagu or any one else ever called Venetia "Pearl." Nor was there any evidence that Venetia had any child but Judith, who was not born until February 1923.

During 1921 and 1922, Venetia traveled a great deal, including some time spent in the winter of 1922 with Clementine Churchill.[6] Nothing was said by Clementine in the many letters she wrote during that time or by any of Venetia's friends concerning any pregnancy of Venetia's. Venetia herself also wrote a great many letters during 1921 and 1922 to Beaverbrook and others and said not a word about a child. In October 1921, moreover, when Montagu was writing to Reading, telling him that "Pearl has just given me a little daughter," Venetia was also writing to Beaverbrook inviting him to luncheons and dinners.[7] It is thus not possible that the daughter Montagu referred to in his letter to Reading was Venetia's child.

Whether Venetia or anyone else knew of either Pearl or the child is a mystery upon which no existing records shed light. What is known is that Lily Montagu, Edwin's sister, as well as Montagu's butler, his secretary, and Venetia all had access to Montagu's letters and memorabilia after his death. Any one of them could have destroyed evidence about Pearl and the daughter.

Lily Montagu was the leading female figure in Liberal Judaism of her day, a distinguished Jewish leader and preacher. She has been described as "very puritanical," someone who "felt that there was something ungodly or, at least, not nice about sex and she could be deeply upset at any instance of sexual misbehavior among members of her youth club."[8] In addition, she also had a great deal of her father's self-righteousness. It is possible that letters showing that her brother had a mistress and an illegitimate child may have been so painful for her that she destroyed those letters.

As for Venetia, in spite of her free style of living, she too may have found embarrassing the prospect that this information might become public and may have thought it wiser to destroy any letters that bore witness to it. As for the butler and the secretary, perhaps they were aware that Venetia did not know about Pearl and decided to protect Montagu by destroying the letters before anyone could go through them.

Montagu's letters to Venetia during 1921 and 1922, while she was traveling extensively, also reveal him to be a little less loving than in earlier years. His letters are largely calendars of his own daily activities, reports of Breccles and the deteriorating political scene he was facing. They did not include the longings for her and the passionate expressions of love that once filled his correspondence to her. They did indicate, however, that he continued to write regularly and was unhappy when she did not respond as frequently.

On January 27, 1922, two months before his forced resignation in March, for example, he wrote that he had been kept enormously busy with the Irish problem, the Geddes Committee, his own office and the Cabinet. He apologized for not having written every day. He also wrote that when Churchill became bored with a subject, he appointed a subcommittee and made Montagu the chairman, "unless I am alert enough to escape it, therefore I dare not be a moment late for any meeting." He described a "man's dinner," which he had recently attended, and confessed that, while he and the other men all "adore" women, there was something about a man's dinner that was special.[9]

On January 31, 1922, he wrote about his strenuous days on the

Geddes Committee, his trip to shoot geese "somewhere between Hunstanton and Wells and just outside the walls of Holkam," and of his visit to Breccles, where "the hens are laying badly" and the "snow drops are just out." "On Monday," he "lunched with Max and dined with Lady Lovat. . . . After dinner he visited Diana in bed with a cold."[10] Relations between Churchill and Montagu continued to worsen. "He [Churchill] has behaved very badly not only coming to the wrong decisions [on Kenya and South Africa] but behaving most trickily."[11]

On February 2, 1922, he admonished Venetia for not writing. He had received only one letter. (She had been away for more than ten days.) His relationship with Churchill was by now so strained that they had to be guarded in their conversation although they were polite and courteous to each other. He then reported on "a terrible tragedy" that happened to him at their house. "The looking glass in the hall had fallen down and smashed itself to smithereens . . . and I am anxious awaiting unfortunate and deplorable incidents."[12] He would not have long to wait.

Four days later, Montagu finally heard from Venetia and replied at once. He wrote that he had become increasingly worried about India and he did not think "the Government is in good spirits."[13] While Venetia may have found such political comments interesting, there is no evidence that they affected her in any way. Instead she continued her travels until the end of February, gambling, playing in tennis tournaments and enjoying the shops and casinos of Paris and the Riviera. Montagu not only accepted this and willingly paid for it, but even seemed to get vicarious pleasure from her vagaries. In his letter of February 7, 1922, he told her he was in the process of getting her jewelry "out of the pawn shop." But in the same letter Montagu told Venetia that he looked forward "to seeing the clothes and hats you describe to me, and I pray not only that your career at the casino is continually meeting with success, but that you have defeated all comers in the tennis tournament, for news of which I look in the daily papers every morning."[14]

For Montagu's sake, one can only hope that Pearl—whoever she was—did exist, and that she and the child she bore him gave him some joy and comfort during these days when his career was hanging by a thread. Clearly, he received no comfort from Venetia.

32

Alone at Eventide,
March–December 1922

The prospect of a general election and the horrors of the next three weeks in Cambridgeshire fills me with unspeakable gloom.

Venetia to Lord Beaverbrook, Oct. 1922

While Montagu lived for two years and eight months after his resignation, his spirit had been broken. He was lonely, bored and depressed. Working for Indian reform had become the focus of his life or, as one friend said after his death, "the deepest conviction of his being."[1] When this was removed, his sense of purpose and direction was destroyed. To make matters worse, he was haunted by the fear that the policies he had fought for in India would be abandoned. All "sense of personal disappointment," his friend later observed, "seemed to be swallowed up in the anguish of fear that the cause he was fighting for would suffer."[2]

Montagu's successor, Lord Robert Peel, a grandson of Queen Victoria's second Prime Minister, was a conservative who was "conscientious and steady going" but "a political nonentity, lacking not only all knowledge of India but also the occasional flash of visionary insight that had made Mr. Montagu so inspiring a colleague."[3] With such a successor, Montagu's fears that reform in India would not be properly implemented were not ungrounded. But beyond his concern with policy, he was most bothered by being "out of things." For the first time in sixteen years he was not at the heart of the political scene, and for the first time since 1910, he was removed from any role relating to India. He was a lonely onlooker, with neither allies nor political friends in the Conservative Party, the Liberal Party or among the Coalition Liberals. And to Lloyd George, he was a "sneak" who had not only caused a constitutional crisis but had had the temerity to publicly attack the Prime Minister's style of government and to expose the dissension within the Cabinet. Montagu himself aptly characterized his political situation to Reading as "having no analogy in loneliness and hopelessness."[4]

An official of the India Office wrote: "My last memory of him [Montagu] is rather pitiful. I was over at the House in the official gallery on some business or other after Edwin's resignation. I saw him wandering about in a homeless and friendless kind of way and eventually he came over to me and had quite a chat about this and that; a thing he would never have dreamt of doing in his great days. A tragic figure."[5] During the months immediately following his resignation, he spent most of his time finishing up his work at the India Office, attending some sessions of Parliament, answering the hundreds of letters that he received from friends in England and India, writing a few letters to the editors of London newspapers and trying to decide what to do with the rest of his life. He followed conditions in India and Turkey with continued interest but as a stranger looking in from the outside.

With Gandhi's arrest on March 10 (the day after Montagu was forced to resign), matters quieted down in India, enough so that Reading could write to Lloyd George in May that "the internal situation has been quieter than at any period since I have been here." Seven months later, he wrote to Peel that the "non-cooperation movement remains more or less stationary. Hindus took little or no interest in the proceedings [of Gandhi's trial]."[6] This was confirmed in a memorandum to Montagu from Victor Lytton, now governor of Bengal, in which he wrote that conditions had so dramatically improved that it was "difficult to believe how short a time ago the whole country was disorganized by political agitation." The non-cooperation movement "was completely collapsed with the arrest of Gandhi." He added that even the Indian Civil Service said that things were considered better. Women can "walk about without fear," he said. He concluded that "only after the government took strong action did matters settle down. . . . Everyone believes if the Government had acted sooner they could have brought order sooner."[7]

These reports supported Montagu's critics in their belief that once he was out of office conditions in India would improve. They also confirmed Montagu's belief that if Reading had arrested Gandhi sooner, the quiet that had now come to India might have come while he was Secretary of State, and thus stripped the Die-Hards of their most effective charge against him. The most Montagu would say to his friend Sir George Lloyd, on June 8, 1922, was: "I never felt much doubt but that when the Government of India asserted itself against Gandhi and his followers, actual law breaking with all its attendant perils would cease."[8] And to his friend Victor Lytton: *"As long as I live people will think I refused to deal with non-cooperation. It is impossible to defend myself without giving others away"* (emphasis added).[9] In this context, he could only have meant Reading. Yet there is no record that he ever directly accused or blamed Reading in public or private, and his letters to Reading continued to be warm and gracious.

He did, however, blame the Indians, whose "disgusting and disgraceful riots and follies" he believed added to the fuel of the Die-Hards. While he was critical of the Indians who were responsible for the riots, moderate Indian leadership continued to venerate him, even to the point of naming a new housing colony in Bombay after him. He responded enthusiastically to the honor, writing to George Lloyd that he was "thrilled by your account of the developing scheme. . . . I cannot tell you how proud I should be to be associated by nomenclature with the work."[10]

This letter revealed, as well, an aspect of Montagu seen only by his dearest friends: his sensitivity to nature. He was sitting at Breccles when he wrote:

In an almost Indian sunshine, enjoying the first roses and wealth of summer flowers. I do not remember any Spring which has been so wonderful as this one. We had a winter prolonged right up till the beginning of May; intense backwardness of everything and the sudden warmth and an almost explosive burst of blossoms. But we have had a May such as has never been equalled. Lilac, chestnut, wisteria all came into flower together.[11]

But sitting at Breccles contemplating nature's beauty was not enough for Montagu, who continued to feel restless and at loose ends, dispirited and alone. In May, he and Venetia decided to visit India the next winter. Spending time traveling and shooting in a country he loved, and which in turn loved and admired him, and visiting his many friends might be just the tonic he needed.

To his surprise, Reading was very unhappy at the prospect of the Montagu visit. "You can never come as just a private gentleman," Reading wrote on May 18. "You will find that you will be Secretary of State still to most people in India. I mean they still think of you in that capacity. I doubt whether you quite realize the hold you have on the Indian public. I shall not say more and merely want to put this view to you."[12]

Montagu would not be put off. He had his heart set on the trip and had no intention of giving it up. In a warm, friendly letter to Reading he wrote:

I welcome your friendship and attach great weight to your advice. Nevertheless my present intention is to come. I have sacrificed everything that I could find to sacrifice for what I conceived to be the interests of India. I have never failed to consider the interests of India as I saw them.

I do not think I feel called upon to debar myself from visiting the country in which I am so profoundly interested and in which I have so many friends. You may be right in what you say about the hold I have on the India public, although I think that a quite momentary ebullition of feeling may make [it] easy to exaggerate it. But if you are right it is far easier for me to visit India when no differences have developed between me and those who govern India than it would be at a later date. Moreover I am free this winter so far as I know at present, and at a later date I might have engagements which would make a visit impossible. I hope I need not assure you that I shall behave myself in such a way as to avoid embarrassment to you.[13]

Reading was as persistent and stubborn as Montagu and replied that a Montagu visit would be "misconstrued." It was bound to cause "embarrassing situations" and he was opposed to it. If Montagu persisted in coming, however, he hoped he would publicize the trip in advance, to emphasize its private nature. He reported that India was quiet, "although there is some attempt to rekindle non-co-operation activities and particularly as they relate to civil disobedience." He did not think this was serious.

Montagu responded that he could not understand Reading's objections. Most of his time would be spent with friends outside of British India. He might come to Delhi to sit in a meeting of the

Legislature, "to see what it looks like." He assured Reading again that he had no intention of attacking his administration or Peel's. But then Montagu's sly sense of humor took over. He dropped a bombshell: Venetia was pregnant.

and now, my dear Rufus, I am going to cheer you up and I am going to take you into my complete confidence. It is more than likely that I shall not be coming to India at all. . . . At the moment of writing I have every reason to hope, at long last, a domestic event which my wife and I have long delayed and prayed for is about to occur. A few days or weeks will make hope certain. . . .

   It amuses me to think how delighted you will be because it will keep us out of India, and you can hope with me that this desirable result will be achieved, not by the expression of a Viceroy's wish but by one of the ordinary incidents of married life.[14]

He warned Reading, however, that while he would not be in India this year, he and Venetia were more determined than ever to visit the Indian jungles "in the following winter."

There you have the whole story—an obstinate, narrow visioned unimaginative ex-Secretary of State, deaf to argument, blind to visions, adamant and disquieting to any Viceroy, but fortunately with a very ordinary chink in his armour which may achieve for the unfortunate Viceroy the purpose he has in view. I shall be sorry not to come to India; I am sorry not to receive from you your reluctant and apprehensive handshake, not to see you bravely fortified as you mask your tremors of apprehension, not to watch you striding your quaking volcano in the unconquerable belief that I have made it rumble and quake yet more. But I am frankly delighted at the cause of my disappointment and if it makes you more comfortable it is all to the good.[15]

   Reading was greatly relieved. While his letters to Montagu were couched in warm and friendly terms, he was troubled by the prospect of a Montagu visit and determined to try to persuade Montagu to abandon it. From an objective point of view, Reading should not have taken this position. He and Montagu agreed on Indian policy and he had no need to fear that Montagu would say anything to harm the direction in which he was moving. And any cheers Montagu would receive from his admiring public in India would have signaled to the Home Government that the Liberal policies Reading supported should not be abandoned. In fact, if Montagu had spoken out on Turkey or Indian policy, it would have been not a hindrance but a help to Reading. The only thing Reading could legitimately have feared was that Montagu might say something critical of Lloyd George and his government. Knowing how Montagu felt about Lloyd George, this was a real possibility. Lloyd George may even have conveyed this fear to Reading and urged him to try to keep Montagu from making the trip. Reading, always the consummate politician, was not likely to ignore this plea, even if it meant opposing the request of an old friend who had put his political life on the line to help him, and who now needed the solace and cheer of India. Montagu's needs were of little concern to Reading, when measured against his own political needs and those of his political protector, Lloyd George.

Montagu suspected that someone was exerting his influence on Reading. On September 29, assuring Reading that he would not pursue the trip, he added, "Somebody seems to me to have imposed upon you very strange and baseless apprehensions."[16] He also felt that Reading "overrated" his (Montagu's) influence in India. But, fortunately, he was spared further arguments with one of his few remaining political friends by what he called "one of the ordinary incidents of married life."

While he gave up his argument with Reading about his trip, he did not give up his keen interest in India, nor his desire to visit the following winter. His correspondence with his many friends and admirers there continued unabated. In a letter to Victor Lytton, who was now the Governor of Bengal, Montagu appeared to have moved away from dyarchy, writing Victor that "the sooner we get away from dyarchy and get a Unified Ministry responsible to the Legislature, carrying on with British assistance, the better we will be."[17] He also disagreed with Lytton about the need to be specific about British goals for India. "I am afraid [that] I wouldn't try and spell out clearer goals now. . . . I am very much afraid that any attempt to arrive at any further clarification would lead, in the temporary reactionary spirit of the world, or at any rate England, to a confusion of the clear ideal which . . . it was thought we had before us. What we have in mind is self-government—in good time, not forced by agitation but warranted by circumstance."

While Montagu may have had second thoughts about dyarchy, his position on Turkey never changed. In time, he had the satisfaction of seeing the peace he had advocated achieved—not, unfortunately, through British diplomatic efforts but by Kemal's armies. "I am amused," he wrote to Reading on September 29, "that the peace which we advocated with Turkey, the peace which I lost office for advocating, now looks like [it is] being achieved but alas with no credit to the British Government."[18]

Chanak

During the summer of 1922, the Greeks began to reinforce their army in Thrace and asked the Allies' permission to enter Constantinople. In August, they were encouraged by the moral support they received in a speech by Lloyd George at the end of the last session of Parliament, in which he had praised the vigor and skill of the Greek army. The speech renewed Greek hopes of gaining Allied support, which they desperately needed. No such support was forthcoming. In the meantime Kemal, alarmed at the prospect of Allied support of the Greeks, launched his long-delayed offensive on August 26. The Greek Army collapsed in retreat. At Izmir, the Greek Army was driven into the sea, and the city was sacked by the victorious Turks, who marched on to Constantinople. Nothing remained between the Turkish Army and the neutral zone around the city of Chanak, a small town on the Asian side of the Bosphorus, where Allied forces under Lt. Gen. Sir Charles Harington stood guard.

The Cabinet met on September 15, 1922, and decided that the Turks must be kept out of Europe and not be allowed to cross the Bosphorus. Lloyd George, with the support of Winston Churchill, was prepared to go to war to implement this decision and convinced the Cabinet that arms and reinforcements must be sent to defend Chanak. They misjudged not only the British public, but also most of the Dominions and the Allies. Hardly anyone was prepared for a renewal of fighting. The memories of Gallipoli were too fresh. And almost no one saw such a conflict as important to British interests. Indeed, like Montagu, most saw it as a detriment to Britain's Muslim interests.

On the instructions of the Cabinet, Curzon was dispatched to Paris on September 18 in an effort to convince the Allies of the need for an International Conference to halt Kemal. The French had no sympathy for the British position and only after protracted arguments did Curzon convince both France and Italy to cable Kemal to invite him to a conference. They agreed to this only after the Cabinet conceded that Turkey's claims to Constantinople and Eastern Thrace should be accepted. This was exactly the position that Montagu had argued for the past four years.

The telegram was sent on September 23. Kemal's troops were well into the neutral zone, close enough to stare at Harington's forces. The situation was tense. Italian and French troops had been withdrawn. Only the British were on the line. Days passed with no reply from Kemal. Lloyd George and Churchill then decided to send their own telegram to Harington, ordering him to inform Kemal that unless his troops were withdrawn at a time fixed by Harington, "all the forces at our disposal, naval, military and air will open fire. . . . The time limit should be short."[19]

There is no question that their cable could have touched off a second world war. Fortunately, Harington ignored it and continued his own negotiations with the Turks, who seemed themselves less than eager to prolong hostilities. A conference at Mudania (on the Sea of Marmora, across from Istanbul, in Turkey) on October 3 was agreed upon, at which British, French, Italian and Greek military leaders would be represented. On October 11, an armistice was signed and the crisis was over.

A peace treaty was signed at Lausanne on July 24, 1923. For Turkey it meant the reestablishment of Turkish sovereignty in almost all the territory included in the present-day Turkish Republic, including Constantinople and eastern Thrace. The freedom of the Straits was guaranteed, with demilitarized zones on both the European and Asian sides; the capitulations long resented by the Turks were abolished; freedom was granted to an entire bloc of Arab countries carved from the Ottoman Empire; and Turkey was granted the right to apply for membership in the League of Nations, under which the protection of Turkish minorities would be guaranteed.

Thus, it took Great Britain five years to catch up to Montagu and to accept the terms he had urged for Turkey at the end of World War I. Had Curzon worked with Montagu and not against him, he might have achieved this agreement years earlier and with far less bloodshed. Whatever sense of vindication Montagu may have felt from the terms of the Treaty of Lausanne may well have been negated by his anger at having lost his political position by advocating a Turkish peace treaty, which in the end was not only adopted, but fashioned by Lord Curzon, who had fought him every inch of the way in his struggle for precisely these treaty terms. Curzon was hailed as a hero for settling the Eastern problem, bringing peace to Turkey, averting a new war and appeasing the Muslims in India. Not a word was written or spoken about a forgotten Jew named Edwin Montagu, who for four years had unremittingly urged this policy and had argued the Muslim case against Curzon and the Foreign Office with logic and persistence.

The End of Lloyd George's Coalition

Chanak not only broke the stalemate in the Greek and Turkish war, it also broke the back of the Lloyd George government. It was the last in a series of crises that persuaded the discontented Conservatives that the time had come to rid themselves of Lloyd George's leadership. They had never trusted him, and by 1922 he no longer served their purpose. His policies were under attack from the left and the right. Prices and taxes were on the rise, the Genoa Conference had been a failure, and the Treaty of Rapallo, signed by Russia and Germany, under which each recognized the other, alarmed both the anti-Germans and the Communists. Violence had again erupted in Ireland, and the breakdown of reparations agreements was having serious repercussions on the economy. Lloyd George's reputation for dishonesty and trickery was finally catching up with him. The Honours scandal, in which Lloyd George was accused of selling nominations to the peerage in exchange for contributions to his campaign chest, did not help. The by-elections, moreover, were beginning to show that Conservatives could win elections without the Liberal votes they had needed in the past. And perhaps most important to the Conservatives was that they now believed that if they did not break away from the Coalition they might be permanently weakened by a fusion party.

Although they were aware of the growing discontent, Lloyd George and his supporters miscalculated its seriousness. They believed that Lloyd George, with his charisma and his past victories and achievements, could continue to disarm his critics. There were no other leaders of his stature and experience on the horizon and they felt secure enough to agree by September 22 that Parliament should be dissolved and a General Election held as soon as possible. The discontents within the Conservative Party, led by Sir George Younger, the Conservative Party Manager, were outraged. Such a course, they believed, would doom the Conservative Party forever.

A meeting of Conservative M.P.'s was called on October 19 at the Carlton Club. Chamberlain believed he could convince the mavericks to stay in line. This was a serious mistake. Hostility to Lloyd George was running high. It was at this meeting that Stanley Baldwin, a relative newcomer to Conservative politics, spoke against Lloyd George, describing him as "a dynamic force," who, if unchallenged, would destroy the Conservative Party, even as he had the Liberal Party.

To the consternation of Chamberlain and Lloyd George, Bonar Law came out of retirement to oppose Lloyd George. Law had strongly disagreed with Lloyd George over the Chanak policy and, on October 6, had written to *The Times* severely criticizing it in what would become his best-known statement: "We cannot act alone as the policeman of the world." He was immediately urged to return to politics, especially by Beaverbrook, who viewed him as the only one who could save the Conservative Party. Law agreed and not only attended the Conservatives' meeting but spoke in favor of disbanding the Coalition.

After a heated debate at the October 19 meeting, by a vote of 185 to 88, the Conservatives resolved to fight the election as an Independent Party with its own leaders and programs, cooperating with Coalition leaders only where and when it was useful to them. Both Lloyd George and Chamberlain resigned that afternoon. Lord Curzon deserted Lloyd George and joined forces with Bonar Law. The King immediately called for Bonar Law to form a Conservative government, and a General Election took place on November 15.

Montagu, too, now faced a General Election, for which he had neither the energy nor the spirit. Venetia described his attitude as well as hers when she wrote to Beaverbrook in October 1922: "The prospect of a general election and the horrors of the next three weeks in Cambridgeshire fill me with unspeakable gloom."[20] In the past Montagu had been supported by both Liberal and Conservative Associations in Cambridgeshire. Technically, a joint Executive Committee, consisting of representatives of both associations, was the vehicle that gave Montagu the joint endorsement. This time, before Montagu had the chance to speak before the Executive Committee, the Conservatives met and decided to recommend a Conservative candidate of their own. Fifty people at the Conservative Association, however, voted for Montagu, including the Vice-President, who moved to support Montagu and pledged that he would speak and campaign for him.

The man chosen to run on the Conservative ticket was Harold Gray, whom Montagu described in a letter to Beaverbrook on October 31[21] as an Irishman by descent, new to politics, who played no part in any community activities and did not belong to the Farmer's Union. He owned horses and was a man of wealth but was not much of a speaker. Gray spoke for only five minutes at the meeting at which he was chosen. He agreed to support the Allies, look after the needs of agriculture and practice economy.

Montagu believed that Gray was the choice of the Die-Hards, who had a hard-working organizer in the district. Montagu also told Beaverbrook that the Cambridgeshire Branch of the National Farmer's Union, "which is an informal body . . . is hostile to Gray. They will support me. But the President won't sign nominating papers because as Vice-President of the Union he can't."[22] "Except for personalities which are running high," Montagu wrote:

I can discover no issue between the Conservative candidate and myself. I can discover nothing in Bonar Law's program which I cannot support. It is well known how profoundly I disagreed with the late Government's Eastern policy and although quite naturally my speeches do not find their way into the London newspapers, I have pointed out that the great weakness, in my opinion, of the new Administration is the continued presence of the expensive Lord Curzon at the Foreign Office, because of his association with this Eastern Policy.

Labour is to be represented by a Labour man of the Cambridgeshire County Council, a Mr. Stubbs (how appropriately named Labour candidates always are) whom I defeated at the last election by 5000.

He [Mr. Stubbs] is having difficulty getting money. If no conservative candidate appeared they would have no Labour candidate.[23]

In this letter, Montagu confessed that he could not guess who would win. Gray had the problem of becoming known in the 131 villages in the constituency. "On the other hand he has an active wife and I have not been as attentive to my constituency as an agricultural candidate is bound to be."[24]

There was a wistfulness in Montagu's comments on Gray's wife. Montagu missed having a wife who was active in politics. While Venetia accompanied Montagu during his campaign for most of the three weeks preceding the election, she hated the entire process and had little or no relationship with the people in his district. She would have much preferred wining, dining and sleeping with Lord Beaverbrook and others to stumping the countryside and making small talk with "country bumpkins."

While he was reluctant to make predictions, Montagu wrote to Beaverbrook that he believed that Gray would not win; he was too inarticulate and the Conservative Party too disorganized. "I think he will be at the bottom," he wrote to Beaverbrook. Stubbs, the Labour candidate, he believed was too "violent" to be a good candidate, but he did have a labour organization which had been working since 1918. "If he polls no more than the last election and Gray polls 5000 votes out of a constituency of 36,000 he [Stubbs] will win."[25]

Montagu continued to feel friendly to Beaverbrook, although the *Daily Express* was supporting all Conservative candidates and, in some cases, Coalition candidates with Conservative support. Thus Beaverbrook, while returning Montagu's expressions of friendship (and in November guaranteeing renewal of a note of £7,000 that Montagu needed to finance his campaign), openly supported Montagu's opponent. He did concede to Montagu that if the Conservatives did not win he hoped that Montagu would get the seat. "This is as high as I can put it," Beaverbrook wrote to Montagu on November 10, "because after all I am out for a Bonar Law majority and in full opposition to any form of Coalition."[26]

Montagu's analysis of his opposition was wrong. The Tory candidate; Harold Gray, came in first with 9,846 votes; Stubbs second, with 9,167; and Montagu third, with only 6,942. The Tories routed the Coalition Liberals not only in Cambridgeshire but throughout the country, gaining 344 seats. The Lloyd George Coalition Liberals won 57 seats, the Asquith Liberals 60, and Labour 138. For the first time Labour became the official opposition party in Parliament.

Bonar Law's slogan of providing "tranquility" to a nation still sore from the ravages of war proved to be a winner. The Liberals who had supported Lloyd George were the most seriously damaged.

Writing to a friend, Asquith permitted himself a rare display of triumphant satisfaction. "For the moment, the thing that gives me the most satisfaction is to gloat over the corpses . . . left on the battlefield, Winston, Hammar Greenwood, Freddie Guest, Montagu, Kellaway—all of them renegades."[27]

While Asquith may have been pleased by the corpses left on the battlefield, he could not have been pleased by the showing of the Asquithian Liberals. They had put up 348 candidates and won only 60 seats. And while this was 3 more than the Lloyd George Liberals, it was too small to matter: "The difference was so small that he [Asquith] could no longer be regarded as the only true guardian of the true Liberal faith. The Anti-Pope was almost as strong as the Pope."[28] Asquith himself had won by only 316 votes, a much narrower margin than in the 1920 by-election.

Asquith's delight over the losses suffered by Churchill and Montagu did not last. It was not in his nature to hold grudges for long. In a short time, his affection for Churchill was renewed, and even when Churchill joined the Conservative government two years later, Asquith wrote: "At lunch we had amongst others Winston Churchill, who was in his best form: he is a Chimborazo or Everest among the sandhills of the Baldwin Cabinet."[29] As for Montagu, Asquith seems to have forgiven him too. "The Spanish Duke and Duchess of Alba," Asquith wrote on October 10, 1923, "came to lunch: also Edwin Montagu, who had not been at our table for at least four years. . . . He is, as he always was, excellent company."[30] It must have been an unusual evening. For after Montagu's defeat in the 1922 election, he was rarely good company. His depression and isolation became increasingly intense. He had lost not only his position in the Cabinet and his involvement with his beloved India, but he had now also lost his seat in Parliament. For the first time since 1906 he was without a political office of any kind.

His last letter of this sad and tragic year was to Beaverbrook, on November 28, 1922, in which he discussed what he should do. Since he had "nothing to do," perhaps he would try to write. The subjects he selected were agriculture, religious communities ("beginning with my own, the Jewish, and dealing with the Church of England, Roman Catholic and Non-Conformist") and Lord Curzon as Foreign Secretary.[31]

But writing would be no substitute for the political action he craved. And while his letters show that he had some skill as a writer, he lacked the temperament. Separated from the excitement and the people of politics, he became increasingly morose. His only solace was that Lloyd George, the man who had been so disloyal to him, had also been turned out of office. There is rarely justice in politics, but occasionally there is retribution.

33

Personal and Political
Darkness, 1923

My mother Judith always said she was the illegitimate child of Eric Dudley.

Anne Montagu Gendel, 1987

The dawn of 1923 held little hope for Edwin Montagu, save for the anticipation that he would soon become a father. This event, which he described to Reading as one he had "long prayed for," took place on February 6, 1923. The child was a girl, named Judith. Venetia was thirty-six years old and Edwin forty-four. Venetia's pregnancy was viewed by the doctors as dangerous for a woman of that age in 1923, but mother and child did well.

Nowhere in Montagu's letters to Venetia or to any of his friends or colleagues written before or after Judith's birth is there any mention of this child or of how he felt about becoming a father, except in the Reading letter postponing his trip to India, and in a letter to his sister, Ethel, thanking her for a present she had sent to "Ruth, Judith, Rebecca, Jessica, Deborah, Bethsheba Montagu. Do not run away with the idea," he jokingly added, "that the luckless infant is to bear all these names, but I thought you would be amused to learn the sort of suggestions that have been made."[1]

He wished Ethel a happy birthday and expressed a sense of love for his family that his letters rarely revealed, as well as a sense of despair which had become more and more pronounced. "I am an old man," he wrote to his sister, "and my memory is treacherous but there is one day in the calendar I never forget and that is your birthday. My thoughts are with you today and I wish you every happiness." The letter was written ten days after Judith was born,

670

and yet it contained no comment about how Venetia and the baby were, how the baby looked, whether she smiled or cried, or any of the usual patter of a new father.

Nor was there any comment about the baby in any of Venetia's letters during her pregnancy or afterward. It was a strange silence from a woman so open on other issues. The letters of her friends, Duff and Diana, Cynthia Asquith, Beaverbrook and others, who were so intimate with her, were also silent about the child. One would expect that letters written to her, especially during February 1923, the month in which Judith was born, would contain some reference to the birth, but they contain not a word.

While the English aristocrats of the period were generally blasé about their children until at least puberty and had them raised by nannies and other household staff, they were not totally disinterested in them. The letters of the Asquiths, the Churchills, Lloyd George and the cold and austere Curzon all contain some references to their children. Even Diana and Duff Cooper's letters refer to the pregnancies of friends, of Diana's desire for a child, and of the pleasure she finally felt when she could write to Duff on January 30, 1929, that she felt so odd "I think I must be with child."[2] In all the hundreds of letters written to and from and about the Montagus, never was the pregnancy or Judith mentioned.

It may be that their friends suspected that the child was not Montagu's and believed that under such circumstances discretion required silence. In her 1980 autobiography, the Duchess of Marlborough wrote that her former husband Eric Dudley (the Earl of Dudley, whom she married in 1943) had had a love affair in his youth with Venetia and that Judith was the child of that union.[3]

The Duchess wrote of this in a matter-of-fact fashion. She described the evening on which she told Eric Dudley that she was planning to leave him to marry someone else. He became furious. The Duchess took refuge with Diana and Duff at the British Embassy in Paris, where Duff was the British Ambassador. "Gerry," she wrote, "took me and my one and only dress to the embassy. I remember so well how funny Duff and Diana were, and it was certainly time for some light relief! Diana was the most practical, saying the staff had scarcely recovered from the ball and that they were going out to dinner and needed an extra man, so Gerry had better go with them, while Venetia Montagu who was staying at the embassy, would have dinner on a tray with me. This arrangement was perfect. *I was nearly dropping on my feet and was fond of Venetia, who was not only a contemporary of Eric's but had had a love affair with him years before which had resulted in a child, Judy Montagu* (later Mrs. Milton Gendel), *who was a great friend of mine.* I thought it would be a chance to talk to Venetia, a woman of the world and of high intelligence. . . . Venetia was far from well (she was in fact dying of cancer but was wonderfully brave). She was most understanding and able to look at all I said with a dispassionate eye" (emphasis added).[4]

Venetia first mentioned Eric Dudley in a letter to Montagu on March 7, 1918, when she casually wrote that she was having lunch with Eric Ednam, who later became the third Earl of Dudley. Eric Dudley was described by the Duchess of Marlborough as twenty years older than the Duchess, about Venetia's age, "very good looking, powerful, in every sense. I found him, on sight, fantastically attractive. He was all-powerful in the world of industry and he had also been a politician. . . . He worked hard and he also played hard. Deep down he was a sad and, in some ways—a sentimental man. . . . Many years before I met him he had married an enchanting woman called Lady Rosemary Leveson-Gower, (the sister of the Duke of Sutherland). She and several others of her generation were killed in an air crash. . . . They had three sons, but the middle one was killed in a horrifying accident. . . . After these tragedies . . . he turned his energy even more feverishly to business—and many love affairs."[5] Since the Duchess did not marry Eric until twenty years later, she appears to have felt no jealousy toward Venetia. The Duchess's comments were presented factually, rather than as gossip.

An inquiry about this was made by the author in 1986 to the Hon. L. H. L. Cohen, a relative of the Montagus, who at the time was living in London. It brought the following response:

I knew both of Venetia's sisters (Sylvia Henley and Blanche Lunared) and never heard a suggestion that Judy was the daughter of anyone but Edwin and Venetia; (although the generation gap between us and the conventions of the time might have discouraged confidence in the subject). Nor did I hear any such suggestion from any of Judy's cousins who I knew (the 4 Serocolds and the two Henley daughters) who were my generation.

I did not know Judy well, though I met her quite often in the period 1944–1949. Despite her animated and lovely face, she was no beauty. She had the muddy complexion and rather jowly looks which I associate with members of the Montagu family (who are all distant relations of mine) such as Lord Swaythling, Ewen Montagu, Joyce Frost (nee Montagu) and David Montagu. On the basis of looks I would have guessed that she was a legitimate Montagu.[6]

Anna Montagu Gendel, Judith's daughter and Venetia's grand-child, not only confirmed the statement of the Duchess of Marlborough, but added that her mother had, in fact, told her that Judith's father was Eric Dudley:

Yes, my mother was the child of Venetia and Eric Dudley. She looked just like Eric's sister Patsy, who is now dead. My mother [Judith] and I always spent Christmas at Peter Wood's. Peter was Eric's younger son (which made him my mother's half-brother). Billy was the older brother. . . . My mother always considered Peter her half brother. . . . Judith, my mother, is buried on Peter Wood's estate—Cornwall Manor, Kingham, Oxford-shire. Breccles had become a pony club and my mother didn't want to be buried there.[7] (emphasis added)

Anna described the family genealogy as follows:

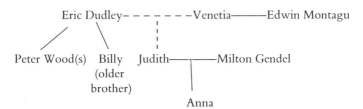

There is no reason to doubt Judith's statement to Anna. The fact that Judith was buried on the estate of Eric Dudley's son, Peter, provides further evidence to support this.

Venetia, who never withheld such matters from Edwin, is likely to have told Montagu the truth. Yet Judith was given the Montagu name and was supported by Montagu as his child during his lifetime and after his death by a trust he established for her. At no time did Montagu or Venetia tell the public or the family otherwise. The secret was kept so well that not only were Venetia's sisters ignorant of this, but Judith's name appears as the child of Venetia and Edwin in *The Samuel Family of Liverpool & London,* painstakingly edited by Ronald J. Hart D'Arcy, a member of the Samuel and Montagu families.[8]

Even in the "Corrupt Coterie" there had been a code of behavior: It was permissible to be sexually promiscuous but not to be indiscreet. In the case of Judith Montagu, even if the Coterie suspected the truth, the code of silence was respected. To do otherwise would not only harm Judith but hurt Venetia and Montagu. The Coterie would not do this to its own.

Trips Planned: Experience Wasted

Montagu lived just a year and a half after Judith's birth. It does not appear that her birth changed the lives of Venetia or Edwin or their marital relations. If anything, their social life and travel increased. Four months after the baby was born, Montagu began to plan again his long-anticipated return to India for the winter of 1924, as well as a one-month trip to South Africa. Venetia would join him on both trips. The baby would be cared for by staff at home.

"I am contemplating a short visit to India this winter," Montagu wrote to Victor Lytton, on June 19, 1923,[9] "getting to India about the beginning of the year [1924]. It is purely a pleasure trip and it is going to be very short, for we are leaving again in the middle of March." His stay in India would last two months. Montagu expressed his deep unhappiness that all his knowledge of India was being ignored and his experience going to waste. "I have not seen Peel [the new Secretary of State for India] since he took office except once," he wrote to Lytton.

I have not met Winterton except at a dinner party. No Indian civilian either employed here or coming from India ever comes to see me. I see the Indians, but they spend most of their time in discussing grievances, in regard to which I cannot help them. I see a good deal of the Indian Princes in this country. I have hardly seen Ronaldshay, and I have had no letters from Reading, Willingdon, or Lloyd recently; in fact when one leaves office I find that there falls down a curtain so impenetrable that its opaqueness is only enhanced by your kindness in writing to me. I cannot tell you how much I appreciate your letters and how much my thoughts are with you in your work. When I went to the India Office my first thoughts were that it was my duty to try and keep a continuity in Indian affairs and I used to send important telegrams and dispatches to Crewe, Chamberlain and even on occasion to Morley and George Hamilton. It would be absurd to suppose that everybody does his work in the same way, and when on occasion I have asked Brown to lunch I find that his embarrassment, if I mention Indian affairs, is so real that I do not pursue it.

Montagu expressed his despair at the continuing disunity among the leaders of the Liberal Party, although there appeared to him to be "real unity in the Liberal ranks." The leadership of the Party, he wrote:

does not trust Lloyd George on the one side, and not even Lloyd George's entourage can say how real is his desire for permanent alliance with Asquith's forces and how long he is prepared for spade work in the desert. In the meantime our relations with France seem to become more and more complicated. The horrors of the occupation of the Ruhr, the dangers of a Bolshevik Germany completely chaotic, seeds of future wars which are involved become more terrifying to me. Although I hold no brief for him, I cannot help thinking that the French would never have succeeded in going into the Ruhr if Lloyd George had remained in office. The fatal step was taken by poor Bonar when he allowed himself to table, in behalf of Great Britain, a scheme [to keep the French out of the Ruhr] and then to permit that it should not be even discussed.

As for the new Prime Minister, Baldwin, Montagu had doubts about his competence. He had the goodwill of the nation but he was a mediocre politician. "Those who know him best," Montagu wrote:

and who watch his success are uneasy at thinking that we are in the hands of a man who loomed not at all in any part of his Parliamentary or official career. The prestige of the Prime Minister's office is so great that anybody will get a chance in it, and there is no doubt that Baldwin is a very likeable fellow. There is no doubt that England is easier to govern than it was a couple of years ago, but nobody can pretend that the Government is a homogeneous or a strong one.

Turning to the negotiations taking place at Lausanne on Turkey and Greece, Montagu confessed to being

absolutely bewildered. It looks as if the Turks and the Greeks want to make peace; that we have abandoned all efforts to protect non-Turkish populations from Turkish Sovereignty; that we have given way on every territorial or minority question; and that the sole obstacle is a purely cash one— the difference between paper Francs and sterling. I do not know how much money is involved, but while it is still being discussed and discussed the Lausanne Delegation must be costing a considerable sum, and we still have our troops in Constantinople.

During September and October of 1923, Montagu continued to plan his trip to India, writing often to Reading and others to make arrangements. Since this was the first time Venetia would visit India he wanted to show her as much of his beloved country as possible "and not rush her off her feet." His brother Lionel (Cardie) would join them.[10]

Montagu asked Reading for a railroad carriage, like the one he had had on his two earlier trips. He would of course pay for it. It "will remind me of the good old times and youth,"[11] he added nostalgically. Of his relations with the new Secretary of State for India, Montagu wrote that they were

neither friendly nor unfriendly because they do not exist. I have not been consulted by the India Office on any matter since I left . . . Therefore, you will understand, with the passionate desire to help . . . that little has occurred to heal my broken heart. But I am learning to suffer patiently what is irreparable. I see Winston occasionally and Asquith rarely. Those are the only remnants of my political life now past.[12]

On November 19, Montagu wrote to Reading that he had to cancel his trip to India. "I am engaged on an important mission to Brazil which it was my duty to undertake in the circumstances of my new life."[13] He also told Reading of the new political efforts in Liberal circles to bring about a reunion of the Lloyd George and Asquith followers, but he had been excluded from this. "Do you remember," he wrote

how often you were convinced of the brightness . . . of my political fate? Well, Liberal reunion has come. You must rejoice in it as much as I do; you must wish our old Party well as I do; but it will amuse you to learn . . . that the reunion does not include me. It has never been suggested to me that I should take any part in the dawning hopes of a united Liberalism, except that this week-end there has been thrown at me, and refused, an off chance of fighting a hopeless rural constituency of no importance! . . . I am quite happy in my new life, but I merely wished to tell who was right![14]

In truth, he was not happy in his new life. As busy as he was in various business ventures and on company boards, his heart was broken by being excluded from politics. He was learning to live without politics, but it did not bring him any real pleasure or satisfaction.

Efforts to Reunite the Liberals

The Liberal reunion to which Montagu referred was the joint effort made by the Coalition and Asquith Liberals in October 1923 to defend free trade, which Baldwin was now attacking. Efforts at reconciliation had in fact begun earlier in the aftermath of the Liberal defeat in 1922. On November 28, 1922, Asquith had written to a friend that there had been "a kind of fraternity gathering last night in one of the Committee rooms between the rank and file of our lot and the ex-Coolie Liberals. The latter seem prepared to 'reunite' on any terms . . . Meanwhile . . . Lloyd George . . . declared he was quite ready to serve with and under me (!) with whom he never had a quarrel and whom he never ceased to admire and respect!"[15] And on March 23 a petition for reunion was signed by seventy-three Liberal backbenchers to dramatize their desire for a united party.

But these and other efforts at the time were fruitless, with "trusted cronies" keeping the "flames of mutual recrimination" burning brightly. There were too many Asquithians who still distrusted Lloyd George, whom they viewed as "the heaviest political liability that any party, especially any party that claims to rest on a moral basis, can assume."[16] And there were others who felt that Asquith was too old and inept to give direction and new life to a reunited Liberal Party.

The catalyst for reunion came, finally, from neither the followers of Lloyd George nor of Asquith. It came in a roundabout manner when Bonar Law resigned because of cancer and Baldwin became Prime Minister. His support of protective tariffs as a means of combating unemployment united the Liberal opposition.

Baldwin had not been expected to become Prime Minister. Most Conservatives, including Lord Curzon himself, expected Curzon to be named. Curzon felt that he had the experience and the intelligence and that he had no equal. On Monday, May 21, he received a telegram from Lord Stamfordham, on behalf of the King, summoning him to London without delay. He was ecstatic. He regarded the message as equal to an offer of the Premiership. On Tuesday, May 22, as he traveled to London with his wife, they discussed their plans. "I shall use No. 10," he said, "only for official purposes." They arrived in London to face the photographers jamming the railroad station and Carlton House, where they were staying. At

3:30, Lord Stamfordham was announced. With some embarrassment he explained that the King had decided to send for Mr. Baldwin. "In an agony of mortification he [Curzon] collapsed into a chair. . . . He wept like a child."[17]

On the advice of Balfour and other aides, the King had appointed Baldwin instead. Curzon was viewed as too arrogant, too elitist and unable to work with the strong Labour opposition. The King was also persuaded that the Prime Minister should not come from the House of Lords.

For Montagu, who always blamed Curzon as much or more than Lloyd George for his forced resignation, this humiliation of Curzon may well have seemed a well-deserved retribution. In fact, Montagu heard the news about Curzon's rejection before the public did. He and Venetia were spending the weekend with the Balfours at Sheringham before Curzon was summoned to London. During that weekend, Balfour was called to Buckingham Palace to advise the King on the next Prime Minister. When he returned to Sheringham, he was besieged by his friends with the question, "And will dear George be chosen?" The answer was, "No, dear George will not."[18]

Baldwin's appointment turned out to be the beginning of a new era. Within five months, he called for an early election in which he made the support of protective tariffs the rallying cry of the Conservative Party. This was the opportunity for which the Liberals had been waiting. Now was their chance to put the pieces of the Liberal Party together again.

The Election of November 1923: Liberals Join with Labour

On November 13, 1923—ten days before Montagu wrote to Reading about his exclusion from efforts at Liberal reunion—Asquith and Lloyd George called on all Liberals, without regard for past differences, to sign a manifesto making the defense of free trade their Party's main plank. Although the Liberals tried to cooperate, internal arguments in local associations and their inability to develop a program to meet the country's economic and social needs resulted in a lackluster and losing campaign.

They managed to win only 158 seats, while Labour won 191 and the Conservatives 258. A "no confidence" amendment was carried against Baldwin. In this crisis, Lloyd George deferred to Asquith over the strategy the Liberals should take. They could join with the Tories against Labour and its leader, Ramsay MacDonald, or throw in their lot with Labour.

On January 22, 1924, Asquith and his followers, with the support of Lloyd George, made a pivotal decision that had an enormous impact on the future of English politics. They threw in with Labour, and Ramsay MacDonald became the first Labour Prime Minister of Great Britain. This must have pleased Montagu. At heart he had always been closer to Labour than to the Liberals, and if he had been part of the decision-making process, he would have supported it. On the other hand, this decision so upset Winston Churchill that five weeks later he left the Liberal Party and ran unsuccessfully for office as an Independent. He lost on March 10, 1924, by 73 votes.

The union between Asquith and the Liberals and Ramsay Mac-Donald and Labour lasted less than a year. MacDonald's attitude toward his Liberal supporters was one of dislike and suspicion and added to the conflict between the parties. "How could Asquith have conjectured that the leader of a great party would have behaved like a jealous, vain, suspicious, ill-tempered actress of the second ranks?" Lloyd George wrote in defense of Asquith in the *Daily Chronicle* on November 1, 1924.[19]

Liberals and Labour Split

Finally, in the face of such treatment, Asquith withdrew his support of Labour, and in the October 1924 election, Labour was turned out of office and the Tories and Baldwin returned. The Tories won 419 seats, Labour 151, and the fading Liberals only 40. In this election Churchill ran again and this time was elected as a Tory for Epping, a seat he held for the rest of his life.

Churchill: Ousted but Unforgettable; Montagu an Outcast

Through all the political efforts to bring Asquith and Lloyd George together, through all the debates on what strategy the Liberals should take in relationship to Labour and the Conservatives, Montagu was totally excluded, even before he became too ill to participate. It is interesting to compare this with Churchill's political position after his three defeats for Parliament and his loss of Cabinet rank. Churchill, like Montagu, had deserted Asquith for a position in the Lloyd George government. Churchill, like Montagu, had incurred the hatred of the Tories (Montagu over India, Churchill over his fight with Fisher and the Admiralty). Churchill changed parties twice; Montagu remained a Liberal all his life. Churchill's position on Kenya was racist and anti-Liberal. On all such issues Montagu was a committed Liberal. Montagu incurred the wrath of part of the British public with his attack against General Dyer; Churchill had incurred its wrath over the Dardanelles, over his almost paranoic position regarding the new Soviet government and over his strong opposition to the Labour Party, which he viewed as disastrous for the future of Britain.

"Even his [Churchill's] wife urged him to take 'a less hostile and negative attitude' toward the socialists. . . . [H]e became the bogey-man of the British left. . . . The *Daily Herald* denounced him for sending to Russia [to fight the Communists] 'munitions which cost over twenty million pounds sterling to produce' all of which has gone down the drain. . . . [H]e was utterly out of touch with public opinion, here as everywhere else."[20] Yet, through all of this, Churchill was never a political outcast, as was Montagu. He continued to have many friends who continuously urged him to join them "in patriotic opposition," and he was offered dozens of seats. Even when Churchill had been defeated in three consecutive elections, Beaverbrook was able to say "he would never be forgotten. He was unforgettable."

Not so for Montagu. He was totally forgotten. Aside from one offer to run for a very undesirable seat in 1923, no one ever urged him to run for office again. His radical economic policies, his record with Reconstruction during the war, in which he had proposed many far-reaching programs in housing and education, his Liberal policies toward India, Kenya and Ireland, his attitude toward reparations and conciliation with Germany, all of these should have made him attractive to the emerging Labour Party or at least have given him a place in the circles of Liberal leaders trying to redesign a program attractive enough to meet the problems of postwar Britain.

But no one trusted him and no party wanted him. He was truly a man without a party. Asquith would never forgive him his desertion. He might invite him to dinner and enjoy his conversation, but he would never view him as a trustworthy political ally. And, whatever Asquith's displays of cordiality, Montagu's marriage to Venetia was also something that he would in his heart never forgive. As for Lloyd George, Montagu's speech at Cambridge was too vicious an attack ever to be forgiven. And to the Tories, Montagu continued to be the Jew who brought nothing but trouble to India.

While no one would suggest that Montagu had the same claim to history as Churchill, it is equally true that in the early 1920s, Churchill's contributions to British history were no more nor less than Montagu's. But Churchhill's personality, abrasive as it was, had a vigor and a strength that made him unforgettable. Montagu had no such charisma. While he had several dear personal friends and a significant following among his colleagues at the India Office and among many of the Indian leaders and Indian Princes, Montagu's personality was not the kind to attract and hold political allies; over the years, instead of gathering supporters, he lost them.

But one should not minimize the fact that Winston Churchill was the son of Randolph Churchill and carried with him the mantle of being a descendant of the great Dukes of Marlborough. Montagu, on the other hand, was the descendant of a Jewish watchmaker from Liverpool. History casts a different light upon those born in the shadows of Blenheim and those raised in the ghettos of the East End and even Kensington Gardens.

34

Despair and Death, 1924

I say that one shall remember me, even afterwards.

Montagu's epitaph

While Montagu was removed from the political fray, he watched with grave misgivings the deterioration of relations between the Liberals and Labour. The alliance he had hoped would be made never was, and relations between the two groups became strained and hostile. But as Montagu had written to Reading, no one asked for his advice; few if any people discussed politics with him and he had to content himself with watching from the sidelines, a silent onlooker upon a scene that wanted no part of him.

He filled his days with his business interests: His new role as Vice-Chairman of De Beers introduced him to the problems of South Africa, in which he became intensely absorbed. He continued his membership on various corporate boards including the Underground Electric Railways and the Board of the Metropolitan and District Railway Companies. But nothing was a substitute for politics. He was sophisticated enough to do well in the financial world. His mind was as sharp as ever, but his heart was not in it. He was especially pleased, therefore, to be made, at the end of 1923, Chairman of a British finance mission to visit Brazil at the request of the Brazilian government, to study the financial conditions of that country. This would permit him to involve himself once again in issues of economic, political and social significance.

The economy of Brazil was of special concern to British businessmen. They had many investments there, as in many other Latin American countries, and a faltering Brazilian economy would have repercussions for Britain. By 1922–23, the value of the Brazilian *milreis* was falling sharply and depreciating considerably in relation to the pound. In addition, the internal economic conditions in the country were becoming more serious, with debt mounting, unemployment a national crisis and inflation threatening the stability of the country.

Montagu asked Lord Lovat to serve on this mission since the two "though of strangely different temperaments and gifts, were close friends."[1] Lovat looked up to Montagu "for his imagination and penetrating intellect while Montagu admired in Lovat those qualities of a man of action which he himself lacked."[2]

The other members of the Mission were Sir Charles Addis, Sir William McLintock and Mr. Hartley Withers—all well-known authorities on economics and finance. Although British influence and prestige in the field of international politics had dwindled to a mere shadow since 1919, they were still high in questions of finance; and the advice of British experts was not only often sought in the period, but even occasionally followed. Unfortunately, however, the finance and economy of a country depend on the political background and on the ideas prevailing in those circles which are of importance politically. In Brazil these had not been favourable to development on sound lines and, though vast amounts of British capital had been sunk in the country, much of it had brought but little profit or security to the investor. Post-War optimism had not evaporated in 1924, and it was hoped that the Montagu Mission would inaugurate a new era of prosperity and progress.[3]

The voyage to Brazil, Lovat wrote, was "non-eventful. Lovely weather every day . . . deck tennis with Venetia . . . Bezique with Edwin whom I always beat, then dinner. After dinner had bridge."[4]

The mission spent two months in Brazil, from December 1923 through January 1924. Montagu's report of it was well received. It recommended that the Brazilian government adopt measures involving banking and financial reforms, which were accepted by the Brazilian government with the promise of implementation. It made other recommendations for putting the finances of the government in order along orthodox economic lines: spending less, increasing gross national productivity, encouraging technological and industrial development and controlling inflation. The report contained some recommendations about the diversification of agriculture, urging that Brazil not depend entirely on a single crop—coffee.[5]

On his return, Montagu began to plan a visit to South Africa in October 1924 with a special commission to inquire into restoring the gold standard as the basis of the currency of South Africa. He had become interested in diamonds and also wanted to see firsthand the De Beers operation in South Africa.[6]

Illness and Death

But soon after he returned home from Brazil, he fell ill and complained to his doctors of a general feeling of malaise. Because of his history of hypochondria, his doctors, his family and his friends underestimated the seriousness of his complaints. They should not have. By June he was absolutely certain that he was dying and on June 7, 1924, he wrote a letter to Venetia to be opened after his death.

Premonitions of death were not new to Montagu. He carried them with him all of his life. His friends teased and joked about this with him but something kept this message of early death always before him. He was right.

In 1917, before he went to India, Montagu had also been sure he would not return and had written to Venetia a "last letter"[7] as he now did in 1924.[8] Both letters were enclosed in a single envelope addressed to "The Hon. Mrs. Montagu—to be opened upon my death."

It is interesting that Montagu did not destroy the 1917 letter when he returned from India; nor did he destroy it when he added the letter of 1924. He obviously felt that the 1917 letter was important enough to be kept as an expression of his great love for Venetia from the early years of their marriage. In 1917 he had written:

Dearest Darling,

This is to say goodbye and my heart is heavy at contemplating such a thing.

You will get this letter only when I am dead and it is just my attempt to say *farewell*.

My life ever since I've known you has been happier than it was before.

My happiness in you as my wife has been beyond belief and potent against all external worries and agonies. It seemed almost too good to last.

I have done everything I could think of for your future and have asked Cardie to look after you.

Darling you were wonderful to me and I loved you more than I can ever show. In the name of everything we have enjoyed together, look for the fun I wanted to give you everywhere. Do what you like, go where you please, anything that brings you fun would be joy to me.

When you and all we loved together are together think of me sometimes, but all I ask of you is to enjoy your life for my sake.

Thank you and bless you.

Yours with tears always,

On June 7, 1924, he wrote:

For some time I have felt all was not right, despite the doctors. If I had more time I could have got out of debt, but it was not to be. I fear you will not have an easy time, but things are not so bad as they were and I have failed in a plan to enjoy things, both of us, while we were young because the end is coming so soon. I am miserable at going. You have always made me very happy and I hope you will be happy always.

Although both letters express Montagu's pleasure at the happiness Venetia brought him, they have a very different tone. The 1917 letter is still the letter of a man very much in love. The 1924 letter is the sad acknowledgment that the dreams he Montagu had had for the two of them had not been fulfilled. He repeated, for the thousandth time, that she had made him "very happy." This, in spite of the fact that she had never reciprocated his deep love, had had other lovers and had given birth to the child of another. He excused all of this. Just being with her, whenever she chose to spend time with him, had made him happy.

As the spring and summer progressed, Montagu grew worse. The doctors were at a loss to diagnose the ailment or find a cure. Finally a diagnosis was made: blood poisoning that he may have acquired in Brazil "following acute rheumatism."[9] Whether or not this was true, or only a guess given to the press by the doctors, because they had no explanation for Montagu's illness, will never be known. Montagu's nephew, Ivor, wrote that Montagu died of "the most virulent of the big First-War epidemics, encephalitis."[10] This is not confirmed by any other source.

Since his resignation, Montagu's will to live had left him. India, the all-consuming passion of his life, had been taken from him. Nothing that he did made up for that loss. The birth of Judith—a reminder of Venetia's extramarital affairs—merely added to his sense of rejection. He had failed in the two areas that meant the most to him: India and gaining Venetia's love. He lost the will to live. He looked and sounded like an old man. During the early fall of 1924, he was placed in a nursing home: His condition had become too critical for him to be treated at home. The doctors now recognized the seriousness of his illness. But it was too late.

And as he lay dying, his beloved Liberal Party was dying too. In October 1924, the Liberal Party, rejected by Labour and by the British public, took a terrible beating at the polls. The Party that had swept Montagu into office in the glorious landslide of 1906, only eighteen years before, was now reduced to an insignificant factor in Parliament with only forty seats. If Montagu had been able to read the newspapers in October, the month before he died, the defeat of the Liberal Party would have added to his sense of loss and depression. Everything in which he had believed was now ending. There was so little left to grasp.

In this state he lingered a little longer, until Saturday, November 15, 1924. He died at the age of forty-five, two months before his forty-sixth birthday.

Universal Grief in India

Death not only brought Montagu relief from pain, mental and physical, but also provided what he craved most in life: recognition and expressions of love. In death he earned the praise that he was denied in life.

India, to which he had given his heart, responded in kind. Sorrow was universal at his death and the obituaries appearing from one end of the vast country to the other were filled with affection and appreciation for this Englishman whom all India now acclaimed "as a sincere friend . . . who had so much vision and whose devotion to her interests was so entirely wholehearted . . . one of the best Secretaries of State . . . whose Reform Act will stand as a striking monument to his great affection for India . . . a striking personality . . . a farsighted and discerning friend . . . whose zeal and passion and commitment to true Liberalism made him unique . . . one who served India with great devotion, with great courage, steadfastness, ability and sympathy. The good work that he has done for India . . . will remain as a shining halo for which his memory will be shrouded."[11]

Typical of the outpouring of feelings for Montagu was the editorial that appeared in the *Rangoon* on Monday, November 17: "It is with the deepest regret,"

. . . that we record the death of Mr. Montagu on the 15th November. Mr. Montagu will live in history as one of the greatest Secretaries of State for India, and few if any of those whose duty and privilege it was to hold charge of the India office had such brilliant abilities and such remarkable powers as those possessed by Mr. Montagu. He was no dreamer of dreams, no visionary but he could see through things and what is more he was intensely practical.[12]

"Of the deep debt of obligation that India owes to him," the *Rangoon* continued:

. . . it is not easy to say much. He will of course be remembered as the joint-author of the Report on Indian Constitutional Reforms popularly known as the Montagu-Chelmsford Report. It was a big experiment no doubt but to one like Mr. Montagu who believed that sincerity, good will and honesty will prevail in the working out of his scheme, there was nothing to look for, but success. And the Montagu method of administering Indian affairs would undoubtedly have been successful had it not been for the fact that, those who are responsible for the carrying out of the Reforms missed—deliberately or otherwise, we are unable to say—his point of view. They have worked the Reforms, according, it may be said to the letter but not to the spirit. Hence the failure of the Reforms to satisfy the Indian aspirations.

If Britain is to maintain the position she now holds, she must produce more Britishers of the type of Mr. Montagu—men intensely patriotic and at the same time possessed of a broad outlook and courage to fight for the rights of the weak, and the governed. Mr. Montagu's death removes from the political world, one whom India could depend upon and look upon as a sincere friend. In his own way and according to his own lights he had done what he thought to be the best for India, and such, his contribution towards leading India to the goal of self-government is neither small nor insignificant.

When all is said and done we have lost in Mr. Montagu a true Britisher of whom history will have to record much, and we mourn to-day his sad and untimely death.[13]

And the *Bengalee,* published in Calcutta, wrote in the beautiful prose of India that is almost poetry: "In the midst of life, we are in death: This is the first feeling with which many of us have received the news of Mr. Montagu's death. Forty-five is youth, according to English standards . . . and what a promise he had as Indian Secretary of State. He was not a mere politician. He had something of that imagination which is the soul of true statesmanship."[14] The *Bengalee* continued:

Mr. Montagu saw that unless Great Britain could organize and use the immense resources in both men and materials of India to effectively carry on the war, her Empire, if not indeed her national freedom itself, was bound to go the fate of older empires. . . . But Indian men and Indian money could not be asked for, to win the war, without removing India's political grievances. Lord Hardinge's statesmanship had saved the situation in the early weeks of the war. Indian statesmanship and the inherent chivalry of the Indian character had refused to exploit England's calamity as India's opportunity. But this first outburst of generosity could not be expected to last unless something was done to support it by substantial appeal to India's enlightened self-interest. This was to our mind the correct genesis of the Parliamentary Announcement of August 20, 1917—which has earned a lasting place for Edwin Samuel Montagu in the history of the evolution of the modern Indian constitution. . . .

Mr. Montagu's place in Indian politics and history will be judged not by the Joint Report . . . but by its central conception. To Mr. Montagu will always belong the full credit of having broadened the foundations of British policy in India for all times. He has helped to remove, if not as yet in deed, but in any case by word, the old badge of serfdom from us. . . . He gave us a word—responsible government . . . and an ideal . . . which really was the same as Swaraj, for which we could fight openly, fearlessly, within the limits of the law. . . . This is no mean gain, and no small credit belongs to Mr. Montagu . . . after the war was over and the need that forced the Announcement of 1917 passed away, and there was a reaction toward the old jingoism in England, Mr. Montagu became an inconvenient idealist in a cabinet that had caught the Prussian spirit even when crushing it. And he had to go out of a Government that was becoming more jingoistic and imperialistic. . . . Mr. Montagu's fall was the precursor of the breakdown of the Coalition. But he fell . . . because of his steadfast loyalty to the ideal of an Empire which shall unite East and West upon terms of perfect equality and honest and honourable co-operation, and be thus the forerunner of that Parliament of Man and Federation of the world which is the dream of all civilized people.[15]

The *Leader* reviewed all that Montagu had done in terms of discrimination against Indians, citing, in addition to the 1917 Proclamation, the Chelmsford-Montagu Report, the Reform Act, his success at removing the racial ban against Indians for commissions in the Army and his success in elevating to the peerage the only Indian baron. Montagu had been instrumental in the appointment of the only Indian Parliamentary Under Secretary and the only Indian Governor of a British Province. The *Leader* also recalled that Montagu had helped set Mrs. Besant free, in spite of the opposition of the Madras Council. "The circumstances in which he had to lay down his office of Secretary of State . . . must still be fresh in the public mind and it should suffice to say that none who was not a friend of India would have found himself in that position. His interest in this country never abated to the end of his days and he will be mourned and his memory blessed and treasured by our countrymen for many a long year."[16]

Even those Indian newspapers that had been critical of Montagu's reforms during his life praised his devotion to his "adopted" country. In an editorial on November 18, the *Englishman,* typical among Montagu's critics, conceded that "even those who like ourselves were most bitterly opposed to Mr. Montagu's policy and who held and still hold that his policy was disastrous for the political development of India on sane and progressive lines, must frankly admit the zeal and the passion, the interest and affection which Mr. Montagu brought to the administration of his great Department of State."[17]

The *Times of India,* which had also not supported Montagu editorially, published the following on November 17, 1924:

Mr. Montagu's work in connection with the Reforms was bound to arouse a great deal of feeling, nor did he care to conciliate his opponents. Pungent expressions such as "sundried bureaucrats" and "lugubrious ex-governors of inconspicuous careers" to which he gave vent in the heat of the moment were taken, and probably rightly, as showing that he had not the same sympathetic understanding of the Europeans in India as of other communities. This was, however, at the time and in the inflamed state of feeling then prevalent, almost the inevitable result of his determination to do his duty by educated Indians. Mr. Montagu had a special claim on the gratitude of Mahomedans, of whose views on Turkey he was as ardent a champion as was the Viceroy and many others in India. *Mr. Montagu and Lord Reading between them were largely responsible for the improvement in the attitude of Mahomedans towards the British and Indian Governments, and perhaps it was as great an achievement as the passing of the Reform Act that he was finally able to defeat the anti-Turkish policy of Mr. Lloyd George, though in the struggle he was forced to resign from the Indian Office.*[18] (emphasis added)

A few weeks later, on December 9, the *Times of India* published a longer story on Montagu, quoting in full from its correspondent in London in a column called "Some Personal Notes," in which the author, writing without a byline, commented on Montagu's life and the relationship between his sense of failure and his death. The writer compared "this brilliant and buffeted career" with that of Canning (Viceroy of India, 1856–62, a difficult time in which the Indian Mutiny occurred). "Both men . . . seemed overborne less by disease than by a sense that they had overbattled their strength against fatality." He suggested that Montagu's depression from the knowledge that he had damaged his Indian scheme by a single rash act was patriotic rather than personal. A similar judgment in the *Times* obituary said that in his last illness Montagu was "depressed at the relative failure of the new order and at the weak-kneed desertion of many of those Indians who had supported its introduction. His plans and hopes with respect to India miscarried and he died a disappointed man."[19] The article continued:

An intimate friend gives . . . testimony in a personal recollection in the *Times* of yesterday. He writes that Montagu's belief in his Indian policy was the deepest conviction of his being; when his downfall came all sense of personal disappointment seemed to be swallowed up in the anguish of fear that the cause he was fighting for would suffer.[20]

This writer added that the deep melancholy of his race lay at his heart, but joined to it were gaiety and the most individual wit.

The Right Honourable T. P. O'Connor, in a personal memoir in the *Daily Telegram,* depicted the scene in the House of Commons when Montagu made his personal explanation after his resignation from the Cabinet. He said, "The explanation was marked not merely by the resentful passion of the man but also by the finer motive of lament at the destruction of his power to complete his great work."[21] The author of this "personal note" had the opportunity to discover, "on unimpeachable authority," what Montagu's last views on India were. "Mr. Montagu felt," he wrote:

. . . that this mission was denied him at a critical time in the fortunes of the reforms, and that if he could have continued to serve India, whether in Whitehall or in the supreme place in India itself the situation would have been to say the least, much less unsatisfactory than it is. I know on unimpeachable authority his latest views on India. He did not accept the view that his famous Act had broken down from any fundamental defect of its own. Its relative failure he took to be due to the wanton removal by Indians themselves to the lynch-pin of the goodwill and the co-operation of Indians elected of the Legislatures. He felt that any further installment of reform by taking Indians into still fuller partnership in carrying on the Government would also depend on goodwill and co-operation; and that since these are lacking no useful purpose could be served in making any attempt to meet the Swarajist demands.[22]

In addition to the tributes paid to Montagu by the Indian press, he received equally glowing tributes from the Legislative Councils throughout India, the Indian Princes and Indian leaders from every political persuasion, including Mrs. Besant, Muslims, University officials, the business community, the Viceroy and the government of India. The government sent a formal telegram to Montagu's family and the India Office, praising "Montagu's intellectual attainments, his sincere attachment to India, his sense of its high destiny in the Empire and his well known sympathy with the aspirations of its people."[23] The local councils were equally laudatory, praising his "courage and enabling ideals" (Madras Council),[24] his "devotion to reform" (Bombay Council)[25] and "his liberalism and devotion to weak nations" (Punjab Council).[26]

In the Calcutta Council, Lord Sinha delivered the principal tribute, describing Montagu as "a passionate lover of India"; in a voice that often broke with emotion, he spoke as a dear friend as well as a colleague:

Knowing him as I did, all I can say is that I do not think any Indian loved India more passionately than Mr. Montagu did, whatever might be said of the particular scheme of reforms for India which he got through Parliament. I know that his one object . . . was the advance of India in the way of self-government.[27]

The resolution of the Calcutta Council adopted on Wednesday, November 19, was also a moving tribute. "In the death of Mr. Montagu," it stated:

India has lost one of her greatest friends, England one of the farsighted and truly liberal-minded statesmen and humanity a champion of liberty and justice. . . .

It could not be denied that he had to secure them [the Montagu-Chelmsford reforms] for India in the face of a great and most organized opposition and racial hatred. It could not be denied that by the inauguration of the Reforms, the late Mr. Montagu laid the most solid foundation for a glorious self-governing India. He was sure that when the diversity of opinion of the present day had passed away Mr. Montagu would be recognized as one of the greatest benefactors of India and would have his place in the master roll of England's greatest statesmen by the side of Gladstone and Bright.[28]

The speaker introducing the resolution spoke of Montagu's contribution during "the darkest days of her suffering over the Punjab affairs" and the fight he waged almost single-handedly for a solution to the Khalifat and Kenya question. "These were enough to command their gratitude."[29]

Another speaker added that "belonging to one of the greatest Asiatic races, he had the noble idealism and imagination by means of which he could feel the heart throb of a subject race even from his distant island home, the new life that was pulsating through this country and that actuated him to take the step which he honestly believed would lead this country towards self-government."[30]

Tributes and expressions of grief were deeply felt among Muhammadans and in the Muslim press. Syed Sirdar Ali Khan wrote:

In the years to come Mr. Montagu's reputation will, I feel certain, be even greater than it is now. He had the sagacity and ability to see far beyond the petty limits of vision granted to most of his contemporaries and it was because of that that he was able to launch India on the course of self-Government and so to give expression to Indian aspirations. No English statesman has been more responsive to Indian expressions of opinion and none has been more eager or more able to voice those opinions in England in a fitting manner. When the full history of the first few post-war years is revealed we shall begin to realise the full extent of the services rendered by Mr. Montagu when he contended with the Cabinet for justice and fairplay for Turkey.

With Lord Reading as Viceroy and Mr. Montagu as Secretary of State for India the Mahomedans of this country had spokesmen in their time of adversity such as they have never had before. The untimely death of one of that illustrious pair is a loss that will bear heavily on us for the rest of our lives; but our sorrow will not prevent us both now and in the future from expressing our thankfulness that such a man was sent to champion our cause.[31]

The Native Princes, too, many of whom had become personal friends, felt Montagu's death deeply. The Chamber of Princes, which Montagu had helped to create, adopted a resolution made up of the individual statements of most of the Princes of India, who spoke of Montagu's "great statesmanship," his "unique relationship to India" and the "special love" the Princes felt for him. "It may be repetition," His Highness, the Maharajah of Bikaner said, "to talk about his friendship to India . . . but it is a repetition [about which] we Indians need not be ashamed. . . . We Indians are nothing if we are not true friends . . . to those who have loved us."[32] A compilation of these tributes was sent to Venetia Montagu on December 16, 1924.[33]

One of the most touching of all the tributes was delivered by the Maharajah Jam Sahib, in Jamnagar at a ceremony where a statue of Montagu, which had been commissioned during his life, was unveiled. The Maharajah was joined by Lord Reading. The statue had been planned as a tribute to Montagu for his role in "advancing the political progress of India and his great services which culminated in the establishment of Indian Princes Chamber." It was the work of the Italian sculptor Riccardi. The *Times of India,* in reporting this event on December 1, 1924, thought it especially fitting that Lord Reading, "another great statesman belonging to his [Montagu's] own race and fully acquainted with his worth and work," would have the honor of actually unveiling the statue. Introducing Lord Reading, the Maharajah Jam Sahib said:

When I solicited from your Excellency the high privilege of unveiling the Montagu Memorial, I never imagined that it would be darkened with a great sorrow and would constitute the earliest posthumous honor offered in India to the beloved memory of a great patriot and statesman whose recent untimely death, we all so deeply deplore. A striking personality has disappeared forever from the public life of England, intellectually the most brilliant statesman and the greatest friend India has ever had since perhaps Edmund Burke. England and the Empire—are the poorer today for this loss. . . .

We owe to Mr. Montagu and Lord Chelmsford the institution of the

Chamber of Princes and we owe it to their recommendations that we now find ourselves in direct relations with your Excellency's Government. . . .

I have lost a dear friend for whom I cherished the sincerest affection, admiration and esteem and who to me personified what is the very best in the British character.

The present function brings into close association three of the greatest names in the history of India—your Excellency [Reading] one of the most gifted and talented Viceroys unveiling the statue of Edwin Samuel Montagu, the noblest of Secretaries of State . . . in the Square opposite the Vegetable Market named after Lord Chelmsford, the third distinguished name connected with India.[34]

Turning to Montagu's place in Indian history, the Maharajah said:

Memories are known to be short and time obliterates footprints on the sands of eternity more rapidly than any process of annihilation in nature's storehouse; epoch making events and persons prominently connected with these events stand out, compelling attention by the solitary grandeur of their survival amidst contemporary crumbling and oblivion. . . . If I may be permitted the privilege of prophecy . . . such an imperishable place in the grateful hearts of the people of India and in her history belongs to the Right Honorable Edwin Montagu and he will stand out, when the present strife and struggle with its factions and feuds is fought out and forgotten as the great Englishman who planted India on the path to liberty.[35]

Jam Sahib then discussed the Reforms as the:

first attempt in the case of a big nation—in the case of any nation except perhaps the American institutions in the Philippines and Cuba—on the part of distant ruling power—to win the hearts and retain the loyalty of its people by means of affection, not force. To the late Mr. Montagu will ever belong the credit and honor of having carried out, in the face of difficulties that would have daunted a lesser man, what is beyond all dispute one of the most remarkable transformations in the government of a vast country. . . .

In grateful appreciation of these achievements which reflect . . . the generous heart of a patriot and statesman . . . unbound by prejudice of creed or color or class—a great mind thinking big thoughts in the service of his King, Country and our Empire and of humanity . . . with a view to keeping ever fresh in the city of Jamnagar . . . the memory of such a beloved name and personality, I request your Excellency [Reading] to do me the honour of unveiling what we believe is the first statue of the Rt. Hon. Edwin Montagu in India.[36]

Reading's response was equally gracious, noting that:

all India is united at this moment in the testimonials paid to the memory of Edwin Montagu. All political parties, all sections of the press have united here in their expression of admiration . . . of gratitude to Mr. Montagu for his labours for India. Human beings sometimes fail to realize the value of their possessions until they have to count up their loss. . . . Mr. Montagu devoted tireless industry, unbounded energy and passionate enthusiasm to the cause for which he labored . . . for an India within the Empire, based on liberty and on justice.[37]

Then the Viceroy, with the appropriate drum roll and trumpet blasts, unveiled the statue, which still stands in Jamnagar. This statue and another of Montagu by Lady Kennet, commissioned by the City of Calcutta in 1927, are among the few statues of Englishmen that the Indians permitted to remain in India after Indian independence.

The newspapers in England were less fulsome in their praise but did publish several long obituaries and tributes. The *Observer*'s editorial was one of the warmest:

The death of Mr. Montagu must be sincerely regretted by all who feel that we have no superfluity of intellectual power in public life. Mr. Montagu's achievements in obtaining confirmation of his Indian program was one of the greatest experiments into which suasion ever led a great power, even if its pathway may have to be retraced for a certain distance.

Mr. Montagu's vision of the future was perhaps over sanguine and over logical but the bridge by which he connected British and Indian ideals cannot wholly disappear.[38]

The Sunday Times, on November 16, deeply regretted Montagu's death and praised:

his brilliance, the courage and the versatility of his race. . . . Had he remained in public life, he might have made a memorable Chancellor of the Exchequer. Even as it was he rendered the country during the war a great but little known financial service. It was he who first suggested and drafted the arrangement with Messrs. J. P. Morgan & Co. which not only ensured to the Allies an abundant supply of munitions and war matériel but also saved them many hundreds of millions on their American purchases. That was a genuine act of commercial statesmanship and it was one for which Mr. Montagu neither claimed nor received the credit that was due to him.[39]

As for his India reforms, *The Sunday Times,* was less complimentary:

By now most people agree that his series of Indian reforms went too far and fast in a democratic direction to be good either for India or for Britain —but it was an error of judgment which sprang from a generous heart.[40]

Tributes from Friends

The men who worked with Montagu at the India Office or in India, like the Indian press and Indian leaders, were deeply saddened. Lord Chelmsford, in a message to *The Times,* deplored that so brilliant a career was so suddenly cut short, and Lloyd Merton wrote that Montagu's death would come "as a shattering blow to all who understood him."[41] Lord Willingdon, in a message to the *Observer,* paid tribute to Montagu "as one of his best and oldest friends and a great statesman," someone who always gave him "constant and loyal support" when Montagu was Secretary of State.[42] Sir George Lloyd, in an interview in the *Observer* of November 16, expressed the belief that Montagu's "generous" affection for the Indian people and his untiring effort for their advance in a manner which he believed to be the best destiny for India, within the orbit of the British Empire, would be long and gratefully remembered in every part of India.[43]

But perhaps the most interesting tribute was the essay on Montagu by John Maynard Keynes, who felt that most of the newspaper accounts did not do justice "to the remarkable personality of Edwin Montagu." In *The Nation and the Athenaeum,* on November 29, 1914, Keynes wrote:

He was one of those who suffer violent fluctuations of mood, quickly passing from reckless courage and self-assertion to abject panic and dejection—always dramatizing life and his part in it, and seeing himself and his own instincts either in the most favourable or in the most unfavourable light, but seldom with a calm and steady view. Thus it was easy for the spiteful to convict him out of his own mouth, and to belittle his name by remembering him only when his face was turned towards the earth. At one moment he would be Emperor of the East riding upon an elephant, clothed in rhetoric and glory; but at the next a beggar in the dust of the road, crying for alms but murmuring under his breath cynical and outrageous wit which pricked into dustier dust the rhetoric and the glory.

That he was an Oriental, equipped nevertheless with the intellectual technique and atmosphere of the West, drew him naturally to the political problems of India, and allowed an instinctive, mutual sympathy between him and its peoples. But he was interested in all political problems and not least in the personal side of politics, and was most intensely a politician. Almost everything else bored him. Some memoir-writers have suggested that he was really a scientist, because with Nature he could sometimes find escape from the footlights. Others, judging from his parentage and from his entering the City in the last two years of his life, make out that he was, naturally, a financier. This also is far from the truth. I saw him intimately in the Treasury and in the financial negotiations of the Peace Conference; and, whilst his general judgment was good, I do not think that he cared, or had great aptitude, for the problems of pure finance. Nor—though he loved money for what it could buy—was he interested in the details of money-making.

Mr. Lloyd George was, of course, the undoing of his political career— as, indeed, Montagu always said that he could be. He could not keep away from that bright candle. But he knew, poor moth, that he would burn his wings. It was from his tongue that I, and many others, have heard the most brilliant, true, and witty descriptions of that (in his prime) undescrib- able. But whilst, behind the scenes, Montagu's tongue was master, his weaknesses made him, in action, the natural tool and victim; for, of all men, he was one of the easiest to use and throw on one side. It used to be alleged that a certain very Noble Lord had two footmen, of whom one was lame and the other swift of foot, so that letters of resignation carried by the one could be intercepted by the other before their fatal delivery at No. 10. Edwin Montagu's letters were not intercepted; but the subtle intelligencer of human weakness, who opened them, knew that by then the hot fit was over and the cold was blowing strong. They could be ignored or used against the writer—at choice.

I never knew a male person of big mind like his who was more addicted to gossip than Edwin Montagu. Perhaps this was the chief reason why he could not bear to be out of things. He was an inveterate gossip in the servant's hall of secretaries and officials. It was his delight to debate, at the Cabinet, affairs of State, and then to come out and deliver, to a little group, a brilliant and exposing parody, aided by mimicry, of what each of the great ones, himself included, had said. But he loved it better when he could push gossip over into intimacy. He never went for long without an intense desire to unbosom himself, even to exhibit himself, and to squeeze out of his confidant a drop of—perhaps reluctant—affection. And then again he would be silent and reserved beyond bearing, sitting stonily with his great hand across his mouth and a staring monocle.

With better health and—what would probably have accompanied it—a more controlled and equable temperament, Edwin Montagu might have rivalled the career of Disraeli; but he was more lovable as he was.

J.M.K.[44]

The *Cambridge Review* also published a very moving editorial, not about Montagu's political career, but about Montagu as a person— his intelligence, determination and great capacity for friendship:

It is the fact that it was Montagu who announced the decision to make an advance towards self-government (in India); but the truth is that the deci- sion to promise such advance had been reached before he resumed office. The part which fell to him was infinitely more difficult—to find the path by which the pledge was to be redeemed and to follow it in the face, not only of open criticism, but of what he at any rate conceived to be a veiled policy of obstruction. Against the open criticism he could bring great intellectual powers, high courage and a ruthless determination that the policy once chosen should be pursued to its logical conclusion; but against suspicion of intrigue he was defenseless and the blow proved mortal. Reference has been made to Montagu's capacity for friendship. A personal recollection appearing in *The Times* of November 19, not ineptly describes it as genius and traces the secret of it to Montagu's power to stimulate response from his friends. To those who did not know him it is peculiarly difficult to convey the real charm of a personality to which at first sight the word "charm" might seem quite inappropriate. But charm there was, a little fantastic, perhaps a little mysterious, but the quality in harmony with the rather mysterious character we knew. Nor is it wholly inappropriate that his life closes, as it were, with a note of sombre interrogation—the work unfinished—judgment suspended.[45]

The longest and most carefully researched tribute to Montagu was in the *Cambridge Independent Press,* in the district with which Montagu was associated for twenty-four years—more than half of his life—first as an undergraduate student of nineteen years and later as the district's representative in Parliament. The article was more than 7,500 words long and covered his entire career, from his job as Parliament Secretary to Asquith to his appointment as Secretary of State for India and the many contributions he made during World War I.

Montagu's great interest in biology and nature, his humor, his enthusiasm for politics, debating and drama, which had begun at

Cambridge, and the pride his district had in his political advancements were all mentioned. "Of his personal characteristics,"

. . . about his ideals, his sensitiveness, his actions and his longing for affection it would be impertinent to write. It is only his public career with which the world is concerned; and when that career seemed to fall in ruins around him in November 1922, it left his work for India standing as a permanent monument to the inherent humanity of his character.

It was in Montagu's heart that his great projects of Indian reform took shape, before they crystallized in his head. With almost a religious fervor did he believe that the educated Indian has rights which our system of paternal government would never recognize, that injustice was being multiplied, and that the only remedy was to force radical change upon British conscience.

He changed the history of India for an ideal; and his name will never be forgotten in the annals of Indian nationalism.[46]

Burial at Breccles

On November 20, amid all this praise and adulation, Montagu was laid to rest at Breccles. He had asked that there be no religious service and that he not be buried in a cemetery. He was granted only one of these requests. He was not buried in a cemetery, but a memorial service was held for him in the West London Synagogue on November 21, and a rabbi officiated at the grave site.

The burial at Breccles was simple and moving, mainly because there was something sad but fitting that Montagu's final resting place was in a garden he had loved so dearly. One of the bridges that he had labored painstakingly to build over one of the streams on the grounds had to be strengthened the day before the burial to bear the weight of the carriage.[47] The grave site itself was one hundred and fifty yards east of Breccles Hall. Montagu had planted a great rhododendron bed which lay between the river and the moat near the Hall, and it was here that the grave had been prepared. By the time the carriage and coffin arrived, the bank on the side of the grave was filled with beautiful flowers that friends and family had brought.

The rabbi, the Rev. Vivian G. Simmons, of the West London Synagogue, offered a brief prayer. A few other burial prayers were recited in accordance with Jewish law, and the mourners walked back to the Hall. The article in the *Eastern Daily Press* on November 20 reported that Breccles had been rented for six months to Captain Birkin, but that he generously let family and friends use it before and after the funeral.

The mourners at the grave site were few, but a considerable gathering, most of whom worked or lived at Breccles or neighboring estates, some who had traveled long distances, stood respectfully at a distance. The pallbearers were all men who worked on the estate. The grave was of brick, lined with greenery and sprigs from autumn shrubs, and the ceremony was described as "simple and dignified."[48]

The mourners included Venetia, Edwin's brothers Lord Swaythling and Lionel Montagu (Gerald was ill and ordered by his doctor not to attend), his sisters Mrs. Franklin and Mrs. Waley, his brothers-in-law Mr. H. Hart D'Arcy and Colonel Stanley, and his nephews Stuart Montagu, Ewen Montagu and Cyril Franklin. Among his friends were Lord and Lady Fisher, Diana and Duff Cooper, Lord and Lady Ednam, Lady Lovat, Prince Singh and several professors and representatives of Cambridge and the Cambridge Union Debating Society. Herbert Henry Asquith was in Egypt.

A circle of stones was placed around the grave. On one were inscribed the words: "I say that one shall remember me even afterwards." While the burial was attended only by the family and very close friends, the memorial service, held, in accordance with Jewish law, the next day, November 21, at the West London Synagogue (a Liberal-Reform Synagogue) was a public event. It was attended by a distinguished roster of business and political leaders and members of the Jewish community. The King was represented by Lord Colebrooke, and Prime Minister Baldwin by Captain Sidney Herbert. All of Montagu's sisters and brothers and their spouses were present, as were other members of the family; Montagu's colleagues, including Grey, Churchill, McKenna, Chelmsford, Birrell, and Beaverbrook; as well as representatives of the great Anglo-Jewish families, the Rothschilds, Montefiores, Samuels, Cohens and Waleys. Cynthia Asquith was the only Asquith present.[49]

Venetia did not attend. She could not have chosen a more public way of expressing her disapproval of a religious service. One can almost hear the heated arguments among the family as to whether a Jewish service should be held, with Venetia reminding the family that Montagu had specifically requested that no religious service be held. The family ignored her pleas and Montagu's last wish. To them, he was in death as in life a Jew, and as such would be given his last farewell in a synagogue, whether he wanted it or not.

If Edwin could have whispered to Venetia from the grave he would have told her not to fight his family over the issue. He would have reminded her of his violent arguments with his father over the same subject, which taught him that on religious issues, the family's bond to Judaism was stronger than the wishes of any of its individual members. He could never win while alive; in death there was even less of a chance, even with so forceful a surrogate as Venetia.

In the days immediately following Montagu's death, Venetia received hundreds of letters of condolence, including letters from the King, the Prince of Wales, Winston Churchill and Lloyd George, the last written in response to a note from Venetia. In spite of the strong mutual dislike of both Montagu and Lloyd George and the role Lloyd George had played in forcing Montagu's resignation, Venetia wrote to the former Prime Minister just three days after Montagu's death in the friendliest of terms, sending him a letter Montagu had written before leaving for India in 1917. "I know in the old days when he was with you at the Treasury how fond he was of you and only about four weeks before he died, when Max asked us to dinner the night of the elections and said you would be there, he was most anxious to be well enough to go and said, 'What fun it will be to see Lloyd George again. I long to hear what he thinks of all this.' "[50]

Lloyd George, who never overcame his dislike of Montagu, responded as a gentleman.

The death of poor Edwin came as a great shock to all his old friends and associates. The disrupting events of the past few years which separated so many friends had the effect of keeping him and myself apart and the letter you were good enough to send me came to me with the solemnity of a message from beyond the tomb. It was written in November 1917, but inasmuch as it refers exclusively to the divisions of the Liberal Party—it comes now with opportune force.

There was much gentleness in his nature and you must miss it.

> With deepest sympathy,
> Ever Sincerely,
> D. Ll. G.[51]

And King George wrote:

Dear Mrs. Montagu,

We, the queen and I have heard with deep regret of the death of Mr. Montagu whom we had the pleasure of knowing throughout his distinguished political career. We offer you our sincere sympathy in your great sorrow.

George R.I.[52]

The Prince of Wales wrote:

Dear Mrs. Montagu,

This is only a line—which please don't trouble to answer—just to say how sorry I am to hear this evening's bad news and to offer my sympathy. It was rather curious that I happened to be playing squash racquets with Cardy this morning when he got an urgent message. So the news wasn't a surprise. It's all too bad and believe me.

Yours sincerely
Edward[53]

The warmest letter came from Winston Churchill who, in spite of all his disagreements with Montagu, liked "our dear Edwin, whose charm, whose tenderness, whose brilliant mind, whose constant friendship was one of the valued treasures of my life. On what a slender thread our brief existence hangs! It is scarcely a month since we were all gathered here in our own living room. And now! My dear I feel for you. I know how devoted you were to Edwin, and I know you will miss him. Dearest Venetia—I know words are useless—even sometimes painful but do believe that the sympathy and sorrow I feel for you comes from my inmost heart. I wish it could be a balm of comfort. Time alone will bring back the daylight. With all my love." It is signed, "your affectionate friend, Winston."[54]

35

Venetia without Edwin,
1924–1948

Dearest, it was with a sad heart and heavy feet that I turned my back on Breccles. I enjoyed every minute of my little visit and long to come again when the flowers are all out.

Asquith to Venetia, Nov. 1927

Venetia in the 1920s

Venetia was thirty-seven years old when Edwin died. She lived twenty-four years more, through the miseries of Hitler and World War II, and died at the age of sixty-one in 1948, after a torturous battle against cancer. Her life during the years immediately following Edwin's death did not seem to alter significantly. He had left her enough money, which, augmented by Beaverbrook's generosity and investment advice, permitted her to continue her travels and the rich social life she enjoyed, although her style of dress and entertaining became more modest.

Soon after Edwin died, Venetia sold 24 Queen Anne's Gate and bought a smaller house at 62 Onslow Gardens in Kensington. She rented it frequently when she was traveling or in need of money. In 1929, for example, she rented it to Winston Churchill when he had to leave the office of Chancellor of the Exchequer and 11 Downing Street following the Tory defeat that year. The Churchills kept the lease until 1931.

In spite of sporadic financial difficulties, she did not sell Breccles. Edwin was buried there. It held too many memories. Besides, she loved the Norfolk country almost as much as Edwin had, and she needed it as an anchor and an escape from the hectic life she led in London and Paris.

The most vivid portrait of her life after Edwin died is captured in the letters she wrote to Beaverbrook, a correspondence that spanned three decades and lasted until the final days of her life. The last letter she wrote to Beaverbrook was dated July 12, 1948, twenty-two days before she died. These letters are augmented by other glimpses of how and with whom she spent her days: in the biography of Clementine Churchill by her daughter Mary Soames, in the letters and books by Duff and Diana Cooper and in other books that her friends and political confidantes wrote about their lives in this period of English history.

One of the first letters she wrote after Montagu's death was to Beaverbrook; she enclosed in it Montagu's watch and cuff links, certain that Montagu would want him to have these as a remembrance.[1]

This may or may not have reflected Montagu's wish. While Beaverbrook was Montagu's friend, one must wonder how he really felt about his wife's lover and whether he would have chosen these intimate possessions to be sent to him. But whether Montagu would have done so, Beaverbrook was deeply moved.

"Darling Venetia," he wrote, "on arriving at Hyde Park on the 4:00 p.m., after an exciting experience in the fog, I found your letter and the watch and cuff links. I cannot write you of my emotion. Everything that I loved in Edwin was so vividly recalled that he seemed to be there with me. Yesterday, as I walked in the . . . House of Lords . . . I overheard two men—strangers to me—speaking of him and his work. I engaged in the conversation, rejoicing that his merits are so widely recognized and his work acknowledged." Beaverbrook selected the watch, "because his monogram is on it. Do let me talk with you about money matters. You know I have a good head for business. Yours forever and a day, Max."[2]

Venetia wrote also, in the days following Montagu's death, to Prime Minister Asquith who was in Egypt. It was the first letter she had written him in nearly ten years. Montagu's death may well have caused Venetia to reflect upon the life she and Montagu had led and to look back upon and reminisce about those people who played important roles in that life. Asquith was surely such a man—playing perhaps the pivotal role in Montagu's life and not an insignificant one in her own.

My dearest Mr. Asquith,

We found this letter for you among Edwin's papers, written I think just before he went to India. I know it is not necessary for me to tell you how deeply he loved you and what a real and lasting grief your political separation was. He always used to say that tho' he was still absorbingly interested in his work after he left you, it was no longer fun.

I feel I am terribly lucky to have had nine and a half such happy years and that I was able, owing to my very unimaginative and unapprehensive frame of mind, to help him sometimes cast off those great fears and glooms which used to torture him. Do you remember how we used to laugh at him in Sicily.

Thank you for all you did for him to make his life happy. He was always grateful to you.

All my love,
Venetia[3]

She wrote again, while Asquith was still in Egypt:

My darling Mr. Asquith,

Edwin asked me to give you something of his and I finally thought you might like this "Hamlet," which I'd given him a long time ago. I've never thanked you for your divine letter, you know how dumb and inarticulate I am, but you do realize, I hope, how glad I was to get it. I hope I may see you sometime when you get back.

Much love always,
Venetia[4]

Over the next years, they continued to exchange a few letters, but none of substance. While Asquith was a memory from her past, Beaverbrook was very much a part of Venetia's present. The letters written immediately after Montagu's death, and throughout the rest of the 1920s, have an intimacy that suggests that they were still lovers. Beaverbrook wrote to Venetia on July 8, 1926: "Will you dine with me at Stornoway House on Wednesday night next? STOP. I can put you up for the night if you will stay. As I am alone in the house, will have double locks put on your doors. Max."[5] On September 6, 1929, he wrote: "The stick is beautiful. . . . Let me hear from you when you come to town. We have a bed and breakfast for you here any night and every morning."[6] And Venetia wrote to Beaverbrook, early in January 1929:

My darling, I never thanked you for your letter. I was still rather emotionally upset and as you know am rather tongue-tied on those matters, but I did love getting it. I think I should miss your love and companionship more than anything in all the world. I've had it now very constantly for nearly eleven years and it's very precious to me.

I've decided to go to New York on the 16th to meet Diana there and stay about three weeks. Couldn't you leave your ship at Havana and come across to Florida where we could all meet?[7]

Beaverbrook was on a cruise to the West Indies with his mistress, Jean Norton. On receiving her note, Beaverbrook wired Venetia on January 16, 1929, while she was on board the SS *Homeric* en route to New York: "Happy journey beloved Venetia. my love goes with you. Max."[8]

In the more than thirty letters that passed between Venetia and Beaverbrook during the 1920s, affection was expressed openly and without reservation. Dates were set, weekends planned, gifts exchanged (with Beaverbrook's gifts always generous). In many letters it was Venetia who asked for time to see him, because she "misses" him, "longs to be with" him and always had "a divine time with him." The fact that it was general gossip in London at the time that Jean Norton was Beaverbrook's official mistress and was "the predominant, though not the only, woman in his life until her death in 1945,"[9] did not diminish Venetia's enthusiasm for him. This was no more a factor in their relationship than the fact that she had had a husband and he a wife (Gladys Beaverbrook did not die until December 1927) when their relationship first began in 1917.

In Venetia's world, being sexually restless and needing several lovers was an accepted way of life, particularly for men. Even Duff Cooper, who was madly in love with beautiful Diana and had wooed her passionately and consistently for several years before she consented to marry him, "could not be content with a single woman and even before the honeymoon was over, was seeking diversions outside their marriage. But such diversions were no more than the gratification of a nagging appetite."[10]

But Beaverbrook's relationship with Venetia was more than a sexual excursion. He genuinely liked her, admired her intelligence and respected her political acumen. She admired his brilliance and political power, and she needed his financial help.

Money as well as power were aphrodisiacs to Venetia. She has been accused of using men and of being ruthless and superficial in her relations with them. That is a harsh judgment. For while she may have enjoyed Asquith's power and never loved him as he loved her, Asquith surely derived as much satisfaction from their affair as she did. And while her marriage to Montagu and her conversion to Judaism were clearly motivated by money, she did not hide this from him or anyone else. She may have used him, but she was open in her motives. Montagu, for his part, knew in advance exactly what he bargained for. Just being with her, even infrequently, was, for many years, enough for him. And Beaverbrook, with a wife, a mistress and other women on the side, was certainly not an exploited victim. He thoroughly enjoyed Venetia's company and, being a very generous man to his friends, found nothing objectionable in Venetia's willingness to accept his largess.

Beaverbrook was not exaggerating when he wrote to Venetia on October 28, 1929: "£10 enclosed as directed. My love is always with you. My worldly goods are at your disposal including my house here and there and elsewhere. Yours ever, Max."[11] Beaverbrook's gifts included not only money and other "worldly goods" but also expensive and lavish trips abroad, not merely for Venetia but for many others who became part of his traveling entourage.

In 1927 Beaverbrook took Venetia, Diana Cooper, Valentine Castlerosse, and Arnold Bennett to Germany. Lord Castlerosse has been described as "gross in appetite and appearance, with nimble wit concealed beneath a buffoon's exterior . . . Beaverbrook's court jester." "What is your handicap?" Nancy Cunard asked him on the golf course. "Drink and debauchery," he answered.[12]

This was exactly the company Venetia loved to keep. Arnold Bennett was reported to have been shocked "by the coarseness of the conversation between Beaverbrook and Castlerosse in front of the women."[13] Venetia and Diana were far from shocked. Their own interest in sex prompted them to go with Castlerosse on a tour of transvestite nightclubs in Berlin.

Bennett liked Venetia and Diana, commenting that they "really do their best to be agreeable and very well succeed, though Venetia has a darting tongue. However, with her stings, she really is witty. Diana less so, but Diana is kinder. . . . [T]he women know about music because it seems to be somehow their job to be companionable in everything, and they must have taken the hell of a lot of pains to be so, and I think they may be mildly interested."[14] "Sefton Delmer, then a junior stringer for the *Express* in Berlin was summoned to the Hotel Adlon. He found Bennett 'sardonic, silent and sallow,' Castlerosse 'fat, flushed and chortling,' Venetia, 'gracious, erect and smiling' and Diana 'brilliant, brittle and blonde.' "[15] The group was in Berlin ostensibly to design a film which Bennett was to write, Beaverbrook to finance and Diana to star in. The group seemed more interested, however, in having a wild time and none of them pursued the film idea with much vigor.

The most exciting trip Beaverbrook took was a cruise to Moscow, Leningrad, Danzig and Stockholm with Arnold Bennett, Michael Wardell, Jean Norton, Lady Louis Mountbatten, Venetia and Diana. It was a fabulous trip, according to Venetia, who wrote:

Darling Max,

I don't know where to begin to thank you for the most wonderful time you have just given me. One would need the whole wealth of adjectives employed by Mr. Hackett to do anything approaching to justice. It was all so very enjoyable. On looking back there are some things which stand out perhaps more than others. Danzig, the horror of Moscow and Leningrad, Stockholm and then four or five meals on the ship at which you were at your very best! I sometimes think after listening to you, it's a pity you made so much money for had you been reduced to becoming a professor of history or literature, your lectures would have been the most inspiring anyone could have listened to.

But your kindness is greater even than your eloquence and you have given me a wealth of wonderful memories which will give me perpetual pleasure.

I hope I shall see you soon.

Much love,
Venetia[16]

One of Beaverbrook's biographers, A. J. P. Taylor, has written: "This was the first visit to Russia by a British privy councillor and ex-minister since the revolution. It was probably also the most luxurious visit of its kind. But as trade relations had already been resumed by the Labour Government, the visit had no political significance."[17]

In addition to the trips sponsored by Beaverbrook, Venetia continued to travel extensively on her own. In January 1926, she took a cruise to North Africa which she described as a "vile expedition," primarily because there was no one on board with whom she could talk. "How I love my friends and hate to travel." This was but a momentary feeling since Venetia traveled all her adult life and, but for this comment, appeared to thoroughly enjoy it. Cardie, Edwin's younger brother, accompanied her on this trip. "Cardie is charming," she wrote, "but I'm not going to marry him as everyone seems to think, because (partly) he hasn't asked me."

Apparently, Venetia had been seeing Cardie in London and gossip had it that they might marry. They did not, probably because Cardie, at that time at least, was a confirmed bachelor. He did not marry until 1944 when he was sixty-one. He died four years later, in 1948. In addition, Cardie was not Venetia's type. While he was a dashing sportsman with impeccable social contacts, he was interested in neither politics nor the arts. On the other hand, he did have money and moved in circles that Venetia enjoyed. But Cardie did not propose, and the issue of whether she would have accepted was moot.

In 1929, Venetia not only visited Russia but also sailed to America and spent several weeks in January and February with Diana in New York City. Beaverbrook was in Trinidad and sent her some "exquisite stockings," which she accepted with "joy."[18] During the late 1920s she often visited Paris and the casinos on the Continent; she spent very little time with her daughter.

In 1928, between her travels, she helped Beaverbrook with his book *Politicians and the War*. She read his galley proofs and continued to send him copies of letters she had received from Asquith, which he used extensively as background material for his book without acknowledging the source. Dr. Brock, discussing Beaverbrook's use of Asquith's letters to Venetia, states:

By 1919, Venetia was reported to be his mistress and at various times made extracts from the letters for him. When forwarding those for March and April 1915 she wrote of Asquith—"I have done him a dirty turn once (tho' I am not fatuous enough to imagine it was more than quite momentary) so I'm very anxious that you should know a lot about him. I'm confident that the more you do the more you will appreciate his very great and exceptional qualities. I wish chance had thrown you together, for I'm sure you wd. have been friends."

Brock continues: "Beaverbrook used these extracts in *Politicians and the War,* Vol. 1 (1928). Neither in this nor in other similar cases did he indicate his source."[19]

Venetia also made substantive comments about the book, especially about Edwin. On April 22, 1928, she wrote:

My darling Max,

Thank you a million times for the book. I finished it last night having read every word with the most absorbed interest. It is quite excellent. Yours is the first book which really gives at all a vivid or true picture of what was going on inside the Government. Up to date everyone has tried to prove that they were right all the time, an obvious impossibility for anyone. To anyone who was at all connected with the people and events in 14–15 you re-create those times with startling clearness. I was delighted with what you said about Edwin, and even Mr. Asquith, who you are bound to criticise, is wonderfully dealt with. My only complaint is that it's too short. Do please get busy with the next vol. I'm sure Winston is delighted, and rightly so.

Life is very pleasant here, up to date lovely weather and a nice party, with an enormous preponderance of women 8–3. Bridget exquisitely dressed, but feeling the honour of Victor always hovering over her (this only a guess and probably quite untrue). Violet Cripps, Rosemarie, Julie, Lady Cranbourne (she's actually just left), Lady Worsley (an old girl of my age who loves Sidney), Diana and me. Sidney I think is really better, he has the eyes of a well man, tho he is immobile owing to having his leg in a splint.

I get back Friday and go to Breccles Saturday late. Is there any chance that you will be in London Saturday? I am staying the night at 3 Belgrave Square with Juliet Duff.

Anyway, Newmarket is a very bright spot.

Have you read *My Mortal Enemy,* by Willa Cather? Very good I thought.

Much love,
Venetia[20]

Beaverbrook respected Venetia sufficiently to write to her on August 27 that he would alter his text "to emphasize Edwin's keen desire to keep Lloyd George and Asquith together." "I will," he added, "also attribute the very brilliant remark about the sinking ship to Edwin."[21] (Venetia must have suggested this orally as there is no written documentation of her suggestion.)

In her April 22 letter Venetia had alluded to her age and the sad recognition that she was no longer a young and attractive girl.

Describing Lady Worsley, Venetia concluded that Worsley is "an *old* girl of my age." Earlier that year, she had referred to herself similarly to Beaverbrook, by asking him to "keep a corner in your overcrowded heart for Venetia, your *old* friend who loves you."[22]

And in a letter to Beaverbrook in which she wrote that she regretted she could not join him on his birthday, May 25, 1929, she reflected on the fact that their friendship had lasted "¼ of her life and ⅕ of his." Time had now become precious. As a woman who enjoyed being sought after by men, growing old was particularly painful. For the first time since her early twenties, when she first met Asquith and Montagu, she did not have a man. As physically unattractive as Montagu was to her, she could not have been unaffected by the intensity of his feelings. Now, with him gone, an important fulcrum in her life had been removed. She was emotionally alone. While she could fill her days with travel and friends, and perhaps superficial flirtations, she could not have failed to feel the difference. Nor could she expect to find another who would adore her as he had.

She mentioned in some of her letters in 1929 that she had luncheon dates with "a Major M. Graham," and also wrote to Beaverbrook that year of a "new boy" she would bring to dinner. But none of this was serious. Dear friends, like Beaverbrook, now became more important than new lovers.

But although Venetia's sexual attractiveness may have been waning, she still retained her enormous capacity for providing a sense of comfort to both men and women during trying times. Beaverbrook now became the recipient of this solicitude during a period in which he was ill and depressed. He wrote: "Sailing home tonight. Your letter is like a bottle of real Scotch Whiskey in New York. I am much better in health and I hope improved in spirits. I turned to you in my despair and you gave me comfort."

Venetia may have had this capacity for comforting friends but she rarely showed it to Montagu or Judith. Montagu had had to face his political crises and his emotional illnesses alone. Venetia had rarely been with him during his worst days in Parliament. As for Judith, she rarely saw her mother as a young child and spent, according to a friend, "a childhood of isolation." She was "a precocious and very smart child, but very lonesome."

Venetia's granddaughter, Anna Gendel, wrote of her mother's relationship with Venetia:

As far as my mother's relations with Venetia, I can remember my mother telling me fantastic stories of her bravery, energy and intelligence . . . and her friendships with powerful men like Lord Beaverbrook. But at the same time my mother also told me how she was intimidated by Venetia and her strictness. When Judy was a child Venetia never allowed her comic books which were instead given her by her nanny who was always presented as an infinitely more accessible and easy character. I think she was called Nanny Perkins.

I know that Venetia brought Mummy up to be as well-read and in-formed as possible, something I believe had been encouraged by my great-grandparents. Here at Tareastock Road I have a portrait of Venetia and her sister Blanche from 1907 by a G. P. Lacomb Hood, which shows them in the library of Alderley, I believe, against an extensive bookshelf. A large globe is in view and Venetia holds an open book. When one thinks of Sargent's sirens, the blue stocking interpretation seems quite conscious.[23]

Anna's comments about Judith's studies are confirmed by a letter Judith wrote to Beaverbrook on February 7, 1930, when she was seven years old, thanking him for a "lovely present" and telling him that she was "very busy" in London. "I ride, swim, dance, paint and I do my ordinary lessons. With love, Judy." But according to Judith's husband, Milton Gendel, an art historian in Rome, Venetia was no more or less indifferent to her child than were other women of her class. He wrote in 1988:

It is part of a class pattern to travel a great deal and to spend a great deal of time with friends. The English aristocracy continued to have their children brought up by staff, upstairs and away. . . . Judy herself felt that her mother was indifferent to her, that she was not beautiful or prompt or talented as her mother might have wished. She was in awe of her and afraid to open her mouth in her presence. She claimed that it was only after her mother's death that she began to speak up in company and make friends. But the night her mother's papers arrived in Rome, Judy woke me at dawn in tears shouting, "My mother *loved* me. Look at these letters she wrote me when I was at school. They are full of love and I never realized it."[24]

Judith's name also appeared in a letter Asquith sent to Venetia, in November 1927, after what was to be his last visit to Breccles and the occasion of his first and only meeting with Judith. It was a sad letter, that of a man who knew that his days were numbered. "Dearest," he wrote:

. . . it was with a sad heart & heavy feet that I turned my back upon Breccles. I had enjoyed every minute of my little visit & long to come again when the flowers are all out. It was most good of you to take me in, a "sheer hulk" in need of refitting in your sheltered and delightful haven. . . . Bluey (as always) imparted his own distinction & stimulating flavour. It is a great refreshment to come within reach of a spray from that pungent and aromatic reservoir.

Asquith continued:

Parkie [his doctor] has just arrived by motor: in most characteristic form. He didn't waste much time over me and my "symptoms."

I haven't grappled yet with *Red Sky in the Morning* but I must soon take it in hand. It looks as if I should be more or less immured here for most of the autumn. Happily, I have occupation. Give my love to your Judith, whose acquaintance I should like to improve. Much love

Yrs always
H[25]

Judith, who was then four years old, remembered years later having seen tears on Asquith's face as he said, "This then is the child." Asquith did not tell Venetia in this letter or during his visit that he was seriously ill. Throughout 1927, he had suffered from a loss of movement in one leg. "When he reached Sutton Courtney from Breccles, this trouble occurred again and he could not get out of the car without help. He never left the Wharf again."[26] He died three months later on February 15, 1928, at seventy-six. His death closed another important chapter in Venetia's life.

After Asquith's death, his widow, Margot, made every effort to restrict knowledge of his affair with Venetia "to the smallest possible circle and to put the best construction on it."[27] In 1932, Desmond MacCarthy published Asquith's letters to Hilda Harrisson, who had become a confidante of Asquith in his later years. "Publication of these letters caused a furore among Nonconformist Liberals,"[28] although they were not as passionate or revealing as Asquith's letters to Venetia. Their publication prompted Margot to send a memorandum about the women in Asquith's life to J. A. Spender, who at the time was writing the official biography of Asquith with Cyril Asquith. In that memorandum Margot attempted to minimize Asquith's love affair with Venetia, causing Daphne Bennett, Margot's biographer, to add that "even at that late date Margot was anxious to suppress knowledge" of this affair "as far as possible. She succeeded remarkably well in protecting her husband's good name."[29]

It was "not till fifteen years after our marriage," Margot wrote, "that he [Asquith] formed two friendships with women that gave him the most pleasure in his life. The first was Venetia Stanley. . . . His other woman friend . . . was Hilda Harrisson."[30] Margot devoted a full paragraph to Hilda Harrisson and half a paragraph to Venetia, describing her merely as a friend of Violet's, the daughter of Lord and Lady Sheffield, who were friends of the family, a clever, good-humored young lady with "a talent for writing letters," whose "genuine attraction" for Asquith attracted him.[31] She downplayed the entire relationship asserting that Asquith developed "a deep affection for Venetia"—nothing more. She equated this relationship with Asquith's "lasting affection for Hilda Harrisson,"[32] although a comparison of the letters Asquith wrote to the two women reveals the evident differences in his feelings. Venetia Stanley was a lover; Hilda Harrisson a friend. Margot was perfectly aware of this, although she did not reveal it in her memorandum to Spender, which ended with the additional disclaimer: "Rumour is always rife over a Prime Minister's reputation, but I have lived long enough in the world to see rumour wrong over almost every political person and event."[33]

Spender, perhaps in deference to the Asquith family and to his coauthor, Asquith's son, accepted Margot's analysis and refrained from additional comment, merely writing:

He discovered a need for some receptive and sympathetic female intelligence, outside, the circle of his family, to which he could communicate as a matter of routine the spontaneous overflow of thought or humour, of fancy or of emotion. A whole succession of women friends responded to this need—Venetia Stanley and latterly Mrs. Harrisson may be cited as examples.[34]

It was only after the publication of Asquith's letters to Venetia, fifty years later, that Asquith's true feelings for Venetia came to light. In 1928, at the time of Asquith's death, these facts were unknown to the public. Only Venetia and a small group of intimate friends and family knew of the intensity of his feelings for her.

A Chance to Become a M.P.

The year 1928 was a memorable one in Venetia's life for another reason. It was the year in which the Liberal Party asked her to run for Parliament in South Norfolk, no small honor for a woman. The *Daily Express* reported:

The Hon. Mrs. Montagu, the widow of Edwin Montagu, who was Secretary of State for India in the Coalition Government, has been invited by the Liberal Party to stand as Liberal Candidate for South Norfolk.

The *Daily Express* understand that Mrs. Montagu has declined the invitation.

It is interesting to recall that in a recent article . . . in the *Sunday Express,* Viscountess Weymouth described Mrs. Montagu, who is a daughter of the Fourth Lord Sheffield, as one of the best women conversationalists.

"She is very knowledgeable, has a wonderful memory and a quaint wit," writes Lady Weymouth. "She desires to please that particular person to whom she is talking and her conversation is coloured with the necessary dash of malice."

Mrs. Montagu's many friends have been speculating on whether she would have achieved in the House of Commons the same reputation as a witty and brilliant speaker as she has built up in her own circle as a conversationalist. [35]

Venetia had declined the offer. She lacked the discipline necessary for sustained work. There was little "fun" in being a Member of Parliament. She had seen the price Edwin had paid for the honor. While she enjoyed discussing politics, she was not prepared to work on behalf of her convictions.

Venetia did undertake one project during this period that took time and effort; she edited, with Alan Parsons, the Indian diary that Edwin had written during his visit to India in 1917 and 1918. It was a tedious job, one that suggests that as Venetia reflected on Edwin after his death, she came to appreciate, more than she had in his lifetime, his political contributions. In her introduction to the book, she wrote:

In one passage he [Edwin] claims . . . that he kept India quiet for six months at a critical period of the war; I hope that the publication of this diary may not only substantiate this claim, but also throw some light on an extraordinarily complex personality whom the great world never understood but his intimate friends . . . knew to be passionately sincere and generous to a fault. [36]

The book was published by William Heinemann Ltd. in 1930, at a time when the struggle over self-government in India was, once again, front page news.

In 1927, a royal commission had been created to review the Montagu-Chelmsford Reforms with a view to suggesting revisions. Chaired by Sir John Simon, the commission was at once boycotted by the Indians, since no Indian had been chosen to sit upon it. To Indian leadership this was yet another affront and triggered yet another wave of violence and rioting. While the commission was continuing its work, Lord Irwin, the Viceroy of India, on leave in England, persuaded the Labour Party and Baldwin to call for a Round Table Conference of all Indian groups on the future of India and to declare that the goal should be dominion status for India.

India—Again

Unfortunately, the call for a conference was attacked both in India and by the Die-Hards at home. As 1930 opened, Gandhi was released from jail insisting that the Indian Congress not attend such a conference unless dominion status was granted first. This was unacceptable to the Viceroy. Violence broke out throughout India, culminating in Gandhi's march to the Indian Ocean and his arrest with that of the two Nehru brothers and thousands of their followers. A year later, Gandhi was released. He began discussions with the Viceroy again. Finally, he agreed that the Indian Congress could participate in the Round Table Conference, and a few more years of peace ensued.

During the bitter debates of 1929, 1930 and 1931 over the Viceroy's permissive attitude toward Gandhi and the Viceroy's support of dominion status for India, Churchill was the principal spokesman for the Die-Hard Conservatives and joined with them in their denunciation of self-government for India. It was not practicable, he believed, to give dominion status to "any nation that treats sixty million of its members, toiling at their side, as 'Untouchables' " and "is a prey to fierce racial and religious dissensions."[37] In holding to his position against self-government for India in 1930 and 1931,

Churchill was opposed not only by Labour but by Baldwin and those Conservatives loyal to him. They might have shared Churchill's feelings, but they did not trust him and feared he might be planning a revolt. They also wanted an end to the discord in India. It was becoming too unpleasant, and they and the public wished for nothing more than that the Indian problem "just fade away." For all of these reasons, they were not prepared to support Churchill, who found himself almost alone, with no Party support and no place to go.

Beaverbrook believed that Churchill's stand revealed "a defect of character" and a willingness to "take up anything as long as it leads to power." He was "trying to make a corner for himself in Indian affairs. He is now taking up the stand of a veritable die-hard."[38] Beaverbrook was wrong: Churchill did not create this position in the 1930s merely to "make a corner for himself." He had believed, as early as when he had debated with Montagu, in white superiority and the inability of India to govern itself. In 1931, Churchill made his break with Baldwin officially and resigned from the shadow cabinet. He now entered the "political wilderness" over India, as Montagu had before him, although for vastly different reasons.

During these days of bitter debate over India, Venetia continued her friendships with both Churchill and Beaverbrook, although the two were at opposite poles in this controversy. From her introduction to Edwin's *Indian Diary,* it is clear that Venetia herself opposed Churchill's virulent anti-Indian statements and was much closer to Beaverbrook's position on India, which was not far from Montagu's. Her letters to Beaverbrook during the 1930s do not, however, contain any references to the political issue or to the Indian debate. There are fewer letters than in the 1920s, and they are largely thank-you notes for presents, dinners and visits to his yacht or his homes. One is a request for Beaverbrook to guarantee Venetia's overdraft at the bank for £10,000. The passion of yesterday was now gone.

Edwin's Will

Venetia's letter to Beaverbrook of June 10, 1934, in which she asked him to guarantee her bank note, reveals that Montagu had divided his estate between Venetia and Judith and that, fearful of Venetia's extravagances, he had left both portions in trust, with annual incomes for both. To thus provide for a child fathered by someone else was another expression of Edwin's enormous kindness, which even Venetia in her introduction to the *Indian Diary* called "generous to a fault." "When Edwin died," Venetia wrote to Beaverbrook:

his money was divided between Judy and me. His trustees decided that if I were to have the use of her share till she came of age, some provision must be made for paying off part at least of the mortgage of this house of £19,000. I therefore took out a 10-year Endowment Policy of £10,000. The last premium on this must be paid in January 1935.

I shall receive £10,000 which will go to pay off the 6% mortgage which Edwin took on this house. But alas, although I have got £10,000—paying those premiums has caused this overdraft. Until now the Board of the North Scotland Bank has been guaranteed by Messrs. Thompson and McIntoch but I heard . . . two days ago that owing to some change in the firm they were not prepared to do so any longer.

If you think you could do this for me, I would propose as security a £10,000 Life Policy. For this I would pay £320 per annum so that with this saving of £600 in mortgage interest and nearly £600 in premium payments, I ought to be able to pay off yearly a fair sum of the overdraft. I have also about £2000 worth of securities held by the Bank. That sum and 108 shares in NY Central and 64 Price Brothers shares are all the capital I have. Last year I managed by letting this house [Breccles] to reduce the overdraft by £200. I have succeeded in letting again this year, so I hope to be able to do the same this year.

I am ashamed of bothering you but please forgive me and must say no and not be angry with me. Much love, Venetia.[39]

From subsequent letters, it is clear that Beaverbrook guaranteed the note. He also continued sending Venetia both cash and jewelry and always remembered her birthday and other special occasions, although he saw her less often.

Pre-Hitler Days: The 1930s

During the 1930s, Beaverbrook became intensely interested in foreign affairs, opposing collective security and the League of Nations. He and his newspapers became exponents of "isolationism," believing, as Bonar Law had said, that "Britain could not be the 'policeman of the world.' " While advocating isolationism, Beaverbrook also supported rearmament and the need to strengthen Britain's ties with the Empire. He strongly opposed agreements with France. "If we make alliances we commit ourselves to a war—a war near or remote—but nevertheless, inevitable," he said. And even after German forces occupied the demilitarized Rhineland he agreed "no war and no sanctions against Germany."

Beaverbrook congratulated Chamberlain on Munich, writing to him on September 28, 1938: "My Dear Neville, My faith is very great, but not so immense as my joy and delight over your reward. Don't answer Yours ever, Max." He was certain that Germany would not "move westward again for some time [it had just captured Czechoslovakia]. They are deeply committed to Eastern operations."[40]

Nowhere in his own writing or in the *Daily Express* did he express any horror at Hitler's plans to exterminate the Jews, although by 1936 Hitler had made no secret of his goal. While Beaverbrook disliked Hitler's fascist dictatorship and "hated so much the regimentation of opinion,"[41] he remained indifferent to the Jewish issue. On December 9, 1938, he wrote that "Neville Chamberlain has lost one chance after another of holding a successful election. . . . His policy of appeasement has been killed by British increased armaments, which upset the Germans, and by German persecution of the Jews which upset everybody."[42]

Beaverbrook blamed the Jews for encouraging war against Germany, adding that "the Jews have got a big position in the press here. I estimate that one third of the circulation of the *Daily Telegram* is Jewish. The *Daily Mirror* may be owned by Jews. The *Daily Herald* is owned by Jews. And the *News-Chronicle* should really be the *Jews Chronicle*. Not because of ownership but because of sympathy. *The Times,* the *Daily Mail,* and the *Express* are the only papers left and I am not sure about the *Mail."* "I have been, for many years, a prophet of no war. But at last I am shaken. The Jews may drive us into war. I do not mean by any conscious purpose of doing so. They do not mean to do it. But unconsciously they are drawing us into war. Their political influence is moving us in that direction."[43]

A. J. P. Taylor, Beaverbrook's biographer, claimed that while this was "a deplorable letter," it was "no more than a passing aberration."[44] Beaverbrook had no sympathy for anti-Semitism. Many years later there was criticism when a Jew was appointed to a high post at one of his newspapers. He reacted sharply:

It would be intolerable if prejudice existed against Scots in England. And certainly much worse for that race if Canadians should object to them. And what is the difference between Scots and Jews.

It may be claimed that the prejudice is unreasoning and nothing can be said to account for it. Certainly that is true. But it is the duty of newspaper editors to refuse to be moved by any such survival of ignorance and prejudice.[45]

Beaverbrook did not view himself as an anti-Semite. He never discriminated in employment or in his friendships. He believed that religious prejudice was the result of ignorance and lack of reasoning. On the other hand, he was not prepared to lift a finger to stop Hitler's massacre of the Jews and was critical of those Jews in the press and in political circles who would do otherwise. He never understood, as Taylor noted, that the British turned against Germany not because of Jewish propaganda but because of Hitler's treatment of the Jews. "The facts made the propaganda by themselves."[46]

But the facts of German genocide and persecution did not move Beaverbrook. In the face of such facts, he believed that Britain should look the other way and remain silent. As late as September 1939, he still argued that Germany and Italy did not want war against France and Britain. His strongest opponent in the House of Commons was Churchill, whom Beaverbrook dismissed as "not an important factor" on this issue and as someone who had "ceased to influence the British public."[47] On September 2, Beaverbrook cabled to Lowell Thomas: "I hope we are going to escape a European war, and in that case I am going back to America at once."[48] The following day, September 3, 1939, at 11 A.M., Great Britain declared war against Germany. As brilliant as Beaverbrook was, he was wrong in his calculations about Germany's intentions and Britain's reactions.

During this period, another of Venetia's dear friends, Duff Cooper, was very much involved in Foreign Office politics, although on the opposite side from isolationists like Beaverbrook. Duff was Secretary of State for War for eighteen months, from November 1935 to March 1937, and then First Lord of the Admiralty from 1937 to 1939. He was an outspoken critic of Chamberlain's and Beaverbrook's advocacy of appeasement. He and Diana loathed what the Nazis were doing to the Jews and were sickened by the stories of persecution which were beginning to filter out of Germany.[49] They were part of a small group, led by Churchill, determined to keep the voice of opposition alive. They were not afraid of expressing themselves in the most outspoken fashion even in the presence of the German Ambassador Joachim von Ribbentrop.

At a supper-party at Emerald Cunard's [it is reported], 'really magnificent stew of German and French and Jews and gentiles and Jockey Club stewards, tarts, duchesses, MPs and idiots'—Diana was sitting next to the German Ambassador, Ribbentrop. He asked if she had been to Berlin lately. "No," she said, but she was going to Paris the next day. To buy dresses? asked the Ambassador archly. "No, to Flanders to see the war cemetery," I said, with a brave stare into his treacherous little eyes. Usually, however, Diana left the more belligerent pronouncements to her husband. At a dinner-party given by Venetia Montagu, where Chips Channon (a rich admirer of Diana's) found the company sadly pro-semite and out of touch, "Crinks" Johnstone toasted the death of Ribbentrop. Diana thought this was going too far, but Duff added the rider that he should die in pain.[50]

When Chamberlain returned from Munich and Duff heard the full terms of this appeasement pact, he threatened to resign. Taylor wrote that after making this threat, Duff waffled and would have remained, but Chamberlain gave him no chance to change his mind. He was only too glad to be rid of so severe a critic. In May 1940, when Chamberlain's government fell and Churchill replaced him, Duff became Minister of Information and, in 1944, Ambassador to France.

Venetia was more in sympathy with the attitude of Duff and Churchill toward Germany than she was with Beaverbrook's. It may have been that her identification with Judaism, as slight as it was, influenced her. She had many Jewish friends, including Victor Rothschild, the Third Baron Rothschild, with whom she was very close. The stories coming out of Germany disturbed her as much as they did the Coopers and the Churchills. Anything that smacked of restraint and authoritarianism was certain to be anathema to her. For all of these reasons her support of the Coopers and Churchill was inevitable.

In spite of this, nothing in her letters to Beaverbrook reveals any dispute between them over this very emotional issue. Her letters indicated a growing concern with the state of the world and the state of his health, but she never commented about his political positions.

Beaverbrook was suffering from asthma and, during these years, sought relief in places such as Miami, the Caribbean and southern France. On her fifty-first birthday in 1938, he sent an extraordinarily beautiful ring which elicited from Venetia an especially loving and sentimental response:

I am now fifty-one, which is very old for a woman and our friendship is now twenty-one years which is I suppose very old for a friendship. At any rate, I have none other which has survived as long. Many of the familiar faces of 1918 are dead and many others I wonder how I could have liked them as much as I did. You are the only one who remains as a tried and always much loved friend. We have so many shared experiences behind us of all kinds and no new friend can ever give you just that. As you can see, I feel very sentimental about you, but you encouraged it by your gift.[51]

War Again: Terror and Trepidation

With Britain's entry into the war, Beaverbrook saw less of Venetia. Putting his isolationism behind him, he plunged into the war effort with his usual energy and began to assume an increasingly important role, not only as a friend and confidant of Churchill but also as the head of a newly created Ministry of Aircraft Production—a post he accepted as a favor to Churchill. At the time, "Hardly anyone then foresaw the turn of events which was to place Beaverbrook among the immortal few who won the battle of Britain."[52] It was his vision that assured the production of the aircraft responsible for defeating the Germans in their effort to bomb Britain into submission.

For Venetia, like all of England, World War II was a sobering and frightening experience. She felt none of the romantic excitement that had characterized her mood in 1914. At the outbreak of World War I, she had been an attractive young woman of twenty-six, the object of a Prime Minister's passion, loved with equal intensity by his brilliant Financial Secretary of the Treasury. The war was a noble adventure, with gallant men from the privileged world in which she lived going off in their dashing uniforms eager to fight for God and the Empire. Such was the idealism of the men who sailed to France and of the women they left behind.

In some cases, as with Venetia and Diana Cooper, the young women volunteered to serve in the hospitals of England and France. But even this, at least at the outset, was motivated more by a romantic notion of helping the boys than by the stark needs of the battlefront. In 1940, no one, especially Venetia, had such illusions. War was hell, and most adults in Britain knew this firsthand. While they faced the war with bravery and determination, they faced it also with trepidation and fear, a fear that arose from experience and a grim respect for Germany's military prowess.

For Venetia, 1914 was light years away from 1939. She was now a woman in her fifties, a widow with a child and no lover in her life. And worst of all, promiscuity, drinking and the wild life she had led, first with the "Corrupt Coterie" and later on her own with Diana and Beaverbrook, had begun to take their toll. Conrad Russell described her in 1940 as part of a "horde of hard-faced tipsy women" who occupied Diana and Duff's suite at the Dorchester from 6:00 P.M. onwards. "Regular habituées were Ann O'Neil, Phyllis de Janzé, Maureen Stanley, Venetia Montagu, Juliet Duff, Moura Budberg, Virginia Cowles and Pamela Berry—some harder-featured and some no doubt tipsier than others."[53]

Duff and Diana's description of Venetia in 1944, on one of her frequent visits to Paris after Duff was made Ambassador to France, confirmed this unflattering picture. Duff wrote that "Venetia Montagu arrived from London to spend a few months and help in some unspecified way with the running of the Embassy—'the witch of Endor,' Diana described her appearance, 'long blue locks, dreadful little hat awry, long blue face, multi-coloured shirts and coats, blue boots: she did look a fright.' She came with alarmist reports of what was being said in London and urged her hostess to be more careful and to occupy herself more conspicuously with ambassadorial good works."[54] As an aside, Diana did not enjoy Venetia's "brief of criticism," but added, "I'm sure Venetia did it for the best, but I suspect the chancery wives here said something to influence her unreliable judgment."[55]

It is interesting that Diana, who for so many years had been so close to Venetia, living for months on end at Breccles, not only described Venetia in such unflattering terms, but described her judgment as "unreliable." The deep attachment the two women had felt for each other had cooled. With the Coopers in Paris totally absorbed in their careers, Venetia did not see them as frequently as before, and their areas of mutual interest became fewer and fewer. Instead of Diana, Venetia began to spend more time with her cousin,

Clementine Churchill. Judith Montagu and Clementine's daughter, Mary, had become good friends and this brought their mothers together more frequently. Clementine, moreover, was often alone, with Winston totally absorbed in his wartime responsibilities, and Venetia, also alone, was good company. The two seemed to enjoy each other and to fill each other's needs.

In 1940, during the London blitz, Mary Churchill was at Breccles. The Churchills insisted she not return to London and as a result she spent many weeks with Venetia and Judith, cementing her friendship with Judith even more strongly. In September 1941, both girls joined the Auxiliary Territorial Service. Mary wrote:

We had become fired with the idea of serving with one of the new "mixed" [men and women] anti-aircraft batteries, which were being formed about this time. Our parents understood our wish to go "a-soldiering" and encouraged us to enlist. So, Judy and I set out on what was, for us a great adventure, our mothers waving us goodbye at Paddington Station. [56]

Mary continued:

While we were first at Aldermaston [the training center near Reading] my mother and Venetia Montagu would come down at the weekends to see their soldier-daughters, bringing vast and delicious picnic luncheons. Judy and I were very nervous lest our mothers should disgrace us by not conforming in the most minute details with the rules and regulations, or by failing to recognize the immense importance in our lives of the Guard Commander. [57]

After basic training, the girls were sent to a huge camp near Oswestory, in Shropshire, to learn the mysteries of antiaircraft instruments. Oswestory was too far for their mothers to visit regularly, but the girls, especially Mary, wrote often of their daily adventures. Life at camp was simple, far different from the comfort and luxury to which they were accustomed.

In 1941, the girls were assigned to a new battery unit at Enfield. Clementine wrote to Winston, who had left for the United States to visit President Roosevelt immediately after Pearl Harbor: "Yesterday Mary's leave came to an end; I took her & Judy in your car & deposited them as night was falling at their new camp near Enfield. In the gathering darkness it looked like a German concentration camp." [58]

No two women, cousins though they were, could have been more different than Clemmie and Venetia in their relationships with their children and husbands. Yet as Venetia grew older she came to appreciate Clementine's character and attitude toward family and marriage and welcomed the opportunity of becoming part of Winston and Clementine's small inner family circle. On Winston's sixty-eighth birthday in 1942, she was one of seven members of the family and closest friends besides Winston and Clementine, and with "the bright gleam of victory"[59] in their grasp the party was especially joyful.

And again, on Winston's seventieth birthday in 1944, with victory even closer, Clementine gave a "glorious dinner party. . . . The guests were Cousin Venetia, Brendan [Bracken] & Max [Beaverbrook] besides the family. . . . Max proposed Papa's health. . . . Papa's reply," Mary Churchill Soames wrote, "made me weep."[60] Although Max was at the party, he had never been a favorite of Clementine's. She openly disliked him and felt he was a bad influence upon Winston. She admired the job he had performed at the Aircraft Production Ministry but did not trust him.[61]

On this subject, as on so many others, Venetia disagreed with Clementine. She liked Beaverbrook, continued her correspondence with him and continued to enjoy his company. On December 18, 1943, she thanked him for a marvelous weekend and wistfully added: "Someone once wrote 'that sorrow's crown of sorrow was remembering happier things.' I've never agreed with this. I find it one of the greatest pleasures to look back on all the *fun*. I've had and with no one have I had more than with you."[62] And on May 10, she wrote that when she was with him she felt she was "still alive."[63]

Beaverbrook, for his part, continued to see Venetia sporadically, between mistresses, travel and politics. He always enjoyed the time they spent together. As busy as he was, he never stopped lavishing presents upon her, which in 1947 included cash that enabled her to buy another cow at Breccles. "Even an unpedigreed . . . breed now costs over £50, so you must congratulate yourself on your well-established herd of Ayrshires," Venetia wrote to Beaverbrook on June 4, 1947. In the same letter she wrote that Judy had enjoyed her journey to Paris very much, "thanks chiefly," to Beaverbrook's help. "It's fun," she wrote wistfully, "seeing the next generation falling under [Paris's] sway and it took me back to 1917."[64]

Cancer

In another letter to Beaverbrook on December 1, 1947, Venetia mentioned the "operation on my neck," the first reference she made to the cancer which had struck her at the end of 1945. She reported that her operation had gone well, that she was healing and "apart from the ugly scar," which she hoped would disappear soon, "she was as good as new." Not only was she facing her illness with confidence, but she had also retained her sense of humor in spite of the tragedy that now hung over her. She wrote of Winston's birthday party: "But on the whole birthday parties should be given by non-family then one can have Tarts and Beauties instead of Nellie, Miss Whyte, Diana Sandys and me! As we used to say in the older days."[65] In truth, Venetia was not "as good as new." Mary Soames, in writing about that same birthday party, reported: "That night we were ten for dinner, all family and faithful friends. Uncle Jack, still looking thin and ill; Venetia Montagu, battered by the course of a mortal illness."[66]

Cancer or no, Venetia was planning to go to Paris to visit Diana and Duff at the Embassy before they left. She was sorry they would be giving up their residence at the British Embassy in Paris. "It will be a great loss to me," she wrote. "I don't know how I shall manage to escape from this prison house [Breccles]. Judy sends you *much* love. She is enjoying herself in London . . . and I think having fun."[67] It was during this visit to Paris that the Duchess of Marlborough took refuge at the Embassy and reported that: "Venetia was far from well (she was in fact dying of cancer, but was wonderfully brave). She was most understanding and able to look at all I said with a dispassionate eye."[68]

Only in the last decade of her life, during the forties, did Venetia spend any significant amount of time with her daughter. This could never make up for the loneliness that marked most of Judith's childhood. A dear friend of Judith's, Patrick Leigh Fermor, recalls that Judith:

wasn't remotely like anyone else. Intelligence and flair and an innate competence at almost everything—except, sometimes, her own interests—

were gifts which, even when she was very young, impressed Prime Ministers, presidential candidates and heads of colleges. She grew up in an active,
sharply faceted world where ability, intellect and wit were prized; and, a
precocious and observant only child, and a lonely one, she absorbed it all
and might have played a vigorous part in the wings of politics, like a
heroine in Disraeli or Trollope. The gifts, inherited and acquired, were
always there; but in any conflict between head and heart, the heart won
every time, and—the mistaken disappointment of elders who looked on
lives as parabolas—her energies took a turning where ambition played no
part. Feelings of early isolation, perhaps, set the companionship of friends,
higher than anything. She loved them and lived for their company. Some
lives must be assessed by the warmth with which friendship is lavished and
returned, and in these rare terms, Judy's was an entire success. Her friendships covered a wide and varied range. They sprang up spontaneously from
affinity or contrast, from the delights of reciprocal stimulus in conversation, from loving warmth and romantic impulse; and all of them, wrapped
in a snowballing mythology of private humour and back-reference, were
fostered by a genius for unpremeditated feasting and fun and improvisation
and a passion for the comic and the odd. In spite of her excellent brain, she
was free of all vanity or arrogance. . . . [S]he was generous and unguarded;
a confident, ungrudging and uncircumspect spirit marked all she did with
headlong zest that was only briefly reined in, now and then, by spells of
depression and languor. She lived at full tilt.[69]

This description could easily have been of Venetia: the intelligence,
the humor, the quest for feasting and fun, the passion for the comic,
the ability to make and hold friends, the instincts that attracted her
to politics, her delight in conversation—and her lack of serious
discipline and ambition. Judy did, however, become a Major in the
Army during World War II, which shows that when she did discipline herself, she could and did succeed.

While Venetia may not have spent much time with Judith, her
daughter not only inherited Venetia's personality and intelligence
but, in the brief time they spent together, saw her mother as a
model. By 1948, Venetia's cancer was very serious. Her courage and
her determination to live a normal life were remarkable. All of her
friends commented on her bravery and fighting spirit. She continued
to plan trips. On January 1, 1948, she wrote to Beaverbrook that
she and Judy were planning to go to South Africa for two months.
Judy, like Venetia, loved to travel, and in the same letter, Venetia
told Beaverbrook that he should not be surprised if Judy "suddenly

turns up in Jamaica as she plans to go to America from South Africa. As I believe the lines goes [sic] by your enchanted isle. Much love and wishes for 1948."[70]

By June 30, 1948, the illness was moving into its final stages, but Venetia was still fighting. She was traveling a little and trying to keep her spirits up by writing and seeing friends. She wrote:

Darling Max,

I see from the *Express* you are back which is very nice news. I have to come to London next Monday for two days and if there is a chance of seeing you, I would very much like it. Either London or Cherkeley whichever suited you. . . . I'm hoping to go to Chantilly to stay with Diana . . . but am not quite sure if I will be able to.

> Much love and longing to see you
> Venetia[71]

Venetia was not able to visit Diana. Instead, Diana visited her at Breccles sometime in July 1948. By then, the doctors had given Venetia only a few weeks to live.[72] Diana wrote that she visited Breccles—a favorite resort for fifteen years, a "place of comfort, beauty, gaiety, shoots, fireworks, picnics and rest. This last visit was like an old woman looking in a glass and seeing her youth's radiance. Very agonizing."[73]

The days were agonizing for Venetia, too. The pain was excruciating. She wrote to Beaverbrook for the last time on July 12, 1948:

My darling,

I was so touched at your ringing me up but maddened that the badness of the line prevented any conversation. As you know, I long to come and see you but just at this moment I've struck a bad patch. This infernal disease has got its teeth into me and the cures for it, such as deep x-ray have the effect of making me feel and be very sick. But luckily, this body is adaptable and this will wear off. (Sez they) In the meantime, I have a nurse to give me lots of morphine at regular intervals so I really don't feel too bad. As soon as I've got over this particular phase I shall hasten to your side, but just now I'm not really fit for anything. . . . Did you buy the aeroplane and fix yourself up with a wonderful crew of three who were really six?

> I long to see you
> Much love, Venetia[74]

She did not see him again. She died on August 3, 1948. In a last act of rebellion against organized religion, she left instructions that her body be cremated (a ceremony not acceptable in the Jewish faith and over which no rabbi can preside) and asked that Judith place her ashes on Edwin's grave. This was done. Thus, in death, she was closer to Edwin than ever she was in life.

Epilogue: The Cycle Is Complete: The End

In 1962, fourteen years after Venetia's death, Judith, at the age of thirty-nine, married Milton Gendel, an art historian who lived in Rome. She fell in love with her adopted city and, unlike Venetia, had nine years of married happiness and joy with Milton. They had a wonderful daughter, Anna, born in January 1963, upon whom Judith lavished all the affection and attention that she was denied in her childhood. Anna became a schoolteacher in London.

Like Edwin, Judith died very young, at the age of forty-eight, of a blood clot, in 1972. Her daughter, Anna, was only nine years old. Judith's friend, Patrick Leigh Fermor concluded:

These Poussin landscapes were a permanent background after her happy marriage to the art-historian, Milton Gendel. Romanesque churches, ruins in mountain villages in Upper Latium, in the Sabine Hills and the Campagna became the goals of exciting hunts for little-known frescoes and abstruse stylistic data: quests that gave rise to picnics by remote sylvan basilicas or crumbling Orsini castles; all the more joyful later on, thanks to their captivating little daughter Anna. (No solitude or isolation here!) Such days ended with after-dinner talk and laughter under the cross-vaults of their house on the Tiber Island above the Fabrician Bridge, and they often lasted till the Tiber was yellow with the Roman dawn, for she hated things to break up.

We know that candles burning at both ends, unlike more careful tapers, may not last the night. But, after the momentary shadows of dismay and loss, the memory of Judy's warm-hearted, spirited, and generous vitality shines brighter than a Christmas tree.[1]

Judith was very much the child of Venetia, and while the Gendel house on the Tiber was not Breccles, the spirits of Edwin and Venetia would have felt very much at home. Thus the cycle of life continues—in its strange and mysterious ways.

Appendix:
The Genealogy of
Edwin S. Montagu

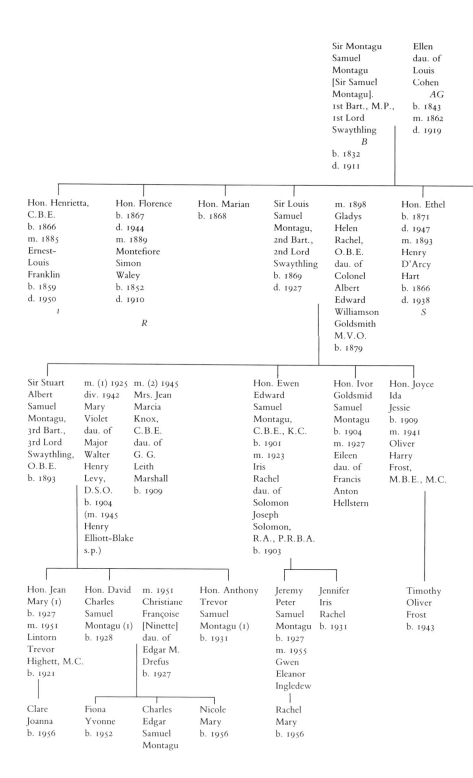

Sir Montagu Samuel Montagu [Sir Samuel Montagu]. 1st Bart., M.P., 1st Lord Swaything B b. 1832 d. 1911

Ellen dau. of Louis Cohen AG b. 1843 m. 1862 d. 1919

Hon. Henrietta, C.B.E. b. 1866 m. 1885 Ernest-Louis Franklin b. 1859 d. 1950 1

Hon. Florence b. 1867 d. 1944 m. 1889 Montefiore Simon Waley b. 1852 d. 1910 R

Hon. Marian b. 1868

Sir Louis Samuel Montagu, 2nd Bart., 2nd Lord Swaything b. 1869 d. 1927

m. 1898 Gladys Helen Rachel, O.B.E. dau. of Colonel Albert Edward Williamson Goldsmith M.V.O. b. 1879

Hon. Ethel b. 1871 d. 1947 m. 1893 Henry D'Arcy Hart b. 1866 d. 1938 S

Sir Stuart Albert Samuel Montagu, 3rd Bart., 3rd Lord Swaything, O.B.E. b. 1893

m. (1) 1925 div. 1942 Mary Violet dau. of Major Walter Henry Levy, D.S.O. b. 1904 (m. 1945 Henry Elliott-Blake s.p.)

m. (2) 1945 Mrs. Jean Marcia Knox, C.B.E. dau. of G. G. Leith Marshall b. 1909

Hon. Ewen Edward Samuel Montagu, C.B.E., K.C. b. 1901 m. 1923 Iris Rachel dau. of Solomon Joseph Solomon, R.A., P.R.B.A. b. 1903

Hon. Ivor Goldsmid Samuel Montagu b. 1904 m. 1927 Eileen dau. of Francis Anton Hellstern

Hon. Joyce Ida Jessie b. 1909 m. 1941 Oliver Harry Frost, M.B.E., M.C.

Hon. Jean Mary (1) b. 1927 m. 1951 Lintorn Trevor Highett, M.C. b. 1921

Hon. David Charles Samuel Montagu (1) b. 1928

m. 1951 Christiane Françoise [Ninette] dau. of Edgar M. Drefus b. 1927

Hon. Anthony Trevor Samuel Montagu (1) b. 1931

Jeremy Peter Samuel Montagu b. 1927 m. 1955 Gwen Eleanor Ingledew

Jennifer Iris Rachel b. 1931

Timothy Oliver Frost b. 1943

Clare Joanna b. 1956

Fiona Yvonne b. 1952

Charles Edgar Samuel Montagu

Nicole Mary b. 1956

Rachel Mary b. 1956

Hon. Lilian Helen, C.B.E. b. 1873 d. 1963	Ruth Frances b. 1875 d. 1877	Hon. Elsie b. 1877 m. 1905 Reginald Abraham Simmons Myer b. 1879 *T* d. 1964	Rt. Hon. Edwin Samuel Montagu, P.C., M.P. b. 1879 d. 1924 m. 1915 Hon. Beatrice Venetia [Stanley] dau. of 4th Lord Sheffield d. 1948	Hon. Gerald Samuel Montagu b. 1880 d. 1956 m. 1909 Florence [Firenza] dau. of Percy Manuel Castello *AO*	Hon. Lionel Samuel Montagu, D.S.O. b. 1883 d. 1948 m. 1944 Mrs. Sybil Stanley dau. of Major Heathfield Butler Dodgson, D.S.O.

Judith Venetia b. 1923 d. 1972 m. 1962 Milton Gendel	Ina Miriam b. 1913 m. 1937 Alexander Poliakoff b. 1910	Bryan de Castro Samuel Montagu b. 1916 m. 1950 Elcie dau. of Johann Weiser b. 1926

Anna b. 1963

Martyn Poliakoff b. 1947	Stephen Poliakoff b. 1952	Lucinda Jane b. 1957	Robert de Castro Samuel Montagu (adopted) b. 1956

Manuscript Sources
and Abbreviations

The compilation of letters between H. H. Asquith and Venetia Stanley, edited by Michael Brock and Eleanor Brock, is the principal source of the Asquith letters used in this book. It is cited as Brock and Brock, *H. H. Asquith Letters to Venetia Stanley*. Only when a letter does not appear in this compilation is the original source cited. The following abbreviations have been used:

AS., MSS.	The Asquith Letters, Bodleian Library, Oxford
M.G.	The letters, manuscripts and other material in the possession of Milton Gendel, husband of the late Judith Montagu Gendel, at his home in Rome, Italy
Montagu F	Material at the India Office, Library and Records, London
Montagu AS	Material in University Library, Cambridge
Parl. Deb.	*Parliamentary Debates*
Cab. Papers	Public Records Office, Cabinet Papers
Margot Asquith, Diaries, Bonham Carter, MSS.	Bonham Carter papers in the possession of Lord Bonham Carter
Lloyd George MSS.	Manuscripts in the Bodleian Library, Oxford
Phillip Sassoon MSS.	Manuscripts at the India Office, Library and Records, London

Notes

1. The *New York Times,* Book Review section, p. 1, Mar. 15, 1987.

1. Roy Jenkins, *Asquith: Portrait of a Man and an Era* (New York, 1964), p. 360.
2. *Dictionary of National Biography (1922–1930),* ed. J. R. H. Weaver (Oxford, 1961).
3. *The Sunday Times,* London, Nov. 16, 1924.
4. Lord Beaverbrook, *Politicians and the War* (London, 1924), p. 66.
5. Id.
6. Proceedings of the Chamber of Princes, Nov. 17, 1924, reprinted in *Edwin S. Montagu,* a compilation of tributes to Montagu printed by his sister Lily H. Montagu at the time of his death. It is among the papers retained by his granddaughter Anna Gendel. See also *Evening News of India,* Summary of Tributes to Montagu, Nov. 18, 1924.
7. The statue in Calcutta was done by Lady Kennet. See Lady Kennet (Lady Scott), *Self-Portrait of an Artist* (London, 1924), p. 254; consists of the diaries of Lady Scott, later Lady Kennet, for the years 1913 onward. The statue in Jamnagar was done by E. Riccardi. See *Dictionary of National Biography* (1922–1930), p. 610.
8. The *Times of India,* Dec. 1, 1924.
9. Henry Fairlie, "Among the Anti-Semites," *The New Republic,* June 8, 1987, p. 24.
10. Id.
11. Cecil Roth, *A History of the Jews in England* (Oxford, 1941); V. D. Lipman, *Social History of the Jews in England, 1850–1950* (London, 1954); V. D. Lipman, *Three Centuries of Anglo-Jewish History* (London, 1961); Israel Finestein, *A Short History of Anglo-Jewry* (World Jewish Congress, London, 1957); Stephen Aris, *The Jews in Business* (London, 1970). See also Samuel Almog, *Patterns of Prejudice,* "Anti-Semitism as a Dynamic Phenomenon: The 'Jewish Question' in England at the End of the First World War," vol. 21, no. 4, 1987, p. 3; and Eugene Black, *The Social Politics of Anglo-Jewry 1880–1920* (Oxford and New York, 1988). For a recent example of the willingness of the British to give their

highest honors to Jews, see the *New York Times,* Dec. 31, 1987, p. A4, which reports that the Chief Rabbi in England, Immanuel Jacobovits, was delegated to the Peerage and now sits in the House of Lords with the Bishops of the Church of England and the representatives of the aristocracy.

1. The Beginning

1. Chaim Bermant, *The Cousinhood* (New York, 1971).
2. Ibid., pp. 39–58.
3. Ivor Montagu, *The Youngest Son* (London, 1970), p. 25.
4. Id.
5. Lily H. Montagu, *Samuel Montagu: First Baron Swaythling* (London, 1911), p. 83.
6. Id.
7. *Gardener's Magazine,* Nov. 19, 1889. After Edwin's mother's death in 1919, the estate in South Stoneham was sold to Southampton University.
8. Id.
9. Montagu, *The Youngest Son,* pp. 41–42.
10. *Bayswater Chronicle,* Oct. 1885.
11. *Ladies' Pictorial,* Oct. 8, 1885. See also *Ladies' Pictorial,* Feb. 24, 1887, for a description of a fancy costume ball given by the Montagus for 400 guests.
12. Montagu, *The Youngest Son,* p. 17.
13. Roth, *A History of the Jews in England,* pp. 162–66. Dr. Roth, in "The Resettlement of Jews in England" in *Three Centuries of Anglo-Jewish History* (Cambridge, England, 1961) reports on a document he uncovered dated March 25, 1656, delivered by Cromwell to the Council of State in June 1656. Roth has new evidence that the Council authorized "Jewish public worship in England, after a lapse of 366 years . . . on Wednesday, 25 June 1656," ibid., p. 15. The minutes for that day's proceedings are missing and Roth's conclusion is based on circumstantial evidence. Not until Aug. 22, 1664, does any written permission exist for Jews to settle in England and enjoy freedom of worship. See note 14 below.
14. This historic "assurance" by the King (Charles II) was given on Aug. 22, 1664. It was the result of an effort by a Mr. Rycaut to warn the Jews that if they held services in their synagogues they were violating the Conventicle Act, which prohibited "assemblies for prayer except in accordance with liturgy of the Church of England" (Roth, *A History of the Jews in England,* p. 170). The Jews petitioned the King, who referred their request to the Privy Council, which gave the Jews a written assurance that "no instructions had been given for disturbing them and they might 'promise themselves the effects of the same favour as formerly they had, soe long as they demeane themselves peaceably & quietly with due obedience to Majesties Lawes & without scandall to his Government.' Thus the residence of the Jews in England was authorized, for the first time, in writing" (ibid., p. 171).
15. Ibid., p. 184.

16. Id.
17. Aris, *The Jews in Business*, pp. 30–52.
18. Lipman, *Social History of the Jews in England*, p. 23.
19. Bermant, *The Cousinhood*, p. 199.
20. Ibid., pp. 199–200.
21. Ronald J. Hart D'Arcy, *The Samuel Family of Liverpool and London* (London, 1958), p. 82.
22. Montagu was the Anglicization of the name Moses.
23. Montagu, *The Youngest Son*, p. 18.
24. Bermant, *The Cousinhood*, p. 200.
25. An account of the development of Samuel Montagu & Co. by S. E. Franklin and Walter L. de'Arcy Hart reports that "every letter and every check had to be signed by the partners." Montagu and Ellis Franklin, his brother-in-law and partner, were such gluttons for work that they lived over the offices on Leadenhall St., to make certain they were never far from work. See letter to author, June 19, 1990, from R. W. Quinn, Samuel Montagu & Co. Ltd.
26. Aris, *The Jews in Business*, p. 70.
27. Id.
28. *Bankers' Magazine*, Sept. 1885.
29. Id.
30. Bermant, *The Cousinhood*, pp. 199–215.
31. Montagu, *The Youngest Son*, p. 25.
32. Bermant, *The Cousinhood*, p. 203.
33. *Eastern Post*, editorial, Feb. 14, 1885.
34. *Topical Times*, Nov. 21, 1885.
35. *East London Observer*, Feb. 7, 1885.
36. *London Figaro*, Mar. 7, 1885.
37. *Eastern Post*, Feb. 14, 1885.
38. *Jewish World*, July 9, 1886, and the *Jewish Chronicle*, July 16, 1886.
39. Bermant, *The Cousinhood*, p. 204.
40. Ibid., pp. 202–203.
41. Montagu, *Samuel Montagu*, pp. 72–73.
42. Ibid., p. 77.
43. Ibid., pp. 78–79.
44. Bermant, *The Cousinhood*, p. 202.
45. Ibid., p. 205.
46. *Jewish Chronicle*, Aug. 20, 1886.
47. Bermant, *The Cousinhood*, p. 201.
48. Ellen Umansky, *Lily Montagu: Sermons, Addresses, Letters, Prayers* (New York and Toronto, 1984), Introduction. In the terminology of Anglo-Jewry, Liberal Judaism is frequently referred to as the Far Left, with the ultra-orthodox as the Far Right. See Stephen Brook, *The Club: The Jews of Modern Britain* (London, 1989), pp. 41, 122, 123, 124, 126–29, 141. Mr. Brook describes English Liberal Judaism as "an offshoot of Reform and the closest thing in Judaism to Unitarianism" (ibid., p. 118). It stresses "individual conscience rather than obedience

to a set of rules. . . . The involvement of Liberal Jews in all the social welfare issues of the '20s and '30s was phenomenal, given their small numbers." (Ibid., p. 130). Doing good deeds was the primary expression of their Judaism.

49. Montagu, *The Youngest Son,* pp. 18, 19.
50. Montagu, *Samuel Montagu,* pp. 48, 54.
51. Aris, *The Jews in Business,* p. 51.
52. Sir David Waley, *Edwin Montagu* (New York and Bombay, 1964) p. 5. See also Bermant, *The Cousinhood,* p. 250.
53. Waley, *Edwin Montagu,* p. 48, fn. 7.
54. Id.

2. Childhood and Early Education

1. Isabel Colgate, *The Shooting Party* (London, 1980).
2. Lipman, *Social History of the Jews in England,* pp. 134–63.
3. Edwin Montagu, letter to his mother, 1881; Montagu AS 5/8/3.
4. Waley, *Edwin Montagu,* p. 4.
5. Ibid., p. 5; Montagu AS 5/8/7.
6. Report Card from Doreck College, Nov. 1, 1889; Montagu AS 5/5/5.
7. Ibid.
8. Report Card from Doreck College, June 6, 1890; Montagu AS 5/4/4.
9. Edwin Montagu, letters to his mother, Feb. 24, 1890; Dec. 31, 1890; Montagu AS 5/8/18.
10. Edwin Montagu, letter to his mother, sometime in 1890; Montagu AS 5/8/18.
11. Waley, *Edwin Montagu,* p. 5.
12. Edwin Montagu, letter to his mother, May 1891; Montagu AS 5/5/15.
13. Id.
14. Edwin Montagu, letter to his mother, May 31, 1891; Montagu AS 5/8/32.
15. Edwin Montagu, letter to his mother, June 9, 1891; Montagu AS 5/2/32.
16. Id.
17. Id.
18. Waley, *Edwin Montagu,* p. 5.
19. Edwin Montagu, letter to his mother, May 3, 1891; Montagu AS 5/2/34.
20. Id.
21. Waley, *Edwin Montagu,* p. 5.
22. Edwin Montagu, letter to his mother, Aug. 11, 1891; Montagu AS 5/5/23.
23. Edwin Montagu, letter to his mother, Oct. 28, 1891; Montagu AS 5/2/80.
24. Bermant, *The Cousinhood,* pp. 208–15.
25. Edwin Montagu, letter to his mother, Dec. 1, 1891; Montagu AS 5/2/25.
26. Edwin Montagu, letter to his mother, Apr. 1, 1892; Montagu AS 5/2/11.
27. Mr. Israel, letters to Mrs. Samuel Montagu: Dec. 29, 1891, Montagu AS 5/2/28; Jan. 16, 1892, Montagu AS 5/2/29.
28. Mr. Israel, letter to Mrs. Samuel Montagu, Dec. 1, 1891; Montagu AS 5/2/25.
29. Mr. Israel, letter to Mrs. Samuel Montagu, Dec. 29, 1891; Montagu AS 5/2/28.
30. Mr. Israel, letter to Mrs. Samuel Montagu, Apr. 1, 1892; Montagu AS 5/2/11.

31. Mr. Israel, letter to Mrs. Samuel Montagu, Feb. 6, 1892; Montagu AS 5/2/22.

32. Mr. Israel, letter to Mrs. Samuel Montagu, Apr. 11, 1892; Montagu AS 5/2/9. The Seder is the traditional Jewish service recited at the Passover dinner.

33. Samuel Raphael Hirsch, *Horeb: A Philosophy of Jewish Laws and Observances* (London, 1962), vol. 1, pp. 175–80.

34. Mr. Israel, letter to Mrs. Samuel Montagu, Feb. 6, 1892; Montagu AS 5/2/22.

35. Edwin Montagu, letter to his mother, Dec. 20, 1891; Montagu AS 5/2/26.

36. Edwin Montagu, letter to his mother, Apr. 1, 1892; Montagu AS 5/2/11.

37. Edwin Montagu, letter to his mother, Apr. 7, 1892; Montagu AS 5/2/10.

38. Id.

39. Id.

40. Edwin Montagu, letter to his mother, May 23, 1892; Montagu AS 5/2/2.

41. Edwin Montagu, letter to his mother, June 19, 1892; Montagu AS 5/8/24.

42. Edwin Montagu, letter to his mother, June or July, 1892; Montagu AS 5/2/5.

43. Edwin Montagu, letter to his mother, July 11, 1892; Montagu AS 5/8/25.

44. Report Card from Clifton College, Oct. 1892; Montagu AS 5/2/6.

45. Edwin Montagu, letter to his mother, Oct. 20, 1892; Montagu AS 5/8/27.

46. Edwin Montagu, letter to his mother, Sept. 14, 1893; Montagu AS 5/7/3.

47. *Cambridge Independent Press,* Nov. 21, 1924.

48. Id.

49. Id.

50. Edwin Montagu, letter to his mother, Aug. 5, 1897; Montagu AS 5/5/73.

51. Edwin Montagu, letter to his mother, Aug. 6, 1897; Montagu AS 5/5/86.

52. Edwin Montagu, letter to his mother, Nov. 7, 1897; Montagu AS 5/5/98.

53. Edwin Montagu, letter to his mother, Nov. 4, 1897; Montagu AS 5/5/97.

54. Edwin Montagu, letter to his mother, Dec. 20, 1896; Montagu AS 5/5/64.

55. Edwin Montagu, letter to his mother, Jan. 2, 1897; Montagu AS 5/3/6.

56. Edwin Montagu, letter to his mother, Aug. 2, 1898; Montagu AS 5/8/71.

57. Edwin Montagu, letter to his father, July 30, 1896; Montagu AS 5/5/60.

58. Id.

59. Edwin Montagu, letter to his mother, Aug. 4, 1897; Montagu AS 5/5/70.

60. Ibid.

61. Edwin Montagu, letter to his mother, Nov. 2, 1897; Montagu AS 5/3/10.

3. Cambridge and the Beginning of a Political Career

1. *Cambridge Independent Press,* story of Edwin Montagu and Cambridge, Nov. 21, 1924; reprinted in *Edwin S. Montagu,* compilation of tributes on his death, printed by Lily H. Montagu (London 1924).

2. Samuel Montagu, letter to Edwin Montagu, Oct. 23, 1898; M.G.

3. Edwin Montagu, letter to his father, Nov. 11, 1898; M.G. See also Montagu AS 5/3/18.

4. Samuel Montagu, letter to Edwin Montagu, Nov. 18, 1898; M.G. See also Montagu, AS 5/3/19.

5. Id.

6. Id.

7. Edwin Montagu, letter to mother, Mar. 18, 1900; Montagu AS 5/5/133.

8. Edwin Montagu, letter to his mother, Mar. 19, 1900; Montagu AS 5/5/134.

9. Edwin Montagu, letter to father, Oct. 14, 1902; Montagu AS 5/4/54.

10. Bill for room and board from Cambridge, dated Mar. 25, 1901; Montagu AS 5/8/123.

11. Edwin Montagu, letter to his mother, Mar. 3, 1899; Montagu AS 5/5/105.

12. Edwin Montagu, letter to his mother, Oct. 19, 1899, Montagu AS 5/3/22.

13. Edwin Montagu, letter to his mother, Nov. 1, 1899; Montagu AS 5/7/113.

14. Edwin Montagu, letter to his mother, June 17, 1899; Montagu AS 3/5/110.

15. Edwin Montagu, letter to his mother, June 10, 1900; Montagu AS 5/5/143.

16. Edwin Montagu, letter to his mother, Mar. 19, 1900; Montagu AS 5/5/136.

17. Edwin Montagu, letter to his mother, May 6, 1900; Montagu AS 5/5/139.

18. Edwin Montagu, letter to his mother, Feb. 6, 1901; Montagu AS 5/3/32.

19. Edwin Montagu, letter to his mother, Jan. 14, 1900; Montagu AS 5/5/121.

20. Edwin Montagu, letter to his mother, Feb. 6, 1901; Montagu AS 5/3/32.

21. Edwin Montagu, letter to his mother, Jan. 29, 1899; Montagu AS 5/7/88.

22. Edwin Montagu, letter to his mother, Dec. 12, 1898, Montagu AS 5/8/83.

23. Edwin Montagu, letter to his mother, Dec. 19, 1899; Montagu AS 5/8/119.

24. Edwin Montagu, letter to his mother, Jan. 7, 1900; M.G.

25. Edwin Montagu, letter to his mother, Aug. 10, 1900; Montagu AS 5/3/26.

26. Edwin Montagu, letter to his mother, Aug. 13, 1900; Montagu AS 5/3/27.

27. Edwin Montagu, letter to his mother, Aug. 19, 1900; Montagu AS 5/3/28.

28. *Cambridge Independent Press,* Nov. 21, 1924.

29. Id.

30. Id.

31. Id.

32. Edwin Montagu, letter to his mother, Oct. 19, 1899; Montagu AS 5/3/22.

33. *Cambridge Independent Press,* Nov. 21, 1924.

34. Id.

35. Id.

36. Id.

37. Robert Skidelsky, *John Maynard Keynes, 1889–1920* (New York, 1986), pp. 113–14.

38. Edwin Montagu, letter to his mother, June 10, 1900; Montagu AS 5/5/143.

39. Edwin Montagu, letter to his mother, Dec. 26, 1900; M.G.

40. Id.

41. Edwin Montagu, letter to his mother, Oct. 2, 1900; M.G.

42. Montagu, *The Youngest Son,* p. 25.

43. *Cambridge Independent Press,* Nov. 21, 1924.

44. Id.

45. Edwin Montagu, letter to his mother, Nov. or Dec. 1901; M.G.

46. Sir Lawrence Jones, *An Edwardian Youth* (New York, 1956), pp. 3–4.

47. Ibid., p. 3.

48. Duff Cooper, *Old Men Forget* (London, 1955), p. 40.

49. Edwin Montagu, letter to his father, June 13, 1902; Montagu AS 5/4/59.

50. Id.
51. Waley, *Edwin Montagu*, pp. 11–12.
52. Edwin Montagu, letter to his mother, Apr. 1902; Waley, *Edwin Montagu*, p. 11.
53. *Cambridge Independent News,* Nov. 21, 1924.
54. Waley, *Edwin Montagu*, p. 12.
55. Edwin S. Montagu and Auberon (Bron) Herbert, *Canada and the Empire* (London, 1904). See also letter in *London Times,* Apr. 26, 1904, p. 2, col. 6, summarizing the findings of this book. Herbert later became Lord Lucas; appointed President of the Ministry of Agriculture in 1914; died at 40 years of age while serving with the R.A.F. in 1916.
56. Id.
57. Edwin Montagu, letter to his father, July 3, 1904; Montagu AS 5/4/30.
58. Edwin Montagu, letter to his mother, Dec. 1904; Waley, *Edwin Montagu*, pp. 13–14.
59. Edwin Montagu, letter to his father, June 14, 1905; M.G.
60. Id.
61. Edwin Montagu, letter to his father, Nov. 2, 1905; M.G., Montagu AS 5/8/161.
62. An authority on the process for selecting candidates for Parliament in England during the late nineteenth and early twentieth centuries, Austin Ronney (*Pathways to Parliament,* Madison, Wis., 1963) makes the observation that one of the aspects of English government that surprises Americans most is the small amount of rivalry that took place for nomination to Parliament, unlike the party nominations for the U.S. Congress, which were often bitterly contested. The reasons given for this are: 1) that constituents were free from strong personal preferences as to individual candidates because of the relative insignificance of the individual M.P., unless he happened to be a minister or senior opposition "front Bencher," 2) that there were a limited number of candidates who were wealthy and desirous of election, 3) the selection process itself minimized sharp conflict. Liberal selection tended to take the form of competitive public speaking before the constituency's Liberal Committee, when the selection was contested. If there was no contest, a good speaker who knew the area and was "a local" (i.e., someone from the neighborhood or whose family had strong and historic ties to the area) generally had no problem in being chosen. David E. Butler and Jennie Freeman, *British Political Facts 1900–1960* (London, 1963); Lawrence Lowell, *The Government of England,* vols. 1 and 2 (London, 1914), p. 46.
63. *Cambridge Independent Press,* Nov. 21, 1924.
64. Id.
65. Id.
66. Edwin Montagu, letter to his mother, Dec. 9, 1905; M.G.
67. Edwin Montagu, letter to his mother, Dec. 14 and 23, 1905; M.G.
68. Edwin Montagu, letter to his mother, Dec. 19, 1899; Montagu AS. 5/8/119
69. Skidelsky, *John Maynard Keynes,* p. 166.

4. The Liberal Party and the Landslide of 1906

1. Finestein, *A Short History of Anglo-Jewry*, pp. 157–58; Geoffrey Adlerman, *The Jewish Community in British Politics* (Oxford, 1983) pp. 1–14. The "Tories" were also called "Unionists" until 1922 and "Conservatives" (Paul Adelman, *The Decline of the Liberal Party, 1910–1931*, Essex, England, 1981, Foreword, p. x).

2. Alderman, *The Jewish Community in British Politics*, p. 42. See also Chris Cook, *A Short History of the Liberal Party, 1900–1976* (New York, 1976), pp. 20–21.

3. Herbert Samuel, *Liberalism* (London, 1902), p. 4.

4. Ibid., p. 31.

5. Cook, *A Short History of the Liberal Party, 1900–1976*, p. 4.

6. Ibid., p. 24. See also Sir Robert Ensor, *The Oxford History of England, 1870–1914* (Oxford, 1936), p. 207.

7. H. V. Emy, *Liberals, Radicals and Social Politics 1892–1914* (Cambridge, 1973), p. 26, 90.

8. Ensor, *The Oxford History of England, 1870–1914*, p. 513.

9. The *Clarion*, open letter by Robert Blatchford, 1893, subsequently published in *Merrie England* (London, 1894); see W. T. Rodgers and Bernard Donoughue, *The People into Parliament* (New York, 1966), p. 45.

10. Robert Rhodes James, *The British Revolution, 1880–1939* (New York, 1977), p. 223.

5. Asquith before 1906

1. Roy Jenkins, *Asquith: Portrait of a Man and an Era* (New York and London, 1964), p. 17.

2. Id.

3. Id.

4. Ibid., p. 18.

5. Id.

6. Ibid., p. 23.

7. Ibid., p. 25.

8. Haldane was elected from the East Lothian, Haddington Division, in 1885.

9. Asquith ran for Parliament for East Fife in northern Scotland in 1886. He held this seat consecutively until 1919.

10. Jenkins, *Asquith*, p. 45.

11. Ibid., p. 74.

12. Angela Lambert, *Unquiet Souls* (London, 1984), p. 21.

13. Ibid., p. 17.

14. Michael Brock and Eleanor Brock, *H. H. Asquith Letters to Venetia Stanley* (Oxford, 1982), p. 9.

15. Jenkins, *Asquith*, p. 63.

16. Ibid., p. 64.

17. Ensor, *The Oxford History of England, 1870–1914*, p. 201.

18. Colin Cross, *The Liberals in Power, 1905–1914*, (London, 1936), p. 37.

19. Id.
20. Jenkins, *Asquith,* p. 42.
21. Stephen Koss, *Asquith* (London, 1976), p. 15.
22. Jenkins, *Asquith,* p. 119.
23. *The Times* (London), Jan. 27, 1906, p. 8.
24. *The Times* (London), Feb. 19, 1906, p. 6, col. 5; *Pall Mall Gazette,* London, Feb. 19, 1906, p. 15.
25. *The Times* (London), Feb. 22, 1906.

6. Parliamentary Private Secretary to the Chancellor of the Exchequer

1. Waley, *Edwin Montagu,* pp. 20–21.
2. The *Daily Mail,* July 27, 1910. This description was printed when Montagu delivered his first Indian Budget Speech.
3. Id.
4. Id.
5. Edwin Montagu, letter to Asquith, Jan. 1907; Montagu AS 1/7/1.
6. Id.
7. Id.
8. Id.
9. Id.
10. Id.
11. Id.
12. Jenkins, *Asquith,* p. 269.
13. Waley, *Edwin Montagu,* p. 22.
14. Ibid., pp. 22–23.
15. Ibid., p. 29.
16. Philip Snowden, *An Autobiography,* vol. 1 (London, 1934), pp. 177–88.
17. Peter de Mendelssohn, *The Age of Churchill, 1874–1911* (New York, 1961), p. 383.
18. Jenkins, *Asquith,* p. 165.
19. Id.
20. Ibid., pp. 166, 167. The pension program adopted in 1908 was "to modern ears . . . cautious and meagre" (ibid., p. 167). It provided for "a non-contributory pension of 5s. a week at seventy for those whose total income did not exceed 10s. a week and who had not disqualified themselves by being criminals or lunatics or (within the previous year) paupers; married couples were to receive 8s. 9d." (id.). In spite of the modest allocations of this plan, Rosebery thought it "so prodigal of expenditure as likely to undermine the whole fabric of the Empire" (id.).
21. Wilhelm Hasbach, *History of the English Agricultural Labourer* (London, 1908), pp. 277–85.
22. Id.
23. Edwin Montagu, letter to Lord Londonderry, Mar. 19, 1907; Montagu AS 1/6/6.
24. Edwin Montagu, letter to Lord Rosebery, Mar. 27, 1907; Montagu AS 1/6/81.

25. Id.
26. Id.
27. Id.
28. *Cambridge Independent Press,* Apr. 26, 1907; Montagu AS 3/7/13.
29. Id.
30. Montagu, *The Youngest Son,* p. 142.
31. Edwin Montagu, Letter to Asquith, Feb. 4, 1908; Montagu AS 1/7/2.
32. Id.
33. Vaughn Nash, letter to Edwin Montagu, Apr. 12, 1908; Montagu AS 1/6/60.
34. Margot Asquith Diaries, Nov. 13, 1911, pp. 172–74; Bonham Carter MSS.
35. Edwin Montagu, letter to Asquith, Apr. 7, 1908; Montagu AS 1/7/10.
36. Waley, *Edwin Montagu,* p. 23.
37. Ibid., p. 31.
38. Ibid., p. 23.
39. Ibid., p. 24.
40. Ibid., p. 25.
41. Id.
42. Ibid., p. 36.
43. Edwin Montagu, letter to his mother, Sept. 20, 1908; Montagu AS 5/6/6.
44. Waley, *Edwin Montagu,* p. 36.
45. Ibid., p. 31.

7. Venetia and the Beginning of a Romance

1. Sir Harold Acton, *More Memoirs of an Aesthete* (London, 1970), p. 35.
2. A. J. P. Taylor, *Beaverbrook* (New York, 1972), p. 178.
3. Philip Ziegler, *Diana Cooper* (London, 1981), p. 58.
4. Raymond Asquith, letter to Diana Cooper, Dec. 18, 1915; M.G.
5. Norman Hignett, "The Stanleys of Alderley," *Cheshire Life* (July 1936), pp. 6–10.
6. Id.
7. Id.
8. Id.
9. Id.
10. See Nancy Mitford, *The Ladies of Alderley* (London, 1968), which consists of letters between Maria Joseph and her daughter-in-law Henrietta Maria during the years 1841–50 and demonstrates the unusual intelligence and strength of the Stanley women even in those early days.
11. Jones, *An Edwardian Youth,* p. 215.
12. Mitford, *The Ladies of Alderley,* Preface, p. xiv. Kate's short life has been lovingly recorded in the *Amberly Papers* by her son Bertrand Russell.
13. Bertrand Russell, *Autobiography* (Boston, 1967), p. 35. See also Brock, *H. H. Asquith Letters to Venetia Stanley,* p. 4.
14. Id.
15. Jones, *An Edwardian Youth,* p. 215. It is rumored within the family that Margaret had a love affair with the 12th Earl of Carlisle (George Howard who

married Venetia's Aunt Rosalind) and that Venetia was the child of that romance. If that is true, Venetia's predilection for extramarital relations came naturally (conversations between the author and G. A. Pitt Rivers, June 18, 1990).

16. Ibid., p. 214.
17. Ibid., pp. 214–15.
18. Id.
19. Ibid., p. 216.
20. Adelaide Stanley Lubbock, *People in Glass Houses* (Melbourne, 1977), p. 13.
21. Ibid., p. 12
22. Jones, *An Edwardian Youth*, p. 214.
23. Brock, *H. H. Asquith Letters to Venetia Stanley*, p. 4.
24. Ziegler, *Diana Cooper*, p. 58.
25. Brock, *H. H. Asquith Letters to Venetia Stanley*, p. 4.
26. Artemis Cooper, *A Durable Fire* (New York, 1984), p. xv.
27. Venetia Stanley, letter to Edwin Montagu, May 2, 1915; M.G.
28. Venetia Stanley, letter to Edwin Montagu, June 30, 1915; M.G.
29. Jones, *An Edwardian Youth*, p. 216.
30. Id.
31. Brock, *H. H. Asquith Letters to Venetia Stanley*, p. 1.
32. Mary Soames, *Clementine Churchill* (Boston, 1979), p. 118.
33. Brock, *H. H. Asquith Letters to Venetia Stanley*, pp. 470–71, chapter of Asquith's autobiography #342, Mar. 1915.
34. Ibid., p. 1. Lillian Tennant was a daughter of one of Margot's cousins. Ibid., p. 16 n. 3.
35. Ibid., p. 307, letter #201, Nov. 3, 1914.
36. Edwin Montagu, letter to Venetia Stanley, Dec. 21, 1909; M.G.
37. Venetia Stanley, letter to Edwin Montagu, Dec. 23, 1909; M.G.
38. Edwin Montagu, letter to Venetia Stanley, Jan. 25, 1910; M.G.
39. Id.
40. Venetia Stanley, letter to Edwin Montagu, Feb. 1, 1910; M.G.

8. The Political Scene

1. Waley, *Edwin Montagu*, p. 32.
2. Edwin Montagu, letter to his mother, Feb. 21, 1909; Montagu AS 5/6/11.
3. Edwin Montagu, letter to Asquith, Jan. 20, 1909; Montagu AS 1/1/21.
4. Waley, *Edwin Montagu*, p. 34.
5. Edwin Montagu, letter to Asquith, Nov. 1909; Montagu AS 1/7/31 (no other date).
6. Id.
7. Id.
8. Edwin Montagu, letter to Asquith, Jan. 20, 1909; Montagu AS 1/1/21.
9. Waley, *Edwin Montagu*, p. 32.
10. Jenkins, *Asquith*, pp. 198, 199.
11. Ensor, *Oxford History of England, 1870–1914*, pp. 413–15. To moderate the

effects of the increase in the income tax, "the principle of children's allowances was introduced for parents with incomes of under £500 a year—another novelty" (Gregg, *Lloyd George: The People's Champion 1902–1911*, p. 177, n. 1). For a full discussion of the People's Budget, see Bruce K. Murray, *The People's Budget 1909–1910: Lloyd George and Liberal Politics* (Oxford, 1980).

12. Mendelssohn, *The Age of Churchill*, p. 484.

13. Jenkins, *Asquith*, p. 199.

14. Edwin Montagu, letter to Asquith, Nov. 1, 1909; Montagu AS 1/7/31. See also Waley, *Edwin Montagu*, p. 35.

15. Koss, *Asquith*, p. 115.

16. Edwin Montagu, letter to Asquith, Nov. 1, 1909; Montagu AS 1/7/3.

17. Jenkins, *Asquith*, p. 202.

18. J. A. Spender and Cyril Asquith, *The Life of Herbert Henry Asquith, Lord Oxford and Asquith* (London, 1932), vol. 1, p. 269.

19. Edwin Montagu, letter to mother, Oct. 22, 1909; M.G.

20. Id.

21. Edwin Montagu, letter to his mother, Dec. 10, 1909; M.G.

22. Edwin Montagu, letter to mother, Dec. 17, 1909; M.G.

23. Edwin Montagu, letter to his mother, Dec. 10, 1909; M.G.

24. Edwin Montagu, letter to mother, May 1910; M.G.

25. Id.

26. Id.

27. Waley, *Edwin Montagu*, p. 35.

28. Edwin Montagu, letter to mother and father, Feb. 17, 1910; Montagu AS 5/9/4.

29. Id.

30. Id.

31. Cross, *The Liberals in Power 1905–14*, p. 113.

32. Jenkins, *Asquith*, p. 210.

33. How Asquith obtained these guarantees from a hostile King, unsophisticated in constitutional issues, makes for a fascinating story that has been told extensively and with justifiable pride by Asquith's biographers. See Jenkins, *Asquith*, pp. 218–32; Koss, *Asquith*, pp. 123–29; Spender and Asquith, *The Life of Herbert Henry Asquith*, vol. 1, pp. 268–328.

34. Jenkins, *Asquith*, p. 222.

9. *Under Secretary of State for India*

1. *Cambridge News*, Nov. 14, 1910, Montagu AS 3/7/105.

2. Id.

3. Durgas Das, *India from Curzon to Nehru and After* (New York, 1970), p. 44.

4. Dr. R. L. Gupta, *Conflict and Harmony, Indo-British Relations* (New Delhi, 1971), p. 12.

5. Waley, *Edwin Montagu*, p. 51.

6. John Morley, Viscount 1908 (1838–1923): journalist; barrister, author; entered

Parliament 1883; Chief Secretary for Ireland 1886 and 1892–1895; Secretary of State for India, 1905–1910.

7. Gilbert John Elliott-Murray-Kynynmound, Earl of Minto 1905 (1845–1914): soldier, Brigadier General, Governor General of Canada, 1898–1904, Viceroy of India, 1905–1910.

8. *Parl. Deb.*, House of Commons, vols 14–19, Feb. 23 to July 29, 1910, pp. 206–2678.

9. The *Review*, Nov. 23, 1910, Montagu AS 3/7/106.

10. Waley, *Edwin Montagu*, p. 39.

11. Frederick Coleridge Mackarness, *The Methods of the Indian Police in the 20th Century*, discussed in *The Times* (London), June 23, 1910, Montagu AS 3/7/5; the *Standard*, June 23, 1910, Montagu AS 3/7/66; the *Daily Express*, June 23, 1910, Montagu AS 3/7/69); the *Times* of India, June 24, 1910, Montagu AS 3/7/5; the *Cambridge News*, Aug. 12, 1910, Montagu AS 3/7/82.

12. *Indian Press Act of 1910*, sec. 12 (1), which prohibited the distribution in India of material designed to ridicule the government of India and hold it up to contempt.

13. *Yorkshire Daily Post*, June 23, 1910, Montagu AS 3/7/61.

14. *Parl. Deb.*, House of Commons, vol. 4, June 22, 1910, p. 250.

15. Id.

16. *Yorkshire Herald*, June 23, 1910; Montagu AS 3/7/62.

17. *Scotsman*, June 22, 1910, Montagu AS 3/7/60. This article described Montagu as "tall, dark, slightly bald with a cautious method of speech and Semitic aspect. His words were carefully chosen." The *Sussex Daily News*, on July 30, 1910, called Montagu a "hard hitting minister [who,] when he gets a little more accustomed to his responsibility will be rough riding over those who got in his way" (Montagu AS 3/7/29).

18. *Parl. Deb.*, House of Commons, vol 4, July 26, 1910, pp. 1950–2063.

19. *Daily Mail*, July 27, 1910; Montagu AS 1/12/30.

20. Id.

21. *Glasgow Evening News*, July 27, 1910; Montagu AS 3/7/15 and Montagu AS 3/7/18.

22. *News of the World*, July 27, 1910; Montagu AS 3/7/33.

23. *Observer*, July 27, 1910; Montagu AS 3/7/35.

24. The *Englishman*, Aug. 3, 1910; Montagu AS 3/7/1.

25. *Punch*, July 27, 1910; Montagu AS 3/7/40.

26. *London Opinion*, July 27, 1910; Montagu AS 3/7/40.

27. *Observer*, July 27, 1910; Montagu AS 3/7/35.

28. The *Englishman*, Aug. 3, 1910; Montagu AS 3/7/1.

29. The *News of the World*, July 31, 1910; Montagu, AS 3/7/33.

30. *London Opinion,* Aug. 6, 1910; Montagu AS 3/7/41.

31. *Wednesday Review*, Aug. 24, 1910; Montagu AS 3/7/99.

32. *Manchester Guardian*, Aug. 8, 1910; Montagu AS 3/7/80.

33. Edwin Montagu, speech at Bishop Auckland, discussed in *Daily Clarion* and *Morning London*, Nov. 3, 1910, Montagu AS 3/7/107. See also *Cambridge Independent Press*, Nov. 18, 1910, Montagu AS 3/7/109.

34. Edwin Montagu, letter to Venetia Stanley, June 18, 1910; M.G.
35. Waley, *Edwin Montagu,* pp. 46–47.
36. Ibid., p. 47.
37. Edwin Montagu, letter to Venetia Stanley, June 18, 1910; M.G.
38. Waley, *Edwin Montagu,* p. 47.
39. Id.
40. Robert Crewe-Milnes, Marquis of Crewe (1858–1945). Succeeded to a peerage at the age of 27. Lord Lieutenant of Ireland, 1892; Lord President of Council, 1905; Secretary for the Colonies, 1908–1911, and 1912–1915; Lord Privy Seal, 1908–1911 and 1912–1915; Secretary of State for India, 1910–1915.
41. Waley, *Edwin Montagu,* p. 46.
42. Ibid., p. 38, n. 2.
43. Margot Asquith Diaries, March 1915; Bonham Carter MSS.
44. Edwin Montagu, letter to Lord Hardinge, Apr. 5, 1911; Montagu AS 1/5/117.
45. Edwin Montagu, letter to Lord Hardinge, Oct. 26, 1911; Montagu AS 2/3/1.
46. *Parl. Deb.,* House of Commons, Vol. 28, July 26, 1911, pp. 1664–1783.
47. *The Times* (London), Montagu, AS 3/7/6. See also the *Leader* (India), July 29, 1911, Montagu AS 3/7/117; East Anglican *Daily News,* July 29, 1911, Montagu, AS 3/7/119; *Indian Spectator,* July 29, 1911, Montagu AS 3/7/116; and the *Times of India,* Aug. 12, 1911; Montagu AS 3/7/139.
48. The *Englishman,* July 28, 1911, Montagu AS 3/7/113. See also the *Outlook,* July 29, 1911, Montagu AS 3/7/126; *Saturday Review,* July 29, 1911, Montagu AS 3/7/22; *Morning Post,* Aug. 1, 1911, Montagu AS 3/7/129.
49. *Justice,* Aug. 5, 1911; Montagu AS 3/7/134.
50. *Parl. Deb.,* House of Commons, vol. 28, July 26, 1911, p. 1677.
51. Ibid., p. 1678.
52. Ibid., p. 1679.
53. *Indian Daily Telegraph,* Aug. 2, 1911; Montagu AS 3/7/130.
54. *Parl. Deb.,* House of Commons, vol 28, July 26, 1911, pp. 1690–1693.
55. Ibid., p. 1693.
56. Ibid., p. 1696.
57. Ibid., p. 1697.
58. Ibid., p. 1672.
59. P. E. Roberts, *History of British India,* ed ed. (Oxford, 1952), pp. 577–78.
60. Ibid., p. 578.
61. Edwin Montagu, letter to Lord Crewe, Dec. 12, 1911; Montagu AS 2/4/4.
62. Id.
63. Id.
64. Edwin Montagu, letter to Lord Crewe, Dec. 14, 1911; Montagu AS 1/4/6.
65. Id.
66. Edwin Montagu, letter to Lord Crewe, Dec. 12, 1911; Montagu AS 2/4/4.
67. Edwin Montagu, letter to Lord Crewe, Dec. 14, 1911; Montagu AS 2.4.6.
68. Edwin Montagu, letter to Lord Crewe, Dec. 26, 1911; Montagu AS 2.4.7.
69. Id.
70. *Parl. Deb.,* House of Commons, vol. 23, Apr. 11, 1911, p. 212.
71. Waley, *Edwin Montagu,* p. 51.

72. Ibid., pp. 51–52.

73. Ibid., p. 52.

74. *Parl. Deb.,* House of Commons, vol. 37, Apr. 22, 1912, p. 812.

75. Waley, *Edwin Montagu,* p. 52.

76. *The Times* (London), June 25, 1912; M.G.

77. Waley, *Edwin Montagu,* p. 52.

78. Ibid., pp. 52–53.

79. Ibid., p. 53.

80. The *Times of India,* July 19, 1912; Montagu AS 3/7/179.

81. Id. The spelling of Sinha's first name is the Indian spelling appearing in the *Times of India.* In London papers it frequently appeared as Satyendra.

82. Waley, *Edwin Montagu,* p. 53. See also *The Times* (London), July 30, 1912; Montagu AS 3/7/9.

83. Id.

84. Waley, *Edwin Montagu,* p. 53.

85. Ibid., p. 51.

86. *Parl.Deb.,* House of Commons, Vol. 37, Apr. 22, 1912, p. 807.

87. Id.

88. The *Observer* and the *Times of India,* June 22, 1912; Montagu AS 3/7/8.

89. Dennis Judd, *Lord Reading* (London, 1982), p. 91. See also pp. 90–103.

90. Jenkins, *Asquith,* p. 252.

91. Ibid., pp. 250–51. See also Dan M. Cregier, *Bounder from Wales* (Missouri, 1976), pp. 200–12.

92. Frank Owen, *Tempestuous Journey: Lloyd George, His Life and Times* (London, 1954), p. 226.

93. Cregier, *Bounder from Wales,* p. 210. See also p. 792, n. 3 of this book.

94. Jenkins, *Asquith,* p. 254.

95. Spender and Asquith, *The Life of Herbert Henry Asquith,* vol. 1, p. 360.

96. Jenkins, *Asquith,* p. 247.

97. Ibid., p. 249.

98. Brock, *H. H. Asquith Letters to Venetia Stanley,* p. 27, letter # 11, Jan. 27, 1913.

99. Venetia Stanley, letter to Edwin Montagu, Jan. 1913; M.G.

100. Edwin Montagu, letter to Venetia Stanley, Jan. 31, 1913; M.G.

101. *Parl. Deb.,* House of Commons, vol. 41, July 30, 1912, pp. 1876–1989.

102. Asquith, letter to Venetia Stanley, July 30, 1912; AS, MSS, #146.

103. *Parl. Deb.,* House of Commons, vol. 41, July 30, 1912, p. 1894.

104. Ibid., p. 1902.

105. Ibid., p. 1887.

106. Ibid., p. 1907.

107. Ibid., pp. 1907, 1908.

108. *India,* Aug. 2, 1912; Montagu AS 3/7/10.

10. A Love Triangle Begins

1. Brock, *H. H. Asquith Letters to Venetia Stanley*, p. 5.
2. Bermant, *The Cousinhood*, p. 252.
3. Cooper, *Old Men Forget*, p. 40.
4. Venetia Stanley, letter to Edwin Montagu, Aug. 18, 1911; M.G.
5. Venetia Stanley, letter to Edwin Montagu, Aug. 1911; M.G.
6. Venetia Stanley, letters to Edwin Montagu, Apr. 4, July 26, Aug. 5 and 17, Sept. 16, 1911; M.G.
7. Venetia Stanley, letter to Edwin Montagu, Apr. 4, 1911; M.G.
8. Edwin Montagu, letter to Venetia Stanley, May 3, 1911; M.G.
9. Venetia Stanley, letter to Edwin Montagu, Aug. 18, 1911; M.G.
10. Edwin Montagu, letters to Venetia Stanley, May 28, June 21 and June 25, 1911; M.G.
11. Id.
12. Edwin Montagu, letter to Venetia Stanley, Sept. 8, 1911; M.G.
13. Edwin Montagu, letter to Venetia Stanley, Oct. 4, 1911; M.G.
14. Venetia Stanley, letter to Edwin Montagu, Oct. 4, 1911; M.G.
15. Ted Morgan, *Churchill, Young Man in a Hurry* (New York, 1982), pp. 518–19.
16. Edwin Montagu, letter to Venetia Stanley, Oct. 4, 1911; M.G.
17. Edwin Montagu, letter to Venetia Stanley, Nov. 1, 1911; M.G.
18. Edwin Montagu, letter to Venetia Stanley, Dec. 16, 1911; M.G.
19. Venetia Stanley, letter to Edwin Montagu, Dec. 24, 1911; M.G.
20. Edwin Montagu, letter to Venetia Stanley, Dec. 27, 1911; M.G.
21. Edwin Montagu, letter to Lord Crewe, Dec. 26, 1911; M.G.
22. Id.
23. Brock, *H. H. Asquith Letters to Venetia Stanley*, p. 532, Item #385, chap. of autobiography by Asquith. It would appear that this was written in Apr. 1915.
24. Id.
25. Ibid., p. 12.
26. Ibid., pp. 12–13.
27. ibid., p. 532.
28. Id.
29. Venetia Stanley, letter to Edwin Montagu, Jan. 1912; M.G.
30. Brock, *H. H. Asquith Letters to Venetia Stanley*, p. 19, letter #2, Apr. 1, 1912, n. 2.
31. Id.
32. Edwin Montagu, letter to Venetia Stanley, Feb. 9, 1912; M.G.
33. Id.
34. Id.
35. Venetia Stanley, letter to Edwin Montagu, Feb. 12, 1912; M.G.
36. Edwin Montagu, letter to Venetia Stanley, Feb. 21, 1912; M.G.
37. Edwin Montagu, letter to his mother, Feb. 6, 1912; M.G.
38. Brock, *H. H. Asquith Letters to Venetia Stanley*, p. 533, letter #386, Apr. 5, 1915.

39. Ibid., p. 532, Item #385, chap. of autobiography by Asquith. It would appear that this was written in April 1915.
40. Asquith, letter to Venetia Stanley, Mar. 20, 1919; AS. MSS, #50.
41. Asquith, letter to Venetia Stanley, no date; AS. MSS., #210.
42. Brock, *H. H. Asquith Letters to Venetia Stanley*, p. 19, letter #2, Apr. 1, 1912.
43. Asquith, letter to Venetia Stanley, Apr. 20, 1912; As. MSS., #210.
44. Venetia Stanley, letter to Edwin Montagu, Mar. 1912; M.G. (letter bears notation "in reply to ESM of March 11, 1912").
45. Edwin Montagu, letter to Venetia Stanley, Mar. 11, 1912; M.G.
46. Venetia Stanley, letter to Edwin Montagu, Mar., 1912; M.G. (letter bears notation "in reply to ESM of March 11, 1912").
47. Edwin Montagu, letter to Venetia Stanley, Apr. 14, 1912; M.G.
48. Venetia Stanley, letter to Edwin Montagu, May 1912; M.G. (no other date).
49. Venetia Stanley, letter to Edwin Montagu, July 15, 1912; M.G.
50. Brock, *H. H. Asquith Letters to Venetia Stanley*, p. 20, letter #3, July 13, 1912.
51. Edwin Montagu, letter to Venetia Stanley, July 22, 1912; M.G.
52. Asquith, letter to Venetia Stanley, July 30, 1912; AS., MSS., #146.
53. Edwin Montagu, letter to Venetia Stanley, Aug. 4, 1912; M.G.
54. Brock, *H. H. Asquith Letters to Venetia Stanley*, p. 22, letter #4, Aug. 14, 1912.
55. Ibid., p. 22 n. 2.
56. Stephen Koss, *Lord Haldane* (New York, 1969), p. 149.
57. Morgan, *Churchill*, p. 520.
58. Edwin Montagu, letter to Venetia Stanley, Aug. 18, 1912; M.G.
59. Edwin Montagu, letter to Venetia Stanley, Aug. 26, 1912; M.G.
60. Id.
61. Waley, *Edwin Montagu*, pp. 57–58.
62. Psychologists frequently point out: "Marriage is regularly used as a means to resolve long-standing, deep seated, unconscious conflicts. Accordingly, a marriage may serve as a vehicle for realizing, in disguised form, unfulfilled daydreams or forbidden gratifications of childhood."

It may be used to right old wrongs, to compensate deprivations, to exact vengeance, to overcome humiliations and disappointments, aggrandize one's image or to elevate one's self-esteem. . . . To a certain man . . . it may be obligatory that the woman he marry be . . . "a celebrity." . . . This attitude may derive from intense unrealistic feelings of worthlessness because he felt unloved by his parents at a critical stage in his life. Marriage to the "proper" woman may satisfy this need and help him overcome neurotic feelings of low self-esteem.

These attitudes are frequently present in Jewish intermarriages, where the "proper" woman or man is seen by a Jewish partner as a Christian—a member of the majority culture. See *Intermarriage, the Psychological Implications,* Proceedings of a Conference (Apr. 1966), ed. Jack J. Zurofsky, printed by the Commission on Synagogue Relations of the Federation of Jewish Philanthropies (New York, 1966), pp. 1–13.
63. Edwin Montagu, letter to Venetia Stanley, Sept. 2, 1912; M.G.
64. Id.

65. Id.
66. Brock, *H. H. Asquith Letters to Venetia Stanley,* p. 23, letter #5, Sept. 14, 1912.
67. Edwin Montagu, letter to Venetia Stanley, Sept. 22, 1912; M.G.
68. Edwin Montagu, letter to Venetia Stanley, Sept. 29, 1912; M.G.
69. Edwin Montagu, letter to Venetia Stanley, Oct. 3, 1912; M.G.

11. The Trip to India

1. *India,* Aug. 23, 1912; Montagu AS 3/7/154.
2. *Englishman,* Aug.19, 1912; Montagu As 3/7/154.
3. *India,* Sept. 20, 1912; Montagu AS 3/7/155.
4. *Times of India,* July 27, 1912; Montagu AS 3/7/150.
5. *Pall Mall Gazette,* Oct. 4, 1912; Montagu AS 3/7/22.
6. Edwin Montagu, letter to Venetia Stanley, Aug. 4, 1912; M.G.
7. Edwin Montagu, letter to Venetia Stanley, Nov. 12, 1912; M.G.
8. Venetia Stanley, letter to Edwin Montagu, Oct. 23, 1912; M.G.
9. Edwin Montagu, letter to Venetia Stanley, Oct. 17, 1912; M.G.
10. Venetia Stanley, letter to Edwin Montagu, Nov. 6, 1912; M.G.
11. Waley, *Edwin Montagu,* section on "The Visit to India" (October 1912–March 1913), pp. 291–333.
12. Ibid., pp. 329–30.
13. Ibid., p. 295.
14. Id.
15. Ibid., pp. 297 and 314.
16. Ibid., p. 308.
17. Ibid., p. 310.
18. Ibid., p. 309.
19. Ibid., pp. 300–301.
20. Ibid., p. 302.
21. Ibid., p. 313.
22. *The Times* (London), Nov. 24, 1912.
23. John Bowle, *Viscount Samuel: A Biography* (London, 1957), p. 101, n. 2.
24. Waley, *Edwin Montagu,* p. 55.
25. Ibid., p. 301.
26. Ibid., p. 310.
27. Ibid., p. 304.
28. Ibid., pp. 332–33.
29. Ibid., p. 311.
30. Ibid., p. 333.
31. Edwin Montagu, letter to Venetia Stanley, Nov. 27, 1912; M.G.
32. Edwin Montagu, letter to Venetia Stanley, Dec. 1919; M.G.
33. Venetia Stanley, letter to Edwin Montagu, Dec. 1912; M.G.
34. Edwin Montagu, letter to Venetia Stanley, Dec. 18, 1912; M.G.
35. Venetia Stanley, letter to Edwin Montagu, Dec. 25, 1912; M.G.
36. Waley, *Edwin Montagu,* p. 56.
37. Venetia Stanley, letter to Edwin Montagu, Dec. 25, 1912; M.G.

38. Brock, *H. H. Asquith Letters Venetia Stanley*, p. 24, letter #6, Jan. 6, 1913; and p. 25, letter #8, Jan. 16, 1913. See also pp. 24–27, letters # 7, 8, 9, 10, and 11, Jan. 7, 16, 20, 22, and 27, 1913.

39. Ibid., p. 28, letter #12, Feb. 18, 1913.

40. Ibid., p. 24, letter #7, Jan. 7, 1913.

41. Ibid., p. 26, letter #9A, Venetia Stanley to Asquith. There is no date on this letter. Venetia's letters to Asquith were all destroyed. This letter survives because Asquith returned it to Venetia on Jan. 20 with some notes on the back, which he used for a speech in the third reading debate on the Home Rule Bill, Jan. 15, 1913. One can assume it was written in Jan. 1913, before the 15th. See Brock, *H. H. Asquith Letters to Venetia Stanley*, pp. 25–26, nn. 1 and 2. The text of Asquith's Jan. 20 letter reads: "It was a real delight to get your dear little pencil letter when I returned from the Coast today. I thought you might like to have the notes, which were purposely put together (in my ramshackle fashion) on the back of a letter of yours which undoubtedly brought them good luck."

42. Venetia Stanley, letter to Edwin Montagu, Nov. 19, 1912; M.G.

43. Venetia Stanley, letter to Edwin Montagu, Nov. 12, 1912; M.G.

44. Brock, *H. H. Asquith Letters to Venetia Stanley*, p. 2.

45. Ibid., p. 9.

46. Ibid., p. 12.

47. Asquith, letter to Venetia Stanley, Dec. 27, 1912; AS. MSS., #193.

48. Edwin Montagu, letter to Venetia Stanley, Jan. 21, 1913; M.G.

49. Id.

12. *The Triangle Is Now in Place*

1. *London Letter,* Mar. 25, 1913; Montagu AS 3/7/157.

2. Venetia Stanley, letter to Edwin Montagu, Mar. 21, 1913; M.G.

3. Asquith, letter to Venetia Stanley, Mar. 22, 1913; AS. MSS., # 24.

4. Brock, *H. H. Asquith Letters to Venetia Stanley*, p. 29, letter #13, Apr. 1913.

5. Ibid., p. 52, letter #41, Mar. 3, 1914.

6. Ibid., p. 29, letter 13, fn. 1, Apr. 1913.

7. Ibid., p. 30, letter #15, Apr. 7, 1913.

8. Edwin Montagu, letter to Venetia Stanley, May 8, 1913; M.G.

9. Edwin Montagu, letter to Venetia Stanley, May 20, 1913; M.G.

10. Edwin Montagu, letter to Venetia Stanley, June 8, 1913; M.G.

11. Asquith, letter to Venetia Stanley, June 11, 1913; AS. MSS., # 156.

12. Edwin Montagu, letter to Venetia Stanley, July 8, 1913; M.G.

13. Venetia Stanley, letter to Edwin Montagu, Aug. 23, 1913; M.G.

14. Waley, *Edwin Montagu*, p. 59.

15. Brock, *H. H. Asquith Letters to Venetia Stanley*, p. 31, a poem, "A Summers Day," item #16, July 1913.

16. *Parl. Deb.,* House of Commons, vol. 56 Aug. 7, 1913, pp. 1780–1908.

17. Ibid., p. 1807.

18. Ibid., pp. 1807, 1808.

19. Ibid., p. 1798.
20. Ibid., p. 1808.
21. Edwin Montagu, letter to Venetia Stanley, Aug. 8, 1913; M.G.
22. Edwin Montagu, letter to Lord Crewe, Feb. 16, 1913; M.G.
23. Lord Crewe, letter to Edwin Montagu, Feb. 14, 1913; M.G.
24. Asquith, letter to Lord Crewe, Feb. 20, 1913; M.G.
25. Brock, *H. H. Asquith Letters to Venetia Stanley*, p. 28, letter #12, Feb. 18, 1913.
26. Edwin Montagu, memorandum on proposals for the reform of India Council and Office organization and procedure, Feb. 19, 1913; Montagu AS 2/7/5.
27. Edwin Montagu, letter to Venetia Stanley, Aug. 8, 1913; M.G.
28. Venetia Stanley, letter to Edwin Montagu, Aug. 11, 1913; M.G.
29. Id.
30. Edwin Montagu, letter to Venetia Stanley, Aug. 14, 1913; M.G.
31. Id.
32. Asquith, letter to Venetia Stanley, Aug. 19, 1913; AS. MSS., # 250.
33. Brock, *H. H. Asquith Letters to Venetia Stanley*, p. 33, letter #17, Aug. 21, 1913.
34. Edwin Montagu, letter to Venetia Stanley, Aug. 29, 1913; M.G.; also Brock, *H. H. Asquith Letters to Venetia Stanley*, pp. 32–33, letter #17, n. 7, Aug. 21, 1913.
35. Id.
36. Id.
37. Brock, *H. H. Asquith Letters to Venetia Stanley*, p. 33, poem, item #18, Aug. 22, 1913.
38. Ibid., p. 34, letter #19, Sept. 3, 1913.
39. Ibid., n. 1.
40. Edwin Montagu, letter to Venetia Stanley, Sept. 14, 1913; M.G.
41. Asquith, letter to Venetia Stanley, Sept. 16, 1913; AS. MSS., #248.
42. Venetia Stanley, letter to Edwin Montagu, Sept. 10, 1913; M.G.
43. Edwin Montagu, letter to Venetia Stanley, Oct. 8, 1912; M.G.
44. Asquith, letter to Venetia Stanley, Oct. 2, 1913; AS. MSS., #280.
45. Venetia Stanley, letter to Edwin Montagu, Nov. 1, 1913; M.G.
46. Edwin Montagu, letter to Venetia Stanley, Nov. 4, 1913; M.G.
47. Edwin Montagu, letter to Venetia Stanley, Nov. 11, 1913; M.G.
48. Brock, *H. H. Asquith Letters to Venetia Stanley*, p. 35, letter #21, Dec. 15, 1913.
49. Asquith, letter to Venetia Stanley, Dec. 17, 1913; AS. MSS., #256.

13. As the War Clouds Gather

1. Brock, *H. H. Asquith Letters to Venetia Stanley*, p. 44, letter #30, Feb. 4, 1914.
2. Ibid., p. 48, letter #35, Feb. 12, 1914.
3. Waley, *Edwin Montagu*, pp. 60–61.
4. John Maynard Keynes, *Essays on Biography* (New York, 1933), p. 56.
5. Sir Thomas W. Heath, *The Treasury* (London, 1927), pp. 9–12.
6. Ibid., pp. 80–81.
7. Edwin Montagu, letter to Venetia Stanley, Feb. 6, 1914; M.G.

8. Brock, *H. H. Asquith Letters to Venetia Stanley,* pp. 50–51, letter #39, Feb. 26, 1914.

9. Ibid., p. 64, letter #57, Apr. 10, 1914.

10. *Parl. Deb.,* March–September 1914, vols. 59–66; 4th session of the 30th Parliament.

11. Cregier, *Bounder from Wales,* p. 206.

12. Skidelsky, *John Maynard Keynes,* p. 300.

13. R. F. Harrod, *The Life of John Maynard Keynes* (New York, 1969), p. 196.

14. Murray, *The People's Budget,* p. 77. Lloyd George not only jumped from issue to issue, but he had no patience with written memoranda. "The truth is he did not always master very thoroughly the financial problems with which he had to deal. There are stories, well authenticated, of Treasury officials who saw with dismay important papers tossed aside, while the Minister invited them to talk to him instead" (Sir Charles Mallet, *Mr. Lloyd George: A Study* (London, 1930), p. 33.

15. Skidelsky, *John Maynard Keynes,* p. 297. In spite of this letter, a major biography of Keynes by Roy Harrod, published in 1951, gave the credit for bringing Keynes to the Treasury during the crisis of August 1914 to Basil Blackett (Harrod, *The Life of John Maynard Keynes,* pp. 195, 196), although at the time this biography was written, the writer had access to the Keynes letter of 1924. While Blackett did write to Keynes on August 2 asking to "pick his brains" (Skidelsky, *John Maynard Keynes,* p. 289) on the crisis, Keynes always believed that this invitation from Blackett came as a result of Montagu's prodding.

It is interesting, too, that the few times Harrod refers to Montagu he describes him as someone who "invited Keynes to speak at Cambridge," a "good Liberal," a "member of a Reparations Committee" and as "Secretary of State for India." He never mentions the fact that Montagu was the Financial Secretary to the Treasury during some of the most critical days of the war— 1914 to 1917. See Harrod, *The Life of John Maynard Keynes,* pp. 15, 60, 241, 248, 354. See also Henry Roseveare, *The Treasury* (New York, 1969), where there is one reference to his tenure at the Treasury; and Kathleen Burk, "The Treasury—From Impotence to Power," in *War and the State,* ed. Kathleen Burk (London, 1982), pp. 84–107, which discusses the role of the Treasury during the war and again does not mention Montagu.

16. Keynes, *Essays on Biography,* p. 56.

17. Frances Stevenson, *Lloyd George: A Diary* (New York, 1971), pp. 51, 139.

18. *Ibid.,* pp. 109–10.

19. *Ibid.,* p. 40.

20. Peter Rowland, *David Lloyd George* (New York, 1975), p. 258.

21. Waley, *Edwin Montagu,* p. 60.

22. Emy, *Liberals, Radicals and Social Politics,* p. 227.

23. Id.

24. *Parl. Deb.,* House of Commons, May 6, 1914, p. 320.

25. Ibid., July 23, 1914, p. 685.

26. Id.

27. Lord Beaverbrook, *Politicians and the War* (London, 1928), p. 66.

28. Keynes, *Essays on Biography*, p. 55.
29. Edwin Montagu, letter to Venetia Stanley, Apr. 21, 1914; M.G.
30. Brock, *H. H. Asquith Letters to Venetia Stanley*, pp. 65–66, letter #59, Apr. 17, 1914.
31. Ibid., p. 66, letter #60, Apr. 18, 1914.
32. Ibid., p. 68, letter #63, May 3, 1914.
33. Edwin Montagu, letter to Asquith, Apr. 17, 1914; Montagu AS 6/11/3.
34. Edwin Montagu, letter to Lloyd George, Apr. 29, 1914; Montagu AS 6/1/1. See also Emy, *Liberals, Radicals and Social Politics*, p. 228.
35. Brock, *H. H. Asquith Letters to Venetia Stanley*, p. 70, letter #64, May 5, 1914.
36. Cregier, *Bounder from Wales*, p. 236.
37. Rowland, *David Lloyd George*, p. 276.
38. Edwin Montagu, letter to Venetia Stanley, June 24, 1914; M.G.
39. Waley, *Edwin Montagu*, p. 61. See also Cregier, *Bounder from Wales*, p. 235.
40. Gregier, *Bounder from Wales*, p. 235.
41. Waley, *Edwin Montagu*, p. 61. The Curragh incident added to the tensions which were mounting rapidly. In view of possible disturbances, troops were sent to guard the arms depot at the Curragh in Ulster. Gen. Paget, the Commander in Chief in Ireland, took the position that a few officers with family ties in Ulster might be excused if disorder broke out, but all the rest were expected to do their duty or be removed. Sixty officers resigned. The War Office became panicky and issued a statement that implied that the Army in Ireland would not be used to enforce Home Rule. Asquith could not permit this to stand. He accepted the resignations of the officers responsible, repudiated their statements, took over the War Office himself and quieted the Army. "His massive common sense . . . proved invaluable" (Jenkins, *Asquith*, p. 315).
42. Id.
43. Ibid., p. 62.
44. Id. It is difficult to reconcile Montagu's belief that Bonar Law would support "any reasonable settlement" when Bonar Law "sedulously exploited the sectarian hatreds in Ulster." Equating "Home Rule" with "Rome Rule," he denounced the government's policy as a "sell out to disloyal and unlawful multitudes, who could be expected to rob proud Ulstermen of their birthright, their prosperity and ultimately their religious heritage" (Koss, *Asquith*, p. 135). It may be that Bonar Law took one posture with his constituents and another behind closed doors.
45. Ibid., p. 63.
46. Brock, *H. H. Asquith Letters to Venetia Stanley*, pp. 108–9, letter #102, July 22, 1914.
47. Id.
48. Ibid., p. 122, letter #103, July 24, 1914.
49. Jenkins, *Asquith*, pp. 324–25.
50. Brock, *H. H. Asquith Letters to Venetia Stanley*, pp. 122–23, letter #103, July 24, 1914.
51. John Grigg, *Lloyd George, From Place to War, 1912–1916* (Great Britain, 1985), p. 151.

52. Burk, *War and the State*, p. 84.

53. Jenkins, *Asquith*, p. 323.

54. Brock, *H. H. Asquith Letters to Venetia Stanley*, p. 146, letter #133, Aug. 2, 1914. Ibid., pp. 111–15.

55. Margot Asquith, *Autobiography* (Boston and Cambridge, 1963), p. 287.

56. Brock, *H. H. Asquith Letters to Venetia Stanley*, p. 7.

57. Ibid., p. 10.

58. Ibid., p. 44, letter #30, Feb. 4; p. 47, letter #33, Feb. 11; p. 50, letter #38, Feb. 19; p. 54, letter #44, Mar. 10; p. 65, letter #58, Apr. 11; p. 71, letter #66, May 11; p. 87, letter #81, June 17; p. 65, letter #59, Apr. 17; p. 97, letter #92, July 8; p. 107, letter #99, July 18. All of these letters were written in 1914.

59. Ibid., p. 13.

60. Morgan, *Churchill*, p. 519.

61. Lambert, *Unquiet Souls*, p. 207.

62. Ziegler, *Diana Cooper* (London, 1981), p. 60.

63. Id.

64. A. J. P. Taylor, *London Review of Books*, Dec. 2–29, 1982, p. 25; review of Brock, *H. H. Asquith Letters to Venetia Stanley*.

66. Id.

67. Godfrey Hodgson, the *New York Times*, Book Review section, Apr. 3, 1983, p. 1; review of Brock, *H. H. Asquith Letters to Venetia Stanley*.

68. Peter Clarke, *The Times* (London), *Higher Education Supplement*, Dec. 14, 1983, p. 13; review of Brock, *H. H. Asquith Letters to Venetia Stanley*.

69. Id.

70. Alastair Forbes, letter to editor, *The Times* (London), Dec. 14, 1982.

71. Michael Brock, letter to the author, May 28, 1989.

72. Nicholas Walter, letter to the editor, *The Times* (London), Jan. 7, 1983.

73. Enoch Powell, *Books & Bookmen*, Jan. 1983; review of Brock, *H. H. Asquith Letters to Venetia Stanley*.

74. Margot Asquith, letter to Montagu, Jan. 1914; AS.MSS., #55.

75. Ibid., Mar. 21, 1914; AS. MSS.

76. Edwin Montagu, letter to Venetia Stanley, Mar. 15, 1914; M.G.

77. Brock, *H. H. Asquith Letters to Venetia Stanley*, p. 59, letter #50, Mar. 22, 1915.

14. Five Months of Military and Naval Disasters

1. Spender and Asquith, *The Life of Herbert Henry Asquith*, vol. 2, p. 114.

2. Margot Asquith Diaries, Oct. 28, 1914; Bonham Carter MSS.

3. Grigg, *Lloyd George, From Peace to War*, p. 159.

4. R. J. Q. Adams, *Arms and the Wizard* (Texas, 1978), p. 5.

5. Spender and Asquith *The Life of Herbert Henry Asquith*, vol. 2, p. 127. See also Grigg, *Lloyd George, From Peace to War*, p. 199.

6. Edwin Montagu, letter to Venetia Stanley, Aug. 7, 1914; M.G.

7. Waley, *Edwin Montagu*, p. 63.

8. Id.

9. Skidelsky, *John Maynard Keynes*, p. 291.

10. Id.
11. Id.
12. Ibid., p. 294.
13. Ibid., pp. 293–94.
14. Grigg, *Lloyd George, From Peace to War*, pp. 187–89.
15. Roseveare, *The Treasury*, p. 237.
16. Lord George Allardice Riddle, *Diaries* (London, 1933–34), vol. 2, p. 42.
17. H. Montgomery Hyde, *Lord Reading* (New York, 1967), p. 176.
18. Id.
19. Roseveare, *The Treasury*, p. 237.
20. Skidelsky, *John Maynard Keynes*, 298; see also Hyde, *Lord Reading*, p. 176.
21. Roseveare, *The Treasury*, p. 237.
22. Burk, *War and the State*, pp. 84–107. See also Grigg, *Lloyd George, From Peace to War*, pp. 152–53; Owen, *Tempestuous Journey*, p. 271; Rowland, *David Lloyd George*, pp. 284–85.
23. Cregier, *Bounder from Wales*, p. 247.
24. David Lloyd George, *War Memoirs* (London, 1938), vol. 1, pp. 61–74.
25. Edwin Montagu, letter to Venetia Stanley, Aug. 7, 1914; M.G.
26. Hyde, *Lord Reading*, p. 184; Judd, *Lord Reading*, p. 124.
27. Edwin Montagu, letters to Asquith, Nov. 26, 1914, and Dec. 1, 1914; M.G.
28. Burk, *War and the State*, p. 96. See also report of the Royal Commission on Civil Service, published in 1914.
29. Ibid., p. 86.
30. G. W. Forster, letter to Asquith, Nov. 29, 1914, in response to Montagu's letter of Nov. 26, 1914; M.G.
31. Edwin Montagu, letter to Asquith, Dec. 1, 1914; M.G.
32. *Daily Chronicle*, Oct. 1, 1914, p. 2.
33. Edwin Montagu, letter to Herbert Samuel, Oct. 1, 1914; M.G.
34. Id.
35. Brock, *H. H. Asquith Letters to Venetia Stanley*, p. 241, letter #159(i), Sept. 16, 1914.
36. Edwin Montagu, letter to Venetia Stanley, Sept. 2, 1914; M.G.
37. Id.
38. Edwin Montagu, letter to Venetia Stanley, Sept. 29, 1914; M.G.
39. Edwin Montagu, letter to Venetia Stanley, Oct. 8, 1914; M.G.
40. Brock, *H. H. Asquith Letters to Venetia Stanley*, pp. 358–59; E.S.M. to B.V.S., Jan. 3, 1915, n. 2.
41. Edwin Montagu, letter to Venetia Stanley, Oct. 15, 1914; M.G.
42. Brock, *H. H. Asquith Letters to Venetia Stanley*, pp. 184–85, letter #127, Aug. 21, 1914.
43. Ibid., p. 281, letter #186, Oct. 21, 1914; p. 178, letter #125, Aug. 19, 1914; p. 265, letter #176, Oct. 7, 1914; p. 275, letter #182, Oct. 13, 1914; p. 290, letter #192, Oct. 28, 1914; p. 295, letter #193, Oct. 29, 1914; p. 311, letter #205, Nov. 6, 1914; p. 326, letter #221, Dec. 5, 1914; p. 335, letter #232, Dec. 26, 1914; p. 339, letter #235, Dec. 25, 1914.
44. Ibid. ["very secret telegram"], p. 339, letter #235, Dec. 25, 1914; ["most

secret"], p. 285, letter #189, Oct. 24, 1914; ["a great secret"], p. 256, letter #168, Sept.29, 1914.

45. Ibid., p. 127, letter #106, July 27, 1914.

46. Morgan, *Churchill*, p. 520.

47. Ibid., p. 519. Robert Blake points out that only 15 letters of the 425 published by the Brocks were actually written during Cabinet or Committee meetings or on the Treasury bench. He points out too that Lloyd George also wrote to his mistress during meetings. *London Review of Books*, Jan. 20–Feb. 3, 1983.

48. Peter Clarke, "Don't Leave This on Your Table," *The Times* (London) *Education Supplement*, Jan. 14, 1983; review of Brock, *H. H. Asquith Letters to Venetia Stanley*.

49. Robert Blake, "Prime Ministers' Pets," *London Review of Books*, Jan. 20–Feb. 3, 1983, review of Brock, *H. H. Asquith Letters to Venetia Stanley*.

50. Philip Ziegler, the *Standard*, Wed. Nov. 24, 1982, p. 19, review of Brock, *H. H. Asquith Letters to Venetia Stanley*.

51. Id.

52. "A Matter of Security," *The Economist*, Jan. 8, 1983, p. 81, review of Brock, *H. H. Asquith Letters to Venetia Stanley*.

53. Godfrey Hodgson, *New York Times*, Book Review section, Apr. 3, 1983, p. 1; review of Brock, *H. H. Asquith Letters to Venetia Stanley*.

54. Bernard Levine, "Love's State Secrets"; review of Brock book; M.G.

55. Brock, *H. H. Asquith Letters to Venetia Stanley*, pp. 219–20, letter #144, Sept. 4, 1914.

56. Ibid., p. 282, letter #187, Oct. 22, 1914.

57. Ibid., p. 318, letter #214, Nov. 21, 1914.

58. Ibid., pp. 358–59, E.S.M. to B.V.S., letter #1, n. 2, Jan. 3, 1915.

59. Ibid., p. 358–59, letter #1; E.S.M. to B.V.S., Jan. 3, 1915.

60. Ibid., p. 345, letter #241 (train), Dec. 30, 1914.

61. Ibid., pp. 347–48, letter #242 (midnight), Dec. 30, 1914(ii).

62. Ibid., pp. 348–50, letter #243, Dec. 31, 1914.

63. Ibid., p. 356, letter #244, Jan. 1, 1915.

15. *Prelude to Political Disaster*

1. H. G. Wells, *Mr. Britling Sees It Through* (1916), pp. 282–83, quoted in Brock, *H. H. Asquith Letters to Venetia Stanley*, p. 354.

2. Barbara Tuchman, *The Proud Tower* (New York, 1966), p. 14. See also *Honours and Titles in Britain*, prepared by the Reference Services, Central Office of Information (London, 1982).

3. Morgan, *Churchill*, p. 535.

4. Id.

5. Edwin Montagu, letter to Venetia Stanley, Feb. 1, 1915; M.G.

6. Brock, *H. H. Asquith Letters to Venetia Stanley*, p. 393, letter #274, Jan. 24, 1915.

7. Id.

8. Id.

9. Venetia Stanley, letter to Edwin Montagu, Jan. 31, 1915; M.G.
10. Id.
11. Brock, *H. H. Asquith Letters to Venetia Stanley*, p. 401, letter #280, Jan. 27, 1915.
12. Id.
13. Id.
14. Ibid., p. 393, letter #274, Jan. 24, 1915.
15. Ibid., pp. 378–79, letter #260, Jan. 14, 1915.
16. Waley, *Edwin Montagu*, p. 64.
17. Edwin Montagu, letter to Asquith, Dec. 22, 1915; M.G.
18. Skidelsky, *John Maynard Keynes*, p. 298.
19. Ibid., pp. 298–99.
20. Ibid., p. 300.
21. Venetia Stanley, letter to Edwin Montagu, May 27, 1915; M.G.
22. Brock, *H. H. Asquith Letters to Venetia Stanley*, p. 356, letter #245, Jan. 1, 1915.
23. Edwin Montagu, letter to Venetia Stanley, Feb. 1, 1915; M.G.
24. Brock, *H. H. Asquith Letters to Venetia Stanley*, p. 356, letter #245, Jan. 1, 1915.
25. Edwin Montagu, letter to Venetia Stanley, Mar. 14, 1915; M.G.
26. Edwin Montagu, letter to Venetia Stanley, Mar. 15, 1915; M.G.
27. Edwin Montagu, letter to his mother, Mar. 20, 1915; M.G.
28. Edwin Montagu, memorandum for the Cabinet on "Postal Servants; Proposal for War Bonus," Mar. 24, 1915; M.G.
29. Brock, *H. H. Asquith Letters to Venetia Stanley*, p. 386, letter #267, Jan. 20, 1915(i).
30. Ibid., p. 426, letter #299, Feb. 11, 1915(i), 11 A.M..
31. Ibid., p. 455, letter #327, Mar. 1, 1915.
32. Ibid., p. 394, letter #275, Jan. 25, 1915.
33. Ibid., p. 396, letter #276, Jan. 26, 1915(i), after lunch.
34. Ibid., p. 359, letter #247, Jan. 5, 1915(i).
35. Ibid., p. 356, letter #244, Jan. 1, 1915, (i).
36. Ibid., pp. 356–58, letter #245, Jan. 1, 1915, (ii).
37. Ibid., p. 366, letter #253, Jan. 9, 1915.
38. Id.
39. Ibid., p. 369, letter #255, Jan. 11, 1915.
40. Ibid., p. 394, letter #275, Jan. 25, 1915.
41. Ibid., p. 417, letter #292, Feb. 7, 1915.
42. Ibid., p. 419, letter #295, Feb. 9, 1915.
43. Margot Asquith, letter to Ettie Desborough, Mar. 31, 1914; M.G.
44. Margot Asquith, letter to Edwin Montagu, Mar. 16, 1915; M.G.
45. Id.
46. Id.
47. Id.
48. Brock, *H. H. Asquith Letters to Venetia Stanley*, p. 548, letter XXII, from H.H.A. to Margot Asquith, Apr. 13, 1915.
49. Id.
50. A. J. P. Taylor, *London Review of Books*, Dec. 29, 1982, p. 25. Gladstone,

according to Taylor, listed as adulterers Prime Ministers Canning, Wellington, Earl Grey, Melbourne, Disraeli, and Palmerston. Taylor suggests the seventh man was Gladstone himself.

51. Lubbock, *People in Glass Houses*, p. 82.
52. Ibid., p. 82.
53. Brock, *H. H. Asquith Letters to Venetia Stanley*, p. 504, letter #365, Mar. 24, 1914(i), 3 P.M.
54. Ibid., p. 436, letter #312, Feb. 18, 1915(i), 11:15 A.M.
55. Ibid., p. 393, letter #274, Jan. 24, 1915.
56. Ibid., p. 472, letter #344, Mar. 11, 1915.
57. Ibid., p. 445, letter #318, Feb. 23, 1915.
58. Ibid., p. 449, letter #322, Feb. 26, 1915.
59. Ibid., p. 490, letter #357, Mar. 19, 1915.
60. Bernard Levin, *Book Review*, "Love's State Secrets," M.G.
61. Brock, *H. H. Asquith Letters to Venetia Stanley*, p. 489, letter #356, "A Portrait," part 3.
62. Ibid., p. 491, letter #358, Mar. 19, 1915.
63. Ibid., pp. 529–30, letter XIV, E.S.M. to B.V.S., [Apr. 3, 1915]. In dating this letter, Prof. Brock states, "The original is lost and the copy made for Mrs. Gendel has no date. The internal evidence strongly suggests 3 Apr." Ibid., n. 1.
64. Id.
65. Ibid., p. 531, letter #384, Apr. 4, 1915.
66. Ibid., p. 538, letter XVIII, B.V.S. to E.S.M., Apr. 13, 1915.
67. Id.
68. Venetia Stanley, letter to Edwin Montagu, Apr. 18, 1915; M.G.
69. Id.
70. Venetia Stanley, letter to Edwin Montagu, Apr. 30, 1915; M.G.
71. Raymond Asquith, letter to Diana Cooper, Dec. 18, 1915; M.G.
72. Id.
73. Venetia Stanley, letter to Edwin Montagu, Apr. 20, 1915, in which she refers to his suggestion that she "gradually free herself"; M.G.
74. Brock, *H. H. Asquith Letters to Venetia Stanley*, p. 543, letter #394, Apr. 16, 1915.
75. Ibid., p. 536, letter #XV, E.S.M. to B.V.S., Apr. 10, 1915.
76. Ibid., p. 537, letter #XVI, B.S.M. to E.S.M., Apr. 12, 1915.
77. Ibid., p. 537, letter #XVII, E.S.M. to B.V.S., Apr. 12, 1915.
78. Ibid., p. 539, letter #XIX, E.S.M. to B.V.S., Apr. 13, 1915.
79. Ibid., p. 539, letter #392, Apr. 14, 1915.
80. Id.
81. Margot Asquith Diaries, Mar. 7, 1915, Bonham Carter MSS.
82. Brock, *H. H. Asquith Letters to Venetia Stanley*, p. 338, letter #234, Dec. 24, 1915.
83. Ibid., pp. 545–46, letter #395, Apr. 16, 1915.
84. Ibid., p. 551, letter #398, Apr. 19, 1915.
85. Ibid., p. 553, letter #399, Apr. 19, 1915(ii).

86. Ibid., p. 555, letter #400, Apr. 20, 1915.

87. Edwin Montagu, letter to Venetia Stanley, Apr. 19, 1915; M.G.

88. Venetia Stanley, letter to Edwin Montagu, Apr. 20, 1915.

89. Kenneth Lindsay, *Contemporary Review, Literary Supplement,* 1983, p. 222; review of Brock, *H. H. Asquith Letters to Venetia Stanley.*

90. Venetia Stanley, letter to Edwin Montagu, Apr. 20, 1915; M.G.

91. Edwin Montagu, letter to Venetia Stanley, no date. Content makes it appear to have been written near the end of Apr. 1915; M.G.

92. Edwin Montagu, letter to Venetia Stanley, Apr. 19, 1915; M.G.

16. Venetia Announces Engagement to Montagu

1. Koss, *Asquith,* p. 161.

2. Jenkins, *Asquith,* p. 349.

3. Arthur Marwick, *The Explosion of British Society* (New York, 1970), Introduction, p. 1.

4. R. J. Q. Adams, *Arms and the Wizard* (Texas, 1978), pp. 13–19.

5. Edwin Montagu, letter to Asquith, Oct. 1, 1914; Montagu AS 1/7/32.

6. Id.

7. Id.

8. Edwin Montagu, letter to Asquith, Dec. 7, 1914; Montagu AS 6/9/19.

9. Edwin Montagu, memorandum to Asquith, enclosed with letter of Dec. 7, 1919; Montagu AS 6/9/19.

10. Brock, *H. H. Asquith Letters to Venetia Stanley,* p. 462, letter #335, Mar. 6, 1915(ii).

11. Id.

12. Ibid., p. 487, letter #355, Mar. 18, 1915, [i] noon.

13. Lloyd George, *War Memoirs,* vol. 1, p. 108.

14. Id.

15. Ibid., p. 109.

16. Brock, *H. H. Asquith Letters to Venetia Stanley,* p. 497, letter #362, Mar. 22, 1915, (ii), 7:15 P.M.

17. Waley, *Edwin Montagu,* p. 65.

18. Lloyd George, *War Memoirs,* vol. 1, p. 111.

19. Adams, *Arms and the Wizard,* p. 22.

20. Marwick, *The Explosion of British Society,* p. 2.

21. Beaverbrook, *Politicians and the War,* p. 66.

22. Ibid., p. 70.

23. Ibid., p. 66. See also Waley, *Edwin Montagu,* p. 65.

24. See Lloyd George, *War Memoirs,* vol. 1, pp. 111–12, in which Lloyd George lists Montagu as a member of the Shell Committee and makes no reference to the fact that he was Executive Secretary. See also Adams, *Arms and the Wizard,* p. 26, in which Montagu is also listed only as a member of the Committee: Sir Frederick Black is reported as the Secretary.

25. Adams, *Arms and the Wizard,* p. 27.

26. Jenkins, *Asquith,* p. 357.

27. Beaverbrook, *Politicians and the War,* pp. 90–91. At the time Repington wrote this story, he was not acting officially as a *Times* reporter; he gathered the information while he was visiting French as a friend.

28. Id.

29. Lloyd George, *War Memoirs,* vol 1, pp. 121, 122.

30. Edwin Montagu, letter to Asquith, Dec. 31, 1914; M.G.

31. William Manchester, *The Last Lion: Winston S. Churchill* (Boston, 1983), p. 517.

32. Jenkins, *Asquith,* p. 351.

33. Ibid., p. 352.

34. Ibid., p. 360.

35. Koss, *Lord Haldane,* pp. 147–56.

36. Ibid., p. 207.

37. Id.

38. Manchester, *The Last Lion,* p. 556.

39. Stevenson, *Lloyd George,* p. 50. See also Manchester, *The Last Lion,* p. 557.

40. Beaverbrook, *Politicians and the War,* p. 95.

41. Koss, *Asquith,* p. 185. Other historians, like Paul Adelman and Martin Pugh, blame Asquith's fear of the prospect of a General Election for the Coalition. Asquith believed, according to their thesis, that "the divided and unsuccessful Liberals were bound to lose. Coalition provided a possible escape route" (Adelman, *The Decline of the Liberal Party,* p. 14).

42. Trevor Wilson, *The Downfall of the Liberal Party, 1914–1915* (Ithaca, N.Y., 1966), p. 40.

43. Koss, *Asquith,* p. 183.

44. Ibid., p. 181.

45. Ibid., p. 183.

46. Ibid., p. 186.

47. Brock, *H. H. Asquith Letters to Venetia Stanley,* p. 598.

48. Koss, *Asquith,* p. 186.

49. Brock, *H. H. Asquith Letters to Venetia Stanley,* p. 353.

50. Ibid., p. 593, letter #425, May 12, 1915.

51. Ibid., p. 586, letter #420, May 7, 1915, (ii), midnight.

52. Id.

53. Ibid., p. 588, letter #422, May 10, 1915, midnight.

54. Ibid., p. 491, letter #358, Mar. 19, 1915, (ii), night.

55. Ibid., p. 596, Asquith to Sylvia Henley, May 12, 1915.

56. Ibid., p. 606, Asquith to Sylvia Henley, July 26, 1916.56.

57. Ibid., p. 596, Asquith to Sylvia Henley, May 12, 1915.

58. Id.

59. Ibid., p. 596, May 14, 1915.

60. Ibid., p. 353.

61. Id.

62. Id.

63. Id.

64. Jenkins, *Asquith,* p. 363.

65. Koss, *Asquith*, p. 186.
66. Jenkins, *Asquith*, p. 366.
67. Brock, *H. H. Asquith Letters to Venetia Stanley*, p. 598. Dr. Brock supports his conclusion that "the evidence cited by Mr. Jenkins is not conclusive" by pointing out that he (Asquith) could not have predicted when Italy would enter the war; he could not have held off an attack in the Commons until the news came from Italy; he did not have a Liberal substitute of sufficient standing to replace Churchill; and it is not clear whether the decision to replace Haldane was due entirely to Conservative pressure (ibid., p. 599). Dr. Brock states further, in the 1982 edition of his book, that while Asquith was worried about his relationship with Venetia weeks before her letter of May 11, during "the May crisis itself he acted *with undeniable skill and vigour*" (emphasis added). In the 1985 revision of his book, Brock softens this last phrase by substituting the following: "Despite the heartbreak he does *not seem to have been much below his usual political form* during the May crisis itself" (Brock, *H. H. Asquith Letters to Venetia Stanley*, paperback edition, 1985, p. 599, emphasis added).
68. Manchester, *The Last Lion*, p. 557.
69. Ibid., p. 558.
70. Brock, *H. H. Asquith Letters to Venetia Stanley*, p. 596, May 17, 1915.
71. Asquith, letter to Venetia Stanley, May 17, 1915; M.G.
72. Lady Cynthia Asquith, *Diaries, 1915–1918* (New York, 1968), p. 42.
73. Brock, *H. H. Asquith Letters to Venetia Stanley*, p. 417, Letter #292, Feb. 7, 1915.

17. Venetia's Escape to France

 1. Asquith, letter to Venetia Stanley, May 20, 1915(ii); M.G.
 2. Id.
 3. Id.
 4. Asquith, letter to Venetia Stanley, May 21, 1915(ii); AS. MSS. #432.
 5. Id.
 6. Asquith, letter to Venetia Stanley, May 21, 1915 (iii); AS. MSS. #433.
 7. Id.
 8. Asquith, Letter to Venetia Stanley, May 22, 1915; AS. MSS. #166.
 9. Edwin Montagu, letter to Venetia Stanley, May 25, 1915; M.G.
10. Asquith, letter to Edwin Montagu, May 18, 1915; M.G.
11. Venetia Stanley, letter to Edwin Montagu, May 24, 1915; AS. MSS. #306.
12. Edwin Montagu, letter to Venetia Stanley, May 25, 1915; M.G.
13. Venetia Stanley, letter to Edwin Montagu, May 24, 1915 (ii); M.G.
14. Edwin Montagu, letter to Venetia Stanley, May 30, 1915; M.G. While there is no date on the letter, its contents indicate that it was probably written on this date.
15. Asquith, Letter to Venetia Stanley, June 3, 1915; AS. MSS. #435.
16. Asquith, letter to Venetia Stanley, June 11, 1915; AS. MSS. #436.
17. Venetia Stanley, letter to Edwin Montagu, June 14, 1915; M.G.
18. Edwin Montagu, letter to Venetia Stanley, May 31, 1915; M.G.

19. Brock, *H. H. Asquith Letters to Venetia Stanley*, p. 600.
20. Asquith, letter to Lord Crewe, Oct. 4, 1913; M.G.
21. Brock, *H. H. Asquith Letters to Venetia Stanley*, p. 364, letter #251, Jan. 7, 1915.
22. Ibid., p. 406, letter #281, Jan. 28, 1915.
23. Ibid., p. 306, letter #200, Nov. 3, 1914.
24. Ibid., p. 600.
25. Asquith, *Diaries, 1915–1918*, p. 50.
26. Stevenson, *Lloyd George*, p. 40.
27. Grigg, *The Young Lloyd George* (London, 1985), p. 260.
28. Id.
29. Lubbock, *People in Glass Houses*, p. 83.
30. Ibid., pp. 83–84.
31. Brock, *H. H. Asquith Letters to Venetia Stanley*, p. 602.
32. Venetia Stanley, letter to Violet Asquith, May 28, 1915; M.G.
33. Violet Asquith, letter to Edwin Montagu, May 24, 1915; M.G.
34. Id.
35. Id.
36. Id.
37. Edwin Montagu, letter to Venetia Stanley, May 31, 1915; M.G.
38. Venetia Stanley, letter to Edwin Montagu, June 6, 1915; M.G.
39. Brock, *H. H. Asquith Letters to Venetia Stanley*, pp. 602–3.
40. Ibid., p. 603.
41. Ibid., p. 602.
42. Margot Asquith, Diaries, July 1916 to Aug. 1917, pp. 185–86; Bonham Carter MSS.
43. Brock, *H. H. Asquith Letters to Venetia Stanley*, p. 603.
44. Lubbock, *People in Glass Houses*, p. 82.
45. Edwin Montagu, letter to Venetia Stanley, June 11, 1915; M.G.
46. Lubbock, *People in Glass Houses*, p. 83.
47. Ibid., p. 83.
48. Id.
49. Id.
50. Edwin Montagu, letter to Venetia Stanley, June 11, 1915; M.G.
51. Edwin Montagu, letters to Venetia Stanley, May 25, 1915, to July 7, 1915; M.G.
52. Venetia Stanley, letter to Edwin Montagu, May 25, 1915; M.G.
53. Venetia Stanley, letter to Edwin Montagu, May 30, 1915; M.G.
54. Venetia Stanley, letter to Edwin Montagu, June 9, 1915; M.G.
55. Venetia Stanley, letter to Edwin Montagu, June 10, 1915; M.G.
56. Venetia Stanley, letter to Edwin Montagu, June 12, 1915; M.G.
57. Edwin Montagu, letter to Venetia Stanley, June 11, 1915; M.G.
58. Venetia Stanley, letter to Edwin Montagu, June 13, 1915; M.G.
59. Edwin Montagu, letter to Venetia Stanley, July 5, 1915; M.G.
60. Asquith, letter to Venetia Stanley, July 14, 1915, midnight; M.G.
61. Edwin Montagu, letter to Venetia Stanley, Apr. 30, 1915, misdated Apr. 29, 1915; M.G.

62. Venetia Stanley, letter to Edwin Montagu, May 27, 1915; M.G.
63. Id.
64. Venetia Stanley, letter to Edwin Montagu, May 28, 1915; M.G.
65. Brock, *H. H. Asquith Letters to Venetia Stanley*, p. 433, Letter #309, February 17, 1915.
66. Venetia Stanley, letter to Edwin Montagu, May 28, 1915; M.G.
67. Venetia Stanley, letter to Edwin Montagu, June 14, 1915; M.G.
68. Brock, *H. H. Asquith Letters to Venetia Stanley*, p. 605.
69. Id. See also Venetia Stanley, letter to Edwin Montagu, July 1, 1915; M.G.
70. Edwin Montagu, letter to Venetia Stanley, June 9, 1915; M.G.
71. Venetia Stanley, letter to Edwin Montagu, June 15, 1915; M.G.
72. Venetia Stanley, letter to Edwin Montagu, July 1, 1915; M.G.
73. Asquith, *Diaries, 1915–1918*, July 13, 1915, p. 54.
74. Diana Cooper, *The Rainbow Comes and Goes* (Boston, 1958), p. 138.
75. Edwin Montagu, letter to Venetia Stanley, July 23, 1915; M.G.
76. Asquith, letter to Venetia Stanley, July 24, 1915; M.G.
77. Jenkins, *Asquith*, p. 365.

18. The Coalition

1. Edwin Montagu, letter to Venetia Stanley, May 26, 1915; M.G.
2. Jenkins, *Asquith*, p. 369.
3. Waley, *Edwin Montagu*, p. 71.
4. Edwin Montagu, letter to Venetia Stanley, May 26, 1915; M.G.
5. Edwin Montagu, letter to Venetia Stanley, May 28, 1915; M.G.
6. Edwin Montagu, letter to Asquith, June 15, 1915; M.G.
7. Edwin Montagu, letter to Venetia Stanley, May 28, 1915; M.G.
8. Jenkins, *Asquith*, p. 362.
9. Edwin Montagu, letter to Venetia Stanley, May 26, 1915; M.G.
10. Asquith, letter to Chief Whip Guilland, May 28, 1915; M.G.
11. Edwin Montagu, letter to Venetia Stanley, June 11, 1915; M.G.
12. F. W. Hirst and J. E. Allen, *British War Budgets* (London: Carnegie Endowment for International Peace, 1926), pp. 36–72.
13. Ibid., p. 56.
14. Edwin Montagu, letter to Venetia Stanley, June 15, 1915; M.G.
15. Edwin Montagu, letter to Venetia Stanley, June 13, 1915; M.G.
16. Edwin Montagu, letter to Venetia Stanley, June 15, 1915; M.G.
17. Waley, *Edwin Montagu*, p. 71.
18. Ibid., pp. 73–74.
19. Ibid., p. 74.
20. For a discussion of protective duties and free trade, see Arthur Marwick, *The Deluge* (Boston, 1965), pp. 172–73.
21. Marwick, *The Explosion of British Society*, p. 2.
22. Hirst and Allen, *British War Budgets*, p. 119. For a full discussion of this budget, see also pp. 73–125.

23. Waley, *Edwin Montagu*, pp. 76–78.
24. Ibid., p. 81.
25. Ibid., p. 79.
26. Id.
27. Id.
28. Ibid., p. 80.
29. Id.
30. Id.
31. Ibid., p. 81.
32. Id.
33. Ibid., p. 82.
34. Stephen McKenna, *Reginald McKenna* (London, 1948), p. 257.
35. Edwin Montagu, letter to Asquith, Jan. 6, 1916; M.G. See also Waley, *Edwin Montagu*, pp. 87–88.
36. Waley, *Edwin Montagu*, p. 82.
37. Raymond Asquith, letter to Diana Cooper, Dec. 18, 1915; M.G.
38. Id.
39. Raymond Asquith, letter to Diana Cooper, Dec. 5, 1915; M.G.
40. Raymond Asquith, letter to Diana Cooper, Nov. 25, 1915; M.G.
41. Raymond Asquith, letter to Diana Cooper, Nov. 19, 1915; M.G.
42. Waley, *Edwin Montagu*, p. 88.
43. Jenkins, *Asquith*, p. 392.
44. Brock, *H. H. Asquith Letters to Venetia Stanley*, p. 607.
45. Waley, *Edwin Montagu*, p. 92.
46. *Dictionary of National Biography (1922–1930)*.
47. Waley, *Edwin Montagu*, p. 92. The "Bertie" referred to in this quote was Viscount Bertie (1844–1919) who was the Ambassador at Paris from 1905 to 1918. When Montagu wrote the letter in Feb. 1916, Bertie was seventy-two years old.
48. Hirst and Allen, *British War Budgets*, p. 149. For a full discussion of this budget, see pp. 126–65.
49. Ibid., p. 143.
50. Waley, *Edwin Montagu*, p. 90.
51. Adams, *Arms and the Wizard*, p. 28.
52. Lloyd George, *Memoirs*, vol. 1, pp. 416–17.
53. Edwin Montagu, letter to Sir Thomas Heath, Feb. 7, 1916; Montagu AS 1/8/18.
54. Id.
55. Id.
56. Waley, *Edwin Montagu*, p. 93. See also Stephen Roskill, *Hankey: Man of Secrets* (New York, 1970), vol. 1, p. 269.
57. Id.
58. Ibid., pp. 93–94.
59. Ibid., p. 94.
60. Id.

61. Brock, *H. H. Asquith Letters to Venetia Stanley*, p. 607.

62. Jenkins, *Asquith*, p. 398.

63. Ibid., p. 401.

19. Montagu at Munitions

1. Waley, *Edwin Montagu*, p. 96, n. 1.

2. Jenkins, *Asquith*, p. 409.

3. Ibid., p. 410.

4. Owen, *Tempestuous Journey*, p. 319.

5. Id.

6. Waley, *Edwin Montagu*, p. 97.

7. Adams, *Arms and the Wizard*, p. 182.

8. Ibid., p. 44.

9. *History of the Ministry of Munitions*, Admin. Pol. and Organ. vol. 2, pt. 1, (London, 1922), p. 160.

10. Ibid., pp. 160–61.

11. Id.

12. Ibid., p. 162.

13. Id.

14. Ibid., p. 162.

15. Id.

16. Ibid., p. 48.

17. Waley, *Edwin Montagu*, p. 99.

18. *History of the Ministry of Munitions*, Admin. Pol. and Organ., vol. 2, pt. 1, p. 167.

19. Waley, *Edwin Montagu*, p. 98.

20. Ibid., pp. 98–99.

21. Ibid., p. 96.

22. *History of the Ministry of Munitions*, Gen. Admin., vol. 2, pt. 1, pp. 47–48. See also pp. 49–74.

23. Gen. Sir C. F. N. Macready, letter to Edwin Montagu, Dec. 9, 1916; Montagu AS 6/2/36.

24. Manchester, *The Last Lion*, p. 510.

25. Id.

26. Edwin Montagu, letter to Asquith, July 3, 1915; M.G.

27. Winston Churchill, letter to Edwin Montagu, Nov. 1916; M.G. Tanks were first used 2 months after Montagu became Minister of Munitions, in the Battle of the Somme on Sept. 15, 1916 (*History of the Ministry of Munitions*, Gen. Admin., vol. 2, pt. 1, p. 56). The British infantry were not prepared to use them properly and the element of surprise was wasted (Manchester, *The Last Lion*, p. 565).

28. Manchester, *The Last Lion*, p. 648.

29. Id.

30. Edwin Montagu, letter to Arthur Henderson, Aug. 4, 1916; Montagu AS 17/40/41.

31. Id.
32. Edwin Montagu, letter to Asquith, Aug. 23, 1916; Montagu AS 17/51/53.
33. Id.
34. Edwin Montagu, letter to Margot Asquith, Aug. 23, 1916; Montagu AS 17/51/53.
35. Edwin Montagu, letter to Margot Asquith, Aug. 8, 1916; Montagu AS 5/1/14. See also Waley, *Edwin Montagu*, pp. 99–100.
36. Id.

20. The Fall of Asquith

1. Jenkins, *Asquith*, p. 412.
2. Ibid., p. 414.
3. Ibid., p. 415. See also the Earl of Oxford and Asquith, K. G., *Memories and Reflections, 1852–1927* (Boston, 1928), vol. 2, pp. 158–59.
4. Ziegler, *Diana Cooper*, pp. 32–33.
5. Ibid., p. 78.
6. Jenkins, *Asquith*, p. 415.
7. Waley, *Edwin Montagu*, p. 102.
8. Jenkins, *Asquith*, p. 417.
9. Ibid., p. 411.
10. Edwin Montagu, memorandum, Dec. 9, 1916; Montagu AS 1/10/1.
11. Jenkins, *Asquith*, pp. 417–19.
12. Ibid., p. 418.
13. Ibid., p. 426.
14. Ibid., pp. 426–27.
15. Ibid., p. 425.
16. Waley, *Edwin Montagu*, pp. 103–4.
17. Jenkins, *Asquith*, pp. 425–26.
18. Ibid., p. 430.
19. Ibid., pp. 430–31.
20. Ibid., p. 431.
21. Jenkins, *Asquith*, p. 432. Based on memorandum prepared by Edwin Montagu, Dec. 9, 1916; Montagu AS 1/10/1.
22. Edwin Montagu, memorandum, Dec. 9, 1916; Montagu AS 1/10/1.
23. Jenkins, *Asquith*, p. 433.
24. Ibid., p. 433.
25. Id.
26. Waley, *Edwin Montagu*, pp. 104–5.
27. Ibid., p. 105.
28. Id.
29. Id.
30. Jenkins, *Asquith*, p. 435.
31. Ibid., p. 436.
32. Ibid., p. 437.
33. Ibid., p. 441.

34. Id.
35. Ibid., p. 442.
36. Ibid., p. 443.
37. Ibid., pp. 441–42.
38. Waley, *Edwin Montagu*, p. 106.
39. Jenkins, *Asquith*, p. 446. Jenkins also reports Hankey wrote that long after the fall of Asquith, Lloyd George had told him that Geoffrey Dawson, the editor of *The Times*, had written this story on his own, without any input from Northcliffe. The specific facts included in the article came from Carson (ibid., p. 445). Jenkins raises serious doubts about this and points out that even if the editor of *The Times* received the information from Carson, the latter could only have received it from Lloyd George.
40. Ibid., p. 448.
41. Ibid., p. 450.
42. Waley, *Edwin Montagu*, p. 107.
43. Jenkins, *Asquith*, p. 452.
44. Ibid., pp. 452–53.
45. Id.
46. Waley, *Edwin Montagu*, p. 110.
47. Jenkins, *Asquith*, pp. 453–54.
48. Waley, *Edwin Montagu*, p. 107.
49. Id.
50. Id.
51. Ibid., p. 108.
52. Ibid., pp. 107–10.
53. Ibid., p. 110.
54. Jenkins, *Asquith*, p. 454.
55. Ibid., p. 455.
56. Id.
57. Koss, *Asquith*, p. 226.
58. Ibid., pp. 225–26.
59. Ibid., p. 227.
60. Stevenson, *Lloyd George*, Introduction by A. J. P. Taylor.
61. Roskill, *Hankey*, vol. 1, p. 172. Edwin Montagu, letter to Hankey, Mar. 22, 1915.
62. Jenkins, *Asquith*, p. 432.
63. Charles Hobhouse, *Inside Asquith's Cabinet* (London, 1977), p. 238.
64. Montagu memorandum, Dec. 9, 1917; Montagu AS 1/10/1.
65. Waley, *Edwin Montagu*, p. 115.
66. Edwin Montagu, memorandum, Dec. 9, 1916; Montagu, AS 1/10/1.
67. Id.
68. Waley, *Edwin Montagu*, p. 113.
69. Ibid., p. 114.
70. Asquith, *Diaries, 1915–1918*, p. 244.
71. Waley, *Edwin Montagu*, p. 115.
72. Id.

73. Edwin Montagu, letter to Lloyd George, Dec. 18, 1916; M.G.
74. Id.
75. Margot Asquith, Diaries, July 1916 to Aug. 1917; Bonham Carter MSS.
76. Even as late as May 1949, 33 years after Asquith's fall and 24 years after Montagu died, Violet's bitterness remained. On May 10, 1949, she sent a copy of Montagu's memorandum of Dec. 9 to a Mr. Roberts. It had been sent to her by Montagu's Private Secretary Alex Berlow, several years after Montagu's death, with the caveat that she "not show it to anyone whose opinion of Edwin S. Montagu would be very much lowered by reading it." (Asquith, MSS, 7.170). After reading the memorandum, Mr. Roberts concluded in a letter to Violet written on May 17, 1949, that Montagu was "disloyal to Asquith" and showed "no consideration for the Liberal Party." It was "not a pretty picture of friend Montagu but characteristic enough." Mr. Roberts wrote:

> He says in his published diary that he felt "hero-worship" for your father. And in a speech of that time he was "inspired with the privilege of intimate friendship with Mr. Asquith." Not much trace of the "worshipper" in this document, merely a cold appraisement of your father's great qualities, if balanced and supplemented by the great qualities of George. Not a line expressing sadness at the passing of a great administration, not a word of personal regret at the fall of one who had given him exceptionally rapid advancement and to whom his debt was great.
>
> And—a lesser count—there is no thought of the blow—an almost mortal blow—that was being dealt to the party to which he owed allegiance: merely a growl that in future he couldn't bring himself to work with members of his party.
>
> He complains that Bonar Law thought only of the interests of his own party. Certainly Montagu wasn't guilty of that.
>
> Of course, it's not a factual account of the events. One small fact I can add. I remember clearly Gulland's heated expostulation when it was thought that he wasn't resigning, and the wave of Montagu's hand as he dismissed Gulland as of no account. He wanted doubtless to leave on record a studied vindication of action which he knew for him was not straight. His mind seems to reveal itself like this: "It is a bit awkward for me to disentangle myself from the fallen fortunes of my hero. But reason is given us to find arguments for what we want—perhaps after a decent brief interval—to do. The war-setbacks, the machinations of Bonar Law and Northcliffe and the perverse malignity of McKenna (was McKenna in his way in getting the Chancellorship?) broke down the Asquith-George combination. I hoped it would be retained as I did my best. George wanted to continue it, so he told me. (No need to ask why he took steps not exactly calculated to preserve it.) Asquith indeed was not a little to blame for the breakdown through bad chairmanship and inability to put things through (the special card George was playing) and through his too hurried resignation contrary to my wish and advice. The combination having collapsed I transfer my allegiance to George. I could have had high office, even the Chancellorship, had I asked for it. Perhaps it wouldn't have been decent at once. Meanwhile I flatter myself on my good work at Munitions. George doubtless understands my restraint. Probably my chance will come again."

> It came soon enough, and he pounced on it. "By this sin fell the angels."

> He had remarkable qualities, but loyalty to a great leader or any consideration for his party, if either stood in the way of his career, were not among his virtues. [Mr. Roberts, letter to Violet Asquith, May 17, 1949; AS., MSS. 7.170]

On May 23, 1949, Violet responded:

> Many thanks for returning the document and for your most interesting letter. I agree with every word you say.
>
> Montagu had practically *lived* in our house for many years. In London, there was not a day on which we did not see him. Failing all else, he would turn up between eleven and twelve at night before we went to bed and pour out a torrent of emotions, thoughts and experiences. His passionate devotion to my father made us forgive him a great deal and we were really fond of him.
>
> After my father's fall from power, Jack Seely lent us, for a few weeks, his house in the Isle of Wight and I wrote to Edwin asking him which weekends he would like to spend with us there. To my amazement, he replied that he was engaged for all of them and could not come at all. This was to me the first shock of realization, and from that moment I understood that his one desire was to get back into the Government, any Government, at any price, and on any terms. This, as you know, he did.
>
> *I always remember Winston's comment when his appointment to the India Office was announced. I met Winston in Palace Yard and he said to me: "I have no right to be squeamish about changes of front—but this!—it is as if one's own lap-dog turned round and bit one." I felt some bitterness at the time. I feel none now because I know that he was, for the rest of his life, a very unhappy man. Still I cannot conceal from myself that knowledge that had he stayed out of the Government and been faithful to his old friends, he would have been still unhappier. Of him it was painfully true that: "Il vaut mieux avoir des remords que des regrets."* [emphasis added]

Yours very sincerely,
Violet Bonham Carter

[Violet Asquith, letter to Mr. Roberts, May 23, 1949; AS., MSS. 7.170]

21. Marriage: The Beginning

1. Asquith, *Diaries, 1915–1918,* Nov. 12, 1915, p. 98.
2. Raymond Asquith, letter to Diana Cooper, Oct. 15, 1915; M.G.
3. Alastair Forbes, letter to *The Times* (London), Dec. 14, 1982.
4. Asquith, *Diaries, 1915–1918,* Nov. 30, 1915, p. 107.
5. Ibid., Apr. 19, 1916, p. 156.
6. Ibid., Apr. 22, 1916, p. 158.
7. Ibid., Nov. 30, 1915, p. 107.
8. Cooper, *The Rainbow Comes and Goes,* p. 148.
9. Ziegler, *Diana Cooper,* p. 23.
10. Lambert, *Unquiet Souls,* p. 152.
11. Cooper, *A Durable Fire,* Introduction, p. xv. See also Lambert, *Unquiet Souls,* pp. 147–66.
12. Cooper, *The Rainbow Comes and Goes,* p. 137.
13. Ibid., p. 138.
14. Id.
15. Id.
16. Ibid., p. 147.
17. Asquith, *Diaries 1915–1918,* Apr. 21, 1916, p. 157.
18. Ziegler, *Diana Cooper,* p. 58.
19. Id.

20. Id.
21. Asquith, *Diaries, 1915–1918*, p. 157.
22. Cooper, *A Durable Fire*, p. 31.
23. Asquith, *Diaries, 1915–1918*, p. 244.
24. Ziegler, *Diana Cooper*, p. 28.
25. Id.
26. Id.
27. Duff Cooper, *Old Men Forget*, p. 45. See also Ziegler, *Diana Cooper*, p. 28, for comment about Billy and Julian Grenfell.
28. Ziegler, *Diana Cooper*, p. 117.
29. Ibid., p. 28.
30. Cooper, *A Durable Fire*, p. 84.
31. Ibid., p. 83.
32. Ziegler, *Diana Cooper*, p. 29.
33. Id.
34. Id.

22. Montagu and Reconstruction

1. Waley, *Edwin Montagu*, pp. 116, 117.
2. A. J. P. Taylor, *English History, 1914–1945* (Oxford History of England, Oxford, 1975), p. 76, points out that "the new departments evolved a system of war socialism" working side by side with the old departments.
3. Ibid., p. 87.
4. Ibid., pp. 88–95.
5. Maurice Hankey, letter to Edwin Montagu, Jan. 21, 1917; Montagu AS 1/12/140.
6. Waley, *Edwin Montagu*, p. 116.
7. Paul Barton Johnson, *Land Fit for Heroes* (Chicago, 1968), p. 10.
8. Ibid., p. 31.
9. Ibid., p. 33.
10. Ibid., p. 36.
11. Id.
12. Ibid., p. 37.
13. Ibid., p. 38.
14. Id.
15. Alfred F. Havighurst, *Twentieth-Century Britain* (New York, 1962), p. 169.
16. Thomas Jones, *Lloyd George* (Cambridge, Mass. 1951), pp. 124–25. Members of the Committee included Dr. Marion Phillips (a member of the Labour Party), Leslie Scott and Major J. W. Hills (both progressive Conservative Members of Parliament), Thomas Jones (Fabian Society, one of Lloyd George's Kitchen Cabinet), B. Seebohm Rowntree (author of study on "Poverty"), Professor W. G. S. Adams (a distinguished economist), Philip Kerr (one of the Prime Minister's secretaries), the Marquis of Salisbury, Sir J. Stevenson (a member of the Ministry of Munitions), J. H. Thomas (Labour Member of Parliament, leader of Trade Union Movement) and Beatrice Webb. Vaughan

Nash was Secretary, assisted by J. L. (Jason) Hammond, Arthur Greenwood and, later, Sir Maurice Bonham Carter (Johnson, *Land Fit for Heroes*, p. 36, n. 2).

17. Johnson refers to Montagu only as one of the secretaries; for example, he states "only the secretaries Montagu and Hammond had served on the old committee," (Johnson, *Land Fit for Heroes*, p. 36). Montagu was not a secretary. He was Vice-Chairman. Again, as in his position on the Munitions Committee, Montagu's role has been minimized.

18. Waley, *Edwin Montagu*, p. 117.

19. Ibid., p. 118.

20. Edwin Montagu, letter to Lloyd George, Mar. 28, 1917; Lloyd George MSS., F/29/3/10.

21. Edwin Montagu, letter to Lloyd George, May 24, 1917; Lloyd George MSS., F/39/3/14.

22. Johnson, *Land Fit for Heroes*, p. 39.

23. Edwin Montagu, letter to Lloyd George, June 5, 1917; Lloyd George MSS., F/39/3/15.

24. Id.

25. Edwin Montagu, letter to Lloyd George, June 5, 1917; 2d letter of the day, written in the afternoon; Lloyd George MSS., F/39/3/16.

26. Johnson, *Land Fit for Heroes*, p. 42.

27. Id.

28. Id.

29. Id.

30. Peter Cline, "Winding Down the War Economy: British Plans for Peacetime Recovery, 1916–19," in Burk, *War and the State*, p. 172.

31. Ibid., p. 173.

32. Ibid., p. 172.

33. Id.

34. Id.

35. Ibid., p. 172. The Sir Edward Carson referred to in this quote was an Ulster leader in the House of Commons, who became First Lord of the Admiralty in Lloyd George's government. He was appointed in 1917 to chair a committee appointed by the War Cabinet which "without prejudice to the effective continuance of the existing Economic Offensive should consider the whole question [of economic strategy during and after the war] with a view to their recommendations being utilized as the basis of further consultations with the Allied governments." Cline, "Winding Down the War Economy," in Burk, *War and the State*, p. 169. Carson believed that the imposition of a blockade against Germany, even if Britain lost, could be leveraged to Britain's advantage.

36. Ibid., pp. 172–73. The Report of the Economic Offensive Committee was submitted to the War Cabinet, Nov. 15, 1917. See also ibid., p. 173, n. 64.

37. Ibid., p. 173.

38. Johnson, *Land Fit for Heroes*, p. 54.

39. Ibid., p. 57.

40. Waley, *Edwin Montagu*, pp. 120–21.

41. Ibid., p. 121.
42. Ibid., p. 122.
43. Ibid., p. 123.
44. Edwin Montagu, memorandum, May 10, 1917; Montagu AS 1/12/10.
45. Id.
46. Id.
47. Edwin Montagu, letter to Lloyd George, May 18, 1917; Montagu AS 6/1/15.
48. Id.
49. Waley, *Edwin Montagu,* p. 126.
50. Edwin Montagu, letter to Lloyd George, June 18, 1917; Montagu AS 6/2/13.
51. Edwin Montagu, letter to H. H. Asquith, June 18, 1917; Montagu AS 18/11/14.
52. H. H. Asquith, letter to Edwin Montagu, June 19, 1917; Montagu AS 6/11/7.
53. Waley, *Edwin Montagu,* p. 127.
54. Id.
55. Id.
56. Edwin Montagu, memorandum to Maurice Hankey, Apr. 21, 1917; Montagu AS 6/2/10.
57. Id.
58. Lloyd George, *War Memoirs,* vol. 1, p. 483.
59. Ibid., p. 484.
60. Edwin Montagu, letter to Lloyd George, July 5, 1917; Montagu AS 6/10/11.
61. Id.
62. Id.
63. Id.
64. Waley, *Edwin Montagu,* p. 127.
65. Ibid., pp. 127, 128.
66. Edwin Montagu, letter to Lloyd George, July 14, 1917; Montagu AS 4/3/5/11.
67. Waley, *Edwin Montagu,* p. 128.
68. Ibid., pp. 128–29.
69. Ibid., p. 129.
70. Id.
71. Id.
72. Id.
73. Id.
74. Lloyd George, letter to Arthur Balfour, July 16, 1917; Lloyd George MSS. F/3/2/25.
75. Arthur Balfour, letter to Lloyd George, July 18, 1917; Lloyd George MSS. F/3/2/26.
76. Waley, *Edwin Montagu,* p. 129.
77. Id.
78. Ibid., pp. 130–31.
79. Ibid., p. 130.
80. Id.
81. Id.
82. Margot Asquith Diaries, July–Aug. 1917, pp. 197–98. Bonham Carter MSS.

83. Ibid., pp. 185–86.
84. Ibid., pp. 207–8.
85. Stevenson, *Lloyd George,* p. 139.
86. Ibid., p. 160.

23. Zionism

1. Leonard Stein, *The Balfour Declaration* (New York, 1961), pp. 75, 76.
2. Stuart A. Cohen, *English Zionists and British Jews* (Princeton, N.J., 1982), p. 167. See also, pp. 161–88.
3. Waley, Edwin Montagu, p. 11.
4. Walter Laqueur, *History of Zionism* (New York, 1972), p. 119. According to Laqueur, the British Zionists were responsible for getting Herzl this invitation.
5. Id.
6. Ibid., p. 126.
7. Ibid., p. 127.
8. Id.
9. Ibid., p. 158.
10. Cohen, *English Zionists and British Jews,* p. 130.
11. Stein, *The Balfour Declaration,* p. 142.
12. Id.; see also pp. 137–46.
13. Ibid., p. 103.
14. Id.
15. Ibid., p. 106.
16. Ibid., p. 112.
17. Ibid., pp. 117–19.
18. Waley, *Edwin Montagu,* p. 139.
19. Stein, *The Balfour Declaration,* p. 111.
20. Ibid., pp. 174–175.
21. Ibid., p. 455.
22. Laqueur, *History of Zionism,* p. 196.
23. Id.
24. Stein, *The Balfour Declaration,* pp. 496–97.
25. Ibid., p. 497.
26. Ibid., p. 486.
27. Ibid., p. 489.
28. Ibid., p. 492. An auxiliary unit of Jewish refugees had been formed by Jabotinsky in Palestine by the end of 1914 called the Jewish Legion. It fought with the British at Gallipoli. In 1916 it was disbanded and about 150 of its ex-members joined the British Army. Eventually they formed the basis of the Jewish unit of the Royal Fusiliers (the 38th Royal Fusiliers).
29. *Edwin Montagu and the Balfour Declaration* (New York: Arab League Office), p. 8. No date appears on this publication. This document is not in the libraries of any of the Jewish organizations in the U.S. It is in the Mocatta Library at University College, London, which includes the Library of the Jewish Histori-

cal Society of England. A copy was given by the author of this book to the Institute of Jewish Affairs of the World Jewish Congress in London.

30. Id.
31. Ibid., pp. 8–10.
32. Ibid., p. 11.
33. Ibid., pp. 12–15. This suggestion was contained in a letter written by Edwin Montagu to Lord Robert Cecil, Ass't. Sec't. for Foreign Affairs, Sept. 14, 1917.
34. Stein, *The Balfour Declaration,* p. 514.
35. Id.
36. Id.
37. Id.
38. Edwin Montagu, memorandum on "Zionism," Oct. 9, 1917, Public Record Office; Cab. Papers, no. 24–28.
39. Id.
40. Ibid., pp. 17–19.
41. Ibid., p. 19.
42. Ibid., p. 19.
43. Ibid., pp. 20–21.
44. Ibid., pp. 21–22.
45. Ibid., p. 22
46. Stein, *The Balfour Declaration,* p. 515.
47. Ibid., p. 516.
48. Id.
49. Ibid., p. 519.
50. Ibid., p. 527.
51. Ibid., p. 528.
52. Ibid., p. 500.
53. Laqueur, *A History of Zionism,* p. 198.
54. Chaim Weizmann, *Trial and Error: An Autobiography* (New York, 1949), p. 206. For a complete analysis of the changes made in the Balfour Declaration, see Stein, *The Balfour Declaration,* pp. 521–56 and p. 664.
55. Stein, *The Balfour Declaration,* pp. 531–32.
56. Ibid., p. 522, n. 17.
57. Id.
58. David Lloyd George, *Memoirs of the Peace Conference* (New Haven, Conn., 1939), vol. 2, p. 733. See also Waley, *Edwin Montagu,* p. 141.
59. Id.
60. Viscount Samuel, *Memoirs* (London, 1945), p. 170.
61. *Parl. Deb.,* House of Commons, vol. 347, May 23, 1939, p. 2173.
62. In commenting on this phase in Montagu's life, Dr. Arthur Hertzberg, noted historian and author of *The Zionist Idea,* has stated:

> The story of Edwin Montagu's struggle against the Balfour Declaration is not merely the story of one man's bitter opposition to the concept of a Jewish people, but is the ultimate demonstration of the illusory nature of Jewish assimilation. It is the story of a rich and powerful Jew who spent a lifetime assimilating into English society only to find that his

pleas to his colleagues to treat him as their equal—as a true and loyal Englishman, were rejected.

There were many reasons for the adoption of the Balfour Declaration, principally England's imperial interests in the Middle East. But one should not underestimate the fact that it was not difficult for the English to accept a Zionist ideology that viewed the Jew as a foreigner, an Oriental, with a homeland in some mysterious place called Palestine. Such a view of Jews was in accord with the attitude of the majority of Englishmen before Herzl touched the shores of England.

Montagu's inability to understand this, according to Dr. Hertzberg, was at the heart of the tragedy which marred his life (conversation between Dr. Hertzberg and the author, March, 1990).

24. Secretary of State for India

1. Sir J. A. R. Marriott, *Modern England 1885–1939* (London, 1941), p. 404.
2. Edwin Montagu, presentation to the House of Commons, *Parl. Deb.*, vol. 109, Aug. 6, 1918, p. 1144.
3. Sir Valentine Chirol, *India* (London, 1930), p. 159.
4. Das, *India from Curzon to Nehru and After*, p. 53.
5. Edwin Montagu, *Indian Diary*, ed. Venetia Stanley Montagu (London, 1930), p. 16.
6. Waley, *Edwin Montagu*, p. 132.
7. Id.
8. Mark Bence-Jones, *The Viceroys of India* (London, 1982), p. 223. For a complete discussion of Chelmsford's critical role in pressing for some statement on and action for providing some form of self-government for India compatible with maintaining British rule, see P. G. Robb, *The Government of India and Reform* (Oxford, 1976), pp. 53–85.
9. Edwin Montagu, letter to Lloyd George, Aug. 1, 1917; Montagu AS 7/10/7.
10. Id.
11. Id.
12. Id.
13. Edwin Montagu, letter to Chamberlain, Aug. 7, 1917; Waley, *Edwin Montagu*, p. 134.
14. Edwin Montagu, letter to Lord Curzon, Aug. 9, 1917; Montagu AS 3/2/1.
15. Edwin Montagu, letter to Lloyd George, Aug. 11, 1917; Montagu AS 7/39/3/29.
16. Waley, *Edwin Montagu*, p. 134.
17. Ibid., p. 136.
18. Leonard Mosley, *The Glorious Fault* (New York, 1960), p. 195.
19. Waley, *Edwin Montagu*, pp. 133–35.
20. Mosley, *The Glorious Fault*, p. 195.
21. Ibid., p. 196.
22. Id.
23. Das, *India from Curzon to Nehru and After*, pp. 58–59. Not only was Curzon

given credit for the Declaration, but a year after its adoption, Montagu told Chelmsford "that Chamberlain regarded himself as the 'father and mother' of the reforms; Chelmsford was glad to hear it—perhaps, he suggested, it was 'the exercise of this dual function' which had prolonged 'the period of gestation' almost to danger point" (Robb, *The Government of India and Reform*, p. 73).

Chelmsford himself believed "that Montagu had entered the reforms discussion 'at a moment when the policy was more or less cut and dried. It only wanted to be developed in detail.' It is easy to see how he came to this conclusion: the central feature of the reforms was the acceptance of the idea of dualism." Chelmsford believed this idea took root "when his Council first tried to relate their proposals to the goal of self-government" (ibid., p. 85).

24. Chirol, *India*, p. 163.
25. Edwin Montagu, letter to Chelmsford, Sept. 21, 1917. Waley, *Edwin Montagu*, pp. 137–38.
26. Edwin Montagu, letter to Chelmsford, Aug. 1917. Waley, *Edwin Montagu*, p. 135.
27. Waley, *Edwin Montagu*, pp. 138–39.
28. Edwin Montagu, letter to Venetia Stanley, Sept. 28, 1917. Waley, *Edwin Montagu*, p. 142.
29. Waley, *Edwin Montagu*, p. 143.
30. Id.
31. Montagu, *Indian Diary*, p. 10.
32. Waley, *Edwin Montagu*, p. 144.
33. Ibid., p. 144.
34. Bence-Jones, *The Viceroys of India*, p. 224.
35. Waley, *Edwin Montagu*, p. 145. Robb's analysis of this period, in *The Government of India and Reform*, unlike Montagu's, gives Chelmsford a major portion of the credit for the reforms and presents a different picture of Chelmsford, showing him as a determined protagonist for reform.
36. Id.
37. Id.
38. Id.
39. Bence-Jones, *The Viceroys of India*, p. 224.
40. Ibid., pp. 224–25.
41. Waley, *Edwin Montagu*, p. 146.
42. Ibid., p. 147.
43. Ibid., p. 151.
44. An entry in Montagu's diary, dated Nov. 10, 1917, indicates that on the ship he and his delegation had discussed the Duke memorandum on dyarchy and had come to the conclusion that with modifications this was the scheme to adopt. "But," Montagu wrote, "it is quite obvious that my role in India must be to disclose nothing of any of these deliberations except possibly quite privately to the Viceroy, until the end, and then . . . let the whole thing come from the Indian Government themselves. . . . But even then I shall drop hints in a pretty effort into voicing my schemes as their own" (Montagu, *Indian*

Diary, p. 1, Nov. 10, 1917). See also S. R. Mehrotra, *The Commonwealth and the Nation* (New Delhi, 1977), p. 87, and Robb, *The Government of India and Reform*, pp. 79–83.

45. Edwin Montagu, letter to Venetia Stanley, Jan. 24, 1918. Waley, *Edwin Montagu*, p. 148.

46. Waley, *Edwin Montagu*, p. 152.

47. Ibid. This is precisely the point Churchill made in defense of Montagu's position in respect to Amritsar, before the House of Commons. See n. 49, chap. 24.

48. Ibid., p. 155.

49. Sir J. A. R. Marriott, *Modern England, 1885–1939: A History of My Own Times* (London, 1941), p. 498.

50. Waley, *Edwin Montagu*, pp. 161, 162.

51. Montagu, *Indian Diary*, p. 362, Apr. 21, 1918. Waley, *Edwin Montagu*, p. 155.

52. Id.

53. A. E. Zimmern, *The Third British Empire* (London, 1926), pp. 13–14.

54. Id.

55. See Bence-Jones, *The Viceroys of India*, pp. 169, 170; see p. 176 as to Curzon's concern with "trifling details." See also Das, *India from Curzon to Nehru*, pp. 47–49; Mosley, *The Glorious Fault*; Kenneth Rose, *Superior Person* (New York, 1960); The Earl of Ronaldshay, *The Life of Lord Curzon* (London and New York, 1928), vols. 1, 2, 3.

56. Id.

57. Waley, *Edwin Montagu*, p. 164.

58. Ibid., p. 165.

59. Id.

60. Mosley, *The Glorious Fault*, p. 196.

61. Waley, *Edwin Montagu*, p. 173.

62. Ibid., pp. 167–68.

63. *Bombay Chronicle*, June 15, 1918.

64. Das, *India from Curzon to Nehru*, p. 61.

65. S. V. Desika Char, *Readings in the Constitutional History of India 1757–1947* (Oxford and Bombay, 1983), pp. 465–66.

66. Edwin Montagu, Presentation of Indian Budget and Indian Constitutional Reforms, August 6, 1918; *Parl. Deb.*, House of Commons, vol. 109, August 6, 1918, pp. 1139–1236.

67. Ibid., p. 1144.

68. Ibid., p. 1146.

69. Ibid., p. 1144.

70. Id.

71. Ibid., p. 1145.

72. Ibid., pp. 1147, 1150.

73. Ibid., p. 1146.

74. Waley, *Edwin Montagu*, p. 168.

75. Id.

76. Id.

77. Ibid., pp. 168–69.

78. Ibid., pp. 169, 170.

79. Ibid., pp. 170–71.

80. Ibid., p. 177.

81. Ibid., p. 178.

82. On May 7, 1918, Major General Sir Frederick Maurice wrote a letter to several newspapers in which he accused Lloyd George of keeping General Haig short of troops, which resulted in terrible casualties at the front and almost lost the war. Jenkins writes: "The suspicion was that Lloyd George, as a counter to Haig's fondness for bloody offensives . . . deliberately kept him short of troops. The commander-in-chief, according to the Prime Minister's plan, would have to save casualties by remaining on the defensive throughout 1918" (Jenkins, *Asquith*, p. 468). This did not work, as the Germans launched two of their most vicious attacks and Haig found himself without sufficient troops to respond effectively. This, the critics of Lloyd George claimed, was another example of how the Prime Minister thought he knew better than the generals.

After the letter was published Asquith raised the issue in the House of Commons. Bonar Law suggested a two-judge committee to inquire into Maurice's allegations. Asquith and others criticized the idea of a judicial inquiry, suggesting a full debate in Commons. Asquith did not get into the substance— merely commenting on process. Lloyd George responded, bitterly and effectively—on substance, as he was determined to avoid a judicial inquiry and further debate. He succeeded brilliantly. He discredited Maurice, stating that his (Lloyd George's) statement on the number of troops on the front was correct. If they were not, it was Maurice's fault, as he had supplied the numbers. He attacked his critics, especially Asquith, as wanting to bring down the government. After Lloyd George's statement he was vindicated by a vote of 295 to 108. Asquith and his followers were beaten. To make matters worse, Lloyd George would never forget their behavior, which he considered tantamount to disloyalty to the government and its war effort.

83. Harry J. Carman and Harold C. Stryett, *A History of the American People* (New York, 1958), p. 418.

84. Id.

85. Taylor, *English History, 1914–1945*, p. 111.

86. Id. One of the main points of concern to the British was freedom of the seas. "On this point the nation is solid," reported Lloyd George (id.). For the French the key issue was their claim "to compensation from Germany" for all damage done to the civilian population of the Allies and to their property "by the aggression of Germany by land, by sea and from the air" (id.). This became a major point of debate and disputation at Versailles.

87. Id.

88. Frank Owen, *Tempestuous Journey*, p. 496.

89. Taylor, *English History, 1914–1945*, p. 114.

90. Lambert, *Unquiet Souls*, p. 222.

91. Asquith, *Diaries, 1915–1918*, p. 480.

92. Waley, *Edwin Montagu*, p. 181.

93. Id.
94. Taylor, *English History, 1914–1945*, p. 125.
95. Id.
96. Ibid., p. 126. See also Jenkins, *Asquith*, p. 477.
97. Waley, *Edwin Montagu*, p. 182.
98. Ibid., p. 185.
99. Ibid., p. 187.
100. Ibid., p. 180.
101. Jenkins, *Asquith*, p. 480.
102. Waley, *Edwin Montagu*, p. 192.

25. The Marriage

1. Cooper, *A Durable Fire*, p. 57.
2. Venetia Stanley, letter to Edwin Montagu, Jan. 20, 1918; M.G.
3. Venetia Stanley, letter to Edwin Montagu, Mar. 21, 1918; M.G.
4. Venetia Stanley, letter to Edwin Montagu, Mar. 7, 1918; M.G.
5. Venetia Stanley, letter to Edwin Montagu, Mar. 21, 1918; M.G.
6. Laura, Duchess of Marlborough, *Laughter from a Cloud* (London, 1980), p. 111.
7. Edwin Montagu, letter to Venetia Stanley, Jan. 11, 1918; Montagu AS.
8. Edwin Montagu, letter to Venetia Stanley, Jan. 24, 1918; Montagu AS.
9. Edwin Montagu, letter to Venetia Stanley, Feb. 7, 1918; Montagu AS.
10. Edwin Montagu, letter to Venetia Stanley, 1918. No other date. From the content, it would appear to be in Mar. 1918; M.G.
11. Edwin Montagu, letter to Venetia Stanley, Apr. 1, 1918; Montagu AS.
12. Asquith, *Diaries, 1915–1918*, p. 456.
13. Ziegler, *Diana Cooper*, p. 59.
14. Sir Matthew Wilson, Lt. Col 4th Bt., Unionist M.P. from Bethnal Green, 1914–22.
15. Lambert, *Unquiet Souls*, p. 214.
16. Id.
17. Asquith, *Diaries, 1915–1918*, p. 460.
18. Cooper, *The Rainbow Comes and Goes*, p. 135.
19. Ibid., p. 189.
20. Cooper, *A Durable Fire*, p. 91.
21. Id.
22. Cooper, *The Rainbow Comes and Goes*, p. 171.
23. Asquith, *Diaries, 1915–1918*, p. 341.
24. Cooper, *The Rainbow Comes and Goes*, p. 179.
25. Ibid., p. 191.
26. Manchester, *The Last Lion*, p. 88.
27. Cooper, *A Durable Fire*, pp. 92–93.
28. Ibid., p. 97.
29. Ibid., pp. 95–96.

26. The Best and Worst of Times

1. Waley, *Edwin Montagu*, p. 193.
2. Id.
3. *The Powers of Signing Declaration*, Jan. 1, 1919; Montagu AS 4/6/260.
4. Waley, *Edwin Montagu*, p. 192.
5. Ibid., p. 194.
6. Id.
7. Id.
8. "The Ottoman Empire and Financial Conditions of Peace," a memorandum prepared by Edwin Montagu, Jan. 1919; Montagu AS 4/4/10.
9. Edwin Montagu, letter to Lloyd George, Feb. 14, 1919; India Office, Montagu F/40/2/35.
10. Manchester, *The Last Lion*, p. 676.
11. Edwin Montagu, memorandum on "Turkish Peace Treaty," Jan. 1919; Montagu AS 4/4/12.
12. Id.
13. Edwin Montagu, memorandum, 1919; Montagu AS 4/4/9.
14. Id.
15. Edwin Montagu, letter to Curzon, Jan. 6, 1919; Montagu AS 3/3/1(7).
16. "Memorandum on Constantinople," prepared by Edwin Montagu, Jan. 8, 1919; Montagu AS 4/6/5.
17. The San Sofia mosque had been built as a church but had been a mosque since 1453 A.D.
18. Edwin Montagu, letter to San Sofia Redemption Committee, Feb. 1919; Montagu AS 4/3/11.
19. Edwin Montagu, letter to Lloyd George, Feb. 24, 1919; Montagu AS 4/3/7.
20. Edwin Montagu, letter to Lloyd George, Feb. 28, 1919; Montagu AS 4/3/8.
21. Aubrey Herbert, letter to Edwin Montagu, Mar. 22, 1919; Montagu AS 4/6/20.
22. Memorandum by Indian Delegation to Peace Conference, Feb. 5, 1919; Montagu AS 4/6/11.
23. Id.
24. Edwin Montagu, letter to Chelmsford, Feb. 18, 1919; Waley, *Edwin Montagu*, p. 196.
25. Waley, *Edwin Montagu*, pp. 196–97.
26. Skidelsky, *John Maynard Keynes*, p. 354.
27. Ibid., pp. 354–55.
28. Ibid., p. 354.
29. Id.
30. Ibid., p. 355.
31. Ibid., p. 356.
32. Ibid., p. 364. Montagu and Keynes were excluded from this Committee. Instead Lord Cunliffe, ex-Governor of the Bank of England, and William M. Hughes, Prime Minister of Australia, two Conservatives, represented Britain.

33. Edwin Montagu, letter to Arthur Balfour, Dec. 20, 1918, Balfour Papers, Public Records Office, Fo800/215 (Foreign Office).
34. Edwin Montagu, letter to Lloyd George, Feb. 24, 1919; India Office, F/40/2/38.
35. Id.
36. Edwin Montagu, letter to Austen Chamberlain, Feb. 27, 1919; Montagu AS 1/12/147.
37. Austen Chamberlain, letter to Edwin Montagu, Mar. 1, 1919; Montagu AS 1/12/146.
38. Skidelsky, *John Maynard Keynes,* p. 364.
39. Id.
40. Id.
41. Ibid., p. 365.
42. Ibid., pp. 365–66.
43. Ibid., p. 366. "Separation allowances" were monies paid to women whose husbands were serving in the army. The amount received depended on a formula that included the number of children at home and other sources of income.
44. Ibid., p. 367.
45. Id.
46. Id.
47. Ibid., p. 371.
48. Id. See Also John Maynard Keynes, "The Economic Consequences of the Peace," in the *Collected Writings of John Maynard Keynes,* 29 vols. (London, 1971), vol. 2.
49. Ibid., p. 372.
50. Edwin Montagu, letter to Maurice Hankey, Mar. 3, 1919; Montagu AS 4/6/12.
51. Edwin Montagu, letter to Maurice Hankey, Mar. 14, 1919; Montagu AS 4/6/14.
52. Id.
53. Edwin Montagu, letter to Maurice Hankey, Mar. 28, 1919; Montagu AS 4/6/275.
54. Edwin Montagu, letter to Arthur Balfour, Mar. 25, 1919; Montagu AS 1/12/108.
55. Id.
56. Edwin Montagu, letter to Maurice Hankey, Mar. 28, 1919; Montagu AS 4/6/275.
57. Maurice Hankey, letter to Edwin Montagu, Mar. 28, 1919; Montagu AS 4/6/276.
58. Edwin Montagu, Memorandum, Apr. 4, 1919; Montagu AS 1/12/18.
59. Id.
60. Id.
61. Edwin Montagu, letter to Lloyd George, Apr. 4, 1919; India Office F/40/2/48.
62. Edwin Montagu, letter to Lloyd George, Apr. 15, 1919; Montagu AS 4/3/17.
63. Id.

64. The Rowlatt Act adopted in 1919 extended the government's wartime emergency powers to deal with conspiracy. It gave the executive increased authority. It was attacked by Indian leadership as "draconian," and a "negation of the rule of law" (Das, *India From Curzon to Nehru*, pp. 63, 64), but it was defended by the British as necessary to promote order and as a defense against terrorism.

65. Bence-Jones, *The Viceroys of India*, pp. 226–27.

66. Ibid., p. 227.

67. Chirol, *India*, pp. 206–7.

68. Waley, *Edwin Montagu*, p. 149.

69. Edwin Montagu, letter to Chelmsford, Mar. 8, 1919; Waley, *Edwin Montagu*, p. 201.

70. Sir Dingel Foot, "Massacre That Started the Ending of the Raj," in the *Observer Magazine* (London), Apr. 5, 1919, pp. 37–38; M.G.

71. Waley, *Edwin Montagu*, p. 205.

72. Ibid., p. 206.

73. Taylor, *English History, 1914–1945*, pp. 152–53.

74. Waley, *Edwin Montagu*, p. 206.

75. Ibid., p. 207.

76. Id.

77. Ibid., p. 208.

78. P. E. Roberts, *History of British India*, 5th ed. (New York and London, 1983), pp. 592, 594; P. G. Robb, *The Government of India and Reform*, pp. 171–219; and notes on *The Case of General Dyer*, Apr. 1920, Montagu AS 3/11/47. See also memorandum on Hunter Committee report (called Report of the Disorders Inquiry Committee, Apr. 1910), Montagu AS 3/4/58; Memorandum from Viceroy on Hunter Committee report, Apr. 13, 1920, Montagu AS 3/4/31.

79. Waley, *Edwin Montagu*, p. 208.

80. Id.

81. Ibid., pp. 208, 209.

82. Edwin Montagu, telegram to Chelmsford, May 14, 1919; Montagu AS 4/4/32.

83. Edwin Montagu, telegram to Chelmsford, May 8, 1919; Montagu AS 4/6/40.

84. Edwin Montagu, telegram to Chelmsford, May 14, 1919; Montagu AS 4/4/32.

85. Waley, *Edwin Montagu*, p. 209.

86. Id.

87. Ibid., pp. 164–75.

88. Ibid., pp. 174, 196.

89. Ibid., pp. 209–10.

90. Ibid., p. 214.

91. Ibid., p. 215.

92. Ibid., pp. 215, 216.

93. Ibid., p. 217.

94. Ibid., pp. 218, 219.

95. Ibid., p. 219.

96. Id.

97. Ibid., p. 220.

98. Id.

99. Id.
100. Id.
101. Ibid., p. 221.
102. Ibid., pp. 221, 222.
103. Edwin Montagu, telegram to Chelmsford, May 8, 1919; Montagu AS 4/6/40.
104. Bernard Lewis, *The Emergence of Modern Turkey* (London, 1961), pp. 234–35.
105. Waley, *Edwin Montagu*, p. 213.
106. Id.
107. Edwin Montagu, letter to Arthur Balfour, June 21, 1919; Montagu AS 1/12/109.
108. Edwin Montagu, memorandum "Lest We Forget," Aug. 28, 1919; Montagu AS 4/6/76.
109. Edwin Montagu, letter to Lloyd George, Sept. 8, 1919; Montagu AS 4/3/29.
110. Peter Rowland, *David Lloyd George* (New York, 1975), p. 565.
111. Edwin Montagu, memorandum to Cabinet, Dec. 18, 1919; Montagu, AS 4/8/96.

27. The Marriage Continues to Deteriorate

1. Brock, *H. H. Asquith Letters to Venetia Stanley*, p. 607.
2. Cooper, *The Rainbow Comes and Goes*, pp. 172–73.
3. Ibid., p. 177.
4. A. J. P. Taylor, *Beaverbrook* (New York, 1972), Introduction, p. 15.
5. Ibid., p. 236.
6. Ibid., p. 164.
7. Ibid., p. 164.
8. David Farrer, *G for God Almighty: A Personal Memoir of Lord Beaverbrook* (New York, 1969), p. 106.
9. Cooper, *A Durable Fire*, p. 131.
10. Ibid., p. 132.
11. Ibid., pp. 131, 132.
12. Ibid., p. 133.
13. Edwin Montagu, letter to Venetia Stanley, Feb. 5, 1919; M.G.
14. Id.
15. Edwin Montagu, letter to Venetia Stanley, Feb. 24, 1919; M.G.
16. Edwin Montagu, letter to Venetia Stanley, May 15, 1919; M.G.
17. Id.
18. Edwin Montagu, letter to Venetia Stanley, Sept. 24, 1919; M.G.
19. Venetia Stanley, letter to Edwin Montagu, Jan. 30, 1919; M.G.
20. Venetia Stanley, letter to Lord Beaverbrook, Apr. 2, 1919; M.G.
21. Id.
22. Id.
23. Venetia Stanley, letter to Lord Beaverbrook, Apr. 23, 1919; M.G.
24. Venetia Stanley, letter to Lord Beaverbrook, Sept. 26, 1919; M.G.
25. Brock, *H. H. Asquith Letters to Venetia Stanley*, pp. 616–17.
26. Venetia Stanley, letter to Lord Beaverbrook, June 12, 1919; M.G.

27. Venetia Stanley, letter to Lord Beaverbrook, Aug. 21, 1919; M.G.
28. Venetia Stanley, letter to Lord Beaverbrook, June 1919 (no other date available); M.G.
29. Venetia Stanley, letter to Lord Beaverbrook, Aug. 21, 1919; M.G.
30. Venetia Stanley, letter to Lord Beaverbrook, Sept. 26, 1919; M.G.
31. Venetia Stanley, letter to Lord Beaverbrook, no date; it appears to be Oct. 1919; M.G.
32. Venetia Stanley, letter to Lord Beaverbrook, Nov. 1919 (no other date available); M.G.
33. Venetia Stanley, letter to Lord Beaverbrook, Dec. 23, 1919; M.G.

28. Censure and Shame

1. Trevor Wilson, *The Downfall of the Liberal Party 1914–1915* (Ithaca, N.Y. 1966), p. 221.
2. Id.
3. Waley, *Edwin Montagu,* p. 224.
4. Ibid., p. 224, n. 1.
5. Edwin Montagu, memorandum on "Proposed Turkish Treaty," Jan. 1, 1920; Montagu AS, folder 6, box 94.
6. Id.
7. David Lloyd George, *Memoirs of the Peace Conference* (New Haven, Conn., 1939), vol. 2, p. 655.
8. Ibid., p. 658.
9. Chirol, *India,* pp. 221–22.
10. Edwin Montagu, letter to Bonar Law, Jan. 8, 1920; Montagu AS 1/12/99.
11. Id.
12. Edwin Montagu, letter to Lloyd George, Jan. 20, 1920; Montagu AS 4/6/107.
13. Edwin Montagu, letter to Lloyd George, Jan. 1920 (no other date available; it appears to have been written on or about January 20); Montagu AS 4/3/32.
14. Id.
15. Id.
16. Violet Bonham Carter, *Winston Churchill, An Intimate Portrait* (New York, 1965), p. 336.
17. Edwin Montagu, letter to H. A. L. Fisher, Feb. 4, 1920; Montagu AS 1/12/98.
18. H. A. L. Fisher, letter to Edwin Montagu, Feb. 5, 1920; Montagu AS 1/12/97.
19. Lloyd George, *Memoirs of the Peace Conference,* vol. 2, p. 821.
20. Waley, *Edwin Montagu,* pp. 224–27.
21. Id.
22. Id.
23. Philip Kerr, letter to Edwin Montagu, Feb. 27, 1920; Montagu AS 2/3/35.
24. Venetia Stanley, letter to Lord Beaverbrook, no date (it appears to have been written in Feb. 1920); M.G.
25. Venetia Stanley, letter to Lord Beaverbrook, Mar. 3, 1920; M.G.
26. Venetia Stanley, letter to Lord Beaverbrook, Mar. 22, 1920; M.G.
27. Edwin Montagu, letter to Lord Beaverbrook, Mar. 15, 1920; M.G.

28. Lloyd George, *Memoirs of the Peace Conference*, vol. 2, p. 821.
29. Lord Curzon, letter to Edwin Montagu, Feb. 18, 1920; Montagu AS 3/3/70.
30. Chelmsford, letter to Edwin Montagu, Apr. 1, 1920. Waley, *Edwin Montagu*, p. 228.
31. Maurice Hankey, letter to Edwin Montagu, Apr. 9, 1920; Montagu AS 4/6/258.
32. Edwin Montagu, letter to Lloyd George, Apr. 15, 1920; Montagu AS 4/3/36.
33. Id.
34. Id.
35. Id.
36. David Lloyd George, letter to Edwin Montagu, Apr. 25, 1920; Montagu AS 1/12/67. Prior to sending this letter, the Prime Minister received a letter from Bonar Law (Apr. 23, 1920; Montagu AS 101/4/41) in which he asked that Lloyd George present "however briefly" the Indian-Montagu position, as he believed that it would hurt the government's relationship with India if Montagu resigned over this issue. "As far as I could judge from his [Montagu's] conversation with me he really does not want to make trouble, but while I entirely agree with you that his resignation on any ordinary issue *would not matter*, his resignation on this issue would be very serious but not from the point of view of its effect upon the Government but from the point of view of its effect on India" (emphasis added).
37. Edwin Montagu, letter to Lloyd George, Apr. 29, 1920; Montagu AS 4/6/254.
38. Edwin Montagu, letter to Lloyd George, Apr. 30, 1920; Montagu AS 4/3/37.
39. Waley, *Edwin Montagu*, p. 227.
40. Ibid., pp. 227–28.
41. Report of the Hunter Commission on Amritsar, officially called Report of the Disorders Inquiry Committee, completed Apr. 7, 1920; published May 26, 1920; Chelmsford Papers, vol. #47. See also General Dyer's condemnation of the report in the *Morning Post* (London, 6/9/1920), p. 6.
42. Waley, *Edwin Montagu*, p. 229.
43. Resolution of government of India, published with Hunter Commission report, May 26, 1920; Montagu AS 3/4/45.
44. Waley, *Edwin Montagu*, p. 230.
45. Sir Michael O'Dwyer, letter to the editor, *Morning Post*, June 9, 1920.
46. Edwin Montagu, letter to the editor, *Morning Post*, June 14, 1920.
47. Id.
48. *Parl. Deb.*, House of Commons, vol. 131, July 8, 1920, p. 1726; see full text of Churchill's strong support of Montagu in this speech, pp. 1726–33. See also Manchester, *The Last Lion*, pp. 692–95.
49. *Parl Deb.*, House of Commons, vol. 131, July 8, 1920, p. 1732.
50. *Parl. Deb.*, House of Commons, vol. 131, July 7, 1920, pp. 1411–19; July 8, 1920, pp. 1706–1814; vol. 130, June 23, 1920, pp. 2150–54; June 25, 1920, pp. 2552–53; June 30, 1920, pp. 411–17. House of Lords Debate, vol. 30, July 19, 1920, pp. 222–307.
51. *Parl. Deb.*, House of Commons, vol. 131, July 7, 1920, p. 1419, and July 8, 1920, p. 1799.

52. Id.
53. T. W. Holderness, letter dated June 30, 1920, entered into *Parliamentary Debates,* vol. 131, July 8, 1920; Montagu AS 3/4/85.
54. Id.
55. Waley, *Edwin Montagu,* pp. 229–30.
56. *Parl. Deb.,* House of Commons, vol. 131, July 7, 1920, p. 1414.
57. Id.
58. Id.
59. Waley, *Edwin Montagu,* p. 230.
60. Manchester, *The Last Lion,* p. 693.
61. Id.
62. *Parl. Deb.,* House of Commons, vol. 131, July 8, 1920, p. 1706.
63. Ibid., p. 1707.
64. Ibid., p. 1708.
65. Ibid., p. 1709.
66. Ibid., p. 1802. For Gwynne's complete statement about Amritsar and Montagu, see pp. 1793–1803.
67. Ibid., p. 1803.
68. Ibid., p. 1806.
69. Ibid., p. 1809.
70. Ibid., p. 1811.
71. Ibid., p. 1812.
72. Robert Blake, *The Unknown Prime Minister* (London, 1955), p. 421.
73. Freddy Guest, letter to Lloyd George, July 9, 1920; Lloyd George MSS. F/22/2/5.
74. Waley, *Edwin Montagu,* p. 233.
75. Ibid., p. 234.
76. Id.
77. Geoffrey Moorhouse, *India Britannica* (London, 1984), p. 173.
78. *Parl. Deb.,* House of Commons, vol. 134, Nov. 17, 1920, p. 1858. A full discussion on this resolution appears on pp. 1859–62.
79. Id.
80. Ibid., p. 1855.
81. Id.
82. Das, *India from Curzon to Nehru and After,* p. 72.
83. Lloyd George, *Memoirs of the Peace Conference,* vol. 2, p. 864.
84. Sir Lord Sinha, letter to Lloyd George, July 11, 1920, Montagu F/60/3/13; M.G.
85. Edwin Montagu, letter to Lloyd George, Aug. 4, 1920; Montagu AS 4/3/42.
86. Edwin Montagu, letter to Lloyd George, Dec. 7, 1920; Montagu AS 4/3/40.
87. Bhupendranath Basu, letter to Lloyd George, Dec. 3, 1920, Montagu AS 7/40/3/35.
88. Edwin Montagu, letter to Lloyd George, Dec. 7, 1920; Montagu AS 4/3/42.
89. Edwin Montagu, letter to Lloyd George, Dec. 16, 1920; Montagu AS 4/3/48.

29. Reading and Montagu

1. Bence-Jones, *The Viceroys of India*, p. 1. See also pp. 1–19.
2. Ibid., p. 231.
3. Rudyard Kipling, *Verse*, inclusive ed., 1885–1932 (Garden City, N.Y., 1934). Comparing the new Lord Chief Justice to Gehazi, the servant of Elisha in the Old Testament, Kipling wrote:

> Whence comest thou, Gehazi,
>   So reverend to behold,
> In scarlet and ermines
>   And chain of England's gold?
> 'From following after Naaman
>   To tell him all is well
> Whereby my zeal hath made me
>   A Judge in Israel.'
>
> Well done, well done, Gehazi!
>   Stretch forth thy ready hand.
> Thou barely 'scaped from judgment,
>   Take oath to judge the land
> Unswayed by gift or money
>   Or privy bribe, more base,
> Of knowledge which is profit
>   In any marketplace.
>
> Search out and probe, Gehazi,
>   As thou of all canst try,
> The truthful, well-weighed answer
>   That tells the blacker lie
> The loud, uneasy virtue,
>   The anger feigned at will,
> To overbear a witness
>   And make the Court keep still.
>
> Take order now, Gehazi
>   That no man talk aside
> In secret with his judges
>   The while his case is tried.
> Lest he should show them—reason
>   To keep a matter hid,
> And subtly lead the questions
>   Away from what he did.
>
> Thou mirror of uprightness,
>   What ails thee at thy vows?
> What means the risen whiteness
>   Of the skin between thy brows?
> The boils that shine and burrow,
>   The sores that slough and bleed—The

> leprosy of Naaman
>> On thee and all thy seed?
> Stand up, stand up, Gehazi,
>> Draw close thy robe and go,
> Gehazi, Judge in Israel,
>> A leper white as snow!

4. Judd, *Lord Reading,* p. 195.
5. Ibid., p. 145.
6. Margot Asquith, letter to Lord Reading, quoted in Judd, *Lord Reading,* p. 90.
7. Waley, *Edwin Montagu,* p. 253.
8. Judd, *Lord Reading,* pp. 198–99.
9. Ibid., p. 199.
10. Chelmsford, telegram to Edwin Montagu, Jan. 26, 1921; Montagu AS 4/8/10.
11. Chelmsford, telegram to Edwin Montagu, Feb. 2, 1921; Montagu AS 4/8/9.
12. Roberts, *History of British India,* p. 594.
13. Das, *India from Curzon to Nehru and After,* p. 79.
14. Edwin Montagu, telegram to Chelmsford, Feb. 16, 1921; Montagu AS 4/8/41.
15. Edwin Montagu, telegram to Chelmsford, Feb. 24, 1921; Montagu AS 4/8/13.
16. Id.
17. Edwin Montagu, letter to Lloyd George, Mar. 11, 1921; Montagu AS 4/8/48.
18. Chelmsford, telegram to Edwin Montagu, Mar. 16, 1922; Montagu AS 4/6/166.
19. Indian delegation, letter to Edwin Montagu, Mar. 26, 1921; Montagu AS 4/8/54.
20. Edwin Montagu, letter to Hassan Imam and other members of the Indian delegation, Mar. 31, 1921; Montagu AS 4/8/55.
21. Waley, *Edwin Montagu,* p. 253.
22. Id.
23. Judd, *Lord Reading,* p. 201.
24. Ibid., p. 221.
25. Waley, *Edwin Montagu,* p. 235.
26. Id.
27. Judd, *Lord Reading,* p. 221.
28. Ibid., p. 206.
29. Ibid., p. 207.
30. Id.
31. Ibid., p. 208.
32. Id.
33. Das, *India From Curzon to Nehru and After,* p. 92.
34. Ibid., p. 91.
35. Judd, *Lord Reading,* p. 222.
36. Edwin Montagu, letter to Winston Churchill, June 17, 1921; Montagu AS 3/5/30.
37. Edwin Montagu, letter to Winston Churchill, June 21, 1921; Montagu AS 3/5/31.

38. Edwin Montagu, letter to Winston Churchill, July 19, 1921; Montagu AS 3/5/27.
39. Winston Churchill, letter to Edwin Montagu, July 20, 1921; Montagu AS 3/5/26.
40. Winston Churchill, letter to Edwin Montagu, July 22, 1921; Montagu AS 3/5/22.
41. Edwin Montagu, letter to Winston Churchill, July 26, 1921; Montagu AS 1/3/2.
42. Lloyd George, Speech Imperial Conference, Aug. 2, 1921; Waley, *Edwin Montagu*, p. 258. See also G. S. Bajpai, "Secret Memorandum on Imperial Conference," Aug. 9, 1921; Montagu AS 3/5/95, also in M.G.
43. Id.
44. Id.
45. Lloyd George, letters to members of Indian delegation to Imperial Conference and to Edwin Montagu, Aug. 19, 1921; Montagu F/41/1/23; F/41/1/22.
46. Indian delegation, letter to Lloyd George, Aug. 3, 1921, signed by Montagu, Maharao Khengarji, and V. Srinivasa Sastri; Montagu AS 3/5/93.
47. Winston Churchill, letter to Edwin Montagu, Oct. 8, 1921; Montagu AS 1/3/3.
48. Edwin Montagu, letter to Winston Churchill, Oct. 12, 1921; Montagu AS 1/12/9.
49. Judd, *Lord Reading*, p. 209.
50. Id.
51. Waley, *Edwin Montagu*, p. 260.
52. Lord Reading, telegram to Edwin Montagu, Oct. 11, 1921; Montagu F/41/1/27.
53. Id.
54. Edwin Montagu, letter to Lloyd George, Oct. 12, 1921; Montagu F/41/1/27.
55. *Islamic News,* published in London, June 7, 1921; M.G.
56. Lord Reading, letters to Edwin Montagu, Apr. 26, and June 11, 1921; M.G.
57. Edwin Montagu, letter to Lord Beaverbrook, Oct. 9, 1921; M.G.
58. Lord Beaverbrook, letter to Edwin Montagu, Oct. 10, 1921; M.G.
59. Judd, *Lord Reading*, pp. 210–11.
60. Ibid., p. 211.
61. Lloyd George to Reading, Oct. 21, 1921; Montagu F/41/1/30.
62. Reading, letter to Montagu, Oct. 23, 1921; Montagu F/61/1/31.
63. Id.
64. Edwin Montagu, letter to Lloyd George, Oct. 25, 1921; Montagu F 61/1/31.
65. Id.
66. Id.
67. *Parl. Deb.,* House of Lords, vol. 47, Oct. 25, 1921, p. 24.
68. Ibid., pp. 24, 25.
69. Ibid., p. 36.
70. Id.
71. Ibid., p. 52, See pp. 46–57 for full text of Chelmsford's remarks.
72. Ibid., p. 79, See pp. 66–80 for full text of Lytton's remarks.

73. Judd, *Lord Reading*, p. 211.
74. Ronaldshay, *The Life of Lord Curzon*, vol. 3, p. 279.
75. Lord Reading, telegram to Edwin Montagu, Nov. 9, 1921; Montagu AS 4/6/202.
76. Id.
77. Edwin Montagu, letter to Lloyd George, Nov. 23, 1921; Montagu AS 4/6/204.
78. Das, *India From Curzon to Nehru and After*, p. 93.
79. H. Montgomery Hyde, *Lord Reading: The Life of Rufus Isaacs, the First Marquess of Reading* (New York, 1967), p. 363.
80. Waley, *Edwin Montagu*, p. 265.
81. Id.
82. Ibid., pp. 262–63.
83. Ibid., pp. 266–67.
84. Lord Curzon, letter to Edwin Montagu, Apr. 1921; Montagu AS 1/12/21.
85. Edwin Montagu, letter to Lord Curzon, Apr. 4, 1921; Montagu AS 1/12/20. See also Waley, *Edwin Montagu*, p. 254.
86. Lord Curzon, letter to Edwin Montagu, May 31, 1921; Montagu AS 6/8/2.
87. Waley, *Edwin Montagu*, p. 249.
88. Id.
89. Edwin Montagu, draft of letter to Lord Curzon, Nov. 23, 1921; Montagu AS 1/12/126. This letter was never sent.
90. Edwin Montagu, letter to Lord Curzon, Nov. 23, 1921; Montagu F/112/221A.
91. Waley, *Edwin Montagu*, p. 250.
92. Edwin Montagu, letter to Sir Edward Gregg, Foreign Office, Dec. 3, 1921; Montagu AS 4/6/239. See also Montagu F/112/221A.
93. Edwin Montagu, letter to Winston Churchill, Dec. 27, 1921; Montagu AS 1/12/11.
94. Harold Nicholson, *Curzon: The Last Phase* (London, 1934), p. 33.
95. Mosley, *The Glorious Fault*, p. 41.
96. Ibid., p. 40.
97. Ibid., p. 32.
98. Waley, *Edwin Montagu*, p. 255.
99. Edwin Montagu, memorandum for Lloyd George, Dec. 9, 1921; Montagu F/141/8/58.
100. Id.
101. Id.
102. Keynes, "The Economic Consequences of the Peace," p. 92. See also Skidelsky, *John Maynard Keynes*, p. 387.
103. Skidelsky, *John Maynard Keynes*, p. 391.
104. Id.
105. Waley, *Edwin Montagu*, p. 255. The reparations crisis erupted again in 1923 when the agreement broke down and the French, in retaliation, occupied the Ruhr.
106. Edwin Montagu, letter to Lord Beaverbrook, Dec. 9, 1921; M.G.

107. Id.
108. Id.

30. The Resignation

1. Lord Curzon, letter to Edwin Montagu, Jan. 2, 1922; Montagu AS 1/12/72.
2. Edwin Montagu, letter to Lord Curzon, Jan. 1, 1922; Montagu F/112/226.
3. Lord Curzon, telegram to Montagu, Jan. 7, 1922; Montagu AS 4/6/230.
4. Id.
5. Id.
6. Edwin Montagu, telegram to Lord Curzon, Jan. 7, 1922; Montagu AS 4/6/228. See also letter from Winston Churchill to Edwin Montagu, Jan. 1, 1922; Montagu AS 1/12/70.
7. Memorandum on "Turkish Treaty & Situation in India," from Governor of Bombay, Jan. 10, 1922; Montagu AS 4/6/234.
8. Id.
9. Correspondence between Stanley Reed, editor of the *Times of India* and Lord Lytton, Under Secretary of State of India, Jan. 12, 1922; Montagu F112/226/13.
10. Edwin Montagu, letter to Winston Churchill, Jan. 13, 1922; Montagu AS 1/12/12.
11. The *Daily Express,* Jan. 16, 1922.
12. *The Times* (London), Jan. 16, 1922.
13. Edwin Montagu, letter to Lord Beaverbrook, Jan. 18, 1922; M.G.
14. Lord Ronaldshay, letter to Edwin Montagu, Dec. 29, 1921; M.G.
15. Edwin Montagu, letter to Lord Beaverbrook, Jan. 18, 1922; M.G.
16. *Daily Express,* Jan. 21, 1922, story on "Gandhi Butchers," by Sir Percival Phillips, *Daily Express* Special Correspondent for the Prince of Wales's visit to India.
17. Lord Beaverbrook, letter to Edwin Montagu, Jan. 23, 1922; M.G.
18. Edwin Montagu, letter to Lord Beaverbrook, Jan. 27, 1922; M.G.
19. Edwin Montagu, telegram to Lord Reading, Jan. 18, 1922; Montagu AS 1/12/85.
20. Judd, *Lord Reading,* p. 224.
21. Edwin Montagu, letter to Winston Churchill, Jan. 27, 1922; Montagu AS 1/12/38.
22. Edwin Montagu, letter to Winston Churchill, Jan. 28, 1922; Montagu AS 3/6/5.
23. Id.
24. *The Times* (London), Jan. 28, 1922.
25. Edwin Montagu, letter to Winston Churchill, Jan. 31, 1922; Montagu AS 1/12/42.
26. Id.
27. Id.
28. Winston Churchill, letter to Edwin Montagu, Feb. 1, 1922; Montagu AS 1/12/48.

29. Edwin Montagu, letter to Winston Churchill, Feb. 1, 1922; Montagu AS 1/12/47.
30. Edwin Montagu, letter to Winston Churchill, Feb. 2, 1922; Montagu AS 1/12/50.
31. Manchester, *The Last Lion,* p. 842.
32. Id.
33. Lord Reading, telegram to Edwin Montagu, Feb. 6, 1922; Montagu F 1112/226B. See also letter from representatives of the Kenya East African Deputation, Feb. 9, 1922; Montagu F 41/2/7.
34. Edwin Montagu, letter to Lord Reading, Feb. 3, 1922; Montagu AS 1/12/59.
35. Winston Churchill, remarks reported in *The Times* (London), Jan. 28, 1922.
36. Waley, *Edwin Montagu,* p. 268.
37. Ibid., p. 269.
38. Edwin Montagu, telegram to Lord Reading, Feb. 6, 1922; Montagu F112/226/B.
39. Id.
40. Edwin Montagu, letter to Reading, Feb. 7, 1922; Montagu AS 1/12/81.
41. Lord Reading, letter to Edwin Montagu, Feb. 9, 1922; Montagu AS 1/12/80.
42. Edwin Montagu, letter to Lloyd George, Feb. 10, 1922; Montagu F 41/2/3.
43. Edwin Montagu, letter to Lord Reading, Feb. 11, 1922; Judd, *Lord Reading,* p. 224.
44. Lord Reading, letter to Edwin Montagu, Feb. 14, 1922; Montagu F 41/12/4.
45. *Parl. Deb.,* House of Commons, vol. 150, Feb. 14, 1922, Motion by Sir W. Joynson-Hicks, to censure Secretary of State for India, pp. 866–975.
46. Id.
47. Ibid., p. 884.
48. Id.
49. Ibid., p. 889.
50. Ibid., pp. 892–98, 899–900, 900–05.
51. Ibid., p. 902.
52. Ibid., pp. 905–6; remarks by Hon. Francis D. Acland, Feb. 14, 1922.
53. Wilson, *The Downfall of the Liberal Party,* p. 221.
54. *Parl Deb.,* House of Commons, vol. 150, Feb. 14, 1922, remarks by Sir D. J. Rees, pp. 914–23.
55. Ibid., p. 919.
56. *Parl. Deb.,* House of Commons, vol. 150, Feb. 14, 1922, p. 954. For full text of Lloyd George's remarks, see pp. 954–66.
57. Ibid., p. 902.
58. Ibid., p. 962–63.
59. Ibid., p. 966.
60. Hyde, *Lord Reading,* p. 370.
61. Id.
62. Ibid., p. 371.
63. Id.
64. Wilson, *The Downfall of the Liberal Party,* p. 221.
65. Id.

66. Edwin Montagu, letter to Lloyd George, Feb. 21, 1922; Montagu F 41/2/5.
67. Id.
68. Venetia Stanley, letter to Lloyd George, Feb. 1922 (no other date available); Montagu F 41/2/12.
69. Lord Reading, telegram to the Cabinet, Mar. 1, 1922; Montagu AS 1/12/100; Hyde, *Lord Reading,* pp. 371–72.
70. Hyde, *Lord Reading,* p. 372.
71. Id.
72. Id.
73. Edwin Montagu, telegram to Lord Reading, Mar. 6, 1922; M.G.
74. Waley, *Edwin Montagu,* p. 273.
75. Id.
76. Ibid., pp. 272–73.
77. Id.
78. Ibid., p. 274.
79. Judd, *Lord Reading,* p. 213.
80. Edwin Montagu, letter to Lord Curzon, Mar. 7, 1922; Montagu AS 1/12/137.
81. Id. This letter bears the notation "Not mailed."
82. Edwin Montagu, letter to Lloyd George, Mar. 9, 1922, letter #1; Montagu AS 6/11/10.
83. Lloyd George, letter to Edwin Montagu, Mar. 9, 1922, letter #1; M.G.
84. Id.
85. Edwin Montagu, letter to Lloyd George, Mar. 9, 1922, letter #2, Montagu F 41/2/9.
86. Lloyd George, letter to Edwin Montagu, Mar. 9, 1922, letter #2, Montagu F 41/2/10.
87. Lloyd George, letter to Edwin Montagu, Mar. 9, 1922, letter #3; Montagu F 41/2/11.
88. Edwin Montagu, letter to His Majesty, King George, Mar. 9, 1922; Montagu AS 6/11/15.
89. Edwin Montagu, address before Liberal Club, Cambridge, Mar. 11, 1922; Montagu AS 1/12/137. See also Waley, *Edwin Montagu,* pp. 277–79.
90. Id.
91. Id.
92. Id.
93. Id.
94. Id.
95. Id.
96. *Parl. Deb.,* House of Commons, vol. 151, Mar. 13, 1922, p. 1760.
97. Ibid., pp. 1760–61.
98. Ibid., p. 1761.
99. Ibid., pp. 1761–62.
100. Ibid., p. 1762. See also comment in *The Times,* (London), Mar. 14, 1922, p. 12.
101. *Parl. Deb.,* House of Lords, vol. 49, Mar. 14, 1922, pp. 464–68, Lord Curzon's rebuttal of Montagu's charges.

102. Ibid., pp. 468–70, Lord Crewe's comments.
103. Austen Chamberlain, letter to Walter Long, Mar. 6, 1922; M.G.
104. Lord Beaverbrook, *The Decline and Fall of Lloyd George* (London, 1963), p. 39.
105. Johnson, *Land Fit for Heroes,* p. 495.
106. *Parl. Deb.,* House of Commons, vol. 151, Mar. 15, 1922, pp. 2300–2301.
107. Ibid., p. 2304.
108. Ibid., p. 2316.
109. Ibid., p. 2317. For Asquith's complete remarks, see pp. 2316–19.
110. Hyde, *Lord Reading,* pp. 373–74.
111. Philip Sassoon, letter to Lloyd George, Mar. 15, 1922; M.G.; Phillip Sassoon MSS A9 F/45/1/9.
112. Phillip Sassoon, letter to Lloyd George, Mar. 16, 1922; Phillip Sassoon MSS A9 F/45/1/10.
113. Sir Walter Lawrence, letter to Lord Curzon, Mar. 14, 1922; Judd, *Lord Reading,* p. 213.
114. Lord Reading, letter to Edwin Montagu, Mar. 10, 1922; Montagu AS 1/12/104.
115. Judd, *Lord Reading,* p. 214.
116. Hyde, *Lord Reading,* p. 370.
117. Judd, *Lord Reading,* p. 214.
118. Id.
119. Lord Reading, telegram to Lloyd George, Mar. 13, 1922. See also Hyde, *Lord Reading,* p. 374.
120. Lord Reading, letter to Edwin Montagu, Mar. 13, 1922. Hyde, *Lord Reading,* p. 374.
121. Edwin Montagu, letter to Lord Reading, Mar. 15, 1922; M.G.
122. Edwin Montagu, letter to Lord Beaverbrook, Mar. 13, 1922; M.G.
123. Aga Khan, statement of Bengal Council, Mar. 17, 1922, Montagu AS 4/5/57; Governor of Madras, Mar. 11, 1922, Montagu AS 4/5/9; telegram from Annie Besant, Mar. 15, 1922, Montagu AS 4/5/35; the President of the All India Conference of Indian Christians, Mar. 17, 1922, Montagu AS 4/5/45; the Maharajah of Bikaner, Mar. 14, 1922, Montagu AS 4/5/30; Sir George Lloyd, Mar. 11, 1922, Montagu AS 4/5/11; the Maharajah Alwar, March 17, 1922, Montagu AS 4/5/43; Bengal Council, Mar. 12, 1922, Montagu AS 4/5/48; Council of Bombay, Mar. 13, 1922, Montagu AS 4/5/59; Moslem Members of Indian Legislature, Mar. 18, 1922, Montagu AS 4/5/15; Indian Merchants Chamber and Bureau, Mar. 20, 1922, Montagu AS 4/5/12; the Executive Committee of the Legislative Council of the Punjab, Mar. 28, 1922, Montagu AS 4/5/24; statement of the Assembly of Delhi, reported in *The Times* (London), Mar. 13, 1922, p. 12.

31. *Some Private Notes: Pearl and the Birth of a Daughter*

1. Edwin Montagu, letter to Lord Beaverbrook, July 15, 1921; M.G.
2. Lord Beaverbrook, letter to Barclay's Bank, May 1, 1922; M.G.
3. Edwin Montagu, letter to Venetia Stanley, Jan. 31, 1922; M.G.

4. Edwin Montagu, letter to Venetia Stanley, Feb. 7, 1922; M.G.
5. Edwin Montagu, letter to Lord Reading, Oct. 11, 1921; Montagu F 118/95.
6. Clementine Churchill, *Winston Churchill*, p. 267.
7. Venetia Stanley, letters to Lord Beaverbrook, Sept., Oct., Nov. 1922; M.G.
8. Bermant, *The Cousinhood*, p. 210.
9. Edwin Montagu, letter to Venetia Stanley, Jan. 27, 1922; M.G.
10. Edwin Montagu, letter to Venetia Stanley, Jan. 31, 1922; M.G.
11. Id.
12. Edwin Montagu, letter to Venetia Stanley, Feb. 3, 1922; M.G.
13. Edwin Montagu, letter to Venetia Stanley, Feb. 7, 1922; M.G.
14. Id.

32. Alone at Eventide

1. The *Times of India*, Dec. 9, 1924.
2. Id.
3. Judd, *Lord Reading*, p. 216.
4. Edwin Montagu, letter to Lord Reading, June 8, 1922; Montagu AS 1/6/69.
5. Waley, *Edwin Montagu*, pp. 283–84.
6. Judd, *Lord Reading*, p. 224.
7. Earl of Lytton (Victor Lytton), letter and memorandum to Edwin Montagu, Aug. 14, 1922; Montagu AS 1/6/14. AS 1/6/15.
8. Edwin Montagu, letter to George Lloyd, June 8, 1922; Montagu AS 1/6/11.
9. Edwin Montagu, letter to Victor Lytton, Sept. 30, 1922; Montagu F/60/25.
10. Edwin Montagu, letter to George Lloyd, June 8, 1922; Montagu AS 1/6/11.
11. Id.
12. Lord Reading, letter to Edwin Montagu, May 18, 1922; Montagu AS 1/6/77.
13. Edwin Montagu, letter to Lord Reading, June 8, 1922; Montagu F 118/95.
14. Edwin Montagu, letter to Lord Reading, July 25, 1922; Montagu F 118/95.
15. Id.
16. Edwin Montagu, letter to Lord Reading, Sept. 29, 1922; Montagu F 118/95.
17. Edwin Montagu, letter to the Earl of Lytton, Sept. 30, 1922; Montagu F 160/25.
18. Edwin Montagu, letter to Lord Reading, Sept. 29, 1922; Montagu F 118/95.
19. Rowland, *Lloyd George*, p. 580.
20. Venetia Stanley, letter to Lord Beaverbrook, Oct. 1922; M.G.
21. Edwin Montagu, letter to Lord Beaverbrook, Oct. 31, 1922; M.G.
22. Id.
23. Id.
24. Id.
25. Id.
26. Lord Beaverbrook, letter to Edwin Montagu, Nov. 10, 1922; M.G.
27. Jenkins, *Asquith*, p. 496.
28. Id.
29. Ibid., p. 497. By that time Bonar Law had resigned because of throat cancer (May 20, 1923) and Baldwin was the Prime Minister.

30. Id.
31. Edwin Montagu, letter to Lord Beaverbrook, Nov. 28, 1922; M.G.

33. Personal and Political Darkness

1. Edwin Montagu, letter to the Hon. Mrs. D'Arcy Hart, Feb. 16, 1923; M.G.
2. Cooper, *A Durable Fire,* p. 264.
3. Laura, Duchess of Marlborough, *Laughter from a Cloud,* p. 111.
4. Ibid., p. 111.
5. Ibid., pp. 33–34.
6. Hon. L. H. L. Cohen, Dovecote House, Swallowfield, Reading, Berkshires, letter to the author, Nov. 25, 1986.
7. Anna Gendel in conversation with the author, Regency Hotel, New York City, July 1987.
8. Hart D'Arcy, *The Samuel Family of Liverpool and London.*
9. Edwin Montagu, letter to the Earl of Lytton, June 19, 1923; Montagu F/60/25.
10. Edwin Montagu, letter to Lord Reading, Sept. 5, 1923; Montagu F/118/95.
11. Edwin Montagu, letter to Lord Reading, Oct. 25, 1923; Montagu F/118/95.
12. Id.
13. Edwin Montagu, letter to Lord Reading, Nov. 19, 1923; Montagu F/118/95.
14. Id.
15. H. H. Asquith, letter to Mrs. Harrison, Nov. 28, 1922; Koss, *Asquith,* p. 259. Mrs. Harrison was the widow of Capt. Harrison, killed in action in 1917. Mrs. Harrison became the dearest friend of Asquith in his old age and the recipient of scores of his letters, which are on file in the Bodleian Library in Oxford.
16. Ibid., p. 260.
17. Nicolson, *Curzon: The Last Phase,* p. 355.
18. Ruddock F. MacKay, *Balfour* (Oxford and New York, 1985), p. 343.
19. *Daily Chronicle* (London), Nov. 1, 1924.
20. Manchester, *The Last Lion,* pp. 740, 741.

34. Despair and Death

1. Sir Francis Lindley, *Lord Lovat* (London, 1935), p. 263.
2. Ibid., p. 264.
3. Id.
4. Id.
5. Ibid., pp. 264–65; Waley, *Edwin Montagu,* p. 285.
6. *Eastern Daily Press,* Nov. 20, 1924.
7. Edwin Montagu, letter to Venetia Stanley, Oct. 16, 1917; M.G.; Waley, *Edwin Montagu,* p. 142.
8. Edwin Montagu, letter to Venetia Stanley, June 7, 1924; M.G.; Waley, *Edwin Montagu,* p. 285.
9. The *Tribune* (published in Lahore), Nov. 18, 1924, editorial, "Mr. Montagu"; M.G.
10. Montagu, *The Youngest Son,* p. 201.

11. *Evening News of India,* roundup of tributes paid to Edwin Montagu, Tues., Nov. 18, 1924 (published in India); M.G.

12. The *Ragoon,* editorial on Edwin Montagu, Mon., Nov. 17, 1924 (published in India); M.G.

13. Id.

14. The *Bengalee,* editorial on Edwin Montagu, Nov. 21, 1924 (published in Calcutta, India); M.G.

15. Id.

16. The *Leader,* Nov. 18, 1924 (published in India); M.G.

17. The *Englishman,* editorial on Edwin Montagu, Nov. 18, 1924 (published in India); M.G.

18. The *Times of India,* Nov. 17, 1924; M.G.

19. The *Times of India,* Dec. 9, 1924; M.G.

20. Id.

21. The *Daily Telegram,* Edwin Montagu, a personal memoir, by T. P. O. Connor, Nov. 24, 1924; M.G.

22. Id.

23. Telegram, Government of India and the Viceroy (Reuters), Nov. 16, 1924; M.G.

24. Madras Council Resolution, Nov. 17, 1924; M.G.

25. Bombay Council Resolution, Nov. 17, 1924; M.G.

26. Punjab Council Resolution (Lahore), Nov. 17, 1924; M.G.

27. Calcutta Council Resolution, Nov. 19, 1924; M.G.

28. Lord Sinha, address at Calcutta Council, Nov. 19, 1924; M.G.

29. Id.

30. Id.

31. The *Times of India,* letter to editor; a Mahomedan tribute. See also the *Civil and Military Gazette,* Nov. 18, 1924; M.G.

32. Tribute, Maharajah of Bikaner in Chamber of Princes, Nov. 17, 1924, sent to Venetia Stanley, Dec. 16, 1924; M.G.

33. Extract of Preceedings of Chamber of Princes, held on Nov. 17, 1924, sent to Venetia Stanley on Dec. 16, 1924; M.G.

34. The *Times of India,* Dec. 1, 1924, on the occasion of the unveiling of the statue of Edwin Montagu, in the town square in Jamnagar; remarks by His Highness, the Maharajah Jam Sahib; M.G.

35. Id.

36. Id.

37. Id., remarks by Lord Reading.

38. The *Observer* (London), editorial on Edwin Montagu, Nov. 16, 1924; M.G.

39. *The Sunday Times* (London), Nov. 16, 1924; M.G.

40. Id.

41. Lord Chelsmford, letter to the editor, *The Times* (London), Nov. 28, 1924; M.G.

42. Lord Willingdon, letter to editor, the *Observer* (London), Nov. 16, 1924; M.G.

43. The *Observer* (London), interview of Sir George Lloyd, about Edwin Montagu, Nov. 16, 1924; M.G.

44. John Maynard Keynes, "Essay on Montagu," *The Nation and the Athenaeum,* Nov. 29, 1924; See also Keynes, *Essays in Biography,* pp. 55–58.

45. The *Cambridge Review,* essay on Edwin Montagu, Nov. 28, 1924; published in a compilation of tributes to Edwin Montagu, by Lily H. Montagu, Apr. 1925; M.G.

46. The *Cambridge Independent Press,* essay on Edwin Montagu, Nov. 21, 1924; M.G.

47. *Eastern Daily Press,* burial of Edwin Montagu, Nov. 20, 1924; M.G.

48. Id.

49. *Daily Telegram,* Nov. 21, 1924; M.G.

50. Venetia Stanley, letter to Lloyd George, Nov. 18, 1924; M.G.

51. Lloyd George, letter to Venetia Stanley, Nov. 21, 1924; M.G.

52. King George, letter to Venetia Stanley, Nov. 16, 1924; M.G.; also Montagu AS 5/10/1.

53. Prince of Wales, letter to Venetia Stanley, Nov. 16, 1924; M.G.; also Montagu AS 5/10/3(2).

54. Winston Churchill, letter to Venetia Stanley, Nov. 16, 1924; M.G.; also Montagu AS 5/10/2(1).

35. *Venetia without Edwin*

1. Venetia Stanley, letter to Lord Beaverbrook, Nov. 18, 1929; M.G.

2. Lord Beaverbrook, letter to Venetia Stanley, Nov. 22, 1924; M.G.

3. Jenkins, *Asquith,* p. 510.

4. Id.

5. Lord Beaverbrook, letter to Venetia Stanley, July 8, 1926; M.G.

6. Lord Beaverbrook, letter to Venetia Stanley, Sept. 6, 1929; M.G.

7. Venetia Stanley, letter to Lord Beaverbrook, Jan. 1929, no other date; M.G.

8. Lord Beaverbrook, telegram to Venetia Stanley, Jan. 16, 1929; M.G.

9. Taylor, *Beaverbrook,* p. 244. After Jean Norton's death, Beaverbrook destroyed all the correspondence between them. Her diaries for the years 1928 to 1931 came into Beaverbrook's hands. He did not destroy these. They show that he and Ms. Norton met nearly every day during these years and that they had a deep and loving relationship.

10. Ziegler, *Diana Cooper,* p. 110.

11. Lord Beaverbrook, letter to Venetia Stanley, Oct. 28, 1929; M.G.

12. Ziegler, *Diana Cooper,* p. 167.

13. Id.

14. Ibid., p. 168.

15. Id.

16. Venetia Stanley, letter to Lord Beaverbrook, Feb. 28, 1929; M.G.

17. Taylor, *Beaverbrook,* p. 264.

18. Venetia Stanley, letter to Lord Beaverbrook, Jan. 23, 1929; M.G.

19. Brock, *H. H. Asquith Letters to Venetia Stanley,* p. 616.

20. Venetia Stanley, letter to Lord Beaverbrook, Apr. 22, 1928; M.G.

21. Lord Beaverbrook, letter to Venetia Stanley, Aug. 27, 1928; M.G.

22. Venetia Stanley, letter to Lord Beaverbrook, Apr. 22, 1928: M.G.
23. Anna Gendel, letter to the author, Nov. 20, 1987.
24. Milton Gendel, letter to the author, Apr. 20, 1988.
25. Brock, *H. H. Asquith Letters to Venetia Stanley*, p. 608.
26. Id.
27. Daphne Bennett, *Margot: A Life of the Countess of Oxford and Asquith* (New York, 1985), p. 252.
28. Id.
29. Ibid., p. 253.
30. Ibid., p. 254.
31. Id.
32. Id.
33. Ibid., p. 255.
34. Spender and Asquith, *The Life of Herbert Henry Asquith*, vol. 1, p. 217.
35. *Daily Express,* Feb. 15, 1928; M.G.
36. Montagu, *Indian Diary,* preface, p. vi.
37. Manchester, *The Last Lion,* p. 845.
38. Ibid., p. 850.
39. Venetia Stanley, letter to Lord Beaverbrook, June 10, 1934; M.G.
40. Taylor, *Beaverbrook,* p. 385.
41. Ibid., p. 366.
42. Ibid., p. 387.
43. Id.
44. Ibid., p. 387.
45. Id.
46. Id.
47. Ibid., p. 386.
48. Ibid., p. 395.
49. Ziegler, *Diana Cooper,* p. 189.
50. Ibid., pp. 186–87.
51. Venetia Stanley, letter to Lord Beaverbrook, Aug. 22, 1938; M.G.
52. Taylor, *Beaverbrook,* p. 413.
53. Ziegler, *Diana Cooper,* p. 201.
54. Ibid., p. 234.
55. Id.
56. Soames, *Clementine Churchill,* p. 406.
57. Id.
58. Ibid., p. 411.
59. Ibid., p. 421.
60. Ibid., p. 477.
61. Ibid., p. 413.
62. Venetia Stanley, letter to Lord Beaverbrook, Dec. 18, 1943; M.G.
63. Venetia Stanley, letter to Lord Beaverbrook, May 10, 1943; M.G.
64. Venetia Stanley, letter to Lord Beaverbrook, June 4, 1947; M.G.
65. Venetia Stanley, letter to Lord Beaverbrook, Dec. 1, 1947; M.G.
66. Soames, *Clementine Churchill,* p. 509.

67. Venetia Stanley, letter to Lord Beaverbrook, May 10, 1943; M.G.

68. Duchess of Marlborough, *Laughter from a Cloud,* p. 111.

69. Brock, *H. H. Asquith Letters to Venetia Stanley,* pp. 611–12.

70. Venetia Stanley, letter to Lord Beaverbrook, Jan. 1, 1948; M.G.

71. Venetia Stanley, letter to Lord Beaverbrook, June 30, 1948; M.G.

72. Ziegler, *Diana Cooper,* p. 272.

73. Id.

74. Venetia Stanley, letter to Lord Beaverbrook, July 12, 1948; M.G.

Epilogue: The Cycle Is Complete: The End

1. Brock, *H. H. Asquith Letters to Venetia Stanley,* pp. 611–12.

Bibliography

Acton, Sir Harold. *More Memoirs of an Aesthete*. London, 1970.

Adams, R. J. Q. *Arms and the Wizard*. Texas, 1978.

Adelman, Paul. *The Decline of the Liberal Party, 1910–1931*. Essex, England, 1981.

Alderman, Geoffrey. *The Jewish Community in British Politics*. Oxford, 1983.

Almog, Samuel. *Patterns of Prejudice*. "Anti-Semitism As a Dynamic Phenomenon: The 'Jewish Question' in England at the End of the First World War," vol. 21, no. 4, 1987.

Aris, Stephen. *The Jews in Business*. London, 1970.

Asquith, H. H. *Fifty Years of British Parliament*. Vols. 1 and 2. Boston, 1926.

Asquith, H. H. *Memories and Reflections, 1852–1927*. Boston, 1928.

Asquith, Lady Cynthia. *Diaries, 1915–1918*. New York, 1968.

Asquith, Margot. Diaries, not yet published. Bonham Carter MSS.

Beaverbrook, Lord. *The Decline and Fall of Lloyd George*. London and Glasgow, 1963.

Beaverbrook, Lord. *Politicians and the War*. London, 1928.

Bence-Jones, Mark. *The Viceroys of India*. London, 1982.

Bennett, Daphne. *Margot: A life of the Countess of Oxford and Asquith*. New York, 1985.

Bermant, Chaim. *The Cousinhood*. New York, 1971.

Black, Eugene. *The Social Politics of Anglo-Jewry, 1880–1920*. Oxford, 1988.

Bonham Carter, Violet. *Winston Churchill, An Intimate Portrait*. New York, 1965.

Brock, Michael, and Eleanor Brock. *H. H. Asquith Letters to Venetia Stanley*. Oxford, 1982.

Burk, Kathleen. "The Treasury—From Impotence to Power." In *War and the State*, ed. Kathleen Burk. London, Boston, and Sydney, 1982.

Carman, Harry J., and Harold C. Stryett. *A History of the American People*. New York, 1958.

Chirol, Sir Valentine. *India*. London, 1930.

Cohen, Stuart A. *English Zionists and British Jews*. Princeton, N.J., 1982.

Colgate, Isabel. *The Shooting Party*. London, 1980.

Cook, Chris. *A Short History of the Liberal Party, 1900–1976*. New York, 1976.

Cooper, Artemis. *A Durable Fire*. New York, 1984.

Cooper, Diana. *The Rainbow Comes and Goes*. Boston, 1958.

Cooper, Duff. *Old Men Forget*. London, 1955.

Cregier, Dan M. *Bounder from Wales*. Missouri and London, 1976.

Cross, Colin. *The Liberals in Power, 1905–1914*. London, 1936.

Dangerfield, George. *The Strange Death of Liberal England*. St. Albans, Great Britain, 1935.

Daniels, Robert V. *Studying History*. Englewood Cliffs, N.J., 1966.

Das, Durgas. *India from Curzon to Nehru and After*. New York, 1970.

Dictionary of National Biography (1901–1911). Ed. Sidney Lee. Oxford, 1963.

Dictionary of National Biography (1922–1930). Ed. J. R. H. Weaver. Oxford, 1961.

Emy, H. V. *Liberals, Radicals, and Social Politics, 1892–1914*. Cambridge, England, 1973.

Ensor, Sir Robert. *The Oxford History of England, 1870–1914*. Oxford, 1936.

Farrer, David. *G for God Almighty: A Personal Memoir of Lord Beaverbrook*. New York, 1969.

Finestein, Israel. *A Short History of Anglo-Jewry*. London: World Jewish Congress, 1957.

Grigg, John. *Lloyd George: From Peace to War, 1912–1916*. Great Britain, 1985.

Grigg, John. *Lloyd George: The People's Champion 1902–1911*. Great Britain, 1985.

Grigg, John. *The Young Lloyd George*. London, 1985.

Gupta, Dr. R. L. *Conflict and Harmony, Indo-British Relations: A New Perspective*. New Delhi, 1971.

Halévy, Elie. *A History of the English People in the Nineteenth Century*. Vol. 6. London, 1965.

Harrod, R. F. *The Life of John Maynard Keynes*. New York, 1969.

Hart D'Arcy, Ronald J. *The Samuel Family of Liverpool and London*. London, 1958.

Hasbach, Wilhelm. *History of the English Agricultural Labourer*. London, 1908.

Havighurst, Alfred F. *Twentieth-Century Britain*. New York, 1962.

Heath, Sir Thomas W. *The Treasury*. London, 1927.

Hirst, F. W., and J. E. Allen. *British War Budgets*. London: Carnegie Endowment for International Peace, 1926.

Hirsch, Samuel Raphael. *Horeb: A Philosophy of Jewish Laws and Observances*. Vols. 1 and 2. London, 1962.

History of the Ministry of Munitions, Administrative Policy and Organization. Vol. 2, part 1. London, 1922.

Hobhouse, Charles. *Inside Asquith's Cabinet*. London, 1977.

Honours and Titles in Britain. Prepared by the Reference Services, Central Office of Information. London, 1982.

Hyde, H. Montgomery. *Lord Reading: The Life of Rufus Isaacs, the First Marquess of Reading*. New York, 1967.

James, Robert Rhodes. *The British Revolution, 1880–1939*. New York, 1977.

Jenkins, Roy. *Asquith: Portrait of a Man and an Era*. New York and London, 1964.

Johnson, Paul Barton. *Land Fit for Heroes*. Chicago and London, 1968.

Jones, Sir Lawrence. *An Edwardian Youth*. New York, 1956.

Jones, Thomas. *Lloyd George*. Cambridge, Mass., 1951.

Judd, Dennis. *Lord Reading*. London, 1982.

Kennet, Lady (Lady Scott). *Self-Portrait of an Artist*. London, 1924.

Keynes, John Maynard. "The Economic Consequences of the Peace." In *Collected Writings of John Maynard Keynes*. 29 vols. London, 1971.

Keynes, John Maynard. *Essays on Biography*. New York, 1933.

Kipling, Rudyard. *Verse*. Inclusive ed., 1885–1932. Garden City, N.Y., 1934.

Koss, Stephen E. *Asquith*. London, 1976.

Koss, Stephen E. *Lord Haldane: Scapegoat for Liberalism*. New York and London, 1969.

Lambert, Angela. *Unquiet Souls*. London, 1984.

Laqueur, Walter. *History of Zionism*. New York, 1972.

Lewis, Bernard. *The Emergence of Modern Turkey*. New York and London, 1961.

Lindley, Sir Frances. *Lord Lovat*. London, 1935.

Lipman, V. D. *Social History of the Jews in England, 1850–1950*. London, 1954.

Lipman, V. D. *Three Centuries of Anglo-Jewish History*. London, 1961.

Lloyd George, David. *Memoirs of the Peace Conference*. Vols. 1 and 2. New Haven, Conn., 1939.

Lloyd George, David. *War Memoirs*. Vols. 1 and 2. London, 1938.

Lubbock, Adelaide Stanley. *People in Glass Houses*. Melbourne, 1977.

MacKay, Ruddock F. *Balfour*. Oxford and New York, 1985.

McKenna, Stephen. *Reginald McKenna*. London, 1948.

Mallet, Sir Charles. *Mr. Lloyd George: A Study*. London, 1950.

Manchester, William. *The Last Lion: Winston S. Churchill*. Boston and Toronto, 1983.

Marlborough, Laura, Duchess of. *Laughter from a Cloud*. London, 1980.

Marriott, Sir J. A. R. *Modern England 1885–1939: A History of My Own Times*. London, 1941.

Marwick, Arthur. *The Deluge*. Boston and Toronto, 1965.

Marwick, Arthur. *The Explosion of British Society*. London and New York, 1970.

Mendelssohn, Peter de. *The Age of Churchill, 1874–1911*. New York, 1961.

Mitford, Nancy. *The Ladies of Alderley*. London, 1968.

Montagu, Edwin S. *Indian Diary*. Edited by Venetia Stanley Montagu. London, 1930.

Montagu, Edwin S., and Auberon (Bron) Herbert. *Canada and the Empire*. London, 1904.

Montagu, Ivor. *The Youngest Son*. London, 1970.

Montagu, Lily H. *Samuel Montagu: First Baron Swaythling*. London, 1911.

Moonman, Jane. *Anglo-Jewry: An Analysis*. London: Institute of Jewish Affairs, Joint Israel Appeal, 1980.

Morgan, Ted. *Churchill, Young Man in a Hurry 1874–1915*. New York, 1982.

Mosley, Leonard. *The Glorious Fault*. New York, 1960.

Murray, Bruce K. *The People's Budget, 1909–1910: Lloyd George and Liberal Politics*. Oxford, 1980.

Nicolson, Harold. *Curzon: The Last Phase*. London, 1934.

Owen, Frank. *Tempestuous Journey: Lloyd George, His Life and Times*. London, 1954.

Peacock, H. L. *History of Modern Britain 1815–1981*. London, 1980.

Pugh, Martin. *The Making of Modern British Politics, 1867–1939*. Oxford, 1982.

Riddle, Lord George Allardice. *Diaries*. Vols. 1 and 2. London, 1933–34.

Robb, P. G. *The Government of India and Reform*. Oxford, 1976.

Roberts, P. E. *History of British India*. 5th ed. New York and London, 1983.

Rodgers, W. T., and Bernard Donoughue. *The People into Parliament*. New York, 1966.

Ronaldshay, Earl of. *The Life of Lord Curzon*. Vols. 1–3. London and New York, 1928.

Roseveare, Henry. *The Treasury*. New York, 1969.

Roskill, Stephen. *Hankey: Man of Secrets*. Vol. 1. New York, 1970.

Roth, Cecil. *A History of the Jews in England*. Oxford, 1941.

Roth, Cecil, "The Resettlement of the Jews of England," in *Three Centuries of Anglo-Jewish History*, edited by V. D. Lipman, London, 1961.

Rowland, Peter. *David Lloyd George*. New York, 1975.

Russell, Bertrand. *Autobiography*. Boston and Toronto, 1967.

Samuel, Herbert. *Liberalism*. London, 1902.

Samuel, Viscount. *Memoirs*. London, 1945.

Scott, C. P. *Diaries*. London, 1970.

Skidelsky, Robert. *John Maynard Keynes, 1883–1920*. New York, 1986.

Snowden, Philip. *An Autobiography*. Vol. 1. London, 1934.

Soames, Mary. *Clementine Churchill: The Biography of a Marriage*. Boston, 1979.

Spender, J. A., and Cyril Asquith. *The Life of Herbert Henry Asquith, Lord Oxford and Asquith*. Vols. 1 and 2. London, 1932.

Stein, Leonard. *The Balfour Declaration*. New York, 1961.

Stevenson, Frances. *Lloyd George: A Diary*. New York, 1971.

Taylor, A. J. P. *Beaverbrook*. New York, 1972.

Taylor, A. J. P. *English History, 1914–1945*. Oxford History of England. Oxford, 1975.

Tuchman, Barbara. *The Proud Tower*. New York and Toronto, 1966.

Umansky, Ellen. *Lily Montagu: Sermons, Addresses, Letters, Prayers*. New York and Toronto, 1984.

Waley, Sir David. *Edwin Montagu*. Bombay, 1964.

Wilson, Trevor. *The Downfall of the Liberal Party, 1914–1915*. Ithaca, N.Y., 1966.

Ziegler, Philip. *Diana Cooper*. London, 1981.

Zimmern, A. E. *The Third British Empire*. London, 1926.

Index

Abbott, Edwin, 75

Acland, Francis D., 624

Acton, Sir Harold, 103

Adams, W. G. S., 775

Addis, Sir Charles, 683

Addison, Christopher: as Minister of Munitions, 353, 354; as Minister of Reconstruction, 405, 409, 416, 538, 604; resigns, 628, 644–45

Adler, Dr. Herman, 422

Adrianople, 499, 549, 558, 600, 630

Afghanistan, 184, 601, 602

Agadir incident, 126

Aga Khan, 190, 259, 454, 517, 525, 585, 603, 610–11, 650

Agricultural Holdings Act, 92

agricultural system, British, 91–92

Airlie, Lady Blanche, 106, 176, 265, 267, 323, 712; on Venetia's engagement, 315

Airlie, Lord, 106

Aisne, 476

Aitken, William Maxwell (1st Baron Beaverbrook), 527–31, 532, 554, 593, 655, 671, 700, 701; anti-Semitism and, 719–20; as author of *Politicians and the War,* 709–10; on Churchill, 680; election of 1922 and, 665, 666, 667, 668; on ESM, 3, 220, 286; ESM seeks advice from, 608; fall of the Asquith government and formation of Coalition and, 292, 366, 369, 371, 375; isolationism of, 718–19, 720; Jean Norton and, 706, 708, 803; on Lloyd George's government, 384;

Ministry of Aircraft Production and, 722, 725; Reading and, 576, 649; self-government for India and, 717; on shell shortage, 286, 287, 292; trips to Germany and Moscow, 707–8; Venetia and, 102, 103, 275, 527, 530–31, 532, 534, 535–37, 545–46, 652, 653, 703, 704, 706, 707, 708, 709–10, 711, 712, 717–18, 721–22, 723, 725–26, 727–28; yellow journalism and, 612–13

Alexander, David L., 432

Ali, Mahommed, 579, 582, 583–84, 590

Ali, Shaukat, 582, 583–84, 590

Aliens Act of 1902, 426

Ali Khan, Syed Sirdar, 692

Alivar, Maharajah of, 571

Allenby, Edmund, 398, 477

All-India-Muslim League, 471

Alverstone, Chief Justice, 159

Alwar, Maharajah, 259, 650

Ambassadors' Conference (1913), 216

Amiens, 358, 476

Ampthill, Lord, 596

Amritsar Massacre, 511–16, 517, 521, 538, 578, 624, 628; Churchill on, 614; Gandhi on, 583; report and debate on, 515–16, 554–57, 558–70, 623, 644

Amsterdam, 11, 12

Anatolia, 522, 570

Anti-Dumping Bill, 604

anti-Semitism: Acland and, 624; Aliens Act of 1902 and, 426; Asquith (Cyn-

anti-Semitism (*Continued*)
thia) and, 391; Asquith (H. H.) and, 160, 177, 193–94, 199, 208, 306–8, 309; Asquith (Margot) and, 208, 314, 419, 420; Balfour Declaration and, 435; Beaverbrook and, 719–20; Belloc and, 14, 158, 309, 312; at Cambridge, 57–58; Chesterton and, 25; the Coterie and, 391–93; Curzon and, 308, 309, 603, 647; in Eastern Europe, 12, 13, 15; ESM and, 4–5, 31, 145, 177, 187, 188, 189, 220, 554; in Great Britain, 4–5, 14–15; Gwynne and, 623, 628; House of Commons and, 562–63, 566, 567, 627; Lloyd George and, 216, 308–9, 574–75; in the Marconi affair, 158, 159; Montagu (Samuel) and, 14–15, 19–20, 21; Montagu-Chelmsford report and, 470; Reading (Lord) and, 573–75; Samuel (Herbert) and, 307; and the Silver Scandal, 159, 187, 188, 189; Stevenson (Frances) and, 216; Tory Party and, 14, 255–56, 308

Arabia, 498, 499, 510
Argyll, Duke of, 450
Armenia, 498, 499, 509, 522
Arnold, Thomas, 14
Arras, 264, 396
Asher, Dr. Asher, 22
Asley, W. J., 503
Asquith, Arthur ("O. C."): on Venetia's engagement and conversion, 313
Asquith, Cynthia, 308, 388, 671, 700; anti-Semitism and, 391; on end of war, 479; on ESM and fall of the Asquith government, 383–84; on ESM's charm, 390; on Montagus' marriage, 386–87, 486; on Queen Anne's Gate, 388; on Venetia's Aarons operation, 534; on Venetia's ambivalence about marriage, 323; on Wilson (Scatters), 487
Asquith, Cyril, 160, 713

Asquith, Helen (née Milland), 77
Asquith, Herbert, 300
Asquith, Herbert Henry (H. H.), 102, 103, 104, 138, 166, 167, 169, 180, 181, 191, 236, 254, 260, 300, 315, 324, 331, 351, 355, 396, 401, 402, 450, 461, 485, 516, 527, 536, 546, 575, 604, 671, 675, 680–81, 698, 700, 711; alcohol and, 231; anti-Semitism and, 160, 177, 193–94, 199, 208, 296, 306–8, 309; appoints ESM Chancellor of the Duchy of Lancaster, 256, 257; appoints ESM Financial Secretary to the Treasury, 210–11; appoints ESM Minister of Munitions, 350; appoints ESM Parliamentary Private Secretary, 81; appoints ESM Privy Councillor (1915), 249, 252; appoints ESM Under Secretary of State for India, 123; appoints Reading Chief Justice, 159; appoints Lloyd George Secretary of War, 350; asks ESM to return to Treasury, 327; Beaverbrook and, 528, 529; becomes Prime Minister, 94, 96; breaks with ESM, 420, 421; Britain's entry into war and, 228–31; budgets of 1906, 1907 and 1908 and, 90–91; budget of 1912 and, 162–63; budget of 1913 and, 203, 204, 205; budget of 1914 and, 220–21, 222, 256; calls ESM "Tante," 171–72, 174, 176, 199, 203; childhood and youth of, 75–76; as Chancellor of the Exchequer, 82, 83, 84, 86, 87, 89, 90–91; Coalition Cabinet and, 328–29; Coalition government and, 1–2, 290, 292–94, 297, 298, 300, 765, 766; Committee on Food Prices and, 262; Committee of Pensions and, 247–48; conscription and, 336–37, 339, 341–42; criticism of, during war, 255–56, 337–39; Dardanelles expedition and, 288, 289–90, 291, 364; death of, 713; death of son Raymond and, 362–63; dismemberment

of Turkey and, 429; dissension in
Cabinet caused by McKenna, 358–
60, 361; drafts Corrupt Practices Act
of 1883, 76–77; early career of, 76–
77; early days of war and, 238–39;
early wartime correspondence with
Venetia of, 248–53; Easter Rebellion
and, 345–49; election of 1899 and,
80; election of 1906 and, 73; election
(1st) of 1910 and, 123, 124; election
of 1918 (coupon election) and, 480,
481, 482–83; election of 1922 and,
667, 668; election travels with Venetia, 112; elevates ESM to the Cabinet, 256, 257, 258; end of war and,
478; entertained at Queen Anne's
Gate during war, 388, 390; envied
by ESM, 172; ESM and Lloyd
George government, 406, 408, 410–
11; on ESM and reorganization of
India Office, 203–4; and ESM's
ambition to be Viceroy, 258–59;
ESM's courtship of Venetia and,
205–8, 252; ESM speaks before at
Cambridge, 51; extravagance of, 76;
fall of the Asquith government and,
366–78, 380, 381, 382, 383, 385,
398, 431; First Reconstruction Committee and, 398, 399–400; Harrisson
(Hilda) and, 713, 714, 801; Home
Rule for Ireland and, 222, 223–26,
228, 758; as Home Secretary, 78–79;
Hunter Committee report and, 560;
intellectual achievements of, 75–76;
King George V and, 126; Kitchener
and, 280; lack of leadership of, 120;
Lansdowne memorandum and, 365–
66; and the law, 76, 99, 121; Liberal
Party and, 344, 676, 677, 678–79;
Lloyd George's government and,
394–95, 397; Marconi affair and,
158, 159, 160, 577; marriages of, 77–
78; Maurice affair and, 783; *Memories
and Reflections,* 362; nature of relationship with Venetia and, 231–35;
Newcastle Programme and, 70; ora-

tory and, 75, 77, 79; overview of career of, 74–75; Oxford career of,
75–76; Palestine as Jewish homeland
and, 430; Parliament Act (1911),
124–25, 126; People's Budget (1909)
and the House of Lords (1910–11),
115–17, 119, 121, 124, 125; personality of, 1; the press and, 366, 378;
Reading and, 577; refers to ESM as
"The Assyrian" and "Mr. Wu,"
177, 179, 193, 199, 200, 201, 205,
206, 210, 213, 220, 221, 252, 257,
261, 273, 283, 285, 295, 306; relationship with Margot and, 265–67;
relationship with Venetia, 169–71,
173–74, 175–76, 179, 193–95, 262–
65, 267–69, 274; resignation of ESM
as Secretary of State and, 643, 646,
647; resigns, 378–79; reveals private
and wartime military information to
Venetia, 210–11, 249–52, 257, 264,
273, 298; seeks Venetia's advice, 160;
Shadow Cabinet and, 332; shell
shortage and, 281, 282–85, 286–87;
Silver Scandal and, 187, 188; social
life of, 79–80; steps leading to war
and, 228–31; the tank and, 357; tendency to delay of, 120; Tory Party
and, 255–56; as traditionalist, 121;
trip to Sicily with Venetia, 170, 195;
Venetia and, after ESM's death,
704–5, 707, 709–10, 712–14; on Venetia and religion, 321; Venetia as
Violet Asquith's friend and, 111,
112; Venetia's engagement and, 2,
292, 294–304, 314, 319; on Venetia's
rejection of ESM, 207; Venetia's
wedding and, 325, 326; visits Venetia in France, 304–6; at Walmer Castle with Venetia and ESM, 272; War
Cabinet meetings and, 363–64; War
Committee crisis and, 366–78; War
Council and, 239; as war leader,
278–80; weakness of, for women,
112; wins first seat in Parliament, 77;
women's suffrage and, 160–62, 169,

Asquith, Herbert Henry (H. H.) (*Cont.*)
193, 483; work style of, 336; as
youthful orator, 38

Asquith, Katharine, 260, 270, 323, 324,
388, 391; on Montagus' marriage,
486; Venetia's engagement and conversion and, 313, 314

Asquith, Margot (née Tennant), 77,
194, 215, 295, 304, 324, 339, 359,
421, 507, 575, 577, 671; anti-Semitism and, 208, 314, 419, 420; on appointment of Lloyd George as Secretary of War, 350–51; Asquith and
other women and, 112, 196, 713–14;
Asquith's trip to Sicily and, 170;
Beaverbrook and, 529; characterized,
78; entertained at Queen Anne's
Gate during war, 388, 390; on ESM
and Britain's entry into war, 230;
ESM and Lloyd George government, 406, 407–8, 419–20; ESM as
friend of, 88–89, 100, 206, 208, 235–
37, 238, 252, 265–66; on ESM as
gossip, 95–96; on ESM's ambition
to be Viceroy, 273; on ESM's extravagance, 488; fall of Asquith government and, 369, 370, 382, 384,
385; health of, 191, 195; Harrisson
(Hilda) and, 713, 714; Lady Sheffield
and, 267; on Lord Crewe and ESM,
143–44; meets and marries Asquith,
77; pedigree of, 78; relationship with
Asquith of, 196, 232, 235, 265–66;
social life of, 79–80; Venetia and,
112, 170, 196, 235–37, 265–67, 314,
420, 713–14; Violet Asquith and,
111, 170, 195–96, 236, 265, 266;
women's movement and, 161

Asquith, Raymond, 323, 324, 388,
389, 393, 478; death of, 362–63;
Diana Cooper and, 103, 271; on the
Montagus' marriage, 387; on trench
warfare, 339–41; on Venetia's engagement and conversion, 313–14;
on Venetia's latent lesbianism, 103,
271, 275

Asquith, Violet (later Mrs. Bonham
Carter), 100, 166, 213, 252, 261,
273, 324, 345, 388, 542; death of
Archibald Gordon and, 111, 113,
114; described, 111; ESM writes to,
about Asquith, 116–17; ESM's desertion of Asquith and, 385, 773–74;
on Francis Henley, 206; Margot Asquith and, 111, 170, 195–96, 236,
265, 266; trip to Sicily with Asquith
and Venetia, 170; Venetia's engagement and conversion and, 310, 311–
12, 314; as Venetia's friend, 111,
112, 191, 393, 714; women's movement and, 161

Astor, Waldorf, 403

Atatürk, Kemal, 525, 547, 558, 620; final offensive against the Greeks of,
662–63

Audithley, Adam de, 104

Audithley, Lyulph, 104

Audithley, William de, 104

Audley, Lord, 104

Australia, 504, 552; Peace Conference
and, 493; self-government and, 454,
468

Austria-Hungary, 226–27, 229, 478,
523; Diaspora Nationalism in, 428;
persecution of Jews in, 13

Baker, Harold Trevor (Bluetooth or
Bluey), 112, 191, 192, 193, 300, 308,
386, 713

Baldwin, Stanley, 668, 700; appointed
Prime Minister, 677, 678, 800; election of 1923 and, 678–79; election of
1924 and, 679; ESM on, 675; free
trade and, 677, 678; self-government
for India and, 716, 717; speaks
against Lloyd George, 665

Balfour, Arthur James, 42, 77, 232,
338, 367, 368, 436, 468, 495, 532,
534; appointed to the Admiralty,
329; Baldwin and, 678; Curzon and,
633–34; Declaration and, 433, 444,
446, 447; as delegate for Peace Con-

ference, 493; election of 1906 and, 72–73, 80; ESM's appointment as Secretary of State for India and, 417, 418, 419; fall of Asquith government and, 369, 371, 372, 375, 376, 377, 378; in Lloyd George's government, 379, 394; Mesopotamian disaster and, 416–17; peace negotiations with Turkey and, 509, 511, 524, 525, 526, 529–40, 541, 550, 600; People's Budget (1909) and, 116; restrictive immigration and, 426; self govern-ment for India and, 454, 456; on Shell Committee, 285; War Council and, 239; Zionism and, 431, 433, 444, 446, 447

Balfour, Gerald, 22

Balfour Declaration: adopted, 447; An-glo-Jewish opposition to, 422–23, 779–80; debated, 435–47; drafted, 433; ESM and, 4, 326, 429, 435–49, 779, 780; Samuel (Herbert) and, 429

Bankers' Magazine, 17

Barnes, George, 493

Barth, Sir James S., 355

Baruch, Bernard, 523, 535

Basu, Bhupendranath, 458, 572, 650

Bayswater Chronicle, 10

Beaconsfield, Lord, 140

Beatty, David, 264

Beauchamp, 259, 273

Beaverbrook, Gladys, 706

Beaverbrook, Lord. *See* Aitken, Max

Belgium, 509; Britain's entry into war and, 228, 229, 230; reparations and, 505

Bell, Gertrude, 110

Bell, Gertrude Lowthian, 439

Belloc, Hilaire: anti-Semitism of, 14, 158, 309, 312; the Coterie and, 392

ben Elijakim Getz, Rabbi. *See* Yates, Benjamin

Bengalee, 688

Benn, Captain W., 564

Bennett, Arnold, 707–8

Bennett, Daphne, 714

Beresford, Dorothy, 112

Berry, Pamela, 723

Berthelat, Philippe, 547

Bertie, Viscount, 343, 769

Bessant, Annie, 451, 452, 459, 462, 518, 525, 650, 689, 691

Bevan, Aneurin, 529

Bikaner, Maharajah of, 259, 454, 493, 525, 650, 693

Billing, Pemberton, 586

Birbeck, Dr., 15

Birkenhead, 1st Earl of, 529, 645

Birkin, Captain, 699–700

Birrell, Augustine, 82, 203, 345, 346, 390, 700; on Breccles, 489

Black, Frederick, 764

Blackett, Basil: Keynes and, 244, 757; on Lloyd George as Chancellor of the Exchequer, 214

Blatchford, Robert, 71

Blow, Detmar, 488

Blowitz, H. G. S. de, 193–94

Bomanjie, S. R., 572

Bombay Chronicle, 470

Bonar Law, Andrew. *See* Law, An-drew Bonar

Bonham Carter, Maurice (Bongie), 261, 306, 308, 323, 324, 345, 372, 399, 776; fall of the Asquith govern-ment and, 369, 385; Shadow Cabinet and, 331–32

Bonham Carter, Violet. *See* Asquith, Violet

Bracken, Brendan, 529, 725

Bradbury, Sir John, 243, 244, 259

Bradford, Dr. Rose, 97

Brazil, 676, 682–84, 685

Breccles Hall. *See* Montagu: RESI-DENCES; Montagu, Venetia

Briand, Aristide, 436, 610, 613

Bright, John, 692

Bristol, 12

British Finance Committee, 495

Brock, Eleanor, 233, 234

Brock, Michael, 193, 235; on Asquith's anxiety about Venetia, 295–96, 298,

Brock, Michael (*Continued*)
766; on Beaverbrook's use of Asquith's letters, 709–10; on nature of relationship between Asquith and Venetia, 231, 232, 233, 234; on Venetia's lack of femininity, 109
Brooke, Rupert, 312, 478
Brown, Lancelot (Capability), 8
Buchan, John, 363
Buckmaster, 324, 379
Budberg, Moura, 723
Bulgaria, 342, 477, 524
Burk, Katherine ("The Treasury"), 244
Burns, John, 82, 230
Butler, Harcourt, 554

Cambridge Independent Press, 52, 64, 698
Cambridge Review, 698
Cambridge Union Society, 575
Campbell, Mrs. Patrick, 490
Campbell-Bannerman, Henry, 42; on Asquith's oratory, 79; becomes Prime Minister, 80; Cabinet of, 82–83; has heart attack and retires, 94, 96; land reform and, 93; Newcastle Programme and, 70; peace and, 217
Canada: ESM's trip to, 60–61; Peace Conference and, 493; racism in South Africa and, 588; self-government and, 468
Canada and the Empire (Herbert and Montagu), 61, 93
Canning, Prime Minister, 690, 763
Caporetto, 396
Carson, Sir Edward: in Admiralty, 379; appointed Attorney General, 329; ESM on appointment of, to Admiralty, 401; fall of Asquith government and, 365, 366, 367, 368, 373, 375–76, 381, 772; Hunter Commission report debate and, 560, 569, 570; as leader of Ulster Unionists, 224, 225, 226; reconstruction and, 405, 776
Casement, Roger, 345
Castlerosse, Valentine, 707–8

Cecil, Robert, 367, 431, 438, 499
Chalmers, Sir Robert, 347
Chamberlain, Austen, 402, 458, 571, 572, 628, 632, 633, 674; budget of 1922 and, 604; election of 1922 and, 665; fall of Asquith government and, 371; Montagu-Chelmsford Report and, 468–70, 472–73; reparations and, 505–6; resignation of, 415, 454, 469, 623, 646; resignation of ESM and, 640, 641–43, 644–45, 646, 648, 650; as Secretary of State for India, 407, 411–12, 413, 414, 453–54; self-government for India and, 453–54, 455, 456, 459, 781; World War I and, 227, 243, 244
Chamberlain, Joseph, 603; imperial preference and, 60–61; Jewish homeland and, 426; National Liberal Federation and, 70; protective tariffs and, 72
Chamberlain, Neville, 719, 720, 721
Champagne-Marne, 476
Chanak, 662–63, 664, 665
Channon, Chips, 721
Charles II, King of England, 11, 738
Chateau-Thierry, 476
Chelmsford, Lord, 211, 459, 460, 481, 492, 493, 502, 521, 539, 555, 561, 567, 571, 572, 582, 592, 624, 693, 694; Amritsar Massacre and, 511–12, 513, 515, 516; described, 452; ESM's death and, 696, 700; ESM's trip to India (1917–18) and, 461–62, 463; on Greece and Turkey, 525; Hunter Commission report and, 568; India debate in House of Lords and, 596; Montagu-Chelmsford report of, 464, 465–68, 469, 470, 471–472, 473, 474, 513; Muslim unrest and, 578, 579, 580; Reform Act of 1919 and, 516, 517, 518, 519, 520; returns to England, 581; relationship with ESM deteriorates, 519, 548; self-government for India and, 453, 454, 456, 457, 465–66, 780, 781

Chesterton, Cecil, 158
Chesterton, G. K., 25
China, 136
Chirol, Sir Valentine, 457; on ESM and peace negotiations with Turkey, 540; on Satyagraha, 512
Churchill, Clementine (née Hozier), 390, 671, 680, 704; on Asquith, 112; Venetia and, 106, 653, 724–25; during World War II, 724–25
Churchill, Lady Gwendoline, 324
Churchill, Mary. See Soames, Mary (née Churchill)
Churchill, Randolph, 94, 450, 681
Churchill, Winston, 96, 100, 106, 177, 203, 231, 232, 324, 350, 627, 645, 654, 671, 676, 703, 710; at the Admiralty, 217, 228, 250, 251, 264; Amritsar and, 614; appointed Chancellor of Duchy of Lancaster, 256, 327; in Baldwin Cabinet, 668; Balfour Declaration and, 449; Beaverbrook and, 528, 529; Bolshevism and, 497, 680; Britain's entry into World War I, and, 229; on British losses in France, 279; as candidate for Viceroy of India, 554, 571; as critic of war policy, 337; Dardanelles expedition and, 255, 287–90, 291, 293, 364, 680; death of ESM and, 700, 701, 702; early career of, compared with ESM's, 679–81; election of 1918 and, 481; election of 1922 and, 668; election of 1923 and, 679; election of 1924 and, 679; end of hostilities with Turkey and Greece and, 662, 663; entertained at Queen Anne's Gate during war, 390; envied by ESM, 172; on ESM's appointment to the India Office, 774; fall of the Asquith government and, 372; Fisher and, 280; formation of coalition government and, 1, 297, 408, 421; Germany in the 1930s and, 720, 721; Home Rule for Ireland and, 223; Hunter Commission report and,

559–60, 561–62, 567; Labour Party and, 680; land reform and, 93–94; on land value tax (1909), 118; Liberal Party and, 72, 291, 576; as Minister of Munitions, 353, 354, 358, 419; as orator, 94, 116; peace negotiations with Turkey and, 603, 609, 610–11, 612, 614; prejudice of, 618; the press and, 366; racism in Kenya and South Africa and, 585–88, 589–90, 614–18, 619, 620, 639, 655, 680; removal of, from Admiralty, 290, 291–92, 294, 298, 302, 329, 766; replaces Chamberlain, 721; restrictive immigration and, 426; self-government for India and, 716–17; Shell Committee and, 282; tanks and, 357–58, 770; Tory Party and, 255, 291, 293; as Under Secretary of the Colonies, 82; unrest in India and, 617–19, 620; War Council and, 239; women's movement and, 161; during World War II, 722, 724, 725, 726
Clarion, 71
Clarke, Peter, 233–34
Clemenceau, Georges, 494, 534, 546, 547, 553; peace negotiations with Turkey and, 550; reparations and, 506
Cline, Peter, 405
Coalition government: conscription and, 335–39; Dardanelles Commission and, 364; Easter Rebellion and, 349; election of 1918 and, 480–83; end of, 538, 567, 641, 644–45, 664–69; formation of, 1–2, 290–94, 297, 298, 300, 328–29, 765, 766; Law (Bonar) as Conservative leader in, 365; Liberal Party and, 641; the press and, 366
Cobbett, William, 14
Cohen, Arthur, 140
Cohen, Benjamin Louis, 18
Cohen, Ellen. See Montagu, Ellen
Cohen, L. H. L., 672
Cohen, Levi Barent, 7, 18

Cohen, Louis, 18, 445
Cohen, Robert Waley (later Sir), 424
Cohen family, 7, 700
Colebrooke, Lord, 700
Collins, Michael, 586
Committee of Imperial Defence, 227, 229, 239
Committee of Pensions, 247–48
Committee on Food Prices, 262
Conjoint Committee, 431–32
Connaught, Duke of, 578–79
Conservative Party: election of 1906 and, 63–64, 72, 80; election (1st) of 1910 and, 123; election of 1922 and, 664–68; election of 1923 and, 678–79; election of 1924 and, 679; ESM and, 681; free trade and, 199; People's Budget (1909) and the House of Lords, 116, 118, 119, 120; protective tariffs and, 678; self-government for India and, 716–17; split of, in 1903, 72
Constantine, King of Greece, 610
Constantinople, 190; Armenian massacre in, 522; Curzon on, 540; Kemal and, 558, 662–63; peace negotiations with Turkey concerning, 498, 499, 500, 501, 502, 508, 511, 517, 524, 525, 539, 543, 544, 547, 600, 601, 610, 630, 634, 675; Treaty of Lausanne and, 663; Treaty of Sèvres and, 570
Conventicle Act, 738
Cooper, Diana, 314, 323, 382, 387, 484, 485, 531, 532, 533, 655, 671, 700, 704, 706, 710, 722; anti-Semitism of, 391–93; on Beaverbrook, 527–28; the Coterie and, 388, 389, 390, 527; ESM makes advances to, 490; on ESM's physical appearance, 391; in France, 723, 726; Germany in the 1930s and, 720–21; on the Montagus' marriage, 459, 486, 490, 491; on nature of relationship between Asquith and Venetia, 232–33, 234; on Norfolk (Breccles), 489, 490;

Raymond Asquith and, 271, 363; travels of, 707–8, 709; Venetia and, 103; on Venetia and Beaverbrook, 530; on Venetia's extravagance, 488; on Venetia's final illness, 728; on Wilson (Scatters), 487
Cooper, Duff, 323, 324, 387, 485, 486, 527, 528, 671, 700, 704; as Ambassador to France, 723, 726; anti-Semitism of, 391–93; on Breccles, 490; the Coterie and, 388, 389, 390; on end of war, 479; on ESM's generosity, 391; on fall of Asquith government, 382; Germany in the 1930s and, 720–21; infidelity of, 706; on Montagus' marriage, 487, 490–91, 531, 533; on nature of relationship between Asquith and Venetia, 232–33
Corn Production Act, 397, 400
Coterie, 110, 478–79, 527, 674, 723; anti-Semitism and, 391–93; Raymond Asquith's death and, 362–63; during the war, 388–93
coupon election, 480–83
Courtney, Lord, 154
Cousinhood, The, 7, 28–29, 100, 316
Cousinhood, The, 18
Cowles, Virginia, 723
Craddock, Sir Reginald, 453
Cranbourne, Lady, 710
Crewe, Lord. See Crewe-Milnes, Robert
Crewe, Peggy, 420
Crewe-Milnes, Robert (1st Marquis of Crew), 145, 150, 169, 180, 181, 191, 210, 307, 343, 674, 750; characterized, 143–44; compared with Morley, 144; discord develops between ESM and, 148, 152, 153–55, 157, 182; Durbar of 1911 and, 149; on ESM as Viceroy, 258, 273; and ESM on Curzon, 151; and ESM on reorganization of India Office, 203–4; fall of the Asquith government and, 372, 379; resignation of ESM and,

644; on self-government for India, 153–55; War Council and, 239

Crimean War, 521

Cripps, Violet, 710

Cromer, Lord, 426

Cromwell, Oliver, 11

Cuba, 618, 694

Cunard, Emerald, 721

Cunard, Nancy, 388, 707

Cunliffe, Sir Walter: fall of the Asquith government and, 369; reparations and, 504, 535, 785; and the Treasury, 227, 244, 359

Curragh incident, 238, 758

Currency and Bank Notes Act, 241

Curzon, George, 133, 134, 181, 198, 402, 407, 452, 458, 487, 671; anti-Semitism and, 308, 309, 603, 647; appointed to the Privy Seal, 329; Balfour Declaration and, 444, 447; Bengal and, 149, 150–51; as critic of war policy, 337; described, 155–56, 603–4, 468; deteriorating relationship between ESM and, 148, 155–56, 157, 601–4; election of 1922 and, 665, 666; end of hostilities with Turkey and, 662–63; on ESM as Viceroy, 544–45; and ESM's appointment as Secretary of State for India, 417, 418, 419; fall of the Asquith government and, 367, 371; India debate in House of Lords and, 595–96; in Lloyd George's government, 379, 394; Mesopotamian disaster and, 416–17; Montagu-Chelmsford report and, 468–70, 472–74, 782; passed over for Prime Minister, 651, 677–78; peace negotiations with Turkey and, 495, 499, 500, 509, 511, 525, 526, 539–40, 541, 543–44, 547, 548–49, 550, 580, 597, 600–601, 602, 609, 610–12, 613–14, 620, 633–34; on Reading as Viceroy, 574; Reading's telegram to ESM and, 632–35; Reform Act of 1919 and, 517, 518; resignation of ESM and, 628, 639–

40, 642, 643–44, 645–46, 647; self-government for India and, 148, 153–54, 155, 454, 455, 456–57, 570, 780–81; Treaty of Lausanne and, 663–64; as Viceroy of India, 130–31; in War Cabinet, 453, 459

Curzon, Gracie, 487

Curzon, Lord. See Curzon, George

Curzon, Mary Victoria (née Leiter), 603

Cyprus, 426

Czechoslovakia, 719

Daily Chronicle, 247, 403, 679

Daily Express, 367, 528, 612, 613, 667, 715, 719

Daily Herald, 680, 719

Daily Mail, 84–85, 137, 138, 166, 338, 362, 363, 367, 719

Daily Mirror, 719

Daily News, 141

Daily Telegram, 690, 719

Damascus, 477

Damascus Blood Libel, 15

Dardanelles expedition, 255, 287–90, 291, 680; commission on, 364

Das, Durga, 457, 579, 584

Davies, J. T., 351, 500

Davies, Norman, 504, 506, 507, 510

Dawson, Geoffrey, 772

death duties, 87, 90, 117, 218

De Beers, 682, 684

Delamere, Lord, 589

Delmer, Sefton, 708

Derby, Earl of (Prime Minister), 450

Derby, Lord: as Director of Recruitment, 337; and ESM's appointment as Secretary of State for India, 419; fall of the Asquith government and, 370, 373, 377; in Lloyd George's government, 394, 475

Derby Scheme, 337, 339

Der Judenstaat (The Jewish State) (Herzl), 424

de Robeck, Admiral, 289, 290

Desborough, Ettie, 265

"Destruction of Sennacherib, The" (Byron), 177
Diaspora Nationalism, 428
Dictionary of National Biography, 331, 342–43
Die-Hards: election of 1922 and, 666; motion to censure ESM and, 622, 625, 626, 627; resignation of ESM and, 609, 614, 617, 629, 640, 641, 644, 645, 658; self-government for India and, 716–17
Dilke, Sir Charles, 90
Dillon, Hon. Henrietta Maria, 105, 106
Disraeli, Benjamin, 28, 138, 307, 521, 534, 698, 763
Donaughoure, Lord, 458
Dorothy, Violet Mouche, 236
Drummond, Eric, 324, 342, 345; fall of Asquith's government and, 371, 385; Shadow Cabinet and, 331–32
Duchy of Lancaster: Churchill and, 256; ESM and, 2, 256
Duckham, Sir Arthur M., 355–56
Dudley, Eric, 275, 485, 671, 672, 673, 700
Duff, Juliet, 710, 723
Duff, Thomas Gordon, 78
Duke, Sir William, 458, 463–64, 781
Dulles, John Foster, 507
Durbar of 1911, 148–50
dyarchy, 202, 463–64, 465, 470, 518, 582–83, 661
Dyer, Gen. Reginald, 514–16, 538, 582, 623, 680; Gandhi on, 583; Hunter Committee report and, 555, 556, 557, 559, 560, 561, 562, 563, 564–65, 566, 567, 568, 569

Eastern Crisis of 1877–78, 521
Eastern Daily Press, 699
Eastern Post, 20
Easter Rebellion (1916), 344–45; aftermath of, 347–49
East India Trading Company, 129–30
East London Observer, 20
Ednam, Eric. *See* Dudley, Eric

Education Act of 1902, 80
Edward I, King of England, 11
Edward VII, King of England, 116; dies, 125–26; Parliament Act (1911) and, 125
Egypt, 544, 559, 601, 639, 644; ESM visits, 459; Palestine's importance to British Empire and, 429, 430; as possible Jewish homeland, 426; unrest in, 136
Elgin, Lord, 616
Elizabeth I, Queen of England, 488; and East India Trading Company, 129–30
Elliot-Murray-Kynynmond, Gilbert (Lord Minto), 132, 145, 471; replaced by Hardinge, 144; on self-government for India, 153
Englishman, 138, 181, 689
Ensor, Sir Robert, 79
Evans, Worthington, 409
Evening News, 338
Evening Standard, 528
Excess Profits Tax, 334, 335, 343
Express, 708
Eye Witness, 158

Farrar, David, 529–30
Federation of Synagogues, 23
Feisul, King, 632
Ferdinand, Archduke Francis, 225
Fermor, Patrick Leigh, 726, 730
Fisher, H. A. L., 468, 543, 544, 554
Fisher, Hayes, 411, 628
Fisher, Lady, 700
Fisher, Lord, 280, 298, 680, 700; Dardanelles expedition and, 288–89, 291; resigns, 287, 290, 292, 293
Fitzgerald, Lt. Col., 331–32
Flanders, 475, 476
Foch, Gen. Ferdinand, 304, 475, 476, 478
Forbes, Alastair: on nature of relationship between Asquith and Venetia, 234; on the Montagus' marriage, 387
Fourteen Points, 477, 494, 502

France, 499, 601, 675, 719, 720, 721;
Agadir incident and, 126; annexation
of Palestine and, 430, 431; Britain's
entry into war and, 228, 229; Diplomatic Service in, 342; end of hostilities between Greece and Turkey,
662–63; entry into war of, 227;
peace negotiations with Turkey and,
546–47, 558, 612, 613; relations with
Great Britain (1914), 217; reparations
and, 502–3, 505, 507; Turkey and,
521, 591
Franchet d'Espérey, 522
Franey, George, 458
Franklin, Cyril, 700
Franklin, Ellis, 54, 739
Franklin, Mrs., 700
Franklin family, 13
free trade, 87, 481, 677, 678; Canada
and, 60–61; Conservative Party
(1909) and, 119; in election of 1906,
72; ESM and, 21; first breach in,
334–35; Samuel Montagu and, 21
French, General, 273, 286–87, 294, 295
French, Lord, 350
French, Sir John, 279
Frost, Joyce (née Montagu), 673
Fry, C. B., 22

Gallipoli. See Dardanelles expedition
Gandhi: Amritsar report and, 556; arrest of, 650–51, 657–58; Churchill
and, 589, 590; civil disobedience
and, 578, 579, 619–20, 621–22, 626,
627; ESM and, 462, 538, 565, 568,
590, 592, 593–94, 595, 614, 623–24,
631; march to the Indian Ocean of,
716; noncooperation and, 512, 514,
554, 569, 570; Prince of Wales's visit
and, 598; Reading and, 582, 583–84,
592, 593–94, 597, 614, 619, 620,
621–22, 624–25, 626, 627, 631, 657,
658
Gardener's Magazine, 9
Gaster, Rabbi Moses, 432
Geddes Committee, 654

"Gehazi" (Kipling), 159, 574, 792–93
Gendel, Anna Montagu, 673, 712, 730,
737
Gendel, Judith (née Montagu), 653,
670–71, 672–74, 686, 717–18, 726–
27, 728, 730; Mary Churchill and,
724; Venetia and, 711–13; during
World War II, 724, 727
Gendel, Milton, 712, 730
Genoa Conference, 664
George V, King of England, 167, 230,
290, 294, 300, 391, 416, 417, 451,
493, 549, 665, 700, 701–2; appoints
Baldwin Prime Minister, 677–78;
Asquith and, 1, 126; Durbar of 1911
and, 149–50; election of 1918 and,
480; fall of the Asquith government
and, 372, 374, 375, 376, 378; Home
Rule for Ireland and, 225–26; India
and, 459; Indian Civil Service and,
163; resignation of ESM and, 637–
38, 646
George, David Lloyd. See Lloyd
George, David
Germany: Agadir incident and, 126;
Britain's entry into war and, 228,
229, 230; British attitude toward,
404–5; entry of, into World War I,
227; in the 1930s, 719, 720, 721; persecution of Jews in, 12; relations
with Great Britain (1914), 216–17;
reparations and, 502–5, 506–7, 523–
24, 606–7, 795; surrenders, 477–78;
Treaty of Rapallo and, 664; Treaty
of Versailles, 524; Turkey and, 522
Gladstone, Herbert: at Home Office,
82
Gladstone, William, 28, 67, 69, 70, 77,
257, 266, 522, 534, 692, 762–63;
Samuel Montagu and, 21, 22
Glasgow Evening News, 138
Glazebrook, Mr., 31
Glyn, Major, 188
gold standard, 241
Goldsmid family, 7
Gordon, Archibald, 111, 113

Gordon, Mrs. Henry Evans, 310, 315–16

Gore, Ormsby, 628

Gournaris, Prime Minister, 597

Government of India Act of 1919. *See* Reform Act of 1919

Graham, Major M., 711

Granard, Beatrice, 420

Granta, 54, 56, 57

Gray, Harold, 666–67

Great Britain: anti-Semitism and, 4–5, 14–15; Diaspora Nationalism in, 428; East India Trading Company and, 129–30; India (1600–1909) and, 129–32; Indian Councils Act (1861), 131; Indian Councils Act (1892), 131; and Indian National Congress, 131; India Office and, 130; Morley-Minto Act (1909), 131–32; poverty in, 71–72; relations with France (1914), 217; relations with Germany (1914), 216–17; reparations and, 502–3, 505–6, 507; steps leading to war and, 228–31; Turkey and, 521–22

Greece, 547, 558, 591, 609; end of hostilities with Turkey and, 662–63; Lloyd George and, 580–81; peace negotiations and, 508, 509; Treaty of Sèvres and, 571; Turkey and, 521, 524, 525–26, 593, 597, 600, 603, 610, 675

Green, Major W. Raymond, 65, 81

Greenfell, Billy, 478

Greenwood, Arthur, 776

Greenwood, Hammar, 668

Grey, Earl, 763

Grey, Sir Edward, 51, 96, 100, 324, 342, 411, 516, 700; Britain's entry into war and, 229; in Coalition Cabinet, 329; conscription and, 339; envied by ESM, 172; fall of Asquith government and, 375, 379; at Foreign Office, 82, 214; and Home Rule for Ireland, 223; in Lloyd George's government, 394; Newcastle Programme and, 70; Palestine as Jewish

homeland and, 429, 430; sends ESM Foreign Office telegrams, 328; War Council and, 239; women's suffrage and, 162

Grigg, John, 308–9

Guest, Freddy, 408, 416, 566, 668

Guilland, John, 329

Gupta, Prince of, 259

Gwynne, Rupert: anti-Semitism and, 623, 628; Gandhi and, 569; Hunter Commission report and, 560, 564–65, 623, 628

Haig, Douglas, 396, 475, 476, 783

Haldane, Richard, 86, 177, 766; Asquith's alcohol consumption and, 231; on Asquith's social life, 79; on Lloyd George's government, 379; Newcastle Programme and, 70; persuades Asquith to run for House of Commons, 77; removal of, from government, 1, 290–91, 294, 298, 302, 329; and Shell Committee, 282; on tax policy, 218–19; Tory Party and, 255; at War Office, 82, 90–91

Hall, Lt. Col. F., 560

Hallifay, F. C. T., 458

Hamilton, George, 204, 674

Hamilton, Ian, 289, 290

Hammond, J. L., 400, 776

Hampshire, 348

Hanbury, Charles Bateman, 488

Hankey, Maurice, 250, 345, 380, 552, 553; on Asquith's defeat in 1918 election, 483; conscription and, 339, 341; Dardanelles expedition and, 288, 291, 364; ESM as Secretary of State for India and, 416; on ESM's cowardice, 346; fall of the Asquith government and, 369–70, 371, 772; in Lloyd George's government, 384, 394; peace negotiations with Turkey and, 499, 508, 509, 548, 549, 550; proposes small War Committee, 338, 366; on Reconstruction Committee, 398; Shadow Cabinet and, 332; War Cabinet and, 363, 412

Harcourt, Lewis, 230, 282, 375, 379

Harcourt, William, 87

Hardie, Keir, 133, 134

Hardinge, Charles, 258, 343, 411, 452, 471, 572, 688; ESM's visit (1912–13) and, 187; India in World War I and, 451, 452; police brutality in India and, 144–45; self-government for India and, 152–53, 155, 453; succeeds Minto, 144

Harington, Charles, 662, 663

Harmsworth, Alfred (Lord Northcliffe), 362, 365, 366, 528; fall of the Asquith government and, 292, 295, 373, 374, 375, 377, 378, 381, 772, 773

Harris, Lord, 518

Harrisson, Hilda, 713, 714, 801

Harrod, R. F., 244

Hart D'Arcy, H., 700

Hart D'Arcy, Ronald J., 673

Heath, Thomas, 345

Henderson, Arthur, 331, 358; fall of the Asquith government and, 374, 376, 378, 379; in Lloyd George's government, 379, 394, 397, 417

Henley, Francis, 206

Henley, Sylvia, 108, 263, 270, 323, 324, 326, 672; Asquith's correspondence with, 296, 297–98, 303, 306, 308

Henry, C., 249

Henry IV, King of England, 104

Henry VII, King of England, 104

Herbert, Auberon (Bron), 60, 61, 324, 743

Herbert, Aubrey, 501

Herbert, Michael, 485

Herbert, Nan, 324

Herbert, Sidney, 485, 532, 700

Hertz, Joseph Herman, 445

Hertzberg, Arthur, 779–80

Herzl, Theodore, 424–27, 428

Hill, Clement, 427

Hills, J. W., 775

Hindus: caste system of, 146–47; ESM and prejudice against, 208; Gandhi and, 512, 650, 657; interest in India and, 201; Muslims and, 147, 581–82, 650–51; peace negotiations with Turkey and, 498, 526, 553, 590, 591; self-government and, 452

History of the Ministry of Munitions, 354

Hitler, 392, 447, 448, 449, 703, 719, 720

Hoare, Samuel, 628

Hobhouse, Charles, 256

Hodgson, Godfrey, 233

Holderness, T. W., 560, 561

Holroyd, Maria Josepha, 105

Home Rule: for India, 414, 418, 451, 453, 461, 462, 467, 481, 570; for Ireland, 21, 67, 217, 221, 222–26, 348–49, 758

Home Rule Bill (1912), 225, 228, 344–45

Honours scandal, 664

Hood, G. P., Lacomb, 712

Hope, Charles, 652–53

Horner, Edward, 478

Horner, Frances, 261

Horner, Katharine, 271

Horner, Lady, 324

House, Col., 506

House of Commons, 175, 416, 419, 492, 538, 607–8, 622, 628; Amritsar and, 515, 516, 557; anti-Semitism in, 627; budget of 1910 and, 135, 137–38; and budget of 1912, 163; Coalition government and, 337; conscription and, 341–42; constitutional issues and, 119, 120–21, 124; end of war and, 478; ESM in, after resignation, 656–58; ESM represents India Office in, 132–33, 168; ESM's resignation and, 641–43, 645–47, 648, 649; Indian affairs and, 414; fall of the Asquith government and, 375; Fisher's resignation and, 293; Hunter Committee report and, 558–67,

House of Commons (*Continued*)
569–70, 571; Jews permitted to sit
in, 14; Law as leader of Conservative
Party in, 365; Mackarness Pamphlet
and, 134; Marconi affair and, 158,
159, 574; motion to censure ESM
and, 622–27; Minister of Munitions
and, 354; Montagu (Samuel) and,
19, 20–21, 22; Montagu-Chelmsford
report and, 471, 472, 474; moving of
Indian capital to Delhi and, 149, 150;
Parliament Act (1911) and, 125; People's Budget (1909) and, 119, 120,
125; police brutality in India and,
144–45, 152; pressure to arrest Gandhi and, 592–94; Reform Act of
1919 and, 517–18, 519–20, 541; reunification of Bengal and, 149, 150;
2d War Budget and, 330; self-government for India and, 153–54; 3d
War Budget and, 334; and women's
suffrage, 162
House of Lords, 492, 607–8, 628; Amritsar and, 515, 516; constitutional
issues and, 116, 119–21, 124, 125;
Crewe and Curzon in, 151; ESM's
resignation and, 643–44; Greece and,
597; Home Rule for Ireland and,
348; Hunter Committee report and,
567; India debate and, 594–97, 600;
Jews permitted to sit in, 14–15;
Montagu (Samuel) and, 22; Montagu-Chelmsford report and, 472,
473, 474; and moving of Indian capital to Delhi, 149, 150; Parliament
Act (1911) and, 125, 126, 279; peace
negotiations with Turkey and, 597;
People's Budget (1909) and, 115–16,
119–20, 125; Reform Act of 1919
and, 517, 518, 519–20, 541; reunification of Bengal and, 149, 150; and
self-government for India, 153–54,
155
Howard, Dorothy, 100, 101, 192; engagement of, 206; marries, 178
Howard, George (Earl of Carlisle), 107

Howard, Rosalind (née Stanley), 106,
107
Hughes, William Morris, 504, 535,
552, 785
Hungary, 524
Hunter, Lord, 515
Hunter Commission report, 515–16,
554–57, 558–70, 623, 644
Hurst, Mr., 506
Hussein, King, 632
Hyde, H. Montgomery, 245, 630

Ibn Saud, 441
Imperial Conference (1921), 585–89
income tax, 118, 218, 219
India: beauty of, 184, 185; Civil Service of, 186–87, 189–90; as delegate
for Peace Conference, 493–94; Delhi
made capital of, 149; Durbar of 1911
and, 149; East India Trading Company and, 129–30; ESM's death and,
3–4, 686–96; ESM's love for, 123;
ESM's postwar goals for, 412;
ESM's pro-Turkish policy and, 21;
ESM's trip to (1912–13), 180–87,
189–91, 196–97; Great Britain
(1600–1909) and, 129–32; Home
Rule for, 414, 418, 451, 453, 461,
462, 467, 481, 570; Hunter Commission report and, 568–69; Indian
Councils Acts and, 131; Indian National Congress and, 131; India Office and, 130; Mackarness pamphlet
banned in, 134; Montagu-Chelmsford report and, 470–71, 474; Morley-Minto Act (1909), 131–32;
Muslim unrest in, 3, 538, 578–81,
618–20, 650–51; nationalism in, 128,
131–32, 147; and partition of Bengal, 149; peace negotiations with
Turkey and, 497–502, 508, 509, 510,
511, 521, 525, 526, 540, 548, 549,
550, 551, 552, 553, 591–92, 629–32,
633, 634, 639, 641–42; police brutality in, 144–45; prejudice in, 208;
Prince of Wales visits, 598–600; rac-

ism in Kenya and South Africa and, 585–90, 615, 616, 617–18; self-government for, 3, 135–36, 152–55, 452, 453–57, 460–61, 462, 463, 471, 518, 570, 716–17; World War I and, 351, 451–52. *See also* Montagu: SECRETARY OF STATE FOR INDIA; Montagu: UNDER SECRETARY OF STATE FOR INDIA

India, 164, 180, 181

India Office, 124; history of, 130. *See also* Montagu: SECRETARY OF STATE FOR INDIA; MONTAGU: UNDER SECRETARY OF STATE FOR INDIA

Indian Councils Acts, 131

Indian Daily Telegraph, 146

Indian Diary (Montagu), 715–16, 717, 718

Indian National Congress, 131

India Reform Act. *See* Reform Act of 1919

Ingles, Robert, 14

inheritance taxes, 218

Inter-Allied Conferences, 214, 215, 259, 495, 578, 580

Inter-Allied Finance Committee, 495

Iraq, 624

Ireland, 544, 559, 591, 664; aftermath of Easter Rebellion, 347–49; Easter Rebellion (1916) in, 344–46; Home Rule for, 21, 67, 217, 221, 222–26, 348–49, 758

Irish Conscription Bill, 397

Irish National Party, 72

Irwin, Lord, 716

Isaacs, Godfrey, 157

Isaacs, Joseph, 575

Isaacs, Rufus (1st Marquis of Reading). 139, 245, 359, 372, 392, 600, 601, 602, 618, 627, 653, 674, 678, 682, 689, 692; agenda for India of, 581–84; appointed Viceroy of India, 147, 571–75; Asquith and, 529, 577; Beaverbrook and, 649; conscription and, 339; Curzon and, 603–4; dyarchy and, 582; early relationship between ESM and, 575–77; ESM's planned trip to India (1922) and, 659–61, 670, 676; ESM's resignation and, 635, 636, 637, 647–50; fall of the Asquith government and, 368, 369–70, 371, 372; Gandhi and, 582, 583–84, 592, 593–94, 597, 598, 614, 619, 620, 621–22, 624–25, 626, 627, 631, 657, 658; Hindus and, 147, 590, 593, 597; India debate in House of Lords and, 595, 596, 597; Lloyd George and, 408, 577; as Lord Chief Justice, 159, 227; Marconi affair and, 157–59, 646; Muslims and, 147, 581, 590, 593, 597; peace negotiations with Turkey and, 591–92, 597, 609, 611–12, 620–21, 629–32, 662; racism in Kenya and South Africa and, 585, 590; self-government for India and, 575, 581; telegram to ESM from, 609, 629–35, 641, 645; Treaty of Sèvres and, 575, 597; unrest in India and, 578, 580, 618, 619, 626, 650–51, 657; unveils statue of ESM in Jamnagar, 693–95; in World War I, 243, 244

Islam: interest of Muslims in, 201, 202

Islamic News, 592, 634

Israel, Israel, 13

Israel, J. D., 33, 34, 35, 183

Italy, 720; Diplomatic Service in, 342; end of hostilities between Greece and Turkey and, 663; peace negotiations with Turkey and, 546, 547, 558; reparations and, 505; Turkey and, 522, 591

Jabotinsky, Mr., 434, 778

Jacobovits, Immanuel, 738

Jallian Wallah Bagh, 511, 514, 559, 561

Jam Sahib, Maharajah, 4, 571, 693, 694

James, Henry, 76

James, William, 321

James I, King of England, 105

Jamnagar, 4, 693–95

Janzé, Phyllis de, 723

Japan: reparations and, 505; unrest in, 136

Jekyll, Pamela, 112

Jenkins, Roy: on fall of the Asquith government, 371, 372, 376; on formation of Coalition government, 298; on War Cabinet, 364

Jerusalem, 398

Jewish Chronicle, 20, 22

Jewish Legion, 433–34, 788

Jewish Press, 15

Jewish World, 20

Jews: education of, 30, 37; in Great Britain in nineteenth century, 7, 9, 13, 14, 15, 28; history of (1290–1800) in Great Britain, 11–13; Liberal Party and, 67–68. *See also* anti-Semitism; Cousinhood, The

Jinnah, Mohammed Ali, 462, 593

Joffre, General, 304

Johnson, Paul Barton, 399–400, 403, 404, 406

Johnstone, "Crinks," 721

Joint Stock Banks, 333

Jones, Lawrence: on Alderley, 108; on first meeting with ESM, 57–58; on friendship of Venetia and Violet Asquith, 111; on Stanley family, 108; on Lady Margaret Stanley, 107–8; on Venetia's tomboyishness, 109; on Violet Asquith, 111

Jones, Thomas, 243, 775

Joseph, Rev. Morris, 316, 321, 323

Joynson-Hicks, Sir William, 628; motion to censure ESM and, 560, 562, 622–23, 625; self-government of India and, 570

Judaism. *See* anti-Semitism; Liberal Judaism; Montagu: RELIGION; Montagu, Samuel

Judd, Dennis, 245, 633

Justice, 145

Kapurthala, Maharajah of, 601, 650

Kemal Pasha. *See* Atatürk, Kemal

Kennet, Lady, 695, 737

Kensington Palace Gardens, 7–8, 99

Kenya, 680, 692; racism in, 208, 585–86, 589–90, 614–18, 619, 621, 655

Kerr, Philip, 445, 511, 545, 775

Keynes, John Maynard, 248; ESM and help with career of, 215, 241, 244, 245, 259–60, 757; on ESM and Lloyd George, 215; ESM as Financial Secretary and, 211–12, 220, 249; in ESM's campaign for House of Commons, 66; on ESM's death, 696–98; financial crisis in early days of war and, 240–41, 244–45; first Inter-Allied Conference and, 259; joins the Treasury, 259–60; leaves government, 244; Lloyd George and, 241, 244, 260; on Lloyd George as Chancellor of the Exchequer, 214; Lloyd George at the Peace Conference and, 508; reparations and, 503, 504, 505, 506, 507–8, 510, 534–35, 606–7, 785; reform of the tax system and, 83; Silver Scandal and, 187; speaks at Cambridge Union, 53–54

Khalifat, 632, 692

Khalifat movement, 569, 578, 582, 590, 611

Kipling, Rudyard, 569, 574, 792

Kisch, Cecil H., 458

Kishnev pogroms, 427

Kitchener, Horatio Herbert (Lord), 250, 251, 259, 293, 338, 542; appointed Secretary of State for War, 238–39; in Coalition Cabinet, 329; conscription and, 280, 336; Dardanelles expedition and, 288, 289, 290, 291, 364; death of, 348, 350; and early conduct of war, 279–80, 451; shell shortage and, 273, 281–85, 286, 287, 294; War Council and, 239

Kitchener Committee, 274, 282–87

Klotz, Louis-Lucien, 507, 532, 535

Koss, Stephen: on anti-Semitism, 177; on formation of Coalition govern-

and, 560, 565–66, 567; isolationism ship between Asquith and Venetia, 234, 235; on shell crisis, 292

Labour Party, 682; as alternative to Liberal Party, 84, 90; Churchill and, 680; election of 1906 and, 72; election of 1918 and, 480, 482; election of 1922 and, 666, 667; election of 1923 and, 678–79; election of 1924 and, 679, 686; formation of, 70; and India, 133; self-government for India and, 716, 717; Socialist Popular Front Peace Conference and, 397
Ladies' Pictorial, 10
Lamb, Charles, 14
Lambert, Angela *(Unquiet Souls),* 232, 234
land reform, 84, 85–86, 91–94; ESM's interest in, 205
land value tax, 118
Lansdowne, Lord (5th Marquess of Lansdowne), 153, 348, 426; and Home Rule for Ireland, 224; memorandum of, 365–66
Lathom, Isabell, 104
Lathom, Thomas, 104
Lausanne. *See* Treaty of Lausanne
Lavery, Hazel, 324
Law, Andrew Bonar, 203, 540, 675; appointed Colonial Secretary, 329; Beaverbrook and, 528, 529; Coalition government and, 1, 290, 298; as Conservative leader in Coalition, 365, 366; as critic of war policy, 337, 338; Dardanelles Commission and, 364; as delegate for Peace Conference, 493; election of 1906 and, 80; election of 1918 and, 480; election of 1922 and, 665, 666, 667; end of war and, 478; fall of the Asquith government and, 369, 370, 371, 372, 373, 374, 375, 376, 377, 378–79, 773; Home Rule for Ireland and, 224, 225, 758; Hunter Commission report

of, 718; in Lloyd George's government, 379, 383, 384, 394; Lloyd George's proposed War Committee and, 366, 367, 368; Maurice affair and, 783; resigns, 677, 800
Lawrence, Walter, 647
Leader, 689
League of Nations, 477, 600, 651, 663, 718
League of Young Liberals (Cambridge), 141
Le Bas, Hedley, 382
Leigh Fermor, Patrick, *See* Fermor, Patrick Leigh
Leiter, Levi Ziegler, 603
Leveson-Gower, Lady Rosemary, 672
Liberal Club (Cambridge), 51
Liberal Judaism, 23, 25–26, 33, 47, 739–40
Liberal League, 93
Liberal Party, 28, 682; anti-Semitism and, 308; and Asquith as Chancellor of Exchequer, 89–90; and budget of 1914, 217; characterized, 67; Churchill and, 291; Coalition government and, 1, 290, 293, 641; conscription and, 335–39; death taxes and, 87; defeat of, in 1886, 69–70, 71; disunity in, in 1923, 675; efforts to reunite, 676, 677–78; election of 1906 and, 72–73, 80–81; election (1st) of 1910 and, 123; election (2d) of 1910 and, 126; election of 1918 and, 480–82; election of 1922 and, 664–68; election of 1923 and, 678–79; election of 1924 and, 679, 686; ESM as candidate for, in West Cambridgeshire, 63–65; ESM as possible head of, 3, 286; ESM speaks for, during Cambridge days, 59–60; ESM's isolation in, 135, 141; free trade and, 60–61, 87, 677, 678; free speech and, 141; Gladstone and, 69, 70; government control and, 344; and Home Rule for Ireland, 222–23; on India, 129; land reform and, 84, 85–86,

Liberal Party (*Continued*)
91–94; on land value tax, 118; Lloyd
George's government and, 394–95,
397; Montagu (Samuel) and, 19, 21;
National Liberal Federation and, 70;
Newcastle Programme and, 70; in
1915, 254; old age pensions and, 84,
85, 86; People's Budget (1909) and
the House of Lords, 120, 121, 125;
philosophy and program of, 68–71,
83; Reading and, 576; self-government and, 141; tax reform and, 84,
85–86; and the vote, 397; on war,
217

Lichnowsky, Count, 216–17

Lister, Laura (Lady Lovat), 487

Lister, Thomas (4th Baron Ribblesdale), 78

Liverpool: Jewish community in, 12–
13, 15

Lloyd, George (Gov. of Bombay),
515, 518, 650, 658, 661, 674, 696

Lloyd George, David, 235, 249, 279,
293, 342, 344, 415, 444, 445, 455,
461, 631, 632, 651, 657, 671, 675,
680, 690, 710; anti-Semitism and,
216, 308–9, 574–75; appoints Reading Viceroy of India, 571–75; and
Asquith's letter writing during Cabinet meetings, 251; attitude of,
toward ESM, 215–16, 284, 286,
420–21; attitude of, toward Keynes,
241, 244; Balfour Declaration and,
446, 447; Beaverbrook and, 528,
529; the Big Four and, 494, 495; at
Board of Trade, 82; Bolshevism and,
496, 497; Britain's entry into war
and, 227–28, 229, 230; British delegation for Peace Conference and,
492, 493; budgets of 1907 and 1908
and, 90; budget of 1914 and, 217,
218, 219–22; budget of 1922 and,
604; as Chancellor of the Exchequer,
91, 213, 214, 757; on Churchill, 291;
Coalition government and, 1, 290,
329; Committee of Pensions and,

248; compared with McKenna, 328,
329–30; conflict with McKenna and,
359–60, 361; criticism of Asquith of,
338, 341; Dardanelles expedition
and, 288, 291; Easter Rebellion and,
344–45, 348–49; election of 1918
and, 480–82, 483; end of Coalition
government and, 664–65, 667, 668,
669, 772; end of hostilities with Turkey and Greece and, 662, 663; end of
war and, 475, 476, 477, 478; on
ESM as gossip, 96; ESM asks to
serve in Ministry of Munitions, 328;
and ESM and motion to censure,
625–26; ESM as Secretary of State
for India and, 416–17, 418–19; ESM
speaks before at Cambridge, 51; and
ESM's ambition to be Viceroy, 258,
541, 542, 543, 544–45; on ESM's
death, 701; and ESM's elevation to
Asquith's Cabinet, 256, 257; ESM's
resignation and, 245, 633, 635–38,
639, 640, 641, 642, 643–44, 645,
646, 647, 648, 650, 681, 697; fall of
the Asquith government and, 366–
79, 380, 381, 382, 383, 385, 398; financial crisis in early days of war
and, 241–45; first Inter-Allied Conference and, 259; government of,
379–80, 384, 385, 394–96, 407, 408,
450, 469, 520; Greece and, 580, 591,
609; and Home Rule for Ireland,
223, 224; Honours scandal and, 664;
Hunter Committee report and, 555–
56, 558, 559, 562, 565, 566, 567,
570; India and, 454, 468; India debate and, 594, 595; Keynes and, 260;
Liberal Party and, 676, 677, 678–79;
Marconi affair and, 157–59, 577,
646; Maurice affair and, 783; *Memoirs
of the Peace Conference,* 447; Mesopotamian disaster and, 413; as Minister
of Munitions, 292, 329, 333, 352–53,
355; oratory of, 462; Palestine and,
309, 429, 430, 431; peace delegation
and, 534–35; peace negotiations with

Turkey and, 499, 500, 501–2, 508, 509–11, 521, 524, 525–26, 538, 539–40, 541, 543, 544, 546, 547, 548–54, 558, 591–92, 597, 600–601, 609, 610, 611, 614; People's Budget (1909) and, 117–19; the press and, 366; pressure to arrest Gandhi and, 594; procedures for Inter-Allied Conference and, 495; progress of war and (1917), 396; racism in South Africa and, 587–89; racism in Kenya and, 618; radicalism of, 83; Reading and, 576, 584; Reconstruction Committee and, 398–99, 400–403, 405, 406, 408–11, 412, 415, 416; reparations and, 504, 505, 506–8, 510, 523, 604, 606, 607; on Russians during war, 250; 2nd War Budget and, 330, 334; as Secretary of War, 350, 351, 361–62, 365; self-government for India and, 456; shell shortage and, 281, 282, 283–84, 285, 286, 287; Stevenson (Frances) and, 298; on tax policy, 218; 3d War Budget and, 343; Treaty of Sèvres and, 570; unrest in India and, 580, 621; War Cabinet end, 338; War Committee crisis and, 366–79; War Council and, 239; *War Memoirs,* 244, 284, 344, 544; War Savings Certificate and, 331; women's movement and, 161; Wood as Under Secretary for India, 628–29; as workingman's hero, 380

Londonderry, Lord, 92

London Figaro, 20

London Opinion, 138, 139

Long, Walter, 329, 644; as critic of war policy, 337; and election of 1906, 80

Loucheur, Louis, 504, 506, 507, 510, 523, 535

Lovat, Lord, 628, 655, 700; trip to Brazil and, 683

Lowther, James W., 161, 226

Lubbock, Adelaide (née Stanley), 108, 267; on Venetia's engagement and conversion, 310, 315

Lucas, Lord, 282

Ludendorff, Erich Von, 475, 476, 477

Lunared, Blanche (née Stanley), 672

Lutyens, Edwin, 485, 488

Luzzati, Luigi, 443

Lyttelton, Alfred, 78; and election of 1906, 80

Lytton, Victor, 571, 572, 596, 611, 628, 657, 658, 661, 674

Macaulay, Thomas, 625, 626

MacCarthy, Desmond, 713

McCarthy, Lillah, 110

MacDonald, Ramsay, 679

Mackarness, Frederick, 134, 135, 140, 141, 145, 181, 199

McKenna, Pamela, 261, 324; on Margot Asquith, 78, 195–96

McKenna, Reginald, 96, 195, 215, 227, 259, 293, 367, 402, 700, 773; appointed Chancellor of the Exchequer, 327, 328, 329; on budget of 1914, 222; ESM's attitude toward, 398; Lloyd George's attitude toward, 398; compared with Lloyd George, 328, 329–30; conflict with ESM at Munitions, 358–60; conflict with Lloyd George, 359–60, 361; conscription and, 339; fall of the Asquith government and, 370, 375, 376, 379, 381–82; 4th War Budget and, 343; 2d War Budget and, 330; Second War Loan and, 331; and Shell Committee, 282; tax policy and, 334–35; 3d War Budget and, 334–35; War Committee and, 367

McLintock, William, 683

McMahon, Henry, 542

Macmillan, Harold, 379

Macready, C. F. N., 357

Magnus, Philip, 424

Magnus, R., 445

Magpie and Stump (Cambridge), 56, 57

Malkin, H. W., 324

Malone, Captain, 585–86

Manchester, William, 562; on Asquith
    and Venetia, 298; on Churchill's
    prejudice, 618
Manchester Guardian, 51, 140, 430
Manners, Diana, 324
Marconi affair, 157–59, 160, 189, 214,
    244, 574, 577, 646
Maria Theresa, Empress, 13
Marlborough, Duchess of, 94, 485,
    671, 672, 673, 726
Mary, Queen of England, 459
Massingham, Henry, 402
Masterman, 256, 257, 294
Mathews, Gen., 324
Maude, Stanley, 413
Maurice, Sir Frederick, 783
Maurice affair, 476, 480
Means, Mr., 528
Mehmed the Conqueror, 522
Meiklejohn, R. S., 221
Melbourne, Lord, 42, 763
Merton, Lloyd, 696
Mesopotamia, 498, 499, 509, 510, 511,
    522, 624; disaster in, 412–13, 451,
    623, 646; report on, 411, 412–15
Messines Ridge, 476
*Methods of the Indian Police in the 20th
    Century* (Mackarness), 134–35, 139,
    140–41
Michelham, Lord, 140
"Millionaires' Row." See Kensington
    Palace Gardens
Milner, Alfred, 438, 475, 509, 532,
    639; in Lloyd George's government,
    379, 394; supports Balfour Declara-
    tion, 444–45, 446; Zionism and, 431
Minto, Lord. See Elliot-Murray-
    Kynynmond, Gilbert
Mitterand, Alexandre, 547
Montagu, Cardy. See Montagu, Lionel
Montagu, Clara, 121
Montagu, David, 673
Montagu, Edwin Samuel, 104, 110;
    birth of, 7, 17; brothers and sisters
    of, 18; genealogy of, 732–33
APPEARANCE: 58, 85, 88, 100, 113, 137,
    138, 139, 165, 166, 296, 316, 390,
    391, 416, 575, 749
CHARACTERISTICS: arrogance, 57, 416,
    461; in childhood, 29–30, 31, 32–33,
    36, 37; as "coward," 220, 346, 459–
    60; directness, force, and candor,
    140, 151; discretion, 252; extrava-
    gance, 76, 487–89; fear of early
    death, 323, 390, 479, 486, 532, 684;
    frankness, 86; as gossipmonger, 95–
    96; hypochrondria, *see* HEALTH *below;*
    idealism, 164; impolitic nature, 84,
    85, 93, 122, 182; insecurity, 57, 62,
    95, 123–24, 248–49, 256; pessimism,
    84, 256, 461; rashness, 92–93; self-
    contempt, 101, 178, 220, 271–72;
    self-deprecation, 172–73; self-pity,
    101; tenderheartedness, 205
CHILDHOOD AND YOUTH: 27–41; affec-
    tion in, 29; anti-Semitism in, 31; Bar
    Mitzvah in, 35; fear of failure in, 32;
    homesickness in, 31, 32–33, 34, 35–
    37; personality in, 29–30, 31, 32–33,
    36, 37; at South Stoneham, 9–10;
    trip around the world (1891–92),
    33–36, 38
DEATH: 684–86; burial of, 699–701; In-
    dian reaction to, 3–4, 686–96; letters
    of condolence about, 701–2; tributes
    from friends, 696–99
EDUCATION: City of London School
    (1893–95), 36, 37–38; Clifton Col-
    lege (1891–93), 30–37; Doreck Col-
    lege (1887–91), 29–30; examinations
    and, 30, 38; interest in politics of,
    38; interest in oratory, 38; interest in
    science, 32, 37, 38, 39, 40–41; reli-
    gious education, 30, 31, 33–35; Uni-
    versity College, London (1895–98),
    38–41
CAMBRIDGE UNIVERSITY (TRINITY COL-
    LEGE) (1898–1902), 41, 42–66; Angli-
    can atmosphere of, 42–43; anti-Sem-
    itism at, 57–58; athletics at, 56;
    chooses law and politics as career,
    49–50; co-editor of *Granta,* 56; com-

pletes B.A., 58–59; dramatics at, 49, 55–56; health at, 48, 52; and Keynes, 54; law studies at, 59–60, 61, 63; Liberal Club, 51; Magpie and Stump, 56; speaks for Liberal Party, 59–60; Union Society, 51–54, 56, 575

FINANCES: dependence on father, 44, 55, 61, 62–63, 97–98, 99–100; in election (1st) of 1910, 122; after father's death, 143; in marriage, 487–88, 489

HEALTH: at Cambridge, 48, 52; in childhood, 29, 30, 31–32, 33, 34, 35, 36, 37, 38; final illness of, 684–86; as Parliamentary Private Secretary, 97, 115, 117, 122–23; as Secretary of State for India, 464, 526, 537, 539, 543, 561; as Under Secretary of State for India, 167

OPINIONS AND ATTITUDES: 21; on free trade, 61, 66, 87; on land reform, 84, 85–86; on the law, 60, 61, 76, 99; on monarchy, 53; as "New Liberal," 83; on old age pensions, 84, 85, 86, 91; on prejudice, racism, and snobbery, 53, 57, 134, 136–37, 155, 163, 164, 186, 189–90, 461, 472, 516; on tax reform, 83, 94, 85–86, 89–90

RECREATION, HOBBIES, SPORTS: Coterie and, 388, 389, 390–91, 392, 393; as cricket player in school, 30; gardening and, 489; as hunter, 30, 39, 98, 185, 464, 654–55, 658; love of nature, 10, 30, 32, 34, 37–38, 39, 184, 185, 658; as ornithologist, 39, 98, 213, 464, 489; as photographer, 39; in Scotland, 178, 179; trip around the world (1891–92), 33–36, 37, 183; trip to Canada, 60–61; trip to Ireland, 114; trip to Spain, 213

RELATIONSHIP WITH FATHER: in childhood, 32, 34, 36, 39–40; conflict over Judaism, 24–25, 43–48, 98; budget speech (1910) and, 138; ca-

reer choice opposed by, 50; disappointment to, 24, 47–48, 54; fear of criticism of, 95; finances and, 44, 55, 61, 62–63, 97–98, 99–100; hostility toward, 101; law practice and, 60, 61, 62, 98

RELATIONSHIP WITH MOTHER: on her death, 509; and pressure to marry cousin, 142, 143; seeks attention from, 31, 32–33, 34, 35–37, 121; writes to, about his father, 40, 49–50, 55, 59, 98–99; writes to, about his fears, 97; writes to, about loneliness, 100; writes to, during war, 240, 261–62; writes to, from India, 183; writes to, throughout her life, 18, 316–17; Venetia's engagement and conversion and, 316

RELATIONSHIP WITH VENETIA STANLEY and, 629; ambivalence about marriage (1915) and, 317, 318–19, 323; and appointment as Privy Councillor, 252; and appointment as Under Secretary of State for India, 124; Baldwin's appointment as Prime Minister and, 678; Beaverbrook and, 527–28, 530–31, 532, 534–37, 545–46, 652; birth of Judith and, 670–71, 672, 673, 674; at Breccles, 485, 488–90, 491; calls ESM "Tante," 171–72; conversion to Judaism and, 276–77, 309–17, 319–22; courtship, 171–73, 174–76, 205–9, 236–37, 248–49, 252, 253, 256, 260–61, 269–71, 272–75; death of ESM and, 684–86, 700–702; election of 1922 and, 665, 667; end of war and, 478, 491; engagement, 2, 254, 275–77, 292, 294–304; and ESM's courtship of his cousin, 142, 143; on fun, 205–6; Hope (Charles) and, 652–53; and Lady Dorothy Howard, 206; married to, 26, 386–88, 393; meets, 111; Pearl and, 653, 655; planned trip to India (1923) and, 676; problems in marriage, 484–91, 530–33, 535, 537;

Montagu, Edwin Samuel (*Continued*)
pregnancy and, 660; proposes to,
176–79, 207; relationship with, 88,
113–14, 115, 141, 165–69, 173; resignation of ESM as Secretary of
State for India, 646–47, 654; and the
sea, 207; sees Asquith correspondence, 252, 269; seeks advice of, 103;
and training as nurse, 260; trip to
Sicily with Asquith and, 169–70;
26th birthday and, 205–6; trip to
Brazil and, 683; urges to break off
with Asquith, 269, 274; visits in
France, 304, 319; at Walmer castle
with Asquith and, 272; wedding of,
323–26; writes last letter to, 684–85;
writes to, from India, 183–84, 191–
93, 196–97, 459, 464, 484–86; writes
to, on death of friend, 205
  RELIGION: ambition to be Viceroy and,
273; anti-Semitism and, 4–5, 31,
159, 177, 187, 188, 189, 208, 220,
259, 306–9, 415–16, 419, 420, 421,
435, 470, 554, 562–63, 566, 567,
647; education in, 30, 31, 33–35; attitude toward Judaism, 5, 19, 23,
24–25, 43–48, 98, 189, 319–22, 425–
26, 575; Balfour Declaration and, 4,
326, 429, 435–49, 779, 780; compares institutions of Judaism with
those of Hinduism, 147; Jewish
women and, 173, 178, 189; as outsider due to, 380; pro-Turkish position and, 540; refuses post of Chief
Secretary of Ireland due to, 345–46;
Zionism and, 4, 326, 422–23, 428–
29, 430–31, 433, 435–49, 779, 780
  RESIDENCES: Breccles, 389, 484, 485,
487, 488–90, 491, 532, 533, 535,
536, 654, 655, 658, 673, 699–700;
desire for country home, 99; Kensington Palace Gardens, 7, 8, 99;
Queen Anne's Gate, 194, 199, 201,
223, 260, 306, 323, 372, 376, 382,
387–88, 389, 390, 488; South Stoneham, 8–10

  PUBLIC LIFE AND POLITICAL CAREER
  CABINET (ASQUITH), 2; and ambition
to be Viceroy, 258–59, 273; and
Committee on Food Prices, 262;
Dardanelles expedition and, 288; elevated to rank of Minister (1915),
256–58; rejoins as Minister of Munitions (1916), 351; as Secretary of the
Shell Committee, 3, 274, 764; shell
shortage and, 280, 281–83, 284–85,
286; war bonuses and, 262; work
schedule and, 261–62
  CABINET (LLOYD GEORGE), 2; appointed to, 314, 433; opposes Balfour Declaration, 4, 326, 435–49,
778–79, 779–80; opposes Jewish legion, 437–38; Palestine and, 4, 326
  CHANCELLOR OF DUCHY OF LANCAS-
TER, 2, 327; appointed, 256–58;
duties as, 256; serves on 1st Reconstruction Committee, 398, 399–400
  FINANCIAL SECRETARY TO THE TREA-
SURY: 2–3, 575; appointed, 209, 210–
12; attitude toward Lloyd George,
215–16, 256; Britain's entry into war
and, 227–28, 230; budget of 1914
and, 217–22; budget (2d) of 1914
and, 242; on Coalition Cabinet, 328–
29; on Committee of Pensions, 247–
48; compares McKenna with Lloyd
George, 328, 329–30; conscription
and, 336–37, 339, 341–42; on critics
of war policy, 337–39; on Diplomatic Service, 342–43; early days of
war and, 238; and financial controls
during the war, 245–48; financial
crisis in early days of war and, 240–
45; financial expertise of, 211–12;
and first Inter-Allied Conference,
259; 4th War Budget and, 343–44;
Home Rule for Ireland and, 223–25;
in House of Commons, 212, 213–
14, 217, 218, 219, 220, 221–22, 242,
330, 334; on Ireland (1916), 345–47;
on Joint Stock Banks, 333; J. P.
Morgan & Co. and, 342–43; leaves

Treasury for Cabinet position, 256;
Keynes and, 211–12, 215, 240, 241,
244, 245, 248, 259–60, 757; on plan
to drive Germans from France, 332;
returns to Treasury, 327–28; 2d War
Budget and, 330, 334; Second War
Loan and, 331; in Shadow Cabinet,
331–34; and social services during
the war, 246–48; tax policy and,
218, 219, 330, 334–35, 343–44; 3d
War Budget and, 334–35; Tory
Party and, 255–56; on war economy, 332–34; War Savings Certificate and, 2, 331
LIBERAL PARTY: 576; disunity in, in
1923, 675; early career in, 59–61,
63–66; efforts to reunite, 676, 677–
78; election of 1922 and, 664–68;
elections of 1923 and 1924 and, 682,
686; ESM as candidate for, in West
Cambridgeshire, 63–65; ESM as
possible head of, 3, 286; ESM speaks
for, during Cambridge days, 59–60;
ESM's isolation in, 135, 141; Lloyd
George's government and, 395, 397,
398, 641
MEMBER OF PARLIAMENT (consolidated
area of Cambridgeshire): 2; campaign for, 480–82; dyarchy and, 661;
election of 1922 and, 665–67, 668,
669; on Gandhi's arrest, 657–58; in
the House, after resignation, 656–58;
peace negotiations with Turkey and,
661–62, 663–64; plans to give up
seat, 545; plans trip to India (1922),
658–61
MEMBER OF PARLIAMENT (West Division of Cambridgeshire): 2; campaign for, 65–66, 83; elected, 80–81;
nominated as candidate for, 63–65;
works for nomination, 60
MINISTER OF MUNITIONS, 2; and Lloyd
George, 350, 361–62, 380; appointed, 350, 351–52; Churchill and,
357–58; conflict with McKenna and,
358–60, 361; Dardanelles Commis-

sion and, 364; fall of the Asquith
government and, 367, 368–78, 380–
85, 398; House of Commons and,
354; Nigerian Land Sales and, 365;
organizes and administers, 352–57;
Raymond Asquith's death and, 362;
tanks and, 357–58, 770; War Cabinet
meetings and, 363–64; War Committee crisis and, 367, 368–78;
weapons for the army in WWI, 3;
women's suffrage and, 352
OUT OF OFFICE: 668–69, 678, 679;
Baldwin's appointment as Prime
Minister and, 678; birth of Judith,
670–71, 672–74; efforts to reunite
the Liberal Party and, 676, 677, 678;
exclusion from politics of, 679–81;
plans trip to South Africa, 684; plans
trip to India, 674–76; trip to Brazil,
676, 682–84
PARLIAMENTARY PRIVATE SECRETARY:
2, 210, 211; appointed, 81; as Asquith becomes Prime Minister, 94–
95, 96; and budgets of 1906, 1907,
and 1908, 90, 91; conduct as, 84–87;
death taxes and, 87; and election
(1st) of 1910, 121–23; free trade and,
87; land reform and, 84, 85–86, 91–
94; memoranda and letters to Asquith, 84, 85, 86–87, 96; old age
pensions, 84, 85, 86, 91; People's
Budget (1909) and the House of
Lords, 115–17, 118, 119, 120, 125;
responsibilities as, 84; romantic interests as, 100–101; spies on colleagues, 95–96; tax reform and, 84,
85–86; Zionist debate and, 428–29
PRIVY COUNCILLOR: 2; appointed
(1915), 249, 252; and New Year's
Honours (1915), 256
RECONSTRUCTION COMMITTEE: 2, 680;
becomes Vice-Chairman, 398–99;
hopes to enter Lloyd George government, 406–8, 410; Mesopotamian
report and, 411, 413–16, 469; suggests Ministry of Reconstruction,

Montague, Edwin Samuel (*Continued*)
407, 408–11, 415, 416; work on,
401–6, 502, 776
SECRETARY OF STATE FOR INDIA: 2,
581, 584; Amritsar massacre and,
511, 512, 513, 515, 516, 521, 554–
57, 582, 680; Anti-Dumping Bill
and, 604; appointed, 401, 416–21,
422, 449, 450, 452, 454; Balfour
Declaration and, 4, 326, 429, 435–
49, 779, 780; on Bolshevism, 496–
97; breaks with Asquith, 420, 421,
481, 483, 577; British Finance Committee and, 495; budget of 1918 and,
471–72; budget of 1922 and, 604–6;
on Chelmsford as Viceroy, 452; chosen as delegate for Peace Conference,
493; desire to be Viceroy and, 541–
43, 544–45, 554, 571; deteriorating
relationship with Curzon and, 601–
4; and discrimination against Indians,
53, 472, 585–90, 614–18; dyarchy
and, 463–64, 465, 470, 518, 582–83,
781; early relationship with Asquith
and, 577; early relationship with
Reading, 575–77; end of war and,
478, 479–80, 491; free trade and,
604; Gandhi and, 462, 538, 565, 568,
590, 592, 593–94, 595, 614, 623–24,
631; House of Commons and, 471,
516, 517–18, 519–20, 538, 541, 557,
558–67, 569–70, 571, 592–94, 607–
8, 621, 622–27, 641–43, 645–47,
648, 649; House of Lords and, 516,
517, 518, 519–20, 541, 567, 592–97,
600, 607–8, 643–44; Hunter Committee report and, 558–70; Inter-Allied Finance Committee and, 495,
532; love of India and, 460, 466–67;
lunches with George V, 459; Montagu-Chelmsford report of, 464,
465–74, 481, 687, 689, 692, 716;
motion to censure and, 622–28;
peace negotiations with Turkey and,
3, 495, 496, 497–502, 508–11, 517,
521, 522, 524–26, 538, 539, 540–41,

543–44, 546–47, 548–54, 558, 591–
92, 600–601, 609–14, 620, 621, 623,
629–32, 633, 634, 639, 644, 790;
Prince of Wales's visit to India and,
597–600; procedures for Inter-Allied
Conference and, 495; racism in
Kenya and South Africa, 585–90,
614–18, 655, 680, 692; Reading appointed Viceroy and, 573–75; reappointed, 492; Reform Act of 1919
and, 511, 515, 516–21, 523, 525,
541, 564, 569, 570, 622, 686, 687,
689, 690, 691, 692, 694, 696; reparations and, 502–8, 510, 523–24, 534–
35, 604, 606–7, 680, 785; resigns,
24, 497, 635–48, 649–50, 651; San
Remo conference and, 548–49, 553,
570; self-government for India and,
3, 454–58, 460–61, 462, 463, 465–
66, 467, 471, 518, 570, 575, 582,
781; telegram from Reading and,
629–35; Treaty of Sèvres and, 570–
71; trip to India (1917–18), 458–68;
unrest in India and, 548, 551–52,
553–54, 578–81, 618–21, 623–24,
627, 650–51; Wood as Under Secretary for India, 628–29
UNDER SECRETARY OF STATE FOR IN-
DIA: 2, 127, 216; appointed, 123–24,
450; budget of 1910 and, 135–40;
budget of 1911 and, 145–48; budget
of 1912 and, 162–64, 172–73, 174;
budget of 1913 and, 201–3; and
court reform, 152; Crewe succeeds
Morley, 143–44; on Curzon, 155–
56; Curzon and reunification of Bengal, 150–51; and discord with
Crewe, 152, 153–55, 157, 182, 203,
204; and discrimination against Indian students, 53, 136–37, 152, 163;
and Durbar of 1911, 149; on education in India, 146, 162, 163, 198,
201, 202; election (2d) of 1910, 126;
and Hardinge dispatch, 152–56;
Hardinge and ESM's visit (1912–13),
187; on Hindu-Muslim relations,

146–47; on Hindus, 201; and Indian Civil Service, 163, 186–87, 189–90, 198; India Council and, 204; and India Office, 203–4; on industrial development in India, 146; and isolation in Liberal Party, 135, 141; Mackarness pamphlet and, 134–35, 139, 140–41; and Marconi affair, 157, 159; on Morley-Minto Reforms, 146; Morley's tutelage and, 132, 141; and moving of capital to Delhi, 149, 150; on Muslims, 156, 190–91, 198, 201–2; nationalism and, 147; police brutality in India and, 144–45, 152, 168, 200, 202; problems facing, 129; reforms and, 152; restlessness as, 205; returns from India (1913), 198–201; and reunification of Bengal, 149, 150–51; and self-government for India, 3, 135–36, 152–55, 198; Silver Scandal and, 159; speaks on Home Rule for Ireland, 172; as spokesman for India Office in House of Commons, 132–33, 168; trip to India (1912–13), 180–87, 189–91, 196–97; women's suffrage and, 160, 161, 162, 169

Montagu, Ellen Cohen (Lady Swaythling) (mother), 319; children of, 18; concern about ESM's love life, 100; death of, 509; ESM and marriage and, 173, 316–17; ESM writes to, from India, 183; and first election of 1910, 121; and Ivor Montagu, 8; letters from ESM, 18; marriage of, 18–19; in old age, 19; pedigree of, 7–8, 18; pressures ESM to marry cousin, 142, 143; relationship with ESM in childhood, 31, 32–33, 34, 35–36, 40; works for ESM's election to House of Commons, 65

Montagu, Elsie (sister), 18, 37

Montagu, Ethel (sister), 18, 670

Montagu, Ewen, 673, 700

Montagu, Florence (sister), 18

Montagu, Gerald (brother), 18, 24, 33, 37, 700; banking career of, 54; engaged, 101

Montagu, Henrietta (sister), 10, 18

Montagu, Ivor (nephew): on Ellen Montagu, 8; on ESM's last illness, 685; on Kensington Palace Gardens, 8; on Samuel Montagu's attitude toward ESM and money, 55; on Samuel Montagu's death, 24; on South Stoneham, 9

Montagu, Judith. See Gendel, Judith

Montagu, Lily (sister), 18, 319, 322; ESM's marriage and, 316; Liberal Judaism and, 23, 25–26, 32, 47, 425; on her father at school, 15; on her father's attitudes toward his children, 24; on her father's politics, 21, 22; nervous breakdown and, 33; Pearl and, 653–54

Montagu, Lionel (Cardy) (brother), 18, 24, 33, 122, 180, 307, 319, 390, 392, 676, 700, 702; banking career of, 54; ESM's marriage and, 316; ESM's wedding and, 325; at school, 54; Venetia and, 709

Montagu, Louis Samuel (brother), 18, 24, 33, 700

Montagu, Marion (sister), 18, 25, 30

Montagu, Samuel (Lord Swaythling) (father), 139, 140, 248, 739; anti-Semitism and, 14–15, 19–20, 21; attitude of, toward ESM, 24, 25, 32, 34, 39–40, 43–48, 54, 55, 61, 62–63, 97–100, 101, 138; attitudes of, toward his children, 24–26, 55, 101; banking career, 16–18, 40; birth of, 13; children of, 18; as collector, 8; death of, 23–24, 143; early life of, 14–16; elevated to the peerage, 14, 22; and ESM's budget speech (1910), 138; and ESM's election to House of Commons, 65, 81; failing health of, 142; financial expertise of, 211; as guardian of Herbert Samuel, 429; helps ESM get law jobs, 60, 61; as host, 10; Jewish education of, 15, 16;

Montagu, Samuel (*Continued*)
    Kensington Palace Gardens and, 7; at
    Mechanics Institute of Liverpool, 15;
    marriage of, 18–19; as millionaire, 7,
    17; name change of, 14; as nature
    lover, 9–10; opposes ESM's career
    choice, 50; as Orthodox Jew, 8, 16,
    19, 21, 22–23, 46, 98; Palestine and,
    425; philanthropy of, 22–23; political
    career and views of, 19–22, 23, 32,
    53, 67, 119; at South Stoneham es-
    tate, 9–10; Zionism and, 424, 425
Montagu, Samuel, and Co., 16–17,
    575, 739; Silver Scandal and, 159,
    187, 188
Montagu, Stuart, 700
Montagu, Venetia Stanley, 88, 101,
    216, 220, 222, 226, 228, 244, 248,
    254, 258, 283, 285, 327, 328, 330,
    331, 345, 369, 372, 382, 383, 629,
    645; Aarons operation and, 534; ad-
    vice of, sought by Asquith (H. H.),
    160; ambivalence about marriage
    and, 317, 318–19, 323; Asquith and,
    after ESM's death, 704–5, 707, 709–
    10, 712–14; Asquith reveals private
    and wartime military information to,
    210–11, 249–53, 257, 264, 273, 298;
    Asquith's (Margo) attitude toward,
    235–37, 265–67; Asquith's (Ray-
    mond) death and, 362; Asquith (Vi-
    olet) and, 111, 112, 191, 310, 311–
    12, 314, 393, 714; Baldwin's ap-
    pointment as Prime Minister and,
    678; Beaverbrook and, 102, 103,
    275, 527–28, 530–31, 532, 534–37,
    545–46, 652, 653, 703, 704, 705–6,
    707, 708, 709–10, 711, 712, 717–18,
    721–22, 723, 725–26, 727–28; birth
    of, 105; Breccles and, 484, 485, 487–
    90, 491, 703, 710, 712, 713, 723,
    724, 725, 726, 728; on budget (1912)
    presentation, 172–73; on budget
    (1913) presentation, 204; calls ESM
    "Tante," 171–72; chance to become
    a M.P. and, 715; characterized, 102–

3, 113; conversational skill of, 103,
    107; conversion to Judaism of, 26,
    107, 276–77, 306, 309–17, 319–22;
    the Coterie and, 110, 388, 389, 390,
    391, 393; courtship of, by ESM,
    171–73, 174–76, 205–9, 236–37,
    248–49, 252, 253, 256, 260–61, 269–
    71, 272–75; death of, 726, 727–29;
    death of ESM and, 684–86, 693,
    700–702; Dudley (Eric) and, 485,
    672, 673; edits *Indian Diary*, 715–16,
    717, 718; election of 1922 and, 665,
    667; election travels with Asquith,
    112; end of war and, 478, 479, 491;
    engagement of, 2, 275–77, 292, 294–
    304; and ESM's appointment as
    Privy Councillor, 252; and ESM's
    appointment as Under Secretary of
    State for India, 124; and ESM's ele-
    vation to Asquith's Cabinet, 256,
    257; ESM's trip to India (1917–18)
    and, 459, 460, 464, 484–86; at family
    christening, 108–9; Germany in the
    1930s and, 721; as hedonist, 108–9,
    110–11, 200–201, 251, 260, 317, 489;
    on Henley (Francis), 206; on illness,
    167; Herbert (Sidney) and, 485;
    Hope (Charles) and, 652–53; intellect
    of, 109–10; Judith and, 670–71, 672,
    711–13, 724, 725, 726, 727; last let-
    ter of ESM to, 684–85; lesbian ten-
    dencies of, 271, 275; love of nature,
    105; on Lloyd George's peace dele-
    gation, 534–35; marriage of, 386–88,
    393; Montagu (Cardie) and, 709; na-
    ture of relationship with Asquith,
    231–35; as nurse, 110–11, 260, 270,
    304–6, 317–18, 722; Pearl and, 653,
    654; pedigree of, 104–8; planned trip
    to India (1923) and, 674, 676; politics
    and, 110; pregnancy of, 660; prob-
    lems in marriage, 484–91, 530–33,
    535, 537; proposed to, 176–79, 207;
    redecorates Queen Anne's Way and
    Breccles, 484–85, 488–89; refers to
    ESM as "The Assyrian" and "Mr.

Wu," 177, 194; relationship with Asquith intensifies, 169–71, 173–74, 175–76, 179, 193–95, 262–65, 267–69, 274; relationship with ESM, 113–14, 115, 141, 165–69, 173; religion and, 173; resignation of ESM as Secretary of State for India and, 646–47, 654; on the sea, 207; sells Queen Anne's Gate, 703; shows correspondence with Asquith to Beaverbrook, 709–10; shows correspondence with Asquith to ESM, 252, 269; as tomboy, 109; travels of, after ESM's death, 707–9; trip to Sicily with Asquith and Montagu, 169–70, 195; twenty-sixth birthday of, 205–6; trip to Brazil and, 683; at Walmer Castle with Montagu and Asquith, 272; wedding of, 323–26; Wilson (Scatters) and, 486–87; women's suffrage and, 161–62; World War II and, 722–26; writes to ESM in India, 183–84, 191–93, 484–85

Montagu-Chelmsford Reforms (1919), 3, 202, 392, 465–74, 687, 688, 689, 692

Montefiore, Claude, 424, 432, 445

Montefiore, Francis, 425

Montefiore, Moses, 7–8, 18

Montefiore family, 7, 700

Moore, George, 295

Morgan, J. P., and Company, 342–43, 695

Morgan, Ted, 177, 251

Morley, John (Lord Morley), 133, 138, 139, 145, 204, 471, 625, 626, 674; as administrator, 132; Britain's entry into war and, 229, 230; compared with Crewe, 144; ESM as protege of, 132, 141; House of Lords and, 132; Indian grievances and, 128–29, 132, 141; on Lord Crewe, 143; Newcastle Programme and, 70; Mackarness pamphlet and, 134; as Secretary of State for India, 82; on self-government for India, 153

Morley-Minto Act (1909), 131–32, 146

Morning Leader, 141

Morning Post, 291, 367, 392, 415, 437, 470, 556, 557, 569, 572, 573, 615

Mountbatten, Lady Louis, 708

Mukerji, 650

Murray, Alec, 157–59

Murray, Bruce K., 214

Murray, General, 264

Murray, Lord, 224

Muslims, 581–82, 583, 590, 592, 595, 650, 689–90; Armenian massacres and, 522; end of hostilities with Turkey and, 662, 664; ESM and prejudice against, 208; on ESM's death, 692–93; Gandhi and, 512; heterogeneity of, 156; interest in Islam and, 201; issue of, in India, 190–91; in North Africa, 202; peace negotiations with Turkey and, 497–502, 511, 517, 521, 522, 524, 525, 526, 540, 544, 550, 551–52, 553, 591, 593, 600, 601, 602, 609, 610–12, 630–31, 632, 641–42, 649; Reading's appointment as Viceroy and, 574; relations of, with Hindus, 147; and reunification of Bengal, 150; self-government and, 452; in Turkey, 190, 198; unrest of, over Turkish peace terms, 578, 579, 580–81

Muslim League, 570

Nair, Sir Sankaran, 453

Napoleonic Wars, 230

Narsimha, Sir B., 584

Nash, Vaughan, 95, 399, 417, 775–76; on promotion for ESM, 123

Nathan, Sir Matthew, 140, 307

Nation, 141

National Liberal Club, 219

National Liberal Federation, 70

Nation and the Athenaeum, The, 696

Nayon-Montdidier, 476

Nehru brothers, 716

Newcastle Programme, 70

News-Chronicle, 719

News of the World, 138, 139
New Witness, 188, 437
New York Times, 233
New Zealand, 468; Peace Conference and, 493; racism in South Africa and, 588
Nicholson, Lord, 186–87
Nigerian Land debate, 364–65, 366, 381
Nitti, Francesco, 547
noncooperation movement, 512, 514, 554, 569, 570, 578, 597, 611; Gandhi's arrest and, 657
Nordau, Max, 427
Norfolk, Duke of, 100
Northcliffe. *See* Harmsworth, Alfred
Norton, Jean, 706, 708, 803

Observer, 138, 156, 403, 695, 696
O'Connor, T. P., 690
O'Dwyer, Michael, 512–13, 515, 568, 583; Amritsar report and, 555, 556–57, 560, 561
old age pensions, 84, 85, 86, 91, 117
Omar Khayyam, 340
O'Neil, Ann, 723
Orlando, Vittorio, 494, 547, 553; peace negotiations with Turkey and, 550
Ottoman Empire. *See* Turkey
Owen, Frank, 351
Owen, Margaret, 105

Paget, General, 758
Pal, Bepin Chandra, 154
Palestine, 624; Balfour Declaration and, 326, 435–37, 440, 442, 443, 444, 445, 446, 447, 448, 449; British imperial interests and, 429, 430, 439, 445; ESM and, 4; Herbert Samuel and, 307; invasion of, 431; as Jewish homeland, 422, 423–24, 426, 427, 428, 433; Lloyd George and, 309; peace negotiations with Turkey and, 498, 499, 509, 510, 601; population of, 440, 446; Samuel Montagu and,

23, 425. *See also* Balfour Declaration; Zionism
Pall Mall Gazette, 182
Palmerston, Lord, 423, 521, 763
Parish, Sir George, 227, 244, 259
Parliament: selection of candidates for, 743. *See also* House of Commons; House of Lords
Parliament Act (1911), 115, 124–25, 126, 223
Parsons, Alan, 176, 387, 388, 458, 715; on Montagus' marriage, 484
Parsons, Viola, 324, 388
Passchendaele, 396–97
Peace Conference (1918–19), 492; British delegates for, 493–94; opening of, 494–96; negotiations with Turkey and, 496, 497–502, 508–11; reparations and, 502–8. *See also* Treaty of Lausanne; Treaty of Versailles; Turkey
Pearl, 653, 654, 655
Peel, Lord Robert, 648, 657, 660, 674; described, 656
Peel, Mr. H., 180
pension program (1908), 745
People, 574
People's Budget, 115–20; goal of, 117; passed, 125; rejected, 120
Pereira, Isaac, 11
Pershing, Gen. John, 475, 476
Persia, 624; Diplomatic Service in, 342; unrest in, 136
Peto, Ruby, 324
Philippines, 694
Phillips, Dr. Marion, 775
Poincaré, Raymond, 613
Polack, Mrs. J., 30
Polack, Rev., 30, 31
Poland: persecution of Jews in, 12, 13; Samuel Montagu and, 22
poverty: in Great Britain, 71–72
Powell, Enoch, 235
Press Act (1910), 134
Primrose, Neil, 373, 408
Prince of Wales, 542, 544, 554, 584

Pringle, W. M. R., 291
Privy Council, 256
Punch, 138

Queen Anne's Gate. *See* Montagu: RES-
    IDENCES

Rangoon, 687
Rapallo. *See* Treaty of Rapallo
Ratcliffe, S. K., 235
Rawlinson, Sir Henry, 106, 250
Reading, Lord. *See* Isaacs, Rufus
Redmond, John, 223, 226
Reed, Stanley, 611, 612
Rees, Sir John David, 133, 181, 624,
    642
Reform Act of 1919, 467, 495, 511,
    515, 516–21, 523, 525, 541, 543,
    564, 569, 570, 578, 622, 648, 686,
    687, 689, 690, 691, 694, 696
Reidel, Rose (Rosie), 29, 34, 240
Reinach, Joseph, 443
reparations, 502–8, 510, 523–24, 534–
    35, 604, 606–7, 680, 785, 795
Repington, Colonel Charles à Court,
    287, 291, 292, 765
*Report of the Royal Commission on Civil
    Service, A,* 246
Report on British War Budgets, 335
Representation of the People Act, 397
Ribbentrop, Joachim von, 721
Riccardi, E., 693, 737
Rice, Spring, 343
Riddle, George Allardice, 534; on bud-
    get of 1914, 222
Ripon, Earl of, 273
Roberts, Charles, 458
Roberts, Mr., 773
Robertson, General, 396
Roger, Alexander, 356
Ronaldshay, Lord, 479, 521, 607, 613,
    674; Indian Reform Act and, 518
Roosevelt, Franklin, 724
Rosebery, Lord, 77, 343; becomes
    Prime Minister, 78; ESM as possible
    successor of, 3, 286; and land re-

form, 93; Newcastle Programme
    and, 70; on pension program of
    1908, 745; People's Budget and, 119;
    Samuel Montagu and, 22; turned out
    of office, 79; writes introduction to
    Canada and the Empire, 61
Roseveare, Henry *(The Treasury),* 243–
    44
Rosie. *See* Reidel, Rose
Ross-Keppel, Chief Commissioner,
    190
Rothermere, Lord, 224, 225
Rothschild, Charles, 424
Rothschild, Leopold, 424
Rothschild, Lionel, 424
Rothschild, Mrs. James, 424
Rothschild, Nathan, 68, 139, 140; in-
    terest in Palestine of, 425; People's
    Budget and, 119; Zionism and, 425,
    426
Rothschild, Victor, 721
Rothschild, Walter, 424, 437, 441;
    Jewish Legion and, 434; supports
    Balfour Declaration, 433, 434, 439,
    445, 446
Rothschild family, 7, 9, 14, 700
Round Table Conference, 716
Rowlatt Act, 512, 555, 787; repeal of,
    651
Rowntree, B. Seebohm, 775
Royal Fusiliers, 778
Runciman, George, 227, 262; conscrip-
    tion and, 339; fall of the Asquith
    government and, 375, 379; and Shell
    Committee, 282
Runciman, Hilda, 101
Runciman, Walter, 100, 101, 113
Russell, Bertrand, 107, 746
Russell, Claude, 388
Russell, Conrad, 313, 314, 723
Russell, Kate (née Stanley), 106, 107,
    746
Russia, 606; Britain's entry into war
    and, 228, 229; Diaspora Nationalism
    in, 428; Gladstone and, 21; Jewish
    immigration from, 427, 428; Samuel

Russia (*Continued*)
  Montagu and, 21, 22–23; Serbia and,
  227; Treaty of Rapallo and, 664;
  Treaty of Sèvres and, 570; Turkey
  and, 521
Russian Revolution, 396, 463, 513

St. Aldwyn, Lord, 243
Salisbury, Marquis of, 79, 402, 450,
  596, 603, 775
Samuel, Edwin (uncle), 16
Samuel, Henrietta Israel (grandmother), 13
Samuel, Herbert (cousin), 122, 139,
  140, 397, 448; anti-Semitism and,
  307; Balfour Declaration and, 429,
  445–46; fall of Asquith government
  and, 379, 431; Jewish Legion and,
  434; Marconi affair and, 157, 158,
  159, 574, 577, 646; on Palestine, 307;
  and social services during the war,
  247; as Under Secretary for Home
  Affairs, 82; Zionism and, 429–30,
  441
Samuel, Louis (grandfather), 13
Samuel, Menachem (great grandfa-
  ther), 13
Samuel, Montagu. *See* Montagu, Sam-
  uel
Samuel, Ralph, 13
Samuel, Stuart (cousin), 21, 445; Silver
  Scandal and, 159, 188
Samuel family, 13, 700
Sandys, Diana, 726
San Remo Peace Conference, 448, 548,
  549, 553, 570
San Sophia Mosque, 500
Sapru, Tej Bahodur, 584, 622
Sarajevo, 225
Sassoon, Philip, 392
Satyagraha, 512. *See also* noncoopera-
  tion movement
Schiff, Jacob, 442, 443
Scott, C. P., 430, 446
Scott, Leslie, 775

Sedgwick, Anne Douglas, 171–72
Seely, Jack, 774
Selbourne, Lord, 474, 518
Serbia, 227, 229
Serocolds, the, 672
Seton, Sir Malcolm, 458
Sèvres. *See* Treaty of Sèvres
Shadow Cabinet, 331–34
Shastri, Shrinivasa, 463
Shaw-Stewart, Patrick, 391, 478
Sheffield, Lady. *See* Stanley, Margaret
Sheffield, Lord. *See* Stanley, Lyulph
Shell Committees, 274, 282–87
Sherwood, Miss, 514, 515
Shortt, Edward, 538, 628
Silesia, 522, 580
Silver Scandal, 159, 187–89, 191, 192,
  193, 203
Simla, 180
Simmons, Vivian G., 699
Simon, Sir John, 227, 230, 249, 716
Singh, Prince, 700
Sinha, Sachedaranda, 154, 454, 691,
  493, 544, 751
Smith, Goldwin, 442
Smith, Masterton, 324, 331–32
Smith, Thomas Graham, 78
Smuts, Jan, 409, 507, 535, 475, 586–
  87, 588, 590
Smyrna, 508, 511, 517, 521, 547, 591,
  597, 600, 610, 630
Snowden, Lord, 89
Soames, Mary (née Churchill), 112,
  704; Judith Montagu and, 724; dur-
  ing World War II, 724, 726
social reform. *See* death duties; land
  reform; tax reform
Soissons, 396
Sokolow, Nathan, 433, 445
Solomon family, 7
Somme, 361, 362, 475, 770
Sommers, E. A., 324
Sonnino, Giorgio, 547
South Africa, 351, 454, 682, 684; Peace
  Conference and, 493; racism in, 208,
  585, 586–89, 655

Southborough, Lord, 474
South Stoneham, 8–10
Spender, J. A., 160, 713, 714
Speyer, Sir Edgar, 140
Spielmann, Adam, 16
Spielmann, Marion, 16
Stamfordham, Lord, 677, 678
Stanley, Adam, 104
Stanley, Albert (Lord Ashfield), 404, 405
Stanley, Algernon, 106, 107
Stanley, Alice, 106
Stanley, Anthony, 321
Stanley, Arthur, 316, 319
Stanley, Beatrice Venetia. See Montagu, Venetia Stanley
Stanley, Blanche. See Airlie, Lady Blanche
Stanley, Colonel, 700
Stanley, Edward, 105, 106
Stanley, Edwin, 310
Stanley, Geoffrey, 321
Stanley, Henry, 104, 106
Stanley, John, 104, 106
Stanley, Lyulph (Lord Sheffield), 104, 105, 106, 107, 108, 172, 313, 714, 715; Venetia's engagement and conversion and, 314, 315, 316
Stanley, Mabella, 104
Stanley, Margaret (Lady Sheffield), 104, 107–8, 313, 323, 714; invites ESM to Alderley, 143; and Venetia's engagement and conversion, 310, 314, 315–16; and Venetia's relationship with Asquith, 267
Stanley, Maude, 106
Stanley, Maureen, 723
Stanley, Oliver, 315, 323
Stanley, Thomas (1st Earl of Derby), 104
Stanley, William de, 104
Statist, 227
Stevenson, Frances (later Mrs. Lloyd George): anti-Semitism of, 216, 308; attitude of, toward ESM, 420–21; on Churchill, 291; on ESM and Lloyd George, 215–16; Lloyd George and, 298
Stevenson, J., 775
Stubbs, Mr., 666, 667
Suasso, Antonio (Isaac) Lopez, 11
Sultan, 497–98, 500, 501, 522, 524, 525, 547, 558, 611, 630, 632
Sumner, Lord, 507, 535
Sunday Express, 528, 593, 715
Sunday Times, The, 695, 696
super tax, 118
Sutherland, Duke of, 672
swaraj, 579, 598, 688
Swaythling, Lord. See Montagu, Samuel
Sydenham, Lord, 493, 595
Sykes, Mark, 433
Syria, 498, 499, 509, 510, 522

Tagore, Rabindranath, 569
Taj Mahal, 185
Tante (Sedgwick), 171–72
Tatler, 310
tax policy: during World War I, 334–35, 343–44
tax reform, 83, 84, 85–86, 89, 90, 481
Taylor, A. J. P., 708, 719, 720, 721; on end of war, 477; on Lloyd George as outsider, 380; on nature of relationship between Asquith and Venetia, 233, 234
Tennant, Charlotte (Charty), 78
Tennant, Frank, 88
Tennant, Laura, 78
Tennant, Lillian, 112
Tennant, Lucy, 78
Tennant, Pauline, 78
Tennant, Charles, 78, 88, 379
Thomas, J. H., 775
Thomas, Lowell, 720
Thrace, 498, 525, 547, 558, 591, 597, 600, 601, 630, 634, 662, 663
Tilak, Bal Gangadhar, 154, 452
Times, The (London), 154, 187, 193, 194, 233, 234, 273, 287, 291, 292,

Times, The (London) (*Continued*)
  295, 338, 362, 363, 367, 373, 432,
  612, 615, 665, 696, 698, 719, 772
Times of India, 154, 156, 181, 611, 689,
  690, 693
Tittoni, 547
Topical Times, 19
Tory Party: anti-Semitism and, 14,
  255–56, 308; Asquith and, 255–56;
  characterized, 67; Churchill and,
  255, 291, 293; Coalition government
  and, 1, 290, 292; imperial preference
  and, 60–61; tax reform and, 256;
  World War I and, 255. *See also* Die-
  Hards
Treaty of Lausanne, 3, 651, 663–64,
  675
Treaty of Rapallo, 664
Treaty of Sèvres, 3, 570–71, 575, 583,
  609, 620, 621, 629, 630, 631, 632,
  634, 639, 649, 651
Treaty of Versailles, 524, 783
Tree, Iris, 388
Tree, Viola, 112, 176, 208, 490, 491
Trench, Le Poer, 20
Turkey, 439; Britain declares war on,
  429; defeat of, 413, 448, 477; Diplomatic Service in, 342; dismemberment of, 429–30; end of hostilities
  with Greece and, 662–64; ESM and,
  21; Germany and, 522; Gladstone
  and, 21; Muslims and, 190, 198, 202,
  578, 579, 580–81; Palestine as Jewish
  homeland and, 423, 424; peace negotiations with, 3, 495, 496–97, 497–
  502, 508–11, 517, 521–22, 524–26,
  538, 539–41, 543–44, 546–47, 548–
  54, 558, 591–92, 592, 597, 600–601,
  602, 603, 609–11, 612, 613–14, 620,
  625, 629–32, 633, 634, 639, 641,
  661–62, 675; Samuel Montagu and,
  21; Treaty of Sèvres and, 3, 570–71;
  unrest in, 136

Uganda, 426, 427
Ulster, 223, 224, 225

Unemployed Workmen's Act, 90
Union Society (Cambridge), 51–54,
  56, 57
United States, 499; enters the war, 398;
  reparations and, 503, 504, 505, 506,
  507, 606; Samuel Montagu travels
  to, 23; Treaty of Sèvres and, 570

Venizélos, Eleuthérios, 525, 547, 558,
  591; Treaty of Sèvres and, 571
Verdun, 339–40, 361
Vernon, George, 478
Versailles. *See* Treaty of Versailles
Victorian society, 27–28
Vimy Ridge, 396
Vincent, Sir William, 458, 579–80

Wales, Prince of, 701, 702; trip to In-
  dia of, 593, 595, 597, 598–600, 612–
  13, 619
Waley, Mrs., 700
Waley family, 7, 700
Walter, Karl, 235
Walter, Nicholas, 235
Walter, W. Grey, 234
Wandsworth, Lord, 140
War Cabinet, 363–64
War Committee, 366–68
War Council, 239, 240
Ward, Miss, 105
Wardell, Michael, 708
War Loan Act, 242, 243
War Savings Certificates, 331
Webb, Beatrice, 775
Wedgwood, Colonel, 642–43
Wednesday Review, 140
Weever, Elizabeth, 104
Weever, Thomas, 104
Weizmann, Chaim, 440; on assimila-
  tion, 432; Balfour Declaration and,
  439, 445, 446; emerges as Zionist
  leader, 427, 430; ESM and, 433;
  Jewish Legion and, 433, 434
Wellington, Duke of, 763
Wells, H. G.: on Beaverbrook, 529; on
  World War I, 254–55

Wemyss, Rosslyn Erskine, 478
West London Synagogue, 699, 700
Weymouth, Lady, 715
Whistler, Rex, 488
White Paper on Palestine, 448
Whyte, Miss, 726
William II, Emperor of Germany, 478
William of Orange, 11–12
William the Conqueror, 104
Willingdon, Lord, 519, 539, 544, 571, 582, 674, 696
Wilson, Arthur, 293
Wilson, Barbara, 487
Wilson, Lady, 536
Wilson, Matthew (Scatters), 486–87, 532, 536, 537
Wilson, Trevor, 627
Wilson, Woodrow, 534, 535, 607; Balfour Declaration and, 438, 444; the Big Four and, 494–95, 496; end of war and, 475, 477; Fourteen Points of, 477, 502; peace negotiations with Turkey and, 508, 509, 547, 550; reparations and, 503, 504, 506, 507, 606
Wimborne, Lady, 324
Wingate, Sir Reginald, 459
"Winston's Folly," 357–58
Winterton, Lord, 628, 674
Withers, Mr. Hartley, 683
Wolfe, Lucien, 431–32, 434
women's suffrage, 159–62, 169, 193, 352, 483
Wood, Edward, 379, 628
Woods, Billy, 673
Woods, Maurice, 103
Woods, Peter, 673
World War I, 110, 554; adumbrations of, 216–17; Asquith as leader in, 278–80; Britain's entry into, 228–31; conscription during, 335–39; course of, in 1915, 254; Dardanelles expedition, 287–90; early days of, 238–39; early military strategy of, 250, 251; end of, 475–80; financial problems in, 227–28, 240–48; formation of Coalition government during, 290–94; India's part in, 451–52; precipitated, 226–27; progress of, in 1917, 396–98; shell shortage and, 3, 280–81, 282–87; tax policy during, 334–35; trench warfare in, 339–41
World War II, 703, 722–23, 724
Worsley, Lady, 710, 711
Wright, Sir Robert Samuel, 76

Yates, Benjamin (Rabbi Benjamin ben Elijakim Getz), 12–13
Yate, Charles Edward, 517, 560, 569, 570
Yorkshire Daily Post, 134
Younger, Sir George, 665
Ypres, 396–97

Ziegler, Philip: on Diana Cooper's anti-Semitism, 391–92; on nature of relationship between Asquith and Venetia, 234
Zionism: Anglo-Jewish opposition to, 422–23, 424–25, 428; Balfour Declaration and, 4, 326, 429, 433, 435–49, 779, 780; British imperial interests and, 429, 430, 439, 445; early development of, 424–28; ESM opposes, 4, 422–23, 430–31, 435; Herzl and, 424–27; increasing support for, 431–32; Jewish Legion and, 433, 434; Samuel Montagu and, 23
Zionist Idea (Hertzberg), 779